Overcoming Obstacles in Drug Discovery and Development

Overcoming Obstacles in Drug Discovery and Development

Surmounting the Insurmountable—Case Studies for Critical Thinking

Edited by

Kan He
Biotranex LLC, Princeton, NJ, United States

Paul F. Hollenberg
University of Michigan Medical School, Ann Arbor, MI, United States

Larry C. Wienkers
Wienkers Consulting, LLC, Bainbridge Island, WA, United States

ACADEMIC PRESS

An imprint of Elsevier

Academic Press is an imprint of Elsevier
125 London Wall, London EC2Y 5AS, United Kingdom
525 B Street, Suite 1650, San Diego, CA 92101, United States
50 Hampshire Street, 5th Floor, Cambridge, MA 02139, United States
The Boulevard, Langford Lane, Kidlington, Oxford OX5 1GB, United Kingdom

ISBN: 978-0-12-817134-9

For information on all Academic Press publications visit our
website at https://www.elsevier.com/books-and-journals

Publisher: Stacy Masucci
Acquisitions Editor: Andre G. Wolff
Editorial Project Manager: Michaela Realiza
Production Project Manager: Punithavathy Govindaradjane
Cover Designer: Christian Bilbow

Typeset by TNQ Technologies

Working together
to grow libraries in
developing countries

www.elsevier.com • www.bookaid.org

Contents

10. Design, conduct, and interpretation of human mass balance studies and strategies for assessing metabolites-in-safety testing (MIST) in drug development

Simon G. Wong and Shuguang Ma

11. Conquering low oral bioavailability issues in drug discovery and development

Timothy J. Carlson

12. Case study of OATP1B DDI assessment and challenges in drug discovery and development—real-life examples

Hong Shen, Jinping Gan and Giridhar S. Tirucherai

13. Investigating the link between drug metabolism and toxicity

W. Griffith Humphreys

18. Kyprolis (carfilzomib) (approved): a covalent drug with high extrahepatic clearance via peptidase cleavage and epoxide hydrolysis

Zhengping Wang, Jinfu Yang and Christopher Kirk

19. Engaging diversity in research: does your drug work in overlooked populations?

Karen E. Brown and Erica L. Woodahl

20. PBPK modeling for early clinical study decision making

Arian Emami Riedmaier

21. Integrated pharmacokinetic/pharmacodynamic/efficacy analysis in oncology: importance of pharmacodynamic/efficacy relationships

Harvey Wong

Contributors

Karim Azer, Axcella Therapeutics, Cambridge, MA, United States

Brian Barnes, Department of Business & Education, Foundation for Critical Thinking, Santa Barbara, CA, United States; Department of Philosophy, University of Louisville, Louisville, KY, United States; Department of Philosophy, Indiana University Southeast, New Albany, IN, United States; Department of Philosophy, Quality Leadership University, Panama City, Panama

Jeff S. Barrett, Critical Path Institute, Tuscon, AZ, United States

Karen E. Brown, Department of Biomedical and Pharmaceutical Sciences, University of Montana, Missoula, MT, United States; L.S. Skaggs Institute for Health Innovation, University of Montana, Missoula, MT, United States

Timothy J. Carlson, Carlson DMPK Consulting, LLC, Belmont, CA, United States

Hsuan Ping Chang, Department of Pharmaceutical Sciences, School of Pharmacy and Pharmaceutical Sciences, The State University of New York at Buffalo, Buffalo, NY, United States

Yuen Kiu Cheung, Department of Pharmaceutical Sciences, School of Pharmacy and Pharmaceutical Sciences, The State University of New York at Buffalo, Buffalo, NY, United States

D.D. Christ, SNC Partners LLC, Annapolis, MD, United States

Upendra P. Dahal, Department of Pharmacokinetics and Drug Metabolism, Amgen Inc., Thousand Oaks, CA, United States

Deepak Dalvie, Bristol Myers Squibb, San Diego, CA, United States

Arian Emami Riedmaier, PBPK Consultancy, Certara, Princeton, NJ, United States

Paul W. Erhardt, DUP Emeritus, Medicinal Chemistry, University of Toledo, Sylvania, OH, United States

Robert S. Foti, ADME & Discovery Toxicology, Merck & Co., Inc., Kenilworth, NJ, United States

Jinping Gan, HiFiBiO Therapeutics, Cambridge, MA, United States; Drug Metabolism and Pharmacokinetics, Bristol Myers Squibb Company, Lawrenceville, NJ, United States

Kan He, Biotranex LLC, Princeton, NJ, United States

Sara C. Humphreys, Pharmacokinetics and Drug Metabolism Department, Amgen Research, South San Francisco, CA, United States

W. Griffith Humphreys, Aranmore Pharma Consulting, Lawrenceville, NJ, United States

Graham Jang, Blaze Bioscience, Seattle, WA, United States

Christopher Kirk, Research and Development, Kezar Life Sciences, South San Francisco, CA, United States

Julie M. Lade, Pharmacokinetics and Drug Metabolism Department, Amgen Research, South San Francisco, CA, United States

Shuguang Ma, Pharmacokinetics and Drug Metabolism, Amgen Inc., South San Francisco, CA, United States

Cynthia J. Musante, Pfizer, Cambridge, MA, United States

Joshua T. Pearson, ADME & Discovery Toxicology, Merck & Co., Inc., Kenilworth, NJ, United States

Chandra Prakash, Department of Drug Metabolism, Pharmacokinetics and Clinical Pharmacology, Agios Pharmaceuticals, Cambridge, MA, United States

Brooke M. Rock, Pharmacokinetics and Drug Metabolism Department, Amgen Research, South San Francisco, CA, United States

Joseph M. Roesner, ADME & Discovery Toxicology, Merck & Co., Inc., Kenilworth, NJ, United States

Dhaval K. Shah, Department of Pharmaceutical Sciences, School of Pharmacy and Pharmaceutical Sciences, The State University of New York at Buffalo, Buffalo, NY, United States

Hong Shen, Drug Metabolism and Pharmacokinetics, Bristol Myers Squibb Company, Lawrenceville, NJ, United States

Sekhar Surapaneni, Bristol Myers Squibb, Summit, NJ, United States

Mai B. Thayer, Pharmacokinetics and Drug Metabolism Department, Amgen Research, South San Francisco, CA, United States

Giridhar S. Tirucherai, Clinical Pharmacology and Pharmacometrics, Bristol Myers Squibb Company, Lawrenceville, NJ, United States

Mirjam Trame, University of Florida, Gainesville, FL, United States

Jan L. Wahlstrom, Department of Pharmacokinetics and Drug Metabolism, Amgen Inc., Thousand Oaks, CA, United States

Zhengping Wang, Nonclinical Development and Clinical Pharmacology, Revolution Medicines, Redwood City, CA, United States

Larry C. Wienkers, Wienkers Consulting, LLC, Bainbridge Island, WA, United States

Harvey Wong, Faculty of Pharmaceutical Sciences, The University of British Columbia., Vancouver, BC, Canada

Simon G. Wong, Drug Metabolism and Pharmacokinetics, Pliant Therapeutics, South San Francisco, CA, United States

Erica L. Woodahl, Department of Biomedical and Pharmaceutical Sciences, University of Montana, Missoula, MT, United States; L.S. Skaggs Institute for Health Innovation, University of Montana, Missoula, MT, United States

Zheng Yang, Metabolism and Pharmacokinetics, Pharmaceutical Candidate Optimization, Bristol Myers Squibb, Princeton, NJ, United States

Jinfu Yang, Research and Development, Zenshine Pharmaceuticals Inc., Burlingame, CA, United States

Preface

Modern drug discovery and development is a highly complex undertaking that, in order to be successful, requires both scientific and professional expertise as well as astute interdisciplinary thinking. Following the identification of a molecular entity that displays potential for treating a medical condition, challenges arise that may alter the further development of the drug at any of its subsequent countless steps. In this process, the team may identify unexpected safety issues, or, on the other hand, uncover new medical conditions the molecular entity might treat. Invariably inherent in drug discovery are missteps, mistakes, and unexpected problems that can derail development and throw timetables into disarray, potentially leading to failure to complete the process for "what might have been" a medically useful drug.

Conquering unexpected challenges requires that scientists involved in discovery and development utilize critical thinking and imaginative problem-solving skills. The process is multidisciplinary in nature, requiring skill in numerous disciplines to facilitate and manage interactions. Fundamental to successful drug discovery and development is a thorough understanding of what critical data are needed to address identified issues and how to best generate these data, taking into account both science and economics, and then how best to interpret the data to make decisions that will further, rather than hinder, successful development.

We believe it is important to gather and share experiences related to drug discovery and development for the educational benefit of both young and established scientists. We have documented many original ideas, thought processes, and unique approaches that have helped drug hunters successfully discover and develop safe and effective medicines. Further, we illustrate how teams may have gone off track, and we relate the approaches they used to "right the ship" and accomplish their original objectives.

We are not aware of any pharmacological books on this subject that are currently available. The vast majority of literature in the field of drug discovery and development focuses primarily on the positive data generated to support moving the molecular entity further along the pipeline and the details of positive experimental approaches. These articles or publications never fully elaborate on mistakes, bottlenecks, misinterpretations of data, or technical failures in specific case studies, or on the innovative approaches that investigators used to overcome such issues.

This book has grown out of a series of sessions titled "Surmounting the Insurmountable: Obstacles in Drug Discovery and Development—Real World Case Studies" that we entered for a competition called the "Big Idea" at ASPET. The proposal was accepted and the first session presented at the Experimental Biology National Meeting in 2017. The purpose of these sessions was to provide a forum for pharmaceutical industry experts in drug discovery and development to present "real-world" stories recounting how drug development challenges that appeared at first glance to be insurmountable were overcome through critical thinking and problem-solving skills. Although we faced some difficulties recruiting speakers (due to company policies of secrecy around their scientific discoveries), we held the symposium for 2 years, receiving excellent feedback.

We were then approached by Dr. Erin Hill-Parks from Elsevier who believed our symposium series could be the basis for a valuable book; she asked us if we would be submit a proposal. Initially, we proposed a wide range of topics in drug discovery and development, but ultimately, it became more realistic to focus on the areas that inevitably affect drug safety, efficacy, and development. These include absorption, distribution, metabolism, pharmacokinetics, and pharmacodynamics.

Working on the outline for the book, it became apparent to us essential to understanding a particular case study would include general topic chapters describing technical background as well as the current state of the art in that given area. Where necessary for comprehension, the general topic chapters are included just before the relevant case study; where a case study requires a general chapter that does not directly precede it, we have directed the reader to the appropriate prefatory chapter(s).

We are grateful to the authors who volunteered to tell their stories and show a side of their research that normally does not appear in published peer-reviewed papers or book chapters. We also thank the executives at various pharmaceutical companies who signed off on these chapters, as there are indeed concerns about publishing work related to proprietary compounds. These executives have graciously allowed their scientists to tell their stories and show their thought processes, thereby contributing to the future of drug discovery.

We intend for this book to help drug hunters understand how to use data to make effective decisions during the drug discovery and development process; to support students and scientists in applying critical thinking and problem-solving skills to solve real-world problems; and to enrich drug discoverers' knowledge and understanding of pharmacological sciences.

Although we too are scientists involved in drug discovery and development, we cannot fully express how fascinating it has been for us to edit these chapters and learn how creative and innovative our colleagues have been in their approaches to solving extremely complex, sometimes confounding, problems. We hope that you will benefit greatly from learning about these novel approaches to problems that initially seemed to be insurmountable.

Kan He
Paul F. Hollenberg
Larry C. Wienkers

Chapter 1

Learning to think critically

Brian Barnes[a, b, c, d]

[a]Department of Business & Education, Foundation for Critical Thinking, Santa Barbara, CA, United States; [b]Department of Philosophy, University of Louisville, Louisville, KY, United States; [c]Department of Philosophy, Indiana University Southeast, New Albany, IN, United States; [d]Department of Philosophy, Quality Leadership University, Panama City, Panama

Some concerns with drug development & discovery

The US Food & Drug Administration offers a 5-part process for drug development and discovery [1]. The five parts are *Discovery and Development* (lab research); *Preclinical Research* (laboratory and animal safety testing); *Clinical Research* (human safety testing); *FDA Review* (where the approval should come); and *FDA Post-Market Safety Monitoring* (monitors public impact of the drug). According to Duxin Sun et al., in their paper, "Why 90% of Clinical Drug Development Fails and How to Improve It," [2] at least 10% of drug failures between 2014 and 2017 were related to "poor strategic planning" [3], a problem that the authors outline in their section regarding optimization of drug studies. The authors refer to "overlooked" aspects of the actual drug interaction process with the body, "failure to adapt" all relevant criteria, and they recommend an additional process (*STAR*), for helping researchers overcome the intellectual problems that are extant in drug development systems. So, the FDA system for maintaining excellence and success, for these authors, would benefit from an additional system that would put potential drugs into categories as a way to aid researchers' thinking.

It is clear that various decision-making problems exist, and this paper's conclusions about the drug development process and the need for improved intellectual processes is not unique among the recent literature. Along with an incredibly large failure rate, and despite, "All pharmaceutical companies [possessing] meticulous development plan[s] with a detailed roadmap and milestones to advance new compounds from the lab through each stage of development [along with a] multidisciplinary project team of experienced experts often work[ing] together in strategic planning with the help of various business models and analytic tools, combined with Artificial Intelligence (AI) [which] has brought state-of-the-art analytical tools that enable pharmaceutical companies to predict patients' needs and market trends in a more efficient and cost-effective way" [4], Nine out of ten drugs that are conceived fail the approval process, wasting huge sums of resources in the process.

This essay suggests that good thinking habits could be developed within those involved in the work, as opposed to the repeated efforts at adding more guidelines to the development and discovery process. Critical thinking theory from Richard Paul and Linda Elder [5] offers an important check on the thinker, rather than modifying the formal processes, though modifications may present themselves while the thinker is considering them. All of the tools explained here can be directly applied by the thinker to their thinking in real time, thus streamlining the process of whatever thinking is being done.

Critical thinking basics

Critical Thinking is a type of thinking, but it differs in important ways from normal thinking. The distinctions between normal thinking and critical thinking are important for the process of drug development, as well as for other organized thinking processes. The first distinction is in the name: *critical* thinking. Richard Paul, one of the pioneers of the academic field of Critical Thinking, pointed out that the meaning of the adjective implies a question: "What kind of thinking is this?" [6] For Paul, it's thinking that uses *criteria*, also known as evidence, data, and information. While all intentional thinking may be thinking about something, not all of that thinking is based in good reasons or high-quality evidence. This latter aspect is what Paul wants us to consider as *critical* thinkers, thinkers who are using *criteria* to arrive at our conclusions, rather than empty or unfounded speculation about facts and states of affairs. Critical thinking demands use of criteria.

Overcoming Obstacles in Drug Discovery and Development. https://doi.org/10.1016/B978-0-12-817134-9.00013-1

Drug development also demands use of criteria. Every single intellectual step is probably governed by the best reasons and evidence — we hope. Paul's concern is that any given thinker may not be sensitive to the nature and disposition of the "evidence" that is being used in their thinking. Learning to look at one's own thinking process and applying relevant criteria can help any thinker detect errors in thinking that cut across many intellectual areas, not just strategic drug development.

The other broad theme that should be present for the thinking in question to be considered *critical* thinking is that the thinker should be able to locate the thinking during metacognition, which Paul and Elder often call *self-reflection* [7]. While *critical* thinking is not the only useful kind of thinking, critical thinking analyzes and assesses itself. Normal thinking does not do this until it chooses to do so, which is one way normal thinking takes on the character of criticality. This idea leads to another important question: "Why is it important that the thinking being done is thinking that the thinker is able to observe?"

Critical thinking contains a variety of micro-skills, each of which can be improved through practice. "Development of the human mind is quite parallel to the development of the human body" [8]. Like a tennis swing, a person's thinking can improved by intentional, consistent, and high-quality practice. Also like a tennis shot during a match, the thinking that is called upon at a moment's notice is used to accomplish something valuable. It is very much a function of the training, or lack of training, that any thinker has put into thinking performance. Sure, a lot of thinkers, like a lot of athletes, have natural ability that carries them a certain distance. The elite thinker, though, like the elite athlete, gains a lot from excellent, targeted training, as well as personal discipline and a variety of useful habits that often are enhanced and developed over time.

When a thinker can observe the thinking being done, the opportunity for training presents itself. Like the tennis player, the thinker can learn to observe thinking in real time and make micro-adjustments that are advantageous for the outcomes of this or that encounter. Also like tennis, there is value in working on my thinking such that I become a better thinker for *any* thinking encounter, not just a particular one. Someone might legitimately question the promising athlete who makes a training decision that will lead to a future limitation on their ability to excel, only for a short-term gain. Thinkers, likewise, can develop habits that will lead to them routinely limiting their own possibilities for the highest quality thinking, typically because gimmicks and short-term manipulation seem to be more valuable than developing better thinking for its own sake, win or lose. Paul and Elder label thinkers with these habits *sophists*, after the ancient teachers of rhetorical devices aimed at achieving immediate goals, like winning a lawsuit or gaining sympathy from a neighbor.

Both of these hallmarks of Paul's and Elder's critical thinking approach— [9] the centrality of criteria for good thinking, and the explicit examining of the thinking process and its components through metacognition— are useful for the drug development process. Vast sums of money are spent annually to shape the intellectual processes involved in drug development, such that outcomes like effectiveness, profit, and safety are achieved. If we take Sun's article above seriously, recent drug development shows that few of the expensive and time-consuming processes for developing medicines result in marketable or profitable products [10].

It is possible to improve thinking processes within the thinker, but only with an understanding of what the thinker is capable of accomplishing in real time, with only the tools of the mind available. The Paul-Elder approach to critical thinking relies upon some foundational abilities being available to the thinker in both real time and in self-reflection. Along with using criteria and locating past thinking during self-reflection, Paul and Elder assume that the thinker will naturally engage in analysis and assessment, that the thinker will develop intellectual habits, and that the thinker is subject to a variety of regular patterns of thinking that could distort the thinking being done. This essay discloses these critical thinking abilities and how any thinker can use them for better thinking in real time and for intellectual training over the long term. While connections are made to drug development, explication of the process is intended to inspire individual experts in this area toward better thinking.

Critical thinking analysis

For the purposes of critical thinking, the mind naturally performs certain functions. The term "naturally" is meant to convey the idea that many minds in fact perform these functions, and many minds can perform certain foundational functions quite well without any explicit awareness of rational process, nor any formal training using it. Memory, for example, falls into this category. A lot of minds seem to possess it, and thinkers use it without any training. Like memory and tennis, though, critical thinking is a skill that can be trained to be more effective.

Paul and Elder suggest that all intentional thinking creates the possibility of eight distinct parts of the thinking becoming identifiable. These separate "Elements of Thought" are always present within the process of thinking about anything, but thinkers rarely focus on the process of thinking as a whole, much less focus on its separate parts. However, a thinker performs intellectual analysis whenever they focus on any of the eight Elements as a way to take their thinking one piece at a time, rather than confronting the whole of it. Analysis allows the thinking to be considered in its different aspects, and most of the time we do this implicitly, rather than explicitly. Since critical thinking wants us to focus on our thinking process, not just on the results of the thinking, it makes the otherwise hidden thinking in our everyday decision-making explicit. For a complete list of Elements of Thought, please see Fig. 1.1 [11].

A thinker might be interested in developing a new drug. While the FDA guidelines mention a variety of motives for drug discovery and development [12], let us assume the purpose that this thinker wants to pursue for drug discovery is primarily motivated by the public good. At some point during the process of discovery and development, other motives will present themselves: profit, power, influence, comfort, etc. These all have value, and each should be considered as a possible primary motive. As each option is considered, the original motive might be displaced or reduced in value relative to a new motive. The thinker who has made their values explicit to themselves can have confidence that they are not straying from or overlooking an important purpose. The thinker who has not made their purpose explicit could waste time, money, and resources in a direction that is not advantageous for the desired outcomes, or even one that contradicts their personal values. While established drug development protocols will likely mandate a purpose for the project, these projects are implemented by individual thinkers, all of whom will possess their own motives and purposes — it behooves all involved to explicitly examine whether institutional and individual purposes align. The recent cases of Shkreli, Holmes, and the Sacklers should suffice to exemplify this suggestion, and many such examples regularly emerge in mainstream media.

Likewise, questions that are made explicit are more easily managed than those left unstated and which, thereby, end up not being pursued. Information used to satisfy my purpose should be made explicit, so that it can be more easily assessed. The same is true for a thinker's inferential processes, which involve how the mind combines concepts, assumptions, information, and other parts of thinking to reach original conclusions. When we have good information, we still may make mistakes in our reasoning, and making this and other parts of my thinking explicit, while challenging and time-consuming, can unlock useful insights into why goals are not being accomplished.

In Fig. 1.1, each of the eight Elements of Thought is presented in a circle. A thinker can begin at any part of the thinking process to engage in explicit analysis. The Elements of Thought are also integrated with one another, so that it is a direct intellectual task to move from one piece of thinking to another (with practice.) So, maybe a partner has raised a question, and that gets the thinking going. Maybe someone has suggested an alternate purpose for the work, maybe new information is being introduced, or maybe the way we value that information is being challenged by stakeholders. Any of these scenarios can benefit from thinkers knowing how to make their purposes, questions, information, and inferences explicit parts of the thinking they are doing, for their own benefit and for the good of the group. Where the thinker starts is completely a function of what is considered important and worth thinking about at the time.

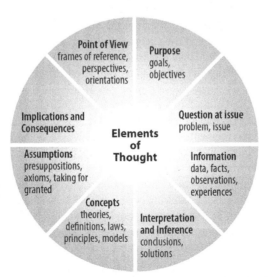

FIGURE 1.1 The Elements of Thought are useful for intellectual analysis on any topic. *Credit: R. Paul, L. Elder. The Miniature Guide to Critical Thinking Concepts and Tools, seventh ed., Rowman & Littlefield, 2008, p. 3.*

Paul and Elder suggest four additional Elements as always being present in thinking implicitly, which means they can be made explicit by the thinker. These are the Point of View, Concepts, Implications and Consequences of the current thinking, and Assumptions. It is obvious that each thinker has an alternate point of view on every situation, even if there is accord among the thinkers present, because each thinker has slightly different processes of inference and different personal narratives surrounding skills and information relative to the discovery process. To ignore the obvious fact that points of view are different is to court disagreement within a team. Likewise, all thinkers have a batch of foundational concepts that can be drilled down into, and it is likely that these fundamental concepts differ from thinker to thinker, creating the possibility for additional dissonance.

All thinking done today has implications for future thinking. Not all of those future implications will actually manifest, but a selection of them will, and these are the intellectual consequences of the thinking that is being done today. If a thinker is not aware of the logical domino effect that is produced by today's thinking for tomorrow's and the future's, thinking, then errors and misunderstandings could infiltrate intellectual processes today, unnoticed, that may do damage somewhere down the line. Allusions to this problem exist in the drug development research offered by Sun et al., from the beginning of this essay.

Assumptions are also potentially damaging and always present in the thinking process. Assumptions are particularly insidious to any intellectual process, because they are ideas thinkers use for decision-making that have never been checked by that thinker. To add to the difficulty, hinkers cannot unravel every instance of assumption, nor all implications of possessing them in our thinking. While no one can know everything, and so some assuming must occur, there is always a risk that a piece of thinking taken for granted could lead to disastrous outcomes for the process.

These eight Elements of Thought are always at play, since any piece of thinking possesses all eight pieces. When a thinker drills down into one Element, it might be discovered that the Element is lacking some useful characteristic, like accuracy or depth. It is incumbent upon the critical thinker to assess the quality of what is produced in any instance of explicit intellectual analysis. Perhaps a piece of important information is so imprecise as to be distorted, an assumption might be illogical, or a question, while interesting to pursue, may lack significance for the project at hand. After all, there is no guarantee that information arrived at during self-reflection will be of high quality. To make that determination, assessment tools are needed.

Critical thinking assessment

In order to think with criteria, thinkers need high-quality standards for their thinking. While it is vital that critical thinkers be able to break thinking into pieces, testing those pieces to make sure they will contribute to the outcomes a thinker is pursuing is a separate proposition. This fundamental set of criteria includes Clarity, Accuracy, Precision, Relevance, Depth, Breadth, Logicalness, Significance, Fairness, Sufficiency, and Completeness [13]. It may also make sense to bring other standards into a specific thinking event, like a drug discovery and development process, since they would be important for checking the quality of the thinking in that context [14].

Without an explicit check, the critical thinker cannot know that these Standards are being met. For better or worse, no one sticks to the strict guidelines critical thinking suggests all of the time. How can a person know that they are being clear to others, that their conclusions are accurate, or that their reasoning is logical, if they don't seek standards outside of their own thinking? Self-deception is dangerous for the best thinking, so strong thinkers need a set of standards to cause them to take a second look at the value of data, of their own assumptions, and to check the relevant characteristics of their points of view.

Each Standard, like each Element, can be used independently by any thinker. If a stakeholder mentions The Precautionary Principle's [15] role in a drug development process, an explicit look at the team's assumptions and concepts might reveal a need for a closer look at risk management, but that will only happen if team members are prompted to make the checking of their thinking explicit. Of course, mistakes can still be made, but knowing that each idea in the critical thinking analysis or assessment process has been scrutinized at the level of each piece of data, each step along the way of analysis, and at each conclusion or assumption is a useful extra check for the thinking being constructed.

Intellectual Standards can be used to assess the thinking of any thinker in self-reflection, but they also can be employed to assess anything else that can be analyzed. This assessment tool is intended to be qualitative, so it is always a question of "more or less" clarity, relevance, logicalness, etc., rather than an absolute standard for any of these. Of course, these ordinary terms are already in use during our assessment of others. As we inevitably do that, critical thinking wants us to always-and-already be applying these tools to ourselves, so that we can be confident that our own thinking adheres to high-quality metrics.

Critical thinking traits

All thinkers develop habits as a result of thinking resolving itself; this is, again, like tennis. Over time, thinkers tend to be more or less selfish, more or less rigorous, more or less autonomous, and other attributes. Thinking is not always the same quality for each characteristic; it occurs on a scale [16]. Paul and Elder identify eight characteristics of thinkers that they call Intellectual Traits [17]. Intellectual Traits develop on a spectrum, such that each thinker possesses each characteristic, but some thinkers are at an extreme, while others are elsewhere. This is not a clinical designation, but it is worthy of some consideration: What tendencies do different thinkers have?

For Paul and Elder, the eight Intellectual Traits are Intellectual Courage, Intellectual Humility, Intellectual Integrity, Intellectual Empathy, Intellectual Autonomy, Intellectual Perseverance, Confidence in Reason, and Fairmindedness [18]. Each of these is integrated, like the Elements, but they also stand alone as language that identifies high-quality intellectual habits [19]. For drug development, it would matter if a thinker was aware of the limitations of their thinking in a discipline core to the process, like chemistry or finance (Intellectual Humility). It could make a huge difference for the project if major stakeholders are open to exploring new ideas (Intellectual Courage), if project managers are willing to stay true to important values in the project (Intellectual Perseverance), or if the standards used to assess one part of the project are identical to standards used in other parts of the project (Intellectual Integrity.) Many other examples are possible.

For critical thinking, the habits of any given thinker are a set of tendencies that are deployed, like the backhand at tennis, in a variety of situations. While Intellectual Traits may be a touchstone for good thinking habits, the fundamentals of critical thinking are based in rational, self-reflective, evidence-based analysis and assessment, all of which promotes the development of Intellectual Traits. Sometimes we need to think quickly and effectively, using the best evidence and skilled methods of arranging that evidence to address an immediate concern. Other times, we can go more slowly and check our thinking in self-reflection along the way. While this may seem obvious, avoidable mistakes occur when the wrong thinking approach is applied, whether in tennis or in thinking about our drug development process.

Working on critical thinking

There are implicit and explicit ways to develop critical thinking habits. Fig. 1.2's three boxes indicate that there is a relationship between each of the major areas of critical thinking — analysis, assessment, and intellectual habit formation. It demonstrates two important approaches, both of which can be something the thinker is trying to accomplish with their thinking (explicit) or something that is being accomplished by thinking that the thinker does not intend, which is a kind of secondary effect (implicit.) How can these mental structures be used for improving thinking?

Self-reflective work is the key here. The thinker can apply the Standards to the Elements explicitly, in order to judge the quality of those Elements. In doing this, the thinker may check the relevance of an assumption. If the motive of the thinker

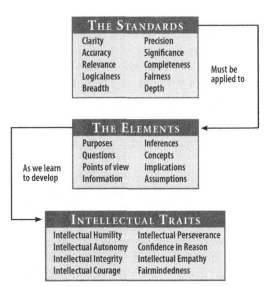

FIGURE 1.2 The Paul-Elder approach to critical thinking contains 3 primary areas, all of which are integrated. *Credit: R. Paul, L. Elder. The Miniature Guide to Critical Thinking Concepts and Tools, seventh ed., Rowman & Littlefield, 2008, p. 19.*

is to seek truth (rather than to sophistically present themselves as a person who checks their thinking in order to satisfy a weak-sense motive), the thinker is holding out the possibility that they could need to alter the relevance of some part of their thinking. Consequently, the thinker is also developing Intellectual Traits in some small ways, intentionally (explicitly) or not (implicitly). When I hold out the possibility that my assumption might be something other than perfect truth, I am applying Intellectual Integrity, in that I am holding myself and other thinkers to some attempt at an objective standard that is greater than my idiosyncratic view on the situation. I am being Intellectually Humble, to some extent, because I am seriously exploring the idea that I may be incorrect. I am being Intellectually Courageous, because I am seriously investigating the idea that I may be doing thinking that is misguided or otherwise flawed. I am being Intellectually Perseverant to the extent that I will follow through on this investigation of my potentially-irrelevant assumption until I am satisfied, for good reasons, that it should remain or should be replaced. My reliance upon criteria and those "good reasons" demonstrates my interest in Confidence in Reason.

Implicitly, how many times performing a repetitive thinking operation would be most useful? If this were advertising, we might appeal to the theory of *impressions*, that each time a consumer thinks about my product due to some subtle prompting, a win has occurred for making that person more comfortable with my product. We can go back to Elizabeth Holmes's public messaging to see examples of how this shows up in drug development rhetoric. Paul's and Elder's point of view is that each instance of examining my thinking with high-quality analysis and assessment tools will exercise some useful combination of Intellectual Traits for me, as well. Arguably, every well-executed backhand contains secondary and tertiary benefits. Why not intellectual exercise?

Explicit work can occur when a thinker looks at a definition of an Intellectual Trait, thinks it through, agrees that it merits further investigation for their thinking, and then begins efforts to emulate the thinking from that definition in their daily thinking habits. Again, like in any physical pursuit, high-quality, intentional practice at being a better thinker, a more careful thinker, a slower thinker, a deeper thinker, or a more considerate thinker can lead to significant gains in areas where thinkers benefit from improvement.

Much of drug development and discovery occurs due to the work of people who are already highly educated in fields that the society deems important and valuable. Many times, sophistic motives to maintain, to change, to signal, and to affect become embedded in the intellectual habits of the highly educated. When a person has studied their whole life to master some set of truths, only the most intellectually-humble and fairminded thinkers will avoid the pitfalls of weak-sense critical thinking or irrational thinking, common in sophistry. Habits will be developed over a lifetime of study and professional work: Good, bad, or ugly. Is the thinker habitually Intellectually Arrogant? Does Intellectual Narrowmindedness make this thinker difficult to work with on a team? What is our risk tolerance if our leader is Intellectually Cowardly? How can we achieve certainty in our process if we do not rely upon evidence and reasoning? What if we exclude others for Unfair reasons?

Biases and conclusion

Merely one instance of failing to take others into account, using one standard for the self and a different standard for others, choosing to go with the gut instead of the intellect, giving up in the face of non-rational opposition, or refusing to look into something that may be suggested by the evidence does not make someone a consistent sophist. The concern is that a pattern could develop that causes a person to make decisions without the best evidence or without a reasoning process. This person may not notice that they make decisions for anything other than the best reasons, since there are a variety of well-known ways to cognitively hide unpleasant facts about myself from myself, even implicitly. This is often called "rationalization." When it comes to the implications of decision-making for a drug development and discovery process, my inability to recognize the limitations of my own thinking could create problems for team dynamics, for stakeholder relations, for FDA interactions, or for a variety of other avoidable problems; if only a person would take the time to think about their thinking and look for hidden biases.

Paul's and Elder's work point to two implicit biases, egocentrism and sociocentrism. Each of these has implications for complex decision making. The egocentric biases are those that I give myself — I decide that something is in my selfish interest; I decide that my group should be supported; I decide that I should follow tradition; I decide that I should believe, even without any evidence: I want to believe it. The untested assumptions I carry through the world around me can cause me to distort reality [20]. Thinkers who fall prey to egocentric biases are assuming that they have figured the world out and that they have done so independently [21]. They decide what to believe, and they don't bow to the fiat of evidence.

A sociocentrically-biased thinker takes their truths from society, but they don't check any of society's pronouncements. The sociocentric thinker knows what is right, who is friendly or not, what is good and not, what is worth the time and not, all because various authorities, subtle and overt, have expressed opinions that the thinker assumed were true. This happens all the time, and its usefulness as a cultural artifact can be seen in the prevalence of speeches, advertising, and media that speak directly to the consumer. Mainly, the thinker is taught to agree without questioning, which leads to the thinker holding beliefs that cannot be justified internally, except through authority and tradition.

One of the dangers of believing egocentrically and sociocentrically is that evidence will not be valuable in this area of thinking when it comes time to deliberate, internally or with the group. The thinkers who cling to sociocentric and egocentric modes of knowing did not arrive at those beliefs through appeal to evidence and a rational process. They believed because they wanted to be part of a group, because they wanted to maintain a set of beliefs, because it seemed like it was in their best interests, or because the dominant group has always held such a belief. When group identity and other values are arrived at irrationally, they will not be dismissed through evidence-based debate. This creates a situation in which even the best thinkers might mistake their biases for their carefully-considered values, and with the result that they stand up for these values in ways that others cannot support in their personal evidence-based process. One result, then, is a mindset that chooses sides, and the dialectical struggle that it entails, without the benefit of agreed-upon standards and evidence.

The struggle to achieve certainty is a consistent struggle. How much evidence is enough? Should we only use rationality to make decisions? Is there any value to non-rational ways of knowing? What is the usefulness of traditional knowledge that does not appeal to evidence? The value of critical thinking for the drug development professional is to make fundamentals explicit, to remind that even the best thinking still might be flawed, and to support the idea that everyone can benefit from practice to become a better thinker.

References

[1] FDA Website.

[2] D. Sun, W. Gao, H. Hu, S. Zhou, Why 90% of clinical drug development fails and how to improve it? Acta Pharm. Sin. B (2022) https://doi.org/10.1016/j.apsb.2022.02.002.

[3] ibid., p. 2.

[4] ibid., p. 4.

[5] www.criticalthinking.org is the home website for this critical thinking theory.

[6] R. Paul, L. Elder, *Critical Thinking: Tools for Taking Charge of Your Learning and Your Life*, second ed., Rowman & Littlefield, 2020, p. 363.

[7] ibid., p. 409.

[8] ibid., p. 76.

[9] The critical thinking theory and practices of Richard Paul, Linda Elder, Gerald Nosich, and other proponents of their work are disseminated through The Foundation for Critical Thinking.

[10] ibid., p. 11.

[11] R. Paul, L. Elder, The Miniature Guide to Critical Thinking Concepts and Tools, eighth ed., Rowman & Littlefield, 2020, p. 14.

[12] FDA Drug Development Website. https://www.fda.gov/patients/learn-about-drug-and-device-approvals/drug-development-process.

[13] R. Paul, L. Elder, The Miniature Guide to Critical Thinking Concepts and Tools, eighth ed., Rowman & Littlefield, 2020, pp. 19−22.

[14] R. Paul, L. Elder, *Critical Thinking: Tools for Taking Charge of Your Learning and Your Life*, second ed., Rowman & Littlefield, 2020, p. 127.

[15] N. Klein, Addicted to Risk, TED Talk, 2010.

[16] R. Paul, L. Elder, *Critical Thinking: Tools for Taking Charge of Your Learning and Your Life*, second ed., Rowman & Littlefield, 2020, p. 24.

[17] ibid., p. 25.

[18] R. Paul, L. Elder, The Miniature Guide to Critical Thinking Concepts and Tools, eighth ed., Rowman & Littlefield, 2020, pp. 23−27.

[19] R. Paul, L. Elder, *Critical Thinking: Tools for Taking Charge of Your Learning and Your Life*, second ed., Rowman & Littlefield, 2020, pp. 22−23.

[20] R. Paul, L. Elder, The Miniature Guide to Critical Thinking Concepts and Tools, eighth ed., Rowman & Littlefield, 2020, p. 38.

[21] ibid., p. 39.

Chapter 2

Leveraging ADME/PK information to enable knowledge-driven decisions in drug discovery and development

Larry C. Wienkers

Wienkers Consulting, LLC, Bainbridge Island, WA, United States

Introduction

Modern drug development is an expensive, arduous journey that is punctuated with colossal risk of failure. However, the journey is a worthwhile endeavor as the successful execution of a drug development program can yield a novel or positively differentiated drug which has the potential to alleviate suffering for grieving patients and enhance quality of life and longevity for thousands of people; both endpoints are certainly worthwhile ambitions by any measure. As the discovery of a new pharmaceutical is so difficult, costly, and risky, application of the highest order of decision-making is crucial for company success [1]. The risk associated with drug development is underscored by three primary factors: an insidiously high attrition rate as molecules transition through the various stages of drug discovery/development continuum; the protracted length of time associated with typical development programs set within an evolving hyper-competitive landscape of which the company has little control; and the inordinate cost required to successfully usher an innovative therapeutic agent from discovery to the market. Therefore, it stands to reason that any BioPharma company that could minimize drug attrition, reduce clinical development timelines, and decrease overall R&D costs would be handsomely rewarded. Obviously, this sentiment isn't original and is embraced by all BioPharma companies agnostic of size and, as a consequence, in addition to searching for novel biological targets and molecules that possess the potential to interdict disease states, companies are also continuously seeking means to improve efficiency by examining mechanisms which might refine their capability to facilitate timely and robust decision-making across the multiple milestones which comprise the drug discovery/development continuum.

While this notion of increasing efficiency in making decisions sounds relatively straight forward for the layperson, decisions made within a BioPharma research and development environment are confounded as most decisions typically must be made under conditions where there is: missing or insufficient data, information that reflects a relatively high degree of uncertainty, institutional dogma/group think and aggressive time constraints which preclude the gathering of additional data; all of which is underscored by the ambiguities associated with human biology. In addition to these uncertainty factors associated with decision-making, the situation is further exasperated by external pressures beyond science which include the economic status of the company and shareholder expectations as well as the overall competitive environment in which there can be several BioPharma companies simultaneously working on the same pharmacological target all sharing the common aspiration of being first to market with their drug candidate.

The intent of this book: "Overcoming Obstacles in Drug Discovery and Development: Surmounting the Insurmountable" is an effort to highlight programmatic decision-making across various stages of drug development as it exists within the boundaries of scientific and business strategies. In this context, the challenge calls for leaders who represent multiple disciplinary functions to review a collection of in-depth scientific information and decide the programmatic fate of a drug candidate within a Go/No Go framework. The fidelity of the decision is based on the aggregation across scientific disciplines and the agreed upon path forward is subject to adaptation or reversal considering dynamic new safety or efficacy findings or changes in the commercial landscape.

Overcoming Obstacles in Drug Discovery and Development. https://doi.org/10.1016/B978-0-12-817134-9.00021-0

This chapter attempts to highlight (albeit hardly comprehensive) some of the important features associated with various decision points and the scientific evidence required for making decisions at various milestones across the drug development continuum. The overarching notion of decision-making in this context is predicated upon the continued awareness and willingness to incorporate knowledge gleaned from the earlier parts of development and aggregate this existing information with new evolving data to help underwrite decisions at later stages. This activity is carried out in a time constrained environment where companies are seeking to reduce development times and aggressively introduce new drugs to help prevent, alleviate and cure diseases which negatively impact the human condition today.

Decision-making stages across the drug discovery/development continuum

As stated earlier, drug development is a high risk, expensive and time-consuming endeavor which does not guarantee a novel therapeutic agent becoming approved or commercially successful for the treatment of a particular disease. Briefly, the drug discovery/development continuum is a multistep process which aims at identifying a novel molecule that may be therapeutically useful in curing and/or treating a particular disease (Fig. 2.1). At a high-level the process begins in the discovery phase which can simplistically be described as the identification of a plausible pharmacological strategy through a novel or established target. This is followed by a search for a potential molecular entity which possesses the structural characteristics to engage the target; which then undergoes an optimization phase of chemical material which can bind the target and also possess the physicochemical features consistent with drug-like features to yield a cadre of chemically unique lead compounds. The newly identified series of compounds are then subject to a series of extensive in vitro and in vivo profiling and screening for safety and therapeutic efficacy. Once a compound has successfully traversed the gauntlet of rigorous preclinical investigations, the drug candidate, if nominated, will enter the process of drug development. The aggregation of all information will be submitted to regulatory agencies in the form of an investigational new drug application (IND), in the case of FDA submissions, and upon approval the initiation of clinical trials. The process of clinical drug development is ultimately aimed at ensuring that the new medicine is viewed as safe, effective, and has met all regulatory expectations required for approval. This process typically proceeds through three stages:

- Phase I studies are carried out where the primary focus is to evaluate pharmacokinetic parameters and tolerance of the new therapeutic, which is generally preformed in healthy volunteers (except in oncology). These studies typically are comprised of initial single-dose studies, dose escalation and short-term repeated-dose studies.
- Phase II clinical studies are limited scale trials to investigate the efficacy and side-effect profile of the new agent usually conducted in 100−250 target patients. During these studies, additional clinical pharmacology and safety studies may also be included at this stage.
- Phase III clinical studies are large scale clinical trials aimed to ensure safety and efficacy of the new drug across a large and diverse patient population. At some point over the course of phase III trials efforts are initiated to prepare regulatory submission documents, depending upon the therapeutic modality as either the Biologics License Application (BLA) or the New Drug Application (NDA).

From the scenario depicted in Fig. 2.1, it is clear that the first critical step in developing a new therapeutic agent is the identification and validation of a drug target [2]. Anything less than a robust understanding of the target undermines its usefulness as a decision-making tool in drug discovery as this information serves as the foundation in the search of a drug

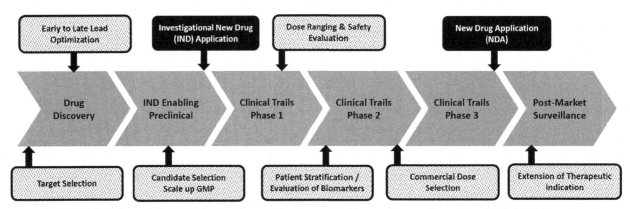

FIGURE 2.1 A linear depiction of the drug discovery/development continuum with a small sampling of critical decision points.

candidate which may someday become clinically useful therapeutic agent in treating patients suffering from grievous illnesses. The term drug target (or target biology) is an umbrella term which can be applied to a broad range of pathophysiological entities with a strong association to a particular disease or condition [3]. The genesis for nomination of a particular target can arise from a variety of avenues which include published academic scientific literature, internally driven investigations into genetic variants linked to disease and from external (competitor) reports [4,5]. Independent of disease area, there exists a simple base case criteria regarding what attributes a good drug target should possess; these include: a reasonable line of sight between anticipated efficacy and predicted toxicity, the proposed target must meet the definition of an unmet clinical need, is aligned with corporate mission and commercial needs, and most importantly is deemed "druggable". For the purposes of this chapter, a druggable target is a defined biological relevant entity which is accessible to a drug molecule, which upon engaging with the target elicits a biological response that is able to be measured in an in vitro and in vivo environment [6]. The process of discovering and validating a novel druggable target is challenging as lack of efficacy is one of the primary reasons for the failure of drug candidates in clinic development [7]. In this instance, failure reflects a circumstance where a promising new mechanism of disease treatment falls short in demonstrating the anticipated impact upon pharmacology surrounding the projects working hypothesis or lack of a link between pharmacology and actual efficacy (i.e., the novel therapeutic binds to the target which subsequently modulates the disease in predicted fashion within a predefined patient population). Interestingly, even with targets which possess a strong genetic link to human disease and has a mechanism supported by a relatively robust understanding of the target biology, success is not guaranteed. In this situation, while the target appeared to be validated, the choice of molecular entity to engage the target may represent the root cause for program failure. For example, inhibition of cholesteryl ester transfer protein (CETP) was considered to represent a most direct means toward raising HDL as a mechanism to prevent HDL from being "diverted" into other lipoprotein forms [8]. Unfortunately, the development of CETP inhibitors represented a black hole of drug development where four large phase III clinical outcome trials (i.e., torcetrapib, dalcetrapib, evacetrapib and anacetrapib) failed either because of safety or lack of a robust efficacy signal [9]. The failure of these programs serves as a harsh reminder that the conduct of drug research is a risky business and late-stage failure has severe financial consequences for Biopharma companies that allocated marked portions of their research budgets toward them [10].

Today, many BioPharma companies, as a means to increase the probability of programmatic success, in addition to generating deep understandings of the target's biological pathways and association to human disease, are expanding their repertoire of possible drug candidates to include novel molecules designed to interact with a specific target which encompass a chemical space far beyond traditional small/chemicals [11]. Therefore, some BioPharma companies which possess the luxury of having the choice of multiple molecular options are subject to addressing the next critical decision; namely, the selection of the most appropriate molecular modality which possesses the characteristics to gain access to and interact with a specific target [12,13]. A quick survey of potential molecular modalities to interact with new targets includes antibodies, antibody-drug conjugates, fusion proteins, peptides, interfering RNA, vaccines, CAR-Ts, etc., all of which currently represent marketed drugs (Fig. 2.2). While the various new biological modalities have some inherent limitations and complexities due to their increased size, these modalities have demonstrated success in treating a wide variety of diseases and disorders [14,15]. Moreover, many of these new modalities exhibit high specificity, low toxicity, and in many cases possess greater efficacy than small-molecule drugs interacting with the same target [16]. Clearly, the treatment of human disease will continue to be dominated by small molecule drugs due to their small size and physiochemical properties which allow them to target extracellular proteins or intracellular receptors in the cytosol, nuclei, and central nervous system [17]. Today, Biopharma companies are focusing on the research and development of next-generation biologics with enhanced characteristics and improved pharmaceutical properties. In fact, next to small molecule drugs, antibody drugs represent a meaningful fraction of the therapeutic landscape today [18]. Again, the success of antibody drugs is reflected in their unique properties, in particular the antibody's exquisite high specificity and selectivity toward a unique target which consequently allows these molecules to be typically devoid of off-target liabilities often observed with small molecules. This reshuffling of potential modalities to treat human disease is reflected in the makeup of recent drug approvals where, of the 55 NMEs approved in 2020 by the Center for Drug Evaluation and Research (CDER) at FDA, 37 medicines were small molecules while the remaining 18 molecules were classified as biologics and [19].

Another decision point early in a program's lifecycle is to determine where the molecule will originate from. Traditionally, identification of chemical substrate within the pharmaceutical industry has primarily been viewed as an in-house activity. However, despite the major advances in the scientific and technological contributions toward facilitating the art of drug discovery research the industry has been plagued with year over year decline in R&D efficiency [20]. To remedy the situation, companies have begun to supplement their internal drug hunting efforts to fill their program pipelines through a variety of creative in-licensing mechanisms. This strategy has led to a renaissance of the BioPharma ecosystem where internal company drug discovery activities are balanced with a robust effort toward leveraging external opportunities to fill

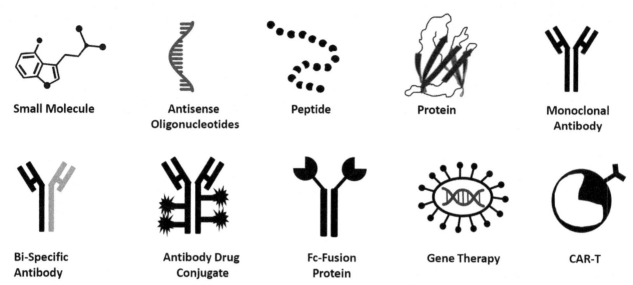

FIGURE 2.2 Short list of existing and emerging drug modalities being applied by the BioPharma industry for targeted therapies.

their respective pipelines (Fig. 2.3). There are two principal drivers that seem to determine the relative appetite regarding how a particular company approaches their external innovation strategy: (1) the company's willingness to embrace risks and (2) the company's overall approach to intellectual property. That said, currently leveraging external opportunities does not appear to represent a significant hurdle for most companies; as in 2018 forty-eight percent of the drugs approved originated from smaller sized BioPharma companies either as licensing deals or direct purchase of the asset [21].

As mentioned at the beginning of this section, independent of molecular modality, successful drugs will be those that satisfy expectations and demonstrate value to a variety of different stakeholders (i.e., regulatory agencies, investors, prescribing physicians and patients). Therefore, the journey from idea to marketed product is comprised of a multitude of milestones representing decision-making opportunities, each underscored with the goal of minimizing failure and maximizing the value of the current asset [22,23]. Typically, as the asset transitions from discovery to clinical development companies are highly focused upon factors that can provide insights toward the mitigation of three implicit risks associated with drug development: (a) failure to gain regulatory approval as the inherit risks of the compound do not to outweigh its therapeutic benefit; (b) stagnation and ultimately discontinuation of a Phase 3 program due to lack of meaningful efficacy; and (c) failure to capture market share after launch due to a lack of differentiation from existing therapies in the same disease area. In a particularly crowded (aka, competitive) therapeutic area, besides durable efficacy, superior safety is a critical differentiation criterion that may be achieved through improved risk/benefit profiles, wider safety margins, fewer contraindications (e.g., drug—drug interactions), and improved patient compliance.

The importance of data in decision-making

Independent of the type of industry we examine, it is safe to say that decision-making is a core activity for every company, as without making decisions (good and timely decisions that is), it is difficult to imagine any company staying

FIGURE 2.3 Depiction of the delicate balance between internal drug discovery efforts and external opportunities.

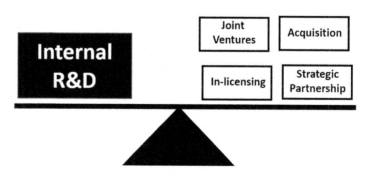

business. No doubt this idea is amplified in the BioPharma industry where companies place significant emphasis toward applying cutting edge science and innovative technologies to generate high value data in support of decision-making opportunities across all aspects of the drug discovery development continuum. To this end, the scientific information used by leadership teams tasked with making decisions must be of the highest possible quality and the team needs to possess an awareness of any possible unconscious biases present to avoid advocating decisions made upon "gut feelings" over scientific first principals [24]. The consequences of promoting decisions based upon unrealistic advocacy or conviction toward advancing a molecule in development in the face of contradictory or ambiguous scientific data typically triggers the freeing up of additional resources which ultimately results in large sums of money spent unnecessarily and, worse yet, a tremendous amount of time is wasted. Indeed, it is easy for undisciplined decision makers to weight one piece of data over all others because it reinforces a conclusion that they had reached *a priori* [25]. Agnostic of company size, programs are destined to fail or minimally be markedly derailed if they do not adhere to fundamental guidelines for decision-making toward program advancement. Restated, decisions must be guided by facts supported by quality data and robust science, coupled with considerable dissent and debate occurring at appropriate time intervals [26]. Factors which undoubtably influence a company's ability to make a reasonable decision are as suggested above: the quality of the information underwriting the decision; the financial impact in enabling the collation of meaningful data; and the time required to curate the appropriate information. This conundrum is to some extent reminiscent of a ternary plot or de Finetti diagram used in undergraduate Physical Chemistry class, which graphically depicts the ratios of the three variables as positions in an equilateral triangle. In a de Finetti diagram, the values of the three variables a, b, and c must sum to some constant, K, and because $a + b + c = K$, no one variable is independent of the other. In the case of decision-making within a BioPharma company, K is essentially the decision, and the three variables are Quality of data; Cost of generating the data; and the Time required to collect the data (Fig. 2.4).

In physical chemistry applications, the advantage of using a de Finetti diagram is that three variables are plotted in a two-dimensional graph. These plots can be applied to create phase diagrams by outlining the composition regions on the plot where different phases may exist but just as importantly defines boundary conditions where the phase cannot exist. In a similar fashion, there are boundary conditions for information to be used for decision-making in a BioPharma environment; however, unlike in a physical chemistry setting, the cross-functional nature of drug programs requires decision-making process to be much more nuanced and hyper-vigilant against bias. Consequently, decision-making across BioPharma companies demands intense interdepartmental cooperation and strict adherence to existing facts. Indeed, without facts, statements regarding advocacy toward program progression is basically relying upon an opinion, fueled by a preexisting perception and may not actually be completely tethered to the reality of the current situation.

Beyond failure due to poor decision-making, programs can also stumble due to the careless conduct of science, usually a consequence of failing to conduct the proper experimental controls and through characterization of comparator molecules, which typically leads to chasing popular findings that are, in reality, false positives for protracted periods. Under these conditions, it's easy and often popular for senior management to unwittingly keep technically flawed drug programs in play [27]. Restated, programs like these are built upon a weak scientific foundation fueled by a weight of evidence approach and have never meaningfully tested the hypothesis through the conduct of what some may call the essential "killer" experiments. As one senior R&D leader exclaimed during a program review "this data is far from being a smoking gun and actually looks more like smoke and mirrors". There is no doubt that killer experiments are critical in supporting early "Go/No Go" decisions in drug development in that they allow organizations to control the extent of

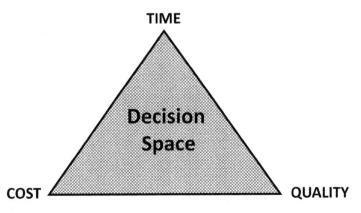

FIGURE 2.4 Representation of a theoretical de Finetti diagram depicting the three variables impacting decision-making (time required to collect the data, cost of generating the data and quality of data generated).

additional investment made toward a particular lead candidate or progression of a program to the next phase of clinical development [28].

In addition to the scientific merits associated with each piece of information that is applied toward making a good decision, there needs to exist a commitment toward aligning the decisions with corporate goals and mission. As mentioned previously, decisions in drug development typically involve multiple stakeholders which under some circumstances may have conflicting objectives. While this statement at first blush appears to be inconsistent, as everyone involved in the decision-making process works for the same company and hence must share common goals. However, upon further scrutiny we can quickly recognize that many times corporate goals may only represent a fraction of the totality goals influencing a particular stakeholder tasked with making decisions and sometimes departmental goals may carry equal weighting as corporate goals in terms of end of year financial considerations [29]. Failing to achieve proper alignment of interests for all stakeholders involved in decision-making through misguided benchmarks of success can introduce an increased complexity in the decision-making environment and more importantly may precipitate untoward consequences for the long-term success of the company.

One mechanism to safeguard against personal biasness and misaligned incentives which may run counter to the best interests of the company and allow for information transparency which aligns with a company's predefined decision criteria and priorities may be achieved by partnering decision-making with artificial intelligence (AI). The application of AI to enhance the fidelity of information being gathered is currently being evaluated with respect to assisting in decision-making across the BioPharma industry [30]. Application of this assistive technology is primarily driven by AIs ability to collect and quickly process large volumes of data through algorithms which can be accessed by scientists to supplement their technical expertize and judgment in support of decision-making at different milestones [31]. This is a natural expansion of domain-specific machine learning approaches which has been successfully applied in molecule design in a drug discovery setting [32]. Obviously, not every research question can be answered utilizing AI, particularly if there is limited or poor-quality data as it could lead to a systematic bias. That said, in many instances this technology should be useful to help extract scientific insights and mitigate institutional biases in the selection of drug candidates with a higher probability of success [33].

Restated, in drug development it is essential to be patient and collect the necessary information that will support an informed, unbiased fact-based decision. The right data at decision stage gates will prevent unsupported data or incorrect information from becoming irreversibly "baked" into a program's narrative and thus build confidence toward clinical conviction for the program. To this end, a balance between focusing on experiments that challenge the hypothesis is required instead of solely conducting experiments that just provide additional weight of evidence support for the working hypothesis. Moreover, decisions must be aligned with the company's business plan and reflect the fundamentals of the firm's stated mission. Thus, there is an obligation on the part of all contributors involved in making decisions that they remain self-aware and vigilant in their efforts to provide a fair appraisal and interpretation of all data throughout every step of drug development, as the fate of the organization's future success is riding upon those decisions.

Product differentiation: first in class versus best in class

For any BioPharma company, charting the course as to where to take their R&D pipeline is a critical and incredibly difficult decision. The first step in this decision-making journey is centered around an existential question as it divides the R&D programmatic mindset into one of two categorical ambitions; namely, do we aspire for our molecule to be first-in-class? The FDA defines a first-in-class drug as one that uses a novel and unique mechanism of action to treat a medical condition; therefore, they are innovative, cutting-edge, and have the potential to produce unprecedented patient outcomes [34]. The company that achieves first-in-class drug status usually gains an advantage in that the drug's brand name becomes synonymous with a new therapeutic class of drugs and is able to secure total market share because of the absence of competitive alternatives [35]. Obviously, a molecule deemed as a first-in-class drug represents tremendous value to patients, particularly if there are no existing therapies for the disease the molecule is intended to treat [36,37]. The attractiveness of first-in-class drugs is that regulatory expectations are bounded in that clinical superiority in efficacy and safety over placebo are the primary requirements for approval and may be able to secure FDA 'priority' designation that can expedite the trial and review process [38,39].

While the follow-on drugs have a high hurdle for approval and commercial success, there are some possible upsides for being second in that the pathway to approval may be more straight forward as the company can in some cases leverage lessons learned from predecessors' development experience. These learnings may also be a reasonable strategy to develop a best-in-class drug by improving upon some of the less desirable attributes of the first to market drug [40]. To this end, decisions made within the framework of drug discovery and development are anchored toward two critical drivers: will the new drug become a first-in-class therapy or can the follow-on molecule exploit the predecessor liabilities and become differentiated compared to the existing therapy. That said, medicines described as follow-on drugs have the burden of competing head-to-head with the first-in-class therapy to achieve approval and must launch into a competitive environment and capture market share. Therefore, in this efficacy centric environment, BioPharma companies must continuously examine their programmatic portfolio with a keen eye toward addressing two questions as part of their decision-making process:

- Does our current program have a realistic chance of achieving first in class status? If first to market, does the molecule possess sufficient therapeutic value to warrant standard of care status?
- If we can't be first, can we rapidly follow on (within X years) with a molecule which possesses characteristics that ensure that it will to be equal to or better than the first-in-class entrant with respect to having therapeutic superiority?

In addition to matching efficacy, there is a second avenue where a follow-on drug can achieve best-in-class status through the reduction of treatment costs and patient burden while maintaining the same therapeutic efficacy/safety. There are a variety of situations which can be envisioned for a new drug to demonstrate a therapeutic advantage over a first-in-class drug and ultimately become viewed as the new gold standard for a particular therapy. Obviously, improved efficacy when compared to a first-in-class is important; however, a best-in-class drug strategy must, besides demonstrating therapeutic superiority, must also demonstrate equal or better safety profiles or enhanced quality of life for patients to be considered the first choice of treatment. Perhaps the poster child of a late entrant achieving best-in-class status is seen with atorvastatin. Although atorvastatin was the fifth statin to obtain marketing approval (trailing lovastatin, the first statin, by more than 9 years), it went on to capture nearly double the combined peak annual sales of other drugs in the statin class, reaching sales at its apex (before patent expiration) of US$13 billion [41]. Other examples of follow-on drugs that secured best-in-class status through therapeutic advantage over its existing competitors include dulaglutide (vs. exenatide) and nab-paclitaxel (vs. docetaxel).

Additional strategies, which can be applied toward capitalizing upon the liabilities to provide a meaningful level of differentiation from of existing therapies beyond creating a drug which is more effective and selective, may be centered around finding a means to reduce dose or frequency of dosing which ultimately leads to improved patient adherence to the treatment regimen and subsequent better outcomes. One such example of product differentiation is seen with the anti-coagulant drug Xarelto developed by Bayer. Despite being second-to-market with a nominal increase effectiveness, Xarelto quickly captured market share over Pradaxa, Boehringer Ingelheim's first-to-market drug. The principal driver for this rapid market replacement primarily centered around the fact that Xarelto offered once-a-day dosing regimen compared with twice-daily dosing for Pradaxa [42]. Additional examples of molecules which surpassed first-in-class molecules based upon increased compliance include doxycycline (vs. oxytetracycline), azithromycin (vs. erythromycin), diltiazem (vs. verapamil) (non-dihydropyridines calcium channel blockers), and adalimumab (vs. infliximab).

Other strategies used to exploit meaningful product differentiation is with a molecule which offers an improved safety profile with similar efficacy to the first-in-class drug. The improvement in safety could come from fewer types of side effects, a lower rate of side effects, or a lower risk of overdose or other treatment complications. Some examples follow-on molecules which became standard-of-care compounds applying this strategy include lisinopril (vs. captopril), rasagiline (vs. selegiline), and tacrolimus (vs. ciclosporin). Therefore, while the notion of product differentiation achieved through efficacy or convenience are commonplace themes in decision-making, drug safety needs to be equally weighted as important with respect to key aspects of product differentiation criterion. Avenues to exploit drug safety may be accomplished through aspects such as expanded safety margins, improved risk/benefit profiles, a reduction in contrain-dications, all of which will ultimately lead to greater patient compliance.

Underwriting drug safety begins with a thorough understanding of the molecular pathways of the disease and the relevance of the pharmacological target as it relates to human pathophysiology and safety. Most programs start with a therapeutic window between target affinity and off target binding of several orders of magnitude. Unfortunately, as graphically detailed in Fig. 2.5, the therapeutic window or index will usually tend to shrink as the program progresses and higher resolution information is generated.

In managing decisions around a molecule's therapeutic index as it relates to safety and tolerability, discussions typically will migrate toward the anticipated patient variability in drug disposition. The degree of interpatient variability manifests itself in the clinic where some patients experience sub-therapeutic exposures of the drug while others may encounter higher "toxic" blood concentrations. A significant source of clinical variability in drug exposure is due to the drug metabolism pathways associated with the drug clearance [43].

Interindividual differences in drug biotransformation as it relates to drug exposure has been a source of scientific inquiry for several decades [44]. Today, it is fully appreciated that interpatient variability in drug exposure is highly

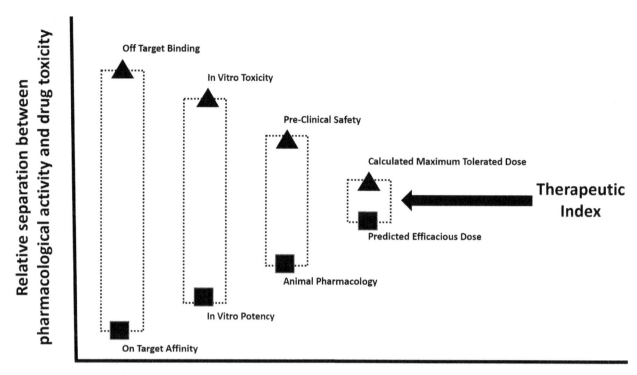

Progression through drug discovery/development continuum

FIGURE 2.5 The diminishing separation between safety and efficacy data generated across the drug development continuum.

influenced by factors such as genetics, age, disease states, diet/lifestyle and drug–drug interactions (Fig. 2.6). It is well understood for drug-metabolizing enzymes that genetic variation can result in the complete absence or enhanced expression of a functional enzyme for example, CYP2D6 and UGT1A1 [45,46]. Factors less understood are associated with upregulation and/or downregulation of gene expression, in response to a particular disease state, which can result in altered metabolic function in a less predictable fashion. Understanding the mechanistic basis for variability in drug disposition and how this impacts drug exposure is essential if we are to move beyond the era of empirical, trial-and-error dose selection and into an age of personalized medicine that will improve outcomes in maintaining health and treating disease [47,48].

A second feature which can support a safety-based differentiation strategy is around possible drug–drug interactions associated with the first-in-class molecules. A drug interaction is defined either as increase or decrease in the therapeutic effect of a specific drug caused by another drug co-administered with the first. Simplistically, the mechanisms of most drug interactions can be divided into two categories: (a) pharmacodynamic interactions, where the pharmacologic efficacy of the first drug is altered by the second, although the drug plasma levels remain unchanged and (b) pharmacokinetic interactions, in which presence of the second drug leads to an increase or reduction in plasma levels

FIGURE 2.6 Intra and inter-individual factors affecting cytochrome P450 mediated drug metabolism.

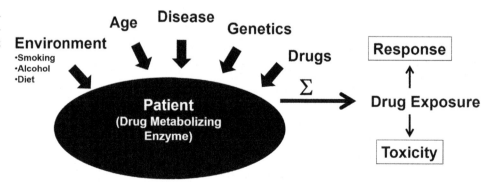

of the first drug. For pharmacokinetic drug—drug interactions, typically one drug affects the metabolic pathway of the other concomitantly administered drug [49,50]. As one might predict, the possibilities of drug interactions increase as the number of drugs being taken by the patient increases. Therefore, patients taking several drugs simultaneously are at the greatest risk for interactions [51]. Therefore, patients with multiple comorbidities are subject to major problems involving drug toxicity due to being prescribed multiple medications in the treatment of multiple diseases. Drug—drug interactions (DDIs) are common; in fact, DDIs and the associated Adverse Drug Reactions (ADRs) represent a marked detriment to public health across the world [52—54].

Despite their prevalence, clinically significant DDIs can be preventable, as long as healthcare providers possess an understanding of the mechanisms of the DDI and have potential alternative therapies to avoid the interaction. Therefore, the impact of product differentiation based upon DDI liability and alternative drug choices is a point of differentiation and is highlighted with the evolution of the H2-antagonists, widely prescribed for the treatment of GERD also known as 'heartburn'. In 1979, the first-in-class H2-antagonist, cimetidine, was approved by the FDA, and despite clinical reports of clinically significant DDIs was the first drug to hit $1 billion in annual sales in 1986. The second H2-antagonist introduced to the market was ranitidine. It was approved by the FDA in 1983 and in just 5 years it had eclipsed cimetidine in sales by becoming the world's best-selling drug largely based upon the fact that it was relatively devoid of serous DDIs. The major differences between cimetidine and ranitidine regarding observed DDIs was that binding affinity toward cytochrome P450 enzymes for ranitidine is about 10 times lower than cimetidine and the daily ranitidine dose was about a quarter of the dose of cimetidine [55].

Clearly there are many instances where follow-on drugs proved to become important medicines in treating a variety of human ailments; however, there are no guarantees that a best-in-class program will produce a drug that is superior to its competitors in a crowded market. For a company to be in a position to exploit the liability of a competitor's molecule, there needs to exist an intellectual framework from which a Go/No Go decision can be derived. This framework will be comprised of various attributes (i.e., modality, efficacy, safety, dose etc.) that the proposed molecule must minimally possess to warrant additional company investment to advance to the next stage of drug development.

Developing and using a target product profile in decision-making

Given the factors discussed above, starting a drug development program with what the end-product should look like is an important first step in creating a strategic decision-making framework for a drug development program and should include details describing what product attributes a successful marketed drug should possess. This will often be comprised of features such as the target indication, patient population(s), therapeutic efficacy and clinical safety, formulations, dosing regimens and administration, drug—drug interactions and contraindications or precautions, among others. An essential feature of this criteria will be a realistic assessment of what the factors are "need to have" versus "nice to have" as this sets the boundary conditions for internal trade-offs. For example, does the drug have pharmacokinetic characteristics that support once-a-day dosing, but the current market will accommodate a twice a day regimen? Implicit in this decision-making framework is the recognition that this molecular criterion is not static and thus to safeguard that a program stays on course, the original rules must be pressure tested with new information from ongoing clinical trials, mechanistic insights gained from nonclinical studies and changes in global regulatory expectations. In other words, it is imperative that decision-making teams have ongoing trade-off discussions which considers all data available at that moment and look to challenge initial assumptions.

Toward the beginning of a drug discovery program, it is easy for BioPharma researchers become highly fixated on the interaction (aka binding affinity) between drug molecules and the target associated with the disease that they may sometimes neglect to examine additional features critically important for the final product. In this instance, developing a Target Product Profile (TPP) for the program is a straightforward mechanism which keeps research teams focused through a collection of programmatic expectations designed to enable the design of all future program activities, such as nonclinical and clinical studies, to ensure that the information required to assess whether the drug has the desired attributes for continued development.

When utilized properly, the TPP becomes a dynamic, living document that ensures all company stakeholders (e.g., research, clinical, regulatory, manufacturing, and commercial) are measuring success from the same agreed upon document. For some companies, the TPP is viewed negatively as they believe such a document is too rigid for the ever-evolving drug development environment. This sentiment may ring true but rather than be too rigid, it may actually be a consequence of a breakdown in incorporating input from all sources or a failure in the past to maintain a more dynamic TPP. Therefore, to be effective, the TPP must be continually updated and revised based on the accumulation of new internal information and changes to the competitive landscape. When companies take a balanced active approach in maintaining their TPP, one that reflects the dynamic nature of drug research and is flexible enough to allow them to adapt it as needed, they introduce structure into drug development program which ultimately facilitates robust Go/No-Go decisions in the future. At first blush it seems like an onerous task to define critical features associated with a novel molecule targeting an unmet medical need 5–10 years from now. Here, the key is to avoid building in rigidity into the development program that does not allow a minor alteration without derailing the entire program every time the landscape changes. Under these circumstances, active monitoring of the competitive landscape allows the team to make real-time adjustments to the TPP and minor modifications to the development program as needed.

Common features found in a TPP document reflect information that is typically found in a package insert. Using the framework of the product insert is useful as it contains all the information necessary for a prescribing physician to effectively prescribe the therapeutic. To this end, thorough knowledge of patient needs, competition and differentiating factors are essential to a credible TPP, as inclusion in the early stages of the decision-making process ensures that the final product reflects the organizations expectations surrounding the investment. Typically, a drug label provides a brief summary of the information that health care practitioners, patients and payers most commonly need to know. In designing the label, the most important information for prescribing a drug safely and effectively is logically organized to facilitate accessibility and retention through the use of various textual and graphic elements (e.g., tables, bulleted lists, boldface, italics). Some of the features commonly associated with drug labels that may be useful in constructing a TPP include:

- Indications and Usage. Listed are the indications for use of a drug, the major limitations to use, the pharmacologic class, and the mechanism of action.
- Dosage and administration. The recommended dosage regimen for the given indications is provided, along with the starting dosage, dosage range, whether the drug should be taken with or without food, critical differences among population subsets, monitoring recommendations, and significant clinical pharmacologic information.
- Contraindications. A listing of circumstances when the drug should be avoided.
- Drug Interactions. The drug interactions are briefly described, for both the drug being a victim or perpetrator.
- Use in Specific Populations. A summary of important information about use in specific populations.

In a nutshell, the TPP provides an interactive roadmap of development in the early stages of drug development. It usually starts at a high level with a description of the characteristics that an 'ideal' drug candidate would possess including what data exists or is needed to support product differentiation and questions whether these features are sufficient to support premium pricing? As stated earlier, the TPP is a living document and changes are necessary to the TPP over the course of drug development as new information emerges during the development program. Considering the dynamic nature of drug development, the TPP besides reflecting the aspirational virtues of the final product, is also a useful tool to evaluate whether these desired characteristics are nice to have or need to have. Depending upon therapeutic area and existing competition, the assessment of the TPP provides the organizational conviction to continue drug development or refocus efforts in earlier discovery to "hunt" for a new potential candidate. Restated, if used properly, the TPP represents a seminal document which supports in the entire drug discovery and development process. The document: (a) facilitates the effective optimization of drug characteristics in the lead candidates; (b) provides for a decision-making framework within the organization, (c) allows for the design of clinical research strategies; and (d) creates a source document.

Finally, it's critical to define the optimal product profile with the end user and market(s) in mind, as this will facilitate strategic decisions that will support programmatic success. Developing a new drug and getting it approved in today's competitive environment is a costly and high-risk enterprise. But developing and using a TPP while proactively updating it can improve the odds of success by facilitating strategic decision-making.

Why drugs fail and the evolution of ADME/PK in drug discovery

For all intent and purposes, there are two reasons drugs fail in development: either the drug is unsafe or doesn't work or at least doesn't provide a suitable risk benefit profile to warrant approval [56]. The root cause for failure due to efficacy can be attributed to a variety of reasons including the pathophysiological basis surrounding the disease (i.e., positive impact of molecular intervention is more straight forward for some diseases than for others). For some therapeutic areas, it is difficult to meaningfully measure the size of the drug effect; this is further exasperated in some instances by the inability to recruit suitable patients in some diseases. In aggregate, these conditions confound developing a robust risk/benefit profile for select diseases when the existing standard of care is effective and thus a new drug brings an iterative improvement where the hurdle is high compared to life-threatening diseases with no standard of care where risk tolerance concerns are less weighted [57]. This notion is borne out where a recent examination of clinical trial data from the period of 2010–2017 revealed that basically four core reasons explained nearly 90% of observed clinical failures of drugs in development. The primary reason for failure was insufficient clinical efficacy (40%–50%), followed by unmanageable toxicity (30%), poor drug-like properties accounted for (10%–15%), and finally about 10% of drug failed due to commercial reasons [7,58].

In addition to the two critical themes described above, there are other factors previously touched upon which serve to underwrite the successful navigation of a drug in development. In particular, the disposition and pharmacokinetics of the drug and the concentration of the molecule at the site of action are seminal underpinnings to drug efficacy [59]. Therefore, understanding the disposition features of a new drug is critical to select the appropriate patient population, optimum dose and associated dosing frequency [60,61]. In this light, decisions regarding moving a novel molecule through the various stages of drug development represents a thoughtful balance between drug efficacy and toxicity and the ultimate clinical dose to deliver the appropriate benefit/risk ratio for patients (Fig. 2.7).

Therefore, a critical activity of DMPKs (Drug Metabolism and Pharmacokinetics) departments within the drug development process is carrying out a wide range of experiments, often referred to as ADMET (Absorption, Distribution, Metabolism, Elimination, Toxicity) studies, as early as possible in drug discovery [62–64]. The aim of these studies is to help underwrite the viability of a drug candidate by addressing these key questions:

- Absorption—How much of the dosed drug is absorbed and how long does it take to gain systemic exposure?
- Distribution—Where is the drug distributed within the body? What factors influence the extent of the drug distribution?
- Metabolism—How quickly is the drug metabolized? What are the principal enzymes associated with metabolism? What is the identity of metabolite formed and does the metabolite possess activity or is it toxic?
- Elimination—How is the drug excreted and how quickly? Are there transporters which facilitate drug excretion?
- Toxicity—Does the drug have a toxic effect on the body or to specific organs? What is the separation between drug concentrations which result in toxicity compared to the concentrations to elicit the desired pharmacologic effect?

It is interesting to place the role of using ADMET information into the greater historical context of decision-making in drug discovery as it is related to drug attrition. Three decades ago, the major root causes for why drug candidates failed in the clinic was due to poor pharmacokinetic characteristics and bioavailability; in fact, these poor ADMET features accounted for ∼40% of all drug attrition [65]. This observation and the increased access to automation and mass spectrometry fueled a technical renaissance within the ADMET scientific community and over the course of the next decade these factors were dramatically reduced as the basis of drug attrition in drug development due to poor ADME/PK reasons accounted for less than 10% of drug attrition [66]. Today, as mentioned above, the root cause of drug attrition in drug development due to ADME/PK reasons is now less than 4% [67].

The marked drop in drug attrition because of poor ADME/PK characteristics in today's drug discovery and development process reflects the parallel evaluation of both therapeutic properties and drug-like features of new chemical entities together as early as possible (Fig. 2.8).

The success of the interdisciplinary partnership between medicinal chemistry and DMPK groups effectively broke up the historical wall between drug discovery and development [68]. This achievement quickly gave rise to the formation of translational teams, comprised of DMPK, Safety Sciences and Biomarker groups which are positioned to navigate the full drug discovery/development continuum from lead optimization to clinical candidate nomination through the launch of the new medicine [69]. In addition to early screening efforts, there was an appreciation and adoption of what drug-like physicochemical features are required for a successful therapeutic. Thanks to the seminal paper by Lipinski, the link

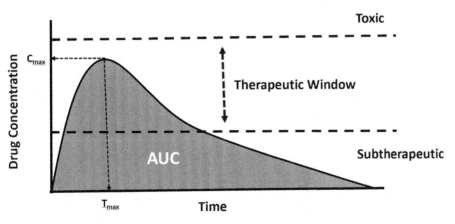

FIGURE 2.7 The therapeutic window is a relationship that compares the blood concentration at which a drug elicits a therapeutic effect compared to the concentration that results in toxicity.

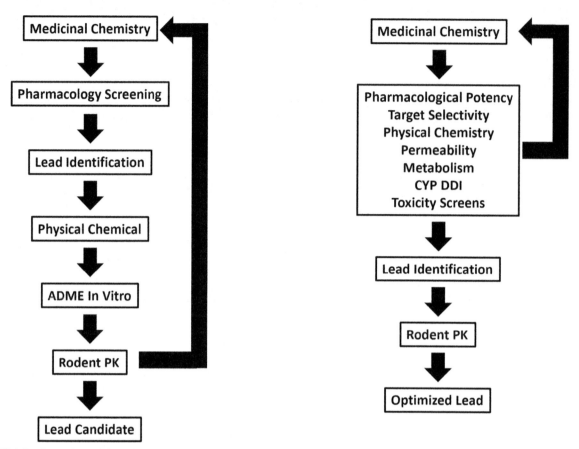

FIGURE 2.8 Comparison of drug discovery "sequential" screening funnels pre-1990s (*left*) versus a funnel reflecting a "parallel optimization" discovery/approach employed today (*right*).

between the size, lipophilicity and H-bonding characteristics of drug molecules and their oral bioavailability was established [70]. In addition to defining boundary conditions for a molecule's physical chemistry attributes, attention was being placed upon avoiding certain sub-molecular functionality group (i.e., Structural Alerts) which are prone to bioactivation to a toxic metabolite [71].

Beyond refining the physical chemical features and avoiding sub structures in drug design, parallel experimental activities were also becoming integrated into the drug discovery testing funnel and included studies designed to predict: drug absorption [72,73]; identification of potential drug transporters and rate of metabolism associated with drug disposition [74,75]; and determination of drug–drug interaction liability [76,77]. It is important to note that clinical drug development failure due to poor drug-like properties was significantly improved through these efforts, which galvanized the role of introducing drug-like properties into the optimization process during drug discovery [78]. Interestingly, as BioPhrama discovery programs evolve to access novel targets, newer modalities (i.e., peptides and protein degraders), represent a departure from the traditional thinking applied toward small molecule drug discovery. To this end, new thinking regarding rule-based decision-making is required to accommodate these large and flexible compounds which extend beyond the boundaries set by the Rule of Five. Today there is an ongoing refinement of computational tools described as beyond the Rule of 5 (bRo5) to help rank drug candidates in the early phases of drug discovery where compounds are often affected by solubility/permeability and thus intestinal absorption and oral bioavailability are program limiting issues [79,80]. Unfortunately, despite the scientific advances in DMPK screening in drug discovery, the overall success rate of clinical drug development has not been significantly improved and remains at a low of 10%−15%. This reflects the previously mentioned concept of drug attrition due to commercial or strategic reasons.

A natural progression of DMPK supporting drug discovery is seen in the utilization of the high-fidelity in vitro information generated toward the prediction of drug pharmacokinetics in a clinical setting. Indeed, in addition to applying simple (allometric and IVIV scaling) pharmacokinetic models [81,82] to judge a lead molecules worthiness in becoming a clinical candidate, there has been an increase in the utilization of the physiological based pharmacokinetic (PBPK)

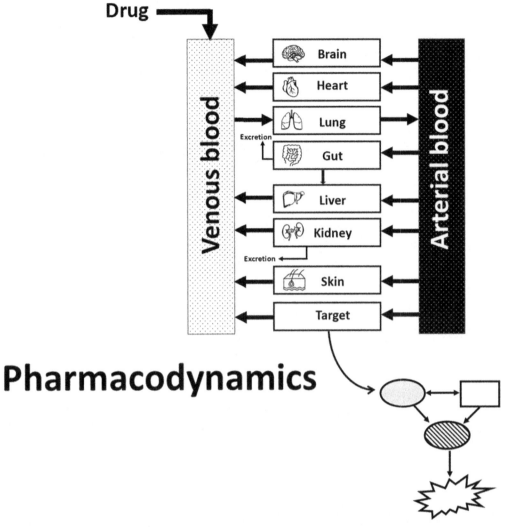

FIGURE 2.9 PBPK models are comprised of compartments representing the different physiological organs of the body, linked by the circulating blood system. In this manner, each compartment is described by approximation of tissue volume and blood flow rate.

modeling approaches to supplement decision-making information as these models are based upon biologically relevant descriptions to describe the disposition of drugs in the body [83]. The application of these PBPK models to predict the time courses of systemic exposure of a molecule using an integrated systems approach allows researchers a means to understand the biological processes that might influence the delivery of drug to its tissue target sites. The schematic depicted in Fig. 2.9 describes how PBPK models may be expanded to integrate streams of information generated across multiple departments, to develop models which reflect pharmacokinetics and the compound's ability to interdict molecular targets [84,85]. The power of PBPK modeling for understanding properties underlying PK and for allowing uncertainty and variability analysis makes this tool valuable in supporting decision-making across multiple stages of the drug development continuum.

Conclusion

This chapter has attempted to provide a very condensed overview on the current challenges associated with decision-making in drug discovery and development. From a high-level point of view, drug development is a highly risky and extremely expensive endeavor, where the commercial success for newly introduced drugs is not guaranteed. Today, through scientific advances and technical achievements, companies have introduced various mitigation strategies where new therapeutic modalities (e.g., biologics) have been successfully introduced and have opened novel avenues for drug therapies which were historically deemed undruggable by small molecules in the past. In addition to new modalities, BioPharma companies have developed internal strategies to minimize drug failure utilizing a variety of key factors for success such as examining opportunities for product differentiation and applying fungible target product profiles to help guide decision-making. Types of information required include the identification of relevant patient populations and various safety issues related to a particular compound in addition to target dependent attributes when deciding upon whether a compound warrants further investment toward achieving the next milestone of drug development. Whereas in the 1990s the drug metabolism pharmacokinetic properties were often the cause of clinical drug failure, today the lack of efficacy, safety and commercial reasons represent the bulk of reasoning behind drug attrition. This chapter focused primarily upon the role of preclinical information outside of pharmacology and chemistry which serve to supplement the intellectual framework used to support decision-making during drug development process. In addition, the chapter highlighted the importance of robust fact-based information to underwrite Go/No Go decisions involved in the progression of a drug candidate through the drug development continuum. Finally, the chapter identified the various stakeholders and the required internal alignment required of goals required for smooth transitions through Go/No Go decision gates present in drug development and hopefully provided an agreement that information beyond drug potency can represent critical factors in supporting decision-making within a BioPharma company.

References

[1] O.J. Wouters, M. McKee, J. Luyten, Estimated research and development investment needed to bring a new medicine to market, 2009—2018, JAMA 323 (9) (2020) 844—853.

[2] J. Knowles, G. Gromo, Target selection in drug discovery, Nat. Rev. Drug Discov. 2 (2003) 63—69.

[3] I. Gashaw, P. Ellinghaus, A. Sommer, K. Asadullah, What makes a good drug target? Drug Discov. Today 17 (2012) S24—S30.

[4] M. Schenone, V. Dančík, B.K. Wagner, P.A. Clemons, Target identification and mechanism of action in chemical biology and drug discovery, Nat. Chem. Biol. 9 (4) (2013) 232—240.

[5] S.K. Thomsen, A.L. Gloyn, Human genetics as a model for target validation: finding new therapies for diabetes, Diabetologia 60 (2017) 960—970.

[6] C.H. Emmerich, L.M. Gamboa, M.C.J. Hofmann, M. Bonin-Andresen, O. Arbach, P. Schendel, et al., Improving target assessment in biomedical research: the GOT-IT recommendations, Nat. Rev. Drug Discov. 20 (2021) 64—81.

[7] H. Dowden, J. Munro, Trends in clinical success rates and therapeutic focus, Nat. Rev. Drug Discov. 18 (7) (2019) 495—496.

[8] A.F. Schmidt, N.B. Hunt, M. Gordillo-Marañón, P. Charoen, F. Drenos, M. Kivimaki, et al., Cholesteryl ester transfer protein (CETP) as a drug target for cardiovascular disease, Nat. Commun. 12 (1) (2021) 5640.

[9] A.R. Tall, D.J. Rader, Trials and tribulations of CETP inhibitors, Circ. Res. 122 (1) (2018) 106—112.

[10] V. Prasad, S. Mailankody, Research and development spending to bring a single cancer drug to market and revenues after approval, JAMA Intern. Med. 177 (11) (2017) 1569—1575.

[11] E. Valeur, S.M. Guéret, H. Adihou, R. Gopalakrishnan, M. Lemurell, H. Waldmann, et al., New modalities for challenging targets in drug discovery, Angew Chem. Int. Ed. Engl. 56 (35) (2017) 10294—10323.

[12] M.J. Espiritu, A.C. Collier, J.P. Bingham, A 21st-century approach to age-old problems: the ascension of biologics in clinical therapeutics, Drug Discov. Today 19 (8) (2014) 1109—1113.

[13] S.T. Sharfstein, Non-protein biologic therapeutics, Curr. Opin. Biotechnol. 53 (2018) 65—75.

[14] B.G. de la Torre, F. Albericio, The pharmaceutical industry in 2019. An analysis of FDA drug approvals from the perspective of molecules, Molecules 25 (3) (2020) 745.

[15] C. Morrison, Fresh from the biotech pipeline-2019, Nat. Biotechnol. 38 (2) (2020) 126—131.

[16] M.S. Kinch, An overview of FDA-approved biologics medicines, Drug Discov. Today 20 (2015) 393—398.

[17] M.J. Blanco, K.M. Gardinier, New chemical modalities and strategic thinking in early drug discovery, ACS Med. Chem. Lett. 11 (2020) 228—231.

[18] D.R. Goulet, W.M. Atkins, Considerations for the design of antibody-based therapeutics, J. Pharm. Sci. 109 (1) (2020) 74—103.

[19] M.S. Kinch, Z. Kraft, T. Schwartz, 2020 in review: FDA approvals of new medicines, Drug Discov. Today 26 (12) (2021) 2794—2799.

[20] J.W. Scannell, A. Alex Blanckley, H. Boldon, B. Warrington, Diagnosing the decline in pharmaceutical R&D efficiency, Nat. Rev. Drug Discov. 11 (3) (2012) 191—200.

[21] A. Bedair, F.R. Mansour, Insights into the FDA 2018 new drug approvals, Curr. Drug Discov. Technol. 18 (2) (2021) 293—306.

[22] A. Kaltenboeck, M. Calsyn, G.W.J. Frederix, J. Lowenthal, D. Mitchell, B. Rector, A. Sarpatwari, Grounding value-based drug pricing in population health, Clin. Pharmacol. Ther. 107 (6) (2020) 1290—1292.

[23] D. Schuster, C. Laggner, T. Langer, Why drugs fail—a study on side effects in new chemical entities, Curr. Pharm. Des. 11 (27) (2005) 3545—3559.

[24] C. Cusimano, T. Lombrozo, Reconciling scientific and commonsense values to improve reasoning, Trends Cogn. Sci. 25 (11) (2021) 937—949.

[25] P. Saffo, Six rules for accurate effective forecasting, Harv. Bus. Rev. 85 (7—8) (2007) 122—123.

[26] D.A. Garvin, M.A. Roberto, What you don't know about making decisions, Harv. Bus. Rev. 79 (8) (2001) 108—116.

[27] D. von Winterfeldt, Bridging the gap between science and decision making, Proc. Natl. Acad. Sci. U.S.A. 110 (Suppl. 3) (2013) 14055—14061.

[28] J. Kuhlmann, Alternative strategies in drug development: clinical pharmacological aspects, Int. J. Clin. Pharmacol. Ther. 37 (12) (1999) 575−583.

[29] R.S. Kaplan, D. Norton, The balanced scorecard: measures that drive performance, Harv. Bus. Rev. 70 (1) (1992) 71−79.

[30] A. Schuhmacher, A. Gatto, M. Kuss, O. Gassmann, M. Hinder, Big Techs and startups in pharmaceutical R&D—a 2020 perspective on artificial intelligence, Drug Discov. Today 26 (10) (2021) 2226−2231.

[31] J. Li, J. Wu, Z. Zhao, Q. Zhang, J. Shao, C. Wang, et al., Artificial intelligence-assisted decision making for prognosis and drug efficacy prediction in lung cancer patients: a narrative review, J. Thorac. Dis. 13 (12) (2021) 7021−7033.

[32] P. Schneider, W.P. Walters, A.T. Plowright, N. Sieroka, J. Listgarten, R.A. Goodnow Jr., et al., Rethinking drug design in the artificial intelligence era, Nat. Rev. Drug Discov. 19 (5) (2020) 353−364.

[33] A. Zhavoronkov, Q. Vanhaelen, T.I. Oprea, Will artificial intelligence for drug discovery impact clinical pharmacology? Clin. Pharmacol. Ther. 107 (4) (2020) 780−785.

[34] C. Scavone, G. di Mauro, A. Mascolo, L. Berrino, F. Rossi, A. Capuano, The new paradigms in clinical research: from early access programs to the novel therapeutic approaches for unmet medical needs, Front. Pharmacol. 10 (2019) 111.

[35] D. Acemoglu, J. Linn, Market size in innovation: theory and evidence from the pharmaceutical industry, Q. J. Econ. 119 (3) (2004) 1049−1090.

[36] M. Lanthier, K.L. Miller, C. Nardinelli, J. Woodcock, An improved approach to measuring drug innovation finds steady rates of first-in class pharmaceuticals, 1987−2011, Health Aff. 32 (2012) 1433−1439.

[37] T.A. Simon, M.S. Khouri, T.D. Kou, A. Gomez-Caminero, Realizing the potential of the patient perspective, Patient Prefer. Adherence 14 (2020) 2001−2007.

[38] J.J. Darrow, J. Avorn, A.S. Kesselheim, FDA approval and regulation of pharmaceuticals, 1983−2018, JAMA 323 (2) (2020) 164−176.

[39] C. McLeod, R. Norman, E. Litton, B.R. Saville, S. Webb, T.L. Snelling, Choosing primary endpoints for clinical trials of health care interventions, Contemp. Clin. Trials Commun. 16 (2019) 100486.

[40] J.A. DiMasi, L.B. Faden, Competitiveness in follow-on drug R&D: a race or imitation? Nat. Rev. Drug Discov. 10 (2011) 23−27.

[41] U. Schulze, M. Ringel, What matters most in commercial success: first-in-class or best-in-class? Nat. Rev. Drug Discov. 12 (6) (2013) 419−420.

[42] E. Perzborn, S. Roehrig, A. Straub, D. Kubitza, F. Misselwitz, The discovery and development of rivaroxaban, an oral, direct factor Xa inhibitor, Nat. Rev. Drug Discov. 10 (1) (2011) 61−75.

[43] R.M. Turner, B.K. Park, M. Pirmohamed, Parsing interindividual drug variability: an emerging role for systems pharmacology, Wiley Interdiscip. Rev. Syst. Biol. Med. 7 (4) (2015) 221−241.

[44] G.R. Wilkinson, Drug metabolism and variability among patients in drug response, N. Engl. J. Med. 352 (2005) 2211−2221.

[45] E. Beutler, T. Gelbart, A. Demina, Racial variability in the UDP-glucuronosyltransferase 1 (UGT1A1) promoter: a balanced polymorphism for regulation of bilirubin metabolism? Proc. Natl. Acad. Sci. U.S.A. 95 (14) (1998) 8170−8174.

[46] M. Ingelman-Sundberg, Genetic polymorphisms of cytochrome P450 2D6 (CYP2D6): clinical consequences, evolutionary aspects and functional diversity, Pharmacogenomics J. 5 (1) (2005) 6−13.

[47] W. Kalow, B.K. Tang, L. Endrenyi, Hypothesis: comparisons of inter- and intra-individual variations can substitute for twin studies in drug research, Pharmacogenetics 8 (4) (1998) 283−289.

[48] S.D. Krämer, B. Testa, The biochemistry of drug metabolism—an introduction: part 7. Intra-individual factors affecting drug metabolism, Chem. Biodivers. 6 (10) (2009) 1477−1660.

[49] M.A. Correia, P.F. Hollenberg, Inhibition of cytochrome P450 enzymes, in: P.R. Ortiz de Montellano (Ed.), Cytochrome P450: Structure, Mechanism, and Biochemistry, fourth ed., Springer, New York, 2015, pp. 177−259.

[50] J.K. Nguyen, M.M. Fouts, S.E. Kotabe, E. Lo, Polypharmacy as a risk factor for adverse drug reactions in geriatric nursing home residents, Am. J. Geriatr. Pharmacother. 4 (2006) 36−41.

[51] D.A. Flockhart, J.R. Oesterheld, Cytochrome P450-mediated drug interactions, Child Adolesc. Psychiatr. Clin. N. Am. 9 (1) (2000) 43−76.

[52] C.A. Jankel, L.K. Fitterman, Epidemiology of drug−drug interactions as a cause of hospital admissions, Drug Saf. 9 (1993) 51−59.

[53] R. Leone, L. Magro, U. Moretti, P. Cutroneo, M. Moschini, D. Motola, et al., Identifying adverse drug reactions associated with drug−drug interactions: data mining of a spontaneous reporting database in Italy, Drug Saf. 33 (2010) 667−675.

[54] M. Pirmohamed, S. James, S. Meakin, C. Green, A.K. Scott, T.J. Walley, et al., Adverse drug reactions as cause of admission to hospital: prospective analysis of 18,820 patients, BMJ 329 (2004) 15−19.

[55] S.R. Smith, M.J. Kendall, J. Lobo, A. Beerahee, D.B. Jack, M.R. Wilkins, Ranitidine and cimetidine; drug interactions with single dose and steady-state nifedipine administration, Br. J. Clin. Pharmacol. 23 (3) (1987) 311−315.

[56] T.J. Hwang, D. Carpenter, J.C. Lauffenburger, Failure of investigational drugs in late-stage clinical development and publication of trial results, JAMA Intern. Med. 176 (12) (2016) 1826−1833.

[57] O. Blin, M.N. Lefebvre, O. Rascol, J. Micallef, Orphan drug clinical development, Therapie 75 (2) (2020) 141−147.

[58] R.K. Harrison, Phase II and phase III failures: 2013–2015, Nat. Rev. Drug Discov. 15 (2016) 817−818.

[59] J. Meza-Junco, M.B. Sawyer, Drug exposure: still an excellent biomarker, Biomark. Med. 3 (6) (2009) 723−731.

[60] B. Bornkamp, F. Bretz, A. Dmitrienko, G. Enas, B. Gaydos, C.H. Hsu, et al., Innovative approaches for designing and analyzing adaptive dose-ranging trials, J. Biopharm. Stat. 17 (6) (2007) 965−995.

[61] S. Habet, Narrow Therapeutic Index drugs: clinical pharmacology perspective, J. Pharm. Pharmacol. 73 (10) (2021) 1285−1291.

[62] Y. Lai, K.E. Sampson, J.C. Stevens, Evaluation of drug transporter interactions in drug discovery and development, Comb. Chem. High Throughput Screen. 13 (2) (2010) 112−134.

[63] A.P. Li, Screening for human ADME/Tox drug properties in drug discovery, Drug Discov. Today 6 (2001) 357−366.

[64] R.J. Riley, I.J. Martin, A.E. Cooper, The influence of DMPK as an integrated partner in modern drug discovery, Curr. Drug Metabol. 3 (5) (2002) 527−550.

[65] T. Kennedy, Managing the drug discovery/development interface, Drug Discov. Today 2 (1997) 436−441.

[66] I. Kola, J. Landis, Can the pharmaceutical industry reduce attrition rates? Nat. Rev. Drug Discov. 3 (8) (2004) 711−715.

[67] M.J. Waring, J. Arrowsmith, A.R. Leach, P.D. Leeson, S. Mandrell, R.M. Owen, et al., An analysis of the attrition of drug candidates from four major pharmaceutical companies, Nat. Rev. Drug Discov. 14 (2015) 475−486.

[68] J.G. Lombardino, J.A. Lowe, The role of the medicinal chemist in drug discovery—then and now, Nat. Rev. Drug Discov. 3 (10) (2004) 853−862.

[69] P. Barton, R.J. Riley, A new paradigm for navigating compound property related drug attrition, Drug Discov. Today 21 (1) (2016) 72−81.

[70] C.A. Lipinski, Drug-like properties and the causes of poor solubility and poor permeability, J. Pharmacol. Toxicol. Methods 44 (1) (2000) 235−249.

[71] A.S. Kalgutkar, M.T. Didiuk, Structural alerts, reactive metabolites, and protein covalent binding: how reliable are these attributes as predictors of drug toxicity? Chem. Biodivers. 6 (2009) 2115−2137.

[72] C.A. Lipinski, F. Lombardo, B.W. Dominy, P.J. Feeney, Experimental and computational approaches to estimate solubility and permeability in drug discovery and development settings, Adv. Drug Deliv. Rev. 46 (1−3) (2001) 3−26.

[73] D. Sun, L.X. Yu, M.A. Hussain, D.A. Wall, R.L. Smith, G.L. Amidon, In vitro testing of drug absorption for drug 'developability' assessment: forming an interface between in vitro preclinical data and clinical outcome, Curr. Opin. Drug Discov. Dev 7 (1) (2004) 75−85.

[74] K.L. Brouwer, D. Keppler, K.A. Hoffmaster, D.A. Bow, Y. Cheng, Y. Lai, et al., International Transporter Consortium, In vitro methods to support transporter evaluation in drug discovery and development, Clin. Pharmacol. Ther. 94 (1) (2013) 95−112.

[75] R. Xu, M. Manuel, J. Cramlett, D.B. Kassel, A high throughput metabolic stability screening workflow with automated assessment of data quality in pharmaceutical industry, J. Chromatogr. A 1217 (10) (2010) 1616−1625.

[76] G. Luo, T. Guenthner, L.S. Gan, W.G. Humphreys, CYP3A4 induction by xenobiotics: biochemistry, experimental methods and impact on drug discovery and development, Curr. Drug Metabol. 5 (6) (2004) 483−505.

[77] R.S. Obach, R.L. Walsky, K. Venkatakrishnan, J.B. Houston, L.M. Tremaine, In vitro cytochrome P450 inhibition data and the prediction of drug−drug interactions: qualitative relationships, quantitative predictions, and the rank-order approach, Clin. Pharmacol. Ther. 78 (6) (2005) 582−592.

[78] M. Davies, R.D.O. Jones, K. Grime, R. Jansson-Löfmark, A.J. Fretland, S. Winiwarter, et al., Improving the accuracy of predicted human pharmacokinetics: lessons learned from the AstraZeneca drug pipeline over two decades, Trends Pharmacol. Sci. 41 (6) (2020) 390−408.

[79] D.A. DeGoey, H.J. Chen, P.B. Cox, M.D. Wendt, Beyond the rule of 5: lessons learned from AbbVie's drugs and compound collection, J. Med. Chem. 61 (7) (2018) 2636−2651.

[80] G. Ermondi, M. Vallaro, G. Goetz, M. Shalaeva, G. Caron, Updating the portfolio of physicochemical descriptors related to permeability in the beyond the rule of 5 chemical space, Eur. J. Pharm. Sci. 146 (2020) 105274.

[81] J.B. Houston, A. Galetin, Progress towards prediction of human pharmacokinetic parameters from in vitro technologies, Drug Metab. Rev. 35 (4) (2003) 393−415.

[82] Q. Huang, J.E. Riviere, The application of allometric scaling principles to predict pharmacokinetic parameters across species, Expert Opin. Drug Metab. Toxicol. 10 (9) (2014) 1241−1253.

[83] H.M. Jones, I.B. Gardner, K.J. Watson, Modelling and PBPK simulation in drug discovery, AAPS J. 11 (1) (2009) 155−166.

[84] E.P. Chen, R.W. Bondi, P.J. Michalski, Model-based target pharmacology assessment (mTPA): an approach using PBPK/PD modeling and machine learning to design medicinal chemistry and DMPK strategies in early drug discovery, J. Med. Chem. 64 (6) (2021) 3185−3196.

[85] P.M. Glassman, J.P. Balthasar, Physiologically-based modeling of monoclonal antibody pharmacokinetics in drug discovery and development, Drug Metabol. Pharmacokinet. 34 (1) (2019) 3−13.

Chapter 3

Systems biology and data science in research and translational medicine

Karim Azer[a], Jeff S. Barrett[b], Mirjam Trame[c] and Cynthia J. Musante[d]

[a]Axcella Therapeutics, Cambridge, MA, United States; [b]Critical Path Institute, Tuscon, AZ, United States; [c]University of Florida, Gainesville, FL, United States; [d]Pfizer, Cambridge, MA, United States

Brief overview of scope of systems biology and applications

I believe that new mathematical schemata, new systems of axioms, certainly new systems of mathematical structures will be suggested by the study of the living world.

Stan Ulam, 1909—84 (Mathematician).

Introduction

Human curiosity has always been intrigued by the "science of life"—how it is understood, defined, and perceived. For centuries, this fundamental tenet of defining life has been a challenge for renowned scientists and philosophers [1,2]. As described recently by Gómez-Márquez, "life is a process that takes place in highly organized organic structures and is characterized by being preprogrammed, interactive, adaptative and evolutionary" [3]. The manifestation of life in four distinct forms such as cells, genes, enzymes, and natural selection (responsible for the evolution of species), has been a driving idea throughout the 19th and 20th centuries [4]. Gradually, these ideas translated into specific and specialized fields of biological science—cell biology, genetics, molecular biology, biochemistry, and evolutionary biology, respectively [4]. In biology, each component such as genes, proteins, ribonucleic acid (RNA), and metabolic products (genomics, proteomics, transcriptomics, and metabolomics—collectively referred to as omics) are assembled and defined to become a part of the "mechanistic model" [5] which helps understand the biological system just like a machine with fixed and defined parts performing repetitive tasks and actions [6,7]. The components of the biological system, once defined, can portray the genotype to phenotype expression relationship [8,9]. The networks of interconnected and mutually dependent components comprise a system [10,11]. The systems approach to biology is a comprehensive, dynamic, interconnected, multidisciplinary approach to deciphering the dynamics of life. The complexity of this approach is informed by interacting cells, genes, and macromolecules to understand the behavior of the entire biological system as an integrated whole [5,12].

Though this approach has a long history, the recent interest in a system-level process is associated with the progress in molecular biology (genome sequencing), high-throughput measurements, biosensors, and nanobiotechnology, which allows the collection of comprehensive datasets on system performance and expand evidence on the structures and functions of biomolecules [13]. The advent of advanced and integrative technology capable of generating comprehensive profiles of biological features, large-scale measurement methods, modern molecular biology imaging techniques, innovative mathematical and engineering concepts, modeling strategies, and computational tools have facilitated tremendous understanding of the biological systems and scientific disciplines to a greater level than was possible even 2 decades ago [5,12,14].

As a result, systems biology has emerged over the past 2 decades, aiming to examine organisms from a systematic and holistic perspective, characterized by big data and advanced computational modeling approaches [15]. Systems biology is essentially a framework for using genome-scale experiments to perform predictive, hypothesis-driven science [16]. In this

Overcoming Obstacles in Drug Discovery and Development. https://doi.org/10.1016/B978-0-12-817134-9.00001-5

chapter, we discuss the evolution of systems biology to investigate and understand disease progression and underlying mechanisms, as well as to identify and advance novel multi-target therapeutic approaches to reversing or improving disease course toward a homeostatic biome.

The origin of systems biology hypothesis

The systems approach to biology will be the dominant theme in medicine.
Leroy Hood, Cofounder, Professor, and Chief Strategy Officer Institute for Systems Biology ISB; Emeritus Science Advisor, Providence.

In the 21st century, the fundamentals of "Systems Biology" have been established [17] with the support of work of many such as Kitano H published in "Science" [18] and "Nature" [19] journals.

A widespread debate exists on the origins of systems biology, with some historians, philosophers, and biologists claiming its early roots emerged in the middle half of the 20th century considering several theories, including that of cybernetics by Wiener in 1948, Noble's heart model in 1960, and Bertalanffy's General Systems Theory [20−22]. Harvey, in 1628, construed blood circulation mechanism using mathematical rationale representing the paradigm of systems biology [23]. One of the most promising statements regarding cellular complexity appeared in the popular [24] paper describing the "one-gene/one-enzyme/one-function" hypothesis [24]. The paper's abstract expressed "how an organism consists essentially of an integrated system of chemical reactions controlled in some manner by genes." Schrödinger was the first to propose a systems approach to biology. In 1943, he opined, "the clue to the understanding of life is that it is based on a pure mechanism and made numerous similar allusions to the living cell as a system" [25]. Schrödinger's book, "What is Life?" continues to inspire scientists and researchers worldwide to decode biological outcomes associated with individual molecules. Subsequently, other researchers and scientists built upon this idea, and a systems view of biology started developing.

The complexity of biological processes was beyond the explanation and scope of the control theory in the 1950s. However, some theorists, especially Bertalanffy and Mesarović, looked at complexity as an essential systems property "in itself" [21,26]. Ultimately, Mesarović coined the term "Systems Biology" by integrating systems theory and biological investigation concepts [27], wherein an organisms' influence on components or subunits or component clusters gives rise to evolutionary and emergent properties, which are usually unpredictable, thereby defining a complex system [10,11,28].

Nevertheless, technologies enabling the generation of large datasets and algorithms for modeling complex systems were established in the 1990s. Conceptually, modern systems biology had its roots in the early 1990s when advanced technologies introduced a deluge of data (big data) to biology. In the absence of mathematical models and computational simulations, the large volumes of reliable data could not be understood adequately. Hood, a pioneer of biological measurement technology, wrote in a book published in 1992 that "the future of biology will depend upon the analysis of complex systems and networks" [29]. Early systems biologists have attempted to develop several algorithms for dealing with substantial datasets and formalisms that model a specific network [30]. Thus, scientific response to the dynamics in the living systems via mathematical modeling and computational analysis became the focus of attention for biologists to interpret and comprehend complexity in living systems.

Systems biology—the approach and scope

Despite varied opinions on the evolution of systems biology, the field is still considered in its infancy compared to other established areas in biology, such as molecular biology, evolutionary biology, cell biology, etc. System-level analyses are valuable in biology since biological systems are multiscale, with multiple levels of organization and continuously transitioning through various states over time. These multiscale systems can be examined from two perspectives: bottom-up and top-down approaches, with their own set of advantages and disadvantages. A bottom-up approach, which involves investigating cellular and molecular components as parts of a system that includes multiple interactions and dynamics, could give mechanistic insight into how the different units collaborate. However, as the system gets more prominent, the details will obscure the overall system capabilities [31].

Contrary to this, the top-down method studies the system and discovers its characteristics and possible capabilities. This gives the design a big picture, which can be comprehensive and integrative. In a top-down method, interactions among units are often determined by correlations, and the complexity of biological systems sometimes indicates that it is difficult to make causal inferences [31]. These two approaches, thus, should not be considered mutually exclusive with regard to the pathway-process distinction (Fig. 3.1).

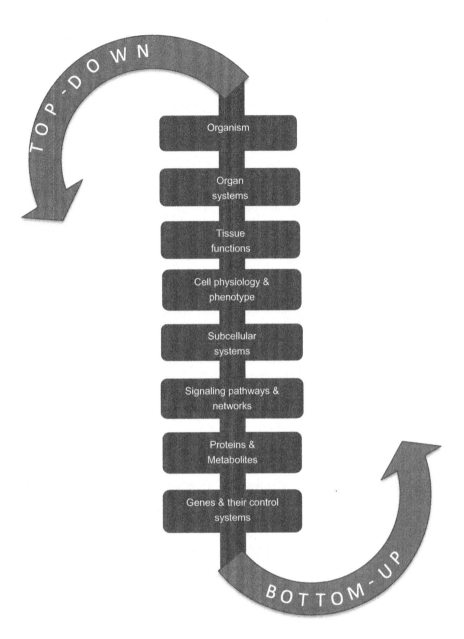

FIGURE 3.1 Systems biology approaches.

Over recent years, the scope of topics covered by systems biology has broadened exponentially and has been the core of significant research progress ranging from pathway-based biomarkers and diagnosis, systematic measurement, and genetic interactions modeling to the classification of disease genes and stem cells [32]. The systems biology framework provides a means of constructing models of biological systems based on systematic measurements [32]. Taking genome-wide measurements (or proteome-wide measurements) on a system has arguably been the single most significant influence enabling the rise of systems biology. It is critical that systems-level models are consistent with and validated by detailed single-molecule measurements and literature. Overall, consistent with the varied definitions for systems biology, its broad scope could be interpreted with a broad definition as "The process of interrogating the genetic, genomic, biochemical, cellular, physiological, and clinical properties of a system to define and create a system pathway or network that can be used to predictively model a biological event(s)" [33].

Hence, a large volume of data is now available. There is a requirement to understand complex and rare diseases which can only be explained by multi-disciplinary interaction within an organism compared with a single gene, cell, or metabolite. A comprehensive perspective of the biological system is required to comprehend the interdependent and dynamic pathway, cellular and network events changing a function of disease predisposition, onset, and progression. The proactive approach of systems biology assists in decoding complex and rare diseases with intricate biological networks making the modeling, perturbation, and prediction of complex networks possible. Moreover, a systematic understanding of such complex networks is needed to diagnose and cure complex diseases [34].

Systems biology and its applications

Over the next ten years, a systems approach will dominate the landscape of understanding all simple and complex diseases.
Leroy Hood, Cofounder, Professor, and Chief Strategy Officer Institute for Systems Biology ISB; Emeritus Science Advisor, Providence.

Systems biology promises to impact most scientific and research areas in biology. A vast amount of experimental and research data has been garnered over the last few decades. The goal is to ensure an accurate and precise interpretation of datasets collected from diverse sources for a meaningful understanding of the complexity of biological systems. Systems biology will play a critical role in analyzing and interpreting such extensive data to decipher the multi-level complexity associated with any biological system. Through its application, system biology may help:

- Understand native biological systems (animals, plants, microorganisms) at the system level, including structures and dynamics, e.g., metabolic, sensitivity, and bifurcation analysis [35].
- Gain a comprehensive systems-level understanding of disease pathophysiology and identify potential therapeutic targets [36,37].
- Advance novel multi-target therapeutics to treat or cure diseases.
- Develop systems-level approaches in biotechnology to create biological systems with desired properties that don't exist in nature [38].

Obstacles in drug discovery and translational medicine, with a focus on new indications/ targets—systems biology as a bridge between discovery and data sciences

The challenges with the conventional drug discovery process and productivity predicament in the pharma industry are well documented [39–41]. The level of innovation, research and analysis performed to alleviate these challenges are ever-evolving. Systems biology-based research efforts are increasingly influencing the drug discovery and development process (Bai et al., [42] CPT Pharmacometrics Syst. Pharmacol. 2021;00:1–6) [43]. Partly, this is accomplished via a systematically integrated approach to generate robust data and information to increase our knowledge of biological functions, system complexity, and biological interactions for making informed decisions.

In the last decade, the estimated average lifetime cost of introducing a new drug in the market via conventional drug discovery and development process has more than doubled as per Tufts Center for the Study of Drug Development (CSDD), Boston, MA. The estimated figures stand at over $2.6 billion (in 2013 dollars), up from $800 million (about $1 billion in 2013 dollars) [44]. Each successful drug will take, on average, 10–12 years to navigate the laborious processes of R&D, quality control, and regulatory oversight before being introduced in the market. The time constraints, scientific effort, personnel involvement, use of technology, and the associated cost(s) play a critical role in defining the success of a new drug in the market. Not to forget the associated role of delayed/flawed decisions and challenges with obtaining meaningful information of biological systems, which also causes hindrance in the drug development process [33]. Before the 1990s, the reductionist approach drove the drug development process, leading to an incomplete understanding of complex biological systems and networks. The 1990s saw the advent of new high throughput technologies and computational tools that could "measure" complex datasets, including genomics, proteomics, metabolomics, etc., making the scientific understanding and interpretation of complex systems possible. Today our focus is to utilize this extensive biological data and convert it into profound information using newer technologies for making informed research and translational medicine decisions [45].

The conventional drug development approach that reduced the complexity of human beings to a single gene, protein targets, metabolic pathways, and treatments to standardize complex functions is no longer efficient for treating complex multifactorial and multigenic diseases, where a multi-targeted drug approach is more likely to be effective [46]. This complexity associated with diseases and multi-molecular interactions calls for a comprehensive understanding of the biological systems uncovering several dynamic and interconnected pathways and networks underlying disease onset and progression. Keeping the biological framework of drugs in mind, systems biology offers novel prospects to address disease mechanisms and approach the drug development process with an ability to translate preclinical discoveries into potential clinical benefits (e.g., new biomarkers and therapies) [47]. Hood and Perlmutter argued that "describing all the elements of the system and defining the appropriate biological networks, (where disease reflects the operation of perturbed networks) and comparing normal versus diseased networks allows critical nodes to be identified. If such nodal points can be reconfigured back toward the norm, this constitutes a treatment of the disease" (Fig. 3.2) [48].

Systems biology as the integration of discovery biology and data sciences

The systems biology-based research approach integrates experimental data with novel database-derived information to discover and validate selected drug candidates, biomarkers, and lead compounds. It aims at understanding physiology and disease from the level of molecular pathways, regulatory networks, cells, tissues, organs, and the whole organism. The complexity of genes, genetic variations, and networks observed in human diseases such as diabetes, cancer, and obesity requires a systematic approach to illustrate the cellular networks, genetic makeup, and other environmental factors to understand how these are interconnected, leading to human diseases. Hood et al. emphasized the systematic disturbances, high-dimensional data generation in biological systems, and integration of these data to arrive at the process driving complex traits [16]. According to Hood, systems biology studies "biological systems by systematically perturbing them (biologically, genetically, or chemically); monitoring the gene, protein, and informational pathway responses; integrating these data; and ultimately, formulating mathematical models that describe the structure of the system and its response to individual perturbations."

Over the past several decades, advancement in biological sciences has led to molecular data generation at the genome, transcriptome, proteome, and metabolome levels. Although identifying all the genes and proteins provides a collection of individual molecular components, it is insufficient to understand the fundamental complexity of biological systems. It is essential to know how individual elements are constructed to form the structure of biological systems, how these interacting components can result in complex system behaviors, and how alterations in conditions may dynamically change these behaviors [49]. The integrated systems biology approach acts as an essential bridge between large amounts of data

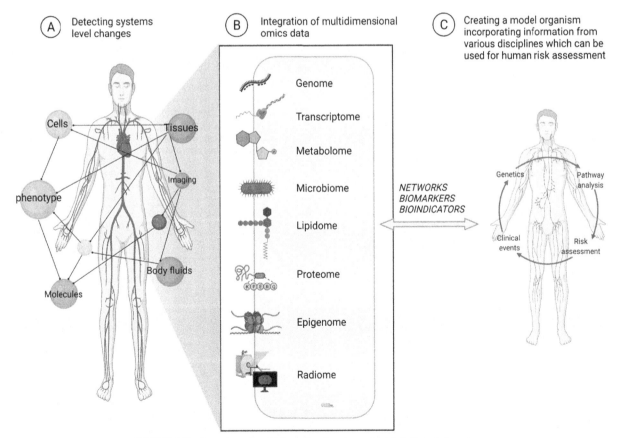

FIGURE 3.2 Overview of multidimensional omics and related clinical phenotypes.

and integrating such information to decode the complexity of biological systems via (a) -omics data (massive datasets of protein, gene, and metabolites), (b) complex cell-level and tissue-level in vitro models, and (c) in silico computer simulations integrating information from the pathway to organism levels [50]. It studies interactions among several components and relies on a combination of experiments that assesses multiple cellular components and computational approaches that helps in analyzing various datasets. As an iterative process, computational modeling proposes nonintuitive hypotheses that can be tested experimentally. The newly obtained quantitative experimental data can then refine the computational model that summarizes the biological system of interest [49]. Systems biology has been broadly considered the natural successor to the Human Genome Project because it caters to integrating complex data sets and provides the tools to carry out physiological studies [51].

There are several critical clinically motivating applications in drug discovery to which systems biology approaches can make significant contributions [49]. Overall, it can be applied to:

- Drug-target networks
- Predictions of drug-target interactions
- Investigations of the mechanism of drug action and potential for adverse effects
- Drug repositioning
- Predictions of drug combination

Quantitative Systems Pharmacology Models—mechanistic virtualization of drug discovery and development processes

Applying a system biology-based approach in translational medical research requires integrating vast -omics data obtained from private or public databases, knowledge of patient diseases, and available clinical data sets, including biomarkers and phenotypic data that bridge preclinical and clinical data (Fig. 3.3). The development of systems-level computational "virtual patient models" will ascertain the likely outcome of various therapies on an individual patient with the potential likelihood of running every step of the drug discovery and development process using virtual trials or virtual patient models [52].

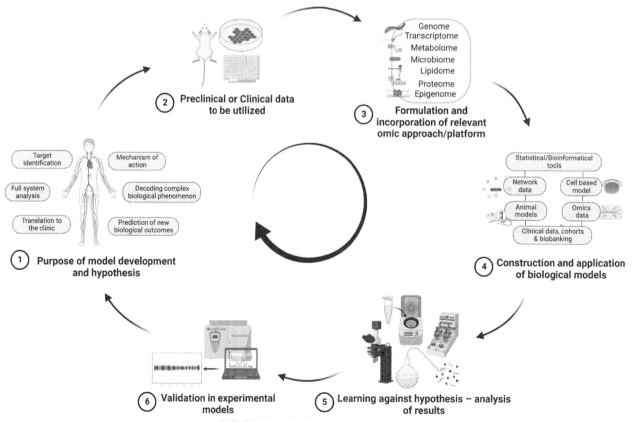

FIGURE 3.3 Schedule of systems biology.

Quantitative Systems Pharmacology (QSP) models integrate mechanistic information derived from experimental data with the knowledge of drug mechanism of action into a representative in-silico framework. Mechanistic models are being extensively utilized to predict the behavior of complex biological systems, exemplified by a vast amount of data generated in the initial research stages [53]. QSP-based 'virtual patient' models offer an opportunity to individualize treatment for patients across diverse areas of medicine; it enables systematic testing of therapies on a 'virtual patient' model representative of a patient and the outcome of therapeutic intervention [54,55]. This virtual patient model is constructed based on the known biological networks in human tissues and is individualized using patients' molecular measurements and disease (Fig. 3.4). QSP models will be beneficial for complex heterogeneous disorders such as cancer or NASH, offering a possibility of developing multi-drug combinations based on the trait(s) under investigation [56]. Using such a predictive modeling system opens the window to test several drug combinations with synergistic or antagonistic effects or scenarios that do not allow testing in preclinical and clinical studies due to logistical, cost, or ethical reasons. Physicians can then utilize such modeling technology to test any therapy on a virtual patient to determine the drug's efficacy and/or safety and narrow it down to an individualized, optimal option based on the patient's condition. Any researcher testing a new drug target in an experimental model will have the advantage of comparing the outcomes with the predicted response in the corresponding computer model and translating it into individual patient responses based on the biological differences between the biology and model environment (cell line, mouse, dog or other animal-based model systems) and that of individual patients.

Similarly, it is possible to conduct a "virtual clinical trial" to potentially enhance the design of the actual trial, optimizing the chances of success while looking to minimize risk and loss of time and associated costs. Such situations will help protect patients from participating in predictably futile trials and reduce failure risk [52]. Systems biology, thus, will not only offer an opportunity to transform complex, deadly, untreatable diseases but provide an option for discovering and developing multi-targeted and personalized treatment options with predictable outcomes that are potentially risk minimized.

Overall, regarding the drug discovery and development process, there is a need to embrace and acknowledge the biological system complexity and simplify the cumbersome "trial-and-error" methodology associated with drug research using intelligent systems via the combination of advanced systems-wide biological readouts, i.e., big data and commensurate mathematical models or computer systems.

In the context of model-informed drug development (MIDD), a family of models developed at different stages of research and development can inform critical decision-making. This goal (improved decision-making) is at the heart of the approach. While systems biology is a broad discipline on its own, one of its primary products is the development of systems biology models or QSP models, which represent a primary asset in the MIDD toolbox.

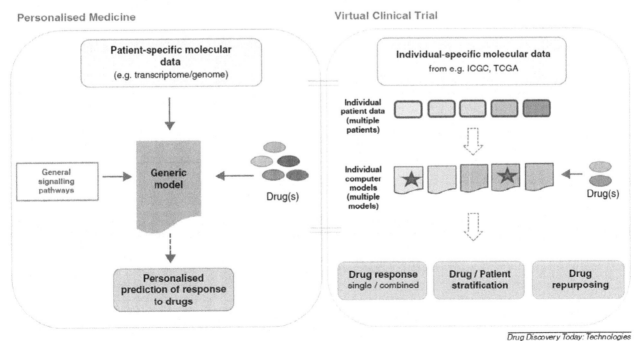

Drug Discovery Today: Technologies

FIGURE 3.4 Virtual patient models—basis for personalized medicine and virtual clinical trials.

Defining the therapeutics mechanism of action

Demonstrating proof-of-concept (POC) is an essential milestone for Phase 2 drug development. The goal of proof-of-concept studies, typically involving a small number of subjects and more latitude in statistical requirements, is to prove that a drug is likely to be successful in later stages of drug development. Although often not published, such studies allow drug developers to make "Go/No Go" decisions about proceeding with larger, more expensive studies [57]. Related concepts include proof-of-principal (POP), which refers to the demonstration of pharmacological impact on the disease in question, and proof-of-mechanism (POM), which refers to the engagement of the active drug entities at the intended site(s) of action.

The lack of specific MOA understanding should not be surprising since this is not a requirement for approval and exists for many approved drugs regardless of therapeutic area. The problem for patients is the myriad of etiologies currently encapsulated in many complex diseases and disease conditions (e.g., Parkinson's disease). The lack of MOA clarity promotes enrollment of patients unlikely to respond to therapy. Thus, low overall response rates, ill-defined clinical endpoints with no mechanistic underpinning, and sampling schemes may be inappropriate as they do not adequately reflect inpatient status and disease progression. Many neurologic conditions and disease states fall into this category, most notably Alzheimer's and Parkinson's disease. Not coincidentally, most drugs approved for these conditions are focused on symptomatic relief and are not disease-modifying. Also, most of these agents list their MOA as unknown or undefined in the drug monograph. The end result is a poor benefit: risk and low expectations for patients. This situation highlights the need for a holistic QSP approach. Fig. 3.5 highlights multiple data sources used in MOA studies defined at multiple biology levels.

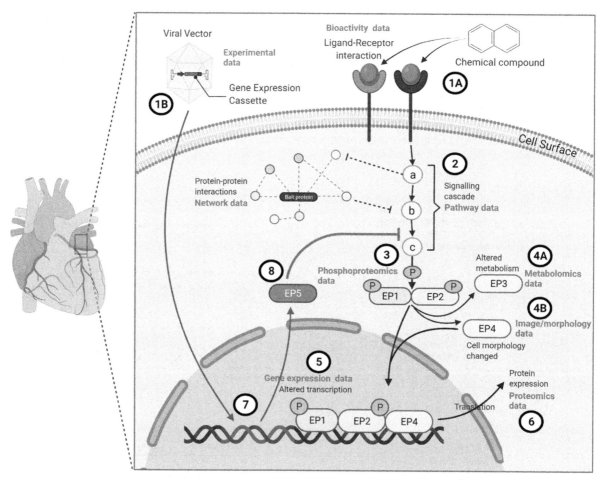

Data sources; a,b,c, signalling cascade; EP, effector proteins; P, phosphorylation; 1A,1B,4A,4B, simultaneous step

FIGURE 3.5 Mechanism of action concept by utilizing multiple data sources.

Systems biology and pharmacology approaches in translational medicine

QSP models represent mechanistically driven, integrated drug and disease models that may be used to inform diverse decisions in the discovery and development of therapies. For example, QSP models have been used in target identification and evaluation, drug design and candidate selection, to understand mechanism of action, in preclinical to clinical translation of efficacy evaluations, in safety assessments, and in the design of preclinical studies and early clinical trials [58,59]. Given the significant uncertainty inherent in early phase development, QSP models seek to increase confidence and mitigate risk in both the compound and the target [60]. This is accomplished by rigorous exploration of uncertainty and variability [61,62] in the characterization of the complex interactions between the biological system, disease processes, and the drug (or combinations of drugs) in a mechanistically-driven quantitative assessment of drug pharmacology.

While some QSP models developed as mechanistic extensions of traditional pharmacokinetic and pharmacodynamic approaches (e.g., Jusko [63] and Pichardo-Almarza and Díaz-Zuccarini [64]), other QSP models are deeply rooted in systems biology and over time have expanded from their use in academic settings to elucidate disease mechanisms, toward identification of novel targets and advancing therapeutic and vaccine candidates in industry [65]. Given the academic and basic science origins to many QSP models, an important component of their overall utility in drug development is their applicability to project milestones, particularly in the evaluation of clinical candidates. One way to ensure this is to require modeling and simulation results to support specific drug development milestones; for example, to support MOA, biomarker strategy, clinical endpoint selection and patient selection [66,65]. Once connected to these milestones, other strategic opportunities may present such as enrichment guidance for clinical trials with targeted agents and a heterogeneous disease population and clinical bridging of related populations or treatment groups where differences in MOA may be theorized or expected.

The utility of a QSP model for such a broad range of deliverables requires that it be adaptable to address evolving questions as a program transitions from discovery to preclinical to clinical development and regulatory submission [67]. This inevitably requires the model structure and parameters be updated as new questions and data emerge. For example, a cell-based model used in exploratory research for target identification/evaluation may track cellular protein concentrations or expression levels over time in response to target inhibition or activation. For this model to be applicable to preclinical efficacy questions, relevant pharmacology and new biological mechanisms or physiology added to reflect tissue, organ, or whole body response to the candidate compound in the animal species of interest. For clinical applications, the preclinical model will need to be modified to reflect human biology and clinical efficacy biomarkers or outcomes of interest. In this way, a QSP model serves as a translational framework from systems biology to preclinical and clinical pharmacology applications. Moreover, at each stage of model modification, the validation requirement increases with decision risk [42].

Three illustrative examples

Rare diseases—development of gene therapies

Gene therapy is a young field with a wide range of challenges. It delivers functional genes into a patient's body to counter or replace malfunctioning genes and can potentially alleviate the underlying cause of genetic and acquired disease lifelong. The gene therapy landscape is especially challenging to navigate, from R&D to regulatory and market access. Gene therapy can have exaggerated and unexpected behavior, and animal models may fail to predict the potential for human toxicity or beneficial immune modulation. In addition, efficacy and safety issues have contributed to unsuccessful regulatory outcomes, creating uncertainty in regulatory pathways, and gene therapies pose pricing and market access challenges as systems wrestle with paying upfront for a lifetime of benefits. Especially challenging is the development of gene therapies for rare diseases when patient recruitment becomes one of the limiting factors due to small populations and low adherence to gene therapy, especially in case of an existing standard of care which often comes with patients having developed pre-existing and treatment-induced immunity to the viral vectors. Rare diseases further come with the challenge of being poorly understood and often lack promising biomarkers and clinical endpoints to predict disease progression, making drug development particularly hard for these diseases. Natural history data play an essential role in rare disease drug development during the IND phase to facilitate efficient clinical development. However, a global lack of pre-competitive disease registries leads to an infrequent application of natural history studies or registry data. Rare diseases often come with considerable heterogeneity leading to poorly understood pheno-genotype correlations, which could be better understood and defined using real-world natural history data, including disease severity sub-types playing an essential role in the successful development of gene therapy.

There are several gene therapy approaches, including gene correction, gene transplantation, gene replacement, and various ways to deliver therapeutic DNA and proteins to target cells. When it comes to gene therapy, non-viral gene delivery methods offer many advantages over viral vectors; they do not cause immunogenicity and carcinogenicity and can efficiently deliver large therapeutic DNA. However, viral vectors have shown to be more efficient in providing therapeutic genetic materials to the target cells and are hence more widely used. The delivery methods range from ex vivo, in situ, to in vivo methods. AAV vectors, lentiviral vectors, and chimeric antigen receptor (CAR)-T cells are examples of different classes of gene and cell therapy products that have already shown to be successful delivery methods.

The main challenge gene therapy approaches have in common is how to best predict the right dose for a first-in-human trial. Current preclinical models are not sufficient in predicting the heterogenic response observed in patients to be used reliably to forecast a therapeutic dose in gene therapy. Additionally, the biodistribution of the viral vector is vastly different in preclinical models compared to humans partly because the fraction of target cells successfully transduced is lower in humans than in small animals. Another challenge comes with ex vivo gene therapy approaches where the traditional dose-escalation studies cannot be performed. In ex vivo gene therapy, the patients' cells are being isolated and transduced with the viral vector outside of the patient's body, and the transduced cells are infused back into the patient via a bone marrow transplantation.

Some of the ultimate needs at hand are (1) to understand how much viral vector is needed to efficiently transduce all cells collected from the patients and are needed to be transduced to carry out complete and long-term engraftment, (2) when can full engraftment be expected and translated into the full clinical benefit ultimately influencing study length and study size, (3) can viral vectors be re-dosed in case of unsuccessful engraftment or immune response, (4) how can off-target effects and insertional mutagenesis be forecasted, and (5) in case of an underlying disease affecting the bone marrow can we assume normal cell counts or is the adjustment for diseases related cell counts needed to adjust the viral vector dose?

Many of these questions could be addressed using systems biology modeling, helping to guide dose selection of viral vectors by exploring predictive and quantitative biomarkers for gene therapy, guiding insights into vector-host cell interactions by complementing cell culture and in vivo integration site analyses to predict potential mutagenesis risks, help identify new targets for gene therapy, predict long-term engraftment and correlation to clinical outcome by computationally predicting expression of gene therapy including inter-individual variability and predicting the biphasic response between gene expression and therapeutic efficacy. Systems biology can further be utilized to support the quantification of the potency assay matrix of the drug product by entangling the complex mechanism of the drug product linking vector copy number, enzyme activity in the drug product, and transduction rates to the underlying disease physiology to forecast long-term outcome.

Understanding the fundamentals of gene therapy utilizing systems biology can provide an advantage for future gene therapy development programs and help shed insight on its full potential. Fully integrated systems approaches have yet to be developed in gene therapy to be leveraged for clinical trial planning, as virtual control arms, and to support market access by showing differentiation to the standard of care on the molecular and target level and to predict long-term benefit automatically significant for regulatory approval and market access.

Global Public Health—challenges specific to public health and opportunities captured versus gaps

A great opportunity exists to employ systems biology approaches to support various Global Health initiatives. There are many obstacles in this effort, not the least of which is the difficulty obtaining quality data and the resources and commitment required to support the research effectively.

An excellent example of the opportunity is the longstanding effort to combat tuberculosis (TB) [68]. A vaccine to prevent *Mycobacterium tuberculosis* (Mtb) infection and stop the disease from developing in the first place would be the ideal tool for young mothers and fathers in low-income countries to help end the TB epidemic. For the one licensed TB vaccine that exists, Bacille Calmette-Guérin (BCG), studies evaluating the effectiveness of a booster dose in older adolescents and adults have shown conflicting results. Further, even though this is the most widely used vaccine globally, there are significant gaps in scientific knowledge. We do not understand: (1) the mechanism by which it provides immunity against TB; (2) if the current dose is the optimal dose; (3) the best way to measure the dose level in the vaccine vial, and (4) whether a booster given in adolescents/young adults can help prevent infection and pulmonary TB. These gaps mesh nicely with the outputs from a well-defined systems biology approach and QSP model.

These gaps exist for many reasons. Specifically, Mtb is an organism that has co-evolved with humans for thousands of years, learning to evade the immune system in most of the hosts it infects. As with most vaccines, the immunologic protection mechanism does not appear to be an antibody, thus leaving no marker by which dosing could be optimized. With historical vaccine development, the dose is determined indirectly by the immune response versus directly measuring the concentration in the blood. Further, once TB was well controlled in high-income countries in the first half of the last century, additional resources were limited to continue studying BCG or developing new vaccines. In the wake of the recent coronavirus-disease 2019 (COVID-19) pandemic, a greater emphasis on tools to challenge such knowledge gaps has been appreciated. Likewise, revisiting study planning, design, and evaluation in the context of new tool availability has opened the door for greater precision.

Cardiovascular diseases—a look back at an area with lots of precedence and model richness—how models enabled evaluation of MOA

Globally, cardiovascular diseases (CVD) are one of the leading causes of morbidity and mortality, with an estimated 17.9 million deaths in 2019, representing 32% of all global deaths; 85% are due to heart attack and stroke [69]. These end-organ dysfunctions are a characteristic feature of the development and progression of CVD, and involving other contributing factors such as cardiac remodeling and co-morbidities such as chronic kidney disease. To elucidate the development and progression of CVD, a detailed understanding of the underlying molecular mechanisms associated with such disease states needs further deep diving. CVDs are typically late-appearing disease manifestations of clinical pathophenotypes (generic endopathophenotypes, including inflammation, immunity, fibrosis, thrombosis, hemorrhage, cell proliferation, apoptosis, and necrosis) within the organ system. The pathophysiological mechanisms underlying CVD are pleotropic, but much progress has been made, with the success of genome-wide association studies [70—73] and sequencing approaches [74], as well as significant investment in development of treatments for CVD. The conventional therapeutic strategies do not focus on the unique target-based determinants but similar clinical pathophenotypes [75]. Progress towards investigation of cardiovascular disease biology and development of novel therapeutics towards unmet medical needs is advancing through various systems biology approaches—the multi-omics approach to CVD are being explored for novel insights and predictions based on a large dataset and cross-platform integration from different analytical techniques [76—78], and the efforts utilizing systems biology approaches to decipher the underlying complexity of CVD for early detection and paving the way for tailored and appropriate treatment strategies [78].

The systems biology approach has profoundly impacted CVD drug discovery and research. They have played a significant role in elucidating physiological regulation mechanisms [79] and pathological processes in complex diseases [80], for example through the construction of gene regulatory networks from large-scale molecular profiles. Moreover, computational and mathematical models coupled with experimental models have contributed to elucidating and efficiently predicting disease biology and risk. There is a significant history and precedence for researcher scientists utilizing systems analysis and modeling parameters to identify potential answers to impending disease risks and outcomes in CVD. Beneken developed one of the first integrated models to describe the heart's pumping characteristics [81,82]. In 1967, Guyton and colleagues developed an analog-computer model to handle the interaction of the control of arterial pressure and cardiac output [83]. Later, in 1972, Guyton and colleagues [84] focused on systems analysis of circulatory regulation by simulating the effects of circulatory stresses on circulatory control. A greater understanding of underlying molecular mechanisms responsible for atherosclerosis development and progression could be achieved via high-throughput sequencing and a systems biology approach [78]. In cardiac remodeling, through systems biology, it might be possible to identify early mechanical stresses and relevant functional modules that underlie ventricular remodeling and complex heart failure pathophysiology [85]. Genome-wide association studies found over 300 genetic variants associated with coronary artery disease with the recent advent of high-throughput sequencing technologies [86,87]. Varshneya and colleagues examined individualized arrhythmia susceptibility by building a computational pipeline combining mechanistic modeling with machine learning analyses [88]. Computational models predicted the effect of bone marrow stem cell transplantation on fibrosis in cardiomyopathy linked to Chagas disease [89] or bioprosthetic heart valve induced platelet activation post-implantation [90]. The McCulloch group used diverse computational models to study cardiac functions, such as the model of focal myofibril disarray to investigate regional septal dysfunction as observed in hypertrophic cardiomyopathy [91] and the effect of biventricular pacing and scar size on left ventricular function [92]. Sheikh et al. studied the influence of myosin regulatory proteins on regulating cardiac muscle contraction [93]. Computational models enabled researchers to develop a high-resolution heart model for the human heart [94] and developed the capability to rapidly simulate cardiac electrophysiology at a high resolution in a human heart [95]. The systems-level computational models could simulate repolarization to improve arrhythmia susceptibility and cardiac risk prediction and improve risk stratification in patients with long QT syndrome [96—98]. Kaiser et al. built a model mitral valve on a design-based elasticity approach, which incorporated anatomical details of a real heart. The simulations in this model were driven by physiologically realistic driving pressures and resulted in physiological responses robust to conditions such as hypertension or hypotension [99]. Varshneya and colleagues [96] combined simulations of pharmacokinetics with QSP modeling of ventricular myocytes to predict the potential effects on cardiac electrophysiology due to drug treatment. Importantly, these systems biology innovations and their application have played an important role in the development of CVD disease biology and mechanisms, and facilitating the discovery and development of novel therapeutics across many CVDs, such as heart failure, dyslipidemia, and hypertension to name a few.

Summary and conclusions

Systems biology has deep academic roots and application in the elucidation of disease mechanism biology and etiology. Results and advancements in disease mechanism and biology have typically relied on the integration of biological sciences with computational and data sciences, and have set the precedence for a multi-disciplinary systems biology approach as the field has found its way into industry. The origins of systems biology stem from the mechanistic model concept e.g., a cell like a machine with many individual parts working together as part of a system. For systems biology, these individual parts constitute the multi-omic components and integrated universe of an organism. The advent of the Human Genome Project, and significant advancement in technology, allowing for large volumes of data to be generated, have played a critical role in the evolution of the field, and its application to investigation of complex, dynamic and interconnected biological processes. Combined with the commensurate advances in computational sciences, biological and data sciences combined represent an inflection point for the opportunity to apply systems biology for elucidating disease mechanisms, and advancing therapeutic and vaccine research and development.

In this chapter, we have reviewed some of the historical notes and origins of the field of systems biology. We built upon this historical framework, which has helped define the opportunity space for the field, as well as the overall approach and ingredients for successful application. After highlighting some of the application in research, and the integration of biological sciences and data sciences as a drug discovery platform, we discussed the challenges of the drug discovery paradigm of single target and single molecular agent, and the opportunities that systems biology can provide for industry throughout the discovery and development life cycle. We described some of the challenges and opportunities, starting with elucidation of a drug's mechanism of action, followed by the utility of a systems biology and pharmacology (QSP) model-based framework in translational medicine to increase the probability of success of molecular candidates entering early clinical development and positioning for successful POC studies. Finally we closed with three examples highlighting the challenges in three distinct areas of drug development, namely global health, gene therapy for rare diseases, and novel drugs for cardiovascular diseases, as well as the precedence and opportunity of applying systems biology approaches in each of these areas. While much progress has been accomplished over the last 2 decades, the opportunity for the field to transform the drug discovery and development landscape is within reach, and calls for scientists across disciplines to bring their respective expertise together under this umbrella of multi-disciplinary systems biology approach, to accelerate the discovery and development of innovative medicines for patients with unmet medical needs.

References

[1] C.E. Cleland, The Quest for a Universal Theory of Life, Cambridge University Press, Cambridge, 2019.

[2] E.V. Koonin, Defining life: an exercise in semantics or a route to biological insights? J. Biomol. Struct. Dyn. 29 (2012) 603–605.

[3] J. Gómez-Márquez, What is life? Mol. Biol. Rep. 48 (8) (2021) 6223–6230.

[4] M. Vidal, A unifying view of 21st century systems biology, FEBS Lett. 583 (24) (2009) 3891–3894.

[5] R. Berlin, R. Gruen, J. Best, Systems medicine-complexity within, simplicity without, J. Healthc. Inform. Res. 1 (1) (2017) 119–137.

[6] A. Levy, W. Bechtel, Abstraction and the organization of mechanisms, Philos. Sci. 80 (2013) 241–261.

[7] A. Levy, Machine-likeness and explanation by decomposition, Philos. Impr. 14 (2014) 1–15.

[8] I. Brigandt, Reductionism in biology, Stanf. Encycl. Philos. (2008). https://plato.stanford.edu/entries/reduction-biology/. (Accessed 20 January 2022).

[9] I. Brigandt, Evolutionary developmental biology and the limits of philosophical accounts of mechanistic explanation, in: P.-A. Braillard, C. Malaterre (Eds.), Explanation in Biology, Springer, Dordrecht, 2015, pp. 135–174.

[10] M. Mesarovic, S. Sreenah, J. Keene, Search for organizing principles: understanding in systems biology, Syst. Biol. 1 (2004) 19–27.

[11] S. Sreenah, M. Mesarovic, R. Soebiyanto, Coordination principles in complex systems biology, IEEE Trans. SysBio Issue (2006). www.systemsbiology.case.edu/publications/submitted/IEEETrans_ SysBioIssue.pdf. (Accessed 20 January 2022).

[12] R. Robeva, Systems biology—old concepts, new science, new challenges, Front. Psychiatry 1 (2020) 1–2.

[13] J.M. Laval, P.E. Mazeran, D. Thomas, Nanobiotechnology and its role in the development of new analytical devices, Analyst 125 (2000) 29–33.

[14] L. Hood, L. Rowen, D. Galas, J. Aitchison, Systems biology at the Institute for systems biology, Brief. Funct. Genom. Proteom. 7 (2008) 239–248.

[15] Y. Zou, M.D. Laubichler, From systems to biology: a computational analysis of the research articles on systems biology from 1992 to 2013, PLoS ONE 13 (7) (2018) e0200929.

[16] T. Ideker, T. Galitski, L. Hood, A new approach to decoding life: systems biology, Annu. Rev. Genom. Hum. Genet. 2 (2001) 343–372.

[17] H. Kitano, Foundations of Systems Biology, MIT Press, Cambridge, MA, 2001.

[18] H. Kitano, Systems biology: a brief overview, Science 295 (2002) 1662–1664.

[19] H. Kitano, Computational systems biology, Nature 420 (2002) 206–210.

[20] N. Wiener, Cybernetics, or Control and Communication in the Animal and the Machine, MIT Press, Cambridge, 1948.

[21] L.V. Bertalanffy, General Systems Theory. Foundations, Development, Applications, George Braziler Inc, New York, 1969.

[22] D. Noble, Cardiac action and pacemaker potentials based on the Hodgkin-Huxley equations, Nature 188 (1960) 495—497.

[23] C. Auffray, D. Noble, Conceptual and experimental origins of integrative systems biology in William Harvey's masterpiece on the movement of the heart and the blood in animals, Int. J. Mol. Sci. 10 (2009) 1658—1669.

[24] G.W. Beadle, E.L. Tatum, Genetic control of biochemical reactions in Neurospora, Proc. Natl. Acad. Sci. U. S. A 27 (1941) 499—506.

[25] E. Schrodinger, What is Life?, Canto Edition, Cambridge University Press, 1967 (Foreword by Roger Penrose).

[26] P. Wellstead, Systems Biology and the Spirit of Tustin. The 2008 Tustin Lecture, The Institution of Engineering and Technology, Savoy Place, London, 2008. SpiritOfTustin.pdf (hamilton. i.e.).

[27] M.D. Mesarović, Systems theory and biology—view of a theoretician, in: Systems Theory and Biology, Springer, Berlin, Heidelberg, 1968, pp. 59—87.

[28] J. Bard, in: Principles of Evolution-Systems, Species, and the History of Life, Garland Science, London, 2017.

[29] D.J. Kevles, L. Hood, The Code of Codes, Harvard University Press, Cambridge, 1992, p. 397.

[30] C. Auffray, S. Imbeaud, M. Roux-RouquieÂ, L. Hood, From functional genomics to systems biology: concepts and practices, C. R. Biol. 326 (10) (2003) 879—892.

[31] F.J. Bruggeman, H.V. Westerhoff, The nature of systems biology, Trends Microbiol. 15 (2007) 45—50.

[32] H.Y. Chuang, M. Hofree, T. Ideker, A decade of systems biology, Ann. Rev. Cell Dev. Biol. 26 (2010) 721—744.

[33] S. Naylor, Systems biology, information, disease and drug discovery, Drug Discovery World (Winter 2004/2005).

[34] M. Sagner, A. McNeil, P. Puska, C. Auffray, N.D. Price, L. Hood, et al., The P4 health spectrum—a predictive, preventive, personalized and participatory continuum for promoting healthspan, Prog. Cardiovasc. Dis. 59 (5) (2017) 506—521.

[35] J.P. Kernevez, E. Doedel, M.C. Duban, J.F. Hervagault, G. Joly, D. Thomas, Spatiotemporal organization in immobilized enzyme systems, Lect. Notes Biomath. 49 (1983) 51—75.

[36] J.E. Bailey, Lessons from metabolic engineering for functional genomics and drug discovery, Nat. Biotechnol. 17 (1999) 616—618.

[37] A. Friboulet, B. Avalle-Bihan, H. Débat, D. Thomas, Compounds capable of modulating the activity an stimulating the production of a catalytic antibody, Patent WO 02/09J015A1 (2002).

[38] J.E. Bailey, Toward a science of metabolic engineering, Science (New York, N.Y.) 252 (5013) (1991) 1668—1675.

[39] F. Pammolli, L. Magazzini, M. Riccaboni, The productivity crisis in pharmaceutical R&D, Nat. Rev. Drug Discov. 10 (2011) 428—438.

[40] B. Munos, Lessons from 60 years of pharmaceutical innovation, Nat. Rev. Drug Discov. 8 (2009) 959—968.

[41] J.W. Scannell, A. Blanckley, H. Boldon, B. Warrington, Diagnosing the decline in pharmaceutical R&D efficiency, Nat. Rev. Drug Discov. 11 (3) (2012) 191—200.

[42] J.P.F. Bai, B.J. Schmidt, K.G. Gadkar, V. Damian, J.C. Earp, C. Friedrich, P.H. van der Graaf, R. Madabushi, C.J. Musante, K. Naik, M. Rogge, H. Zhu, FDA-industry scientific exchange on assessing quantitative systems pharmacology models in clinical drug development: a meeting report, summary of challenges/gaps, and future perspective, AAPS J 23 (3) (2021) 60, https://doi.org/10.1208/s12248-021-00585-x. PMID: 33931790.

[43] E.C. Butcher, E.L. Berg, E.J. Kunkel, Systems biology in drug discovery, Nat. Biotechnol. 22 (10) (2004) 1253—1259.

[44] Drug development costs jump to $2.6 billion, Cancer Discov., AACR 5 (2) (2015) OF2.

[45] J.P. Galizzi, B.P. Lockhart, A. Bril, Applying systems biology in drug discovery and development, Drug Metabol. Drug Interact. 28 (2) (2013) 67—78.

[46] E.L. Berg, Systems biology in drug discovery and development, Drug Discov. Today 19 (2) (2014) 113—125.

[47] A. Pujol, R. Mosca, J. Farrés, P. Aloy, Unveiling the role of network and systems biology in drug discovery, Trends Pharmacol. Sci. 31 (3) (2010) 115—123.

[48] L. Hood, R.M. Perlmutter, The impact of systems approaches on biological problems in drug discovery, Nat. Biotechnol. 22 (10) (2004) 1215—1217.

[49] J. Zou, M.W. Zheng, G. Li, Z.G. Su, Advanced systems biology methods in drug discovery and translational biomedicine, BioMed Res. Int. 2013 (2013) 742835.

[50] E.J. Kunkel, Systems biology in drug discovery, in: Conference Proceedings: Annual International Conference of the IEEE Engineering in Medicine and Biology Society. IEEE Engineering in Medicine and Biology Society. Annual Conference, 2006, 2006, p. 37.

[51] A.M. Henney, Who will take up the gauntlet? Challenges and opportunities for systems biology and drug discovery, EMBO Rep. 10 (Suppl 1) (2009) S9—S13.

[52] C. Wierling, T. Kessler, L.A. Ogilvie, B.M. Lange, M.L. Yaspo, H. Lehrach, Network and systems biology: essential steps in virtualizing drug discovery and development, Drug Discov. Today. Technol. 15 (2015) 33—40.

[53] B. Regierer, V. Zazzu, R. Sudbrak, A. Kühn, H. Lehrach, Future of medicine: models in predictive diagnostics and personalized medicine, Adv. Biochem. Eng. Biotechnol. 133 (2013) 15—33.

[54] B.J. Schmidt, F.P. Casey, T. Paterson, et al., Alternate virtual populations elucidate the type I interferon signature predictive of the response to rituximab in rheumatoid arthritis, BMC Bioinformatics 14 (2013) 221. https://doi.org/10.1186/1471-2105-14-221.

[55] R. Allen, T. Rieger, C. Musante, Efficient generation and selection of virtual populations in quantitative systems pharmacology models: generation and selection of virtual populations, CPT Pharmacometrics Syst Pharmacol 5 (2016) 140—146. https://doi.org/10.1002/psp4.12063.

[56] B. Al-Lazikani, U. Banerji, P. Workman, Combinatorial drug therapy for cancer in the post-genomic era, Nat. Biotechnol. 30 (7) (2012) 679—692.

[57] S.H. Preskorn, The role of proof of concept (POC) studies in drug development using the EVP-6124 POC study as an example, J. Psychiatr. Pract. 20 (1) (2014) 59—60.

[58] E.L. Bradshaw, M.E. Spilker, R. Zang, L. Bansal, H. He, R.D.O. Jones, K. Le, M. Penney, E. Schuck, B. Topp, A. Tsai, C. Xu, M.J.M.A. Nijsen, J.R. Chan, Applications of quantitative systems pharmacology in model-informed drug discovery: Perspective on impact and opportunities, CPT Pharmacometrics Syst Pharmacol 8 (11) (2019) 777−791, https://doi.org/10.1002/psp4.12463, 2019 Oct 25. PMID: 31535440; PMCID: PMC6875708.

[59] A. Kondic, D. Bottino, J. Harrold, J.D. Kearns, C.J. Musante, A. Odinecs, S. Ramanujan, J. Selimkhanov, B. Schoeberl, Navigating between right, wrong, and relevant: The use of mathematical modeling in preclinical decision making, Front Pharmacol 13 (2022) 860881, https://doi.org/10.3389/fphar.2022.860881. PMID: 35496315; PMCID: PMC9042116.

[60] P. Vicini, P.H. van der Graaf, Systems pharmacology for drug discovery and development: paradigm shift or flash in the pan? Clin Pharmacol Ther 93 (5) (2013) 379−381, https://doi.org/10.1038/clpt.2013.40. PMID: 23598453.

[61] C.M. Friedrich, A model qualification method for mechanistic physiological QSP models to support model-informed drug development, CPT Pharmacometrics Syst Pharmacol 5 (2) (2016) 43−53, https://doi.org/10.1002/psp4.12056. Epub 2016 Jan 26. PMID: 26933515; PMCID: PMC4761232.

[62] K. Gadkar, D. Kirouac, N. Parrott, S. Ramanujan, Quantitative systems pharmacology: a promising approach for translational pharmacology, Drug Discov Today Technol (2016) 957−965, https://doi.org/10.1016/j.ddtec.2016.11.001. Epub 2016 Nov 24. PMID: 27978989.

[63] W.J. Jusko, Moving from basic toward systems pharmacodynamic models, J Pharm Sci 102 (9) (2013) 2930−2940, https://doi.org/10.1002/jps.23590. Epub 2013 May 16. PMID: 23681608; PMCID: PMC3743951.

[64] C. Pichardo-Almarza, V. Diaz-Zuccarini, From PK/PD to QSP: Understanding the dynamic effect of cholesterol-lowering drugs on atherosclerosis progression and stratified medicine, Curr Pharm Des 22 (46) (2016) 6903−6910, https://doi.org/10.2174/1381612822666160905095402. PMID: 27592718; PMCID: PMC5403958.

[65] K. Azer, C. Kaddi, J.S. Barrett, J. Bai, S. McQuade, N. Merrill, et al., History and future perspectives on the discipline of QSP modeling and its applications, Accepted Front. Physiol. Syst. Pharmacol. (2021).

[66] E. Bradley, Incorporating biomarkers into clinical trial designs: points to consider, Nat. Biotechnol. 30 (2012) 596−599.

[67] J.P.F. Bai, J.C. Earp, D.G. Strauss, H. Zhu, A perspective on quantitative systems pharmacology applications to clinical drug development, CPT Pharmacometrics Syst Pharmacol 9 (12) (2020) 675−677, https://doi.org/10.1002/psp4.12567. Epub 2020 Nov 7. PMID: 33159491; PMCID: PMC7762807.

[68] P.M. Heaton, J.S. Barrett, From patient to molecule: in pursuit of universal treatments for TB, Clin. Transl. Sci. (2019), https://doi.org/10.1111/cts.12718. PMID: 31782618.

[69] Cardiovascular diseases, 2022. WHO.int. https://www.who.int/health-topics/cardiovascular-diseases/ (Accessed 10 March 2022).

[70] C.P. Nelson, A. Goel, A.S. Butterworth, S. Kanoni, T.R. Webb, E. Marouli, et al., Association analyses based on false discovery rate implicate new loci for coronary artery disease, Nat. Genet. 49 (9) (2017) 1385−1391. Epub 2017/07/18.

[71] J.M.M. Howson, W. Zhao, D.R. Barnes, W.K. Ho, R. Young, D.S. Paul, et al., Fifteen new risk loci for coronary artery disease highlight arterial-wall-specific mechanisms, Nat. Genet. 49 (7) (2017) 1113−1119. Epub 2017/05/23.

[72] P.L. Auer, N.O. Stitziel, Genetic association studies in cardiovascular diseases: do we have enough power? Trends Cardiovasc. Med. 27 (6) (2017) 397−404. Epub 2017/05/01.

[73] M. Nikpay, A. Goel, H.H. Won, L.M. Hall, C. Willenborg, S. Kanoni, et al., A comprehensive 1,000 genomes-based genome-wide association meta-analysis of coronary artery disease, Nat. Genet. 47 (10) (2015) 1121−1130. Epub 2015/09/08.

[74] J. Erdmann, K. Stark, U.B. Esslinger, P.M. Rumpf, D. Koesling, C. de Wit, et al., Dysfunctional nitric oxide signalling increases risk of myocardial infarction, Nature 504 (7480) (2013) 432−436. Epub 2013/11/12.

[75] J. Loscalzo, A.L. Barabasi, Systems biology and the future of medicine, Wiley Interdiscip. Rev. Syst. Biol. Med. 3 (6) (2011) 619−627, https://doi.org/10.1002/wsbm.144.

[76] A. Joshi, M. Rienks, K. Theofilatos, M. Mayr, Systems biology in cardiovascular disease: a multiomics approach, Nat. Rev. (2020).

[77] M. Santolini, M.C. Romay, C.L. Yukhtman, C.D. Rau, S. Ren, J.J. Saucerman, et al., A personalized, multiomics approach identifies genes involved in cardiac hypertrophy and heart failure, NPJ Syst. Biol. Appl. 4 (12) (2018), https://doi.org/10.1038/s41540-018-0046-3.

[78] S. Doran, M. Arif, S. Lam, A. Bayraktar, H. Turkez, M. Uhlen, et al., Multi-omics approaches for revealing the complexity of cardiovascular disease, Brief. Bioinform. 22 (5) (2021) 1−19.

[79] K.D. Bromberg, A. Ma'ayan, S.R. Neves, R. Iyengar, Design logic of a cannabinoid receptor signaling network that triggers neurite outgrowth, Science (New York, N.Y.) 320 (5878) (2008) 903−909, https://doi.org/10.1126/science.1152662.

[80] M.S. Carro, W.K. Lim, M.J. Alvarez, R.J. Bollo, X. Zhao, E.Y. Snyder, et al., The transcriptional network for mesenchymal transformation of brain tumours, Nature 463 (7279) (2010) 318−325, https://doi.org/10.1038/nature08712.

[81] J.E.W. Beneken, A Mathematical Approach to Cardiovascular Function, The Uncontrolled Human System Institute of Medical Physics Report no. 2-4-5/6 Utrecht, the Netherlands, 1965.

[82] J. Beneken, B.A. DeWIT, Physical approach to hemodynamic aspects of the human cardiovascular system, in: Physical Bases of Circulatory Transport: Regulation and Exchange, W.B. Saunders, Philadelphia, PA, 1967.

[83] A.C. Guyton, T.G. Coleman, Long-term regulation of the circulation: Interrelationships with body fluid volumes, in: E.B. Reeve, A.C. Guyton (Eds.), Physical Bases of Circulatory Transport, W.B. Saunders, Philadelphia, PA, 1967, pp. 179−201.

[84] A.C. Guyton, T.G. Coleman, H.J. Granger, Circulation: overall regulation annual review of physiology, Annu. Rev. Physiol. 34 (1972) 13−46.

[85] G.E. Louridas, K.G. Lourida, Systems biology and biomechanical model of heart failure, Curr. Cardiol. Rev. 8 (2012) 220−230.

[86] EPIC-CVD Consortium, A. Goel, A.S. Butterworth, et al., Association analyses based on false discovery rate implicate new loci for coronary artery disease, Nat. Genet. 49 (2017) 1385−1391.

[87] The CARDIoGRAMplusC4D Consortium, A comprehensive 1000 genomes—based genome-wide association meta analysis of coronary artery disease, Nat. Genet. 47 (2015) 1121−1130.

[88] M. Varshneya, I. Irurzun-Arana, C. Campana, R. Dariolli, A. Gutierrez, T.K. Pullinger, E.A. Sobie, Investigational treatments for COVID-19 may increase ventricular arrhythmia risk through drug interactions, CPT Pharmacometrics Syst. Pharmacol. 10 (2) (2021) 100−107, https://doi.org/10.1002/psp4.12573.

[89] V. Galvao, J.G. Miranda, R. Ribeiro-dos-Santos, Development of a two-dimensional agent-based model for chronic chagasic cardiomyopathy after stem cell transplantation, Bioinformatics 24 (2008) 2051−2056.

[90] E. Sirois, W. Sun, Computational evaluation of platelet activation induced by a bioprosthetic heart valve, Artif. Organs 35 (2010) 157−165.

[91] T. Usyk, J. Omens, A. McCulloch, Regional septal dysfunction in a three-dimensional computational model of focal myofiber disarray, Am. J. Physiol. Heart Circ. Physiol. 281 (2001) H506−H514.

[92] R.C. Kerckhoffs, A.D. McCulloch, J.H. Omens, L.J. Mulligan, Effects of biventricular pacing and scar size in a computational model of the failing heart with left bundle branch block, Med. Image Anal. 13 (2009) 362−369.

[93] F. Sheikh, K. Ouyang, S. Campbell, R. Lyon, J. Chuang, D. Fitzsimons, et al., Integrative mouse and computational models link altered myosin kinetics to early events in cardiac disease, J. Clin. Invest. 122 (2012) 1209−1221.

[94] V. Gurev, P. Pathmanathan, J.L. Fattebert, H.F. Wen, J. Magerlein, R.A. Gray, et al., A high-resolution computational model of the deforming human heart, Biomech. Model. Mechanobiol. 14 (4) (2015) 829−849, https://doi.org/10.1007/s10237-014-0639-8.

[95] D.F. Richards, J.N. Glosli, E.W. Draeger, A.A. Mirin, B. Chan, J.L. Fattebert, et al., Towards real-time simulation of cardiac electrophysiology in a human heart at high resolution, Comput. Methods Biomech. Biomed. Eng. 16 (7) (2013) 802−805, https://doi.org/10.1080/10255842.2013.795556.

[96] M. Varshneya, X. Mei, E.A. Sobie, Prediction of arrhythmia susceptibility through mathematical modeling and machine learning, Proc. Natl. Acad. Sci. U. S. A. 118 (37) (2021), https://doi.org/10.1073/pnas.2104019118 e2104019118.

[97] C. Jons, J. O-Uchi, A.J. Moss, M. Reumann, J.J. Rice, I. Goldenberg, et al., Use of mutant-specific ion channel characteristics for risk stratification of long QT syndrome patients, Sci. Transl. Med. 3 (76) (2011) 76ra28, https://doi.org/10.1126/scitranslmed.3001551.

[98] R. Hoefen, M. Reumann, I. Goldenberg, A.J. Moss, J. O-Uchi, Y. Gu, et al., In silico cardiac risk assessment in patients with long QT syndrome: type 1: clinical predictability of cardiac models, J. Am. Coll. Cardiol. 60 (21) (2012) 2182−2191, https://doi.org/10.1016/j.jacc.2012.07.053.

[99] A.D. Kaiser, D.M. McQueen, C.S. Peskin, Modeling the mitral valve [published correction appears in Int J Numer Method Biomed Eng. 2020 Sep;36(9):e3349], Int. J. Numer. Method Biomed. Eng. 35 (11) (2019) e3240, https://doi.org/10.1002/cnm.3240.

Chapter 4

ADME considerations for siRNA-based therapeutics

Mai B. Thayer, Sara C. Humphreys, Julie M. Lade and Brooke M. Rock

Pharmacokinetics and Drug Metabolism Department, Amgen Research, South San Francisco, CA, United States

Introduction

Synthetic oligonucleotides used to control disease at the transcriptional level have emerged as a new class of promising therapeutics-offering unique targeting capabilities to diseases once thought to be undruggable. Harnessing the unique pathway of RNA interference (RNAi) synthetic oligonucleotides neutralize their mRNA targets and inhibit protein transcription. Traditional drug development strategies have been re-evaluated with this novel approach. In this chapter, we examine the required ADME (absorption, distribution, metabolism and excretion) tools critical to the development of oligonucleotide drugs and discuss their applicability to the translational development of new chemical entities. Our aim is to review the current practices of the field and to highlight areas of possible improvement.

Two major therapeutic classes have emerged to exploit two distinct endogenous RNAi pathways [1−3] for pharmacologic applications. In the first approach, small interfering RNAs (siRNA) engages the RNA-induced silencing complex (RISC) to silence complementary endogenous RNA targets such as mRNA. In the second, antisense oligonucleotide (ASO) binds its RNA complement via recruitment of RNase H to inhibit protein synthesis [4−11]. Although siRNA and ASOs are both oligonucleotides, their physicochemical properties diverge given that siRNA is double-stranded RNA and ASOs are single stranded DNA and/or RNA. These differences are further exacerbated in the therapeutic design space, with distinct chemical modifications being applied to the backbone, sugars and bases of each class to increase specific activity. To ensure depth and focus, in this chapter, we have elected to focus primarily on siRNA.

The natural function of RNAi is to regulate gene expression in a two-step manner—the first step involves an RNase-like degradation of double stranded RNA into 21−25 nucleotide pieces resulting in small interfering RNAs. In the subsequent step, siRNA molecules associate with an RNA-induced silencing protein complex (RISC) which acts upon a complimentary RNA sequence for degradation [12]. This mechanism of transcriptional interference was discovered in the 1900s in eukaryotes and over the last decade, monumental advances in delivery strategy and oligonucleotide chemistry have allowed for the application of this technology as a therapeutic [13−16]. Key characteristics of these molecules make them stand out from their traditional small and large molecule counterparts. Synthetic siRNAs are generally ∼15,000 Da in size and highly negatively charged, posing a challenge for delivery as well as for the development of novel ADME assays. Furthermore, combined advancements in delivery and chemistry have had a dramatic impact on efficacy leading to reduction in dose. Consequently, bioanalytical sensitivity has emerged as a new challenge for quantification and characterization.

In this chapter, we focus namely on publicly available information pertaining to the approved siRNA drugs. Lack of technique standardization across the field can lead to many issues including experimental design flaws, reproducibility, and data comparability issues. Without controlled experimental procedures in place, translational development can also be impacted. The fate of a molecule and its absorption, distribution, metabolism, and excretion characteristics is directly tied to the quality of the assays used to measure the drug. Relationships between pharmacokinetics and pharmacodynamics are also critical in the selection of a drug candidate and in understanding species differences. Herein, we discuss the tools that exist, highlight their strengths and limitations, and propose workflows moving forward in a tool-kit development for siRNA therapeutics.

Overcoming Obstacles in Drug Discovery and Development. https://doi.org/10.1016/B978-0-12-817134-9.00024-6

Deep dive on RNAi mechanism of action

RNA interference is a highly evolutionarily conserved process to modulate RNA concentration and translation at the post-transcriptional level [17]. The mechanism in eukaryotes was elucidated in the 1990s, and in 2006, Fire and Mello were awarded the Nobel Prize in Physiology for their contribution to this work [13]. From the onset, RNAi promised to revolutionize personalized medicine by bridging the gap between the genetic code and targeted therapeutics; bringing to reality an exciting new therapeutic modality to battle undruggable diseases. Despite this potential, early pioneers encountered significant hurdles relating to delivery, stability, efficacy, and toxicity. Over the last two decades, this novel drug modality has gained traction. Many early development obstacles have been overcome via advances in delivery strategy, structure-activity relationships (SAR), and oligonucleotide chemistry [14−16].

Many of these early obstacles were overcome through understanding of the RNAi mechanistic pathway. Specifically, siRNA is bioactivated through selective loading of the antisense strand into the Argonaute (Ago), a principal component of RISC. Ago-mediated strand selection is governed by the relative thermodynamic stability of the dsRNA termini [18]. Silencing occurs via Ago2-mediated target RNA degradation or Ago "stalling" through sterically blocking translational machinery access [17]. The molecular mechanism of siRNA follows a complex scheme of: siRNA binding to Argonaute 2 (Ago2); sense strand dissociation that may be driven by via Ago2-mediated site-specific cleavage of the phosphodiester (PO) bond directly across from nucleotides 10−11 of the antisense strand (counting from the 5′ terminus), resulting in RISC-activated antisense; RISC-activated antisense locating and hybridizing to its target RNA via Watson-Crick base-pairing complementarity; Ago2-mediated cleavage of the target mRNA via an RNAse H-like hydrolysis mechanism [17]; and catalytic cycling of activated RISC through many rounds of target RNA degradation. Target RNA specificity is achieved via full- or partial Watson-Crick base-pair complementarity of the antisense strand. In contrast to SM therapeutics, which typically act via binding-mediated pharmacology, siRNA and a growing number of other emerging therapeutic modalities such as proteolysis-targeting chimeras (PROTACs) exhibit event driven pharmacology [19]. This is an important concept to consider when attempting to understand the relationship between PK and PD, since a linear application of the free drug hypothesis does not apply.

Measurement of siRNA drug exposure

Essential to translating lead molecules to promising therapies—precise quantification of siRNA therapeutics within systemic and site of action exposures is required. To this end, various bioanalytical assays have been developed. They can be broadly classified into the following categories: hybridization-based plate-assays, hybridization-based liquid chromatography (LC) fluorescence assays, and chromatographic assays. Relying on Watson-Crick base pairing mechanisms, hybridization assays function as indirect analyses using a probe oligonucleotide to hybridize to the target nucleotide analyte of interest. Hybridization complexes formed are then directed for quantification on appropriate platforms including hybridization ELISA or immunoassay, quantitative PCR (qPCR), in situ hybridization, northern blot, microarray or next-generation sequencing [20]. For chromatographic assays, detection is direct—usually involving liquid chromatographic separation followed by detection of target molecule using UV, fluorescence or mass spectrometry (MS). In general, chromatographic assays are known for their specificity, whereas hybridization for its sensitivity.

Hybridization-based assays use an oligonucleotide comprised probe instead of an antigen-based detection, as is the case with typical ELISA and immunoassays, and are capable of being carried out in a high-throughput, plate-based formats. Plate-based processes typically involves immobilization of the hybridization product with complementary oligonucleotide probe, and the addition of a detection probe for assay signaling. One important advantage of this approach is the ability for analyte detection without the removal of biological matrices involved with extraction steps or the need for rounds of target amplification, as with PCR. They have been widely implemented for the quantitative analyses of oligonucleotides to support discovery and regulatory information gathering in efforts of toxicokinetic (TK) and pharmacokinetic (PK) evaluations and are particularly useful for terminal phase PK assessment [21,22]. Various types of hybridization-based ligand binding assays have been reported in the literature and patent space to support drug exposures including sandwich-hybridization assay, hybridization-ligation, nuclease-based hybridization assay, competitive hybridization assay, hybridization-based fluorescence assay, and triplex forming oligonucleotide assay [21−25].

Hybridization-based LC-fluorescence assays build upon the traditional hybridization ELISA principles (high sensitivity and lack of sample preparation) and conventional high-performance liquid chromatography and ultra violet (HPLC/UV) fluorescence assays (high accuracy/precision and specificity) [26,27]. Two main steps are involved with this method, the first is to hybridize our target oligonucleotide strand to a fluorescence-labelled sequence-specific probe oligonucleotide. The second step is then to subject the fluorescence-labelled duplex to a strong-anion exchange HPLC (SAX-HPLC) analysis via a fluorescence detector. In the published assays, a ligation step is often added to aid in hybridization stability and specificity [28−30].

Liquid chromatography with tandem mass spectrometry (LC-MS/MS) assays are most commonly used chromatographic assays to quantify oligonucleotide therapeutics in biological matrices. LC-MS/MS offers one of the most specific bioanalytical methods for oligonucleotides as it offers chromatographic separation, molecular weight identification, and product ion characterization [31]. Another advantage includes its application to the identification of oligonucleotide metabolites—which we discuss in a later section of this chapter. One major limitation of this approach is the challenge of detection sensitivity within complex biological matrices—especially with oligonucleotide therapeutics where understanding of distribution within target tissues is critical to understanding delivery and efficacy. While coupling MS/MS with ultra-performance LC (UPLC) has been shown to improve chromatographic resolution and sharper peaks, routine analysis out of biological samples exhausts the short lifespan of UPLC columns [32].

As with all mentioned assays, hybridization or chromatography, and coupled assays are denaturing assays—having either a stand-alone denaturing step or secondary denaturation due to column heat. For siRNA therapeutics, this means for the individual analysis of each strand separately, with no assays in place specific to "duplex siRNA." At this point in time, there is no published assay for the measurement of duplex or intact siRNA. This limitation in bioanalytical assays, requires two assays to measure "intact" siRNA drug.

Biodistribution of siRNA

As more similar with large molecule therapeutics, biodistribution is fundamental to anticipating safety and efficacy in target organs—allowing for more integrated human predictions within a whole body. In the exploratory drug discovery space, there is often limited human data, imparting the importance of relevant species consideration in biodistribution studies for both systemically and locally administered therapeutic. Similar to pharmacokinetic studies, siRNA itself may be qualitatively tracked using hybridization, secondary-antibody, PCR, or MS methods, however these methods do not inform the distribution of the molecule within the specific tissue(s). Organ collection related to these methods may be extremely tedious.

Alternate, indirect methods are more commonly implemented for siRNA biodistribution studies including tracking of surrogate signals of dyes or radioactive elements incorporated into the molecule. Non-invasive methods for tracing siRNA *in vivo* are key to understanding the biodistribution of these therapeutics, especially in humans. As such, molecular imaging techniques can serve as powerful tools for tracking siRNA delivery *in vivo*. Optical imaging (fluorescence and bioluminescence), magnetic resonance imaging (MRI), radionuclide-based imaging (single photon emission computed tomography—SPECT and positron emission tomography—PET), and ultrasound have been employed for the assessment of various siRNA delivery techniques [33,34].

Two strategies for optical imaging of siRNA are labeling of the siRNA or labeling of their carriers. Due to its many advantages, such as easy labeling, choice of dyes, and whole body real-time read out, optical imaging is the most convenient way for preclinical study of RNAi knockdown [34]. Chang et al. describes an siRNA-based molecular beacon incorporating a fluorescence resonance energy transfer (FRET) fluorophore pair (Cy3/Cy5) developed to detect and knockdown telomerase expression in human breast cancer cells [35]. This strategy had impressive gene silencing efficiency and allowed for fluorescence imaging. There have been many examples where quantum dots are used to label siRNA carriers. For example, cationic liposomes to deliver quantum dots and siRNA to murine fibroblasts [36], incorporated a polyethylene glycol-modified quantum dot core with siRNA and tumor-homing peptides [37]. Lastly, encapsulated quantum dots in chitosan nanoparticles to deliver and monitor HER2 siRNA [38]. However, due to poor tissue penetration and lack of quantitation capability, optical imaging has limited clinical potential. Uniquely, a dual-purpose probe that consisted of magnetic nanoparticles and Cy5.5 dye conjugated to a synthetic siRNA duplex was the first example of multimodality imaging using a nanoparticle. Through their experiments, they found they were able to monitor probe delivery *in vivo* by optical imaging and MRI [39].

Radionuclide-based imaging are more suitable for *in vivo* imaging of siRNA delivery than MRI and optical imaging due to their sensitive, quantitative, and tomographic characteristics. ^{99m}Tc and ^{111}In have been used to determine the biodistribution of siRNAs with SPECT, however, it is not known if there was any correlation with efficacy [40,41]. PET imaging remains the method of choice for assessing the pharmacokinetics of new therapeutic agents [42]. Fluorine-18 appears often as the radionuclide of choice for the preparation of short-lived positron-emitter radiotracers. The low positron energy and short ranges in tissues lead to a high image resolution [43]. Recent advances in 18F-labeling may greatly facilitate future research of siRNA pharmacokinetics and biodistribution [44].

Ultrasound is widely used to evaluate the structure, function, and blood flow of organs. However, it requires contrast agents such as microbubbles to increase imaging accuracy [34]. Microbubbles have poor tissue penetration due to its size which prompted development of smaller contrast agents with better tissue penetration properties (nanobubbles, nanoparticles, and nanoscale liposomes) [45]. Ultrasound is limited to imaging soft tissue only.

The advances in noninvasive imaging techniques to understand the mechanism and pharmacokinetics of siRNA *in vivo* has led to significant contributions to the field. As the field continues to grow, further improvements in imaging probes, contrast agents, and imaging devices would greatly add to the understanding of siRNA.

Considerations for metabolic pathways of siRNA

Measurement of oligonucleotide concentrations as well as identification and quantitation of their metabolites in both *in vitro* and *in vivo* studies are essential during drug development, as they can provide critical information to evaluate pharmacokinetic profiles and elucidate metabolic pathways. A robust, selective, and sensitive bioanalytical method is the key to achieve successful measurement of oligonucleotides and their metabolites in a variety of biological matrices. Traditionally, PCR- or ELISA-based assays have been the gold standard for oligonucleotide quantitation due to their high sensitivity; however, it is quite challenging to differentiate metabolites from the full-length oligonucleotides in these assays. Recently, scientists have developed several LC-MS-based methods to analyze oligonucleotides which can offer better specificity and achieve simultaneous detection/quantitation of full-length strands as well as their metabolites while providing reasonable sensitivity [46−57]. Ion-pairing (IP) reversed-phase LC coupled with ESI high resolution MS (HRMS) in negative ion mode has been the most preferred approach nowadays. The roles of IP reagents (e.g., TEA, DIEA), counter anions (e.g., HFIP), other additives (e.g., EDTA) and pH in mobile phases have been extensively investigated for the separation and ionization of oligonucleotides [58−62]. HRMS can not only offer high selectivity for target oligonucleotide quantitation, but also provide information related to metabolites. It is important to note that a high-recovery extraction method is also essential to increase the sensitivity of analyzing oligonucleotides in plasma, urine, tissues, and other complex biological samples. Various sample preparation techniques such as liquid-liquid extraction and anion-exchange solid phase extraction have been developed to enrich oligonucleotides from complex biological matrices prior to LC-MS analysis [63−65]. To account for any loss that might happen during sample preparation, a surrogate oligonucleotide that matches the chemistry and stereochemistry of the target analyte can be spiked in as an internal standard.

Compared to small molecules, the metabolism of oligonucleotides can be more predictable. They are mainly metabolized via cleavage of the phosphodiester bonds by intracellular endo- and exonucleases to produce chain-shortened oligonucleotide metabolites. Cleavage at the 3′-terminus by exonucleases is the major metabolic route for oligonucleotides, followed by 5′-exonuclease and endonuclease cleavage events [47,50]. The chemical modifications on the backbone of oligonucleotides determine enzymatic activities leading to the generation of metabolites. In addition, oligonucleotides can be conjugated to other entities to enhance desired target delivery. The metabolism of these entities should also be characterized. For example, triantennary GalNAc is often conjugated to oligonucleotide for hepatic target delivery as it can be recognized and internalized by asialoglycoprotein receptor, a major cell surface receptor on hepatocytes. Oligonucleotide with such ligand is mainly metabolized by loss of GalNAc sugars and their linkers [51]. Oligonucleotide metabolites can be identified by high resolution accurate mass (HRAM) measurement in full scan mode; the observed mass should be of ≤10 ppm mass error from the exact mass of the predicted metabolite. The identification can be further confirmed with MS/MS spectra; however, MS/MS data interpretation is quite difficult and time-consuming due to the large number of fragment ions generated from oligonucleotides. Fortunately, this issue has been alleviated through advances in software such as automated deconvolution [47,51,66]. Moreover, MS/MS analysis can also aid in the characterization of novel metabolites [53].

During early stage of drug discovery, reference compounds may not available for absolute quantitation of metabolites. In this case, the abundance of each metabolite can be reported as the percentage of peak area/intensity of individual metabolite to that of the parent oligonucleotide [47,49]. Each analyte may have a different ionization efficiency, and thus the relative percentage is only an estimation of their relative abundance. But this estimation can provide critical insights on whether a more accurate quantitative assay is needed or not.

Similar to small molecule therapeutics, understanding cross species metabolism can aid in toxicology species selection, and re-design of more metabolically stable entities.

Measurement of plasma protein binding (PPB)

siRNA plasma protein binding (PPB) is a measure of the unbound fraction (f_u) of siRNA in plasma at equilibrium. A PPB report is required for small molecule regulatory filing because according to the free drug hypothesis, $f_{u,plasma}$ is equivalent to the unbound drug concentration at the site of action at steady state. There is currently no clear guidance about PPB filing for siRNA. To date, two methods describing siRNA PPB quantification have been published. One approach employs ultrafiltration (UF) to separate the unbound fraction via a size-selective membrane, the other uses an electrophoretic mobility shift assay (EMSA) to separate based on size and charge [67,68]. A comparison of the methods indicates that across the therapeutic range of 1.5−15 μg/mL siRNA, $f_{u,plasma}$ ranges from approximately 0.1−0.25 for ultrafiltration and 0.1−0.65 for EMSA.

Advantages of UF are that it can be performed in neat plasma, and low non-specific binding is achievable when the filter is pre-treated with a detergent such as Tween 20 or CHAPS. Limitations of UF are that GalNAc-conjugated 21−23-mer siRNA appear to be close to the upper limit to freely flow through a 50 MWCO filter, so longer siRNA or siRNA with bulky ligands may result in lower recoveries. Also, the filter does not explicitly separate unbound siRNA from all protein species in plasma; anything with a hydrodynamic radius smaller than the filter pore size can get through. Consequently, although the contribution was shown to be negligible, it is theoretically possible for siRNA bound to small molecular weight protein species to result in overprediction of PPB.

Advantages of EMSA is that it is relatively faster than ultrafiltration because $f_{u,plasma}$ is quantifiable directly from a gel image, rather than PCR- or hybridization-based quantitation. Disadvantages of EMSA are that nucleic acid staining is not linear across a wide range of concentrations, and nucleic acid contaminants in plasma mean that percent recovery measurements are confounded.

The pharmacological role of PPB and the effects on pharmacokinetics and pharmacodynamic is not clearly defined in the literature. In general, measure of PPB for siRNA is completed as a regulatory obligation, and no direct link between the relative amount of free drug and efficacy has been defined. Namely because the amount of bound siRNA drug is relatively low, and the relationship between free drug in plasma and free drug at the site of action is not linear.

siRNA and de-risking drug-drug interactions

There is limited literature precedent of drug-drug interaction (DDI) assessments designed specifically for the siRNA modality. At present, the majority of oligonucleotide DDI strategies are based largely on a workflow indicated for traditional small molecule therapeutics. This strategy is exemplified in recent examinations of GalNAc-conjugated siRNAs [69] and 2′-O-(2-methoxyethyl)-modified antisense oligonucleotides (2-MOE-ASOs) [70]. In these studies, a panel of siRNA molecules were examined for their ability to time-dependently inhibit and/or compete for CYP active sights in purified protein or pooled liver microsomes. The proteins of interest were reflective of typical small molecule metabolizers, namely the CYP isoforms 1A2, 2B6, 2C8, 2C9, 2C19, 2D6, 2E1, 3A4, and 3A5. Similar analyses were performed by Yu, Geary [71], who demonstrated a lack of pharmacokinetic interactions between CYP1A2, 2C9, 2C19, 2D6, and 3A4 with mipomersen (an antisense oligonucleotide) in cryo-preserved human hepatocytes. Each of these three studies summarily dismiss the likelihood that major drug-metabolizing CYPs are susceptible to problematic outcomes pertinent to drug-drug interactions.

Additional experiments were carried out to examine induction of CYP1A2, 2B6, and 3A4. Probe turnover and mRNA concentrations were measured in response to concentrations of 2-MOE-ASOs. Here, human hepatocytes were incubated with up to 100 μM or 100 μg/mL 2-MOE-ASOs or positive control small molecule inducers (omeprazole for 1A2, phenobarbital for 2B6, or rifampicin for 3A4). CYP activity was then measured using isoform-specific probe substrates in aliquots of supernatant from the culture plate. The remaining cells were treated to assess the mRNA concentrations of the three CYP isoforms. While the 2-MOE-ASOs were associated with some induction in both activity (up to 2.28-fold in the case of 3A4) and mRNA concentration (up to 2.01-fold in the case of 1A2), the relative magnitudes of these effects in comparison to the control inducers led the authors to conclude a low likelihood of clinical risk.

Additional investigations into siRNA DDI have taken plasma protein binding competition and displacement into account. It is unlikely that siRNAs will be able to saturate the plasma protein compartment at therapeutic concentrations. As a result, publications have commented on the low likelihood that siRNAs would displace small molecule drugs bound to plasma proteins and therefore alter their pharmacodynamics to produce a drug-drug interaction. Ultracentrifugation to measure the free fraction of an antisense phosphorothiorated oligodeoxynecleotide (PS-ODN, 7 or 70 μg/mL) in the presence of seven highly bound small molecule substrates. No significant free fraction difference or substrate displacement was observed in either whole human plasma or human serum albumin from these experiments, which may indicate that siRNAs bind to non-competitive sites in comparison to hydrophobic small molecule drugs [72]. This statement is a feasible branching point for the field of DDI risk assessment. It seems that reports indicating a lack of interactions between siRNAs and small molecule metabolizers leave open the question of whether general siRNA structures are feasible substrates for the enzymes traditionally thought to be critical for DDI. A biophysical investigation into the nature of siRNA binding to drug metabolizing enzymes, transporters, and plasma proteins is necessary to guide future research on this emerging field.

Immunogenicity of siRNA molecules

To develop therapeutics in RNAi, overcoming toxicity that is not originated from the therapeutics' on-target activity has been a challenge. Sometimes it is also needed to find whether the therapeutic outcomes come from siRNA-mediated specific gene silencing or from non-specific innate immune response stimulated by siRNA. Up to date four types of non-target specific toxicity have been known: immunogenicity to the therapeutics through innate immune response, toxicity (either from immunogenicity or non-immunogenicity) from chemical excipients, off-target effect by the therapeutics, and the drugs' effects on targets that reside in other targets as well [73]. The anti-drug antibodies (ADAs) can recognize endogenous nucleic acids in systemic circulation, for instance in systemic lupus erythematosus where it leads to increased cytokine production and kidney inflammation. It is also known that the presence of the nucleic acid-binding proteins can lead an immune response to different directions by modifying a cellular pathway [74]. Although the investigation of immunogenicity against the biological drugs are both essential and critical nowadays, there have been only limited amount of works done regarding siRNA drugs so far.

In the innate immune response, siRNA is recognized by so-called pattern recognition receptors (PRR) that mediate stimulation of the innate immune response. There are two groups of PRRs: toll-like receptors (TLRs) and cytoplasmic receptors (TLR-independent). TLRs mediate innate immune response mostly in endosomal compartments and on cell membrane especially for TLR3. TLR3 is known to recognize double-stranded RNA (dsRNA), and TLR7 and TLR8 to recognize single-stranded RNA (ssRNA). They all respond to siRNAs since siRNAs are dsRNAs composed of two ssRNAs, resulting in increased productions of various cytokines such as IFN-α, IFN-β, TNF-a, IL-1, and IL-6. The receptors in the cytoplasm include double-stranded RNA-dependent protein kinase (PKR) and retinoic acid-inducible gene 1 protein (RIG-1). PKR can be activated by both traditional siRNA and blunt siRNA and inhibits translation of proteins and increase responses of interferons. RIG-1 reacts to uncapped 5$'$ end of siRNA or blunt siRNA leading to elevated responses of interferons. All these PRRs therefore are shown to mediate the innate immune response through their unique mechanisms after responding to siRNA in various cell types and cell locations [75,76]. Various techniques are currently available to measure level of the immune response caused by siRNA such as measurement of cytokine levels, mRNA level measurement of IFIT1 gene that is an upstream indicator of IFN expression, or inclusion of control siRNA in a study.

The immunogenicity is able to influence on the activity of the drugs and there are reported sources of toxicity from siRNA treatment [73]. On the other hand some expect synergistic therapeutic effects from the gene silencing plus the innate immune response by siRNA, which can be beneficial in treatment of a certain disease such as cancer [76]. Therefore, it is crucial to carefully design siRNA molecules or studies in regard to several factors that are known to modulate the degree of the immune responses, such as chemical sequence/sequence modification, structure, delivery agents, cell types or selection of animal species so that toxic effect of siRNA is controlled, and the beneficial effect of the immune response can be utilized.

Characterizing target engagement of siRNA

To establish pharmacology of siRNA therapeutics, the measurement of direct target RNA knockdown, or of subsequent translational inhibition of protein production is required. In the ideal scenario where disease state has a secreted protein of interest, traditional ligand-based assays, such as ELISAs, or mass spectrometry (MS) can be utilized. Alternatively, quantitative assessment of circulating levels of RNA is possible using circulating extracellular RNA detection (cERD). When soluble proteins are not available and/or target RNA expression levels are too low or variable for cERD, efficacy measurements require more invasive approaches. In preclinical studies, biopsies or target tissues are assessed for target knockdown. Various methods including PCR, Northern blots, RNase protection analysis, serial analysis of gene expression and microarrays have been developed for measuring RNA in different biological samples [77,78]. The extreme sensitivity of PCR has made it the technique of choice for quantification, especially with low abundance species. Knockdown of RNA is readily quantified using reverse transcription-polymerase chain reaction (RT-PCR) and quantitative RT- PCR, after sample extraction steps, generation of cDNA, and the addition of an internal standard [79,80]. Droplet digital PCR (ddPCR) improves upon the fundamentals of PCR amplification by partitioning and offering robustness independent of reaction efficiency [81,82]. ddPCR provides absolute quantification of message by partitioning reaction mixtures into aqueous droplets in oil. The readout of positive reactions per droplet enables digitization can be fit Poisson's distribution, can be used to produce high-confidence measurements, removing the need for rate-based measurements (CT values) and the need of calibration curves [83].

An additional technique employed is the branched DNA (bDNA) technology. bDNA relies on hybridization amplification methods with the unique approach of quantification without purification and PCR amplification [84,85]. The bDNA assay uses a sandwich nucleic acid hybridization assay based on pooled oligonucleotides that function to capture, bind amplification sites, and stabilize the mRNA of interest. Next, label extenders and amplifiers are added in a branching order to directly amplify your target molecule. In contrast to RT-PCR, where amplification efficiency in a reference/calibration sample can be different from your experimental sample, bDNA calculates the absolute numbers of mRNA transcripts from a known reference sample. Coupling this technology with a Luminex platform offers extreme sensitivity and the expansion into multiplexing [84].

Moving to support clinical studies, collection of biological samples of target tissues is often not available. It has been shown that messenger and micro RNAs synthesized from various tissues can circulate through biological fluids protected from degradation via vesicular structures such as exosomes and ribonucleoprotein particles [86–88]. Tissue-specific gene silencing can be monitored with the circulation extracellular mRNA detection (cERD) assay. In short, biological fluids are subjected to high-speed centrifugation to extract total RNA from the resulting pellet. Following further enrichment with LiCl, samples are measured with RT-qPCR [89]. This assay has been applied with givosiran where mRNA levels were measured in serum and urine to evaluate nonclinical pharmacology.

Independent of the bioanalytical technique employed to measure target engagement of an siRNA molecule, understanding the amount of mRNA knockdown is key to drive the desire pharmacodynamic response. Understanding the pharmacodynamic response in relationship to drug dose is key in design of the new chemical entities.

Conclusions

The siRNA field went from being non-existent to the first approval for treatment of human disease in just over 20 years. For a completely novel therapeutic approach employing biophysically idiosyncratic drug molecular architecture, this clinical achievement was remarkable. However, while hurdles encountered by early pioneers concerning minimal stability, delivery, efficacy and safety requirements have been largely overcome, the field is now at an important junction. It may be tempting to treat siRNA or oligonucleotide therapeutics like small molecules for regulatory filing purposes, but the field must continue to develop novel tools for this new modality. Questions as: can siRNA be utilized in personalized medicine, and how we can improve the translatability to increase speed to patients, must continued to be asked.

Unsurprisingly, these questions go hand-in-hand as they both relate to our ability to fine-tune the ADME properties of these molecules to achieve an optimal therapeutic index profile toward a given target RNA. Major considerations for siRNA therapeutics today still concern stability, delivery, efficacy and safety, but the focus has shifted from identifying the minimal requirements to homing in on optimal properties.

The simplest optimization of current siRNA involves evolving structure-activity relationships understanding to select for enhanced potency and duration of effect. However, we caution that this strategy alone may not be enough. Instead, we invite the field to reconsider their idea of what an ideal drug candidate PK-PD profile looks like for this modality. Is it perhaps possible to synthesize molecules that are too stable, and bind RISC too tightly? Perhaps there is a fundamental threshold of the endogenous RISC machinery that we should avoid saturating to decrease toxicity? Could we possibly further tweak siRNA design to increase efficiency of systemic delivery to organs beyond the liver, enhance endosomal escape?

To address these questions, we need to gain better understanding of siRNA mechanistic ADME. We need to play catch-up with the small- and large-molecule fields and begin to conduct systematic investigations into siRNA in the preclinical setting such as: (1) identify meaningful *in vitro-in vivo* correlations and use them to establish and advance *in vitro* drug candidate screening funnels; (2) understand species differences at the biodistribution level, at the clearance pathway level, at the RISC machinery level, and (3) use this information to identify the most relevant preclinical animal pharmacology models to aid in construction of PK-PD models for efficacious human dose predictions.

The importance of establishing a bioanalytical toolkit to accurately characterize parent drug, bioactivated drug, and catabolites, as well and monitoring secondary drug-related perturbations to biological systems cannot be underestimated. Having the ability to spatiotemporally track these molecular entities *in vivo* and *in vitro* with high sensitivity and specificity is paramount to furthering siRNA drug development, and emphasis should be placed on standardizing robust methods to aid reproducibility and comparability of data across studies. Finally, while comprehensive mechanistic ADME studies are necessary for general field advancement, so too, are robust regulatory guidelines for clinical translation.

References

[1] M.D. de Smet, C.J. Meenken, G.J. van den Horn, Fomivirsen - a phosphorothioate oligonucleotide for the treatment of CMV retinitis, Ocul. Immunol. Inflamm. 7 (3−4) (1999) 189−198.

[2] D.J. Rader, J.J. Kastelein, Lomitapide and mipomersen: two first-in-class drugs for reducing low-density lipoprotein cholesterol in patients with homozygous familial hypercholesterolemia, Circulation 129 (9) (2014) 1022−1032.

[3] D. Adams, et al., Patisiran, an RNAi therapeutic, for hereditary transthyretin amyloidosis, N. Engl. J. Med. 379 (1) (2018) 11−21.

[4] S.M. Hammond, Dicing and slicing: the core machinery of the RNA interference pathway, FEBS Lett. 579 (26) (2005) 5822−5829.

[5] J.J. Song, et al., Crystal structure of Argonaute and its implications for RISC slicer activity, Science 305 (5689) (2004) 1434−1437.

[6] X. Shen, D.R. Corey, Chemistry, mechanism and clinical status of antisense oligonucleotides and duplex RNAs, Nucleic Acids Res. 46 (4) (2018) 1584−1600.

[7] T.A. Vickers, S.T. Crooke, The rates of the major steps in the molecular mechanism of RNase H1-dependent antisense oligonucleotide induced degradation of RNA, Nucleic Acids Res. 43 (18) (2015) 8955−8963.

[8] J. Minshull, T. Hunt, The use of single-stranded DNA and RNase H to promote quantitative 'hybrid arrest of translation' of mRNA/DNA hybrids in reticulocyte lysate cell-free translations, Nucleic Acids Res. 14 (16) (1986) 6433−6451.

[9] H. Nakamura, et al., How does RNase H recognize a DNA.RNA hybrid? Proc. Natl. Acad. Sci. U. S. A. 88 (24) (1991) 11535−11539.

[10] R.M. Crooke, et al., Metabolism of antisense oligonucleotides in rat liver homogenates, J. Pharmacol. Exp. Therapeut. 292 (1) (2000) 140−149.

[11] R.S. Geary, Antisense oligonucleotide pharmacokinetics and metabolism, Expet Opin. Drug Metabol. Toxicol. 5 (4) (2009) 381−391.

[12] N. Agrawal, et al., RNA interference: biology, mechanism, and applications, Microbiol. Mol. Biol. Rev. 67 (4) (2003) 657−685.

[13] A. Fire, et al., Potent and specific genetic interference by double-stranded RNA in *Caenorhabditis elegans*, Nature 391 (6669) (1998) 806−811.

[14] S.F. Dowdy, Overcoming cellular barriers for RNA therapeutics, Nat. Biotechnol. 35 (3) (2017) 222−229.

[15] A. Khvorova, J.K. Watts, The chemical evolution of oligonucleotide therapies of clinical utility, Nat. Biotechnol. 35 (3) (2017) 238−248.

[16] X. Chi, P. Gatti, T. Papoian, Safety of antisense oligonucleotide and siRNA-based therapeutics, Drug Discov. Today 22 (5) (2017) 823−833.

[17] A.J. Pratt, I.J. MacRae, The RNA-induced silencing complex: a versatile gene-silencing machine, J. Biol. Chem. 284 (27) (2009) 17897−17901.

[18] A. Khvorova, A. Reynolds, S.D. Jayasena, Functional siRNAs and miRNAs exhibit strand bias, Cell 115 (2) (2003) 209−216.

[19] A.C. Lai, C.M. Crews, Induced protein degradation: an emerging drug discovery paradigm, Nat. Rev. Drug Discov. 16 (2016) 101.

[20] G.A. Tremblay, P.R. Oldfield, Bioanalysis of siRNA and oligonucleotide therapeutics in biological fluids and tissues, Bioanalysis 1 (3) (2009) 595−609.

[21] J.R. Deverre, et al., A competitive enzyme hybridization assay for plasma determination of phosphodiester and phosphorothioate antisense oligonucleotides, Nucleic Acids Res. 25 (18) (1997) 3584−3589.

[22] R.Z. Yu, et al., Development of an ultrasensitive noncompetitive hybridization−ligation enzyme-linked immunosorbent assay for the determination of phosphorothioate oligodeoxynucleotide in plasma, Anal. Biochem. 304 (1) (2002) 19−25.

[23] S.C. Humphreys, et al., Quantification of siRNA-antibody conjugates in biological matrices by triplex-forming oligonucleotide ELISA, Nucleic Acid Therapeut. 29 (2019) 161−166.

[24] M.B. Thayer, et al., Application of locked nucleic acid oligonucleotides for siRNA preclinical bioanalytics, Sci. Rep. 9 (1) (2019) 3566.

[25] K.K. Chan, et al., A novel ultrasensitive hybridization-based ELISA method for 2-methoxyphosphorothiolate microRNAs and its in vitro and in vivo application, AAPS J. 12 (4) (2010) 556−568.

[26] L. Wang, Bioanalysis of oligonucleotide therapeutics, Genet. Eng. Biotechnol. News 31 (2) (2011) 14−27.

[27] A.C. McGinnis, B. Chen, M.G. Bartlett, Chromatographic methods for the determination of therapeutic oligonucleotides, J. Chromatogr. B 883−884 (2012) 76−94.

[28] V. Arora, et al., Bioavailability and efficacy of antisense morpholino oligomers targeted to c-myc and cytochrome P-450 3A2 following oral administration in rats, J. Pharmaceut. Sci. 91 (4) (2002) 1009−1018.

[29] G.R. Devi, et al., In vivo bioavailability and pharmacokinetics of a c-MYC antisense phosphorodiamidate morpholino oligomer, AVI-4126, in solid tumors, Clin. Cancer Res. 11 (10) (2005) 3930.

[30] Q. Tian, et al., Quantitative determination of a siRNA (AD00370) in rat plasma using peptide nucleic acid probe and HPLC with fluorescence detection, Bioanalysis 9 (11) (2017) 861−872.

[31] L. Wang, Oligonucleotide bioanalysis: sensitivity versus specificity, Bioanalysis 3 (12) (2011) 1299−1303.

[32] V.B. Ivleva, Y.-Q. Yu, M. Gilar, Ultra-performance liquid chromatography/tandem mass spectrometry (UPLC/MS/MS) and UPLC/MSE analysis of RNA oligonucleotides, Rapid Commun. Mass Spectrom. 24 (17) (2010) 2631−2640.

[33] H. Hong, Y. Zhang, W. Cai, In vivo imaging of RNA interference, J. Nucl. Med. Off. Publ. Soc. Nuclear Med. 51 (2) (2010) 169−172.

[34] J. Wang, et al., Imaging-guided delivery of RNAi for anticancer treatment, Adv. Drug Deliv. Rev. 104 (2016) 44−60.

[35] E. Chang, M.-Q. Zhu, R. Drezek, Novel siRNA-based molecular beacons for dual imaging and therapy, Biotechnol. J. 2 (4) (2007) 422−425.

[36] A.A. Chen, et al., Quantum dots to monitor RNAi delivery and improve gene silencing, Nucleic Acids Res. 33 (22) (2005) e190.

[37] A.M. Derfus, et al., Targeted quantum dot conjugates for siRNA delivery, Bioconjugate Chem. 18 (5) (2007) 1391−1396.

[38] W.B. Tan, S. Jiang, Y. Zhang, Quantum-dot based nanoparticles for targeted silencing of HER2/neu gene via RNA interference, Biomaterials 28 (8) (2007) 1565−1571.

[39] Z. Medarova, et al., In vivo imaging of siRNA delivery and silencing in tumors, Nat. Med. 13 (3) (2007) 372−377.

[40] N. Liu, et al., Radiolabeling small RNA with technetium-99m for visualizing cellular delivery and mouse biodistribution, Nucl. Med. Biol. 34 (4) (2007) 399−404.

[41] O.M. Merkel, et al., In vivo SPECT and real-time gamma camera imaging of biodistribution and pharmacokinetics of siRNA delivery using an optimized radiolabeling and purification procedure, Bioconjugate Chem. 20 (1) (2009) 174−182.

[42] T. Jones, The role of positron emission tomography within the spectrum of medical imaging, Eur. J. Nucl. Med. 23 (2) (1996) 207−211.

[43] W. Heindel, et al., The diagnostic imaging of bone metastases, Deutsches Arzteblatt Int. 111 (44) (2014) 741−747.

[44] T.R. Nayak, L.K. Krasteva, W. Cai, Multimodality imaging of RNA interference, Curr. Med. Chem. 20 (29) (2013) 3664−3675.

[45] Q.-L. Zhou, et al., Ultrasound-mediated local drug and gene delivery using nanocarriers, BioMed Res. Int. 2014 (2014) 963891.

[46] L. Gong, J.S. McCullagh, Analysis of oligonucleotides by hydrophilic interaction liquid chromatography coupled to negative ion electrospray ionization mass spectrometry, J. Chromatogr. A 1218 (32) (2011) 5480−5486.

[47] J. Liu, et al., Oligonucleotide quantification and metabolite profiling by high-resolution and accurate mass spectrometry, Bioanalysis 11 (21) (2019) 1967−1980.

[48] M. Meng, et al., Quantitative determination of AVI-7100 (Radavirsen), a phosphorodiamidate morpholino oligomer (PMOplus((R))), in human plasma using LC-MS/MS, Bioanalysis 9 (10) (2017) 827−839.

[49] J. Kim, et al., Metabolite profiling of the antisense oligonucleotide eluforsen using liquid chromatography-mass spectrometry, Mol. Ther. Nucleic Acids 17 (2019) 714−725.

[50] N. Post, et al., Metabolism and disposition of volanesorsen, a 2'-O-(2 methoxyethyl) antisense oligonucleotide, across species, Drug Metab. Dispos. 47 (10) (2019) 1164−1173.

[51] C.S. Shemesh, et al., Elucidation of the biotransformation pathways of a galnac3-conjugated antisense oligonucleotide in rats and monkeys, Mol. Ther. Nucleic Acids 5 (2016) e319.

[52] L. Ramanathan, H. Shen, LC-TOF-MS methods to quantify siRNAs and major metabolite in plasma, urine and tissues, Bioanalysis 11 (21) (2019) 1983−1992.

[53] J. Li, et al., Discovery of a novel deaminated metabolite of a single-stranded oligonucleotide in vivo by mass spectrometry, Bioanalysis 11 (21) (2019) 1955−1965.

[54] S. Studzinska, R. Rola, B. Buszewski, Development of a method based on ultra high performance liquid chromatography coupled with quadrupole time-of-flight mass spectrometry for studying the in vitro metabolism of phosphorothioate oligonucleotides, Anal. Bioanal. Chem. 408 (6) (2016) 1585−1595.

[55] N.M. Elzahar, et al., Degradation product characterization of therapeutic oligonucleotides using liquid chromatography mass spectrometry, Anal. Bioanal. Chem. 410 (14) (2018) 3375−3384.

[56] A. Goyon, P. Yehl, K. Zhang, Characterization of therapeutic oligonucleotides by liquid chromatography, J. Pharm. Biomed. Anal. 182 (2020) 113105.

[57] A. Goyon, K. Zhang, Characterization of antisense oligonucleotide impurities by ion-pairing reversed-phase and anion exchange chromatography coupled to HILIC/MS using a versatile 2D-LC setup, Anal. Chem. 92 (2020) 5944−5951.

[58] L. Gong, J.S. McCullagh, Comparing ion-pairing reagents and sample dissolution solvents for ion-pairing reversed-phase liquid chromatography/ electrospray ionization mass spectrometry analysis of oligonucleotides, Rapid Commun. Mass Spectrom. 28 (4) (2014) 339−350.

[59] R. Liu, et al., The role of fluoroalcohols as counter anions for ion-pairing reversed-phase liquid chromatography/high-resolution electrospray ionization mass spectrometry analysis of oligonucleotides, Rapid Commun. Mass Spectrom. 33 (7) (2019) 697−709.

[60] B. Basiri, et al., The role of fluorinated alcohols as mobile phase modifiers for LC-MS analysis of oligonucleotides, J. Am. Soc. Mass Spectrom. 28 (1) (2017) 190−199.

[61] R.E. Birdsall, et al., Reduction of metal adducts in oligonucleotide mass spectra in ion-pair reversed-phase chromatography/mass spectrometry analysis, Rapid Commun. Mass Spectrom. 30 (14) (2016) 1667−1679.

[62] S. Studzinska, B. Buszewski, Effect of mobile phase pH on the retention of nucleotides on different stationary phases for high-performance liquid chromatography, Anal. Bioanal. Chem. 405 (5) (2013) 1663−1672.

[63] B. Chen, M. Bartlett, A one-step solid phase extraction method for bioanalysis of a phosphorothioate oligonucleotide and its 3' n-1 metabolite from rat plasma by uHPLC-MS/MS, AAPS J. 14 (4) (2012) 772−780.

[64] L. Sips, et al., LC-MS quantification of oligonucleotides in biological matrices with SPE or hybridization extraction, Bioanalysis 11 (21) (2019) 1941−1954.

[65] S. Franzoni, et al., Development and validation of a bioanalytical method for quantification of LNA-i-miR-221, a 13-mer oligonucleotide, in rat plasma using LC-MS/MS, J. Pharm. Biomed. Anal. 150 (2018) 300−307.

[66] C. Husser, et al., Identification of GalNAc-conjugated antisense oligonucleotide metabolites using an untargeted and generic approach based on high resolution mass spectrometry, Anal. Chem. 89 (12) (2017) 6821−6826.

[67] S.C. Humphreys, et al., Plasma and liver protein binding of N-acetylgalactosamine-conjugated small interfering RNA, Drug Metab. Dispos. 47 (10) (2019) 1174−1182.

[68] C. Rocca, et al., Evaluation of electrophoretic mobility shift assay as a method to determine plasma protein binding of siRNA, Bioanalysis 11 (21) (2019) 1927−1939.

[69] D. Ramsden, et al., In vitro drug-drug interaction evaluation of GalNAc conjugated siRNAs against CYP450 enzymes and transporters, Drug Metabol. Dispos. 47 (10) (2019) 1183−1194.

[70] C.S. Shemesh, et al., Assessment of the drug interaction potential of unconjugated and GalNAc(3)-conjugated 2'-MOE-ASOs, Mol. Ther. Nucleic Acids 9 (2017) 34−47.

[71] R.Z. Yu, et al., Lack of pharmacokinetic interaction of mipomersen sodium (ISIS 301012), a 2'-O-methoxyethyl modified antisense oligonucleotide targeting apolipoprotein B-100 messenger RNA, with simvastatin and ezetimibe, Clin. Pharmacokinet. 48 (1) (2009) 39–50.

[72] W. Yin, M. Rogge, Targeting RNA: a transformative therapeutic strategy, CTS-Clin. Translat. Sci. 12 (2) (2019) 98–112.

[73] R.L. Setten, J.J. Rossi, S.P. Han, The current state and future directions of RNAi-based therapeutics, Nat. Rev. Drug Discov. 18 (6) (2019) 421–446.

[74] J. Wang, et al., Oligonucleotide-based drug development: considerations for clinical pharmacology and immunogenicity, Ther. Innov. Regul. Sci. 49 (6) (2015) 861–868.

[75] R.L. Kanasty, et al., Action and reaction: the biological response to siRNA and its delivery vehicles, Mol. Ther. 20 (3) (2012) 513–524.

[76] K.A. Whitehead, et al., Silencing or stimulation? siRNA delivery and the immune system, Annu. Rev. Chem. Biomol. Eng. 2 (2011) 77–96.

[77] A. Válóczi, et al., Sensitive and specific detection of microRNAs by northern blot analysis using LNA-modified oligonucleotide probes, Nucleic Acids Res. 32 (22) (2004) e175.

[78] A.M. Krichevsky, et al., A microRNA array reveals extensive regulation of microRNAs during brain development, RNA 10 (3) (2004) 551.

[79] K. Holmes, et al., Detection of siRNA induced mRNA silencing by RT-qPCR: considerations for experimental design, BMC Res. Notes 3 (2010) 53.

[80] K. Reue, mRNA quantitation techniques: considerations for experimental design and application, J. Nutr. 128 (11) (1998) 2038–2044.

[81] C.M. Hindson, et al., Absolute quantification by droplet digital PCR versus analog real-time PCR, Nat. Methods 10 (10) (2013) 1003–1005.

[82] S.A. Bustin, T. Nolan, Pitfalls of quantitative real-time reverse-transcription polymerase chain reaction, J. Biomol. Tech. 15 (3) (2004) 155–166.

[83] R.T. Hayden, et al., Comparison of droplet digital PCR to real-time PCR for quantitative detection of cytomegalovirus, J. Clin. Microbiol. 51 (2) (2013) 540.

[84] M. Flagella, et al., A multiplex branched DNA assay for parallel quantitative gene expression profiling, Anal. Biochem. 352 (1) (2006) 50–60.

[85] Z. Zheng, Y. Luo, G.K. McMaster, Sensitive and quantitative measurement of gene expression directly from a small amount of whole blood, Clin. Chem. 52 (7) (2020) 1294–1302.

[86] R.C. Kamm, A.G. Smith, Nucleic acid concentrations in normal human plasma, Clin. Chem. 18 (6) (2020) 519–522.

[87] M.P. Hunter, et al., Detection of microRNA expression in human peripheral blood microvesicles, PLoS One 3 (11) (2008) e3694.

[88] N.R. Smalheiser, Exosomal transfer of proteins and RNAs at synapses in the nervous system, Biol. Direct 2 (2007) 35.

[89] A. Sehgal, et al., Tissue-specific gene silencing monitored in circulating RNA, RNA (New York, N.Y.) 20 (2) (2014) 143–149.

Chapter 5

Drug development of covalent inhibitors

Upendra P. Dahal and Jan L. Wahlstrom

Department of Pharmacokinetics and Drug Metabolism, Amgen Inc., Thousand Oaks, CA, United States

Introduction to covalent drugs

The major difference between reversible (noncovalent) and irreversible (covalent) inhibitors is their mechanism of inhibition. Reversible inhibitors bind with enzymes via non-covalent interactions such as hydrogen bonding, hydrostatic, and van der Walls forces. A reversible enzyme-inhibitor complex is formed, which is characterized by inhibition potency, K_i, as shown in Fig. 5.1. K_i is a key parameter for optimization during the drug discovery process to ensure complete inhibition of the biological target. Kuntz and coworkers have determined an approximate limit for K_i of 10 pM for reversible inhibitors based on non-covalent interactions [1]. Covalent inhibitors also form an enzyme inhibitor complex, but the inhibition mechanism involves a second step to form an irreversible covalent bond with the target protein of interest, characterized by K_I, also shown in Fig. 5.1. Most often, covalent bond formation is not reversible and the target enzyme is inhibited until it is degraded. Due to this unique characteristic of the inhibition mechanism, covalent inhibitors often exhibit high biochemical efficiency, limited competition from endogenous ligands or cofactors, a potential disconnect between circulating plasma concentrations and biological effect (where the biological effect lasts longer than drug exposure), the potential to avoid some resistance mechanisms due to total and prolonged inhibition of target, and less frequent dosing [2]. Covalent inhibitors have the theoretical potential to cause idiosyncratic drug interactions or toxicities due to haptenization of endogenous proteins [3]. Thus far, however, targeted covalent inhibitors have demonstrated reasonable safety and have not shown toxicity profiles markedly different from their reversible inhibitor counterparts [4].

Therapeutic areas

Covalent drugs have existed since the late 1800s, although the mechanism of action for many of these drugs was not known until much later. A timeline outlining the progression of covalent inhibitors is shown in Fig. 5.2. Aspirin is an early example of a covalent inhibitor; the mechanism of acyl transfer to inactivate its cyclooxygenase target was not elucidated until the mid-1970s [5]. Other early examples of covalent inhibitors include the discovery of antibiotic aminolactams, such as penicillin, in the 1920s. Later examples of drugs that act as covalent inhibitors include warfarin, the proton pump inhibitors omeprazole, lansoprazole and pantoprazole, as well as the platelet inhibitor clopidogrel. These drugs were discovered through traditional potency screening, not structure-based design, because their mechanisms of action were unknown at the time [6]. Key intellectual advances were made in the mid to late 2000s, with Robertson recognizing

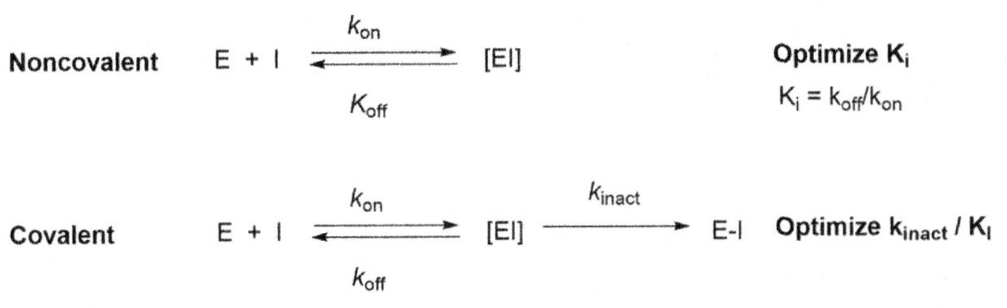

Noncovalent	E + I $\underset{k_{off}}{\overset{k_{on}}{\rightleftarrows}}$ [EI]	**Optimize K_i** $K_i = k_{off}/k_{on}$
Covalent	E + I $\underset{k_{off}}{\overset{k_{on}}{\rightleftarrows}}$ [EI] $\xrightarrow{k_{inact}}$ E-I	**Optimize k_{inact} / K_I**

FIGURE 5.1 Mechanism of action for covalent drugs.

Overcoming Obstacles in Drug Discovery and Development. https://doi.org/10.1016/B978-0-12-817134-9.00009-X

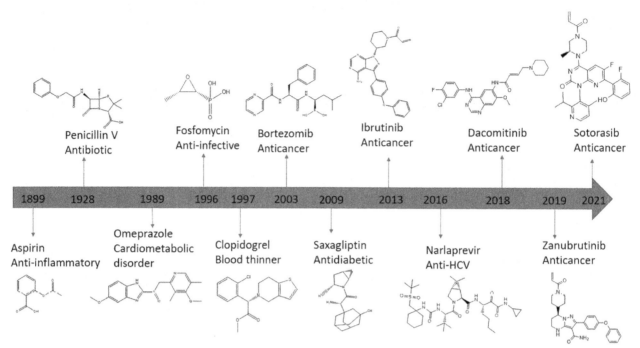

FIGURE 5.2 Timeline of FDA approved covalent drugs (reactive warheads are depicted in *blue*).

covalent inhibitors as a distinct class of therapeutic agents and Potashman and Duggan realizing the potential for covalent inhibitors as an orthogonal approach to traditional drug design [7,8].

The emergence of targeted covalent inhibitors (TCIs) specifically designed and optimized to react with a protein target occurred in the early 2000s and was heralded by the approval of ibrutinib (targeting Bruton's tyrosine kinase, BTK) and afatinib (targeting epidermal growth factor receptor, EGFR) by the US Food and Drug Administration in 2013 [9]. While the TCI approach has been associated with oncology more recently, covalent inhibitors have been approved and used clinically across multiple therapeutic areas (TAs). Fig. 5.3 shows a breakdown of currently marketed covalent inhibitors based on TA [6].

Chemical considerations for TCI design

A key consideration of appropriate biological targets for TCIs is the presence of a nucleophilic residue such as cysteine, lysine, histidine, serine, tyrosine, threonine, or the carboxylate group of glutamic or aspartic acid, generally in close proximity to the target enzyme active site or a site critical to protein-protein interactions [10,11]. The unique nucleophilic characteristics of cysteine, as well as its infrequent presence in many proteins, makes it the most common choice for site of reactivity with TCIs [12]. Bioinformatic approaches have been used to identify proteins containing cysteine residues that are likely to confer selectivity with TCIs [13]. Accessibility of the cysteine thiol group and its acidity constant (represented

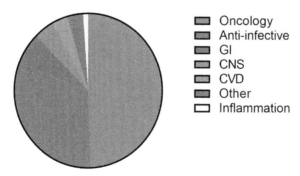

FIGURE 5.3 FDA approved covalent drugs by therapeutic area.

through its negative log value, pKa) may have marked influence on cysteine reactivity, where higher nucleophilic reactivity is associated with lower pKa. Hemoglobin is an example of the dramatic influence that protein microenvironment can have on cysteine reactivity. The thiolate anion (reactive form) of cysteine 125 of the β-subunit of rat hemoglobin is stabilized by an adjacent serine residue. This stabilization results in a lower pKa (6.5) and a 4000-fold increase in reactivity with electrophiles when compared to dog or human hemoglobin, where the cysteine pKa ranges from 8.5 to 9.0 [14,15].

Warhead selection is a critical issue for structure-based design of a TCI. The reactivity of nucleophiles is generally governed by the principles of hard and soft acids and bases [16]. Hard nucleophiles and electrophiles have localized charge density that is not polarizable; hard nucleophiles tend to react with hard electrophiles. Examples of hard nucleophiles present on proteins are the amino-side chains of lysine residues or the hydroxyl moiety of serine. Hard electrophiles include boronic acids, epoxides and sulfonyl fluorides. Soft nucleophiles and electrophiles are characterized by diffuse and polarizable charge density. The thiolate anion of cysteine is an example of a soft nucleophile associated with proteins; α,β-unsaturated carbonyl (acrylamide) moieties are soft electrophiles that are the most commonly selected warhead for TCIs [3].

Warhead reactivity may be assessed in vitro through reaction with various nucleophiles. Dahal and coworkers characterized the reactivity of several electrophilic warheads to assess whether lysine residues may be a suitable residue to target on proteins by comparing reactivity of glutathione (a cysteine containing peptide) or N-α-acetyllysine (NAL) with acrylamide, cyanamide, nitrile, or sulfonamide-based warhead analogs [17]. Using a nonphysiological pH of 10 due to limited reactivity of lysine at physiological pH, cysteine was generally still more reactive than lysine with most chemical warheads. Vinyl sulfones were an exception with higher observed reactivity with NAL than the other functional groups tested. Reactivity of the warhead could be tuned by altering the electron density of the acrylamide moiety, where electron withdrawing groups generally increased reactivity and electron donating groups reduced reactivity. Cee and coworkers studied the subtle effects of altering aryl substitution on a series of thirty-four compounds synthesized to examine the effects of electron withdrawing and electron donating substituents on acrylamide warheads substituted with aryl groups [18]. Linear correlations were observed for substitution at all aryl positions, which enabled prospective use of computation techniques to tune inhibitor reactivity. Members of the same team also characterized the effect of direct substitution on either the alpha or beta position of the acrylamide [19]. Generally, electron donating substitution on either position increased warhead reactivity, while electron withdrawing substitution decreased reactivity, although solvation of the transition state also played a marked role in predicting reactivity with glutathione.

Reversible TCIs have been developed due to concerns around warhead selectivity and potential immunological responses to haptenized proteins [20]. For acrylamide-based warheads, this has generally meant the introduction of a cyano moiety to tune competing β-elimination with protein adduction. As an added benefit, the structure-based design of reversible covalent inhibitors may facilitate the adoption of a fragment-based approach to inhibitor design. Fragment-based design can be more challenging with irreversible covalent inhibitors, as warhead reactivity may obscure noncovalent interactions with the protein. Taunton and coworkers used the fragment-based approach as a starting point to develop inhibitors of mitogen- and stress activated kinase 1 (MSK1), where screening hits were not available to begin a rational synthesis campaign [21]. Noncovalent interactions such as van der Waals and hydrogen bonding were essential to increasing binding affinity in conjunction with covalent interactions. In this case, the stability of the fragment complexes was found to be inversely coordinated to carbanion affinity.

ADME considerations

Optimizing the absorption, distribution, metabolism, and excretion (ADME) properties of TCIs is critical in the drug discovery and development process [22]. A cornerstone of this optimization is characterizing and improving drug stability in physiological systems. The liver is a key organ for drug metabolism. Many drugs undergo metabolism by drug metabolizing enzymes such as the cytochrome P450s (CYPs) or UDP-glucuronosyl transferases (UGTs) that are present in the liver. Liver microsomal fractions are used routinely in drug discovery to characterize the metabolic stability of drugs with enzymes that reside in the endoplasmic reticulum, such as CYPs and flavin mono-oxygenases (FMOs). The use of whole liver cells (hepatocytes) may be required when a more complete set of hepatic enzymes is involved in metabolism of a drug. Specifically for TCIs, warheads may react directly with endogenous thiol-containing nucleophiles such as glutathione or proteins such as hemoglobin or serum albumin [23]. Reaction with glutathione may occur due to intrinsic chemical reactivity (Michael reaction) or may be assisted by enzymes known as glutathione transferases (GSTs). The contribution of GST to glutathione adduct formation may be quantified by comparing rates of reactivity of the TCI in buffer containing physiologically relevant levels of glutathione to reactions with added liver fractions. The GST selective inhibitor acivicin may also be used for in vitro or in vivo experiments to quantify the contribution of GSTs to glutathione adduct formation [23].

Extrapolation of in vitro results to the in vivo situation for TCIs may be particularly confounding due to the contribution of extrahepatic enzymes to drug clearance. As a first step for drugs cleared through metabolism, in vitro drug stability results using liver microsomes or hepatocytes are translated to the in vivo situation using species-specific scaling factors for liver weight, drug metabolizing enzyme content, and blood flow. Because TCIs may react with endogenous nucleophiles or proteins that are outside of the liver, an additional term may be added to the extrapolation using blood stability (as a surrogate for reaction with GSTs residing in blood or reaction with serum albumin) or reactivity rates with GSH in buffer alone (or in the presence of GSTs) to account for this extrahepatic component. Leung and coworkers used this approach to predict the in vivo clearance of a series of eighteen TCIs targeting Janus kinase 3 (JAK3), with hepatocytes representing metabolism in the liver and whole blood stability or recombinant GST P1-1 representing extrahepatic metabolism [24]. An empirical scaling factor was developed in rat and used to extrapolate clearance to other species. Pharmacokinetic (PK) data for two of the JAK3 TCIs were available across preclinical species. Use of the empirical scaling factor enabled clearance predictions within 2-fold of observed values across species, although the authors noted that the empirical scaling factor may be chemotype specific. A similar approach using hepatocytes in serum was used to predict observed clearance in rat, dog, nonhuman primate and humans for afatinib, ibrutinib, and neratinib; reasonable agreement was obtained between actual in vivo and scaled in vitro results [25].

Unique assays critical for covalent drug discovery and development

Although conceptually promising and possessing several potential advantages when compared to traditional reversible inhibitors, design of covalent inhibitors is challenging. The three key steps of drug discovery for a TCI are: identification of a target protein with appropriate nucleophile (e.g., serine, cystine, etc.), identification of a binding core chemotype (motif) with acceptable affinity so that TCI can bind to the target, and an appropriately positioned warhead (electrophile) attached to the chemotype core structure. The right balance of warhead reactivity and selectivity are important to maintain efficacy and minimize toxicity of a TCI. To support these key steps and characterize the TCIs, several non-traditional assays need to be established. Since these non-traditional assays are time and resource consuming, refinement and development of high throughput assays has not been fully established, but attempts have been discussed in the literature to support development of structure-activity relationships (SARs) for covalent drug design. Some of the key assays that are important and specific to covalent drug development are discussed briefly below.

A critical criterion for a covalent drug target is the presence of a nucleophilic residue (cysteine, serine, etc.) in the binding site of the target protein that can react with an electrophilic moiety of the TCI to form a covalent bond that should ultimately interfere the activity of the target protein. The intrinsic reactivity of the warhead electrophile of the TCI with the protein residue nucleophile should be optimized. The intrinsic reactivity of the warhead should not be so high that it reacts non-specifically with similar amino acid residues on other proteins to avoid off-target effects or potential toxicity. However, the reactivity should be fast enough to form a covalent bond between the TCI warhead and corresponding amino acid nucleophile when the drug binds to the binding pocket of the target and brings them in close proximity. Several reports are documented in literature discussing importance of intrinsic reactivity of nucleophiles and surrogate nucleophiles were used to monitor as well as fine tune or rank order reactivity of the warheads. Reports are abundant using cysteine or glutathione as a surrogate nucleophile [18,26−28]; reports using other surrogate nucleophiles (primarily lysine) are available as well [29,30]. The published reports highlight the benefit of computational methods for reactivity assessment of both the warhead and nucleophiles when experimental data are abundant to validate the reactivity estimations [18,26,27].

Another important criterion for TCI development is half-life (turnover rate) estimation of the target protein. The advantages of covalent drugs are due to complete inactivation of the target protein. Once the target protein is inactivated by a covalent drug, the activity of the protein can generally only be restored after the target protein is re-synthesized. Proteins may exhibit half-lives on a scale from hours to days or longer [31]. Hence, target resynthesis rate will dictate the frequency of drug administration. A longer half-life of the target protein will enable a covalent drug to be administered less frequently and may be helpful to avoid non-target related toxicity due to the lower body burden based on dosing regimen. Target resynthesis rate estimation can be surrogated by measuring the protein degradation rate or degradation half-life using in vitro assays. The most commonly employed approach for estimation of protein degradation rate (half-life) is the stable isotope labeling of amino acids in cell culture (SILAC) method. The SILAC technique uses mass spectrometry to detect differences in protein abundance using non-radioactive isotopic labeling. Briefly, a protein is cultured in vitro using a specific stable label amino acid for incorporation. Upon full stable label incorporation into the protein, the cell culture conditions are changed to remove the stable label source from the in vitro system. As new protein is synthesized without the stable label present, the ratio of stable label protein to unlabeled protein can be measured over time, providing an estimate of degradation rate. Detailed discussion of the SILAC technique has been provided in recent reviews [32,33]. Of note, the SILAC method requires extensive expertize with cell culture, protein analysis and LC/MS methods to successfully generate protein degradation data.

Traditional reversible drug discovery approaches rely on IC_{50} (drug concentration at half-maximal inhibition) values to estimate target coverage and related pharmacological effects. Covering IC_{50} or K_i does not generally predict pharmacological outcome accurately for covalent drugs, because covalent inhibitors exert their effects differently than reversible inhibitors [34]. In the first step, a covalent drug binds non-covalently with the target protein where the strength of binding affinity is usually measured by inhibition constant K_I. In the second step the covalent drug forms a covalent bond with the target protein and the strength of chemical reactivity is measured in terms of rate of inactivation, k_{inact}. Hence, k_{inact} and K_I are the key parameters for SAR and inhibitor optimization efforts for covalent drugs. Since covalent inhibition is time-dependent and separately but intrinsically related to both affinity (K_I) and reactivity (k_{inact}), use of biochemical IC_{50} (or K_i) to assess potency of a covalent drug and rank order covalent inhibitors is not an appropriate practice, because IC_{50} values of a covalent drug depends on length of incubation with target. Estimation of k_{inact} and K_I requires additional expertize, but is more time consuming and resource intensive. Since k_{inact} and K_I determinations are multistep and potentially low throughput, alternative approaches have been discussed in the literature, such as time-dependent IC_{50} experiments or competition-based assays using irreversible probe substrates [35−37].

Covalent drugs exert their physiological or pharmacological effects mainly by inactivation of target protein through formation of a covalent bond with the target protein. Hence, confirmation of covalent bond formation and target occupancy both in vitro and in vivo is critical. Confirmation of adduction of a covalent drug to a target protein can be achieved by mass spectrometry (MS)-based technologies. The MS based technologies can quantitate target occupancy by determining the fraction of the target protein that is adducted by a covalent drug using targeted peptide analysis after protein digestion or by intact protein quantitation. The targeted peptide analysis can also confirm the covalent reaction is taking place at the desired amino acid site and is able to rule out the non-specific reaction with other undesired residues. Percent target occupancy (%TO) can be estimated using the equation %TO = covalently adducted target protein*100/total target protein and can be estimated from a single study sample as described by Hansen et al. [38]. The %TO may be used to rank order lead compounds as well as to apply in modeling efforts to estimate pharmacodynamic (PD) and efficacy using in silico methods. In addition to estimation of target occupancy, it is also advised to perform proteomic analysis to confirm the selectivity of the covalent drugs with the target protein in biological matrices, which can also be performed using LC-MS based technologies.

PK/PD establishment

A disconnect between PK and PD is commonly observed for TCIs. For a reversible drug, PD outcome depends on concentration of the drug available to reversibly and dynamically bind with the target protein. Once drug is depleted at the site of action, no PD effect is expected since the protein is now functional and there is no drug to exert inhibitory effect. However, for a covalent drug, the PD effect can last long after disappearance of the covalent drug from the site of action or from the body. The PD effect of the covalent drug is exerted by covalent binding of the drug with a target protein and thereby completely inactivating the target protein from performing its function as long as covalent drug is bound to the target protein. There is no need for continuous presence of covalent drug at the site of action once the target protein is inactivated. The catalytic function of the target protein can only be restored once the new target protein is resynthesized. The length of PD effect of covalent drugs lasts until the resynthesis of target protein is completed and hence PD effect depends on the resynthesis rate of the target protein. The protein resynthesis rate also dictates frequency of dosing of covalent drugs to get desired PD effect, where longer target half-life enables less frequent dosing. Overall, the PD effect of the covalent drug not solely depends on the exposure (drug concentration), but also the protein synthesis rate and determination of protein half-life is essential part of covalent drug discovery and development strategies. Because of dependency on protein synthesis as well as potency, the PD effect may not be directly estimated using the IC_{50} or K_i coverage which is a common practice for reversible drugs. Use of the time dependent parameters K_I, k_{inact} and protein resynthesis rate need to be incorporated in potency estimation or PK/PD modeling.

IC_{50} is the most commonly used parameter for ranking potency of reversible inhibitors in drug discovery, where IC_{50} is the concentration of compound required to produce 50% inhibition of activity of the target protein at a fixed time point. However, for the covalent inhibitors, the inhibition is time-dependent and IC_{50} decreases as the length of incubation increases, as shown in Fig. 5.4A. The IC_{50} of a covalent drug depends on affinity (K_I), reactivity (k_{inact}) and incubation duration (time) as depicted in Fig. 5.4B. Hence, ranking of covalent inhibitors based on IC_{50} values may give misleading

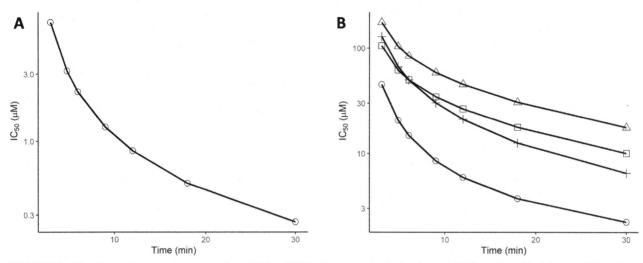

FIGURE 5.4 IC_{50} of a covalent drug changes over time: (A) Plot of IC50 values versus incubation time and (B) Illustration of the influence of K_I and k_{inact} on the time-dependence of the IC_{50} ($\bigcirc$: $K_I = 10$ μM, $k_{inact} = 100$ h^{-1}; $\square$: $K_I = 10$ μM, $k_{inact} = 10$ h^{-1}; $\triangle$: $K_I = 20$ μM, $k_{inact} = 10$ h^{-1} and +: $K_I = 20$ μM, $k_{inact} = 30$ h^{-1}).

information; the use of IC_{50} for covalent drug SAR is discouraged [34,35,39,40]. However, despite sub-optimal performance using IC_{50}, the parameter has been used for ranking the potency of the covalent inhibitors in select instances. It has been demonstrated that the IC_{50} of all covalent inhibitors will be approximately equal to half of the enzyme concentration in the assay if the incubation is long enough [34,41]. Several reports have demonstrated successful use of k_{inact}/K_I parameters to predict the PD outcomes as well as in PK/PD modeling although poor translation of k_{inact}/K_I to in vivo outcome cannot be ruled out [34,40]. The possible explanations for poor translation of k_{inact}/K_I to cellular assays or in vivo studies from biochemical assays may be incorrect protein or protein complex concentrations/conditions in the biochemical assays; hence, more physiologically or disease relevant conditions (appropriate cellular concentration of target protein, appropriate substrate concentration such as high ATP concentration in a kinase targets) should be used in the biochemical assays to estimate k_{inact} and K_I parameters. Despite the success and rationale use of k_{inact}/K_I, IC_{50} values have also been used to rank order the potency due to ease and scale at which the IC_{50} assays can be performed. It has also been reported that in specific instances IC_{50} may be able to rank order covalent inhibitors [37].

PK/PD modeling to assist SAR development and to predict human dose corresponding to efficacy is an important aspect for all drug discovery projects. PK of a drug depends on the ADME properties of the drug, while the PD of a drug depends on drug concentration and binding kinetics at the site of action. PK/PD models can be developed to predict the time course of PD effects from drug doses and exposure. Due to complexity of action of covalent drugs, several in vitro as well as in vivo parameters should be incorporated in PK/PD modeling. A mechanistic PK/PD model can be applied where drug concentration at the site of action is used to predict target occupancy. Percent target occupancy can then be used along with other kinetic parameters to estimate PD effect as well as efficacy as depicted in Fig. 5.5 for a hypothetical drug.

Use of quantitative mechanistic PK/PD models has been successfully applied to predict PK/PD of covalent drugs [42,43]. Daryaee et al. used a mechanistic PK/PD model to quantitatively correlate the engagement to Brutan's tyrosine kinase by a covalent inhibitor CC-292 and predicted drug efficacy (reduction of ankle swelling in preclinical model). The authors used key input parameters for the PK/PD modeling from both in vitro as well in vivo data and discussed the role of kinetic and thermodynamic parameters such as k_{inact} and K_I, rate of target turnover, substrate concentration and target vulnerability. Based on modeling, the authors concluded that in addition to commonly measured parameters (k_{inact}, K_I, target resynthesis rate), target vulnerability (relating target occupancy to PD effect) was an important parameter and postulated that BTK exhibited a relatively low target vulnerability, where high labels of engagement must be maintained to achieve a good therapeutic outcome. The target vulnerability informs the sensitivity of target engagement to efficacy of a drug (Fig. 5.6). Since target vulnerability defines the threshold and strength of target occupancy with PD effect (and ultimately efficacy), high vulnerability targets are easier to develop drug than the low vulnerability targets as shown in Fig. 5.6.

Some controversy exists as to whether C_{max} or area under the plasma concentration versus time curve (AUC) drives the pharmacodynamics of covalent drugs. Although the field is emerging and more detailed studies investigating C_{max} versus AUC driven PD for covalent drugs have yet to be conducted, limited reports indicate that the PD effect of covalent drugs is

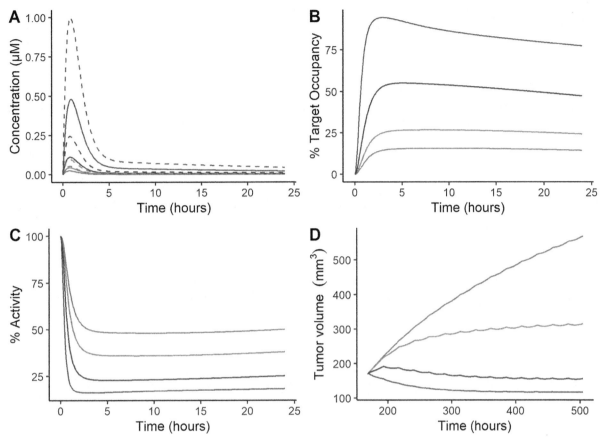

FIGURE 5.5 Mechanistic PK/PD model predictions for a hypothetical covalent inhibitor (A) Plasma (*dashed*) and tumor (*solid*) unbound concentration, (B) Target occupancy, (C) Percent phosphorylated ERK, and (D) Tumor volume following 10 (*orange*), 15 (*blue*), 30 (*red*), and 100 (*green*) mg/kg dosing in tumor xenografted mice. (For interpretation of the references to colour in this figure legend, the reader is referred to the web version of this chapter.)

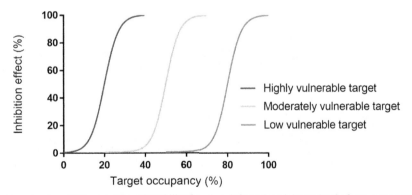

FIGURE 5.6 Hypothetical target vulnerability plot. The vulnerability functions inform the minimum level of target engagement required to initiate PD effect and the target engagement required to exhibit maximum PD effect.

driven by AUC. A perspective published by Strelow discussed the importance of k_{inact}/K_I parameters and explained that IC_{50} can be misleading in ranking of the covalent drugs [34]. The criticality of using free (unbound) drug concentration to estimate the PD effect was also highlighted. According to the free drug hypothesis, unbound drug concentrations should be similar when comparing plasma to tissue concentrations in many cases; however, this is not the case for all drugs [44,45]. Examples where this is not the case include morphine, gabapentin and atenolol, where unbound brain concentrations were significantly lower than in plasma [46−48]. In those instances, differing unbound concentration of drug in tissues (e.g. brain) compared to plasma can be explained by expression of transporters (both efflux and uptake transporters) in the tissues/organs [47,49,50]. Presence of efflux transporters in the tissue can lead to lower unbound tissue (e.g., brain, tumor etc.) concentration compared to plasma; presence of uptake transporter may lead to higher unbound tissue concentration to that of plasma. Hence caution should be taken to use appropriate unbound concentrations in tissues to estimate PD effect. Other instances where the free drug hypothesis may not apply include pH gradients, unique distribution systems (nanoparticles), and receptor-mediated uptake of protein therapeutics [51].

Strelow applied modeling and simulation to explain the role of C_{max} and AUC and concluded unbound AUC would be better predictor for PD effects [34]. At higher concentration of inhibitor (when $C_{max} > K_I$), covalent bond formation is faster and more than 95% of target occupancy can be achieved if the drug concentration is above K_I for five half-lives of protein inactivation ($T_{1/2} = ln2/k_{inact}$). However, at lower inhibitor concentration, covalent bond formation will continue but at slower rate, hence the unbound exposure of the drug over time will be better predictor of the target occupancy (and thereafter PD effect) which can be estimated by the equation (% Target Occupancy $= 100*(1 - exp(-(k_{inact}/K_I)(AUC_u)))$. It should be noted that the derived equation is an oversimplification of a much more complex process of covalent bond formation and did not account for many factors including target protein resynthesis rate; however, this simplified equation can be applied to estimate the percent target occupancy of a covalent drug based on covalent bond formation kinetics and unbound AUC. Similarly, Brachmann et al. concluded AUC but not C_{max} driven efficacy for an in vivo mouse xenograft study where the authors used a continuous delivery of a drug using mini-pump administration [52].

Emerging data have demonstrated several advantages of covalent dugs and the covalent modality has been proven to be successful strategy to develop drugs even for targets that were previously considered undruggable. A very recent example is approval of Sotorasib (AMG 510) for non-small cell lung cancer with KRASG12C mutation by several regulatory agencies, including the US Food and Drug Administration [53−55]. This is an excellent example of application of a TCI-approach for a target (KRAS), where drug discovery efforts had been prosecuted for over 30 years. Despite multiple approvals of covalent drugs (as well as many ongoing clinical trials) which demonstrate the potential for TCIs through clinical development [56], concerns persist about application of a covalent approach in drug discovery and development. One of the key concerns for covalent modifiers is due to the theoretical concern for potential toxicity due to haptenization and non-selective off target reaction with biologically important proteins [57]. Although haptenization and potential immunological consequences may occur and have been observed in limited instances [4], several decades of successful use of covalent drugs in the clinic have informed that there are low frequencies of observed toxicity of covalent drugs in clinical practice. In contrast to reactive metabolites that may be responsible for protein adduct formation that is often highly reactive and non-selective, the reactivity of warhead of the covalent drugs is low and selectivity was designed into the drug discovery program through SAR relationships. Additionally, if the TCIs are dosed appropriately, the risk due to off target binding can be reduced or avoided. Low daily dose is one of the strategies proposed to de-risk potential toxicity of covalent drug due to off-target reactivity [3,58]. While low dose is generally considered a good strategy to mitigate adverse drug reactions, there are several covalent drugs whose recommended daily dose in human is several hundred milligrams (i.e., aspirin, orlistat, ibrutinib) and are in clinical use without apparent drug-limiting toxicity. This suggests the mechanism and reaction of covalent drug with biomolecules may play critical role for idiosyncratic or off-target toxicity of TCIs.

The human liver is exposed to many foreign molecules in daily basis from food, the environment, as well as occupational exposures. Many of these molecules are inherently reactive and undergo biotransformation to form reactive intermediates or metabolites which have the potential to form covalent bonds with macromolecules. Not all of these compounds are toxic, however. The human body has detoxification mechanisms to reduce potential toxicity due to these reactive intermediate or metabolites. Dahal et al. analyzed a set of covalent drugs which are in clinical use to estimate daily body burden limit and proposed an estimated daily body burden of 10 mg/day as a cut off to mitigate potential toxicity due to covalent binding to biomolecules [59]. As evident from these studies, it is worthy to note that not all protein adduct formation is toxic and there can be a limitation to tolerate body burden due to covalent drug protein adduct formation. It is also interesting to note that many approved acrylamide based covalent drugs such as afatinib [60], osimertinib [61] and neratinib [62] were found to form adducts with serum proteins in addition to the target protein in human, but these drugs were well tolerated. All of these observations indicate that covalent drug-protein adduction may not end up with immunological or toxicological effects, but caution needs to be taken to understand the possible effect of protein adduct formation of covalent drugs. More research in this area is evolving to guide the covalent drug discovery and development programs and to mitigate potential toxicity as well as to apply more rigorous tools in early stage of drug discovery stages to select better candidates for clinical use.

The off-target reactivity of a warhead of the covalent drug with macromolecules is one reason for potential toxicity; another is bioactivation of covalent drugs to form reactive metabolites that can form adducts with macromolecules and may cause toxicity. The bioactivation of drugs to form reactive metabolites is not a unique property of covalent drugs, but is a potential risk for all small molecule drugs. Bioactivation of reversible drugs to cause toxicity is well documented in literature and a structural alert approach that identifies potential moieties of concern and related strategies to assess bioactivation potential is discussed in detail elsewhere [63–65]. Here, covalent drug toxicity concerns are briefly discussed that are specifically related to the α,β-unsaturated arylamide, the most commonly used warhead in targeted covalent drug design (10 of 14 FDA-approved TCIs from 2011 to 2019 contained an α,β-unsaturated acrylamide as electrophilic warhead) [56]. It is interesting to note that many foods that we consume in daily basis such as coffee, cereal, chips, bread, crackers, fries and prune juice contain acrylamide [66,67]. The unsaturated acrylamide from our food can react with glutathione (GSH) or cysteine in tissues and cellular compartments to form GSH or cysteine adducts. The GSH adducts can eventually be converted to cysteine adduct through biotransformation pathways which is susceptible to undergo either a detoxication mercapturic acid pathway or potentially toxic lyase pathway. It has been argued that when the concentration of cysteine adduct is high then the mercapturic acid pathway can be saturated and β-lyase pathway can yield reactive thiols which may be demonstrated to be toxic [68]. The β-lyase-mediated reactive thiol pathway is proposed as a mechanism for rat specific renal toxicity observed with sotorasib where the concentration of mercapturate/β-lyase pathway metabolites were present in rat kidney in higher extent than other species [69,70]. A similar mechanism was proposed for ibrutinib-mediated nephrotoxicity when the oxidative pathway was compromised [71]. Ibrutinib is metabolized by oxidation (cytochrome P450 mediated) as well as a glutathione/cysteine adduct pathway; when the oxidative pathway was inhibited, the glutathione/cysteine-adduct pathway became the prominent metabolic route yielding high concentrations of reactive thiol via a β-lyase pathway, which is proposed as the mechanism for renal toxicity [72]. These observations suggest to closely monitor the formation of GSH and cysteine adducts; efforts should be applied to minimize formation of such adducts, if possible.

As depicted in Fig. 5.7, covalent drugs with unsaturated acrylamide can get adducted with glutathione either by intrinsic reaction or by catalysis through the glutathione S-transferase (GST) enzyme system [70]. High reactivity with glutathione can lead to cellular stress due to glutathione pool depletion causing hepatotoxicity similar to the toxicity of acetaminophen [73]. This type of risk can be monitored using in vivo studies characterizing organ toxicity in nonclinical species [74]. The involvement of GSTs in the metabolism of covalent drugs may impact both clearance and potential detoxification. GST-mediated glutathione conjugation can have species specific ramification since the expression of GST isoforms can be different between nonclinical species and human. It has been documented that GST levels may be different in disease conditions when compared to healthy subjects, for example increased levels of GST alpha isozymes in patients with liver diseases [75], deficiency in GST isoforms in human population due to genetic polymorphism [76] and over-expression of GSTs in tumors [77]. Hence the role of GSTs in metabolism of covalent drug and their expression in normal

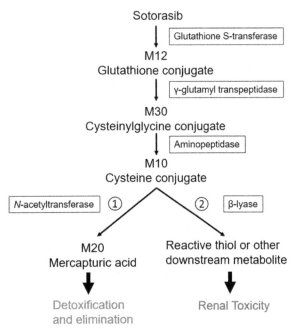

FIGURE 5.7 Two competing pathways of metabolism of unsaturated acrylamides. *Credit: J.A. Werner, R. Davies, J. Wahlstrom, U.P. Dahal, M. Jiang, J. Stauber, et al. Mercapturate pathway metabolites of sotorasib, a covalent inhibitor of KRAS(G12C), are associated with renal toxicity in the Sprague Dawley rat. Toxicol. Appl. Pharmacol. 423 (2021) 115578.*

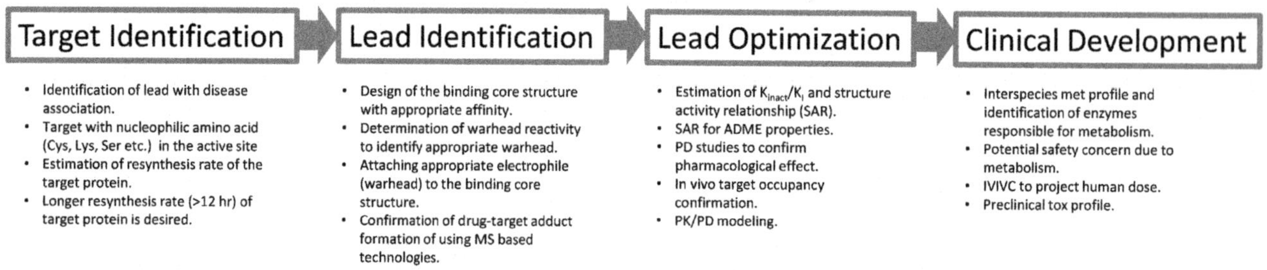

Target Identification	Lead Identification	Lead Optimization	Clinical Development
• Identification of lead with disease association. • Target with nucleophilic amino acid (Cys, Lys, Ser etc.) in the active site • Estimation of resynthesis rate of the target protein. • Longer resynthesis rate (>12 hr) of target protein is desired.	• Design of the binding core structure with appropriate affinity. • Determination of warhead reactivity to identify appropriate warhead. • Attaching appropriate electrophile (warhead) to the binding core structure. • Confirmation of drug-target adduct formation of using MS based technologies.	• Estimation of K_{inact}/K_i and structure activity relationship (SAR). • SAR for ADME properties. • PD studies to confirm pharmacological effect. • In vivo target occupancy confirmation. • PK/PD modeling.	• Interspecies met profile and identification of enzymes responsible for metabolism. • Potential safety concern due to metabolism. • IVIVC to project human dose. • Preclinical tox profile.

FIGURE 5.8 Flow scheme for covalent inhibitor discovery and development.

and disease conditions need to be considered to understand the extent of glutathione adduct formation by GSTs as well as the potential ramifications of different expression levels of GSTs in humans.

Conclusion

Application of the targeted covalent inhibitor approach continues to expand the available space of druggable targets. Adoption and implementation of appropriate computational and experimental paradigms will aid in the design and selection of clinical candidates through the drug discovery and development process. While a well-defined steps for development of targeted covalent drugs is evolving, a general strategy for discovery and development of TCIs is presented in Fig. 5.8. Further clinical experience with the use of TCIs will refine our understanding of PK/PD and its relationship to efficacy in the clinical setting. The resurgence of covalent inhibitors as a viable approach continues to expand and impact patients, especially for those targets which had previously been deemed as undruggable.

Acknowledgment

The authors thank Nashid Farhan for generating Fig. 5.4 and 5.5.

References

[1] I.D. Kuntz, K. Chen, K.A. Sharp, P.A. Kollman, The maximal affinity of ligands, Proc. Natl. Acad. Sci. U. S. A. 96 (1999) 9997–10002.

[2] R.A. Bauer, Covalent inhibitors in drug discovery: from accidental discoveries to avoided liabilities and designed therapies, Drug Discov. Today 20 (2015) 1061–1073.

[3] T.A. Baillie, Targeted covalent inhibitors for drug design, Angew Chem. Int. Ed. Engl. 55 (2016) 13408–13421.

[4] T.A. Baillie, Approaches to mitigate the risk of serious adverse reactions in covalent drug design, Expert Opin. Drug Discov. 16 (2021) 275–287.

[5] G.J. Roth, N. Stanford, P.W. Majerus, Acetylation of prostaglandin synthase by aspirin, Proc. Natl. Acad. Sci. U. S. A. 72 (1975) 3073–3076.

[6] J. Singh, R.C. Petter, T.A. Baillie, A. Whitty, The resurgence of covalent drugs, Nat. Rev. Drug Discov. 10 (2011) 307–317.

[7] J.G. Robertson, Mechanistic basis of enzyme-targeted drugs, Biochemistry 44 (2005) 5561–5571.

[8] M.H. Potashman, M.E. Duggan, Covalent modifiers: an orthogonal approach to drug design, J. Med. Chem. 52 (2009) 1231–1246.

[9] E. De Vita, 10 years into the resurgence of covalent drugs, Future Med. Chem. 13 (2021) 193–210.

[10] M. Hagel, D. Niu, T. St Martin, M.P. Sheets, L. Qiao, H. Bernard, et al., Selective irreversible inhibition of a protease by targeting a noncatalytic cysteine, Nat. Chem. Biol. 7 (2011) 22–24.

[11] J.S. Martin, C.J. MacKenzie, D. Fletcher, I.H. Gilbert, Characterising covalent warhead reactivity, Bioorg. Med. Chem. 27 (2019) 2066–2074.

[12] E. Awoonor-Williams, C.N. Rowley, How reactive are druggable cysteines in protein kinases? J. Chem. Inf. Model. 58 (2018) 1935–1946.

[13] M.S. Cohen, C. Zhang, K.M. Shokat, J. Taunton, Structural bioinformatics-based design of selective, irreversible kinase inhibitors, Science 308 (2005) 1318–1321.

[14] R. Rossi, D. Barra, A. Bellelli, G. Boumis, S. Canofeni, P. Di Simplicio, et al., Fast-reacting thiols in rat hemoglobins can intercept damaging species in erythrocytes more efficiently than glutathione, J. Biol. Chem. 273 (1998) 19198–19206.

[15] R. Rossi, A. Milzani, I. Dalle-Donne, F. Giannerini, D. Giustarini, L. Lusini, et al., Different metabolizing ability of thiol reactants in human and rat blood: biochemical and pharmacological implications, J. Biol. Chem. 276 (2001) 7004–7010.

[16] R.M. Lopachin, T. Gavin, A. Decaprio, D.S. Barber, Application of the hard and soft, acids and bases (HSAB) theory to toxicant-target interactions, Chem. Res. Toxicol. 25 (2012) 239–251.

[17] U.P. Dahal, A.M. Gilbert, R.S. Obach, M.E. Flanagan, J.M. Chen, C. Garcia-Irizarry, et al., Intrinsic reactivity profile of electrophilic moieties to guide covalent drug design: N-α-acetyl-L-lysine as an amine nucleophile, Med. Chem. Commun. 7 (2016) 864–872.

[18] V.J. Cee, L.P. Volak, Y. Chen, M.D. Bartberger, C. Tegley, T. Arvedson, et al., Systematic study of the glutathione (GSH) reactivity of N-arylacrylamides: 1. Effects of aryl substitution, J. Med. Chem. 58 (2015) 9171–9178.

[19] A. Birkholz, D.J. Kopecky, L.P. Volak, M.D. Bartberger, Y. Chen, C.M. Tegley, et al., Systematic study of the glutathione reactivity of N-phenylacrylamides: 2. Effects of acrylamide substitution, J. Med. Chem. 63 (2020) 11602–11614.

[20] I.M. Serafimova, M.A. Pufall, S. Krishnan, K. Duda, M.S. Cohen, R.L. Maglathlin, et al., Reversible targeting of noncatalytic cysteines with chemically tuned electrophiles, Nat. Chem. Biol. 8 (2012) 471–476.

[21] R.M. Miller, V.O. Paavilainen, S. Krishnan, I.M. Serafimova, J. Taunton, Electrophilic fragment-based design of reversible covalent kinase inhibitors, J. Am. Chem. Soc. 135 (2013) 5298–5301.

[22] M.F. Moghaddam, Y. Tang, Z. O'Brien, S.J. Richardson, M. Bacolod, P. Chaturedi, et al., A proposed screening paradigm for discovery of covalent inhibitor drugs, Drug Metabol. Lett. 8 (2014) 19–30.

[23] U.P. Dahal, B.M. Rock, J. Rodgers, X. Shen, Z. Wang, J.L. Wahlstrom, Absorption, distribution, metabolism and excretion of [(14)C]-sotorasib in rats and dogs: interspecies differences in absorption, protein conjugation and metabolism, Drug Metab. Dispos. 50 (2022) 600–612.

[24] L. Leung, X. Yang, T.J. Strelevitz, J. Montgomery, M.F. Brown, M.A. Zientek, et al., Clearance prediction of targeted covalent inhibitors by in vitro-in vivo extrapolation of hepatic and extrahepatic clearance mechanisms, Drug Metab. Dispos. 45 (2017) 1–7.

[25] Y. Shibata, M. Chiba, The role of extrahepatic metabolism in the pharmacokinetics of the targeted covalent inhibitors afatinib, ibrutinib, and neratinib, Drug Metab. Dispos. 43 (2015) 375–384.

[26] M.E. Flanagan, J.A. Abramite, D.P. Anderson, A. Aulabaugh, U.P. Dahal, A.M. Gilbert, et al., Chemical and computational methods for the characterization of covalent reactive groups for the prospective design of irreversible inhibitors, J. Med. Chem. 57 (2014) 10072–10079.

[27] R. Lonsdale, J. Burgess, N. Colclough, N.L. Davies, E.M. Lenz, A.L. Orton, R.A. Ward, Expanding the armory: predicting and tuning covalent warhead reactivity, J. Chem. Inf. Model. 57 (2017) 3124–3137.

[28] L. Petri, P. Abranyi-Balogh, P.R. Varga, T. Imre, G.M. Keseru, Comparative reactivity analysis of small-molecule thiol surrogates, Bioorg. Med. Chem. 28 (2020) 115357.

[29] S.M. Hacker, K.M. Backus, M.R. Lazear, S. Forli, B.E. Correia, B.F. Cravatt, Global profiling of lysine reactivity and ligandability in the human proteome, Nat. Chem. 9 (2017) 1181–1190.

[30] R. Liu, Z. Yue, C.C. Tsai, J. Shen, Assessing lysine and cysteine reactivities for designing targeted covalent kinase inhibitors, J. Am. Chem. Soc. 141 (2019) 6553–6560.

[31] P. Zhou, Determining protein half-lives, Methods Mol. Biol. 284 (2004) 67–77.

[32] X. Chen, S. Wei, S. Ji, X. Guo, F. Yang, Quantitative proteomics using SILAC: principles, applications, and developments, Proteomics 15 (2015) 3175–3192.

[33] A.B. Ross, J.D. Langer, M. Jovanovic, Proteome turnover in the spotlight: approaches, applications, and perspectives, Mol. Cell. Proteom. 20 (2021) 100016.

[34] J.M. Strelow, A perspective on the kinetics of covalent and irreversible inhibition, SLAS Discov 22 (2017) 3–20.

[35] B.F. Krippendorff, R. Neuhaus, P. Lienau, A. Reichel, W. Huisinga, Mechanism-based inhibition: deriving K(I) and k(inact) directly from time-dependent IC(50) values, J. Biomol. Screen 14 (2009) 913–923.

[36] I. Miyahisa, T. Sameshima, M.S. Hixon, Rapid determination of the specificity constant of irreversible inhibitors (kinact/KI) by means of an endpoint competition assay, Angew Chem. Int. Ed. Engl. 54 (2015) 14099–14102.

[37] A. Thorarensen, P. Balbo, M.E. Banker, R.M. Czerwinski, M. Kuhn, T.S. Maurer, et al., The advantages of describing covalent inhibitor in vitro potencies by IC50 at a fixed time point. IC50 determination of covalent inhibitors provides meaningful data to medicinal chemistry for SAR optimization, Bioorg. Med. Chem. 29 (2021) 115865.

[38] R. Hansen, S.J. Firdaus, S. Li, M.R. Janes, J. Zhang, Y. Liu, P.P. Zarrinkar, An internally controlled quantitative target occupancy assay for covalent inhibitors, Sci. Rep. 8 (2018) 14312.

[39] H.J. Burt, A. Galetin, J.B. Houston, IC50-based approaches as an alternative method for assessment of time-dependent inhibition of CYP3A4, Xenobiotica 40 (2010) 331–343.

[40] F. Daryaee, Z. Zhang, K.R. Gogarty, Y. Li, J. Merino, S.L. Fisher, P.J. Tonge, A quantitative mechanistic PK/PD model directly connects Btk target engagement and in vivo efficacy, Chem. Sci. 8 (2017) 3434–3443.

[41] G.A. Holdgate, T.D. Meek, R.L. Grimley, Mechanistic enzymology in drug discovery: a fresh perspective, Nat. Rev. Drug Discov. 17 (2018) 115–132.

[42] F. Daryaee, P.J. Tonge, Pharmacokinetic-pharmacodynamic models that incorporate drug-target binding kinetics, Curr. Opin. Chem. Biol. 50 (2019) 120–127.

[43] Z. Yang, Achieving a low human dose for targeted covalent drugs: pharmacokinetic and pharmacodynamic considerations on target characteristics and drug attributes, Biopharm. Drug Dispos. 42 (2021) 150–159.

[44] K. Van Belle, S. Sarre, G. Ebinger, Y. Michotte, Brain, liver and blood distribution kinetics of carbamazepine and its metabolic interaction with clomipramine in rats: a quantitative microdialysis study, J. Pharmacol. Exp. Therapeut. 272 (1995) 1217–1222.

[45] X. Liu, K. Van Natta, H. Yeo, O. Vilenski, P.E. Weller, P.D. Worboys, M. Monshouwer, Unbound drug concentration in brain homogenate and cerebral spinal fluid at steady state as a surrogate for unbound concentration in brain interstitial fluid, Drug Metab. Dispos. 37 (2009) 787–793.

[46] Y. Wang, D.F. Welty, The simultaneous estimation of the influx and efflux blood-brain barrier permeabilities of gabapentin using a microdialysis-pharmacokinetic approach, Pharm. Res. 13 (1996) 398–403.

[47] J.H. Lin, M. Yamazaki, Clinical relevance of P-glycoprotein in drug therapy, Drug Metab. Rev. 35 (2003) 417–454.

[48] K. Tunblad, E.N. Jonsson, M. Hammarlund-Udenaes, Morphine blood-brain barrier transport is influenced by probenecid co-administration, Pharm. Res. 20 (2003) 618–623.

[49] M.J. Dresser, M.K. Leabman, K.M. Giacomini, Transporters involved in the elimination of drugs in the kidney: organic anion transporters and organic cation transporters, J. Pharm. Sci. 90 (2001) 397–421.

[50] R.B. Kim, Transporters and xenobiotic disposition, Toxicology 181–182 (2002) 291–297.

[51] D. Zhang, C. Hop, G. Patilea-Vrana, G. Gampa, H.K. Seneviratne, J.D. Unadkat, et al., Drug concentration asymmetry in tissues and plasma for small molecule-related therapeutic modalities, Drug Metab. Dispos. 47 (2019) 1122–1135.

[52] S.M. Brachmann, A. Weiss, D.A. Guthy, K. Beyer, J. Voshol, M. Maira, et al., JDQ443, a covalent irreversible inhibitor of KRAS G12C, exhibits a novel binding mode and demonstrates potent anti-tumor activity and favorable pharmacokinetic properties in preclinical models [abstract]. In: proceedings of the AACR-NCI-EORTC virtual international conference on molecular targets and cancer therapeutics, Mol. Cancer Therapeut. 20 (2021) P124.

[53] J. Canon, K. Rex, A.Y. Saiki, C. Mohr, K. Cooke, D. Bagal, et al., The clinical KRAS(G12C) inhibitor AMG 510 drives anti-tumour immunity, Nature 575 (2019) 217–223.

[54] B.A. Lanman, J.R. Allen, J.G. Allen, A.K. Amegadzie, K.S. Ashton, S.K. Booker, et al., Discovery of a covalent inhibitor of KRAS(G12C) (AMG 510) for the treatment of solid tumors, J. Med. Chem. 63 (2020) 52–65.

[55] E.C. Nakajima, N. Drezner, X. Li, P.S. Mishra-Kalyani, Y. Liu, H. Zhao, et al., FDA approval summary: sotorasib for KRAS G12C-mutated metastatic NSCLC, Clin. Cancer Res. 28 (2021) 1482–1486.

[56] F. Sutanto, M. Konstantinidou, A. Domling, Covalent inhibitors: a rational approach to drug discovery, RSC Med Chem 11 (2020) 876–884.

[57] A.J. Smith, X. Zhang, A.G. Leach, K.N. Houk, Beyond picomolar affinities: quantitative aspects of noncovalent and covalent binding of drugs to proteins, J. Med. Chem. 52 (2009) 225–233.

[58] J. Uetrecht, Mechanistic studies of idiosyncratic DILI: clinical implications, Front. Pharmacol. 10 (2019) 837.

[59] U.P. Dahal, R.S. Obach, A.M. Gilbert, Benchmarking in vitro covalent binding burden as a tool to assess potential toxicity caused by nonspecific covalent binding of covalent drugs, Chem. Res. Toxicol. 26 (2013) 1739–1745.

[60] S. Wind, D. Schnell, T. Ebner, M. Freiwald, P. Stopfer, Clinical pharmacokinetics and pharmacodynamics of afatinib, Clin. Pharmacokinet. 56 (2017) 235–250.

[61] P.A. Dickinson, M.V. Cantarini, J. Collier, P. Frewer, S. Martin, K. Pickup, P. Ballard, Metabolic disposition of osimertinib in rats, dogs, and humans: insights into a drug designed to bind covalently to a cysteine residue of epidermal growth factor receptor, Drug Metab. Dispos. 44 (2016) 1201–1212.

[62] J. Wang, X.X. Li-Chan, J. Atherton, L. Deng, R. Espina, L. Yu, et al., Characterization of HKI-272 covalent binding to human serum albumin, Drug Metab. Dispos. 38 (2010) 1083–1093.

[63] A.F. Stepan, D.P. Walker, J. Bauman, D.A. Price, T.A. Baillie, A.S. Kalgutkar, M.D. Aleo, Structural alert/reactive metabolite concept as applied in medicinal chemistry to mitigate the risk of idiosyncratic drug toxicity: a perspective based on the critical examination of trends in the top 200 drugs marketed in the United States, Chem. Res. Toxicol. 24 (2011) 1345–1410.

[64] C. Limban, D.C. Nuta, C. Chirita, S. Negres, A.L. Arsene, M. Goumenou, et al., The use of structural alerts to avoid the toxicity of pharmaceuticals, Toxicol. Rep. 5 (2018) 943–953.

[65] A.S. Kalgutkar, Designing around structural alerts in drug discovery, J. Med. Chem. 63 (2020) 6276–6302.

[66] R.J. Foot, N.U. Haase, K. Grob, P. Gonde, Acrylamide in fried and roasted potato products: a review on progress in mitigation, Food Addit. Contam. 24 (Suppl. 1) (2007) 37–46.

[67] E.J. Konings, P. Ashby, C.G. Hamlet, G.A. Thompson, Acrylamide in cereal and cereal products: a review on progress in level reduction, Food Addit. Contam. 24 (Suppl. 1) (2007) 47–59.

[68] A. Cooper, M. Hanigan, Enzymes involved in processing glutathione conjugates, Compr. Toxicol. (2010) 323–366.

[69] K. Ishida, J.A. Werner, R. Davies, F. Fan, B. Thomas, J. Wahlstrom, et al., Nonclinical safety profile of sotorasib, a KRAS(G12C)-specific covalent inhibitor for the treatment of KRAS p.G12C-mutated cancer, Int. J. Toxicol. 40 (2021) 427–441.

[70] J.A. Werner, R. Davies, J. Wahlstrom, U.P. Dahal, M. Jiang, J. Stauber, et al., Mercapturate pathway metabolites of sotorasib, a covalent inhibitor of KRAS(G12C), are associated with renal toxicity in the Sprague Dawley rat, Toxicol. Appl. Pharmacol. 423 (2021) 115578.

[71] C. Markoth, I. File, R. Szasz, L. Bidiga, J. Balla, J. Matyus, Ibrutinib-induced acute kidney injury via interstitial nephritis, Ren. Fail. 43 (2021) 335–339.

[72] J.J.M. Rood, A. Jamalpoor, S. van Hoppe, M.J. van Haren, R.E. Wasmann, M.J. Janssen, et al., Extrahepatic metabolism of ibrutinib, Invest. New Drugs 39 (2021) 1–14.

[73] S.S. Kalsi, P.I. Dargan, W.S. Waring, D.M. Wood, A review of the evidence concerning hepatic glutathione depletion and susceptibility to hepatotoxicity after paracetamol overdose, Open Access Emerg. Med. 3 (2011) 87–96.

[74] A.S. Kalgutkar, D.K. Dalvie, Drug discovery for a new generation of covalent drugs, Expert Opin. Drug Discov. 7 (2012) 561–581.

[75] G.J. Beckett, J.D. Hayes, Glutathione S-transferases: biomedical applications, Adv. Clin. Chem. 30 (1993) 281–380.

[76] P.G. Board, Biochemical genetics of glutathione-S-transferase in man, Am. J. Hum. Genet. 33 (1981) 36–43.

[77] S. Zhong, A.H. Wyllie, D. Barnes, C.R. Wolf, N.K. Spurr, Relationship between the GSTM1 genetic polymorphism and susceptibility to bladder, breast and colon cancer, Carcinogenesis 14 (1993) 1821–1824.

Chapter 6

Denosumab: dosing and drug interaction challenges on the path to approval

Graham Jang

Blaze Bioscience, Seattle, WA, United States

Introduction

Denosumab, a fully human monoclonal antibody (mAb) to the Receptor Activator of Nuclear Factor Kappa B (RANK) Ligand (RANKL), had worldwide sales in fiscal year 2021 of ~$3.2 billion as Prolia and ~$2.0 billion as XGEVA—two Amgen drugs that represent the same mAb administered very differently across multiple indications. This chapter summarizes some of the clinical pharmacology-related experiences and challenges that were faced by the denosumab clinical development teams as the molecule progressed through Phase 2 and 3 clinical trials and during US Food and Drug Administration (FDA) review of the Biologics Licensing Applications (BLAs).

RANKL is critical in osteoclast maturation and function and therefore its inhibition can rapidly and profoundly inhibit bone resorption. Accordingly, denosumab was being developed for the treatment of post-menopausal osteoporosis (PMOs), to reverse bone loss associated with hormone ablation therapies in breast and prostate cancer patients, and to reduce the risk of skeletal related events (SREs) in advanced cancer patients. At the time, these were among the highest priority programs at Amgen. Given the importance of such programs at any biotech or pharma company, they are afforded the most resources and oversight by senior management, and this was certainly true for the two denosumab programs, which were grouped by the bone loss (reduction in fracture risk associated with PMO and bone loss with hormone ablation therapies) and SRE indications.

These two sets of potential therapeutic uses for denosumab were evaluating markedly different dose regimens in the ongoing clinical trials: 60 mg administered every 6 months (Q6M) in the bone loss phase 3 trials and 30–180 mg administered every 4 weeks (Q4W) or 12 weeks (Q12W) in the advanced cancer phase 2 study. Any End-of-Phase 2 (EOP2) meeting discussion with the FDA will include as a necessary and key component the justification of the dose regimen planned or used in the pivotal clinical trial(s). At the time this author joined the advanced cancer development team, discussions were ongoing to determine the optimal dose regimen for planned phase 3 trials, which was to be discussed with FDA at the face-to-face EOP2 meeting in approximately 2 months. It was therefore a particularly challenging time to be joining the team, attempting to get up-to-speed on the fast-paced program, and helping determine and then represent the justification for what would turn out to be a 12-fold higher (overall) dose level of 120 mg Q4W in the advanced cancer versus bone loss trials. This marked dose level discrepancy between indications for the same molecule represented a unique and challenging aspect in the regulatory interactions and filings for denosumab, complicated further by the decisions to transition from weight-based (mg/kg) doses in Phase 1 to "fixed" (mg) doses in the Phase 2 and 3 trials.

An additional and relatively new (at the time) consideration that complicated the initial BLA submission and approvals for denosumab in the bone loss indications involved a potential drug-disease interaction. During the characterization of RANKL and its receptor RANK, it was determined that they shared roughly 20%–30% sequence homology with various members of the tumor necrosis factor (TNF) ligand and receptor families and were involved in T-lymphocyte and dendritic cell interactions; RANKL was thus classified as a cytokine [1–3]. In the years preceding and coinciding with the initial BLA submission, potential interactions between therapeutic proteins, including monoclonal antibodies, and small molecule drugs were of increased interest to drug regulatory agencies and industry sponsors [4–6]. Focus was on the downregulation of some cytochrome P450 (CYP) enzymes by proinflammatory cytokines such as several interleukins (IL-1, IL-6, and

Overcoming Obstacles in Drug Discovery and Development. https://doi.org/10.1016/B978-0-12-817134-9.00006-4

IL-10) and TNFα, as evidenced by lower CYP expression and activity in some inflammatory disease states [7—10]. In theory, a therapeutic protein that neutralizes or reduces the action of an inflammatory cytokine could reverse suppression of (or normalize) CYP expression, leading to faster elimination of concomitant small molecule drugs that are substrates of the affected CYPs. The initial BLA for denosumab and responses to FDA during its review therefore involved an assessment of the potential for denosumab (as a "cytokine" modulator) to alter CYP expression in patients, with important implications for its use with concomitant medicines in all planned patient populations, as well as related language in its prescribing information.

The summaries below describe the interesting challenges faced in devising and justifying the dose regimens used for denosumab in the pivotal clinical trials and the interactions with FDA on its drug interaction potential.

Justifying the dose regimen for bone loss indications

In the initial phase 1 trials, denosumab was found to have clinical pharmacokinetic (PK) properties that were clearly indicative of apparent target-mediated drug disposition (TMDD), whereby clearance or elimination of the drug occurs via a target-mediated pathway, and as higher doses and systemic concentrations are reached, this target-mediated pathway becomes saturated. For monoclonal antibodies with this property, PK properties such as clearance and half-life at higher doses resemble those typical for mAbs that do not display such "non-linear" (with dose) behavior. Such non-linear PK is sometimes considered undesirable for a drug candidate, since it can potentially introduce greater inter-subject variability in systemic exposures, which also increase greater than dose-proportionally (in fact, this is key evidence of TMDD), sometimes markedly so, such as a 10-fold increase in exposure for a doubling in dose.

This behavior is illustrated in Fig. 6.1, which shows the mean serum denosumab concentration-time profiles from a phase 1 study in healthy post-menopausal women, in which a wide (300-fold) range of single subcutaneous (SCs) doses from 0.01 to 3 mg/kg were evaluated (FDA Clinical Pharmacology Review, Prolia). It is evident from the mean profiles that serum levels decline much more rapidly for the lower dose levels, whereas for higher doses such as 0.3 and 1 mg/kg, serum concentrations decline more slowly initially, until they reach an apparent threshold of $\sim 10^3$ ng/mL (1 μg/mL), below which the slopes of decline in serum concentrations are steeper and similar to those at the lower dose levels.

With the assumption that the non-linear PK for denosumab reflected saturation of binding to RANKL, it was reasonable to then consider that the threshold for apparent saturation was therefore a proxy for target occupancy. In other words, if a potential therapeutic goal was to cover the target for all or a majority of the dosing interval, tailoring the dose level and dosing frequency to achieve and maintain serum levels above the threshold could be useful to guide dosing.

Fortunately, such empirical rationalizations based on the PK data were strongly supported in this case by well-established pharmacodynamic (PD) markers of bone resorption that were readily measurable in clinical trial subjects

FIGURE 6.1 FDA Clinical Pharmacology Review, Prolia (p. 28).

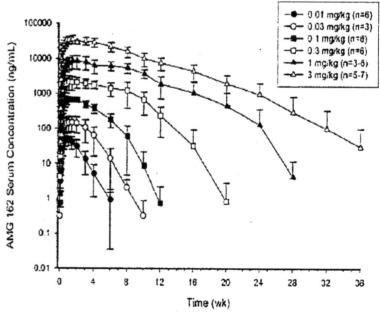

and patients. As osteoclasts resorb bone, this liberates evidence of this activity in the form of fragments of collagen (from the bone matrix), measured for example as the collagen type I C-terminal peptide in serum (sCTX1) or the N-terminal peptide in urine (uNTX). Others had established that measured reductions in sCTX1 during the treatment of osteoporosis with bisphosphonates such as alendronate correlated well with increases in bone mineral density (BMD) that resulted from inhibition of osteoclasts and reduced bone resorption [11]. Given this, sCTX1 and/or uNTX were measured in the majority of clinical studies conducted with denosumab.

Another fortunate aspect was the rigor with which the phase 2 trial for denosumab in post-menopausal women with low BMD was conducted. In this trial [12], denosumab was administered SC using *eight* dose regimens with two dosing schedules (6, 14, and 30 mg every 3 months (Q3M) and 14, 30, 60, 100, and 210 mg Q6M), along with placebo and active control (70 mg alendronate weekly) groups, in a total of over 400 subjects. Focusing on the Q6M regimens (the approved bone loss dose frequency), the lowest dose level (14 mg) resulted in less complete reductions in sCTx over a 6 month period compared to the higher doses, while the 60 mg dose led to maximal reductions (by >90%) in sCTx over most of the dose interval, similar to the 100 and 210 mg doses, but with some evidence of reversibility in the effects after ~5 months of the dose interval. These extents and durations of inhibition of bone resorption, as measured by sCTx, translated to changes in lumbar spine BMD that were less robust at 14 mg and similar at 60, 100, and 210 mg (Fig. 6.2).

On this basis, the 60 mg Q6M dose regimen was selected for pivotal phase 3 trials investigating the following potential indications for denosumab: (1) the treatment of post-menopausal osteoporosis; (2) the treatment and prevention of bone loss in patients undergoing hormone ablation for breast cancer; and (3) the treatment and prevention of bone loss in patients undergoing hormone ablation for prostate cancer. In the FREEDOM (Fracture REduction Evaluation of Denosumab in Osteoporosis every 6 Months) trial, which enrolled ~7800 subjects, treatment with denosumab for 3 years significantly reduced the risk of new vertebral, non-vertebral, and hip fractures (vs. placebo) in women with post-menopausal osteoporosis [13]. The 60 mg Q6M dose regimen also increased BMD at lumbar spine and multiple other sites evaluated after 12 and 24 months relative to placebo in ~250 women with breast cancer receiving adjuvant aromatase inhibitor therapy [14]. Denosumab treatment (vs. placebo in ~1500 subjects) in men with prostate cancer receiving androgen deprivation therapy increased BMD at the lumbar spine, femoral neck, and hip at 24 and 36 months, and moreover, was associated with significant decreases in the incidences of new vertebral fracture at 12, 24, and 36 months [15].

Despite clearly successful outcomes for these pivotal trials, it was still critical that the BLA seeking approval in these indications include a discussion and justification of the dose regimen. As illustrated in Fig. 6.3 (US FDA Clinical Pharmacology Review, Prolia), data from the phase 2 trial in postmenopausal women with low bone mineral density enabled a strong rationale based on PK and both PD measures; as serum denosumab levels decline below ~1 μg/mL, the levels of sCTx that were rapidly and extensively reduced shortly after dosing showed reversibility (i.e., increased) in the last 2 months of the dose interval, while lumbar spine BMD increased continuously. Importantly, the BMD gains with 60 mg Q6M dosing were similar to those at higher dose levels (Fig. 6.2), indicating that this represented the lowest dose that

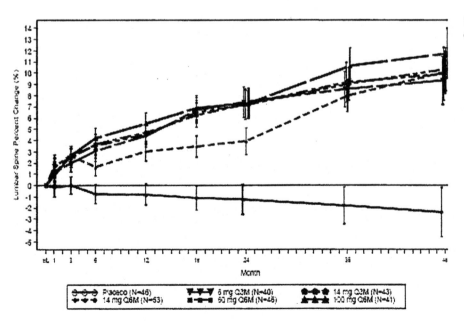

FIGURE 6.2 FDA Clinical Pharmacology Review, Prolia (p. 12).

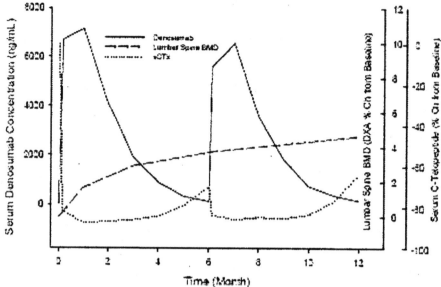

FIGURE 6.3 US FDA Clinical Pharmacology Review, Prolia (p. 14).

provides maximal gains in BMD, while evidence of reversibility was important given concerns with "over-suppression" of bone resorption.

Lastly, the use of fixed versus weight-based doses was supported by analyses of data in the pivotal trials demonstrating that fracture risk reduction in PMO or gains in BMD were independent of body weight quartile (i.e., treatment benefits were the same, regardless of body weight). This example illustrates how a robust phase 2 trial design, with strong PK and PD data collected across a wide dose range, enabled a relatively straightforward dose selection that led to multiple successful pivotal trials and approvals in numerous indications. The decisions and rationale for dosing in the advanced cancer trials would not be as straightforward.

Justifying the dose regimen for the advanced cancer indications

Bone metastases are common in advanced cancer, occurring in ~70%–80% of patients with breast or prostate cancer and 30%–40% of patients with lung cancer or other solid tumors [16]. In these patients, this can lead to SREs, which include pathological fractures (i.e., fractures caused by an underlying disease), spinal cord compression, or the need for surgery or radiation to bone. Bisphosphonates are approved to delay or prevent SREs, but their effectiveness is incomplete, they can cause adverse effects, and their use can be limited (e.g., in renally impaired patients). Given the effectiveness of denosumab at inhibiting bone resorption, it was hypothesized that denosumab would improve upon the effectiveness of bisphosphonates at delaying or preventing SREs.

In the initial phase 1 trial in advanced cancer patients [17], denosumab PK was similar to that in post-menopausal women, though there was evidence that the extent and duration of inhibition of bone resorption was different. Mean uNTx reductions in breast cancer patients with bone metastases at 1.0 mg/kg were not as extensive as those at 3.0 mg/kg; this contrasts with apparent maximal reductions in sCTX at the roughly equivalent fixed doses of 60 and 210 mg in post-menopausal women. This observation alone indicated that a 1.0 mg/kg or 60 mg dose of denosumab would likely not provide maximal inhibition of bone resorption in subjects with advanced cancer, while a 3.0 mg/kg or 180 mg dose appeared to provide maximal effects.

In the phase 2 study in subjects with advanced cancer, fixed SC denosumab doses of 30, 120 and 180 mg Q4W and 60 or 180 mg Q12W were evaluated alongside an active comparator group of intravenous bisphosphonate Q4W, with approximately 40 patients per group [18]. The median changes in uNTx/Cr over time for these dose regimens are shown in Fig. 6.4 (FDA Clinical Pharmacology Review, Xgeva), with the 120 and 180 mg Q4W regimens providing the greatest overall reductions over 12 weeks of treatment, including when compared to the bisphosphonate group. But a similarly important observation is the notable inter-patient variability indicated by the error bars representing the first and third quartiles, demonstrating that some patients on these dose regimens have less extensive reductions in bone resorption based on this biomarker.

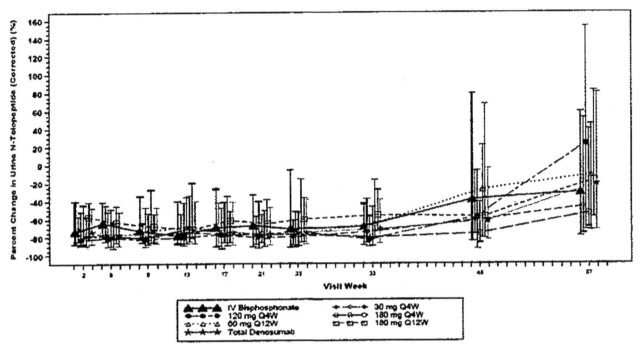

FIGURE 6.4 FDA Clinical Pharmacology Review Xgeva.

The patient populations for the advanced cancer versus bone loss indications are clearly very different with regard to disease severity and the goals of treatment. To prevent or treat bone loss, a dose regimen that leads to strong increases in BMD, with a favorable safety profile and evidence of reversibility, was a reasonable goal that appeared readily accepted by regulatory agencies. In contrast, the goal in advanced cancer was to select a dose regimen that resulted in a near-maximal or maximal reduction in bone resorption in the highest proportion of treated patients, in an effort to disrupt what is sometimes referred to as a "vicious cycle" of bone metastases, in which metastases-induced bone destruction enables further tumor proliferation. Thus, by virtue of this fundamental difference in treatment intent, a more intensive dose regimen in advanced cancer versus bone loss was likely appropriate. But how would this be justified on a quantitative basis?

In common with the bone loss program, the phase 2 trial in advanced cancer was robust, in that it evaluated a wide range in dose level and different dosing frequencies. Using the data from the Phase 2 study, population PKPD modeling was performed [18] to characterize individual patient PK and PD properties for denosumab in the advanced cancer population. The varied dose levels and frequencies evaluated in ~160 patients enabled this analysis to provide what was considered a meaningful representation of denosumab PK and PD in this patient population. The individual PK and PD properties from the modeling (i.e., variability in individual patient estimates for PK and PD parameters in the model) then enabled Monte Carlo simulations to be performed; in essence, the PKPD model and population PK and PD estimates were used to simulate denosumab PK and PD profiles for various denosumab dosing regimens tested in hypothetical phase 3 study designs. Because there was evidence that the Q12W dose regimens allowed some "release" in the inhibition of bone resorption (based on uNTx/Cr values), the simulations were performed only for Q4W dose regimens ranging from 30 to 180 mg, including intermediate dose regimens that had not been evaluated in the phase 2 study. In the modeling, the serum denosumab concentration leading to >90% of the maximal inhibition of uNTx/Cr was estimated for each individual patient, and variability in serum denosumab pharmacokinetics was used to estimate serum denosumab PK and exposures for a hypothetical group of 2000 patients for each dose level evaluated. From these simulated exposures, it was then estimated what proportion of patients at each dose level had serum denosumab exposures exceeding the concentration necessary to reduce uNTx/Cr by 90% or more of the maximal extent. Dose levels of 30 and 60 mg Q4W were predicted to lead to serum denosumab exposures that maintain uNTx/Cr suppression above 90% (of maximum) in approximately 85% −90% of treated patients over time. Dose levels of 120−180 mg Q4W were predicted to lead to similar proportions (~95%) of treated patients maintaining serum denosumab concentrations associated with >90% of the maximal inhibition of uNTx/Cr. Although ~95 versus 90% of treated patients (120 vs. 60 mg Q4W) maintaining the target uNTx/Cr reduction may not appear to be a meaningful difference, it indicates that 5 out of every 100 patients treated at the lower dose level would potentially benefit from receiving the higher dose level. In addition, and importantly, the overall profile of denosumab in the phase 1 and 2 trials suggested that this greater level of inhibition of bone resorption for the 120 mg versus lower doses would be associated with acceptable safety and tolerability and would therefore have a favorable benefit to risk profile.

At the EOP2 meeting with FDA, the above rationale was discussed and the Agency agreed that overall the 120 mg Q4W dose regimen appeared appropriate for the planned phase 3 trials of denosumab in advanced cancer. Another critical discussion topic was the non-inferiority margin for denosumab treatment compared to zoledronic acid (ZA), which was approved in these indications and as a result was to be the required active comparator in the pivotal trials. The need to demonstrate non-inferiority of denosumab treatment effects to those of ZA meant that much larger studies would be needed, as compared to a study in which a placebo control was used, and the studies were further powered to potentially demonstrate superiority of denosumab to ZA.

Together the 3 pivotal SRE trials enrolled nearly 6000 patients. In the study conducted in over 2000 patients with advanced breast cancer [19], denosumab was superior to ZA in delaying the time to first on-study SRE, as well as the time to first and subsequent SREs. Similarly, denosumab was superior to ZA in delaying the time to first on-study SRE in the study conducted in ~1900 patients with castration-resistant prostate cancer [20]. Lastly, denosumab was non-inferior to ZA in delaying the time to first on-study SRE in a study conducted in nearly 1800 patients with other (non-breast or prostate) advanced cancer or multiple myeloma [21]; there was a trend for superiority of denosumab for this endpoint that just missed statistical significance (P = 0.06).

The dose regimen of 120 mg Q4W denosumab therefore yielded 3 successful pivotal trials that demonstrated it was non-inferior or superior to ZA in delaying SREs in patients with advanced cancer.

In hindsight, it's informative to assess how accurately the modeling based on phase 2 data predicted the effects of this dose regimen in suppressing the bone turnover marker uNTx/Cr, which was evaluated in a subset of patients in each trial. Table 6.1 summarizes the median % decrease from baseline in uNTX/Cr for denosumab and ZA across the three trials; denosumab had consistently greater effectiveness at reducing uNTX/Cr, which is in turn consistent with its superiority to ZA in 2 of the 3 trials (and trend in the third) in delaying the time to first on-study SRE. As noted above, the modeling of the phase 2 study data [18] predicted that the 120 mg Q4W dose regimen would result in ~95% of patients with uNTX/Cr reductions >90% of their individual, model-predicted maximal extent. Importantly, the population estimate for the maximal extent was ~78%. In other words, the modeling predicted that the 120 mg Q4W dose regimen would lead to ~95% of treated patients with reductions in uNTX/Cr of ~70% from baseline on average. The results shown in Table 6.1 are consistent with the model prediction, in that they indicate at least 50% of the denosumab-treated patients in each trial had 76%−84% reductions in uNTX/Cr from baseline. Subsequent population PKPD modeling at Amgen [22] was performed that employed a different PD model structure and method for dealing with uNTX/Cr values below the lower limit of quantitation, and further incorporated data from the phase 3 trials. This work confirmed that the 120 mg Q4W dosing regimen provides the targeted level of uNTX/Cr inhibition in a proportion of treated patients that is similar to those predicted for higher dose levels, meaning it is the lowest dose level providing maximal effects.

Inhibition of RANKL and the potential for drug-disease interactions

It was recognized over 30 years ago that inflammation associated with lipopolysaccharide (LPS) challenge in rodents led to a decrease in CYP2C11 levels [23]. Progress in the field continued steadily and it was demonstrated by the early 2000s that, in humans, proinflammatory cytokines such as interleukin 6 (IL-6) lower CYP expression and activity in some inflammatory disease states [7−10]. It follows then that, in theory, a therapeutic protein that neutralizes or reduces the action of an inflammatory cytokine such as IL-6 could reverse suppression of (or "normalize") the expression of CYPs, leading to faster elimination of concomitant drugs that are substrates of the affected enzymes. For an impacted drug, this would result

TABLE 6.1 Median % decrease from baseline in uNTx/Cr at Week 13 in the pivotal advanced cancer trials with denosumab.

Patient population	Denosumab	Zoledronic acid	References
Breast cancer	80	68	[19]
Prostate cancer	84	69	[20]
Other solid tumors or multiple myeloma	76	65	[21]

in lower exposures, which could potentially lead to reduced efficacy (if the magnitude of the effects are marked and the drug has a narrow range of therapeutic exposures at the approved dose), but would have low probability of causing *greater* toxicity. In other words, such a drug-disease interaction is unlikely to have safety implications.

The initial BLA for tocilizumab (Actemra), which binds to the IL-6 receptor and therefore antagonizes the effects of IL-6, was filed November 19, 2007 for the treatment of rheumatoid arthritis (RA). In the FDA Clinical Pharmacology Review document (Actemra, BLA 125276), it is stated that a clinical drug-disease interaction study was ongoing at the time of the BLA filing that evaluated the effects of tocilizumab on the pharmacokinetics of the CYP3A4 substrate simvastatin and methotrexate, which is not a CYP3A4 substrate, but would be a common co-administered drug in the RA population. The results of this study were not published until several years later [24], but were provided to FDA in July of 2008, during review of the BLA. In the study, 24 subjects with RA were enrolled, with 12 (Group 1) receiving an oral (40 mg) dose of simvastatin on Day 1, a 10 mg/kg IV infusion of tocilizumab on Day 8, oral 40 mg doses of simvastatin on Days 15 and 43, and once-weekly methotrexate throughout the study period. Group 2 (the other 12 patients) did not receive simvastatin, but otherwise received the same treatments to assess potential tocilizumab effects on methotrexate PK, which were found not to be notable or clinically meaningful. For Group 1, it was found that: (1) mean C_{max} and AUC values for simvastatin on Day 1 were approximately 4- to 9-fold higher than those observed in healthy subjects for a 40 mg dose; (2) simvastatin exposures on Day 15 (1 week after the tocilizumab dose) were reduced by 57% when compared to Day 1; and (3) simvastatin exposures on Day 43 (5 weeks after the tocilizumab dose) were reduced by ~40% relative to Day 1, indicating persistent yet waning effects of the tocilizumab dose on CYP3A4 activity. Similar effects (though lower in magnitude) were observed for exposures of the active metabolite of simvastatin (simvastatin acid) with respect to higher exposures in subjects with RA (vs. healthy subjects) and the effects of tocilizumab treatment.

These results demonstrated several key points: (1) elevated IL-6 (and likely other inflammatory cytokine) levels in subjects with RA appear to lead to markedly reduced CYP3A4 expression and activity; (2) while the effects of tocilizumab treatment were readily detectable, they were relatively modest; and (3) those effects were associated with simvastatin exposures in these subjects with RA that were still higher than those observed in healthy subjects. The latter observation indicates that IL-6 inhibition by tocilizumab did not lead to "normalized" CYP3A4 expression and activity, potentially due to continued suppressive effects of other inflammatory cytokines in the study subjects. This, in turn, would suggest that the effects of any therapeutic protein that inhibits a single inflammatory cytokine may be limited in magnitude and would be unlikely to "normalize" CYP3A4 activity in subjects with inflammatory disease to that observed in healthy subjects.

As an aside, while the US prescribing information for simvastatin (Zocor) lists several medications that should be avoided when taking simvastatin because they lead to ~1.4- to 6-fold increases in simvastatin exposures (e.g., verapamil, gemfibrozil, nelfinavir), it does not disclose ~4- to 9-fold higher simvastatin exposures in RA (vs. healthy subjects) or suggest that dose reductions should be considered in this population [25].

The tocilizumab results described above very likely impacted the regulatory experience for denosumab, given that the results of the study were provided to FDA approximately 5 months before the BLA submission for denosumab in the bone loss indications (December 2008). In addition, FDA clinical pharmacology reviewers published articles related to biologics and cytokine-related clinical disease-drug interactions prior to and shortly after this period [5,26], thus it is clear that such interactions were of increasing importance to FDA at the time. Indeed, during the FDA review of the bone loss submission, we were asked to address the potential for denosumab, via inhibition of RANKL, to lead to altered CYP3A4 expression and activity in post-menopausal women with osteoporosis.

We considered and proposed to FDA that the risk of denosumab provoking CYP3A4-related, drug-disease interactions was low, for several key reasons: (1) available data suggested that CYP3A4 expression and activity was not different in post-menopausal osteoporosis, thus there were no altered or disease-related effects to "normalize"; (2) RANKL is not a proinflammatory cytokine with demonstrated effects on CYP3A4 expression; and (3) an indirect effect via denosumab altering inflammatory cytokine levels was also unlikely, based on preclinical and clinical data.

It had been demonstrated that age and menopause do not affect CYP3A4 activity in women based on studies with midazolam [27], triazolam [28], or erythromycin [29]. At the time, no published studies had evaluated whether osteoporosis impacts CYP3A4, although it had been shown that it was not associated with increased levels of proinflammatory cytokines such as IL-6 [30]. This indicated that unlike RA, post-menopausal osteoporosis is not an inflammatory disease in which cytokines impact CYP3A4 activity.

We acknowledged that, while a direct effect of RANKL on CYP expression had not been demonstrated or to our knowledge evaluated, this lack of evidence did not of course indicate a lack of effect. But importantly, based on mRNA levels, its receptor RANK did not appear to be expressed in human liver, in contrast to receptors for inflammatory cytokines (e.g., IL-6) that impact CYP3A4 expression through their activation on hepatocytes. Thus, we proposed that there was very low likelihood that RANK is directly involved in CYP regulation in the liver, and that as a consequence, inhibition of RANKL would likely not impact CYP expression.

It was possible that inhibition of RANKL could lead to secondary effects on CYPs by altering circulating levels of proinflammatory cytokines known to impact CYP expression. However, the lifelong inhibition of RANKL in rats and mice, via over-expression of the natural RANKL inhibitor osteoprotegerin, did not alter circulating levels of IL-1, IL-6, IL-10, or TNFα [31], and the pharmacologic inhibition of RANKL did not have significant effects on circulating levels of TNFα or IL-1β in rodent models of arthritis [32]. Moreover, in a phase 2 study in subjects with RA [33], denosumab treatment for 1 year at 60 or 180 mg every 6 months did not alter circulating levels of C-reactive protein (Amgen Inc., unpublished data), which is regulated primarily by IL-6 [34]. These preclinical and clinical data indicated that denosumab does not alter levels of circulating inflammatory cytokines and was thus unlikely to indirectly impact CYPs.

In the context of the tocilizumab drug-disease interaction and increased awareness and concern with such interactions, the FDA reviewers were not convinced by the above arguments. Several of their counterarguments are summarized in the FDA Clinical Pharmacology Review for Prolia, but key concerns were (1) still unknown effects of RANKL inhibition on CYP enzymes; (2) a potential interaction having safety-related implications (though examples of increased vs. decreased exposures with an interaction were given); and (3) the fact that denosumab would be first-in-class and used in a population likely to receive concomitant drugs.

Prolia was approved in June of 2010, with the approval letter indicating that Amgen was to conduct a clinical drug-disease interaction study as a Post-Marketing Requirement (PMR):

Finally, we have determined that only a clinical trial … will be sufficient to identify an unexpected serious risk of drug interactions of Prolia (denosumab) with CYP3A4 substrates. Therefore, based on appropriate scientific data, FDA has determined that you are required, to conduct the following: an in vivo drug-drug interaction clinical trial with a CYP3A4 substrate (e.g., midazolam) in postmenopausal female patients with osteoporosis to characterize the potential risk of drug interactions of Prolia (denosumab) with CYP3A4 substrates.

The clinical study enrolled 30 post-menopausal women with osteoporosis, randomized to 21 and 9 subjects in Groups A and B, respectively [35]. Group A received a 2 mg oral dose of the commonly used, CYP3A4 substrate midazolam on Day 1, followed by a 60 mg SC dose of denosumab on Day 2, with a subsequent 2 mg oral dose of midazolam on Day 16. This study design therefore evaluated the potential impact of RANKL inhibition on midazolam PK 2 weeks after the SC dose of denosumab, which was considered sufficient time to enable absorption of the dose (median time to maximal serum levels is 10 days) and de-suppression or "normalization" of CYP3A4, if it was to occur. Group B received only the midazolam oral doses on Days 1 and 16 to evaluate a potential period effect, which was not observed.

The mean midazolam plasma concentration-time profiles for Group A prior to and following denosumab administration were virtually superimposable, as illustrated in Fig. 6.5. Accordingly, the point estimates for the ratios of the least square means for AUC and C_{max} values (Day 16 vs. Day 1) ranged from 1.02 to 1.04 and all 90% confidence intervals were well within the pre-specified range of 0.80−1.25, illustrating a clear lack of effects of denosumab on midazolam PK and therefore CYP3A4 activity.

Incidentally, the mean C_{max} and AUC values for the 2 mg oral dose of midazolam on Day 1 in Groups A and B ranged from 11.3 to 11.6 ng/mL and 31.0−35.6 ng* h/mL, respectively. These values are very similar to reported mean values in healthy men and women (19−46 years of age) of 11.9 ng/mL and 32.1 ng* h/mL, respectively [36]. This strongly implies that CYP3A4 is not altered in post-menopausal osteoporosis due to a disease-related, RANKL or other cytokine-mediated impact on its expression; in other words, our supposition to FDA during the Prolia BLA review that there was likely not altered CYP3A4 activity in this patient population to "normalize" was eventually shown to be accurate. Nonetheless, the conduct of the study was worthwhile in the interest of patient safety and advancing our collective understanding of potential CYP3A4-related, drug-disease interactions provoked by a therapeutic protein.

The current US prescribing information for Prolia [37] indicates in the Clinical Pharmacology section that "Denosumab did not affect the pharmacokinetics of midazolam, which is metabolized by cytochrome P450 3A4 (CYP3A4). This indicates that denosumab should not alter the pharmacokinetics of drugs metabolized by CYP3A4 in postmenopausal women with osteoporosis."

In the years since publication of the tocilizumab and denosumab studies, several additional clinical drug-disease interaction studies have been performed, with results confirming the relatively modest effects of an IL-6 inhibitor on CYP3A4 activity and no apparent effects of inhibitors of IL-23 and IL-17 (Table 6.2).

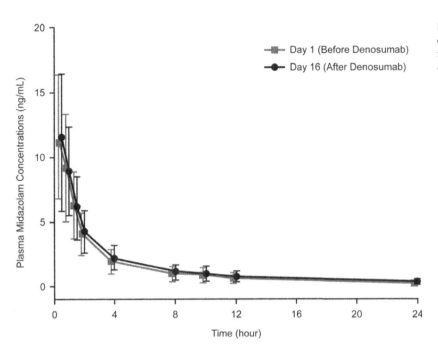

FIGURE **6.5** Mean midazolam plasma concentration-time profiles in women with post-menopausal osteoporosis before and after denosumab administration are virtually superimposable [35].

TABLE 6.2 Clinical therapeutic protein-disease interaction studies with CYP3A4 substrates conducted in various patient populations.

Therapeutic protein	Target	Patient population	CYP3A4 substrate	Magnitude of effects on exposure	References
Tocilizumab	IL-6	Rheumatoid arthritis	Simvastatin	↓ 57%	[24]
Denosumab	RANKL	Post-menopausal osteoporosis	Midazolam	None	[35]
Sirukumab	IL-6	Rheumatoid arthritis	Midazolam	↓ 30%–35%	[38]
Sarilumab	IL-6	Rheumatoid arthritis	Simvastatin	↓ 45%	[39]
Tildrakizumab	IL-23	Psoriasis	Midazolam	None	[40]
Secukinumab	IL-17	Psoriasis	Midazolam	None	[41]

Closing perspectives

The above summaries represent just a few outcomes from countless internal team meetings and strategic discussions with senior management at Amgen and both written and in-person interactions with FDA, but leave out numerous interactions with other health authorities around the world. They of course represent only a small fraction of the work of hundreds of individuals that contributed to the advancement of denosumab from discovery through preclinical and clinical development. The collective effort ultimately enabled the approval of two highly effective drugs that are benefitting thousands of patients around the world every year. Now over 12 years removed from the initial approval of Prolia to treat osteoporosis, the author remains extremely grateful to have been given the opportunity to represent the Pharmacokinetics and Drug Metabolism Department and Clinical Pharmacology function on the denosumab development teams and to have gained the tremendous personal and professional experiences and growth that came from the work. Assuming these responsibilities was intimidating, exciting, and motivating, given the importance of the programs to the company and the potential that denosumab had to make a meaningful difference in the treatment of multiple diseases. This importance was naturally accompanied by close oversight and support of the teams by all levels of management, and significant pressure on the teams and their individual members. As a relatively junior scientist at the time, with ∼7 years of industry experience (the majority on small molecule discovery and early development teams), the request by my management to join the denosumab teams was surprising, but represented confidence in my abilities to grow and meet the scientific, strategic, organizational and regulatory challenges of such a role. Along with this confidence was excellent advice and mentoring, as well as resources (e.g., consultants, headcount) to meet the considerable needs of the programs. Readers are encouraged to frequently assess their management and leadership for how well they provide such opportunities for development and growth, and to seek them out whenever possible, despite the accompanying uncertainty and discomfort of new challenges.

Comparing the dose rationales for the osteoporosis/bone loss versus advanced cancer indications summarized above illustrates a couple interesting points. For one, an empirical, logical approach for justifying the 60 mg Q6M dose regimen in the bone loss indications was straightforward, intuitive (based on sCTX and BMD changes and a desire to demonstrate reversibility), and readily accepted by the FDA and other regulatory agencies. Thorough characterization of dose-response relationships in phase 1 and 2 studies enabled this relatively simple and effective dose rationale, and it seems unlikely that more extensive pharmacometric assessments would have markedly improved the strength of justification. In contrast, an inherently more aggressive treatment paradigm for the advanced cancer patient populations was also readily accepted by regulatory agencies, but the use of population PKPD modeling and clinical trial simulations was instrumental in enabling quantitative arguments in support of the 12-fold higher dose level in the SRE (vs. bone loss) indications. While today such approaches are routine in drug development, the practice was still emerging ∼15 years ago. The numerous internal discussions and interactions with regulatory agencies (including an Oncologic Drugs Advisory Committee meeting) on such key development and regulatory issues taught and reinforced the value of clear and concise verbal and written communication—getting key points and arguments across in simple terms and backing them up judiciously with data and relevant (literature or regulatory) precedent. This approach can be challenging to some scientists, who may be naturally inclined to elaborate in detail about experimental or study design and the intricacies or caveats in the data and their interpretation.

Lastly, the disease-drug interaction challenges faced during the Prolia BLA review taught valuable lessons in dealing with the FDA or other health authorities. Although we strongly considered that denosumab had very little potential to provoke a disease-drug interaction for the above-noted reasons, which we thought were convincingly communicated to the Agency, we were unsuccessful in swaying their opinion, resuling in a PMR. In retrospect, given the growing concern among the scientific and regulatory communities about the possibility of such interactions, one can conclude in hindsight that conducting a clinical disease-drug interaction study was the only possible outcome from the debate with FDA. Our inability to convince the reviewers otherwise wasn't a failure and our arguments were sound (and eventually proven to be correct), but at the time there was an obvious need for additional clinical data to inform the field's understanding of the magnitude of such interactions. As such, the "negative" outcome of the study, which incidentally led a journal to reject publication of the manuscript, should be viewed as very positive in contributing to our collective understanding on this issue. FDA was ultimately viewed from this broader perspective as a partner (rather than adversary) in advancing denosumab. Along with optimizing the dose regimens used in pivotal clinical trials, a clear understanding of its drug interaction potential contributed signficantly to the shared (industry and regulator) goal of making a safe and effective therapeutic available to patients.

References

[1] D.M. Anderson, E. Maraskovsky, W.L. Billingsley, W.C. Dougall, M.E. Tometsko, E.R. Roux, et al., A homologue of the TNF receptor and its ligand enhance T-cell growth and dendritic-cell function, Nature 390 (1997) 175–179.

[2] D.L. Lacey, E. Timms, H.L. Tan, M.J. Kelley, C.R. Dunstan, T. Burgess, et al., Osteoprotegerin ligand is a cytokine that regulates osteoclast differentiation and activation, Cell 93 (1998) 165–176.

[3] B.R. Wong, J. Rho, J. Arron, E. Robinson, J. Orlinick, M. Chao, et al., TRANCE is a novel ligand of the tumor necrosis factor receptor family that activates c-Jun N-terminal kinase in T cells, J. Biol. Chem. 272 (1997) 25190–25194.

[4] S.M. Huang, H. Zhao, J.I. Lee, K. Reynolds, L. Zhang, R. Temple, et al., Therapeutic protein-drug interactions and implications for drug development, Clin. Pharmacol. Ther. 87 (2010) 497–503.

[5] J.I. Lee, L. Zhang, A.Y. Men, L.A. Kenna, S.M. Huang, CYP-mediated therapeutic protein-drug interactions: clinical findings, proposed mechanisms and regulatory implications, Clin. Pharmacokinet. 49 (2010) 295–310.

[6] H. Zhou, H.M. Davis, Risk-based strategy for the assessment of pharmacokinetic drug-drug interactions for therapeutic monoclonal antibodies, Drug Discov. Today 14 (2009) 891–898.

[7] A.E. Aitken, T.A. Richardson, E.T. Morgan, Regulation of drug-metabolizing enzymes and transporters in inflammation, Annu. Rev. Pharmacol. Toxicol. 46 (2006) 123–149.

[8] E.T. Morgan, Regulation of cytochrome p450 by inflammatory mediators: why and how? Drug Metab. Dispos. 29 (2001) 207–212.

[9] E.T. Morgan, T. Li-Masters, P.Y. Cheng, Mechanisms of cytochrome P450 regulation by inflammatory mediators, Toxicology 181−182 (2002) 207−210.

[10] E.T. Morgan, Impact of infectious and inflammatory disease on cytochrome P450-mediated drug metabolism and pharmacokinetics, Clin. Pharmacol. Ther. 85 (2009) 434−438.

[11] S.L. Greenspan, N.M. Resnick, R.A. Parker, Early changes in biochemical markers of bone turnover are associated with long-term changes in bone mineral density in elderly women on alendronate, hormone replacement therapy, or combination therapy: a three-year, double-blind, placebo-controlled, randomized clinical trial, J. Clin. Endocrinol. Metab. 90 (5) (2005) 2762−2767.

[12] E.M. Lewiecki, P.D. Miller, M.R. McClung, S.B. Cohen, M.A. Bolognese, Y. Liu, et al., Two-year treatment with denosumab (AMG 162) in a randomized phase 2 study of postmenopausal women with low BMD, J. Bone Miner. Res. 22 (2007) 1832−1841.

[13] S.R. Cummings, J. San Martin, M.R. McClung, E.S. Siris, R. Eastell, I.R. Reid, et al., Denosumab for prevention of fractures in postmenopausal women with osteoporosis, N. Engl. J. Med. 361 (2009) 756−765.

[14] G.K. Ellis, H.G. Bone, R. Chlebowski, D. Paul, S. Spadafora, J. Smith, et al., Randomized trial of denosumab in patients receiving adjuvant aromatase inhibitors for nonmetastatic breast cancer, J. Clin. Oncol. 26 (30) (2008) 4875−4882.

[15] M.R. Smith, B. Egerdie, N. Hernández Toriz, R. Feldman, T.L. Tammela, F. Saad, , et al.Denosumab HALT Prostate Cancer Study Group, Denosumab in men receiving androgen-deprivation therapy for prostate cancer, N. Engl. J. Med. 361 (8) (2009) 745−755.

[16] A. Lipton, J.R. Berenson, J.J. Body, B.F. Boyce, O.S. Bruland, M.A. Carducci, et al., Advances in treating metastatic bone cancer: summary statement for the First Cambridge Conference, Clin. Cancer Res. 12 (20 Pt 2) (2006) 6209s−6212s.

[17] J.J. Body, T. Facon, R.E. Coleman, A. Lipton, F. Geurs, M. Fan, et al., A study of the biological receptor activator of nuclear factor-kappaB ligand inhibitor, denosumab, in patients with multiple myeloma or bone metastases from breast cancer, Clin. Cancer Res. 12 (4) (2006) 1221−1228.

[18] A. Lipton, G.G. Steger, J. Figueroa, C. Alvarado, P. Solal-Celigny, J.J. Body, et al., Randomized active controlled phase II study of denosumab efficacy and safety in patients with breast cancer-related bone metastases, J. Clin. Oncol. 25 (28) (2007) 4431−4437.

[19] A.T. Stopeck, A. Lipton, J.J. Body, G.G. Steger, K. Tonkin, R.H. de Boer, et al., Denosumab compared with zoledronic acid for the treatment of bone metastases in patients with advanced breast cancer: a randomized, double-blind study, J. Clin. Oncol. 28 (35) (2010) 5132−5139.

[20] K. Fizazi, M. Carducci, M. Smith, R. Damião, J. Brown, L. Karsh, et al., Denosumab versus zoledronic acid for treatment of bone metastases in men with castration-resistant prostate cancer: a randomised, double-blind study, Lancet 377 (9768) (2011) 813−822.

[21] D.H. Henry, L. Costa, F. Goldwasser, V. Hirsh, V. Hungria, J. Prausova, et al., Randomized, double-blind study of denosumab versus zoledronic acid in the treatment of bone metastases in patients with advanced cancer (excluding breast and prostate cancer) or multiple myeloma, J. Clin. Oncol. 29 (9) (2011) 1125−1132.

[22] S. Doshi, L. Sutjandra, J. Zheng, W. Sohn, M. Peterson, G. Jang, et al., Denosumab dose selection for patients with bone metastases from solid tumors, Clin. Cancer Res. 18 (9) (2012) 2648−2657.

[23] E.T. Morgan, Suppression of constitutive cytochrome P-450 gene expression in livers of rats undergoing an acute phase response to endotoxin, Mol. Pharmacol. 36 (5) (1989) 699−707.

[24] C. Schmitt, B. Kuhn, X. Zhang, A.J. Kivitz, S. Grange, Disease-drug-drug interaction involving tocilizumab and simvastatin in patients with rheumatoid arthritis, Clin. Pharmacol. Ther. 89 (2011) 735−740.

[25] ZOCOR, Simvastatin Tablets. Full Prescribing Information, Merck & Co., Inc., Whitehouse Statin, NJ, 2022.

[26] I. Mahmood, M.D. Green, Drug interaction studies of therapeutic proteins or monoclonal antibodies, J. Clin. Pharmacol. 47 (12) (2007) 1540−1554.

[27] J.C. Gorski, S. Vannaprasaht, M.A. Hamman, W.T. Ambrosius, M.A. Bruce, B. Haehner-Daniels, et al., The effect of age, sex, and rifampin administration on intestinal and hepatic cytochrome P450 3A activity, Clin. Pharmacol. Ther. 74 (2003) 275−287.

[28] D.J. Greenblatt, J.S. Harmatz, L.L. von Moltke, C.E. Wright, R.I. Shader, Age and gender effects on the pharmacokinetics and pharmacodynamics of triazolam, a cytochrome P450 3A substrate, Clin. Pharmacol. Ther. 76 (2004) 467−479.

[29] R.Z. Harris, S.M. Tsunoda, P. Mroczkowski, H. Wong, L.Z. Benet, The effects of menopause and hormone replacement therapies on prednisolone and erythromycin pharmacokinetics, Clin. Pharmacol. Ther. 59 (1996) 429−435.

[30] B. Ozmen, C. Kirmaz, K. Aydin, S.O. Kafesciler, F. Guclu, Z. Hekimsoy, Influence of the selective oestrogen receptor modulator (raloxifene hydrochloride) on IL-6, TNF-alpha, TGF-beta1 and bone turnover markers in the treatment of postmenopausal osteoporosis, Eur. Cytokine Netw. 18 (2007) 148−153.

[31] M. Stolina, D. Dwyer, M.S. Ominsky, T. Corbin, G. Van, B. Bolon, et al., Continuous RANKL inhibition in osteoprotegerin transgenic mice and rats suppresses bone resorption without impairing lymphorganogenesis or functional immune responses, J. Immunol. 179 (2007) 7497−7505.

[32] M. Stolina, G. Schett, D. Dwyer, S. Vonderfecht, S. Middleton, D. Duryea, et al., RANKL inhibition by osteoprotegerin prevents bone loss without affecting local or systemic inflammation parameters in two rat arthritis models: comparison with anti-TNFalpha or anti-IL-1 therapies, Arthritis Res. Ther. 11 (2009) R187.

[33] S.B. Cohen, R.K. Dore, N.E. Lane, P.A. Ory, C.G. Peterfy, J.T. Sharp, et al., Denosumab treatment effects on structural damage, bone mineral density, and bone turnover in rheumatoid arthritis: a twelve-month, multicenter, randomized, double-blind, placebo-controlled, phase II clinical trial, Arthritis Rheum. 58 (2008) 1299−1309.

[34] C.M. Eklund, Proinflammatory cytokines in CRP baseline regulation, Adv. Clin. Chem. 48 (2009) 111−136.

[35] G. Jang, A. Kaufman, E. Lee, L. Hamilton, S. Hutton, O. Egbuna, D. Padhi, A clinical therapeutic protein drug-drug interaction study: coadministration of denosumab and midazolam in postmenopausal women with osteoporosis, Pharmacol. Res. Perspect. 2 (2) (2014) e00033.

[36] H. Winter, E. Egizi, N. Erondu, A. Ginsberg, D.J. Rouse, D. Severynse-Stevens, et al., Evaluation of pharmacokinetic interaction between PA-824 and midazolam in healthy adult subjects, Antimicrob. Agents Chemother. 57 (2013) 3699−3703.

[37] Prolia, Denosumab Injection for Subcutaneous Use. Full Prescribing Information, Amgen Inc., Thousand Oaks, CA, 2022.

[38] Y. Zhuang, D.E. de Vries, Z. Xu, S.J. Marciniak Jr., D. Chen, F. Leon, et al., Evaluation of disease-mediated therapeutic protein-drug interactions between an anti-interleukin-6 monoclonal antibody (sirukumab) and cytochrome P450 activities in a phase 1 study in patients with rheumatoid arthritis using a cocktail approach, J. Clin. Pharmacol. 55 (12) (2015) 1386−1394.

[39] E.B. Lee, N. Daskalakis, C. Xu, A. Paccaly, B. Miller, R. Fleischmann, et al., Disease-drug interaction of sarilumab and simvastatin in patients with rheumatoid arthritis, Clin. Pharmacokinet. 56 (6) (2017) 607−615.

[40] S. Khalilieh, A. Hussain, D. Montgomery, V. Levine, P.M. Shaw, I. Bodrug, et al., Effect of tildrakizumab (MK-3222), a high affinity, selective anti-IL23p19 monoclonal antibody, on cytochrome P450 metabolism in subjects with moderate to severe psoriasis, Br. J. Clin. Pharmacol. 84 (10) (2018) 2292−2302.

[41] G. Bruin, A. Hasselberg, I. Koroleva, J. Milojevic, C. Calonder, R. Soon, et al., Secukinumab treatment does not alter the pharmacokinetics of the cytochrome P450 3A4 substrate midazolam in patients with moderate to severe psoriasis, Clin. Pharmacol. Ther. 106 (6) (2019) 1380−1388.

Chapter 7

Discovery and development of ADCs: obstacles and opportunities

Hsuan Ping Chang, Yuen Kiu Cheung and Dhaval K. Shah

Department of Pharmaceutical Sciences, School of Pharmacy and Pharmaceutical Sciences, The State University of New York at Buffalo, Buffalo, NY, United States

Historical perspective

Antibody-drug conjugate (ADC) is one of the fastest-growing drug classes in oncology and a proven approach for treating cancer patients. Back in 1907, Paul Ehrlich, a German chemist and founder of chemotherapy, came up with the idea of *Zauberkugel*, which was translated to "magic bullet" in English [1]. With this idea, Ehrlich envisioned agents that go straight to their identified targets without harming the organism. More than a century later, antibody-based "magic bullets" are the most promising targeted agents that exist today. However, monoclonal antibody (mAb) alone demonstrates limited cytotoxic potency. To increase the cytotoxic power of these molecules, it was hypothesized that traditional chemotherapy and cytotoxic small molecules can be attached to mAbs to enhance their therapeutic effectiveness. These "enhanced" magic bullets will utilize the selectivity of mAb and possess potent cytotoxic small molecules that can kill the cancer cells. ADCs are essentially the realization of this concept and modern "magic bullets."

Early development

As shown in Fig. 7.1, researchers have been trying to make ADCs for over 100 years. However, there was not much progress in this field for the first 50 years after the "magic bullet" concept was introduced [2]. This was because of the difficulties in isolating, purifying, and producing large quantities of mAbs. Pioneering studies in the field used partially purified antibody preparations to make drug conjugates, and demonstrated the possibility of using an antibody as a targeted carrier to treat different cancers. The first ADC can be traced back to 1957, where Mathé reported that an antileukemia 1210 antigen immunoglobulins (IgGs) conjugated with methotrexate (MTX) via a diazo coupling reaction could achieve target-specific antiproliferation activity [3]. Although Mathé did not further investigate his work on the MTX conjugate, several other researchers extended his ADC work in the late 1960s to early 1970s, providing the foundation for the existing studies in the field. During this period, studies demonstrated that after IgGs (mostly originated from rabbits or goats) and cytotoxic agents are linked (via covalent or noncovalent bond), they could achieve superior tumor inhibition in vitro and in vivo, compared to IgGs or cytotoxic drugs given alone [4,5].

ADCs were tested in patients in several studies in the mid-1970s and showed promising results (Fig. 7.1). For example, Ghose et al. found objective tumor regression in neuroblastoma patients after treatment of chlorambucil-linked IgG, despite the relatively small sample size (<5 patients) [5]. Ghose and Blair published the first review paper for ADCs in 1978, which covers ADC studies before 1977 [6]. Not only did the review discuss the considerations of antibody production in the early days (i.e., isolated from animal serum), but it also brought up various topics such as payload selection, conjugation method, linker chemistry, antibody-antigen specificity, sufficient drug exposure at the site-of-action, immunogenicity, and possible resistance in certain tumor cell populations, all of which are still existing critical problems for ADC development today. Although previously developed ADCs were tested in human, they were not widely adopted because their targets failed to show differential expression between tumors and normal tissues. The first "formal" clinical trial with ADC was conducted in 1983 [7]. The vindesine-anti-CEA ADC was investigated in patients with advanced metastatic

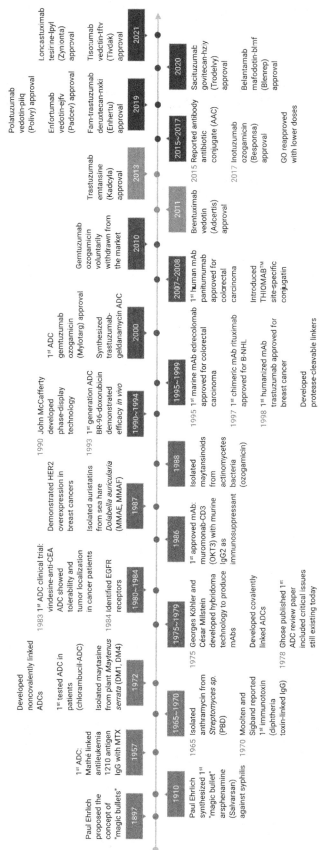

FIGURE 7.1 Timeline of ADCs since 1897 that shows the long history and improvements made throughout the development of ADCs.

carcinoma (four colorectal and four ovarian). The drug was tolerated in all patients and able to localize in the tumors, suggesting the feasibility of a vindesine-conjugated ADC to treat cancer patients.

In the late 1980s, switching from murine mAb to chimeric, humanized, and human mAb marked the start of the mainstream ADC journey in oncology (Fig. 7.1) [8]. The advances in antibody engineering enabled the production of humanized mAbs with reduced immunogenicity in humans compared with the murine mAbs used for early ADCs. With more and more reliable studies in the 1990s, ADCs became a mature research area in immunotherapy [1]. Since then, the development of ADCs has gone through three generations [9].

First-generation ADCs

The first-generation ADCs typically utilized clinically approved chemotherapeutic drugs with well-established mechanism-of-action as payloads, such as antimetabolites (MTX and 5-fluorouracil), DNA crosslinkers (mitomycin), and anti-microtubule agents (vinblastine) [10]. One of the significant issues with these ADCs was the insufficiency potency of the payloads. Despite the clinical success of these traditional chemotherapeutic drugs, a lack of potency was observed when they were conjugated to a mAb along with the attainment of low concentrations in the tumors. BR96-doxorubicin conjugate, a mAb targeting Lewis-Y antigen linked to doxorubicin molecules, was an early example [11]. Although curative efficacy was observed in human tumor xenograft models, the relatively low potency of doxorubicin required high drug-to-antibody ratio (DAR, eight molecules per mAb) and high doses of ADC were needed to achieve the antitumor activity. Unstable linker was another issue for the first-generation ADCs [9]. Linkers designed to be cleaved under certain physiological conditions, such as an acidic environment, could lead to the early release of payloads in blood circulation and consequently significant toxicity. As found in Gemtuzumab Ozogamicin (GO) clinical trials, an acid-labile hydrazone linker could cause severe toxicity due to instability of the linker resulting in premature payload release [12,13]. This first-ever ADC was initially approved for the treatment of relapsed acute myeloid leukemia (AML) for older patients (>60 years old) in 2000. However, in 2010, GO was withdrawn due to raised concerns on its safety profiles (notably life-threatening hepatic veno-occlusive disease) and its clinical risk over benefit. After 7 years of GO withdrawal, it was reapproved with a lower dosing schedule (3 mg/m^2 on days 1, 4, 7) (Fig. 7.1) [14].

Second-generation ADCs

Development of second-generation ADCs was inspired by the limitations found in the first-generation ADCs. Generally speaking, the second-generation ADCs have more stable linkers, higher potency payloads, and better characterization and optimization of ADC formulations [9]. Trastuzumab emtansine (T-DM1) and brentuximab vedotin (BV) are two representative examples of second-generation ADCs. The lessons learned from GO, where instability of linkers could cause severe toxicities, led to the exploration of more stable linkers for second-generation ADCs, including non-cleavable linkers (i.e., used in T-DM1) and cleavable linkers (i.e., used in BV) [15]. BV employs the valine-citrulline (vc) dipeptide linker, connecting to a spacer molecule (para-aminobenzyl carbamate, PABC) with the self-cleavage capacity and thus facilitates the release of the naked payload. In addition, most of the second-generation ADCs utilize more potent payloads such as monomethyl auristatin E (MMAE), monomethyl auristatin F (MMAF), DM1, and DM4 [9]. For example, MMAE is 100−1000 times more potent than doxorubicin [16]. Furthermore, the introduction of state-of-art analytical methodology enabled better characterization of critical quality attributes of ADCs and further optimization of ADC formulations (Fig. 7.1) [17]. Consequently, second-generation ADCs have relatively lower levels of unconjugated mAbs [18] and more optimized formulation properties [9].

Despite improvements, there are still some problems remaining in second-generation ADCs. Off-target toxicity is one of the main reasons for the suboptimal therapeutic index of second-generation ADCs, which is attributed to molecular structures used for their bioconjugation [19]. For example, a maleimide linkage employed in the second-generation vc-based cleavable ADC could undergo deconjugation through a retro-Michael reaction in plasma. The generated maleimide-payload conjugate could then be bound to other plasma thiols (i.e., albumin), resulting in off-target toxicity [20]. This could be observed in approved ADCs such as BV, polatuzumab vedotin, and enfortumab vedotin (Fig. 7.1) [9]. Another concern for the second-generation ADCs is the inability to precisely control the conjugation between mAb and the payload, resulting in the heterogeneous mixture of ADCs (i.e., variable numbers of payloads at various places on mAb) [21]. Indeed, the random mixtures of DAR could significantly influence hydrophobicity and pharmacokinetics/pharmacodynamics (PK/PD) of ADCs. An ADC with higher DAR tends to be more hydrophobic and prone to aggregation. Additionally, an ADC with a higher average drug loading demonstrates higher in vivo clearance than an ADC with a lower average drug loading, resulting in reduced plasma exposure and lower efficacy [21,22].

Third-generation ADCs

The notable progress in third-generation ADCs involves the discovery of highly potent payloads and site-specific methodologies to generate more homogenous products [9]. Some of the novel cytotoxic payloads in third-generation ADCs include pyrrolobenzodiazepines (PBD) and indolinobenzodiazepines (IGN), with at least 10 PBD-based ADCs and one IGN-based ADC tested in clinical trials since 2013 [9]. The dimerization of two PBD units forms a PBD-dimer, which has the capability of crosslinking DNA. The PBD-dimers are $\sim 50-100$ times more potent than the commonly used payloads such as MMAE and DM1, exhibiting picomolar activity against many human tumor cell lines (IC50 $\sim$ 2–7 pM) [23]. Similarly, IGN is another highly potent payload, which has the capability of alkylating single-strand DNA with picomolar activity (IC50 $\sim$ 4–20 pM) [24]. IMGN779 is an IGN-based ADC developed to balance efficacy (i.e., maintain DNA-alkylating activity) and tolerability (without having DNA-cross-linking properties that are associated with systemic toxicity) [24,25]. Furthermore, since both PBD and IGN are not substrates for MDR1, they may provide benefits for the treatment of MMAE- or DM1-ADC resistant tumors [9]. Site-specific conjugation of ADCs enhances their homogeneity with uniform DAR [26]. The homogenous ADCs have reduced drug deconjugation rate, increased tolerability, and lower systemic toxicity compared to the heterogeneous ADC formulations [27]. While the improvement of conjugation technology can provide enhanced efficacy to ADCs, it may also change their toxicity profile. For example, DCDSO780A, a site-specific MMAE-based ADC showed ocular toxicities as dose-limited toxicity in the phase 1 clinical study, which was distinct from the most observed toxicities of MMAE-based ADC, namely peripheral neuropathy [28]. Recently, Dxd-based ADCs, which incorporate an enzymatic cleavable linker with a self-immolative spacer to reduce hydrophobicity and increase plasma stability, enable high drug loading (average DAR $\sim$ 8) and good homogeneity. Dxd-based ADCs demonstrate a wider therapeutic index and trastuzumab deruxtecan, approved by the FDA in 2020, is an example of Dxd-based ADC [29].

While the concept of ADCs seems straightforward theoretically, each component of these complex molecules plays an essential role in making it an efficacious and safe therapeutic agent. With 12 approved ADCs and more than 100 additional currently under clinical development (Fig. 7.1) [30], we have just begun to understand the challenges associated with ADC development, and how to fine-tune each ADC component to optimize the safety, efficacy, and therapeutic index of ADCs. Below we have discussed these components in depth.

Learning through experience

The three main components of an ADC include: mAb, linker, and payload, whose optimization has led the birth of successful ADCs (Fig. 7.2). Failures and challenges throughout the development of ADCs arise because of issues related to one or more of these components.

Antibodies: the ones that put it together

Early ADCs utilized murine mAbs, which became problematic as high immunogenicity was evoked. Patients' immune system would recognize the mouse-origin mAbs as foreign substances and develop human anti-murine antibodies [31]. Consequently, rapid ADC elimination, short half-life, and reduced efficacy limited the usage of these ADCs. Further advances in mAb engineering enabled the production of chimeric, humanized, or fully human mAbs, minimizing the immunogenicity issue of early ADCs. A chimeric mAb combines the variable regions of mouse mAbs with constant regions of human mAbs, thus the interaction of mAb and immune cells mediated by human constant regions reduces immunogenicity [32]. BV and indatuximab ravtansine are ADCs that use chimeric mAbs. However, human anti-chimeric antibodies could still develop, and the immunogenicity problem remains. Humanized mAbs, where only the complementary determining regions of murine (or other non-humans) antibodies are inserted into the human mAb framework, can further reduce the immunogenicity risk. T-DM1, polatuzumab vedotin, belantamab mafodotin, trastuzumab deruxtecan, and sacituzumab govitecan are the examples of ADCs with humanized mAb. More recently, with the help of phage display technology and transgenic mice technology, fully human mAbs are generated. These full human mAbs produce little immunogenicity. Enfortumab vedotin is an ADC containing fully human anti-nectin-4 mAb [33].

Linkers: the ones that hold the ADC together

The choice of linker plays an important role in ADC activity. Ideally, a linker should be stable in blood circulation with limited premature release of the payload in non-target tissues, while it should efficiently release the drugs at the target site to maximize the therapeutic effect [34]. Besides, linker types and linker technologies determine DAR, which is another critical factor for ADC activity [34]. There are two types of linkers, cleavable and non-cleavable; both of which have been proven safe and effective in the clinic. A cleavable linker takes advantage of the differential environment between the

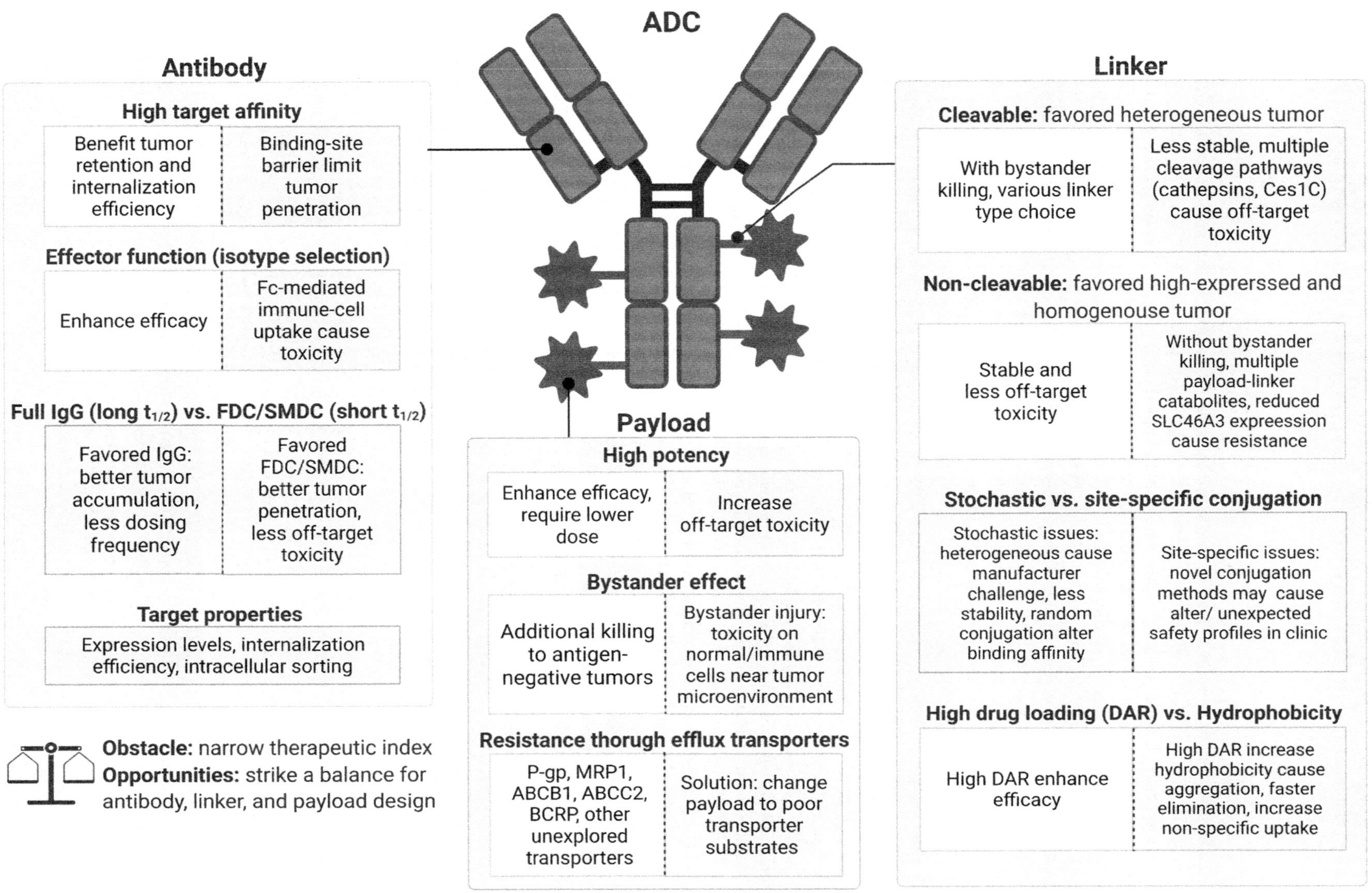

ADC

Antibody

High target affinity

| Benefit tumor retention and internalization efficiency | Binding-site barrier limit tumor penetration |

Effector function (isotype selection)

| Fc-mediated immune-cell uptake cause toxicity | Enhance efficacy |

Full IgG (long $t_{1/2}$) vs. FDC/SMDC (short $t_{1/2}$)

| Favored IgG: better tumor accumulation, less dosing frequency | Favored FDC/SMDC: better tumor penetration, less off-target toxicity |

Target properties

| Expression levels, internalization efficiency, intracellular sorting |

Linker

Cleavable: favored heterogeneous tumor

| With bystander killing, various linker type choice | Less stable, multiple cleavage pathways (cathepsins, Ces1C) cause off-target toxicity |

Non-cleavable: favored high-exprssed and homogenouse tumor

| Stable and less off-target toxicity | Without bystander killing, multiple payload-linker catabolites, reduced SLC46A3 expreession cause resistance |

Stochastic vs. site-specific conjugation

| Stochastic issues: heterogeneous cause manufacturer challenge, less stability, random conjugation alter binding affinity | Site-specific issues: novel conjugation methods may cause alter/ unexpected safety profiles in clinic |

High drug loading (DAR) vs. Hydrophobicity

| High DAR enhance efficacy | High DAR increase hydrophobicity cause aggregation, faster elimination, increase non-specific uptake |

Payload

High potency

| Enhance efficacy, require lower dose | Increase off-target toxicity |

Bystander effect

| Additional killing to antigen-negative tumors | Bystander injury: toxicity on normal/immune cells near tumor microenvironment |

Resistance thorugh efflux transporters

| P-gp, MRP1, ABCB1, ABCC2, BCRP, other unexplored transporters | Solution: change payload to poor transporter substrates |

Obstacle: narrow therapeutic index
Opportunities: strike a balance for antibody, linker, and payload design

FIGURE 7.2 The summary of the characteristics of each component of an ADC: antibody, linker and payload. The figure emphasizes the importance of striking a balance between all three components of an ADC in order to overcome obstacles throughout the development of ADCs, notably the narrow therapeutic index.

plasma and intracellular compartment in cancer cells. Following receptor-mediated endocytosis of an ADC, a cleavable linker would be cleaved and release the payloads within the tumor cells [35]. On the other hand, rather than relying on the intracellular conditions of the tumor cells, a non-cleavable linker requires lysosomal degradation of an ADC to release the payload.

Cleavable linkers

One would expect a cleavable linker to be less stable than a non-cleavable linker. In fact, the stability issue of cleavable linkers was observed in the pH-dependent hydrazone linkers. GO, the first-ever approved ADC, is an example ADC that utilized this linker. Theoretically, hydrazone linkers should be stable in blood circulation at physiological pH and can only be hydrolyzed at low pH within the endosomes (pH 5.0—6.5) and lysosomes (pH 4.5—5.0) [36]. However, the excitement for GO slowly faded when the highly toxic profile was observed, mainly due to the instability of the hydrazone linker, leading to the premature release of the toxic payload in plasma [34].

Disulfide linker is another group of chemically cleavable linkers developed earlier, which undergo reductive cleavage by intracellular glutathione through nucleophilic attack of thiols [34]. Due to the differential environment between intracellular space and plasma, and between tumor cells and healthy tissues, disulfide linkers are designed to selectively release the payload in the tumor cells while remaining stable in the blood circulation. Glutathione concentration is high in tumor cells as they are involved in promoting cell survival and tumor growth, and glutathione is highly produced under oxidative stress. In contrast, glutathione levels are low in healthy tissues [34]. In addition, glutathione concentration is relatively higher in the cytoplasm (1—10 mM) than the concentration in the blood (2—20 μM) [37]. However, it should be noted that the presence of low concentrations of glutathione and cysteine (~ 8 μM) in systemic circulation may contribute to payload release, which could be more impactful on drugs with long-circulation time such as ADCs. Currently, the stability of disulfide linkers is improved by adding methyl groups surrounding disulfide bonds to create steric hindrances [38]. For examples, many ADCs that use modified disulfide linkers with different levels of hindrances to improve stability, such as mirvetuximab soravtansine, lorvotuzumab mertansine, coltuximab ravtansine, indatuximab ravtansine, anetumab ravtansine, and SAR566658 are in phase 2 and 3 clinical trials [34,39,40].

Protease cleavable linkers are the most widely used ADC linkers [34]. Owing to the relatively higher expression of lysosomal proteases like cathepsin B in tumor cells than in normal cells, protease-sensitive linkers are selectively cleaved by intracellular enzymes following ADC internalization in the target cells. A variety of protease cleavable linkers, such as vc, phenylalanine-lysine, and valine-alanine, have been explored, with vc linkers being the most commonly used in clinical research [41]. One special note regarding the combination of vc-linker and MMAE is that due to the bulky structure of the payload, a spacer between this dipeptide linker and the payload is required. A spacer helps separate the cytotoxic payload from the vc sequence, allowing cathepsin B to access the cleavage better, thus more effectively exerting the protease cleavage. PABC is one of the most used spacers, which has the self-cleavage capability. Following protease cleavage, PABC undergoes self-immolation, resulting in the release of the "pure" payload (i.e., free MMAE) in the tumors [34]. Despite the success of cleavable linkers, it is still difficult to strike a balance between good linker stability in the circulation and efficient cleavage upon delivery into the tumor cells. Therefore, the design of optimized linkers and the discovery of orthogonal conjugation chemistries are warranted.

Non-cleavable linkers

In the initial stages of ADC development, non-cleavable linkers containing an amide group or amide/ester group with a succinate spacer were used to attach traditional cytotoxic drugs (i.e., MTX, daunorubicin, vinca alkaloids, mitomycin C) to different murine mAbs. Although the mAb-antigen interactions were maintained for these conjugates, the potency of the cytotoxic drugs decreased after conjugation compared to unconjugated cytotoxic drugs. For example, the conjugated MTX showed 80—90% lower cytotoxicity than the unconjugated MTX [42]. This may partly be explained by the overly stable linkage of the payloads [43].

When it comes to the success of non-cleavable linkers, T-DM1 was the first approved non-cleavable ADC. Several interesting discoveries were made throughout its development [42,44,45]. Initially, the conjugation of DM1 to trastuzumab was made using a disulfide cleavable linker or a thioether non-cleavable linker [46]. Surprisingly, DM1 conjugated to trastuzumab via a thioether non-cleavable linker (succinimidyl-4-(N-maleimidomethyl)-cyclohexane-1-carboxylate, SMCC) demonstrates superior efficacy, PK and reduced toxicity compared to disulfide cleavable linkers (i.e., N-succinimidyl-4-(2-pyridyldithio) pentanoate, SPP) [45,46]. In vivo efficacy of trastuzumab ADC with the two types of linkers was evaluated in the trastuzumab-resistant MMTV-HER2 Fo5 syngeneic mammary tumor model. Trastuzumab-MMC-DM1 showed increased antitumor activity over trastuzumab-SPP-DM1 after a single 10 mg/kg intravenous (IV) dose. This finding was surprising, as other disulfide-linked maytansinoid-containing ADCs showed better efficacy than using the thioether design. Of note, a subsequent study comparing in vivo efficacy of trastuzumab-MMC-DM1 and trastuzumab-SPP-DM1 in BT-474EEI (trastuzumab-resistant) mice xenograft model failed to show an observable difference in antitumor activity [45]. Regarding the PK of ADC analytes, trastuzumab-SPP-DM1 exhibited faster clearance ($\sim$40 versus 19 mL/d/kg) and shorter half-life (2.7 versus 5.7 days) than trastuzumab-MMC-DM1, which is expected since non-cleavable linkers are more stable [47]. However, *in vivo* maytansinoid catabolites in the tumors showed similar concentration profiles between the two conjugates, though trastuzumab-SPP-DM1 displayed faster plasma clearance [47]. Perhaps the most important factor for T-DM1 linker selection (SMCC versus SPP linkers) is the tolerability of the two conjugates, which was evaluated in Sprague–Dawley rats. In the single-dose acute toxicity study, treatment of SPP-linked conjugate at a dose of 22 mg/kg resulted in significant ($\sim$10%) body weight loss, while the SMCC-linked conjugate could be dosed as high as 50 mg/kg without any observable weight loss [45]. Evidently, the non-cleavable SMCC linker could afford at least twofold better tolerability and therapeutic index as trastuzumab-DM1 conjugate compared to the cleavable SPP linker [44]. Consequently, the SMCC linker was chosen for clinical development of T-DM1.

Payloads: small but mighty

A critical factor for achieving optimal ADC is the selection of the right payload. Difficulty in meeting this criterion was demonstrated during the early development of ADCs. Early ADCs utilized clinically approved chemotherapeutic drugs with established mechanism-of-actions as their payloads [48]. However, they failed to show benefit in clinical trials, which was likely due to the insufficient potency of these cytotoxic agents. Most of them had IC50 in the micromolar range. In contrast, the current ADCs approved in the market utilize more toxic payloads with IC50 in the subnanomolar or picomolar range [43]. A highly toxic payload is needed for an ADC because each mAb can only accommodate a limited number of payload molecules, and only a small fraction (i.e., $\sim$0.01%) of administered ADCs can reach the tumor site [15]. Therefore, highly toxic payloads are necessary to kill cancer cells. In addition, some payloads have the ability to exert bystander effects, mainly contributed by cleavable linkers and the payloads' characteristics of membrane permeability. Bystander killing effect allows for additional cytotoxicity, but it may also cause safety concerns.

Moving forward

Each generation of ADCs is born from previous failures. Improvement in the stability of cleavable linkers, design of functional non-cleavable linkers, discovery of payloads with sufficient potency, and reduction of mAb immunogenicity, all have paved the way for better ADCs with improved therapeutic window. However, there is still room for improvement, and therapeutic index of ADCs still remains close to 1. To further optimize ADCs, it is important to go back to basics. It is important to better understand the properties of each ADC component, the factors and mechanisms that determine ADC efficacy and toxicity, and each component's PK/PD behavior in vitro and in vivo. The dedication from past and current researchers have led to a bright future for ADCs, but efforts are still needed to resolve current and emerging problems in the field.

Current critical problems for ADCs

As our experience with ADCs continues, each of the three ADC components has been presenting critical problems that remain to be addressed. We have discussed these component-specific problems below (Fig. 7.2).

The antibodies

One of the critical aspects of developing ADCs for cancer is selecting a unique antigenic target and its corresponding specific mAb (Fig. 7.2). The mAb component of an ADC serves as a carrier of cytotoxic agents to the tumor cells and requires both target specificity and affinity. The high specificity of mAbs to the targets ensures minimal cross-reactivity with healthy cells, and high target affinity is essential to achieve durable tumor retention and efficient internalization of the ADC-antigen complex into the tumor cells. However, a very high affinity of mAb might limit the tumor penetration due to a "binding-site barrier," where ADCs primarily bind to cellular antigens located near the extravasation site, leading to limited ADC exposure to the tumor cells located at less accessible interior regions [49]. Therefore, an optimal binding affinity of a mAb or utilizing novel strategies such as transient competitive inhibition of ADC-antigen binding may enhance the tumor penetration and efficacy of ADCs [50].

Although mAbs themselves may have antitumor actions through decreasing signal transduction of the targets or exerting Fc-mediated effector functions, the activity of the naked mAb is not necessary to develop an active ADC [51]. Human IgG consists of four subclasses (IgG1, IgG2, IgG3, and IgG4), which differ in solubility, serum half-lives, and affinity to different Fcγ receptors [32]. Although IgG1 is used in the majority of ADCs due to its serum stability and greater complement activation and Fc receptor (FcR) binding affinity, the section of IgG backbone may vary case by case [51–53]. For example, it was found that the binding of T-DM1 to FcRIIa was followed by internalization into the megakaryocytes, leading to thrombocytopenia [51]. The binding of LOP628 ADC, which comprises IgG1 mAb conjugated to maytansine, to FcRI and FcRII on mast cells was found to result in mast cell degranulation and hypersensitivity reactions in patients [54]. On the other hand, IgG4 could be a preferred mAb backbone if the recruitment of effector functions is least required [51]. For example, GO and inotuzumab ozogamicin are both built upon the IgG4 backbone.

The linker

The selection of linker for an ADC affects its stability in blood circulation, the rate of lysosomal processing and catabolism, and the potential bystander effect toward neighboring tumor cells through the catabolites released from the target cell (Fig. 7.2) [55]. The mechanisms of linker cleavage include proteolytic degradation of mAb component for non-cleavable linkers, protease cleavage for peptide linkers, acid hydrolysis for hydrazone linkers, and cytosolic reductive cleavage for disulfide linkers [34].

Non-cleavable linkers

For ADC with non-cleavable linkers, the released catabolite is the linker-cytotoxic agent attached to an amino acid residue [43]. For example, lysine-SMCC-DM1 and SMCC-DM1 are the major catabolites for T-DM1, which is an ADC with a non-cleavable thioether linker [47]. These two catabolites account for 72% and 13% of the metabolites in bile, respectively [47]. No further metabolic modification compound was detected, suggesting that lysine-SMCC-DM1 would not undergo further catabolic transformation [47]. The release of the amino acid-linker-payload generated from a non-cleavable ADC in the lysosome may also require lysosomal membrane transporter such as SLC46A3 to transfer the catabolite from the lysosome to the cytoplasm [56]. In fact, it has been observed that reduced expression of SLC46A3 might impair the release of lysine-MCC-DM1 into the cytoplasm, resulting in resistance to the ADC T-DM1 [57]. A study also supports SLC46A3 as a potential predictive biomarker for T-DM1 efficacy [58]. In sum, for a non-cleavable ADC, one should consider both its parent drug and the potential catabolites, since a payload could be potent in its parent form but may not be suitable for efficacy following derivatization with a non-cleavable linker [59].

Cleavable linkers

The cleavage of these linkers depends on differences in physiological conditions and the differential environment between tumors and normal tissues. Acid-labile linkers such as hydrazone are often associated with the premature release of payload since acidic conditions could be found in various areas of the body. Dipeptide linkers such as a vc-linker can be cleaved by cathepsin B, which is a lysosomal cysteine protease. However, more protease enzymes have recently been identified as contributors to the cleavage of this dipeptide linker as well. Multiple cleavage pathways could increase the possibilities of payload release in blood circulation or non-target tissues, leading to off-target toxicities. Studies show that cathepsin B is upregulated in cancer cells, especially in metastatic tumors, and is expected to have a rare presence in the extracellular space [60]. However, it is reported that cathepsin B could be secreted into normal tissue before cells metastasis, which might lead to the cleavage of linkers within normal tissues, triggering adverse effects [61]. In addition, lysosomal cleavage of dipeptide linkers can result from not only cathepsin B but also various proteases such as cathepsin K, cathepsin L, and cathepsin S, which may be expressed in normal tissues [62]. Indeed, the lack of specificity toward cathepsin B cleavage was emphasized in the in vitro isolated enzyme incubation studies, where cathepsin S was found to be the most active enzyme among the cathepsin family toward vc-linker containing ADCs [63]. Furthermore, when vc-MMAE ADC was tested in cathepsin B-suppressed and cathepsin B-expressed cells, no difference in the efficiency of MMAE release or ADC potency was observed [61], suggesting that a vc-linker has multiple pathways to generate catabolites. Therefore, one would expect that an ADC whose dipeptide linker is designed to be more exclusively cleaved by cathepsin B would release its payload more selectively and efficiently in the tumor microenvironment, as cathepsin B is commonly involved in tumor progression and overexpressed in a wide range of cancers. For example, a cyclobutane-1,1-dicarboxamide (cBu)-citrulline linker is more selectively hydrolyzed by cathepsin B than a vc-linker and has shown equivalent efficacy and stability in vivo. One would hypothesize that cBu-citrulline linker's selectivity toward cathepsin B would enhance its specificity of cleavage by tumor-specific/enhanced protease, and thus improve the safety margin of ADCs with this linker [64].

Apart from cathepsins, it is reported that the extracellular enzyme carboxylesterase 1c (Ces1C), which is expressed abundantly in the plasma and liver and has lesser expressions in the kidney, lung, intestine, testis, heart, monocyte, and macrophage, is responsible for dipeptide linker cleavage, causing extracellular hydrolysis and ADC instability [35,65–68]. In Ces1C knockout mice, a vc-linker ADC was completely stable, confirming that Ces1C contributes to the instability of vc-linkers in vivo [67].

Linker selection: cleavable or non-cleavable

Based on previous experience, some generalizations may be made when selecting between cleavable and non-cleavable linkers. Cleavable linkers are found to work better for a broader range of targets (Fig. 7.2). They may especially provide greater advantages for the targets with heterogenous expression in terms of intensity and distribution, which are more evident in solid tumors (i.e., mesothelin antigen in lung cancer, prostate stem cell antigen in prostate cancer) than in hematological malignancies [69]. Bystander killing mediated by cleavable linkers contributes to such benefit. Following internalization, an ADC with a cleavable linker is cleaved and able to release the "free" drug (i.e., without linker attached). The resulting free drug can directly kill the target cells; in addition, it can also diffuse out of the target cell and be taken up by and kill surrounding or bystander cells, which may not express the target antigens. The versatility of cleavable linkers makes them popular in current ADC development. On the other hand, non-cleavable linkers could be preferable for safety reasons for some specific targets (Fig. 7.2). Considering their increased stability in blood circulation and the limited bystander effect, a non-cleavable ADC may serve as a good choice for a target that is highly and homogenously expressed throughout the tumors, as the released catabolites can be efficacious without the need for bystander killing.

Hydrophobicity: the dilemma of DAR, payload, and hydrophobicity

Another crucial issue during ADC development is the hydrophobicity of these conjugates, and the polarity of the linker plays a vital role in determining the biophysical properties of an ADC [70]. Inadequate hydrophilicity of ADCs can lead to faster elimination, increased non-specific uptake, aggregation, and off-target toxicity issues (Fig. 7.2) [41,70,71]. Several studies have shown that higher ADC hydrophobicity is associated with higher clearance of total mAb of an ADC. Hamblett published the first study in 2004, where they found that vc-MMAE ADCs with higher DAR exhibited faster clearance and lower efficacy [72]. A subsequent study was able to preserve the clearance for a DAR8 ADC by using a hydrophilic β-glucuronide linker with PEG element to decrease the hydrophobicity, resulting in the DAR8 ADC exhibiting comparable clearance to that of the unmodified mAb [71]. Another study demonstrated that conjugation to a highly exposed site (C-terminal of the heavy chain) resulted in higher hydrophobicity and higher clearance of an ADC. In contrast, conjugation to a "shielded" site (C-terminal of the kappa chain) leads to an ADC with lower hydrophobicity and lower clearance [73].

Recently a variety of novel payloads have been discovered, and most of these payloads are highly hydrophobic compounds since lipophilicity is found to be essential for high potency. This brings up the issues of conjugation liabilities and aggregation. Currently, the problem can somehow be mitigated by optimizing the linker-payload design. For example, a highly hydrophilic linker can be designed to accommodate a highly hydrophobic payload (i.e., amatoxins, BCL-XL inhibitors, PBD, CBI dimers). Several strategies have been proposed to design a polar linker, such as utilizing extended polyethylene glycol (PEG) units, charged amino acids, incorporating quaternary ammonium salts, and addition of phosphate or sulfate groups [70].

Theoretically, the dose potency of an ADC should increase as the DAR increases. However, as observed in the case of Hamblett's study, increasing DAR and thereby increasing ADC hydrophobicity could lead to higher plasma clearance, lower systemic exposure of an ADC, and reduced in vivo efficacy [72]. The dilemma of greater DAR and less hydrophobicity could be modulated by introducing a hydrophilic linker design to facilitate high DAR ADCs (Fig. 7.2). Examples of linkers used to increase drug loading include β-glucuronide linker (resulting in DAR ~ 8), monodisperse polysarcosine (DAR ~ 8) [60], hydroxymethylethylene hydroxymethylformal (PHF, DAR ~ 15–20), and other various dendrimers and polymers [70]. Thus, optimal linker design is a challenge but also provides opportunities to optimize the PK and therapeutic index of an ADC (Fig. 7.2).

The payloads

Bystander effect: favorable or not

Although the emergence of the highly toxic payloads could resolve the problem of inadequate ADC potency, it could also raise a safety issue since the majority of ADC toxicities are attributed to the payloads (Fig. 7.2). As mentioned above, premature release of the unconjugated drugs in circulation may cause widespread toxicities, which may be attenuated through a stable linker-payload design. On the other hand, ADCs with cleavable linkers and membrane-permeable payloads tend to contribute to additional antitumor activity through bystander killing [55,74]. However, at the same time, the bystander effect may also cause toxicities on normal cells or immune cells located in or near the tumor microenvironment [55,74,75]. Whether the benefit of bystander effect on ADC efficacy outweighs the potential risk of toxicity has no conclusion, and it may depend on the selection of the target, linker, and payload [75] (Fig. 7.2). Although many studies reported that the bystander effect is beneficial, the bystander effect was found unfavorable in a small number of cases. For example, a study compared conventional MMAE-based ADCs with dipeptide cleavable linkers to MMAE-based ADCs with ionized cysteine non-cleavable linkers. It was found that non-cleavable ADCs with lower bystander effect could maintain similar potency to free MMAE while providing an improved safety profile in vitro and in vivo. It was observed that mice treated with non-cleavable MMAE-ADC had similar maximum tolerated doses (MTDs, ~160 mg/kg) compared to mice treated with naked mAb [76]. Another example of bystander effect with disfavor is found in the phase 1 study of cantuzumab mertansine, an ADC targeting CanAg tumor antigen, with cleavable disulfide linker (SPP) and DM1. Although hepatic transaminases elevation was a common toxicity for cantuzumab mertansine, it was observed that patients with hepatic metastasis were at the highest risk of developing this toxicity, even though they had normal or near-normal transaminases before treatment [77]. This suggested that as cantuzumab mertansine localizes at hepatic metastases, it may cause bystander effect to adjacent normal hepatocytes, resulting in bystander injury [19].

Payload resistance: efflux transporters matter

Resistance to ADCs can lead to treatment failure or reduced treatment effectiveness (Fig. 7.2). Resistance may be developed after ADC treatment (acquired resistance) or be present at the beginning of the treatment (*de novo* resistance) [78]. Several mechanisms of acquired resistance to ADCs have been proposed, such as downregulation of antigen expression, alternation of intracellular trafficking, and payload resistance through upregulating the ATP-binding cassette (ABC) efflux transporters [15,55,78]. The latter mechanism arises through the increase of efflux transporter expression, resulting in the elimination of cytotoxic payloads from the cytoplasm to the extracellular space. As a payload is a driver for ADC potency, resistance developed to this "warhead" is detrimental to the ADC efficacy (Fig. 7.2). Some commonly used ADC payloads such as MMAE, DM-1, and ozogamicin are substrates to ABC transporters [78]. Therefore, alternations of ABC transporter family expression, including P-glycoprotein (P-gp), multidrug resistance protein 1 (MRP1), ATP binding cassette subfamily B member 1 (ABCB1), ABCC2, and breast cancer resistance protein (BCRP), could lead to ADC resistance [55,78−80]. Here we have provided some examples of resistance to three clinical approved and commonly used ADCs (GO, BV, and T-DM1) due to drug efflux transporters, which is supported by in vitro, preclinical and clinical data.

1. Resistance to GO

In vitro experiment have shown that despite sufficient expression of CD33 target the expression of P-gp in AML cell could lead to resistance to GO [81]. A similar in vitro result was found in inotuzumab ozogamicin, which also uses calicheamicin as a payload [82]. Moreover, clinical data suggested that P-gp activity is significantly associated with GO treatment outcomes in patients with AML. It was found that AML blasts from the responders to GO have a significantly lower P-gp activity compared with GO non-responders [83]. Besides, it was also observed that patients with lower levels of MRP1 had better responses to GO [84], while the contribution of MRP1 to GO clinical resistance can only be observed when P-gp resistance concurrently occurred [85].

2. Resistance to BV

Chronic treatment of BV could result in the upregulation of P-gp expression and thereby leading to resistance to BV [55]. In vitro experiment showed increased P-gp expression and decreased intracellular accumulation of MMAE in BV-resistance Hodgkin lymphoma (HL) cell lines (L428-R, KMH2-R) as well as tumor samples from patients with BV-resistant HL [86]. Further studies demonstrated that the competitive inhibition of P-gp using P-gp inhibitors (cyclosporine and verapamil) could overcome the resistance to BV in a xenograft mouse model and in clinic [87]. In a phase 1 study, the combination of BV and cyclosporine resulted in an overall and complete response rate of 75% and 42% in the patient population who were refractory to BV treatment, respectively [87]. Another study used the anti-CD22-VC-MMAE-resistant cell lines derived from in vivo xenograft tumors and confirmed the overexpression of P-gp (but not other ABC transporters like MRP1, ABCC3, and BCRP1) was the major driver for resistance to VC-MMAE-based ADCs in non-HL [88].

3. Resistance to T-DM1

The catabolite of T-DM1, Lys-MCC-DM1, is the substrate of several ABC transporters, and thus the resistance to T-DM1 could be associated with the expression and activity of these transporters [79]. Several studies have demonstrated the upregulation of P-gp [44], MRP1 [89], ABCC2 [90], and BCRP [90] in various cancer cell lines that were resistant to

T-DM1. Further inhibition of these transporters could restore T-DM1 sensitivity [91]. Apart from the resistances owing to efflux transporters, other potential mechanisms of resistance to T-DM1 are: alternations in HER2 expression or structure (i.e., low HER2 levels, truncated forms, MUC4 expression, *ERBB2* mutations); defective HER2 trafficking (i.e., decreased internalization, increased recycling); changes in lysosome processing (increased pH, reduced enzyme activity); alternations in proteins involved in signaling pathways (i.e., low PTEN levels); and defective cytotoxic effect of the released tubulin inhibitor payload. The mechanisms of T-DM1 resistance have recently been reviewed in Ref. [79].

In the light of the data presented above, a straightforward approach to circumvent ADC resistance linked to drug efflux transporters is to change the payloads to poor ABC transporter substrates (Fig. 7.2) [79]. Several such attempts have been successfully employed in both preclinical and clinical settings. For example, changing auristatin-based ADCs (anti-CD22-vc-MMAE, anti-CD79b-vc-MMAE) to an anthracycline-based ADCs (anti-CD22-NMS249) showed efficacy in xenograft models that are resistance to microtubule inhibitor-based ADCs such as MMAE-ADCs [88]. Another good example is the accelerated FDA approval of trastuzumab deruxtecan (DS-8201a) in 2019 for pretreated patients with HER2-positive metastatic breast cancer [92]. Trastuzumab deruxtecan, a HER2-targeted ADC using topoisomerase I inhibitor as its payload, showed durable antitumor activity in patients who previously received treatment with T-DM1 [92,93]. Therefore, the success of trastuzumab deruxtecan marked one of the first strategies to overcome resistance to T-DM1 and highlighted the value of using different cytotoxic agents for an ADC to bypass multidrug resistance [94].

Novel technologies

New technologies and innovative strategies have propelled the refinement of each ADC component in the last decade. However, these innovations may also bring some new challenges. We have briefly discussed these innovations below.

The antibodies

Fragment-drug conjugates (FDCs)

To date, there are 12 approved products and more than 100 ADCs in clinical trials. This ADC pipeline mainly focuses on the use of the whole IgG structure format. However, treating solid tumors with whole-IgG format ADCs remains challenging, as revealed by the greater success of ADCs for hematological cancers compared to solid tumors. To effectively treat solid tumors, mAbs need to overcome two challenges: sufficient drug exposure at the tumor site and selective widespread tumor penetration [95,96]. The former is associated with several biological barriers such as poor vascular supply, transport across the capillary wall (extravasation), high pressure in the tumor interstitial fluid, and diffusion through the dense stroma [95,97]. The latter is influenced by many factors such as antigen density, binding affinity, antigen internalization rate, and conjugate molecule size [97,98]. Such challenges of IgG-based ADCs motivate researchers to seek conjugates with a smaller structural format, which may have faster tumor extravasation, diffusion, and penetration due to lower molecular weight (MW) [95,97,98]. With advances in modern biotechnology, novel smaller format conjugates may provide an alternative to the more established ADCs in solid tumors (Fig. 7.2). From PK aspects, the delivery of different drug conjugate formats can be classified into three groups [95,97]. First, a conventional ADC (MW > 150 kDa), which could accumulate and penetrate into tumors over days, and its longer elimination half-life over weeks enables less frequent dosing but a higher risk of off-target toxicity [95]. Second, antibody FDC with MW $\sim$ 12.5−80 kDa, which have higher tumor uptake and penetration kinetics (hours), and their faster elimination may reduce non-specific exposure time while requiring strategies for higher drug delivery such as higher DAR or more frequent/higher dosing regimen [97] (Fig. 7.2). Examples of such FDC include Fab-drug conjugates, diabody-drug conjugates, and scFv-drug conjugates [97]. Kim et al. [99] demonstrated that an anti-CD30 diabody conjugated to four molecules of MMAF in Karpas-299 xenografts could lead to complete responses at well-tolerated doses. When comparing to the corresponding IgG1-MMAF conjugate, the clearance of diabody was $\sim$ 30-fold higher while a similar in vivo potency was observed. This implies that improving tumor extravasation and penetration via FDC may benefit antitumor activity. Third, a small molecule drug conjugate (SMDC) (<5 kDa) may have very rapid and more complete uptake and penetration kinetics while being eliminated within hours. These molecules may require strategies to improve the exposure at the target site-of-action [97]. Examples of SMDC include affibody-drug conjugates, fibronectin type III-drug conjugate, Designed Ankyrin Repeat (DARPin)-drug conjugates, cysteine knot-drug conjugates, abdurin-drug conjugates, pentarin-drug conjugates, and bicyclic peptide (bicycle)-drug conjugates [95,97]. The bicycle-drug conjugates are the most advanced as there are currently three products in phase 1/2 clinical trials. These include BT5528-vc-MMAE targeting EphA2 [100,101], BT8009-vc-MMAE targeting Nectin-4 [102], and BT1718-cleavable DM1 targeting MT1-MMP [103,104]. It is hypothesized that improved tumor penetration and rapid systemic clearance of these conjugates could provide a wider therapeutic window than the larger ADCs, which take days to reach peak accumulation and weeks to clear from the body [100].

The linkers

Site-specific conjugation

Until recently, most ADCs were prepared using the traditional random conjugation methods via reaction with either surface-exposed lysine residues ($\sim$70$-$90 per mAb) or cysteine residues from the interchain disulfide bonds (8 per IgG1) [27]. These lysine and cysteine-based methods generate heterogeneous products with varied numbers of drugs coupled across several possible sites, which can raise several issues [27]. First, the heterogeneous formulations create challenges in the process consistency, and product characterization and developability [105]. Second, the potential modifications at or near complementarity-determining region (CDR) in mAbs may reduce antigen binding and specificity [106]. In addition, the understanding of the relationships between the site/extent of drug loading and ADC attributes (efficacy, toxicity, PK, immunogenicity, etc.) is limited [26]. On the other hand, site-specific conjugation methods have been explored and developed to help reinforce the more homogenous mixture of ADCs [106] (Fig. 7.2). Several side-by-side comparisons between site-specific and random approaches have demonstrated that site-specific ADCs have enhanced plasma stability, enhanced binding efficiency, less variability in dose-dependent studies (especially in lower dose group), and increased tumor uptake [9,107].

Various strategies have been developed to make site-specific ADCs using engineered mAbs or native (non-engineered) mAbs [27]. While protein engineering is feasible and commonly used, it requires detailed optimization to determine appropriate insertion/conjugation sites. It brings up the issues of scale-up and reproducibility, which sometimes provides opportunities for making site-specific ADC using native mAb [106]. Generally, the site-specific conjugation includes protein engineering techniques to introduce the designated conjugation site with unique reactivity, which can be achieved by engineering reactive cysteine residues, incorporating sugars or unnatural amino acids with bioorthogonal functional groups, or genetically encoding peptide tags for further enzymatic or chemical conjugation. The tagged mAbs can be conjugated to linker-payload molecules through bioorthogonal transformation or enzyme-mediated conjugation [107]. Three well-established methods to construct site-specific ADCs and their examples are discussed below.

1. Cysteine-based conjugation

This method utilizes unique reactive cysteine residues, which are engineered into a mAb as the target sites for conjugation. In 2008, THIOMAB, a homogeneous ADC prepared by conjugation to an IgG with special "hot" cysteines whose positions have been preselected and optimized, was disclosed by Genentech [108]. THIOMAB is produced by the reduction of capped engineered cysteine residues and interchain disulfides, followed by oxidation in the presence of CuSO4 or dehydroascorbic acid to regenerate the interchain disulfide bonds, then conjugation of the reactive cysteine thiol to maleimide containing linker payload (i.e., vc-MMAE). This method generates ADC with high purity and homogeneous DAR values (i.e., 92.1% ADC with DAR two in the formulation). An anti-MUC16-MMAE ADC (DAR $\sim$ 1.6) prepared by the THIOMAB approach was shown to be as efficacious as a conventional thiol-conjugated ADC (DAR $\sim$ 3.1) in mouse xenograft models. Importantly, this THIOMAB ADC was tolerated at higher doses than the conventional ADC in rats and monkeys [108]. Subsequent studies found that conjugation sites HC-A118, LC-K149, and HC-A140 provide better stability in the plasma due to less solvent accessibility [109]. THIOMAB method has been successfully applied to different mAbs and linkers, such as anti-HER2-DM1 [110] and anti-CD70-PBD [111], demonstrating comparable efficacy, superior safety, and better stability in preclinical models. The success of THIOMAB opened up the trend of producing site-specific ADCs. Currently, DCDSO780A, an anti-CD79BTHIOMAB MMAE-ADC with DAR of 2 [28], and DMUC4064A, an anti-MUC16 THIOMAB MMAE-ADC [112], and DSTA4637S, an anti-*Staphylococcus aureus* TIO-MAB antibody-antibiotic conjugate [113] are examples of such ADCs in clinical trials. It is worth mentioning that the recent findings of DCDSO780A in the phase 1 study demonstrated ocular toxicities as dose-limited toxicity, distinct from the most observed toxicities of MMAE-based ADC, namely peripheral neuropathy [28]. This indicates that while the improvement of conjugation method and production of homogenous ADCs could provide enhanced efficacy, it can also change the toxicity profile of the ADC.

2. Glycoconjugation

The production of homogenous ADCs can also be done through the modification of mAb glycan residues. Human IgGs have a conserved glycosylation site at each N297 residue in the CH2 domain, and these N-glycans serve as a convenient target for site-specific conjugation [107]. Glycan-mediated conjugation typically involves enzymatic transglycosylation and installation of an unnatural sugar moiety containing a handle for bioconjugation [107]. Studies showed that trastuzumab-DM1 ADC prepared via site-specific glycan-mediated conjugation resulted in a more homogenous product and favorable in vitro and in vivo efficacy profiles compared to T-DM1 [106,114]. Furthermore, at least two ADCs that utilize glycan-medicated conjugation have entered phase 1 clinical trials, including mipasetamab uzoptirine (ADCT-601), an anti-human AXL mAb conjugated to PBD dimer with a DAR of 2 [115], and XMT-1592, an anti-Napi2b mAb conjugated to a proprietary auristatin payload (DolaLock) with a DAR of 6 [116]. However, the heterogeneous nature of glycosylation and immunogenicity associated with glycoengineering should be considered when it comes to implementing glycan-based site-specific conjugation method for ADCs [107].

3. Transglutaminase-mediated and unnatural amino acid incorporation

Transglutaminase-mediated conjugation is another approach for site-specific conjugation. In this chemo-enzymatic approach, microbial transglutaminase catalyzes amide bond formation between glutamine side chain within a deglycosylated IgG1 and a primary amine within linkers [117]. PF-06664178 is an ADC composed of an anti-Trop-2 mAb conjugated with an auristatin-based payload (Aur0101) [118]. It was engineered using transglutaminase-mediated conjugation with a homogeneous DAR of 2. PF-06664178 was initially proceeded to a phase I study; however, it was terminated due to high toxicity and limited efficacy. Conjugation methods based on the incorporation of unnatural amino acids (UAA) into a mAb is another site-specific conjugation method, which offers the most flexibility compared to other site-specific conjugation preparation [107]. Current technology can insert UAA at any selected site within a mAb, and the resulting mAb can then be readily conjugated to a cytotoxic payload [27]. ADCs produced via UAA incorporation are still in preclinical development [119,120].

Although all the currently approved ADCs employ conventional conjugation approaches, the promising results observed from various site-specific strategies will no doubt open a new door for ADCs and an important therapeutic platform in the future. However, as observed with THIOMAB technology, the refinement of the conjugation method may also bring different and unexpected toxicity profiles.

The payloads

Novel payloads

1. Pyrrolobenzodiazepines (PBD)

The evolution of ADC demands the development of a variety of novel payloads with different mechanisms-of-action to fulfill unmet needs for various types of cancers. One of the promising new payloads is PBDs. PBDs are sequence-selective DNA minor-groove binding agents that belong to a class of antitumor antibiotics. The first PBD monomer, anthramycin, was discovered in the 1960s, and the best-known PBD dimer was synthesized in the 1990s. PBD dimers have two alkylating functionalities to induce DNA cross-linking and form DNA adducts, resulting in cytotoxicity and antitumor activity. Due to its additional types of DNA adducts, PBD dimers have significantly greater cytotoxicity than PBD monomers. Therefore, PBD dimers are being used as payloads for ADCs with a DAR of 2 [121]. PBD dimer is the most potent payload employed in a marketed ADC to date [30], with cytotoxicity in the picomolar range against various cancer cell types. In April 2021, the FDA granted accelerated approval for the first PBD-dimer containing ADC, Zynlonta® (loncastuximab tesirine-lpyl), for the treatment of relapsed or refractory non-HL. PBD dimer-related toxicities include edema or effusion, altered liver function tests, skin-related events, myelosuppression, and fatigue, all of which are clinically manageable [122]. With a different cellular target than the auristatin and maytansinoid (i.e., tubulin inhibitors) and a different mode of DNA damage than other DNA interacting payloads (i.e., calicheamicin), PBD dimers offer opportunities for patients who develop resistance to other classes of payloads [123]. By 2022, more than 20 PBD dimer-containing ADCs have entered the clinic, and over 40 clinical trials have been completed or ongoing [123].

2. mRNA targeting payloads

Another group of payloads is designed to target mRNAs such as amanitin and thailanstatin A. Amanitins is a member of the amatoxin natural toxic compounds, which work by inhibition of RNA polymerase II and leads to cell death [124]. HDP-101 is a new amanitin-based ADC targeting B cell maturation antigen (BCMA) [125]. HDP-101 has entered a phase 1 clinical trial in February 2022 for the treatment of relapsed/refractory multiple myeloma [126]. Thailanstatin A works by a novel mechanism-of-action, where it binds to spliceosome and inhibits mRNA splicing, resulting in an antiproliferative activity [127]. Since the spliceosomes of cancer cells are more active than those of normal cells, it serves as suitable anti-tumor target. Thailanstatin-based ADCs have shown superior efficacy in preclinical studies compared to T-DM1 and could overcome MDR phenotype of ADCs with microtubule inhibitors as payloads [127]. Thus, the discovery of new payloads can prompt the development of new ADCs and potentially help overcome the resistance of conventional ADCs.

Non-traditional payloads

Instead of searching for potent payloads to kill cancer cells, researchers have also switched gears to an innovative non-traditional approach where payloads target the body's immune system. Rather than linking the mAbs with potent cytotoxic agents, mAbs have been conjugated to immune stimulators such as Toll-like receptors (TLR) agonists [128] and stimulator of interferon genes (STING) [129], forming the "immune-stimulating antibody conjugates" [130]. This therapeutic modality combines the precision of mAb targeting with the tumor-killing capability of the innate and adaptive immune systems into a single molecule [130].

1. TLR agonists

Considering the motive for ADC development is to deliver agents that are too toxic to be administrated systemically, the scope of potential payloads can be much wider. Traditionally, systemic administration of TLR agonists was found to lead to systemic toxicities due to widespread immune activation. In contrast, the TLR-based ADCs are designed to solely activate localized immune cells in the tumor microenvironment and minimize other off-target immune activation by requiring multiple steps for immune activation, including tumor antigen recognition, FcγR-dependent phagocytosis, and TLR-mediated activation [130]. Currently, there are two immune-stimulating ADCs in clinical development. BDC-1001 is an ADC consisting of HER2-targeting biosimilar trastuzumab conjugated to a TLR7/8 agonist with a non-cleavable linker [79,130,131]. The drug is designed to activate the innate immune system, inducing antibody-dependent cellular phagocytosis and a durable adaptive immune response. Preliminary results from an ongoing phase 1/2 study of BDC-1001 in patients with advanced HER2-expressing solid tumors show that BDC-1001 appears to be well-tolerated up to the tested dose of 5 mg/kg and demonstrates evidence of clinical efficacy [131]. Another example is SNT6050, an ADC comprised of an anti-HER2 mAb conjugated with a TLR8 agonist [79]. SNT6050 is currently being investigated in two clinical trials to evaluate its activity in HER2+ solid tumors when administered as monotherapy versus in combination with other anti-HER2 [132] or immune therapies [133].

2. STING agonists

STING, an endoplasmic protein that can induce the production of pro-inflammatory cytokines such as type I interferons, is another potential target that can augment the anti-tumor immune response [129]. Therefore, STING agonists have become potential immunotherapeutic agents to stimulate the innate antitumor immune response [129]. However, many small-molecule STING agonists developed in the past require intra-tumoral injection due to the systemic toxicity when administered via IV injection. The targeted delivery property of ADC allows systemic administration of these molecules with limited toxicity and circumvents the limitation of intra-tumoral delivery. XMT-2056, the first STING-agonist ADC targeting HER2, has shown promising preclinical results [134], and is expected to enter a phase 1 dose-escalation clinical trial in 2022.

The data for ADC development: how to generate, how to use

Perhaps all the obstacles encountered during the discovery and development of ADCs can be attributed to their narrow therapeutic window. Therefore, a comprehensive and quantitative evaluation of an ADC through a series of in vitro, in vivo, and clinical studies is essential to optimize the ADC design and ultimately provide a safer and more efficacious treatment for patients. Utilizing in vitro and preclinical data helps one understand the mechanism-of-action for ADCs' efficacy, toxicities, resistance, etc. Whenever a new strategy or hypothesis is proposed aiming to improve the therapeutic index of an ADC, the preclinical setting can be used for proof-of-concept studies. The preclinical information can then be translated into the clinical study design. Mathematical modeling approaches enable further quantitative evaluation of all the ADC data generated throughout the discovery and development stages, and enables objective evaluation and preclinical-to-clinical translation of ADCs. Below, we have outlined how in vitro, in vivo, and clinical studies can be employed to address critical problems encountered during the discovery and development of ADCs.

In vitro studies

Cytotoxicity assay

Cytotoxicity assay is the essential first step for the development of ADCs. It provides a tool to select promising ADC candidates, predict in vivo efficacy, and evaluate the cell specificity of ADCs. The most important information obtained from the cytotoxicity assay would be the change in the number of live and dead cells after ADC treatment [135]. Knowing that membrane integrity is the feature to differentiate live and dead cells, molecules that exist in the cytoplasm of viable cells but leak out into the culture medium upon cell death can serve as dead cell markers [136]. On the other hand, molecules that exist naturally or can represent cell metabolism or enzyme activity can serve as markers for live cells. Assays that utilize dead/live cell markers include tetrazolium reduction (i.e., MTT, MTS assays), resazurin reduction (alamarBlue assay), LDH release, glucose-6-phosphate dehydrogenase release, protease viability markers, ATP detection, etc. [135,136]. Besides, dyes that are not permeable in live cells but can enter the dead cells can serve as an indicator for dead cells. Examples are trypan blue and many fluorogenic DNA binding dyes, where DNA binding dyes are largely used in flow cytometry or image cytometry experiments [135].

Tetrazolium reduction assays are routinely used to evaluate the efficacy of ADCs with high throughput and low cost. There are several tips that should be considered when conducting cytotoxicity assays for ADCs [137]. First, drug loading or DAR needs to be considered when deciding the concentration range of an ADC in the experiment. Conceptually, an ADC with higher DAR would show more cytotoxicity than one with a lower DAR. Therefore, payload concentration (i.e., multiply ADC concentration with DAR) rather than ADC concentration may be a better predictor when determining the concentration range for the cytotoxicity assay based on payload IC50. Second, ADC incubation time could depend on the types of cytotoxic payloads. For the two main classes of payloads, microtubule-disrupting agents and DNA-damaging agents, it usually requires at least $\sim$3$-$5 days to evaluate the cytotoxicity of these agents. Lastly, it is always important to include control groups (i.e., untreated cells, medium only, non-targeted ADC, etc.) and relate live and dead cell numbers by a normalization process to provide more robust results and enable better triaging of potential ADC candidates.

Bystander effect

As mentioned before, bystander effect can benefit the efficacy of a cleavable ADC, while it may also increase the risk of toxicity in non-target cells. Therefore, a quantitative understanding of the bystander effect is needed to support the discovery and development of novel cleavable ADCs [138]. In an in vitro system, bystander effect can be characterized by using co-culture methods that contain antigen-positive (Ag+) and antigen-negative (Ag−) cells [138,139] or conditioned medium transfer assay [140]. In the co-culture method, Ag+ and Ag− cells are cultured together, and the viability of Ag− cells in the co-culture system is compared with the viability of Ag− in the monoculture system treated with the same ADC concentrations. If the cytotoxicity of Ag− cells in the co-culture system is greater than that in the monoculture system, it indicates that the ADC tested can elicit the bystander effect. Methods to measure the viability of Ag− cells in the co-culture system include loading Ag− cells with artificial measurable markers (i.e., calcein-AM [^{51}Cr]), genetically engineering Ag− cells to express luciferase or fluorescent protein, and using a fluorescent-labeled mAb targeting Ag− cells measured via flow cytometry [137]. One can also design different experiments to quantitatively evaluate the bystander effect. For example, combine different ratios of Ag+ and Ag− cells in the co-culture system (i.e., 50% Ag+ and 50% Ag−), or treat the cells with different ADC concentrations or incubation time. We have introduced the "bystander effect coefficient," which represents the percentage (%) killing of Ag− cells at a given ratio of Ag+ and Ag− cells [138]. By plotting the bystander effect coefficient versus the % of Ag+ in the co-culture system, one can evaluate the relationship between the extent of bystander effect and antigen availability. When it comes to medium transfer assay, Ag + cells are first treated with ADC for different periods. Then, the conditioned medium is transferred to Ag− cells and after incubation period Ag− cell viability is measured. Notably, one can utilize the in vitro bystander effect data to build a PD model and mathematically describe the bystander killing of ADCs. The PD model can further be integrated with the systems PK model to make a mechanistic PK/PD model, which can facilitate the development of ADCs with optimal bystander killing capabilities [141].

Antigen expression

Understanding the PK of ADCs and payloads at the cellular level is essential to evaluate the relationship between target expression and ADC exposure inside cancer cells. This provides crucial information for antigen selection and target patient population during the discovery and development of ADCs [142]. Given the mechanism-of-action of an ADC, it can be assumed that patients with higher target expression are more responsive than low or non-expressers. However, the relationship between target expression and ADC efficacy reported from the literature is inconsistent, making the antigen expression level as a criterion for selecting target patient population ambiguous [143]. Therefore, exploring cellular PK of ADCs and cytotoxic payloads may enable better understanding of the relationship between biomeasures (i.e., antigen expression) and ADC efficacy [142,144].

To investigate the cellular PK of ADCs [145], one may start from the cellular disposition study of a plain payload (e.g., MMAE), where payload concentration in medium and cell samples is measured after incubated with the plain payload for a given time. Then, an ADC cellular disposition study is performed, where concentrations of different analytes of an ADC (i.e., total antibody, unconjugated payloads, total payload etc.) in medium and cell samples are measured after treatment of cells with ADC for different period of time. By utilizing cell lines expressing different target levels, the relationship between target expression and cellular exposure of different analytes of an ADC can be analyzed. For example, we have found a positive linear relationship between HER2 receptor count and the released MMAE exposure inside the cancer cells, after treating different HER2-expressing breast cancer cell lines with a tool ADC, trastuzumab-vc-MMAE [142]. The finding may support the concept of antigen expression screening in patients to achieve the maximum therapeutic benefit from ADCs.

The cellular PK data of different ADC analytes can be used to develop a mechanistic cell-level PK model for ADCs, which can simultaneously predict the concentrations of ADC and its payload inside the cancer cells [146]. The in vitro cell-level model can further be integrated into an in vivo PK/PD model or a PBPK model, allowing prediction of tumor payload concentrations and efficacy in vivo and in the clinic. These cell-level models can ultimately facilitate clinical translation and optimization of ADC dosing regimens [147].

Intracellular trafficking of ADCs

ADCs can be viewed as prodrugs, which need to be processed and metabolized inside the tumor cells before exerting their activity [55]. The ADC-target complexes undergo internalization and lysosomal trafficking to release the payloads and exert anticancer activity [51]. Therefore, the degree of endocytosis, recycling, and lysosomal trafficking for the ADC-target complexes are important contributors to ADC activity. However, based on a recent review, the information of endocytosis mechanism for the receptor targeted by the currently approved ADC is limited [148]. Therefore, quantitative evaluation of the intracellular trafficking of ADCs in vitro can facilitate the design and optimization of novel ADCs.

Several in vitro assays have been employed to assess the intracellular trafficking of ADCs. First, the cellular accumulation assay investigates the accumulation of ADC intracellularly. Cells are exposed to ADCs labeled with a pH-sensitive dye, which exhibits minimal fluorescence at neutral pH but only shows fluorescence at acidic pH. The properties of the dye allow for tracing of ADC trafficking into acidic endosomes and lysosomes. Second, an internalization assay investigates the uptake and endocytosis of ADCs, and the results can be used to calculate the internalization rate [149]. Cells are surface-labeled with fluorescent-labeled ADCs and then incubated at 37 °C for different time intervals for the internalization of surface fluorescence. Next, cells will be incubated on ice for 30 min with (quenched) or without (non-quenched) anti-fluorescence mAb, followed by flow cytometry analysis. The extent of ADC internalization can be calculated from quenched and non-quenched sample data [149]. Furthermore, it is known that several receptors such as HER2 undergo rapid and efficient recycling following ADC-receptor complex endocytosis rather than entry into the lysosomal degradative pathway [150]. Therefore, a recycling assay can be used to track the recycling kinetics, where the pulse and chase approach is applied.

The intracellular disposition data of ADCs can provide insight into key pathways for ADC activity and allow one to advance the cell-level ADC PK models by incorporating endosomal and lysosomal compartments to describe the intracellular processing of ADCs. As previously mentioned, linker chemistries can affect the stability of an ADC, and they can also have a significant impact on the subcellular trafficking of an ADC. Therefore, the advanced cellular ADC PK model can be utilized to evaluate and optimize different types of linkers. In addition, the model can also be used to evaluate novel strategies that aim to enhance the intracellular delivery of ADCs. Several examples are provided here: a tetravalent biparatopic ADC targeting distinct epitopes on HER2, which can induce receptor clustering and promote internalization and degradation [151]; a bispecific ADC targeting HER2 and prolactin receptor, where prolactin receptor is believed to trigger faster degradation of HER2 [152]; co-administration of an ADC with geldanamycin, a heat shock protein 90 inhibitor, which was able to disrupt HER2 endosomal recycling and increase lysosomal trafficking [149].

In vivo studies

A comprehensive nonclinical evaluation of ADCs is essential as it provides opportunities to better predict the efficacy and safety profiles in clinical and increase the chance of clinical success of ADCs. Nonclinical study plan should consider individual components (i.e., mAb or payload) and ADC as a whole. Key factors that need to be considered during nonclinical studies include: (1) identifying appropriate animal species with better translatability of the nonclinical findings; (2) PK and PD of mAb, payload, and ADC conjugate; and (3) toxicity profile of an ADC. Thus, common studies that should be included during the preclinical phase of ADC development are PK, PD, and toxicology studies.

Bioanalysis: multiple formats

A quantitative understanding of the systemic PK and tissue distribution of an ADC is essential for establishing the exposure-response relationship, determining appropriate doses for the pivotal toxicology studies, and evaluating the safety profile of ADCs. However, characterization of an ADC's PK is challenging as it requires multiple assay formats to measure different analytes [153]. Total mAb (conjugated mAb + naked mAb), total payload (conjugated payload + unconjugated payload), conjugated mAb, conjugated payload, and unconjugated payload are typically measured analytes for ADCs. Therefore, the bioanalysis strategy for ADCs usually requires ligand binding assays (i.e., ELISA) for large molecules and LC-MS/MS methods for small molecules [154,155]. Ligand binding assays such as ELISA can be used to quantify total mAb, conjugated mAb, or conjugated drug depending on the types of capture and detection reagents. For example, using capture and detection reagents that bind to the mAb component of an ADC enables the quantification of total mAb, applying a capture and a detection reagent that bind to conjugated drug and mAb component respectively can quantify conjugated mAb, or utilizing a reagent that captures mAb and use anti-drug mAb can quantify conjugated drug [154]. Of note, ELISA is sensitive to the choice of the anti-drug mAb when it comes to the quantification of conjugated mAb for an ADC with heterogenous DAR values [156]. Hence, the important aspect in the assay development is to identify an anti-drug mAb that is minimally influenced by the drug loading (i.e., DAR) [157]. Moreover, based on our experience, ELISA to quantify total mAb for an ADC should have a standard curve made with ADC stock solutions (e.g., trastuzumab-vc-MMAE ADC) but not pure mAb (i.e., trastuzumab). We found that the signals of standard curves generated using pure mAb stock solutions are higher than those using ADC stock solutions. Therefore, one can erroneously report lower concentrations of total mAb in an ADC sample if the standard curves are generated using pure mAb [154].

Liquid chromatography with tandem mass spectrometry (LC-MS/MS) is usually utilized to analyze payloads or ADC catabolites. For an ADC with a cleavable linker, unconjugated and total (unconjugated + conjugated) payloads are usually measured, where the total payload is quantified after linker cleavage. For example, ADCs with vc-linker and disulfide linker can be treated with protease (i.e., cathepsin B and papain) and reducing agent (i.e., DTT, TCEP), respectively [158]. On the other hand, for ADCs conjugated with non-cleavable linkers, the cleavage products may not be pure payloads. For example, multiple catabolites of T-DM1 apart from DM1, such as MCC-DM1 and lysine-MCC-DM1, are also observed. Therefore, additional considerations are needed for the bioanalysis of payload, payload-linker complex, or payload-partial linker complex, depending on the mechanism of release [159]. One also needs to consider that the released payload may contain a reactive group such as maytansinoid. A validated DM1 catabolite LC-MS/MS assay has been reported, designed with a reduction step to measure the free DM1 present in circulation or any disulfide bound forms of released DM1 (i.e., dimers, glutathione, cysteine, and albumin adducts) while excluding MCC-DM1 and lysine-MCC-DM1 [160,161]. Because DM1 contains a free sulfhydryl, the released DM1 from T-DM1 could undergo dimerization or react with other thiol-containing molecules in plasma. Therefore, to avoid under-quantifying the released DM1, plasma samples are treated with a reducing agent (TCEP) to release disulfide-bound DM1. The free thiol is then blocked with N-ethylmaleimide (NEM) to prevent further reactions. Finally, DM1-NEM is quantified by LC-MS/MS. Therefore, it is crucial to thoroughly understand the catabolism of ADCs and biotransformation of ADC catabolites and incorporate this information into assay development for in vivo PK, PD, and toxicity studies [160].

Another important attribute to an ADC formulation is DAR, which may affect the stability, PK, and efficacy of an ADC. Current analytical methods that have been reported to measure average DAR include UV–visible spectroscopy, hydrophobic interaction chromatography (HIC), LC-MS, reversed phase-HPLC (RP-HPLC), and LC-electrospray ionization assay MS (LC-ESI-MS) [162].

In vivo PK data

Preclinical in vivo studies are the foundation of ADC development and translation, which bridge in vitro studies with first-in-human clinical trials. Quantitatively understanding the PK of an ADC is essential for establishing the exposure-response relationship and evaluating the safety profile of an ADC.

1. Understanding of payload PK

It is generally believed that the toxicities of an ADC stem from the pharmacological effects of the payload, and thereby knowledge of the PK and biodistribution of a payload itself is indispensable. However, this information is often less emphasized or even lacking during ADC development. Additionally, it is impossible to conduct PK studies of a plain payload in humans due to its inherent toxicity. Therefore, preclinical PK studies for the free payload alone can be of great value for developing a novel ADC, especially for cleavable ADCs that can release payload as the free form (e.g., MMAE), and facilitate their preclinical-to-clinical translation [163].

2. Understanding systemic and tissue PK

Another significance of the preclinical experiment is investigating the whole-body PK of ADCs, which is almost impossible to conduct in clinical. The observations from several clinical trials suggest that the plasma PK alone may not be sufficient to represent the toxicity/efficacy of an ADC. For example, in the phase 2 study of BV, the probability of objective response rate (ORR) decreased with increased MMAE trough concentration, and adverse events of ADC increased with decreased MMAE trough concentrations. Another example is the exposure-response (E-R) analysis of T-DM1 reported from the FDA [164]. Based on the pooled phase 3 data of T-DM1, the E-R relationship showed a higher incidence of grade 3+ adverse events in patients in the low-exposure quartiles than patients in the high-exposure quartiles. Subsequently, exposure-response analysis was also performed for the most commonly observed adverse events that cause T-DM1 dose adjustments, including hepatotoxicity, thrombocytopenia, and peripheral neuropathy. The results found a higher incidence of hepatotoxicity in patients with lower T-DM1 exposure, while no clinically meaningful relationships for thrombocytopenia and peripheral neuropathy. Therefore, it is imperative to investigate the PK of an ADC in plasma and different tissues.

3. Understanding of different ADC analytes

Regarding quantification of the whole-body PK of an ADC, the best practice is to measure different analytes of an ADC (i.e., total mAb, conjugated mAb, unconjugated payload) in order to adequately determine the overall biodistribution in vivo. It is known that conjugation of the payload to a mAb could cause change in the PK of an ADC due to the modification of the physicochemical property of the molecule. Our group also found that mAb-mediated delivery of a payload may lead to alternation in the tissue distribution profile of the payload [165]. For example, in mice biodistribution studies, upon administration of plain MMAE, the exposure of MMAE in the heart was ~ 18-fold higher than in plasma, which reduced to ~ 1.5-fold higher upon administration of MMAE as a conjugate with a mAb (i.e., trastuzumab-vc-MMAE). In contrast, MMAE exposure in the liver was about 2.5-fold higher than in plasma, which increased to 10-fold higher when MMAE was administered as a conjugate with mAb. Therefore, solely analyzing individual analytes would overlook the effect of conjugation on the disposition of mAb and payload components of an ADC.

Another reason for the requirement of quantifying multiple analytes is that there is currently no consensus on which ADC analyte from which biological matrices is better for building exposure-response relationships for ADCs, since each analyte provides insights into different aspects of the overall PK of ADC [160]. However, an analysis using clinical data for eight vc-MMAE ADCs from phase 1 clinical trials suggested that the conjugated MMAE is a better indicator for efficacy and safety profiles. Thus the measurement of conjugated MMAE alone may be sufficient to support later phase clinical development [166]. However, such a conclusion may not be applicable to other ADCs with different linkers-payload designs.

We believe that the best execution for PK studies during preclinical development is to comprehensively evaluate the PK of different analytes of an ADC in plasma, tissues, and the site-of-action, using suitable bioanalytical methods that are planned beforehand.

In vivo PD data

Despite utilizing a variety of animal models, the translation of efficacy and PD results from bench-to-bedside remains relatively challenging compared to PK results [167]. Moreover, the development of complicated molecules (i.e., ADCs) for cancer therapy makes the prediction of clinical outcomes from preclinical settings more difficult.

1. Selection of animal models

Different types of animal models are needed during preclinical development to evaluate the efficacy and toxicity of ADCs. For example, human xenograft mouse models are commonly used to measure drug efficacy since mouse cell lines are often less sensitive to ADC payloads. Humanized or syngeneic mouse models are needed to investigate the contribution of the immune system in humans. Non-human primates are often used to test toxicity since most mAbs developed in murine systems typically do not cross-react with mouse antigens, and antigen expression levels are different in rodent species. Ocular toxicity was reported as dose-limit toxicity for many ADCs (i.e., cantuzumab ravtansine, mirvetuximab soravtansine, coltuximab ravtansine, etc.), which can only be detected in rabbit models [19]. Obviously, no single model that can incorporate all these factors, and there are known issues with the preclinical models (e.g., species-specific metabolic pathways, faster clearance in animals, immune system differences between species) that make the clinical translation ADC PD more challenging.

Regardless of the limitations mentioned, the preclinical models still serve as a useful tool to examine different hypotheses or strategies aiming to improve the therapeutic index of ADCs. It can also be used to examine different ADC designs (i.e., linker types, linker chemistry, conjugation methodology, drug loading, mAb backbone) and help select optimal ADC formulations. Here we have provided two examples where preclinical PD studies are designed to examine novel strategies devised to improve the narrow therapeutic index of ADCs.

2. Overcoming of the binding-site barrier

It is known that mAbs/ADCs exhibit heterogeneous distribution in solid tumors due to the "binding-site-barrier" effect. The rapid binding of mAbs relative to their tumor penetration rate leads to receptor saturation in the perivascular cells.

Additionally, mAb must go into tumors in order to penetrate deeper into the tissue; however, administration of higher doses of ADCs is not feasible as they have much lower MTDs than unconjugated mAbs. Cilliers and colleagues have developed a novel strategy that utilizes parental antibody (e.g., trastuzumab) as a competitor that can be coadministration with the ADC (e.g., T-DM1) [168]. Upon coadministration of mAb and ADC the perivascular cells would receive a smaller payload dose while more cells in deeper tissue could receive therapeutic doses of payload. To test this hypothesis, an in vivo efficacy study was conducted in a mouse xenograft model that is insensitive to trastuzumab. They found that coadministration of trastuzumab with a therapeutic dose of T-DM1 at 3:1 and 8:1 ratio significantly improved in vivo efficacy and resulted in a twofold improvement in median survival compared with T-DM1 monotherapy, which suggest that the combination was synergistic. Subsequently, a proof-of-principal clinical study in head and neck cancer patients has demonstrated that an antibody-dye conjugate co-administered with a loading dose of parent mAb can improve the intratumoral distribution and decreases the healthy tissue uptake of the antibody-dye conjugate [169]. Since the antibody-dye conjugate serves as a surrogate for ADCs, this clinical finding supports the feasibility of applying coadministration strategy to improve the therapeutic index of ADCs in solid tumors. This example demonstrated the utilization of an in vivo efficacy study for proof-of-concept and design of a proof-of-principle clinical study, which is an important first step toward the translation of dosing strategy into cancer patients [169]. However, antibody coadministration regimens may not always be applicable to different clinical settings, and often they can only be beneficial under certain conditions [170]. Therefore, preclinical experiments serve as a useful tool to broadly test the novel strategies in all the scenarios and identify the benefits and risks of the strategies.

3. Evaluation of effector functions

The second example is to investigate the role of the Fc effector function on ADC efficacy in vivo. The mAb component of an ADC can recruit and activate immune effector cells and/or complements into tumors to mediate effector functions [12,78]. However, for ADCs, no conclusion has been made as some suggests that effector functions could provide advantages, disadvantages, or minimal effect. The effector functions have the potential to enhance ADC's antitumor activity [51]. For example, Belantamab Mafodotin, which utilizes afucosylated IgG1 as its mAb backbone resulting in increased FcγRIIIa binding, demonstrated potent antitumor activity in multiple myeloma [171]. In contrast, some studies identified Fc receptor engagement as a possible cause of adverse events. For example, the internalization of T-DM1 by megakaryocytes via FcγRIIa binding contributes to T-DM1 induced thrombocytopenia [172]. Alternatively, it is suggested that the mAb internalization and payload release in the target cells serve as the primary mechanism-of-action for ADCs, which is considerably more potent than the effector function. Thus, the enhancement of effector functions can have little impact on ADC efficacy [173]. For example, the anti-Trop-2 ADC IMMU-132, which has ~70% lower antibody-dependent cellular cytotoxicity (ADCC) activity than the unconjugated mAb, still demonstrated significant antitumor effects in preclinical and clinical studies [174].

Preclinical in vivo mouse models can serve as useful systems to objectively evaluate the contribution of effector function on ADC efficacy. However, traditionally used human cell line xenograft models in immune-compromised mice cannot be used in this case. Fortunately, the number and diversity of available mouse models that can depict human immune system and can be used to evaluate ADCs with altered effector function have increased dramatically. Several immunocompetent mouse model systems are currently well-established, including transplantable, genetically engineered, and humanized mouse tumor models, and each has its advantages and disadvantages, reviewed elsewhere [175,176]. For example, genetically engineered models may better recapitulate tumor progression and tumor microenvironment as well as more closely resemble tumor-induced tolerance and immunosuppression in human cancers. However, tumor formation in transgenic animals tends to be more variable and requires a longer period of time. Humanized mouse models may directly represent human immune systems and could capture the heterogenicity of patient response. However, the efficiency of the reconstituted human cells to exert immune function is unknown, and the interaction between mouse-derived immune factors and human immune cells may complicate the interpretation of experimental results. Implantable tumor models where mouse-originated cells are inoculated into syngeneic mice serve as an initial model system to evaluate immunotherapy strategies (i.e., ADC with enhanced effector function). These models are relatively convenient [176], though the rapid growth rate of many cell lines may limit the syngeneic models for long-term studies [175]. It is known that preclinical data provide a wide range of responses to a single agent, and hence the therapeutic effects of ADCs should be evaluated in multiple models [177]. Syngeneic models can help achieve this goal since various cell lines for a single disease are readily available [178,179]. This example highlights the importance of selecting an appropriate preclinical model to test novel hypotheses.

Toxicity and safety

The objective of preclinical toxicity studies may be classified as: (1) to generate the safety data to inform the first-in-human dose and identify potential human risks of a novel ADC, or (2) to address mechanistic problems related to ADC toxicity (such as investigation of the effect of different linker chemistry, conjugation site, DAR, dosing regimens, etc. on ADC toxicity) [180−183]. For the first objective, preclinical studies should at least follow the ICHS6(R1) and ICHS9 regulatory guidance to support the investigational new drug (IND) submission. Generally, it includes GLP toxicity studies in relevant species (i.e., one rodent and one non-rodent, usually in non-human primates), in vitro stability in human and tested preclinical species plasma, tissue cross-reactivity, toxicokinetics, subchronic and chronic toxicity, and genotoxicity studies [180].

Several considerations that are unique to ADCs when conducting preclinical toxicity studies are emphasized as follows. First, it is important to utilize the available data from ADCs with the same payloads (i.e., auristatins, maytansines, calicheamicins) or the same linkers. Many ADCs employ the same mAb or cytotoxic drug, some of which have been approved for use alone (i.e., trastuzumab, taxane, MTX). Thus, considerable nonclinical and clinical data may already exist. Second, each component of an ADC can contribute to the observed toxicities and should be considered when designing or interpreting the preclinical toxicity studies. For example, low-level expression of an antigen on normal tissues may result in more specific toxicities, while the premature release of payload can lead to more widespread toxicities. It is thought that ADC toxicities mainly come from the payload, while Fc-mediated immune cell uptake through the interaction of the mAb component of an ADC with immune cells can also cause off-target toxicity. One should also be aware of payload class-wide toxicities [19], such as: peripheral neuropathy and neutropenia caused by MMAE; thrombocytopenia and ocular toxicities induced by MMAF; ocular toxicity associated with DM4; thrombocytopenia and hepatotoxicity through calicheamicin, etc. Third, the duration of dosing and exposure of an ADC in preclinical toxicity studies should be long enough to allow for the detection of the onset of toxicities. A classic example is that peripheral neuropathy from vc-MMAE ADCs observed in clinic was not predicted in preclinical toxicity studies in monkeys or rats [184]. After evaluation, it was believed that inadequate exposure duration of the drug is the most likely reason for the lack of translatability of peripheral neuropathy for vc-MMAE [184]. Based on the onset of peripheral neuropathy observed in patients (20−32 weeks), the dosing/exposure in cynomolgus monkeys (Q3W for four to five dosing cycles, 15 weeks exposure) and rats (4 weeks exposure) may not be long enough to observe the evidence of peripheral neuropathy (i.e., axonal degeneration).

Apart from the considerations mentioned, it is also important to investigate how and why ADCs exert the observed toxicities on different cell types and why toxicity profiles are inconsistent between the same types of ADCs (i.e., same payload, linker). A comprehensive assessment of ADC toxicities during preclinical development will increase the chance of clinical success of an ADC. Preclinical toxicity studies can also be used to guide the selection of optimal dosing strategy or favorable ADC design, which are relatively different from the regulatory toxicity studies [181]. For example, evidence has demonstrated that manipulating the dosing regimens can improve the tolerability of ADCs, and one can utilize the preclinical toxicity studies to examine the feasibility of different dosing regimens. As demonstrated in Hinrichs et al. study, they found that fractionated dosing (0.33 mg/kg QW for three doses) of a PBD-conjugated ADC significantly reduces systemic toxicity compared to a single dose of 1 mg/kg while maintaining similar tumor growth inhibition in rats and monkeys [185]. Of note, data from these types of preclinical toxicity studies should be interpreted in conjunction with data from parallel in vivo PK/PD studies, and/or combined with modeling and simulation approaches to assess the overall impact of dosing regimen on the therapeutic index of ADCs.

Clinical data

Considerations for clinical pharmacology beyond guidance

Comprehensive understanding of clinical data is very important for ADC development since it helps guide the final dosing regimen for ADCs and provides an opportunity to deliver safer and more efficacious pharmacotherapy in each patient population [186]. The complex nature of an ADC requires unique considerations, dedicated clinical pharmacology strategies, and quantitative approaches to support the development and approval of an ADC. Based on the 2022 FDA guidance, clinical pharmacology considerations for ADCs include bioanalytical methods, dosing strategies (PK/PD), dose-response and exposure-response analysis, intrinsic factors (i.e., organ dysfunction, pharmacogenomics, body weight, age, gender, race), QTc assessments, immunogenicity, and drug-drug interactions (DDIs) [187]. Here, we discuss some of these clinical considerations while highlighting the factors that are unique to ADCs.

To characterize the clinical PK of ADCs, multiple analytes are measured. The commonly measured ADC analytes include conjugated mAb, conjugated payload, total mAb, unconjugated mAb, and unconjugated payload. However, clinical PK is limited to plasma data, unlike preclinical PK studies that may include biodistribution data. PK data from the phase 1 dose-escalation study can be dose-normalized and superimposed to assess PK linearity. Plasma concentrations of different analytes of ADCs are first analyzed through non-compartmental analysis (NCA). While NCA seems to be a simple method, comparing PK parameters of different ADC analytes calculated from NCA can be very informative. Here, we use the cleavable vc-MMAE ADCs as an example to demonstrate how PK parameters can provide insights into the PK characteristics of an ADC. First, by comparing the total mAb clearance of an ADC to the clearance of typical mAbs (i.e., normal IgG1), one can identify whether conjugation affects the PK of the mAb component. In fact, it was reported that the non-specific cellular uptake (via Kupffer cells, hepatic sinusoidal endothelium, and myeloid lineage cells) and extracellular enzyme-based hydrolysis (via carboxylesterase 1c) could lead to the "conjugated-induced clearance," which is unique for an ADC but not for a mAb [188]. Second, conjugated payload/mAb often shows faster clearance compared to total mAb analyte, which may indicate the elimination of conjugates is driven by two processes: deconjugation and proteolytic degradation, where the degradation process solely drives the total mAb clearance. Third, the exposure of unconjugated payload is usually much lower than total mAb or conjugates (i.e., >100-fold lower), as it may serve as an indicator of ADC stability in the systemic circulation. Fourth, a time delay in reaching maximum concentration plus prolonged half-life of the unconjugated payload would suggest formation rate-limited kinetics of the released drug [189]. In addition, one should check if the difference of maximum-observed concentration (C_{max}) between conjugated payload and conjugated mAb (or total mAb) corresponds to the DAR in the ADC dosing formulation (i.e., C_{max} of conjugated MMAE is fourfold higher than the conjugated ADC for an ADC with a DAR of 4).

It has also been observed that the PK parameters of different analytes for an ADC may be generalized to another ADC with a similar payload-linker design. For example, Li et al. have demonstrated that PK profiles and PK parameters of the three different analytes (total mAb, conjugated MMAE, unconjugated MMAE) are remarkably similar across eight vc-MMAE ADCs at 2.4 mg/kg in phase 1 clinical trials, regardless of their target and indications [166]. We have expanded the analysis to 18 vc-MMAE ADCs under clinical development with wider dosing ranges, frequencies (i.e., Q3W and QW), targets, and indications, and found similar results, validating the generalizability of ADC PK, at least for vc-MMAE ADCs, which is one of the most used drug-linker platforms. Current ADCs under clinical development (or approved) typically exploit established conjugation methods, linkers design, and payloads that have been used in other approved ADCs, while simply selecting distinct targets for different indications. Therefore, one may easily compare the PK parameters of different ADC analytes between these molecules and make use of the reported values to predict human PK of a novel ADC with a similar linker-payload.

Clinical PK data are also analyzed using compartmental approaches such as the population PK modeling. Population PK modeling enables quantitative characterization of ADC PK in plasma and assessment of the effect of intrinsic and extrinsic factors on ADC PK. A better practice is to develop a PK model that is able to simultaneously characterize all analytes of an ADC measured during clinical trial. Unfortunately, the current population PK models of the approved ADCs used in submission packages do not meet this criterion. For example, these population PK models only included two analytes (i.e., total mAb/ADC/conjugated payload and unconjugated payload) or one analyte (i.e, ADC), as shown in Ref. [186]. Therefore, development of population PK models that incorporate compartments for all measured analytes is warranted.

When it comes to exposure-response analysis, it serves as a critical tool for dose selection in pivotal studies. As mentioned before, it remains uncertain which ADC analyte drives efficacy and/or safety. Based on the data of current approved ADCs, the ADC analyte (i.e., conjugated antibody or conjugated drug) tends to correlate better in exposure-efficacy analysis. In contrast, no apparent exposure-safety relationship is observed in most ADCs, while the conjugated mAb rather than unconjugated payload tends to have a better correlation to adverse events in some ADCs. This exposure-safety relationship may be counterintuitive since the release of the highly potent payload would possibly cause toxicity. Therefore, such clinical observations may again emphasize the fact that plasma PK may not represent the whole-body PK of different ADC analytes, and thus a bottom-up modeling approach such as physiologically-based PK (PBPK) modeling may facilitate the prediction of biodistribution of ADCs [165,190].

Evaluation of the effect of intrinsic and extrinsic factors on ADC PK mostly focus on their impact on the unconjugated payload exposure. The recommendations for each factor during the clinical development of an ADC are provided in the FDA guidance [191]. Here, we expand some points and provide some additional thoughts that are not mentioned in the guidance. First, although adjustment of ADC doses in renal/hepatic impairment patients to match the desired unconjugated payload concentrations seems reasonable, it can also cause altered exposure of other analytes (i.e., ADC), resulting in altered efficacy. Therefore, dose adjustments should be employed after the assessment of the benefit-risk profile. This concept may also be applied to dose adjustments for other special populations such as pediatrics and geriatrics. Second, plasma/tissue protein binding and red blood cell partition of the payload should be considered. Based on our PBPK model simulations for a vc-MMAE ADC, change of MMAE protein binding significantly affect plasma and tissue PK of unconjugated MMAE [165]. Notably, hepatic or renal impairment can cause hypoalbuminemia [192], resulting in altered protein binding of the payload, and consequently changing the distribution and elimination of the drug due to organ impairment. Third, cancer patients who are immunocompromized may present different immunogenicity profiles. In addition, the immunocompromized status may induce ADC uptake into nontarget organs via Fc receptor-mediated uptake. The decrease of endogenous IgG in immunocompromized patients creates less competition for Fc receptor binding with ADCs, which may eventually lead to nonspecific uptake of ADCs in the bones, liver, and spleen, while less uptake in the tumors [193]. Thus, implementation of robust clinical pharmacology strategies along with ADC and patient-specific considerations are bound to increase the clinical success of ADCs.

Mathematical modeling: a quantitative approach

Quantitative evaluation of the PK and PD of an ADC is challenging as it requires simultaneous considerations of the properties of three components of the ADC: mAb, linker, and payload. One of the useful tools to conquer this challenge is PK/PD modeling and simulation approach, which enables simultaneous integration of PK/PD properties of each ADC component in a quantitative manner. Previously we have discussed how to generate in vitro, in vivo, and clinical data to answer the questions encountered during ADC development. Further quantitative analysis of these data through the development of mathematical PK/PD models will facilitate model-based drug development and preclinical-to-clinical translation of ADCs [194,195]. Here we outline some applications of PK/PD modeling and simulation strategies throughout different stages of ADC development (i.e., discovery, preclinical and clinical development) to facilitate rational decision making.

Modeling of in vitro data

During drug discovery, PK/PD modeling and simulation strategies can be used to triage lead ADC candidates, identify critical parameters to optimize ADC design, evaluate different potential targets, investigate attributes of ADC efficacy (i.e., the bystander effect), or examine different hypotheses or strategies (i.e., strategies to enhance intracellular delivery of ADCs, methods to overcome binding site barrier). This can be achieved by developing cell-level systems PK models for ADCs using in vitro PK data for different ADC analytes generated in cancer cells [145]. The cellular disposition model can help estimate key parameters that are difficult to measure experimentally (i.e., payload efflux rate from cancer cells) or identify critical parameters that would affect the cellular disposition of different ADC analytes (i.e., mAb binding affinity, payload binding affinity to its pharmacological target) through sensitivity analysis. On the other hand, in vitro PD data can be used to establish in vitro PK/PD models, which can be used to derive secondary parameters representing the efficacy of an ADC (i.e., *in vitro* tumor static concentration, TSC) [196]. Such parameters (i.e., TSC values) can be compared across different ADCs to triage ADC candidates as well.

Modeling of in vivo data

Mechanistic models

Since relatively more data can be obtained from preclinical studies compared to the clinical setting, various dedicated PK/PD models have been developed to mechanistically characterize in vivo PK/PD of ADCs and answer different questions encountered during ADC development. For example, a multi-scale mechanistic-based tumor disposition model for ADCs has been developed by us to *a priori* predict tumor concentration of different ADC analytes [146,189]. The model accounts for key disposition mechanisms of an ADC inside the tumors, such as: tumor size-dependent permeability/diffusion exchange of ADC and payload, ADC-antigen interaction, ADC degradation followed by payload generation within the tumor cells, and payload-intracellular target (i.e., tubulin) interaction. One can use this model to predict the tumor exposure of an ADC that targets a novel antigen by changing the antigen-related parameters (i.e., antigen expression, internalization, mAb binding affinity), or can simulate tumor exposure of an ADC conjugated with different payloads if payload-related information is available (i.e., intracellular payload binding capacity and affinity). Additionally, the tumor PK model can be linked with a PD model, where the intertumoral payload concentrations can be used to drive the efficacy of an ADC [189].

PBPK models

Many studies have demonstrated the ability of mechanistic PK/PD models to predict the concentrations of ADC analytes at the target sites and their utility in establishing a reliable exposure-efficacy relationship of an ADC in humans. However, these mechanistic models may not be sufficient to establish a translatable exposure-toxicity/safety relationship of an ADC. In order to establish an accurate exposure-toxicity relationship, the concentration of different analytes of an ADC in the toxicity-prone tissues is required. Therefore, a PBPK model of an ADC, which allows for the characterization of the PK of multiple ADC analytes in the whole body, can be a solution. However, developing a PBPK model for an ADC could be uniquely challenging as one needs to simultaneously account for the disposition (distribution, metabolism, and excretion) of both the large and small molecules, which are driven by distinct physiological processes, and connect them mechanistically (i.e., payload release mechanism). This also requires one to understand the biodistribution of just the payload itself in preclinical experiments.

Nevertheless, PBPK models for T-DM1 [190] and an MMAE-based ADC [165] have been reported, which could characterize the whole-body PK of different ADC analytes reasonably well in lower species. The ability of these models to *a priori* predict the human PK of different ADC analytes has also been demonstrated. In the ADC PBPK models, the mAb PBPK model and the payload PBPK model are connected in a mechanistic manner (i.e., deconjugation and degradation processes). These PBPK models serve as a flexible platform, where tissue-specific processes of ADCs can be added to advance the model once more information is available. For example, in specific tissues, immune cell-mediated ADC uptake [197], extracellular enzyme-based hydrolysis of ADC [67,198,199], or non-specific tissue uptake [19] of the ADC can be incorporated. Similarly, plasma or tissue protein binding, red blood cell partition, transporters (i.e., P-gp, SLC46A3) mediated exchange, and formation of linker-payload albumin adducts [200] can be incorporated in the PBPK model for the payload component.

As one of the most translatable models, the ADC PBPK models have several applications. For example, one can use an ADC PBPK model for *a priori* prediction of plasma and tissues PK of different ADC components in higher species and humans by changing species-specific physiological parameters without estimating any parameters. Second, the ADC PBPK model can also help evaluate clinical drug-drug interactions and may facilitate regulatory submission, as in the case of Polatuzumab vedotin [201]. Third, the ADC PBPK model may assist in predicting PK of different ADC analytes in special populations such as pediatrics, geriatrics, patients with organ impairment, or obesity. Indeed, acquiring insights into the influence of physiological changes in these special populations on payload disposition is essential, as the highly toxic payloads are often the main driver for ADC toxicities. Moreover, the ADC PBPK models may be more advantageous over compartmental models in terms of exploring different dosing regimens such as fractionated dosing schedules. For example, dosing of ADC using different dosing intervals and amounts but totaling a fixed total dose (i.e., 3 mg/kg Q3W versus 1 mg/kg QW) may result in similar plasma PK yet significantly different tissue distribution of ADC analytes. In this case, the ADC PBPK model can serve as a valuable tool to compare the safety profiles of an ADC administrated via different dosing regimens.

Model advancement

PK/PD modeling and simulation can be applied throughout the development of ADCs. For a complex biochemical modality like ADCs, quantitative and mechanistically oriented modeling approaches may be more beneficial to address a variety of research questions during ADC development. Notably, ADC-immune cell interaction, which is an emerging topic in ADCs, may significantly contribute to ADC efficacy (i.e., payload-induced immunogenic cell death, mAb effector function) and toxicity (i.e., immune cell uptake). However, efforts to develop mathematical models for ADC-immune cell interaction are lacking. Several mathematical models regarding immune cell-cancer cell interaction have recently become available [202]. Incorporating such immune system-tumor cell interactions into the PK/PD models of ADCs will provide a new era for model-based drug development for ADCs.

Emerging opportunities

ADC combination therapy

ADC-IO

Efforts are being made to augment ADC activity and enhance the ADC therapeutic index, and combining ADCs with other therapeutic modalities has become an exciting topic in preclinical and clinical development. One of the strategies being examined in numerous clinical trials is combining ADCs with immune-oncology (IO) agents, based on the rationale of the immunomodulatory properties of the payloads used in ADCs [203,204]. Payloads including microtubule inhibitors (i.e., auristatins, maytansinoids, tubulysins) and DNA-targeting agents (i.e., calicheamicin, PBD) have been shown to induce immunogenic cell death (ICD), resulting in potent stimulation of effector T-cell activation and their recruitment into the tumors. Additionally, the tubulin depolymerizing payloads such as MMAE and DM1 can directly induce dendritic cell activation and maturation. These previously underemphasized immunomodulatory effects of ADCs suggest the potential synergism of ADC and IO combination. Indeed, preclinical data for ADCs conjugated with auristatins, maytansinoids, and tubulysins have proved several possible mechanisms for the enhanced anti-tumor activity observed in ADC-IO combination treatment [203]; justifying the evaluation of the therapeutic potential for this combination strategy in the clinic. Currently, a significant number of clinical studies have been investigating ADC-IO combination therapy using approved or experimental immunotherapies. However, most of these trials are still ongoing, and only limited data are available currently.

Based on our review of the preliminary data from some of these studies, the benefit of ADC-IO combinations compared to ADC monotherapy in terms of efficacy may not be as promising as expected from the preclinical results for both hematological malignancies and solid tumors. Also, this inferior efficacy is on top of risking patients to additional toxicities associated with individual drugs in the combination therapy or amplification of overlapping toxicities. As an example of ADC-IO treatment in hematological malignancies, BV plus nivolumab (PD-1 inhibitor) was evaluated in a phase 2 trial for the treatment of HL in older patients who were considered unsuitable for standard chemotherapy [205]. However, the interim analysis showed an overall response rate of 64%, lower than the predefined criteria of 80%, and thus the trial was closed. Moreover, the overall response rate for ADC-IO was lower than the one reported for the BV monotherapy, and more dose reductions and delays due to drug-related toxicities (primarily neurotoxicity) were found. The combination did not show improvement of the toxicity profile since peripheral neuropathy (48% of patients) remained challenging in this patient population. Another example for the use of ADC-IO combination therapy in solid tumors is telisotuzumab vedotin (MMAE-ADC targeting c-Met) combined with nivolumab, which was evaluated in a phase 1b study for the treatment of non-small cell lung cancer (NSCLC) [206]. However, the combination of telisotuzumab vedotin and nivolumab in NSCLC patients showed the least benefit than either telisotuzumab vedotin or nivolumab monotherapy. The overall response rate for the combination therapy was 7.4%, which is relatively lower than reported in nivolumab monotherapy (19%) or telisotuzumab vedotin monotherapy (23%). In addition, the occurrence of peripheral neuropathy was still evident, with 10 of the 23 patients without baseline neuropathy developing neuropathy during the study. Therefore, until more data from clinical studies are available, no conclusions can be drawn on the clinical benefit of ADC-IO combinations. This also highlights the complexity of ADC-IO strategies. Whether ADC-IO can enhance (or diminish) antitumor activity would depend on payloads, targets, tumor indications, or dosing regimens (i.e., dose levels and dosing sequence).

Other combinations

Several other combination strategies to potentiate ADC anti-tumor activity have also been proposed. The first approach is combining ADC with a drug that can modulate antigen expression or dynamics on tumor cells, thus sensitizing tumor cells to ADC treatment. For example, cotreatment of an anti-HER2 ADC with an irreversible pan-HER inhibitor (i.e., neratinib) enables enhanced HER2 receptor ubiquitination and internalization of ADCs [207]. The combination of T-DM1 and neratinib improved the efficacy of T-DM1 in preclinical studies and showed favorable responses in patients with metastatic HER2-positive breast cancer [208], though further comparison of this combination to T-DM1 monotherapy efficacy in patients with T-DM1−refractory breast cancer is warranted.

The second strategy is combining two drugs for differential targeting of different tumor populations, aiming to overcome intratumor heterogeneity, which a factor that often leads to treatment failure. The combination of enapotamab vedotin and MAPK pathway inhibitors [i.e., trametinib (MEK inhibitor), vemurafenib and dabrafenib (BRAF inhibitors)] employs this strategy to eliminate heterogeneous melanoma. Enapotamab vedotin is an MMAE-based ADC targeting AXL, a receptor tyrosine kinase frequently overexpressed in different types of cancer, including melanoma [209]. However, the phase 2 trial results that investigated enapotamab vedotin monotherapy in patients with solid tumors did not meet stringent criteria for proof-of-concept, and thus the development of this ADC was discontinued [210,211]. Alternatively, the enapotamab vedotin-based combination therapy could possibly bring some hope to this ADC to treat melanoma. In resistant melanoma, two distinct tumor cell populations would frequently exist, including AXL-high cells resistant to MAPK pathway inhibitors but sensitive to AML-targeted therapies, and AXL-low cells, which are MAPK pathway inhibitor-sensitive [212]. Therefore, cooperatively targeting these two cell populations through ADC-MAPK inhibitors combination may provide benefit for treating the heterogeneous tumors.

More and more rational combination strategies have been proposed and tested in preclinical settings. Apart from concrete rationales, factors such as dosing amount, sequence of administration, time to incorporate the partner drug, and target patient populations should be considered. Most importantly, the effect of second agents on ADC toxicity profiles should always be evaluated.

ADC beyond oncology

The success of ADCs in oncology has attracted interest in expanding the therapeutic use of ADCs to other therapeutic areas. The up-and-coming therapeutic area where the concept of ADC can be put into good use includes infectious diseases, autoimmune diseases, and atherosclerosis [213,214].

Infectious diseases

Infections with *S. aureus* have become a challenge for the infectious disease community due to the emergence and rapid spread of methicillin-resistant *S. aureus* (MRSA), which is resistant to all existing β-lactam antibiotics, including linezolid and daptomycin, and reduced susceptibility to vancomycin [215]. The ADC concept and technology gave rise to antibody-antibiotic conjugate (AAC), in which the anti-cancer drug is replaced by an antibiotic [215]. DSTA4637S is one of the first examples of AAC, which consist of an anti-*S. aureus* THIOMAB-type IgG1 linked to a novel rifamycin-class antibiotic (4-dimethylaminopiperidino-hydroxybenzoxazino rifamycin, dmDNA31) via a protease-cleavable vc-linker with a DAR of 2 [215,216]. DSTA4637S specifically targets the β-N-acetylglucosamine sugar modification of wall teichoic acid (β-WTA), a major cell wall component of *S. aureus*. Upon binding to β-WTA, the ADC-bound bacteria are phagocytosed by phagocytic cells, which serve as intracellular reservoirs for *S. aureus* resistant to conventional antibiotics. After phagocytosis, intracellular cathepsins cleave the vc-linker, releasing the antibiotic dmDNA31 to kill the intracellular bacteria via the mechanism of DNA-dependent RNA polymerase inhibition. DSTA4637S has successfully completed a phase 1 trial in healthy volunteers [113], and has been evaluated in a phase I trial in patients with MRSA bacteremia where DSTA4637S was given in addition to standard-of-care antibiotics [217]. The AACs' ability to facilitate intracellular bacteria elimination is an encouraging aspect for the infectious disease area, which supports its development as a novel therapy for the treatment of MRSA infections.

Immunological diseases

ADC platform has also been applied to autoimmune diseases. Glucocorticoids are widely used to treat autoimmune and chronic inflammatory diseases. However, the adverse effects after long-term treatment remain the main drawbacks of this class of drug. To deliver steroids specifically to the pathogenic cells within sites of inflammation and limit systemic toxicity, scientists have come up with a new approach to conjugate glucocorticoids to a targeted mAb. Efforts have been made to identify potent glucocorticoid payloads with desired glucocorticoid receptor binding affinity and linker-payload design, which is recently discussed in Ref. [218]. A good example is ABBV-3373 ADC, which is composed of an anti-TNFα mAb, adalimumab, conjugated with the glucocorticoid payload [219]. It was found that the transmembrane form of TNFα is frequently expressed on the activated immune cells. Moreover, anti-TNF mAb can bind to transmembrane TNFα followed by endocytosis and lysosomal trafficking [220]. This feature suggests transmembrane TNFα as a potential target to facilitate ADC intracellular processing. Currently, ABBV-3373 has demonstrated clinical efficacy for patients with rheumatoid arthritis in a phase 2a study, and there are plans to move forward the ADC to later clinical development and expand to other immune-mediated diseases [221,222].

As shown in above examples, the current clinical readout of ADCs in infectious disease and autoimmune diseases reinforces the endless potential of ADCs for the treatment of many diseases.

Summary

The maturation of ADCs epitomizes the advances in various research fields (i.e., chemistry, biology, bioanalysis, clinical diagnosis, etc.) and the evolution of novel technologies. However, the "immature" side of the development of ADCs still requires tackling, which can be summarized as narrow therapeutic index. In this book chapter, we first provide a comprehensive review of the discovery and development of ADCs from historical perspectives (Fig. 7.1). The previous experience serves as the cornerstone for the development of next-generation ADCs and, more importantly, can inspire the innovations for ADCs.

In our opinion, the optimization of an ADC to tackle its "narrow therapeutic index" issue is indeed the exercise of how one can strike a balance during the design of each component of an ADC, namely mAb, linker, and payload (Fig. 7.2). For mAb design, one should evaluate: (1) the benefit of high mAb-antigen binding affinity versus the consequence of binding-site-barrier; (2) the enhancement of efficacy via mAb effector function versus non-specific immune cell uptake; (3) PK properties of antibody-based conjugates versus small-molecule drug conjugates; and (4) relationship between target expression levels versus target internalization efficiency and intracellular sorting (i.e., recycling, lysosomal trafficking). For linker design, one should assess: (1) the benefit of bystander killing of cleavable linkers versus preferable safety profiles of a stable non-cleavable linker; (2) the hydrophobicity of an ADC versus DAR and payload selection; and (3) the risk of altered or unexpected toxicities from novel conjugation method versus problems of heterogeneous mixtures from conventional random conjugation. For payload selection, one should weigh: (1) the advantages and disadvantages of bystander effect; (2) the high potency of a payload versus increased off-target toxicity, and (3) considerations of resistance development. Moreover, consideration of enhanced efficacy versus the risk of additional toxicities should be kept in mind with proposed strategies such as ADC combination therapy. Unfortunately, these trade-offs can be case-by-case bases for individual ADCs, and thorough evaluation of these aspects throughout different stages of ADC development is warranted.

One can utilize in vitro and in vivo data generated from dedicated experiments to better understand the mechanisms of ADCs at cellular, tissue, and systemic levels. Comprehensive preclinical data and rigorous analysis of clinical data facilitate the assessment of the pros and cons of ADC during development and optimization. Mathematical modeling approaches should be employed during all stages of ADC development, as they enable quantitative evaluation of the data to make objective conclusions during decision making and provide *a priori* prediction of clinical outcomes for ADCs.

References

[1] K. Strebhardt, A. Ullrich, Paul Ehrlich's magic bullet concept: 100 years of progress, Nat. Rev. Cancer 8 (6) (2008) 473–480.

[2] J. Wang, W.-C. Shen, J.L. Zaro, Antibody-Drug Conjugates: The 21st Century Magic Bullets for Cancer, Springer International Publishing AG, Cham, SWITZERLAND, 2015.

[3] G. Mathe, L.O. Tran Ba, J. Bernard, [Effect on mouse leukemia 1210 of a combination by diazo-reaction of amethopterin and gamma-globulins from hamsters inoculated with such leukemia by heterografts], C. R. Hebd. Seances Acad. Sci. 246 (10) (1958) 1626–1628.

[4] T. Ghose, S.P. Nigam, Antibody as carrier of chlorambucil, Cancer 29 (5) (1972) 1398–1400.

[5] T. Ghose, A. Guclu, J. Tai, Suppression of an AKR lymphoma by antibody and chlorambucil, J. Natl. Cancer Inst. 55 (6) (1975) 1353–1357.

[6] T. Ghose, A.H. Blair, Antibody-linked cytotoxic agents in the treatment of cancer: current status and future Prospects2, J. Natl. Cancer Inst.: J. Natl. Cancer Inst. 61 (3) (1978) 657–676.

[7] C.H. Ford, et al., Localisation and toxicity study of a vindesine-anti-CEA conjugate in patients with advanced cancer, Br. J. Cancer 47 (1) (1983) 35–42.

[8] G. KÖHler, C. Milstein, Continuous cultures of fused cells secreting antibody of predefined specificity, Nature 256 (5517) (1975) 495–497.

[9] A. Beck, et al., Strategies and challenges for the next generation of antibody–drug conjugates, Nat. Rev. Drug Discov. 16 (5) (2017) 315–337.

[10] G.A. Pietersz, K. Krauer, Antibody-targeted drugs for the therapy of cancer, J. Drug Target. 2 (3) (1994) 183–215.

[11] A.W. Tolcher, et al., Randomized phase II study of BR96-doxorubicin conjugate in patients with metastatic breast cancer, J. Clin. Oncol. 17 (2) (1999) 478–484.

[12] C. Peters, S. Brown, Antibody-drug conjugates as novel anti-cancer chemotherapeutics, Biosci. Rep. 35 (4) (2015).

[13] S. Coats, et al., Antibody-drug conjugates: future directions in clinical and translational strategies to improve the therapeutic index, Clin. Cancer Res. 25 (18) (2019) 5441–5448.

[14] S. Sukumaran, et al., Mechanism-based pharmacokinetic/pharmacodynamic model for THIOMAB™ drug conjugates, Pharm. Res. (N. Y.) 32 (6) (2015) 1884–1893.

[15] P. Khongorzul, et al., Antibody-drug conjugates: a comprehensive review, Mol. Cancer Res. 18 (1) (2020) 3–19.

[16] A. Maderna, C.A. Leverett, Recent advances in the development of new auristatins: structural modifications and application in antibody drug conjugates, Mol. Pharm. 12 (6) (2015) 1798–1812.

[17] A. Beck, et al., Cutting-edge mass spectrometry methods for the multi-level structural characterization of antibody-drug conjugates, Expert Rev. Proteomics 13 (2) (2016) 157–183.

[18] I. Garrido-Laguna, et al., First-in-human, phase I study of PF-06647263, an anti-EFNA4 calicheamicin antibody-drug conjugate, in patients with advanced solid tumors, Int. J. Cancer 145 (7) (2019) 1798–1808.

[19] H. Donaghy, Effects of antibody, drug and linker on the preclinical and clinical toxicities of antibody-drug conjugates, mAbs 8 (4) (2016) 659–671.

[20] P.A. Szijj, C. Bahou, V. Chudasama, Minireview: addressing the retro-Michael instability of maleimide bioconjugates, Drug Discov. Today Technol. 30 (2018) 27–34.

[21] N. Joubert, et al., Antibody-drug conjugates: the last decade, Pharmaceuticals 13 (9) (2020).

[22] R.G.E. Coumans, et al., A platform for the generation of site-specific antibody-drug conjugates that allows for selective reduction of engineered cysteines, Bioconjugate Chem. 31 (9) (2020) 2136–2146.

[23] S. Ponziani, et al., Antibody-drug conjugates: the new frontier of chemotherapy, Int. J. Mol. Sci. 21 (15) (2020) 5510.

[24] M.L. Miller, et al., A new class of antibody-drug conjugates with potent DNA alkylating activity, Mol. Cancer Therapeut. 15 (8) (2016) 1870–1878.

[25] R.V. Chari, M.L. Miller, W.C. Widdison, Antibody-drug conjugates: an emerging concept in cancer therapy, Angew Chem. Int. Ed. Engl. 53 (15) (2014) 3796–3827.

[26] S. Panowski, et al., Site-specific antibody drug conjugates for cancer therapy, mAbs 6 (1) (2014) 34–45.

[27] Q. Zhou, Site-specific antibody conjugation for ADC and beyond, Biomedicines 5 (4) (2017) 64.

[28] A.F. Herrera, et al., Anti-CD79B antibody-drug conjugate DCDS0780A in patients with B-cell non-hodgkin lymphoma: phase 1 dose-escalation study, Clin. Cancer Res. 28 (7) (2022) 1294−1301, https://doi.org/10.1158/1078-0432.Ccr-21-3261.

[29] T. Nakada, et al., The latest research and development into the antibody-drug conjugate, [fam-] trastuzumab deruxtecan (DS-8201a), for HER2 cancer therapy, Chem. Pharm. Bull. (Tokyo) 67 (3) (2019) 173−185.

[30] J.T.W. Tong, et al., An insight into FDA approved antibody-drug conjugates for cancer therapy, Molecules 26 (19) (2021).

[31] Y.-J. Wang, et al., Marine antibody-drug conjugates: design strategies and research progress, Mar. Drugs 15 (1) (2017) 18.

[32] U. Hafeez, et al., Antibody−drug conjugates for cancer therapy, Molecules 25 (20) (2020).

[33] A.V. Kamath, S. Iyer, Preclinical pharmacokinetic considerations for the development of antibody drug conjugates, Pharm. Res. (N. Y.) 32 (11) (2015) 3470−3479.

[34] R. Sheyi, B.G. de la Torre, F. Albericio, Linkers: an assurance for controlled delivery of antibody-drug conjugate, Pharmaceutics 14 (2) (2022).

[35] J.D. Bargh, et al., Cleavable linkers in antibody-drug conjugates, Chem. Soc. Rev. 48 (16) (2019) 4361−4374.

[36] P.D. Senter, Potent antibody drug conjugates for cancer therapy, Curr. Opin. Chem. Biol. 13 (3) (2009) 235−244.

[37] H. Liu, et al., Metabolism of bioconjugate therapeutics: why, when, and how? Drug Metabol. Rev. 52 (1) (2020) 66−124.

[38] G. Saito, J.A. Swanson, K.-D. Lee, Drug delivery strategy utilizing conjugation via reversible disulfide linkages: role and site of cellular reducing activities, Adv. Drug Deliv. Rev. 55 (2) (2003) 199−215.

[39] B.A. Kellogg, et al., Disulfide-linked antibody−maytansinoid conjugates: optimization of in vivo activity by varying the steric hindrance at carbon atoms adjacent to the disulfide linkage, Bioconjugate Chem. 22 (4) (2011) 717−727.

[40] M.A. Socinski, et al., Phase 1/2 study of the CD56-targeting antibody-drug conjugate lorvotuzumab mertansine (IMGN901) in combination with carboplatin/etoposide in small-cell lung cancer patients with extensive-stage disease, Clin. Lung Cancer 18 (1) (2017) 68−76.e2.

[41] K. Tsuchikama, Z. An, Antibody-drug conjugates: recent advances in conjugation and linker chemistries, Protein Cell 9 (1) (2018) 33−46.

[42] N. Endo, et al., Target-selective cytotoxicity of methotrexate conjugated with monoclonal anti-MM46 antibody, Cancer Immunol. Immunother. 25 (1) (1987) 1−6.

[43] F. Dosio, P. Brusa, L. Cattel, Immunotoxins and anticancer drug conjugate assemblies: the role of the linkage between components, Toxins 3 (7) (2011) 848−883.

[44] J.M. Lambert, R.V.J. Chari, Ado-trastuzumab emtansine (T-DM1): an antibody−drug conjugate (ADC) for HER2-positive breast cancer, J. Med. Chem. 57 (16) (2014) 6949−6964.

[45] G.D. Lewis Phillips, et al., Targeting HER2-positive breast cancer with trastuzumab-DM1, an antibody-cytotoxic drug conjugate, Cancer Res. 68 (22) (2008) 9280−9290.

[46] H.K. Erickson, et al., The effect of different linkers on target cell catabolism and pharmacokinetics/pharmacodynamics of trastuzumab maytansinoid conjugates, Mol. Cancer Therapeut. 11 (5) (2012) 1133−1142.

[47] H.K. Erickson, J.M. Lambert, ADME of antibody-maytansinoid conjugates, AAPS J. 14 (4) (2012) 799−805.

[48] J. Dott, B. Abila, J.U. Wuerthner, Current trends in the clinical development of antibody-drug conjugates in oncology, Pharm. Med. 32 (4) (2018) 259−273.

[49] G.P. Adams, et al., High affinity restricts the localization and tumor penetration of single-chain fv antibody molecules, Cancer Res. 61 (12) (2001) 4750−4755.

[50] B.M. Bordeau, Y. Yang, J.P. Balthasar, Transient competitive inhibition bypasses the binding site barrier to improve tumor penetration of trastuzumab and enhance T-DM1 efficacy, Cancer Res. 81 (15) (2021) 4145−4154.

[51] R.M. Hoffmann, et al., Antibody structure and engineering considerations for the design and function of Antibody Drug Conjugates (ADCs), OncoImmunology 7 (3) (2018) e1395127.

[52] U. Hafeez, H.K. Gan, A.M. Scott, Monoclonal antibodies as immunomodulatory therapy against cancer and autoimmune diseases, Curr. Opin. Pharmacol. 41 (2018) 114−121.

[53] J.G. Salfeld, Isotype selection in antibody engineering, Nat. Biotechnol. 25 (12) (2007) 1369−1372.

[54] L. L'Italien, et al., Mechanistic insights of an immunological adverse event induced by an anti-KIT antibody drug conjugate and mitigation strategies, Clin. Cancer Res. 24 (14) (2018) 3465−3474.

[55] J.Z. Drago, S. Modi, S. Chandarlapaty, Unlocking the potential of antibody−drug conjugates for cancer therapy, Nat. Rev. Clin. Oncol. 18 (6) (2021) 327−344.

[56] K.J. Hamblett, et al., SLC46A3 is required to transport catabolites of noncleavable antibody maytansine conjugates from the lysosome to the cytoplasm, Cancer Res. 75 (24) (2015) 5329−5340.

[57] F.W. Hunter, et al., Mechanisms of resistance to trastuzumab emtansine (T-DM1) in HER2-positive breast cancer, Br. J. Cancer 122 (5) (2020) 603−612.

[58] K. Kinneer, et al., SLC46A3 as a potential predictive biomarker for antibody−drug conjugates bearing noncleavable linked maytansinoid and pyrrolobenzodiazepine warheads, Clin. Cancer Res. 24 (24) (2018) 6570−6582.

[59] J.R. McCombs, S.C. Owen, Antibody drug conjugates: design and selection of linker, payload and conjugation chemistry, AAPS J. 17 (2) (2015) 339−351.

[60] Z. Su, et al., Antibody−drug conjugates: recent advances in linker chemistry, Acta Pharm. Sin. B 11 (12) (2021) 3889−3907.

[61] N.G. Caculitan, et al., Cathepsin B is dispensable for cellular processing of cathepsin B-cleavable antibody−drug conjugates, Cancer Res. 77 (24) (2017) 7027−7037.

[62] P.L. Salomon, et al., Optimizing lysosomal activation of antibody–drug conjugates (ADCs) by incorporation of novel cleavable dipeptide linkers, Mol. Pharm. 16 (12) (2019) 4817–4825.

[63] J.D. Bargh, et al., Cleavable linkers in antibody–drug conjugates, Chem. Soc. Rev. 48 (16) (2019) 4361–4374.

[64] B. Wei, et al., Discovery of peptidomimetic antibody–drug conjugate linkers with enhanced protease specificity, J. Med. Chem. 61 (3) (2018) 989–1000.

[65] R.D. Jones, et al., Carboxylesterases are uniquely expressed among tissues and regulated by nuclear hormone receptors in the mouse, Drug Metab. Dispos.: The Biological Fate of Chemicals 41 (1) (2013) 40–49.

[66] S. Oda, et al., A comprehensive review of UDP-glucuronosyltransferase and esterases for drug development, Drug Metabol. Pharmacokinet. 30 (1) (2015) 30–51.

[67] M. Dorywalska, et al., Molecular basis of valine-citrulline-PABC linker instability in site-specific ADCs and its mitigation by linker design, Mol. Cancer Therapeut. 15 (5) (2016) 958–970.

[68] Y. Anami, et al., Glutamic acid–valine–citrulline linkers ensure stability and efficacy of antibody–drug conjugates in mice, Nat. Commun. 9 (1) (2018) 2512.

[69] N. Chen, et al., Driving CARs on the uneven road of antigen heterogeneity in solid tumors, Curr. Opin. Immunol. 51 (2018) 103–110.

[70] N.L. Tumey, S. Han, ADME considerations for the development of biopharmaceutical conjugates using cleavable linkers, Curr. Top. Med. Chem. 17 (32) (2017) 3444–3462.

[71] R.P. Lyon, et al., Reducing hydrophobicity of homogeneous antibody-drug conjugates improves pharmacokinetics and therapeutic index, Nat. Biotechnol. 33 (7) (2015) 733–735.

[72] K.J. Hamblett, et al., Effects of drug loading on the antitumor activity of a monoclonal antibody drug conjugate, Clin. Cancer Res. 10 (20) (2004) 7063–7070.

[73] L.N. Tumey, et al., Site selection: a case study in the identification of optimal cysteine engineered antibody drug conjugates, AAPS J. 19 (4) (2017) 1123–1135.

[74] Y. Jin, et al., Stepping forward in antibody-drug conjugate development, Pharmacol. Ther. 229 (2022) 107917.

[75] H. Tang, et al., The analysis of key factors related to ADCs structural design, Front. Pharmacol. 10 (2019) 373.

[76] Y. Wang, et al., Antibody-drug conjugate using ionized cys-linker-MMAE as the potent payload shows optimal therapeutic safety, Cancers 12 (3) (2020).

[77] A.W. Tolcher, et al., Cantuzumab mertansine, a maytansinoid immunoconjugate directed to the CanAg antigen: a phase I, pharmacokinetic, and biologic correlative study, J. Clin. Oncol. 21 (2) (2003) 211–222.

[78] S. García-Alonso, A. Ocaña, A. Pandiella, Resistance to antibody-drug conjugates, Cancer Res. 78 (9) (2018) 2159–2165.

[79] E. Díaz-Rodríguez, et al., Novel ADCs and strategies to overcome resistance to anti-HER2 ADCs, Cancers 14 (1) (2021) 154.

[80] L. Shefet-Carasso, I. Benhar, Antibody-targeted drugs and drug resistance—challenges and solutions, Drug Resist. Updates 18 (2015) 36–46.

[81] T. Matsumoto, et al., Importance of inducible multidrug resistance 1 expression in HL-60 cells resistant to gemtuzumab ozogamicin, Leuk. Lymphoma 53 (7) (2012) 1399–1405.

[82] A. Takeshita, et al., CMC-544 (inotuzumab ozogamicin) shows less effect on multidrug resistant cells: analyses in cell lines and cells from patients with B-cell chronic lymphocytic leukaemia and lymphoma, Br. J. Haematol. 146 (1) (2009) 34–43.

[83] R.B. Walter, et al., CD33 expression and P-glycoprotein–mediated drug efflux inversely correlate and predict clinical outcome in patients with acute myeloid leukemia treated with gemtuzumab ozogamicin monotherapy, Blood 109 (10) (2007) 4168–4170.

[84] R.B. Walter, et al., Multidrug resistance protein attenuates gemtuzumab ozogamicin–induced cytotoxicity in acute myeloid leukemia cells, Blood 102 (4) (2003) 1466–1473.

[85] M. Cianfriglia, et al., Multidrug transporter proteins and cellular factors involved in free and mAb linked calicheamicin-gamma1 (gentuzumab ozogamicin, GO) resistance and in the selection of GO resistant variants of the HL60 AML cell line, Int. J. Oncol. 36 (6) (2010) 1513–1520.

[86] R. Chen, et al., CD30 downregulation, MMAE resistance, and MDR1 upregulation are all associated with resistance to brentuximab vedotin, Mol. Cancer Therapeut. 14 (6) (2015) 1376–1384.

[87] R. Chen, et al., Inhibition of MDR1 overcomes resistance to brentuximab vedotin in Hodgkin lymphoma, Clin. Cancer Res. 26 (5) (2020) 1034–1044.

[88] S.-F. Yu, et al., A novel anti-CD22 anthracycline-based antibody–drug conjugate (ADC) that overcomes resistance to auristatin-based ADCs, Clin. Cancer Res. 21 (14) (2015) 3298–3306.

[89] F. Loganzo, et al., Tumor cells chronically treated with a trastuzumab–maytansinoid antibody–drug conjugate develop varied resistance mechanisms but respond to alternate treatments, Mol. Cancer Therapeut. 14 (4) (2015) 952–963.

[90] N. Takegawa, et al., DS-8201a, a new HER2-targeting antibody–drug conjugate incorporating a novel DNA topoisomerase I inhibitor, overcomes HER2-positive gastric cancer T-DM1 resistance, Int. J. Cancer 141 (8) (2017) 1682–1689.

[91] F.W. Hunter, et al., Mechanisms of resistance to trastuzumab emtansine (T-DM1) in HER2-positive breast cancer, Br. J. Cancer 122 (5) (2020) 603–612.

[92] S. Modi, et al., Trastuzumab deruxtecan in previously treated HER2-positive breast cancer, N. Engl. J. Med. 382 (7) (2020) 610–621.

[93] K. Tamura, et al., Trastuzumab deruxtecan (DS-8201a) in patients with advanced HER2-positive breast cancer previously treated with trastuzumab emtansine: a dose-expansion, phase 1 study, Lancet Oncol. 20 (6) (2019) 816–826.

[94] A. Ocaña, E. Amir, A. Pandiella, HER2 heterogeneity and resistance to anti-HER2 antibody-drug conjugates, Breast Cancer Res. 22 (1) (2020) 15.

[95] M.P. Deonarain, Q. Xue, Tackling solid tumour therapy with small-format drug conjugates, Antib. Ther. 3 (4) (2020) 237–245.

[96] S. Jin, et al., Emerging new therapeutic antibody derivatives for cancer treatment, Signal Transduct. Targeted Ther. 7 (1) (2022) 39.

[97] M.P. Deonarain, et al., Small-format drug conjugates: a viable alternative to ADCs for solid tumours? Antibodies 7 (2) (2018).

[98] M.P. Deonarain, G. Yahioglu, Current strategies for the discovery and bioconjugation of smaller, targetable drug conjugates tailored for solid tumor therapy, Expet Opin. Drug Discov. 16 (6) (2021) 613−624.

[99] K.M. Kim, et al., Anti-CD30 diabody-drug conjugates with potent antitumor activity, Mol. Cancer Therapeut. 7 (8) (2008) 2486−2497.

[100] G. Bennett, et al., MMAE delivery using the bicycle toxin conjugate BT5528, Mol. Cancer Therapeut. 19 (7) (2020) 1385−1394.

[101] J.C. Bendell, et al., BT5528-100 phase I/II study of the safety, pharmacokinetics, and preliminary clinical activity of BT5528 in patients with advanced malignancies associated with EphA2 expression, J. Clin. Oncol. 38 (15_Suppl. l) (2020). TPS3655-TPS3655.

[102] M. McKean, et al., Association of combined phase I/II study of a novel bicyclic peptide and MMAE conjugate BT8009 in patients with advanced malignancies with Nectin-4 expression, J. Clin. Oncol. 39 (15_Suppl. l) (2021). TPS2668-TPS2668.

[103] H. Harrison, et al., Abstract 5144: BT1718, a novel bicyclic peptide-maytansinoid conjugate targeting MT1-MMP for the treatment of solid tumors: design of bicyclic peptide and linker selection, Cancer Res. 77 (13_Suppl. ment) (2017), 5144-5144.

[104] N. Cook, et al., 464P - pharmacokinetic (PK) assessment of BT1718: a phase I/II a study of BT1718, a first in class bicycle toxin conjugate (BTC), in patients (pts) with advanced solid tumours, Ann. Oncol. 30 (2019) v174.

[105] K. Yamada, Y. Ito, Recent chemical approaches for site-specific conjugation of native antibodies: technologies toward next-generation antibody−drug conjugates, Chembiochem 20 (21) (2019) 2729−2737.

[106] A. Sadiki, et al., Site-specific conjugation of native antibody, Antib. Ther. 3 (4) (2020) 271−284.

[107] P. Agarwal, C.R. Bertozzi, Site-specific antibody-drug conjugates: the nexus of bioorthogonal chemistry, protein engineering, and drug development, Bioconjugate Chem. 26 (2) (2015) 176−192.

[108] J.R. Junutula, et al., Site-specific conjugation of a cytotoxic drug to an antibody improves the therapeutic index, Nat. Biotechnol. 26 (8) (2008) 925−932.

[109] R. Ohri, et al., High-throughput cysteine scanning to identify stable antibody conjugation sites for maleimide- and disulfide-based linkers, Bioconjugate Chem. 29 (2) (2018) 473−485.

[110] J.R. Junutula, et al., Engineered thio-trastuzumab-DM1 conjugate with an improved therapeutic index to target human epidermal growth factor receptor 2-positive breast cancer, Clin. Cancer Res. 16 (19) (2010) 4769−4778.

[111] S.C. Jeffrey, et al., A potent anti-CD70 antibody-drug conjugate combining a dimeric pyrrolobenzodiazepine drug with site-specific conjugation technology, Bioconjugate Chem. 24 (7) (2013) 1256−1263.

[112] J. Liu, et al., An open-label phase I dose-escalation study of the safety and pharmacokinetics of DMUC4064A in patients with platinum-resistant ovarian cancer, Gynecol. Oncol. 163 (3) (2021) 473−480.

[113] M. Peck, et al., A phase 1, randomized, single-ascending-dose study to investigate the safety, tolerability, and pharmacokinetics of DSTA4637S, an anti-Staphylococcus aureus thiomab antibody-antibiotic conjugate, in healthy volunteers, Antimicrob. Agents Chemother. 63 (6) (2019) 1−12, https://doi.org/10.1128/aac.02588-18. PMC6535527.

[114] R. van Geel, et al., Chemoenzymatic conjugation of toxic payloads to the globally conserved N-glycan of native mAbs provides homogeneous and highly efficacious antibody-drug conjugates, Bioconjugate Chem. 26 (11) (2015) 2233−2242.

[115] Safety, Tolerability, Pharmacokinetics, and Antitumor Study of ADCT-601 to Treat Advanced Solid Tumors. Available from: https://ClinicalTrials.gov/show/NCT03700294.

[116] First-in-Human Study of XMT-1592 in Patients With Ovarian Cancer and NSCLC Likely to Express NaPi2b. Available from: https://ClinicalTrials.gov/show/NCT04396340.

[117] Y. Anami, K. Tsuchikama, Transglutaminase-mediated conjugations, Methods Mol. Biol. 2078 (2020) 71−82.

[118] G.T. King, et al., A phase 1, dose-escalation study of PF-06664178, an anti-Trop-2/Aur0101 antibody-drug conjugate in patients with advanced or metastatic solid tumors, Invest. N. Drugs 36 (5) (2018) 836−847.

[119] D. Jackson, et al., In vitro and in vivo evaluation of cysteine and site specific conjugated herceptin antibody-drug conjugates, PLoS One 9 (1) (2014) e83865.

[120] X. Li, et al., Stable and potent selenomab-drug conjugates, Cell Chem. Biol. 24 (4) (2017) 433−442.e6.

[121] J. Mantaj, et al., From anthramycin to pyrrolobenzodiazepine (PBD)-containing antibody−drug conjugates (ADCs), Angew. Chem. Int. Ed. 56 (2) (2017) 462−488.

[122] H. Saber, et al., An FDA oncology analysis of toxicities associated with PBD-containing antibody-drug conjugates, Regul. Toxicol. Pharmacol. 107 (2019) 104429.

[123] J.A. Hartley, Antibody-drug conjugates (ADCs) delivering pyrrolobenzodiazepine (PBD) dimers for cancer therapy, Expet Opin. Biol. Ther. 21 (7) (2021) 931−943.

[124] A. Pahl, C. Lutz, T. Hechler, Amanitins and their development as a payload for antibody-drug conjugates, Drug Discov. Today Technol. 30 (2018) 85−89.

[125] V. Figueroa-Vazquez, et al., HDP-101, an anti-BCMA antibody-drug conjugate, safely delivers amanitin to induce cell death in proliferating and resting multiple myeloma cells, Mol. Cancer Therapeut. 20 (2) (2021) 367−378.

[126] Study to Assess Safety of HDP-101 in Patients With Relapsed Refractory Multiple Myeloma. Available from: https://ClinicalTrials.gov/show/NCT04879043.

[127] S. Puthenveetil, et al., Natural product splicing inhibitors: a new class of antibody-drug conjugate (ADC) payloads, Bioconjugate Chem. 27 (8) (2016) 1880−1888.

[128] S. Adams, Toll-like receptor agonists in cancer therapy, Immunotherapy 1 (6) (2009) 949–964.

[129] A. Amouzegar, et al., STING agonists as cancer therapeutics, Cancers 13 (11) (2021) 2695.

[130] S.E. Ackerman, et al., Immune-stimulating antibody conjugates elicit robust myeloid activation and durable antitumor immunity, Nat. Cancer 2 (1) (2021) 18–33.

[131] M. Sharma, et al., Preliminary results from a phase 1/2 study of BDC-1001, a novel HER2 targeting TLR7/8 immune-stimulating antibody conjugate (ISAC), in patients (pts) with advanced HER2-expressing solid tumors, J. Clin. Oncol. 39 (15_Suppl. l) (2021), 2549-2549.

[132] A Safety and Activity Study of SBT6050 in Combination With Other HER2-directed Therapies for HER2-positive Cancers. Available from: https://ClinicalTrials.gov/show/NCT05091528.

[133] A Study of SBT6050 Alone and in Combination With PD-1 Inhibitors in Subjects With Advanced HER2 Expressing Solid Tumors. Available from: https://ClinicalTrials.gov/show/NCT04460456.

[134] R.A. Bukhalid, et al., Abstract 6706: systemic administration of STING agonist antibody-drug conjugates elicit potent anti-tumor immune responses with minimal induction of circulating cytokines, Cancer Res. 80 (16_Suppl. ment) (2020), 6706-6706.

[135] T. Riss, A. Niles, R. Moravec, et al., Cytotoxicity assays: in vitro methods to measure dead cells, Internet, in: S. Markossian, A. Grossman, K. Brimacombe, et al. (Eds.), Assay Guidance Manual, Eli Lilly & Company and the National Center for Advancing Translational Sciences; 2004, Bethesda (MD), May 1, 2019. Available from: https://www.ncbi.nlm.nih.gov/books/NBK540958/.

[136] T.L. Riss, et al., Cell viability assays, in: S. Markossian, et al. (Eds.), Assay Guidance Manual, Eli Lilly & Company and the National Center for Advancing Translational Sciences, Bethesda (MD, 2004.

[137] S. Wu, D.K. Shah, Determination of ADC cytotoxicity in immortalized human cell lines, in: L.N. Tumey (Ed.), Antibody-Drug Conjugates: Methods and Protocols, Springer US, New York, NY, 2020, pp. 329–340.

[138] A.P. Singh, S. Sharma, D.K. Shah, Quantitative characterization of in vitro bystander effect of antibody drug conjugates, J. Pharmacokinet. Pharmacodyn. 43 (6) (2016) 567–582.

[139] N.M. Okeley, et al., Intracellular activation of SGN-35, a potent anti-CD30 antibody-drug conjugate, Clin. Cancer Res. 16 (3) (2010) 888–897.

[140] C. Szot, et al., Tumor stroma-targeted antibody-drug conjugate triggers localized anticancer drug release, J. Clin. Invest. 128 (7) (2018) 2927–2943.

[141] A.P. Singh, D.K. Shah, A "dual" cell-level systems PK-PD model to characterize the bystander effect of ADC, J. Pharm. Sci. 108 (7) (2019) 2465–2475.

[142] S. Sharma, et al., Evaluation of quantitative relationship between target expression and antibody-drug conjugate exposure inside cancer cells, Drug Metab. Dispos. 48 (5) (2020) 368–377.

[143] D. Li, et al., DCDT2980S, an anti-CD22-monomethyl auristatin E antibody–drug conjugate, is a potential treatment for non-hodgkin lymphoma, Mol. Cancer Therapeut. 12 (7) (2013) 1255–1265.

[144] D. Bussing, et al., Quantitative evaluation of the effect of antigen expression level on antibody-drug conjugate exposure in solid tumor, AAPS J. 23 (3) (2021) 56.

[145] A.P. Singh, D.K. Shah, Measurement and mathematical characterization of cell-level pharmacokinetics of antibody-drug conjugates: a case study with trastuzumab-vc-MMAE, Drug Metab. Dispos. 45 (11) (2017) 1120–1132.

[146] D.K. Shah, et al., A priori prediction of tumor payload concentrations: preclinical case study with an auristatin-based anti-5T4 antibody-drug conjugate, AAPS J. 16 (3) (2014) 452–463.

[147] D.K. Shah, N. Haddish-Berhane, A. Betts, Bench to bedside translation of antibody drug conjugates using a multiscale mechanistic PK/PD model: a case study with brentuximab-vedotin, J. Pharmacokinet. Pharmacodyn. 39 (6) (2012) 643–659.

[148] M. Hammood, A.W. Craig, J.V. Leyton, Impact of endocytosis mechanisms for the receptors targeted by the currently approved antibody-drug conjugates (ADCs)-A necessity for future ADC research and development, Pharmaceuticals 14 (7) (2021) 674.

[149] C.D. Austin, et al., Endocytosis and sorting of ErbB2 and the site of action of cancer therapeutics trastuzumab and geldanamycin, Mol. Biol. Cell 15 (12) (2004) 5268–5282.

[150] A. Sorkin, L.K. Goh, Endocytosis and intracellular trafficking of ErbBs, Exp. Cell Res. 314 (17) (2008) 3093–3106.

[151] J.Y. Li, et al., A biparatopic HER2-targeting antibody-drug conjugate induces tumor regression in primary models refractory to or ineligible for HER2-targeted therapy, Cancer Cell 29 (1) (2016) 117–129.

[152] J. Andreev, et al., Bispecific antibodies and antibody-drug conjugates (ADCs) bridging HER2 and prolactin receptor improve efficacy of HER2 ADCs, Mol. Cancer Therapeut. 16 (4) (2017) 681–693.

[153] S. Kaur, et al., Bioanalytical assay strategies for the development of antibody-drug conjugate biotherapeutics, Bioanalysis 5 (2) (2013) 201–226.

[154] H.P. Chang, D.K. Shah, Determination of ADC concentration by ligand-binding assays, Methods Mol. Biol. 2078 (2020) 361–369.

[155] D.K. Shah, et al., Key bioanalytical measurements for antibody–drug conjugate development: PK/PD modelers' perspective, Bioanalysis 5 (9) (2013) 989–992.

[156] J.-P. Stephan, et al., Anti-CD22-MCC-DM1 and MC-MMAF conjugates: impact of assay format on pharmacokinetic parameters determination, Bioconjugate Chem. 19 (8) (2008) 1673–1683.

[157] B. Gorovits, et al., Bioanalysis of antibody-drug conjugates: American association of pharmaceutical scientists antibody-drug conjugate working group position paper, Bioanalysis 5 (9) (2013) 997–1006.

[158] X. Zhu, et al., Current LC-MS-based strategies for characterization and quantification of antibody-drug conjugates, J. Pharm. Anal. 10 (3) (2020) 209–220.

[159] Y. Liu, et al., LC-MS/MS method for the simultaneous determination of Lys-MCC-DM1, MCC-DM1 and DM1 as potential intracellular catabolites of the antibody-drug conjugate trastuzumab emtansine (T-DM1), J. Pharm. Biomed. Anal. 137 (2017) 170–177.

[160] O.M. Saad, et al., Bioanalytical approaches for characterizing catabolism of antibody-drug conjugates, Bioanalysis 7 (13) (2015) 1583–1604.

[161] R. Dere, et al., PK assays for antibody-drug conjugates: case study with ado-trastuzumab emtansine, Bioanalysis 5 (9) (2013) 1025–1040.

[162] Y. Tang, et al., Real-time analysis on drug-antibody ratio of antibody-drug conjugates for synthesis, process optimization, and quality control, Sci. Rep. 7 (1) (2017) 7763.

[163] H.P. Chang, Y.K. Cheung, D.K. Shah, Whole-body pharmacokinetics and physiologically based pharmacokinetic model for monomethyl auristatin E (MMAE), J. Clin. Med. 10 (6) (2021).

[164] J. Wang, et al., Exposure–response relationship of T-DM1: insight into dose optimization for patients with HER2-positive metastatic breast cancer, Clin. Pharmacol. Therapeut. 95 (5) (2014) 558–564.

[165] H.-P. Chang, Z. Li, D.K. Shah, Development of a physiologically-based pharmacokinetic model for whole-body disposition of MMAE containing antibody-drug conjugate in mice, Pharmaceut. Res. 39 (1) (2022) 1–24.

[166] C. Li, et al., Clinical pharmacology of vc-MMAE antibody-drug conjugates in cancer patients: learning from eight first-in-human Phase 1 studies, mAbs 12 (1) (2020) 1699768.

[167] S. Dong, et al., Predictive simulations in preclinical oncology to guide the translation of biologics, Front. Pharmacol. 13 (2022).

[168] C. Cilliers, et al., Improved tumor penetration and single-cell targeting of antibody–drug conjugates increases anticancer efficacy and host survival, Cancer Res. 78 (3) (2018) 758–768.

[169] G. Lu, et al., Co-administered antibody improves penetration of antibody–dye conjugate into human cancers with implications for antibody–drug conjugates, Nat. Commun. 11 (1) (2020) 5667.

[170] A.P. Singh, et al., Antibody coadministration as a strategy to overcome binding-site barrier for ADCs: a quantitative investigation, AAPS J. 22 (2) (2020) 28.

[171] R. Montes de Oca, et al., Belantamab mafodotin (GSK2857916) drives immunogenic cell death and immune-mediated antitumor responses in vivo, Mol. Cancer Therapeut. 20 (10) (2021) 1941–1955.

[172] H. Zhao, et al., Inhibition of megakaryocyte differentiation by antibody–drug conjugates (ADCs) is mediated by macropinocytosis: implications for ADC-induced thrombocytopenia, Mol. Cancer Therapeut. 16 (9) (2017) 1877.

[173] D. Leung, et al., Antibody conjugates-recent advances and future innovations, Antibodies 9 (1) (2020).

[174] T.M. Cardillo, et al., Sacituzumab govitecan (IMMU-132), an anti-trop-2/SN-38 antibody–drug conjugate: characterization and efficacy in pancreatic, gastric, and other cancers, Bioconjugate Chem. 26 (5) (2015) 919–931.

[175] S.E. Gould, M.R. Junttila, F.J. de Sauvage, Translational value of mouse models in oncology drug development, Nat. Med. 21 (5) (2015) 431–439.

[176] G. Dranoff, Experimental mouse tumour models: what can be learnt about human cancer immunology? Nat. Rev. Immunol. 12 (1) (2011) 61–66.

[177] T.T. Junttila, et al., Antitumor efficacy of a bispecific antibody that targets HER2 and activates T cells, Cancer Res. 74 (19) (2014) 5561–5571.

[178] S.I.S. Mosely, et al., Rational selection of syngeneic preclinical tumor models for immunotherapeutic drug discovery, Cancer Immunol. Res. 5 (1) (2017) 29.

[179] S. Wang, et al., Effective antibody therapy induces host-protective antitumor immunity that is augmented by TLR4 agonist treatment, Cancer Immunol. Immunother. 61 (1) (2012) 49–61.

[180] J.A. Lansita, et al., An introduction to the regulatory and nonclinical aspects of the nonclinical development of antibody drug conjugates, Pharm. Res. (N. Y.) 32 (11) (2015) 3584–3592.

[181] M.J. Hinrichs, R. Dixit, Antibody drug conjugates: nonclinical safety considerations, AAPS J. 17 (5) (2015) 1055–1064.

[182] J.E. Fisher Jr., Considerations for the nonclinical safety evaluation of antibody-drug conjugates, Antibodies 10 (2) (2021).

[183] G.G. Bornstein, Antibody drug conjugates: preclinical considerations, AAPS J. 17 (3) (2015) 525–534.

[184] N.J. Stagg, et al., Peripheral neuropathy with microtubule inhibitor containing antibody drug conjugates: challenges and perspectives in translatability from nonclinical toxicology studies to the clinic, Regul. Toxicol. Pharmacol. 82 (2016) 1–13.

[185] M.J.M. Hinrichs, et al., Fractionated dosing improves preclinical therapeutic index of pyrrolobenzodiazepine-containing antibody drug conjugates, Clin. Cancer Res. 23 (19) (2017) 5858–5868.

[186] S.N. Liu, C. Li, Clinical pharmacology strategies in supporting drug development and approval of antibody-drug conjugates in oncology, Cancer Chemother. Pharmacol. 87 (6) (2021) 743–765.

[187] Research, U.S.F.a.D.A.C.f.D.E.a., Clinical Pharmacology Considerations for Antibody-Drug Conjugates, Guidance for Industry, 2022.

[188] D.W. Meyer, et al., An in vitro assay using cultured kupffer cells can predict the impact of drug conjugation on in vivo antibody pharmacokinetics, Mol. Pharm. 17 (3) (2020) 802–809.

[189] D.K. Shah, N. Haddish-Berhane, A. Betts, Bench to bedside translation of antibody drug conjugates using a multiscale mechanistic PK/PD model: a case study with brentuximab-vedotin, J. Pharmacokinet. Pharmacodyn. 39 (6) (2012) 643–659.

[190] A. Khot, et al., Development of a translational physiologically based pharmacokinetic model for antibody-drug conjugates: a case study with T-DM1, AAPS J. 19 (6) (2017) 1715–1734.

[191] U.S. Food and Drug Administration, Clinical Pharmacology Considerations for Antibody-Drug Conjugates Guidance for Industry, 2022.

[192] J. Lang, et al., Association of serum albumin levels with kidney function decline and incident chronic kidney disease in elders, Nephrol. Dial. Transplant. 33 (6) (2018) 986–992.

[193] S.K. Sharma, et al., Fc-mediated anomalous biodistribution of therapeutic antibodies in immunodeficient mouse models, Cancer Res. 78 (7) (2018) 1820–1832.

[194] A.P. Singh, Y.G. Shin, D.K. Shah, Application of pharmacokinetic-pharmacodynamic modeling and simulation for antibody-drug conjugate development, Pharmaceut. Res. 32 (11) (2015) 3508–3525.

[195] A. Singh, D. Shah, Utility of PK-PD Modeling and Simulation to Improve Decision Making for Antibody-Drug Conjugate Development, 2018, pp. 73–97.

[196] D.K. Shah, et al., Establishing in vitro-in vivo correlation for antibody drug conjugate efficacy: a PK/PD modeling approach, J. Pharmacokinet. Pharmacodyn. 45 (2) (2018) 339–349.

[197] B. Gorovits, C. Krinos-Fiorotti, Proposed mechanism of off-target toxicity for antibody-drug conjugates driven by mannose receptor uptake, Cancer Immunol. Immunother. 62 (2) (2013) 217–223.

[198] Y. Anami, et al., Glutamic acid-valine-citrulline linkers ensure stability and efficacy of antibody-drug conjugates in mice, Nat. Commun. 9 (1) (2018) 2512.

[199] R.D. Jones, et al., Carboxylesterases are uniquely expressed among tissues and regulated by nuclear hormone receptors in the mouse, Drug Metab. Dispos. 41 (1) (2013) 40–49.

[200] C. Wei, et al., Where did the linker-payload go? A quantitative investigation on the destination of the released linker-payload from an antibody-drug conjugate with a maleimide linker in plasma, Anal. Chem. 88 (9) (2016) 4979–4986.

[201] D. Samineni, et al., Physiologically based pharmacokinetic model-informed drug development for polatuzumab vedotin: label for drug-drug interactions without dedicated clinical trials, J. Clin. Pharmacol. 60 (Suppl. 1) (2020) S120–s131.

[202] A. Sancho-Araiz, V. Mangas-Sanjuan, I.F. Trocóniz, The role of mathematical models in immuno-oncology: challenges and future perspectives, Pharmaceutics 13 (7) (2021) 1016.

[203] P. Müller, et al., Combining ADCs with immuno-oncology agents, in: M. Damelin (Ed.), Innovations for Next-Generation Antibody-Drug Conjugates, Springer International Publishing, Cham, 2018, pp. 11–44.

[204] H.P. Gerber, et al., Combining antibody-drug conjugates and immune-mediated cancer therapy: what to expect? Biochem. Pharmacol. 102 (2016) 1–6.

[205] B.D. Cheson, et al., Brentuximab vedotin plus nivolumab as first-line therapy in older or chemotherapy-ineligible patients with Hodgkin lymphoma (ACCRU): a multicentre, single-arm, phase 2 trial, Lancet Haematol. 7 (11) (2020) e808–e815.

[206] D.R. Camidge, et al., A phase 1b study of telisotuzumab vedotin in combination with nivolumab in patients with NSCLC, JTO Clin. Res. Rep. 3 (1) (2022) 100262.

[207] B.T. Li, et al., HER2-Mediated internalization of cytotoxic agents in ERBB2 amplified or mutant lung cancers, Cancer Discov. 10 (5) (2020) 674–687.

[208] J. Abraham, et al., Safety and efficacy of T-DM1 plus neratinib in patients with metastatic HER2-positive breast cancer: NSABP foundation trial FB-10, J. Clin. Oncol. 37 (29) (2019) 2601–2609.

[209] L.A. Koopman, et al., Enapotamab vedotin, an AXL-specific antibody-drug conjugate, shows preclinical antitumor activity in non-small cell lung cancer, JCI Insight 4 (21) (2019) e128199.

[210] S. Ramalingam, et al., OA02.05 first-in-human phase 1/2 trial of anti-AXL antibody–drug conjugate (ADC) enapotamab vedotin (EnaV) in advanced NSCLC, J. Thorac. Oncol. 14 (2019) S209.

[211] Enapotamab Vedotin (HuMax-AXL-ADC) Safety Study in Patients With Solid Tumors. Available from: https://ClinicalTrials.gov/show/NCT02988817.

[212] J. Boshuizen, et al., Cooperative targeting of melanoma heterogeneity with an AXL antibody-drug conjugate and BRAF/MEK inhibitors, Nat. Med. 24 (2) (2018) 203–212.

[213] M.J. McPherson, A.D. Hobson, Pushing the envelope: advancement of ADCs outside of oncology, Methods Mol. Biol. 2078 (2020) 23–36.

[214] C. Theocharopoulos, et al., Antibody-drug conjugates: functional principles and applications in oncology and beyond, Vaccines 9 (10) (2021).

[215] S.M. Lehar, et al., Novel antibody–antibiotic conjugate eliminates intracellular *S. aureus*, Nature 527 (7578) (2015) 323–328.

[216] H. Cai, et al., Characterization of tissue distribution, catabolism, and elimination of an anti–*Staphylococcus aureus* THIOMAB antibody-antibiotic conjugate in rats, Drug Metabol. Dispos. 48 (11) (2020) 1161.

[217] Study to Investigate the Safety, Tolerability, and Pharmacokinetics of DSTA4637S in Participants With Staphylococcus Aureus Bacteremia Receiving Standard-of-Care (SOC) Antibiotics. Available from: https://ClinicalTrials.gov/show/NCT03162250.

[218] P.S. Dragovich, Antibody–drug conjugates for immunology, J. Med. Chem. 65 (6) (2022) 4496–4499, https://doi.org/10.1021/acs.jmedchem.2c00339.

[219] M.J. McPherson, A.D. Hobson, M.E. Hayes, C.C. Marvin, D. Schmidt, W. Waegell, C. Goess, J.Z. Oh, A. Hernandez Jr., J.T. Randolph, Preparation of Glucocorticoid Receptor Agonist and Immunoconjugates WO2017210471A1, 2017.

[220] A. Deora, et al., Transmembrane TNF-dependent uptake of anti-TNF antibodies, mAbs 9 (4) (2017) 680–695.

[221] B. Stoffel, et al., Pos0365 anti-tnf glucocorticoid receptor modulator antibody drug conjugate for the treatment of autoimmune diseases, Ann. Rheum. Dis. 80 (2021) 412.2–413.

[222] A Study to Evaluate the Safety, Tolerability, Pharmacokinetics, and Efficacy of ABBV-3373 in Participants With Moderate to Severe Rheumatoid Arthritis (RA). Available from: https://ClinicalTrials.gov/show/NCT03823391.

Chapter 8

How to reduce risk of drug induced liver toxicity from the beginning

Jinping Gan[a], Kan He[b] and W. Griffith Humphreys[c]

[a]HiFiBiO Therapeutics, Cambridge, MA, United States; [b]Biotranex LLC, Princeton, NJ, United States; [c]Aranmore Pharma Consulting, Lawrenceville, NJ, United States

Introduction

Drug discovery is a long and resource-intensive process. We not only have to find molecules that bind and act on the target in the desired fashion to be therapeutically effective, but these molecules should also have the right properties to be dosed in patients, which include being safe in acute and chronic dosing regimens. For drug safety, there are a battery of liability tests in discovery, from cardiac ion channels to off-target GPCRs. Some of these tests are straightforward, have high predictive value (such as hERG flux for QTc prolongation [1]), or have clear regulatory path (such as Ames assay for genotoxicity [2]), however some of the more complex safety liabilities such as liver toxicities, remain challenging to screen for, both in vitro and in vivo.

Liver toxicity, or Drug Induced Liver Injury (DILI), is one of the leading causes of drug development failures at all stages of drug discovery and development process. Although DILI failures can occur in preclinical toxicology studies and in early clinical study, it is the failures in late clinical trials and post-approval that are the most troublesome and cause the largest impact. What makes DILI unique is that it is not a singular clinical presentation, but covers a wide variety of manifestations such as acute hepatitis, cholestatic jaundice, hepatocellular hyperplasia, sinusoidal obstruction, steatohepatitis, etc. Indeed, there have been various nomenclatures proposed to attempt to discriminate different aspects of the disease into early and delayed presentation with acute versus idiosyncratic being the most common terminology. The underlying mechanisms for DILI are poorly understood and rarely translatable from one molecule to another, or from preclinical species to human. All of these make the prediction of DILI in humans a daunting and almost impossible task.

The most challenging part of DILI risk assessment is the prediction of idiosyncratic DILI, which is unpredictable without clear dose response, low frequency of occurrence, and often of delayed onset. Depending on the frequency of severe presentation of idiosyncratic DILI, it may not be possible to be detected until later stages of clinical trials or even until after marketing authorization. All of these contributed to significant health and safety burden to patients and major financial and regulatory risks to drug developers.

The presentation of DILI in humans is likely a combination of drug-related properties and host-related risk factors (Scheme 8.1). Also, the current thinking is that most drugs that cause DILI engage both the innate and adaptive immune responses to provoke a response. Drugs such as acetaminophen seem to engage predominately the innate response while drugs such as halothane engage predominately the adaptive system, however, these drugs are more the exception rather than the rule. The drug itself and/or its metabolites could interact with its molecular targets on any cell type in the liver, eliciting either on or off-target pharmacological/toxicological activity. For example, many drugs are known inhibitors of bile salt extrusion protein (BSEP) on hepatocytes to block the excretion of bile acids into the bile, which could lead to severe cholestatic toxicity. The drug or its metabolites could also be metabolized into an unstable reactive species that readily react with critical cellular redox factors such as glutathione or cellular proteins including the metabolizing enzyme itself. Downstream to these processes can get really complicated which includes cellular redox response,

Overcoming Obstacles in Drug Discovery and Development. https://doi.org/10.1016/B978-0-12-817134-9.00010-6

107

SCHEME 8.1 The many factors contributing to the DILI susceptibility in humans.

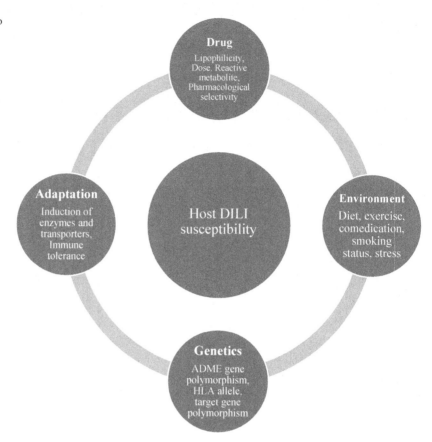

upregulation of many protective enzymes and factors, generation of DAMP signals, mitochondria damage, apoptosis, and presentation of neoantigens, etc. It is now realized that host factors play an important role in the presentation of DILI, as many genome-wide association studies helped to identify correlations between specific human leukocyte antigen (HLA) serotypes and DILI occurrences [3–5].

For the last 20 years, the pharmaceutical industry has adopted a philosophy of avoidance to screen out certain features of molecules that are associated with DILI [6], such as chemical structure alerts [7,8], reactive metabolite formation [9], covalent protein binding [10], BSEP inhibition [11–13], and mitochondria toxicity [14]. The industry and individual companies have also devised various predictive algorithms to come up with a screening tree to flag the compounds that are most likely to cause DILI. There is also heightened vigilance among pharmaceutical companies and the regulatory agencies in the early detection of potential DILI risks in human trials such as the wide adoption of eDISH (evaluation of Drug Induced Serious Hepatotoxicity) plots in pharmacovigilance [15].

Despite all these efforts, there are still experimental drug attritions due to liver toxicities in either preclinical toxicology studies or various stages of clinical development, with increasing costs along the drug development timeline. This is not necessarily a failure of the respective discovery efforts to minimize the properties thought to drive DILI, rather a reflection of the complexity of DILI and the lack of translation of the preclinical screens to DILI prediction.

In this chapter, we will try to simplify the screening strategies in drug discovery, focusing on the dose optimization, reactive metabolite reduction, and maintenance of bile acid homeostasis.

Dose

There is a common understanding that the total dose is very relevant regarding liver toxicity. This was initially highlighted by Uetrecht in 2001 [16], and further corroborated by US and European DILI datasets in the decade following Uetrecht's seminal publication [17]. Chen et al. further explored the relationship of drug properties and DILI risk, leading to the "rule of two" theory that the combination of high dose and high lipophilicity are sufficient to predict the likelihood of clinical DILI [18]. It was later demonstrated that adding the formation of reactive metabolites could further improve the predictive power [19].

The realization of dose being a key predictor of DILI should not come as a surprise. After all, liver is the most important detoxification and clearance organ for most drugs. In the case of oral drugs, the initial concentration of drug presented at the hepatic portal vein can reach tens of micromolar (μM) for an oral dose of 100 mg and above. If such drug happens to be a substrate of hepatic uptake transporter such as OATP, the intracellular concentration in hepatocytes could be further increased. These concentrations are high enough to bind to irrelevant targets, and high enough to disrupt essential cellular processes such as redox potential if oxidative stress is induced by the drug or its reactive metabolites. In some literature, the total amount of reactive metabolites was found to be correlative with DILI, and total daily burden of reactive species were compared with total hepatic reserve of glutathione to corroborate the importance of daily dose threshold [20].

The association of dose with DILI frequency does somewhat fly in the face of the commonly asserted notion that idiosyncratic DILI is completely dose independent. This fact does seem to point toward a mechanism that is driven by a relatively dose-dependent component and a relatively dose-independent component. This concept fits nicely with the idea of the engagement of the innate immune system being dose-dependent and the engagement of the adaptive immune system as being relatively dose-independent.

It is relatively easier to optimize on the daily dose than to predict DILI risk. In fact, DMPK scientists have mastered an impressive toolbox of in vitro, in vivo, and in silico approaches to improve PK exposure and dose projection, in close collaboration with medicinal chemists, biologists, and pharmacologists. Briefly it involves the optimization of absorption, intrinsic clearance (metabolism), distribution, and sometimes transport-mediated elimination. The key to success is the close collaboration among discovery scientists to optimize the compounds to ensure best possible PK while having potent in vivo PD effect leading to robust efficacy in a human disease relevant model. It is worth noting that there is a fallacy in the improvement of in vitro potency without consideration of protein binding and cellular potency which could lead the medicinal chemistry to a chemical space that are high hydrophobic and highly protein bound. Many of those molecules will ultimately lead to higher efficacious doses due to the low free fraction engaging the target. High lipophilicity also leads to promiscuity in target binding which could lead to undesired toxicity consequences.

Reactive metabolite screening

Although there is substantial circumstantial evidence of a causal relationship between reactive metabolites and DILI, there is no commonly accepted hypothesis for the underlying mechanism linking the two [21,22]. Bioactivation is believed to be the initial step toward drug induced host injury by many drugs and the primary mechanism typically cited for the engagement of both the innate and adaptive immune systems. Although the sequence of events following bioactivation is still unclear, it does nonetheless seem to be a central mechanism at least for the most of hepatotoxic drugs. For these reasons, the formation of a reactive metabolite is considered a potential liability in the development of new chemical entities (NCEs) [10].

Bioactivation of drugs can be mediated by various host cells (hepatocytes, neutrophils) and enzymatic systems (cytochrome P450s, FMO, esterases, peroxidases, UDP-glucuronosyl transferases) and can lead to different reactive species including epoxides, Michael acceptors, free radicals, acyl glucuronides, and hard electrophiles such as iminium ions [23].

To minimize DILI liabilities, preclinical screening for reactive metabolites has been adopted by many companies. The first step is to simply examine for the presence of structure alerts, i.e. chemical substructures that have been shown to have a propensity to form reactive species [7,24,25]. The next stage is to screen for the formation of reactive species through covalent protein binding studies and/or the use of chemical trapping agents [9,26]. Reduced glutathione (GSH) has been widely used as an in vitro chemical trapping agent for the characterization and mechanistic study of reactive metabolites [27]. GSH is an important cellular component that is crucial for the cellular homeostasis of redox potential and a natural defense against oxidative stress [28,29]. Glutathione also serves as the primary intracellular nucleophile. It reacts with many known reactive metabolites, and the resulting GSH adducts are usually nontoxic and readily excreted, although in some cases, the formation of GSH adducts has been associated with kidney and bile duct toxicities after further processing of the adducts [30,31].

Screening assays typically involve incubation of the candidate compound with liver microsomes in the presence of GSH. GSH adducts of NCEs can be identified, and the molecular mass of the GSH adduct can be determined by various LC-MS techniques such as neutral loss LC-MS/MS. Detailed structural characterization can be accomplished by further LC-MS/MS and NMR studies. Although a qualitative understanding of GSH adduct formation can be useful in screening studies, it is also important to gain quantitative information regarding the extent of adduct formation to fully characterize the adduct. A quantitative assay allows for the determination of the magnitude of the reactive intermediate trapping as well as enabling measurements such as the effects of various substitution patterns on the amount of adduct formed for structure-activity relationship (SAR) development around a problematic NCE. With this information, it may be possible to formulate a working hypothesis of the bioactivation mechanism that, in turn, would enable chemistry efforts attempting to block the route of metabolism leading to reactive metabolite formation. One of the methods to gain quantitative information on the extent of reactive metabolite formation is trapping with dansylated glutathione (dGSH). The detection of a fluorescence signal with dGSH adducts enables semiquantitative measurement of thiol-reactive metabolite formation and makes it possible for the broad screening of highly prescribed drugs described in this study without the use of radiolabeled materials. Another feature of dGSH is that it does not serve as cofactor for glutathione S-transferases, so the trapping by dGSH measures the extent of chemical reactivity between reactive metabolites and dGSH [32]. The semiquantitative nature of this assay enables a rapid test of hypotheses on bioactivation pathways by substitutions at suspected sites without the costly and time-consuming synthesis of radiolabeled analogues.

One downside to the use of thiol-containing reagents such as glutathione is that they can only react with a subset of reactive species such as epoxides and Michael acceptors. For this reason, the trapping by an additional nucleophile such as cyanide is often added to allow a complete characterization of the potential for reactive metabolite formation [33].

Covalent protein binding studies measure the extent of protein-bound drug-related material after incubation of radiolabeled compounds with an in vitro bioactivation system or through direct in vivo dosing to experimental animals [10,34,35]. The quantitation of the level of covalent protein binding has been proposed to minimize the risk of reactive metabolite-mediated toxicity. The method can be applied both to provide rank ordering information on a series of compounds or as an absolute measurement of binding versus reference standards. However, the use of this technique is often limited due to the prerequisite need for the synthesis of radiolabeled material for every compound of interest.

The results of these assays must be put into proper context to allow sound decision making. The finding of formation of some level of GSH adduct should be considered as a "hazard identification" and any actions based on the finding should only occur along with a "risk assessment" step. The risk assessment step should include things like the severity of disease state targeted by the NCE, acute versus chronic dosing, and perhaps most importantly the projected daily dose. Many companies use the combination of the level of reactive metabolite formed along with a projected dose to determine the total body burden of reactive metabolites during a dosing interval [20,36,37]. Along with the projected dose, this method requires a quantitative determination of reactive metabolite formation along with a predicted fraction of dose that follows that pathway. While it is by no means perfect, the total body burden of reactive metabolite is considered the best value for judging risk of DILI through this pathway.

A recent challenge in the field has been that many NCEs from modern drug discovery efforts have been optimized for slow metabolic clearance in vitro. This presents challenges as these compounds are often slowly cleared in vivo as well, however, the predominant clearance pathway is through metabolism. In these cases, it is important to consider the fractional of metabolism to yield reactive metabolites versus to yield other metabolites. This can then be extrapolated to give a better idea of the total body burden.

Screening for drug-induced dysfunction of liver transporters

Transporters are expressed in hepatocytes on both sinusoidal (basolateral) and canalicular (apical) membranes [38,39]. They play critical roles in liver function by regulating the uptake and excretion of endobiotic and xenobiotic substances in hepatocytes. As shown in Fig. 8.1, the sinusoidal transporters consist of the uptake transporters OATP1B1, OATP1B3, OCTP2B1, NTCP, OCT1, OCT3 and OAT2, and the efflux transporters MRP3, MRP4 and MRP6. OSTα/β, ENT1, ENT2 and OCTN2 are bidirectional transporters. Canalicular transporters BSEP, MDR3, MDR1, BCRP, MRP2 and ABCG5/G8 are exclusively efflux, except for MATE1 and ENT1. Both MATE1 and ENT1 can function bidirectionally, but in most circumstances they act as biliary efflux transporters. ATP8B1 is not a transporter by definition, but a flippase with a function complimentary to MDR3 in regulating the phospholipid asymmetry of the canalicular membrane of hepatocytes and is therefore also discussed in this chapter.

Among all the hepatic transporters, BSEP, MDR3 and ATP8B1 have been shown to be critical for normal liver function. Loss-of-function mutations for these transporter lead to severe liver diseases and potentially to liver failure and death in early age [40,41], indicating that the function of these transporters is not fully compensated for by other mechanisms in liver.

Dysfunction of BSEP and bile acid homeostasis

Glycine and taurine conjugates of cholic and chenodeoxycholic acids are the primary bile salts found in human and mammals [42,43]. Bile acids are synthesized starting from cholesterol in hepatocytes by multiple enzyme processes. The

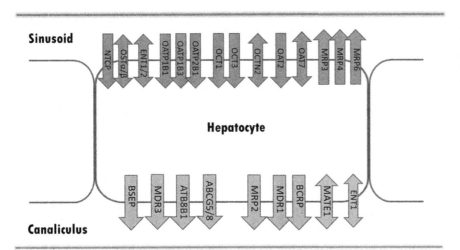

FIGURE 8.1 Major transporters in hepatocytes. Note: ATP8B1 is not a transporter by definition, but a flippase with a function complimentary to MDR3 in regulating the phospholipid asymmetry of canalicular membrane of hepatocytes.

bile acids are further conjugated with glycine and taurine by the enzyme bile acid-CoA:amino acid N-acyltransferase (BAAT) to form the respective bile salts. Once formed, the bile salts are exported from the hepatocytes into bile, then temporarily stored in the gallbladder, and eventually excreted into the small intestine. More than 95% of the bile salts are reabsorbed and taken up by the hepatocytes where they can be again excreted into bile. This process is generally referred to as enterohepatic recirculation. Approximately 2—4 g of bile salts recycle 6—10 times daily with only about 15%—30% of the bile salts being excreted out of the body. The total amount of bile salts in the body is tightly regulated and remains at steady state. In addition to the primary bile salts, there are secondary bile salts which are predominantly glycine and taurine conjugates of deoxycholic acid and lithocholic acid. They are formed from de-conjugated primary bile salts by gut microbiota.

Bile salts play a critical role in the absorption of dietary lipids and fat-soluble nutrients and vitamins through solubilization and emulsification [43]. They are essential in biliary secretion of cholesterol, and are the driving force for bile flow, which eliminates bilirubin and other catabolites, xenobiotics and metabolites. Furthermore, bile salts are potent in transcriptional and posttranscriptional regulations of many genes in the liver and intestines. They activate the nuclear receptor farnesoid X receptor (FXR) and increase FGF19, and ultimately regulate their own synthesis and excretion. Bile salts also interact with pregnane X receptor (PXR), vitamin D receptor (VDR) and G-protein-coupled bile acid receptor-1 such (GPBAR-1). In addition, the high concentration of bile salts in canaliculi results in inward diffusion of solutes.

The intracellular concentrations of bile salts are tightly regulated in hepatocytes. Since bile salts are not membrane permeable, uptake and efflux transporters are required to transport bile salts across cell membranes. OSTα/β and NCTP are involved in absorption and uptake of bile salts. BSEP is responsible for biliary excretion of bile salts and is the rate-limited step in enterohepatic circulation of bile salts [40].

BSEP, encoded by human *ABCB11*, is an ATP-binding cassette (ABC) membrane transporter primarily located on the hepatocyte canalicular membrane [44]. The primary role of BSEP is to export bile salts from hepatocytes into the biliary canaliculi, which is the driving force for enterohepatic circulation of bile salts and bile flow. BSEP functions as a vacuum cleaner to intracellular bile salts, keeping the intracellular concentrations at very low levels. BSEP is responsible for approximately 99% of bile salt exports in liver [45]. BSEP can also export some xenobiotics and drugs such as pravastatin and vinblastine [12]. Dysfunction of BSEP leads to defective bile flow and intracellular accumulation of bile salts, and eventually liver injury. Bile salts have detergent-like properties damaging mitochondria at higher intracellular concentrations. It is important to note that individuals carrying certain BSEP mutations may increase the susceptibility to drug-induced BSEP inhibition, thus are more prone to DILI [40,46].

Several studies with benchmark drugs demonstrated that BSEP inhibition is highly associated with DILI, especially cholestatic, and mixed cholestatic and hepatocellular liver injury [11,12,47—52]. However, there are also drugs that inhibit BSEP in vitro, but are not associated with DILI. The clinical consequence may not be related to the intrinsic inhibition activity alone, but also to the intracellular drug concentration in the hepatocytes and the duration of the inhibition. A more detailed discussion is presented in the below section entitled "How to use BSEP Inhibition Data."

There are various types of in vitro assays that have been developed to assess the potential for drugs or other chemical entities to inhibit BSEP activity. Detailed comparison of these assays can be found elsewhere [53]. Of these, the most commonly used in vitro models in drug discovery and development are the BSEP transfected membrane vesicle assay and the hepatocyte-based models [53]. Which assay to be used will depend on factors such as questions to be addressed, the stage in drug discovery and development, relevance to in vivo inhibition, species difference, throughput, reproducibility and cost.

Membrane vesicles are an artificial inside-out system prepared from cells that over-expressed BSEP, such as from the insect *Spodoptera frugiperda* (sf9 or sf21), CHO, MDCK, LLC-PK1, HeLa and HEK cells [53]. The membrane vesicle-based BSEP inhibition assay tests the inhibition of the uptake of bile salts in the membrane vesicles. It has been widely used in drug discovery paradigms because of its flexibility to be used in a high throughput screening format. However, potential concerns with this type of assay include: (1) lack of a metabolism function, thereby not allowing for the effect of metabolites on BSEP inhibition to be assessed, (2) lack of uptake transporters which could lead to underestimating inhibition potency due to potential drug accumulation in hepatocytes, and (3) lack of physiological relevance due to the artificial nature of the system, thereby making it difficult to do in vivo extrapolation of the BSEP inhibition data.

Compared with the membrane vesicles-based assays, the more physiological hepatocyte-based assays are in general superior platforms for studying BSEP inhibition with respect to in vivo relevance [47,51,53]. Primary hepatocytes are considered as the "gold standard" for drug metabolism and hepatic transporter studies. The sandwich-cultured-hepatocyte platform (SCH) has been used to assess BSEP inhibition. The primary hepatocytes are cultured in two layers of gelled collagen or biomatrix/Matrigel in a sandwich configuration which facilitates the formation of gap junctions and functional bile canalicular networks over days in the culture. For the BSEP assay, SCH are incubated with taurocholic acid or other bile salts [12]. A fraction of taurocholic acid is excreted into bile canaliculi during the incubation and is released into the medium upon depletion of extracellular calcium. The BSEP activity expressed as a biliary excretion index for the bile salt is calculated by using the percentage of the bile salt excreted in the canalicular pocket compared to the total amount in both the intra-hepatocytes and the canalicular pockets. The SCH method is generally used for investigating BSEP inhibition issues with a limited number of compounds because of issues related to complexity in the preparation, reproducibility, length of time, and relatively high cost.

An in vitro assay (BSEP*cyte*®) using primary hepatocytes in suspension has been shown to be accurate, reproducible, and flexible platform to investigate BSEP inhibition [47]. This assay involves the incubation of hepatocytes in suspension with bile acids in the presence or absence of a test compound followed by a specific LC-MS/MS determination of bile salts in the extracellular media. During the incubation, bile acids are rapidly taken up by hepatocytes and converted into intracellular bile salts that are subsequently pumped out of the hepatocytes by BSEP, which is responsible for export of approximately 99% of bile salts. The assay form is extremely flexible with (1) a variety of bile acids can be used including cholic acid, chenodeoxycholic acid, deoxycholic acid or lithocholic acid, (2) hepatocytes from mouse, rat, dog, monkey and human can be used, (3) pooled or individual, fresh or cryopreserved hepatocytes can be used and (4) the platform can be configured for higher-throughput studies or detailed kinetic analysis investigations. Therefore, the BSEP-suspension inhibition assay platform offers the opportunity to be used in various stages of drug discovery and development.

In addition to the in vitro assays, efforts have been made to identify appropriate biomarkers for assessing the effect of BSEP inhibition in animal or clinical studies. These biomarkers include various bile acids and bile salts which can be measured by LC-MS/MS in plasma or serum samples. If there is a BSEP inhibition concern based on in vitro study, it would be helpful to monitor plasma/serum concentrations of bile acid or salts to assess the potential clinical implications.

How to use BSEP inhibition data: Given the importance of bile salts in physiological functions, inhibition of BSEP would appear to have no apparent benefit but having only potentially harmful effects. Therefore, efforts should be made to identify the potential of a drug candidate to inhibit or interfere with BSEP function. However, as discussed in the above section, not all drugs that inhibit BSEP function are associated with DILI, and not all DILI drugs inhibit BSEP function, thus creating challenges on how to interpret the BSEP inhibition data to address drug discovery and development concerns. These challenges are mainly derived from these following three questions: (1) how to accurately extrapolate the in vitro BSEP inhibition to in vivo effect, (2) whether the potential effects caused by BSEP inhibition are manageable in clinical settings, and (3) how predictable is a biomarker for BSEP inhibition for assessing liver injury. It is important to avoid false positive and negative results by choosing the right in vitro models.

The in vivo effect of BSEP inhibition depends on the intrinsic potency of the compound, the intracellular concentration(s) of the compound and its inhibitory metabolite(s), and the duration of the inhibition by the compound. Other biological effects that may play a role BSEP inhibition include a predisposition to BSEP inhibition due to genetic and environmental factors. As you can see, in vitro assays provide only the intrinsic potency, however, there are other factors that contribute to the in vivo outcomes, including the disposition, metabolism and pharmacokinetic properties of the inhibitor, and the sensitivity of an individual to BSEP inhibition. Practically it is not possible to know precisely the intracellular concentrations of the inhibitor and its inhibitory metabolite(s) in hepatocytes with time, and the duration of the

BSEP inhibition. A great deal of efforts have been taken to develop PBPK and quantitative systems toxicology models such as DILIsym to fill the gap between in vitro findings and in vivo potential effects [54].

Several studies have attempted to develop cut-off limits for BSEP inhibition IC$_{50}$ values to support compound selection in the discovery stage, but the values are conflicting. For example, the IC$_{50}$ cutoff values of 25 μM [49] and 300 μM [11] have been proposed in two separate studies in which BSEP inhibitions were independently assessed as a risk factor for DILI using inside-out membrane vesicle assays. An issue with a 300 μM cutoff is a high false negative rate. In a recent study, 50 μM for BSEP inhibition was proposed as the most optimal cutoff following maximizing the difference of total DILI reports [50]. An empirical cutoff (5 μM) for BSEP inhibition was established based on a relationship between BSEP IC$_{50}$ values and the calculated maximal unbound concentration at the inlet of the human liver [51]. Efforts have been made to combine BSEP IC$_{50}$ with inhibition of other transporters such as MRPs, MW and Log P, but the improvement was limited [50,51].

Several groups are looking at using the ratio of BSEP IC50 to plasma concentration (Cmin or Cmax) derived from a set of benchmark drugs to identify potential cutoff values for a compound's potential to cause DILI. However, this has proven to be challenging as IC50 values can be dependent on the in vitro system used to generate IC$_{50}$ values and inter-laboratory differences. The potential for over 200 drugs to inhibit human BSEP activity was determined using primary hepatocyte-based BSEP inhibition assay [47,55]. In these studies, BSEP inhibition was demonstrated to be highly correlated with cholestatic and mixed cholestatic and hepatocellular liver injury. There were 25 drugs with Cmax/IC$_{50}$ ratio >0.1, among them eight drugs withdrawn from the market or discontinued from further development (troglitazone, fasiglifam, benziodarone, benzbromarone, lumiracoxib, bromfenac, ciglitazone and fipexide), 12 drugs associated with most-DILI-concern (ritonavir, deferasirox, cyclosporine, indinavir, ketoconazole, etodolac, bosentan, leflunomide, disulfiram, diclofenac, itraconazole, ticlopidine), and five drugs with less-DILI-concern (saquinavir, rosiglitazone, pioglitazone, chlorpromazine, trazodone).

A rank order approach has been used for in vitro BSEP inhibition for discovery programs. Usually, the data is compared to benchmark positive controls. A large number of compounds are screened, and false positive and negative results can be tolerated at this stage.

Dysfunction of MDR3 and phospholipid homeostasis

Phosphatidylcholines (PC) are the principal biliary phospholipids found in human and animals, comprising more than 95% of the total biliary phospholipids. The major biliary PC species are 1-palmitoyl 2-linoleyl (16:0-18:2) and 1-palmitoyl 2-oleol (16:0-18:1) [56]. The PC species are critical in the process of solubilizing biliary cholesterol. The PC species form mixed micelles with bile salts in such a way the cholesterol solubility is increased by more than a million-fold compared to simple bile salt micelles. The mixed micelles containing bile salts, PC species and cholesterol are excreted into bile flow. In addition, the PC containing mixed micelles dramatically reduce the cytotoxicity of free bile salts.

PC is transported from the inner leaflet to the outer leaflet of the canalicular membrane by MDR3 [57]. MDR3 is a 1279 amino acid transmembrane protein encoded by the human gene ABCB4 [57]. It is primarily expressed in the canalicular membrane of hepatocytes, although low levels of MDR3 mRNA can be found in the adrenal gland, muscle, tonsil, spleen, placenta, testis, and ileum. Mdr2 is the analog of human MDR3 in mice. MDR3 functions as a type of floppase by translocating PC from the inner leaflet to the outer leaflet of the canalicular membrane of hepatocytes. It is activated by bile salts and bile salt micelles. The PC species on the outer leaflet of the canalicular membrane can be extracted by bile salts micelles to form the mixed micelles which further incorporate cholesterol. A proposed mechanism of action of MDR3 is shown in Fig. 8.2.

Dysfunction or decreased activity of the MDR3 transporter leads to reduced biliary PC levels, which results in crystallization and precipitation of cholesterol in the bile and cytotoxic effect of free bile salts on hepatocytes and biliary epithelium cells [58]. In addition, MDR3 dysfunction may disturb the phospholipid asymmetry of hepatocyte membranes and thereby affecting hepatocyte function. Loss-of-function mutations in human ABCB4 gene have been associated with a wide spectrum of liver diseases including progressive familial intrahepatic cholestasis type 3 (PFIC-3), low phospholipid-associated cholelithiasis (LPAC), ICP, mild chronic cholangiopathy, primary biliary cirrhosis, and DILI [46,58].

Inhibition of MDR3 has been associated with DILI [58,59]. In order to investigate the potentials for drugs to inhibit MDR3 activity, several in vitro assays have been developed that employ MDR3-tranfected LLC-PK and HEK293 cells, Mdr3-expressed yeast secretory vesicles, and MDR3-over expressed SF9 insect cell membrane vesicles. Itraconazole and ticlopidine were demonstrated to inhibit MDR3 activity in ABCB4-tranfected LLC-PK cells [60,61]. Furthermore, itraconazole and ticlopidine were observed to decrease biliary secretion of phospholipids through inhibition of Mdr3 in rat. The inhibition was hypothesized to be an underlying mechanism of DILI caused by these drugs. It was noteworthy that

FIGURE 8.2 Proposed mechanism of action of MDR3 and the formation of mixed micelles.

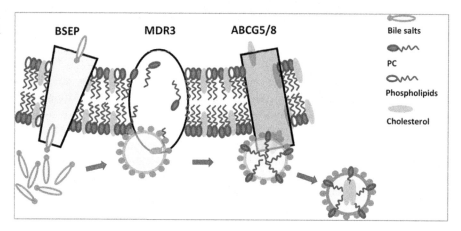

some artificial probe substrates for MDR3 such as 7-nitro-2,1,3-benzoxadiazol (NBD), a PC analog containing a fluorescence group, are used in some in vitro assays [59]. However, the major issue is that they are not readily available for flopping by MDR3 if they are not incorporated into the cell phospholipid bilayer membrane. The mechanism of action of MDR3 makes it difficult to develop a valid in vitro assay than many other drug transporters.

Recently, an in vitro assay platform has been developed using primary hepatocytes [59]. The assay involves *in situ* biosynthesis of deuterium-labeled PC in primary hepatocytes and LC-MS/MS determination of extracellular d_9-PC. Several drugs associated with DILI were found to inhibit MDR3 activity including chlorpromazine, imipramine, itraconazole, haloperidol, ketoconazole, saquinavir, clotrimazole, ritonavir, and troglitazone. This study suggested that MDR3 inhibition may play an important role in drug-induced cholestasis and vanishing bile duct syndrome.

The investigation was further expanded to include a group of 125 benchmark drugs (70 of Most- and 55 of No-DILI-concern from the United States Food and Drug Administration Liver Toxicity Knowledge Base) [62]. Of the compounds tested, 41% of Most-DILI- (29 of 70) and 47% of No-DILI- (26 of 55) concern drugs had MDR3 IC_{50} values < 50 μM. Many No-DILI-concerns drugs with MDR3 inhibition had relatively low systemic exposures. It was noted that several antihistamine drugs (brompheniramine, clemastine, loratadine, and doxylamine) and antidepressants (fluvoxamine and protriptyline) were potent MDR3 inhibitors ($IC_{50} < 10$ μM), but they are No-DILI-concern. It was not clear if the MDR3 activity was affected by the pharmacological action on membrane receptors. Nine Most-DILI-concern drugs caused potent inhibition of both MDR3 and BSEP activities ($IC_{50} < 20$), including four withdrawn (tasosartan, benziodarone, benzbromarone, and troglitazone), four boxed warning (tipranavir, ketoconazole, nefazodone, and lapatinib), and one liver injury warning (ritonavir) in their current approved label, suggesting that multiple inhibitory mechanisms governing bile formation (bile acid and phospholipid efflux) may confer additional risk factors that play into more severe forms of clinical liver injury.

Better distinction across DILI classifications were observed when systemic exposure was taken into account where safety margins of 50-fold had low sensitivity (0.29), but high specificity (0.96). For all drugs causing MDR3 inhibition with $IC_{50} < 100$ μM, the total plasma C_{max}/IC_{50} ratio of the most-DILI-concern drugs were much higher than the no-DILI-concern drugs (1.27 vs. 0.04) [63]. There were 18 drugs with C_{max}/IC_{50} ratio of >0.2, among them nine drugs withdrawn from market (benzbromarone, benzarone, benziodarone, troglitazone, benoxaprofen, pirprofen, zimeldine, ebrotidine, tasosartan), eight drugs with boxed warning (tipranavir, pazopanib, ketoconazole, leflunomide, nefazodone, lapatinib, tolcapone and methotrexate), and one drug with warnings and precautions (ritonavir). This study suggested that MDR3 inhibition is associated with DILI, and the plasma C_{max}/IC_{50} ratio >0.2 appeared to be association with severe DILI.

Dysfunction of other liver transporters

ATP8B1 (FIC1) is a member of the type 4 subfamily of P-type ATPases (P4 ATPase), and is responsible for flipping phosphatidylserine and phosphatidylethanolamine from the outer leaflet to inner leaflet of hepatocyte canalicular membranes [41,64]. ATP8B1, together with MDR3, plays an important role in maintaining the phospholipid asymmetry of the canalicular membrane where PC and sphingomyelin are mainly located in the outer leaflet while phosphatidylserine and phosphatidylethanolamine are mainly located in the inner (cytoplasmic) leaflet. Phospholipid asymmetry plays an important role in cell functions. While ATP8B1 is not technically classified as a hepatic transporter, a discussion on

ATP8B1 is included in this chapter because of recent concerns that ATP8B1 mutations and potential inhibition by drugs may also lead to DILI.

ATP8B1 contributes to the formation of a liquid-ordered state in the canalicular membrane which makes the membrane extremely resistant to bile salt—mediated cytotoxicity [41]. ATP8B1 also regulates BSEP function through maintaining the optimum lipid and cholesterol compositions of the canalicular membranes. Loss-of-function mutations of ATP8B1 cause progressive familial intrahepatic cholestasis 1 (PFIC-1) [41,65]. PFIC-1 patients develop cholestasis in early infancy which could progress to liver failure before adulthood. ATP8B1 mutations can also lead to benign recurrent intrahepatic cholestasis-1 (BRIC-1). To our knowledge, there have been no extensive investigations on the possible inhibition of ATP8B1 by drugs, this being largely the result of the lack of appropriate in vitro and in vivo study models. It is also possible that ATP8B1 mutations may predispose the patients to DILI.

MRP2 is expressed in the canalicular membrane of hepatocytes and on the apical membrane of epithelial cells in the intestines, renal proximal tubules, and gallbladder, and is encoded by the human *ABCC2* gene [40,66]. MRP2 plays a primary role in biliary excretion of phase II metabolites (glucuronide, sulfate, and glutathione conjugates). MRP2 also transports some unconjugated drugs and endogenous substances. Dysfunction of MRP2 is implicated in the development of acquired and hereditary jaundice [40]. Loss-of-function mutations of MRP2 can cause Dubin-Johnson syndrome which is characterized by a mild conjugated hyperbilirubinemia. MRP2 has been reported to be active in transporting bile salts, tetrahydroxylated bile acids, and sulfate conjugates of bile acids. However, the contribution of MRP2 to biliary excretion of bile salts is considered to be minimal, possible less than 1% based on the finding that the biliary excretion of bile salts was reduced by approximately 99% in PFIC-2 patents having normal expression levels of MRP2 [45]. MRP3 and MRP4 are involved in sinusoidal excretion of bile salts, but they are a minor pathways in the overall disposition of bile salts [67]. Therefore, the impaired BSEP function in PFIC-2 patients is not compensated by mechanisms involving MRPs. A recent study demonstrated that addition of MRP inhibition data in a multifactorial approach to predicting DILI provided little predictive advantage over just BSEP inhibition alone [50,51]. Nevertheless, interference of MRP function may contribute to DILI in some cases, possibly due to the mechanisms involving alteration of the drug disposition.

NTCP and OSTs are involved in the uptake and absorption of bile salts. However, dysfunctions of these transporters are not associated with severe impairment of liver function, which may be due to compensatory mechanisms for their functions and the fact that they are not involved in the rate limiting step in the disposition of bile salts. Other hepatocyte transporters such as OATP1B1, OATP1B3, OATP2B1, OCT1, OAT2, OAT3, OAT7, ENT1, ENT2, P-gp, BCRP and MATE1 appear to not be directly associated with DILI, nevertheless, they may contribute to a drug's accumulation in hepatocytes and alteration of drug disposition that could potentially increase the risk for DILI in some cases [40,68].

Immune-mediated liver toxicity

When we talk about immune-mediated liver toxicity, the most popular belief has been the involvement of adaptive immune system in the recognition of MHC complex on antigen presentation cells, either by neoantigen presentation after covalent modification of proteins or by direct alteration of MHC complex, to elicit T cell mediated immune response [69—71]. Over the past 2 decades, genome wide association studies have revealed positive associations between specific HLA serotypes and liver toxicities of a handful of drugs, including ticlopidine, ximelagatran, lapatinib, flucloxacillin, terbinafine, and amoxicillin.

It is extremely difficult to predict which drug will cause immune-mediated liver toxicity, and if it does, whether people with a specific HLA serotype will be more susceptible. Current in vitro models are quite primitive, typically of co-cultures of hepatocytes and Kupffer cells, which is hardly a model of adaptive immune system. But a bigger question is whether such models, assuming they could be developed, could be effectively used. After all, for many of the drugs mentioned above, only a very small fraction of patients develop severe liver toxicity, even in patients with the specific HLA serotype. There are hundreds of variant alleles for each of the HLA subtypes, including HLA-A, B, and C in the MHC class I family, and HLA-DP, DQ, and DR in the MHC class II family, with each allele presenting its unique antigens.

In addition, a wide variety of studies have linked acetaminophen hepatotoxicity with several cell types in the innate immune system, including Kupffer cells, neutrophils, and NK cells [72]. It is believed that these inflammatory responses are merely consequences of severe hepatocyte necrosis induced by acetaminophen via the formation of reactive metabolites, it is plausible the subsequent release of cytokines and chemokines from these inflammatory responses could exacerbate the liver injury.

So, if we cannot predict it, can we minimize it? The answer is maybe. First of all, most of these drugs are used in high doses. Secondly, most of them form covalent adducts in vitro. An exception to these general statements is ximelagatran and its active metabolite, melagatran. Short term uses (<12 days) of ximelagatran (36 mg) was generally safe, however,

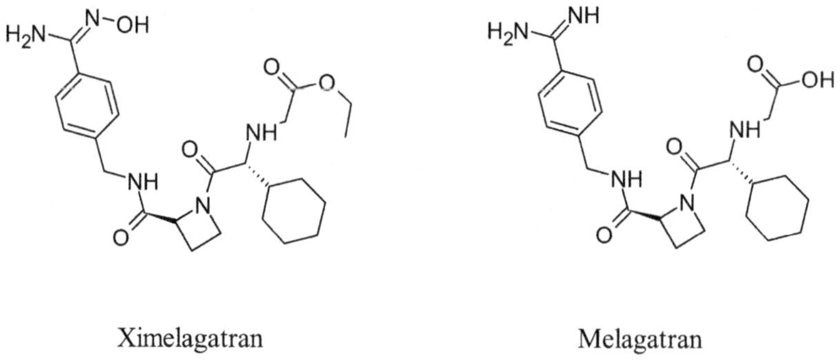

FIGURE 8.3 Chemical structures of ximelagatran and its active metabolite melagatran.

Ximelagatran

Melagatran

>35 days of ximelagatran use was associated with higher frequency of liver enzyme elevations (3x ULN) as compared with placebo. In rare cases (0.5%), accompanying bilirubin increases (2x ULN) were also observed, indicating potential severe liver toxicity with the chronic use of ximelagatran [73]. Subsequent to these findings, ximelagatran was withdrawal from European market in 2006. Pharmacogenomic data later revealed potential association of HLA alleles DRB1*07 and DQA1*02 [73]. In any case, there were no reports of preclinical liver toxicity nor reactive metabolite formation nor hepatic transporter inhibition [74,75]. Therefore, ximelagatran represents a curious case of idiosyncratic DILI that warrants further investigation. The contrasting physiochemical properties of ximelagatran and its active drug melagatran perhaps holds some clues. Ximelagatran is a double prodrug of melagatran, aiming at increasing lipophilicity and reducing basicity of melagatran (Fig. 8.3). It is reported that ximelagatran is 80-fold more permeable than melagatran [76]. Metabolite conversion of a permeable ximelagatran inside the hepatocyte leads to an essentially impermeable melagatran. It is plausible that the chronic dosing could lead to accumulation of melagatran leading to undesired liver toxicities.

Finally, we need to be aware of therapeutic targets that may interfere with the immune system, either directly as an immune agonist such as a CD40 agonist [77] or indirectly blocking an immune suppressive pathway such as anti-PD-1/PD-L1 agents [78,79]. In the case of anti-PD-1 checkpoint inhibitors, special attention is needed when it is to be combined with small molecule targeted therapies that may have underlining liver enzyme signals in the clinic.

Thinking beyond hepatocytes

Traditional 2D hepatocyte models can be used early in the drug discovery process for hazard identification. These models are amenable to high throughput screening and high content image analysis. The use of hepatocyte cultures, however, are limited in its duration as the enzymatic and transporter activity deteriorate with time during culture. The availability of longer-term culture medium may extend the use time of these cultures, but these cells gradually lose hepatocyte phenotype and morphology in culture. Moreover, hepatocyte monolayers suffer from the lack of tight junction and canaliculi formation, therefore missing a major part of the hepatocyte function which is the maintenance of bile acid homeostasis. Modifications to these 2D monolayer cultures such as the matrix overlay (sandwich culture) enables bile canaliculi formation, and it is commonly used for the study of biliary clearance of drugs [80]. Micropatterned fibroblast co-cultures can stay in culture for up to 7 days, while maintaining drug metabolizing enzyme activities [81,82]. Newer models of 3D hepatocyte cultures including spheroids, bioprinted liver, and liver-on-chip can be sustained for much longer time in culture with appropriate culture media and right flow/oxygenation in the case of liver-on-chip [83]. Hepatocyte monolayers and liver spheroids were tested side by side for their ability to predict DILI risk. Liver spheroids cultured for 7 days marginally performed better in the prediction [84]. Theoretically, Liver-on-chip, especially those derived from iPSC cells, could be the ultimate model system to test for DILI on a population basis. However, Liver-on-chip is still at its infancy stage and far from everyday use due to its complex setup, lofty expense, and lack of reproducibility.

Signal detection in preclinical species and translation to humans

Before a NCE is introduced to first-in-human clinical trials, it must undergo various toxicity testing to ensure the safety of healthy volunteers and patients. Although we strive for minimal usage of animals in safety assessment, acute and long-term toxicity studies are still required to have a systemic assessment of safety pharmacology, expected and unexpected target organ toxicity, and toxicities that may arise upon repeated dosing. Recent literature has been mixed concerning the utility of animal models in accurate prediction of human risk of hepatotoxicity, however it is impossible to obtain a true account of the translational value of animal testing for liver toxicity assessment, because the number of candidates that were terminated due to liver toxicity in animals is proprietary and often are not shared among stakeholders. In a recent analysis by the IQ Consortium, 16 of 182 NCEs caused liver injury in animals, with a sensitivity of 65% in rodent, 50% in dogs, and 27% in nonhuman primate [85,86]. When combining the results of safety evaluation in two species, the positive predictive value is still only 62%. There are many reasons for the differences in hepatotoxicity across the species. For example, there are major inter-species differences in bile acid profiles and their corresponding hydrophobicity characteristics [87], as well as hepatic drug transporter expression [88], in addition to the differences in the metabolite profile and bioactivation across species.

It is generally understood that, upon finding of liver toxicity, comprehensive evaluation of liver toxicity signals is warranted, taking into consideration of the ADME properties of the NCE and potential species differences thereof, the exposure multiples, the histopathological manifestation of the liver findings, and general consideration of the indication and associated benefit/risk assessment. In some cases, it may be valuable to ascertain the contribution of drug metabolism to liver toxicity by conducting toxicity testing with and without the administration of 1-aminobenzotriazole (ABT) [89]. If no liver toxicity is observed in ABT-treated animals, follow-up studies are needed to determine the similarity or difference in metabolism across species, and to inform any backup efforts to minimize certain metabolic pathways. If cholestasis is involved in the liver injury, it is possible to compare the dose, exposure, and bile acid transporter inhibition potency with that is expected in humans to fully assess the risk of such injuries in humans. Physiologically based pharmacokinetic models could be employed to further refine the handling of drugs and metabolites across species and therefore enable more reliable risk assessment [90]. Last but not least, it is desirable to use early predictive biomarkers in the serum/plasma to inform potential liver injuries, preferably more selective and sensitive than the typical liver enzyme panel including ALT, AST, alkaline phosphatase, gamma glutamyl transferase, and total bilirubin. Recent literature has shown utilities of GLDH and miR-122 in the early detection of liver injuries in animal toxicity testing [91].

Concluding remarks

After decades of intense research and debate about DILI in the academia, biopharmaceutical industry, and the regulatory agency, it remains to be one of the most prominent challenges in the R&D of novel therapeutics, especially for small molecules. In this chapter, we have laid out a simplified and practical strategy in the minimization and mitigation of DILI risk in drug discovery, and we hope this will provide a reference point for discovery scientists. Scheme 8.2 is the proposed general workflow.

Briefly, any target nominated to enter the discovery pipeline should be evaluated for on-target toxicities including liver toxicity, integrating data from genetic knockout animals, clinical features of functional genetic polymorphisms, and preclinical or clinical toxicity profiles of existing agents targeting the same or similar pathways. Any potential hazard identified in this step needs to be verified in subsequent in vitro and in vivo experiments. This exercise needs to be performed for closely related targets so that appropriate recommendations on target selectivity criterion can be set.

As the project progresses into medicinal chemistry, routine screenings on reactive metabolite formation and bile acid transporter (e.g. BSEP and MDR3) inhibition are recommended. LC-MS characterization of reactive metabolite trapping products is usually recommended to guide the chemical modifications to reduce or eliminate any bioactivation. SAR of bile acid transporter inhibition is mostly empirical in nature, therefore routine screening with appropriate controls is needed to identify potential liabilities.

As was discussed earlier, low dose is seldomly associated with clinically significant DILI. Therefore, optimization of pharmacological potency should parallel the efforts in optimization of bioavailability, clearance, and volume of distribution to ensure sufficient drugs on target in the target organ at a relatively low dose. Often attention should be made on the free drug concentration across species to ensure any differences in plasma protein binding are taken into account when

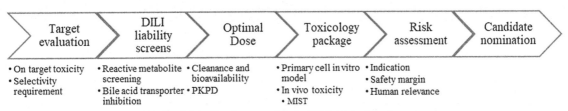

SCHEME 8.2 Roadmap to minimize DILI risk in drug discovery.

projecting the human dose. PKPD and PBPK modeling are now routinely performed to improve the translational power of animal models.

Once a pharmacologically active compound is identified with reasonable projected dose, acute and repeated dose toxicity studies in rodent and non-rodent species are to be done to determine the safety and tolerability. Any changes of liver enzymes and signs of histopathological changes in the liver must be evaluated, and if necessary, investigative studies need to be completed to further understand the mechanism of such toxicity. The understanding of such mechanism will help determine the translatability to humans and inform the backup efforts. *In vitro* evaluations in primary hepatocytes in suspension, 2D, or more complex 3D cultures are often used at this stage, to obtain a comprehensive understanding of cytotoxicity across species and its relationship to metabolic clearance and metabolite profiles.

Ultimately, risk assessment needs to be made in the context of the overall package of pharmacological activities, toxicology package, and projected human dose and indications. Hopefully, the recommendations detailed in this chapter will serve as a general guide toward minimizing DILI risks in drug discovery to maximize the success of clinical development.

References

[1] D.M. Roden, Drug-induced prolongation of the QT interval, N. Engl. J. Med. 350 (2004) 1013−1022.

[2] ICH Guideline S2 (R1) on Genotoxicity Testing and Data, June 2012. Available from: https://www.ema.europa.eu/en/documents/scientific-guideline/ich-guideline-s2-r1-genotoxicity-testing-data-interpretation-pharmaceuticals-intended-human-use-step_en.pdf.

[3] A.K. Daly, P.T. Donaldson, P. Bhatnagar, Y. Shen, I. Pe'er, A. Floratos, et al., HLA-B*5701 genotype is a major determinant of drug-induced liver injury due to flucloxacillin, Nat. Genet. 41 (7) (2009) 816−819.

[4] A.K. Daly, Human leukocyte antigen (HLA) pharmacogenomic tests: potential and pitfalls, Curr. Drug Metabol. 15 (2) (2014) 196−201.

[5] P. Nicoletti, G.P. Aithal, E.S. Bjornsson, R.J. Andrade, A. Sawle, M. Arrese, et al., Association of liver injury from specific drugs, or groups of drugs, with polymorphisms in HLA and other genes in a genome-wide association study, Gastroenterology 152 (5) (2017) 1078−1089.

[6] R.J. Weaver, E.A. Blomme, A.E. Chadwick, I.M. Copple, H.H.J. Gerets, C.E. Goldring, et al., Managing the challenge of drug-induced liver injury: a roadmap for the development and deployment of preclinical predictive models, Nat. Rev. Drug Discov. 19 (2) (2020) 131−148.

[7] A.S. Kalgutkar, I. Gardner, R.S. Obach, C.L. Shaffer, E. Callegari, K.R. Henne, et al., A comprehensive listing of bioactivation pathways of organic functional groups, Curr. Drug Metabol. 6 (3) (2005) 161−225.

[8] F.P. Guengerich, J.S. MacDonald, Applying mechanisms of chemical toxicity to predict drug safety, Chem. Res. Toxicol. 20 (3) (2007) 344−369.

[9] W.G. Chen, C. Zhang, M.J. Avery, H.G. Fouda, Reactive metabolite screen for reducing candidate attrition in drug discovery, Adv. Exp. Med. Biol. 500 (2001) 521−524.

[10] D.C. Evans, A.P. Watt, D.A. Nicoll-Griffith, T.A. Baillie, Drug-protein adducts: an industry perspective on minimizing the potential for drug bioactivation in drug discovery and development, Chem. Res. Toxicol. 17 (1) (2004) 3−16.

[11] S. Dawson, S. Stahl, N. Paul, J. Barber, J.G. Kenna, In vitro inhibition of the bile salt export pump correlates with risk of cholestatic drug-induced liver injury in humans, Drug Metab. Dispos. 40 (1) (2012) 130−138.

[12] J.M. Pedersen, P. Matsson, C.A. Bergstrom, J. Hoogstraate, A. Noren, E.L. LeCluyse, et al., Early identification of clinically relevant drug interactions with the human bile salt export pump (BSEP/ABCB11), Toxicol. Sci. Off. J. Soc. Toxicol. 136 (2) (2013) 328−343.

[13] J.L. Woodhead, K. Yang, S.Q. Siler, P.B. Watkins, K.L. Brouwer, H.A. Barton, et al., Exploring BSEP inhibition-mediated toxicity with a mechanistic model of drug-induced liver injury, Front. Pharmacol. 5 (2014) 240.

[14] Y. Will, J. Dykens, Mitochondrial toxicity assessment in industry−a decade of technology development and insight, Expert Opin. Drug Metabol. Toxicol. 10 (8) (2014) 1061−1067.

[15] P.B. Watkins, M. Desai, S.D. Berkowitz, G. Peters, Y. Horsmans, D. Larrey, et al., Evaluation of drug-induced serious hepatotoxicity (eDISH): application of this data organization approach to phase III clinical trials of rivaroxaban after total hip or knee replacement surgery, Drug Saf. 34 (3) (2011) 243−252.

[16] J. Uetrecht, Prediction of a new drug's potential to cause idiosyncratic reactions, Curr. Opin. Drug Discov. Dev. 4 (1) (2001) 55−59.

[17] C. Lammert, S. Einarsson, C. Saha, A. Niklasson, E. Bjornsson, N. Chalasani, Relationship between daily dose of oral medications and idiosyncratic drug-induced liver injury: search for signals, Hepatology 47 (6) (2008) 2003−2009.

[18] M. Chen, C.-W. Tung, Q. Shi, L. Guo, L. Shi, H. Fang, et al., A testing strategy to predict risk for drug-induced liver injury in humans using high-content screen assays and the 'rule-of-two' model, Arch. Toxicol. 88 (7) (2014) 1439−1449.

[19] M. Chen, J. Borlak, W. Tong, A model to predict severity of drug-induced liver injury in humans, Hepatology 64 (3) (2016) 931−940.

[20] N. Kakutani, T. Nanayama, Y. Nomura, Novel risk assessment of reactive metabolites from discovery to clinical stage, J. Toxicol. Sci. 44 (3) (2019) 201−211.

[21] J.P. Uetrecht, New concepts in immunology relevant to idiosyncratic drug reactions: the "danger hypothesis" and innate immune system, Chem. Res. Toxicol. 12 (5) (1999) 387−395.

[22] B.K. Park, N.R. Kitteringham, H. Powell, M. Pirmohamed, Advances in molecular toxicology-towards understanding idiosyncratic drug toxicity, Toxicology 153 (1−3) (2000) 39−60.

[23] J. Gan, S. Ma, D. Zhang, Non-cytochrome P450-mediated bioactivation and its toxicological relevance, Drug Metab. Rev. 48 (4) (2016) 473−501.

[24] E. Fontana, P.M. Dansette, S.M. Poli, Cytochrome p450 enzymes mechanism based inhibitors: common sub-structures and reactivity, Curr. Drug Metabol. 6 (5) (2005) 413−454.

[25] A.F. Stepan, D.P. Walker, J. Bauman, D.A. Price, T.A. Baillie, A.S. Kalgutkar, et al., Structural alert/reactive metabolite concept as applied in medicinal chemistry to mitigate the risk of idiosyncratic drug toxicity: a perspective based on the critical examination of trends in the top 200 drugs marketed in the United States, Chem. Res. Toxicol. 24 (9) (2011) 1345−1410.

[26] Z. Yan, G.W. Caldwell, Stable-isotope trapping and high-throughput screenings of reactive metabolites using the isotope MS signature, Anal. Chem. 76 (23) (2004) 6835−6847.

[27] K. Samuel, W. Yin, R.A. Stearns, Y.S. Tang, A.G. Chaudhary, J.P. Jewell, et al., Addressing the metabolic activation potential of new leads in drug discovery: a case study using ion trap mass spectrometry and tritium labeling techniques, J. Mass Spectrom. 38 (2) (2003) 211−221.

[28] W. Davis Jr., Z. Ronai, K.D. Tew, Cellular thiols and reactive oxygen species in drug-induced apoptosis, J. Pharmacol. Exp. Therapeut. 296 (1) (2001) 1−6.

[29] A. Meister, M.E. Anderson, Glutathione, Ann. Rev. Biochem. 52 (1) (1983) 711−760.

[30] P.A. Jean, R.A. Roth, Naphthylisothiocyanate disposition in bile and its relationship to liver glutathione and toxicity, Biochem. Pharmacol. 50 (9) (1995) 1469−1474.

[31] A.E. Mutlib, R.J. Gerson, P.C. Meunier, P.J. Haley, H. Chen, L.S. Gan, et al., The species-dependent metabolism of efavirenz produces a nephrotoxic glutathione conjugate in rats, Toxicol. Appl. Pharmacol. 169 (1) (2000) 102−113.

[32] J. Gan, T.W. Harper, M.M. Hsueh, Q. Qu, W.G. Humphreys, Dansyl glutathione as a trapping agent for the quantitative estimation and identification of reactive metabolites, Chem. Res. Toxicol. 18 (5) (2005) 896−903.

[33] G. Meneses-Lorente, M.Z. Sakatis, T. Schulz-Utermoehl, C. De Nardi, A.P. Watt, A quantitative high-throughput trapping assay as a measurement of potential for bioactivation, Anal. Biochem. 351 (2) (2006) 266−272.

[34] R. Sawamura, N. Okudaira, K. Watanabe, T. Murai, Y. Kobayashi, M. Tachibana, et al., Predictability of idiosyncratic drug toxicity risk for carboxylic acid-containing drugs based on the chemical stability of acyl glucuronide, Drug Metab. Dispos. Biol. Fate Chem. 38 (10) (2010) 1857−1864.

[35] U.A. Boelsterli, Specific targets of covalent drug-protein interactions in hepatocytes and their toxicological significance in drug-induced liver injury, Drug Metab. Rev. 25 (4) (1993) 395−451.

[36] W.G. Humphreys, Overview of strategies for addressing BRIs in drug discovery: impact on optimization and design, Chem. Biol. Interact. 192 (1−2) (2011) 56−59.

[37] R.A. Thompson, E.M. Isin, Y. Li, L. Weidolf, K. Page, I. Wilson, et al., In vitro approach to assess the potential for risk of idiosyncratic adverse reactions caused by candidate drugs, Chem. Res. Toxicol. 25 (8) (2012) 1616−1632.

[38] A. Jetter, G.A. Kullak-Ublick, Drugs and hepatic transporters: a review, Pharmacol. Res. 154 (2020) 104234.

[39] M.J. Zamek-Gliszczynski, M.E. Taub, P.P. Chothe, X. Chu, K.M. Giacomini, R.B. Kim, et al., Transporters in drug development: 2018 ITC recommendations for transporters of emerging clinical importance, Clin. Pharmacol. Therapeut. 104 (5) (2018) 890−899.

[40] F.J. Cuperus, T. Claudel, J. Gautherot, E. Halilbasic, M. Trauner, The role of canalicular ABC transporters in cholestasis, Drug Metab. Dispos. Biol. Fate Chem. 42 (4) (2014) 546−560.

[41] S. Amirneni, N. Haep, M.A. Gad, A. Soto-Gutierrez, J.E. Squires, R.M. Florentino, Molecular overview of progressive familial intrahepatic cholestasis, World J. Gastroenterol. 26 (47) (2020) 7470−7484.

[42] R. Coleman, Bile salts and biliary lipids, Biochem. Soc. Trans. 15 (Suppl. 1) (1987) 68S−80S.

[43] A. Di Ciaula, G. Garruti, R. Lunardi Baccetto, E. Molina-Molina, L. Bonfrate, D.Q. Wang, et al., Bile acid physiology, Ann. Hepatol. 16 (Suppl. 1) (2017) S4−S14.

[44] S.Y. Cai, L. Wang, N. Ballatori, J.L. Boyer, Bile salt export pump is highly conserved during vertebrate evolution and its expression is inhibited by PFIC type II mutations, Am. J. Physiol. Gastrointest. Liver Physiol. 281 (2) (2001) G316−G322.

[45] P.L. Jansen, S.S. Strautnieks, E. Jacquemin, M. Hadchouel, E.M. Sokal, G.J. Hooiveld, et al., Hepatocanalicular bile salt export pump deficiency in patients with progressive familial intrahepatic cholestasis, Gastroenterology 117 (6) (1999) 1370−1379.

[46] G. Vitale, S. Gitto, R. Vukotic, F. Raimondi, P. Andreone, Familial intrahepatic cholestasis: new and wide perspectives, Dig. Liver Dis. Off. J. Italian Soc. Gastroenterol. Italian Assoc. Study Liver 51 (7) (2019) 922−933.

[47] J. Zhang, K. He, L. Cai, Y.C. Chen, Y. Yang, Q. Shi, et al., Inhibition of bile salt transport by drugs associated with liver injury in primary hepatocytes from human, monkey, dog, rat, and mouse, Chem. Biol. Interact. 255 (2016) 45−54.

[48] R.E. Morgan, C.J. van Staden, Y. Chen, N. Kalyanaraman, J. Kalanzi, R.T. Dunn 2nd, et al., A multifactorial approach to hepatobiliary transporter assessment enables improved therapeutic compound development, Toxicol. Sci. Off. J. Soc. Toxicol. 136 (1) (2013) 216−241.

[49] R.E. Morgan, M. Trauner, C.J. van Staden, P.H. Lee, B. Ramachandran, M. Eschenberg, et al., Interference with bile salt export pump function is a susceptibility factor for human liver injury in drug development, Toxicol. Sci. Off. J. Soc. Toxicol. 118 (2) (2010) 485−500.

[50] R.W. Yucha, K. He, Q. Shi, L. Cai, Y. Nakashita, C.Q. Xia, et al., In vitro drug-induced liver injury prediction: criteria optimization of efflux transporter IC50 and physicochemical properties, Toxicol. Sci. Off. J. Soc. Toxicol. 157 (2) (2017) 487−499.

[51] M.J. Hafey, R. Houle, K.Q. Tanis, I. Knemeyer, J. Shang, Q. Chen, et al., A two-tiered in vitro approach to de-risk drug candidates for potential bile salt export pump inhibition liabilities in drug discovery, Drug Metab. Dispos. Biol. Fate Chem. 48 (11) (2020) 1147−1160.

[52] M.D. Aleo, Y. Luo, R. Swiss, P.D. Bonin, D.M. Potter, Y. Will, Human drug-induced liver injury severity is highly associated with dual inhibition of liver mitochondrial function and bile salt export pump, Hepatology 60 (3) (2014) 1015−1022.

[53] Y. Cheng, T.F. Woolf, J. Gan, K. He, In vitro model systems to investigate bile salt export pump (BSEP) activity and drug interactions: a review, Chem. Biol. Interact. 255 (2016) 23−30.

[54] P.B. Watkins, The DILI-sim initiative: insights into hepatotoxicity mechanisms and biomarker interpretation, Clin. Transl. Sci. 12 (2) (2019) 122−129.

[55] K. He, E. Qian, Q. Shi, L. Cai, Prediction of drug-induced liver toxicity using ratio of plasma C_{max} to IC_{50} for BSEP inhibition, in: 24th International Symposium on Microsomes and Drug Oxidations and 13th International ISSX Meeting, 2022. #P180.

[56] S.Y. Morita, A. Kobayashi, Y. Takanezawa, N. Kioka, T. Handa, H. Arai, et al., Bile salt-dependent efflux of cellular phospholipids mediated by ATP binding cassette protein B4, Hepatology 46 (1) (2007) 188−199.

[57] S.Y. Morita, T. Terada, Molecular mechanisms for biliary phospholipid and drug efflux mediated by ABCB4 and bile salts, BioMed Res. Int. 2014 (2014) 954781.

[58] A.F. Stattermayer, E. Halilbasic, F. Wrba, P. Ferenci, M. Trauner, Variants in ABCB4 (MDR3) across the spectrum of cholestatic liver diseases in adults, J. Hepatol. 73 (3) (2020) 651−663.

[59] K. He, L. Cai, Q. Shi, H. Liu, T.F. Woolf, Inhibition of MDR3 activity in human hepatocytes by drugs associated with liver injury, Chem. Res. Toxicol. 28 (10) (2015) 1987−1990.

[60] T. Yoshikado, T. Takada, T. Yamamoto, H. Yamaji, K. Ito, T. Santa, et al., Itraconazole-induced cholestasis: involvement of the inhibition of bile canalicular phospholipid translocator MDR3/ABCB4, Mol. Pharmacol. 79 (2) (2011) 241−250.

[61] T. Yoshikado, T. Takada, H. Yamamoto, J.K. Tan, K. Ito, T. Santa, et al., Ticlopidine, a cholestatic liver injury-inducible drug, causes dysfunction of bile formation via diminished biliary secretion of phospholipids: involvement of biliary-excreted glutathione-conjugated ticlopidine metabolites, Mol. Pharmacol. 83 (2) (2013) 552−562.

[62] M.D. Aleo, F. Shah, K. He, P.D. Bonin, A.D. Rodrigues, Evaluating the role of multidrug resistance protein 3 (MDR3) inhibition in predicting drug-induced liver injury using 125 pharmaceuticals, Chem. Res. Toxicol. 30 (5) (2017) 1219−1229.

[63] K. He, E. Qian, Q. Shi, L. Cai, Prediction of drug-induced liver toxicity using ratio of plasma Cmax to IC50 for MDR3 inhibition, 2022 ISSX/MDO meeting, in: 24th International Symposium on Microsomes and Drug Oxidations and 13th International ISSX Meeting, 2022. #P180.

[64] L.W. Klomp, J.C. Vargas, S.W. van Mil, L. Pawlikowska, S.S. Strautnieks, M.J. van Eijk, et al., Characterization of mutations in ATP8B1 associated with hereditary cholestasis, Hepatology 40 (1) (2004) 27−38.

[65] J.S. Nayagam, P. Foskett, S. Strautnieks, K. Agarwal, R. Miquel, D. Joshi, et al., Clinical phenotype of adult-onset liver disease in patients with variants in ABCB4, ABCB11, and ATP8B1, Hepatol. Commun. 6 (2022) 2654−2664.

[66] G. Jedlitschky, U. Hoffmann, H.K. Kroemer, Structure and function of the MRP2 (ABCC2) protein and its role in drug disposition, Expert Opin. Drug Metabol. Toxicol. 2 (3) (2006) 351−366.

[67] P. Borst, C. de Wolf, K. van de Wetering, Multidrug resistance-associated proteins 3, 4, and 5, Pflueg. Arch. Eur. J. Physiol. 453 (5) (2007) 661−673.

[68] C. Pauli-Magnus, P.J. Meier, Hepatobiliary transporters and drug-induced cholestasis, Hepatology 44 (4) (2006) 778−787.

[69] A. Mak, J. Uetrecht, Immune mechanisms of idiosyncratic drug-induced liver injury, J. Clin. Transl. Res. 3 (1) (2017) 145−156.

[70] M. Mosedale, P.B. Watkins, Drug-induced liver injury: advances in mechanistic understanding that will inform risk management, Clin. Pharmacol. Therapeut. 101 (4) (2017) 469−480.

[71] S.H. Kim, D.J. Naisbitt, Update on advances in research on idiosyncratic drug-induced liver injury, Allergy Asthma Immunol. Res. 8 (1) (2016) 3−11.

[72] Z.X. Liu, S. Govindarajan, N. Kaplowitz, Innate immune system plays a critical role in determining the progression and severity of acetaminophen hepatotoxicity, Gastroenterology 127 (6) (2004) 1760−1774.

[73] M. Keisu, T.B. Andersson, Drug-induced liver injury in humans: the case of ximelagatran, Handb. Exp. Pharmacol. 196 (2010) 407−418.

[74] E.K. Ainscow, J.E. Pilling, N.M. Brown, A.T. Orme, M. Sullivan, A.C. Hargreaves, et al., Investigations into the liver effects of ximelagatran using high content screening of primary human hepatocyte cultures, Expert Opin. Drug Saf. 7 (4) (2008) 351−365.

[75] K. Kenne, I. Skanberg, B. Glinghammar, A. Berson, D. Pessayre, J.P. Flinois, et al., Prediction of drug-induced liver injury in humans by using in vitro methods: the case of ximelagatran, Toxicol. Vitro 22 (3) (2008) 730−746.

[76] O.S. Gudmundsson, Case study: ximelagatran: a double prodrug of melagatran, in: V.J. Stella, R.T. Borchardt, M.J. Hageman, R. Oliyai, H. Maag, J.W. Tilley (Eds.), Prodrugs: Challenges and Rewards Part 1, Springer New York, New York, NY, 2007, pp. 1395−1402.

[77] J. Medina-Echeverz, C. Ma, A.G. Duffy, T. Eggert, N. Hawk, D.E. Kleiner, et al., Systemic agonistic anti-CD40 treatment of tumor-bearing mice modulates hepatic myeloid-suppressive cells and causes immune-mediated liver damage, Cancer Immunol. Res. 3 (5) (2015) 557−566.

[78] T. Affolter, H.P. Llewellyn, D.W. Bartlett, Q. Zong, S. Xia, V. Torti, et al., Inhibition of immune checkpoints PD-1, CTLA-4, and IDO1 coordinately induces immune-mediated liver injury in mice, PLoS One 14 (5) (2019) e0217276.

[79] D. Zhang, J. Hart, X. Ding, X. Zhang, M. Feely, L. Yassan, et al., Histologic patterns of liver injury induced by anti-PD-1 therapy, Gastroenterol. Rep. (Oxf) 8 (1) (2020) 50−55.

[80] K. Yang, C. Guo, J.L. Woodhead, R.L.S. Claire, P.B. Watkins, S.Q. Siler, et al., Sandwich-cultured hepatocytes as a tool to study drug disposition and drug-induced liver injury, J. Pharmaceut. Sci. 105 (2) (2016) 443−459.

[81] O. Ukairo, M. McVay, S. Krzyzewski, S. Aoyama, K. Rose, M.E. Andersen, et al., Bioactivation and toxicity of acetaminophen in a rat hepatocyte micropatterned coculture system, J. Biochem. Mol. Toxicol. 27 (10) (2013) 471−478.

[82] O.J. Trask Jr., A. Moore, E.L. LeCluyse, A micropatterned hepatocyte coculture model for assessment of liver toxicity using high-content imaging analysis, Assay Drug Dev. Technol. 12 (1) (2014) 16−27.

[83] A.R. Baudy, M.A. Otieno, P. Hewitt, J. Gan, A. Roth, D. Keller, et al., Liver microphysiological systems development guidelines for safety risk assessment in the pharmaceutical industry, Lab Chip 20 (2) (2020) 215−225.

[84] W.R. Proctor, A.J. Foster, J. Vogt, C. Summers, B. Middleton, M.A. Pilling, et al., Utility of spherical human liver microtissues for prediction of clinical drug-induced liver injury, Arch. Toxicol. 91 (8) (2017) 2849−2863.

[85] L.D. Butler, P. Guzzie-Peck, J. Hartke, M.S. Bogdanffy, Y. Will, D. Diaz, et al., Current nonclinical testing paradigms in support of safe clinical trials: an IQ Consortium DruSafe perspective, Regul. Toxicol. Pharmacol. 87 (Suppl. 3) (2017) S1−S15.

[86] T.M. Monticello, T.W. Jones, D.M. Dambach, D.M. Potter, M.W. Bolt, M. Liu, et al., Current nonclinical testing paradigm enables safe entry to First-In-Human clinical trials: the IQ consortium nonclinical to clinical translational database, Toxicol. Appl. Pharmacol. 334 (2017) 100−109.

[87] K. Ashby, E.E. Navarro Almario, W. Tong, J. Borlak, R. Mehta, M. Chen, Review article: therapeutic bile acids and the risks for hepatotoxicity, Aliment. Pharmacol. Ther. 47 (12) (2018) 1623−1638.

[88] X. Chu, K. Bleasby, R. Evers, Species differences in drug transporters and implications for translating preclinical findings to humans, Expert Opin. Drug Metabol. Toxicol. 9 (3) (2013) 237−252.

[89] L. Huang, Y. Li, H. Pan, Y. Lu, X. Zhou, F. Shi, Cortex dictamni-induced liver injury in mice: the role of P450-mediated metabolic activation of furanoids, Toxicol. Lett. 330 (2020) 41−52.

[90] S.H. Jeong, J.H. Jang, H.Y. Cho, Y.B. Lee, Human risk assessment of 4-n-nonylphenol (4-n-NP) using physiologically based pharmacokinetic (PBPK) modeling: analysis of gender exposure differences and application to exposure analysis related to large exposure variability in population, Arch. Toxicol. 96 (10) (2022) 2687−2715.

[91] S.E. Roth, M.I. Avigan, D. Bourdet, D. Brott, R. Church, A. Dash, et al., Next-generation DILI biomarkers: prioritization of biomarkers for qualification and best practices for biospecimen collection in drug development, Clin. Pharmacol. Therapeut. 107 (2) (2020) 333−346.

Chapter 9

Optimization for small volume of distribution leading to the discovery of apixaban

Kan He

Biotranex LLC, Princeton, NJ, United States

Apixaban, sold under the brand name Eliquis®, is a potent and selective small molecule inhibitor of coagulation Factor Xa (FXa). Medical indications include reducing the risk of stroke and systemic embolism in patients with nonvalvular atrial fibrillation, prophylaxis and treatment of deep vein thrombosis (DVT), treatment of pulmonary embolism (PE), and reducing the risk of recurrent DVT and PE following initial therapy. The discovery of apixaban is the result of a nearly two-decades long effort of one company searching for a best-in-class new oral anticoagulant. This chapter will focus on how the strategy of limiting the volume of distribution—critical in minimizing the potential for toxicity and optimizing the efficacy of FXa inhibitors—resulted in the discovery of apixaban.

Milestones and pitfalls in early discovery of FXa inhibitors

The FXa discovery program was initiated in the mid-1990s at DuPont Pharmaceuticals Company. At that time, warfarin, an oral vitamin K antagonist, was the standard of care for venous thrombotic diseases. Warfarin therapy is associated with a high rate of serious and even fatal bleeding due to its narrow therapeutic window. Patients on warfarin therapy require frequent monitoring of prothrombin time with dosing adjusted accordingly [1]. DuPont, along with many other companies, sought to discover a replacement for warfarin, one with a wider therapeutic window. I joined the discovery team in May 2000, when the FXa discovery program was well advanced. To follow are some important milestones the team had achieved in the early discovery phase [2,3].

Selection of FXa over thrombin as the therapeutic target for new oral anticoagulant drugs

Among all the coagulation factors, thrombin was the drug target that most companies focused on in the 1990s [2]. Initially, an anti-thrombin program was also pursued for a brief time at DuPont, but this program was dropped in favor of focusing on the discovery of novel FXa inhibitors. DuPont was one of the first companies to initiate a small molecule FXa discovery program [2].

FXa catalyzes the conversion of prothrombin to thrombin, which is crucial for both intrinsic and extrinsic coagulation pathways (Fig. 9.1). Early experiments with recombinant hirudin (a specific thrombin inhibitor isolated from the medicinal leech *Hirudo medicinalis*) and tick anticoagulant peptide (TAP, a specific FXa inhibitor from the soft tick *Ornithodoros moubata*), both demonstrated that FXa inhibition results in less bleeding time compared to that produced by thrombin inhibition, while both compounds produced equal antithrombotic efficacy [4,5]. FXa inhibition was also considered more efficient than direct thrombin inhibition, as one FXa molecule leads to the formation of more than a thousand thrombin molecules [6]. More important, FXa inhibition does not interfere with residual thrombin activity that may contribute to the maintenance of hemostasis via activation of the high-affinity platelet thrombin receptor. In addition, the low molecular weight heparin (LMWH) enoxaparin, with its anticoagulation mechanism of action, involves mainly inhibition of FXa, and has demonstrated clinical efficacy with an acceptable safety profile. Considering these

Overcoming Obstacles in Drug Discovery and Development. https://doi.org/10.1016/B978-0-12-817134-9.00023-4

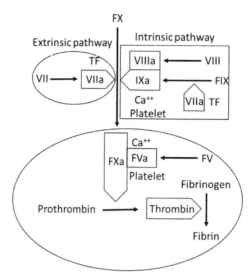

FIGURE 9.1 Central role of factor Xa (Fxa) in the coagulation cascade at the point of convergence of the intrinsic and extrinsic pathways.

factors, the discovery team at DuPont believed that FXa inhibition would result in a wider therapeutic index than thrombin inhibition [2].

Screening of the DuPont library of glycoprotein IIb/IIIa (GPIIb/IIIa) inhibitors pointed to the discovery of lead molecule SN429

When the program started in the mid-1990s, there were only a few known small molecule FXa inhibitors. Unfortunately, these dibasic compounds lacked selectivity over other serine proteases and had poor oral bioavailability. An initial effort by the DuPont team using a molecular modeling rational design approach resulted in the discovery of a novel bis-phenylamidine series of FXa inhibitors [7]. However, these early compounds failed to address selectivity and oral bioavailability issues [3].

A breakthrough was made with the screening of the DuPont library of GPIIb/IIIa inhibitors. DuPont scientists had invested a great amount of effort in the discovery of GPIIb/IIIa inhibitors as potential anti-platelet agents. The rationale behind this screening effort was the realization that the FXa recognition motif in prothrombin, Glu-Gly-Arg, mimics the core moiety of GPIIb/IIIa inhibitors Arg-Gly-Asp. Screening of this chemical library identified weak leads with FXa binding affinity in the range of 30–40 μM [8].

Extensive optimization of these weak leads quickly led to the discovery of a lead molecule SN429, which showed potent in vitro anti-FXa activity with a Ki of 13 pM and good antithrombotic activity in a rabbit model of thrombosis [9]. (Fig. 9.2). However, SN429 was found to have poor oral bioavailability, attributed to the polar benzamidine moiety. The high potency of SN429 allowed the team to pursue a strategy of trading binding affinity for oral bioavailability and selectivity by replacing the benzamidine with other functional groups with less basicity.

Innovative biological screening approaches

Simple chromogenic assays were established for screening a large number of chemicals for anti-FXa activity [2]. Because trypsin-like serine proteases are ubiquitous and are involved in many biological processes, selectivity screening was incorporated into the program from the very beginning in order to assess the potential for off-target toxicity. Molecular modeling and structural-based drug design were employed to optimize potency and selectivity. A rabbit AV shunt disease model was extensively used to evaluate in vivo efficacy [10]. Plasma concentrations were measured and used to calculate EC_{50} values to address concerns about a potential species difference in rabbit pharmacokinetics and protein binding.

At this point, the discovery effort was focused on addressing issues related to oral bioavailability and plasma concentration peak/trough ratio. A large number of compounds were synthesized, with their permeability values determined using a Caco-2 cell permeability screen. Pharmacokinetic profiles were determined in dogs using an "N-in-1" approach [11]. The "N-in-1" approach, based on a carefully considered study design, provided quick turnaround of pharmacokinetic

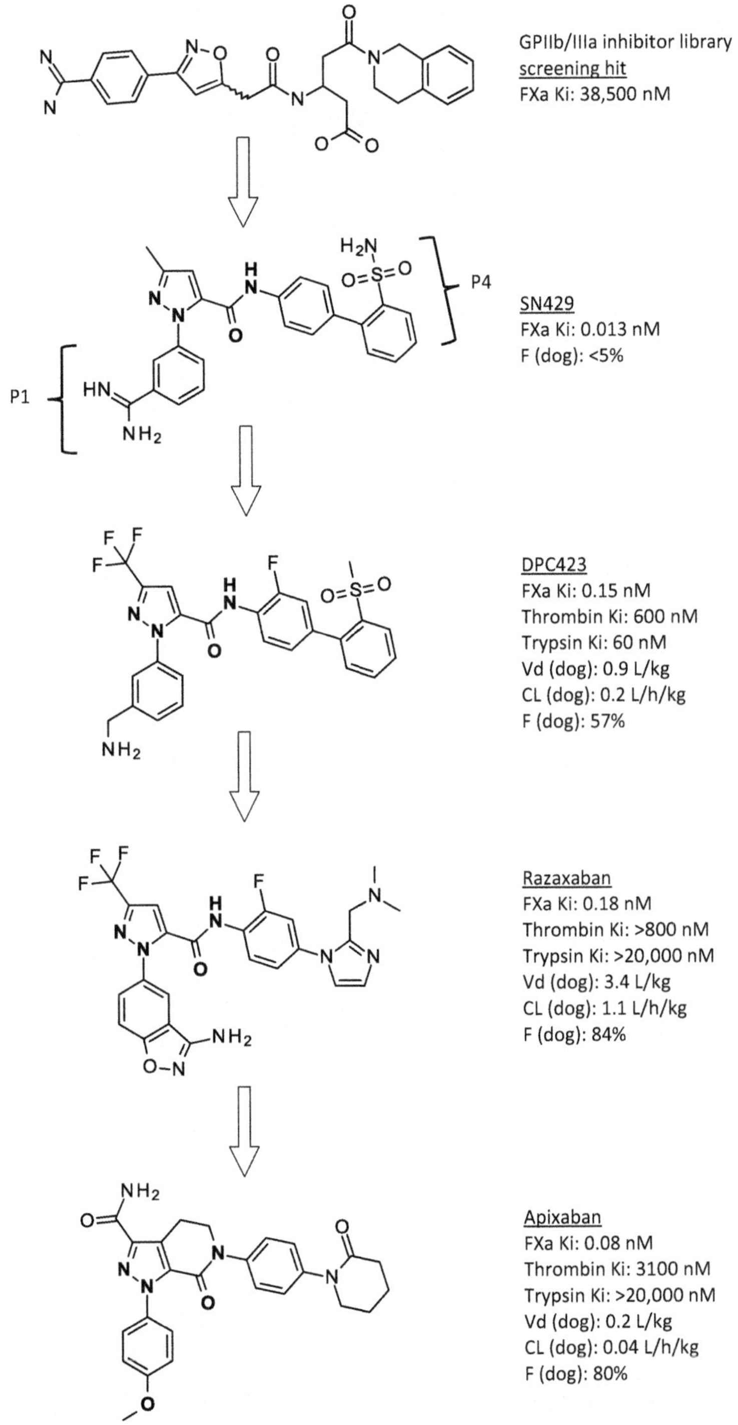

FIGURE 9.2 Evolution of FXa inhibitors discovered at DuPont Pharmaceuticals, Inc.

results, allowing the team to rapidly optimize lead compounds with improved pharmacokinetic profiles. Another important aspect of the screening approach was the use of chimpanzees in pharmacokinetic studies for selected compounds, providing more clinically relevant pharmacokinetic information than other animal models. The chimpanzee model has been evaluated as an appropriate surrogate for human PK prediction for certain compounds due to genetic, physiological, and biochemical similarities between chimpanzee and human [12].

The discoveries of DPC-423 and DPC-906 (razaxaban)

In general, benzamidine-containing compounds have poor Caco-2 cellular permeability and limited oral bioavailability. This is believed to be a result of the polar basic amidine moiety, with a pKa value of approximately 11, being positively charged in intestinal fluids. Successful replacement of the benzamidine moiety with a less basic P1 benzylamine led to the discovery of 1-[3-(aminomethyl)phenyl]-N-3-fluoro-2'-(methylsulfonyl)-[1,1'-biphenyl]-4-yl]-3-(trifluoromethyl)-1H-pyrazole-5-carboxamide (DPC-423) (Fig. 9.2) [9]. DPC-423 is a potent FXa inhibitor (Ki: 0.15 nM) that exhibited good permeability in Caco-2 cells (P_{app}: 4.86×10^{-6} cm/s). DPC-423 had improved oral bioavailability in dogs (F%: 57%, $t_{1/2}$: 7.5 h) and demonstrated efficacy in the rabbit thrombosis A−V shunt model (ID_{50}: 1.1 µmol/kg/h). DPC-423 also exhibited excellent selectivity over thrombin and many other serine proteases (>10,000-fold) except for trypsin and plasma kallikrein (at approximately 400-fold selectivity). DPC-423 was advanced to Phase I clinical trials and showed desirable plasma exposure concentrations and a $t_{1/2}$ of about 30 h, which represented the first small-molecule FXa inhibitor tested in humans. However, further advancement of DPC-423 was curtailed due to preclinical toxicity issues.

After the discovery of DPC-423, a deep backup strategy was adopted focusing on optimizing enzyme selectivity profiles to minimize the potential for off-target toxicity. Selectivity was observed to be significantly improved with a DPC-423 analog in which the benzamidine moiety was replaced with an aminobenzisoxazole group. However, permeability and solubility were dramatically reduced. Further optimization was focused on permeability, solubility, protein binding, and pharmacokinetic profiles. These cumulated efforts led to the discovery of 1-(3'-aminobenzisoxazole-5'-yl)-3-trifluoromethyl-N-[2-fluoro-4-[(2'-dimcthylaminomethyl)imidazole-1-yl]phenyl]-1H-pyrazole 5 carboxyamide (razaxaban, DPC-906, BMS-561389) (Fig. 9.2) [13]. Razaxaban was the first small-molecule oral FXa inhibitor to establish the clinical proof of concept for the FXa mechanism in Phase II clinical trials. Unfortunately, it was discontinued in further development due to preclinical toxicity findings.

After joining the FXa discovery group in May 2000, I was involved in the nomination of two backup candidate compounds which were advanced for preclinical development. Despite the team's great hope for these two compounds, they both exhibited preclinical toxicities and were discontinued from further development. The toxicities with the FXa inhibitors discovered in the early phase of the program included biliary toxicity and hepatotoxicity, seizures, retinal lesions, and pulmonary toxicity. Although some of these toxicities were overcome with chemical modifications, the modifications led to new toxicities. The discovery team became challenged with toxicity issues. After careful consideration and extensive discussions with other team members, I proposed that FXa inhibitors might be optimized for a small volume of distribution (V_d) to minimize the potential for organ toxicity and to maximize in vivo efficacy (Fig. 9.3). This idea contradicted the previous strategy in which the optimization for long $t_{1/2}$ often resulted in compounds with a large volume of distribution. Additional screening of cytotoxicity was also included in the screening strategy.

It is important to point out that high peak/trough ratio of plasma drug concentration is detrimental for FXa inhibitors because the peak drug concentration is related to bleeding potential and trough drug concentration to efficacy. Long $t_{1/2}$ is essential to maintain a low peak/trough ratio.

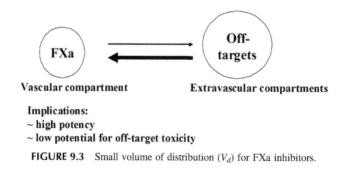

FIGURE 9.3 Small volume of distribution (V_d) for FXa inhibitors.

Why small V_d for anti-FXa drugs

The question became: why was a small V_d essential for FXa inhibitor drugs? Before we answer this question, let's discuss where FXa is distributed in the human body and what the biological implication of V_d is. FXa is primarily generated in blood by the activation of Factor X, a vitamin K-dependent zymogen synthesized in the liver and secreted into the blood. The activation of Factor X involves two principal pathways: (1) the extrinsic pathway, which involves Factors VII/VIIa in complex with tissue factor (TF) and is responsible for the initiation of coagulation, and (2) the intrinsic pathway, which involves Factor IXa in complex with Factor VIIIa on the surface of platelets and is responsible for amplifying the coagulation process (Fig. 9.1). Once formed, FXa activates prothrombin to thrombin, the final clotting protease responsible for the conversion of soluble fibrinogen to insoluble fibrin, which leads to blood clotting. Thrombin is activated on the surface of activated platelets by FXa in a prothrombinase complex with the platelet phospholipids, Ca^{2+}, and Factor V_a cofactor. As you can see, FXa is formed and functions almost exclusively in blood. Therefore, theoretically, FXa inhibitors need only be present in blood for anticoagulation to take effect.

Then the question became: how to estimate how much drug stays in blood in a simple and practical way to support FXa inhibitor drug discovery? Blood contains plasma and blood cells. For most drugs, the plasma-to-blood partition ratio is approximately one. For the following discussion, I will focus on plasma, assuming the plasma-to-blood partition ratio is one. The fraction of drug in plasma can be assessed using the following equation [14]:

$$\text{Fraction of drug in plasma} = V_p/V_d \qquad (9.1)$$

where V_p is the volume of plasma, a physiological constant, and V_d is the apparent volume of distribution, a mathematical volume in which drug distributes in the body. As shown by this equation, the only variable that determines the fraction of drug in plasma is V_d. Therefore, the smaller the V_d, the larger the fraction of drug residing in the plasma. Conceptionally, the smaller the V_d, the higher the in vivo efficacy FXa inhibitor will exhibit.

Theoretically, $V_d = V_p + V_t \times K_p$, where $V_t \times K_p$ is a mathematical volume in which drug distributes in all tissues outside of plasma, representing the sum of the apparent volume of all tissues. V_t is the physiological volume of a tissue or organ of the body and K_p is the tissue-to-plasma partition coefficient ratio or tissue distribution ratio. Both V_t and K_p vary among tissues for a drug. Since $K_p = C_t/C_p = f_u/f_{ut}$, where C_t is the drug concentration in tissue and C_p is the drug concentration in plasma, f_u is the unbound fraction in plasma and f_{ut} is the unbound fraction in tissue, V_d can be expressed in the following equation [14]:

$$V_d = V_p + V_t \times C_t/C = V_p + V_t \times f_u/f_{ut} \qquad (9.2)$$

As you can see from Eq. (9.2), the higher the V_d is, the higher the drug concentration is in tissue, indicating higher tissue binding. Tissue binding can be specific or nonspecific. Nonspecific tissue binding may be related to the binding of membrane components, cellular proteins, trapped-in cell, and/or subcellular organelles. In some cases, nonspecific tissue binding is associated with unwanted off-target biological toxicities. Specific binding is generally associated with biological effects. For FXa inhibitors, all the tissue binding should be considered off-target binding. Therefore, FXa inhibitors with a large V_d would have increased potential for off-target toxicities.

Conventionally, drug candidates are screened using in vitro binding assays against a broad range of biological targets to minimize the potential for off-target toxicities. For the FXa program, we screened candidates for binding to trypsin, thrombin, plasma kallikrein, chymotrypsin, activated protein C, FIXa, FVIIIa, FXIa, urokinase, plasmin, and tPA. We also screened candidates for interactions with various known biological targets using commercially available screening panels; however, screening panels are limited, as there are millions of unknown biological targets in the body as potential off-targets. Therefore, a broader approach to minimizing off-target toxicity potential was needed to incorporate tissue distribution or plasma selectivity. Fortunately, for FXa inhibitors, we could use the V_d to estimate the plasma selectivity in order to reduce the potential for off-target toxicity.

Given the above rationale, drawing the benefits of a small V_d strategy was communicated to the team (Fig. 9.3) [15], and it was agreed to incorporate the strategy for optimization of small V_d in the selection of FXa inhibitors.

The small V_d strategy

V_d is a result of complex interactions between a drug molecule and all biological molecules in the body. Based on Eq. (9.2), plasma protein binding is a key determinant of V_d. In general, drugs with high plasma protein binding tend to have a smaller V_d. [16,17] However, in the case of FXa inhibitors, it is the unbound compound that directly inhibits FXa activity. High plasma protein binding reduces the efficacy of FXa inhibitors. Therefore, we could not simply optimize small V_d for FXa inhibitors at the expense of high protein binding.

V_d is one of the two parameters that determine $t_{1/2}$ as shown in the following equation: $t_{1/2} = V_d/CL$, where CL refers to systemic clearance. A small V_d results in a short $t_{1/2}$, which in turn results in increased plasma peak/trough concentration ratios. The anticoagulation efficacy is related to the trough drug concentration, while the peak drug concentration is related to bleeding side effects. Therefore, a short $t_{1/2}$ is detrimental to FXa inhibitors. It was clear that the only solution to overcome this issue was to reduce the CL to a very low or extremely low level while maintaining a small V_d.

The small V_d strategy included three primary components: (1) minimizing V_d, (2) reducing the CL to a very low or extremely low level, and (3) avoiding high plasma protein binding. These three components might appear to be conflicting; the challenge was to find an optimum balance. We also had to focus on achieving good oral bioavailability and avoiding polymorphic metabolism to reduce potential individual variations in efficacy and bleeding potentials, while maintaining high FXa binding affinity, high selectivity, and efficacy as shown in the rabbit A–V shunt model. This represented a significant discovery challenge: to obtain the right balance of all of these key target compound parameters.

Another significant challenge was determining how to generate biological data that would be predictive of a human biological profile in a manner that would meet the team's throughput demand for discovery screening. There are several methods to predict human V_d [18]. Among them is preclinical species extrapolation. Previous studies have demonstrated that human V_d could be reasonably predicted using allometric scaling based on animal body weight. The formula for this allometric scaling is $Y = {_a}\mathrm{BW}^b$, where a and b are the coefficients generated using different animal species, and BW is body weight. The allometric exponents for V_d range from 0.75 to 1. The V_d was determined in pharmacokinetic studies in dog and used to rank order compounds. In order to improve the throughput, the compounds were tested using an N-in-1 format [11].

It is well recognized that, in contrast to V_d, significant species differences in metabolic clearance can occur, making extrapolation to humans more complicated. The reason for this includes, among other differences, the expression of cytochrome P450 isoforms across species. Therefore, we used an intrinsic clearance approach to estimate human metabolic clearance by screening compounds with human liver microsomes [19]. Human pharmacokinetic profiles were estimated using a hybrid approach combining the in vitro-projected human intrinsic CL and the pharmacokinetic parameters obtained from in vivo dog studies. Protein binding was measured in human plasma, as well as in animal species used for efficacy and PK investigations.

This approach allowed us to screen several hundred compounds for structure activity relationships (SAR), optimization, and selection of candidates for further characterization. It is noteworthy that our accumulated experience on how to optimize compounds to reduce the CL to a very or extremely low-level enabled our ultimate success.

Discovery of apixaban

The discovery of apixaban started with the aim of finding a structurally diverse backup to razaxaban. Medicinal chemistry efforts leading to apixaban are summarized in papers published elsewhere [3,20]. Briefly, the initial medicinal chemistry effort focused on designing rigid pyrazole scaffolds to replace the 5-carboamido linker that connected the pyrazole ring and the P4 moiety (Fig. 9.2). There was concern that the 5-carboamido linker could be cleaved metabolically or chemically to generate a potentially mutagenic aniline fragment. To achieve this goal, a dual strategy was adopted. The first strategy involved tying back the amide NH onto the P4 inner phenyl ring, while the second involved cyclizing the amide moiety onto the pyrazole ring [3]. Compounds generated using the first strategy (tying back the amide NH) were found to be potent and highly selective inhibitors of FXa; however, these compounds exhibited poor oral bioavailability and weak clotting times. It was surmised that the weak clotting times were related to high protein binding for these compounds. Therefore, the first strategy was abandoned. The second strategy led to the discovery of pyrazolopyrimidinone and dihydropyrazolopyridinone derivatives, which had high FXa binding affinity, potency in the clotting assay, and good oral bioavailability. However, the pyrazolopyrimidinone analogs were not stable under acidic conditions, and therefore were dropped from further consideration. The dihydropyrazolopyridinone derivatives, on the other hand, were stable under acidic conditions and showed good versatility in tolerating a broader range of functional groups; this group was selected as the chemical scaffold for further optimization.

Initially, the aminobenzisoxazole P1 group was maintained unchanged, while extensive modifications on the P4 moiety were explored. This chemical modification led to several potent compounds with high FXa binding affinities (Ki < 0.05 nM) and potent in vivo efficacy [3]. However, these compounds also had high CL and high V_d properties. Additionally, a preclinical development candidate from this chemical series was stopped from further development due to toxicities observed in preclinical safety assessment studies. The concern about the aminobenzisoxazole P1 moiety also came from the findings that razaxaban caused liver toxicity in the dog chronic dose studies. I hypothesized that the liver toxicity was caused by an accumulation of an impermeable benzamidine metabolite in hepatocytes, resulting from the extensive metabolic ring opening reduction of the aminobenzisoxazole moiety (Fig. 9.4) [21]. Indeed, this metabolite was found to accumulate to a significant level in the chronic-dose toxicity studies of dog liver samples.

Given the above concerns, the chemistry focus was shifted to finding a replacement for the aminobenzisoxazole P1 group. As part of this effort, a p-methoxyphenyl P1 group was introduced [3,20]. The C-3 position of the pyrazole ring was targeted to optimize FXa binding, polarity, and plasma protein binding (Table 9.1, Fig. 9.2). The C-3 carboxamide analogs

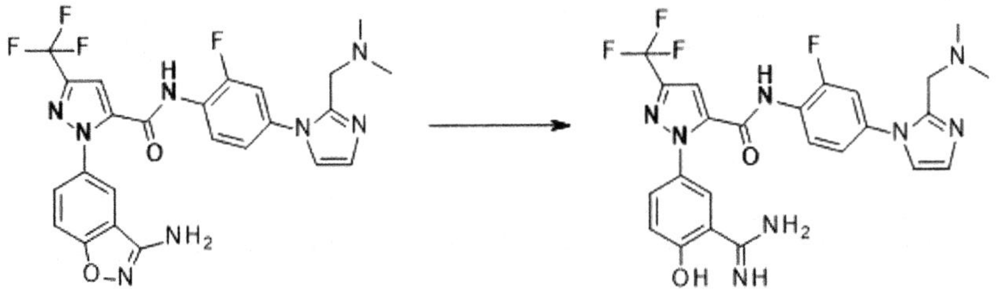

FIGURE 9.4 The major metabolic pathway of razaxaban in rat, dog, and human.

TABLE 9.1 Effects of P4 substituents on volume of distribution (V_d) and systemic clearance (CL) in dog.[a]

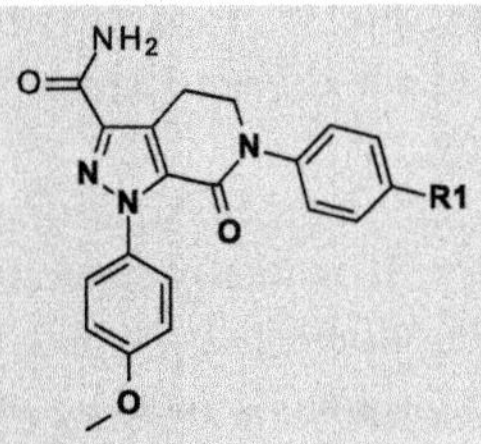

R1	FXa Ki (nM)[b]	V_d (L/kg)	CL (L/h/kg)	F%
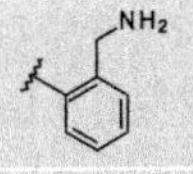	0.97	N/A	N/A	N/A
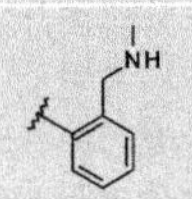	0.14	7.4	1.3	56
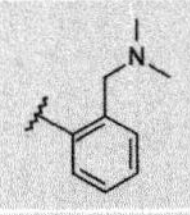	0.24	6.1	2.0	56
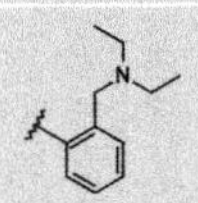	0.08	6.5	2.4	20
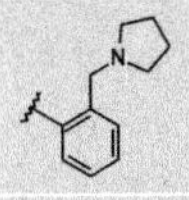	0.30	5.6	1.5	53
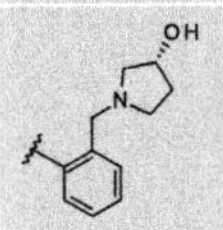	0.07	1.6	0.3	100
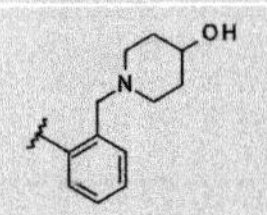	0.29	1.0	0.1	55
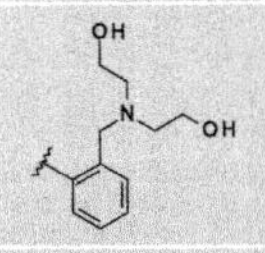	0.36	1.1	0.5	15
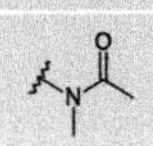	0.54	1.7	2.8	56
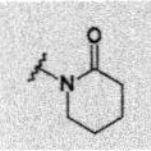	0.08	0.2	0.02	58

N/A: not available.
[a]Pharmacokinetic parameters were obtained in dogs following a single dose of intravenous (0.4 mg/kg) and oral (0.2 mg/kg) administration in N-in-1 format.
[b]Ki values were obtained with purified human FXa.

showed smaller V_d (1.6 versus 3.7—4.9 L/kg), lower CL (0.32 versus 2.5—2.6 L/h/kg), and higher bioavailability (100% versus 7%—24%) than the C-3 triazole analogs. In general, a large V_d was associated with a cationic structure (Table 9.1, Fig. 9.2). We also observed that reducing the basicity resulted in lower V_d.

To further minimize V_d, we explored polar non-basic functional modifications on the P4 position (Table 9.1, Fig. 9.2) [20]. The substituted amino compounds exhibited high V_d in dogs (6—7 L/kg). While the pyrrolidine analog showed similar V_d to the substituted amino compounds, the hydroxypyrrolidinyl and hydroxyperidinyl analogs exhibited much lower V_d (1—1.6 L/kg). In a parallel effort, a compound containing a P4 nitrogen atom at the point of attachment was also prepared and tested (Table 9.1). An N-methylacetyl group, which differed from all previous pendent P4 functionalities, was identified; however, it was found to have a moderate V_d (1.7 L/kg) in the dog. Cyclization of the P4 N-methylacetyl group to form a lactam analog dramatically reduced the V_d and CL, while improving the FXa binding affinity. The C-3 carboxamide moiety is important to reduce plasma protein binding. All these chemical modification efforts culminated in the discovery of 1-(4-methoxyphenyl)-7-oxo-6-(4-(2-oxopiperidin-1-yl)phenyl)-4,5,6,7-tetrahydro-1H-pyrazolo[3,4-c]pyridine-3-carboxamide (apixaban, BMS-562247, DPC-0023) (Table 9.1, Figs. 9.2, 9.5).

Up to this point, approximately 4000 compounds had been synthesized for FXa affinity screening, and approximately 500 compounds were tested for PK profiles in dog.

Apixaban is a potent, reversible, and selective inhibitor of FXa with a Ki of 0.08 nM for human FXa and a 30,000-fold selectivity over other human coagulation proteases. It is totally neutral (no ionizable groups), in contrast to earlier FXa inhibitors. Its x-ray structure shows a similar binding orientation in the FXa active site compared with earlier FXa inhibitors (Fig. 9.5) [3]. Apixaban is efficacious in multiple thrombotic models, including the arterial-venous shunt, the tissue-stasis venous, the electrically or $FeCl_2$-induced vena cava, and the carotid artery thrombosis rat and rabbit models [10]. The plasma concentration-time profile of apixaban was significantly improved, compared with earlier clinical development candidates (Fig. 9.6). Detailed preclinical pharmacology profiles of apixaban are summarized elsewhere [10].

The V_d value of apixaban was found to be similar in rat, dog, and chimpanzee, ranging from approximately 0.2—0.5 L/kg, less than the total body water volume in these species (Table 9.2) [22,23]. In addition, apixaban was found to be equally distributed between plasma and blood. Compared to average blood volumes, approximately 20%, 40%, and 50% of apixaban remained in the blood in rat, dog, and chimpanzee, respectively. This small V_d for apixaban is unlikely to be related to protein binding in these species, as the protein binding was very low, with unbound fractions ranging from 4% to 9%. The small V_d of apixaban suggests that the compound remains largely in blood, the site for the therapeutic target FXa, compared to earlier FXa inhibitors that were extensively distributed to other tissues (Fig. 9.2). A drug's distribution primarily to the same tissue compartment as the drug target can result in high potency while reducing the potential for off-

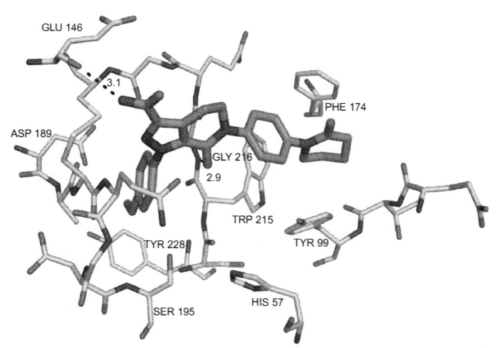

FIGURE 9.5 X-ray structure of apixaban bound in the active site of FXa [3].

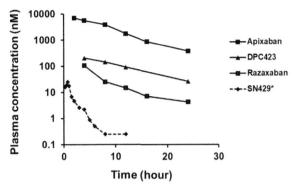

FIGURE 9.6 Time-plasma concentration profiles of DPC-423, razaxaban and apixaban in chimpanzee following a single oral dose of 1 mg/kg *SN429 was dosed orally in dog at 1 mg/kg for comparison purpose.

TABLE 9.2 Volume of distribution at steady state (V_d), systemic clearance (CL), and oral bioavailability (F) of apixaban in rat, dog, chimpanzee, and human.

	Rat ($n = 4$)	Dog ($n = 3$)	Chimpanzee ($n = 1/2$)[a]	Human ($n = 6$)
V_d (L/kg)	0.5 ± 0.2	0.2 ± 0.02	0.17	$0.24-0.37$[b]
CL (L/h/kg)	0.9 ± 0.2	0.04 ± 0.0	0.018	$0.04-0.05$[b]
F (%)	48 ± 8	80 ± 9	43/59	66

[a]$n = 1$ for V_d and CL, $n = 2$ for F.
[b]Normalized by 70 kg as average body weight for a healthy human adult.

target effects (Fig. 9.3). To compare to the previous clinical development candidates, the V_d for DPC-423 and razaxaban in chimpanzee were 2.6 and 2.4 L/kg, respectively [12,23]. As a result, we predicted low potential for apixaban to cause off-target toxicity.

As discussed above, low clearance is essential for a drug with a small V_d to maintain adequate $t_{1/2}$. Apixaban has a very low clearance in dog and chimpanzee, accounting for less than 2% of the hepatic blood flow (Table 9.2) [23]. Consistent across species, the intrinsic metabolic clearance is very low, with no appreciable disappearance in dog, chimpanzee, or human liver microsomes and hepatocytes. Renal clearance values are also very low across species, being less than the protein binding-adjusted glomerular filtration rates. Based on the preclinical profile, we predicted that apixaban would have a desirable PK profile in humans with good oral bioavailability, a small V_d, a low CL, low potential for drug-drug interactions due to multiple clearance pathways, and lack of polymorphic metabolism. A more detailed discussion of apixaban's preclinical pharmacokinetic profile is reported elsewhere [23].

The human dose of apixaban was estimated based on projected human PK and unbound EC_{50} values. The human PK profile was projected using the chimpanzee PK data, given that there was no substantial difference in vitro clearance and the consistent PK profiles in the animals tested. Apixaban unbound peak and trough concentrations at steady state were estimated by PK modeling for multiple dosing and normalized by human plasma protein binding to yield the unbound peak and trough concentration. The EC_{50} values generated from the disease animal models were normalized by animal plasma protein binding to yield the unbound EC_{50}. The human dose was projected to achieve the unbound trough concentration, which was equal to the unbound EC_{50} value in human. With this approach, we projected the apixaban dose to be between 5 and 20 mg with once- or twice-daily dosing. This human dose projection was found to be extremely valuable in dose selections for both Phase I and Phase II clinical trials. Apixaban was nominated as the backup candidate of razaxaban for development, and a Phase I clinical trial was initiated in 2002.

Development of apixaban

Nonclinical safety assessment

Apixaban was tested in multiple safety studies in several animal species [24]. The oral LD_{50} for apixaban was found to be greater than 4000 mg/kg (maximum dose) in single-dose toxicology studies in mice and rats. There were no toxicity findings except pharmacological activity-related effects such as prolongation of coagulation parameters and evidence of bleeding in the chronic repeat dose 6-month and 12-month toxicology studies in rats and dogs at oral doses up to 600 and 100 mg/kg, respectively. The safety margins were 3.5−4 and 20−28 comparing the systemic exposures at the no-observed-adverse-effect level (NOAEL) of 600 mg/kg/day in rats and 100 mg/kg/day in dogs to the human exposure of apixaban at a dose of 5 mg twice a day, respectively.

There were no statistically significant findings for other studies, including the carcinogenicity study in CD-1 male and female mice (3000 mg/kg/day) and Sprague Dawley rats (600 mg/kg/day) at doses up to 1500, 3000, and 600 mg/kg/day, respectively; oral fertility and early embryo development study in male and female rats at doses up to 600 mg/kg/d; and oral embryo-fetal development study in mice at doses up to 1500 mg/kg/day. These preclinical findings, consistent with our prediction based on the small V_d profile, established the safety profiles to support the clinical development and use of apixaban.

Clinical pharmacology

The pharmacokinetic and pharmacodynamic properties of apixaban were investigated in human following single and multiple oral dose, and intravenous dose administration [25]. The pharmacodynamic effect of apixaban is closely correlated with apixaban plasma concentrations, consistent with direct reversible inhibition of FXa. Apixaban is rapidly absorbed with an absolute oral bioavailability of approximately 50%. Apixaban showed a small V_d in human, approximately 21 L or 0.3 L/kg, assuming the average body weight of 70 kg for a male adult [26]. Apixaban is uniformly distributed between plasma and red blood cells. In heathy subjects given apixaban, the plasma protein binding of apixaban is approximately 87% in vitro in human plasma, and 93% in plasma samples. Apixaban showed a low plasma clearance in human, approximately 3.3 L/h or 0.05 L/h/kg [26]. Elimination involves multiple pathways, including metabolic and biliary (∼50%), renal elimination of the unchanged parent drug (∼25%), and direct intestinal excretion (∼25%). The apparent elimination half-life ($t_{1/2}$) is approximately 12 h. The metabolic pathways for apixaban include O-demethylation, hydroxylation, and sulfation of hydroxy O-desmethyl apixaban, with metabolism primarily occurring via cytochrome P450 (CYP) 3A4/5 [27]. Apixaban is not an inhibitor or inducer of CYP enzymes or drug transporters [28]. The pharmacokinetics of apixaban are consistent across a broad range of patients, and apixaban has limited clinically relevant interactions with most commonly prescribed medications. All these results were consistent with our projections based on the preclinical models.

However, it was not anticipated that the sulfate metabolite of apixaban would be a major circulating metabolite in human which was defined as >10% of total drug related exposure [27,29,30]. Apixaban undergoes O-demethylation and subsequently sulfation to form desmethyl apixaban sulfate (Fig. 9.7). This sulfate metabolite represented 24%−27% of the total apixaban plasma exposure in human. We proactively approached the regulatory agencies to address this issue based on the then newly published FDA guidance on *Safety Testing of Drug Metabolites Guidance for Industry* (2008) [30]. Although the desmethyl apixaban sulfate is chemically stable, concerns arose because some sulfate metabolites are highly labile metabolites, and may covalently bind to proteins, RNA, and DNA. We performed extensive literature searches and authored a white paper on this subject.

We also completed a thermodynamic analysis of the apixaban sulfate metabolite and concluded that this metabolite is stable, biologically inert and inactive against human FXa, and therefore should not pose any clinical concerns. We were able to convince the regulatory agencies that separate genotoxicity testing and direct in vivo testing of the O-desmethyl apixaban sulfate was not necessary based on (1) desmethyl apixaban sulfate being a phenol sulfate conjugate with no pharmacological activity and no structural alerts; (2) adequate levels of the desmethyl apixaban being formed with rat liver S9; and (3) rats and dogs tested had low circulating levels of desmethyl apixaban sulfate and its precursor, desmethyl

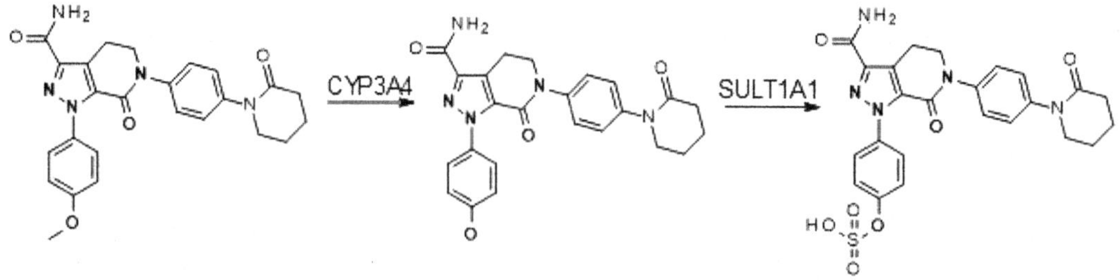

FIGURE 9.7 Major metabolic pathway of apixaban in human.

apixaban. However, the total (%) exposure to desmethyl apixaban sulfate and desmethyl apixaban in dogs was higher than the exposure in man.

Clinical development

Apixaban testing was conducted in multiple clinical studies for safety and efficacy [31]. The dose selection posed a challenge for some indications such as atrial fibrillation (AF), in which the stroke rates are so low that the difference between doses could only possibly be observed in studies that are the same size as those in a typical Phase III trial. To inform dosing in subsequent trials, an extensive Phase II study was conducted in patients following total knee replacement because: (1) the primary efficacy outcome, a composite of VTE (mandatory venography) and all-cause mortality during treatment, has substantially greater frequency in orthopedic surgery patients than stroke in AF patients; and (2) the primary safety outcome, major bleeding, is sufficiently high for evaluation of dose-limited toxicity.

A total of 1238 patients were randomized to one of six double-blind apixaban doses, 5, 10, or 20 mg/day administered as a single (QD) or a twice-daily divided dose (BID), enoxaparin (30 mg BID) or open-label warfarin (titrated to an International Normalized Ratio of 1.8–3.0). The study concluded that apixaban in doses of 2.5 mg BID or 5 mg QD has a promising benefit-risk profile compared with the current standards of care [32].

Another Phase II dose-ranging study was conducted in 520 consecutive patients with symptomatic deep vein thrombosis, including apixaban 5 mg twice-daily, 10 mg twice-daily, or 20 mg once-daily, compared with low molecular weight heparin (LMWH) followed by a vitamin K antagonist [33]. A model-based approach was also used to integrate data from a Phase II study in order to provide a quantitative rationale for selecting the apixaban dosage regimen for a Phase III trial [34]. The analysis showed that BID dosing offered greater avoidance of thrombotic or bleeding events than QD dosing. Therefore, apixaban BID dosing was selected for Phase III studies across all indications [31]. An extensive review about the clinical development can be found elsewhere [31].

Apixaban achieved superiority versus vitamin K antagonist on the primary efficacy and safety outcomes in Phase III clinical trials [35–38]. The FDA approved apixaban to reduce the risk of stroke and blood clots in patients with non-valvular atrial fibrillation in 2012; and in 2014, the FDA approved apixaban to reduce risk of blood clots following hip or knee replacement surgery and for the treatment of deep vein thrombosis and pulmonary embolism. Recently, "real-world" data demonstrated that use of apixaban produces significantly fewer major bleeding events in patents than other direct oral anticoagulants [39–41].

Conclusion

Today, apixaban is an important medicine for patients with non-valvular atrial fibrillation, deep vein thrombosis, and pulmonary embolism, and is best-in-class in oral anticoagulants. It took more than 18 years to discover and develop apixaban at DuPont and BMS. More than 10,000 compounds were synthesized and tested for biological activities, of which several hundreds were tested in vivo in animals, and five entered clinical trials. It was one of the so called "must-win" projects at Bristol Myers Squibb, representing a deep back-up strategy and strong commitment. The success of the program was afforded by three processes: (1) the selection of the right target for efficacy and acceptable mechanism-based toxicity, (2) the discovery of the right compound with optimal profile, and (3) the execution of the right development program. Our scientific understandings of FXa inhibition and optimal profile of FXa inhibitor were accumulated through extensive preclinical and clinical studies with multiple development candidates. During this process, the small V_d strategy, developed through integration of knowledge across disciplines in the context of physiology of the therapeutic target, drug tissue distribution, pharmacokinetics, pharmacodynamics, and toxicology, successfully led to the discovery of apixaban by reducing the potential for off-target toxicity and increasing efficacy.

Acknowledgment

The author was an employee of the legacy DuPont Pharmaceutical Co. and Bristol-Myers Squib Co. from 2000 to 2008, working on the discovery and development of apixaban. The author would like to thank former or current BMS colleagues Drs. Scott J. Grossman, Robert M. Knabb, Donald J. Pinto, and Joseph M. Luettgen for their comments and suggestions on the manuscript. The author would also like to thank Dr. Thomas F. Woolf, Ms. Mary McTique and Ms. Yanping Wang for their editorial comments on the manuscript.

References

[1] M. Pirmohamed, Warfarin: almost 60 years old and still causing problems, Br. J. Clin. Pharmacol. 62 (2006) 509−511, https://doi.org/10.1111/j.1365-2125.2006.02806.x.

[2] R.M. Knabb, R.R. Wexler, From basic science to life-saving therapy: the rationale, and drug discovery efforts that led to the direct factor Xa inhibitor eliquis, J. Thromb. Thrombolysis 52 (2021) 403−407, https://doi.org/10.1007/s11239-021-02529-w.

[3] D.J.P. Pinto, P.C. Wong, R.M. Knabb, R.R. Wexler, Case History: Eliquis (Apixaban), a Potent and Selective Inhibitor of Coagulation Factor Xa for the Prevention and Treatment of Thrombotic Diseases, vol 47, Elsevier Inc., 2012, pp. 123−141.

[4] R.B. Wallis, Hirudins: from leeches to man, Semin. Thromb. Hemost. 22 (1996) 185−196, https://doi.org/10.1055/s-2007-999007.

[5] L. Waxman, D.E. Smith, K.E. Arcuri, G.P. Vlasuk, Tick anticoagulant peptide (TAP) is a novel inhibitor of blood coagulation factor Xa, Science 248 (1990) 593−596, https://doi.org/10.1126/science.2333510.

[6] K.G. Mann, K. Brummel, S. Butenas, What is all that thrombin for? J. Thromb. Haemostasis 1 (2003) 1504−1514, https://doi.org/10.1046/j.1538-7836.2003.00298.x.

[7] T.P. Maduskuie Jr., K.J. McNamara, Y. Ru, R.M. Knabb, P.F. Stouten, Rational design and synthesis of novel, potent bis-phenylamidine carboxylate factor Xa inhibitors, J. Med. Chem. 41 (1998) 53−62, https://doi.org/10.1021/jm970485a.

[8] M.L. Quan, R.R. Wexler, The design and synthesis of noncovalent factor Xa inhibitors, Curr. Top. Med. Chem. 1 (2001) 137−149, https://doi.org/10.2174/1568026013395407.

[9] D.J. Pinto, et al., Discovery of 1-[3-(aminomethyl)phenyl]-N-3-fluoro-2'-(methylsulfonyl)-[1,1'-biphenyl]-4-yl]-3- (trifluoromethyl)-1H-pyrazole-5-carboxamide (DPC423), a highly potent, selective, and orally bioavailable inhibitor of blood coagulation factor Xa, J. Med. Chem. 44 (2001) 566−578, https://doi.org/10.1021/jm000409z.

[10] P.C. Wong, D.J. Pinto, D. Zhang, Preclinical discovery of apixaban, a direct and orally bioavailable factor Xa inhibitor, J. Thromb. Thrombolysis 31 (2011) 478−492, https://doi.org/10.1007/s11239-011-0551-3.

[11] K. He, et al., N-in-1 dosing pharmacokinetics in drug discovery: experience, theoretical and practical considerations, J. Pharmaceut. Sci. 97 (2008) 2568−2580, https://doi.org/10.1002/jps.21196.

[12] H. Wong, et al., The chimpanzee (*Pan troglodytes*) as a pharmacokinetic model for selection of drug candidates: model characterization and application, Drug Metabol. Dispos.: The Biological Fate of Chemicals 32 (2004) 1359−1369, https://doi.org/10.1124/dmd.104.000943.

[13] M.L. Quan, et al., Discovery of 1-(3'-aminobenzisoxazol-5'-yl)-3-trifluoromethyl-N-[2-fluoro-4- [(2'-dimethylaminomethyl)imidazole-1-yl]phenyl]-1H-pyrazole-5-carboxyamide hydrochloride (razaxaban), a highly potent, selective, and orally bioavailable factor Xa inhibitor, J. Med. Chem. 48 (2005) 1729−1744, https://doi.org/10.1021/jm0497949.

[14] M. Rowland, T.N. Tozer, Distribution, third ed., Lippincott Williams & Wilkins, 1995, pp. 137−155.

[15] K. He, et al., Preclinical pharmacokinetic and metabolism of apixaban, a potent and selective factor Xa inhibitor, Blood 108 (2006).

[16] F. Lombardo, G. Berellini, R.S. Obach, Trend analysis of a database of intravenous pharmacokinetic parameters in humans for 1352 drug compounds, Drug Metabol. Dispos.: The Biological Fate of Chemicals 46 (2018) 1466−1477, https://doi.org/10.1124/dmd.118.082966.

[17] D.A. Smith, K. Beaumont, T.S. Maurer, L. Di, Volume of distribution in drug design, J. Med. Chem. 58 (2015) 5691−5698, https://doi.org/10.1021/acs.jmedchem.5b00201.

[18] K. Holt, S. Nagar, K. Korzekwa, Methods to predict volume of distribution, Curr. Pharmacol. Rep. 5 (2019) 391−399, https://doi.org/10.1007/s40495-019-00186-5.

[19] R.S. Obach, Prediction of human clearance of twenty-nine drugs from hepatic microsomal intrinsic clearance data: an examination of in vitro half-life approach and nonspecific binding to microsomes, Drug Metabol. Dispos. 27 (1999) 1350−1359.

[20] D.J. Pinto, et al., Discovery of 1-(4-methoxyphenyl)-7-oxo-6-(4-(2-oxopiperidin-1-yl)phenyl)-4,5,6,7-tetrahydro-1H -pyrazolo[3,4-c]pyridine-3-carboxamide (apixaban, BMS-562247), a highly potent, selective, efficacious, and orally bioavailable inhibitor of blood coagulation factor Xa, J. Med. Chem. 50 (2007) 5339−5356, https://doi.org/10.1021/jm070245n.

[21] D. Zhang, et al., Reductive isoxazole ring opening of the anticoagulant razaxaban is the major metabolic clearance pathway in rats and dogs, Drug Metabol. Dispos. 36 (2008) 303−315, https://doi.org/10.1124/dmd.107.018416.

[22] B. Davies, T. Morris, Physiological parameters in laboratory animals and humans, Pharmaceut. Res. 10 (1993) 1093−1095, https://doi.org/10.1023/a:1018943613122.

[23] K. He, et al., Preclinical pharmacokinetics and pharmacodynamics of apixaban, a potent and selective factor Xa inhibitor, Eur. J. Drug Metabol. Pharmacokinet. 36 (2011) 129−139, https://doi.org/10.1007/s13318-011-0037-x.

[24] Apixaban, Pharmacology/Toxicology NDA Review and Evaluation. https://www.accessdata.fda.gov/drugsatfda_docs/nda/2012/202155Orig1s000PharmR.pdf.

[25] W. Byon, S. Garonzik, R.A. Boyd, C.E. Frost, Apixaban: a clinical pharmacokinetic and pharmacodynamic review, Clin. Pharmacokinet. 58 (2019) 1265−1279, https://doi.org/10.1007/s40262-019-00775-z.

[26] C. Frost, S. Garonzik, A. Shenker, Y.C. Barrett, F. LaCreta, Apixaban single-dose pharmacokinetics, bioavailability, renal clearance, and pharmacodynamics following intravenous and oral administration, Clin. Pharmacol. Drug Develop. 10 (2021) 974−984, https://doi.org/10.1002/cpdd.990.

[27] N. Raghavan, et al., Apixaban metabolism and pharmacokinetics after oral administration to humans, Drug Metabol. Dispos.: The Biological Fate of Chemicals 37 (2009) 74−81, https://doi.org/10.1124/dmd.108.023143.

[28] L. Wang, et al., In vitro assessment of metabolic drug-drug interaction potential of apixaban through cytochrome P450 phenotyping, inhibition, and induction studies, Drug Metabol. Dispos.: The Biological Fate of Chemicals 38 (2010) 448−458, https://doi.org/10.1124/dmd.109.029694.

[29] D. Zhang, et al., Comparative metabolism of 14C-labeled apixaban in mice, rats, rabbits, dogs, and humans, Drug Metabol. Dispos.: The Biological Fate of Chemicals 37 (2009) 1738−1748, https://doi.org/10.1124/dmd.108.025981.

[30] FDA, Safety Testing of Drug Metabolites—Guidance for Industry, 2008. https://www.federalregister.gov/documents/2008/02/15/E8-2827/guidance-for-industry-on-safety-testing-of-drug-metabolites-availability.

[31] M.S. Hanna, et al., Development of apixaban: a novel anticoagulant for prevention of stroke in patients with atrial fibrillation, Ann. N. Y. Acad. Sci. 1329 (2014) 93−106, https://doi.org/10.1111/nyas.12567.

[32] M.R. Lassen, et al., The efficacy and safety of apixaban, an oral, direct factor Xa inhibitor, as thromboprophylaxis in patients following total knee replacement, J. Thromb. Haemostasis : JTH 5 (2007) 2368−2375, https://doi.org/10.1111/j.1538-7836.2007.02764.x.

[33] W.C. Botticelli Investigators, H. Buller, D. Deitchman, M. Prins, A. Segers, Efficacy and safety of the oral direct factor Xa inhibitor apixaban for symptomatic deep vein thrombosis. The Botticelli DVT dose-ranging study, J. Thromb. Haemostasis : JTH 6 (2008) 1313−1318, https://doi.org/10.1111/j.1538-7836.2008.03054.x.

[34] T.A. Leil, C. Frost, X. Wang, M. Pfister, F. LaCreta, Model-based exposure-response analysis of apixaban to quantify bleeding risk in special populations of subjects undergoing orthopedic surgery, CPT Pharmacometrics Syst. Pharmacol. 3 (2014) e136, https://doi.org/10.1038/psp.2014.34.

[35] C.B. Granger, et al., Apixaban versus warfarin in patients with atrial fibrillation, N. Engl. J. Med. 365 (2011) 981−992, https://doi.org/10.1056/NEJMoa1107039.

[36] M.R. Lassen, et al., Apixaban versus enoxaparin for thromboprophylaxis after knee replacement (ADVANCE-2): a randomised double-blind trial, Lancet 375 (2010) 807−815, https://doi.org/10.1016/S0140-6736(09)62125-5.

[37] M.R. Lassen, et al., Apixaban versus enoxaparin for thromboprophylaxis after hip replacement, N. Engl. J. Med. 363 (2010) 2487−2498, https://doi.org/10.1056/NEJMoa1006885.

[38] M.R. Lassen, et al., Apixaban or enoxaparin for thromboprophylaxis after knee replacement, N. Engl. J. Med. 361 (2009) 594−604, https://doi.org/10.1056/NEJMoa0810773.

[39] A. Slomski, Apixaban vs rivaroxaban for preventing recurrent VTE, JAMA 327 (2022) 314, https://doi.org/10.1001/jama.2021.25108.

[40] M.A. Mamas, et al., Meta-analysis comparing apixaban versus rivaroxaban for management of patients with nonvalvular atrial fibrillation, Am. J. Cardiol. 166 (2022) 58−64, https://doi.org/10.1016/j.amjcard.2021.11.021.

[41] W.A. Ray, et al., Association of rivaroxaban vs apixaban with major ischemic or hemorrhagic events in patients with atrial fibrillation, JAMA 326 (2021) 2395−2404, https://doi.org/10.1001/jama.2021.21222.

Chapter 10

Design, conduct, and interpretation of human mass balance studies and strategies for assessing metabolites-in-safety testing (MIST) in drug development

Simon G. Wong[a] and Shuguang Ma[b]

[a]Drug Metabolism and Pharmacokinetics, Pliant Therapeutics, South San Francisco, CA, United States; [b]Pharmacokinetics and Drug Metabolism, Amgen Inc., South San Francisco, CA, United States

Introduction

The definitive characterization of ADME (absorption, distribution, metabolism, and excretion) remains a critical component to the development of new medicines. Unambiguous elucidation of how a new chemical entity is eliminated and a comprehensive understanding of its metabolite profile are paramount to evaluating both the safety and efficacy of new medicines. The human mass balance study remains the pivotal clinical read-out for definitive AME (absorption, metabolism, and excretion) assessment. In this chapter, the design, conduct and interpretation of the human mass balance (or human AME) study will be presented, and recommendations on how to address common issues will be reviewed. Micro-radioactive dosing as an alternative to traditional radiometric designs for mass balance and metabolite profiling will be discussed. In addition, analytical strategies for assessment of human metabolites-in-safety testing (MIST) are reviewed and new approaches to the determination of coverage of human drug metabolites in preclinical species are discussed. Novel approaches toward understanding AME and absolute bioavailability (ABA), leveraging the latest bioanalytical techniques, will be proposed.

Objectives of the mass balance study

The importance of the human mass balance study to regulatory submissions cannot be understated [1]. The human mass balance study has been the topic of several comprehensive reviews [2–4]. Consistent across these reports is agreement on the two key broad objectives of the study:

- Quantitative determination of metabolic pathways and clearance mechanisms
- Identification of the complete metabolic profile in circulation and excreta

It is useful to consider the relationship between these objectives and the corresponding impact on the clinical pharmacology, safety assessment, and bioanalytical plans as a molecule proceeds toward registration. Overall, clear understanding of the clearance mechanisms provides insight on the appropriate design of drug-drug interaction studies and the need to investigate the pharmacokinetics in certain special (renal or hepatic impaired) populations. The complete metabolic profile in circulation allows for the assessment of metabolites-in-safety testing (MIST) guidance—specifically if there is adequate coverage in preclinical toxicology studies to conclude that exposure to the metabolites is sufficient to ascertain the

Overcoming Obstacles in Drug Discovery and Development. https://doi.org/10.1016/B978-0-12-817134-9.00004-0

potential safety concerns in humans. Regarding MIST, it is important to appreciate that the definitive metabolic profile must be determined at steady-state, i.e., after multiple doses, in both human and preclinical species. Since a typical AME study is conducted after a single radioactive dose, the MIST guidance cannot be adequately addressed, unless there is an assumption that the single dose metabolic profile is representative of steady-state.

Timing of the human mass balance study

Recognizing the importance of a thorough understanding the AME properties of a compound in development, it is tempting to assume that a mass balance study would be scheduled as early as possible. However, cost, resources, and lead-time for the synthesis of radioactive material remain the key drivers for delaying the human AME study to phase II after proof of concept and, a more robust understanding of the efficacious dose. This sentiment is supported by a review of industry practices [5], which indicated that all of the pharmaceutical companies surveyed conduct the radiolabeled human AME study in the middle of phase II, likely after critical proof of clinical efficacy has been established. FDA guidelines recommend human in vivo studies, including mass balance, to be conducted prior to large scale phase II or III studies, and the EMA expects these data to be available prior to phase III trials, but there has been recent interest in conducting earlier. This guidance is consistent with the overall goal to understand the metabolic and excretory fates of a new medicine prior to its administration to a larger patient population, where the potential to identify more rare drug interactions, variable PK in selected sub-populations, or safety concerns may be more likely than in smaller trials.

Review of mass balance in literature: methodology

To investigate trends in the design, conduct and interpretation of the human AME study over the past 2 decades, a comprehensive review of the published literature was conducted. The PubMed database was queried for common search terms related to the AME study and over 215 human studies were identified (2000—2021), with key characteristics summarized in Table 10.1. Overall, trends included increased adoption of new techniques, such as micro-radioactive dose with accelerator mass spectrometry (AMS), combined IV-microtracer/PO dosing to determine absolute bioavailability (ABA), and dual labeled studies for mass balance and ABA.

Experimental methods and study design

Review of the literature on published human AME studies reveals general consistency around the study design. Several general trends and recommendations will be discussed below.

Subject selection: patients versus healthy volunteers

The distribution of AME studies conducted in patients or healthy participants is summarized in Table 10.1. Overall, across all studies, 74.4% were conducted in healthy males, and 47% of all studies utilized six subjects. Few studies (4.6%) were conducted in healthy participants of mixed gender and only 1.8% were conducted in exclusively healthy females. Reviewing only studies on oncology medications, 60% were conducted in healthy volunteers and 40% were conducted in patients. In general, for oncology indications, it has been recommended to conduct an AME study in patients [2], and due to concerns associated with exposing healthy volunteers to potentially mutagenic, carcinogenic, or teratogenic anticancer medications, oncology patients may indeed be more appropriate for an AME study than healthy volunteers. Additional rationale for conducting the study in the target disease population includes the potential for differences in AME between the critically ill and healthy subjects [217] and reported variability in PK in cancer patients [218]. There are also potential advantages of conducting AME studies in patients with the same tumor type to reduce variability or increase the accuracy of estimated pharmacokinetic parameters [125]. Despite these rationale for conducting AME studies in the target patient population, practical considerations are likely reasons why most AME studies, even in for oncology indications, are conducted in healthy volunteers. In our analysis, 60% of the AME studies for oncology compounds were conducted in healthy volunteers, and for non-oncology indications, nearly all of the studies were not conducted in patients. The high frequency of AME studies conducted in healthy volunteers is likely due to the difficulty in recruiting oncology patients [219], long enrollment time [150] or ethical concerns regarding their enrollment in a mass balance study. Of the studies reviewed for the present analysis, the majority of studies utilized six heathy male subjects, regardless of indication. It should be noted that as no statistics are generated, increasing the number of participants only serves to increase confidence in the study objectives, i.e., understanding different excretory and metabolic profiles. Therefore, compounds with previously identified high variability in pharmacokinetics, or known substrates to polymorphic metabolism may benefit from more customized subject selection.

TABLE 10.1 Summary of mass balance studies from 2000 to 2021.

Compound	Indication	% Urine	% Feces	% Total	Parent $t_{1/2}$	TRA $t_{1/2}$	Method	Dose	Subjects	Reference
Aclidinium bromide	COPD	64.7	32.5	97.2	3.4	NA	Traditional	40 µCi	12HM	[6]
JNJ-53718678	Antiviral	19.9	70.6	90.5	9	17	Traditional	88.5 µCi	6HM	[7]
5-CNAC	Osteoarthritis	90	<1	90	1.52	13.9	Traditional	100 µCi	6HF	[8]
Abiraterone	Oncology	5.3	87.9	93.2	11.2	4.8	Traditional	97.8 µCi	8HM	[9]
Acalabrutinib	Oncology	12	83.5	96	1.57	46.5	Traditional	1000 µCi	8HM	[10]
ACT-541468	Insomnia	27.9	56.6	84.5	6.5	NA	Traditional	250 µCi	6HM	[11]
Afatinib	Oncology	4.29	85.4	89.5	33.9	118	Traditional	60.8 µCi	8HM	[12]
Alectinib	Oncology	0.456	97.8	98.2	17.5	65.1	Traditional	67 µCi PO; 500 nCi IV (AMS)	6HM	[13]
Aleglitazar	Acute coronary syndrome	66.3 69.7	9.7	93	5–16	60.2	Traditional	90 µCi	3HM 3HF	[14]
Alisertib	Oncology	2.7	87.8	90.5	23.4	42	Traditional	80 µCi	2MP 1FP	[15]
Almonertinib	Oncology	5.44	84.75	90.19	25	863	Traditional	50 µCi	4HM	[16]
Alpelisib	Oncology	13.1	79.8	94.5	13.7	18	Traditional	75 µCi	4HM	[17]
Alpelisib	Oncology	12.3	83.7	90	13.7	18	Traditional	75 µCi	4HM	[18]
Amenamevir	Antiviral	20.6	74.6	95.3	7.65	8.03	Traditional	48 µCi	6HM	[19]
Amiselimod	Autoimmune	35.32	55.84	91.16	451	468	Traditional	80 µCi	8HM	[20]
Amisulpride	Antiemetic	73.6	22.8	96.4	3.7	NA	Traditional	48 µCi	6HM	[21]
Amprenavir	Antiviral	14	75	89	4.7	11.49	Traditional	95.76 µCi	6HM	[22]
Anlotinib	Oncology	13.51	48.52	62.03	64–167	NA	Traditional	80 µCi	6PM	[23]
Apalutamide	Oncology	64.6	24.3	88.9	148	257	AMS	AMS 250 nCi IV; PO; 1000 µCi for AME	12HM	[24]
Apixaban	Thrombosis	Intact: 24.5 Bile: 28.8	Intact: 56 Bile: 46.7	Intact: 80	12.7	8.2	Traditional	108 µCi	10HM	[25]
Apremilast	Psoriasis	58	39	97	6.8	50.4	Traditional	100 µCi	6HM	[26]
Aprocitentan	Hypertension	52.1	24.8	77	~49	NA	NA	N/A	6HM	[27]
ASA404	Oncology	53.9	33.3	86.9	27.2	157	Traditional	60 µCi	1MP 6FP	[28]

Continued

TABLE 10.1 Summary of mass balance studies from 2000 to 2021.—cont'd

Compound	Indication	% Urine	% Feces	% Total	Parent $t_{1/2}$	TRA $t_{1/2}$	Method	Dose	Subjects	Reference
Asenapine	Schizophrenia	50	40	90	27.5	39.3	Traditional	55.9 µCi	6HM	[29]
ASP015K	Anti-inflam	36.8	56.6	93.4	12	3.1	Traditional	100 µCi	6HM	[30]
ASP7991	Hyperparathyroidism	30.08	49.31	79.39	2.27	7.39	AMS	500 nCi	6HM	[31]
Avibactam	Antibacterial	0	93	93	2.8	NA	Traditional	300 µCi	6HM	[32]
Axitinib	Oncology	22.7	37	59.7	10.6	12.9	Traditional	100 µCi	8HM	[33]
AZD8931	Oncology	13.4	71.4	80.3	35	NA	Traditional	200 µCi	6HM	[34]
Barasertib	Oncology	27	51	72-82	44.6-162	66	Traditional	250 µCi	3MP 3FP	[35]
Basimglurant	Major depressive disorder	73.4	26.5	99.9	77.2	178	Traditional	60 µCi	6HM	[36]
Batefenterol	COPD	6.3	77.6	83.9	IV: 3.9	IV: 8.5 PO: 32.1	AMS	IV: 168 nCi PO:8.4 µCi	6HM	[37]
Bazedoxifene	Osteoporosis	0.81	84.7	85.6	32	10.2	Traditional	200 µCi	6HF	[38]
Belinostat	Oncology	84.8	9.7	94.5	1.58	NA	Traditional	100 µCi	4MP 2FP	[39]
Bendamustine	Oncology	45.5	25.2	76	0.65	197	Traditional	80-95 µCi	3MP, 3FP	[40]
BI 425809	Schizophrenia	48	48	96.7	32.9	48	AMS	IV: 300 nCi	6HM	[41]
BMS-690514	Oncology	34	51	90.28	16-18	>170	AMS	80 µCi	9HM	[42]
Brivanib	Oncology	12.2	81.5	93.7	13.8	105	Traditional	100 µCi	3MP, 1 FP	[43]
Cabazitaxel	Oncology	3.7	76	79.7	155	10.3	Traditional	50 µCi	3MP, 1 FP	[44]
Cabozantinib	Oncology	27.29	53.79	81.09	102	NA	Traditional	100 µCi	8HM	[45]
Canagliflozin	Diabetes	34.1	34.5	68.6	11.6	9.5	AMS	200 nCi	9HM	[46]
Capmatinib	Oncology	21.8	77.9	99.7	10.6	7.8	Traditional	150 µCi	6HM	[47]
Casopitant	Nausea and vomiting	<8	83.8	93	15.6	78.6	Traditional	35 µCi	6HM	[48]
CC-223	Oncology	57.6	38.9	97	5	NA	AMS	200 nCi	6HM	[49]
Cefiderocol	Antibacterial	98.7	~0	101	2.3	2.7	Traditional	100 µCi	6HM	[50]
Cenerimod	Lupus	4.6-12	58 ∼100	84	170-199	NA	Traditional	100 µCi	6HM	[51]

Cenobamate	Seizures	88	5.2	93	38.7	84.6	Traditional	50 µCi	6HM	[52]
Cerlapirdine	Alzheimer's	28	70.3	98.3	59.6	90	AMS	177 nCi	6HM	[53]
Cetagliptin	Diabetes	72.88	18.81	91.68	8–14	NA	Traditional	50 µCi	HM	[54]
Cipargamin	Malaria	0	~85	85	33.4	24 −35.1	Traditional	65 µCi	6HM	[55]
Cobimetinib	Oncology	17.8	76.5	94.3	75.5	141	Traditional	200 µCi	6HM	[56]
Copanlisib	Oncology	41	64	86	52.1	NA	Traditional	75 µCi	6HM	[57]
Crizotinib	Cancer	22	63	85	94	134	Traditional	100 µCi	6HM	[58]
Dabrafenib	Oncology	22.7	71.1	93.8	5.3	26.4	Traditional	80 µCi	3MP, 1FP	[59]
Dacomitinib	Oncology	3.2	78.8	82	54.58	182.3	Traditional	100 µCi	6HM	[60]
Darolutamide	Oncology	63.4	32.4	95.9	10.6	11.5	Traditional	146 µCi	6HM	[61]
Darunavir	Antiviral	12.2	81.7	93.9	29.4	4.1	Traditional	40.5 µCi	4HM	[62]
Dasotraline	ADHD	68.3	22.4	90.7	61.3	114	Traditional	110 µCi	8HM	[63]
Deferasirox	Anemia	8	84	91.5	9.4	9.6	Traditional	70 µCi	3MP, 2FP	[64]
Delafloxacin	Antibacterial	66	29	95	2.35	2.29	Traditional	100 µCi	6HM	[65]
Deleobuvir	HCV	0.137	95.1	95.2	2.84	NA	Traditional	100 µCi	12HM	[66]
Dexlansoprazole	Erosive esophagitis Gastro-esophageal reflux	50.69	47.59	98.28	2.24	11.9	Traditional	100 µCi	6HM	[67]
Dolutegravir	HIV	31.6	64	95.6	15.6	15.7	Traditional	80 µCi	6HM	[68]
Doravirine	HIV	10.8	90.4	100	22.95	NA	Traditional	200 µCi	6HM	[69]
Dovitinib	Oncology	16	61	77	32.2	58.2	Traditional	50 µCi	1MP, 3FP	[70]
Edoxaban	Antithrombotic	35.4	62.2	97	7.4	4.4	Traditional	59.4 µCi	6HM	[71]
Eltrombopag	Thrombocytopenia	31	59	90	32	49	Traditional	100 µCi	6HM	[72]
Empagliflozin	Diabetes	54.4	41.1	95.5	15.9	9.2	Traditional	100 µCi	8HM	[73]
Enarodustat	Anemia	10.9	77.1	88	25.9	69	Traditional	100 µCi	6MP	[74]
Ensartinib	Oncology	10.21	91	101.2	18.3	27.2	Traditional	100 µCi	6HM	[75]
Eravacycline	Intra abdominal infection	34	47.8	82.8	14	NA	Traditional	105 µCi (IV infusion over 60 min)	5HM	[76]
Eribulin	Oncology	8.9	81.5	90.4	45.6	42.3	Traditional	80–90 µCi	6P	[77]
Erlotinib	Oncology	8.1	83	91	8.1	10	Traditional	91 µCi	4HM	[78]

Continued

TABLE 10.1 Summary of mass balance studies from 2000 to 2021.—cont'd

Compound	Indication	% Urine	% Feces	% Total	Parent $t_{1/2}$	TRA $t_{1/2}$	Method	Dose	Subjects	Reference
Ertugliflozin	Diabetes	50.2	40.9	91	16.87	17.25	Traditional	100 µCi	6HM	[79]
Etamicastat	Cardiovascular disorders	58.5	33.3	94	22.9	136.9	Traditional	98 µCi	4HM	[80]
Etelcalcetide	Chronic kidney disease			67.2	72–120	861	AMS	710 nCi	3MP 3FP	[81]
Etoperidone	Antidepressants	78.8	9.6	88.4	21.7	21.7	Traditional	100 µCi	6HM	[82]
Evobrutinib	Oncology	20.6	71	91.6	381	NA	Traditional	100 µCi	6HM	[83]
Faldaprevir	HCV	0.113	98.7	98.3	30.3	22.3	Traditional	61.7 µCi	8HM	[84]
Febuxostat	Gout	49	45	94	10.8	6.5	Traditional	100 µCi	6HM	[85]
Fevipiprant	Asthma	42.1	51.9	93.9	12.3	254	Traditional	85 µCi	4HM	[86]
Fingolimod	Multiple sclerosis	20	10	62	162	382	Traditional	58.3 µCi	4HM	[87]
Formestane	Breast cancer	95.1	3.9	98.9	0.3		Traditional	50 µCi	7FP	[88]
Fotemustine	Oncology	50.1; 61.3	6.8; 0.3	57.0; 61.7	80	NA	Traditional	30 µCi	2MP	[89]
Fruquintinib	Oncology	60.31	29.8	90.11	33.4	41.1	Traditional	100 µCi	6HM	[90]
furmonertinib	Oncology	6.63	71.2	77.8	37.2	333	Traditional	97.9 µCi	6HM	[91]
Galunisertib	Oncology	36.8	64.5	101.3	8.6	10	Traditional	100 µCi	6HM	[92]
Gedatolisib	Oncology	11.53 −14.75	63.443 −73.04	80.45 −85.07	36.92	125.9	AMS	60 µCi	6HM	[93]
Gefitinib	Oncology	4	86	90	48	NA	Traditional	166 µCi	6HM	[94]
Gemigliptin	Diabetes	63.4	27.1	90.5	30.8	NA	Traditional	146 µCi	6HM	[95]
Glasdegib	Oncology	49	42	91	18.6	14.2	Traditional	100 µCi	6HM	[96]
GSK2140944	Antibacterial	IV: 59.2 PO: 31.2	IV: 32.8 PO: 42.5	IV: 92 PO: 84	12.6	94.5	AMS	IV: 22.5 µCi Oral: 45 µCi	6HM	[97]
Guadecitabine	Oncology	86.7	0	90.5	<1	NA	Traditional	30 µCi	3MP, 2FP	[98]
Henagliflozin	Diabetes	33.9	40.6	74.5	~11	NA		N/A	12HM	[99]
HR011303	Hyperuricemia, gout	81.5	10.26	91.75	16.6	24.2	Traditional	80 µCi	6HM	[100]
HSK3486	Anesthetic	84.6	2.65	87.3	1.5	61.2	Traditional	47–57 µCi	6HM	[101]
Idasanutlin	Oncology	0.1	91.5	91.6	31.2	38	Traditional	100 µCi	8P	[102]

Imatinib	Oncology	13	67	80	13	57.3	Traditional	31.9 µCi	4HM	[103]
Imidafenacin	Overactive bladder	65.6	29.4	95	2.9	72	Traditional	46 µCi	6HM	[104]
INCB018424	Oncology	74	22	96	2.32	5.81	Traditional	90 µCi	7HM, 2HF	[105]
Irinotecan	Oncology	62.1	63.7	95.8	6–12	NA	Traditional	100 µCi	8P	[106]
Irofulven	Oncology	71.2	2.9	74.1	0.3	116.5	Traditional	100 µCi	2MP, 1FP	[107]
Isavuconazonium	Invasive mold disease	45.5	46.1	91.6	141.9	160.5	Traditional	NA	6HM	[108]
Ivosidenib	Oncology	17	77	94	53.4	71.7	Traditional	200 µCi	8HM	[109]
Ixabepilone	Oncology	21.4	64.9	86.2	50.3	73.1	AMS	80 nCi	3MP, 5FP	[110]
Ixabepilone	Oncology	25.1	52.18	77.28	50.3	73	AMS	22.8 nCi	3MP, 5FP	[111]
Ixazomib	Oncology	62.1	21.8	83.9	4–9 d	228	AMS	500 nCi	2MP, 5FP	[112]
KD101	Obesity	78	7.3	85.2	45.5	152.8	AMS	184 nCi	6HM	[113]
Lacosamide	Epilepsy	96.8	0.3	97	13–16	15.04	Traditional	40 µCi	5HM	[114]
Lanicemine	Antidepressants	93.8	1.9	95	16.1	16.9	Traditional	150 µCi	6HM	[115]
Lapatinib	Oncology	91.8	1.16	93.1	14.8	5.59	Traditional	89.1 µCi	3HM, 3HF	[116]
Lenalidomide	Anemia	90	4	94	2.78	2.97	Traditional	85 µCi	6HM	[117]
Leniolisib	autoimmune	23	42.4	65.5	~10 h	4.8	F18 NMR	N/A	4M, 1F	[118]
Lenvatinib	Oncology	25	64	89	34.5	10.8	Traditional	100 µCi	3MP, 3FP	[119]
Lersivirine	Antiviral	80	23	103	5.83	9.41	Traditional	62 µCi	4HM	[120]
Linerixibat	Cholestatic pruritus in primary biliary cholangitis	20	80	100	6.76	6.25	Traditional	250 nCi (IV) 134.1 µCi (PO)	6HM	[121]
Linsitinib	Oncology	5.44	76.4	81.8	2.4	4.51	Traditional	100 µCi	3MP, 2FP	[122]
Liraglutide	Diabetes	20.1	6.2	26.3	15.60	NA	Traditional	383 µCi	7HM	[123]
Lixivaptan	Polycistic kidney disease	20.5	63.7	84.2	341	387	Traditional	200 µCi	6HM	[124]
Lurbinectedin	Oncology	5.6	88.7	94.3	47	NA	Traditional	100 µCi	6P	[125]
Lusutrombopag	Thrombocytopenia	1	83	84	25.7	70.7	Traditional	100 µCi	7HM	[126]
LY3202626	Alzheimer's	44.2	31.3	75.4	24.5	32.5	Traditional	100 µCi	6HM	[127]

Continued

TABLE 10.1 Summary of mass balance studies from 2000 to 2021.—cont'd

Compound	Indication	% Urine	% Feces	% Total	Parent $t_{1/2}$	TRA $t_{1/2}$	Method	Dose	Subjects	Reference
Macitentan	Pulmonary arterial hypertension	49.7	23.9	73.6	15	103	Traditional	75 µCi	6HM	[128]
Mavoglurant	Parkinson disease-associated levodopa-induced dyskinesia	36.7	58.6	95.3	12	17.9	Traditional	43.5 µCi i	4HM	[129]
Mirabegron	Overactive bladder	55	34	89.2	47.9	28.2	Traditional	50 µCi	4HM	[130]
Mirogabalin	Neuropathic pain		1.21	98.06	3.76	7.63	Traditional	150 µCi	6HM	[131]
Molidustat	Renal anemia	90.7	6.27	97	11.5	NA	Traditional	96.5 µCi	4HM	[132]
Momelotinib	Oncology	27.5	69.3	96.7	3.7	4	Traditional	100 µCi	6HM	[133]
Naldemedine	Opioid-induced constipation	57.3	34.8	92	10.6	20.4	Traditional	140 µCi	12HM	[134]
Naloxegol	Pain	16	67	84.2	7.88	7.28	Traditional	78–95 µCi	6HM	[135]
Napabucasin	Oncology	23.8	57.2	81.1	7.92	11.8	Traditional	100 µCi	8HM	[136]
Navoximod	Oncology	80.4	7.44	87.8	9.41	206	Traditional	600 µCi	8HM	[137]
Nefopam	Analgesic	79.3	13.4	92.6	8.08	15.4	Traditional	100 µCi	8HM	[138]
Nemiralisib	Respiratory diseases	6	79	85	58.4	50.8	AMS	IV: 0.6 µCi PO: 50 µCi	6HM	[139]
Niraparib	Oncology	47.5	38.8	86.3	87.4	92.5	Traditional	100 µCi	6FP	[140]
Omarigliptin	Diabetes	74.4	3.4	78	132	159	AMS	2.1 µCi	6HM	[141]
Osimertinib	Oncology	14.2	67.8	81.9	61.2	474	AMS	1 µCi	6HM	[142]
Ozanimod	Multiple sclerosis	26	37	63	20.78	98.61	AMS	37 µCi	6HM	[143]
P2Y12	Acute coronary syndrome	2.4	92.5	94.9	4.7	8.2	Traditional	100 µCi	6HM	[144]
Pamapimod	Oncology	76.5	23.9	100	7.2	NA	Traditional	NA	6HM	[145]
Pamiparib	Oncology	57.8	26.9	84.7	29.2	21.6	Traditional	100 µCi	3MP, 1FP	[146]
Panobinostat	Oncology	40.6	54.3	87	30.7	75.3	Traditional	50 µCi	2MP, 2FP	[147]
Pasireotide	Cushing's disease	7.63	48.3	84	7.8	211	AMS	232 nCi	4HM	[148]
Patupilone	Oncology	14.4	31.3	45.8	137	NA	Traditional	29.7 µCi	2MP, 3FP	[149]
Pazopanib	Oncology	2.6	82	62–97	43.9	33.6	Traditional	65 µCi	3MP	[150]
Pevonedistat	Oncology	41	53	94	8.4	15.6	Traditional	65–85 µCi	3MP, 5FP	[1551]

Drug	Indication						Method	Dose		Ref.
Pictilisib	Oncology	1.1	94.2	95.3	1.6	10.9	Traditional	100 µCi	5HM	[152]
Pimasertib	Oncology	52.8	30.7	83.5	6.3	3.5	AMS	250 nCi	6MP	[153]
Pimecrolimus	Inflammation	2.5	78.4	80.9	62	145	Traditional	NA	4HM	[154]
Pomalidomide	Multiple myeloma, sclerosis	73	15	88	8.9	11.2	Traditional	100 µCi	8HM	[155]
Ponatinib	Oncology	5.4	86.6	92	27.4	66.4	Traditional	36.7 µCi	6HM	[156]
Ponesimod	Autoimmune	10.3 −18.4	57.3 −79.6	77.9	32	80.2	Traditional	102 µCi	6HM	[157]
Prucalopride	Constipation	84.2	13.3	97.5	20.6	19.7	AMS	200 nCi	6HM	[158]
PTZ601	Antimicrobial	73.9	18.1	92	1.59	108	Traditional	79.2 µCi	6HM	[159]
Pyronaridine	Antimalarial	23.7	47.8	71.5	5.03	804	AMS	800 nCi	6HM	[160]
Pyrotinib	Oncology	1.7	90.9	92.6	29.3	47.9	Traditional	150 µCi	6HM	[161]
Quizartinib	Oncology	1.64	76.3	77.94	>36 h	NA	Traditional	100 µCi	6HM	[162]
Ralfinamide	Neuropathic pain	93.6	1.13	95	14.70	59.2	Traditional	55.4 µCi	6HM	[163]
Raltitrexed	Oncology	28.75	14.4	43.15	257	NC	Traditional	14.25 µCi	6MP, 3FP	[164]
Regorafenib	Oncology	19.3	71.2	90.5	48.6	37.6	Traditional	100 µCi	4HM	[165]
Remogliflozin	Diabetes	92.8	2.58	95.5	1.57	6.57	Traditional	106 µCi	8HM	[166]
Revefenacin	Chronic obstructive pulmonary disease	4.7	88	92.7		56.65	AMS	10 µCi	3HM	[167]
Revexepride	GERD	38.2	57.3	95.5	11	10.9	AMS	200 nCi	6HM	[168]
Rezafungin	Fungal disease	27	73	88.3	341	387	Traditional	200 µCi	9HM	[169]
Ribociclib	Oncology	22.6	69.1	91.7	54.7	293	AMS	NA	6HM	[170]
Rolapitant	Nauseau and vomiting	14.2	72.7	86.9	186	NA	Traditional	100 µCi	6HM	[171]
Rovatirelin	Spinocerebellar degeneration	36.8	50.1	89	14.9	32.1	Traditional	58.3 µCi	6HM	[172]
Rucaparib	Oncology	17.4	71.9	89.3	25.9	30.4	Traditional	35 µCi	6FP	[173]
S-777469	Anti-atopic dermatitis	25	67	93	7.3	5.1	Traditional	100 µCi	6HM	[174]
Sacubitril/ valsartan	Heart failure	60.7	41.8	102.5	Valsartan (20.8) Sacubitril (1.31)	10.2	Traditional	75 µCi	4HM	[175]
Saxagliptin	Diabetes	74.9	22.1	97	2.45	2.77	Traditional	91.5 µCi	6HM	[176]
Selatogrel	Acute coronary syndrome	2.4	92.5	94.9	4.74	8.25	Traditional	100 µCi	6HM	[144]
Seletalisib	Autoimmune	11.3	74.6	86.1	23.1	27.6	AMS	2 µCi	3HM 3HF	[177]

Continued

TABLE 10.1 Summary of mass balance studies from 2000 to 2021.—cont'd

Compound	Indication	% Urine	% Feces	% Total	Parent $t_{1/2}$	TRA $t_{1/2}$	Method	Dose	Subjects	Reference
Selumetinib	Oncology	33	59	93	13.7	56.8	Traditional	200 µCi	6HM	[178]
Semaglutide	Diabetes	53	18.6	75.1	168	201	Traditional	450 µCi	7HM	[179]
Siponimod	Multiple sclerosis	3.56	82.3	85.9	56.6	171	Traditional	100 µCi	4HM	[180]
Sirolimus	Immunosuppressive	2.2	91	93.2	63	59.8	Traditional	100 µCi i	6HM	[181]
Solithromycin	Pneumonia	14.1	74.4	90.6	7.82	NA	Traditional	100 µCi	8HM	[182]
Sonidegib	Oncology	1.2	92.1	93.3	319	978	AMS	2 µCi	6HM	[183]
Sunitinib	Oncology	16	61	77	50.9	28.2	Traditional	100 µCi	6HM	[184]
Talazoparib	Oncology	68.7	19.7	88.4	89.8	77.6	Traditional	100 µCi	6 MP	[185]
Tapentadol	Analgesic	99	1	99	4	3.93	Traditional	50 µCi	4HM	[186]
TAS-102	Oncology	55	3	59.8	2	40	AMS	200 nCi	8MP, 2FP	[187]
Tedizolid	Antibacterial	18	81.5	99.5	10.6	11.5	Traditional	100 µCi	6HM	[188]
Telavancin	Antibacterial	76	1	77	7.08	94.2	Traditional	47 µCi	6HM	[189]
Tepotinib	Oncology	13.61	77.87	91.9	33	37.8	AMS	72 µCi PO 1.4 µCi IV (AMS)	6HM	[190]
Ticagrelor	Acute coronary syndrome	26.5	57.8	84.3	8.4	6.3	Traditional	60 µCi	6HM	[191]
Tivantinib	Oncology	19	68.2	87.2	0.5	NA	Traditional	250 µCi	6HM	[192]
Tivozanib	Oncology	11.8	79.3	91	87	99.1	Traditional	160 µCi	8HM	[193]
Tofogliflozin	Diabetes	77	22	99	12.9	NA	Traditional	100 µCi	6HM	[194]
Tofogliflozin	Diabetes	77	21.7	98.7	6.3	6.3	Traditional	100 µCi	6HM	[195]
Tozadenant	Parkinson disease	30.5	55.1	85.6	15	NA	AMS	2.2 µCi	6HM	[196]
TPA023	Anxiety	53.2	29.4	82.6	6.7	7.7	Traditional	99 µCi	5HM	[197]
Trabectedin	Oncology	5.9	55.5	61.4	54	54	Traditional	57–81 µCi	5MP, 3FP	[198]
Trametinib	Oncology	18.6; 5.6	39.2; 35	48.2; 37.1	152–303	189–370	Traditional	79 µCi	2MP	[199]
Triamcinolone acetonide	Asthma	39.5	54.1	93.7	6.6	20.2	Traditional	100 µCi	6HM	[200]
Tropifexor	NASH	29	65	94	13.5	NA	Traditional	NA	4HM	[201]
Vadimezan (ASA404)	Oncology	53.9	33.3	86.9	27.2	157	Traditional	60 µCi	1MP, 6FP	[28]

Drug	Therapeutic area						Method	Dose	Metabolite	Ref.
Vandetanib	Oncology	25	44	69	176–315	246.6	Traditional	60 µCi	4HM	[202]
Vatalanib	Oncology	13–29	42–74	67–96	4.6	23.4	Traditional	27.16 µCi	4MP, 4FP	[203]
Velsecorat	Asthma	24.4	51.6	76	26.9	18.4	AMS	180 nCi	2HM, 4HF	[204]
Vemurafenib	Oncology	<1	94.1	95	57	71.1	Traditional	69.2 µCi	3MP, 4FP	[205]
Vericiguat	Chronic heart failure	53.1	45.2	98.3	30	NA	Traditional	N/A	6HM	[206]
Vernakalant	Antiarrhythmic	EM: 91.4 PM: 81.7	EM: 7.7 PM: 6.5	EM: 98.7 PM: 88.2		EM: 4.21 PM: 7.78	Traditional	78.96 µCi	8HM	[207]
Vicagrel	Myocardial infarction	68.03	28.67	96.7	12–14	37.3	Traditional	120 µCi	6HM	[208]
Vilaprisan	Uterine fibroids	13.1	73.5	86.6	42.4	62.2	Traditional	62 µCi	6HF	[209]
Vismodegib	Oncology	4.43	82.2	86.6	224	227	AMS	1 µCi	6HF	[210]
Vistusertib	Oncology	10	80	92	3.7	29	Traditional	100 µCi	1MP, 4FP	[211]
Volixibat	Nonalcoholic steatohepatitis	0.01	92.3	92.31	NA	NA	Traditional	5.95 µCi	8HM	[212]
Z-215	Proton pump inhibitor	59.61	31.36	90.97	1.51	16.7	Traditional	100 µCi	6HM	[213]
Zibotentan	Oncology	83.3	9.7	93	8.17	NA	Traditional	90 µCi	3HM, 3HF	[214]
Ziritaxestat	IPF	7	77	84	7	47.8	Traditional	100 µCi	6HM	[215]
Zoliflodacin	Antibacterial	18.2	79.6	97.8	6.5	7.5	Traditional	500 µCi	6HM	[216]

Special considerations for subject selection: use of genotyped subjects for AME study

CYP2D6 has been identified as polymorphic [220], with extensive metabolizers (EM) or poor metabolizers (PM) exhibiting enhanced or reduced metabolism and clearance of CYP2D6 substrates, respectfully. Mao et al. reported on the human AME for vernakalant, a novel antiarrhythmic drug, that was studied in five subjects genotyped as EM and two subjects genotyped as PM [207]. Consistent with initial pharmacokinetic studies [221], the disposition and metabolic profile was different in EM versus PM participants. Importantly, the metabolic profile was dependent on the CYP2D6 genotype, with a 4-O-demethylated metabolite followed by subsequent glucuronidation predominating in EMs, whereas direct glucuronidation predominated in PMs. Interestingly, mean radioactivity recovery in urine was slightly higher in EMs than PMs after both IV and oral administration of vernakalant, whereas fecal recovery was similar. Consistent with reduced CYP2D6-mediated metabolism, unchanged vernakalant contributed to a higher percentage of urinary recovery in PMs (21.9%) than EMs (3.5%). The example of vernakalant emphasizes the value of adequate reaction phenotyping prior to the human AME study, since CYP2D6 had been previously identified as the primary CYP isoform responsible for the vernakalant's clearance. In addition, genotype-specific metabolic profiles may need to be considered to address MIST guidance, in scenarios where the metabolic profile warrants further evaluation in preclinical species due to disproportionate metabolites. A detailed understanding of the metabolic pathways involved can inform on the potential utility of using genotyped subjects, as there are several examples where no differences in disposition or metabolic profile were observed. Interestingly, a human AME of ivosidenib was also conducted in both CYP2D6 PM and EM subjects, but there were no differences in excretion mass balance or metabolic profile, likely due to the contribution of multiple CYP isoforms to the elimination [109]. Morris et al. reported on the mass balance of pyronaridine using genotyped subjects and also saw no appreciable difference in excretion based on CYP2D6 metabolizer status [160]. Investigators at AstraZeneca [222] cited an example of compound F, which is metabolized by CYP2D6 and converted to an O-dealkylated metabolite M1 in EMs, but not in PMs, and was also not appreciably formed in preclinical safety studies. Had development of compound F continued, further studies would be required to evaluate the safety of the disproportionate M1 metabolite formed by EMs. These examples underscore the need to fully understand the metabolic pathways involved and the potential contribution of a polymorphic enzyme (CYP2D6) to the overall metabolic profile to adequately address the MIST guidance.

The metabolism of several proton pump inhibitors involves CYP2C19, and the frequency of PM varies among different racial and ethnic populations [223]. In the AME study for dexlansoprazole, a proton pump inhibitor, 5/6 subjects were genotyped as CYP2C19 EM status and 1/6 as a PM status [67]. Clearance (CL/F) of parent dexlansoprazole was 8.5-fold higher in EM versus PM, but the overall excretion pathways were similar, with mean recoveries of 50.7% in urine and 45.6% in feces. Consistent with the much lower clearance, formation of the primary metabolite (5-hydroxydexlansoprazole) in plasma from PM subjects was only 13% of the mean value from EM subjects. Interestingly, an alternate metabolite, dexlansoprazole sulfone (formed mainly by CYP3A4) was 228-fold higher in the PM subject compared to the EM subjects, likely due to the reduced activity of CYP2C19 to from 5-hydroxydexlansoprasole.

The exposure of the experimental anti-obesity compound KD101 was >60% lower in a subject who carried the variant type single-nucleotide polymorphisms in UGT2B7 compared to a subject with wild type [113]. Interestingly, the subject with variant types of UGT1A1, UGT2A4, and UGT2B7 (i.e., an extensive metabolizer) displayed the highest metabolic burden as evidenced by the high ratio of AUC of total radioactivity compared to parent molecule, and the highest urinary recovery of >90%.

Etamicastat, a novel dopamine-β-hydroxylase inhibitor has high interindividual pharmacokinetic variability which was attributed to polymorphic N-acetyltransferase type 1 (NAT1) and type 2 (NAT2) [224–226]. To further investigate the contribution of these enzymes to the metabolic profile and excretion profile, the AME study enrolled NAT1 and NAT2 genotyped subjects. Subject 1 was identified as a NAT1 poor acetylator and a NAT2 rapid acetylator. Conversely, subjects 2, 3, and 4 were NAT1 rapid acetylators and NAT2 poor acetylators. Consistent with data indicating that NAT2 was the primary enzyme involved, the NAT2 rapid acetylator (subject 1) had the highest urinary recovery of the N-acetylated metabolite (BIA 5−961) and lowest exposure of parent drug. In addition, as noted for the other examples of genotyped subjects in AME studies, the overall recovery in feces versus urine was not different in the poor versus rapid acetylators, although, at least qualitatively, the initial rate of excretion may have been higher in the rapid NAT2 acetylator. In this example AME data in genotyped subjects confirmed the contribution of NAT1/NAT2 polymorphism to the interindividual variability of etamicastat.

Although the frequency of AME studies utilizing genotyped subjects was relatively low, understanding the metabolic profile and excretion pathways in subpopulations of poor or extensive metabolizers can be useful. Known classes of drugs may be susceptible to metabolism via polymorphic enzymes, and should be considered when planning an AME study. Importantly, MIST guidelines still technically apply for subpopulations, and thus the formation of a genotype-specific metabolite would still require adequate coverage in preclinical safety studies. Thus, for compounds known to be susceptible to metabolism by polymorphic enzymes, it is indeed prudent to enroll subjects based on genotype status.

Subject selection: gastrointestinal status

Recognizing the potential contribution of issues related to fecal or gastrointestinal status to overall recovery, an important consideration for subject selection is to exclude participants with a history of stomach or intestinal surgery, stomach disease, or resection that could potentially alter absorption/excretion. In addition, participants with irregular defecation pattern or acute constipation problems within 2−3 weeks of day 1 should be excluded. Additional exclusion criteria include ongoing GI pathology or a history of GI surgery, bowel perforation, fecal incontinence, GI obstruction, chronic idiopathic constipation, clinically important diverticular disease, or any other active disorder associated with chronic diarrhea or intermittent loose stools or constipation.

Sample collection time and discharge criteria

As the concept of "mass balance" involves recovery from excreta (i.e., urine, feces, or in some cases, expired CO_2), subjects are confined for a pre-defined duration and are discharged after defined criteria are met. Pragmatically, the goal is to collect excreta over a sufficient interval to achieve the maximum acceptable overall recovery. Similarly, plasma must be collected over a sufficient interval to allow characterization of the metabolite profile that includes late or persistent metabolites. These goals are achieved by using a predetermined recovery from excreta (such as >90%) in conjunction with a minimum excretion rate (such as <1% recovered in excreta for two consecutive days) [3]. Achieving these endpoints becomes challenging for compounds with long half-lives (parent or total radioactivity) since it is not practical to confine subjects longer than 14 days, which could reduce the likelihood of achieving the desired recovery or characterize the metabolite profile. Alternative designs can address these limitations, by confining subjects for up to 2 weeks, followed by weekly visits to the study center for additional collection. This approach was used for vismodegib, which has a half-life of 227 h. Subjects were confined for 14 days (336 h) and returned for overnight visits at weeks 3−8 [210]. The overall recovery in this study was 86.6%. While it is likely that a parent compound's plasma half-life has been determined in a typical first in human single ascending dose (SAD) study (prior to the AME study design phase), the half-life for total radioactivity (TRA), which represents the sum the parent and all drug-related metabolites, is not known. Therefore, it is difficult to predict the adequate sampling time to characterize the terminal half-life for TRA (for this reason, the half-life for total radioactivity may not be reported due to insufficient time points for extrapolation).

Traditional approaches to AME versus microtracer

A key requirement prior to conducting a traditional human AME study (i.e., one that uses a radioactive dose in the range of 20−100 µCi) with ^{14}C material is an estimation of the radioactive exposure to human tissues, which is accomplished in a tissue distribution study (whole-body autoradiography; quantitative whole-body autoradiography, QWBA) in preclinical species (typically rat) [227,228]. Limits on the total human exposure to radiolabeled materials vary with the organ (US code of Federal Regulations)—3000 mrem for the whole body, active blood forming organs, lens of the eye and gonads. With conventional radioactive doses, quantitative profiling of metabolites in circulation and excreta can be accomplished with HPLC−MS coupled with online radiometric detector or offline radiodetectors after HPLC fractionation. In rare cases, if the tissue residence of radioactivity is extensive and prolonged, the amount of radioactivity that can be safely dosed to humans may be too small to practically carry out the study with conventional radiodetectors, micro radioactive dose (<1 µCi) has to be used in human AME studies. In fact, there is a recent trend of conducting human AME studies with micro radioactive dose which offers distinct advantages [4]. A micro radioactive dose (typically 0.1−1.0 µCi) does not require preclinical QWBA data for dosimetry calculation, since the overall radioactive exposure is low. In addition, GMP radioactive material may not be required due to the overall low contribution (<1%) to the total (cold) administered dose which is GMP material. The obvious drawback is the need of ultrasensitive ^{14}C-detection techniques (such as accelerator mass spectrometry (AMS) or cavity ring-down spectroscopy (CRDS)) to support micro radioactive dose AME studies.

AMS is an isotope counting technique that measures the ratio of carbon isotopes ($[^{14}C{:}^{12}C]$) in biological samples and offers superior sensitivity [229−232]. The major disadvantage of AMS technology is its labor-intensive sample processing procedures. The analyte of interest must be separated and isolated from all other drug-related material by HPLC fractionation prior to AMS analysis. The sample preparation process is not amenable to automation and, thus, suffers from longer turnaround compared to the conventional liquid scintillation counter. The cost of AMS analysis is typically high, however this should be balanced by the savings in time and resources associated with not requiring GMP material and/or a preclinical QWBA study.

While the number of AMS studies has steadily increased over the past decade, emerging technology may further enable more widespread adoption of these techniques in AME studies, by increasing throughput and reducing cost. Quantification of ^{14}C by cavity ring-down spectroscopy (CRDS) offers an alternative ultra-sensitive approach that eliminates many of the shortcomings of an AMS in biomedical research [233,234]. In CRDS, the beam from a single-frequency laser diode enters a cavity defined by two or more high reflectivity mirrors. When the laser is on, the cavity quickly fills with circulating laser light, and then the laser is shut off starting the "ring-down" event. Some radiation leaks out an end mirror on each bounce, and the stored radiant energy inside the optical cavity decays exponentially with time. When a gas sample is introduced inside the optical cavity, the ring-down lifetime is shortened [235], allowing for the quantitation of the gas concentration. The gain in sensitivity is a result of the long effective pathlength (10s of kilometers) the light travels during circulation [236]. The analysis of total radioactivity in samples derived from a human microtracer study of YH12852 (1 µCi radioactive dose) was conducted using CRDS and the result was compared with that from AMS to assess the viability of CRDS as an instrument to support human microtracer studies. The data using CRDS method closely reproduced that from AMS method for total ^{14}C concentration in plasma and urine [237]. Importantly, CRDS represents a potential savings in resources, time, and cost. Throughput of CRDS is approximately 100 samples a day and the cost of the instrument will be substantially less than that of a conventional AMS system.

Human only approach—an argument against conducting preclinical ^{14}C mass balance studies

The original paradigm adopted by the pharmaceutical industry, in general, involved the AME studies first conducted in preclinical species, and an assessment of whole-body quantitative radiology and dosimetry-based estimate of the human radioactive exposure. However, Obach et al. (2012) suggest that traditional mass-balance studies in animals should no longer be conducted as a routine requirement for drug development. Specifically, they recommend focus on ensuring that human metabolites are present in animals at equal or greater quantity and downplay the need for exhaustive (and complete) characterization of the preclinical metabolite profile (which may include metabolites of no relevance to humans). Fundamentally, the crux of the proposal relies on the ability to demonstrate coverage of the key human metabolites ($>10\%$ of the total drug related material in circulation) in preclinical species without radiolabeled material (see MIST section). Once the key human metabolites are identified in the human AME study, sufficient coverage in the preclinical species can be accomplished via a variety of methods without the need for preclinical radiolabel studies.

Arguments against a "human only" ADME approach justify the utility of animal ADME data assuming the translatability of preclinical ADME to humans. As such [238], acknowledge that preclinical mass balance data may be useful in the following scenarios: (1) interpreting preclinical toxicity data, (2) assessing the potential of biliary excretion, (3) predicting oral absorption, (4) predicting if low mass balance and recovery may occur in humans, (5) assessment of the potential for covalent binding, (6) identification of reactive intermediates, and (7) early assessment of elimination pathways [239]. Further discuss the utility of animal mass balance data, suggesting that at least one of these seven scenarios is relevant to every development candidate molecule.

With respect to translating preclinical excretion data to humans, it is important to recognize species differences in metabolism [240] and transporters associated with biliary secretion [241,242]. Notably, rats have higher rates of bile flow [243], canalicular efflux transport [244] and higher efflux transporter expression [245,246], leading to more rapid biliary excretion than humans [247]. Roffey et al. [248] noted that overall recovery in AME studies was higher in preclinical species than humans and cited higher biliary excretion rate as an important contributor. This tendency for more rapid excretion via feces in preclinical species was also observed by Roffel et al. [249]; who attributed higher rodent biliary excretion in rats as a contributor to the low overall translatability of preclinical mass balance studies to human, in their analysis of 34 human AME studies.

The decision to conduct AME studies in preclinical species therefore depends on the perceived translatability of the animal data to human and practical considerations associated with the need to support a traditional or microtracer study (i.e., AMS). As discussed, a microtracer study does not require a dosimetry data from a preclinical QWBA study, and thus the need for a preclinical AME study may be diminished based on the clinical development plan. Despite the species differences in AME, it is tempting to leverage preclinical data to help context data from the human AME study, for example to make qualitative conclusions on stability of metabolites or comment on consistency across species for excretion pathways. In addition, the preclinical AME study can confirm stability of the radiolabel and may also provide early information on issues that may arise in the human AME study.

Common issues with AME studies

As the metabolism and excretion of a new chemical entity can be complex, achieving the primary goal of the AME study is often challenging, and it may be difficult to make definitive conclusions from the available data. Regulatory agencies are tasked with evaluating the readouts from AME study and identifying deficiencies, which in some cases may require repeating the study. A comprehensive review by Coppola et al. [1] noted that of 472 new drug applications reviewed by the EMA from 2013 to 2017, 10 ($\sim$2%) had major objection related to AME or metabolism data. In general deficiencies can be broadly divided into two categories: (1) insufficient characterization of metabolites or (2) insufficient characterization of elimination pathways.

Issues related to metabolite characterization were related to identification of the relevant metabolites, and importantly, over the appropriate time course. Despite clear guidance from regulatory agencies, in several cases, components contributing to more than 10% of the total radioactive AUC were not characterized. Another common deficiency was metabolite profiling based only the first 24 h for compounds with a much longer half-life for total radioactivity. Overall, the metabolite profile should be determined over the time interval that covers >90% of the total AUC of radioactive material in plasma, or >90% of dose excreted in excreta. Poor extraction efficiency from excreta (typically feces) and/or plasma can also contribute to inadequate characterization of the metabolic profile. Finally, insufficient preclinical safety data on disproportionate human metabolites (i.e., MIST guidance) or inadequate characterization of a potentially active metabolite were also highlighted as deficiencies in several cases. In addition to overcoming potential technical challenges, it is clear that more careful adherence to regulatory guidelines and recognition of the radioactivity half-life could help mitigate issues associated with insufficient metabolite characterization.

Issues related to characterization of elimination pathways were largely due to incomplete mass balance data resulting in ambiguous conclusions on the contribution of excretion mechanisms. Inadequate recovery, for example, complicates conclusions due to the uncertainty around how the unaccounted drug-related material is excreted. Notably, in cases where large percentage of unchanged parent is recovered in feces, it is difficult to differentiate what was simply unabsorbed, excreted, or potentially formed from unstable metabolites (i.e., gut microbiome metabolism). Determination of absolute bioavailability and calculation of fraction absorbed is the most definitive way to interpret % unchanged parent drug in feces. However, the minimum fraction absorbed (Fa) can be estimated based on the sum of the % total radioactivity recovered in urine and the % radioactivity attributed to metabolites in feces. This estimation does not account for parent drug that was absorbed and excreted back into feces via intestinal secretion, and it also assumes that all metabolites (and parent drug) are stable in feces (i.e., no metabolites detected in feces are formed via gut microbiota). Acknowledging these caveats, the detection of a large percentage of unchanged drug in feces, without Fa or bioavailability data, remains challenging to interpret and could reduce the confidence in understanding the excretion pathways. Although the regulatory agencies may be reluctant to reject an AME study with incomplete understanding of elimination pathways due to the limited data, restrictive and overly conservative language around the potential for drug-drug interactions (DDI's) may be enforced in cases where the true extent of transporter-mediated excretion pathways remain ambiguous or unknown.

As highlighted by Coppola et al. [1], the recovery of a high percentage unchanged parent in feces remains a potentially difficult endpoint to interpret in a traditional AME study. In the present analysis (2000−2021) more than half of the compounds had >50% excretion via feces, and with few exceptions, no IV data to estimate absolute bioavailability. In many of these cases, qualitative arguments based on in vitro and preclinical data were made to support conclusions on the elimination pathways leading to the fecal recovery of unchanged parent. Of the studies reviewed, faldaprevir had the highest recovery in feces (98.3%) [84], which was distributed almost evenly between unchanged parent (51.9%) and two hydroxylated metabolites. Although IV data was not available, the recovery of oxidative metabolites in feces together with the total dose recovered in urine suggested that at least $\sim$50% of dose was absorbed. Although faldaprevir and its major metabolites were previously identified as substrates of P-gp, the extent of biliary secretion of unchanged parent (or metabolites) cannot be deduced from this AME study, and therefore the susceptibility to victim DDI due to P-gp inhibition remained unanswered. Therefore, the key objectives of elucidating the elimination pathways (and importantly, susceptibility as victim to transporter-mediated drug interactions) were not completely achieved. Notably, the propensity for DDI was further assessed several years later by Huang et al. [250] who showed that cyclosporine increased steady-state faldaprevir C_{max} by 41% and AUC_{tau} by 23%, confirming contributions from both CYP3A4 and P-gp to the elimination of faldaprevir. In contrast to the faldaprevir example, the utility of a combined absolute bioavailability and mass balance study is highlighted by the example of alectinib [13], which also demonstrated a high recovery of unchanged parent in feces (84%). Importantly, IV administration enabled the determination of both absolute bioavailability (F = 36.9%), hepatic extraction ($E_h = \sim$0.14), which were used to estimate fraction absorbed (Fa $\sim$ 25%, assuming Fg = 1). Therefore, $\sim$75% of the dose was accounted as unabsorbed parent drug in the feces, with the remaining $\sim$10% attributed to biliary/intestinal secretion. In this example, estimation of fraction absorbed assisted in the conclusion that contribution of biliary/intestinal secretion pathways was minima to the overall elimination of alectinib, and, notably, the key objective of the AME study was achieved without ambiguity.

Interpretation of AME studies with high fecal recovery are likely to be more complex for compounds that are susceptible to glucuronidation and/or direct intestinal secretion of parent drug. Glucuronide conjugates are known to be converted back to the parent by gut bacterial β-D-glucuronidases to parent drug, therefore, glucuronide metabolites are rarely detected in feces. Fundamentally, estimation of the % of unchanged parent that is biliary excreted versus back-converted from an unstable glucuronide metabolite remains challenging, due to technical difficulties associated with sampling bile. Strategies to better understand biliary excretion were reviewed by Ghibellini et al. [251]; and in general involve various techniques to sample bile or duodenal fluid. In the studies reviewed from 2000 to 2021, the majority of studies did not sample bile or duodenal fluid to help context the % recovery of parent and/or metabolites in feces, perhaps due to the difficulty associated with the sampling and the potential for inconclusive data (since fraction absorbed may still be required to interpret a high % of parent drug detected in feces).

To assist in the interpretation of high % of parent drug in feces, Remmerie et al. [7] described an approach utilizing duodenal sampling to determine the contribution of different metabolic and excretion pathways to the high fecal recovery of JNJ-53718678 (rilematovir). Importantly, the authors noted that a traditional AME study would be unable to differentiate between the unabsorbed parent drug from biliary secreted parent or back-conversion of secreted N-glucuronide metabolite (M8) to parent drug in the intestine. Using a nasoduodenal tube, duodenal fluid samples were collected at 2.5 and 3.75 h post dose, following gallbladder contraction. The biliary clearance of the N-glucuronide M8 was determined to be 84-fold higher than the parent drug and contributed to 10.4% of the total radioactivity in duodenal fluid. Assessment of the glucuronide metabolite formation and clearance in duodenal fluid confirmed that the very low amount of M8 detected in excreta was due to rapid conversion to parent drug. Of note, the overall contribution of glucuronidation was estimated to be low, in contrast to in vitro data indicating N-glucuronidation of the parent drug was a significant clearance pathway.

The example of regorafenib reveals additional ex vivo techniques to help context parent and metabolites detected in feces [165]. Although no bile or duodenal fluid was sampled in this study, the stability of the N-oxide (M2) or N-glucuronide (M7) metabolites were determined ex vivo in fecal samples under anaerobic conditions. Rapid reduction of the N-oxide metabolite M2 resulting in parent regorafenib indicated that M2 was susceptible to fecal degradation, consistent with its lack of detection in the excreted feces from all subjects in the study. Conversely, ex vivo conversion of M7 back to parent was slow in fecal incubations, consistent with the detection of M7 in only two out of four subjects. While this technique does not help quantitate the contribution of these metabolic pathways to the elimination of regorafenib, assessing the fecal metabolic stability ex vivo can assist in the interpretation of a high percentage of parent drug detected in feces and the absence of expected metabolites.

Compounds with low recovery

An often-cited parameter for judging the success of a human AME study is the overall total percent recovery or "mass balance" with some investigators [2] recommending greater than 90% recovery as an adequate cut-off. Conceptually, the desire for so-called "complete" mass balance (i.e., approaching 100% recovery from excreta) is understandable—if the fate of a large percentage of radioactive dose is unknown, how can there be confident elucidation of the elimination pathways? Seminal analysis by Roffey et al. [248] challenged the assumption that key objectives of the mass balance study could only be achieved by near complete recovery. Rather than focus on % recovery as a metric for success, the authors recommended a more pragmatic approach to holistically evaluate if the key goals of the AME study were achieved—namely, understanding elimination pathways and metabolic profile. While lower recoveries can reduce the confidence in the determination of the relative contribution of different clearance pathways, qualitative conclusions are still possible even with incomplete recovery. Nevertheless, low and, frequently observed, variable recovery remains a common observation across AME studies, and of studies (2000−2021), 31 (14%) had less than 80% recovery, encompassing a wide range of therapeutic indications (oncology, multiple sclerosis, kidney disease, diabetes, hypertension, asthma, and autoimmune diseases). Review of these with low recovery revealed several interesting trends, which are discussed below.

Problems with fecal recovery

Nine studies attributed low overall recovery to inconsistent recovery of radioactivity in feces across subjects, and identified at least one outlier due to low fecal recovery and, reported evidence for constipation or altered bowel movements (ixabepilone [110], axitinib [33], barasertib [35], linsitinib [122], sonidegib [183], enarodustat [74], vistusertib [211], pazopanib [150], and saxagliptin [176]). It is important to note that across these studies, the subject outliers with low total and fecal recovery did not have inconsistent urine recovery or altered metabolism or pharmacokinetics of parent drug or metabolites, compared to subjects with good recovery. Therefore inconsistent (or poor) recovery in fecal samples is likely driven by issues related to feces production and collection, and are not mechanistic driven (i.e., related to specific, altered clearance mechanisms in the subjects with low recovery). Slow fecal excretion was noted as a key contributor to the overall low recovery of fingolimod [87], which has a half-life of 137 h (parent) and 382 h (radioactivity). It is useful to consider whole-gut transit time (WGTT), which has been reported to be ~30 h (median) in healthy subjects and almost two-fold higher (59.3 h) in constipated subjects [252]. Of note, WGTT was significantly ($P < 0.0001$) slower in healthy women (33.9 h) compared to healthy men (25.6 h), but no gender difference among constipated subjects. This gender difference should therefore be considered for enrollment, as a study conducted in only males or females may have more consistent fecal recovery than a mixed gender study. Recognizing that unabsorbed parent should be complete excreted via feces after completing gut transit, recovery of parent material post ~30 h may represent secreted parent compound. However, due to the variability in WGTT, it is difficult to make quantitative conclusions. Overall, complications related to fecal recovery were also noted by Roffey et al. [248] who suggest that prolonged excretion into feces represents a huge technical barrier, confounded by non-homogenous samples and irregularity of defecation. In addition, AME studies of oncology medications may be at increased risk of poor recovery due to irregular bowel movements, which have been shown to be common patients with advanced cancer [253].

Long plasma half-life

Trends with respect to the half-life and total recovery for mass balance studies were investigated for the studies conducted from 2000 to 2021. The majority of compounds (79%) with short TRA half-lives (<15 h) had greater than 85% total recovery. For compounds a long half-life (>75 h), the percentage of studies achieving >85% recovery was reduced to 61%, which is higher than previously reported by Roffey et al. [248]; who noted only 28% achieved this recovery level for long half-life compounds. The increase in overall recovery for compounds with long-half in our present study compared to the previous one by Roffey et al. may have resulted from recent improvements in study conduct/study design, longer confinement or collection times, and the increased use of more sensitive analytical technique (i.e., AMS). Notably the majority (~60%) of studies utilizing AMS had half-lives > 50 h, indicating that investigators may be choosing this more sensitive detection method for compounds with a long half-life. Further, seven AMS studies on compounds with TRA half-life >75 h (ixazomib, sonidegib, ribociclib, apalutamide, vismodegib, KD101, gedatolisib and cerlapirdine) had total recoveries of >80%, suggesting this approach may indeed improve the recovery for slowly excreted compounds. Although in general AMS appears to be a promising technique to improve overall recovery, there were several AMS studies which had <80% recovery. Pyronaridine [160] had an overall recovery of 71.5%, and had a long half-life of 33.5 days. Excretion in urine and feces displayed two distinct phases, an in initial phase of 19% (urine) and 59% (feces) in the first 168 h, followed by a much slower rate until the end of the study. Continued recovery through final sampling period suggested that the cumulative percentage of drug recovery would continue beyond 87 days post dose. Ozanimod [143] also had a long TRA half-life of 98.6 h and low overall recovery of 63%, which was attributed to long-lived stable metabolites in plasma and a loss of ^{14}C label as carbon dioxide in expired air due to anaerobic microbial reductive metabolism. These two examples highlight that very slowly excreted compounds or unaccounted loss of label as CO_2 could remain as potential challenges that AMS techniques cannot resolve.

Recovery for irreversibly or covalently bound drugs

To investigate a potential relationship between drugs known to bind irreversibly or covalently to proteins (either non-specifically or specifically to intended targets) and % recovery, AME studies for compounds of this class (typically for oncology indications) were reviewed separately. Pyrotinib is a novel irreversible epidermal growth factor receptor/human epidermal growth factor receptor 2 inhibitor that also binds nonspecifically and covalently to protein [161]. Optimized extraction procedures yielded >95% extraction efficiency from feces but a maximum of only ~50% extraction recovery was achieved in plasma, which was attributed to nonspecific covalent binding to plasma proteins. Despite the difficulty in extraction radioactivity from plasma, the overall recovery was 92.6%, which suggests that the overall mass balance is driven by the higher relative radioactivity associated with excreta (in this case, feces) than that retained in systemic circulation or bound to tissues proteins. Two other targeted covalent inhibitors that target various kinases also demonstrated good recovery: evobrutinib [83] and acalabrutinib [10] achieving total recoveries of >90%. Good recovery for this class of compounds that bind irreversibly is consistent with previous analysis [248] where known covalent binders also did not demonstrate a trend for low or incomplete recovery [248]. These authors also concluded that since the overall binding to tissue macromolecules and proteins represents a low percentage of the total radioactivity administered, losses due to this binding does not impact the overall recovery.

Recommendations for addressing poor recovery and long half-life compounds

Review of the studies with lower recoveries in the past 2 decades revealed no trends with respect to target indication, mechanism of action or propensity to bind macromolecules. Improvements in achieving higher total recovery, in particular for compounds with long half-life may be achieved by ultrasensitive radiodetection technique (e.g., AMS). AMS offers two key advantages: (1) reduction in the radioactive dose (and burden) to subjects and (2) long sampling duration for excreta to ensure improved recovery for compounds with long half-life. As noted in several studies, greater contribution of fecal excretion may predispose a study to have reduced recovery, whereas compounds with short half-lives and predominantly renal excretion are most likely to have the highest recoveries. The somewhat frequent observation of outlier subjects with lower fecal recovery suggests that study-related (i.e., non-mechanistic) may be contributing to the low recovery. A commonly cited explanation for inconsistent fecal recovery is incomplete collection of excreta or missing samples (lost collection or inadequate sampling protocols). Alternatively, variability in a subject's GI status, in particular frequency of bowel movements appears to be a key contributor to the inconsistent recovery in feces, in light of the high frequency of "outlier" subjects. Therefore, review of study exclusion criteria selection of subjects with strict guidance no prior GI related issues (i.e., related to bowel movements) may reduce the likelihood of issues related to feces sampling and improve the overall recovery. In addition, as poor recovery could result from a variety of study-related issues (incorrect dose, missing samples, etc.) improved adherence to clinical study conduct could help improve the recovery.

Metabolites in safety testing (MIST)

The ICH M3(R2) [254] (http://www.ema.europa.eu/docs/en_GB/document_library/Scientific_guideline/2009/09/WC500002720.pdf) and FDA [255] (http://www.fda.gov/downloads/drugs/guidancecomplianceregulatoryinformation/guidances/ucm079266.pdf) guidance on metabolites-in-safety testing (MIST) require exposures of major human circulating metabolites to be compared to the exposures observed in non-clinical safety testing at steady state. The guidance defines a major metabolite as one whose abundance is greater than or equal to 10% of the total drug-related exposure and outline specific criteria for evaluation of the relevant major metabolites. If this drug metabolite is formed at adequate exposure levels in at least one animal test species, it can be concluded that the metabolite's contribution to the overall toxicity assessment has been established, as described in the decision tree flow diagram (Fig. 10.1). Characterization of metabolite toxicity would generally be considered adequate when animal exposure is at least 50% the exposure seen in

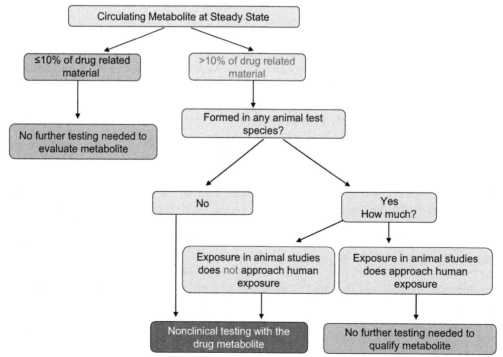

FIGURE 10.1 Decision tree flow diagram for assessing metabolites in safety testing (MIST).

humans. In some cases, for example when a metabolite composes the majority of the total human exposure, it is appropriate for exposure to the metabolite in animals to exceed that in humans. In this latter case it is important to achieve a higher exposure to the metabolite in animals because this metabolite constitutes the bulk of human exposure (ICH guideline M3 (R2)—questions and answers. https://www.ema.europa.eu/en/documents/other/international-conference-harmonisation-technical-requirements-registration-pharmaceuticals-human-use_en.pdf).

Traditionally, human metabolites are identified and quantified in a single-dose radiolabeled (^{14}C) study during phase II clinical development or after proof-of-concept is achieved. The information generated from the ^{14}C-AME study in humans may therefore be inadequate to assess metabolism at steady state, and since it is generated late in the development programs, may delay large scale clinical trials if any human metabolite requires safety evaluation. For example, lack of safety information about an active metabolite of ozanimod, called CC112273, caused significant delay of drug's approval. The major human disproportionate metabolite CC112273 was not identified until late in the development when the radiolabeled study was conducted. After identification of CC112273 as a major circulating, disproportionate, and active metabolite with long half-life, steady-state exposures were determined in multiple-dose studies in patients with relapsing multiple sclerosis, which showed that metabolite CC112273 accumulated approximately 11- to 13-fold upon repeat dosing. The identification of disproportionate metabolites late in the development presented challenges for the metabolites in safety testing assessment, pharmacokinetic-pharmacodynamic and exposure-response, and drug-drug interaction assessment in clinical pharmacology studies [143]. The major human circulating metabolite of momelotinib, M21 (a morpholino lactam), was observed in disproportionately higher amounts in human plasma than in rat or dog, the rodent and nonrodent species used for the general nonclinical safety assessment. This discrepancy needed to be resolved with an additional nonclinical safety study by a combination dosing of parent and M21 to boost M21 exposure in rats in a 104-week study to meet the regulatory guidance on MIST [133].

Prediction of circulating metabolites from in vitro data

The evolution of in vitro systems (mainly microsomes and hepatocytes) for the generation of metabolites has prompted several retrospective analyses by large pharmaceutical companies to determine if it is possible to predict which metabolites will circulate and become relevant in vivo. Analysis reported by [256] (Pfizer), [257] (Eli Lilly), and [258] (Astra Zeneca) revealed that in vitro systems adequately predicted in vivo metabolites for 41%, 33%, and 33−54% of the selected studies, respectively. This low accuracy was attributed to the observation that multistep biotransformation reactions (both conjugative and multiple, subsequent oxidative reactions) were prone to underprediction. Insufficient reaction time, due to limited viability of hepatocytes in vitro, was cited as a potential contributor for the trend for the underprediction of metabolite formation arising from more complex, multi-step processes involving several enzyme systems. Accordingly, advances in long-term hepatocyte culture may prove to help address this issue in the future, and preliminary data is indeed promising [259−262]). Another key conclusion from these retrospective reports is the overall poor success rate to predict the quantity of metabolite formed, and thus in vivo exposure and metabolic profile. In addition, the Astra Zeneca analysis revealed that species differences in transporter activity, secondary metabolism, and enzyme kinetics may contribute to the formation of disproportionate or human-specific metabolites. Overall, while qualitative prediction of the primary metabolites may be possible, prediction of the quantity and extent of circulating metabolites based on in vitro data is not possible. Physiochemical properties of the parent compound, in particular high permeability, appear to be good predictors on the potential for metabolites to circulate [263]. Due to relatively minor structural changes via oxidative, reductive or hydrolytic processes, metabolites of compounds with high lipoidal permeability are likely to circulate, in particular if they are converted to more stable forms than the parent. Conversely, compounds or metabolites (i.e., conjugates such as glucuronides) with low lipoidal permeability depend on active transport (efflux) from the liver to circulate. Pragmatically, information of efflux transport may be a key predictor for the propensity for circulating metabolites with poor permeability, whereas metabolites of highly permeable parent molecules may be assumed to also circulate. Despite these broad trends, it is generally recognized that prediction of circulating human metabolites is challenging, and due to species differences in metabolism the preclinical in vivo metabolite profiling may not offer any additional information on clinically relevant metabolites.

Metabolite profiling from single dose versus multiple dose studies

It is clear that the MIST guidance refers to the metabolic profile at steady state, and therefore AME studies based on a single dose may not adequately describe the metabolites that require sufficient coverage in preclinical safety studies. Notably, the level and ratio of metabolites at steady state may be different from that after a single dose, due to a variety of factors. For example, some metabolites may have a much longer half-life in the systemic circulation than their parent drug [264,265]. Three novel metabolites of AZD7325, M9, M10, and M42, were either minor or absent in circulation after a single dose; however, they were all major circulating metabolites after repeated doses in humans and preclinical animals [265]. From the venetoclax human AME study, analysis of pooled plasma ($AUC_{0-48 h}$) showed that an oxidative metabolite, M27, represented 12% of the total drug related material; however, the terminal phase elimination half-life of M27 (58.8 h) was 2.5-fold longer than that of venetoclax; and, at 48 h and beyond, M27 was the major drug related component in the plasma. Therefore, M27 level was expected to be significantly higher after repeated doses [5,264]. The observation of circulating metabolites with long $t_{1/2}$ demonstrates the need to collect plasma samples at steady state after multiple doses when conducting metabolite analysis for the safety testing of drug metabolites.

Assuming no time-dependent changes in the pharmacokinetics of parent or metabolites following repeated doses, the steady-state metabolic profile can be modeled from a single dose study. Prakash et al [124] demonstrated successful prediction of the steady-state metabolic profile of lixivaptan by modeling the available single dose data and simulating multiple-dose data. However, induction or inhibition of metabolism, or other time-dependent changes (caused by parent or metabolite) may yield a different metabolic profile at steady-state, and therefore a metabolite profile following single dose might be inadequate to address MIST.

Two approaches have been proposed to obtain human steady-state metabolite profiles [238]. Multiple dosing of un-labeled material is done in an attempt to reach a predicted steady-state for total drug-related material before a carbon-14 labeled dose is given on the final dosing interval. Plasma metabolite profiling obtained represents the steady-state profile assuming no metabolite or parent drug accumulation. As repeated administration of unlabeled drug would theoretically achieve the true steady-state metabolic status (i.e., induced and/or inhibited enzymes), it may provide a more relevant metabolite profile with respect to MIST guidance. However, since the plasma metabolite profile obtained by measuring ^{14}C only reflects the last radioactive dose, metabolites which have accumulated throughout the study will not be captured. One way to definitively assess the steady-state radioprofile is to administrate multiple microtracer doses of ^{14}C labeled material (~ 10 nCi daily) to reach steady-state for total drug-related material. On the final dose, plasma is collected during the dosing interval period, and the metabolite profiles obtained by analysis of ^{14}C in plasma following fractionation by HPLC and use of AMS will be representative of the steady-state profile.

Recognizing the ethical and practical limitations of conducting a repeated dose radioactivity study in humans, an appealing alternative approach to comply with the regulatory authority's MIST guidelines is to assess metabolism in early drug development with phase I multiple ascending dose (MAD) studies in humans. Plasma samples from these studies can be used for metabolite identification and quantification at steady state, thus allowing for an early estimation of whether any human metabolite that exceeds 10% of the total drug-related material has been adequately tested in safety evaluation experiments. Later in a radiolabeled study in humans an assessment can be made if all major metabolites have been appropriately detected and characterized adequately in earlier studies [266].

Strategies for addressing MIST guidance: tiered approaches

A key limitation of utilizing samples obtained at steady-state from multiple doses, non-AME study is that the material is not radiolabeled, making quantitation difficult. Authentic metabolite standards and a validated bioanalytical method are eventually required to assess exposure of clinically relevant metabolites, but in early clinical development these standards are likely not available. Since the publication of the MIST guidance, several strategic papers addressing these concerns around metabolite quantitation and determination of exposure coverage have been published [222,266–269]. Overall, these commentaries discuss how to balance the objectives of the MIST guidance with the available bioanalytical methodology, within the context of the overall plans of clinical development programs. Importantly, definitive measurement of preclinical and clinical metabolite concentrations with authentic standard across multiple studies is a large resource burden and may result in delays in drug development. Metabolite structures need to be fully characterized and preparation of adequate quantities of authentic standards of drug metabolites can be difficult and sometimes is impossible. Additionally, developing and validating bioanalytical assays for multiple metabolites in multiple matrices can be very lab-intensive [270,271]. Recognizing these challenges, pharmaceutical industry scientists propose to rethink the questions of "when do we need a validated assay for metabolite quantitation" and "how can we fully utilize alternative bioanalytical approaches to generate reliable data for enabling decision-making," with a focus on minimizing resource intensive validated bioanalysis [272,273].

Critical to implementing an optimized strategy for metabolite profiling is understanding which metabolites should be quantified, at which phase of clinic development, and with what level of scientific and regulatory rigor. The general consensus from the bioanalytical community is that a tiered approach is needed to balance the resource burden and requirements for method validation and data quality. This has resulted in three tiers proposed for metabolite quantification during drug discovery and development: screening methods, qualified methods, and validated methods [271,274], with each tier offering increasing confidence in quantitation.

The decision on which tier should be applied to a particular metabolite and at what stage of drug development will depend on the amount and the nature of the metabolite. For example, if a metabolite retains pharmacological activity, data may be required ascertain its pharmacokinetics and impact on pharmacodynamic response or to determine the drug's safety and efficacy, or make dosing adjustments. In this situation, routine quantitation with a fully validated method is recommended [271]. In cases where the metabolite is not active but is disproportionate in humans, qualified bioanalytical methods may be more appropriate in line with the stage of development. This tiered-approach to metabolite quantification in drug development has gained in popularity and can potentially save tremendous resources in the regulated bioanalytical laboratories in three areas: reducing the number of metabolites being monitored in toxicology studies; avoiding full validation of metabolite assays in early clinical studies; and avoiding a commitment to long-term monitoring of human metabolites that are of no concern in large scale clinic trials [269]. The result of this strategy would be fewer resources utilized, but potential MIST issues still fully addressed early in a drug development program.

Indeed, the MIST guidance does not require the absolute concentrations of circulating metabolites to be known, but it is necessary to demonstrate that non-clinical safety species have exposure levels that at least approach, and ideally exceed, those in humans. The guidance does not specify how much the safety species exposures should exceed the human exposures. Therefore, a fully validated bioanalytical method to quantitate the metabolite may be, in most cases, excessive. A variety of novel methods have been developed and employed to estimate the exposure of circulating drug metabolites in humans and animals, including those which do not require an authentic standard of the metabolite.

Semi-quantitation of drug metabolites

Metabolism results in structural changes that may appreciably alter the ionization efficiency of individual metabolite; therefore, it is necessary to first calibrate the mass spectrometric response of metabolites relative to that of the parent drug to semi-quantify the metabolite level in biological matrices. Various methods have been developed to determine a metabolite's response factor, including mass spectrometry response calibration with authentic standard or radioactivity and quantitative NMR.

Radiometric calibration approach determines a correction factor based on the ^{14}C radioactive response and the LC−MS response for a given metabolite (generated from in vitro or in vivo samples) and applies the same correction factor to studies conducted without a radiolabel. Therefore, based on LC−MS response (i.e., peak area alone), metabolites detected from clinical samples can be quantitated based on radio-calibration from studies conducted with radiolabel. Yu et al. [275] validated this approach by successfully determining the relative proportion of four metabolites (M7, M10, M17, and M28) of GSK-A. In this example the correction factors for M10 and M17 were determined in vitro by incubating ^{14}C-GSK-A in dog hepatocytes, whereas for M7 and M28, in vivo ^{14}C rat bile samples were used [276]. Further developed the approach by recommending the use of a pseudo-internal standard (PIS; typically the parent drug of interest, which has validated bioanalytical detection method) to address potential issues with sample preparation and assay-related variability. Conceptually, the key difference compared to the original approach by Yu et al. (2007) is that both the MS and radioactive responses of the metabolite of interest are first normalized to the PIS response prior to determining the correction factor. Since the PIS is present in both radioactive reference and the cold (nonradioactive unknown) samples, metabolite exposures in the unknown samples can be estimated from the measured PIS exposure using a relative molar ratio established between the metabolite and the PIS.

$$RCF = [CPM \text{ metabolite}/CPM \text{ PIS}]/[MS \text{ area of metabolite}/MS \text{ area of PIS}]$$

Radio-calibration approach can also be useful for determining metabolite exposure in preclinical safety studies where a validated method for a metabolite is not available. Human ^{14}C AME studies revealed that a prominent metabolite (M3) of compound LY05 represented 21% of the radioactivity associated with parent drug in plasma, but its generation, isolation and synthesis proved to be challenging [257,276]. A radio-calibration approach was utilized to estimate preclinical M3 exposure, and address the MIST guidance, since a validated bioanalytical method was not available. A more recent application of the radio-calibration approach was reported by Xu et al. [277] who determined the metabolic profile of 6-chloro-9-(4-methoxy-3, 5-dimethylpyridin-2-ylmethyl)-9H-purin-2-ylamine (BIIB021) in human (non-radioactive) clinical samples obtained from phase I multiple ascending dose studies based on preclinical in vivo data in rat conducted with radiolabel. It is important to note that since BIIB021, which was under development as an oral HSP90 inhibitor for treatment of breast cancer, is clastogenic, and therefore a traditional AME study in healthy subjects was not possible.

Further, the metabolic profile at steady-state following multiple ascending dose was determined to be the most relevant to consider for MIST guidance, and the radiocalibration approach enabled this assessment from cold (non-radio labeled) studies.

If a metabolite reference standard is available, the metabolite's response factor can be directly determined by spiking the metabolite standard and the parent drug into plasma and measuring the peak area ratio by LC/MS. The response factor can then be applied to determine the amounts of metabolites in human plasma samples. This is a cost effective means to identify if any metabolite requires MIST evaluation early in the clinical development programs.

NMR is a traditional analytical tool for definitive structural characterization. With recent improvements in sensitivity especially the availability of cryoprobes—NMR is increasingly able to estimate the concentrations of drug metabolites present in biological matrices. Application of quantitative NMR for pharmaceutical applications has been reviewed [278] and discussion how this technology can support metabolite profiling has been summarized elsewhere [279,280]. Prior to its application for addressing MIST guidance, NMR has been used to unambiguously identify and quantitate biologically synthesized metabolites [279,281], and the utility of NMR as powerful quantitative tool was initially demonstrated through the measurement of endogenous compounds in metabolomic studies, with urine as the typical matrix. Improvements in sensitivity due to the development of cryoprobe technology [282,283] enabled further development of NMR to support quantitative metabolite profiling from early phase I clinical studies [284], and its application has been reported [279,284–287]. In 2014, investigators from GlaxoSmithKline [288] indicated that quantitative NMR was the preferred choice for metabolite quantification. James et al. [18] reported successful use of 19F NMR with good correlation with ^{14}C data for alpelisib, but noted several potential limitations including sensitivity (related to the number of fluorine atoms) and potential issues around sample extraction efficiency. A more recent example was reported by Pearson et al. [118] who used this technique to quantify the metabolic profile of leniolisib, a novel oral phosphatidylinositol-3-kinase (PI3K) delta inhibitor, which was under investigation for treatment inflammatory and autoimmune disease. Overall recovery of leniolisib was only 65%, potentially due to insufficient collection time which was 120 h for a 7-h half-life compound. Key limitations in NMR-based approaches to metabolite profiling include the overall lower sensitivity compared to radioactive and LC—MS/MS approaches. These factors likely contribute to the small number of literature reports utilizing this technique in recent years (2011–21), despite the initial enthusiasm.

Mixed matrix method (MmM) for early assessment of metabolite exposures

The mixed matrix method (MmM) was developed for assessing human metabolite exposure coverage in preclinical species without using reference standards or radiolabeled compounds [267,289,290]. This approach is accomplished by mixing equal volume of dosed human plasma sample with blank animal plasma and vice versa. Since the matrices in both plasma samples are essentially identical, the effect of matrix difference across species on the LC—MS response is eliminated. With "Hamilton" pooling [291,292], the concentrations of parent and metabolites in the pooled sample are proportional to the area under the curve (AUCs). Thus, the animal-to-human exposure multiples of parent or metabolites can be calculated from their peak area ratios versus an internal standard (IS) from LC—MS analysis, as described in the equation below:

$$\text{Exposure Multiples (Parent)} = \frac{\left(A_a^p / A_a^{IS}\right)}{\left(A_h^p / A_h^{IS}\right)} \text{ and Exposure Multiples (Metabolite)} = \frac{\left(A_a^m / A_a^{IS}\right)}{\left(A_h^m / A_h^{IS}\right)}$$

where A_a^p and A_h^p are the peak area of the parent drug in animal and human, A_a^{IS} and A_h^{IS} are the peak area of the internal standard in animal and human, A_a^m and A_h^m are the peak area of metabolite in animal and human, respectively. An internal standard (stable labeled parent drug or analog) is spiked into the pooled plasma to account for the run-to-run differences from sample processing and analysis. If a metabolite has comparable or greater exposure in one of the toxicology species than in humans, then it is considered to have sufficient coverage for safety assessment. However, one should note that at this point, it may remain undetermined whether or not the metabolite is, in fact, 10% or more of total drug-related material exposures to qualify it as a major human metabolite.

Several investigators have reported success using the MmM approach. Gao et al. demonstrated that a quantitative comparison of metabolite levels in animals versus humans can be obtained from the peak area ratios of the metabolites versus internal standard from multiple reaction monitoring (MRM) experiments [289]. Ma et al. developed a similar approach to Gao et al., but obtained quantitative data using full scan high resolution mass spectrometry (HRMS) and demonstrated that the exposure multiples of the parent and its metabolites determined from MmM were all within ±15% to those obtained with validated LC—MS/MS measurements [290]. Takahashi et al. further demonstrated the accuracy of

MmM by comparing the results to those obtained from validated bioanalysis for the parent drugs and their metabolites from multiple development programs [293]. Overall, the exposure multiples of the parent drugs and their metabolites determined from the MmM agreed remarkably well (within ±20%) to those obtained from validated bioanalytical methods. The accuracy remains consistent for compounds with diverse physicochemical properties and several standard toxicological species (rats, dogs, rabbits, and monkeys). As shown in Fig. 10.2, the accuracy was also independent of the exposure multiple values, indicating the method has a reasonable dynamic range (>2 order of magnitude). The results provided high confidence that MmM reliably assesses metabolite exposure coverage and can remove the necessity for absolute quantification of drug metabolites to address coverage in accordance to the MIST guidance. Accurate mass full scan LC−MS analysis provides an advantage of capturing data for all metabolites; therefore, this approach is applicable to assess the coverage of any metabolite of interest without knowing the definitive structure of the metabolite, as well as allowing later queries of data for other analytes that become of interest.

The application of alternative approaches to assessing metabolite coverage by no means obviates the need for a radiolabeled AME study in humans, which is still considered the "gold" standard for metabolite detection and quantification and is necessary to determine metabolite exposure relative to the total drug-related material. In addition, it provides excretion and mass balance information and confirms if in earlier "first-in-human" studies all metabolites have been detected and coverage determined as appropriate [3]. Thus, the radiolabeled human study will remain an important and necessary study in drug development but one that should be performed at an appropriate time. The obvious limitation of the data generated from the human mass balance study is that they may not be adequate to assess the steady state exposure of the metabolites, as discussed in previous sections.

Toxicology studies for assessing the safety of human unique/disproportional metabolites

If the metabolite is formed only in humans or is present at higher levels in humans than in the animal species used in the standard toxicology testing, the safety of such a disproportionate drug metabolite has not been adequately evaluated during nonclinical safety studies ([255] (http://www.fda.gov/downloads/drugs/guidancecomplianceregulatoryinformation/guidances/ucm079266.pdf). Demonstrating that a metabolite is pharmacologically inactive at the target receptor is not sufficient to ensure that the metabolite is not toxic, therefore, testing of drug metabolite alone in nonclinical toxicity studies may be warranted. These studies include general toxicity studies, genotoxicity studies, embryo-fetal development toxicity studies, and carcinogenicity studies, which should be completed prior to beginning large-scale clinical trials. However, the number and type of nonclinical studies for the drug metabolites can be modified on a case-by-case basis for those drugs for serious or life-threatening diseases that lack an approved effective therapy.

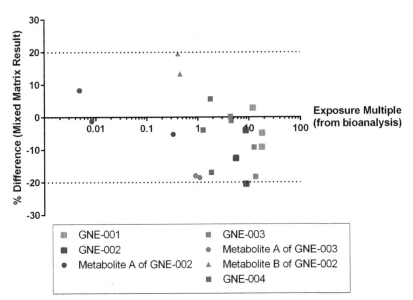

FIGURE 10.2 Comparison of exposure multiples of parent drugs and their metabolites determined from mixed matrix method to those obtained from validated LC−MS/MS bioanalytic methods.

Absolute bioavailability (ABA)

As discussed previously, in cases where a large fraction of the drug is found unchanged in feces, knowledge about the oral bioavailability (and importantly, estimation of the fraction absorbed) can be critical to interpreting % parent and metabolites recovered in feces and understanding the role of biliary and/or gut wall secretion to drug elimination [1]. Bioavailability (BA) is a measurement of the rate and extent to which the active moiety of a drug is absorbed, reaches the systemic circulation and becomes available at the site of action. While there is no direct guidance on the inclusion of an IV arm in a traditional AME study, absolute bioavailability (ABA) is increasingly requested by the EMEA for new chemical entities (NCEs) [1], and is required for new drug application (NDA) submission to Australian Therapeutic Goods Administration (TGA) since 2006.

Traditionally, the absolute bioavailability (%F) for drugs intended for extravascular administration is obtained using a two-period cross-over study design, in which an extravascular dose and an intravascular (IV) dose are administrated separately to each subject with a washout period in between. The drug concentration in circulation is then measured by traditional LC−MS/MS methods. This type of study design is often expensive and time consuming because it requires an additional safety toxicology data in rodent for the IV route and a suitable formulation for IV dosing. Formulation development for IV dosing at an equivalent exposure dose could be very challenging especially for poorly soluble drugs [294]. Conducting toxicology studies for IV dosing for ABA assessment has the potential for undesired safety findings that may not be relevant to the intended route of administration. In addition, the possibility of introducing variables between two dosing periods and nonlinear pharmacokinetics that might affect the pharmacokinetic data exists. As a result, apparent ABA in excess of 100% and errors in the determination of ABA due to non-equivalent CL were reported [294,295].

To address these drawbacks, the IV microtracer approach, first introduced in 1975 as an efficient alternative to the crossover design [296], has emerged and been widely accepted by the pharmaceutical industry as a cost effective way to obtain ABA data in clinical studies. With this approach, subjects are administered a therapeutic dose of drug via the non-IV route, then a microtracer (either radiolabeled drug or stable isotope labeled drug) is typically given via the IV route at 1/100th of therapeutic dose or less than 100 µg at the expected T_{max}. Since the dose of the microtracer is very low, supporting IV toxicology studies are not needed. Formulation development work is also limited. Even very insoluble compounds can be easily formulated with physiological concentration of saline or glucose at such a low dose. The IV microtracer is administered at the peak concentration of the non-IV route at which time the body is already behaving in the therapeutic dose range, therefore, the possibility of nonequivalent kinetics that might otherwise occur between separate dosing occasions is virtually eliminated. In addition, microtracer study with a single dosing period shortens the study duration and eliminates inter-occasion variability present in crossover study design.

When a radiolabeled drug (often [14]C-) is used as the microtracer, either accelerator mass spectrometry (AMS) [41,121,204,297] or cavity ring-down spectroscopy (CRDS) is required for quantifying the drug concentration. As discussed previously, the major disadvantage of these techniques is its labor-intensive sample processing procedures.

Stable isotope labeled (SIL) microtracer with LC−MS/MS analysis is an alternative, cost- and time-effective approach for supporting ABA studies if sufficiently low limit of quantitation (LLOQ) can be achieved to determine the drug concentrations in plasma via IV dosing. Besides LLOQ requirements, feasibility and cost of the chemical synthesis of drug labeled with multiple stable isotopes need to be considered and potentials for isotopic interferences with the LC−MS/MS detection [298] and kinetic isotope effect on drug disposition need to be assessed before choosing stable isotope label microtracer approach [299−301].

With the recent advancement of mass spectrometry technologies with superior robustness, improved scan speed and ionization efficiency, and enhanced ion transmission and detection, the LLOQ of selected reaction monitoring (SRM) has been improved to low pg/mL level with optimization of sample clean up, enrichment procedures and mass spectrometry conditions [302−304]. This sensitivity makes it possible to accurately measure the drug concentration in plasma following an IV administration of a SIL microtracer. The assay's sensitivity requirement is mainly determined by the dose, volume of distribution and clearance of the drug. Typically, it is necessary to quantitate plasma drug concentrations for four to five half-lives to robustly characterize PK profile of a drug. For example, following a 100 µg IV administration of a drug with an estimated volume of distribution of 100 L in humans, the drug concentration is calculated to be 31.3 pg/mL at $5 \times t_{1/2}$ and an assay with a LLOQ at 10−20 pg/mL would be necessary. Allometry (animal-to-human scaling methods), semi-physiological methods and full physiologically-based pharmacokinetics (PBPK) models have also been developed for predicting IV PK parameters and concentration-time profile shape [305], which can provide C_{min} requirement of the LC−MS/MS assay development.

Due to improvement in LC−MS technologies it is becoming clear that as an alternative to AMS, conventional LC−MS/MS will continue to play an important role in microtracer studies. Most recently, several ABA studies published in the literature have used stable isotope labeled drug as microtracer. The ABA of daclatasvir [299] was determined in healthy subjects who received a 60 mg tablet orally followed by a 100 μg [$^{13}C_2$,$^{15}N_4$]-daclatasvir intravenous dose. The LC–MS/MS selected reaction monitoring (SRM) method using $^{13}C_{10}$-daclatasvir as internal standard (IS) had a LLOQ of 20 pg/mL. The accuracy and precision was sufficient to cover analysis up to 72 h (>5 half-lives). In this comprehensive study, the authors initially evaluated isotope contribution to SIL and the IS using theoretical isotope distribution pattern analysis followed by an in vivo study in the monkeys to assure complete lack of isotopic interference. The ABA of evacetrapib [306] and ibrutinib [307] was determined in healthy subjects by administration of 130 mg evacetrapib orally or 175 μg [$^{13}C_8$]-evacetrapib intravenously and 560 mg ibrutinib orally and 100 μg [$^{13}C_6$]-ibrutinib intravenously, respectively. In both cases, LC–MS/MS methods were developed and fully validated to quantify [$^{13}C_8$]-evacetrapib and [$^{13}C_6$]-ibrutinib with sufficiently LLOQ to cover up to at least 4× of $t_{1/2}$. More recently, the ABA of venetoclax was determined in female subjects receiving a single oral dose of 100 mg venetoclax followed by a 100-μg i.v. dose of $^{13}C_7$-venetoclax at the oral time of maximum concentration. The LLOQ for ^{13}C-venetoclax was 30 pg/mL. The [$^{13}C_7D_8$]-venetoclax internal standard did not affect the accuracy or precision of the assay. The absolute bioavailability of venetoclax was estimated at 5.4% and hepatic extraction ratio was estimated to be 0.06, suggesting that the fraction transferred from the enterocytes into the liver is limiting venetoclax bioavailability [308].

The microtracer approach has opened up and simplified the clinical study design to obtain absolute bioavailability data. Recently, LC–MS/MS assays are commonly approaching to the detection limit of low pg/mL, which makes it the preferred bioanalytical tool of choice for supporting SIL microtracer absolute BA studies due to its simplicity, robustness, high throughput analysis, time and cost effectiveness, and superior selectivity. The technology is now ripe to face the challenges of the increased regulatory requirements to provide ABA data for registration of pharmaceuticals [309].

Novel study design: duo-tracer for ABA and mass balance in a single-period study

For most drugs, ^{14}C-AME (mass balance) and ABA studies are performed separately using conventional trial designs, as described above. Using a novel duo-tracer approach, an oral dose of ^{14}C-radiolabeled drug mixed with unlabeled (^{12}C) drug and an intravenous microtracer of stable isotopically labeled drug are administered to a study subject to determine both mass balance and ABA during a single trial. For mass balance, the total amount of radioactivity in the circulation and excreta can be analyzed using LSC, in the same way as for a conventional ^{14}C-AME trial. For ABA, the intravenously administered stable isotopically labeled microtracer can be distinguished from orally administered $^{14}C/^{12}C$ drug by virtue of their different molecular masses, using simultaneous LC–MS/MS detection. The advantage of such a study design is that it requires less subjects and dose events, therefore, shortens the study duration [310]. Schwab et al. reported a combination of traditional mass balance study with absolute bioavailability of tofogliflozin [194]. In this study six healthy subjects received 20 mg [$^{12}C/^{14}C$]-tofogliflozin orally and a concomitant 100 μg [$^{13}C_6$]-tofogliflozin intravenously. The ^{13}C-drug was quantified by LC–MS/MS in the concentration range of 10 pg/mL to 100 ng/mL using a D_4-hydroxyl-metabolite as internal standard. This LC–MS/MS method was able to quantify plasma drug concentration up to 24 h post dose (~5 half-lives). The same approach was applied for basimglurant [36] and idasanutlin [102], whereby ^{14}C-radiolabeled drug was orally administered at the therapeutic dose while a microdose (~100 μg) of stable isotopically labeled drug was administered intravenously at the T_{max}. This study design represents a novel concept of obtaining total AME and ABA data in a single, one-period study.

Conclusions

The human mass balance study is a key study in the Clinical Pharmacology package of new drug applications. It ascertains a drug's elimination routes and extent, elucidates major metabolic pathways and clearance mechanisms, and identifies and quantifies metabolites in circulation and excreta. The results are critical to design further clinical studies, for example, subjects with organ impairment and/or any clinical drug–drug interaction (DDI) studies. Ultrasensitive detection methodology afforded by AMS has enabled much lower radioactive dose and exposure, which allows for longer excreta collection time and potentially improved total recovery. A high percentage of unchanged parent in feces complicates conclusions around a drug's absorption and clearance mechanism in the absence of bioavailability data, but biliary or duodenal sampling techniques, preclinical AME data, or ex vivo stability data in feces, can help interpret the fecal metabolic profile. Importantly, the utility of the double-tracer approach enables the flexibility to evaluate absolutely bioavailability simultaneously with excretion mass balance, and unambiguous interpretation of the drug's clearance mechanism. Mixed-matrix approach provides an elegant solution to comparing human and preclinical metabolite exposures at steady-state, in the absence of reference standards or radiolabeled material, to address MIST guidance.

References

[1] P. Coppola, A. Andersson, S. Cole, The importance of the human mass balance study in regulatory submissions, CPT Pharmacomet. Syst. Pharmacol. 8 (2019) 792−804.

[2] J.H. Beumer, J.H. Beijnen, J.H. Schellens, Mass balance studies, with a focus on anticancer drugs, Clin. Pharmacokinet. 45 (2006) 33−58.

[3] N. Penner, L.J. Klunk, C. Prakash, Human radiolabeled mass balance studies: objectives, utilities and limitations, Biopharm. Drug Dispos. 30 (2009) 185−203.

[4] D.K. Spracklin, D. Chen, A.J. Bergman, E. Callegari, R.S. Obach, Mini-review: comprehensive drug disposition knowledge generated in the modern human radiolabeled ADME study, CPT Pharmacomet. Syst. Pharmacol. 9 (2020) 428−434.

[5] S. Schadt, B. Bister, S.K. Chowdhury, C. Funk, C. Hop, W.G. Humphreys, F. Igarashi, A.D. James, M. Kagan, S.C. Khojasteh, A.N.R. Nedderman, C. Prakash, F. Runge, H. Scheible, D.K. Spracklin, P. Swart, S. Tse, J. Yuan, R.S. Obach, A decade in the MIST: learnings from investigations of drug metabolites in drug development under the "metabolites in safety testing" regulatory guidance, Drug Metab. Dispos. 46 (2018) 865−878.

[6] S. Ortiz, S. Flach, J. Ho, F. Li, C.F. Caracta, E.G. Gil, J.M. Jansat, Mass balance and metabolism of aclidinium bromide following intravenous administration of [^{14}C]-aclidinium bromide in healthy subjects, Biopharm. Drug Dispos. 33 (2012) 39−45.

[7] B. Remmerie, M. van den Boer, T. Van Looy, I. Wynant, S. Rusch, D. Huntjens, M. De Meulder, M. Stevens, Integrating duodenal sampling in a human mass balance study to quantify the elimination pathways of JNJ-53718678, a respiratory syncytial virus fusion protein inhibitor, Adv. Ther. 37 (2020) 578−591.

[8] H.P. Gschwind, U. Glaenzel, F. Waldmeier, B. Wirz, H.D. Sabia, F. Picard, H.M. Weiss, L. Choi, P.J. Swart, A. Vasudevan, M. Azria, Metabolism and disposition of the oral absorption enhancer 14C-radiolabeled 8-(N-2-hydroxy-5-chlorobenzoyl)-amino-caprylic acid (5-CNAC) in healthy postmenopausal women and supplementary investigations in vitro, Eur. J. Pharmaceut. Sci. 47 (2012) 44−55.

[9] M. Acharya, M. Gonzalez, G. Mannens, R. De Vries, C. Lopez, T. Griffin, N. Tran, A phase I, open-label, single-dose, mass balance study of ^{14}C-labeled abiraterone acetate in healthy male subjects, Xenobiotica 43 (2013) 379−389.

[10] T. Podoll, P.G. Pearson, J. Evarts, T. Ingallinera, E. Bibikova, H. Sun, M. Gohdes, K. Cardinal, M. Sanghvi, J.G. Slatter, Bioavailability, biotransformation, and excretion of the covalent bruton tyrosine kinase inhibitor acalabrutinib in rats, dogs, and humans, Drug Metabol. Dispos. 47 (2019) 145−154.

[11] C. Muehlan, J. Heuberger, P.E. Juif, M. Croft, J. van Gerven, J. Dingemanse, Accelerated development of the dual orexin receptor antagonist ACT-541468: integration of a microtracer in a first-in-human study, Clin. Pharmacol. Therapeut. 104 (2018) 1022−1029.

[12] P. Stopfer, K. Marzin, H. Narjes, D. Gansser, M. Shahidi, M. Uttereuther-Fischer, T. Ebner, Afatinib pharmacokinetics and metabolism after oral administration to healthy male volunteers, Cancer Chemother. Pharmacol. 69 (2012) 1051−1061.

[13] P.N. Morcos, L. Yu, K. Bogman, M. Sato, H. Katsuki, K. Kawashima, D.J. Moore, M. Whayman, K. Nieforth, K. Heinig, E. Guerini, D. Muri, M. Martin-Facklam, A. Phipps, Absorption, distribution, metabolism and excretion (ADME) of the ALK inhibitor alectinib: results from an absolute bioavailability and mass balance study in healthy subjects, Xenobiotica 47 (2017) 217−229.

[14] S. Sturm, M. Seiberling, I. Weick, A. Paehler, C. Funk, T. Ruf, Metabolism, excretion, and pharmacokinetics of [^{14}C]-radiolabeled aleglitazar: a phase I, nonrandomized, open-label, single-center, single-dose study in healthy male volunteers, Clin. Therapeut. 34 (2012) 420−429.

[15] X. Zhou, S. Pusalkar, S.K. Chowdhury, S. Searle, Y. Li, C.D. Ullmann, K. Venkatakrishnan, Mass balance, routes of excretion, and pharmacokinetics of investigational oral [^{14}C]-alisertib (MLN8237), an Aurora A kinase inhibitor in patients with advanced solid tumors, Invest. N. Drugs 37 (2019) 666−673.

[16] C. Zhou, L. Xie, W. Liu, L. Zhang, S. Zhou, L. Wang, J. Chen, H. Li, Y. Zhao, B. Zhu, S. Ding, C. Zhang, F. Shao, Absorption, metabolism, excretion, and safety of [^{14}C]almonertinib in healthy Chinese subjects, Ann. Transl. Med. 9 (2021a) 867.

[17] A. James, L. Blumenstein, U. Glaenzel, Y. Jin, A. Demailly, A. Jakab, R. Hansen, A. Hazell, A. Mehta, L. Trandafir, P. Swart, Absorption, distribution, metabolism, and excretion of [^{14}C]BYL719 (alpelisib) in healthy male volunteers, Cancer Chemother. Pharmacol. 76 (2015) 751−760.

[18] A.D. James, C. Marvalin, A. Luneau, A. Meissner, G. Camenisch, Comparison of ^{19}F NMR and ^{14}C measurements for the assessment of ADME of BYL719 (alpelisib) in humans, Drug Metab. Dispos. 45 (2017) 900−907.

[19] K. Kato, M. den Adel, D. Groenendaal-van de Meent, Y. Ohtsu, A. Takada, M. Katashima, An open-label, single-dose, human mass balance study of amenamevir in healthy male adults, Clin. Pharmacol. Drug. Dev. 8 (2019) 595−602.

[20] T. Kifuji, S. Inoue, M. Furukawa, B. Perez Madera, T. Goto, H. Kumagai, S.J. Mair, A. Kawaguchi, Absorption, disposition and metabolic pathway of amiselimod (MT-1303) in healthy volunteers in a mass balance study, Xenobiotica 49 (2019) 1033−1043.

[21] G.M. Fox, A.F. Roffel, J. Hartstra, L.A. Bussian, S.P. van Marle, Metabolism and excretion of intravenous, radio-labeled amisulpride in healthy, adult volunteers, J. Clin. Pharmacol. 11 (2019) 161−169.

[22] B.M. Sadler, G.E. Chittick, R.E. Polk, D. Slain, T.M. Kerkering, S.D. Studenberg, Y. Lou, K.H. Moore, J.L. Woolley, D.S. Stein, Metabolic disposition and pharmacokinetics of [^{14}C]-amprenavir, a human immunodeficiency virus type 1 (HIV-1) protease inhibitor, administered as a single oral dose to healthy male subjects, J. Clin. Pharmacol. 41 (2001) 386−396.

[23] Y. Liu, L. Liu, L. Liu, T. Wang, L. Guo, Y. Wang, Z. Gao, Y. Shu, A phase I study investigation of metabolism, and disposition of [^{14}C]-anlotinib after an oral administration in patients with advanced refractory solid tumors, Cancer Chemother. Pharmacol. 85 (2020) 907−915.

[24] R. de Vries, F. Jacobs, G. Mannens, J. Snoeys, F. Cuyckens, C. Chien, P. Ward, Apalutamide absorption, metabolism, and excretion in healthy men, and enzyme reaction in human hepatocytes, Drug Metabol. Dispos. 47 (2019) 453−464.

[25] N. Raghavan, C.E. Frost, Z. Yu, K. He, H. Zhang, W.G. Humphreys, D. Pinto, S. Chen, S. Bonacorsi, P.C. Wong, D. Zhang, Apixaban metabolism and pharmacokinetics after oral administration to humans, Drug Metabol. Dispos. 37 (2009) 74−81.

[26] M. Hoffmann, G. Kumar, P. Schafer, D. Cedzik, L. Capone, K.L. Fong, Z. Gu, D. Heller, H. Feng, S. Surapaneni, O. Laskin, A. Wu, Disposition, metabolism and mass balance of [^{14}C]apremilast following oral administration, Xenobiotica 41 (2011) 1063−1075.

[27] P.N. Sidharta, H. Fischer, J. Dingemanse, Absorption, distribution, metabolism, and excretion of aprocitentan, a dual endothelin receptor antagonist, in humans, Curr. Drug Metabol. 22 (2021) 399−410.

[28] M.J. McKeage, P.C. Fong, X. Hong, J. Flarakos, J. Mangold, Y. Du, C. Tanaka, H. Schran, Mass balance, excretion and metabolism of [^{14}C] ASA404 in cancer patients in a phase I trial, Cancer Chemother. Pharmacol. 69 (2012) 1145−1154.

[29] S.F. van de Wetering-Krebbers, P.L. Jacobs, G.J. Kemperman, E. Spaans, P.A. Peeters, L.P. Delbressine, M.L. van Iersel, Metabolism and excretion of asenapine in healthy male subjects, Drug Metabol. Dispos. 39 (2011) 580−590.

[30] K. Oda, Y.J. Cao, T. Sawamoto, N. Nakada, O. Fisniku, Y. Nagasaka, K.Y. Sohda, Human mass balance, metabolite profile and identification of metabolic enzymes of [^{14}C]ASP015K, a novel oral janus kinase inhibitor, Xenobiotica 45 (2015) 887−902.

[31] D. Miyatake, N. Nakada, A. Takada, K. Kato, Y. Taniuchi, M. Katashima, T. Sawamoto, A phase I, open-label, single-dose micro tracer mass balance study of ^{14}C-labeled ASP7991 in healthy Japanese male subjects using accelerator mass spectrometry, Drug Metabol. Pharmacokinet. 33 (2018) 118−124.

[32] K. Vishwanathan, S. Mair, A. Gupta, J. Atherton, J. Clarkson-Jones, T. Edeki, S. Das, Assessment of the mass balance recovery and metabolite profile of avibactam in humans and in vitro drug-drug interaction potential, Drug Metabol. Dispos. 42 (2014) 932−942.

[33] B.J. Smith, Y. Pithavala, H.Z. Bu, P. Kang, B. Hee, A.J. Deese, W.F. Pool, K.J. Klamerus, E.Y. Wu, D.K. Dalvie, Pharmacokinetics, metabolism, and excretion of [^{14}C]axitinib, a vascular endothelial growth factor receptor tyrosine kinase inhibitor, in humans, Drug Metabol. Dispos. 42 (2014) 918−931.

[34] P. Ballard, H.C. Swaisland, M.D. Malone, S. Sarda, S. Ghiorghiu, D. Wilbraham, Metabolic disposition of AZD8931, an oral equipotent inhibitor of EGFR, HER2 and HER3 signalling, in rat, dog and man, Xenobiotica 44 (2014) 1083−1098.

[35] M. Dennis, M. Davies, S. Oliver, R. D'Souza, L. Pike, P. Stockman, Phase I study of the Aurora B kinase inhibitor barasertib (AZD1152) to assess the pharmacokinetics, metabolism and excretion in patients with acute myeloid leukemia, Cancer Chemother. Pharmacol. 70 (2012) 461−469.

[36] E. Guerini, S. Schadt, G. Greig, R. Haas, C. Husser, M. Zell, C. Funk, T. Hartung, A. Gloge, N.L. Mallalieu, A double-tracer technique to characterize absorption, distribution, metabolism and excretion (ADME) of [^{14}C]-basimglurant and absolute bioavailability after oral administration and concomitant intravenous microdose administration of [(13)C6]-labeled basimglurant in humans, Xenobiotica 47 (2017) 144−153.

[37] C. Ambery, G. Young, T. Fuller, A.L. Lazaar, A. Pereira, A. Hughes, D. Ramsay, F. van den Berg, P. Daley-Yates, Pharmacokinetics, excretion, and mass balance of [^{14}C]-batefenterol following a single microtracer intravenous dose (concomitant to an inhaled dose) or oral dose of batefenterol in healthy men, Clin. Pharmacol. Drug. Dev. 7 (2018) 901−910.

[38] A. Chandrasekaran, W.E. McKeand, P. Sullivan, W. DeMaio, R. Stoltz, J. Scatina, Metabolic disposition of [^{14}C]bazedoxifene in healthy post-menopausal women, Drug Metabol. Dispos. 37 (2009) 1219−1225.

[39] E. Calvo, G. Reddy, V. Boni, L. Garcia-Canamaque, T. Song, J. Tjornelund, M.R. Choi, L.F. Allen, Pharmacokinetics, metabolism, and excretion of ^{14}C-labeled belinostat in patients with recurrent or progressive malignancies, Invest. N. Drugs 34 (2016) 193−201.

[40] A.C. Dubbelman, H. Rosing, M. Darwish, D. D'Andrea, M. Bond, E. Hellriegel, P. Robertson Jr., J.H. Beijnen, J.H. Schellens, Pharmacokinetics and excretion of ^{14}C-bendamustine in patients with relapsed or refractory malignancy, Drugs R 13 (2013) 17−28.

[41] U. Burkard, M. Desch, Y. Shatillo, G. Wunderlich, S.R. Mack, C. Schlecker, A.M. Teitelbaum, P. Liu, T.S. Chan, The absolute bioavailability, absorption, distribution, metabolism, and excretion of BI 425809 administered as an oral dose or an oral dose with an intravenous microtracer dose of [^{14}C]-BI 425809 in healthy males, Clin. Drug Invest. 42 (2022) 87−99.

[42] L.J. Christopher, H. Hong, B.J. Vakkalagadda, P.L. Clemens, H. Su, V. Roongta, A. Allentoff, H. Sun, K. Heller, C.T. Harbison, R.A. Iyer, W.G. Humphreys, T. Wong, S. Zhang, Metabolism and disposition of [^{14}C]BMS-690514, an ErbB/vascular endothelial growth factor receptor inhibitor, after oral administration to humans, Drug Metabol. Dispos. 38 (2010) 2049−2059.

[43] T. Mekhail, E. Masson, B.S. Fischer, J. Gong, R. Iyer, J. Gan, J. Pursley, D. Patricia, D. Williams, R. Ganapathi, Metabolism, excretion, and pharmacokinetics of oral brivanib in patients with advanced or metastatic solid tumors, Drug Metabol. Dispos. 38 (2010) 1962−1966.

[44] L. Ridoux, D.R. Semiond, C. Vincent, H. Fontaine, C. Mauriac, G.J. Sanderink, C. Oprea, L. Kelly, S. Clive, A phase I open-label study investigating the disposition of [^{14}C]-cabazitaxel in patients with advanced solid tumors, Anti Cancer Drugs 26 (2015) 350−358.

[45] S. Lacy, B. Hsu, D. Miles, D. Aftab, R. Wang, L. Nguyen, Metabolism and disposition of cabozantinib in healthy male volunteers and pharmacologic characterization of its major metabolites, Drug Metabol. Dispos. 43 (2015) 1190−1207.

[46] D. Devineni, J. Murphy, S.S. Wang, H. Stieltjes, P. Rothenberg, E. Scheers, R.N. Mamidi, Absolute oral bioavailability and pharmacokinetics of canagliflozin: a microdose study in healthy participants, Clin. Pharmacol. Drug. Dev. 4 (2015) 295−304.

[47] U. Glaenzel, Y. Jin, R. Hansen, K. Schroer, G. Rahmanzadeh, U. Pfaar, J. Jaap van Lier, H. Borell, A. Meissner, G. Camenisch, S. Zhao, Absorption, distribution, metabolism, and excretion of capmatinib (INC280) in healthy male volunteers and in vitro aldehyde oxidase phenotyping of the major metabolite, Drug Metabol. Dispos. 48 (2020) 873−885.

[48] M. Pellegatti, E. Bordini, P. Fizzotti, A. Roberts, B.M. Johnson, Disposition and metabolism of radiolabeled casopitant in humans, Drug Metabol. Dispos. 37 (2009) 1635−1645.

[49] Z. Tong, C. Atsriku, U. Yerramilli, X. Wang, J. Nissel, Y. Li, S. Surapaneni, Absorption, distribution, metabolism, and excretion of mTOR kinase inhibitor CC-223 in rats, dogs, and humans, Xenobiotica 49 (2019) 43−53.

[50] S. Miyazaki, T. Katsube, H. Shen, C. Tomek, Y. Narukawa, Metabolism, excretion, and pharmacokinetics of [^{14}C]-Cefiderocol (S-649266), a siderophore cephalosporin, in healthy subjects following intravenous administration, J. Clin. Pharmacol. 59 (2019) 958−967.

[51] M.L. Boof, J.J. van Lier, S. English, H. Fischer, M. Ufer, J. Dingemanse, Absorption, distribution, metabolism, and excretion of cenerimod, a selective S1P1 receptor modulator in healthy subjects, Xenobiotica 50 (2020) 947−956.

[52] L. Vernillet, S.A. Greene, H.W. Kim, S.M. Melnick, K. Glenn, Mass balance, metabolism, and excretion of cenobamate, a new antiepileptic drug, after a single oral administration in healthy male subjects, Eur. J. Drug Metab. Pharmacokinet. 45 (2020) 513−522.

[53] S. Tse, L. Leung, S. Raje, M. Seymour, Y. Shishikura, R.S. Obach, Disposition and metabolic profiling of [^{14}C]cerlapirdine using accelerator mass spectrometry, Drug Metabol. Dispos. 42 (2014) 2023−2032.

[54] J. Lu, Y. Bian, H. Zhang, D. Tang, X. Tian, X. Zhou, Z. Xu, Y. Xiong, Z. Gu, Z. Yu, T. Wang, J. Ding, Q. Yu, J. Ding, The metabolism and excretion of the dipeptidyl peptidase 4 inhibitor [^{14}C] cetagliptin in healthy volunteers, Xenobiotica (2021) 1−12.

[55] S.E. Huskey, C.Q. Zhu, A. Fredenhagen, J. Kuhnol, A. Luneau, Z. Jian, Z. Yang, Z. Miao, F. Yang, J.P. Jain, G. Sunkara, J.B. Mangold, D.S. Stein, KAE609 (cipargamin), a new spiroindolone agent for the treatment of malaria: evaluation of the absorption, distribution, metabolism, and excretion of a single oral 300-mg dose of [^{14}C]KAE609 in healthy male subjects, Drug Metabol. Dispos. 44 (2016) 672−682.

[56] R.H. Takahashi, E.F. Choo, S. Ma, S. Wong, J. Halladay, Y. Deng, I. Rooney, M. Gates, C.E. Hop, S.C. Khojasteh, M.J. Dresser, L. Musib, Absorption, metabolism, excretion, and the contribution of intestinal metabolism to the oral disposition of [^{14}C]cobimetinib, a MEK inhibitor, in humans, Drug Metabol. Dispos. 44 (2016) 28−39.

[57] M. Gerisch, T. Schwarz, D. Lang, G. Rohde, S. Reif, I. Genvresse, S. Reschke, D. van der Mey, C. Granvil, Pharmacokinetics of intravenous pan-class I phosphatidylinositol 3-kinase (PI3K) inhibitor [^{14}C]copanlisib (BAY 80-6946) in a mass balance study in healthy male volunteers, Cancer Chemother. Pharmacol. 80 (2017) 535−544.

[58] T.R. Johnson, W. Tan, L. Goulet, E.B. Smith, S. Yamazaki, G.S. Walker, M.T. O'Gorman, G. Bedarida, H.Y. Zou, J.G. Christensen, L.N. Nguyen, Z. Shen, D. Dalvie, A. Bello, B.J. Smith, Metabolism, excretion and pharmacokinetics of [^{14}C]crizotinib following oral administration to healthy subjects, Xenobiotica 45 (2015) 45−59.

[59] D.A. Bershas, D. Ouellet, D.B. Mamaril-Fishman, N. Nebot, S.W. Carson, S.C. Blackman, R.A. Morrison, J.L. Adams, K.E. Jurusik, D.M. Knecht, P.D. Gorycki, L.E. Richards-Peterson, Metabolism and disposition of oral dabrafenib in cancer patients: proposed participation of aryl nitrogen in carbon-carbon bond cleavage via decarboxylation following enzymatic oxidation, Drug Metabol. Dispos. 41 (2013) 2215−2224.

[60] C.L. Bello, E. Smith, A. Ruiz-Garcia, G. Ni, C. Alvey, C.M. Loi, A phase I, open-label, mass balance study of [^{14}C] dacomitinib (PF-00299804) in healthy male volunteers, Cancer Chemother. Pharmacol. 72 (2013) 379−385.

[61] P. Taavitsainen, O. Prien, M. Kahkonen, M. Niehues, T. Korjamo, K. Denner, P. Nykanen, A. Vuorela, N.A. Jungmann, C.J. von Buhler, M. Koskinen, C. Zurth, H. Gieschen, Metabolism and mass balance of the novel nonsteroidal androgen receptor inhibitor darolutamide in humans, Drug Metabol. Dispos. 49 (2021) 420−433.

[62] M. Vermeir, S. Lachau-Durand, G. Mannens, F. Cuyckens, B. van Hoof, A. Raoof, Absorption, metabolism, and excretion of darunavir, a new protease inhibitor, administered alone and with low-dose ritonavir in healthy subjects, Drug Metabol. Dispos. 37 (2009) 809−820.

[63] Y.L. Chen, E. Skende, J. Lin, Y. Yi, P.L. Wang, S. Wills, H.S. Wilkinson, K.S. Koblan, S.C. Hopkins, Absorption, distribution, metabolism, and excretion of [^{14}C]-dasotraline in humans, Pharmacol. Res. Perspect. 5 (2017) e00281.

[64] F. Waldmeier, G.J. Bruin, U. Glaenzel, K. Hazell, R. Sechaud, S. Warrington, J.B. Porter, Pharmacokinetics, metabolism, and disposition of deferasirox in beta-thalassemic patients with transfusion-dependent iron overload who are at pharmacokinetic steady state, Drug Metabol. Dispos. 38 (2010) 808−816.

[65] A. McEwen, L. Lawrence, R. Hoover, L. Stevens, S. Mair, G. Ford, D. Williams, S. Wood, Disposition, metabolism and mass balance of delafloxacin in healthy human volunteers following intravenous administration, Xenobiotica 45 (2015) 1054−1062.

[66] L.Z. Chen, J.P. Sabo, E. Philip, L. Rowland, Y. Mao, B. Latli, D. Ramsden, D.A. Mandarino, R.S. Sane, Mass balance, metabolite profile, and in vitro-in vivo comparison of clearance pathways of deleobuvir, a hepatitis C virus polymerase inhibitor, Antimicrob. Agents Chemother. 59 (2015b) 25−37.

[67] B. Grabowski, R.D. Lee, Absorption, distribution, metabolism and excretion of [^{14}C]dexlansoprazole in healthy male subjects, Clin. Drug Invest. 32 (2012) 319−332.

[68] S. Castellino, L. Moss, D. Wagner, J. Borland, I. Song, S. Chen, Y. Lou, S.S. Min, I. Goljer, A. Culp, S.C. Piscitelli, P.M. Savina, Metabolism, excretion, and mass balance of the HIV-1 integrase inhibitor dolutegravir in humans, Antimicrob. Agents Chemother. 57 (2013) 3536−3546.

[69] R.I. Sanchez, K.L. Fillgrove, K.L. Yee, Y. Liang, B. Lu, A. Tatavarti, R. Liu, M.S. Anderson, M.O. Behm, L. Fan, Y. Li, J.R. Butterton, M. Iwamoto, S.G. Khalilieh, Characterisation of the absorption, distribution, metabolism, excretion and mass balance of doravirine, a non-nucleoside reverse transcriptase inhibitor in humans, Xenobiotica 49 (2019) 422−432.

[70] A.C. Dubbelman, A. Upthagrove, J.H. Beijnen, S. Marchetti, E. Tan, K. Krone, S. Anand, J.H. Schellens, Disposition and metabolism of ^{14}C-dovitinib (TKI258), an inhibitor of FGFR and VEGFR, after oral administration in patients with advanced solid tumors, Cancer Chemother. Pharmacol. 70 (2012b) 653−663.

[71] M.S. Bathala, H. Masumoto, T. Oguma, L. He, C. Lowrie, J. Mendell, Pharmacokinetics, biotransformation, and mass balance of edoxaban, a selective, direct factor Xa inhibitor, in humans, Drug Metabol. Dispos. 40 (2012) 2250−2255.

[72] Y. Deng, A. Madatian, M.B. Wire, C. Bowen, J.W. Park, D. Williams, B. Peng, E. Schubert, F. Gorycki, M. Levy, P.D. Gorycki, Metabolism and disposition of eltrombopag, an oral, nonpeptide thrombopoietin receptor agonist, in healthy human subjects, Drug Metabol. Dispos. 39 (2011) 1734−1746.

[73] L.Z. Chen, A. Jungnik, Y. Mao, E. Philip, D. Sharp, A. Unseld, L. Seman, H.J. Woerle, S. Macha, Biotransformation and mass balance of the SGLT2 inhibitor empagliflozin in healthy volunteers, Xenobiotica 45 (2015a) 520−529.

[74] S.M. Pai, J. Connaire, H. Yamada, S. Enya, B. Gerhardt, M. Maekawa, H. Tanaka, R. Koretomo, T. Ishikawa, A mass balance study of ^{14}C-labeled JTZ-951 (enarodustat), a novel orally available erythropoiesis-stimulating agent, in patients with end-stage renal disease on hemodialysis, Clin. Pharmacol. Drug. Dev. 9 (2020) 728−741.

[75] S. Zhou, W. Liu, C. Zhou, L. Zhang, L. Xie, Z. Xu, L. Wang, Y. Zhao, L. Guo, J. Chen, L. Ding, L. Mao, Y. Tao, C. Zhang, S. Ding, F. Shao, Mass balance, metabolic disposition, and pharmacokinetics of [^{14}C]ensartinib, a novel potent anaplastic lymphoma kinase (ALK) inhibitor, in healthy subjects following oral administration, Cancer Chemother. Pharmacol. 86 (2020) 719−730.

[76] J.V. Newman, J. Zhou, S. Izmailyan, L. Tsai, Mass balance and drug interaction potential of intravenous eravacycline administered to healthy subjects, Antimicrob. Agents Chemother. 63 (2019).

[77] A.C. Dubbelman, H. Rosing, R.S. Jansen, M. Mergui-Roelvink, A.D. Huitema, B. Koetz, M. Lymboura, L. Reyderman, A. Lopez-Anaya, J.H. Schellens, J.H. Beijnen, Mass balance study of [^{14}C]eribulin in patients with advanced solid tumors, Drug Metabol. Dispos. 40 (2012a) 313−321.

[78] J. Ling, K.A. Johnson, Z. Miao, A. Rakhit, M.P. Pantze, M. Hamilton, B.L. Lum, C. Prakash, Metabolism and excretion of erlotinib, a small molecule inhibitor of epidermal growth factor receptor tyrosine kinase, in healthy male volunteers, Drug Metabol. Dispos. 34 (2006) 420−426.

[79] Z. Miao, G. Nucci, N. Amin, R. Sharma, V. Mascitti, M. Tugnait, A.D. Vaz, E. Callegari, A.S. Kalgutkar, Pharmacokinetics, metabolism, and excretion of the antidiabetic agent ertugliflozin (PF-04971729) in healthy male subjects, Drug Metabol. Dispos. 41 (2013) 445−456.

[80] A.I. Loureiro, J.F. Rocha, C. Fernandes-Lopes, T. Nunes, L.C. Wright, L. Almeida, P. Soares-da-Silva, Human disposition, metabolism and excretion of etamicastat, a reversible, peripherally selective dopamine beta-hydroxylase inhibitor, Br. J. Clin. Pharmacol. 77 (2014) 1017−1026.

[81] R. Subramanian, X. Zhu, M.B. Hock, B.J. Sloey, B. Wu, S.F. Wilson, O. Egbuna, J.G. Slatter, J. Xiao, G.L. Skiles, Pharmacokinetics, biotransformation, and excretion of [^{14}C]etelcalcetide (AMG 416) following a single microtracer intravenous dose in patients with chronic kidney disease on hemodialysis, Clin. Pharmacokinet. 56 (2017) 179−192.

[82] G.W. Caldwell, W.N. Wu, J.A. Masucci, Evaluation of the absorption, excretion and metabolism of [^{14}C] etoperidone in man, Xenobiotica 31 (2001) 823−839.

[83] H. Scheible, M. Dyroff, A. Seithel-Keuth, E. Harrison-Moench, N. Mammasse, A. Port, A. Bachmann, J. Dong, J.J. van Lier, W. Tracewell, D. Mitchell, Evobrutinib, a covalent Bruton's tyrosine kinase inhibitor: mass balance, elimination route, and metabolism in healthy participants, Clin. Transl. Sci. 14 (2021) 2420−2430.

[84] L.Z. Chen, P. Rose, Y. Mao, C.L. Yong, R. St George, F. Huang, B. Latli, D. Mandarino, Y. Li, Mass balance and metabolite profiling of steady-state faldaprevir, a hepatitis C virus NS3/4 protease inhibitor, in healthy male subjects, Antimicrob. Agents Chemother. 58 (2014) 2369−2376.

[85] B.A. Grabowski, R. Khosravan, L. Vernillet, D.J. Mulford, Metabolism and excretion of [^{14}C] febuxostat, a novel nonpurine selective inhibitor of xanthine oxidase, in healthy male subjects, J. Clin. Pharmacol. 51 (2011) 189−201.

[86] D. Pearson, H.M. Weiss, Y. Jin, J. Jaap van Lier, V.J. Erpenbeck, U. Glaenzel, P. End, R. Woessner, F. Eggimann, G. Camenisch, Absorption, distribution, metabolism, and excretion of the oral prostaglandin D2 receptor 2 antagonist fevipiprant (QAW039) in healthy volunteers and in vitro, Drug Metabol. Dispos. 45 (2017) 817−825.

[87] M. Zollinger, H.P. Gschwind, Y. Jin, C. Sayer, F. Zecri, S. Hartmann, Absorption and disposition of the sphingosine 1-phosphate receptor modulator fingolimod (FTY720) in healthy volunteers: a case of xenobiotic biotransformation following endogenous metabolic pathways, Drug Metabol. Dispos. 39 (2011) 199−207.

[88] P.E. Lonning, J. Geisler, D.C. Johannessen, H.P. Gschwind, F. Waldmeier, W. Schneider, B. Galli, T. Winkler, W. Blum, H.P. Kriemler, W.R. Miller, J.W. Faigle, Pharmacokinetics and metabolism of formestane in breast cancer patients, J. Steroid Biochem. Mol. Biol. 77 (2001) 39−47.

[89] R.M. Ings, A.J. Gray, A.R. Taylor, B.H. Gordon, M. Breen, M. Hiley, R. Brownsill, N. Marchant, R. Richards, D. Wallace, et al., Disposition, pharmacokinetics, and metabolism of ^{14}C-fotemustine in cancer patients, Eur. J. Cancer 26 (1990) 838−842.

[90] S. Zhou, F. Shao, Z. Xu, L. Wang, K. Jin, L. Xie, J. Chen, Y. Liu, H. Zhang, N. Ou, A phase I study to investigate the metabolism, excretion, and pharmacokinetics of [^{14}C]fruquintinib, a novel oral selective VEGFR inhibitor, in healthy Chinese male volunteers, Cancer Chemother. Pharmacol. 80 (2017) 563−573.

[91] J. Meng, H. Zhang, J.J. Bao, Z.D. Chen, X.Y. Liu, Y.F. Zhang, Y. Jiang, L.Y. Miao, D.F. Zhong, Metabolic disposition of the EGFR covalent inhibitor furmonertinib in humans, Acta Pharmacol. Sin. 43 (2022) 494−503.

[92] K.C. Cassidy, I. Gueorguieva, C. Miles, J. Rehmel, P. Yi, W.J. Ehlhardt, Disposition and metabolism of [^{14}C]-galunisertib, a TGF-betaRI kinase/ALK5 inhibitor, following oral administration in healthy subjects and mechanistic prediction of the effect of itraconazole on galunisertib pharmacokinetics, Xenobiotica 48 (2018) 382−399.

[93] B.E. Houk, C.W. Alvey, R. Visswanathan, L. Kirkovsky, K.T. Matschke, E. Kimoto, T. Ryder, R.S. Obach, C. Durairaj, Distribution, metabolism, and excretion of gedatolisib in healthy male volunteers after a single intravenous infusion, Clin. Pharmacol. Drug. Dev. 8 (2019) 22−31.

[94] D. McKillop, M. Hutchison, E.A. Partridge, N. Bushby, C.M. Cooper, J.A. Clarkson-Jones, W. Herron, H.C. Swaisland, Metabolic disposition of gefitinib, an epidermal growth factor receptor tyrosine kinase inhibitor, in rat, dog and man, Xenobiotica 34 (2004) 917−934.

[95] N. Kim, L. Patrick, S. Mair, L. Stevens, G. Ford, V. Birks, S.H. Lee, Absorption, metabolism and excretion of [^{14}C]gemigliptin, a novel dipeptidyl peptidase 4 inhibitor, in humans, Xenobiotica 44 (2014) 522−530.

[96] J.L. Lam, A. Vaz, B. Hee, Y. Liang, X. Yang, M.N. Shaik, Metabolism, excretion and pharmacokinetics of [^{14}C]glasdegib (PF-04449913) in healthy volunteers following oral administration, Xenobiotica 47 (2017) 1064−1076.

[97] K. Negash, C. Andonian, C. Felgate, C. Chen, I. Goljer, B. Squillaci, D. Nguyen, J. Pirhalla, M. Lev, E. Schubert, C. Tiffany, M. Hossain, M. Ho, The metabolism and disposition of GSK2140944 in healthy human subjects, Xenobiotica 46 (2016) 683−702.

[98] J. Roosendaal, H. Rosing, L. Lucas, A. Gebretensae, A.D.R. Huitema, M.G. van Dongen, J.H. Beijnen, A. Oganesian, Mass balance and metabolite profiling of ^{14}C-guadecitabine in patients with advanced cancer, Invest. N. Drugs 38 (2020b) 1085−1095.

[99] Z.D. Chen, Q. Chen, Y.T. Zhu, Y.F. Zhang, Y. Zhan, X.F. Chen, X. Liang, J.Y. Jia, C. Yu, H.Y. Liu, J.J. Zou, Y.M. Liu, D.F. Zhong, Effects of food on the pharmacokinetic properties and mass balance of henagliflozin in healthy male volunteers, Clin. Therapeut. 43 (2021) e264−e273.

[100] Y. Zheng, H. Zhang, M. Liu, G. Li, S. Ma, Z. Zhang, H. Lin, Y. Zhan, Z. Chen, D. Zhong, L. Miao, X. Diao, Pharmacokinetics, mass balance, and metabolism of the novel URAT1 inhibitor [^{14}C]HR011303 in humans: metabolism is mediated predominantly by UDP-glucuronosyltransferase, Drug Metabol. Dispos. 50 (6) (2022) 798−808.

[101] Y. Bian, H. Zhang, S. Ma, Y. Jiao, P. Yan, X. Liu, S. Ma, Y. Xiong, Z. Gu, Z. Yu, C. Huang, L. Miao, Mass balance, pharmacokinetics and pharmacodynamics of intravenous HSK3486, a novel anaesthetic, administered to healthy subjects, Br. J. Clin. Pharmacol. 87 (2021) 93−105.

[102] Z. Papai, L.C. Chen, D. Da Costa, S. Blotner, F. Vazvaei, M. Gleave, R. Jones, J. Zhi, A single-center, open-label study investigating the excretion balance, pharmacokinetics, metabolism, and absolute bioavailability of a single oral dose of [^{14}C]-labeled idasanutlin and an intravenous tracer dose of [^{13}C]-labeled idasanutlin in a single cohort of patients with solid tumors, Cancer Chemother. Pharmacol. 84 (2019) 93−103.

[103] A.V. Boddy, J. Sludden, M.J. Griffin, C. Garner, J. Kendrick, P. Mistry, C. Dutreix, D.R. Newell, S.G. O'Brien, Pharmacokinetic investigation of imatinib using accelerator mass spectrometry in patients with chronic myeloid leukemia, Clin. Cancer Res. 13 (2007) 4164−4169.

[104] S. Ohmori, M. Miura, C. Toriumi, Y. Satoh, T. Ooie, Absorption, metabolism, and excretion of [^{14}C]imidafenacin, a new compound for treatment of overactive bladder, after oral administration to healthy male subjects, Drug Metabol. Dispos. 35 (2007) 1624−1633.

[105] A.D. Shilling, F.M. Nedza, T. Emm, S. Diamond, E. McKeever, N. Punwani, W. Williams, A. Arvanitis, L.G. Galya, M. Li, S. Shepard, J. Rodgers, T.Y. Yue, S. Yeleswaram, Metabolism, excretion, and pharmacokinetics of [^{14}C]INCB018424, a selective Janus tyrosine kinase 1/2 inhibitor, in humans, Drug Metabol. Dispos. 38 (2010) 2023−2031.

[106] J.G. Slatter, L.J. Schaaf, J.P. Sams, K.L. Feenstra, M.G. Johnson, P.A. Bombardt, K.S. Cathcart, M.T. Verburg, L.K. Pearson, L.D. Compton, L.L. Miller, D.S. Baker, C.V. Pesheck, R.S. Lord 3rd, Pharmacokinetics, metabolism, and excretion of irinotecan (CPT-11) following I.V. infusion of [^{14}C]CPT-11 in cancer patients, Drug Metabol. Dispos. 28 (2000) 423−433.

[107] A. Paci, K. Rezai, A. Deroussent, D. De Valeriola, M. Re, S. Weill, E. Cvitkovic, C. Kahatt, A. Shah, S. Waters, G. Weems, G. Vassal, F. Lokiec, Pharmacokinetics, metabolism, and routes of excretion of intravenous irofulven in patients with advanced solid tumors, Drug Metabol. Dispos. 34 (2006) 1918−1926.

[108] R. Townsend, K. Kato, C. Hale, D. Kowalski, C. Lademacher, T. Yamazaki, S. Akhtar, A. Desai, Two phase 1, open-label, mass balance studies to determine the pharmacokinetics of ^{14}C-labeled isavuconazonium sulfate in healthy male volunteers, Clin. Pharmacol. Drug. Dev. 7 (2018) 207−216.

[109] C. Prakash, B. Fan, S. Altaf, S. Agresta, H. Liu, H. Yang, Pharmacokinetics, absorption, metabolism, and excretion of [^{14}C]ivosidenib (AG-120) in healthy male subjects, Cancer Chemother. Pharmacol. 83 (2019) 837−848.

[110] J.H. Beumer, R.C. Garner, M.B. Cohen, S. Galbraith, G.F. Duncan, T. Griffin, J.H. Beijnen, J.H. Schellens, Human mass balance study of the novel anticancer agent ixabepilone using accelerator mass spectrometry, Invest. N. Drugs 25 (2007) 327−334.

[111] S.N. Comezoglu, V.T. Ly, D. Zhang, W.G. Humphreys, S.J. Bonacorsi, D.W. Everett, M.B. Cohen, J. Gan, J.H. Beumer, J.H. Beijnen, H.M. Schellens, G. Lappin, Biotransformation profiling of [^{14}C]ixabepilone in human plasma, urine and feces samples using accelerator mass spectrometry (AMS), Drug Metabol. Pharmacokinet. 24 (2009) 511−522.

[112] N. Gupta, S. Zhang, S. Pusalkar, M. Plesescu, S. Chowdhury, M.J. Hanley, B. Wang, C. Xia, X. Zhang, K. Venkatakrishnan, D.R. Shepard, A phase I study to assess the mass balance, excretion, and pharmacokinetics of [^{14}C]-ixazomib, an oral proteasome inhibitor, in patients with advanced solid tumors, Invest. N. Drugs 36 (2018) 407−415.

[113] A. Kim, S.R. Dueker, J.G. Hwang, J. Yoon, S.W. Lee, H.S. Lee, B.Y. Yu, K.S. Yu, H. Lee, An investigation of the metabolism and excretion of KD101 and its interindividual differences: a microtracing mass balance study in humans, Clin. Transl. Sci. 14 (2021) 231−238.

[114] W. Cawello, H. Boekens, R. Bonn, Absorption, disposition, metabolic fate and elimination of the anti-epileptic drug lacosamide in humans: mass balance following intravenous and oral administration, Eur. J. Drug Metab. Pharmacokinet. 37 (2012) 241−248.

[115] J. Guo, D. Zhou, S.W. Grimm, K.H. Bui, Pharmacokinetics, metabolism and excretion of [^{14}C]-lanicemine (AZD6765), a novel low-trapping N-methyl-d-aspartic acid receptor channel blocker, in healthy subjects, Xenobiotica 45 (2015) 244−255.

[116] S. Castellino, M. O'Mara, K. Koch, D.J. Borts, G.D. Bowers, C. MacLauchlin, Human metabolism of lapatinib, a dual kinase inhibitor: implications for hepatotoxicity, Drug Metabol. Dispos. 40 (2012) 139−150.

[117] N. Chen, L. Wen, H. Lau, S. Surapaneni, G. Kumar, Pharmacokinetics, metabolism and excretion of [^{14}C]-lenalidomide following oral administration in healthy male subjects, Cancer Chemother. Pharmacol. 69 (2012) 789−797.

[118] D. Pearson, M. Garnier, A. Luneau, A.D. James, M. Walles, ^{19}F-NMR-based determination of the absorption, metabolism and excretion of the oral phosphatidylinositol-3-kinase (PI3K) delta inhibitor leniolisib (CDZ173) in healthy volunteers, Xenobiotica 49 (2019) 953−960.

[119] A.C. Dubbelman, H. Rosing, C. Nijenhuis, A.D. Huitema, A. Mergui-Roelvink, A. Gupta, D. Verbel, G. Thompson, R. Shumaker, J.H. Schellens, J.H. Beijnen, Pharmacokinetics and excretion of ^{14}C-lenvatinib in patients with advanced solid tumors or lymphomas, Invest. N. Drugs 33 (2015) 233−240.

[120] M. Vourvahis, M. Gleave, A.N. Nedderman, R. Hyland, I. Gardner, M. Howard, S. Kempshall, C. Collins, R. LaBadie, Excretion and metabolism of lersivirine (5-{[3,5-diethyl-1-(2-hydroxyethyl)(3,5-14C2)-1H-pyrazol-4-yl]oxy}benzene-1,3-dic arbonitrile), a next-generation non-nucleoside reverse transcriptase inhibitor, after administration of [^{14}C]Lersivirine to healthy volunteers, Drug Metabol. Dispos. 38 (2010) 789−800.

[121] M.J. Zamek-Gliszczynski, D. Kenworthy, D.A. Bershas, M. Sanghvi, A.I. Pereira, J. Mudunuru, L. Crossman, J.L. Pirhalla, K.M. Thorpe, J. Dennison, M.M. McLaughlin, M. Allinder, B. Swift, R.L. O'Connor-Semmes, G.C. Young, Pharmacokinetics and ADME characterization of intravenous and oral [^{14}C]-Linerixibat in healthy male volunteers, Drug Metabol. Dispos. 49 (2021) 1109–1117.

[122] S. Poondru, J. Chaves, G. Yuen, B. Parker, E. Conklin, M. Singh, M. Nagata, S. Gill, Mass balance, pharmacokinetics, and metabolism of linsitinib in cancer patients, Cancer Chemother. Pharmacol. 77 (2016) 829–837.

[123] M. Malm-Erjefalt, I. Bjornsdottir, J. Vanggaard, H. Helleberg, U. Larsen, B. Oosterhuis, J.J. van Lier, M. Zdravkovic, A.K. Olsen, Metabolism and excretion of the once-daily human glucagon-like peptide-1 analog liraglutide in healthy male subjects and its in vitro degradation by dipeptidyl peptidase IV and neutral endopeptidase, Drug Metabol. Dispos. 38 (2010) 1944–1953.

[124] C. Prakash, Z. Li, C. Orlandi, L. Klunk, Assessment of exposure of metabolites in preclinical species and humans at steady state from the single-dose radiolabeled absorption, distribution, metabolism, and excretion studies: a case study, Drug Metabol. Dispos. 40 (2012) 1308–1320.

[125] P. Aviles, R. Altares, L. van Andel, R. Lubomirov, S. Fudio, H. Rosing, F.M. Marquez Del Pino, M.M. Tibben, G. Benedit, L. Nan-Offeringa, X.E. Luepke Estefan, A. Francesch, A. Zeaiter, C. Cuevas, J.H.M. Schellens, J.H. Beijnen, Metabolic disposition of lurbinectedin, a potent selective inhibitor of active transcription of protein-coding genes, in nonclinical species and patients, Drug Metabol. Dispos. 50 (4) (2022) 327–340.

[126] T. Kawachi, M. Ninomiya, T. Katsube, T. Wajima, T. Kanazu, Human mass balance, metabolism, and cytochrome P450 phenotyping of lusutrombopag, Xenobiotica 51 (2021) 287–296.

[127] K. Katyayan, P. Yi, S. Monk, K. Cassidy, Excretion, mass balance, and metabolism of [^{14}C]LY3202626 in humans: an interplay of microbial reduction, reabsorption, and aldehyde oxidase oxidation that leads to an extended excretion profile, Drug Metabol. Dispos. 48 (2020) 698–707.

[128] S. Bruderer, G. Hopfgartner, M. Seiberling, J. Wank, P.N. Sidharta, A. Treiber, J. Dingemanse, Absorption, distribution, metabolism, and excretion of macitentan, a dual endothelin receptor antagonist, in humans, Xenobiotica 42 (2012) 901–910.

[129] M. Walles, T. Wolf, Y. Jin, M. Ritzau, L.A. Leuthold, J. Krauser, H.P. Gschwind, D. Carcache, M. Kittelmann, M. Ocwieja, M. Ufer, R. Woessner, A. Chakraborty, P. Swart, Metabolism and disposition of the metabotropic glutamate receptor 5 antagonist (mGluR5) mavoglurant (AFQ056) in healthy subjects, Drug Metabol. Dispos. 41 (2013) 1626–1641.

[130] S. Takusagawa, J.J. van Lier, K. Suzuki, M. Nagata, J. Meijer, W. Krauwinkel, M. Schaddelee, M. Sekiguchi, A. Miyashita, T. Iwatsubo, M. van Gelderen, T. Usui, Absorption, metabolism and excretion of [^{14}C]mirabegron (YM178), a potent and selective beta(3)-adrenoceptor agonist, after oral administration to healthy male volunteers, Drug Metabol. Dispos. 40 (2012) 815–824.

[131] N. Yamamura, J. Mendel-Harary, K. Brown, M. Uchiyama, Y. Urasaki, M. Takahashi, V. Warren, V. Vashi, Metabolism, excretion, and pharmacokinetics of [^{14}C]mirogabalin, a novel alpha2delta ligand, in healthy volunteers following oral administration, Xenobiotica 51 (2021) 549–563.

[132] S. Lentini, D. van der Mey, A. Kern, U. Thuss, A. Kaiser, K. Matsuno, M. Gerisch, Absorption, distribution, metabolism and excretion of molidustat in healthy participants, Basic Clin. Pharmacol. Toxicol. 127 (2020) 221–233.

[133] J. Zheng, Y. Xin, J. Zhang, R. Subramanian, B.P. Murray, J.A. Whitney, M.R. Warr, J. Ling, L. Moorehead, E. Kwan, J. Hemenway, B.J. Smith, J.A. Silverman, Pharmacokinetics and disposition of momelotinib revealed a disproportionate human metabolite-resolution for clinical development, Drug Metabol. Dispos. 46 (2018) 237–247.

[134] S. Ohnishi, K. Fukumura, R. Kubota, T. Wajima, Absorption, distribution, metabolism, and excretion of radiolabeled naldemedine in healthy subjects, Xenobiotica 49 (2019) 1044–1053.

[135] K. Bui, F. She, M. Hutchison, A. Brunnstrom, M. Sostek, Absorption, distribution, metabolism, and excretion of [^{14}C]-labeled naloxegol in healthy subjects, Int. J. Clin. Pharmacol. Therapeut. 53 (2015) 838–846.

[136] X. Dai, M.D. Karol, M. Hitron, M.L. Hard, J.E. Blanchard, N. Eraut, N. Rich, B.T. Gufford, Mass balance and pharmacokinetics of an oral dose of ^{14}C-napabucasin in healthy adult male subjects, Pharmacol. Res. Perspect. 9 (2021) e00722.

[137] S. Ma, J. Suchomel, E. Yanez, E. Yost, X. Liang, R. Zhu, H. Le, N. Siebers, L. Joas, R. Morley, S. Royer-Joo, A. Pirzkall, L. Salphati, J.A. Ware, K.M. Morrissey, Investigation of the absolute bioavailability and human mass balance of navoximod, a novel Ido1 inhibitor, Br. J. Clin. Pharmacol. 85 (2019) 1751–1760.

[138] M. Sanga, J. Banach, A. Ledvina, N.B. Modi, A. Mittur, Pharmacokinetics, metabolism, and excretion of nefopam, a dual reuptake inhibitor in healthy male volunteers, Xenobiotica 46 (2016) 1001–1016.

[139] A.W. Harrell, R. Wilson, Y.L. Man, K. Riddell, E. Jarvis, G. Young, R. Chambers, L. Crossman, A. Georgiou, A. Pereira, D. Kenworthy, C. Beaumont, M. Marotti, D. Wilkes, E.M. Hessel, W.A. Fahy, An innovative approach to characterize clinical ADME and pharmacokinetics of the inhaled drug nemiralisib using an intravenous microtracer combined with an inhaled dose and an oral radiolabel dose in healthy male subjects, Drug Metabol. Dispos. 47 (2019) 1457–1468.

[140] L. van Andel, Z. Zhang, S. Lu, V. Kansra, S. Agarwal, L. Hughes, M.M. Tibben, A. Gebretensae, L. Lucas, M.J.X. Hillebrand, H. Rosing, J.H.M. Schellens, J.H. Beijnen, Human mass balance study and metabolite profiling of ^{14}C-niraparib, a novel poly(ADP-Ribose) polymerase (PARP)-1 and PARP-2 inhibitor, in patients with advanced cancer, Invest. N. Drugs 35 (2017) 751–765.

[141] S. Xu, D. Tatosian, I. McIntosh, M. Caceres, C. Matthews, K. Samuel, D. Selverian, S. Kumar, E. Kauh, Absorption, metabolism and excretion of [^{14}C]omarigliptin, a once-weekly DPP-4 inhibitor, in humans, Xenobiotica 48 (2018) 584–591.

[142] P.A. Dickinson, M.V. Cantarini, J. Collier, P. Frewer, S. Martin, K. Pickup, P. Ballard, Metabolic disposition of osimertinib in rats, dogs, and humans: insights into a drug designed to bind covalently to a cysteine residue of epidermal growth factor receptor, Drug Metabol. Dispos. 44 (2016) 1201–1212.

[143] S. Surapaneni, U. Yerramilli, A. Bai, D. Dalvie, J. Brooks, X. Wang, J.V. Selkirk, Y.G. Yan, P. Zhang, R. Hargreaves, G. Kumar, M. Palmisano, J.Q. Tran, Absorption, metabolism, and excretion, in vitro pharmacology, and clinical pharmacokinetics of ozanimod, a novel sphingosine 1-phosphate receptor modulator, Drug Metabol. Dispos. 49 (2021) 405−419.

[144] M. Ufer, C. Huynh, J.J. van Lier, E. Caroff, H. Fischer, J. Dingemanse, Absorption, distribution, metabolism and excretion of the P2Y12 receptor antagonist selatogrel after subcutaneous administration in healthy subjects, Xenobiotica 50 (2020) 427−434.

[145] X. Zhang, S. Fettner, E. Winter, M. Masjedizadeh, G. Hisoire, Metabolism and excretion of a novel p38 MAP kinase inhibitor pamapimod in healthy male subjects, Int. J. Clin. Pharmacol. Therapeut. 49 (2011) 345−352.

[146] S. Mu, D. Palmer, R. Fitzgerald, C. Andreu-Vieyra, H. Zhang, Z. Tang, D. Su, S. Sahasranaman, Human mass balance and metabolite profiling of [^{14}C]-Pamiparib, a poly (ADP-Ribose) polymerase inhibitor, in patients with advanced cancer, Clin. Pharmacol. Drug. Dev. 10 (2021) 1108−1120.

[147] S. Clive, M.M. Woo, T. Nydam, L. Kelly, M. Squier, M. Kagan, Characterizing the disposition, metabolism, and excretion of an orally active pan-deacetylase inhibitor, panobinostat, via trace radiolabeled ^{14}C material in advanced cancer patients, Cancer Chemother. Pharmacol. 70 (2012) 513−522.

[148] T.H. Lin, K. Hu, J. Flarakos, M. Sharr-McMahon, J.B. Mangold, H. He, Y. Wang, Assessment of the absorption, metabolism and excretion of [^{14}C] pasireotide in healthy volunteers using accelerator mass spectrometry, Cancer Chemother. Pharmacol. 72 (2013) 181−188.

[149] K.R. Kelly, M. Zollinger, F. Lozac'h, E. Tan, A. Mita, F. Waldmeier, P. Urban, S. Anand, Y. Wang, P. Swart, C. Takimoto, M. Mita, Metabolism of patupilone in patients with advanced solid tumor malignancies, Invest. N. Drugs 31 (2013) 605−615.

[150] Y. Deng, C. Sychterz, A.B. Suttle, M.M. Dar, D. Bershas, K. Negash, Y. Qian, E.P. Chen, P.D. Gorycki, M.Y. Ho, Bioavailability, metabolism and disposition of oral pazopanib in patients with advanced cancer, Xenobiotica 43 (2013) 443−453.

[151] X. Zhou, F. Sedarati, D.V. Faller, D. Zhao, H.M. Faessel, S. Chowdhury, J. Bolleddula, Y. Li, K. Venkatakrishnan, Z. Papai, Phase I study assessing the mass balance, pharmacokinetics, and excretion of [^{14}C]-pevonedistat, a NEDD8-activating enzyme inhibitor in patients with advanced solid tumors, Invest. N. Drugs 39 (2021b) 488−498.

[152] Q. Yue, S.C. Khojasteh, S. Cho, S. Ma, T. Mulder, J. Chen, J. Pang, X. Ding, A. Deese, J.D. Pellet, N. Siebers, L. Joas, L. Salphati, J.A. Ware, Absorption, metabolism and excretion of pictilisib, a potent pan-class I phosphatidylinositol-3-Kinase (PI3K) inhibitor, in rats, dogs, and humans, Xenobiotica 51 (2021) 796−810.

[153] O. von Richter, G. Massimini, H. Scheible, I. Udvaros, A. Johneet, Pimasertib, a selective oral MEK1/2 inhibitor: absolute bioavailability, mass balance, elimination route, and metabolite profile in cancer patients, Br. J. Clin. Pharmacol. 82 (2016) 1498−1508.

[154] M. Zollinger, F. Waldmeier, S. Hartmann, G. Zenke, A.G. Zimmerlin, U. Glaenzel, J.P. Baldeck, A. Schweitzer, S. Berthier, T. Moenius, M.A. Grassberger, Pimecrolimus: absorption, distribution, metabolism, and excretion in healthy volunteers after a single oral dose and supplementary investigations in vitro, Drug Metabol. Dispos. 34 (2006) 765−774.

[155] M. Hoffmann, C. Kasserra, J. Reyes, P. Schafer, J. Kosek, L. Capone, A. Parton, H. Kim-Kang, S. Surapaneni, G. Kumar, Absorption, metabolism and excretion of [^{14}C]pomalidomide in humans following oral administration, Cancer Chemother. Pharmacol. 71 (2013) 489−501.

[156] Y.E. Ye, C.N. Woodward, N.I. Narasimhan, Absorption, metabolism, and excretion of [^{14}C]ponatinib after a single oral dose in humans, Cancer Chemother. Pharmacol. 79 (2017) 507−518.

[157] M. Reyes, M. Hoch, P. Brossard, W. Wagner-Redeker, T. Miraval, J. Dingemanse, Mass balance, pharmacokinetics and metabolism of the selective S1P1 receptor modulator ponesimod in humans, Xenobiotica 45 (2015) 139−149.

[158] S. Flach, G. Scarfe, J. Dragone, J. Ding, M. Seymour, M. Pennick, T. Pankratz, S. Troy, J. Getsy, A phase I study to investigate the absorption, pharmacokinetics, and excretion of [^{14}C]prucalopride after a single oral dose in healthy volunteers, Clin. Therapeut. 38 (2016b) 2106−2115.

[159] J. Flarakos, L.S. Ting, Y. Du, D.S. Stein, C.V. Reynolds, M. Patel, S. Roy, J.B. Mangold, Disposition and metabolism of [^{14}C]PTZ601 in healthy volunteers, Xenobiotica 43 (2013) 283−292.

[160] C.A. Morris, S.R. Dueker, P.N. Lohstroh, L.Q. Wang, X.P. Fang, D. Jung, L. Lopez-Lazaro, M. Baker, S. Duparc, I. Borghini-Fuhrer, R. Pokorny, J.S. Shin, L. Fleckenstein, Mass balance and metabolism of the antimalarial pyronaridine in healthy volunteers, Eur. J. Drug Metab. Pharmacokinet. 40 (2015) 75−86.

[161] J. Meng, X.Y. Liu, S. Ma, H. Zhang, S.D. Yu, Y.F. Zhang, M.X. Chen, X.Y. Zhu, Y. Liu, L. Yi, X.L. Ding, X.Y. Chen, L.Y. Miao, D.F. Zhong, Metabolism and disposition of pyrotinib in healthy male volunteers: covalent binding with human plasma protein, Acta Pharmacol. Sin. 40 (2019) 980−988.

[162] M. Sanga, J. James, J. Marini, G. Gammon, C. Hale, J. Li, An open-label, single-dose, phase 1 study of the absorption, metabolism and excretion of quizartinib, a highly selective and potent FLT3 tyrosine kinase inhibitor, in healthy male subjects, for the treatment of acute myeloid leukemia, Xenobiotica 47 (2017) 856−869.

[163] M. Bauer, H. Bliesath, C. Leuratti, E. Lackner, W. Dieterle, M. Muller, M. Brunner, Disposition and metabolism of ralfinamide, a novel Na-channel blocker, in healthy male volunteers, Pharmacology 86 (2010) 297−305.

[164] P. Beale, I. Judson, J. Hanwell, C. Berry, W. Aherne, T. Hickish, P. Martin, M. Walker, Metabolism, excretion and pharmacokinetics of a single dose of [^{14}C]-raltitrexed in cancer patients, Cancer Chemother. Pharmacol. 42 (1998) 71−76.

[165] M. Gerisch, F.T. Hafner, D. Lang, M. Radtke, K. Diefenbach, A. Cleton, J. Lettieri, Mass balance, metabolic disposition, and pharmacokinetics of a single oral dose of regorafenib in healthy human subjects, Cancer Chemother. Pharmacol. 81 (2018) 195−206.

[166] J.F. Sigafoos, G.D. Bowers, S. Castellino, A.G. Culp, D.S. Wagner, M.J. Reese, J.E. Humphreys, E.K. Hussey, R.L. O'Connor Semmes, A. Kapur, W. Tao, R.L. Dobbins, J.W. Polli, Assessment of the drug interaction risk for remogliflozin etabonate, a sodium-dependent glucose cotransporter-2 inhibitor: evidence from in vitro, human mass balance, and ketoconazole interaction studies, Drug Metabol. Dispos. 40 (2012) 2090−2101.

[167] D.L. Bourdet, S. Yeola, S.S. Hegde, P.J. Colson, C.N. Barnes, M.T. Borin, Revefenacin absorption, metabolism, and excretion in healthy subjects and pharmacological activity of its major metabolite, Drug Metabol. Dispos. 48 (2020) 1312–1320.

[168] S. Flach, M. Croft, J. Ding, R. Budhram, T. Pankratz, M. Pennick, G. Scarfe, S. Troy, J. Getsy, Pharmacokinetics, absorption, and excretion of radiolabeled revexepride: a phase I clinical trial using a microtracer and accelerator mass spectrometry-based approach, Drug Des. Dev. Ther. 10 (2016a) 3125–3132.

[169] V. Ong, S. Wills, D. Watson, T. Sandison, S. Flanagan, Metabolism, excretion, and mass balance of [^{14}C]-rezafungin in animals and humans, Antimicrob. Agents Chemother. (2021) AAC0139021.

[170] A.D. James, H. Schiller, C. Marvalin, Y. Jin, H. Borell, A.F. Roffel, U. Glaenzel, Y. Ji, G. Camenisch, An integrated assessment of the ADME properties of the CDK4/6 Inhibitor ribociclib utilizing preclinical in vitro, in vivo, and human ADME data, Pharmacol. Res. Perspect. 8 (2020) e00599.

[171] Z.Y. Zhang, J. Wang, V. Kansra, X. Wang, Absorption, metabolism, and excretion of the antiemetic rolapitant, a selective neurokinin-1 receptor antagonist, in healthy male subjects, Invest. N. Drugs 37 (2019) 139–146.

[172] K. Kobayshi, Y. Abe, A. Kawai, T. Furihata, H. Harada, T. Endo, H. Takeda, Human mass balance, pharmacokinetics and metabolism of rovatirelin and identification of its metabolic enzymes in vitro, Xenobiotica 49 (2019) 1434–1446.

[173] M. Liao, S. Jaw-Tsai, J. Beltman, A.D. Simmons, T.C. Harding, J.J. Xiao, Evaluation of in vitro absorption, distribution, metabolism, and excretion and assessment of drug-drug interaction of rucaparib, an orally potent poly(ADP-ribose) polymerase inhibitor, Xenobiotica 50 (2020) 1032–1042.

[174] K. Sekiguchi, K. Fukumura, H. Hasegawa, T. Kanazu, The metabolism and pharmacokinetics of [^{14}C]-S-777469, a new cannabinoid receptor 2 selective agonist, in healthy human subjects, Xenobiotica 45 (2015) 150–157.

[175] J. Flarakos, Y. Du, T. Bedman, Q. Al-Share, P. Jordaan, P. Chandra, D. Albrecht, L. Wang, H. Gu, H.J. Einolf, S.E. Huskey, J.B. Mangold, Disposition and metabolism of [^{14}C] sacubitril/valsartan (formerly LCZ696) an angiotensin receptor neprilysin inhibitor, Xenobiotica vol 46 (2016) 986–1000.

[176] H. Su, D.W. Boulton, A. Barros Jr., L. Wang, K. Cao, S.J. Bonacorsi Jr., R.A. Iyer, W.G. Humphreys, L.J. Christopher, Characterization of the in vitro and in vivo metabolism and disposition and cytochrome P450 inhibition/induction profile of saxagliptin in human, Drug Metabol. Dispos. 40 (2012) 1345–1356.

[177] E. Helmer, J.M. Nicolas, J. Long, A.F. Roffel, E. Jones, H. Chanteux, N. Diaz, H. Garratt, T. Bosje, A dual-administration microtracer technique to characterize the absorption, distribution, metabolism, and excretion of [^{14}C]seletalisib (UCB5857) in healthy subjects, J. Clin. Pharmacol. 57 (2017) 1582–1590.

[178] A.W. Dymond, C. Howes, C. Pattison, K. So, G. Mariani, M. Savage, S. Mair, G. Ford, P. Martin, Metabolism, excretion, and pharmacokinetics of selumetinib, an MEK1/2 inhibitor, in healthy adult male subjects, Clin. Therapeut. 38 (2016) 2447–2458.

[179] L. Jensen, H. Helleberg, A. Roffel, J.J. van Lier, I. Bjornsdottir, P.J. Pedersen, E. Rowe, J. Derving Karsbol, M.L. Pedersen, Absorption, metabolism and excretion of the GLP-1 analogue semaglutide in humans and nonclinical species, Eur. J. Pharmaceut. Sci. 104 (2017) 31–41.

[180] U. Glaenzel, Y. Jin, R. Nufer, W. Li, K. Schroer, S. Adam-Stitah, S. Peter van Marle, E. Legangneux, H. Borell, A.D. James, A. Meissner, G. Camenisch, A. Gardin, Metabolism and disposition of siponimod, a novel selective S1P1/S1P5 agonist, in healthy volunteers and in vitro identification of human cytochrome P450 enzymes involved in its oxidative metabolism, Drug Metabol. Dispos. 46 (2018) 1001–1013.

[181] L.Y. Leung, H.K. Lim, M.W. Abell, J.J. Zimmerman, Pharmacokinetics and metabolic disposition of sirolimus in healthy male volunteers after a single oral dose, Ther. Drug Monit. 28 (2006) 51–61.

[182] C. MacLauchlin, S.E. Schneider, K. Keedy, P. Fernandes, B.D. Jamieson, Metabolism, excretion, and mass balance of solithromycin in humans, Antimicrob. Agents Chemother. 62 (2018).

[183] M. Zollinger, F. Lozac'h, E. Hurh, C. Emotte, H. Bauly, P. Swart, Absorption, distribution, metabolism, and excretion (ADME) of ^{14}C-sonidegib (LDE225) in healthy volunteers, Cancer Chemother. Pharmacol. 74 (2014) 63–75.

[184] B. Speed, H.Z. Bu, W.F. Pool, G.W. Peng, E.Y. Wu, S. Patyna, C. Bello, P. Kang, Pharmacokinetics, distribution, and metabolism of [^{14}C] sunitinib in rats, monkeys, and humans, Drug Metabol. Dispos. 40 (2012) 539–555.

[185] Y. Yu, C.H. Chung, A. Plotka, K. Quinn, H. Shi, Z. Papai, L. Nguyen, D. Wang, A phase 1 mass balance study of ^{14}C-labeled talazoparib in patients with advanced solid tumors, J. Clin. Pharmacol. 59 (2019) 1195–1203.

[186] R. Terlinden, J. Ossig, F. Fliegert, C. Lange, K. Gohler, Absorption, metabolism, and excretion of ^{14}C-labeled tapentadol HCl in healthy male subjects, Eur. J. Drug Metab. Pharmacokinet. 32 (2007) 163–169.

[187] J.J. Lee, S. Seraj, K. Yoshida, H. Mizuguchi, S. Strychor, T. Fiejdasz, T. Faulkner, R.A. Parise, P. Fawcett, L. Pollice, S. Mason, J. Hague, M. Croft, J. Nugteren, C. Tedder, W. Sun, E. Chu, J.H. Beumer, Human mass balance study of TAS-102 using ^{14}C analyzed by accelerator mass spectrometry, Cancer Chemother. Pharmacol. 77 (2016) 515–526.

[188] V. Ong, S. Flanagan, E. Fang, H.J. Dreskin, J.B. Locke, K. Bartizal, P. Prokocimer, Absorption, distribution, metabolism, and excretion of the novel antibacterial prodrug tedizolid phosphate, Drug Metabol. Dispos. 42 (2014) 1275–1284.

[189] J.P. Shaw, J. Cheong, M.R. Goldberg, M.M. Kitt, Mass balance and pharmacokinetics of [^{14}C]telavancin following intravenous administration to healthy male volunteers, Antimicrob. Agents Chemother. 54 (2010) 3365–3371.

[190] A. Johne, H. Scheible, A. Becker, J.J. van Lier, P. Wolna, M. Meyring, Open-label, single-center, phase I trial to investigate the mass balance and absolute bioavailability of the highly selective oral MET inhibitor tepotinib in healthy volunteers, Invest. N. Drugs 38 (2020) 1507–1519.

[191] R. Teng, S. Oliver, M.A. Hayes, K. Butler, Absorption, distribution, metabolism, and excretion of ticagrelor in healthy subjects, Drug Metabol. Dispos. 38 (2010) 1514–1521.

[192] T. Murai, H. Takakusa, D. Nakai, E. Kamiyama, T. Taira, T. Kimura, T. Jimbo, M. Bathala, F. Pickersgill, H. Zahir, T. Tokui, R.E. Savage, M.A. Ashwell, T. Izumi, Metabolism and disposition of [^{14}C]tivantinib after oral administration to humans, dogs and rats, Xenobiotica 44 (2014) 996−1008.

[193] M.M. Cotreau, C.L. Hale, L. Jacobson, C.S. Oelke, A.L. Strahs, R.G. Kochan, M. Sanga, W. Slichenmyer, D.L. Vargo, Absorption, metabolism, and excretion of [^{14}C]-Tivozanib, a vascular endothelial growth factor receptor tyrosine kinase inhibitor, in healthy male participants: a phase I, open-label, mass-balance study, Clin. Pharmacol. Drug. Dev. 1 (2012) 102−109.

[194] D. Schwab, A. Portron, Z. Backholer, B. Lausecker, K. Kawashima, A novel double-tracer technique to characterize absorption, distribution, metabolism and excretion (ADME) of [^{14}C]tofogliflozin after oral administration and concomitant intravenous microdose administration of [^{13}C] tofogliflozin in humans, Clin. Pharmacokinet. 52 (2013) 463−473.

[195] M. Zell, C. Husser, O. Kuhlmann, D. Schwab, T. Uchimura, T. Kemei, K. Kawashima, M. Yamane, A. Pahler, Metabolism and mass balance of SGLT2 inhibitor tofogliflozin following oral administration to humans, Xenobiotica 44 (2014) 369−378.

[196] V. Mancel, F.X. Mathy, P. Boulanger, S. English, M. Croft, C. Kenney, T. Knott, A. Stockis, M. Bani, Pharmacokinetics and metabolism of [^{14}C]-tozadenant (SYN-115), a novel A2a receptor antagonist ligand, Xenobiotica vol 47 (2017) 705−718.

[197] S.L. Polsky-Fisher, S. Vickers, D. Cui, R. Subramanian, B.H. Arison, N.G. Agrawal, T.V. Goel, L.K. Vessey, M.G. Murphy, K.C. Lasseter, R.C. Simpson, J.M. Vega, A.D. Rodrigues, Metabolism and disposition of a potent and selective GABA-Aalpha2/3 receptor agonist in healthy male volunteers, Drug Metabol. Dispos. 34 (2006) 1004−1011.

[198] J.H. Beumer, J.M. Rademaker-Lakhai, H. Rosing, L. Lopez-Lazaro, J.H. Beijnen, J.H. Schellens, Trabectedin (Yondelis, formerly ET-743), a mass balance study in patients with advanced cancer, Invest. N. Drugs 23 (2005) 429−436.

[199] M.Y. Ho, M.J. Morris, J.L. Pirhalla, J.W. Bauman, C.B. Pendry, K.W. Orford, R.A. Morrison, D.S. Cox, Trametinib, a first-in-class oral MEK inhibitor mass balance study with limited enrollment of two male subjects with advanced cancers, Xenobiotica 44 (2014) 352−368.

[200] D. Argenti, B.K. Jensen, R. Hensel, K. Bordeaux, R. Schleimer, C. Bickel, D. Heald, A mass balance study to evaluate the biotransformation and excretion of [^{14}C]-triamcinolone acetonide following oral administration, J. Clin. Pharmacol. 40 (2000) 770−780.

[201] L. Wang-Lakshman, Z. Miao, L. Wang, H. Gu, M. Kagan, J. Gu, E. McNamara, M. Walles, R. Woessner, G. Camenisch, H.J. Einolf, J. Chen, Evaluation of the absorption, metabolism, and excretion of a single oral 1-mg dose of tropifexor in healthy male subjects and the concentration dependence of tropifexor metabolism, Drug Metabol. Dispos. 49 (2021) 548−562.

[202] P. Martin, S. Oliver, S.J. Kennedy, E. Partridge, M. Hutchison, D. Clarke, P. Giles, Pharmacokinetics of vandetanib: three phase I studies in healthy subjects, Clin. Therapeut. 34 (2012) 221−237.

[203] L.M. Jost, H.P. Gschwind, T. Jalava, Y. Wang, C. Guenther, C. Souppart, A. Rottmann, K. Denner, F. Waldmeier, G. Gross, E. Masson, D. Laurent, Metabolism and disposition of vatalanib (PTK787/ZK-222584) in cancer patients, Drug Metabol. Dispos. 34 (2006) 1817−1828.

[204] A.A. Holmberg, L. Weidolf, S. Necander, P. Bold, S. Sidhu, M. Pelay-Gimeno, R.A.F. de Ligt, E.R. Verheij, A. Jauhiainen, I. Psallidas, U. Wahlby Hamren, S. Prothon, Characterization of clinical absorption, distribution, metabolism, and excretion and pharmacokinetics of velsecorat using an intravenous microtracer combined with an inhaled dose in healthy subjects, Drug Metabol. Dispos. 50 (2022) 150−157.

[205] S.M. Goldinger, J. Rinderknecht, R. Dummer, F.P. Kuhn, K.H. Yang, L. Lee, R.C. Ayala, J. Racha, W. Geng, D. Moore, M. Liu, A.K. Joe, S.P. Bazan, J.F. Grippo, A single-dose mass balance and metabolite-profiling study of vemurafenib in patients with metastatic melanoma, Pharmacol. Res. Perspect. 3 (2015) e00113.

[206] M. Boettcher, M. Gerisch, M. Lobmeyer, N. Besche, D. Thomas, M. Gerrits, J. Lemmen, W. Mueck, M. Radtke, C. Becker, Metabolism and pharmacokinetic drug-drug interaction profile of vericiguat, A soluble guanylate cyclase stimulator: results from preclinical and phase I healthy volunteer studies, Clin. Pharmacokinet. 59 (2020) 1407−1418.

[207] Z.L. Mao, A. Alak, J.J. Wheeler, J. Keirns, Disposition and mass balance of [^{14}C]vernakalant after single intravenous and oral doses in healthy volunteers, Drug Metabol. Lett. 5 (2011) 114−125.

[208] Y.D. Zheng, H. Zhang, Y. Zhan, Y.C. Bian, S. Ma, H.X. Gan, X.J. Lai, Y.Q. Liu, Y.C. Gong, X.F. Liu, H.B. Sun, Y.G. Li, D.F. Zhong, L.Y. Miao, X.X. Diao, Pharmacokinetics, mass balance, and metabolism of [^{14}C]vicagrel, a novel irreversible P2Y12 inhibitor in humans, Acta Pharmacol. Sin. 42 (2021b) 1535−1546.

[209] M.H. Schultze-Mosgau, J. Hochel, O. Prien, T. Zimmermann, A. Brooks, J. Bush, A. Rottmann, Characterization of the pharmacokinetics of vilaprisan: bioavailability, excretion, biotransformation, and drug-drug interaction potential, Clin. Pharmacokinet. 57 (2018) 1001−1015.

[210] R.A. Graham, B.L. Lum, G. Morrison, I. Chang, K. Jorga, B. Dean, Y.G. Shin, Q. Yue, T. Mulder, V. Malhi, M. Xie, J.A. Low, C.E. Hop, A single dose mass balance study of the Hedgehog pathway inhibitor vismodegib (GDC-0449) in humans using accelerator mass spectrometry, Drug Metabol. Dispos. 39 (2011) 1460−1467.

[211] A. MacDonald, G. Scarfe, D. Magirr, T. Sarvotham, J. Charlton, W. Brugger, E. Dean, Phase I study of orally administered ^{14}Carbon-isotope labelled-vistusertib (AZD2014), a dual TORC1/2 kinase inhibitor, to assess the absorption, metabolism, excretion, and pharmacokinetics in patients with advanced solid malignancies, Cancer Chemother. Pharmacol. 83 (2019) 787−795.

[212] N. Siebers, M. Palmer, D.G. Silberg, L. Jennings, C. Bliss, P.T. Martin, Absorption, distribution, metabolism, and excretion of [^{14}C]-Volixibat in healthy men: phase 1 open-label study, Eur. J. Drug Metab. Pharmacokinet. 43 (2018) 91−101.

[213] R. Toda, T. Miyagawa, Y. Masuda, Y. Hoshino, K. Yoshii, M. Hirayama, M. Shibuya, Y. Kawabata, Mass balance and metabolism of Z-215, a novel proton pump inhibitor, in healthy volunteers, Xenobiotica 48 (2018) 1006−1020.

[214] J.A. Clarkson-Jones, A.S. Kenyon, J. Kemp, E.M. Lenz, S.D. Oliver, H. Swaisland, Disposition and metabolism of the specific endothelin A receptor antagonist zibotentan (ZD4054) in healthy volunteers, Xenobiotica 42 (2012) 363−371.

[215] E. Helmer, A. Willson, C. Brearley, M. Westerhof, S. Delage, I. Shaw, R. Cooke, S. Sidhu, Pharmacokinetics and metabolism of ziritaxestat (GLPG1690) in healthy male volunteers following intravenous and oral administration, Clin. Pharmacol. Drug. Dev. 11 (2) (2022) 246—256.

[216] J. O'Donnell, K. Lawrence, K. Vishwanathan, V. Hosagrahara, J.P. Mueller, Single-dose pharmacokinetics, excretion, and metabolism of zoli-flodacin, a novel spiropyrimidinetrione antibiotic, in healthy volunteers, Antimicrob. Agents Chemother. 63 (2019).

[217] D.J. Roberts, R.I. Hall, Drug absorption, distribution, metabolism and excretion considerations in critically ill adults, Expet Opin. Drug Metabol. Toxicol. 9 (2013) 1067—1084.

[218] S.D. Undevia, G. Gomez-Abuin, M.J. Ratain, Pharmacokinetic variability of anticancer agents, Nat. Rev. Cancer 5 (2005) 447—458.

[219] N. Bushby, J. Bergin, J. Harding, [^{14}C]-AZD1152 drug substance manufacture: challenges of an IV-infusion dosed human mass balance study in patients, J. Label. Compd. Radiopharm. 59 (2016) 250—254.

[220] J. Kirchheiner, A. Seeringer, Clinical implications of pharmacogenetics of cytochrome P450 drug metabolizing enzymes, Biochim. Biophys. Acta 1770 (2007) 489—494.

[221] I.G. Stiell, J.S. Roos, K.M. Kavanagh, G. Dickinson, A multicenter, open-label study of vernakalant for the conversion of atrial fibrillation to sinus rhythm, Am. Heart J. 159 (2010) 1095—1101.

[222] J. Haglund, M.M. Halldin, A. Brunnstrom, G. Eklund, A. Kautiainen, A. Sandholm, S.L. Iverson, Pragmatic approaches to determine the exposures of drug metabolites in preclinical and clinical subjects in the MIST evaluation of the clinical development phase, Chem. Res. Toxicol. 27 (2014) 601—610.

[223] J.F. Rogers, A.N. Nafziger, J.S. Bertino Jr., Pharmacogenetics affects dosing, efficacy, and toxicity of cytochrome P450-metabolized drugs, Am. J. Med. 113 (2002) 746—750.

[224] T. Nunes, J.F. Rocha, M. Vaz-da-Silva, B. Igreja, L.C. Wright, A. Falcao, L. Almeida, P. Soares-da-Silva, Safety, tolerability, and pharmaco-kinetics of etamicastat, a novel dopamine-beta-hydroxylase inhibitor, in a rising multiple-dose study in young healthy subjects, Drugs R 10 (2010) 225—242.

[225] T. Nunes, J.F. Rocha, M. Vaz-da-Silva, A. Falcao, L. Almeida, P. Soares-da-Silva, Pharmacokinetics and tolerability of etamicastat following single and repeated administration in elderly versus young healthy male subjects: an open-label, single-center, parallel-group study, Clin. Ther-apeut. 33 (2011) 776—791.

[226] J.F. Rocha, M. Vaz-Da-Silva, T. Nunes, B. Igreja, A.I. Loureiro, M.J. Bonifacio, L.C. Wright, A. Falcao, L. Almeida, P. Soares-Da-Silva, Single-dose tolerability, pharmacokinetics, and pharmacodynamics of etamicastat (BIA 5-453), a new dopamine beta-hydroxylase inhibitor, in healthy subjects, J. Clin. Pharmacol. 52 (2012) 156—170.

[227] E.G. Solon, L. Kraus, Quantitative whole-body autoradiography in the pharmaceutical industry. Survey results on study design, methods, and regulatory compliance, J. Pharmacol. Toxicol. Methods 46 (2001) 73—81.

[228] E.G. Solon, Use of radioactive compounds and autoradiography to determine drug tissue distribution, Chem. Res. Toxicol. 25 (2012) 543—555.

[229] G. Lappin, R.C. Garner, The use of accelerator mass spectrometry to obtain early human ADME/PK data, Expet Opin. Drug Metabol. Toxicol. 1 (2005) 23—31.

[230] R.C. Garner, Practical experience of using human microdosing with AMS analysis to obtain early human drug metabolism and PK data, Bio-analysis 2 (2010) 429—440.

[231] F. Lozac'h, S. Fahrni, D. Maria, C. Welte, J. Bourquin, H.A. Synal, D. Pearson, M. Walles, G. Camenisch, Evaluation of cAMS for 14C microtracer ADME studies: opportunities to change the current drug development paradigm, Bioanalysis 10 (2018) 321—339.

[232] M.A. Seymour, Accelerator MS: its role as a frontline bioanalytical technique, Bioanalysis 3 (2011) 2817—2823.

[233] A.D. McCartt, T. Ognibene, G. Bench, K. Turteltaub, Measurements of carbon-14 with cavity ring-down spectroscopy, Nucl. Instrum. Methods Phys. Res. B 361 (2015) 277—280.

[234] A.D. McCartt, T.J. Ognibene, G. Bench, K.W. Turteltaub, Quantifying carbon-14 for biology using cavity ring-down spectroscopy, Anal. Chem. 88 (2016) 8714—8719.

[235] R.N. Zare, Analytical chemistry: ultrasensitive radiocarbon detection, Nature 482 (2012) 312—313.

[236] N.A. Kratochwil, S.R. Dueker, D. Muri, C. Senn, H. Yoon, B.Y. Yu, G.H. Lee, F. Dong, M.B. Otteneder, Nanotracing and cavity-ring down spectroscopy: a new ultrasensitive approach in large molecule drug disposition studies, PLoS One 13 (2018) e0205435.

[237] A. Kim, S.R. Dueker, F. Dong, A.F. Roffel, S.W. Lee, H. Lee, Human ADME for YH12852 using wavelength scanning cavity ring-down spectroscopy (WS-CRDS) after a low radioactivity dose, Bioanalysis 12 (2020) 87—98.

[238] R.S. Obach, A.N. Nedderman, D.A. Smith, Radiolabelled mass-balance excretion and metabolism studies in laboratory animals: are they still necessary? Xenobiotica 42 (2012) 46—56.

[239] R.E. White, D.C. Evans, C.E. Hop, D.J. Moore, C. Prakash, S. Surapaneni, F.L. Tse, Radiolabeled mass-balance excretion and metabolism studies in laboratory animals: a commentary on why they are still necessary, Xenobiotica 43 (2013) 219—225, discussion 226-217.

[240] J.H. Lin, Species similarities and differences in pharmacokinetics, Drug Metab. Dispos. 23 (1995) 1008—1021.

[241] H. Ishizuka, K. Konno, T. Shiina, H. Naganuma, K. Nishimura, K. Ito, H. Suzuki, Y. Sugiyama, Species differences in the transport activity for organic anions across the bile canalicular membrane, J. Pharmacol. Exp. Therapeut. 290 (1999) 1324—1330.

[242] H. Wang, E.L. LeCluyse, Role of orphan nuclear receptors in the regulation of drug-metabolising enzymes, Clin. Pharmacokinet. 42 (2003) 1331—1357.

[243] B. Davies, T. Morris, Physiological parameters in laboratory animals and humans, Pharmaceut. Res. 10 (1993) 1093—1095.

[244] M. Li, H. Yuan, N. Li, G. Song, Y. Zheng, M. Baratta, F. Hua, A. Thurston, J. Wang, Y. Lai, Identification of interspecies difference in efflux transporters of hepatocytes from dog, rat, monkey and human, Eur. J. Pharmaceut. Sci. 35 (2008) 114—126.

[245] N. Li, J. Palandra, O.V. Nemirovskiy, Y. Lai, LC-MS/MS mediated absolute quantification and comparison of bile salt export pump and breast cancer resistance protein in livers and hepatocytes across species, Anal. Chem. 81 (2009a) 2251−2259.

[246] N. Li, Y. Zhang, F. Hua, Y. Lai, Absolute difference of hepatobiliary transporter multidrug resistance-associated protein (MRP2/Mrp2) in liver tissues and isolated hepatocytes from rat, dog, monkey, and human, Drug Metabol. Dispos. 37 (2009b) 66−73.

[247] E. Kimoto, Y.A. Bi, R.E. Kosa, L.M. Tremaine, M.V.S. Varma, Hepatobiliary clearance prediction: species scaling from monkey, dog, and rat, and in vitro-in vivo extrapolation of sandwich-cultured human hepatocytes using 17 drugs, J. Pharmaceut. Sci. 106 (2017) 2795−2804.

[248] S.J. Roffey, R.S. Obach, J.I. Gedge, D.A. Smith, What is the objective of the mass balance study? A retrospective analysis of data in animal and human excretion studies employing radiolabeled drugs, Drug Metab. Rev. 39 (2007) 17−43.

[249] A. Roffel, J.J.V. Lier, G. Rozema, E.J. van Hoogdalem, Predictability of elimination and excretion of small molecules from animals to humans, and impact on dosimetry for human ADME studies with radiolabeled drugs, Curr. Clin. Pharmacol. 17 (1) (2022) 26−38.

[250] F. Huang, C. Voelk, M. Trampisch, L. Rowland, A. Schultz, J.P. Sabo, Pharmacokinetic interaction between faldaprevir and cyclosporine or tacrolimus in healthy volunteers: a prospective, open-label, fixed-sequence, crossover study, Basic Clin. Pharmacol. Toxicol. 123 (2018) 84−93.

[251] G. Ghibellini, E.M. Leslie, K.L. Brouwer, Methods to evaluate biliary excretion of drugs in humans: an updated review, Mol. Pharm. 3 (2006) 198−211.

[252] S.S. Rao, B. Kuo, R.W. McCallum, W.D. Chey, J.K. DiBaise, W.L. Hasler, K.L. Koch, J.M. Lackner, C. Miller, R. Saad, J.R. Semler, M.D. Sitrin, G.E. Wilding, H.P. Parkman, Investigation of colonic and whole-gut transit with wireless motility capsule and radiopaque markers in constipation, Clin. Gastroenterol. Hepatol. 7 (2009) 537−544.

[253] A. Tuca, E. Guell, E. Martinez-Losada, N. Codorniu, Malignant bowel obstruction in advanced cancer patients: epidemiology, management, and factors influencing spontaneous resolution, Cancer Manag. Res. 4 (2012) 159−169.

[254] Guidance on nonclinical safety studies for human clinical trials and marketing authorization for pharmaceuticals M3(R2), International Conference on Harmonisation, EMA, London, UK, 2009, http://www.ema.europa.eu/docs/en_GB/document_library/Scientific_guideline/2009/09/WC500002720.pdf. (Accessed 13 November 2022).

[255] U.S. Food and Drug Administration, Safety Testing of Drug Metabolites: Guidance for Industry, FDA, Silver Spring, 2016. http://www.fda.gov/downloads/drugs/guidancecomplianceregulatoryinformation/guidances/ucm079266.pdf. (Accessed 13 November 2022).

[256] D. Dalvie, R.S. Obach, P. Kang, C. Prakash, C.M. Loi, S. Hurst, A. Nedderman, L. Goulet, E. Smith, H.Z. Bu, D.A. Smith, Assessment of three human in vitro systems in the generation of major human excretory and circulating metabolites, Chem. Res. Toxicol. 22 (2009) 357−368.

[257] S. Anderson, D. Luffer-Atlas, M.P. Knadler, Predicting circulating human metabolites: how good are we? Chem. Res. Toxicol. 22 (2009) 243−256.

[258] J. Iegre, M.A. Hayes, R.A. Thompson, L. Weidolf, E.M. Isin, Database extraction of metabolite information of drug candidates: analysis of 27 AstraZeneca compounds with human absorption, distribution, metabolism, and excretion data, Drug Metabol. Dispos. 44 (2016) 732−740.

[259] T.S. Chan, H. Yu, A. Moore, S.R. Khetani, D. Tweedie, Meeting the challenge of predicting hepatic clearance of compounds slowly metabolized by cytochrome P450 using a novel hepatocyte model, HepatoPac, Drug Metabol. Dispos. 41 (2013) 2024−2032.

[260] D. Ramsden, D.J. Tweedie, R. St George, L.Z. Chen, Y. Li, Generating an in vitro-in vivo correlation for metabolism and liver enrichment of a hepatitis C virus drug, faldaprevir, using a rat hepatocyte model (HepatoPac), Drug Metabol. Dispos. 42 (2014) 407−414.

[261] I. Hultman, C. Vedin, A. Abrahamsson, S. Winiwarter, M. Darnell, Use of HmuREL human coculture system for prediction of intrinsic clearance and metabolite formation for slowly metabolized compounds, Mol. Pharm. 13 (2016) 2796−2807.

[262] T.E. Ballard, N. Kratochwil, L.M. Cox, M.A. Moen, F. Klammers, A. Ekiciler, A. Goetschi, I. Walter, Simplifying the execution of HepatoPac MetID experiments: metabolite profile and intrinsic clearance comparisons, Drug Metabol. Dispos. 48 (2020) 804−810.

[263] D.A. Smith, D. Dalvie, Why do metabolites circulate? Xenobiotica 42 (2012) 107−126.

[264] H. Liu, M.J. Michmerhuizen, Y. Lao, K. Wan, A.H. Salem, J. Sawicki, M. Serby, S. Vaidyanathan, S.L. Wong, S. Agarwal, M. Dunbar, J. Sydor, S.M. de Morais, A.J. Lee, Metabolism and disposition of a novel B-cell lymphoma-2 inhibitor venetoclax in humans and characterization of its unusual metabolites, Drug Metabol. Dispos. 45 (2017) 294−305.

[265] C. Gu, M. Artelsmair, C.S. Elmore, R.J. Lewis, P. Davis, J.E. Hall, B.T. Dembofsky, G. Christoph, M.A. Smith, M. Chapdelaine, M. Sunzel, Late-occurring and long-circulating metabolites of GABAAalpha2,3 receptor modulator AZD7325 involving metabolic cyclization and aromatization: relevance to MIST analysis and application for patient compliance, Drug Metabol. Dispos. 46 (2018) 303−315.

[266] S. Ma, S.K. Chowdhury, Analytical strategies for assessment of human metabolites in preclinical safety testing, Anal. Chem. 83 (2011) 5028−5036.

[267] L. Leclercq, F. Cuyckens, G.S. Mannens, R. de Vries, P. Timmerman, D.C. Evans, Which human metabolites have we MIST? Retrospective analysis, practical aspects, and perspectives for metabolite identification and quantification in pharmaceutical development, Chem. Res. Toxicol. 22 (2009) 280−293.

[268] H. Gao, R.S. Obach, Addressing MIST (Metabolites in Safety Testing): bioanalytical approaches to address metabolite exposures in humans and animals, Curr. Drug Metabol. 12 (2011) 578−586.

[269] A.F. Aubry, L.J. Christopher, J. Wang, M. Zhu, G. Tirucherai, M.E. Arnold, Reflecting on a decade of metabolite screening and monitoring, Bioanalysis 6 (2014) 651−664.

[270] W.G. Humphreys, S.E. Unger, Safety assessment of drug metabolites: characterization of chemically stable metabolites, Chem. Res. Toxicol. 19 (2006) 1564−1569.

[271] P. Timmerman, S. Blech, S. White, M. Green, C. Delatour, S. McDougall, G. Mannens, J. Smeraglia, S. Williams, G. Young, Best practices for metabolite quantification in drug development: updated recommendation from the European Bioanalysis Forum, Bioanalysis 8 (2016) 1297−1305.

[272] H. Yu, D. Bischoff, D. Tweedie, Challenges and solutions to metabolites in safety testing: impact of the International Conference on Harmonization M3(R2) guidance, Expet Opin. Drug Metabol. Toxicol. 6 (2010) 1539−1549.

[273] B. Booth, When do you need a validated assay? Bioanalysis 3 (2011) 2729−2730.

[274] S. Ma, S.K. Chowdhury, A tiered approach to address regulatory drug metabolite-related issues in drug development, Bioanalysis 6 (2014) 587−590.

[275] C. Yu, C.L. Chen, F.L Gorycki, T.G. Neiss, A rapid method for quantitatively estimating metabolites in human plasma in the absence of synthetic standards using a combination of liquid chromatography/mass spectrometry and radiometric detection, Rapid Commun. Mass Spectrom 21 (4) (2007) 497−502.

[276] P. Yi, D. Luffer-Atlas, A radiocalibration method with pseudo internal standard to estimate circulating metabolite concentrations, Bioanalysis 2 (2010) 1195−1210.

[277] L. Xu, C. Woodward, J. Dai, C. Prakash, Metabolism and excretion of 6-chloro-9-(4-methoxy-3,5-dimethylpyridin-2-ylmethyl)-9H-purin-2-ylamine, an HSP90 inhibitor, in rats and dogs and assessment of its metabolic profile in plasma of humans, Drug Metabol. Dispos. 41 (2013) 2133−2147.

[278] U. Holzgrabe, Quantitative NMR spectroscopy in pharmaceutical applications, Prog. Nucl. Magn. Reson. Spectrosc. 57 (2010) 229−240.

[279] K. Vishwanathan, K. Babalola, J. Wang, R. Espina, L. Yu, A. Adedoyin, R. Talaat, A. Mutlib, J. Scatina, Obtaining exposures of metabolites in preclinical species through plasma pooling and quantitative NMR: addressing metabolites in safety testing (MIST) guidance without using radiolabeled compounds and chemically synthesized metabolite standards, Chem. Res. Toxicol. 22 (2009) 311−322.

[280] A. Mutlib, R. Espina, J. Atherton, J. Wang, R. Talaat, J. Scatina, A. Chandrasekaran, Alternate strategies to obtain mass balance without the use of radiolabeled compounds: application of quantitative fluorine (19F) nuclear magnetic resonance (NMR) spectroscopy in metabolism studies, Chem. Res. Toxicol. 25 (2012) 572−583.

[281] G.S. Walker, J.N. Bauman, T.F. Ryder, E.B. Smith, D.K. Spracklin, R.S. Obach, Biosynthesis of drug metabolites and quantitation using NMR spectroscopy for use in pharmacologic and drug metabolism studies, Drug Metabol. Dispos. 42 (2014) 1627−1639.

[282] H.C. Keun, O. Beckonert, J.L. Griffin, C. Richter, D. Moskau, J.C. Lindon, J.K. Nicholson, Cryogenic probe 13C NMR spectroscopy of urine for metabonomic studies, Anal. Chem. 74 (2002) 4588−4593.

[283] M. Spraul, A.S. Freund, R.E. Nast, R.S. Withers, W.E. Maas, O. Corcoran, Advancing NMR sensitivity for LC-NMR-MS using a cryoflow probe: application to the analysis of acetaminophen metabolites in urine, Anal. Chem. 75 (2003) 1536−1541.

[284] G.J. Dear, A.D. Roberts, C. Beaumont, S.E. North, Evaluation of preparative high performance liquid chromatography and cryoprobe-nuclear magnetic resonance spectroscopy for the early quantitative estimation of drug metabolites in human plasma, J. Chromatogr. B: Anal. Technol. Biomed. Life Sci. 876 (2008) 182−190.

[285] R. Espina, L. Yu, J. Wang, Z. Tong, S. Vashishtha, R. Talaat, J. Scatina, A. Mutlib, Nuclear magnetic resonance spectroscopy as a quantitative tool to determine the concentrations of biologically produced metabolites: implications in metabolites in safety testing, Chem. Res. Toxicol. 22 (2009) 299−310.

[286] A. Mutlib, R. Espina, K. Vishwanathan, K. Babalola, Z. Chen, C. Dehnhardt, A. Venkatesan, T. Mansour, I. Chaudhary, R. Talaat, J. Scatina, Application of quantitative NMR in pharmacological evaluation of biologically generated metabolites: implications in drug discovery, Drug Metabol. Dispos. 39 (2011) 106−116.

[287] G.S. Walker, T.F. Ryder, R. Sharma, E.B. Smith, A. Freund, Validation of isolated metabolites from drug metabolism studies as analytical standards by quantitative NMR, Drug Metabol. Dispos. 39 (2011) 433−440.

[288] C. Beaumont, G.C. Young, T. Cavalier, M.A. Young, Human absorption, distribution, metabolism and excretion properties of drug molecules: a plethora of approaches, Br. J. Clin. Pharmacol. 78 (2014) 1185−1200.

[289] H. Gao, S. Deng, R.S. Obach, A simple liquid chromatography-tandem mass spectrometry method to determine relative plasma exposures of drug metabolites across species for metabolite safety assessments, Drug Metab. Dispos. 38 (2010) 2147−2156.

[290] S. Ma, Z. Li, K.J. Lee, S.K. Chowdhury, Determination of exposure multiples of human metabolites for MIST assessment in preclinical safety species without using reference standards or radiolabeled compounds, Chem. Res. Toxicol. 23 (2010) 1871−1873.

[291] R.A. Hamilton, W.R. Garnett, B.J. Kline, Determination of mean valproic acid serum level by assay of a single pooled sample, Clin. Pharmacol. Therapeut. 29 (1981) 408−413.

[292] C.E. Hop, Z. Wang, Q. Chen, G. Kwei, Plasma-pooling methods to increase throughput for in vivo pharmacokinetic screening, J. Pharmaceut. Sci. 87 (1998) 901−903.

[293] R.H. Takahashi, C. Khojasteh, M. Wright, C. Hop, S. Ma, Mixed matrix method provides A reliable metabolite exposure comparison for assessment of metabolites in safety testing (MIST), Drug Metabol. Lett. 11 (2017) 21−28.

[294] G. Lappin, Approaches to intravenous clinical pharmacokinetics: recent developments with isotopic microtracers, J. Clin. Pharmacol. 56 (2016) 11−23.

[295] K.W. Ward, L.B. Hardy, J.R. Kehler, L.M. Azzarano, B.R. Smith, Apparent absolute oral bioavailability in excess of 100% for a vitronectin receptor antagonist (SB-265123) in rat. II. Studies implicating transporter-mediated intestinal secretion, Xenobiotica 34 (2004) 367−377.

[296] J.M. Strong, J.S. Dutcher, W.K. Lee, A.J. Atkinson Jr., Absolute bioavailability in man of N-acetylprocainamide determined by a novel stable isotope method, Clin. Pharmacol. Therapeut. 18 (1975) 613−622.

[297] O. Schueller, E. Skucas, G. Regev, I. Shaw, N. Singh, M. Sanghvi, M. Croft, L. Lohmer, A. Alabanza, J. Patel, Absolute bioavailability, mass balance, and metabolic profiling assessment of [(14) C]-Belumosudil in healthy men: a phase 1, open-label, 2-part study, Clin. Pharmacol. Drug. Dev. 11 (7) (2022) 786−794.

[298] H. Jiang, C. Titsch, J. Zeng, B. Jones, P. Joyce, Y. Gandhi, W. Turley, R. Burrell, A.F. Aubry, M.E. Arnold, Overcoming interference with the detection of a stable isotopically labeled microtracer in the evaluation of beclabuvir absolute bioavailability using a concomitant microtracer approach, J. Pharm. Biomed. Anal. 143 (2017) 9−16.

[299] H. Jiang, J. Zeng, W. Li, M. Bifano, H. Gu, C. Titsch, J. Easter, R. Burrell, H. Kandoussi, A.F. Aubry, M.E. Arnold, Practical and efficient strategy for evaluating oral absolute bioavailability with an intravenous microdose of a stable isotopically-labeled drug using a selected reaction monitoring mass spectrometry assay, Anal. Chem. 84 (2012) 10031−10037.

[300] X.S. Xu, H. Jiang, L.J. Christopher, J.X. Shen, J. Zeng, M.E. Arnold, Sensitivity-based analytical approaches to support human absolute bioavailability studies, Bioanalysis 6 (2014) 497−504.

[301] B. Chen, P. Lu, D. Freeman, Y. Gao, E. Choo, K. DeMent, S. Savage, K. Zhang, D. Milanwoski, L. Liu, B. Dean, Y. Deng, Practical strategies when using a stable isotope labeled microtracer for absolute bioavailability assessment: a case study of a high oral dose clinical candidate GDC-0810, J. Pharm. Biomed. Anal. 154 (2018) 116−122.

[302] A.F. Aubry, LC-MS/MS bioanalytical challenge: ultra-high sensitivity assays, Bioanalysis 3 (2011) 1819−1825.

[303] P. Keski-Rahkonen, R. Desai, M. Jimenez, D.T. Harwood, D.J. Handelsman, Measurement of estradiol in human serum by LC-MS/MS using a novel estrogen-specific derivatization reagent, Anal. Chem. 87 (2015) 7180−7186.

[304] M.E. Wieder, S.W. Paine, P.R. Hincks, C.M. Pearce, J. Scarth, L. Hillyer, Detection and pharmacokinetics of salbutamol in thoroughbred racehorses following inhaled administration, J. Vet. Pharmacol. Therapeut. 38 (2015) 41−47.

[305] H.M. Jones, M. Dickins, K. Youdim, J.R. Gosset, N.J. Attkins, T.L. Hay, I.K. Gurrell, Y.R. Logan, P.J. Bungay, B.C. Jones, I.B. Gardner, Application of PBPK modelling in drug discovery and development at Pfizer, Xenobiotica 42 (2012) 94−106.

[306] E.A. Cannady, A. Aburub, C. Ward, C. Hinds, B. Czeskis, K. Ruterbories, J.G. Suico, J. Royalty, D. Ortega, B.W. Pack, S.L. Begum, W.F. Annes, Q. Lin, D.S. Small, Absolute bioavailability of evacetrapib in healthy subjects determined by simultaneous administration of oral evacetrapib and intravenous [$^{13}C_8$]-evacetrapib as a tracer, J. Label. Compd. Radiopharm. 59 (6) (2016) 238−244.

[307] R. de Vries, J.W. Smit, P. Hellemans, J. Jiao, J. Murphy, D. Skee, J. Snoeys, J. Sukbuntherng, M. Vliegen, L. de Zwart, E. Mannaert, J. de Jong, Stable isotope-intravenous microdose for absolute bioavailability and effect of grapefruit juice on ibrutinib in healthy adults, Br. J. Clin. Pharmacol. 81 (2) (2016) 235−245.

[308] A. Alaarg, R. Menon, D. Rizzo, Y. Liu, J. Bien, T. Elkinton, T. Grieme, L.R. Asmus, A.H. Salem, A microdosing framework for absolute bioavailability assessment of poorly soluble drugs: a case study on cold-labeled venetoclax, from chemistry to the clinic, Clin. Transl. Sci. 15 (2022) 244−254.

[309] S. Ma, S.K. Chowdhury, The use of stable isotope-labeled drug as microtracers with conventional LC-MS/MS to support human absolute bioavailability studies: are we there yet? Bioanalysis 8 (2016) 731−733.

[310] J. Roosendaal, H. Rosing, J.H. Beijnen, Combining isotopic tracer techniques to increase efficiency of clinical pharmacokinetic trials in oncology, Drugs R 20 (2020a) 147−154.

Chapter 11

Conquering low oral bioavailability issues in drug discovery and development

Timothy J. Carlson

Carlson DMPK Consulting, LLC, Belmont, CA, United States

Introduction

For an oral drug to be successful, it must overcome many barriers and obstacles to reach the site of action and exert its activity. Initially, the drug must be swallowed and survive the transition to the site of absorption, which is typically the gastrointestinal (GI) tract. In the GI tract, the drug must be dissolved into solution, and begin the process of absorption across the gut wall. Here the barrier can be failure to cross the wall, or the drug can be removed by metabolic enzymes in the enterocytes. If the drug survives and makes it to the portal vein, it is transported to the liver. The liver is the major site of metabolism for pharmaceutical compounds, and the molecule can be metabolized to another entity in the liver, or it can be excreted into the bile. Only if the molecule escapes these fates can it then be returned to the blood for distribution to other tissues including the site of action.

The bioavailability of a drug is a measure of the extent to which that drug becomes available to the systemic circulation. Oral bioavailability is a function of both the absorption process and also first pass metabolism and elimination, and can be considered to be dependent on three serial steps: the fraction of dosed drug that is absorbed (F_A); the fraction escaping intestinal metabolism (F_G); and the fraction that escapes liver extraction (F_H) as it passes from the portal vein through the liver to the systemic circulation. Bioavailability can be expressed mathematically as:

$$F_{oral} = F_A \times F_G \times F_H$$

Although absorption is an important component of bioavailability, it is important to distinguish between absorption and bioavailability, in that oral exposure is determined not only by absorption through the membranes of the GI tract but also by the extent to which the organs just after absorption are able to extract the compound. The most important organs causing first pass extraction are the liver (which extracts by metabolism, uptake transport and biliary secretion) and the intestine (which extracts mainly by metabolism). Although the lung, heart, and blood are also tissues where first pass metabolism can occur, it is generally viewed that the GI tract and the liver are more important in first pass metabolism that limits the systemic exposure of an orally administered drug.

The oral route of dosing is often preferred due to it being less invasive and easy to administer, resulting in a higher degree of patient compliance. As a result the assessment and understanding of oral bioavailability is of vital importance in drug discovery and development. Low bioavailability can be the main factor that limits the success of a new drug candidate during the clinical development process. Inadequate systemic exposure, and therefore inadequate exposure at the site of action, prevents the biological activity of the compound from being exerted and therefore prevents therapeutic benefit to the patient. In addition to not providing hoped-for benefit to patients, low exposure also does not allow for proper testing of the clinical experiment during drug development, that is, the proof of concept of the therapeutic hypothesis. Several retrospective studies have revealed that low exposure, or low confidence in exposure, led to a significant number of clinical failures that did not test the mechanism adequately [1−3]. Conducting clinical studies with compounds that are unlikely to provide a clear result due to poor drug exposure is inefficient and expensive.

Oral bioavailability is one of the most important determinants of the dosing regimen for drugs. The extent to which a drug fails to be absorbed or is removed by first pass extraction helps determine how large a dose must be administered.

Overcoming Obstacles in Drug Discovery and Development. https://doi.org/10.1016/B978-0-12-817134-9.00007-6

Additionally, poor bioavailability is associated with larger interindividual variability in bioavailability [4], which has important implications to clinical development. Because of the larger interindividual variability in bioavailability, the consequence is likely that low bioavailable drugs will show more patient-to-patient variability than more bioavailable drugs, in turn requiring larger clinical trials with more patients to yield information. Caution would also need to be taken when prescribing low bioavailability drugs with large interindividual variability, as these are drugs for which previous clinical experience are less likely to apply to a new patient. This is particularly true when considering low bioavailability drugs with a narrow therapeutic index, that is, those drugs for which there is a small difference in the exposure required for efficacy relative to the exposure that would lead to toxicity.

Overall, the optimization of bioavailability is a vital way to reduce underlying risks in drug development and increase the likelihood of a drug candidate to have therapeutic benefit. The goal of this chapter is to summarize current methodologies and approaches to assess bioavailability and overcome bioavailability issues in the drug discovery and development process. The first section is on the characterization of bioavailability. This section will cover in vivo and in vitro assessments, and will target the key processes involved in bioavailability, that is, solubility, permeability, and metabolic stability. The section will also describe different approaches depending on the stage in the discovery-development continuum in which they are typically used. The second section will cover compound design aspects to optimize bioavailability. This will include some rule-based guidelines that have been developed and applied to compound design, as well as computational approaches that have been used for design of compounds with optimal bioavailability. The third section will cover ways of optimizing and managing bioavailability through formulation or other technologies. The overall goal of the chapter is to provide useful information covering current approaches to optimize oral bioavailability to increase the likelihood of success in drug discovery and development.

Characterization of bioavailability

In order to focus drug discovery project efforts, it is important to develop a target product profile (TPP) as early in the process as possible. The TPP serves to identify and define a desired therapeutic profile of a drug candidate. Pharmacokinetic (PK) properties of a drug candidate are critical to achieving success, and the targeted PK properties for a particular project are dependent on the intended and desired use of the compound. For example, oral delivery and once a day dosing are often desired in terms of the intended use of the drug. Having a desired PK profile in turn defines the compound attributes that are needed, for example goals regarding bioavailability and metabolic stability.

With a focus on the TPP and other project goals, a strategy can be built for evaluating compounds. This typically takes the form of a screening cascade, or iterative evaluation cycles, and defines the specifics and sequence of experiments to be performed to evaluate candidate compounds. There are several excellent reviews that describe the development and the details of strategies that discovery project teams can implement [1,5,6]. Screening cascades differ and evolve depending on the different stages of the discovery and development continuum, as the experiments will change depending on the question being asked. Generally, in the earlier stages, after hits have been identified, the focus is on chemical scaffolds and identifying and understanding the issues with those scaffolds. In the later stages (e.g. lead optimization), the focus shifts to careful characterization of individual compounds and on resolving issues. The experiments will generally increase in complexity as the project progresses to later stages.

In vivo approaches

Oral bioavailability is a function of multiple mechanisms, including solubility, permeability, and metabolic stability. Due to its dependence on multiple mechanisms and complex physiology, the only way to actually measure bioavailability is with in vivo studies. Practically, bioavailability is calculated from the results of the pharmacokinetic data (plasma concentration-time curve) following oral and intravenous doses. Oral bioavailability is expressed as the ratio of dose-corrected area under the curve (AUC) following an oral dose to the AUC following an intravenous dose. In the earlier stages of drug discovery, the strategy for in vivo studies to assess bioavailability focuses on many compounds being evaluated in a single species (typically rat). The focus at this early stage is on identifying issues, in this case, whether oral bioavailability is a significant issue for a particular chemical scaffold or series. Later, in the lead optimization stages, the focus shifts to more detailed experimentation and evaluation, for example a single compound would be evaluated for PK characteristics in multiple species.

Although animal PK studies are routinely done in various preclinical species prior to human clinical studies, it should be emphasized that to date animal bioavailability has not been shown to be quantitively predictive of bioavailability in human. Analysis of data from a broad range of 184 compounds indicated that there were no strong or predictive correlations to human bioavailability for any preclinical species, individually or combined [7]. This lack of cross-species predictability is consistent with the fact that there are considerable interspecies differences in first-pass intestinal and liver metabolism, and that these differences would prevent any conclusion about a level of overall bioavailability in humans based on the animal data.

Where animal data have shown predictive value is on the absorption component of bioavailability. Despite the considerable complexity of the absorption process, animal models have been successfully used to estimate human absorption. Rats have been reported to be effective as a good model for predicting oral absorption in humans [8,9], and there have also been reports using monkeys as a successful predictor of human absorption [10,11] and mixed results using dog in vivo studies [12,13]. The cost and ethical concerns would limit the use of the monkey and dog to late stage discovery, where they can be used for characterizing a select, few compounds.

The safety of an oral drug must be evaluated in animals prior to dosing in humans, and so an understanding of clinical candidate's PK, including bioavailability, must be obtained in preclinical animals. Typically, this would be done for both a rodent and a non-rodent species. For this reason, as well as the fact that animal models can be predictive of the absorption component of human bioavailability, it is likely that drug discovery efforts will continue to include animal models as an important component of the candidate's bioavailability evaluation. It is the combination of in vivo data from preclinical animals with data obtained from in vitro experiments, and the resulting synthesis of that information, that has led to the best predictions of human pharmacokinetics [14,15].

In vitro approaches

Solubility, permeability and metabolic stability are three parameters that can be assessed with in vitro model systems and that provide valuable information on oral bioavailability. Solubility and permeability together provide information on the absorption of a compound, and metabolic stability provides information on the potential of first pass extraction. In vitro experiments offer multiple advantages relative to in vivo studies. In vitro approaches allow for increased efficiency with lower cost and a higher throughput compared to in vivo approaches, enabling the evaluation of more molecules. Additionally, in vitro systems aid in the implementation of the principle of the 3Rs (reduction, refinement, and replacement) through the decreased use of animal experiments in preclinical research. Finally, through the isolation of cell or enzymatic systems, in vitro approaches can provide tools that address mechanistic questions and either avoid or evaluate species differences.

Solubility and permeability

The characterization of solubility and permeability together form the basis of classification systems, like the Biopharmaceutical Classification System (BCS) and Biopharmaceutical Drug Disposition Classification System (BDDCS), that are widely used to describe a compound's attributes and are used in decision-making in drug discovery and development [16—18]. The BCS classifies compounds into four different categories based on their solubility and permeability (Table 11.1). Class 1 compounds are high solubility and high permeability, class 2 compounds are low solubility and high permeability, class 3 compounds are high solubility and low permeability, and class 4 compounds are both low solubility and low permeability. The classification systems can provide medicinal chemists with a framework and opportunity to design molecules with better physicochemical properties to achieve more optimal solubility and permeability and thereby increase chances of higher bioavailability. The design aspects are discussed more in the following section. The BCS is also used throughout the drug discovery and development continuum and can help companies save time and development costs

TABLE 11.1 Summary of the biopharmaceutical classification system.

Classification	Solubility	Permeability
Class 1	High solubility	High permeability
Class 2	Low solubility	High permeability
Class 3	High solubility	Low permeability
Class 4	Low solubility	Low permeability

[19,20]. The system has been adopted by the FDA and the EMEA for setting standards of bioavailability and bioequivalence for oral drug product approvals.

To optimize bioavailability, the goal is to have a highly soluble compound, as the compound must be in solution in order to be absorbed across the intestinal wall. The BCS defines "highly soluble" as when the highest recommended dose is soluble in 250 mL or less of aqueous media over the pH range of 1.2–7.5. There are various approaches, including kinetic, semi-equilibrium, and equilibrium methods, that have been developed to assess solubility during drug discovery and development. Generally, kinetic methods are high throughput and applicable during the earlier stages of drug discovery. In these kinetic determinations, the compound is generally in a dissolved state in DMSO and then precipitated in aqueous buffer at pH levels that mimic intestine (pH 6.5) or blood (pH 7.4). The kinetic solubility value is the concentration preceding precipitation. An example of a semi-equilibrium approach is for removal of DMSO by evaporation leaving a solid material to which to add the buffer for solubility determination. These methods are very efficient, due to their amenability to high throughput, as well as their requirement for low amounts of compound. However, the kinetic methods have been shown to overestimate solubility compared with the gold-standard thermodynamic methods, and so caution should be used when interpreting the results [21]. The thermodynamic methods involve dispersion of excess powder into aqueous media and measurement after equilibrium is reached. These equilibrium experiments are typically done in late stage discovery or early development for full characterization of a drug candidate's solubility.

Another approach for solubility assessment is to determine solubility in simulated intestinal fluid (SIF), which has been used as a key component in considering a compound's potential to be a successful oral drug [1]. Analysis of successful marketed drugs led to the development of a classification system, in which a solubility greater than 100 µg/mL in SIF was defined as desirable. The solubility value, along with permeability and projected dose, was then used to place compounds into high risk, moderate risk, or desirable categories to aid decision making and prioritization. Of course, a challenge with this kind of analysis is that it is based on dose, or a projected highest marketed dose strength, and this information may be years away from when a compound is initially made and evaluated. A practical guideline that has been proposed for initial evaluation of a compound suggests using 200 µg/mL as a solubility cut-off, where compounds with greater than 200 µg/mL solubility would be classified as high solubility (either Class 1 or 3) and less soluble compounds as low solubility (either Class 2 or 4) [17,22].

The evaluation of permeability is critical to the assessment of oral drug candidates, and it can vary based on the stage of the project. The permeability assessments done in early drug discovery can be used to pursue objectives such as: (1) exclusion, or deprioritization, of poorly permeable compounds, (2) development of structure-property relationships for chemical scaffolds, or (3) identification of structural elements of molecules associated with poor permeability that can be optimized in a later phase. The focus of these early-stage assessments is on identifying potential permeability issues with a chemical series. In the later lead optimization stage, other objectives can be focused on, for example: (1) optimization of the required permeability in relation to other requirements like metabolism, dose, potency, and solubility, (2) establishment of in vitro/in vivo correlations using animals and prediction of human F_A, and (3) evaluation of dose linearity.

The main in vitro tool for assessing permeability is the cell-based Caco-2 assay [23,24]. The Caco-2 cell line has been well studied and widely used, and it has been shown to correlate well with fraction absorbed in humans for some series of compounds. The Madin-Darby canine kidney (MDCK) cell line, often transfected with the multi-drug resistance 1 polypeptide (MDR1) gene, as well as the parallel artificial membrane permeability assays (PAMPA) are also well used tools [25,26].

Permeability is generally described in terms of units of molecular movement distance per unit time (e.g. cm/s). Compounds with an apparent permeability (P_{app}) value less than 1×10^{-6} cm/s are poorly permeable, compounds with P_{app} between 1 and 10×10^{-6} cm/s are considered moderately permeable, and P_{app} greater than 10×10^{-6} cm/s are considered highly permeable. Permeability assessment with Caco-2 cells are well suited for relatively high throughput, so it can be positioned relatively early in drug discovery if absorption and/or permeability is found to be an issue in the project. If more detailed evaluation of absorption is needed, more physiological models, such as sections of intestinal tissue in an Ussing chamber, or transfected cell lines that overexpress particular transporters, may be employed to test certain hypotheses in order to assist with lead optimization.

As mentioned previously, solubility and permeability can be used together to classify compounds in the BCS or other system, as a decision support framework regarding pharmacokinetics and bioavailability. The Biopharmaceutics Drug Disposition Classification System (BDDCS) can serve as a basis for predicting the importance of transporters in the pharmacokinetic profile of a compound. For example, BDDCS class 1 compounds are highly soluble, highly permeable, and extensively metabolized. Because of their high solubility, they are present in high concentrations in the gut, can saturate transporters, and transporter effects are expected to be minimal and not clinically important. BDDCS class 2 compounds, due to their high permeability readily are passively absorbed. However, due to their low solubility they are unlikely to saturate transporters, and so efflux transport may be important to their disposition. Finally, class 3 compounds are poorly permeable, so influx may play an important role, while for class 4 compounds (poor solubility and poor permeability) both influx and efflux transporters may play a significant role in their absorption. A compound that is a substrate for intestinal efflux transporters may show dose-dependent bioavailability, which is critical to consider in terms of the potential effect on ascending dose studies in the clinic. The risk of having low exposure from efflux is highest for those compounds with a low predicted dose, or low solubility, as the low gut concentration would be below the K_m of the transporter.

There are several ways that solubility and permeability assessments are used together to assess potential human absorption and help decision making in drug discovery and development. For example, there are reviews that describe useful recommendations on targeting aqueous solubility as a function of permeability categories and three different hypothetical doses (0.1 mg/kg, 1.0 mg/kg, and 10 mg/kg) [27]. For example, at the extremes of the hypothetical doses, for a compound that has medium permeability with an expected dose of 10 mpk, the solubility would need to be approximately 520 μg/mL. For a compound with medium permeability and an expected dose of 0.1 mg/kg, a requirement for aqueous solubility would only need to be approximately 5 μg/mL. The bracketing of a wide range of doses allow for guidelines that are useful for targeting sufficient solubility and permeability early in drug discovery, to increase the chances of good oral absorption and therefore the potential for good bioavailability.

More confident predictions of human absorption are obtained when in vitro permeability and solubility assessments are coupled with in vivo pharmacokinetic data from preclinical animals [14]. In vivo data in rat and/or dog can be obtained on compounds from a scaffold of interest to establish an in vivo-in vitro correlation. A poor correlation may lead to further studies to investigate mechanistic explanations. In later stages, and at the time of clinical candidate selection, all in vitro and in vivo data and information should be incorporated into decision making. If the in vitro data and in vivo data from preclinical species are conflicting, then any prediction of human absorption will carry increased uncertainty. Additionally, compounds with low fraction absorbed tend to have more variable absorption, and this is borne out in the relationship between low bioavailability and interindividual variability in bioavailability discussed earlier. For these reasons, a high F_A (typically greater than 50%) is usually targeted in drug discovery.

First pass metabolism

First pass metabolism and extraction are the other major limitations to oral bioavailability. As discussed earlier, the liver and the intestine are the major organs of metabolic extraction. For most oral drug candidates, it is likely that hepatic metabolism will be the major route of elimination, and this has been established and summarized for oral marketed drugs [6]. A key activity and priority in drug discovery is the prediction of in vivo hepatic clearance, a measure of the liver's ability to metabolize a compound, and a major determinant of a compound's oral exposure as well as half-life. There are well established in vitro methods, using either liver microsomes or hepatocytes, that are routinely used to experimentally determine metabolic stability of new compounds, and using that data to predict hepatic clearance (Cl_H) and hepatic extraction ratio (E_H). These calculations are most commonly based on a well-stirred model of the liver, which has been extensively reviewed, along with other models of hepatic extraction [28–30]. Generally, the in vitro experiment provides an in vitro intrinsic clearance value for the compound, which can be extrapolated to yield an in vivo intrinsic clearance. The intrinsic clearance can then be used, along with values of plasma protein binding (f_u) and hepatic blood flow (Q_H), to calculate hepatic clearance and extraction ratio (Eqs. 11.1 and 11.2). E_H provides an estimate of F_H, a key component of oral bioavailability.

$$CL_H = Q_H \times E_H = Q_H(f_u \times CL_{int})/(Q_H + f_u(CL_{int})) \qquad 11.1$$

$$F_H = 1 - E_H \qquad 11.2$$

Both liver microsomes and hepatocytes have been shown to be useful models for the prediction of hepatic clearance [31]. Liver microsomes contain many of the key drug metabolizing enzymes, including cytochrome P450 (CYP) enzymes and flavin-containing monooxygenases, and these microsomal enzymes metabolize most small molecule drugs. Microsomes are very convenient to use, as they can be stored frozen for long periods of time without compromising enzyme activity. Hepatocytes have the full complement of liver enzymes, including conjugation enzymes like uridine 5′-diphospho-glucuronosyltransferases (UGTs), and they retain an overall intact cell structure. Due to these features, and their availability and relative ease of use with modern cryopreservation techniques, hepatocytes are generally considered the gold standard systems for in vitro metabolism studies. Many compounds have been shown to be extensively metabolized directly by conjugation reactions, resulting in low bioavailability. Examples of compounds with extensive conjugation and poor bioavailability include morphine, propofol, and raloxifene [32–34]. The methodologies used with either in vitro model are consistently being fine-tuned to increase their quantitative predictivity. One example is the incorporation of empirical correction factors to account for a systematic underprediction that is sometimes observed with these models.

Predictions of hepatic clearance from either microsomes or hepatocytes yield important decision-making information across drug discovery and development stages. In early stages, the focus is to obtain the metabolic stability data and the hepatic clearance prediction for a large number of compounds over ideally multiple chemical series and a broad range of structural space. This data allows for the prioritization of compounds or chemical series, that have predicted clearance values that are significantly below liver blood flow, in order to increase chances of low hepatic extraction and high bioavailability. The data also allows for the building of SAR in order to aid the redesign of molecules with increased metabolic stability. Two main approaches are often used to increase metabolic stability: (1) decrease lipophilicity, or (2) block "metabolic soft spots", which can be obtained experimentally or by prediction based on likely biotransformation pathways.

In later stages of discovery, the focus turns more to individual compounds. In these latter stages, the emphasis is on establishing in vitro-in vivo correlations in multiple species, ensuring predictability in preclinical species to strengthen confidence in human prediction, and to further understand the quantitative role of F_H to oral bioavailability. A significant role of F_H would lead further optimization efforts toward decreasing metabolic clearance, while a relatively low contribution of F_H to oral bioavailability would point any further optimization efforts toward optimizing absorption (F_A), or potentially intestinal metabolic extraction (F_G). It should be emphasized that there are significant species differences in drug metabolizing enzymes, and the resulting species differences in metabolism can translate to significant species differences in oral bioavailability. There are numerous examples of marketed drugs, including reboxetine, diazepam and indinavir, that have poor bioavailability in rodents yet good bioavailability in human. Project teams need to keep their primary focus on the projected clearance in human to not miss out on such compounds. However, as toxicology studies are necessary to perform prior to the conduct of any clinical studies, identifying compounds with sufficient bioavailability in the toxicology species (typically rat and dog) is necessary.

Intestinal metabolism is known to play an important role in the bioavailability of many oral drugs. Examples of drugs that are limited in bioavailability by intestinal metabolism include CYP3A substrates midazolam, lovastatin, and cyclosporine, and the UGT substrates raloxifene and lamotrigine. For many years, the liver was thought to be the predominant site of first pass metabolism, largely due to its capacity for drug metabolism and elimination. For example, most data indicate that CYP3A4, a major contributor to the drug metabolizing capacity of the intestine, is expressed at significantly lower levels in the intestine relative to the liver. However, the intestine is positioned as the first organ to encounter a drug following oral dosing, so the intestine may be exposed to high concentrations of the drug during the absorption phase prior to the passage through the liver. It is now well understood the intestinal metabolism is an important contributor to limiting F_G and by extension oral bioavailability; one analysis of hundreds of drugs indicated that approximately 30% of the drugs exhibited greater than 20% intestinal extraction [35].

There are multiple experimental model systems for studying intestinal metabolism in vitro. These include tissue slices, enterocyte preparations and intestinal microsomes. Microsomes, and some of the cell preparations, are amenable to relatively high throughput and can be used to interrogate intestinal metabolism at early and late stages of drug discovery. The in vitro model systems can be used to identify intestinal metabolic stability issues with certain chemical scaffolds, and the data can be used to prioritize compound or series with less of this liability. In vitro intestinal systems have also been used to mechanistically probe the underlying causes of poor oral exposure in the rat animal models early in a discovery program, enabling troubleshooting to help redesign of compounds and chemical series to avoid the issue [5,14]. In later stages of discovery, intestinal in vitro models can be used to establish in vitro-in vivo correlations, understand species differences in metabolism and bioavailability, all with the goal of predicting human bioavailability and pharmacokinetics.

In general, the intestinal models have more challenges than do the liver counterparts [36,37,38]. One of the challenges is that there is heterogenous expression of enzymes along the GI tract, causing significant variability between preparations and laboratories. Often in vitro intestinal preparations have been shown to have lower levels of drug metabolism enzyme expression and/or activity than that in human small intestine in vivo [39,40]. Additionally, compared to the liver, less is known about the physiological scaling factors necessary for extrapolation of in vitro to in vivo. However, recently there are numerous reports of advances in the development of in vitro intestinal models, including cryopreserved human enterocytes and cryopreserved human intestinal mucosal epithelium (CHIM), and the use of these and other intestinal models in drug discovery and development have been recently reviewed [41−43]. CHIM have the advantage of possessing virtually all cell types in the intestinal mucosal epithelium, while cryopreserved enterocytes can be used to resolve and define enterocyte specific questions and issues.

Another focus of recent in vitro model development for the intestine, and other organs, is the organoid, which represents a model that incorporates more of the real-life complexity of the in vivo intestine [44]. Although the Caco-2 model has been effectively and widely used in drug candidate permeability screening, this model does have some limitations. Caco-2 cells have a low expression of drug metabolizing enzymes and an overall expression pattern that is more like the colon than the small intestine [45], while the small intestine is where most drug compounds are absorbed. Additionally, Caco-2 cells exhibit tighter junctions compared to small intestine of humans [46], and Caco-2 cells do not appear to be appropriate for active, carrier-mediated drug absorption due to altered transporter expression patterns [47]. Intestinal organoids can be generated from induced pluripotent stem cells (iPSCs) and/or from isolated crypts from biopsies, and the resultant ex vivo intestinal culture represents a useful model for the intestinal epithelium. Organoids are compatible with nearly all methods that are used to analyze cells or tissue samples, and intestinal organoids have been shown to be useful for drug absorption and oral bioavailability studies [48,49].

The development of organoids is an example of a broader effort to develop microphysiological systems (MPS) to study absorption, metabolism, distribution, and excretion (ADME) processes. The goal of MPS development to help evaluate the ADME characteristics of new compounds is to recreate a portion of an organ that retains a physiologically relevant phenotype relevant to test and understand exposures to drug candidate compounds. Recent technological advances, for example with cell culture techniques, fluid delivery systems, and materials engineering, have made it feasible to evaluate ADME parameters, like bioavailability, with a stand-alone or interconnected organ system [50]. The major driving forces for the continual effort to improve MPS and human in vitro systems in general, are three-fold: (1) to improve the predictability of a drug's disposition in human, (2) to understand and overcome issues with species differences, and (3) to continue to move toward a decrease in the use of preclinical animals, consistent with the principle of the 3Rs (refinement, reduction, and replacement).

Design of molecules for optimizing bioavailability

One of the best and most efficient ways of resolving issues is of course to minimize those issues to begin with. To design molecules with the best chance of having optimal, or at least sufficient, oral bioavailability, it is necessary to have predictive tools to aid with the design. There have been three general computational strategies used to model and predict oral bioavailability: (1) development of rule-based approaches, (2) development of quantitative structure-property relationships (QSPR), and (3) application of physiologically based pharmacokinetic modeling. In this section of the chapter, these approaches will be discussed, with emphasis on their application, along with the challenges and opportunities with each approach.

Rule-based approaches to design

The rule-based approach centers on the idea that to maximize the chances of good absorption and bioavailability, the starting point is to ensure that the physicochemical properties of the molecule or chemical series are in an optimal space. A landmark assessment of the physicochemical properties associated with oral absorption and bioavailability was reported by Lipinski and colleagues at Pfizer, and it was codified as the "rule of 5." [51]. The rules predicted that a compound was more likely to exhibit good absorption if it had the following characteristics: (1) less than or equal to five hydrogen bond donors, (2) less than or equal to 10 hydrogen bond acceptors, (3) a MW less than or equal to 500, and (4) LogP less than or equal to 5. The rules were built on an analysis of >2000 drugs and related the potential for good oral absorption to various physicochemical boundaries. A fundamental reason for the utility of rules for guiding design is that the chemical space that defines ADME is relatively simple, in that the variability amongst ADME parameters can be described by relatively few unique descriptors. These descriptors typically are related to size, polarity, lipophilicity, charge status, and H-bonding status. Because these descriptors do a reasonable job describing the chemical space of ADME parameters, simple rules or filters have proven very useful in describing characteristics that increase the potential for good ADME properties, including oral bioavailability [52].

Subsequent analyses have provided additional insights regarding useful rules for optimizing oral bioavailability. In particular, the number of rotatable bonds in a molecule, as well as polar surface area have been shown to be associated with good oral bioavailability. For example, an initial study indicated that a total of <10 rotatable bonds, combined with a polar surface area (PSA) of less than 140, was associated with a high probability of having an oral bioavailability of greater than 20% in rat [53]. Subsequent analyses have generally supported an important role of rotatable bonds and PSA, although the recommended placement of boundaries varies among studies [54,55].

Measures of molecular complexity have also garnered interest in terms of helping design molecules with optimal ADME properties [27]. The number of aromatic rings and the fraction of carbons that are sp3 hybridized both influence solubility, which impacts oral bioavailability. Generally, the fewer aromatic rings in a compound means that compound is more developable, with the presence of more than three aromatic rings in a compound correlating with more ADME issues and greater attrition in the clinic [56]. Lipophilicity and aromaticity have been shown to independently influence ADME properties, and this has led to a proposed composite measure of hydrophobicity called the property forecast index (PFI), which is composed of logP (as a measure of lipophilicity) plus the number of aromatic rings [1]. Generally increasing PFI adversely affects solubility and permeability, and therefore lowers the chances of good oral bioavailability.

The analyses that resulted in the establishment of the rule of 5, as well as the additional descriptors described above, were primarily focused on the absorption component of oral bioavailability. Further work has focused on separating out the three components of oral bioavailability: absorption, first-pass intestinal metabolism and first pass hepatic extraction. Lipophilicity has generally been found to be the physicochemical parameter that has the biggest impact on metabolism, both at the intestine and the liver. The trends with lipophilicity highlight the importance of balancing properties to achieve good oral bioavailability. For example, enough lipophilicity is needed to ensure good membrane permeability, but too much lipophilicity will cause high hepatic and intestinal extraction due to metabolism. Additionally, it has been well established that ensuring minimal, yet sufficient, lipophilicity benefits multiple small molecule ADME properties, including increased potential of metabolic stability and decreased potential of causing CYP inhibition [57,58].

There have been multiple ways that have been described for the application of physicochemical property, rule-based design. One intriguing application is the proposal of modifying the rule of 5 based on the different stages of drug discovery and optimization. This proposal extends the rule of 5 concepts to lead molecules and fragments with more stringent rules being applied to leads versus drug candidates, and even more stringent rules being applied to fragments that are used in drug design campaigns (Table 11.2). Other applications have been to identify rules that describe optimal in vitro experimental results — one such approach found that a relationship between logD and MW could map to optimal permeability and metabolic stability. At MW of 450, the acceptable log D was a fairly narrow range between 1 and 2; as MW decreases, the lipophilicity range for satisfying permeability and metabolic stability goals increases, such that at MW of 200, the acceptable range of log D was between −2 and 5. Another example of a rule-based approach for optimizing overall ADME parameters focuses on a combination of projected parameters and measured parameters: projected dose, solubility in simulated intestinal fluid, and a measure of lipophilicity (PFI, as mentioned above). Guidelines and boundary conditions are described which demonstrate that a composite of these three parameters are consistent with physicochemical space that is occupied by successful oral drugs. An extension of this proposal is to emphasize an individual parameter at different stages of drug discovery: PFI for hit identification and selection, solubility in hit to lead stage, and projected dose for lead optimization [1].

All the analyses and rule-based design relationships have reinforced the idea that attaining good oral bioavailability requires a balancing act among physicochemical properties. The trends and rules can be used in the design of compounds, and aid in the decision making about altering molecule properties, to achieve sufficient bioavailability. However, while these rules are useful guidelines, there are numerous examples of successful oral drugs that lie outside the optimal physicochemical space, and these exceptions serve to teach us more about the bioavailability process. Most of the successful exceptions to the general rule-of-5 (RO5) physicochemical space occur with natural products. As a class of compounds, natural products contain more macrocycles (rings that contain 12 or more atoms) than do typical collections of synthetic compounds. Additionally, natural products have multiple hydrogen bonding possibilities and conformational mobility that aid in their membrane permeability. Cyclosporine is a natural product that lies well outside the RO5 space, with a MW of 1203 and log P of 7.5, and yet it is orally bioavailable. Cyclosporine has been shown to have markedly

TABLE 11.2 Summary of an adaptation of Lipinski's rule of 5 for different stages of drug discovery (as described in [27]).

	Rule of 3	Rule of 4	Rule of 5
Application	Fragments	Leads	Drug candidates
MW	≤300	≤400	≤500
Log P	≤3	≤4	≤5
H-bond donors	≤3	≤4	≤5
H-bond acceptors	≤3	≤8	≤10
PSA (A^2)	≤60	≤120	≤140

different intramolecular hydrogen bonding patterns and shape depending on whether it is found in aqueous or non-aqueous medium, and this physical flexibility has been speculated to be important to its permeability.

Drugs that are targeted at protein-protein interactions (PPI) represent a class of compounds that are a challenge for physicochemical property optimization. In general terms, the PPI interface can be quite large and lipophilic, requiring a compound that is aimed at such a target to lie outside the optimal RO5 space. For a long time, such targets were thought to be undruggable, although there are recent examples of some success. Navitoclax is a drug that is directed at a PPI target that is orally bioavailable, although it lies outside optimal physicochemical space with a MW of 975 and a logP of 9.6. Navitoclax serves as a great case study for the challenges that such a compound poses, and for the skill and resources required to advance and develop such a compound [59].

Rule-based design is widely used, and analysis of successful drugs has revealed that the most efficient path to good oral bioavailability is to start with good physicochemical properties. However, there are limitations to the rule-based approach. The rule-based guidelines generally bin compounds together as favorable or not, or as outliers in 1, or 2, or 3 categories, and as such the rule-based approach doesn't distinguish between compounds within the same bin. There are some chemical modifications used in compound design that have profound effect on oral bioavailability but without much change on physicochemical properties. An example would be small modifications that affect metabolism by blocking a specific site on a molecule. Each chemical series will have specific structural elements that can impact bioavailability and other ADME properties, and as a result it is beneficial to focus on these structural elements in generating useful structure-activity relationships within that series to optimize human bioavailability.

Computational modeling

Given the importance of bioavailability, a reliable quantitative prediction of oral bioavailability would be valuable for drug discovery project teams. However, the computational prediction of bioavailability has proven challenging because of the mechanistic complexity of bioavailability, in that it involves numerous processes, like solubility, permeability, and ability to escape metabolism. Despite these challenges, numerous reports have detailed the development and application of quantitative structure-property relationships (QSPR) for bioavailability. The generation of these predictive models follow three key steps: (1) selection of an experimental dataset, (2) calculation of molecular descriptors, and (3) construction of a statistical model. There have been diverse statistical and artificial intelligence techniques applied, as well as the calculation and application of 2-D and 3-D descriptors, to the development of the computational models [60]. Some efforts to improve the predictability of the models have focused on using experimental data, like animal PK data, as descriptor input [61,62]. One of the most promising approaches has been to build multiple QSPR models, with each model describing a discrete step of the bioavailability process, for example, dissolution, solubility, permeability and metabolic stability. Once the results of the separate models are obtained, they can be used subsequently as new descriptors for the development of a final bioavailability QSPR model [63].

A final approach worth highlighting is the incorporation of physiologically-based pharmacokinetic (PBPK) modeling in the effort to predict oral bioavailability. PBPK models are mathematical models that integrate information about physiological processes (e.g. organ blood flow, GI transit time) along with properties of the molecule of interest to simulate complex biological outcomes, like a plasma-concentration time profile of a compound. One of the valuable applications of a PBPK model is to use such a model to predict a PK profile in a preclinical species, which can then be tested against experimental data. Such an evaluation can be used in an iterative manner to improve the model prior to any prediction of human PK. The PBPK approach, which combines experimental data along with the computational, has been used in late stage discovery for candidate selection and optimization [64]. Although in general QSPR modeling and PBPK modeling have been used independently, a recent trend has been to use a hybrid QSPR-PBPK approaches, where QSPR models have been used to predict input properties with PBPK models. This hybrid approach has opened up some perspectives for the development of tools from different or orthogonal approaches, all in the service of improving the prediction of oral bioavailability.

Formulation strategies to optimize bioavailability

As has been discussed, the most efficient manner of drug discovery and development for an orally administered compound is to design, optimize, and select a clinical candidate that has optimal properties, including those that provide a high likelihood of good oral bioavailability. Unfortunately, it is very difficult to optimize all features, combining desired properties related to efficacy, safety, and pharmaceutical properties, in a single molecule. In the balancing act, a property or properties related to oral bioavailability may be compromised. In such a situation, there have been multiple formulation technologies that have been developed and can be applied to improve bioavailability. Most of the enabling formulation technologies have been developed to improve a molecule's absorption, by improving a compound's solubility and/or permeability. Examples of the technologies used are particle size reduction, solid dispersion, complexation, and lipid formulations. Often, application of a combination of the technologies has resulted in excellent results for successful drugs.

Particle size reduction is used to increase the rate of dissolution of poorly water-soluble drugs by increasing the surface area of the drug. Reducing the particle size to less than 1 μm can improve bioavailability and improve the safety of oral delivery by increasing the distribution uniformity in the GI fluid and avoiding high, prolonged local concentrations [65]. Nanocrystals can be formulated in a wide variety of nanoparticulate systems, often with a modified surface. Nitrendipine, when its nanocrystals were surface-modified with chitosan, exhibited increased bioavailability compared with unmodified crystals [66]. Docetaxel, a drug used in chemotherapy, was shown to have increased oral delivery by using thiolated chitosan. Many polymers, including polyethylene glycol (PEG), polyvinyl pyrollidine (PVP), polyglycolic acid (PGA), and poly-lactide-co-glycoside (PLGA), have been used to create polymeric nanoparticles to improve the properties and therapeutic value of BCS class 2 and class 4 drugs.

Another formulation technique is complexation with cyclodextrins. Cyclodextrins are cyclic oligosaccharides containing typically 6–10, or sometimes more alpha-D-glucopyranose subunits. Due to its chemical properties, including a lipophilic interior and hydrophilic exterior, cyclodextrins are able to form complexes with many drugs, and increase the solubility of the drug. Numerous studies have reported the enhancement of the dissolution rate of poorly soluble drugs by cyclodextrin complexation, including clonazepam [67] and ibuprofen [68].

Solid dispersion formulations involve the dispersion of the drug in an inert matrix. The active ingredient can be in a solubilized form, an amorphous state, or the crystalline state. Various synthetic or natural origin polymers have been utilized as carriers for solid dispersions, and surfactants and emulsifiers can also be used as carriers. Examples of drugs for which solid dispersion formulations have shown enhancement of oral bioavailability include atorvastatin [69], tranilast [70], and tacrolimus [71].

Lipid-based drug delivery systems have shown great promise to aid in the delivery of poorly soluble and poorly permeable drugs. Lipid-based formulations can have a positive effect on absorption through many of the mechanisms of the absorption process — by increasing solubility, enhancing membrane permeability, inhibiting efflux transporters, and increasing lymphatic transport [72,73]. Lipid colloidal drug delivery systems like liposomes, solid-lipid nanoparticles (SLN), and nanostructured lipid carriers are further examples of lipid-based formulation systems, and these can not only enhance bioavailability, but also have been shown to provide controlled release of the active drug [74,75]. Examples of drugs for which lipid-based delivery systems have been applied successfully include paclitaxel, montelukast, and saquinavir [76–78].

Overall, a deep knowledge of the compound and its classification per the BCS is a necessary first step in the selection of the appropriate formulation strategy. Additionally, an understanding of the fundamentals of the technology options assists in the matching of the compound, and the needs of the therapeutic product, with the appropriate formulation technology. For solubility issues, techniques like particle size reduction, solid dispersion and complexation can be useful approaches. For poorly permeable compounds, approaches like lipid-based systems, surface modifications, and polymeric conjunctions can prove to be helpful.

Conclusion

Optimizing oral bioavailability is a critical aspect of drug discovery and development. Sufficient oral bioavailability provides for the systemic exposure that is needed for the drug to reach its site of action and deliver its therapeutic benefit. Good bioavailability also has the value of decreasing interindividual variability between patients. Early in clinical drug development process, achieving good oral bioavailability is vital in order to properly conduct the key clinical proof of concept experiment. Drugs that fail early in drug development due to inadequate exposure to the target tissue are a huge opportunity lost in terms of not being able to adequately test whether intervention of the target has any therapeutic value.

There are many tools, technologies, and strategies available to address and overcome issues with oral bioavailability. Numerous in vitro, ex vivo, and in vivo assays can be applied to characterize bioavailability, and many of these are appropriately built for application at different stages of drug discovery and development. Focused experimentation can reveal the mechanisms by which bioavailability may be limiting, and this knowledge can then enable a strategy and workflow for resolving the issue. Substantial research and analysis have revealed a great deal of information about the properties of molecules that are associated with good bioavailability, and this knowledge can be translated into guidelines, rules, and even predictive models for the design, and iterative re-design, of molecules with high potential for good oral bioavailability. Finally, there is an increasing number of technologies and formulation strategies that have been developed and are available for managing the bioavailability issues of a compound that is therapeutically promising but has suboptimal properties (e.g. poor solubility). Many of these formulation strategies have been used with great success to enhance the oral bioavailability of such compounds. Overall, the complexity of the oral bioavailability process, as well as the wealth of tools and technologies available to address bioavailability issues, highlight the high degree of expertize and skill that are required to implement the proper strategy and workflow in order to successfully discovery and develop a therapeutic molecule with optimal properties.

References

[1] M.K. Bayliss, J. Butler, P.L. Feldman, D.V.S. Green, P.D. Leeson, M.R. Palovich, A.J. Taylor, Quality guidelines of oral drug candidates: dose, solubility and lipophilicity, Drug Discov. Today 21 (2016) 1719−1727.

[2] D. Cook, D. Brown, R. Alexander, R. March, P. Morgan, G. Satterthwaite, M.N. Pangalos, Lessons learned from the fate of AstraZeneca's drug pipeline: a five-dimensional framework, Nat. Rev. Drug Discov. 13 (2014) 419−431.

[3] P. Morgan, P.H. Van Der Graaf, J. Arrowsmith, D.E. Feltner, K.S. Drummond, C.D. Wegner, S.D.A. Street, Can the flow of medicines be improved? Fundamental pharmacokinetic and pharmacological principles toward improving phase II survival, Drug Discov. Today 17 (2012) 419−424.

[4] E.T. Hellriegel, T.D. Bjornsson, W.W. Hauck, Interpatient variability in bioavailability is related to the extent of absorption: implications for bioavailability and bioequivalence studies, Clin. Pharm. Ther. 60 (1996) 601−607.

[5] P. Ballard, P. Brassil, K.H. Bui, C. Petersson, A. Tunek, P.J.H. Webborn, The right compound in the right assay at the right time: an integrated discovery DMPK strategy, Drug Metab. Rev. 44 (3) (2012) 224−252.

[6] V.H. Thomas, S. Bhattachar, L. Hitchingham, P. Zocharski, M. Naath, N. Surendran, C.L. Stoner, A. El-Kattan, The road map to oral bioavailability: an industrial perspective, Expet Opin. Drug Metabol. Toxicol. 2 (2006) 591−608.

[7] H. Musther, A. Olivares-Morales, O.J.D. Hatley, B. Liu, A. Rostami-Hodjegan, Animal versus human oral drug bioavailability: do they correlate? Eur. J. Pharmaceut. Sci. 57 (2014) 280−291.

[8] X. Cao, S.T. Gibbs, L. Fang, H.A. Miller, C.P. Landowski, H.-C. Shin, H. Lennernas, Y. Zhong, G.L. Amidon, L.X. Yu, D. Sun, Why is it challenging to predict intestinal drug absorption and oral bioavailability in human using rat model? Pharm. Res. 23 (2006) 1675−1686.

[9] W.L. Chiou, A. Barve, Linear correlation of the fraction of oral dose absorbed of 64 drugs between humans and rats, Pharm. Res. 15 (1998) 1792−1795.

[10] J.M. DeSesso, A.L. Williams, Chapter 21 − contrasting the gastrointestinal tracts of mammals: factors that influence absorption, Annu. Rep. Med. Chem. 43 (2008) 353−371.

[11] M. Takahashi, T. Washio, N. Suzuki, K. Igeta, S.J. Yamashita, The species differences of intestinal drug absorption and first-pass metabolism between cynomolgus monkeys and humans, J. Pharm. Sci. 98 (2009) 4343−4353.

[12] W. Chiou, C. Ma, S.M. Chung, T. Wu, H.Y. Jeong, Similarity in the linear and non-linear oral absorption of drugs between human and rat, Int. J. Clin. Pharmacol. Ther. 38 (2000) 532−539.

[13] M.N. Martinez, A. El-Kattan, E. Awji, M. Papich, Reconciling human-canine differences in oral bioavailability: looking beyond the biopharmaceutics classification system, AAPS J. 21 (2019) 99.

[14] K.H. Grime, P. Barton, D.F. McGinnity, Application of in silico, in vitro and preclinical pharmacokinetic data for the effective and efficient prediction of human pharmacokinetics, Mol. Pharm. 10 (2013) 1191−1206.

[15] A. Sjoberg, M. Lutz, C. Tannergren, C. Wingolf, A. Borde, A.-L. Ungell, Comprehensive study on regional human intestinal permeability and prediction of fraction absorbed of drugs using the Ussing chamber technique, Eur. J. Pharmaceut. Sci. 48 (2013) 166−180.

[16] G.L. Amidon, H. Lennernas, V.P. Shah, J.R. Crison, A theoretical basis for a biopharmaceutic Drug Classification: the correlation of in vitro drug product dissolution and in vivo bioavailability, Pharm. Res. 12 (1995) 413−420.

[17] L.Z. Benet, The role of BCS (biopharmaceutics classification system) and BDDCS (biopharmaceutics drug disposition classification system) in drug development, Pharmaceut. Sci. 102 (2013) 34−42.

[18] P.B. Shekhawat, V.B. Pokharkar, Understanding peroral absorption: regulatory aspects and contemporary approaches to tackling solubility and permeability hurdles, Acta Pharm. Sin. B 7 (2017) 260−280.

[19] J.A. Cook, H. Bockbrader, An industrial implementation of the biopharmaceutics classification system, Dissolution Technol. 9 (2002) 6−9.

[20] J.A. Cook, B.M. Davis, J.E. Polli, Impact of biopharmaceutics classification system-based biowaivers, Mol. Pharm. 7 (2010) 1539−1544.

[21] C. Saal, A.C. Petereit, Optimizing solubility: kinetic versus thermodynamic solubility temptations and risks, Eur. J. Pharmaceut. Sci. 47 (2012) 589−595.

[22] M.V. Varma, I. Gardner, S.J. Steyn, P. Nkansah, C.J. Rotter, C. Whitney-Pickett, H. Zhang, L. Di, M. Cram, K.S. Fenner, A.F. El-Kattan, pH-Dependent solubility and permeability criteria for provisional biopharmaceutics classification (BCS and BDDCS) in early drug discovery, Mol. Pharm. 9 (2012) 1199−1212.

[23] P. Artursson, K. Palm, K. Luthman, Caco-2 monolayers in experimental and theoretical predictions of drug transport, Adv. Drug Deliv. Rev. 46 (2001) 27−43.

[24] A.-L. Ungell, P. Artursson, in: H. Van de Waterbeemd, B. Testa (Eds.), Drug Bioavailability, second ed., Wiley-VCH, Weinheim, Germany, 2009, pp. 133−159.

[25] A. Avdeef, The rise of PAMPA, Expet Opin. Drug Metabol. Toxicol. 1 (2005) 325−342.

[26] F. Tang, K. Horie, R.T. Borchardt, Are MDCK cells transfected with the human MDR1 gene a good model of the human intestinal mucosa? Pharm. Res. 19 (2002) 765–772.

[27] N.A. Meanwell, Improving drug candidates by design: a focus on physicochemical properties as a means of improving compound disposition and safety, Chem. Res. Toxicol. 24 (2011) 1420–1456.

[28] J. Dong, M.S. Park, Discussions on the hepatic well-stirred model: re-derivation from the dispersion model and re-analysis of the lidocaine data, Eur. J. Pharmaceut. Sci. 124 (2018) 46–60.

[29] L. Liu, K.S. Pang, An integrated approach to model hepatic drug clearance, Eur. J. Pharmaceut. Sci. 29 (2006) 215–230.

[30] J.K. Sodhi, H.-J. Wang, L.Z. Benet, Are there any experimental perfusion data that preferentially support the dispersion and parallel-tube models over the well-stirred model of organ elimination? Drug Metab. Dispos. 48 (2020) 537–543.

[31] R.S. Obach, J.G. Baxter, T.E. Liston, B.M. Silber, B.C. Jones, F. MacIntyre, D.J. Rance, P. Wastall, The prediction of human pharmacokinetic parameters from preclinical and in vitro metabolism data, J. Pharmacol. Exp. Therapeut. 283 (1997) 46–58.

[32] H. Hiraokah, K. Yamamoto, N. Okano, T. Morita, F. Goto, R. Horiuchi, Changes in drug plasma concentrations of an extensively bound and highly extracted drug, propofol, in response to altered plasma binding, Clin. Pharm. Ther. 75 (2004) 324–330.

[33] D.C. Kemp, P.W. Fan, J.C. Stevens, Characterization of raloxifene glucuronidation in vitro: contribution of intestinal metabolism to presystemic clearance, Drug Metab. Dispos. 30 (2002) 694–700.

[34] D. Westerling, C. Persson, P. Hoglund, Plasma concentrations of morphine, morphine-3-glucuronide, and morphine-6-glucuronide after intravenous and oral administration to healthy volunteers: relationship to nonanalgesic actions, Ther. Drug Monit. 17 (1995) 287–301.

[35] M.V.S. Varma, R.S. Obach, C. Rotter, H.R. Miller, G. Chang, S.J. Steyn, A. El-Kattan, M.D. Troutman, Physicochemical space for optimum oral bioavailability: contribution of human intestinal absorption and first-pass elimination, J. Med. Chem. 53 (2010) 1098–1108.

[36] Z.E. Barter, M.K. Bayliss, P.H. Beaunne, A.R. Boobis, D.J. Carlile, R.J. Edwards, J.B. Houston, B.G. Lake, J.C. Lipscomb, O.R. Pelkonen, G.T. Tucker, A. Rostami-Hodjegan, Scaling factors for the extrapolation of in vivo metabolic drug clearance from in vitro data: reaching a consensus on values of human microsomal protein and hepatocellularity per gram liver, Curr. Drug Metabol. 8 (2007) 33–45.

[37] M.B. Fisher, G. Laissiere, The role of the intestine in drug metabolism and pharmacokinetics: an industry perspective, Curr. Drug Metabol. 8 (2007) 694–699.

[38] C.R. Jones, O.J.D. Hatley, A.-L. Ungell, C. Hilgendorf, S.A. Peters, A. Rostami-Hodjegan, Gut wall metabolism: application of preclinical model for the prediction of human drug absorption and first pass metabolism, AAPS J. 18 (2016) 589–604.

[39] W. Lu, E. Rettenmeier, M. Paszek, M.-F. Yueh, R.H. Tukey, J. Trottier, O. Barbier, S. Chen, Crypt organoid culture as an in vitro model in drug metabolism and cytotoxicity studies, Drug Metab. Dispos. 45 (2017) 748–754.

[40] S.F. Vaessen, M.M. van Lipzig, R.H. Peters, C.A. Krul, H.M. Wortelboer, E. van de Steeg, Regional expression levels of drug transporters and metabolizing enzymes along the pig and human intestinal tract and comparison with Caco-2 cells, Drug Metab. Dispos. 45 (2017) 353–360.

[41] A.P. Li, N. Alam, K. Amaral, M.-C.D. Ho, C. Loretz, W. Mitchell, Q. Yang, Cryopreserved human intestinal mucosal epithelium: a novel in vitro experimental system for the evaluation of enteric drug metabolism, cytochrome P450 induction, and enterotoxicity, Drug Metab. Dispos. 46 (2018) 1562–1571.

[42] A. Sawant-Basak, R.S. Obach, Emerging models of drug metabolism, transporters, and toxicity, Drug Metab. Dispos. 46 (2018) 1556–1561.

[43] S. Wong, U. Doshi, P. Vuong, N. Liu, S. Tay, H. Le, M. Kosaka, J.R. Kenny, A.P. Li, Z. Yan, Utility of pooled cryopreserved human enterocytes as an in vitro model for assessing intestinal clearance and drug-drug interactions, Drug Metabol. Lett. 12 (2018) 3–13.

[44] T. Zietek, W.A.D. Boomgaarden, E. Rath, Drug screening, oral bioavailability, and regulatory aspects: a need for human organoids, Pharmaceutics 13 (2021) 1280.

[45] A.M. Calcagno, J.A. Ludwig, J.M. Fostel, M.M. Gottesman, S.V. Ambudkar, Comparison of drug transporter levels in normal colon, colon cancer, and Caco-2 cells: impact on drug disposition and discovery, Mol. Pharm. 3 (2006) 87–93.

[46] P. Matsson, C.A. Bergstrom, N. Nagahara, S. Tavelin, U. Norinder, P. Artursson, Exploring the role of different drug transport routes in permeability screening, J. Med. Chem. 48 (2005) 604–613.

[47] N. Jezyk, C. Li, B.H. Stewart, X. Wu, H.N. Bockbrader, D. Fleisher, Transport of pregabalin in rat intestine and Caco-2 monolayers, Pharm. Res. 16 (1999) 519–526.

[48] T. Takahashi, Organoids for drug discovery and personalized medicine, Annu. Rev. Pharmacol. Toxicol. 59 (2019) 447–462.

[49] A. Skardal, J. Aleman, S. Forsythe, S. Rajan, S. Murphy, M. Devarasetty, N. Pourhabibi Zarandi, G. Nzou, R. Wicks, H. Sadri-Ardekani, C. Bishop, S. Soker, A. Hall, T. Shupe, A. Atala, Drug compound screening in a single and integrated multi-organoid body-on-a-chip systems, Biofabrication 12 (2020) 025017.

[50] K.P. Van Ness, F. Cesar, C.K. Yeung, J. Himmelfarb, E.J. Kelly, Microphysiological systems in absorption, distribution, metabolism, and elimination sciences, Clin. Transl. Sci. 15 (2022) 9–42.

[51] C.A. Lipinski, F. Lombardo, B.W. Dominy, P.J. Feeney, Experimental and computational approaches to estimate solubility and permeability in drug discovery and development settings, Adv. Drug Deliv. Rev. 23 (1997) 3–25.

[52] C.A. Lipinski, Drug-like properties and the causes of poor solubility and poor permeability, J. Pharmacol. Toxicol. Methods 44 (2000) 235–249.

[53] D.F. Veber, S.R. Johnson, H.Y. Cheng, B.R. Smith, K.W. Ward, K.D. Kopple, Molecular properties that influence the oral bioavailability of drug candidates, J. Med. Chem. 45 (2002) 2615–2623.

[54] J.J. Lu, K. Crimin, J.T. Goodwin, P. Crivori, C. Orrenius, L. Xing, P.J. Tandler, T.J. Vidmar, B.M. Amore, A.G.E. Wilson, P.F.W. Stouten, P.S. Burton, Influence of molecular flexibility and polar surface area metrics on oral bioavailability in the rat, J. Med. Chem. 47 (2004) 6104–6107.

[55] S. Tian, Y. Li, J. Wang, J. Zhang, T. Hou, ADME evaluation in drug discovery. 9. Prediction of oral bioavailability in humans based on molecular properties and structural fingerprints, Mol. Pharm. 8 (2011) 841–851.

[56] T.R. Ritchie, S.J.F. Macdonald, The impact of aromatic ring count on compound developability – are too many aromatic rings a liability in drug design, Drug Discov. Today 14 (2009) 1011–1120.

[57] C. Hansch, J.P. Bjorkroth, A.J. Leo, Hydrophobicity and central nervous system agents: on the principle of minimal hydrophobicity in drug design, J. Pharm. Sci. 76 (1987) 663–687.

[58] M.J. Waring, Lipophilicity in drug discovery, Expert. Opin. Drug Discov. 5 (2010) 235–248.

[59] M.D. Wendt, The discovery of navitoclax, a Bcl-2 family inhibitor, in: Protein-Protein Interactions, part of the Topics in Medicinal Chemistry book series, volume 8, 2012, pp. 231–258.

[60] M.A. Cabrera-Perez, H. Pham-The, Computational modeling of human oral bioavailability: what will be next, Expet Opin. Drug Discov. 13 (2018) 509–521.

[61] H. Imawaka, K. Ito, Y. Kitamura, K. Sugiyama, Y. Sugiyama, Prediction of human bioavailability from human oral administration data and animal pharmacokinetic data without data from intravenous administration of drugs in human, Pharm. Res. 26 (2009) 1881–1889.

[62] Z. Wang, A. Yan, Q. Yuan, J. Gasteiger, Explorations into modeling human oral bioavailability, Eur. J. Med. Chem. 43 (2008) 2442–2452.

[63] M.A. Cabrera-Perez, H. Pharm-The, M. Bermejo, I.G. Alvarez, M.G. Alvarez, T.M. Garrigues, QSPR in oral bioavailability: specificity or integrality? Mini Rev. Med. Chem. 12 (2012) 534–550.

[64] P. Espie, D. Tytgat, M.-L. Sargentini-Maier, I. Poggesi, J.-B. Watelet, Physiologically based pharmacokinetics (PBPK), Drug Metab. Rev. 41 (2009) 391–407.

[65] P.P. Desai, A.A. Date, V.B. Patravale, Overcoming poor oral bioavailability using nanoparticle formulations – opportunities and limitations, Drug Discov. Today Technol. 9 (2012) e87–e95.

[66] P. Quan, K. Shi, H. Piao, H. Piao, N. Liang, D. Xia, F. Cui, A novel surface modified nitrendipine nanocrystals with enhancement of bioavailability and stability, Int. J. Pharm. 430 (2012) 366–371.

[67] N. Mennini, M. Bragagni, F. Maestrelli, P. Mura, Physicochemical characterization in solution and in the solid state of clonazepam complexes with native and chemically-modified cyclodextrins, J. Pharm. Biomed. Anal. 89 (2014) 142–149.

[68] P.J. Salustio, G. Feio, J.L. Figueirinhas, H.M. Cabral-Marques, P.C. Costa, J.F. Pinto, Release profile of ibuprofen in beta-cyclodextrin complexes from two different solid dosage forms, Powder Technol. 221 (2012) 245–251.

[69] A. Choudhary, A.C. Rana, G. Aggarwal, V. Kumar, F. Zakir, Development and characterization of an atorvastatin solid dispersion formulation using skimmed milk for improved bioavailability, Acta Pharm. Sin. B 2 (2012) 421–428.

[70] Y. Kawabata, K. Yamamoto, K. Debari, S. Onoue, S. Yamada, Novel crystalline solid dispersion of tranilast with high photostability and improved bioavailability, Eur. J. Pharmaceut. Sci. 39 (2010) 256–262.

[71] T. Yoshida, I. Kurimoto, K. Yoshihara, UmejimaH, N. Ito, S. Watanabe, K. Sako, A. Kikuchi, Aminoalkyl methacrylate copolymers for improving the solubility of tacrolimus. I: evaluation of solid dispersion formulations, Int. J. Pharm. 428 (2012) 18–24.

[72] F. Carriere, Impact of gastrointestinal lipolysis on oral lipid-based formulations and bioavailability of lipophilic drugs, Biochimie 125 (2016) 297–305.

[73] J.A. Yanez, S.W. Wang, I.W. Knemeyer, M.A. Wirth, K.B. Alton, Intestinal lymphatic transport for drug delivery, Adv. Drug Deliv. Rev. 63 (2011) 923–942.

[74] G.P. Kumar, P. Rajeshwarrao, Nonionic surfactant vesicular systems for effective drug delivery – an overview, Acta Pharm. Sin. B 1 (2011) 208–219.

[75] D. Pandita, S. Kumar, N. Poonia, V. Lather, Solid lipid nanoparticles enhance oral bioavailability of resveratrol, a natural polyphenol, Food Res. Int. 62 (2014) 1165–1174.

[76] A. Beloqui, M.A. Solinis, A.R. Gascon, A. del Pozo-Rodriguez, A. Rieux, V. Preat, Mechanism of transport of saquinavir-loaded nanostructured lipid carriers across the intestinal barrier, J. Contr. Release 166 (2013) 115–123.

[77] A. Patil-Gadhe, V. Pokharkar, Montelukast-loaded nanostructured lipid carriers: part I oral bioavailability improvement, Eur. J. Pharm. Biopharm. 88 (2014) 160–168.

[78] M.A. Videira, A.G. Arranja, L.F. Gouveia, Experimental design towards an optimal lipid nanosystem: a new opportunity for paclitaxel-based therapeutics, Eur. J. Pharmaceut. Sci. 49 (2013) 302–310.

Chapter 12

Case study of OATP1B DDI assessment and challenges in drug discovery and development—real-life examples

Hong Shen[a], Jinping Gan[a],* and Giridhar S. Tirucherai[b]

[a]Drug Metabolism and Pharmacokinetics, Bristol Myers Squibb Company, Lawrenceville, NJ, United States; [b]Clinical Pharmacology and Pharmacometrics, Bristol Myers Squibb Company, Lawrenceville, NJ, United States

Background

It is now widely understood that organic anion transporting polypeptides (OATP) 1B1 and OATP1B3, expressed on the sinusoidal membrane of the hepatocytes, play an important role in uptake of many clinically important anionic and zwitterionic drugs in hepatocytes [1–4]. OATP1B1 and OATP1B3 have been suggested to be important loci of drug-drug interactions (DDIs). Indeed, increased area under the plasma concentration-time curve (AUC) of statin drugs and greater risk of myopathy and rhabdomyolysis occurred in patients who received co-administration of OATP1B inhibitor gemfibrozil or those carrying decreased functional OATP1B1 genetic mutations [5,6]. Therefore, the ability to quantitatively predict OATP1B-mediated DDI is essential to minimize unexpected clinical study readouts and manage the associated adverse risks. However, unlike the prediction of DDIs involving cytochrome P450 (CYP) enzymes, there is a lack of reliable approaches for quantitative prediction of OATP1B-mediated DDIs although tremendous strides in several areas of drug transporters have been made in the last two decades.

A conservative risk assessment of OATP1B-mediated DDI is often made using a static model recommended by US Food and Drug Administration (FDA), European Medicines Agency (EMA), and Japanese Pharmaceutical and Medical Devices Agency (PMDA) (https://www.fda.gov/regulatory-information/search-fda-guidance-documents/vitro-drug-interaction-studies-cytochrome-p450-enzyme-and-transporter-mediated-drug-interactions; https://www.ema.europa.eu/en/documents/scientific-guideline/guideline-investigation-drug-interactions-revision-1_en.pdf; https://www.pmda.go.jp/files/000228122.pdf). This approach relies on the translatability of the in vitro inhibition potency measured by half-maximal inhibitory concentration (IC_{50}) or inhibition constant (K_i), in connection with predicted unbound maximum plasma liver inlet concentration ($I_{in,max,u}$) after oral administration of the inhibitor. According to the FDA final guidance published in January 2020, if an investigational drug is inhibiting OATP1B and its $I_{in,max,u}$ is equal to or greater than 10% of the IC_{50} value [i.e., the predicted ratio of OATP1B victim drug AUC in the presence and absence of inhibitor (R-value) (R-value $= 1 + I_{in,max,u}/IC_{50}) \geq 1.1$], then an in vivo OATP1B DDI risk is likely and a clinical DDI study using recommended probe drugs, such as rosuvastatin and atorvastatin, is recommended. Additionally, EMA recommends performing a dedicated OATP1B DDI study if K_i is less than or equal to a concentration of 25-fold the $I_{in,max,u}$ (i.e., R-value ≥ 1.04). Although these cutoff values generally minimize false-negative predictions, the method often yields high false-positive prediction rates [4], leading to unnecessary clinical DDI studies. Additionally, there is still no census on which unbound drug fraction (f_u) should be used for an investigational drug that binds to plasma protein highly (i.e., $f_u < 1\%$). According to regulatory guidance, the f_u should be set to 1% if it is determined to be <1%. However, it has been suggested that the experimentally determined f_u values may better describe free portal drug concentrations and OATP1B inhibition potential for highly plasma binding drugs [4]. On the other hand, a static model does not account for the

---

* Current affiliation: HiFiBiO Therapeutics, Cambridge, MA, United States

involvement of other mechanisms, such as CYP enzymes and intestinal breast cancer resistance protein (BCRP) and P-glycoprotein (P-gp), to the OATP1B DDIs. While the magnitudes of rosuvastatin DDIs were not captured satisfactorily by either OATP1B or the BCRP static model, the combined static model incorporating both OATP1B and BCRP inhibition provides a better approach to quantitatively predict the magnitude of transporter-mediated DDI for rosuvastatin [7,8]. Cynomolgus monkey is a valuable model to assess OATP1B DDI in drug discovery and development with many successful reports [9]. However, quantitative prediction of OATP1B DDIs is often hindered by species-dependent differences in the absorption, distribution, metabolism, and excretion of substrate and inhibitor drugs between monkey and human [10–13], therefore requiring data from OATP1B DDI studies using established probe drugs that share similar clearance mechanisms between the species [14,15]. Additionally, understanding the discrepancies related to the OATP1B inhibition properties, and inhibitor pharmacokinetic properties between species (e.g., achieving equivalent exposure, elimination routes, protein binding, metabolic profiles, etc.) could be valuable for cross-species translation.

BMS-919373

Atrial fibrillation (AF) is the most common type of sustained cardiac arrhythmia and is an important contributor to population morbidity and mortality. AF has an associated higher risk of stroke because of thromboembolism, and patients have reduced quality of life [16]. Bristol Myers Squibb (BMS)-919373 is an investigational IKur inhibitor for the treatment of AF [17]. Since patients with AF often receive statins, the substrates of OATP1B1 and OATP1B3, to manage cardiovascular complications [18], it is important to assess the OATP1B DDI risk for a new agent developed for this indication.

To investigate the potential of BMS-919373 to inhibit the human and cynomolgus monkey OATP1B1 and OATP1B3, a transporter inhibition study was performed using stably transfected human embryonic kidney (HEK) 293 cells that individually overexpressed human and cynomolgus monkey OATP1B1 and OATP1B3. The experiments are described in the previous publications by our laboratory [14,19,20], Initial assessment indicated that BMS-919373 was a potent inhibitor of human OATP1Bs. BMS-919373 inhibited human OATP1B1- and OATP1B3-mediated cellular uptake of rosuvastatin with IC_{50} of 0.24 ± 0.12 and 0.65 ± 0.30 μM, respectively, using human HEK293 cells overexpressing these transporter proteins (Table 12.1). Additionally, using [$^{3-}$H]estradiol-17β-glucuronide and [^{3}H]cholecystokinin-8 as a probe of OATP1B1 and OATP1B3, respectively, it was confirmed that BMS-919373 was a potent inhibitor of human OATP1B1 and OATP1B3, with IC_{50} of 0.49 ± 0.26 and 0.22 ± 0.11 μM, respectively (Table 12.1). These results mean that BMS-919373 might affect the clearance of OATP1B substrates, necessitating more detailed transporter studies in accordance with regulatory guidance.

Consequently, the uptake by HEK293 cells transfected with cynomolgus monkey OATP1B in the presence of various concentrations of BMS-919373 was evaluated. Derived IC_{50} values were comparable for OATP1B1 (0.24 ± 0.12 μM and 0.15 ± 0.08 μM) with respect to rosuvastatin uptake by human and monkey transporters (Table 12.1). However, there was approximately 3-fold difference in IC_{50} for OATP1B3 between the species (0.65 ± 0.30 μM and 2.2 ± 1.0 μM). In addition, the BMS-919373 IC_{50} values for human and monkey OATP1B1 (0.49 ± 0.26 μM and 0.22 ± 0.09 μM) and OATP1B3 (0.22 ± 0.11 μM and 0.76 ± 0.27 μM), using ^{3}[H]estradiol-17β-glucuronide and ^{3}[H]cholecystokinin-8 as

TABLE 12.1 IC_{50} (μM) for inhibition by BMS-919373 and cyclosporine A of rosuvastatin, ^{3}[H]estradiol-17β-glucuronide, and ^{3}[H]cholecystokinin-8 uptake by HEK293 cells transfected with individual human and monkey OATP1Bs.

Cell line	OATP1B1		OATP1B3	
	BMS-919373	Cyclosporine A	BMS-919373	Cyclosporine A
Rosuvastatin				
Human	0.24 ± 0.12	0.21 ± 0.10	0.65 ± 0.30	ND
Monkey	0.15 ± 0.08	0.28 ± 0.11	2.2 ± 1.0	ND
	[^{3}H]Estradiol-17β-glucuronide		[^{3}H]Cholecystokinin-8	
	BMS-919373	Cyclosporine A	BMS-919373	Cyclosporine A
Human	0.49 ± 0.26	0.39 ± 0.11	0.22 ± 0.11	0.1 ± 0.05
Monkey	0.22 ± 0.09	0.20 ± 0.07	0.76 ± 0.27	0.08 ± 0.01

ND, not done.

probe of OATP1B1 and OATP1B3, respectively, were generally similar to those determined using rosuvastatin (Table 12.1). These results confirm the appropriateness of the in vivo DDI comparison (see below).

The known human OATP1B inhibitor cyclosporine A reduced the probe uptake values in all OATP1B-expressing cells in a concentration-dependent manner: IC_{50} values for cyclosporine A on human OATP1B1 and OATP1B3 cells ranged from 0.08 to 0.39 μM (Table 12.1). The transporter inhibition by cyclosporine A indicated that human and monkey OATP1B1/HEK and OATP1B3/HEK cell lines were functioning as expected under the conditions used for the evaluation of OATP1B inhibition in this study.

Estimation of drug interaction potential for BMS-919373 using in vitro data

The assessment using mechanistic static model suggested that the OATP1B drug interaction potential for BMS-919373 was significant (Table 12.2). In these calculations, several factors contribute to the complexity in the risk assessment of human and monkey OATP1B DDI between BMS-919373 and OATP1B substrates using the R-value approach. First, BMS-919373 is highly bound to plasma protein(s), with a free fraction (f_u) of less than 1%. BMS-919373 was 99.4% bound to cynomolgus monkey serum proteins and 99.7% bound to human serum proteins. Depending on whether the default or experimental f_u was used (1% and 0.3%, respectively), the R-value varied significantly (1.4 vs. 1.1). Second, there were considerable species-dependent differences in the absorption, distribution, metabolism and excretion of BMS-919373. For example, the apparent clearance following oral administration of BMS-919373 in humans was significantly smaller than monkeys. Lastly, the in vitro inhibition potential of BMS-919373 toward human and monkey OATP1Bs were different although the difference in IC_{50} is less than approximately 3-fold (Table 12.1).

To predict the DDI potential for BMS-919373, we used the f_u value of 1% recommended by FDA and EMA. This value provides an R-value, based on clinical efficacious dose of 30 mg BMS-919373, of 1.4 in humans (Table 12.2). Since the clearance rate for BMS-919373 is relatively high in monkeys compared to humans, the R-values, for doses in the monkey targeting the clinical C_{max} and $I_{in,max}$ in humans for a clinical dose of 30 mg, are predicted to be 9.1 and 1.4, respectively (Table 12.2). The R-value based on $I_{in,max}$ in monkeys for a 1 mg/kg dose that targeted similar portal vein exposures in the monkey as the human clinical dose was similar to that in human. These values suggest that the DDI potential is high, as an R-value of 1.1 or 1.04 could result in clinically significant drug interactions. Due to the uncertainty mentioned above, to better quantitate the potential DDI risk between BMS-919373 and OATP1B substrates, we performed a series of translational studies utilizing in vivo monkey studies targeting either human equivalent systemic exposure or portal vein concentration, and finally a clinical study with both rosuvastatin and atorvastatin, two widely prescribed statins that are substrates of the OATP1B transporter.

Pharmacokinetcs of rosuvastatin and BMS-919373 in cynomolgus monkeys

Based on in vitro IC_{50} values and the static R-value approach, predicted DDI for rosuvastatin coadministration were 9.1 at a dose of 20 mg/kg in monkeys (Table 12.2). This dose was anticipated to generate the human equivalent maximum systemic concentration in monkeys as an oral dose of 30 mg in humans and the projected R-values in both monkeys and humans indicated the need for an in vivo study. Four male cynomolgus monkeys aged 2–6 years were used in all studies. We used a 3-period cross-over design with at least a 1-week washout period to determine the inhibitory effect of BMS-919373 on the pharmacokinetics of rosuvastatin. BMS-919373 vehicle (61.5% polyethylene glycol 400, 8.5% Tween 80, 20% α-tocopherol polyethylene glycol 1000 succinate, and 10% propylene glycol) was administered orally on day 1. Oral

TABLE 12.2 C_{max} and predicted R-values for the BMS-919373 doses used in the monkey and human.

Species	Dose	C_{max} (μM)	$f_u{}^a$ (%)	Predicted $I_{in,max}$ (μM)	Estimated R-value
Monkey	20 mg/kg	12.3	1	111.2	9.1
Monkey	1.0 mg/kg	0.5	1	5.45	1.4
Human	30 mg	6.0	1	10.27	1.4
Human	30 mg	6.0	0.3	10.27	1.1

C_{max}, maximum plasma concentration; $I_{in,max}$, predicted unbound maximum plasma liver inlet concentration.
^{a}In these calculations, the unbound fractions (f_{iu}) were set to 1% although the determined f_{iu} values of BMS-919373 were <1% (0.6% and 0.3% in monkey and human serum samples, respectively).

doses of BMS-919373 of 20 mg/kg were given on day 8, and doses of 1 mg/kg BMS-919373 on day 34. One hour (h) after each dose of BMS-919373 or vehicle, each animal received rosuvastatin 3 mg/kg dissolved in water by oral gavage followed by a sterile water rinse. Blood was withdrawn to determine plasma concentrations of rosuvastatin and BMS-919373, at 0.25, 0.5, 0.75, 1, 2, 3, 5, 7, 24, and 48 h after each rosuvastatin dose in K2-EDTA-containing tubes, centrifuged for 3 min at 13,000 rpm, and the resultant plasma stored at $-20°C$ until bioanalysis.

(A) BMS-919373 20 mg/kg

Following an oral dose of 20 mg/kg BMS-919373 in the cynomolgus monkeys, plasma concentrations reached maximum concentration (C_{max}) of 12.3 µM, with a time to C_{max} (T_{max}) of 5.5 h. The area under the concentration versus time curve over a 48-h ($AUC_{(0-48h)}$) period was 245 ± 79.3 µM h. The C_{max} of BMS-919373 following the 20 mg/kg dose was approximately 2-fold greater than that of a 30 mg daily dose in human subjects (i.e., 12.3 vs. 6.0 µM, Table 12.2). In contrast, the predicted maximum plasma liver inlet concentration ($I_{in,max}$) of BMS-919373 in the monkey after a 20 mg/kg dose was 111.2 µM, whereas in humans after a 30 mg dose, it was estimated to be 10.27 µM, an order of magnitude lower (Table 12.2).

When BMS-919373 was administered 1 h before the dosing of rosuvastatin in the monkey, the rosuvastatin C_{max} increased from 10.1 ± 9.9 to 144.6 ± 63.5 nM and the rosuvastatin $AUC_{(0-48h)}$ increased by 11.5-fold (Table 12.3). The extent of increase in systemic exposure to rosuvastatin following pre-treatment with BMS-919373 20 mg/kg confirmed the strong inhibition of both OATP1B1 and 1B3 observed in vitro. In addition, the observed increases were in the range of projected increases for the co-administration based on the static R-value approach (11.5 vs. 9.1).

(B) BMS-919373 1 mg/kg

Given that the magnitude of increase in rosuvastatin exposure based on targeting human equivalent systemic concentrations was large (i.e., $\sim 12\times$), we then assessed the interaction with a lower dose (i.e., a 1 mg/kg dose) of BMS-919373 in monkeys. This dose was chosen to produce a predicted portal vein concentration in monkeys that was much closer to that in humans (Table 12.2).

When rosuvastatin was administered in combination with BMS-919373 1 mg/kg, the mean systemic concentrations were still greater than when rosuvastatin was administered alone (Fig. 12.1), but these increases were much less than those seen with 20 mg/kg BMS-919373. The rosuvastatin C_{max} was increased from 10.1 ± 9.9 to 41.5 ± 63.7 nM using a dose of 1 mg/kg BMS-919373. The resulting $AUC_{(0-48h)}$ ratio was 2.22-fold higher than rosuvastatin alone following coadministration of BMS-919373 1 mg/kg (Table 12.3).

Pharmacokinetics of statins and BMS-919373 in human subjects

This single-center, open-label, single sequence, drug-interaction study (Clinicaltrials.gov; NCT02089061) was approved by the IntegReview LTD Institutional Review Board/Independent Ethics Committee (Austin, TX USA). The study was

TABLE 12.3 Pharmacokinetic parameters (mean ± SD) of single-dose rosuvastatin 3 mg/kg in cynomolgus monkeys ($n = 4$) administered with and without oral doses of BMS-919373 1 mg/kg or 20 mg/kg.

	BMS-919373 dose (mg/kg)		
Parameter	0	1	20
C_{max} (nM)	10.1 ± 9.89	41.5 ± 63.7[a]	144.6 ± 63.5[a]
Fold change (90% CI)	–	2.95 (1.02–5.80)	26.0 (5.4–56.9)
$AUC_{(0-48h)}$ (nM·h)	105 ± 57	206 ± 121[a]	944 ± 290[a]
Fold change (90% CI)	–	2.22 (0.97–3.94)	11.5 (4.2–22.3)
T_{max} (h)	1.81 ± 2.14	3.50 ± 2.52	3.75 ± 1.50

$AUC_{(0-48h)}$, area under the plasma rosuvastatin concentration-time curve from time of dosing to 48 h; C_{max}, maximum plasma rosuvastatin concentration; CI, confidence interval; SD, standard deviation.
[a]P < .05, Student's t-test comparing the pharmacokinetic parameters between coadministration of BMS-919373 and rosuvastatin with rosuvastatin alone.

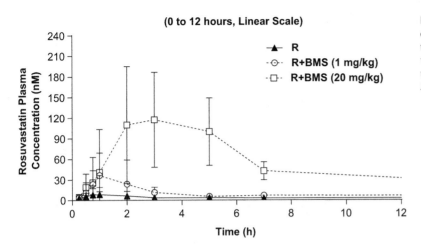

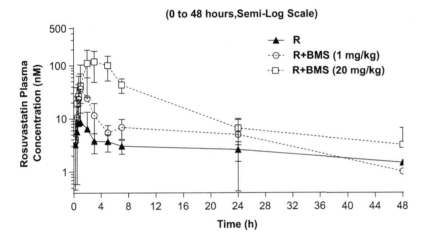

FIGURE 12.1 Mean plasma concentration of single-dose rosuvastatin in cynomolgus monkeys ($n = 4$) after a single oral dose of rosuvastatin 3 mg/kg with and without oral doses of BMS-919373 (1 and 20 mg/kg) up to 12 (up panel) and 48 h (down panel) postdose. *BMS*, BMS-919373; *R*, rosuvastatin.

conducted at PPD Development, LP (Austin, TX, USA), and undertaken in compliance with the Good Clinical Practice guidelines of the International Conference on Harmonization of Technical Requirements for Registration of Pharmaceuticals for Human Use and the principles of the Declaration of Helsinki. Consenting healthy male and female subjects aged 18−55 years with a body mass index of 18−32 kg/m² underwent screening up to 21 days prior to day -2, were admitted to the clinical facility on day -2, and remained confined to the clinical facility until discharge on day 10. They received either rosuvastatin 10 mg (CRESTOR®, AstraZeneca) or atorvastatin 40 mg (LIPITOR®, Pfizer, Inc.) as single oral doses on day 1 followed by a loading dose of BMS-919373 100 mg as a suspension on day 4. On day 5, all patients received their assigned statin dose plus BMS-919373 30 mg. Patients were then maintained on BMS-919373 30 mg on days 6 and 7 without further statin administration. All doses of study drug were administered after an overnight fast of ≥10 h and subjects continued to fast until 4 h after each study drug administration. Blood samples were collected from before study drug administration and at regular intervals for up to 120 h after study drug administration.

Of the 55 subjects who enrolled in the clinical study, 26 subjects entered the treatment period (13 subjects in each cohort). All 13 subjects in the rosuvastatin and atorvastatin cohort received all study treatments and completed the study. Most subjects were men (96.2%), 57.7% were white, 42.3% were black, and the mean age was 34 years (range, 21−52 years). Subject demographics at baseline were similar across both cohorts.

After administration of rosuvastatin 10 mg in combination with BMS-919373 30 mg, plasma rosuvastatin concentrations increased compared to administration of rosuvastatin alone (Fig. 12.2A). Geometric mean rosuvastatin C_{max}, $AUC_{(0-T)}$, and $AUC_{(0-\infty)}$ values were all higher in the presence of BMS-919373 (Table 12.4). The ratio of geometric means of rosuvastatin pharmacokinetic parameters (rosuvastatin plus BMS-919373 vs. rosuvastatin alone) was used as an estimate of relative systemic exposure. C_{max}, $AUC_{(0-T)}$, and $AUC_{(0-\infty)}$ values were 38%, 47%, and 45% higher in the presence of

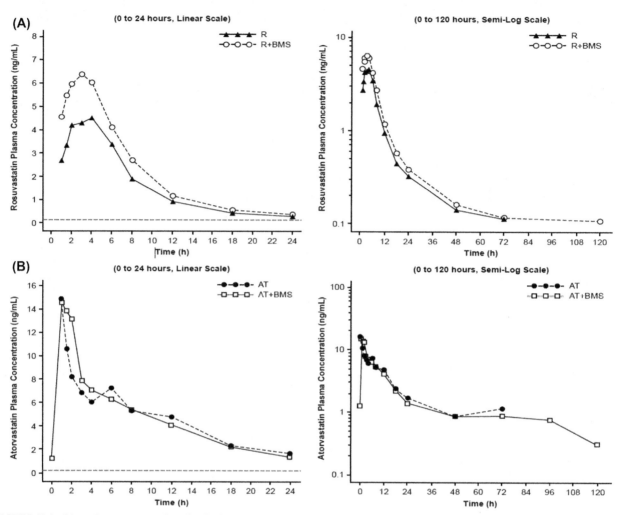

FIGURE 12.2 Mean plasma concentration of statins in the presence and absence of BMS-919373 up to 24 (left panel) and 120 h (right panel) postdose. (A) Rosuvastatin and (B) Atorvastatin in healthy volunteers ($n = 12$ per group). *AT*, atorvastatin; *BMS*, BMS-919373; *R*, rosuvastatin.

BMS-919373 (Table 12.4). The observed increases in *AUC* for rosuvastatin were consistent with the projected increases in humans (*R*-value of 1.4) using the static model and estimated portal vein concentrations.

BMS-919373 did not influence the pharmacokinetics of atorvastatin to the same extent as it did rosuvastatin (Fig. 12.2B). Table 12.4 shows that the atorvastatin C_{max} value was 18% higher in the presence of BMS-919373, although total systemic exposure (based on *AUC* values) to atorvastatin was unaffected by BMS-919373 coadministration.

Safety

Five of thirteen subjects (38.5%) in the rosuvastatin group and four of thirteen subjects (30.8%) in the atorvastatin group experienced ≥ 1 adverse effect (AE). The most frequently reported AE was diarrhea, reported by two subjects (15.4%) after rosuvastatin and BMS-919373 were coadministered. Most AEs reported were of mild intensity, and all AEs resolved by the end of the study. There were no notable findings or trends in clinical laboratory, ECG, 24-h telemetry, vital signs, or physical examination results. No deaths or serious AEs occurred during the study, and no subjects were discontinued from the study due to AEs.

Discussion

Collective findings from current preclinical and clinical studies confirmed the inhibitory effects of BMS-919373 on OATP1B-mediated hepatic uptake of statins and the translational value of monkey OATP1B DDI model. First, in

TABLE 12.4 Summary of plasma pharmacokinetic parameters of rosuvastatin and atorvastatin following the administration of each statin alone (day 1) and coadministered with BMS-919373 (day 5) in healthy volunteers.

Parameter	Rosuvastatin 10 mg alone ($n = 13$)	Rosuvastatin 10 mg + BMS-919373 30 mg ($n = 13$)	Atorvastatin 40 mg alone ($n = 13$)	Atorvastatin 40 mg + BMS-919373 30 mg ($n = 13$)
C_{max} (ng/mL)	4.63 (34)	6.40 (31)	13.5 (69)	15.9 (69)
Fold change (90% CI)[*]	1.38 (1.16−1.64)		1.18 (1.01−1.37)	
T_{max} (h)	4.0 (2.0−6.0)	3.00 (1.0−6.1)	1.00 (1.0−6.0)	1.0 (1.0−2.0)
$AUC_{(0-T)}$ (ng·h/mL)	38.7 (38)	56.8 (25)	81.6 (157)	82.9 (160)
Fold change (90% CI)[*]	1.47 (1.27−1.71)		1.02 (0.93−1.11)	
$AUC_{(0-\infty)}$ (ng·h/mL)	41.9 (36)	60.6 (25)	85.5 (159)	86.5 (157)
Fold change (90% CI)[*]	1.45 (1.26−1.67)		1.01 (0.93−1.10)	
$t_{1/2}$ (h)	12.9 (7.38)	17.2 (8.19)	8.93 (3.34)	9.88 (4.32)
CL_T/F (mL/min)	3981 (34)	2752 (26)	7793 (62)	7711 (52)

Data are geometric mean (geometric CV [%]) for C_{max}, AUCs, and CL_T/F, median (range) for T_{max}, and mean (SD) for $t_{1/2}$.
A linear mixed-effects model with treatment as a fixed effect and subject as repeated measures was fitted to the log-transformed pharmacokinetic parameters for use in estimation of effects and construction of CIs.
$AUC_{(0-T)}$, area under the plasma statin concentration-time curve from the time of dosing to the last quantifiable concentration; $AUC_{(0-\infty)}$, AUC from time of dosing extrapolated to infinity; CL_T/F, apparent total plasma clearance after oral dosing; C_{max}, maximum observed statin concentration; $t_{1/2}$, apparent terminal elimination half-life; T_{max}, time to reach C_{max}.
*$P < 0.05$ statistically significantly different from the pharmacokinetic parameter in statin alone.

transfected cell systems, BMS-919373 was an in vitro inhibitor of human and cynomolgus monkey OATP1B1 and OATP1B3 based on IC_{50} values required to inhibit the uptake of rosuvastatin, estradiol-17β-glucuronide, and cholecystokinin-8 (Table 12.1). The calculated R-factor based on the IC_{50} values and estimated efficacious dose (i.e., 30 mg) indicated a modest risk of a DDI between BMS-919373 and statins in humans (i.e., $R = 1.4$) (Table 12.2). A monkey model was then nevertheless deployed to monitor disposition of rosuvastatin in the presence and absence of BMS-919373 at doses targeting human equivalent systemic or portal vein concentrations that revealed a significant difference in rosuvastatin $AUC_{(0\ 48h)}$ ratio (11.5 vs. 2.22) (Table 12.3). Finally, the clinical DDI studies between BMS-919373 and statins demonstrated 1.47- and 1.02-fold increase of the $AUC_{(0-T)}$ of rosuvastatin and atorvastatin, respectively (Table 12.4).

Given the differences in pharmacokinetics between monkeys and humans, the dose that generated similar systemic concentrations in monkeys and humans also generated 10.8-fold greater portal vein concentrations in monkeys relative to humans (Table 12.2). Therefore, an approach for an in vivo study in monkeys where the dose was selected to achieve similar systemic exposures in monkeys and humans grossly over-estimated the magnitude of a potential clinical interaction (11.5-fold vs. 1.02- to 1.47-fold AUC changes) (Tables 12.3 and 12.4). When followed up with a dose that generated similar portal vein concentrations (estimated) in monkeys and humans, the magnitude of the interaction was much less (2.22-fold vs. 1.02- to 1.47-fold AUC changes). This study demonstrated that understanding and accounting for species-dependent differences in pharmacokinetics is important in translational DDI studies. This study, when performed at doses targeting similar systemic concentrations, indicated severe risk of interactions, and could have potentially stopped development of the molecule if the DDI assessment was not performed at a lower dose targeting similar portal vein concentrations. Therefore, while studying a dose that generates similar systemic concentrations in monkey as in humans would seem logical and conservative, it is important to be aware of the false positive signal that could come with this approach, based on the potential differences between monkey and human pharmacokinetics. This case study showed that targeting similar portal vein concentrations in monkeys as in humans is not only important for the sake of translational value of the DDI studies, but also important to avoid a false no-go signal during early development. These results support the use of free maximum portal vein concentration for OATP1B DDI prediction [4,21].

Another important concept is the impact of plasma protein binding on transporter DDI prediction [22,23]. Specifically, the use of unbound fraction of 1%, instead of experimentally determined unbound fraction for highly protein bound drugs, remains controversial within the pharmaceutical industry. The FDA final guidance for drug interaction studies published in January 2020 recommended that the unbound fraction should be set to 1% if actually determined to be <1% since nonspecific binding could be considered also in testing systems. This case study provides some insight into the utility of using unbound concentrations in OATP1B DDI analyses. Table 12.2 shows the R-values when f_u of 1% is used with IC_{50} values from different OATP1B cell models. Assuming that the free maximum portal vein drug concentration hypothesis is appropriate, experimentally determined f_u provides a worse estimate of the DDI magnitude compared to the assumed f_u value. Using the determined f_u values obtained from serum protein binding experiment, a R-value of 1.1 would be calculated for human OATP1B DDI whereas those of 3.2 and 1.1 for 20 and 1 mg/kg BMS-919373, respectively, are estimated in monkeys, resulting in a under-prediction in DDI potential compared to observed DDIs in humans and monkeys (Tables 12.3 and 12.4). Since it takes time (e.g., 10 h) for a highly plasma bound drug to reach binding equilibrium following oral absorption [24], it may be reasonable to use f_u of 1% for the OATP1B estimation of highly protein bound drugs. It is worth noting that the increase in rosuvastatin C_{max} is greater than that of rosuvastatin $AUC_{(0\ 48h)}$ by 20 mg/kg BMS-919373 in monkeys (26.0-fold vs. 11.5-fold) (Table 12.3). The inhibition potential of BMS-919373 toward cynomolgus monkey BCRP has not been assessed.

The phase 1 clinical study results showed that inhibition of OATP1B1 and OATP1B3 by BMS-919373 may have consequences for the pharmacokinetics of some xenobiotics that are eliminated primarily by the hepatobiliary system, thereby affecting their efficacy and/or toxicity. However, in this study, the extent of increase in statin exposure due to coadministration of BMS-919373 30 mg/day in humans was modest and did not represent a safety concern from the standpoint of concomitant statin use. In the monkey, the difference between BMS-919373 1 mg/kg, mimicking the portal vein concentration, and 20 mg/kg to achieve the estimated systemic C_{max} in humans, confirmed the importance of drug concentration at the site of action (portal vein), reconfirming the usefulness of static R-value calculation.

An established limitation of detecting and quantifying OATP1B-mediated DDIs is the lack of specific inhibitors or probes needed to dissect the relative contribution of transporters affecting drug uptake while at the same time controlling for oxidative metabolism [25]. Our clinical results with atorvastatin and rosuvastatin were important in this regard, as rosuvastatin is eliminated primarily in the feces by transporter-mediated biliary excretion of unchanged drug while atorvastatin undergoes a significant amount of CYP-mediated metabolism [7,26]. While it is important to discharge the risk of a signal during early development using a sensitive substrate like rosuvastatin to inform on the maximum increase in exposure of statins, it is likewise important to determine if these effects may be mitigated by the use of other statins (such as atorvastatin) that are substrates of OATP1B and oxidative metabolism enzymes. In such instances, the use of a different statin may provide an alternative path for development, should a more acceptable profile be observed, although OATP1B-mediated transport may be the rate-determining step for statin hepatic clearance. In fact, in our clinical DDI study of BMS-919373 and atorvastatin, a relatively smaller increase in atorvastatin than in rosuvastatin exposure due to BMS-919373 coadministration in humans was observed, with little to no change in exposure.

The monkey model is able to calibrate human OATP1B IVIVE and thus translate in vitro inhibition to in vivo DDI predictions [9,14,15,19,27−30]. However, further understanding of the absorption, distribution, metabolism, and excretion of the investigational drug under study is required in both species (monkey and human), as significant inter-species differences in drug disposition may result in incorrect predictions, especially where differences in intestinal metabolism and bioavailability may exist [10,13,31] (Fig. 12.3). Nevertheless, as long as the species-dependent differences are understood, they can be accounted for when translating monkey data to clinical outcomes [9]. The differences would be used for mechanism-informed understanding when the monkey model is not applicable. Our results in this case study emphasize the importance of targeting the portal vein concentration rather than the systemic concentration for studying compounds metabolized in the hepatic system (Tables 12.2, 12.3, and 12.4).

While in this study OATP1B monkey model was used to assess in vivo OATP1B inhibition, endogenous biomarkers such coproporphyrin I (CPI) are also emerging as useful tool to offer insight and gain confidence in quantitative OATP1B DDI predictions [32−34]. It has been reported that biomarker model-based approach provides prospective predictions of OATP1B DDIs. The robust signal of CPI in tracking OATP1B activity supports its utility in verifying in vivo OATP1B inhibition, which can then enable reliable quantitative predictions of DDIs with probe drugs or comedications

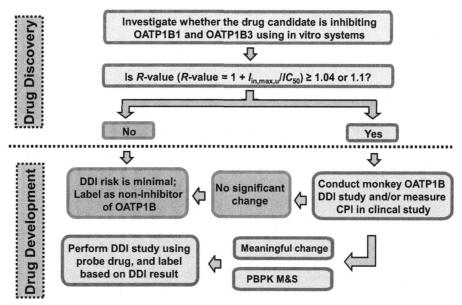

FIGURE 12.3 A schematic of OATP1B DDI risk assessment in drug development based on the current learning from mechanistic static, monkey model, endogenous biomarker, and PBPK analyses. R-value cutoff is based on FDA and EMA recommended criteria. Obtaining monkey pharmacokinetic DDI and clinical CPI data, and subsequent PBPK modeling and simulation may help predict clinical OATP1B inhibition risk. *CPI*, coproporphyrin I; *DDI*, drug-drug interaction; *EMA*, European Medicines Agency; *FDA*, US Food and Drug Administration; *OATP*, organic anion transporting polypeptide; *R-value*, the predicted ratio of OATP1B victim drug *AUC* in the presence and absence of inhibitor.

(e.g., statins). Identification and validation of endogenous biomarkers of OATP1B and physiologically-based pharmacokinetic modeling (still not matured) are important developmental tools for OATP1B DDI predictions in the future (Fig. 12.3).

Conclusion

BMS-919373 is a potent in vitro inhibitor of OATP1B1 and OATP1B3. While assessing the risk of potential interaction with OATP1B substrates in humans, IVIVE translation in cynomolgus monkeys was utilized to further elucidate the translational value of the monkey model in OATP1B inhibition risk assessment. Our findings emphasize the translational value of the cynomolgus monkey OATP1B DDI model in complementing the static mathematic IVIVE approach, but also stresses the need for appropriate dose selection approaches to inform the actual risk in clinical development. In addition, our study demonstrates the importance of selecting the proper probe substrates, especially during early development, so as to avoid making a no-go decision based on observations for one probe that may not apply for all.

References

[1] M. Niemi, Role of OATP transporters in the disposition of drugs, Pharmacogenomics 8 (7) (2007) 787—802.

[2] Y. Shitara, K. Maeda, K. Ikejiri, K. Yoshida, T. Horie, Y. Sugiyama, Clinical significance of organic anion transporting polypeptides (OATPs) in drug disposition: their roles in hepatic clearance and intestinal absorption, Biopharm Drug Dispos. 34 (1) (2013) 45—78.

[3] K. Maeda, Organic anion transporting polypeptide (OATP)1B1 and OATP1B3 as important regulators of the pharmacokinetics of substrate drugs, Biol. Pharmaceut. Bull. 38 (2) (2015) 155—168.

[4] J. Vaidyanathan, K. Yoshida, V. Arya, L. Zhang, Comparing various in vitro prediction criteria to assess the potential of a new molecular entity to inhibit organic anion transporting polypeptide 1B1, J. Clin. Pharmacol. 56 (Suppl. 7) (2016) S59—S72.

[5] S.C. Group, E. Link, S. Parish, J. Armitage, L. Bowman, S. Heath, F. Matsuda, I. Gut, M. Lathrop, R. Collins, SLCO1B1 variants and statin-induced myopathy–a genomewide study, N. Engl. J. Med. 359 (8) (2008) 789—799.

[6] J.T. Backman, C. Kyrklund, M. Neuvonen, P.J. Neuvonen, Gemfibrozil greatly increases plasma concentrations of cerivastatin, Clin. Pharmacol. Therap. 72 (6) (2002) 685—691.

[7] R. Sane, K.W.K. Cheung, P. Kovacs, T. Farasyn, R. Li, A. Bui, L. Musib, E. Kis, E. Plise, Z. Gaborik, Calibrating the in vitro-in vivo correlation for OATP-mediated drug-drug interactions with rosuvastatin using static and PBPK models, Drug Metab. Disposition Biol. Fate Chem. 48 (12) (2020) 1264—1270.

[8] C. Costales, J. Lin, E. Kimoto, S. Yamazaki, J.R. Gosset, A.D. Rodrigues, S. Lazzaro, M.A. West, M. West, M.V.S. Varma, Quantitative prediction of breast cancer resistant protein mediated drug-drug interactions using physiologically-based pharmacokinetic modeling, CPT Pharmacometrics Syst. Pharmacol. 10 (9) (2021) 1018−1031.

[9] H. Shen, Z. Yang, A.D. Rodrigues, Cynomolgus monkey as an emerging animal model to study drug transporters: in vitro, in vivo, in vitro-to-in vivo translation, Drug Metab. Disposition Biol. Fate Chem. 50 (2021) 299−319.

[10] T. Akabane, K. Tabata, K. Kadono, S. Sakuda, S. Terashita, T. Teramura, A comparison of pharmacokinetics between humans and monkeys, Drug Metab. Disposition Biol. Fate Chem. 38 (2) (2010) 308−316.

[11] C. Emoto, N. Yoda, Y. Uno, K. Iwasaki, K. Umehara, E. Kashiyama, H. Yamazaki, Comparison of p450 enzymes between cynomolgus monkeys and humans: p450 identities, protein contents, kinetic parameters, and potential for inhibitory profiles, Curr. Drug Metabol. 14 (2) (2013) 239−252.

[12] L. Wang, B. Prasad, L. Salphati, X. Chu, A. Gupta, C.E. Hop, R. Evers, J.D. Unadkat, Interspecies variability in expression of hepatobiliary transporters across human, dog, monkey, and rat as determined by quantitative proteomics, Drug Metab. Disposition Biol. Fate Chem. 43 (3) (2015) 367−374.

[13] K. Ball, T. Jamier, Y. Parmentier, C. Denizot, A. Mallier, M. Chenel, Prediction of renal transporter-mediated drug-drug interactions for a drug which is an OAT substrate and inhibitor using PBPK modelling, Eur. J. Pharmaceut. Sci. Off. J. Eur. Federation Pharmaceut. Sci. 106 (2017) 122−132.

[14] H. Shen, H. Su, T. Liu, M. Yao, G. Mintier, L. Li, R.M. Fancher, R. Iyer, P. Marathe, Y. Lai, A.D. Rodrigues, Evaluation of rosuvastatin as an organic anion transporting polypeptide (OATP) probe substrate: in vitro transport and in vivo disposition in cynomolgus monkeys, J. Pharmacol. Exp. Therapeut. 353 (2) (2015) 380−391.

[15] R.E. Kosa, S. Lazzaro, Y.A. Bi, B. Tierney, D. Gates, S. Modi, C. Costales, A.D. Rodrigues, L.M. Tremaine, M.V. Varma, Simultaneous assessment of transporter-mediated drug-drug interactions using a probe drug cocktail in cynomolgus monkey, Drug Metab. Disposition Biol. Fate Chem. 46 (8) (2018) 1179−1189.

[16] P. Kirchhof, The future of atrial fibrillation management: integrated care and stratified therapy, Lancet 390 (10105) (2017) 1873−1887.

[17] S.R. Wisniewski, J.M. Stevens, M. Yu, K.J. Fraunhoffer, E.O. Romero, S.A. Savage, Utilizing native directing groups: synthesis of a selective IKur inhibitor, BMS-919373, via a regioselective C-H arylation, J. Org. Chem. 84 (8) (2019) 4704−4714.

[18] I. Savelieva, N. Kakouros, A. Kourliouros, A.J. Camm, Upstream therapies for management of atrial fibrillation: review of clinical evidence and implications for European Society of Cardiology guidelines. Part I: primary prevention, Europace 13 (3) (2011) 308−328.

[19] H. Shen, Z. Yang, G. Mintier, Y.H. Han, C. Chen, P. Balimane, M. Jemal, W. Zhao, R. Zhang, S. Kallipatti, S. Selvam, S. Sukrutharaj, P. Krishnamurthy, P. Marathe, A.D. Rodrigues, Cynomolgus monkey as a potential model to assess drug interactions involving hepatic organic anion transporting polypeptides: in vitro, in vivo, and in vitro-to-in vivo extrapolation, J. Pharmacol. Exp. Therapeut. 344 (3) (2013) 673−685.

[20] Y.H. Han, D. Busler, Y. Hong, Y. Tian, C. Chen, A.D. Rodrigues, Transporter studies with the 3-O-sulfate conjugate of 17alpha-ethinylestradiol: assessment of human liver drug transporters, Drug Metab. Disposition Biol. Fate Chem. 38 (7) (2010) 1072−1082.

[21] C. International Transporter, K.M. Giacomini, S.M. Huang, D.J. Tweedie, L.Z. Benet, K.L. Brouwer, X. Chu, A. Dahlin, R. Evers, V. Fischer, K.M. Hillgren, K.A. Hoffmaster, T. Ishikawa, D. Keppler, R.B. Kim, C.A. Lee, M. Niemi, J.W. Polli, Y. Sugiyama, P.W. Swaan, J.A. Ware, S.H. Wright, S.W. Yee, M.J. Zamek-Gliszczynski, L. Zhang, Membrane transporters in drug development, Nat. Rev. Drug Discov. 9 (3) (2010) 215−236.

[22] L. Di, An update on the importance of plasma protein binding in drug discovery and development, Expet Opin. Drug Discov. 16 (12) (2021) 1453−1465.

[23] C.M. Bowman, L.Z. Benet, An examination of protein binding and protein-facilitated uptake relating to in vitro-in vivo extrapolation, Eur. J. Pharmaceut. Sci. Off. J. Eur. Federation Pharmaceut. Sci. 123 (2018) 502−514.

[24] L. Di, C. Breen, R. Chambers, S.T. Eckley, R. Fricke, A. Ghosh, P. Harradine, J.C. Kalvass, S. Ho, C.A. Lee, P. Marathe, E.J. Perkins, M. Qian, S. Tse, Z. Yan, M.J. Zamek-Gliszczynski, Industry perspective on contemporary protein-binding methodologies: considerations for regulatory drug-drug interaction and related guidelines on highly bound drugs, J. Pharmaceut. Sci. 106 (12) (2017) 3442−3452.

[25] T. Prueksaritanont, X. Chu, C. Gibson, D. Cui, K.L. Yee, J. Ballard, T. Cabalu, J. Hochman, Drug-drug interaction studies: regulatory guidance and an industry perspective, AAPS J. 15 (3) (2013) 629−645.

[26] R. Elsby, C. Hilgendorf, K. Fenner, Understanding the critical disposition pathways of statins to assess drug-drug interaction risk during drug development: it's not just about OATP1B1, Clin. Pharmacol. Therap. 92 (5) (2012) 584−598.

[27] H. Eng, Y.A. Bi, M.A. West, S. Ryu, E. Yamaguchi, R.E. Kosa, D.A. Tess, D.A. Griffith, J. Litchfield, A.S. Kalgutkar, M.V.S. Varma, Organic anion-transporting polypeptide 1B1/1B3-mediated hepatic uptake determines the pharmacokinetics of large lipophilic acids: in vitro-in vivo evaluation in cynomolgus monkey, J. Pharmacol. Exp. Therapeut. 377 (1) (2021) 169−180.

[28] X. Chu, G.H. Chan, R. Evers, Identification of endogenous biomarkers to predict the propensity of drug candidates to cause hepatic or renal transporter-mediated drug-drug interactions, J. Pharmaceut. Sci. 106 (9) (2017) 2357−2367.

[29] T. De Bruyn, A. Ufuk, C. Cantrill, R.E. Kosa, Y.A. Bi, M. Niosi, S. Modi, A.D. Rodrigues, L.M. Tremaine, M.V.S. Varma, A. Galetin, J.B. Houston, Predicting human clearance of organic anion transporting polypeptide substrates using cynomolgus monkey: in vitro-in vivo scaling of hepatic uptake clearance, Drug Metab. Disposition Biol. Fate Chem. 46 (7) (2018) 989−1000.

[30] Y. Cheng, X. Liang, J. Hao, C. Niu, Y. Lai, Application of a PBPK model to elucidate the changes of systemic and liver exposures for rosuvastatin, carotegrast, and bromfenac followed by OATP inhibition in monkeys, Clin. Transl. Sci. 14 (2021) 1924−1934.

[31] X. Chu, S.J. Shih, R. Shaw, H. Hentze, G.H. Chan, K. Owens, S. Wang, X. Cai, D. Newton, J. Castro-Perez, G. Salituro, J. Palamanda, A. Fernandis, C.K. Ng, A. Liaw, M.J. Savage, R. Evers, Evaluation of cynomolgus monkeys for the identification of endogenous biomarkers for

hepatic transporter inhibition and as a translatable model to predict pharmacokinetic interactions with statins in humans, Drug Metab. Disposition Biol. Fate Chem. 43 (6) (2015) 851−863.

[32] X. Chu, M. Liao, H. Shen, K. Yoshida, A.A. Zur, V. Arya, A. Galetin, K.M. Giacomini, I. Hanna, H. Kusuhara, Y. Lai, D. Rodrigues, Y. Sugiyama, M.J. Zamek-Gliszczynski, L. Zhang, C. International Transporter, Clinical probes and endogenous biomarkers as substrates for transporter drug-drug interaction evaluation: perspectives from the international transporter consortium, Clin. Pharmacol. Therap. 104 (5) (2018) 836−864.

[33] H. Shen, A pharmaceutical industry perspective on transporter and CYP-mediated drug-drug interactions: kidney transporter biomarkers, Bioanalysis 10 (9) (2018) 625−631.

[34] A.D. Rodrigues, K.S. Taskar, H. Kusuhara, Y. Sugiyama, Endogenous probes for drug transporters: balancing vision with reality, Clin. Pharmacol. Therap. 103 (3) (2018) 434−448.

Chapter 13

Investigating the link between drug metabolism and toxicity

W. Griffith Humphreys

Aranmore Pharma Consulting, Lawrenceville, NJ, United States

Introduction

A full understanding of the pharmacology and toxicology of a new drug must account for the activities not just of the new drug molecule but of all metabolites as well. It is well documented that metabolites can contribute to the pharmacological activity of a drug [1−3]. It is also well documented that metabolic reactions and products thereof are responsible for some fraction of the off-target toxicology seen during drug development and marketing [4−9]. Metabolism-mediated toxicity, often manifest as organ-specific toxicity, is seen at all stages of discovery and development process. As toxicity (non-clinical and clinical) is the largest cause of drug attrition due to toxicity [10], the understanding of the role of metabolism (or lack of a role) in any toxicity finding is often critical to successful drug development programs.

The toxicities that have been demonstrated to be linked to metabolism can be broken down into three general categories: (1) the formation of reactive metabolites that provoke a wide range of deleterious responses due to binding to cellular components, (2) the formation of a metabolite that produces a pharmacology unique from the parent molecule, and (3) the formation of a metabolite that has different physicochemical characteristics than the parent and is thus prone to local accumulation. Polymorphic metabolic clearance can also play a role in toxicity, however, in these cases it is the parent that is the causative agent, *e.g.* terfenadine.

The study of metabolism-related liabilities often begins in the lead optimization phase through the screening for reactive intermediates [7] along with a variety of other safety-associated liability screens [11]. While the screening is meant to reduce risk of metabolite-mediated issues downstream, at this stage the screens are run without a direct toxicological correlate. As programs progress toward candidate nomination and early development, new drug candidates often produce some type of toxicological finding of concern. Determining the mechanism of action of these toxicities often includes questions such as: is the mechanism due to an on-target receptor interaction? off-target interactions? is the mechanism parent or metabolite related? are reactive metabolites involved? These efforts often become high priority activities, especially in cases where there is a species-specific toxicity found, whether that be in one of the toxicology species or in human.

Some degree of species-related differences in metabolism profiles is typically seen for new drug candidates [12]. This is most often manifest in quantitative differences in cross-species metabolite levels, however, qualitative differences are also not uncommon. These differences, where specific metabolite levels are highly variable between species, are what often form the basis for hypotheses regarding toxicity mechanisms.

The investigation of metabolism-mediated toxicology becomes a critical activity if there are toxicology observations in an animal and/or human study that are significant enough to impact the drug candidates' progression. A thorough investigation of whether metabolism is involved in the mechanism of action leading to toxicity will likely be required in these cases. In many cases these investigations will not provide any mechanistic insight, however, if a metabolism-related mechanism can be identified and characterized across species, then a risk assessment for human can be completed. In some cases this may lead to a favorable assessment and allow program progression. Alternatively, the understanding of the mechanism may lead to the selection of a backup compound without the same liability. In many cases there will be the conclusion reached that metabolism is not playing a role in the toxicology finding. This conclusion can help to refine the mechanism of action studies examining direct on- and off-target activity of the parent compound.

Overcoming Obstacles in Drug Discovery and Development. https://doi.org/10.1016/B978-0-12-817134-9.00013-1

This chapter will cover the utility of investigative metabolism studies throughout discovery and development, methodology for conduct of such studies, and finally examples from the literature of these types of studies applied to drug candidates.

Utility of metabolite-mediated toxicity information in discovery and development

Discovery studies

The characterization and optimization of the metabolism properties of new candidates is part of most modern discovery efforts [13]. These studies likely begin with simple metabolic stability studies designed to optimize metabolic clearance. Studies progress to more involved metabolism studies as lead compounds get closer to a nomination. Cross-species in vitro metabolism studies are conducted to characterize the profile and examine whether there are differences in metabolic profile between species with a focus on whether all significant human metabolites are also represented in animals. Other key considerations are whether observed metabolites may have on- or off-target pharmacology.

A common metabolism related property that is investigated in early studies is the presence of metabolites originating from reactive intermediates [7]. This screening study is almost always done without any in vivo correlate and is purely conducted based on the history of compound failure due to organ specific toxicology thought to be due to reactive metabolite formation. It is a relatively easy study to conduct in a qualitative fashion, but without any quantitative information it is difficult to incorporate the information in a manner that truly drives rational drug design. If conducted, the reactive metabolite screen is best interpreted as part of a multiparameter optimization scheme that includes other mechanisms associated with potential for toxicity [14–16].

It is rarer that there will be an actual toxicology finding during the early discovery phase, i.e., before repeat dose studies at supra-pharmacological doses are performed. This is not always the case and there are certainly many examples of toxicology findings in efficacy models that raise questions regarding the viability of the target and/or the chemotype. In these instances, there may be a need to conduct metabolism-mediated toxicity investigations at this stage of the program. This is illustrated by the first two examples in the case-study section.

Development studies

Metabolites in safety testing considerations

After candidate selection a compound moves into the characterization phase which is accompanied by more rigorous metabolism studies. The studies typically involve more definitive in vitro studies and progress toward a clinical study using a radiolabeled analog of the drug candidate (often referred to as the human Absorption, Disposition, Metabolism and Excretion (ADME) study). The goals of these studies are to: (1) characterize the profile of metabolites circulating in human as well as the major clearance pathways including pathways arising from metabolism and (2) determine if the major metabolites (defined as a metabolite that circulates at >10% of the drug-related material Area-Under-the-Curve) found in human are adequately represented in the toxicology species. These studies are necessary for new chemical entities to meet the requirements laid out in the Metabolites in Safety Testing (MIST) guidance [17]. There have been recent reviews on the topic of MIST and its impact on drug development [18,19].

Metabolism by nature is always somewhat species specific in terms of the exact profile and extent of metabolites formed. However, it is relatively rare for there to be truly human specific metabolite, i.e., not present in animals, that circulates in quantities sufficient to be characterized as major. If this situation arises then there may be a need to conduct specific toxicology studies to examine the effects of the human metabolite in the toxicology species. A much more typical situation is the presence of human metabolites with at least some level of coverage in the animal species at no effect doses. The major questions regarding the major human circulating metabolites are typically around on- and off-target pharmacology. Thus, the characterization studies focus on on-target, safety pharmacology and drug-drug interaction screening. A challenging step in the process is moving from qualitative plasma profiling by LC-MS/MS to some measure of quantity of the metabolite (either absolute or relative to the level in a plasma sample from a comparator species) and finally measures of target pharmacological activity and perhaps off-target pharmacological activity. NMR quantitation, relative MS response in mixed-matrix and other analytical tools are valuable methods to streamline this process [20–22].

As the set of studies aiming to address MIST issues focus on circulating and excreted metabolites, they are often not the best for investigating organ-specific toxicology. However, they can often provide information that can be incorporated into an investigative effort and/or risk assessment.

Species specific metabolism-related toxicology

As pointed out above, it is common to observe qualitative and quantitative differences in metabolite profiles when doing cross-species in vitro experiments. This sometimes manifests in significant differences in circulating and/or excreta profiles between key species and humans, although typically major human metabolites are covered to some extent by levels in animals. If there is a significant toxicity found in an animal study or in the clinic then the cross-species profiling results will be an excellent place to begin to examine whether there appears to be a link between metabolism and the observed toxicity. This information is especially valuable if there is a species-specific toxicity found. The subsequent sections will describe methodology for studies beyond plasma profiling and provide examples of drug candidates that displayed species-specific effects.

Metabolism-related toxicology during clinical development

Clinical toxicity findings can occur at all stages of development and may be due to metabolism related issues. If the toxicity is found at doses close to the efficacious dose and seen at a significant frequency, then the progression of the candidate would obviously be in jeopardy. On the other hand, if the toxicity is not severe or very infrequent then there may be a path forward for the candidate. In either case, investigations that successfully determine the mechanism of action can help determine risks of moving the candidate further in clinical development and alternatively could serve to help the advancement of a back-up compound.

One of the most common toxicities found in clinical trials and also post-marketing is drug-induced liver injury (DILI) [23]. The prevailing understand of DILI mechanism is that it arises from a combination of a response from the innate and adaptive branches of the immune system [23,24]. There has been significant progress into characterization of different aspects of the cellular responses through the study of the inhibition of hepatic transporters by drug candidates, formation of reactive metabolites with associated oxidative stress, mitochondrial toxicity, etc. [25–28]. Tools such as the DILIsym program can help integrate these findings and make predictions regarding toxicity biomarkers [29].

Methods to investigate metabolite-mediated toxicology

Investigations of an observed toxicology should always begin with a very open consideration of all possible mechanisms of action that may be responsible for the findings. Potential contributions should be considered from information such as known or hypothesized on-target effects, potential on- and off-target pharmacology of known stable/circulating metabolites, potential metabolic pathways that generate reactive intermediates, what is known about the levels of parent and metabolites at the site of toxicity. Other important considerations include whether it is organ specific, species-specific, clinical or non-clinical, time to onset, etc. An immediate need for any investigational program is the determination of whether there are in vitro or in vivo models for the toxicity. Ideal these models can recapitulate the finding and do so in a time frame consistent with the needs of the investigational program.

Exposure at site of action

Exploration of what drug-related species are present at the site of action should be an early focus of the investigational plan. These studies should be conducted with eye toward a complete qualitative analysis with as much quantitative information as feasible. The studies are typically conducted through collection of tissues after single or short-term drug administration. Collection at multiple time points after the last drug administration can be very useful. Drug and metabolite characterization can be accomplished after tissue homogenate preparation and analysis via LC-MS/MS or radiodetection.

For drug candidates causing hepatotoxicity there may already be some knowledge of the species present from in vitro studies with hepatic models (microsomes and hepatocytes), however, studies in vivo are important to look for relative levels of the in vitro metabolites over time with special focus on metabolites that may be prone to accumulation. This work can also uncover metabolites not seen in the in vitro metabolite studies as the pathways were not well represented in the in vitro systems or because the metabolites were the results of multiple metabolic transformations. If the toxicology is seen in non-hepatic tissue, then study of drug-related compounds in the target tissue give important information on what circulating metabolites are distributed and whether there are any extra-hepatic metabolic steps that may be important. In any case, a qualitative and quantitative understanding of drug-related species at the site of action will allow refinement and focus of hypotheses around on- and off-target mechanisms of action.

Additional information on compound distribution can be gained with techniques that allow spatial resolution within an organ of interest. Matrix assisted laser desorption (MALDI)-MS and laser capture microdissection in tandem with traditional LC-MS are both techniques that allow resolution that can localize compound distribution to various zones of an organ of interest. MALDI paired with histology has been shown to be a very powerful addition to studies attempting to determine what drug-related species are at the site of action [30,31].

In vitro methods

The first set of investigative experiments will typically involve in vitro studies to better define metabolic transformations, measure on- or off-target potencies of parent and/or metabolites, characterize physicochemical properties of metabolites (stability, solubility, etc.). These studies should always attempt to characterize properties of parent/metabolites in model systems from species that display the observed toxicology as well as in species that do not. Models should only be progressed in so far as they can provide explanation for the full breadth of the findings, both positive and negative.

In vitro systems provide an optimal method of not only testing what drug-related species are being formed at the site of action, but what enzymes are responsible for formation and what are potential consequences of metabolites. LC-MS/MS based metabolite search and identification strategies have been worked out that allow rapid identification and partial structural identification of metabolites from typical in vitro systems [32,33]. Understanding of the profile of drug-related species at the site of action, especially if there are metabolites present that track in cross-species study with the toxicology findings, can focus further efforts.

Additional in vitro investigations can be conducted to investigate: (1) what enzymes are involved in metabolite formation, (2) can the enzyme pathways be modulated through inhibition or induction, (3) are the metabolites substrates or inhibitors of transporters. These types of study are important to solidify hypotheses as well plan for in vivo studies as described below. There are established tools for much of this type of work, especially for human and rat CYP enzymes [34−37]. There is more limited information on modulation of UGT and other drug metabolizing enzymes [38,39]. For specific oxidative transformations, it may be possible slow the metabolite formation rate with specific deuterium substitution that take advantage of the deuterium isotope effect [40−42].

The use of microphysiological systems (MPS) as predictive models for in vitro evaluation of toxicity shows tremendous promise [43−48]. Models for many organs are available and there is active research to determine the predictive potential of these systems. Future MPS may allow for the examination of multiple organs in a single system, often referred to as a lab-on-a-chip.

In vivo methods

The next phase of study would typically be to test hypotheses that emerge from the tissue distribution and in vitro mechanism of action studies in an in vivo model. These studies are obviously dependent on the identification of a suitable in vivo model. This is not an issue if toxicity is seen after short-term administration but becomes a more significant issue as the length of exposure prior to a finding increases. For examples where the toxicology is observed only after long-term dose administration, there may be early biomarkers of that change that may be reliable predictors with greater sensitivity and be seen after shorter-term administration. Having a short-term administration model that is predictive of the long-term toxicology is a key part of successful investigational studies.

With a short-term in vivo model in place experiments can be run to determine if the toxicity (or toxicity marker) is impacted by modulating the pathway responsible for the toxicity response. This is typically done with inhibitors and/or inducers of the enzyme or transporter thought to be involved. There are many examples of CYP inhibitors being administered to impact the toxic response to drugs/natural products/chemicals that are bioactivated via oxidation [49−56]. Methods are also available for other enzymes and transporters. In some instances, there may be transgenic models that may be useful [57,58]. Results from these in vivo experiments that fit with expectations, *e.g.* inhibition of bioactivation reduces toxicity, add significantly to the weight of evidence argument that links the molecular pathway to the observed toxicology.

In some cases it may not be practically possible to drive the suspected pathway to an extent sufficient to elicit toxicity after administration of the parent. This is especially common when the suspect pathway involves a secondary metabolite that may take time to build up. In these cases, there may be benefit to administration of the metabolite directly. Although this may be an effective way to drive the suspected pathway, it does entail risks that new toxicities may be present as the metabolite may distribute differently after direct administration. This is especially true if the metabolite requires parenteral administration due to low oral bioavailability. These factors should be carefully considered before employing this method.

Examples of metabolite-mediated toxicity

General

The history of investigation of metabolism-mediated toxicology very much parallels the history of the understanding of cytochrome P450 enzymes [8]. Early work on chemical carcinogenesis [56] and hepatotoxicity caused by acetaminophen [50−63] formed the basis for how drug metabolism could influence drug and environmental chemical toxicity. Other drugs from this early period where links were established between metabolism and toxicity were thalidomide [64] and furosemide [65−67]. This history is covered in depth in a recent review by Guengerich [8].

Efavirenz (Sustiva™) is an early example where a toxicity was found during the development stage and studies were conducted to determine mechanism of action, determine species-specificity and perform overall risk assessment. Efavirenz was developed by Dupont-Merck Pharmaceuticals as a HIV therapeutic. During long term toxicology studies the compound was found to produce severe renal injury in male rats at high dose. This toxicity was not observed in female rats or cynomolgus monkey. Also, it had not been observed in human in early clinical trials, however, due to the severity of the finding was still a significant clinical safety concern. A series of investigative metabolism studies was conducted [68−70] and demonstrated a complex metabolic pathway found only in male rats (Fig. 13.1). The pathway ultimately led to the generation of a reactive metabolite in kidney. Multiple methods were used to perturb the reactive metabolite generation pathway and thus gain confidence in the link between metabolism and toxicity, one of the methods involved a deuterium substitution that slowed metabolism at that site which was the first step in the bioactivation pathway (site denoted by arrow in first panel of Fig. 13.1). This example is covered in depth in a subsequent chapter in this book.

The literature examples where toxicity has been demonstrated to be linked to metabolism can be broken down into three general categories: (1) the formation of reactive metabolites that provoke a wide range of deleterious responses due to binding to cellular components, (2) the formation of a metabolite that produces a pharmacology unique from the parent molecule, and (3) the formation of a metabolite that has different physicochemical characteristics than the parent and is thus prone to local accumulation. The first mechanism of action is the most common and is found at all stages of drug development [4−8]. The second mechanism of action, i.e., a metabolite that causes toxicity through a unique pharmacology, is surprisingly rare. There is data to support this type of mechanism with drug-drug interactions via CYP inhibition [71]. An area where this may become more commonplace is toxicity and drug-drug interactions caused by transporter inhibition [72], especially by drug conjugates. There are some examples where this type of interaction has been hypothesized to play a role in toxicity but it has been difficult to demonstrate conclusively due to potential contributions from multiple contributing mechanisms [73]. The final mechanism has been demonstrated or hypothesized to involved in the toxicity seen with multiple drugs due the effect of parent and metabolites, with the most commonly observed toxicity being renal and sometimes referred to as crystal nephropathy [74].

The following examples illustrate the methodologies used to investigate metabolism-mediated toxicity and how the investigation can impact the discovery and development process. The first two examples are from programs that were in the discovery/optimization phase where metabolite-mediated toxicity information was used to: (1) confirm that the target pharmacology was not related to the finding and (2) make changes in the chemotype that would reduce or eliminate the

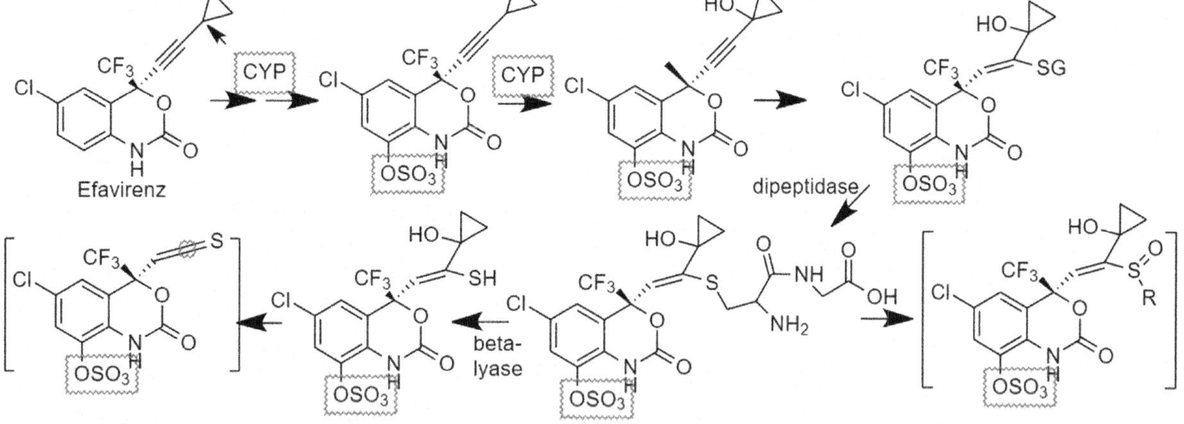

FIGURE 13.1 Proposed metabolism and bioactivation scheme of efavirenz. The multiple steps are thought to result in two potential toxicants (thioketene, bottom left; sulfoxide, bottom right) formed in male rat kidney that result in toxicity. Arrow denotes the site of deuterium substitution [68−70].

bioactivation and associated toxicity. The final three examples are post candidate nomination and arise from findings in toxicology studies that led to the need to determine whether the findings posed a risk for the administration of the candidate drug to human.

Amgen PI3K inhibitor program

A series of phosphatidylinositol 3-kinase (PI3Ks) inhibitors was being explored by Amgen as potential antitumor agents [75]. A lead compound was found that had potent and selective target inhibition, acceptable drug-like properties and was active in tumor models. However, when the compound was tested in a short-term rat toxicity study it was found to cause hepatocellular and hepatobiliary toxicity. The toxicity was shown to be metabolism dependent through co-administration of CYP inhibitor 1-aminobenzotriazole (ABT). Metabolite identification studies in rats led to the determination of the primary oxidative metabolite and a pathway for metabolic bioactivation was proposed. As depicted in Fig. 13.2, two structural changes were introduced that slowed were designed to slow overall metabolism (fluorine substitution) or directly block the oxidative bioactivation (methylation). The two changes in tandem did indeed provide the desired results as the molecule did not produce hepatotoxicity when tested in the rat model. The resultant compound also retained good on-target pharmacological properties and was nominated as a clinical candidate.

This above example is an excellent example of the type of approach that is often used in the candidate optimization phase to reduce risk of toxicity issue in later stages. In this example, medicinal chemistry approaches were used to reduce observed hepatotoxicity. More commonly, the approach is used to attempt to reduce the level of reactive intermediates detected in in vitro experiments (prior to even testing for hepatotoxicity) or even earlier by altering the structure to avoid inclusion of "structural alerts" (substructures that have been demonstrated to be susceptible to bioactivation) [76—79].

Bristol-Myers Squibb MET kinase inhibitor

BMS-A was a MET kinase inhibitor in late discovery at Bristol-Myers Squibb as an anticancer agent, an analogue from a series of potent MET kinase inhibitors. The compound was found to induce atrophy of the adrenal cortex (zona fasciculata and zona reticularis) in rats during early efficacy and toxicology studies [80]. A series of studies was conducted to attempt to determine mechanism of action in order to assess: (1) whether this was a compound, chemotype of target related toxicity and (2) risk of this in other species including human.

Initial experiments sought to establish an in vivo and in vitro model for the toxicology finding. BMS-A was administered to rats as a single dose and vacuolar degeneration with single cell necrosis in the adrenal gland cortex was observed. As the adrenal is a very active metabolic organ, these initial experiments included co-administration of BMS-A with ABT. ABT co-administration prevented the toxicity as measured by histology. Additionally, BMS-A was administered to cultures of two adrenal cell lines, Y-1 (mouse) and H295R (human). Cytotoxicity was observed in both lines and could be monitored by following early signals of apoptosis.

A radiolabeled version of BMS-A was synthesized, and the metabolism and disposition examined in the rat. A high level of radioactivity was found in adrenal tissue and was found to be non-extractable, *i.e.* covalently bound to cell components, and the binding could be reduced by co-administration of ABT. The radioactivity could be further localized within the adrenal tissue to the mitochondrial fraction. The major CYP enzymes in adrenal mitochondria are CYP11A1 and 11B1/2. Additional studies with specific inhibitors of CYP11A1 and siRNA knock down of CYP11A1 expression in the adrenal cell lines gave solid evidence that the bioactivation leading to the adrenal lesions were mediated via CYP11A1 metabolism. A scheme for bioactivation of BMS-A was proposed (Fig. 13.3).

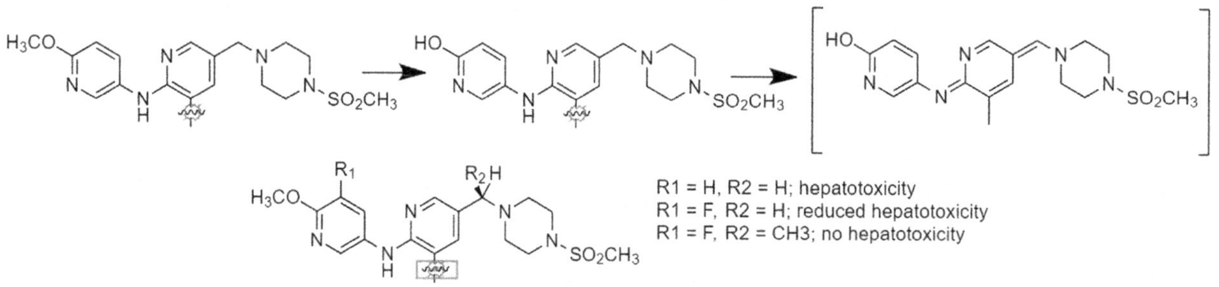

R1 = H, R2 = H; hepatotoxicity
R1 = F, R2 = H; reduced hepatotoxicity
R1 = F, R2 = CH3; no hepatotoxicity

FIGURE 13.2 Proposed bioactivation of lead phosphatidylinositol 3-kinase (PI3Ks) inhibitor. Top row shows successive oxidations leading to reactive intermediate. Second row shows medicinal chemistry substitutions that modulated metabolism and eliminated hepatotoxicity [75].

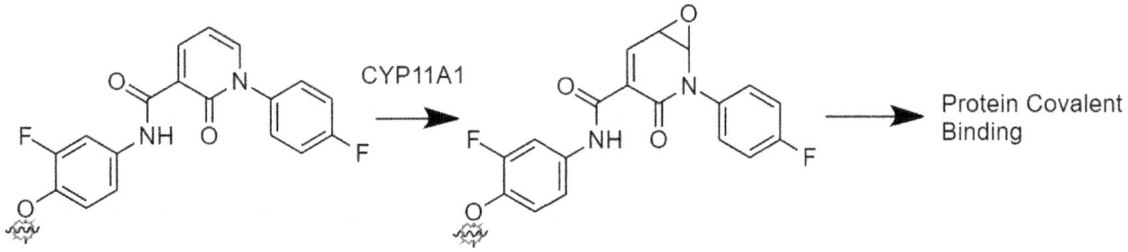

FIGURE 13.3 Proposed bioactivation of lead MET kinase inhibitor. The compound was found to induce atrophy of the adrenal cortex in rats due to bioactivation by CYP11A1 [80].

The investigative studies provided very sound evidence that the adrenal toxicity was specific to a bioactivation pathway for BMS-A and was not related to inhibition of target. It also gave evidence that it may occur in analogs that contained the same pyrazone ring system but would not be anticipated to impact the entire chemotype.

Saxagliptin

Saxaglipin (Onglyza™) was developed by Bristol-Myers Squibb/Astra Zeneca as an antidiabetic agent. During the development program there was a significant toxicity found during the carcinogenicity assessment, a severe CNS lesion was found in male rats when administered a high dose for an extended period [81,82]. CNS toxicity was not seen is female rats, mice or cynomolgus monkeys, however, due to the severity of the lesion there was still significant concern over human safety.

Saxagliptin is a dipeptidyl peptidase-4 (DPP-4) inhibitor that also had some activity against other related enzymes. As such, it had the potential to alter the processing of peptidic signaling molecules other than its pharmacological target, glucagon like peptide-1 (GLP-1). At high doses there was concern that saxagliptin may be altering signaling, especially of neuropeptides, and this could be the mechanism of toxicity. A series of studies was designed to examine whether this may be the case. In parallel, a series of studies was conducted to examine the interspecies differences in metabolism of saxagliptin.

The initial focus of the studies was the major human circulating metabolite, a pharmacologically active hydroxylated version of saxagliptin that had very significant exposure in human and much lower multiples of coverage than the parent in toxicology models. The human enzyme responsible for formation of the hydroxylated metabolite was CYP3A4 and an experiment was conducted to determine the rat CYP enzymes involved. The rat CYP3A enzymes, CYP3A1/2, were both found to form the hydroxylated metabolite, however, CYP2C11 was found to metabolize saxagliptin rapidly but not produce the characterized hydroxylated metabolite. The new CYP2C11-mediated metabolite was quickly characterized as having been formed through α-hydroxylation adjacent to the cyano moiety of saxagliptin with subsequent loss of cyanide and finally internal cyclization (Fig. 13.4).

Cross-species liver microsome experiments quickly showed that this new metabolic pathway was not completely unique to the male rat but was >10 fold more efficient when tested at 1 μM saxagliptin than in any other system. The question of whether the CNS lesion could be the result of exposure to cyanide was posed as it would explain the species and gender selectivity. It was not immediately obvious from the literature on cyanide intoxication that a lesion such as that observed could be the result of long-term subacute cyanide exposure. However, there was some literature that showed CNS lesions after chronic cyanide exposure in rat [83]. There was also literature on CNS effects in humans of chronic low-level cyanide exposure from a diet including unprocessed cassava [84,85]. Taken together, the evidence was certainly enough to elevate this hypothesis to a high priority and proceed to additional with follow-ups including in vivo experiments.

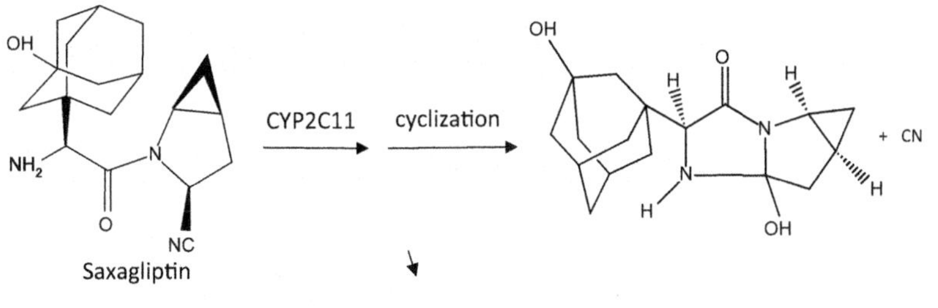

Saxagliptin

FIGURE 13.4 Metabolism of saxagliptin by CYP2C11 that results in the liberation of cyanide and the male rat specific CNS lesion [81,82].

Additional studies in vivo showed measurable levels of cyanide and thiocyanate in male rats after exposure to saxagliptin. An acute model showed impacts of cyanide exposure were apparent at doses above 2-fold those that caused the original CNS lesion. Cyanide and thiocyanate levels could be modulated by co-administration of agents that modified CYP2C11 activity such as cimetidine. The weight of evidence from these investigational studies led to the conclusion that cyanide was the causative agent of the male rat CNS lesions.

A final step was to perform risk assessment for human exposure and associated toxicity produced through the cyanide-formation pathway after administration of saxagliptin. That exercise showed that due to the much lower clinical dose relative to the toxic dose in rat and the lower fractional clearance through that pathway that humans would be exposed to minimal cyanide at the recommended clinical dose.

Empagliflozin

Empagliflozin (Jardiance™) is a potent inhibitor of the sodium-dependent glucose transporter 2 (SGLT2) and was developed as an anti type 2 diabetic agent by Boehringer Ingelheim. As part of a 2-year carcinogenicity study, empagliflozin was orally administered to male and female CD-1 mice at doses up to 1000 mg/kg/day. Male mice displayed renal tubular injury along with renal tubular adenomas and carcinomas at the highest dose administered, while these finding were not detected at lower doses in male mice or at any dose level in female mice (up to 1000 mg/kg/day) or in male or female Han Wistar rats (up to 700 mg/kg/day). A series of investigative studies was conducted to attempt to determine the mechanism of action for the kidney findings and determine the likelihood that the mechanism would also be found in human [86,87].

The initial hypotheses for mechanism of action centered around renal tissue accumulation due to differences in renal excretion between male and female mice. There are known difference in transporter expression in mice between males and females, however, no differences were noted for empagliflozin uptake in kidney slices.

The second set of studies involved cross-species in vitro metabolism studies of empagliflozin. Incubations with hepatic and renal microsomes from male and female mice, rats, and humans demonstrated a hydroxylated metabolite of empagliflozin (M+16, hemiacetal structure), predominantly formed in male mouse kidney microsomes. Formation of this metabolite in male mouse kidney microsomes was 20−31-fold higher relative to the amounts found in female mouse kidney or other species. The hemiacetal M+16 metabolite is unstable and spontaneously degrades to yield a phenol and 4-hydroxycrotonaldehyde (Fig. 13.5). 4-hydroxycrotonaldehyde is a reactive α,β unsaturated ketone that would react with thiols, including glutathione. Indeed, a 4-hydroxycrotonaldehyde-GSH adduct could be observed in incubations of empagliflozin with male mouse kidney microsomes. High levels of crotonaldehyde formation were hypothesized to cause local oxidative stress response. This level of chronic stress response was sufficient to cause the renal injury and eventually lead to tumor formation. These data in total made a convincing case that the pathway to form 4-hydroxycrotonaldehyde was the mechanism of action for the toxicity findings and that it was selectively expressed in the male mouse kidney. Risk to human was judged to very low as the metabolism pathways were very different and the formation of a 4-hydoxycrotonaldehyde was very minor.

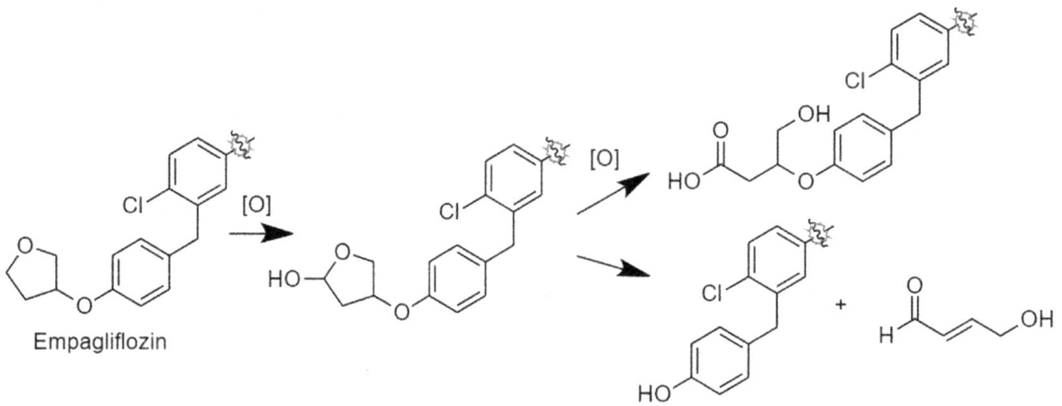

FIGURE 13.5 Metabolism of empagliflozin showing formation of hydroxycrotonaldehyde subsequent to a CYP-catalyzed oxidation. The oxidation depicted was found predominately in male mouse kidney microsomes and is thought to cause the renal tubular injury found in male mice [86].

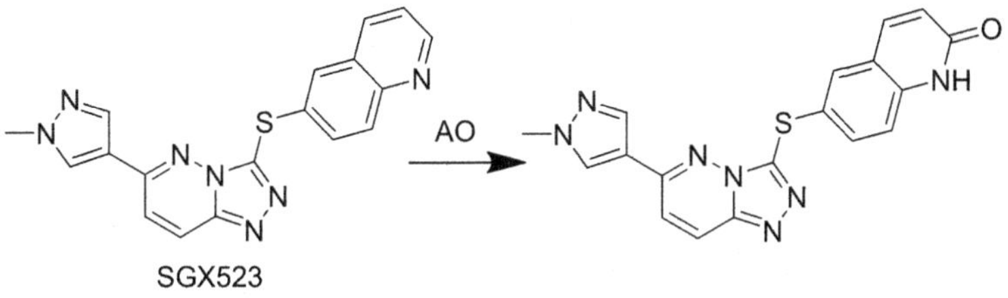

FIGURE 13.6 Biotransformation of SGX523 showing formation of lactam metabolite [89].

SGX523

SGX523 is an orally bioavailable, potent, and selective small molecule inhibitor of c-MET that was in development at Incyte as an antitumor agent [88,89]. The compound was studied in multiple in vitro and in vivo models prior to initiation of clinical trials. The species chosen for IND-enabling toxicity studies were rat and dog. The design for the first in human study was to explore escalating doses on a continuous or intermittent dosing schedule. Although doses of 20−60 mg were tolerated, all six patients administered doses of ≥80 mg developed renal failure, as measured by a rise of serum blood urea nitrogen and creatinine [88].

Studies were conducted to further probe the metabolism of SGX523 in human in vitro systems and from clinical samples [89]. Incubations with liver S9 fraction demonstrated a non-NADPH dependent metabolite formed in human and cynomolgus monkey but was not formed in rat or dog. The metabolite had and LC retention time greater than parent, which aided in the identification of the metabolite as a product of oxidation of the quinoline moiety to a lactam (Fig. 13.6). Aldehyde oxidase was identified as the enzyme responsible for the formation of the lactam. Analysis of human plasma showed the metabolite at levels above those in rat or dog toxicology studies. Profiling of the metabolite physiochemical properties showed it had significantly lower solubility than parent and led to the hypothesis that the renal toxicity may be due to crystallization of the metabolite in the renal tubules [89].

As the metabolite was observed in monkey in vitro, multiple dose toxicology were conducted to determine if the human findings could be recapitulated. The circulating metabolite profile and clinical signs of renal toxicity were observed. Importantly, monkey kidney histology showed the presence of crystals in the renal tubules [88,89].

Taken as a whole, the investigations gave convincing evidence that the renal toxicity seen in clinical studies with SGX523 was due to the formation of a lactam metabolite that crystalized in the renal tubule. The toxicity was not observed in the species used for preclinical evaluation due to the low expression of aldehyde oxidase in those species.

Conclusions

The pharmacology and toxicology of a new drug candidate will be determined by the behavior of the drug and all of its metabolites. There are certain metabolite characterization studies that are dictated by guidance to understand metabolism in human and also determine how the human metabolite profile compares to that in the key toxicology species. These studies are important in understanding the contributions metabolites and metabolite pathways have on the properties of a new drug and are particularly important in understand the contributions to on-target pharmacology and drug-drug interactions. These studies will often not be sufficient to understand the full impact of metabolic pathways on the toxicology profile. To gain an understanding of how metabolites play a role in observed toxicology there is often a need to conduct a set of investigation metabolism studies.

These investigations are ideally conducted with a series of studies following this general pattern: (1) determination of the drug-related molecules at the site of action, (2) proposals of how the parent, metabolites and inferred intermediates may be producing the observed toxicity, e.g. through a bioactivation step to a reactive intermediate, (3) establishment of an in vitro system that mimics the key elements of the pathways proposed in step (2), (4) additional in vitro experiments to determine if the pathways can be modulated, e.g. through addition of a metabolic inhibitor, (5) establishment of an in vivo model that allows direct measurement of the toxicity or some biomarker of toxicity within a time frame commensurate with the needs of the program and (6) in vivo experiments with and without the modulation of the pathways as determined in step (4). This systematic approach can then be used to complete risk assessment through cross-species studies.

The examples provided illustrate how the framework outlined above for conduct of investigations of metabolism-mediated toxicity can be applied to real world drug candidates. The case-studies were all detailing work conducted in response to a significant animal toxicology finding, either thought to be species-specific or cross-species. Each example showed how in vitro experiments can be paired with in vivo toxicology studies to confirm in vitro finding and add weight of evidence in support of a proposed mechanism of action. Also demonstrated is the importance of modulation of the pathway in question in in vivo experiments to gain full confidence in the proposed mechanism of action. The examples also show that if mechanism of action studies can successfully demonstrate that significant toxicities in animals are metabolism-mediated and not relevant to human, then candidates can progress and become successful drugs.

Abbreviations

ABT 1-aminobenzotriazole
ADME absorption, disposition, metabolism and excretion
CNS central nervous system
CYP cytochrome P450
DILI drug-induced liver injury
GSH reduced glutathione
LC-MS/MS liquid chromatography-tandem mass spectrometry
MALDI-MS matrix assisted laser desorption-mass spectrometry
MIST metabolites in safety testing
MPS microphysiological systems
UGT uridine 5′-diphospho-glucuronosyltransferase

References

[1] A. Fura, Y.Z. Shu, M. Zhu, R.L. Hanson, V. Roongta, W.G. Humphreys, Discovering drugs through biological transformation: role of pharmacologically active metabolites in drug discovery, J. Med. Chem. 47 (18) (2004) 4339−4351.

[2] A. Fura, Role of pharmacologically active metabolites in drug discovery and development, Drug Discov. Today 11 (3−4) (2006) 133−142.

[3] R.S. Obach, Pharmacologically active drug metabolites: impact on drug discovery and pharmacotherapy, Pharmacol. Rev. 65 (2) (2013) 578−640.

[4] D.C. Liebler, F.P. Guengerich, Elucidating mechanisms of drug-induced toxicity, Nat. Rev. 4 (2005) 410−420.

[5] L. Leung, A.S. Kalgutkar, R.S. Obach, Metabolic activation in drug-induced liver injury, Drug Metab. Rev. 44 (1) (2012) 18−33.

[6] T. Cho, J. Uetrecht, How reactive metabolites induce an immune response that sometimes leads to an idiosyncratic drug reaction, Chem. Res. Toxicol. 30 (1) (2017) 295−314.

[7] R.A. Thompson, E.M. Isin, M.O. Ogese, J.T. Mettetal, D.P. Williams, Reactive metabolites: current and emerging risk and hazard assessments, Chem. Res. Toxicol. 29 (4) (2016) 505−533.

[8] F.P. Guengerich, A history of the roles of cytochrome P450 enzymes in the toxicity of drugs, Toxicol. Res. 37 (1) (2020) 1−23.

[9] J. Gan, S. Ma, D. Zhang, Non-cytochrome P450-mediated bioactivation and its toxicological relevance, Drug Metab. Rev. 48 (4) (2016) 473−501.

[10] I. Kola, J. Landis, Can the pharmaceutical industry reduce attrition rates? Nat. Rev. Drug Discov. 3 (8) (2004) 711−715.

[11] W.G. Humphreys, Y. Will, F.P. Guengerich, Toxicology strategies for drug discovery - present and future: introduction, Chem. Res. Toxicol. 29 (4) (2016) 437 (and additional manuscripts within this special issue).

[12] T.A. Baillie, A.E. Rettie, Role of biotransformation in drug-induced toxicity: influence of intra- and inter-species differences in drug metabolism, Drug Metabol. Pharmacokinet. 6 (1) (2011) 15−29.

[13] J. Shanu-Wilson, L. Evans, S. Wrigley, J. Steele, J. Atherton, J. Boer, Biotransformation: impact and application of metabolism in drug discovery, ACS Med. Chem. Lett. 11 (11) (2020) 2087−2107.

[14] A.V. Stachulski, T.A. Baillie, B.K. Park, R.S. Obach, D.K. Dalvie, D.P. Williams, A. Srivastava, S.L. Regan, D.J. Antoine, C.E. Goldring, A.J. Chia, N.R. Kitteringham, L.E. Randle, H. Callan, J.L. Castrejon, J. Farrell, D.J. Naisbitt, M.S. Lennard, The generation, detection, and effects of reactive drug metabolites, Med. Res. Rev. 33 (5) (2013) 985−1080.

[15] R.A. Thompson, E. M Isin, Y. Li, R. Weaver, L. Weidolf, I. Wilson, A. Claesson, K. Page, H. Dolgos, J.G. Kenna, Risk assessment and mitigation strategies for reactive metabolites in drug discovery and development, Chem. Biol. Interact. 192 (1−2) (2011) 65−71.

[16] A.F. Stepan, D.P. Walker, J. Bauman, D.A. Price, T. A Baillie, A.S. Kalgutkar, M.D. Aleo, Structural alert/reactive metabolite concept as applied in medicinal chemistry to mitigate the risk of idiosyncratic drug toxicity: a perspective based on the critical examination of trends in the top 200 drugs marketed in the United States, Chem. Res. Toxicol. 24 (9) (2011) 1345−1410.

[17] https://www.fda.gov/regulatory-information/search-fda-guidance-documents/safety-testing-drug-metabolites.

[18] S. Schadt, B. Bister, S.K. Chowdhury, C. Funk, C.E.C.A. Hop, W.G. Humphreys, F. Igarashi, A.D. James, M. Kagan, S.C. Khojasteh, A.N.R. Nedderman, C. Prakash, F. Runge, H. Scheible, D.K. Spracklin, P. Swart, S. Tse, J. Yuan, R.S. Obach, A decade in the MIST: learnings from investigations of drug metabolites in drug development under the "metabolites in safety testing" regulatory guidance, Drug Metab. Dispos. 46 (6) (2018) 865−878.

[19] T. Minagawa, K. Nakano, S. Furuta, T. Iwasa, K. Takekawa, K. Minato, T. Koga, T. Sato, K. Kawashima, Y. Kurahashi, H. Onodera, S. Naito, K. Nakamura, Perspectives on non-clinical safety evaluation of drug metabolites through the JSOT workshop, J. Toxicol. Sci. 37 (4) (2012) 667−673.

[20] R. Espina, L. Yu, J. Wang, Z. Tong, S. Vashishtha, R. Talaat, J. Scatina, A. Mutlib, Nuclear magnetic resonance spectroscopy as a quantitative tool to determine the concentrations of biologically produced metabolites: implications in metabolites in safety testing, Chem. Res. Toxicol. 22 (2) (2009) 299–310.

[21] K. Vishwanathan, K. Babalola, J. Wang, R. Espina, L. Yu, A. Adedoyin, R. Talaat, A. Mutlib, J. Scatina, Obtaining exposures of metabolites in preclinical species through plasma pooling and quantitative NMR: addressing metabolites in safety testing (MIST) guidance without using radiolabeled compounds and chemically synthesized metabolite standards, Chem. Res. Toxicol. 22 (2) (2009) 311–322.

[22] M.A. Cerny, A.S. Kalgutkar, R.S. Obach, R. Sharma, D.K. Spracklin, G.S. Walker, Effective application of metabolite profiling in drug design and discovery, J. Med. Chem. 63 (12) (2020) 6387–6406.

[23] R.J. Andrade, N. Chalasani, E.S. Björnsson, A. Suzuki, G.A. Kullak-Ublick, P.B. Watkins, H. Devarbhavi, M. Merz, M.I. Lucena, N. Kaplowitz, G.P. Aithal, Drug-induced liver injury, Nat. Rev. Dis. Prim. 5 (1) (2019) 58.

[24] M. Mosedale, P.B. Watkins, Drug-induced liver injury: advances in mechanistic understanding that will inform risk management, Clin. Pharmacol. Ther. 101 (4) (2017) 469–480.

[25] R. J Weaver, E.A. Blomme, A.E. Chadwick, I.M. Copple, H.H.J. Gerets, C.E. Goldring, A. Guillouzo, P.G. Hewitt, M. Ingelman-Sundberg, K.G. Jensen, S. Juhila, U. Klingmüller, G. Labbe, M.J. Liguori, C.A. Lovatt, P. Morgan, D.J. Naisbitt, R.H.H. Pieters, J. Snoeys, B. van de Water, D.P. Williams, B.K. Park, Managing the challenge of drug-induced liver injury: a roadmap for the development and deployment of preclinical predictive models, Nat. Rev. Drug Discov. 19 (2) (2020) 131–148.

[26] J.C. Fernandez-Checa, P. Bagnaninchi, H. Ye, P. Sancho-Bru, J.M. Falcon-Perez, F. Royo, C. Garcia-Ruiz, O. Konu, J. Miranda, O. Lunov, A. Dejneka, A. Elfick, A. McDonald, G.J. Sullivan, G.P. Aithal, M.I. Lucena, R.J. Andrade, B. Fromenty, M. Kranendonk, F.J. Cubero, L.J. Nelson, Advanced preclinical models for evaluation of drug-induced liver injury - consensus statement by the European Drug-Induced Liver Injury Network [PRO-EURO-DILI-NET], J. Hepatol. 75 (4) (2021) 935–959.

[27] A. Sawant-Basak, R.S. Obach, Emerging models of drug metabolism, transporters, and toxicity, Drug Metab. Dispos. 46 (11) (2018) 1556–1561 (and additional manuscripts within this special issue).

[28] J.G. Kenna, K.S. Taskar, C. Battista, D.L. Bourdet, K.L.R. Brouwer, K.R. Brouwer, D. Dai, C. Funk, M.J. Hafey, Y. Lai, J. Maher, Y.A. Pak, J.M. Pedersen, J.W. Polli, A.D. Rodrigues, P.B. Watkins, K. Yang, R.W. Yucha, International transporter consortium, can bile salt export pump inhibition testing in drug discovery and development reduce liver injury risk? An international transporter consortium perspective, Clin. Pharmacol. Ther. 104 (5) (2018) 916–932.

[29] P.B. Watkins, The DILI-sim initiative: insights into hepatotoxicity mechanisms and biomarker interpretation, Clin. Transl. Sci. 12 (2) (2019) 122–129.

[30] S. Castellino, M.R. Groseclose, J. Sigafoos, D. Wagner, M. de Serres, J.W. Polli, E. Romach, J. Myer, B. Hamilton, Central nervous system disposition and metabolism of fosdevirine (GSK2248761), a non-nucleoside reverse transcriptase inhibitor: an LC-MS and Matrix-assisted laser desorption/ionization imaging MS investigation into central nervous system toxicity, Chem. Res. Toxicol. 26 (2) (2013) 241–251.

[31] S. Castellino, N.M. Lareau, M.R. Groseclose, The emergence of imaging mass spectrometry in drug discovery and development: making a difference by driving decision making, J. Mass Spectrom. 56 (8) (2021) e4717.

[32] M. Zhu, H. Zhang, W.G. Humphreys, Drug metabolite profiling and identification by high-resolution mass spectrometry, J. Biol. Chem. 286 (29) (2011) 25419–25425.

[33] S. Ma, S.K. Chowdhury, Data acquisition and data mining techniques for metabolite identification using LC coupled to high-resolution MS, Bioanalysis 5 (10) (2013) 1285–1297.

[34] https://www.fda.gov/drugs/drug-interactions-labeling/drug-development-and-drug-interactions-table-substrates-inhibitors-and-inducers.

[35] C. Emoto, N. Murayama, A. Rostami-Hodjegan, H. Yamazaki, Methodologies for investigating drug metabolism at the early drug discovery stage: prediction of hepatic drug clearance and P450 contribution, Curr. Drug Metabol. 11 (8) (2010) 678–685.

[36] M.A. Correia, P.F. Hollenberg, Inhibition of cytochrome P450 enzymes, in: P.R. Ortiz de Montellano (Ed.), Cytochrome P450: Structure, Mechanism, and Biochemistry, fourth ed., 2015, pp. 177–259.

[37] J. Hakkola, J. Hukkanen, M. Turpeinen, O. Pelkonen, Inhibition and induction of CYP enzymes in humans: an update, Arch. Toxicol. 94 (11) (2020) 3671–3722.

[38] J.O. Miners, A. Rowland, J.J. Novak, K. Lapham, T.C. Goosen, Evidence-based strategies for the characterisation of human drug and chemical glucuronidation in vitro and UDP-glucuronosyltransferase reaction phenotyping, Pharmacol. Ther. 218 (2021) 107689.

[39] U.A. Argikar, P.M. Potter, J.M. Hutzler, P.H. Marathe, Challenges and opportunities with non-CYP enzymes aldehyde oxidase, carboxylesterase, and UDP-glucuronosyltransferase: focus on reaction phenotyping and prediction of human clearance, AAPS J. 18 (6) (2016) 1391–1405.

[40] A.E. Mutlib, Application of stable isotope-labeled compounds in metabolism and in metabolism-mediated toxicity studies, Chem. Res. Toxicol. 21 (9) (2008) 1672–1689.

[41] T. Pirali, M. Serafini, S. Cargnin, A.A. Genazzani, Applications of deuterium in medicinal chemistry, J. Med. Chem. 62 (11) (2019) 5276–5297.

[42] F.P. Guengerich, Kinetic deuterium isotope effects in cytochrome P450 reactions, Methods Enzymol. 596 (2017) 217–238.

[43] S. Fowler, W.L.K. Chen, D.B. Duignan, A. Gupta, N. Hariparsad, J.R. Kenny, W.G. Lai, J. Liras, J.A. Phillips, J. Gan, Microphysiological systems for ADME-related applications: current status and recommendations for system development and characterization, Lab Chip 20 (3) (2020) 446–467.

[44] S. Youhanna, A.M. Kemas, L. Preiss, Y. Zhou, J.X. Shen, S.D. Cakal, F.S. Paqualini, S.K. Goparaju, R.Z. Shafagh, J.U. Lind, C.M. Sellgren, V.M. Lauschke, Organotypic and microphysiological human tissue models for drug discovery and development-current state-of-the-art and future perspectives, Pharmacol. Rev. 74 (1) (2022) 141–206.

[45] J.X. Shen, S. Youhanna, R. Zandi Shafagh, J. Kele, V. M Lauschke, Organotypic and microphysiological models of liver, gut, and kidney for studies of drug metabolism, pharmacokinetics, and toxicity, Chem. Res. Toxicol. 33 (1) (2020) 38−60.

[46] J.A. Phillips, T.S.P. Grandhi, M. Davis, J.C. Gautier, N. Hariparsad, D. Keller, R. Sura, T.R. Van Vleet, A pharmaceutical industry perspective on microphysiological kidney systems for evaluation of safety for new therapies, Lab Chip 20 (3) (2020) 468−476.

[47] A.R. Baudy, M.A. Otieno, P. Hewitt, J. Gan, A. Roth, D. Keller, R. Sura, T.R. Van Vleet, W.R. Proctor, Liver microphysiological systems development guidelines for safety risk assessment in the pharmaceutical industry, Lab Chip 20 (2) (2020) 215−225.

[48] A.K. Kopec, R. Yokokawa, N. Khan, I. Horii, J.E. Finley, C.P. Bono, C. Donovan, J. Roy, J. Harney, A.D. Burdick, B. Jessen, S. Lu, M. Collinge, R.B. Sadeghian, M. Derzi, L. Tomlinson, J.E. Burkhardt, Microphysiological systems in early stage drug development: perspectives on current applications and future impact, J. Toxicol. Sci. 46 (3) (2021) 99−114.

[49] P.R.O. de Montellano, 1-aminobenzotriazole: a mechanism-based cytochrome P450 inhibitor and probe of cytochrome P450 biology, Med. Chem. 8 (3) (2018) 038.

[50] T.J. Strelevitz, R.S. Foti, M. B Fisher, In vivo use of the P450 inactivator 1-aminobenzotriazole in the rat: varied dosing route to elucidate gut and liver contributions to first-pass and systemic clearance, J. Pharmaceut. Sci. 95 (2006) 1334−1341.

[51] M.O. Boily, N. Chauret, J. Laterreur, F.A. Leblond, C. Boudreau, M.C. Duquet, J.F. Lévesque, L. Ste-Marie, V. Pichette, In vitro and in vivo mechanistic studies toward understanding the role of 1-aminobenzotriazole in rat drug-drug interactions, Drug Metab. Dispos. 43 (2015) 1960−1965.

[52] K.E. Parrish, J. Mao, J. Chen, A. Jaochico, J. Ly, Q. Ho, S. Mukadam, M. Wright, In vitro and in vivo characterization of CYP inhibition by 1-aminobenzotriazole in rats, Biopharm. Drug Dispos. 37 (2016) 200−211.

[53] R.A. Stringer, E. Weber, B. Tigani, P. Lavan, S. Medhurst, B. Sohal, 1-Aminobenzotriazole modulates oral drug pharmacokinetics through cytochrome P450 inhibition and delay of gastric emptying in rats, Drug Metab. Dispos. 42 (2014) 1117−1124.

[54] R.A. Stringer, S. Ferreira, J. Rose, S. Ronseaux, Application of osmotic pumps for sustained release of 1-aminobenzotriazole and inhibition of cytochrome P450 enzymes in mice: model comparison with the hepatic P450 reductase null mouse, Drug Metab. Dispos. 44 (2016) 1213−1216.

[55] S.K. Balani, T. Zhu, T.J. Yang, Z. Liu, B. He, F.W. Lee, Effective dosing regimen of 1- aminobenzotriazole for inhibition of antipyrine clearance in rats, dogs, and monkeys, Drug Metab. Dispos. 30 (2002) 1059−1062.

[56] S.K. Balani, P. Li, J. Nguyen, H. Zeng, D.X. Mu, J.T. Wu, L.S. Gan, F.W. Lee, Effective dosing regimen of 1-aminobenzotriazole for inhibition of antipyrine clearance in Guinea pigs and mice using serial Sampling, Drug Metab. Dispos. 32 (2004) 1092−1095.

[57] Y. Wei, X. Zhou, C. Fang, L. Li, K. Kluetzman, W. Yang, Q.Y. Zhang, X. Ding, Generation of a mouse model with a reversible hypomorphic cytochrome P450 reductase gene: utility for tissue-specific rescue of the reductase expression, and insights from a resultant mouse model with global suppression of P450 reductase expression in extrahepatic tissues, J. Pharmacol. Exp. Therapeut. 334 (1) (2010) 69−77.

[58] L. Ding, L. Li, S. Liu, X. Bao, K.G. Dickman, S.S. Sell, C. Mei, Q.-Y. Zhang, J. Gu, X. Ding, Proximal tubular vacuolization and hypersensitivity to drug-induced nephrotoxicity in male mice with decreased expression of the NADPH-cytochrome P450 reductase, Toxicol. Sci. 173 (2) (2020) 362−372.

[59] J.A. Miller, Carcinogenesis by chemicals: an overview. G.H.A Clowes memorial lecture, Cancer Res. 30 (1970) 559−576.

[60] W.Z. Potter, D.C. Davis, J.R. Mitchell, D.J. Jollow, J.R. Gillette, B.B. Brodie, Acetaminophen-induced hepatic necrosis. III. Cytochrome P-450-mediated covalent binding in vitro, J. Exp. Pharmacol. Ther. 187 (1973) 203−210.

[61] J.R. Mitchell, D.J. Jollow, W.Z. Potter, J.R. Gillette, B.B. Brodie, Acetaminophen-induced hepatic necrosis. IV. Protective role of glutathione, J. Exp. Parmacol. Therap. 187 (1973) 211−217.

[62] J.R. Mitchell, D.J. Jollow, W.Z. Potter, D.C. Davis, J.R. Gillette, B.B. Brodie BB, Acetaminophen-induced hepatic necrosis. I. Role of drug metabolism, J. Exp. Pharmacol. Ther. 187 (1973) 185−194.

[63] D.J. Jollow, M.R. Mitchell, W.Z. Potter, D.C. Davis, J.R. Gillette, B.B. Brodie, Acetaminophen-induced hepatic necrosis. II. Role of covalent binding in vivo, J. Exp. Pharmacol. Ther. 187 (1973) 195−202.

[64] H. Schumacher, R.L. Smith, R.T. Williams, The metabolism of thalidomide: the fate of thalidomide and some of its hydrolysis products in various species, Br. J. Pharmacol. Chemother. 25 (1965) 338−351.

[65] J.R. Mitchell, W.Z. Potter, J.A. Hinson, D.J. Jollow, Hepatic necrosis caused by furosemide, Nature 251 (1974) 508−511.

[66] P.J. Wirth, C.J. Bettis, W.L. Nelson, Microsomal metabolism of furosemide evidence for the nature of the reactive intermediate involved in covalent binding, Mol. Pharmacol. 12 (1976) 759−768.

[67] R.J. McMurtry, J.R. Mitchell, Renal and hepatic necrosis after metabolic activation of 2-substituted furans and thiophenes, including furosemide and cephaloridine, Toxicol. Appl. Pharmacol. 42 (1977) 285−300.

[68] A.E. Mutlib, H. Chen, G.A. Nemeth, J.A. Markwalder, S.P. Seitz, L.S. Gan, D.D. Christ, Identification and characterization of efavirenz metabolites by liquid chromatography/mass spectrometry and high field NMR: species differences in the metabolism of efavirenz, Drug Metab. Dispos. 27 (11) (1999) 1319−1333.

[69] A.E. Mutlib, R.J. Gerson, P.C. Meunier, P.J. Haley, H. Chen, L.S. Gan, M.H. Davies, B. Gemzik, D.D. Christ, D.F. Krahn, J.A. Markwalder, S.P. Seitz, R.T. Robertson, G.T. Miwa, The species-dependent metabolism of efavirenz produces a nephrotoxic glutathione conjugate in rats, Toxicol. Appl. Pharmacol. 169 (1) (2000) 102−113.

[70] A.E. Mutlib, J. Shockcor, R. Espina, N. Graciani, A. Du, L.S. Gan, Disposition of glutathione conjugates in rats by a novel glutamic acid pathway: characterization of unique peptide conjugates by liquid chromatography/mass spectrometry and liquid chromatography/NMR, J. Pharmacol. Exp. Therapeut. 294 (2) (2000) 735−745.

[71] C. Zetterberg, F. Maltais, L. Laitinen, S. Liao, H. Tsao, A. Chakilam, N. Hariparsad, VX-509 (decernotinib)-mediated CYP3A time-dependent inhibition: an aldehyde oxidase metabolite as a perpetrator of drug-drug interactions, Drug Metab. Dispos. 44 (8) (2016) 1286−1295.

[72] J.J. Beaudoin, J. Bezençon, N. Sjöstedt, J.K. Fallon, K.L.R. Brouwer, Role of organic solute transporter alpha/beta in hepatotoxic bile acid transport and drug interactions, Toxicol. Sci. 176 (1) (2020) 34−35.

[73] M.A. Otieno, J. Snoeys, W. Lam, A. Ghosh, M.R. Player, A. Pocai, R. Salter, D. Simic, H. Skaggs, B. Singh, H.K. Lim, Fasiglifam (TAK-875): mechanistic investigation and retrospective identification of hazards for drug induced liver injury, Toxicol. Sci. 163 (2) (2018) 374−384.

[74] S.G. Yarlagadda, M.A. Perazella, Drug-induced crystal nephropathy: an update, Expert Opin. Drug Saf. 7 (2008) 147−158.

[75] B.A. Lanman, A.B. Reed, V.J. Cee, F.T. Hong, L.H. Pettus, R.P. Wurz, K.L. Andrews, J. Jiang, J.D. McCarter, E.L. Mullady, T. San Miguel, R. Subramanian, L. Wang, D.A. Whittington, T. Wu, L. Zalameda, N. Zhang, A.S. Tasker, P.E. Hughes, M.H. Norman, Phosphoinositide-3-kinase inhibitors: evaluation of substituted alcohols as replacements for the piperazine sulfonamide portion of AMG 511, Bioorg. Med. Chem. Lett. 24 (24) (2014) 5630−5634.

[76] S. Kumar, K. Mitra, K. Kassahun, T.A. Baillie, Approaches for minimizing metabolic activation of new drug candidates in drug discovery, Handb. Exp. Pharmacol. 196 (2010) 511−544.

[77] D. Dalvie, A.S. Kalgutkar, W. Chen, Practical approaches to resolving reactive metabolite liabilities in early discovery, Drug Metab. Rev. 47 (1) (2015) 56−70.

[78] N.A. Meanwell, Improving drug candidates by design: a focus on physicochemical properties as a means of improving compound disposition and safety, Chem. Res. Toxicol. 24 (9) (2011) 1420−1456.

[79] A.S. Kalgutkar, Designing around structural alerts in drug discovery, J. Med. Chem. 63 (12) (2020) 6276−6302.

[80] D. Zhang, O. Flint, L. Wang, A. Gupta, R.A. Westhouse, W. Zhao, N. Raghavan, J. Caceres-Cortes, P. Marathe, G. Shen, Y. Zhang, A. Allentoff, J. Josephs, J. Gan, R. Borzilleri, W.G. Humphreys, Cytochrome P450 11A1 bioactivation of a kinase inhibitor in rats: use of radioprofiling, modulation of metabolism, and adrenocortical cell lines to evaluate adrenal toxicity, Chem. Res. Toxicol. 25 (3) (2012) 556−571.

[81] https://www.accessdata.fda.gov/drugsatfda_docs/nda/2009/022350s000_PharmR_P1.pdf.

[82] https://www.ema.europa.eu/en/documents/assessment-report/onglyza-epar-public-assessment-report_en.pdf.

[83] B. Soto-Blanco, P.C. Marioka, S.L. Górniak, Effects of long-term low-dose cyanide administration to rats, Ecotoxicol. Environ. Saf. 53 (1) (2002) 37−41.

[84] T. Tylleskär, M. Banea, N. Bikangi, R.D. Cooke, N.H. Poulter, H. Rosling, Cassava cyanogens and konzo, an upper motoneuron disease found in Africa, Lancet 339 (8787) (1992) 208−211.

[85] E. Kashala-Abotnes, D. Okitundu, D. Mumba, M.J. Boivin, T. Tylleskär, D. Tshala-Katumbay, Konzo: a distinct neurological disease associated with food (cassava) cyanogenic poisoning, Brain Res. Bull. 145 (2019) 87−91.

[86] M.E. Taub, E. Ludwig-Schwellinger, N. Ishiguro, W. Kishimoto, H. Yu, K. Wagner, D. Tweedie, Sex-, species-, and tissue-specific metabolism of empagliflozin in male mouse kidney forms an unstable hemiacetal metabolite (M466/2) that degrades to 4-hydroxycrotonaldehyde, a reactive and cytotoxic species, Chem. Res. Toxicol. 28 (1) (2015) 103−115.

[87] J.D. Smith, Z. Huang, P.A. Escobar, P. Foppiano, H. Maw, W. Loging, H. Yu, J.A. Phillips, M. Taub, W.W. Ku, A predominant oxidative renal metabolite of empagliflozin in male mice is cytotoxic in mouse renal tubular cells but not genotoxic, Int. J. Toxicol. 36 (6) (2017) 440−448.

[88] J.R. Infante, T. Rugg, M. Gordon, I. Rooney, L. Rosen, K. Zeh, R. Liu, H.A. Burris, R.K. Ramanathan, Unexpected renal toxicity associated with SGX523, a small molecule inhibitor of MET, Invest. N. Drugs 31 (2) (2013) 363−369.

[89] S. Diamond, J. Boer, T.P. Maduskuie Jr., N. Falahatpisheh, Y. Li, S. Yeleswaram, Species-specific metabolism of SGX523 by aldehyde oxidase and the toxicological implications, Drug Metab. Dispos. 38 (8) (2010) 1277−1285.

Chapter 14

Overcoming nephrotoxicity in rats: the successful development and registration of the HIV-AIDS drug efavirenz (Sustiva®)

D.D. Christ

SNC Partners LLC, Annapolis, MD, United States

In memory of Gerald T. Miwa Ph.D., scientist, mentor, friend

Background and introduction

All drugs encounter obstacles on the road to approval. The successful development and registration of efavirenz (also referred to in the literature as L-743,726 and DMP266, Fig. 14.1), a non-nucleoside reverse transcriptase inhibitor (NNRTI) and a cornerstone in the effective treatment of HIV AIDS is an excellent example of the critical integration of traditional drug development and discovery departments and the teamwork necessary to solve complex scientific problems. While these concepts may be self-evident now (but still aren't universal), it's important to remember that the studies described here occurred in the 1990s, when many pharmaceutical organizations operated in a "silo" model where "discovery" was distinct from "development" and departments (toxicology, DMPK), were not always well integrated.

Efavirenz was first synthesized at Merck and profiled by their pharmacology and DMPK groups. Dupont Merck was formed as a joint venture in 1991, and in 1994 efavirenz was brought into the new company by the new senior R&D leadership from Merck, taking leadership roles in the joint venture. It was a time of transition and growth. This case study describes the background and the science behind the successful effort to eliminate a nonclinical toxicity as an obstacle to clinical studies and drug registration. There are three key messages to emphasize from this example that are still important and applicable;

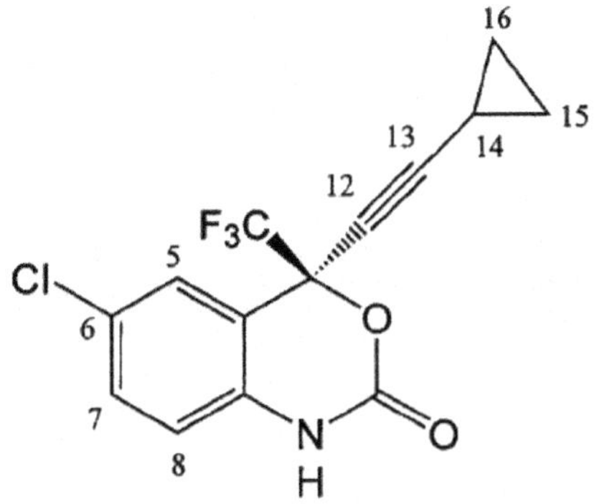

FIGURE 14.1 Chemical structure of efavirenz. Oxidation at the 8′ position of the phenyl ring with subsequent glucuronidation and sulfation and oxidation at the 14′ methine of the cyclopropyl sidechain substituent are key metabolic reactions.

Overcoming Obstacles in Drug Discovery and Development. https://doi.org/10.1016/B978-0-12-817134-9.00006-4

- Experienced, engaged scientific leadership is necessary to making correct decisions. Is this a problem worth solving? Is it one we *can* solve, scientifically and from a regulatory review perspective and in a practical timeframe? What resources (intellectual and physical) do we need and do we have them?
- Teams, across and within *all* organizational departments, must be formed rapidly; integration is essential, not optional and a strong sense of urgency is expected, not desired. Are there intellectual and technical resources available in other departments that can help solve the problem? Are there key experts that can help us think about this?
- Hypotheses, clear plans, and experiments coupled to strong communication must be established yet revised. How do the latest data confirm or refute our understanding and affect the plans for what's next based on these data?

It's important to recognize that while this narrative is linear, many of the experiments described below were done in parallel since time was critical. The ability to adjust rapidly based on the latest data and recruit additional resources were key to the success.

Background and the problem

You know it's a bad day when pathology slides look like this (Fig. 14.2):

Efavirenz was in the clinic after completing GLP-compliant, 1-month repeat dose toxicity studies with rats and monkeys and 3-month toxicity studies were in progress. Rats were dying in the 3-month studies of nephrotoxicity, specifically acute renal cortical tubular epithelial necrosis, producing the histology seen in the figure above. There was no nephrotoxicity in monkeys nor was there any evidence of renal toxicity in humans. Differences in systemic exposure to efavirenz didn't explain the species difference in nephrotoxicity since pharmacokinetics revealed both Cmax and AUC were higher in monkeys and in humans than in rats. But given the poorly understood relationship of the nephrotoxicity in rats to potential human safety, clinical dosing was suspended and a team of toxicologists and scientists from the DMPK department was assembled. *Here was the first key hurdle and organizational decision point; Is this a problem worth solving and do we have the team that can do it?*

Recall that in the 1980s and 1990s there were far fewer effective treatments for HIV-AIDS; the nucleoside analog AZT was introduced in 1987 and the first protease inhibitor saquinavir was available in 1995. Nivirapine, the first NNRTI, was approved in 1996. Efavirenz had excellent virological properties and good preliminary human safety and tolerability, and was clearly a needed therapeutic option for a devastating disease. Toxicology departments in pharmaceutical companies are not for the faint of heart; their job is to reveal a molecule's toxicity and *place toxicity in perspective regarding human safety*. The location of the lesion, potentially reversibility, and whether an easily measured, clearly relevant clinical marker is available must be considered when toxicity is observed. Seasoned, scientifically driven leadership is critical in evaluating nonclinical toxicities, placing findings in perspective, and advising senior management (including clinical development) on next steps. Here another part of the first question was answered; the experienced senior scientific leadership in R&D, Safety Assessment and DMPK, recently established at DuPont Merck from Merck and Glaxo (GTM), had a demonstrated track record of successfully integrating drug disposition and metabolism in addressing animal toxicities. The DMPK department at DuPont Merck had scientists with expertize in structure elucidation of metabolites, enzymology and pharmacokinetics, both nonclinical and clinical, and more were being hired to complement the existing expertize in these areas. The Safety Assessment department, already experienced in addressing these issues in Merck's programs, was also adding experienced toxicologists and pathologists at all levels. There were also excellent scientists from medicinal chemistry, chemical and

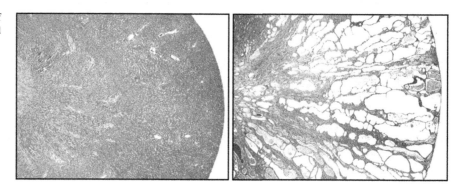

FIGURE 14.2 H&E stained sections of kidney cortex from control (left) and efavirenz-treated (right) rats.

physical sciences, pharmaceutics and analytical R&D available. *This was a problem worth solving and the expertize was present and growing.*

What was known

The toxicokinetics and metabolism of efavirenz are complex. Biochemical (Western blotting and CYP substrate assay) and TK data showed that efavirenz induced hepatic CYP2B and 3A isozymes in rats after a single dose and accelerated its metabolism producing lower plasma concentrations after multiple daily oral doses. Preliminary in vitro metabolism studies, both at Merck and DuPont Merck had shown efavirenz to be a low-turnover substrate in subcellular fractions from all species and that phenolic 8′-hydroxyefavirenz was the major metabolite produced, primarily by CYP2B1 and CYP2B6 in humans. Incubation with microsomes from rats treated with efavirenz to induce metabolism and liver and kidney slices from animals or humans produced 8′-hydroxyefavirenz and the phenolic glucuronide and sulfate conjugates. While other minor metabolites would be identified, the major metabolite in all species was the glucuronide conjugate of 8′-hydroxyefavirenz. But these conjugates weren't reactive, so what was their role, if any, in producing the nephrotoxicity? Were there important exposure differences in these metabolites associated with toxicity, or was an uncharacterized species-specific reactive metabolite responsible? More and more detailed metabolism studies and synthesis of authentic 8′-hydroxyefavirenz and glucuronide and sulfate conjugates by the medicinal chemists, were accelerated. The availability of authentic standards of primary and secondary metabolites in large quantities for in vitro and in vivo studies cannot be overemphasized. Recruiting medicinal chemists, classically a "discovery department" to the team early greatly facilitated in vitro and in vivo experiments in both safety assessment and DMPK. *Here the second key message is illustrated: while the team was led by scientists in toxicology and DMPK (both nonclinical and clinical groups), medicinal chemists, spectroscopists from chemical sciences, and scientists from pharmaceutics and analytical R&D were rapidly brought onto the team and contributed important expertise.*

Hypotheses and experimental attack

While a biochemical mechanism producing the toxicity was a credible hypothesis, like in all good mysteries another suspect was identified that would complicate the plot. The toxicologists had noted distinct off-white, crystalline material in the urine from some high-dose rats with nephrotoxicity and wondered if formation or disposition of these crystals (Fig. 14.3) in the nephron could be responsible for the toxicity. But were they drug-related?

To address this question, rats were given multiple 500 mg/kg oral doses of efavirenz and urine containing the crystals was collected and filtered. The crystals were harvested after careful washing, dissolved, analyzed by HPLC-MS/MS and ^{1}H-NMR and identified as the major metabolite, 8′-hydroxyefavirenz glucuronide. The structure was confirmed with authentic standards and plasma and urine assays were developed and used to quantitate 8′-hydroxyefavirenz glucuronide in rat, cynomolgus monkey, and human plasma and urine.

The potential for 8′-hydroxyefavirenz glucuronide to be filtered by rat kidney and precipitate as crystals in the microenvironment of the cortex causing damage was plausible because plasma concentrations of 8′-hydroxyefavirenz glucuronide in rats given nephrotoxic doses of efavirenz were extremely high, with a mean Cmax and AUC_{0-24h} of

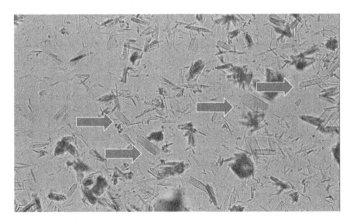

FIGURE 14.3 Crystals of drug-related material isolated from the urine of rats given nephrotoxic doses of efavirenz.

1.3 mM and 15.4 mM h, respectively. The appearance of 8′-hydroxyefavirenz glucuronide crystals in urine was also suggestive, as concentrations in the 0−24 urine from rats given 500 mg/kg/day for 14 days were also high, approximately 3 mM, and it's likely urine concentrations were greater earlier in the collection period. Plasma concentrations in cynomolgus monkeys and humans given the highest oral doses of efavirenz (75 mg/kg/day or 600 mg, respectively) were much lower, with mean Cmax values of 25 and 17 μM, respectively. Urine concentrations of 8′-hydroxyefavirenz glucuronide excreted by rats given 500 mg/kg/day for 2 weeks ranged from 3 to 6 mM and approximately 26% of the dose was recovered in the urine as 8′-hydroxyefavirenz glucuronide. Both the plasma Cmax and urine concentrations in rats were lower than the aqueous pH 7.3 solubility of 8′-hydroxyefavirenz glucuronide determined by the pharmaceutics and analytical R&D department, 18.3 mM. Any contribution of 8′-hydroxyefavirenz glucuronide crystals to the observed nephrotoxicity seemed unlikely.

While the 8′-hydroxyefavirenz glucuronide crystals were being isolated and identified to test that hypothesis, studies to define potential species-specific reactive metabolite formation were ongoing. In vivo and in vitro studies to test this hypothesis were being designed, facilitated by the availability of authentic standards. The steps were clear; generate a comprehensive metabolite profile from all species, identify primary and secondary metabolites suggesting formation of reactive intermediates, propose a pathway relating metabolism and toxicity, and manipulate metabolism and toxicity in vivo. *Here the third key lesson is illustrated: generate hypotheses, design experiments, reprioritize based on data, and communicate plans and progress clearly. Experimental data from these hypothesis-driven studies would be key in the regulatory approval of efavirenz.*

Defining the rat-specific nephrotoxic metabolic pathway

The metabolite profile was determined by LC-MS/MS and coupled LC-NMR using bile and urine collected from rats dosed with parent or authentic 8′-hydroxyefavirenz and 8′-hydroxyefavirenz sulfate metabolites [1]. Novel, mixed diconjugates including M9, a glutathione adduct of the 8′-hydroxyefavirenz sulfate, were identified and the structures defined unambiguously (Fig. 14.4), aided by the presence of the chlorine M+2 isotope clusters in the mass specta. Moreover, a cysteinyl-glycine metabolite (M10) was found in urine, consistent with the well-known renal processing of glutathione conjugates. Interestingly, no mercapturic acid metabolite was found. The structure of the glutathione adduct and cys-gly metabolite was unusual; sulfation of the phenol at the 8′ position of the phenyl ring and hydroxylation of the cyclopropyl methine to a cyclopropanol. Diconjugates had been identified previously (e.g. bilirubin diglucuronide, glutathione-glucuronide conjugate of valproic acid), but these were and are often difficult to characterize structurally because of their highly polar nature.

The presence of the cyclopropanol, demonstrating two metabolic oxidations, was intriguing. Consultants from academia with expertize in reactive intermediate chemistry and mechanisms of CYP oxidation were brought in to provide mechanistic insight into these novel structures. A step-wise mechanism was proposed for the ultimate production of M9 based on IV dosing or in vitro incubations with authentic parent, 8′-hydroxyefavirenz, and 8′-hydroxyefavirenz sulfate. These studies confirmed that initial oxidation at the 8′ position was followed by sulfation then oxidation to the cyclopropanol with subsequent addition of glutathione by glutathione S-transferase to the activated alkyne. Oxidation of the 8′-hydroxyefavirenz sulfate *per se* was shown after incubating authentic 8′-hydroxyefavirenz sulfate with rat liver microsomes and after IV dosing with the metabolite and identifying the cyclopropanol glutathione adduct from microsomal supernatants and rat bile. Now, the findings from these careful metabolite ID and in vitro studies with rats needed to be applied to monkeys and humans where nephrotoxicity was not apparent.

Urinary metabolites from several species including cynomolgus monkeys and humans were characterized by LC-MS/MS, LC-NMR, and high field NMR techniques [2]. In vitro studies with hepatic and renal subcellular fractions and purified enzymes (e.g. glutathione S-transferase) were also completed to confirm the sequential formation of the putative obligate nephrotoxic metabolite M9 and to define the species selectivity in its formation. While much of the focus was on urinary metabolites, plasma metabolite profiles, including in humans, were also determined. These studies demonstrated two key findings:

1. No glutathione or glutathione metabolites (cys-gly) were found in urine from humans or cynomolgus monkeys dosed with efavirenz.
2. No 8′-hydroxyefavirenz sulfate or metabolites containing the 8′-hydroxyefavirenz sulfate were found in human urine. Trace amounts of the sulfate conjugate of the 7′-hydroxy isomer on the phenyl ring were found, in addition to the expected 8′-hydroxyefavirenz glucuronide, suggesting that humans preferentially conjugate the 8′-hydroxy efavirenz with glucuronic acid rather than sulfate.

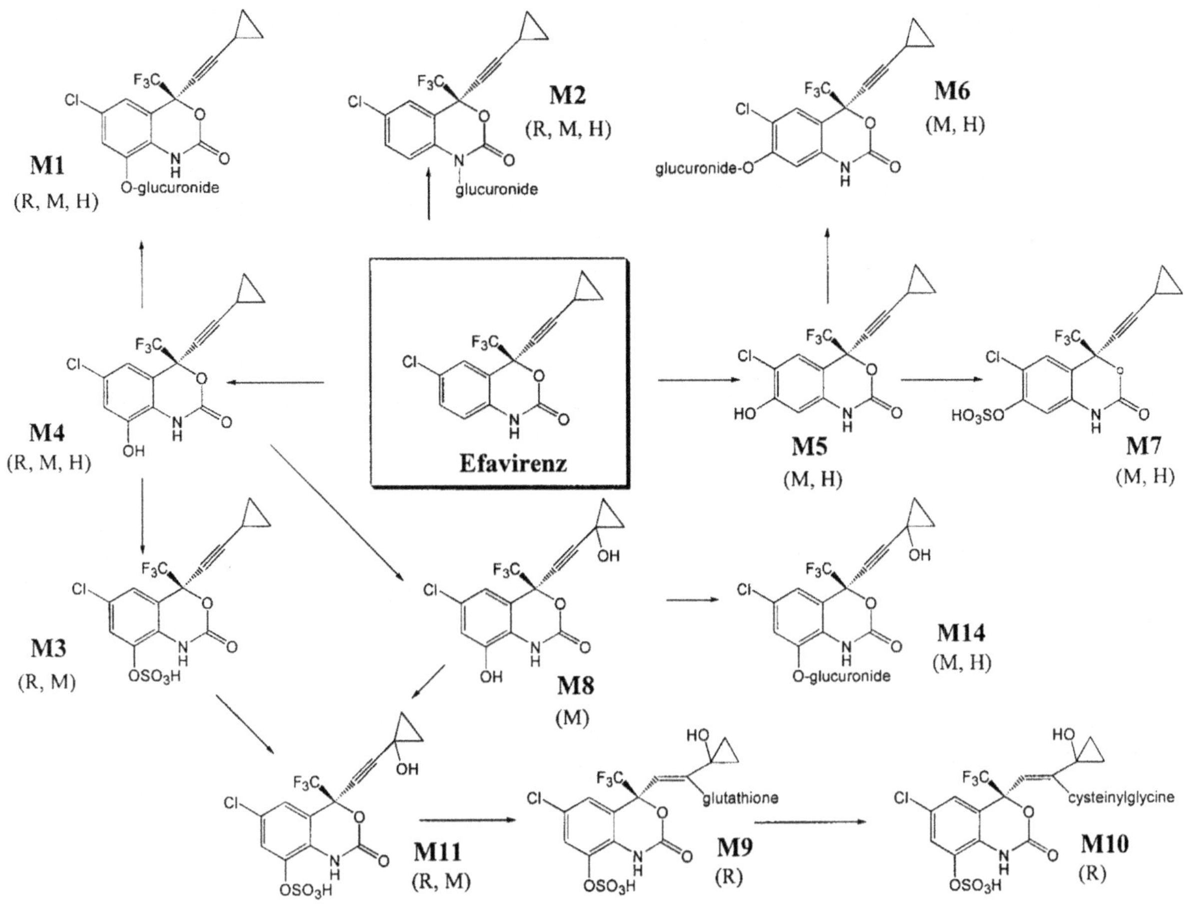

FIGURE 14.4 Pathways of formation and chemical structures for the metabolites of efavirenz in different species. *Reproduced from A.E. Mutlib, R.J. Gerson, P.C. Meunier, P.J. Haley, H. Chen, L. Gan, M.H. Davies, B. Gemzik, D.D. Christ, D.F. Krahn, J.A. Markwalder, S.P. Seitz, R.T. Robertson, G.T. Miwa, The species-dependent metabolism of efavirenz produces a nephrotoxic conjugate in rats, Toxicol. Appl. Pharmacol. 169 (2000) 102—113 with permission.*

Glutathione conjugation is classically a detoxification pathway for reactive electrophiles, although the intra-renal processing of glutathione conjugates by the γ-glutamyltranspeptidase/β-lyase pathway is a well-characterized activation cascade producing nephrotoxicity from halogenated alkenes, described in the 1980s by Drag Anders and colleagues. With a plausible biochemical mechanism proposed for the rat-specific nephrotoxicity, i.e. rat specific formation of M9, followed by renal metabolism of the glutathione conjugate and ultimate reaction with tissue nucleophiles to produce cortical necrosis, the next steps were clear; manipulate metabolism and determine the effect on nephrotoxicity in vivo.

Reducing the formation of reactive intermediate and interrupting the biochemical processing leading to tissue damage from these reactive intermediates was critical to establishing actual as opposed to theoretical causality. And essential to this effort was establishing a model that reproduced the renal tubular necrosis observed in the GLP-compliant studies. In vitro kidney slices were considered but were deprioritized in favor of the in vivo lesion. But any in vivo model had to satisfy two key criteria; the time frame for reproducing histological damage must be practical (short), and the quantitative scale for defining the damage (histology) must be robust. Capitalizing on the CYP induction of metabolism after even a single dose, toxicology and pathology developed a 5-day oral dosing with efavirenz study design, with a 3-day, low oral dose (30 mg/ kg) induction phase followed by a single, high oral dose (700 mg/kg). This regimen produced a reliable, graded histology score for nephrotoxicity ranging from 0 (no lesions) to 3 (moderate lesions defined as 25%—40% necrotic cells or tubules) or 4 (severe lesions defined as >40% necrotic cells or tubules) using four to nine rats per group. Establishing this reliable and robust model in a short time was a remarkable achievement.

Both chemical and biochemical tools were used to manipulate metabolism of efavirenz. Deuterium substitution to block or diminish CYP-mediated oxidation is a classic tool in the study of enzyme kinetics or the role of oxidation in the formation of reactive intermediate and subsequent toxicity. The availability of efavirenz deuterated at the C14 cyclopropyl methine position in sufficient quantities to support in vivo dosing greatly facilitated both in vivo and in vitro experiments demonstrating that oxidation at this position was critical in the formation of the ultimate nephrotoxicant. The potent and selective γ-glutamyltranspeptidase inhibitor acivicin was used to interrupt the renal processing of the glutathione conjugate by the γ-glutamyltranspeptidase/β-lyase pathway. Renal histology was evaluated and scored by pathologists blinded with respect to animal treatment with either deuterated efavirenz or acivicin, and urinary concentrations of the cys-gly metabolite (M10), 8′-hydroxyefavirenz glucuronide, and 8′-hydroxyefavirenz sulfate were also measured by LC-MS/MS. These were the key studies linking species-specific metabolism and toxicity, and while the ultimate cellular targets hit by the proposed reactive intermediate species weren't identified, the data would provide key mechanistic support for the continued safe human dosing with efavirenz in pivotal clinical trials.

Pretreating rats with acivicin before dosing with efavirenz or dosing with deuterated efavirenz decreased both the magnitude of nephrotoxicity (as expressed by a weighted histology score, Fig. 14.5) and the severity of the renal lesion (as expressed by the number of animals rated with moderate or severe histological lesions). The incidence of cortical epithelial necrosis was 100% (9 of 9 rats) with equal distribution among grades 1, 2, and 3 given efavirenz alone, and was shifted markedly after pretreatment with acivicin, where only 5 of 9 rats had scores of 1 (4 of 9) or 3 (1 of 9) while the other 4 rats had no lesions. Dosing with deuterated efavirenz also shifted the severity distribution in a statistically significant way, with 2 of 10 rats presenting no lesions (0) and 4 of 10 presenting minimal lesions [1]. No rats dosed with deuterated efavirenz had a grade 4 lesion.

This mitigation of toxicity was accompanied by statistically significant decreases in the concentration and amount of the cys-gly metabolite M10 excreted in urine after either acivicin or deuterated efavirenz treatment. The following scheme (Fig. 14.6) was proposed for the processing of the rat-specific nephrotoxic M10 based on the animal model results, the extensive metabolite profiling work demonstrating the absence of any glutathione-related metabolites in human or cynomolgus monkey excreta, and the lack of any glutathione adducts formed in vitro by human or cynomolgus monkey liver or kidney preparations. Whether the absence of glutathione adducts in monkeys or humans results from species differences in GST isozymes or species differences in substrate selectivity for M11 is unknown.

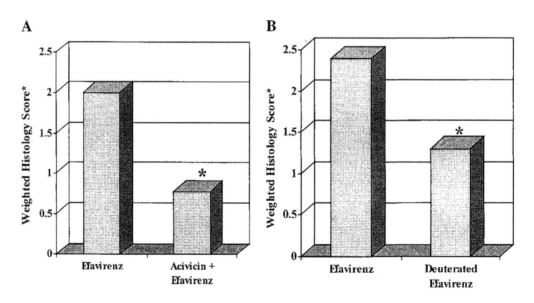

Weighted Histology Score = (Sum of Individual Histology Scores ÷ N)

Histology *Score of 0 = unaffected, 1 = minimal, 2 = mild, 3 = moderate, 4 = marked

FIGURE 14.5 Effects of dosing deuterated efavirenz, or proto efavirenz after pretreatment of rats with acivicin on the observed nephrotoxicity in rats. *Reproduced from A.E. Mutlib, R.J. Gerson, P.C. Meunier, P.J. Haley, H. Chen, L. Gan, M.H. Davies, B. Gemzik, D.D. Christ, D.F. Krahn, J.A. Markwalder, S.P. Seitz, R.T. Robertson, G.T. Miwa, The species-dependent metabolism of efavirenz produces a nephrotoxic conjugate in rats, Toxicol. Appl. Pharmacol. 169 (2000) 102–113 with permission.*

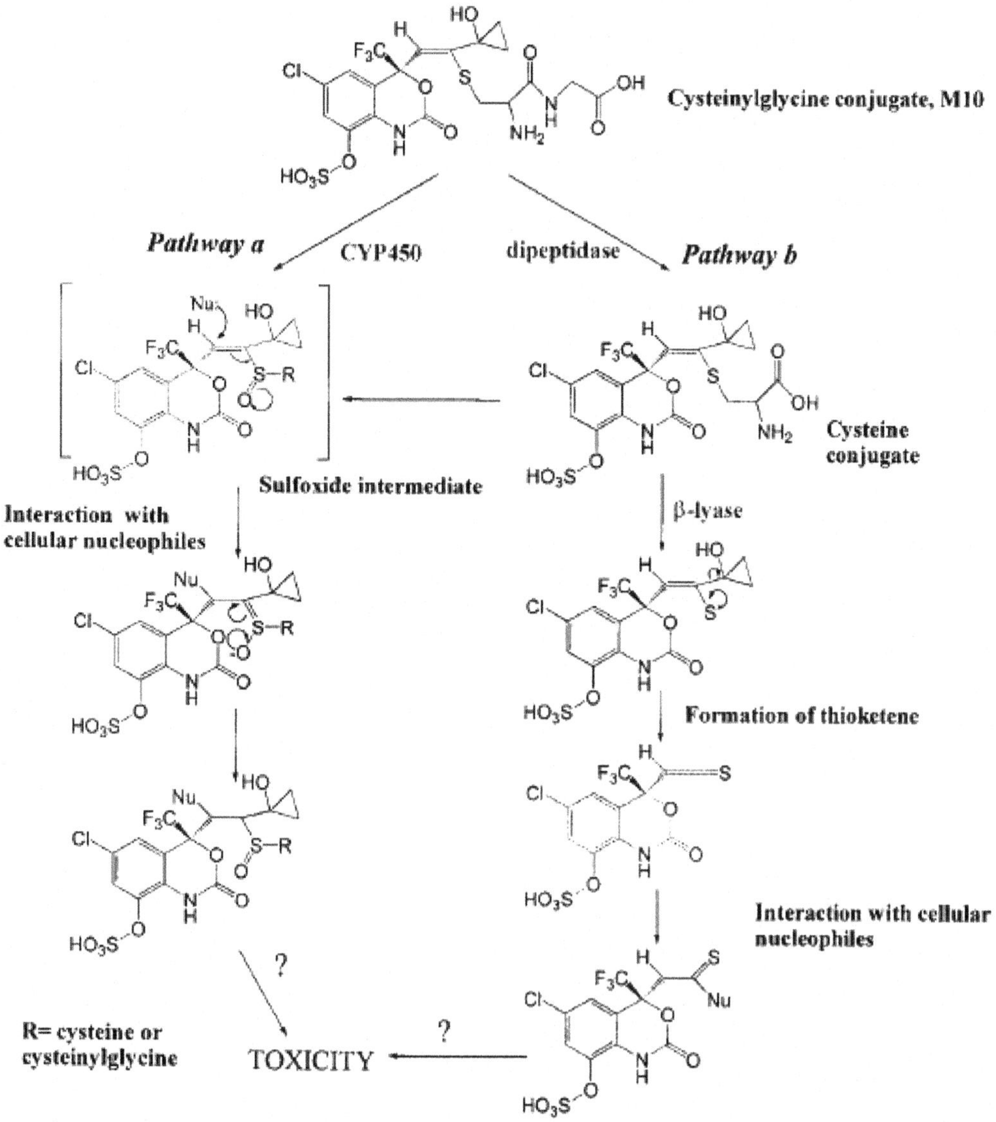

SCHEME 3. Postulated mechanisms of efavirenz glutathione-induced nephrotoxicity in rats.

FIGURE 14.6 Proposed pathway by which the rat-specific nephrotoxic metabolite M10 could produce renal cortical tubular necrosis in rats given efavirenz. *Reproduced from A.E. Mutlib, R.J. Gerson, P.C. Meunier, P.J. Haley, H. Chen, L. Gan, M.H. Davies, B. Gemzik, D.D. Christ, D.F. Krahn, J.A. Markwalder, S.P. Seitz, R.T. Robertson, G.T. Miwa, The species-dependent metabolism of efavirenz produces a nephrotoxic conjugate in rats, Toxicol. Appl. Pharmacol. 169 (2000) 102–113 with permission.*

Impact

While clinical development was initially paused until the relevance of the rat nephrotoxicity was better understood, development resumed once it became apparent there was little risk to patients. Efavirenz was approved by the FDA in 1998 and the extensive studies summarized here (including the identification of urinary crystals) were cited in the FDA's review and conclusions of the adequacy of the nonclinical safety package submitted for approval [4]. While not the only example, the work described here illustrates the power of dedicated scientific teams in overcoming a critical hurdle in drug development, and supporting approval of an important new drug.

Acknowledgments

Gerald Miwa's unexpected passing was a great loss to his family, many friends and the drug metabolism community. I was flattered to be asked to step in and summarize a great deal of effort and good science by many, many people. It really was a company-wide effort for scientists, clinicians, and staff across the organization involved in this project and I'm sure I will miss acknowledging some and I apologize; every contribution was important and deserves recognition. Some key people however, need to be named. Suresh Balani, Jiunn Lin and colleagues did the early metabolism and TK studies during discovery at Merck. Paul Friedman, Rick Robertson and Gerald Miwa provided the science-driven leadership and perspective to start and then guide these efforts. Ron Gerson, Paul Meunier, Brad Barnes, Brian Gemzik, Dave Krahn, Pat Haley and Mark Davies from Safety Assessment drove these and many other studies, especially the short-term nephrotoxicity rat model. Abdul Mutlib, Hao Chen, Lawrence Gan, Sharon Diamond, Mary Grubb and others worked out the metabolism story while Bill Fiske, Barbara Massello, Amita Joshi and others from the clinical DMPK group added the pharmacokinetic and toxicokinetic data for animals and humans dosed in the many studies cited here and others that were not discussed. Classic discovery chemistry support from Paul Anderson's department was essential, innovative, and timely. Steve Seitz, Jay Markwalder, Greg Nemeth, and George Trainor provided the synthetic expertize and analytical characterization necessary to provide standards of complex metabolites. External company consultants like Tom Baille and Paul Ortiz de Montellano were brought in to comment on chemical structure, activation, and reactivity.

I accept the responsibility for any and all errors and omissions in this narrative, and while I believe I have the metabolism-toxicology story right, I'm sure there was much going on in other critical areas I didn't see, especially the adjustments to the clinical, regulatory, and drug supply programs necessitated by these studies that I haven't covered.

References

[1] A.E. Multib, H. Chen, G. Nemeth, L. Gan, D.D. Christ, LC/MS and high field NMR characterization of novel mixed diconjugates of the non-nucleoside HIV-1 reverse transcriptase inhibitor, efavirenz, Drug Metab. Dispos. 27 (1999) 1045−1056.

[2] A.E. Multib, H. Chen, G.A. Nemeth, J.A. Markwalder, S.P. Seitz, L.S. Gan, D.D. Christ, Identification and characterization of efavirenz metabolites by LC/MS and high field NMR. Species differences in the metabolism of efavirenz, Drug Metab. Dispos. 27 (1999) 1319−1333.

[3] A.E. Mutlib, R.J. Gerson, P.C. Meunier, P.J. Haley, H. Chen, L. Gan, M.H. Davies, B. Gemzik, D.D. Christ, D.F. Krahn, J.A. Markwalder, S.P. Seitz, R.T. Robertson, G.T. Miwa, The species-dependent metabolism of efavirenz produces a nephrotoxic conjugate in rats, Toxicol. Appl. Pharmacol. 169 (2000) 102−113.

[4] Pharmacologist's review, CDER application no. 20-972. Available online at: https://www.accessdata.fda.gov/drugsatfda_docs/nda/98/20972pharmtox_review.pdf.

Chapter 15

Disproportionate drug metabolites: challenges and solutions

Chandra Prakash

Department of Drug Metabolism, Pharmacokinetics and Clinical Pharmacology, Agios Pharmaceuticals, Cambridge, MA, United States

Introduction

Metabolites, products of in vivo biotransformation, have a significant impact in drug development because they can modulate the safety and efficacy of drugs. There are many cases in which metabolites can cause on-target and/or off-target toxicity, which result in drug withdrawals or black box warnings [1]. Therefore, safety evaluation of metabolites, in addition to the parent drug, is of high interest in the pharmaceutical industry.

The common practice used to assess parent drug safety in clinical trials is comparing systemic exposure of the parent drug's systemic exposure in humans to that achieved in animals used for long-term toxicity assessments. When the metabolic profile is similar across species, monitoring parent drug exposure only in nonclinical and clinical settings gives a good estimate of the drug safety profile. However, when a metabolite either is formed exclusively in humans or its exposure is significantly higher than in the nonclinical species, the safety of the parent drug cannot be fully characterized in standard toxicology studies. To provide guidance on how to address key issues regarding the role of metabolites in the overall safety profile of the parent drug, the FDA issued a draft guidance on the safety testing of drug metabolites in 2008 [2]. In an industry-wide push for regulatory harmonization, the FDA revised the guidance to closely align with the ICH M3(R2) [3,4] and finalized the guidance in 2020 [5]. The FDA guidance introduces the concept of "disproportionate drug metabolites," defining them as "metabolites identified only in humans or present at higher plasma concentrations in humans than in any of the animal species used during standard nonclinical toxicology testing" [2–5]. Human metabolites that can raise a safety concern are those present at greater than 10% of total drug-related exposure at steady state [5] and are referred to as "major metabolites". The guidance recommended the following:

1. Qualitative and quantitative characterization of metabolism across species
2. Establishing in vitro-in vivo correlation of metabolism in nonclinical species
3. Conducting in vivo human metabolism studies as early as possible to avoid drug development delays due to the identification of disproportionate metabolites
4. Initiating discussions with the FDA about the safety assessment of major or unique metabolites or the adequacy of using metabolite exposure in other matrices such as urine, bile, feces, when measurements cannot be made in plasma of the test species for any reason.

While the formation of human-specific metabolites is relatively rare, there are many examples in which the level of a circulating metabolite or metabolites is higher than 10% of the total drug related exposure. It is possible that a metabolite is considered major in humans but minor (i.e., less 10% of total drug-related exposure at steady state) in nonclinical species. Such metabolites could be at a greater risk of being considered disproportionate metabolites. However, nonclinical studies are often conducted at dose levels that are far greater than those in humans when normalized by weight and these major human metabolites may still provide adequate coverage in animal species and therefore no further toxicology studies on the metabolites would be warranted.

In cases where safety studies are needed with a disproportionate metabolite, it is highly recommended to consider (1) the pharmacological and chemical/structural similarity of the metabolite to its parent drug, (2) solubility, (3) stability via

Overcoming Obstacles in Drug Discovery and Development. https://doi.org/10.1016/B978-0-12-817134-9.00017-9

intended route of administration, (4) whether the metabolite is a phase I or phase II metabolite, and (5) the relative amount of metabolite formed in humans compared to that in animals.

The guidance states that sponsors can consider 2 general approaches to assess the safety of drug metabolite(s):

1. Identify an animal species that form the metabolite at exposures equivalent to or greater than the human exposure and use this species for the long-term safety assessment.
2. Synthesize the metabolite and directly administer it to the test system, preferably via the intended clinical route before initiation of large Phase 3 clinical trials.

Various in vitro and vivo systems and analytical approaches have been reported to characterize and assess the exposure ratios of metabolites between toxicology species and humans at the different stages of drug discovery and development. This chapter summarizes these analytical techniques, as well as the challenges and solutions associated with the analysis of disproportionate metabolites. In addition, several case studies of disproportionate metabolites are described.

Tools for the characterization of drug metabolites

In vitro systems

Liver microsomes, liver S9 fraction, and hepatocytes

In vitro models typically derived from human and animal livers, such as S9 fractions, microsomes and hepatocytes, are routinely used in early discovery to determine metabolite profiles. The data from these experiments are mostly used to guide a selection of appropriate nonclinical species for investigational new drug (IND)-enabling toxicology studies and to evaluate the profile of metabolites for potential human-specific metabolites. Dalvie et al. assessed the performance of these 3 in vitro systems in predicting in vivo metabolic profiles using the data from 27 compounds in the Pfizer database and 21 additional commercially available compounds for which the human metabolism data were available [6]. The results from this analysis suggest that all 3 systems reasonably predicted human primary excretory and circulating metabolites. While the success in predicting primary metabolites and metabolic pathways was high (>70%), these systems were not successful in predicting complex metabolites formed via multi-step processes [6]. Using a small group of compounds (n = 12), Anderson et al. showed that in vitro systems correctly predicted 41% of metabolites [7]. In this study, these systems failed to predict in vivo profiles of low clearance compounds. Therefore, these systems cannot solely mitigate the risk of disproportionate circulating secondary metabolites in humans and may need to be supplemented with metabolic profiling from single ascending dose, multiple ascending dose, and human radiolabeled studies.

Cultured hepatocytes

Coculture hepatocyte systems and plateable hepatocytes have been used to predict human metabolites for compounds with very low turnover/low clearance since these systems allow for a much longer incubation time than do cryopreserved hepatocytes in suspension (≥7-days) [8].

Micropatterned cocultured (MPCC) hepatocytes have been shown to recapitulate in vivo qualitative metabolic profiles. The MPCC model retains phenotypic stability over several weeks, enabling long-term biotransformation studies and generating multi-steps metabolites. Wang et al. evaluated the ability of this novel coculture system to generate human in vivo metabolites [9]. The MPCC system generated 82% of the excretory metabolites and 75% of the circulating metabolites, better than the performance of hepatocyte suspension incubations and other in vitro systems [6,7].

Kamel et al. examined the metabolic profiles of a low-clearance compound TAK-041 using suspended cryopreserved hepatocytes and HepatoPac micropatterned coculture hepatocytes from rats, dogs, monkeys, and humans [10]. Fewer metabolites of TAK-041 were detected in suspended hepatocytes than were detected in the corresponding HepatoPac incubations, and extensive and unusual downstream metabolites were detected in the HepatoPac incubations. Predominant in vitro metabolites were similar to those reported in humans and nonclinical species from in vivo studies [10].

Burton et al. compared the metabolic profiles of 4 commercial drugs following incubations in both suspended cryopreserved human hepatocytes and the HμREL hepatocyte coculture model [11]. The HμREL coculture model generated a more robust metabolite profile over 7 days than that which was observed following incubation using conventional hepatocyte suspension for all 4 drugs. Only 1 or 2 minor metabolites were detected in suspension hepatocytes, but multiple relevant human metabolites were detected in the corresponding HμREL incubations [11].

Ballard et al. reported the use of a recently developed human hepatocyte relay method for predicting human drug metabolite profiles [12]. The hepatocyte relay method generated 75% of human in vivo metabolites including those arising from both oxidative and conjugative reactions and metabolites that required sequential reactions. These data suggest that the hepatocyte relay assay method can be successfully used in the generation of relevant human metabolites.

Liver-on-A-chip models

There are reports on the evaluation of 2 promising liver-on-a-chip models, micro engineered organ-chips, and 3-D hepatic spheroids, that asse the metabolism of acetaminophen, fialuridine, and cytochrome 450 (CYP) probe substrate metabolites [13,14]. Metabolic turnover of CYP probe substrates, acetaminophen and fialuridine was maintained over the 10-day exposure period. Both models demonstrated integrated drug metabolism and similar sensitivity to the known hepatotoxins at clinically relevant concentrations and could be used to mimic the in vivo metabolic profiles in humans.

In vivo methods

PXB mice

The PXB mouse model is a useful in vivo model used to predict human hepatic metabolism and clearance. Bateman et al. evaluated this chimeric mouse model with humanized liver on a uPA/SCID background to predict the human metabolites of 4 model drugs (lamotrigine, diclofenac, MRK-A, and propafenone) [15]. The results from this study demonstrated that PXB mice produced human-specific metabolites covering both phase I and phase II metabolic pathways for 3 of the 4 drugs (lamotrigine, diclofenac, and MRK-A) and therefore could be a useful tool for the prediction of human-specific metabolism of xenobiotics.

Kato et al., also evaluated the PXB mouse model as a predictor of human hepatic metabolism using 4 model compounds, desloratadine, carbazeran, mianserin, and cyproheptadine [16]. All these compounds formed disproportionate metabolites. Desloratadine, 3-hydroxydesloratadine and its O-glucuronide were observed as the predominant metabolites in both the plasma and urine of PXB mice, similar to those of disproportionate metabolites (Fig. 15.1). Neither of these metabolites were detected in the control SCID mice. 4-Hydroxy carbazeran was the predominant metabolite of carbazeran in the plasma of PXB mice, but it was only observed as a minor peak in SCID mice (Fig. 15.1). Similarly, for the other 2 compounds, mianserin, cyproheptadine, all disproportionate metabolites were detected at a high level in PXB mice, suggesting that this in vivo model can be used in the evaluation of possible disproportionate metabolites prior to conducting clinical studies.

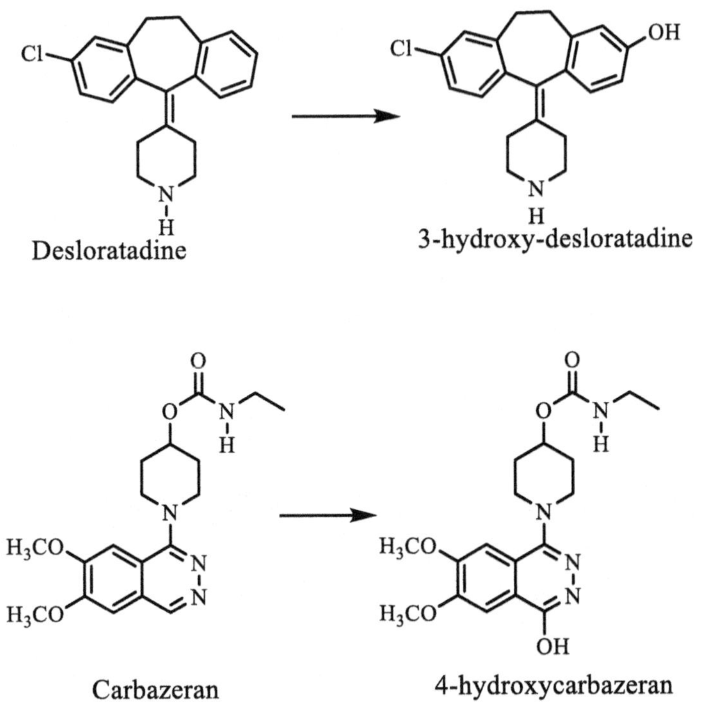

FIGURE 15.1 Metabolites of desloratadine and carbazeran. *Modified from S. Kato, A. Shah, M. Plesescu, Y. Miyata, J. Bolleddula, S. Chowdhury, X. Zhu, Prediction of human disproportionate and biliary excreted metabolites using chimeric mice with humanized liver. Drug Metab. Dispos. 48 (10) (2020) 934–943.*

Desloratadine

3-hydroxy-desloratadine

Carbazeran

4-hydroxycarbazeran

Samples from first-in-human and toxicology studies

Another approach used to assess qualitative and quantitative coverage of metabolites across species in the early stages of drug development is analysis of plasma samples from first-in-human (FIH) and nonclinical good laboratory practice (GLP)-toxicology studies. During Phase 1 clinical studies, plasma samples from single dose and multiple dose studies are routinely used in the detection of circulating metabolites. Comparing metabolite profiles from plasma samples between nonclinical toxicology species and humans at steady state allows for assessment of whether a metabolite has the necessary coverage.

PF-04937319, a partial activator of glucokinase, was in Phase 2 clinical trials for the treatment of type 2 diabetes mellitus. It is metabolized via oxidative and hydrolytic pathways in rat, dog, and human hepatocytes. N-Desmethyl-M1 is the major metabolite in human but not in rat or dog hepatocytes (Fig. 15.2) [17]. The metabolite profiles of plasma samples from a 14-day multiple dose clinical trial were obtained. M1 was identified as the principal component, accounting for 65% of the drug-related material at steady state in human plasma. M1 was then quantified in plasma samples from 3-month toxicology studies in rats and dogs at the no-observed-adverse-effect level (NOAEL). Although circulating levels of M1 were very low in dogs and female rats, there was adequate coverage of 3.6-fold (based on the area under the concentration time curve [AUC]) at the NOAEL in male rats, fulfilling the regulatory requirements [17].

Tong et al. utilized in vitro studies and plasma samples from non-clinical species for vabicaserin to select a species for toxicology studies [18,19]. In vitro, vabicaserin is extensively metabolized in animal species and in humans [18,19]. The predominant metabolite identified was vabicaserin carbamoyl glucuronide, referred to as M6. Metabolite profiling in early clinical trials showed that M6 was the major circulating component, with concentrations much higher than the parent drug. Analysis of M6 in nonclinical species revealed that systemic exposure was less than human exposure, with the highest exposures found in mice, dogs, and monkeys and the lowest exposures found in rats and rabbits. Based on this observation, rats were selected as the rodent species for chronic toxicology studies.

Quantitation of human metabolites

Several methods such as LC-MS/MS, LC-UV, and NMR have been utilized to compare metabolite exposures in animals to humans [6,20−33].

LC-MS/MS

Due to its high speed, enhanced resolution, and greater sensitivity and specificity, liquid chromatography-tandem mass spectrometry (LC-MS/MS), it is the method of choice for the -rapid and sensitive determination of metabolites in biological fluids. However, determining the absolute amounts of metabolites from in vitro and in vivo cold (ie, non-radiolabeled) studies remains considerably challenging. Metabolism results in structural changes that may alter the ionization efficiency of individual metabolites. In addition, the presence of endogenous components in the biological matrices and the constantly changing composition of background ions due to gradient elution used for metabolism studies could vary the suppression ionization of the parent drug and its metabolites. Therefore, it is necessary to first calibrate the MS response of metabolites relative to that of the parent drug in biological matrices using either a synthetic standard or radio calibrant. This response factor can then be used to estimate the amount of a metabolite using the formula below:

$$\% \text{ Metabolite} = \% \text{ Metabolite} (LC - MS / MS) \times \text{Response Factor}$$

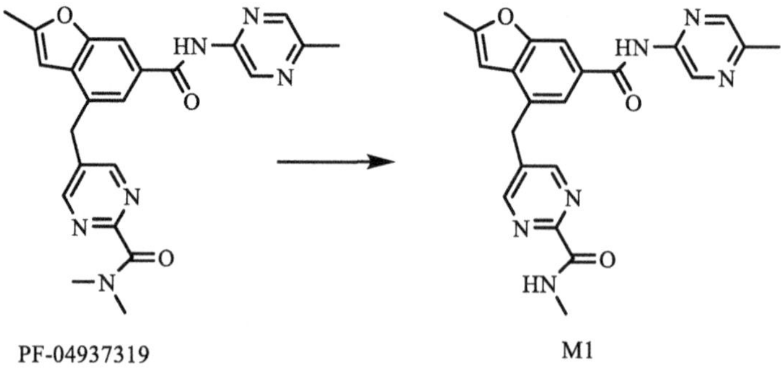

FIGURE 15.2 Major metabolite of PF-04937319. *Modified from R. Sharma, J. Litchfield, K. Atkinson, H. Eng, N.B. Amin, W.S. Denney, J.C. Pettersen, T.C. Goosen, L. Di, E. Lee, J.A. Pfefferkorn, D.K. Dalvie, A.S. Kalgutkar, Metabolites in safety testing assessment in early clinical development: a case study with a glucokinase activator. Drug Metab. Dispos. 42 (11) (2014) 1926 −1939.*

PF-04937319   M1

If the synthetic standard of a metabolite is available, the response factor can be directly determined by spiking the metabolite standard and the parent drug into plasma (or other biological matrix) and measuring the peak area ratio by LC-MS [20–28]. The synthetic standards for metabolites are generally not available in early discovery. Walker et al. have developed biosynthetic methods coupled with quantitative NMR spectroscopy to generate solutions of metabolites of known structure and concentration to be used as analytical standards for bioanalytical work to estimate exposure in humans [29].

Another approach used to normalize MS response is to use biological samples from in vitro or nonclinical species obtained from radiolabeled absorption, distribution, metabolism, and excretion (ADME) studies [30,31]. The relative radioactive response of each metabolite to the parent drug and the relative MS response of each metabolite to the parent drug can be used to generate correction factors as follows:

$$\text{Correction Factor} = (\text{RAmetabolite} / \text{RAparent}) / (\text{MSmetabolite} / \text{MSparent})$$

Where $\text{RA}_{\text{metabolite}}$ and $\text{RA}_{\text{parent}}$ are the radioactivity peak areas of each metabolite and parent compound, respectively, as determined by radiometric detection, and $\text{MS}_{\text{metabolite}}$ and $\text{MS}_{\text{parent}}$ are the peak areas of each metabolite and the parent compound as determined by MS detection.

Xu et al. used plasma samples containing parent compound and 4 metabolites from a radiolabeled rat ADME study [31]. The pooled plasma samples were spiked into control human plasma at a concentration of 10% by volume. The spiked samples were analyzed by LC-MS with radiometric detection. The correction factors were applied to the percent peak area calculations for each metabolite by multiplying the MS peak area response of the metabolite by the respective correction factor. The estimated concentrations in 5 out of 6 patients were 70% of the measured concentrations [31].

Recently, Gao et al. developed a method that eliminated the need for response correction in the assessment of exposure multiples of metabolites in nonclinical species [25]. An equal volume of plasma from humans dosed with drug was mixed with blank animal plasma and plasma from animals dosed with drug was mixed with blank human plasma. Samples were extracted and analyzed by LC-MS/MS. The results from this study demonstrated that a quantitative comparison of metabolite levels in animals and humans is possible from the peak area ratios of the metabolites versus an internal standard [25].

LC-UV

UV-based techniques are routinely used to determine the abundance of metabolites from in vitro studies in the discovery stage [6]. For UV-based quantitation, the parent compound and its metabolites must have good UV chromophores, as well as similar maximum UV absorption [6].

Nuclear magnetic resonance (NMR)

NMR is routinely used for the unambiguous structural characterization of metabolites, but its utility for quantitative estimation has been limited in the past due to its low sensitivity compared to MS. There recent reports on the use of NMR as an analytical tool to provide quantitative information on drug metabolites [32,33]. Vishwanathan et al. used the 1HNMR approach together with LC-UV-MS to obtain exposure values for metabolites in plasma samples from short-term toxicology studies. The results from this study were in excellent agreement with the data generated by a traditional LC-MS assay [32].

Radiolabeled human ADME study

The radiolabeled ADME studies performed in nonclinical species and human volunteers provide the total fate of the drug-derived radioactivity including the relative abundance of metabolites. There was debate if radiolabeled ADME studies in animals are still necessary [34,35]. Although there is no regulatory requirements for conducting such studies in laboratory animals, these studies, especially those conducted in bile-duct cannulated animals, provide very valuable information such as the extent of absorption and quantitative estimation of both excreted (biliary) and circulating metabolites prior to the exposure of large numbers of human subjects to investigative drugs [35].

A radiolabeled study in humans, one of the principle studies in drug development programs, is a gold standard for understanding the overall disposition of a drug candidate, including mass balance, excretion pattern, and metabolite profiles in circulation and excreta [36–38]. It is also required by health authorities for new drug registration applications [39]. These studies are typically conducted using a single dose of radiolabeled drug. It has been reported that the level and ratio of metabolites at steady state may vary from those after a single dose, especially for metabolites that may have a much longer half-life in systemic circulation than the parent drug [40−42]. Prakash et al. have reported that a well-designed single-dose radiolabeled study in humans could provide the exposure of metabolites at the steady state [43]. In this study, the C_{max} and AUC of parent drug and 2 major metabolites were simulated at steady state using the data from a single dose radiolabeled study in humans. The simulated exposures of parent drug and the 2 metabolites were similar to those from a 7-day clinical trial that were quantified using a validated LC-MS assay, suggesting that a well-designed single-dose radiolabeled human study can help in addressing the metabolites in safety testing-related issues [43].

The use of a ^{14}C microtracer in early human studies and the detection and quantification of metabolites using a combination of LC/MS and accelerator mass spectrometry (AMS) can be an alternative approach to obtain the relative abundance of metabolites and MIST coverage early in the development programs [44,45].

Case studies of disproportionate metabolites

While the formation of human-specific metabolites is relatively rare, there are several examples in the literature in which the level of a circulating metabolite is greater than 10% of the total drug related radioactivity in humans but much less in animal species [46,47]. Some of these examples are described below.

Case study Example 1

Ribociclib, a CDK4/6 inhibitor was being developed for the treatment of hormone-receptor positive, human epidermal growth factor-2-negative advanced breast cancer. In an exploratory in vivo clinical study, a total of 24 metabolites were detected in circulation. Two metabolites were estimated to be >10% of the total drug-related material [22,48].

The exposure of these metabolites was estimated in plasma AUC_{0-24hr} pools from 15-week rat and dog toxicology studies and a single-dose AUC_{0-24hr} pool from humans using a mixed plasma matrix method [22,48]. The exposures of these two metabolites were $\geq$2-fold higher in male rats compared to humans.

Case study Example 2

BILR355 is an inhibitor of the human immunodeficiency virus-1. It is extensively metabolized by CYP3A in vitro. Metabolite profiling was performed using human plasma samples obtained from a with concomitant administration of BILR355 and a CYP3A4 inhibitor, ritonavir (RTV). A disproportionate metabolite, BILR516, was detected during this metabolite profiling study and had higher exposure than the parent compound at steady state (Fig. 15.3). BILR 516 was not detected in human plasma when BILR355 was administered alone [49].

Case study Example 3

Canagliflozin is an oral antihyperglycemic agent used for the treatment of type 2 diabetes mellitus. In vivo biotransformation of canagliflozin was studied in intact and bile duct-cannulated (BDC) mice and rats and in intact dogs and humans [50]. The primary metabolic pathways of canagliflozin were oxidation in animals and direct glucuronidation in humans (Fig. 15.4). In human plasma, 2 O-glucuronide conjugates of canagliflozin, M5 and M7, represented >10% of total drug-related exposure and were considered major human metabolites (Fig. 15.4). Plasma concentrations of M5 and M7 in mice and rats from repeat-dose toxicology studies were lower than those in humans given canagliflozin at the maximum recommended dose of 300 mg. However, these metabolites were present in the bile of rodents, suggesting that mouse and rat livers had significant exposure to M5 and M7.

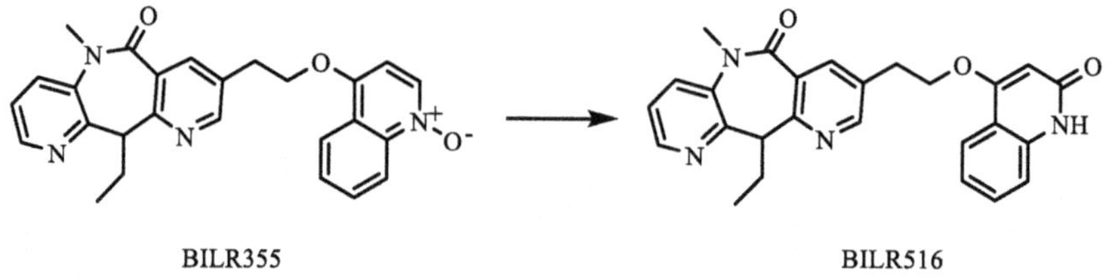

FIGURE 15.3 Metabolite of BILR 355. *Modified from Y. Li, W.G. Lai, A. Whitcher-Johnstone, C.A. Busacca, M.C. Eriksson, J.C. Lorenz, D.J. Tweedie, Metabolic switching of BILR 355 in the presence of ritonavir. Identifying an unexpected disproportionate human metabolite. Drug Metab. Dispos. 40 (6) (2012) 1122−1129.*

BILR355   BILR516

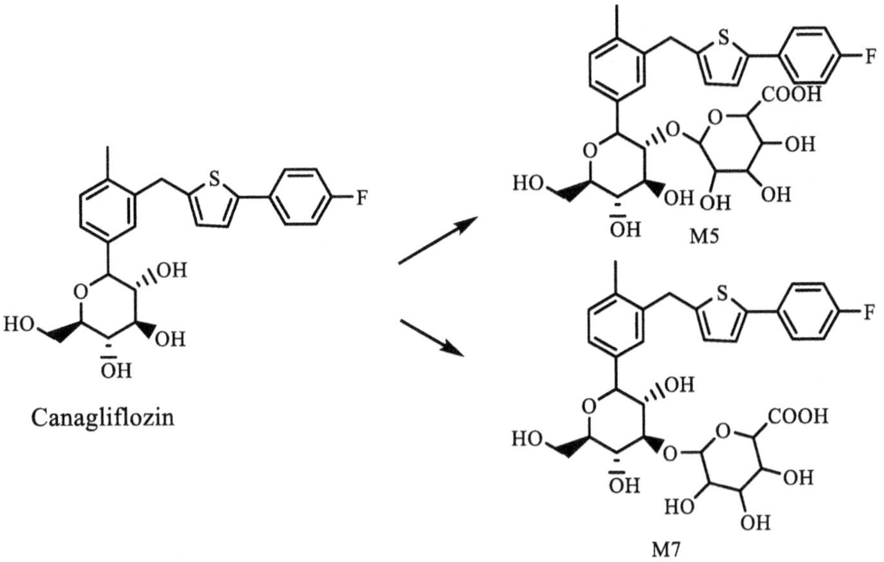

FIGURE 15.4 Disproportionate metabolites of canagliflozin. *Modified from N.V.S M. Rao, F. Cuyckens, J. Chen, E. Scheers, D. Kalamaridis, R. Lin, J. Silva, S. Sha, D.C. Evans, M.F. Kelley, D. Devineni, M.D. Johnson, H.K. Lim, Metabolism and excretion of canagliflozin in mice, rats, dogs, and humans. Drug Metab. Dispos. 42 (5) (2014) 903–916.*

Case study Example 4

Lesogaberan, a $GABA_B$ receptor agonist, has been developed for the treatment of patients with gastroesophageal reflux disease. It was shown to be stable in vitro in human and animal hepatocytes but it is extensively metabolized in humans in vivo and a total of 6 metabolites were identified [51]. The exposure of these metabolites was determined in plasma from humans, rats, and dogs using samples from clinical and nonclinical studies. Two metabolites, M4 and M5 were present at >10% of total drug related exposure at steady state (Fig. 15.5). Absolute exposure to M5 was greater in rats than the highest exposure observed in humans at steady state. In contrast, exposure to M4 in rats was less than 50% of the highest exposure observed in humans. Further safety testing of this metabolite would therefore be required.

Case study Example 5

Sharma et al. used plasma samples from a 14-day multiple ascending dose study to examine human circulating metabolites of a hepatoselective glucokinase activator, PF-04991532 [52]. The molecule did not undergo any metabolic turnover in liver microsomes and hepatocytes from nonclinical species and humans suggesting that metabolism would not play a major role in its clearance in vivo. However, analysis of plasma samples from a clinical study revealed the formation of a glucuronide (M1) and 3 monohydroxylated metabolites (M2*a* and M2*b*/M2*c*), which were estimated to be greater than 10% of the total drug-related material based on UV response (Fig. 15.6). These monohydroxylated metabolites were not detected in the plasma from rats or dogs following administration of [14C]PF-04991532 and therefore, determination of absolute amounts (total/unbound) of systemic exposures of these metabolites in humans and toxicology studies will be needed to meet the regulatory requirements [52].

Case study Example 6

R483, a peroxisome proliferator–activated receptor γ agonist, was in development for the treatment of type 2 diabetes. In vitro metabolite profiles of R483 were qualitatively comparable across species. It was extensively metabolized in human liver microsomes, and 3 metabolites (M1, M2 and M4) were identified in these incubations (Fig. 15.7). Analysis of plasma samples from the single dose study in humans revealed the presence of a major metabolite (M4) accounting for greater than 50% of total drug-related material based on HPLC-UV and exposure was not covered in the 2 species of animals used in the general toxicology studies (rats and cynomolgus monkeys) and therefore, it was considered a disproportionate metabolite [53]. To assess the safety of this metabolite, a general toxicology study, an embryo-fetal development study, and carcinogenicity studies were conducted in rats after oral administration of M4.

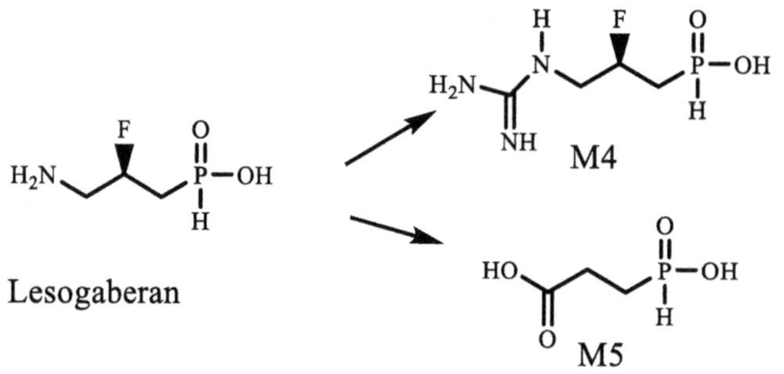

FIGURE 15.5 Major human metabolites of lesogaberan. *Modified from A.A. Holmberg, A. Ekdahl, L. Weidolf, Systemic exposure to the metabolites of lesogaberan in humans and animals: a case study of metabolites in safety testing. Drug Metab. Dispos. 42 (6) (2014) 1016–1021.*

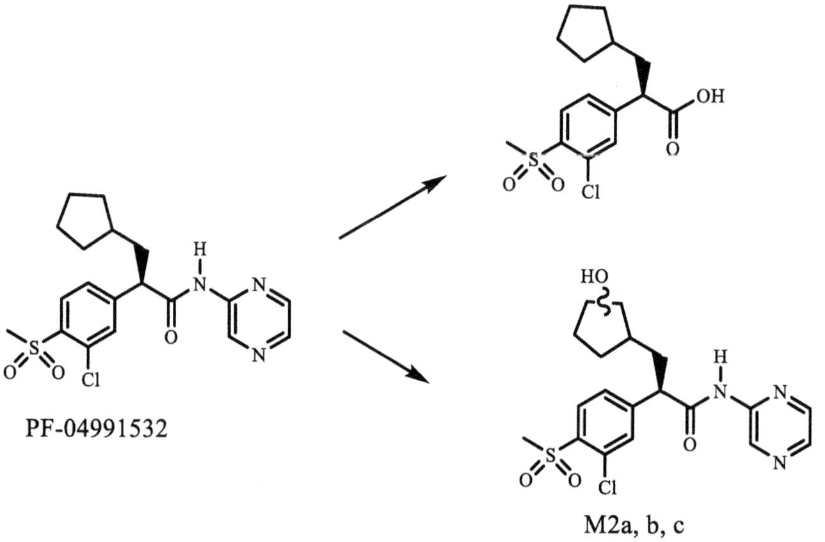

FIGURE 15.6 Proposed major metabolic pathways of PF-04991532. *Modified from R. Sharma, J. Litchfield, A. Bergman, K. Atkinson, D. Kazierad, S.M. Gustavson, L. Di, J.A. Pfefferkorn, A.S. Kalgutkar, Comparison of the circulating metabolite profile of PF-04991532, a hepatoselective glucokinase activator, across preclinical species and humans: potential implications in metabolites in safety testing assessment. Drug Metab. Dispos. 43 (2) (2015) 190–198.*

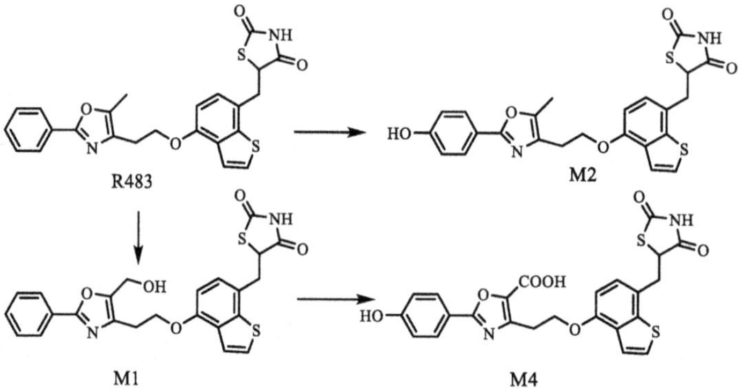

FIGURE 15.7 In vitro metabolites of R483. *Modified from K. Bogman, M. Silkey, S.P. Chan, B. Tomlinson, C. Weber, Influence of CYP2C19 genotype on the pharmacokinetics of R483, a CYP2C19 substrate, in healthy subjects and type 2 diabetes patients. Eur. J. Clin. Pharmacol. 66 (2010) 1005–1015.*

Case study Example 7

Azilsartan medoxomil, a prodrug of azilsartan, is an angiotensin II receptor antagonist for the treatment of hypertension. In healthy human subjects, M2 was a major circulating metabolite, accounting for 10% of the total radioactivity [46,47] (Fig. 15.8). In rats and dogs, after oral administration of [^{14}C]azilsartan medoxomil, a small amount of M2 was present at ≤2.4% of the exposure to azilsartan, suggesting that M2 was a disproportionate metabolite [46,47]. Subsequently,

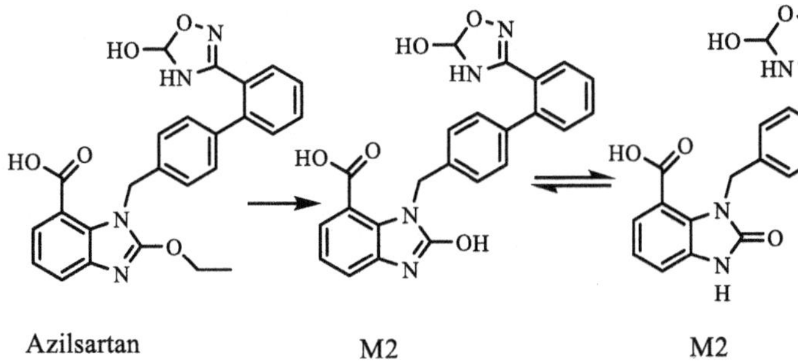

FIGURE 15.8 Disproportionate metabolite of azilsartan. *Modified from S. Schadt, B. Bister, S.K. Chowdhury, C. Funk, C.E.C.A. Hop, W.G. Humphreys, F. Igarashi, A.D. James, M. Kagan, S. Cyrus Khojasteh, A. Nedderman, C. Prakash, F. Runge, H. Scheible, D.K. Spracklin, P. Swart, S. Tse, J. Yuan, R.S. Obach, A decade in the MIST: learnings from investigations of drug metabolites in drug development under the "metabolites in safety testing" regulatory guidance. Drug Metab. Dispos. 46 (6) (2018) 865–878.*

additional safety studies including 26-week Tg.rasH2 mouse and 2-year rat studies, an Ames bacterial reverse mutation assay, a Chinese hamster ovary cell forward mutation assay, a mouse lymphoma gene mutation assay, and an in vivo mouse and rat bone marrow micronucleus assay were conducted by directly administering metabolite M2 as part of the azilsartan drug development program.

Case study Example 8

Momelotinib (MMB), an inhibitor of Janus kinase (JAK)1/2 and of activin A receptor type 1 (ACVR1), is in clinical development for the treatment of myeloproliferative neoplasms. The disposition of MMB was determined in healthy subjects following a single oral dose of [^{14}C]MMB [54]. A total of 6 metabolites (M5, M8, M19, M20, M21 and M28) were identified in human plasma. The parent drug and M21 accounted for 17.3% and 64.2% of the AUC of total radioactivity in human plasma, respectively. Other metabolites were <10% of the AUC of total circulating radioactivity (Table 15.1).

In single-dose mass-balance studies in rats and dogs, the parent drug accounted for most of the circulating radioactivity and M21 was not detected in either species (Fig. 15.9).

TABLE 15.1 The relative abundance of metabolites in humans, rats, and dogs.

Metabolite	% of [^{14}C] AUC		
	Humans	Rats	Dogs
MMB	17.3	83.4	43.4
M21	64.2	ND	ND
M8	5.8	ND	ND
M19	5.2	6.9	54.9
M5	2.7	ND	ND
M28	2.5	ND	ND
M20	2.3	ND	ND

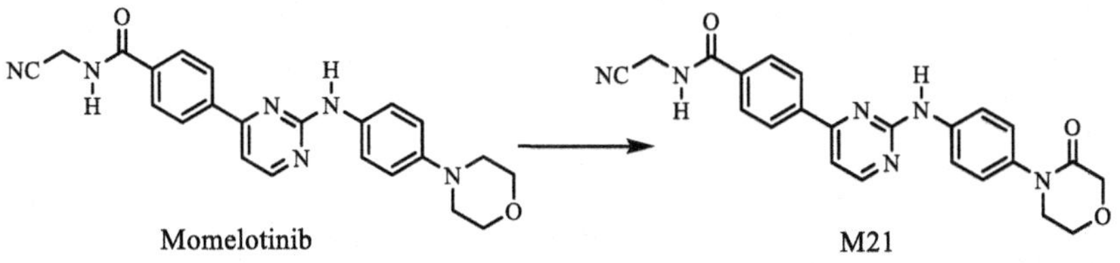

FIGURE 15.9 Disproportionate metabolite of momelotinib.

The exposure of M21 was also determined at steady state in rats, dogs, and humans and systemic exposure of M21 was higher in humans than in rats and dogs and therefore, it was considered a disproportionate metabolite. A combination dosing approach, i.e., coadministration of both M21 (25 mg/kg) and MMB (5 mg/kg) was used to increase M21 systemic AUC exposure in rats. The M21 AUC in rats reached 50% of the M21 overall mean AUC in humans, and was considered sufficient to allow for M21 safety assessment. This combination dosing approach was adopted in a subsequent 104-week rat toxicology study to meet regulatory requirements.

Case study Example 9

Venetoclax, a selective and potent Bcl-2 inhibitor, is approved for the treatment of chronic lymphocytic leukemia and other hematologic oncology indications. Analysis of pooled plasma (AUC_{0-48hr}) from a single-dose human mass balance study using [^{14}C]venetoclax showed that an oxidative metabolite, at 12% of the total drug-related material [55]. The terminal phase elimination half-life of this metabolite was >2-fold longer than that of venetoclax; and, at 48 h and beyond, it was the major drug-related component in the plasma. It was less abundant in the plasma from 2 toxicology species (mice and dogs) compared to human plasma. Further, the exposure of this metabolite was estimated in humans and toxicology studies using a qualified assay. The human steady-state AUC of the metabolite at the therapeutic dose in humans was much higher than the AUCs in the toxicologic species (mice, dogs), confirming that this is a disproportionate human metabolite.

Case study Example 10

Lemborexant is a novel dual orexin receptor antagonist recently approved for the treatment of insomnia. It is eliminated primarily by metabolism in nonclinical species and humans. After single oral administration of [^{14}C]lemborexant, one metabolite, M10, accounted for >10% of total drug-related exposure (Fig. 15.10). It was not detected in rats and was <3% of the total radioactivity in monkeys after oral administration of [^{14}C]lemborexant and therefore it was considered a disproportionate metabolite [56,57].

The exposure of M10 was determined in toxicology studies at steady state using a validated assay [57]. M10 had limited systemic exposure in rats at a no-observable-adverse-effect level (NOAEL), but exposure at the lowest dose tested in monkeys exceeded that at the maximum recommended 10 mg dose in humans (Table 15.2). These results indicated that higher exposure to M10 was achieved at a NOAEL dose in at least one species of the nonclinical toxicological species and therefore, no additional toxicology studies were needed from the perspective of metabolite safety.

Case study Example 11

Ozanimod is a small molecule that exhibits potent agonism at sphingosine 1-phosphate (S1P) 1 and S1P5 receptors. Ozanimod was found to be very stable in microsomes, S9 and hepatocytes of humans and nonclinical species. Three metabolites, N-dealkyl-ozanimod, a carboxy metabolite, and an N-acetylated metabolite were identified in vitro and in vivo in rats [58,59]. A human radiolabeled study of ozanimod was conducted late in development concurrent to Phase 3 studies. After oral administration of a single dose of [^{14}C]ozanimod to humans, the parent drug represented only <10% of circulating radioactivity indicating that most of the circulating radioactivity was attributable to metabolites. A total of 6 metabolites were identified in human plasma (Table 15.3).

Two metabolites, CC112273 and CC1084037 (both active) and one metabolite, RP101124 (inactive) accounted for 33.2, 5.48 and 14.5% of the circulating total radioactivity (Fig. 15.11). Further analysis of steady-state PK samples showed that ozanimod and its 2 active metabolites CC112273, and CC1084037 were 6%, 73%, and 15% of circulating total drug

FIGURE 15.10 Disproportionate metabolite of lemborexant. *Modified from T. Ueno, T. Ishida, K. Kusano, Disposition and metabolism of [14C]lemborexant, a novel dual orexin receptor antagonist, in rats and monkeys. Xenobiotica 49 (2019) 688−697. T. Ueno, T. Ishida, J. Aluri, M. Suzuki, C.T. Beuckmann, T. Kameyama, S. Asakura, K. Kusano, Disposition and metabolism of [14C]lemborexant in healthy human subjects and characterization of its circulating metabolites. Drug Metab. Dispos. 49 (2021) 31 −38.*

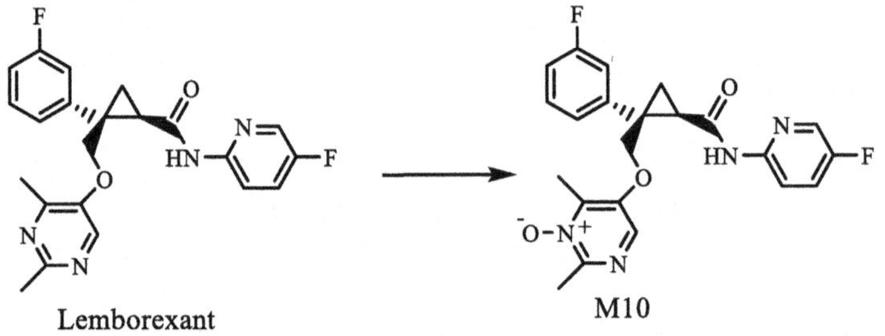

Lemborexant   M10

TABLE 15.2 Comparison of plasma exposures of lemborexant and its major metabolite, M10 in humans and animals.

| Species | Sex | Dose | AUC$_{(0-24hr)}$ | | Exposure multiple |
| | | | Lemborexant | M10 | |
			ng h/mL		M10
Humans	Male	10 mg/subject	431 ± 226	259 ± 110	—
Rats	Female	10 mg/kg	584	1.76	0.007
	Male	30 mg/kg	2630	9.85	0.038
	Male	100 mg/kg	16,500	74.1	0.286
	Female	100 mg/kg	39,100	204	0.788
	Male	1000 mg/kg	40,000	259	1
	Female	1000 mg/kg	223,000	3070	11.9
Monkeys	Male	10 mg/kg	4090	353	1.36
	Female	10 mg/kg	3820	320	1.24
	Male	100 mg/kg	94,000	3650	14.1
	Female	100 mg/kg	88,300	3210	12.4
	Male	1000 mg/kg	74,000	2820	10.9
	Female	1000 mg/kg	162,000	6780	26.2

TABLE 15.3 Relative abundance of ozanimod and its metabolites in human plasma.

Metabolites	Plasma (% of AUC$_{0-96hr}$ for [^{14}C] related drug materials)	Plasma (% of AUC at steady state relative to drug materials)
Ozanimod	6.7	6
CC112273	33.2	73
CC1084037	5.48	15
RP101124	14.5	<6[a]
RP101988	6.98	—
RP101075	5.4	—
RP112289	4.69	—
RP112509	3.92	—

[a]All remaining metabolites combined.

exposure, respectively. The remaining metabolites together, including RP101124, contributed to the remaining 6% of circulating radioactivity.

CC112273 and CC1084037 were not detected either in vitro or in vivo in toxicology species after oral administration of [^{14}C]ozanimod and were considered disproportionate metabolites [58,59]. Therefore, chronic, reproductive, and carcinogenicity toxicology studies, and bridging repeat-dose good laboratory practice PK studies in nonclinical species (rats, mice,

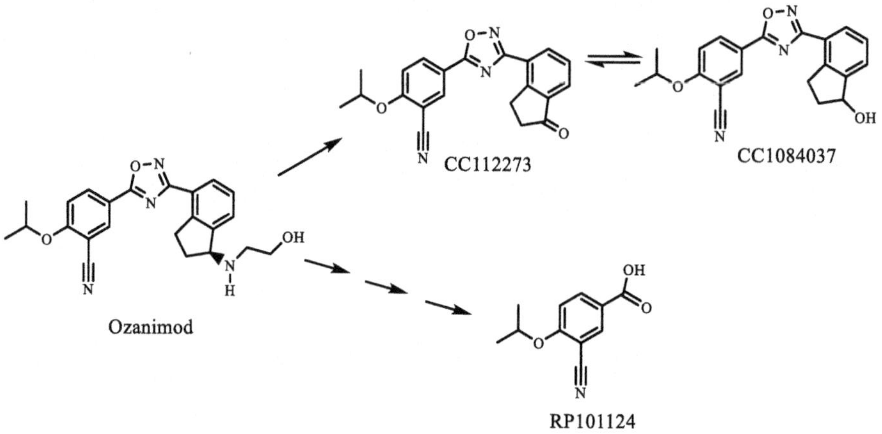

FIGURE 15.11 Disproportionate metabolites of ozanimod. *Modified from S. Surapaneni, U. Yerramilli, A. Bai, D. Dalvie, J. Brooks, X. Wang, J.V. Selkirk, Y.G. Yan, P. Zhang, R. Hargreaves, G. Kumar, M. Palmisano, J.Q. Tran, Absorption, metabolism, and excretion, in vitro pharmacology, and clinical pharmacokinetics of ozanimod, a novel sphingosine 1-phosphate receptor modulator. Drug Metab. Dispos. 49 (5) (2021) 405−419.*

rabbits, and monkeys) were triggered to demonstrate the exposure in these species. In addition, a standard battery of nonclinical studies was conducted additional following oral administration of major human metabolite CC112273 [58].

The systemic exposures to the 2 major human metabolites (CC112273 and CC1084037) were lower in nonclinical species than in humans at the maximum recommended human dose (0.92 mg/day). However, for the most abundant metabolite (CC112273), the sponsor demonstrated that higher exposures were not achieved with direct oral administration (doses up to 100 mg/kg). Studies with direct administration of CC1084037 were not conducted.

Case study Example 12

DS-1971a, Na$_V$1.7 inhibitor is under development for the treatment of neuropathic pain. The major metabolites in human plasma were mono-oxidized metabolites M1 and M2 representing 27% and 10% of total drug-related exposure, respectively [60]. M1 and M2 were also identified as the predominant metabolites in vitro in liver microsomes and S9 fraction of humans (Fig. 15.12). Therefore, plasma M1 and M2 exposure levels were compared between humans and nonclinical species to determine whether these metabolites were disproportionate metabolites.

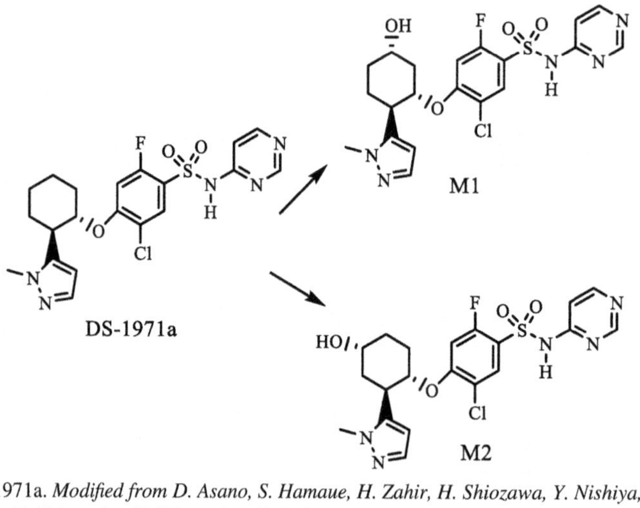

FIGURE 15.12 Metabolites of DS-1971a. *Modified from D. Asano, S. Hamaue, H. Zahir, H. Shiozawa, Y. Nishiya, T. Kimura, M. Kazui, N. Yamamura, M. Ikeguchi, T. Shibayama, S. Inoue, T. Shinozuka, T. Watanabe, C. Yahara, N. Watanabe, K. Yoshinari, CYP2C8-mediated formation of a human disproportionate metabolite of the selective NaV1.7 inhibitor DS-1971a, a mixed cytochrome P450 and aldehyde oxidase substrate. Drug Metab. Dispos. 50 (3) (2022) 235-242. https://doi.org/10.1124/dmd.121.000665.*

The exposure of M1 was considerably higher (>2-fold) in humans than in mice, rats, dogs, and monkeys whereas the exposure of M2 was lower in humans than in the nonclinical species. Therefore, M1 but not M2 was considered a human disproportionate metabolite, requiring further characterization under the MIST guidance.

Summary

The regulatory guidance on MIST has highlighted the importance of identifying the differences in drug metabolism between humans and animals used in nonclinical safety assessments as early as possible during the drug development process. However, approaches on how to mitigate MIST-related risks and avoid delays in clinical programs due to metabolite-related findings differ significantly among major pharmaceutical companies. There is an agreement across the pharmaceutical industry that a tiered approach should be used to address MIST issues. In early discovery during lead optimization, in vitro metabolism in rat and human liver microsomes is used to assist chemists in improving the metabolic stability of new molecular entities (NMEs). Similar experiments with cofactors, GSH or cyanide can determine the potential of the NMEs to form reactive metabolites [61]. The next step is to compare the metabolic profiles of a development candidate in hepatocytes of nonclinical species (rats, dogs, and monkeys) and humans to guide the selection of an appropriate nonclinical species for toxicology studies. These in vitro systems are less reliable in predicting circulating metabolites [62], especially metabolites formed by sequential metabolism events. The poor prediction by these in vitro systems is likely due to short incubation time and low metabolic capacity of the drug metabolizing enzymes in the system.

In the last decade, several in vitro systems such as MPCC, HμREL coculture and the hepatocyte relay method have been developed and used for generating the metabolite profiles [8−13]. These in vitro systems offer the ability to carry out incubations for several days without changing the medium and are therefore better suited for compounds that are slowly but extensively metabolized and/or expected to undergo multiple sequential metabolism. Recently, 3-dimensional spheroid cultures of primary human hepatocytes and liver-on-a-chip devices have been used for predicting hepatotoxicity and are being examined for their utility in generating human metabolite profiles that are more realistic than the in vivo profile.

Although advancement in LC-MS/MS technology combined with other analytical approaches (LC-NMR, wet chemistry and H/D exchange techniques) have greatly improved our capabilities to detect and identify metabolites [63,64], accurate quantification of metabolites from in vitro or cold clinical studies without authentic metabolite standards is often challenging due to differences in UV absorbance, MS ionization efficiency of metabolite versus parent drug and/or matrix effect. Several recent publications addressing quantitative comparison of exposure to circulating metabolites between toxicology species and FIH studies with cold parent drug have demonstrated the significant advances made in this challenging field. Plasma pooling methods, combined with NMR, LC-UV-MS, and radio calibrant has also produced reliable exposure estimates of circulating metabolites in nonclinical toxicology studies and humans.

Regardless of how much metabolism information is available from cold in vitro and FIH studies, definitive information about mass balance and metabolite profiles can only be obtained after administration of the radiolabeled drug. Additionally, there is always a risk that major drug-related entities could be missed in cold studies. Several examples described in this chapter illustrate the need for conducting timely radiolabeled human ADME studies for characterization of disproportionate metabolites and assessment of exposure coverage during drug development. These studies not only provide information about metabolites but also generate a more complete package that includes information on mass balance, absolute bioavailability, and major elimination pathways. In the past, these studies were conducted after Phase 2 or after achieving proof-of-concept but recently there has been a shift to conduct human mass balance studies earlier in clinical development, i.e., before the demonstration of efficacy.

While very important, the FDA guidance on disproportionate metabolites in drug safety should be viewed as a recommendation only. Additional studies examining metabolite coverage should always be performed on case-by-case basis.

Acknowledgments

I thank Allyson Jenkins, Agios, for her editorial assistance.

References

[1] K.E. Lasser, P.D. Allen, S.J. Woolhandler, D. U Himmelstein, S.M. Wolfe, D.H. Bor, Timing of new black box warnings and withdrawals for prescription medications, JAMA 287 (17) (2002) 2215−2220.

[2] Food and Drug Administration (FDA), Guidance for Industry: Safety Testing of Drug Metabolites, US Department of Health and Human Services FDA, Center for Drug Evaluation and Research, Silver Spring, MD, 2008.

[3] International Conference on Harmonization (ICH) *M3(R2) Nonclinical Safety Studies for the Conduct of Human Clinical Trials and Marketing Authorization of Pharmaceuticals*, The International Council for Harmonization of Technical Requirements for Pharmaceuticals for Human Use, Geneva, Switzerland, 2010.

[4] FDA Guidance for Industry: Safety Testing of Drug Metabolites, US Department of Health and Human Services FDA, Center for Drug Evaluation and Research, Silver Spring, MD, 2016.

[5] FDA Guidance for Industry: Safety Testing of Drug Metabolites Guidance for Industry, U.S. Department of Health and Human Services Food and Drug Administration, Center for Drug Evaluation and Research, Silver Spring, MD, 2020.

[6] D. Dalvie, R.S. Obach, P. Kang, C. Prakash, C.M. Loi, S. Hurst, A. Nedderman, L. Goulet, E. Smith, H.Z. Bu, Assessment of three human in vitro systems in the generation of major human excretory and circulating metabolites, Chem. Res. Toxicol. 22 (2009) 357−368.

[7] S. Anderson, D. Luffer-Atlas, M.P. Knadler, Predicting circulating human metabolites: how good are we? Chem. Res. Toxicol. 22 (2009) 243−256.

[8] J.M. Hutzler, B.J. Ring, S.R. Anderson, Low-turnover drug molecules: a current challenge for drug metabolism scientists, Drug Metab. Dispos. 43 (2015) 1917−1928.

[9] W.W. Wang, S.R. Khetani, S. Krzyzewski, D.B. Duignan, R.S. Obach, Assessment of a micropatterned hepatocyte coculture system to generate major human excretory and circulating drug metabolites, Drug Metab. Dispos. 38 (2010) 1900−1905.

[10] A. Kamel, S. Bowlin, N. Hosea, D. Arkilo, A. Laurenza, In vitro metabolism of slowly cleared TAK-041, Drug Metabol. Dispos. 49 (2) (2021) 121−132.

[11] R.D. Burton, T. Hieronymus, T. Chamem, D. Heim, S. Anderson, X. Zhu, J.M. Hutzler, Assessment of the biotransformation of low turnover drugs in the HμREL human hepatocyte coculture model, Drug Metab. Dispos. 46 (2018) 1617−1622.

[12] T.E. Ballard, C. C Orozco, R.S. Obach, Generation of major human excretory and circulating drug metabolites using a hepatocyte relay method, Drug Metab. Dispos. 42 (5) (2014) 899−902.

[13] J. Riede, B.M. Wollmann, E. Molden, M. Ingelman-Sundberg, Primary human hepatocyte spheroids as an in vitro tool for investigating drug compounds with low hepatic clearance, Drug Metab. Dispos. 49 (7) (2021) 501−508.

[14] A.J. Foster, B. Chouhan, S.L. Regan, et al., Integrated in vitro models for hepatic safety and metabolism: evaluation of a human liver-chip and liver spheroid, Arch. Toxicol. 93 (2019) 1021−1037.

[15] J.T. Bateman, V.G.B. Reddy, M. Kakuni, Y. Morikawa, S. Kumar, Application of chimeric mice with humanized liver for study of human-specific drug metabolism, Drug Metab. Dispos. 42 (6) (2014) 1055−1065.

[16] S. Kato, A. Shah, M. Plesescu, Y. Miyata, J. Bolleddula, S. Chowdhury, X. Zhu, Prediction of human disproportionate and biliary excreted metabolites using chimeric mice with humanized liver, Drug Metab. Dispos. 48 (10) (2020) 934−943.

[17] R. Sharma, J. Litchfield, K. Atkinson, H. Eng, N.B. Amin, W.S. Denney, J.C. Pettersen, T.C. Goosen, L. Di, E. Lee, J.A. Pfefferkorn, D.K. Dalvie, A.S. Kalgutkar Metabolites, Safety testing assessment in early clinical development: a case study with a glucokinase activator, Drug Metab. Dispos. 42 (11) (2014) 1926−1939.

[18] Z. Tong, A. Chandrasekaran, W. DeMaio, R. Jordan, H. Li H, R. Moore, N. Poola, P. Burghart, T. Hultin, J. Scatina, Species differences in the formation of vabicaserin carbamoyl glucuronide, Drug Metab. Dispos. 38 (2010a) 581−590.

[19] Z. Tong, A. Chandrasekaran, W. DeMaio, R. Espina, W. Lu, R. Jordan, J. Scatina, Metabolism of vabicaserin in mice, rats, dogs, monkeys, and humans, Drug Metab. Dispos. 38 (2010b) 2266−2277.

[20] D. Walker, J. Brady, D. Dalvie, J. Davis, J.D. Matin, J.N. Duncan, A. Nedderman, R.S. Obach, P. Wright, A holistic strategy for characterizing the safety of metabolites through drug discovery and development, Chem. Res. Toxicol. 22 (10) (2009) 1653−1662.

[21] S. Ma, Z. Li, K.-J. Lee, S.K. Chowdhury, Determination of exposure multiples of human metabolites for MIST assessment in preclinical safety species without using reference standards or radiolabeled compounds, Chem. Res. Toxicol. 23 (2010) 1871−1873.

[22] H. Gao, S. Deng, R.S. Obach, A simple liquid chromatography-tandem mass spectrometry method to determine relative plasma exposures of drug metabolites across species for metabolite safety assessments, Drug Metab. Dispos. 38 (2010) 2147−2156.

[23] S. Schadt, L.Z. Chen, D. Bischoff, Evaluation of relative LC/MS response of metabolites to parent drug in LC/nanospray ionization mass spectrometry: potential implications in MIST assessment, J. Mass Spectrom. 46 (12) (2011) 1281−1286.

[24] N. Penner, J. Zgoda-Pols, C. Prakash, Early assessment of exposure of drug metabolites in humans using mass spectrometryin Handbook of metabolic pathways of xenobiotics. Edited by P.W. Lee, H. Aizawa, L.L. Gan, Chandra Prakash, and Dafang Zhong, John Wiley & Sons.

[25] H. Gao H, R.S. Obach, Data-driven approach for cross-species comparative metabolite exposure assessment: how to establish fundamental bioanalytical parameters for the peak area ratio method, Bioanalysis 6 (5) (2014) 641−650.

[26] J. Haglund, M.M. Halldin, A. Brunnström, G. Eklund, A. Kautiainen, A. Sandholm, S.L. Iverson, Pragmatic approaches to determine the exposures of drug metabolites in preclinical and clinical subjects in the MIST evaluation of the clinical development phase, Chem. Res. Toxicol. 27 (4) (2014) 601−610.

[27] P. Timmerman, S. Blech, S. White, M. Green, C. Delatour, S. McDougall, G. Mannens, J. Smeraglia, S. Williams, G. Young, Best practices for metabolite quantification in drug development: updated recommendation from the European Bioanalysis Forum, Bioanalysis 8 (2016) 1297−1305.

[28] R.H. Takahashi, C. Khojasteh, M. Wright, C.E.C.A. Hop, S. Ma, Mixed matrix method provides a reliable metabolite exposure comparison for assessment of metabolites in safety testing (MIST), Drug Metabol. Lett. 11 (2017) 21−28.

[29] G.S. Walker, J.N. Bauman, T.F. Ryder, E.B. Smith, D.K. Spracklin, R.S. Obach, Biosynthesis of drug metabolites and quantitation using NMR spectroscopy for use in pharmacologic and drug metabolism studies, Drug Metab. Dispos. 42 (2014) 1627−1639.

[30] P. Yi P, D. Luffer-Atlas, A radiocalibration method with pseudo internal standard to estimate circulating metabolite concentrations, Bioanalysis 2 (7) (2010) 1195–1210.

[31] L. Xu, C. Woodward, J. Dai, C. Prakash C., Metabolism, and excretion of 6-chloro-9-(4-methoxy-3,5-dimethylpyridin-2-ylmethyl)-9H-purin-2-ylamine (BIIB021), an HSP90 inhibitor, in rats and dogs, and assessment of its metabolic profile in plasma of humans, Drug Metab. Dispos. 41 (2013) 2133–2147.

[32] K. Vishwanathan, K. Babalola, J. Wang, R. Espina, L. Yu, A. Adedoyin, R. Talaat, A. Mutlib, J. Scatina, Obtaining exposures of metabolites in preclinical species through plasma pooling and quantitative NMR: addressing metabolites in safety testing (MIST) guidance without using radiolabeled compounds and chemically synthesized metabolite standards, J. Chem. Res. Toxicol. 22 (2) (2009) 311–322.

[33] J. Caceres-Cortes, M.D. Reily, NMR spectroscopy as a tool to close the gap on metabolite characterization under MIST, Bioanalysis 2 (7) (2010) 1263–1276.

[34] R. Obach, A. Nedderman, D. Smith, Radiolabeled mass-balance excretion, and metabolism studies in laboratory animals: are they still necessary? Xenobiotica 42 (2012) 46–56.

[35] R.E. White, D.C. Evans, C.E. Hop, D.J. Moore, C. Prakash, S. Surapaneni, F.L. Tse, Radiolabeled mass-balance excretion and metabolism studies in laboratory animals: a commentary on why they are still necessary, Xenobiotica 43 (2013) 219–225.

[36] N. Penner, L.J. Klunk, C. Prakash, Human radiolabeled mass balance studies: objectives, utilities and limitations, Biopharm. Drug Dispos. 30 (4) (2009) 185–203.

[37] N. Penner, L. Xu, C. Prakash, Radiolabeled absorption, distribution, metabolism, and excretion studies in drug development: why, when, and how? Chem. Res. Toxicol. 25 (3) (2009) 513–531.

[38] D.K. Spracklin1, D. Chen, A.J. Bergman, E. Callegari, R.S. Obach, Mini-review: comprehensive drug disposition knowledge generated in the modern human radiolabeled ADME study, CPT Pharmacometrics Syst. Pharmacol. 9 (2020) 428–434.

[39] P. Coppola1, A. Andersson, S. Cole, The importance of the human mass balance study in regulatory submissions, CPT Pharmacometrics Syst. Pharmacol. 8 (2019) 792–804.

[40] P. Griffini, A.D. James, A.D. Roberts, M. Pellegatti, Metabolites in safety testing: issues and approaches to the safety evaluation of human metabolites in a drug that is extensively metabolized, J. Drug Metabol. Toxicol. 1 (2010) 1000102.

[41] J. Gong J, T. Eley, B. He, V. Arora, T. Philip, H. Jiang, J. Easter, W.G. Humphreys, R.A. Iyer, W. Li, Characterization of ADME properties of [^{14}C] asunaprevir (BMS-650032) in humans, Xenobiotica 46 (2016) 52–64.

[42] C. Gu, M. Artelsmair, C.S. Elmore, R.J. Lewis, P. Davis, J.E. Hall, B.T. Dembofsky, G. Christoph, M.A. Smith, M. Chapdelaine, M. Sunzel, Late-occurring and long-circulating metabolites of GABAAa2,3 receptor modulator AZD7325 involving metabolic cyclization and aromatization: relevance to MIST analysis and application for patient compliance, Drug Metab. Dispos. 46 (2018) 303–315.

[43] C. Prakash, Z. Li, C. Orlandi, L. Klunk, Assessment of exposure of metabolites in preclinical species and humans at steady state from the single-dose radiolabeled absorption, distribution, metabolism, and excretion studies: a case study, Drug Metab. Dispos. 40 (7) (2012) 1308–1320.

[44] A.F. Roffel, S.P. van Marle, J.J. van Lier, J. Hartstra, E.-J. van Hoogdalem, An evaluation of human ADME and mass balance studies using regular or low doses of radiocarbon, J. Label. Compd. Radiopharm. 59 (2016) 619–626.

[45] G. Lappin, M. Seymour, G. Gross, M. Jørgensen, M. Kall, L. Kværnø, Meeting the MIST regulations: human metabolism in Phase I using AMS and a tiered bioanalytical approach, Bioanalysis 4 (4) (2012) 407–416.

[46] D. Luffer-Atlas, A. Atrakchi A, A decade of drug metabolite safety testing: industry and regulatory shared learning, Expet Opin. Drug Metabol. Toxicol. 13 (2017) 897–900.

[47] S. Schadt, B. Bister, S.K. Chowdhury, C. Funk, C.E.C.A. Hop, W.G. Humphreys, F. Igarashi, A.D. James, M. Kagan, S. Cyrus Khojasteh, A. Nedderman, C. Prakash, F. Runge, H. Scheible, D.K. Spracklin, P. Swart, S. Tse, J. Yuan, R.S. Obach, A decade in the MIST: learnings from investigations of drug metabolites in drug development under the "metabolites in safety testing" regulatory guidance, Drug Metab. Dispos. 46 (6) (2018) 865–878.

[48] C. Yu, C.L. Chen, F.L. Gorycki, T.G. Neiss, A rapid method for quantitatively estimating metabolites in human plasma in the absence of synthetic standards using a combination of liquid chromatography/mass spectrometry and radiometric detection, Rapid Commun. Mass Spectrom. 21 (2007) 497–502.

[49] Y. Li, W.G. Lai, A. Whitcher-Johnstone, C.A. Busacca, M.C. Eriksson, J.C. Lorenz, D.J. Tweedie, Metabolic switching of BILR 355 in the presence of ritonavir. Identifying an unexpected disproportionate human metabolite, Drug Metab. Dispos. 40 (6) (2012) 1122–1129.

[50] N.V.S.M. Rao, F. Cuyckens, J. Chen, E. Scheers, D. Kalamaridis, R. Lin, J. Silva, J. Sha, D.C. Evans, M.F. Kelley, D. Devineni, M.D. Johnson, H.K. Lim, Metabolism and excretion of canagliflozin in mice, rats, dogs, and humans, Drug Metab. Dispos. 42 (5) (2014) 903–916.

[51] A.A. Holmberg, A. Ekdahl, L. Weidolf, Systemic exposure to the metabolites of lesogaberan in humans and animals: a case study of metabolites in safety testing, Drug Metab. Dispos. 42 (6) (2014) 1016–1021.

[52] R. Sharma, J. Litchfield, A. Bergman, K. Atkinson, D. Kazierad, S.M. Gustavson, L. Di, J.A. Pfefferkorn, A.S. Kalgutkar, Comparison of the circulating metabolite profile of PF-04991532, a hepatoselective glucokinase activator, across preclinical species and humans: potential implications in metabolites in safety testing assessment, Drug Metab. Dispos. 43 (2) (2015) 190–198.

[53] K. Bogman, M. Silkey, S.P. Chan, B. Tomlinson, C. Weber, Influence of CYP2C19 genotype on the pharmacokinetics of R483, a CYP2C19 substrate, in healthy subjects and type 2 diabetes patients, Eur. J. Clin. Pharmacol. 66 (2010) 1005–1015.

[54] J. Zheng, Y. Xin, J. Zhang, R. Subramanian, B.P. Murray, J.A. Whitney, M.R. Warr, J. Ling, L. Moorehead, E. Kwan, J. Hemenway, B.J. Smith, J.A. Silverman, Pharmacokinetics and disposition of momelotinib revealed a disproportionate human metabolite—resolution for clinical development, Drug Metab. Dispos. 46 (2018) 237–247.

[55] H. Liu, M.J. Michmerhuizen, Y. Lao, K. Wan, A.H. Salem, J. Sawicki, M. Serby, S. Vaidyanathan, S.L. Wong, An B-cell lymphoma-2 inhibitor venetoclax in humans and characterization of its unusual metabolites, Drug Metab. Dispos. 45 (2017) 294–305.

[56] T. Ueno, T. Ishida, K. Kusano, Disposition and metabolism of [14C]lemborexant, a novel dual orexin receptor antagonist, in rats and monkeys, Xenobiotica 49 (2019) 688–697.

[57] T. Ueno, T. Ishida, J. Aluri, M. Suzuki, C.T. Beuckmann, T. Kameyama, S. Asakura, K. Kusano, Disposition and metabolism of [14C]lemborexant in healthy human subjects and characterization of its circulating metabolites, Drug Metab. Dispos. 49 (2021) 31–38.

[58] https://www.accessdata.fda.gov/scripts/cder/daf/index.cfm?event=overview.process&ApplNo=209899.

[59] S. Surapaneni, U. Yerramilli, A. Bai, D. Dalvie, J. Brooks, X. Wang, J.V. Selkirk, Y.G. Yan, P. Zhang, R. Hargreaves, G. Kumar, M. Palmisano, J.Q. Tran, Absorption, metabolism, and excretion, in vitro pharmacology, and clinical pharmacokinetics of ozanimod, a novel sphingosine 1-phosphate receptor modulator, Drug Metab. Dispos. 49 (5) (2021) 405–419.

[60] D. Asano, S. Hamaue, H. Zahir, H. Shiozawa, Y. Nishiya, T. Kimura, M. Kazui, N. Yamamura, M. Ikeguchi, T. Shibayama, S. Inoue, T. Shinozuka, T. Watanabe, C. Yahara, N. Watanabe, K. Yoshinari, CYP2C8-mediated formation of a human disproportionate metabolite of the selective Na_v 1.7 inhibitor DS-1971a, a mixed cytochrome P450 and aldehyde oxidase substrate, Drug Metab. Dispos. 50 (3) (2022) 235–242.

[61] C. Prakash, R. Sharma, M. Gleave, A. Nedderman, In vitro screening techniques for reactive metabolites for minimizing the bioactivation potential in drug discovery, Curr. Drug Metabol. 9 (9) (2008) 952–964.

[62] D.A. Smith, D. Dalvie, Why do metabolites circulate? Xenobiotica 42 (1) (2012) 107–126.

[63] A. Kamel, S. Harriman, C. Prakash, Strategies for the identification of unusual and novel metabolites using derivatization, hydrogen-deuterium exchange (HDX) and liquid chromatography-nuclear magnetic resonance (LC-NMR) spectroscopy, techniques in handbook of metabolic pathways of xenobiotics, in: P.W. Lee, H. Aizawa, L.L. Gan (Eds.), Chandra Prakash, and Dafang Zhong, John Wiley & Sons, 2013.

[64] C. Prakash, C. Shaffer, A. Nedderman, Analytical strategies for identifying drug metabolites, Mass Spectrom. Rev. 26 (2007) 340–369.

Chapter 16

Disposition and metabolism of ozanimod—Surmounting the unanticipated challenge late in development

Deepak Dalvie[a] and Sekhar Surapaneni[b]

[a]Bristol Myers Squibb, San Diego, CA, United States; [b]Bristol Myers Squibb, Summit, NJ, United States

Ozanimod (Zeposia) (Fig. 16.1), is a sphingosine-1-phosphate (S1P) receptor modulator that binds selectively to S1P receptor subtypes 1 (S1P$_1$) and 5 (S1P$_5$) with high affinity [1–4].

It acts as a functional antagonist of S1P$_1$ receptor by promoting sustained receptor internalization and resulting in a reduction of a number of circulating lymphocytes which express this receptor [1]. To date, ozanimod has been approved in the USA for the treatment of adults with relapsing forms of multiple sclerosis and in Europe for the treatment of adults with relapsing-remitting MS [4–6]. While the mechanism of the therapeutic effect of ozanimod for MS is unknown, it involves the reduction of lymphocyte migration into the central nervous system. More recently, it was approved in the US for the treatment of ulcerative colitis and is in clinical development for the treatment of Crohn's disease [7–9]. Ozanimod also demonstrates activity against S1P$_5$ receptor, which supports oligodendrocyte progenitor extension and survival and contributes to blood brain barrier integrity [10,11].

Ozanimod demonstrated good PK, efficacy and safety profile in humans. The safety, pharmacokinetics (PK) and pharmacodynamics of this drug has been studied following single oral doses up to 3 mg and following multiple oral doses up to 2 mg once daily as a part of the phase I study in healthy volunteers [12–15]. Following single or multiple oral doses it is well-tolerated up to 3 mg with no severe or dose limiting toxicities. Single and multiple dose studies in the clinic suggests that the pharmacokinetics (PK) of ozanimod in the clinic is very desirable and makes this drug amenable to once a day dosing. It exhibits linear PK with dose proportional increases in exposure and low to moderate inter-subject variability and exhibits a large steady state volume of distribution (81.9 L/kg) and moderate oral clearance (233 L/h) leading to an elimination half-life of approximately 17–20 h, thus supporting once-a-day dosing [12]. Following multiple administration of ozanimod at doses of 0.3–2.0 mg for seven or 0.3–1.5 mg for 28 days, the steady state peak to trough concentration

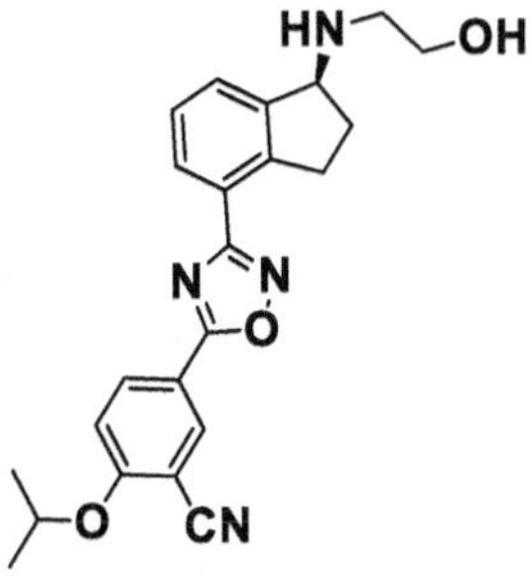

Ozanimod

FIGURE 16.1 Structure of ozanimod.

Overcoming Obstacles in Drug Discovery and Development. https://doi.org/10.1016/B978-0-12-817134-9.00016-7

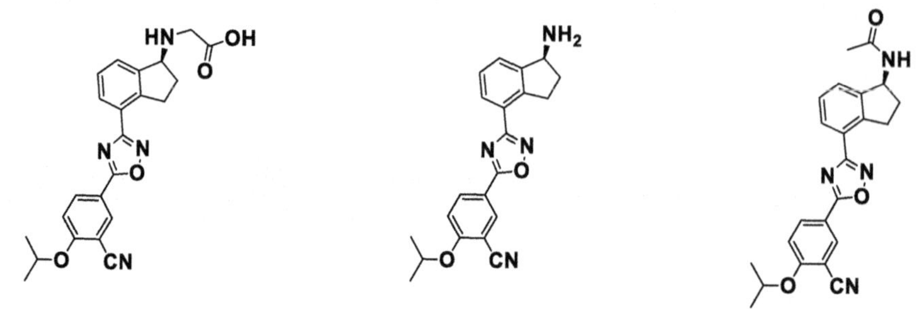

FIGURE 16.2 Structures of three active metabolites that were identified earlier in the preclinical species.

RP101988

Carboxylic acid
derivative of ozanimod

RP101075

Indaneamine

RP101442

N-Acetylindaneamine

TABLE 16.1 Half-maximal concentrations (EC_{50}) of ozanimod, RP101988, RP101075, RP 101442 and CC112273 toward $S1P_1$ and $S1P_5$ [17].

	EC_{50} for $S1P_1$ (nM)	EC_{50} for $S1P_5$ (nM)
Ozanimod	1.03	10.66
RP101988	0.33	29.15
RP101075	0.35	4.49
RP101442	3.3	69.0
CC112273	2.99	29.32

ratio and drug accumulation ratio is approximately 2.0 [15], which is consistent with it's half-life. Ozanimod is also shown to exhibit a robust pharmacodynamic response at 1.0 and 1.5 mg doses after 28 days of dosing. The lymphocyte count reductions were 65% and 68% for the two doses, respectively, and showed selectivity for lymphocytes subtypes with greater effect on $CD4^+$, $CCR7^+$ and $CD8^+$ and $CCR7^+$ T cells [12]. Overall, good PK properties and a robust PD response makes ozanimod a promising immunomodulatory agent for the treatment of chronic inflammatory diseases.

Early in vitro and in vivo metabolism studies in preclinical species led to the identification of three pharmacologically active metabolites, namely the carboxylic acid metabolite, RP101988, the indaneamine, RP101075 and N-acetyl indaneamine, RP101442 (Fig. 16.2) [16].

All three metabolites had equivalent potency and selectivity when compared to ozanimod (Table 16.1) [17]. While ozanimod exhibited an EC_{50} of 1.03 and 10.66 nM for $S1P_1$ and $S1P_5$ receptors, respectively, the half-maximal effective concentration values of RP101988, RP101075 and RP101442 toward $S1P_1$ were 0.33, 0.35 and 3.3 nM and those toward $S1P_5$ were 29.15, 4.49 and 69 nM, respectively [17]. Assessment of concentrations and the PK parameters of the three metabolites in early clinical studies (phase I studies) following single and multiple doses of ozanimod to healthy human subjects revealed that while RP101442 was present in very low concentrations in human plasma. However, RP101988 and RP101075 exhibited pharmacokinetics similar to that of ozanimod in these studies and were present at similar exposures as parent ozanimod [16].

As a part of a drug development plan, absorption, metabolism and excretion (AME) of ozanimod in humans was also investigated using radiolabeled ozanimod [17]. Following a single oral dose of 1 mg [^{14}C]-ozanimod hydrochloride to six healthy male subjects, the total mean recovery of the administered radioactivity by the end of the sampling period (240 h for urine and 504 h for feces) was 63%, with 26% recovered from the urine and 37% recovered from the feces [17]. Investigation into the circulating radioactivity and circulating ozanimod levels in this study revealed that total circulating radioactivity was quantifiable from the first sampling point (1 h) in all subjects. Maximum total radioactivity concentrations occurred between 8 and 24 h and then declined in a multi-phasic manner. While the plasma PK parameters for ozanimod were consistent with what was observed in other studies, the $t_{1/2}$ for total radioactivity ranged from 84 to 117 h with a mean $t_{1/2}$ of 99 h [17]. Ozanimod represented ~5% and 12% of circulating radioactivity in terms of AUC_{last} and C_{max}, respectively, indicating that most of the circulating radioactivity was attributable to metabolites. As in the previous studies, RP101988 and RP101075 showed PK properties that were similar to that of ozanimod, with similar T_{max} and $t_{1/2}$.

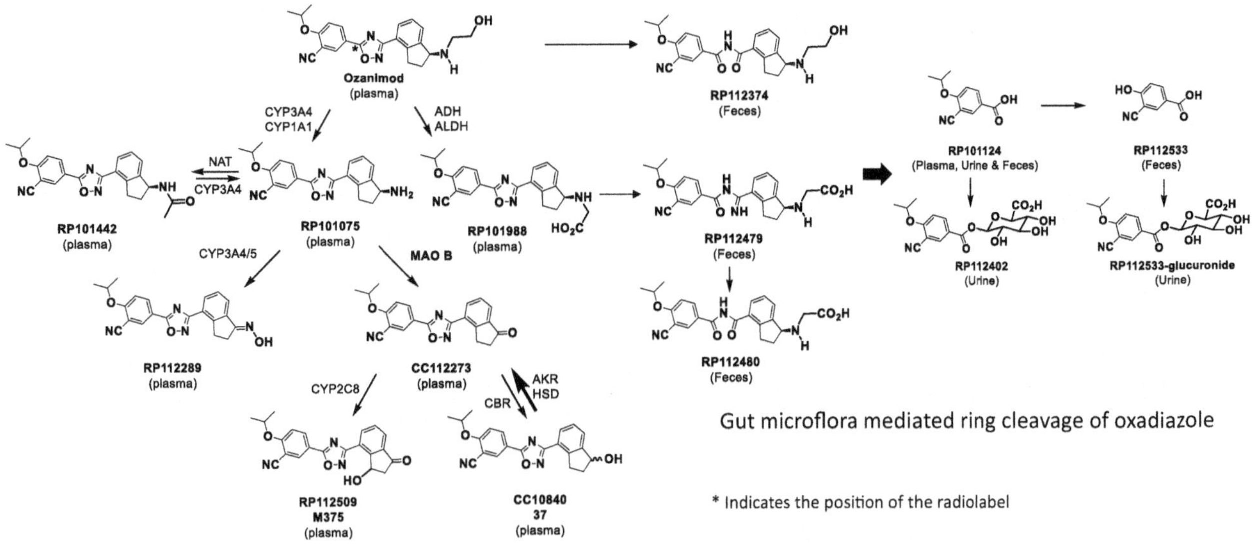

FIGURE 16.3 Proposed metabolic scheme of ozanimod in humans [17]. *ADH*, alcohol dehydrogenase; *AKR*, aldo-keto reductase; *ALDH*, aldehyde dehydrogenase; *CBR*, carbonyl reductase; *HSD*, 11β-hydroxysteroid dehydrogenase; *MAO B*, monoamine oxidase B.

The AME study revealed that metabolism was a primary route of clearance and ozanimod was extensively metabolized in humans since very little unchanged drug was detected in the excreta. Up to fourteen metabolites identified in plasma, urine, and feces. Fig. 16.3 shows the metabolic scheme of ozanimod and presents the metabolites detected in the excreta and plasma, in humans.

The predominant components recovered in the excreta were RP112374, RP112479 and RP112480 (Fig. 16.3) that were formed via reductive N—O bond cleavage of the oxadiazole ring of ozanimod by gut-microflora, as well as the benzoic acid metabolites RP101124 and RP112533, along with the glucuronide conjugates, RP112402 and RP112253-glucuronide that were formed via hydrolysis the of imide or acylamidine bond of RP112402, RP112533 and RP112480. The ring cleavage of the oxadiazole ring led to inactivity and loss of potency. RP101988 was the only intact oxadiazole recovered in urine accounting for approximately 4% of the dose.

In contrast to the excretory metabolites, most circulating components in plasma were intact oxidative metabolites and were similar in potency to that of ozanimod, except for the benzoic acid derivative, RP101124. Ozanimod, RP101988, RP101075, CC1084037, RP112289, RP112509 and RP101124 together accounted for approximately 33.6% of the circulating total radioactivity, while CC112273 accounted for 33% of the total circulating radioactivity. This suggesting that the indanone, which was not identified in the preclinical species, was the major circulating metabolite [17]. Table 16.2 presents the amount of each metabolite and is presented as % of circulating radioactivity and percentage of dose in the excreta.

As noted above, CC112273 was the major circulating metabolite in humans and exhibited different PK properties compared to the parent ozanimod. The plasma concentration-time profile of CC112273 paralleled to that of the total radioactivity plasma concentration-time profile with its concentration peaking at 18 h and with an elimination half-life of 195 h [17]. Following multiple oral doses, CC112273 exposure constituted ~73% of the total active drug exposure (parent and metabolites) [14,15]. The levels of CC112273 were not only high following multiple doses of ozanimod but its mean terminal elimination half-life was ~10 days, resulting in 11 to 13-fold accumulation [15]. A dose proportional increase in the exposure was observed for CC112273 and the increase in exposure correlated well with the alcohol metabolite, CC1084037. Comparison of the exposure of CC112273 with its exposure in the preclinical species used in ozanimod development, showed significant interspecies differences (https://www.accessdata.fda.gov/drugsatfda_docs/nda/2020/209899Orig1s000ClinPharmR.pdf). A radiolabeled study with ozanimod in the rat also confirmed this and failed to identify this metabolite prior to human AME results [17]. CC112273 was present at low levels in this study either due to its minimal formation and/or its high clearance.

Characterizing CC112273 formation

Among all circulating metabolites of ozanimod, CC112273 was the most important metabolite given its disproportionality in humans. Moreover, it was similar in potency to ozanimod toward S1P$_1$ and S1P$_5$ receptors (Table 16.2). Since

TABLE 16.2 Amount of ozanimod metabolites in the plasma (presented as % of total circulating radioactivity) and excreta (presented as % of dose) [17].

Metabolites	Plasma	Feces	Urine
	% Total radioactivity	% Dose	% Dose
Ozanimod	6.7	–	–
CC112273	33.2	–	–
RP101024	14.5	5.53	0.73
RP101988	6.98	–	3.54
RP101075	5.4	–	–
RP101442	Trace	–	–
CC1084037	5.48	–	–
RP112289	4.69		
RP112509	3.92		
RP112402	–		15.70
RP112533	–	7.67	
RP112480	–	12.23	
RP112374	–	5.30	
RP112479	–	2.54	
M339	–		2.58

regulatory agencies require that metabolites that are greater than 25% in circulation be characterized, in vitro studies were initiated to identify the enzymes responsible for the formation of CC112273, and its elimination in humans and assess its inhibitory potential.

Early in vitro experiments with ozanimod indicated that it was quite stable in liver microsomes and human hepatocytes. The in vitro metabolic profile showed only two primary pathways, one leading to the carboxylic acid RP101988 and second leading to RP101075 via oxidative dealkylation of hydroxyethylamine. Very little CC112273 was formed in these incubations. Subsequent phenotyping studies using recombinant CYP450 enzymes and co-incubation with selective CYP450 inhibitors suggested that RP101075 was primarily catalyzed by CYP3A4. Inhibition of formation of RP101075 in incubations, which contained CYP3A4 inhibitors, further confirmed the contribution of CYP3A4. On the other hand, formation of the carboxylic acid was catalyzed by non-CYP enzymes, alcohol dehydrogenase (ADH) and aldehyde dehydrogenase (ALDH). ADH converted the hydroxyethylamine to aminoaldehyde intermediate, which was trapped using semicarbazide to yield the corresponding semicarbazone in human liver microsomes. Furthermore, co-incubation of ozanimod with ALDH inhibitor, disulfiram along with an ADH inhibitor, 4-methylpyrazole inhibited the formation of RP101988. In vitro incubations with all fourteen recombinant CYPs indicated that the aldehyde intermediate nor the carboxylic acid was formed by CYP450. Overall, detection of minor amounts of CC112273 in incubation of ozanimod with liver microsomes and hepatocytes suggested that the indanone was not directly formed from ozanimod and that it was a secondary metabolite.

Since studies with ozanimod did not produce a satisfactory yield of CC112273, a next set of experiments were conducted with the indaneamine RP101075 to investigate the potential involvement of enzymes involved in CC112273 formation. Enzymatic formation of ketones from primary and secondary amines via oxidative deamination is well-known and has been observed in the biotransformation of amines, such as serotonin, epinephrine, amphetamine and fenfluramine (Fig. 16.4) [18−20].

Although several oxidative enzymes can catalyze these reactions, the two primary enzymes that catalyze such deamination reactions of amine containing xenobiotics, include the CYP450s and monoamine oxidases (MAO). Preliminary incubations were conducted with human liver microsomes in the presence and absence of the cofactor (NADPH) and CYP450 chemical inhibitors, including the non-selective CYP450 inhibitor, 1-aminobenzotriazole. Although the

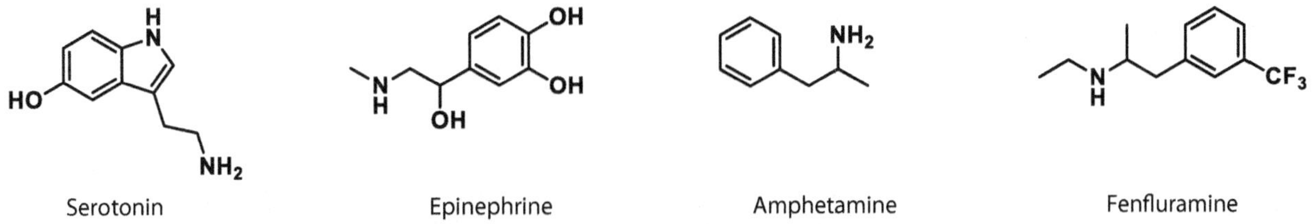

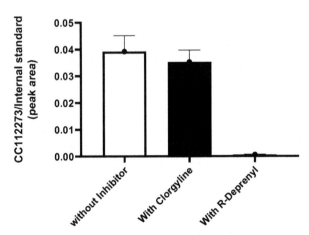

Serotonin   Epinephrine   Amphetamine   Fenfluramine

FIGURE 16.4 Structures of primary and secondary amines undergoing enzymatic oxidative deamination.

turnover of the amine in these incubations was low, coincubations with CYP450 inhibitors had no effect on the depletion of the substrate suggesting that CYP450 enzymes did not play a role in the formation of CC112273 [17].

Since P450 did not catalyze formation of CC112273, RP101075 was incubated with different subcellular fractions, including mitochondria in the presence of MAO A and MAO B inhibitors clorgyline and *R*-deprenyl (selegiline), respectively. Both these inhibitors have been previously used to identify the MAO enzymes involved in the metabolism of amine containing compounds [21,22]. The formation of CC112273 in the mitochondrial fractions and in incubation mixtures containing clorgyline, but its absence in incubation mixtures containing *R*-deprenyl suggested that CC112273 formation was primarily catalyzed by MAO and specifically by MAO B and not MAO A (Fig. 16.5).

The involvement of MAO B was further confirmed following incubation of RP101075 with human recombinant MAO B. On the other hand, recombinant human MAO A did not catalyze the formation of CC112273. This suggested that the overall biotransformation process in the formation of CC112273 involved CYP34A-catalyzed dealkylation of ozanimod to the amine as the first step followed by oxidative deamination to the ketone by MAO B (Fig. 16.3). Furthermore, the MAO catalyzed deamination was specifically carried out by MAO B only.

MAO A and MAO B are mitochondrial flavoenzymes that play an important role in the oxidative deamination of several structurally diverse amines, including biogenic amines and xenobiotics [20,23−28]. Both the enzymes catalyze the deamination reaction by cleavage of the C−H bond from the α-carbon and reducing the flavin moiety (FAD to FADH$_2$) by transfer of a hydride equivalent from the amine (Fig. 16.6). In the process, the amine is converted to an unstable imine intermediate, which is hydrolyzed non-enzymatically to aldehyde or ketone.

Despite the commonalities, these enzymes are biochemically differentiated by their substrate and inhibitor specificities [21,22,29−43]. Representative substrates and inhibitors of MAO A and B are shown in Fig. 16.7. The two isozymes are present in most mammalian tissues, but their proportions vary from tissue to tissue [44,45]. Some human tissues express only one form of MAO. For instance, fibroblasts and the placenta only express MAO A, whereas platelets and lymphocytes express only MAO B [46].

As mentioned earlier, remarkable interspecies differences were observed in the exposure of CC112273 suggesting species difference in MAO B catalyzed oxidative deamination. This was investigated further with studies using liver mitochondrial fractions from humans and preclinical species. In these studies, the Michaelis-Menten parameters (K_M and V_{max}) as well as the intrinsic clearance (Cl_{int}) for CC112273 formation were estimated and compared (Table 16.3) [47].

FIGURE 16.5 Incubation of RP101075 with human liver mitochondrial fraction with and without MAO A and B inhibitors, clorgyline and *R*-deprenyl, respectively [17].

FIGURE 16.6 Mechanism of oxidation of amines by MAO.

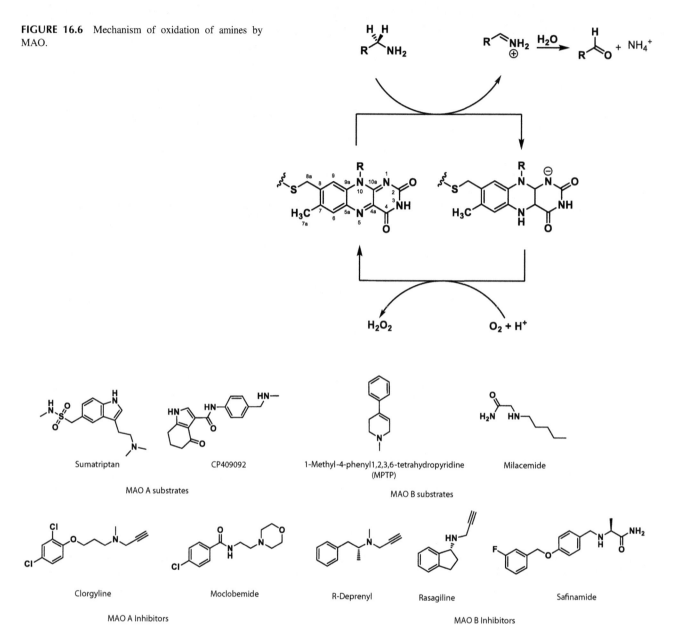

FIGURE 16.7 Structures of MAO A and B substrates and inhibitors.

TABLE 16.3 Mean kinetic parameters (K_M, Vmax and Cl_{int}) for CC112273 formation from RP101075 using human, monkey, rat and mouse liver mitochondrial fractions [47].

Species	K_M (µM)	V_{max} (pmols/min/mg protein)	Cl_{int} (µL/min/mg protein)
Human	4.8 ± 2.18	50.3 ± 7.42	12.0 ± 4.93
Monkey	3.0 ± 0.09	80.6 ± 0.4	27.2 ± 0.8
Rat	35 ± 4.8	114 ± 9.7	3.25 ± 0.18
Mouse	33 ± 8.27	37.3 ± 4.1	1.14 ± 0.15

These estimates indicated that the monkey was 2-fold more efficient and the mouse and rat was 11- and 4-fold less efficient than humans in forming CC112273. This disparity was primarily attributed to KM of the substrate in these species. The KM of RP101075 in rodents was ~7-fold higher than that in humans suggesting weak interactions with mouse and rat MAO B. On the other hand, a less than 2-fold difference in the KM between monkey and human suggested possible similarities in the MAO B binding pocket in these two species. A comparison of Clint estimates for CC112273 formation from in vitro studies, with CC112273 levels in preclinical and clinical studies after ozanimod administration, suggested good concordance. As reported in the summary basis of approval of Zeposia, the systemic exposures of CC112273 in mouse, rat, monkey, and human were 2.4%, 6%, 48%, and 73% of the total active drug related material at steady-state, respectively, and this was consistent with higher and lower efficiency of CC112273 formation observed in the primates and rodents, respectively. Although such a comparison can be challenging, the CC112273 exposures in the rodents and primates trended with the Clint values of CC112273 formation.

Inhibition of MAO B by CC112273

In vitro studies were also conducted to assess the inhibition of MAO A and B by CC112273. Using recombinant MAO enzymes, the results showed that CC112273 selectively inhibited MAO B over MAO A [15]. The half maximal inhibitory concentration (IC_{50}) value of CC112273 to inhibit MAO B was 5.72 nM, whereas the IC_{50} value for MAO A was greater than 10,000 nM. It is well known that MAO inhibition reduces the breakdown of important endogenous amines serotonin, norepinephrine, and dopamine. Increase in the concentration of these endogenous amines can have a deleterious side effects, like increase in blood pressure following increase in norepinephrine. Although this effect is elicited mainly by MAO A inhibitors mostly, high levels of MAO B inhibitors can also lead to the same effect due to their loss of selectivity and inhibition of MAO A at higher concentrations. For instance, drugs used for treatment of depression (e.g. phenelzine, tranylcypromine) or Parkinson's disease (e.g. safinamide, rasagiline, selegiline) can interact with sympathomimetic drugs, like pseudoephedrine can lead to hypertensive crises [15]. Pseudoephedrine, a sympathomimetic agent, which is found in many over the counter medicines used to relieve nasal congestion acts by releasing norepinephrine. Inhibition of MAO can reduce the deamination of norepinephrine leading to pressor effect enhancement of pseudoephedrine. For example, co-administration of a weak MAO A and B inhibitor linezolid, with pseudoephedrine has shown to increase the blood pressure response in humans [48,49]. To that end, an in vitro interaction study using CC112273 with and without known MAO-B inhibitors, selegiline, safinamide, phenelzine and linezolid, was conducted in human platelets. The results indicated that CC1122273 inhibited MAO-B activity with an IC50 value of 446 nM and did not potentiate the effect of MAO-B inhibitors activity in presence of CC112273 (unpublished results). In addition, a clinical study was conducted to evaluate the effect of ozanimod on the pressor response to a single dose administration of pseudoephedrine and on the PK of pseudoephedrine [15]. The results of this study demonstrated that there was no effect on the exposure of pseudoephedrine [15]. The lack of drug-drug interaction was ascribed to high plasma protein binding of CC112273 in humans (99.8%). Estimation of free C_{max} concentrations indicated that these levels were less than 1% and 0.001% of the IC_{50} for MAO A and MAO B, respectively [15].

Conclusion

Overall, ozanimod represents an interesting case study that highlights the importance of conducting a radiolabeled human AME study of developmental candidates at the right time during the drug development. While early in vitro studies led to the identification of some metabolites that were eventually monitored in preclinical and clinical studies, the major disproportionate metabolite CC112273 was not identified until late in development when the radiolabeled study was conducted. This presented formidable challenges and delays for the metabolites in safety testing assessment. To demonstrate the exposure coverage in chronic, reproductive and carcinogenicity studies, bridging and repeat dose good laboratory practice PK studies were conducted using ozanimod in preclinical studies (rat, mouse, rabbit and monkey) and the exposures of CC112273 were measured to calculate the safety multiples. In addition, there was need for determining the exposure of this active metabolite on the overall pharmacokinetic-pharmacodynamic effect of ozanimod and drug-drug interaction characterization in the clinic. The results of these studies also reiterate that not only is it important to assess the metabolic profile of drug candidates in animal species in vitro prior to selection of an animal model for a pharmacology or toxicology study, but also necessary to identify the enzymes involved in generating key metabolites, especially if the metabolite is pharmacologically active. This case study emphasize the need for conducting thorough absorption, metabolism and excretion studies early in the clinical development for assessing any disproportionate human metabolites.

References

[1] F.L. Scott, B. Clemons, J. Brooks, E. Brahmachary, R. Powell, H. Dedman, H.G. Desale, G.A. Timony, E. Martinborough, H. Rosen, E. Roberts, M.F. Boehm, R.J. Peach, Ozanimod (RPC1063) is a potent sphingosine-1-phosphate receptor-1 (S1P1) and receptor-5 (S1P5) agonist with autoimmune disease-modifying activity, Br. J. Pharmacol. 173 (2016) 1778−1792.

[2] P.S. Sorensen, Ozanimod: a better or just another S1P receptor modulator? Lancet Neurol. 15 (2016) 345−347.

[3] K.R. Taylor Meadows, M.W. Steinberg, B. Clemons, M.E. Stokes, G.J. Opiteck, R. Peach, F.L. Scott, Ozanimod (RPC1063), a selective S1PR1 and S1PR5 modulator, reduces chronic inflammation and alleviates kidney pathology in murine systemic lupus erythematosus, PLoS One 13 (2018) e0193236.

[4] S. Harris, J.Q. Tran, H. Southworth, C.M. Spencer, B.A.C. Cree, S.S. Zamvil, Effect of the sphingosine-1-phosphate receptor modulator ozanimod on leukocyte subtypes in relapsing MS, Neurol. Neuroimmunol. Neuroinflamm. 7 (2020) e839.

[5] J.A. Cohen, G. Comi, D.L. Arnold, A. Bar-Or, K.W. Selmaj, L. Steinman, E.K. Havrdova, B.A. Cree, X. Montalban, H.P. Hartung, V. Huang, P. Frohna, B.E. Skolnick, L. Kappos, R.T. Investigators, Efficacy and safety of ozanimod in multiple sclerosis: dose-blinded extension of a randomized phase II study, Mult. Scler. 25 (2019) 1255−1262.

[6] G. Lassiter, C. Melancon, T. Rooney, A.M. Murat, J.S. Kaye, A.M. Kaye, R.J. Kaye, E.M. Cornett, A.D. Kaye, R.J. Shah, O. Viswanath, I. Urits, Ozanimod to treat relapsing forms of multiple sclerosis: a comprehensive review of disease, drug efficacy and side effects, Neurol. Int. 12 (2020) 89−108.

[7] W.J. Sandborn, B.G. Feagan, Ozanimod treatment for ulcerative colitis, N. Engl. J. Med. 375 (2016) e17.

[8] W.J. Sandborn, B.G. Feagan, D.C. Wolf, G. D'Haens, S. Vermeire, S.B. Hanauer, S. Ghosh, H. Smith, M. Cravets, P.A. Frohna, R. Aranda, S. Gujrathi, A. Olson, T.S. Group, Ozanimod induction and maintenance treatment for ulcerative colitis, N. Engl. J. Med. 374 (2016) 1754−1762.

[9] B.G. Feagan, W.J. Sandborn, S. Danese, D.C. Wolf, W.J. Liu, S.Y. Hua, N. Minton, A. Olson, G. D'Haens, Ozanimod induction therapy for patients with moderate to severe Crohn's disease: a single-arm, phase 2, prospective observer-blinded endpoint study, Lancet Gastroenterol. Hepatol. 5 (2020) 819−828.

[10] V.E. Miron, C.G. Jung, H.J. Kim, T.E. Kennedy, B. Soliven, J.P. Antel, FTY720 modulates human oligodendrocyte progenitor process extension and survival, Ann. Neurol. 63 (2008) 61−71.

[11] R. van Doorn, P.G. Nijland, N. Dekker, M.E. Witte, M.A. Lopes-Pinheiro, B. van het Hof, G. Kooij, A. Reijerkerk, C. Dijkstra, P. van van der Valk, J. van Horssen, H.E. de Vries, Fingolimod attenuates ceramide-induced blood-brain barrier dysfunction in multiple sclerosis by targeting reactive astrocytes, Acta Neuropathol. 124 (2012) 397−410.

[12] J.Q. Tran, J.P. Hartung, R.J. Peach, M.F. Boehm, H. Rosen, H. Smith, J.L. Brooks, G.A. Timony, A.D. Olson, S. Gujrathi, P.A. Frohna, Results from the first-in-human study with ozanimod, a novel, selective sphingosine-1-phosphate receptor modulator, J. Clin. Pharmacol. 57 (2017) 988−996.

[13] J.Q. Tran, J.P. Hartung, C.A. Tompkins, P.A. Frohna, Effects of high- and low-fat meals on the pharmacokinetics of ozanimod, a novel sphingosine-1-phosphate receptor modulator, Clin. Pharmacol. Drug Dev. 7 (2018b) 634−640.

[14] J.Q. Tran, P. Zhang, A. Ghosh, L. Liu, M. Syto, X. Wang, M. Palmisano, Single-dose pharmacokinetics of ozanimod and its major active metabolites alone and in combination with gemfibrozil, itraconazole, or rifampin in healthy subjects: a randomized, parallel-group, open-label study, Adv. Ther. 37 (2020) 4381−4395.

[15] J.Q. Tran, P. Zhang, S. Walker, A. Ghosh, M. Syto, X. Wang, S. Harris, M. Palmisano, Multiple-dose pharmacokinetics of ozanimod and its major active metabolites and the pharmacodynamic and pharmacokinetic interactions with pseudoephedrine, a sympathomimetic agent, in healthy subjects, Adv. Ther. 37 (2020b) 4944−4958.

[16] J.Q. Tran, J.P. Hartung, A.D. Olson, B. Mendzelevski, G.A. Timony, M.F. Boehm, R.J. Peach, S. Gujrathi, P.A. Frohna, Cardiac safety of ozanimod, a novel sphingosine-1-phosphate receptor modulator: results of a thorough QT/QTc study, Clin. Pharmacol. Drug Dev. 7 (2018) 263−276.

[17] S. Surapaneni, U. Yerramilli, A. Bai, D. Dalvie, J. Brooks, X. Wang, J.V. Selkirk, Y.G. Yan, P. Zhang, R. Hargreaves, G. Kumar, M. Palmisano, J.Q. Tran, Absorption, metabolism, and excretion, in vitro pharmacology, and clinical pharmacokinetics of ozanimod, a novel sphingosine 1-phosphate receptor agonist, Drug Metab. Dispos. 49 (2021) 405−419.

[18] N.C. Marchant, M.A. Breen, D. Wallace, S. Bass, A.R. Taylor, R.M. Ings, D.B. Campbell, J. Williams, Comparative biodisposition and metabolism of 14C-(+/-)-fenfluramine in mouse, rat, dog and man, Xenobiotica 22 (1992) 1251−1266.

[19] H. Yamada, S. Shiiyama, T. Soejima-Ohkuma, S. Honda, Y. Kumagai, A.K. Cho, K. Oguri, H. Yoshimura, Deamination of amphetamines by cytochromes P450: studies on substrate specificity and regioselectivity with microsomes and purified CYP2C subfamily isozymes, J. Toxicol. Sci. 22 (1997) 65−73.

[20] H. Gaweska, P.F. Fitzpatrick, Structures and mechanism of the monoamine oxidase family, Biomol. Concepts 2 (2011) 365−377.

[21] C.M. Dixon, G.R. Park, M.H. Tarbit, Characterization of the enzyme responsible for the metabolism of sumatriptan in human liver, Biochem. Pharmacol. 47 (1994) 1253−1257.

[22] A. Kamel, R.S. Obach, E. Tseng, A. Sawant, Metabolism, pharmacokinetics and excretion of the GABA(A) receptor partial agonist [(14)C]CP-409,092 in rats, Xenobiotica 40 (2010) 400−414.

[23] T.P. Singer, Perspectives in MAO: past, present, and future. A review, J. Neural. Transm. Suppl. 23 (1987) 1−23.

[24] R.F. Squires, Discovery of monoamine oxidase forms A and B, Vopr. Med. Khim. 43 (1997) 433−439.

[25] M. Strolin Benedetti, K.F. Tipton, Monoamine oxidases and related amine oxidases as phase I enzymes in the metabolism of xenobiotics, J. Neural. Transm. Suppl. 52 (1998) 149−171.

[26] A.S. Kalgutkar, D.K. Dalvie, N. Castagnoli Jr., T.J. Taylor, Interactions of nitrogen-containing xenobiotics with monoamine oxidase (MAO) isozymes A and B: SAR studies on MAO substrates and inhibitors, Chem. Res. Toxicol. 14 (2001) 1139–1162.

[27] D.E. Edmondson, A. Mattevi, C. Binda, M. Li, F. Hubalek, Structure and mechanism of monoamine oxidase, Curr. Med. Chem. 11 (2004) 1983–1993.

[28] D.E. Edmondson, C. Binda, J. Wang, A.K. Upadhyay, A. Mattevi, Molecular and mechanistic properties of the membrane-bound mitochondrial monoamine oxidases, Biochemistry 48 (2009) 4220–4230.

[29] J.P. Johnston, Some observations upon a new inhibitor of monoamine oxidase in brain tissue, Biochem. Pharmacol. 17 (1968) 1285–1297.

[30] D.L. Murphy, Substrate-selective monoamine oxidases–inhibitor, tissue, species and functional differences, Biochem. Pharmacol. 27 (1978) 1889–1893.

[31] R.M. Cawthon, X.O. Breakefield, Differences in A and B forms of monoamine oxidase revealed by limited proteolysis and peptide mapping, Nature 281 (1979) 692–694.

[32] N.A. Garrick, D.L. Murphy, Species differences in the deamination of dopamine and other substrates for monoamine oxidase in brain, Psychopharmacology (Berl) 72 (1980) 27–33.

[33] A.J. Trevor, N. Castagnoli Jr., P. Caldera, R.R. Ramsay, T.P. Singer, Bioactivation of MPTP: reactive metabolites and possible biochemical sequelae, Life Sci. 40 (1987) 713–719.

[34] A.J. Trevor, T.P. Singer, R.R. Ramsay, N. Castagnoli Jr., Processing of MPTP by monoamine oxidases: implications for molecular toxicology, J. Neural. Transm. Suppl. 23 (1987) 73–89.

[35] P.C. Waldmeier, Amine oxidases and their endogenous substrates (with special reference to monoamine oxidase and the brain), J. Neural. Transm. Suppl. 23 (1987) 55–72.

[36] P. Janssens de Varebeke, E. Schallauer, W.D. Rausch, P. Riederer, M.B. Youdim, Milacemide, the selective substrate and enzyme-activated specific inhibitor of monoamine oxidase B, increases dopamine but not serotonin in caudate nucleus of rhesus monkey, Neurochem. Int. 17 (1990) 325–329.

[37] N.P. Nair, S.K. Ahmed, N.M. Kin, Biochemistry and pharmacology of reversible inhibitors of MAO-A agents: focus on moclobemide, J. Psychiatry Neurosci. 18 (1993) 214–225.

[38] I.J. Kopin, Monoamine oxidase and catecholamine metabolism, J. Neural. Transm. Suppl. 41 (1994) 57–67.

[39] K.F. Tipton, Monoamine oxidase inhibition, Biochem. Soc. Trans. 22 (1994) 764–768.

[40] N. Hauptmann, J. Grimsby, J.C. Shih, E. Cadenas, The metabolism of tyramine by monoamine oxidase A/B causes oxidative damage to mitochondrial DNA, Arch. Biochem. Biophys. 335 (1996) 295–304.

[41] M.B. Youdim, A. Gross, J.P. Finberg, Rasagiline [N-propargyl-1R(+)-aminoindan], a selective and potent inhibitor of mitochondrial monoamine oxidase B, Br. J. Pharmacol. 132 (2001) 500–506.

[42] C. Caccia, R. Maj, M. Calabresi, S. Maestroni, L. Faravelli, L. Curatolo, P. Salvati, R.G. Fariello, Safinamide: from molecular targets to a new anti-Parkinson drug, Neurology 67 (2006) S18–S23.

[43] J.P. Finberg, J.M. Rabey, Inhibitors of MAO-A and MAO-B in psychiatry and neurology, Front. Pharmacol. 7 (2016) 340.

[44] J.C. Shih, K. Chen, M.J. Ridd, Monoamine oxidase: from genes to behavior, Annu. Rev. Neurosci. 22 (1999) 197–217.

[45] K.F. Tipton, S. Boyce, J. O'Sullivan, G.P. Davey, J. Healy, Monoamine oxidases: certainties and uncertainties, Curr. Med. Chem. 11 (2004) 1965–1982.

[46] J.C. Shih, K. Chen, Regulation of MAO-A and MAO-B gene expression, Curr. Med. Chem. 11 (2004) 1995–2005.

[47] A. Bai, V. Shanmugasundaram, J.V. Selkirk, S. Surapaneni, D. Dalvie, Investigation into MAO B-mediated formation of CC112273, a major circulating metabolite of ozanimod, in humans and preclinical species: stereospecific oxidative deamination of (S)-enantiomer of indaneamine (RP101075) by MAO B, Drug Metab. Dispos. 49 (2021) 601–609.

[48] E.J. Antal, P.E. Hendershot, D.H. Batts, W.P. Sheu, N.K. Hopkins, K.M. Donaldson, Linezolid, a novel oxazolidinone antibiotic: assessment of monoamine oxidase inhibition using pressor response to oral tyramine, J. Clin. Pharmacol. 41 (2001) 552–562.

[49] P.E. Hendershot, E.J. Antal, I.R. Welshman, D.H. Batts, N.K. Hopkins, Linezolid: pharmacokinetic and pharmacodynamic evaluation of coadministration with pseudoephedrine HCl, phenylpropanolamine HCl, and dextromethorpan HBr, J. Clin. Pharmacol. 41 (2001) 563–572.

Chapter 17

Application of reaction phenotyping to address pharmacokinetic variability in patient populations

Robert S. Foti, Joseph M. Roesner and Joshua T. Pearson

ADME & Discovery Toxicology, Merck & Co., Inc., Kenilworth, NJ, United States

Introduction

Characterization of drug metabolism pathways and their quantitative importance is a major component in the determination of the pharmacokinetic properties of most xenobiotics [1,2]. The basis of these drug metabolism studies resides in multiple disciplines including physiology, enzymology, metabolic biotransformation, in silico modeling and toxicology, among others [3]. As such, the identification of the enzymes involved in the metabolism of a new compound, characterization of the metabolic stability and primary biotransformation pathways of the compound and determination of the ability of the new compound to inhibit or induce drug metabolizing enzymes are all major facets of the drug discovery and development continuum.

Though a great deal of progress has been made in understanding the factors which contribute to variations in pharmacokinetic profiles across populations, differences in anticipated versus observed drug exposure still result in adverse drug reactions, drug-drug interactions or lack of efficacy in certain patients [4]. Covariates such as impaired hepatic or renal capacity, weight or body surface area, age, gender, progression of disease state or nutritional and smoking habits are commonly invoked to explain such variations in pharmacokinetics [5]. While all plausible causes in their own right, the primary focus of this book chapter will be to describe the various roles that drug metabolizing enzymes and transporters play in altering a drug's pharmacokinetic profile in one patient versus another.

The fields of pharmacogenetics (studying the effect of altering a single gene on the pharmacokinetics or pharmacology of a drug) and pharmacogenomics (studying the effect of the entire genome on the pharmacology of a drug, often across a population) and their impact on studying drug metabolizing enzymes and transporters have significantly evolved since the initial identification of drug metabolizing enzymes, transporters and their associated genetic properties. Improvements and access to genetic testing together with an increased focus on personalized medicine have all driven a greater understanding of the roles that polymorphic enzymes and transporters play in the disposition of a drug. Examples of drugs with altered pharmacokinetic or pharmacodynamic profiles due to polymorphic enzymes or transporters include repaglinide (CYP2C8), nortriptyline, debrisoquine and desipramine (CYP2D6), multiple statins (CYP3A5), isoniazid (NAT2) and metformin (OCT1) [6−10].

Drug metabolizing enzymes

The biotransformation of xenobiotics into generally more polar metabolites is catalyzed by a variety of enzyme families in the liver and throughout the body. The metabolic reactions are often categorized into either Phase I (oxidation, reduction and hydrolysis) or Phase II (conjugation) reactions [11]. Enzyme families that are involved in Phase I drug metabolism include the cytochrome P450s, flavin monooxygenases, aldehyde and xanthine oxidases, monoamine oxidases, carboxylesterases, epoxide hydrolases and ketoreductases [12−17]. The Phase II drug metabolizing enzymes include UDP-glucuronosyltransferases, sulfotransferases, glutathione transferases, N-acetyltransferases, acyl-CoA synthetases and methyltransferases [2,18−23]. The relative expression levels of the cytochrome P450 drug metabolizing enzymes in the human liver together with the primary elimination routes for commonly prescribed drugs are depicted in Fig. 17.1. Excellent reviews are available on the chemistry and reaction mechanisms governing each of the metabolic processes, and as such, only a brief review of the cytochrome P450 family will be covered below [2,24−29].

The cytochrome P450s are a well-studied superfamily of heme-containing drug metabolizing enzymes that catalyze the oxidation or reduction of the vast majority of small molecule drugs currently in use today [30]. Nearly 60 individual isozymes have been characterized within the family, though approximately 10 of those enzymes are considered to be the 'primary' enzymes involved in xenobiotic metabolism (CYP1A1, CYP1A2, CYP2B6, CYP2C8, CYP2C9, CYP2C19, CYP2D6, CYP2E1, CYP3A4 and CYP3A5) [31]. Cytochrome P450s enzymes are expressed ubiquitously throughout the body, with key tissues including the liver, intestine, lung, kidney, brain and nasal mucosa cells [32]. The catalytic cycle of cytochrome P450 enzymes utilizes a transfer of electrons from NADPH, a mechanism facilitated by key protein-protein interactions cytochrome P450 reductase (CPR) and cytochrome b5 [33−35]. Within the cytochrome P450 family, CYP3A4 and CYP3A5 together are believed to account for approximately one-third of hepatic P450 expression [31] (Fig. 17.1A). It is important to note that the absolute and relative expression levels of the different P450 isoforms will be dependent upon the genotype and phenotype of the individuals and vary considerably depending on both ethnic and patient

FIGURE 17.1 (A) Estimated expression levels of cytochrome P450 enzymes as a percentage of total hepatic P450 content. (B) The relative contribution of different elimination pathways for the top 200 prescribed drugs in the United States for 2012. The relative importance of the elimination pathways was determined using the data (product labels, pharmacogenetic studies and drug-drug interaction studies) available for all of the clearance pathways of the top 200 drugs. Each clearance pathway was weighted for the individual drug by the fraction metabolized or excreted and incorporated into the overall calculation. The relative importance of each elimination pathway is expressed as a percentage of total elimination pathways for all of the drugs in the data set. "Other" refers to elimination by minor enzymes such as CYP2E1, xanthine oxidase, aldo-keto reductase, etc. *(A) The expression data was collected from multiple literature sources [39,40,175−188].*

a.

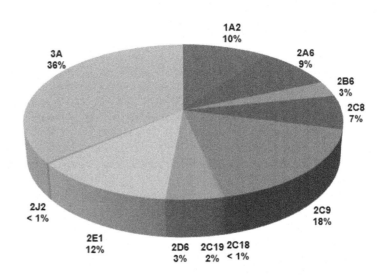

b.

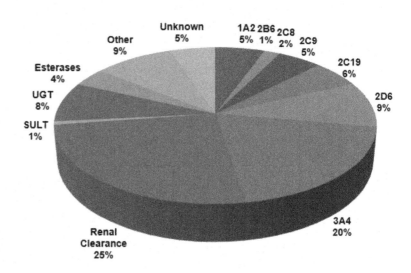

(i.e., disease state) populations [36]. Cytochrome P450 protein expression differs somewhat in the proximal small intestine, with CYP3A (combined CYP3A4 and CYP3A5) accounting for over 80% of total intestinal P450 expression [37]. CYP2C9, CYP2C19 and CYP2J2 expression have also been readily detected in the small intestine. CYP3A expression on a per-milligram basis has been shown to be higher in the intestine versus the liver and as such, the intestinal contribution to drug metabolism may be significant [38]. In general, expression analysis of other Phase I and Phase II drug metabolizing enzymes has been limited to measuring mRNA expression as selective antibodies are not as readily available as they are for the cytochrome P450s. Recent advancements in proteomics coupled with mass spectrometry have begun to explore the expression levels of other families of enzymes such as the UDP-glucuronosyltransferases, and may provide additional expression data as the analytical methods continue to evolve [39,40].

Tissue distribution of drug metabolizing enzymes

While the liver is generally considered to be the primary organ that contributes to drug metabolism, the enzymes involved in metabolizing xenobiotics are expressed in numerous tissues throughout the human body. For example, in addition to hepatic cytochrome P450 expression, these enzymes are also readily expressed in extra-hepatic tissues such as the intestine, lung, kidney, heart, nasal mucosa, brain and testes, as well as most other tissues [32]. In a similar fashion, while UGTs are also highly expressed in the liver, they are also found in the small intestine, stomach, brain, esophagus, kidneys and prostate [41−44]. Quite often, the tissue localization of a given drug metabolizing enzyme results from its role in homeostatic regulation, as is the case with CYP17, CYP19 or the P450 enzymes involved in the metabolism of arachidonic or retinoic acid [45−50].

Subcellular localization of drug metabolizing enzymes

In regard to the subcellular localization of drug metabolizing enzymes, the cytochrome P450s, UGTs and many others are localized within the microsomal membranes of the endoplasmic reticulum [51,52]. In addition to the endoplasmic reticulum, the mitochondria also serves as a depot for many drug metabolizing enzymes, with some P450 isoforms residing in both subcellular locations [47,53]. Interestingly, when cytochrome P450 distribution was studied in brain tissue, enzyme concentrations were more than nine times greater in the mitochondria as compared to the microsomal fractions [54]. Expression of drug metabolizing enzymes has also been observed in plasma membranes and lysosomes, though there is limited knowledge of the role of P450s in these locations in the metabolism of either xenobiotics or endogenous compounds [55−61]. Finally, many of the Phase II drug metabolizing enzymes are readily expressed in hepatic cytosol fractions. These cytosolic enzymes include the glutathione S-transferases, sulfotransferases, N-acetyltransferases, carboxylesterases, xanthine and diamine oxidases, and the epoxide and alcohol dehydrogenases [62].

Ontogeny of drug metabolizing enzymes

The ontogeny of drug metabolizing enzymes, especially the cytochrome P450s, has received a great deal of attention over the past decade. The expression patterns of drug metabolizing enzymes can vary significantly from the fetus through childhood and into adult subjects, resulting in altered pharmacokinetics from one age group to the next [63−66]. The end result is the potential to have different efficacy and toxicity profiles across age groups as well as the need to restrict the use of certain xenobiotics in a given age range. In general, total cytochrome P450 expression levels are thought to be approximately 10%−40% of adult liver content in the fetal liver through the first year after birth, though expression levels of the individual isoforms can greatly vary (or even be absent) with respect to each other and across prenatal trimesters [67−69]. With respect to the P450s, the ontogeny of the CYP3A family has probably received the most attention. While CYP3A4 has been identified as the major CYP3A isoform in the adult liver and intestine, it is CYP3A7 that accounts for the majority of CYP3A expression in the fetus [67,70]. In addition to CYP3A, CYP1A2 has also been shown to have differential expression levels when adult livers are compared to fetal liver samples. While CYP1A2 expression represents approximately 10%−13% of total adult liver P450 expression, multiple studies have reported that the enzyme is absent in fetal livers [67,71−73]. An analysis of the enzyme activity of CYP1A2, CYP2E1, CYP3A4 and UGT2B7 revealed relatively low activity levels for each of the enzymes (approximately 30% or less of adult values) in the neonate with CYP3A4, CYP2E1 and UGT2B7 activities being equal to adult activity by 1 year post birth [63,74]. It was not until 10 years of age that CYP1A2 enzyme activity was equal to that found in adults. CYP2C8, CYP2C9 and CYP2D6 activities were observed to be near adult levels within the first few months post birth.

The ontogeny of other drug metabolizing enzymes has also been evaluated [75]. Hepatic flavin monooxygenase expression, for example, switches from primarily FMO1 in fetal livers to predominantly FMO3 in adult liver tissue [76—78]. Similar to P450 expression patterns, UDP-glucuronosyltransferase, sulfotransferase and glutathione S-transferase expression patterns also appear to be isoform dependent with respect to age. While UGT1A1 and UGT1A6 appear to be absent in fetal livers, UGT1A3, UGT2B7 and UGT2B17 all appear to be readily expressed in the fetus [79—83]. More recently, it has been observed that UGT2B15 and UGT2B17 may represent the major UGT2B isoforms in the fetal liver, though fetal expression of UGT2B7, UGT2B15 and UGT2B17 were still 13—36 times lower than that observed in adult livers [84]. With respect to the sulfotransferase family of drug metabolizing enzymes, SULT1A1 and SULT1A3 appear to be expressed by the second trimester, though SULT2A1 expression appears to be primarily relegated to the third trimester of fetal development [85—88]. Finally, within the glutathione S-transferase family, while GSTA1, GSTA2 and GSTM appear to be expressed throughout all stages from fetal development through adulthood, glutathione S-transferase GSTP1 appears to be limited to the fetal and neonatal developmental periods, with no GSTP1 expression in adult livers [89—92].

In vitro systems to catalyze metabolic pathways

Understanding the drug metabolism properties of a given drug often relies upon in vitro systems designed to characterize the drug with respect to in vitro clearance, metabolite identification, reaction phenotyping and drug interactions, experiments which generate data on the rate, metabolites and enzymes involved in a drug's metabolism. The aforementioned studies can be accomplished using a host of well characterized reagents including whole cell systems such as hepatocytes or individual cell lines, subcellular fractions including microsomes, S9 or isolated cytosol, and individual recombinant enzymes expressed in *E. coli* or baculovirus-infected insect cells and will discussed in more detail below [15,93—96]. Factors that affect choice of in vitro systems include (but are not limited to) physiological relevance, assay endpoints (i.e., inhibition vs. induction assessment) and general throughput requirements.

Hepatocytes

Complex systems such as isolated perfused livers, liver slices and hepatocytes are generally considered to be more physiologically relevant when compared to other in vitro systems [62]. Of the three, hepatocytes are the most commonly used owing to recent advancements in culture, plating and cryopreservation techniques. Hepatocytes can be kept viable in culture for one to 3 weeks, allowing for the assessment of properties such as the regulation of drug metabolizing enzymes and interactions with hepatic transporters [97—100]. Cultured hepatocytes may also provide greater physiological relevance from the standpoint of protein interactions between drug metabolizing enzymes. When utilizing hepatocytes, one must also factor in the fact that all relevant enzymes and cofactors are generally active and available in cultured hepatocytes resulting in a mixture of primary and secondary metabolite formation [42]. An evolving area of research in the use of cultured cell systems for drug metabolism purposes involves the use of human embryonic stem cells and induced pluripotent stem cell derived hepatocytes [101,102]. Stem cell systems have the potential to provide a virtually inexhaustible supply of hepatocytes with very limited variability. However, a number of issues such as long-term viability in culture, cellular uniformity and the fetal-like phenotype of the derived hepatocytes, as well as ethical considerations still need to be addressed.

Microsomal systems

Perhaps one of the most commonly used in vitro systems in today's drug metabolism laboratory are hepatic microsomes (either from human or various preclinical species). In additional to the liver, microsomes can be prepared from additional organs including the intestine, lung and kidneys. The subcellular fraction is prepared by tissue homogenization followed by differential centrifugation and consists essentially of isolated vesicles from the endoplasmic reticulum. Though simpler than some of the aforementioned in vitro systems such as hepatocytes, cofactors such as NADPH (for cytochrome P450 and other enzymatic activity) or UDPGA (for UGT activity) must be added to microsomes to initiate the enzymatic reaction.

Recombinantly expressed single enzyme systems

The simplest of the commonly used in vitro systems are the recombinant drug metabolizing enzymes expressed either in baculovirus-infected insect cells, yeast or *E. coli* [93,103]. Single-enzyme systems are often used in reaction phenotyping studies to determine the percent contribution of a given enzyme to the overall clearance of the drug in question.

Recombinant systems are also useful for determining kinetic parameters for a drug that may be a substrate of multiple enzymes. Single-enzyme systems have proven useful in the prediction of metabolic clearance, but various scaling approaches such as relative abundance and relative activity factors must be accounted for [104–107]. However, the lack of physiologically relevant protein interactions, altered ratios of accessory proteins and matrix effects all need to be considered when attempting to extrapolate data from recombinant enzyme systems to in vivo endpoints.

Sources of in vitro variability

As previously mentioned, one of the potential differences between in vitro systems is the presence and relative concentrations of accessory proteins such as cytochrome P450 reductase and cytochrome b5 [93]. Cytochrome P450 reductase facilitates the transfer of electrons from the cofactor (NADPH) to the catalytically active cytochrome P450 while cytochrome b5 has been implicated in the transfer of the second electron in the cytochrome P450 cycle as well as in potential protein-protein interactions with cytochrome P450s that result in conformational changes [108–111]. Ratios of cytochrome P450 to P450 reductase and b5 can vary between in vitro systems and often differ from physiologically relevant concentrations, which can affect overall reaction rates in the individual systems and thus their applicability to in vivo predictions [108]. Additional experimental factors that can differ and affect the comparison of one in vitro system to the next include nonspecific binding (i.e., free fraction of the test compound in the in vitro system), the choice of buffer, percent of organic solvent and inclusion of divalent cations such as Mg^{2+}.

Reaction phenotyping approaches

To better understand the metabolic fate of investigational drugs during the drug discovery process, it is imperative to identify those enzymes that contribute to drug metabolism as well as the extent of involvement from each enzyme. This process is known as in vitro reaction phenotyping. Proper reaction phenotyping is key to informing on liabilities such as the potential for drug-drug interactions (victim or perpetrator) or involvement of polymorphic enzymes, which can lead to safety and/or toxicity concerns in the clinic [112]. While drug metabolism can occur in multiple organs throughout the body, the vast majority of metabolism occurs in the liver and intestine. As hepatic metabolism is primarily driven by the family of cytochrome P450 enzymes (CYPs), it is important to identify those enzymes that contribute to metabolism and the potential liabilities associated with them. Current FDA guidelines recommend determination of whether the investigational drug is either a substrate, inducer, or inhibitor of metabolizing enzymes. This can be further followed up with determining whether the metabolites of the investigational drug are also substrates or inhibitors of drug-metabolizing enzymes. FDA recommendations on reaction phenotyping are structured to determine the proper clinical studies that will need to be performed to ensure development of safe and efficacious drug.

The determination of the quantitative contribution (f_m, fraction metabolized) of a given reaction or enzyme toward a specific metabolic route or the overall elimination of a drug can be an extremely challenging task, albeit one for which a number of in vitro approaches currently exist. As multiple enzymes and multiple products are usually observed, the f_m by a specific enzyme versus through a specific metabolic pathway are usually not the same number. It is also important to distinguish an f_m value that quantifies the fraction of drug metabolism going through a specific enzymatic pathway versus the percentage of a drug's elimination that is through metabolism as opposed to excretion. While quantitatively accurate f_m determinations are challenging, it is often relatively simple to determine whether a given enzyme is a major contributor to a substrate clearance. Often, an initial approach involves screening a drug against a panel of recombinant enzymes and measuring substrate depletion or metabolite formation, with the latter often being critically important for the estimation of enzyme kinetic parameters. Subsequently, K_m and V_{max} values may be determined in several donor livers, preferably in a set that includes multiple polymorphic expression profiles for enzymes such as CYP2D6, CYP2C19 and CYP3A5. Similar kinetic values across multiple lots of human liver microsomes suggest that a polymorphic enzyme is not contributing to the metabolic route in question. If a polymorphic enzyme is a major contributor to the substrate turnover, substrate turnover kinetics in poor metabolizer livers should be significantly affected depending on the nature of the polymorphism. If multiple enzymes contribute to substrate metabolism, the importance of the low and high affinity enzymes varies from donor to donor. Missing a high affinity component that contributes to a drug's clearance will lead to misidentification of the relevant enzymes contributing to the clearance of the drug. Furthermore, irreversible inhibitors and/or enzyme specific antibodies should inhibit the reaction by >80% at any substrate concentration. Selective inhibitors can be further used to separate high affinity from lower affinity pathways, allowing more complete characterization of the latter. As the pharmacological potency of new compounds increases and target circulating concentrations decrease the necessity to identify high affinity clearance pathways becomes increasingly important.

In vitro reaction phenotyping approaches

As mentioned above, there are a variety of orthogonal in vitro approaches which can be used to identify those enzymes which contribute to the metabolism of a drug. As described in previous sections, there are a number of in vitro reagents and tools that are commercially available, including recombinant CYP proteins, microsomes, and hepatocytes. While each in vitro system can provide information on CYP metabolism, understanding the utility of each system is imperative to ensure proper experimental design [113]. Table 17.1 highlights the benefits and limitations of each in vitro system. An added benefit with the use of microsomes and hepatocytes include the availability of pooled, individual, and genotyped donor lots highlighting specific polymorphisms which can be used for further delineation of CYP-mediated metabolism. The most straight-forward reaction phenotyping technique to identify metabolic contributors is the use of recombinant CYPs (rCYPs). Initial studies are typically run at higher CYP concentrations using lower substrate concentrations assuming that the substrate concentration will be below the K_m. Higher CYP concentrations are selected to maximize identification of minor metabolic pathways [114]. At a minimum, general guidance recommends investigating a primary human CYP panel including CYP1A2, CYP2B6, CYP2C8, CYP2C9, CYP2C19, CYP2D6, and CYP3A. Additional follow-up may be required with less commonly investigated isoforms including CYP1A1, CYP2A6, CYP2E1, CYP2J2, and CYP4F2. These initial studies can be executed by sampling at a single time point and monitoring substrate depletion relative to control incubations. By comparing the two incubations, the percent of substrate depleted by a given CYP isoform can be calculated. General acceptance criteria would classify any isoform showing greater than a 20% loss in substrate as a metabolic contributor. As the 20% cut-off is an arbitrary value, further evaluation of those enzymes showing any significant depletion of parent drug may be warranted. Where substrate depletion is too low to be monitored, or for cases where a higher degree of rigor is required, metabolite formation by each CYP isoform can also be characterized. Ideally, this approach is based on the results from previously conducted metabolite elucidation studies and synthetic metabolite standards, though an initial evaluation can be accomplished using mock LC-MS/MS transitions for anticipated metabolites (i.e., MW + 16) [115].

Upon identifying the isoforms potentially involved in the metabolism of a new drug, the next step is to estimate the intrinsic clearance for each isoform. While initial substrate depletion experiments are directional, the intrinsic clearance data will ultimately be used to calculate the fraction of drug metabolized by each P450 (f_m). Intrinsic clearance (Cl_{int}) can be assessed by generating time course data at appropriate CYP and substrate concentrations to produce an initial slope following linear kinetics as shown in Fig. 17.2. Also shown in Fig. 17.2 is simulated data from an incubation assayed with too high of a CYP concentration leading to uncertainty in the initial slope since only the first two time points are able to be

TABLE 17.1 Properties of in vitro systems used in reaction phenotyping approaches.

In vitro system	Physiological relevance	Permeability limited	Enzymes present	Cofactor supplementation needed	System viability
rCYP	+	No	Single enzyme	Yes	<60 min
Microsomes	++	No	Phase I/II	Yes	<120 min
Hepatocytes	+++	Yes	Phase I/II	No	Hrs—Weeks

FIGURE 17.2 Representative graph showing intrinsic clearance data sets plotted as natural log of percent substrate remaining versus time. Ideal reaction conditions (appropriate enzyme and substrate concentrations) result in a high degree of confidence fitting the initial slope of the substrate depletion curve. Alternatively, utilization of too high a substrate concentration (enzyme saturation) or too high a protein concentration (significant substrate depletion) results in difficulty accurately estimating the initial slope of the substrate depletion curve.

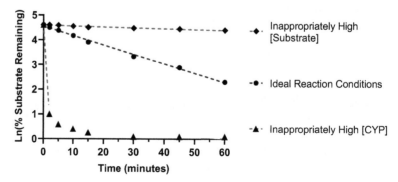

used, or from an incubation conducted at too high a substrate concentration, where metabolism is saturated. An additional consideration when selecting CYP concentrations is understanding the protein levels of each reagent lot and how non-specific binding may skew the apparent Cl_{int} for each isoform. This will be most prevalent for highly bound compounds and as the unbound fractions in the recombinant system are not likely known at this stage, it is beneficial to normalize protein levels across all isoforms that are being used. This can be accomplished by using the same protein levels for all isoforms or by normalizing CYP concentrations and then adjusting the protein levels in the incubations using blank vector control cells. For example, if using Supersomes as the recombinant system, protein levels can range anywhere from 2 mg/mL up to 15 mg/mL depending on which isoforms are selected. Based on the disparity between these concentrations, if protein normalization is not taken into account, significant bias could be incorporated into the data interpretation of highly bound substrates.

Methods for scaling in vitro phenotyping data (RAF, REF, ISEF)

Intrinsic clearance assays in recombinant systems are typically performed using lots that have been classified with either a relative activity factor (RAF) or intersystem extrapolation factor (ISEF). These recombinant enzymes provide an alternative approach than other in vitro systems such as microsomes or hepatocytes for quantitative in vitro-in vivo extrapolation (IVIVE) and provide an estimation of the extent of in vivo hepatic clearance [107,116]. The RAF approach uses a predetermined value (pmol/mg) generated from either V_{max} or CL_{int} data that is then applied to rCYP intrinsic clearance data [117]. This application will convert the intrinsic clearance from a rate per unit enzyme to a rate per mg microsomal protein [118]. One limiting aspect to the RAF approach is a lack of application toward population IVIVE as RAFs do not account for CYP abundance in microsomes or the activity per unit of enzyme. This can lead to potential ambiguity with IVIVE predictions. Improving upon the RAF approach, the ISEF approach expands on the RAF by factoring in the microsomal CYP abundance resulting in a unitless factor. Historically, abundance values were determined by quantitation from Western blotting, but with continued analytical improvements, proteomics approaches using liquid chromatography-mass spectrometry provide more reliable quantitation than past methodologies [119]. By accounting for CYP abundance, more accurate assessments of in vitro-in vivo correlations, drug interactions and metabolic variability can be made. Ultimately these approaches combine to provide a more robust understanding of the fraction metabolized per CYP enzyme and how this will translate into clinical outcomes [120]. One caveat with the ISEF approach is the potential to generate substrate-dependent ISEF values. Recent studies have shown that for certain isoforms, a substantial range of ISEF values can be calculated depending on the substrate used [121]. This discrepancy across substrates can lead to either over or underestimation of f_m values [122]. A commonly accepted approach to minimize estimation inaccuracies is to use multiple substrates to determine ISEF values and then use the average value for application.

Applying the ISEF approach, the intrinsic clearance values determined in rCYPs are scaled to physiological relevance relating to in vivo liver CYP activity by incorporating CYP abundance in the liver, amount of protein per gram of liver, and liver weight. Once the intrinsic clearances have been scaled, the fraction metabolized pertaining to each isoform can be calculated as shown in Fig. 17.3. This is an important step in drug discovery as this information will help guide the timing and nature of clinical DDI and pharmacogenomic studies [36,123]. Additionally, these data can be used to facilitate the prediction of pharmacokinetic parameters.

Chemical inhibitors and monoclonal antibodies

Given the number of caveats noted for the aforementioned reaction phenotyping experiments, it is recommended to utilize orthogonal approaches to verify the recombinant results in a different in vitro system [124]. The most common approach is using either selective chemical inhibitors or inhibitory monoclonal antibodies with human liver microsomal incubations. Table 17.2 lists commonly used chemical inhibitors. Relying on the selective nature of the inhibitors allows for a determination of the fraction of drug metabolized by P450s [125]. A key challenge with the inhibitor approach is ensuring that the inhibitors are selective and that sufficient inhibition of metabolic activity can be obtained. Under ideal conditions, it is recommended to run inhibitor studies by monitoring either metabolite formation or using radiolabeled substrates, but depending on the extent of metabolism for the substrate of interest, monitoring substrate depletion may also be acceptable as metabolite standards are typically unavailable in early drug discovery. When using metabolite formation, incubations are conducted at a single time point with one substrate concentration, typically near the predicted human Cmax if known or at a concentration that will ensure formation and monitoring of primary metabolites. The optimized parameters will also need to ensure 10%−20% substrate depletion under initial linear rate conditions. Similar to the use of recombinant systems, inhibition data from human liver microsomes can be used to calculate the specific fraction metabolized by each P450. A

a.

$$\boxed{\mu L/min/pmol\ CYP_j}$$

$$\boxed{\begin{array}{c}\text{mg microsomal}\\\text{protein/g liver}\end{array}}$$

$$CL_{int,h_j} = ISEF_j \times CL_{int,rCYP_j} \times [CYP\ Abundance]_j \times MPPGL \times LW$$

$$\boxed{\mu L/min/kg}$$

$$\boxed{\begin{array}{c}\text{pmol CYP}_j/\text{mg}\\\text{microsomal protein}\end{array}}$$

$$\boxed{\begin{array}{c}\text{g liver/kg}\\\text{body weight}\end{array}}$$

b.

$$Percent\ Contribution_j = \left(\frac{CL_{int,h_j}}{\sum CL_{int,h}}\right) \times 100$$

FIGURE 17.3   ISEF calculations are used to scale in vitro data to physiological relevant units and determine fraction metabolized per CYP enzyme. (A) Scaling calculation using the ISEF approach where j represents each CYP isoform of interest. (B) The equation used to determine the percent contribution from each CYP isoform of interest.

TABLE 17.2 Common chemical inhibitors used in reaction phenotyping assays with human liver microsomes.

Targeted CYP isoform	Chemical inhibitor	Pre-incubation required
CYP1A2	Furafylline	Yes
CYP2B6	ThioTEPA	Yes
CYP2C8	Montelukast	No
CYP2C9	Tienilic acid	Yes
CYP2C19	(S)-(+)-N-3-Benzylnirvanol	No
CYP2D6	Quinidine	No
CYP3A	Ketoconazole	No
CYP3A4	CYP3cide	No

majority of these chemical inhibitors and inhibitory antibodies are commercially available. The downside with some of these is the lack of complete P450 inhibition which can lead to skewed fractions metabolized [126]. Improving upon the inhibitory approach, it has been shown that superior inhibition profiles can be achieved when using a combination of chemical inhibitors and inhibitory antibodies. In the case of CYP3A metabolism of midazolam or testosterone, inhibition by selective inhibitors or antibodies along results in approximately 20% activity still remaining under selective inhibitor conditions, but when used in combination complete inhibition of CYP3A was observed [127]. While a significant amount of information of selective inhibitors has been published, this approach still requires multiple steps to optimize ideal parameters to ensure appropriate conditions are being used to generate accurate f_m values. When used appropriately, the inhibitory reaction phenotyping method can provide additional support to the validity of recombinant reaction phenotyping.

Correlation analysis

One final approach to reaction phenotyping is correlation analysis, using human liver microsomes from multiple individual donors with varying expression levels of drug metabolizing enzymes [128]. In this instance, the formation of metabolites from the drug candidate is compared to the activity of enzyme-selective metabolic reactions across the panel of donors. For best results, the use of at least 15 individual donors is often recommended. This approach can also be accomplished by comparing the metabolic rates of the drug candidate to the immunoquantified concentrations of the individual lots of human liver microsomes [129]. Complicating factors often encountered when performing a correlation analysis include the inherent correlation between enzymes in the set of human liver microsomes and the prevalence of polymorphic enzymes which can often bias the results if immunoquantitation is the method of choice. The combination of correlation analysis and selective inhibitors can further be used to elucidate the contributions of multiple enzymes to the metabolism of a drug.

Role of transporters in pharmacokinetic variability

In addition to drug metabolizing enzymes, pharmacokinetic variability can also be influenced by the role of drug transporters in the disposition of a drug. The expression patterns of drug transporters are regulated by many of the same mechanisms as noted for drug metabolizing enzymes, including nuclear receptors such as the pregnane X receptor (PXR), the constitutive androstane receptor (CAR), the farnesoid X receptor (FXR) and the peroxisome proliferator-activated receptor γ (PPARγ) [130]. For example, P-glycoprotein (P-gp), a well-studied efflux transporter involved in the transport of many commonly used drugs, has been shown to be inducible via activation of PXR and CAR [131,132]. Similarly, the breast cancer resistance protein (BCRP), another efflux transporter that is widely expressed throughout the body and has been shown to limit the efficacy of anti-cancer agents in tumor cells, is regulated by multiple nuclear receptors, including PPARγ, hypoxia inducible factor 1α and the estrogen receptor [133]. In a similar fashion, uptake transporters such as those belonging to the organic anion-transporting polypeptide (OATP) family are regulated by numerous cytokines and nuclear receptors, including PXR, CAR, FXR, the liver X receptor (LXR) and hepatocyte nuclear factor 4α (HNF-4α) [134]. The resulting changes in the expression patterns of drug transporters can have a direct effect on the amount of drug crossing the brush border of the intestinal epithelia, the local drug concentration in specific tissues such as brain or tumor and the extent of renal excretion of a drug [135].

Multiple examples of the role of drug transporters in pharmacokinetic and/or pharmacodynamic variability have been noted, including examples where the change in transporter expression or activity is the direct result of disease state progression [136]. Drugs such as simvastatin (P-gp), digoxin (P-gp), sulfasalazine (BCRP), pravastatin (OATP1B1) and metformin (OCT2) all have been shown to exhibit significant changes in either AUC or Cmax due to polymorphic expression of their respective transporters [135]. For narrow therapeutic index drugs such as digoxin, co-administration with a P-gp inhibitor such as verapamil may also result in altered exposure and a clinically relevant drug-drug interaction [137]. Finally, as noted above, the onset and progression of disease state, especially when associated with altered liver function, can affect the activity and expression of drug transporters. For example, increases in the protein expression of OATP1B1, MRP1, MRP3, MRP4 and BCRP has been noted in patients diagnosed with nonalcoholic steatohepatitis (NASH), while OATP1B3 expression appears to decrease in the same patients [136]. Similarly, the pharmacokinetic profiles of drugs such as metformin, nelfinavir, and methotrexate have been shown to be altered in patients diagnosed with cholestasis, hepatitis C or NASH, respectively [138−140]. As such, drug developers must account for potential differences in drug exposure when conducting clinical trials in healthy volunteers versus patients.

The increased focus on drug transporters in recent years as a major cause of pharmacokinetic variability has resulted in the development of new approaches to study drug transporters and their associated effects on drug disposition. Membrane and cell-based assays have been available for years and can be used to determine if a drug is a substrate or inhibitor of a given transporter, determine the overall contribution of a transporter to a drug's disposition (f_t; analogous to f_m) and determine kinetic parameters which can later be used in pharmacokinetic and drug-interaction predictions [141]. Membrane-based assays are generally divided into ATPase and vesicle assays, while commonly used cell lines to study transporter effects include Caco-2, LLC-PK1 (Lewis-lung cancer porcine kidney 1), MDCK (Madin-Darby canine kidney) or HEK293 (human embryonic kidney) cells. Of utmost importance is the fact that transporter profiles can differ significantly between species and as such, translation of transporter data derived from preclinical species (either in vitro or in vivo) should be extrapolated to clinical outcomes cautiously [142]. Other factors which can introduce variability into transporter data include the physicochemical properties of the test substrates themselves, number of passages of a given cell line, and whether an assay is performed using fresh or frozen cells [143]. Clinical methods to assess transporter activity and variability will be discussed in Clinical assessment of metabolic and transport pathways section.

In vivo assessment of elimination pathways

As described above, most reaction phenotyping approaches in drug discovery involve in vitro experiments. While in vivo studies specifically aimed at understanding pharmacokinetic variability in patient studies are limited, a number of options in either preclinical species or in clinical studies do exist and are routinely used when warranted.

Preclinical characterization of routes of elimination

Preclinical studies aimed at elucidating the contributions of specific metabolic or transport pathways to the elimination and pharmacokinetic variability of a new chemical entity must be interpreted carefully due to well-characterized species differences in drug metabolizing enzymes and transporters [144]. While the aforementioned species differences generally preclude the use of preclinical in vivo studies to estimate human f_m values, higher level information can be gained from these experiments. In vivo ADME studies in bile duct cannulated rats (often utilizing radiolabeled test compounds) can be used to estimate the fraction of a drug eliminated as unchanged drug or metabolites in urine, bile and feces, providing valuable information on routes of elimination and potential sources of pharmacokinetic variability [145]. In a similar fashion, the use of the P450 inactivator 1-aminobenzotriazole (1-ABT) has been shown to be a useful tool in determining the fraction of a molecule eliminated by oxidative metabolism and, when dosed IV and orally, can be used to estimate hepatic versus intestinal contributions to the metabolism of the test molecule [146]. The contribution of transporters to the disposition of a molecule can also be estimated by co-dosing with chemical inhibitors such as elacridar, which can be used to characterize transporter effects on oral bioavailability as well as brain uptake [147]. While less commonly utilized, genetically modified animal models (humanized liver, P450 reductase knockout, transporter knockouts, etc.) can also be used to assess sources of variability and contributions of various pathways to a molecule's disposition. Finally, by comparing drug exposure after the first and last dose from multiple-dose studies such as 4, 7 or 14 day safety studies (often incorporating high doses), the potential for auto-induction or auto-inhibition to lead to variable pharmacokinetic profiles in clinical studies can be inferred and subsequently modeled for therapeutically relevant doses.

Clinical assessment of metabolic and transport pathways

All of the previously described studies are aimed at providing the maximum possible amount of information about a molecule's disposition prior to clinical trials, allowing early design of the necessary clinical trials needed to adequately characterize the ADME and drug interaction properties of a drug. Clinical pharmacokinetics can be affected by numerous factors, many of which can be accounted for or anticipated based on data from in vitro or preclinical studies. In addition to polymorphic enzyme and transporter expression, other factors which can lead to variability include co-administered medications, disease state, hepatic or renal impairment, patient-specific descriptors (age, gender, weight) as well as diet [5]. The first evaluation of a test compound's pharmacokinetics occurs during first-in-human trials, where single ascending dose (SAD) and multiple ascending dose (MAD) study designs will be used to evaluate the safety and pharmacokinetic profiles of the molecule. Information collected from patients or healthy volunteers in these studies can be used to begin to characterize sources of pharmacokinetic variability in the clinic.

More definitive studies can be used to add additional information around a molecule's disposition. The gold standard experiment to characterize routes of elimination in humans remains the ^{14}C human ADME study which, similar to the ADME studies described in preclinical species, can provide information on the fraction of unchanged drug and metabolites in circulation as well as in excreta [148]. When polymorphic enzymes or transporters are thought to be involved in a molecule's disposition, studies in genotyped volunteers are often useful to more accurately determine an f_m via the polymorphic pathway [149]. Similarly, when a significant fraction of a molecule's elimination is via hepatic metabolism or renal excretion, clinical trials in hepatically or renally impaired subjects, respectively, may be required. Population PK modeling approaches can often be used to incorporate information from multiple clinical trials to more adequately characterize sources of pharmacokinetic variability in patients.

Case examples

Montelukast

Montelukast (Singulair) is a selective leukotriene D4 receptor antagonist prescribed for the treatment of asthma. It has also been shown to selectively and potently inhibit CYP2C8, and as such, is often used as a tool when conducting reaction phenotyping assessments on new molecular entities [150]. Initial reaction phenotyping experiments conducted during the development of the molecule suggested CYP3A4 (montelukast 21-hydroxylation) and CYP2C9 (montelukast 36-hydroxylation) as the primary drug metabolizing enzymes involved in the clearance of montelukast [151]. As noted in In vitro reaction phenotyping approaches section, understanding the enzyme kinetics of a given metabolic pathway and conducting reaction phenotyping at clinically relevant concentrations is key when trying to determine the contribution of a given enzyme to the clearance of a drug. The aforementioned reaction phenotyping experiments for montelukast were conducted at a substrate concentration of between 100 and 500 μM, while total circulating drug concentrations in humans after a therapeutically relevant dose are generally less than 1 μM [152]. Subsequent in vitro phenotyping experiments conducted at clinically relevant concentrations of montelukast identified a significant role for CYP2C8 in the oxidative metabolism of montelukast (Fig. 17.4A) [153,154]. Further supporting the in vitro role of CYP2C8, clinical trials in healthy subjects were used to determine that CYP2C8 is the primary CYP isoform involved in the clearance of montelukast (not CYP3A4 or CYP2C9), with an observed f_m of approximately 0.8 based on interactions with the CYP2C8 inhibitor gemfibrozil [155]. The CYP3A4 inhibitor itraconazole does not significantly alter the pharmacokinetics of montelukast in vivo.

Warfarin

The anticoagulant warfarin (Coumadin) is an inhibitor of the vitamin K epoxide reductase complex 1 (VKORC1) and arguably one of the most studied drugs with regard to clearance pathways and their subsequent roles in contributing to the highly variable pharmacokinetic and pharmacodynamic profiles of the drug. Further, given the multiple enzymes involved in the clearance of warfarin, it is also the victim of multiple drug and food interactions, thus further adding to variability in the exposure of warfarin and often resulting in the need for altered dosing regimens [156]. Warfarin is dosed as a racemate

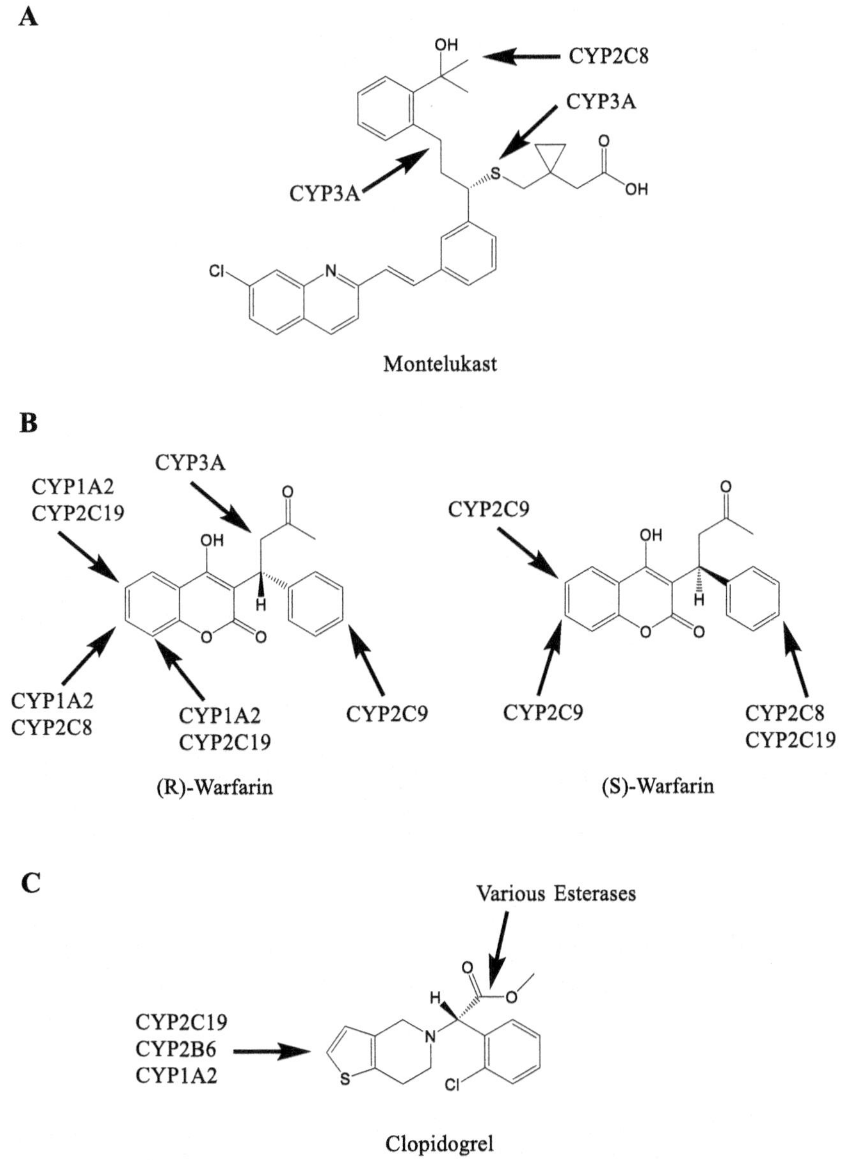

FIGURE 17.4 Primary enzymes contributing to the major sites of metabolism for montelukast (A), (R)-warfarin and (S)-warfarin (B) and clopidogrel (C).

of R- and S-warfarin (Fig. 17.4B), with the S-enantiomer being the more potent of the two with regard to its anticoagulative properties [157]. Both enantiomers undergo P450-catalyzed oxidation at multiple positions with (S)-6-hydroxywarfarin (CYP2C9), (S)-7-hydroxywarfarin (CYP2C9) and (R)-10-hydroxywarfarin (CYP3A4) being the most abundant metabolites formed [158–160]. Seminal studies on the metabolic pathways of warfarin and its in vitro drug interaction profile also identified roles for CYP1A2 in the hydroxylation of R-warfarin at the 6- and 8-positions and CYP2C19 in the formation of (R)-8-hydroxywarfarin [161–163]. The polymorphic nature of CYP2C9 as well as that of VKORC1 combine to result in the highly variable pharmacokinetic profile of warfarin [164]. Presence of a CYP2C9*2 (R144C) allele results in an approximate 30% decrease in CYP2C9 activity, while the CYP2C9*3 allele (I359L) results in over 75% loss of activity, thus leading to potential increased concentrations of warfarin [165–167]. As such, blood testing (INR) is commonly conducted after warfarin dosing to ensure exposure is in the safe and efficacious range, and patient genotyping of VKORC1 and CYP2C9 has been proposed, though its use in clinical practice is limited.

Clopidogrel

The oral antiplatelet medication clopidogrel (Plavix) is an irreversible inhibitor of $P2Y_{12}$ that is used to treat cardiac disease and stroke patients. The drug has a well-studied history of variable pharmacokinetic and pharmacodynamic outcomes in patients [168]. Clopidogrel itself is a prodrug, requiring a two-step bioactivation process in order to elicit a pharmacological effect [169]. The first step, catalyzed by CYP2C19, CYP2B6 and CYP1A2 involves oxidation of the thiophene ring in clopidogrel to a thiolactone (2-oxo-clopidogrel). The second step in the bioactivation of clopidogrel, catalyzed by CYP2C19, CYP2C9, CYP3A4 and CYP2B6, is ring opening of the thiolactone moiety to the resulting thiol via a sulfenic acid intermediate (Fig. 17.4C). Clopidogrel is also a substrate of P-glycoprotein [170]. The mechanism of action of clopidogrel suggests that any alteration to the bioactivation pathways of the drug could have significant effects on its safety and efficacy. Indeed, clopidogrel carries an FDA black box warning for CYP2C19 poor metabolizers, for whom clopidogrel may be much less efficacious due to decreased levels of the active thiol metabolite. Beyond CYP2C19 polymorphisms (CYP2C19*2 and CYP2C19*3), it has also been postulated that loss-of-function mutations in CYP2C9 (*3) or CYP2B6 (*5) may also result in lower efficacy for clopidogrel, while gain-of-function mutations such as CYP2C19*17, CYP1A2*1C and CYP3A4*16 result in a stronger antiplatelet effect due to greater circulating levels of the active thiol [171]. While inconclusive, studies have also suggested a role for P-gp polymorphisms (ABCB1 C3435T) in the observed clinical response variability to clopidogrel [172]. The clopidogrel story also provides an example of the use of reaction phenotyping and accurate determination of metabolic pathways in order to reduce population variability in second-generation therapies. Similar to clopidogrel, prasugrel is a pro-drug, however rather than being catalyzed primarily by CYP2C19, the bioactivation of prasugrel occurs mainly through intestinal hydrolysis (carboxylesterases) followed by CYP2B6 and CYP3A4 oxidation, leading to a decrease in the observed clinical variability for prasugrel relative to clopidogrel [173]. In a similar, and perhaps even simpler fashion, ticagrelor is a reversible inhibitor of $P2Y_{12}$ that has on-target activity itself, but is also metabolized into an active metabolite by CYP3A [174].

Conclusion

The identification of the enzymes involved in the metabolism of a molecule is a critical step in advancing the molecule from pre-clinical studies into clinical trials. Understanding the individual contributions of each enzyme through well-designed reaction phenotyping experiments can aid in the understanding and anticipation of potential drug-drug interactions, pharmacokinetic variability and adverse drug reactions. As described throughout this chapter, a number of approaches are available for the drug discovery scientist to utilize, each with their own advantages and caveats, some of which can be overcome by combining multiple approaches in the evaluation of a molecule. Ultimately, the ability to bring safe, effective and well-characterized drugs to patients will continue increase as our understanding of the properties of drug metabolizing enzyme and transporters continues to expand.

References

[1] L.C. Wienkers, T.G. Heath, Predicting in vivo drug interactions from in vitro drug discovery data, Nat. Rev. Drug Discov. 4 (2005) 825–833.

[2] R.S. Foti, D.A. Rock, L.C. Wienkers, J.L. Wahlstrom, Mechanisms of drug metabolism, Encycl. Drug Metab. Interact. (2011) 1–68.

[3] J. Lee, R.S. Obach, M.B. Fisher, Drug Metabolizing Enzymes: Cytochrome P450 and Other Enzymes in Drug Discovery and Development, Taylor & Francis, 2003.

[4] J.H. Lin, Pharmacokinetic and pharmacodynamic variability: a daunting challenge in drug therapy, Curr. Drug Metab. 8 (2007) 109–136.

[5] E. Reyner, B. Lum, J. Jing, M. Kagedal, J.A. Ware, L.J. Dickmann, Intrinsic and extrinsic pharmacokinetic variability of small molecule targeted cancer therapy, Clin. Transl. Sci. 13 (2020) 410−418.

[6] M. Niemi, J.B. Leathart, M. Neuvonen, J.T. Backman, A.K. Daly, P.J. Neuvonen, Polymorphism in CYP2C8 is associated with reduced plasma concentrations of repaglinide, Clin. Pharmacol. Ther. 74 (2003) 380−387.

[7] M. Ingelman-Sundberg, Genetic polymorphisms of cytochrome P450 2D6 (CYP2D6): clinical consequences, evolutionary aspects and functional diversity, Pharmacogenomics J. 5 (2005) 6−13.

[8] K.T. Kivisto, M. Niemi, E. Schaeffeler, K. Pitkala, R. Tilvis, M.F. Fromm, M. Schwab, M. Eichelbaum, T. Strandberg, Lipid-lowering response to statins is affected by CYP3A5 polymorphism, Pharmacogenetics 14 (2004) 523−525.

[9] V. Leiro-Fernandez, D. Valverde, R. Vazquez-Gallardo, L. Constenla, A. Fernandez-Villar, Genetic variations of NAT2 and CYP2E1 and isoniazid hepatotoxicity in a diverse population, Pharmacogenomics 11 (2010) 1205−1206 (Author reply 1207−8).

[10] Y. Shu, S.A. Sheardown, C. Brown, R.P. Owen, S. Zhang, R.A. Castro, A.G. Ianculescu, L. Yue, J.C. Lo, E.G. Burchard, C.M. Brett, K.M. Giacomini, Effect of genetic variation in the organic cation transporter 1 (OCT1) on metformin action, J. Clin. Invest. 117 (2007) 1422−1431.

[11] R.T. Williams, The fate of foreign compounds in man and animals, Pure Appl. Chem. 18 (1969) 129−141.

[12] J.R. Cashman, Role of flavin-containing monooxygenases in drug development, Expert Opin. Drug Metab. Toxicol. 4 (2008) 1507−1521.

[13] M. Decker, M. Arand, A. Cronin, Mammalian epoxide hydrolases in xenobiotic metabolism and signalling, Arch. Toxicol. 83 (2009) 297−318.

[14] E. Garattini, M. Terao, The role of aldehyde oxidase in drug metabolism, Expert Opin. Drug Metab. Toxicol. 8 (2012) 487−503.

[15] S. Rendic, F.J. Carlo, Human cytochrome P450 enzymes: A status report summarizing their reactions, substrates, inducers, and inhibitors, Drug Metab. Rev. 29 (1997) 413−580.

[16] T. Satoh, M. Hosokawa, Structure, function and regulation of carboxylesterases, Chem. Biol. Interact. 162 (2006) 195−211.

[17] M.S. Benedetti, FAD-dependent enzymes involved in the metabolic oxidation of xenobiotics, in: Annales Pharmaceutiques Francaises, Elsevier, 2011, pp. 45−52.

[18] D. Dourado, P.A. Fernandes, M.J. Ramos, Mammalian cytosolic glutathione transferases, Curr. Protein Pept. Sci. 9 (2008) 325−337.

[19] G.J. Dutton, Raising the colors: personal reflections on the glucuronidation revolution 1950−1970, Drug Metab. Rev. 29 (1997) 997−1024.

[20] M. Michio, H. Hiroshi, Biochemistry and molecular biology of drug-metabolizing sulfotransferase, Int. J. Biochem. 26 (1994) 1237−1247.

[21] R.S. Foti, U.A. Argikar, UDP-glucuronosyltransferases, in: Handbook of Drug Metabolism, CRC Press, 2019.

[22] B. Riddle, W.P. Jencks, Acetyl-coenzyme A: arylamine N-acetyltransferase: role of the acetyl-enzyme intermediate and the effects of substituents on the rate, J. Biol. Chem. 246 (1971) 3250−3258.

[23] R.M. Weinshilboum, D.M. Otterness, C.L. Szumlanski, Methylation pharmacogenetics: catechol O-methyltransferase, thiopurine methyltransferase, and histamine N-methyltransferase, Annu. Rev. Pharmacol. Toxicol. 39 (1999) 19−52.

[24] B. Burchell, C. Brierley, G. Monaghan, D. Clarke, The structure and function of the UDP-glucuronosyltransferase gene family, in: Advances in Pharmacology, Elsevier, 1997.

[25] D.K. Dalvie, A.S. Kalgutkar, S.C. Khojasteh-Bakht, R.S. Obach, J.P. O'donnell, Biotransformation reactions of five-membered aromatic heterocyclic rings, Chem. Res. Toxicol. 15 (2002) 269−299.

[26] J.R. Halpert, T.L. Domanski, O. Adali, C.P. Biagini, J. Cosme, E.A. Dierks, E.F. Johnson, J.P. Jones, P.O. DE Montellano, R.M. Philpot, Structure-function of cytochromes P450 and flavin-containing monooxygenases: implications for drug metabolism, Drug Metab. Dispos. 26 (1998) 1223−1231.

[27] S.D. Nelson, W.F. Trager, The use of deuterium isotope effects to probe the active site properties, mechanism of cytochrome P450-catalyzed reactions, and mechanisms of metabolically dependent toxicity, Drug Metab. Dispos. 31 (2003) 1481−1497.

[28] P. Riley, R. Hanzlik, Electron transfer in P450 mechanisms. Microsomal metabolism of cyclopropylbenzene and p-cyclopropylanisole, Xenobiotica 24 (1994) 1−16.

[29] W.F. Trager, Stereochemistry of cytochrome P-450 reactions, Drug Metab. Rev. 20 (1989) 489−496.

[30] P.R. Ortiz De Montellano, J.J. De Voss, Oxidizing species in the mechanism of cytochrome P450, Nat. Prod. Rep. 19 (2002) 477−493.

[31] F.P. Guengerich, Human cytochrome P450 enzymes, in: P.R. Ortiz De Montellano (Ed.), Cytochrome P450: Structure, Mechanism, and Biochemistry, Springer US, Boston, MA, 2005.

[32] X. Ding, L.S. Kaminsky, Human extrahepatic cytochromes P450: function in xenobiotic metabolism and tissue-selective chemical toxicity in the respiratory and gastrointestinal tracts, Annu. Rev. Pharmacol. Toxicol. 43 (2003) 149−173.

[33] T. Iyanagi, H.J. Mason, Properties of hepatic reduced nicotinamide adenine dinucleotide phosphate-cytochrome c reductase, Biochemistry 12 (1973) 2297−2308.

[34] J.B. Schenkman, I. Jansson, Interactions between cytochrome P450 and cytochrome b5, Drug Metab. Rev. 31 (1999) 351−364.

[35] J. Vermilion, D. Ballou, V. Massey, M.J. Coon, Separate roles for FMN and FAD in catalysis by liver microsomal NADPH-cytochrome P-450 reductase, J. Biol. Chem. 256 (1981) 266−277.

[36] A. Rostami-Hodjegan, G.T. Tucker, Simulation and prediction of in vivo drug metabolism in human populations from in vitro data, Nat. Rev. Drug Discov. 6 (2007) 140−148.

[37] M.F. Paine, H.L. Hart, S.S. Ludington, R.L. Haining, A.E. Rettie, D.C. Zeldin, The human intestinal cytochrome P450 "pie", Drug Metab. Dispos. 34 (2006) 880−886.

[38] O. Von Richter, O. Burk, M.F. Fromm, K.P. Thon, M. Eichelbaum, K.T. Kivistö, Cytochrome P450 3A4 and P-glycoprotein expression in human small intestinal enterocytes and hepatocytes: a comparative analysis in paired tissue specimens, Clin. Pharm. Ther. 75 (2004) 172−183.

[39] S. Ohtsuki, O. Schaefer, H. Kawakami, T. Inoue, S. Liehner, A. Saito, N. Ishiguro, W. Kishimoto, E. Ludwig-Schwellinger, T. Ebner, T. Terasaki, Simultaneous absolute protein quantification of transporters, cytochromes P450, and UDP-glucuronosyltransferases as a novel approach for the characterization of individual human liver: comparison with mRNA levels and activities, Drug Metab. Dispos. 40 (2012) 83–92.

[40] O. Schaefer, S. Ohtsuki, H. Kawakami, T. Inoue, S. Liehner, A. Saito, A. Sakamoto, N. Ishiguro, T. Matsumaru, T. Terasaki, T. Ebner, Absolute quantification and differential expression of drug transporters, cytochrome P450 enzymes, and UDP-glucuronosyltransferases in cultured primary human hepatocytes, Drug Metab. Dispos. 40 (2012) 93–103.

[41] M.W. Coughtrie, M.B. Fisher, The role of sulfotransferases (SULTs) and UDP-glucuronosyltransferases (UGTs) in human drug clearance and bioactivation, in: Drug Metabolizing Enzymes, CRC Press, 2003.

[42] R.S. Foti, M.B. Fisher, UDP-Glucuronosyltransferases: pharmacogenetics, functional characterization, and clinical relevance, J. Encycl. Drug Metab. Interact. (2011) 1–71.

[43] A. Nakamura, M. Nakajima, H. Yamanaka, R. Fujiwara, T. Yokoi, Expression of UGT1A and UGT2B mRNA in human normal tissues and various cell lines, Drug Metab. Dispos. 36 (2008) 1461–1464.

[44] R.H. Tukey, C.P. Strassburg, Human UDP-glucuronosyltransferases: metabolism, expression, and disease, Annu. Rev. Pharmacol. Toxicol. 40 (2000) 581–616.

[45] J.H. Capdevila, J.R. Falck, The CYP P450 arachidonic acid monooxygenases: from cell signaling to blood pressure regulation, Biochem. Biophys. Res. Commun. 285 (2001) 571–576.

[46] A.E. Enayetallah, R.A. French, M.S. Thibodeau, D.F. Grant, Distribution of soluble epoxide hydrolase and of cytochrome P450 2C8, 2C9, and 2J2 in human tissues, J. Histochem. Cytochem. 52 (2004) 447–454.

[47] M. Seliskar, D. Rozman, Mammalian cytochromes P450—importance of tissue specificity, Biochim. Biophys. Acta Gen. Subj. 1770 (2007) 458–466.

[48] J.E. Thatcher, N. Isoherranen, The role of CYP26 enzymes in retinoic acid clearance, Expert Opin. Drug Metab. Toxicol. 5 (2009) 875–886.

[49] J.E. Thatcher, A. Zelter, N. Isoherranen, The relative importance of CYP26A1 in hepatic clearance of all-trans retinoic acid, Biochem. Pharmacol. 80 (2010) 903–912.

[50] M. Akhtar, J.N. Wright, P. Lee-Robichaud, A review of mechanistic studies on aromatase (CYP19) and 17α-hydroxylase-17, 20-lyase (CYP17), J. Steroid Biochem. Mol. Biol. 125 (2011) 2–12.

[51] S. Bar-Nun, G. Kreibich, M. Adesnik, L. Alterman, M. Negishi, D.D. Sabatini, Synthesis and insertion of cytochrome P-450 into endoplasmic reticulum membranes, Proc. Natl. Acad. Sci. U.S.A. 77 (1980) 965–969.

[52] M. Sakaguchi, K. Mihara, R. Sato, Signal recognition particle is required for co-translational insertion of cytochrome P-450 into microsomal membranes, Proc. Natl. Acad. Sci. 81 (1984) 3361–3364.

[53] D.R. Nelson, D.C. Zeldin, S.M. Hoffman, L.J. Maltais, H.M. Wain, D.W. Nebert, Comparison of cytochrome P450 (CYP) genes from the mouse and human genomes, including nomenclature recommendations for genes, pseudogenes and alternative-splice variants, Pharmacogenetics Genom. 14 (2004) 1–18.

[54] J.-F. Ghersi-Egea, R. Perrin, B. Leininger-Muller, M.-C. Grassiot, C. Jeandel, J. Floquet, G. Cuny, G. Siest, A. Minn, Subcellular localization of cytochrome P450, and activities of several enzymes responsible for drug metabolism in the human brain, Biochem. Pharmacol. 45 (1993) 647–658.

[55] J. Loeper, V. Descatoire, M. Maurice, P. Beaune, J. Belghiti, D. Houssin, F. Ballet, G. Feldmann, F.P. Guengerich, D. Pessayre, Cytochromes P-450 in human hepatocyte plasma membrane: recognition by several autoantibodies, Gastroenterology 104 (1993) 203–216.

[56] J. Loeper, V. Descatoire, M. Maurice, P. Beaune, G. Feldmann, D. Larrey, D. Pessayre, Presence of functional cytochrome P-450 on isolated rat hepatocyte plasma membrane, Hepatology 11 (1990) 850–858.

[57] E.P. Neve, M. Ingelman-Sundberg, Molecular basis for the transport of cytochrome P450 2E1 to the plasma membrane, J. Biol. Chem. 275 (2000) 17130–17135.

[58] M.-A. Robin, V. Descatoire, M. Le Roy, A. Berson, F.-P. Lebreton, F. Maratrat, F. Ballet, J. Loeper, D. Pessayre, Vesicular transport of newly synthesized cytochromes P4501A to the outside of rat hepatocyte plasma membranes, J. Pharmacol. Exp. Ther. 294 (2000) 1063–1069.

[59] M.-A. Robin, M. Maratrat, J. Loeper, A.-M. Durand-Schneider, M. Tinel, F. Ballet, P. Beaune, G. Feldmann, D. Pessayre, Cytochrome P4502B follows a vesicular route to the plasma membrane in cultured rat hepatocytes, Gastroenterology 108 (1995) 1110–1123.

[60] M.J. Ronis, I. Johansson, K. Hultenby, J. Lagercrantz, H. Glaumann, M. Ingelman-Sundberg, Acetone-regulated synthesis and degradation of cytochrome P4502E2 and cytochrome P4502B1 in rat liver, Eur. J. Biochem. 198 (1991) 383–389.

[61] D. Wu, A.I. Cederbaum, Presence of functionally active cytochrome P-450IIE1 in the plasma membrane of rat hepatocytes, Hepatology 15 (1992) 515–524.

[62] P. Fasinu, P. J Bouic, B. Rosenkranz, Liver-based in vitro technologies for drug biotransformation studies-a review, Curr. Drug Metab. 13 (2012) 215–224.

[63] T.N. Johnson, A. Rostami-Hodjegan, G.T. Tucker, Prediction of the clearance of eleven drugs and associated variability in neonates, infants and children, Clin. Pharmacokinet. 45 (2006) 931–956.

[64] R.N. Hines, Ontogeny of human hepatic cytochromes P450, J. Biochem. Mol. Toxicol. 21 (2007) 169–175.

[65] R.N. Hines, D.G. Mccarver, The ontogeny of human drug-metabolizing enzymes: phase I oxidative enzymes, J. Pharmacol. Exp. Ther. 300 (2002) 355–360.

[66] M.J. Blake, L. Castro, J.S. Leeder, G.L. Kearns, Ontogeny of drug metabolizing enzymes in the neonate, in: Seminars in Fetal and Neonatal Medicine, Elsevier, 2005, pp. 123–138.

[67] T. Shimada, H. Yamazaki, M. Mimura, N. Wakamiya, Y.-F. Ueng, F.P. Guengerich, Y. Inui, Characterization of microsomal cytochrome P450 enzymes involved in the oxidation of xenobiotic chemicals in human fetal liver and adult lungs, Drug Metab. Dispos. 24 (1996) 515–522.

[68] T. Cresteil, P. Beaune, P. Kremers, C. Celier, F.P. Guengerich, J.P. Leroux, Immunoquantification of epoxide hydrolase and cytochrome P-450 isozymes in fetal and adult human liver microsomes, Eur. J. Biochem. 151 (1985) 345–350.

[69] J.M. Treluyer, G. Cheron, M. Sonnier, T. Cresteil, Cytochrome P-450 expression in sudden infant death syndrome, Biochem. Pharmacol. 52 (1996) 497–504.

[70] D. Lacroix, M. Sonnier, A. Moncion, G. Cheron, T. Cresteil, Expression of CYP3A in the human liver—evidence that the shift between CYP3A7 and CYP3A4 occurs immediately after birth, Eur. J. Biochem. 247 (1997) 625–634.

[71] J. Hakkola, M. Pasanen, R. Purkunen, S. Saarikoski, O. Pelkonen, J. Mäenpää, A. Rane, H. Raunio, Expression of xenobiotic-metabolizing cytochrome P450 forms in human adult and fetal liver, Biochem. Pharmacol. 48 (1994) 59–64.

[72] H.-Y.L. Yang, M.J. Namkung, M.R. Juchau, Expression of functional cytochrome P4501A1 in human embryonic hepatic tissues during organogenesis, Biochem. Pharmacol. 49 (1995) 717–726.

[73] J. Mäenpää, A. Rane, H. Raunio, P. Honkakoski, O.J.B.P. Pelkonen, Cytochrome P450 isoforms in human fetal tissues related to phenobarbital-inducible forms in the mouse, Biochem. Pharmacol. 45 (1993) 899–907.

[74] F. Bouzom, B. Walther, Pharmacokinetic predictions in children by using the physiologically based pharmacokinetic modelling, Fundam. Clin. Pharmacol. 22 (2008) 579–587.

[75] D.G. Mccarver, R.N. Hines, The ontogeny of human drug-metabolizing enzymes: phase II conjugation enzymes and regulatory mechanisms, J. Pharmacol. Exp. Ther. 300 (2002) 361–366.

[76] C.T. Dolphin, T.E. Cullingford, E.A. Shephard, R.L. Smith, I.R. Phillips, Differential developmental and tissue-specific regulation of expression of the genes encoding three members of the flavin-containing monooxygenase family of man, FMO1, FMO3 and FMO4, Eur. J. Biochem. 235 (1996) 683–689.

[77] S.B. Koukouritaki, P. Simpson, C.K. Yeung, A.E. Rettie, R.N. Hines, Human hepatic flavin-containing monooxygenases 1 (FMO1) and 3 (FMO3) developmental expression, Pediatr. Res. 51 (2002) 236–243.

[78] C.K. Yeung, D.H. Lang, K.E. Thummel, A.E. Rettie, Immunoquantitation of FMO1 in human liver, kidney, and intestine, Drug Metab. Dispos. 28 (2000) 1107–1111.

[79] S. Alam, R. Roberts, L.J. Fischer, Age-related differences in salicylamide and acetaminophen conjugation in man, J. Pediatr. 90 (1977) 130–135.

[80] B. Burchell, M. Coughtrie, M. Jackson, D. Harding, S. Fournel-Gigleux, J. Leakey, R. Hume, Development of human liver UDP-glucuronosyltransferases, Dev. Pharmacol. Ther. 13 (1989) 70–77.

[81] J. Leakey, R. Hume, B. Burchell, Development of multiple activities of UDP-glucuronyltransferase in human liver, Biochem. J. 243 (1987) 859–861.

[82] G. Pacifici, J. Säwe, L. Kager, A. Rane, Morphine glucuronidation in human fetal and adult liver, Eur. J. Clin. Pharmacol. 22 (1982) 553–558.

[83] D. Rollins, C. Von Bahr, H. Glaumann, P. Moldeus, A. Rane, Acetaminophen: potentially toxic metabolite formed by human fetal and adult liver microsomes and isolated fetal liver cells, Science 205 (1979) 1414–1416.

[84] L. Ekström, M. Johansson, A. Rane, Tissue distribution and relative gene expression of UDP-glucuronosyltransferases (2B7, 2B15, 2B17) in the human fetus, Drug Metab. Dispos. 41 (2013) 291–295.

[85] E.V. Barker, R. Hume, A. Hallas, W. Coughtrie, Dehydroepiandrosterone sulfotransferase in the developing human fetus: quantitative biochemical and immunological characterization of the hepatic, renal, and adrenal enzymes, Endocrinology 134 (1994) 982–989.

[86] R.A. Gilissen, R. Hume, J.H. Meerman, M.W. Coughtrie, Sulphation of N-hydroxy-4-aminobiphenyl and N-hydroxy-4-acetylaminobiphenyl by human foetal and neonatal sulphotransferase, Biochem. Pharmacol. 48 (1994) 837–840.

[87] A.L. Jones, R. Hume, K.J. Bamforth, M.W. Coughtrie, Estrogen and phenol sulfotransferase activities in human fetal lung, Early Hum. Dev. 28 (1992) 65–77.

[88] G. Pacifici, M. Kubrich, L. Giuliani, M. DE Vries, A.J. Rane, Sulphation and glucuronidation of ritodrine in human foetal and adult tissues, Eur. J. Clin. Pharmacol. 44 (1993) 259–264.

[89] G. Beckett, A. Howie, R. Hume, B. Matharoo, C. Hiley, P. Jones, R. Strange, Human glutathione S-transferases: radioimmunoassay studies on the expression of alpha-, mu-and pi-class isoenzymes in developing lung and kidney, Biochim. Biophys. Acta Gen. Subj. 1036 (1990) 176–182.

[90] D. Cossar, J. Bell, M. Lang, R. Hume, Development of human fetal lung in organ culture compared with in utero ontogeny, In Vitro Cell. Dev. Biol. Anim. 29 (1993) 319–324.

[91] C. Hiley, J. Bell, R. Hume, R. Strange, Differential expression of alpha and pi isoenzymes of glutathione S-transferase in developing human kidney, Biochim. Biophys. Acta Gen. Subj. 990 (1989) 321–324.

[92] R.C. Strange, B.A. Davis, C.G. Faulder, W. Cotton, A. Bain, D. Hopkinson, R. Hume, The human glutathione S-transferases: developmental aspects of the GST1, GST2, and GST3 loci, Biochem. Genet. 23 (1985) 1011–1028.

[93] R.S. Foti, L.C. Wienkers, J.L. Wahlstrom, Application of cytochrome P450 drug interaction screening in drug discovery, Comb. Chem. High Throughput Screen. 13 (2010) 145–158.

[94] L.C. Eriksson, J.W. Depierre, G. Dallner, Preparation and properties of microsomal fractions, Pharmacol. Ther. Part A Chemother. Toxicol. Metab. Inhib. 2 (1978) 281–317.

[95] F. Guengerich, Analysis and characterization of enzymes, Princ. Methods Toxicol. (1994).

[96] P. Graham Somers, In Vitro Techniques for Investigating Drug Metabolism, 2004.

[97] A. Guillouzo, F. Morel, D. Ratanasavanh, C. Chesne, C. Guguen-Guillouzo, Long-term culture of functional hepatocytes, Toxicol. In Vitro 4 (1990) 415−427.

[98] O. Luttringer, F.-P. Theil, T. Lavé, K. Wernli-Kuratli, T.W. Guentert, A. De Saizieu, Influence of isolation procedure, extracellular matrix and dexamethasone on the regulation of membrane transporters gene expression in rat hepatocytes, Biochem. Pharmacol. 64 (2002) 1637−1650.

[99] J. Sahi, S. Grepper, C. Smith, Hepatocytes as a tool in drug metabolism, transport and safety evaluations in drug discovery, Curr. Drug Discov. Technol. 7 (2010) 188−198.

[100] S. Wang, D. Nagrath, P.C. Chen, F. Berthiaume, M.L. Yarmush, Three-dimensional primary hepatocyte culture in synthetic self-assembling peptide hydrogel, Tissue Eng. Part A 14 (2008) 227−236.

[101] D.C. Hay, S. Pernagallo, J.J. Diaz-Mochon, C.N. Medine, S. Greenhough, Z. Hannoun, J. Schrader, J.R. Black, J. Fletcher, D. Dalgetty, Unbiased screening of polymer libraries to define novel substrates for functional hepatocytes with inducible drug metabolism, Stem Cell Res. 6 (2011) 92−102.

[102] H. Inoue, S. Yamanaka, The use of induced pluripotent stem cells in drug development, Clin. Pharmacol. Ther. 89 (2011) 655−661.

[103] L. Di, E.H. Kerns, S.Q. Li, G.T. Carter, Comparison of cytochrome P450 inhibition assays for drug discovery using human liver microsomes with LC−MS, rhCYP450 isozymes with fluorescence, and double cocktail with LC−MS, Int. J. Pharm. 335 (2007) 1−11.

[104] L. Becquemont, M.A. LE Bot, C. Riche, C. Funck-Brentano, P. Jaillon, P. Beaune, Use of heterologously expressed human cytochrome P450 1A2 to predict tacrine-fluvoxamine drug interaction in man, Pharmacogenetics 8 (1998) 101−108.

[105] A. Galetin, C. Brown, D. Hallifax, K. Ito, J.B. Houston, Utility of recombinant enzyme kinetics in prediction of human clearance: impact of variability, CYP3A5, and CYP2C19 on CYP3A4 probe substrates, Drug Metab. Dispos. 32 (2004) 1411−1420.

[106] M.G. Soars, H.V. Gelboin, K.W. Krausz, R.J. Riley, A comparison of relative abundance, activity factor and inhibitory monoclonal antibody approaches in the characterization of human CYP enzymology, Br. J. Clin. Pharmacol. 55 (2003) 175−181.

[107] R.A. Stringer, C. Strain-Damerell, P. Nicklin, J.B. Houston, Evaluation of recombinant cytochrome P450 enzymes as an in vitro system for metabolic clearance predictions, Drug Metab. Dispos. 37 (2009) 1025−1034.

[108] M. Hutzler, D.M. Messing, L.C. Wienkers, Predicting drug-drug interactions in drug discovery: where are we now and where are we going? Curr. Opin. Drug Discov. Dev. 8 (2005) 51−58.

[109] I. Jansson, J.B. Schenkman, Substrate influence on interaction between cytochrome P450 and cytochrome b5in microsomes, Arch. Biochem. Biophys. 325 (1996) 265−269.

[110] J.B. Schenkman, I. Jansson, The many roles of cytochrome b5, Pharmacol. Ther. 97 (2003) 139−152.

[111] G. Vergeres, L. Waskell, Cytochrome b5, its functions, structure and membrane topology, Biochimie 77 (1995) 604−620.

[112] H. Zhang, C.D. Davis, M.W. Sinz, A.D. Rodrigues, Cytochrome P450 reaction-phenotyping: an industrial perspective, Expert Opin. Drug Metab. Toxicol. 3 (2007) 667−687.

[113] A.Y. Lu, R.W. Wang, J.H. Lin, Cytochrome P450 in vitro reaction phenotyping: a re-evaluation of approaches used for P450 isoform identification, Drug Metab. Dispos. 31 (2003) 345−350.

[114] R. Yuan, S. Madani, X.X. Wei, K. Reynolds, S.M. Huang, Evaluation of cytochrome P450 probe substrates commonly used by the pharmaceutical industry to study in vitro drug interactions, Drug Metab. Dispos. 30 (2002) 1311−1319.

[115] B. Prasad, A. Garg, H. Takwani, S. Singh, Metabolite identification by liquid chromatography-mass spectrometry, TrAC Trends Anal. Chem. 30 (2011) 360−387.

[116] E.M. Howgate, K. Rowland Yeo, N.J. Proctor, G.T. Tucker, A. Rostami-Hodjegan, Prediction of in vivo drug clearance from in vitro data. I: impact of inter-individual variability, Xenobiotica 36 (2006) 473−497.

[117] K. Venkatakrishnan, L.L. Von Moltke, D.J. Greenblatt, Application of the relative activity factor approach in scaling from heterologously expressed cytochromes p450 to human liver microsomes: studies on amitriptyline as a model substrate, J. Pharmacol. Exp. Ther. 297 (2001) 326−337.

[118] H.K. Crewe, Z.E. Barter, K.R. Yeo, A. Rostami-Hodjegan, Are there differences in the catalytic activity per unit enzyme of recombinantly expressed and human liver microsomal cytochrome P450 2C9? A systematic investigation into inter-system extrapolation factors, Biopharm. Drug Dispos. 32 (2011) 303−318.

[119] C. Seibert, B.R. Davidson, B.J. Fuller, L.H. Patterson, W.J. Griffiths, Y. Wang, Multiple-approaches to the identification and quantification of cytochromes P450 in human liver tissue by mass spectrometry, J. Proteome Res. 8 (2009) 1672−1681.

[120] K.A. Youdim, A. Zayed, M. Dickins, A. Phipps, M. Griffiths, A. Darekar, R. Hyland, O. Fahmi, S. Hurst, D.R. Plowchalk, J. Cook, F. Guo, R.S. Obach, Application of CYP3A4 in vitro data to predict clinical drug-drug interactions; predictions of compounds as objects of interaction, Br. J. Clin. Pharmacol. 65 (2008) 680−692.

[121] S. Wang, X. Tang, T. Yang, J. Xu, J. Zhang, X. Liu, L. Liu, Predicted contributions of cytochrome P450s to drug metabolism in human liver microsomes using relative activity factor were dependent on probes, Xenobiotica 49 (2019) 161−168.

[122] A.L. Dantonio, A.C. Doran, R.S. Obach, Intersystem extrapolation factors are substrate-dependent for CYP3A4: impact on cytochrome P450 reaction phenotyping, Drug Metab. Dispos. 50 (2022) 249−257.

[123] M. Jamei, G.L. Dickinson, A. Rostami-Hodjegan, A framework for assessing inter-individual variability in pharmacokinetics using virtual human populations and integrating general knowledge of physical chemistry, biology, anatomy, physiology and genetics: a tale of 'bottom-up' vs 'top-down' recognition of covariates, Drug Metabol. Pharmacokinet. 24 (2009) 53−75.

[124] J.M. Margolis, R.S. Obach, Impact of nonspecific binding to microsomes and phospholipid on the inhibition of cytochrome P4502D6: implications for relating in vitro inhibition data to in vivo drug interactions, Drug Metab. Dispos. 31 (2003) 606−611.

[125] X. Cai, R.W. Wang, R.W. Edom, D.C. Evans, M. Shou, A.D. Rodrigues, W. Liu, D.C. Dean, T.A. Baillie, Validation of (-)-N-3-benzyl-phenobarbital as a selective inhibitor of CYP2C19 in human liver microsomes, Drug Metab. Dispos. 32 (2004) 584−586.

[126] N.N. Bumpus, U.M. Kent, P.F. Hollenberg, Metabolism of efavirenz and 8-hydroxyefavirenz by P450 2B6 leads to inactivation by two distinct mechanisms, J. Pharmacol. Exp. Ther. 318 (2006) 345−351.

[127] D.A. Rock, R.S. Foti, J.T. Pearson, The combination of chemical and antibody inhibitors for superior P450 3A inhibition in reaction phenotyping studies, Drug Metab. Dispos. 36 (2008) 2410−2413.

[128] L.C. Wienkers, J.C. Stevens, Cytochrome P450 reaction phenotyping, in: Drug Metabolizing Enzymes, CRC Press, 2003.

[129] N. Raghavan, D. Zhang, M. Zhu, J. Zeng, L. Christopher, CYP2D6 catalyzes 5-hydroxylation of 1-(2-pyrimidinyl)-piperazine, an active metabolite of several psychoactive drugs, in human liver microsomes, Drug Metab. Dispos. 33 (2005) 203−208.

[130] B.L. Urquhart, R.G. Tirona, R.B. Kim, Nuclear receptors and the regulation of drug-metabolizing enzymes and drug transporters: implications for interindividual variability in response to drugs, J. Clin. Pharmacol 47 (2007) 566−578.

[131] B. Greiner, M. Eichelbaum, P. Fritz, H.-P. Kreichgauer, O. Von Richter, J. Zundler, H.K. Kroemer, The role of intestinal P-glycoprotein in the interaction of digoxin and rifampin, J. Clin. Invest. 104 (1999) 147−153.

[132] O. Burk, K.A. Arnold, A. Geick, H. Tegude, M. Eichelbaum, A role for constitutive androstane receptor in the regulation of human intestinal MDR1 expression, Biol. Chem. 386 (2005) 503−513.

[133] T. Nakanishi, D.D. Ross, Breast cancer resistance protein (BCRP/ABCG2): its role in multidrug resistance and regulation of its gene expression, Chin. J. Cancer 31 (2012) 73−99.

[134] M. Svoboda, J. Riha, K. Wlcek, W. Jaeger, T. Thalhammer, Organic anion transporting polypeptides (OATPs): regulation of expression and function, Curr. Drug Metab. 12 (2011) 139−153.

[135] Y. Lai, M. Varma, B. Feng, J.C. Stephens, E. Kimoto, A. EL-Kattan, K. Ichikawa, H. Kikkawa, C. Ono, A. Suzuki, M. Suzuki, Y. Yamamoto, L. Tremaine, Impact of drug transporter pharmacogenomics on pharmacokinetic and pharmacodynamic variability—considerations for drug development, Expert Opin. Drug Metab. Toxicol. 8 (2012) 723−743.

[136] N. Thakkar, J.R. Slizgi, K.L.R. Brouwer, Effect of liver disease on hepatic transporter expression and function, J. Pharm. Sci. 106 (2017) 2282−2294.

[137] K.V. Ledwitch, R.W. Barnes, A.G. Roberts, Unravelling the complex drug-drug interactions of the cardiovascular drugs, verapamil and digoxin, with P-glycoprotein, Biosci. Rep. 36 (2016).

[138] H.E. Jin, S.S. Hong, M.K. Choi, H.J. Maeng, D.D. Kim, S.J. Chung, C.K. Shim, Reduced antidiabetic effect of metformin and down-regulation of hepatic Oct1 in rats with ethynylestradiol-induced cholestasis, Pharm. Res. 26 (2009) 549−559.

[139] M. Regazzi, R. Maserati, P. Villani, M. Cusato, P. Zucchi, E. Briganti, R. Roda, L. Sacchelli, F. Gatti, P. Delle Foglie, G. Nardini, P. Fabris, F. Mori, P. Castelli, L. Testa, Clinical pharmacokinetics of nelfinavir and its metabolite M8 in human immunodeficiency virus (HIV)-positive and HIV-hepatitis C virus-coinfected subjects, Antimicrob. Agents Chemother. 49 (2005) 643−649.

[140] R.N. Hardwick, J.D. Clarke, A.D. Lake, M.J. Canet, T. Anumol, S.M. Street, M.D. Merrell, M.J. Goedken, S.A. Snyder, N.J. Cherrington, Increased susceptibility to methotrexate-induced toxicity in nonalcoholic steatohepatitis, Toxicol. Sci. 142 (2014) 45−55.

[141] D.A. Volpe, Transporter assays as useful in vitro tools in drug discovery and development, Expert Opin. Drug Discov. 11 (2016) 91−103.

[142] X. Chu, K. Bleasby, R. Evers, Species differences in drug transporters and implications for translating preclinical findings to humans, Expert Opin. Drug Metab. Toxicol. 9 (2013) 237−252.

[143] S. Bhoopathy, C. Bode, V. Naageshwaran, E. Weiskircher-Hildebrandt, V. Mukkavilli, I.J. Hidalgo, Principles and experimental considerations for in vitro transporter interaction assays, Methods Mol. Biol. 2342 (2021) 339−365.

[144] C. Lu, L. Di, In vitro and in vivo methods to assess pharmacokinetic drug−drug interactions in drug discovery and development, Biopharm. Drug Dispos. 41 (2020) 3−31.

[145] M. Pellegatti, Preclinical in vivo ADME studies in drug development: a critical review, J. Expert Opin. Drug Metab. Toxicol. 8 (2012) 161−172.

[146] T.J. Strelevitz, R.S. Foti, M.B. Fisher, In vivo use of the P450 inactivator 1-aminobenzotriazole in the rat: varied dosing route to elucidate gut and liver contributions to first-pass and systemic clearance, J. Pharm. Sci. 95 (2006) 1334−1341.

[147] R.P. Dash, R. Jayachandra Babu, N.R. Srinivas, Therapeutic potential and utility of elacridar with respect to P-glycoprotein inhibition: an insight from the published in vitro, preclinical and clinical studies, Eur. J. Drug Metab. Pharmacokinet. 42 (2017) 915−933.

[148] A. Mcewen, The human ADME study, J. Drug Discov. Eval. Methods Clin. Pharmacol. (2020) 773−806.

[149] M. Ingelman-Sundberg, M. Oscarson, R.A. Mclellan, Polymorphic human cytochrome P450 enzymes: an opportunity for individualized drug treatment, Trends Pharmacol. Sci. 20 (1999) 342−349.

[150] R.L. Walsky, R.S. Obach, E.A. Gaman, J.-P.R. Gleeson, W.R. Proctor, Selective inhibition of human cytochrome P4502C8 by montelukast, Drug Metab. Dispos. 33 (2005) 413−418.

[151] M. Chiba, X. Xu, J.A. Nishime, S.K. Balani, J.H. Lin, Hepatic microsomal metabolism of montelukast, a potent leukotriene D4 receptor antagonist, in humans, Drug Metab. Dispos. 25 (1997) 1022−1031.

[152] T. Karonen, A. Filppula, J. Laitila, M. Niemi, P.J. Neuvonen, J.T. Backman, Gemfibrozil markedly increases the plasma concentrations of montelukast: a previously unrecognized role for CYP2C8 in the metabolism of montelukast, Clin. Pharmacol. Ther. 88 (2010) 223−230.

[153] B.M. Vandenbrink, R.S. Foti, D.A. Rock, L.C. Wienkers, J.L. Wahlstrom, Evaluation of CYP2C8 inhibition in vitro: utility of montelukast as a selective CYP2C8 probe substrate, Drug Metab. Dispos. 39 (2011) 1546−1554.

[154] A.M. Filppula, J. Laitila, P.J. Neuvonen, J.T. Backman, Reevaluation of the microsomal metabolism of montelukast: major contribution by CYP2C8 at clinically relevant concentrations, Drug Metab. Dispos. 39 (2011) 904−911.

[155] T. Karonen, P.J. Neuvonen, J.T. Backman, CYP2C8 but not CYP3A4 is important in the pharmacokinetics of montelukast, Br. J. Clin. Pharmacol. 73 (2012) 257−267.

[156] A.M. Holbrook, J.A. Pereira, R. Labiris, H. Mcdonald, J.D. Douketis, M. Crowther, P.S. Wells, Systematic overview of warfarin and its drug and food interactions, Arch. Intern. Med. 165 (2005) 1095−1106.

[157] J. Hirsh, V. Fuster, J. Ansell, J.L. Halperin, American Heart Association/American College of Cardiology, F, American Heart Association/American College of Cardiology foundation guide to warfarin therapy, J. Am. Coll. Cardiol. 41 (2003) 1633−1652.

[158] A.E. Rettie, A.C. Eddy, L.D. Heimark, M. Gibaldi, W.F. Trager, Characteristics of warfarin hydroxylation catalyzed by human liver microsomes, Drug Metab. Dispos. 17 (1989) 265−270.

[159] A.E. Rettie, K.R. Korzekwa, K.L. Kunze, R.F. Lawrence, A.C. Eddy, T. Aoyama, H.V. Gelboin, F.J. Gonzalez, W.F. Trager, Hydroxylation of warfarin by human cDNA-expressed cytochrome P-450: a role for P-4502C9 in the etiology of (S)-warfarin-drug interactions, Chem. Res. Toxicol. 5 (1992) 54−59.

[160] J.S. Ngui, Q. Chen, M. Shou, R.W. Wang, R.A. Stearns, T.A. Baillie, W. Tang, In vitro stimulation of warfarin metabolism by quinidine: increases in the formation of 4'- and 10-hydroxywarfarin, Drug Metab. Dispos. 29 (2001) 877−886.

[161] K.L. Kunze, L.C. Wienkers, K.E. Thummel, W.F. Trager, Warfarin-fluconazole. I. Inhibition of the human cytochrome P450-dependent metabolism of warfarin by fluconazole: in vitro studies, Drug Metab. Dispos. 24 (1996) 414−421.

[162] D.J. Black, K.L. Kunze, L.C. Wienkers, B.E. Gidal, T.L. Seaton, N.D. Mcdonnell, J.S. Evans, J.E. Bauwens, W.F. Trager, Warfarin-fluconazole. II. A metabolically based drug interaction: in vivo studies, Drug Metab. Dispos. 24 (1996) 422−428.

[163] L.C. Wienkers, C.J. Wurden, E. Storch, K.L. Kunze, A.E. Rettie, W.F. Trager, Formation of (R)-8-hydroxywarfarin in human liver microsomes. A new metabolic marker for the (S)-mephenytoin hydroxylase, P4502C19, Drug Metab. Dispos. 24 (1996) 610−614.

[164] E.A. Sconce, T.I. Khan, H.A. Wynne, P. Avery, L. Monkhouse, B.P. King, P. Wood, P. Kesteven, A.K. Daly, F. Kamali, The impact of CYP2C9 and VKORC1 genetic polymorphism and patient characteristics upon warfarin dose requirements: proposal for a new dosing regimen, Blood 106 (2005) 2329−2333.

[165] C.L. Crespi, V.P. Miller, The R144C change in the CYP2C9*2 allele alters interaction of the cytochrome P450 with NADPH: cytochrome P450 oxidoreductase, Pharmacogenetics 7 (1997) 203−210.

[166] K. Takanashi, H. Tainaka, K. Kobayashi, T. Yasumori, M. Hosakawa, K. Chiba, CYP2C9 Ile359 and Leu359 variants: enzyme kinetic study with seven substrates, Pharmacogenetics 10 (2000) 95−104.

[167] M.K. Higashi, D.L. Veenstra, L.M. Kondo, A.K. Wittkowsky, S.L. Srinouanprachanh, F.M. Farin, A.E. Rettie, Association between CYP2C9 genetic variants and anticoagulation-related outcomes during warfarin therapy, JAMA 287 (2002) 1690−1698.

[168] C. Combescure, P. Fontana, N. Mallouk, P. Berdague, C. Labruyere, I. Barazer, J.C. Gris, S. Laporte, P. Fabbro-Peray, J.L. Reny, I.E.M.-A.S.G. Clopidogrel & Vascular, Clinical implications of clopidogrel non-response in cardiovascular patients: a systematic review and meta-analysis, J. Thromb. Haemost. 8 (2010) 923−933.

[169] M. Kazui, Y. Nishiya, T. Ishizuka, K. Hagihara, N.A. Farid, O. Okazaki, T. Ikeda, A. Kurihara, Identification of the human cytochrome P450 enzymes involved in the two oxidative steps in the bioactivation of clopidogrel to its pharmacologically active metabolite, Drug Metab. Dispos. 38 (2010) 92−99.

[170] D. Taubert, N. Von Beckerath, G. Grimberg, A. Lazar, N. Jung, T. Goeser, A. Kastrati, A. Schomig, E. Schomig, Impact of P-glycoprotein on clopidogrel absorption, Clin. Pharmacol. Ther. 80 (2006) 486−501.

[171] A. Alkattan, E. Alsalameen, Polymorphisms of genes related to phase-I metabolic enzymes affecting the clinical efficacy and safety of clopidogrel treatment, Expert Opin. Drug Metabol. Toxicol. 17 (2021) 685−695.

[172] T. Simon, C. Verstuyft, M. Mary-Krause, L. Quteineh, E. Drouet, N. Meneveau, P.G. Steg, J. Ferrieres, N. Danchin, L. Becquemont, French Registry of Acute, S. T. E., Non, S. T. E. M. I. I., Genetic determinants of response to clopidogrel and cardiovascular events, N. Engl. J. Med. 360 (2009) 363−375.

[173] M.J. Sorich, A. Vitry, M.B. Ward, J.D. Horowitz, R.A. Mckinnon, Prasugrel vs. clopidogrel for cytochrome P450 2C19-genotyped subgroups: integration of the TRITON-TIMI 38 trial data, J. Thromb. Haemost. 8 (2010) 1678−1684.

[174] R. Teng, S. Oliver, M.A. Hayes, K. Butler, Absorption, distribution, metabolism, and excretion of ticagrelor in healthy subjects, Drug Metab. Dispos. 38 (2010) 1514−1521.

[175] J.K. Coller, N. Krebsfaenger, K. Klein, K. Endrizzi, R. Wolbold, T. Lang, A. Nussler, P. Neuhaus, U.M. Zanger, M. Eichelbaum, T.E. Murdter, The influence of CYP2B6, CYP2C9 and CYP2D6 genotypes on the formation of the potent antioestrogen Z-4-hydroxy-tamoxifen in human liver, Br. J. Clin. Pharmacol. 54 (2002) 157−167.

[176] M.H. Hofmann, J.K. Blievernicht, K. Klein, T. Saussele, E. Schaeffeler, M. Schwab, U.M. Zanger, Aberrant splicing caused by single nucleotide polymorphism c.516G>T [Q172H], a marker of CYP2B6*6, is responsible for decreased expression and activity of CYP2B6 in liver, J. Pharmacol. Exp. Ther. 325 (2008) 284−292.

[177] H. Kawakami, S. Ohtsuki, J. Kamiie, T. Suzuki, T. Abe, T. Terasaki, Simultaneous absolute quantification of 11 cytochrome P450 isoforms in human liver microsomes by liquid chromatography tandem mass spectrometry with in silico target peptide selection, J. Pharmaceut. Sci. 100 (2011) 341−352.

[178] K. Klein, S. Winter, M. Turpeinen, M. Schwab, U.M. Zanger, Pathway-targeted pharmacogenomics of CYP1A2 in human liver, Front. Pharmacol. 1 (2010) 129.

[179] S.B. Koukouritaki, J.R. Manro, S.A. Marsh, J.C. Stevens, A.E. Rettie, D.G. Mccarver, R.N. Hines, Developmental expression of human hepatic CYP2C9 and CYP2C19, J. Pharmacol. Exp. Ther. 308 (2004) 965−974.

[180] V. Lamba, J. Lamba, K. Yasuda, S. Strom, J. Davila, M.L. Hancock, J.D. Fackenthal, P.K. Rogan, B. Ring, S.A. Wrighton, E.G. Schuetz, Hepatic CYP2B6 expression: gender and ethnic differences and relationship to CYP2B6 genotype and CAR (constitutive androstane receptor) expression, J. Pharmacol. Exp. Ther. 307 (2003) 906–922.

[181] E. Langenfeld, U.M. Zanger, K. Jung, H.E. Meyer, K. Marcus, Mass spectrometry-based absolute quantification of microsomal cytochrome P450 2D6 in human liver, Proteomics 9 (2009) 2313–2323.

[182] Y.S. Lin, A.L. Dowling, S.D. Quigley, F.M. Farin, J. Zhang, J. Lamba, E.G. Schuetz, K.E. Thummel, Co-regulation of CYP3A4 and CYP3A5 and contribution to hepatic and intestinal midazolam metabolism, Mol. Pharmacol. 62 (2002) 162–172.

[183] S.B. Naraharisetti, Y.S. Lin, M.J. Rieder, K.D. Marciante, B.M. Psaty, K.E. Thummel, R.A. Totah, Human liver expression of CYP2C8: gender, age, and genotype effects, Drug Metab. Dispos. 38 (2010) 889–893.

[184] A.E. Rettie, J.P. Jones, Clinical and toxicological relevance of CYP2C9: drug-drug interactions and pharmacogenetics, Annu. Rev. Pharmacol. Toxicol. 45 (2005) 477–494.

[185] T. Shimada, H. Yamazaki, M. Mimura, Y. Inui, F.P. Guengerich, Interindividual variations in human liver cytochrome P-450 enzymes involved in the oxidation of drugs, carcinogens and toxic chemicals: studies with liver microsomes of 30 Japanese and 30 Caucasians, J. Pharmacol. Exp. Ther. 270 (1994) 414–423.

[186] A. Westlind-Johnsson, S. Malmebo, A. Johansson, C. Otter, T.B. Andersson, I. Johansson, R.J. Edwards, A.R. Boobis, M. Ingelman-Sundberg, Comparative analysis of CYP3A expression in human liver suggests only a minor role for CYP3A5 in drug metabolism, Drug Metab. Dispos. 31 (2003) 755–761.

[187] U.M. Zanger, J. Fischer, S. Raimundo, T. Stuven, B.O. Evert, M. Schwab, M. Eichelbaum, Comprehensive analysis of the genetic factors determining expression and function of hepatic CYP2D6, Pharmacogenetics 11 (2001) 573–585.

[188] U.M. Zanger, M. Schwab, Cytochrome P450 enzymes in drug metabolism: regulation of gene expression, enzyme activities, and impact of genetic variation, Pharmacol. Ther. 138 (2013) 103–141.

Chapter 18

Kyprolis (carfilzomib) (approved): a covalent drug with high extrahepatic clearance via peptidase cleavage and epoxide hydrolysis

Zhengping Wang[a], Jinfu Yang[b] and Christopher Kirk[c]

[a]Nonclinical Development and Clinical Pharmacology, Revolution Medicines, Redwood City, CA, United States; [b]Research and Development, Zenshine Pharmaceuticals Inc., Burlingame, CA, United States; [c]Research and Development, Kezar Life Sciences, South San Francisco, CA, United States

In July 2012, Carfilzomib (Kyprolis), a second-generation proteasome inhibitor, gained accelerated approval in the United States as a single agent for the treatment of relapsed and/or refractory (RR) multiple myeloma (MM) [1]. Carfilzomib is a tetrapeptide epoxyketone, structurally distinct from the first-generation dipeptide boronate proteasome inhibitor bortezomib (Velcade) [2]. The electrophilic epoxyketone warhead forms two covalent bonds with the catalytic N-terminal threonine (Thr) in the active sites of the proteasome, resulting in irreversible inactivation of the target. The covalent irreversible mechanism of action (MOA) leads to high potency and selectivity of carfilzomib to the proteasome. Moreover, carfilzomib can overcome resistance to bortezomib in patients with RRMM. At the time of carfilzomib approval, interests in targeted covalent inhibitors (TCIs) just started to resurge after years of concerns over potential toxicities driven by off-target effects [3]. Several TCIs were in late-stage clinical development with encouraging efficacy [4–6]. Important insights into optimal pharmacokinetic (PK) properties, safety profiles, and the benefit/risk of covalent MOA were still emerging [7–9].

Over the past decade, multiple carfilzomib-based therapies became available for the treatment of patients with RRMM [10–13]. Notably, in a randomized phase 3 head-to-head trial (ENDEAVOR) [11], carfilzomib ($20/56$ mg/m^2, dosed twice weekly on Days 1 and 2) in combination with dexamethasone significantly extended progression-free survival (PFS) and overall survival (OS) compared to bortezomib (1.3 mg/m^2, dosed twice weekly on Days 1 and 4) plus dexamethasone. The median PFS was 18.7 months for carfilzomib compared to 7.6 months for bortezomib ($P < .0001$), and the median OS was 47.6 months for carfilzomib compared to 40.0 months for bortezomib ($P = .010$).

The discovery of carfilzomib is an elegant story of the transformation of a natural product into an effective medicine. Carfilzomib originated from a tetrapeptide epoxyketone natural product epoxomicin (Fig. 18.1), which was discovered from an unidentified microbial actinomycetes strain in the 1980s by scientists at Bristol-Myers Squibb in Japan. Although epoxomicin showed promising anti-tumor activity against B16 melanoma tumors [14], a lack of understanding of its mechanism and the apparent poor drug-like properties made it unappealing as a drug lead. In addition, no synthetic strategy was available at the time for compound production, further hindering the potential optimization of this scaffold. Almost a decade later in late 1990s, Dr. Craig Crews from Yale University, attracted by the potent biological activity of the natural product, set out to identify its intracellular target and hope to uncover novel signaling pathways crucial for tumor growth. They successfully accomplished the total synthesis of epoxomicin [15]. In addition, they also prepared a biotin-tagged version of epoxomicin, which they used as an affinity reagent to identify potential intracellular target proteins. Utilizing modern chemical biology tools, the Crews lab determined that epoxomicin exerts anti-tumor activity through inhibition of the proteasome [16], a large multi-subunit protease complex and a critical component of the ubiquitin proteasome system (UPS) responsible for the degradation of ~80% of all proteins in eukaryotic cells [17]. While investigating epoxomicin's

Overcoming Obstacles in Drug Discovery and Development. https://doi.org/10.1016/B978-0-12-817134-9.00011-8

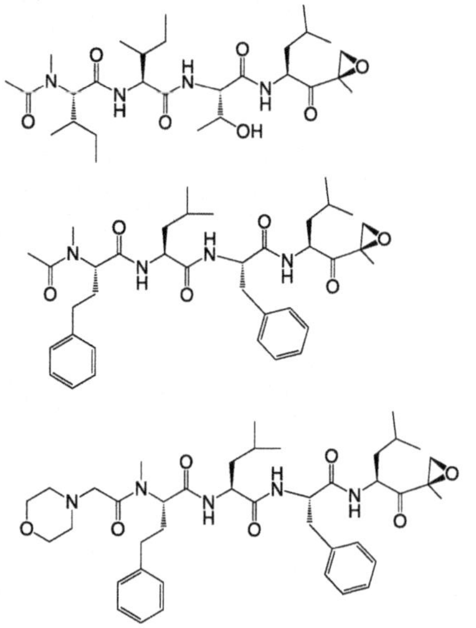

FIGURE 18.1 Chemical structure of epoxomicin, YU-101 and carfilzomib.

activity against common proteases, they were intrigued by its unprecedented specificity for the proteasome [16]. Further X-ray crystallographic studies revealed the irreversible formation of a six-membered morpholino ring between epoxyketone moiety and the N-terminal Thr of the proteasome [18]. The interaction is unique to the N-terminal Thr residues, as epoxyketone does not form stable intermediates with catalytic residues of serine and cysteine proteases that do not contain a free α-amino group. Armed with the knowledge, they initiated a structure activity relationship (SAR) campaign and synthesized a series of analogs. Among which, YU-101 (Fig. 18.1) [19] stood out with improved potency relative to epoxomicin while maintaining high selectivity and was later adopted as an improved tool molecule to gain deeper insight into the effect of proteasome inhibition. YU-101 also served as the starting point of the lead discovery program for Proteolix Inc, a startup biotech founded in South San Francisco in 2003. Scientists at Proteolix generated and screened several hundreds of YU-101 derivatives, and ultimately nominated PR-171 (now carfilzomib, Fig. 18.1), an analog with a morpholino moiety added to the N-terminal side of YU-101, as the development candidate. This seemingly minor change to YU-101 led to over three orders of magnitude increase in aqueous solubility, enabled further in vivo preclinical studies, and eventually clinical testing.

Proteasome as a drug target for the treatment of multiple myeloma

Multiple myeloma is a cancer of the antibody-generating plasma cells and the second most common hematological malignancy, with about 34,920 new cases and approximately 12,410 deaths annually in the United States according to the American Cancer Society estimates [20]. It remains an incurable disease, but the availability of new drugs, including proteasome inhibitors (PIs) [1,2,21], immunomodulatory drugs (IMiDs) [22], monoclonal antibodies (mAbs) [23−25], and BCMA-targeted CAR T-cell therapy [26], has greatly improved the long-term prognosis of MM patients. The approval of bortezomib in 2003 provided the first clinical validation supporting the proteasome as a viable drug target [2,27]. Since then, carfilzomib and an orally bioavailable proteasome inhibitor ixazomib [21] have been approved in 2012 and 2015, respectively. Proteasome inhibitors have become the backbone and used in combination with IMiDs and mAbs for the treatment of patients with RRMM.

Regulated intracellular protein degradation via the UPS was discovered at the beginning of 1980s by three researchers [28], Aaron Ciechanover, Avram Hershko and Irwin Rose, who shared the Nobel Prize in Chemistry in 2004. Proteins in eukaryotic cells are degraded via the UPS to maintain homeostasis and to regulate cellular function and phenotypic differentiation. A protein targeted for recognition and subsequent degradation by the proteasome is first ubiquitinated via a multistep process: activation, conjugation, and ligation [17,29,30]. Ubiquitin is activated by enzyme E1, then transferred to a ubiquitin-conjugating enzyme (E2) before it is coupled to the substrate protein by a ubiquitin-protein ligase (E3). The typical ubiquitination pattern for recognition by the proteasome comprises a chain of at least four ubiquitins with the first one attaching to a surface lysine (Lys) of the substrate protein. After conjugation, the protein moiety of the adduct is degraded by the proteasome complex, and the ubiquitin is removed and recycled.

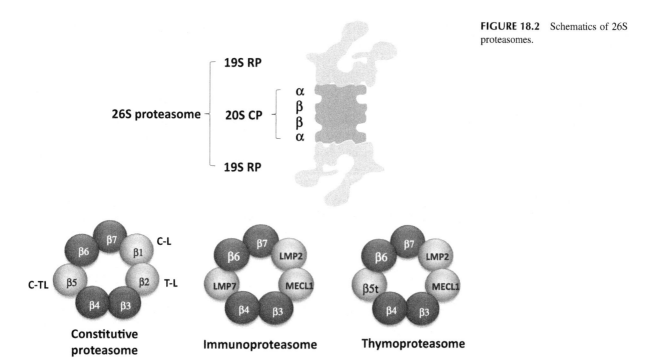

FIGURE 18.2 Schematics of 26S proteasomes.

The 26S proteasome (Fig. 18.2) is a large complex with a total molecular weight of about 2.5 MDa and is at the center of the UPS protein degradation regulatory network. The most prominent and well characterized form constitutes two 19S regulatory caps (RPs) and a 20S core particle (CP) in a 19S−20S−19S setup [31,32]. The 20S CP contains four homologous rings (two inner ß rings and two outer α rings) forming a hollow barrel-shaped structure with each ring containing seven subunits [32]. The proteolytic chamber resides in the ß rings, with β1, β2, and β5 subunits exhibiting caspase-like (C-L), trypsin-like (T-L), and chymotrypsin-like (CT-L) activities, respectively. The active sites of proteasome are unique in that their catalytic nucleophile is the N-terminal Thr residue. Only one other N-terminal Thr protease, taspase, is not a proteasome active site. Access to the central proteolytic chamber is tightly controlled. The 19S RP is responsible for recognizing, unfolding, and translocating polyubiquitinated substrates into the 20S CP. The narrow entry port in the α-ring of 20S CP limits access to the proteolytic chamber to unfolded polypeptides. There are three different proteasomes: constitutive proteasome, immunoproteasome, and thymoproteasome [33]. Each is defined by distinct proteolytic subunits in the β rings. The abundant constitutive proteasome is present in all tissues, whereas the immunoproteasome exists predominantly in immune cells such as monocytes and lymphocytes but is also inducible in non-immune cells following exposure to inflammatory cytokines such as interferon gamma (IFN-γ). Instead of β1, β2, and β5 active sites for constitutive proteasome, the active sites in 20S CP of immunoproteasome are LMP2 (β1i), MECL1 (β2i), and LMP7 (β5i). Finally, in the thymoproteasome, which is exclusively found in cortical thymic epithelial cells, a unique β5t, along with LMP2 and MECL1, is expressed.

Inhibition of proteasome was initially thought to be too toxic as a viable therapeutic treatment strategy, considering the essential function of proteasome in all eukaryotic cells. However, it was later discovered that highly proliferative cancer cells generally are more susceptible to proteasome inhibition than non-transformed normal cells [34−36], possibly due to increased needs for protein turnover. MM cells are particularly sensitive to proteasome inhibition as they generate large amounts of abnormal immunoglobins that need to be continuously broken-down and cleared by the UPS. Brief inhibition of the proteasome in MM cells triggers apoptosis while normal cells are not significantly perturbed, rendering an acceptable safety margin for proteasome inhibitors [36].

Carfilzomib irreversibly inactivates proteasome with high specificity

As discussed early, for a long time, drug developers have deliberately avoided to apply covalent mode of action in rational drug design, largely due to concerns about potential liabilities related to undesired off-target reactivity. Although initially epoxomicin was used as a tool to understand biologic pathways, its exquisite specificity for the proteasomes inspired Dr. Crews' team to explore peptide epoxyketones as potential cancer treatments.

Compared to epoxomicin, carfilzomib has higher potency and improved pharmaceutical properties while maintaining high selectivity for the proteasome. Carfilzomib primarily targets the CT-L subunits in both the constitutive proteasome (β5) and immunoproteasome (LMP7). Parlati el al [37] discovered that, in MM tumor cells, inhibition of both β5 and LMP7 are necessary and sufficient to induce proapoptotic sequelae and cell death. In vitro in cell-based assays, carfilzomib also inhibits other catalytic subunits (T-L and C-L) in a dose- and time-dependent manner. For example, a brief 1-h treatment of HT-29 colorectal adenocarcinoma cells with carfilzomib results in a higher sensitivity toward CT-L activity (IC_{50}: 9 nM) compared to T-L and C-L activities (IC_{50} values: 150−200 nM). When the length of compound exposure was extended from 1 to 6 h, greater inhibition was observed for all three subunits.

The high selectivity of carfilzomib is attributed to its unique mode of covalent interaction with the active site N-terminal Thr residue of the proteasome. The peptide backbone selectively binds in the substrate binding pocket(s) of the proteasome with high affinity, positioning the epoxyketone warhead in a close juxtaposition to the catalytic N-terminal Thr residue to facilitate the formation of two covalent bonds [38]. Two MOAs for dual covalent adduct formation (Fig. 18.3), both via a 2-step process, were proposed for epoxomicin and the class of epoxyketone proteasome inhibitors [18,38−40]. First, the catalytical hydroxyl group attacks the carbonyl of epoxyketone to produce a hemiacetal intermediate. Subsequently, the free α-amine of the Thr attacks and opens the epoxide ring to complete intramolecular cyclization. Early X-ray crystallographic studies [18,38,39] suggest that the second nucleophilic attack involves the α-carbon of epoxide and results in a six-membered morpholino ring. However, a recent study by Schrader et al. [40] suggests a different intracellular cyclization mechanism involving the β-carbon of epoxide to form a seven-membered oxazepane ring. Regardless of the cyclization mechanism, the dual covalent adduct formation requires both side chain hydroxyl and free α-amino groups of the N-terminal Thr residue of the proteasome. It is expected that other proteases lacking both nucleophiles cannot form the dual covalent ring structure with carfilzomib.

Different from carfilzomib, the first generation proteasome inhibitor bortezomib forms a tetrahedral bond between the boronate warhead and the catalytical hydroxyl group of the N-terminal Thr [41]. Similar interaction also can occur between boronnate warhead and serine proteases, which likely contributes to its dose limiting toxicity of bortezomib, an often-irreversible sensory peripheral neuropathy (PN), in MM patients when used as a single agent [42,43]. Although PN may be partly associated with MM driven by immunonoglobulin deposition on peripheral nerves, the rate of PN in MM patients treated with carfilzomib was significantly lower (1/5th) and was at reduced severities compared to bortezomib in the EDEAVOR study [10]. To investigate whether PN is a class effect, Kapur et al. [44] treated SH-SY5Y cells (neuroblastoma) differentiated to produce neurons with neurite outgrowth with the two inhibitors to achieve equivalent proteasome inhibition (~80%). They found that exposure to bortezomib, but not carfilzomib, resulted in neurite degeneration and cell death. In pre-differentiated cells, bortezomib potently inhibited the activity of HtrA2/omi, a protease shown to have a pro-survival activity in neurons. The in vitro model of neurodegeneration also suggests that the neuropathic effects of bortezomib are likely related to off-target activity, rather than proteasome inhibition. Kapur et al. also assessed nonproteasomal targets of the two structurally and mechanistically distinct proteasome inhibitors utilizing an activity-based probe (ABP) approach. Bortezomib was found to inhibit several proteases, including cathepsins A and G, dipeptidyl

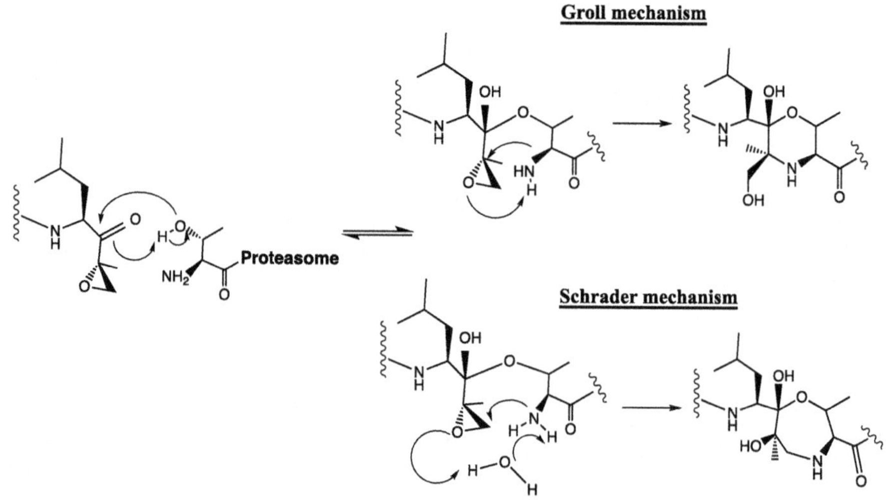

FIGURE 18.3 Mechanisms of dual covalent adduct formation between carfilzomib and the active site N-terminal Thr residue of the proteasome.

peptidase II, chymase, and HtrA2/omi at IC_{50} values that were near or equivalent to inhibition of the proteasome. Further experiments confirmed that inhibition of serine proteases is a generalized property of peptide boronates. When boronate warhead was added to the tetrapeptide backbone (hPhe-Peu-Phe-Leu) of carfilzomib, the resulting compound also potently inhibited serine proteases. On the other hand, the epoxyketone with bortezomib peptide backbone had no activity against these serine proteases.

The high selectivity of carfilzomib was also demonstrated in HepG2 cells. Federspiel el al [45] used click chemistry approach to identify potential off-target proteins of carfilzomib. They incubated an alkynyl analog of carfilzomib in HepG2 cells, followed streptavidin-based immunoprecipitation and shotgun tandem mass spectrometry analysis. The in vitro study identified two potential off-target proteins, cytochrome P450 27A1 (CYP27A1) and glutathione S-transferase omega 1 (GSTO1). Quantitative estimates of adductions suggests that these proteins are much less efficiently modified by carfilzomib than proteasomal targets in the same study.

Taken together, the results of these preclinical studies as well as the head-to-head clinical trial of the two agents, strongly suggests that carfilzomib, by nature of its chemical warhead, induces a more selective inhibition of the proteasome relative to boronate-based proteasome inhibitors.

Carfilzomib displayed a high systemic clearance primarily mediated by peptidase and epoxide hydrolase metabolism

The presence of a peptide backbone and the epoxyketone warhead, both susceptible to metabolic hydrolysis, renders carfilzomib extremely metabolically labile. In preclinical studies, carfilzomib displayed systemic clearance (CL) values higher than hepatic blood flows, with a short plasma half-life of about 5–20 min [46] and unpublished data. Following intravenous (IV) bolus administration, plasma concentrations declined sharply across species in the first few minutes. In rats at 5 min post-dose, the mean plasma concentration was about 20-fold lower than that immediately at the end of injection (Fig. 18.4). Scientists at Proteolix recognized the importance of early plasma sampling to appropriately characterize the PK profiles of carfilzomib and other peptide epoxyketone-based proteasome inhibitors following IV bolus dosing. For example, the first plasma PK sample should be taking as quickly as feasible, typically within 10 s of dosing to prevent significant under-estimation of the maximum plasma concentration (C_{max}) and area under the plasma concentration curve (AUC). The initial sharp decline in plasma concentration is partly due to rapid conversion of carfilzomib to hydrolyzed metabolites, and partly due to extensive tissue distribution. Consistent with preclinical observations, carfilzomib also shows a high systemic CL and a short half-life (~1 h) in patients [46] (Fig. 18.5). In both preclinical species and humans, major metabolites M14, M15 and M16, formed immediately after IV administration (Figs. 18.4–18.6). These metabolites formed by peptidase cleavage and epoxide hydrolysis are inactive against proteasome subunits. We also observed a dipeptide epoxyketone (M11) at low levels, which further converted to single amino acids and other secondary metabolites [46,47]. Although bearing the warhead, the dipeptide epoxyketone is not active as a proteasome inhibitor [48]. In vitro, these major metabolites were observed in hepatocytes and in tissue homogenate incubations from rat lung, liver, heart,

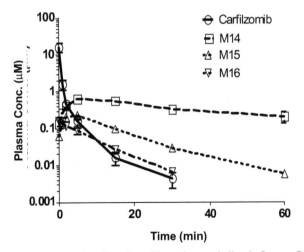

FIGURE 18.4 Plasma concentration over time profiles of carfilzomib and its major metabolites in Sprague-Dawley rats following a single IV bolus administration at 2 mg/kg.

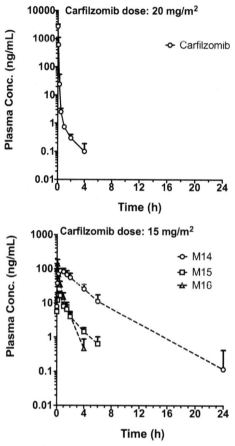

FIGURE 18.5 PK of carfilzomib and its major metabolites following a single dose of carfilzomib to patients with multiple myeloma via IV infusion over 2–10 min at 15 or 20 mg/m^2.

FIGURE 18.6 Major metabolic pathways for carfilzomib.

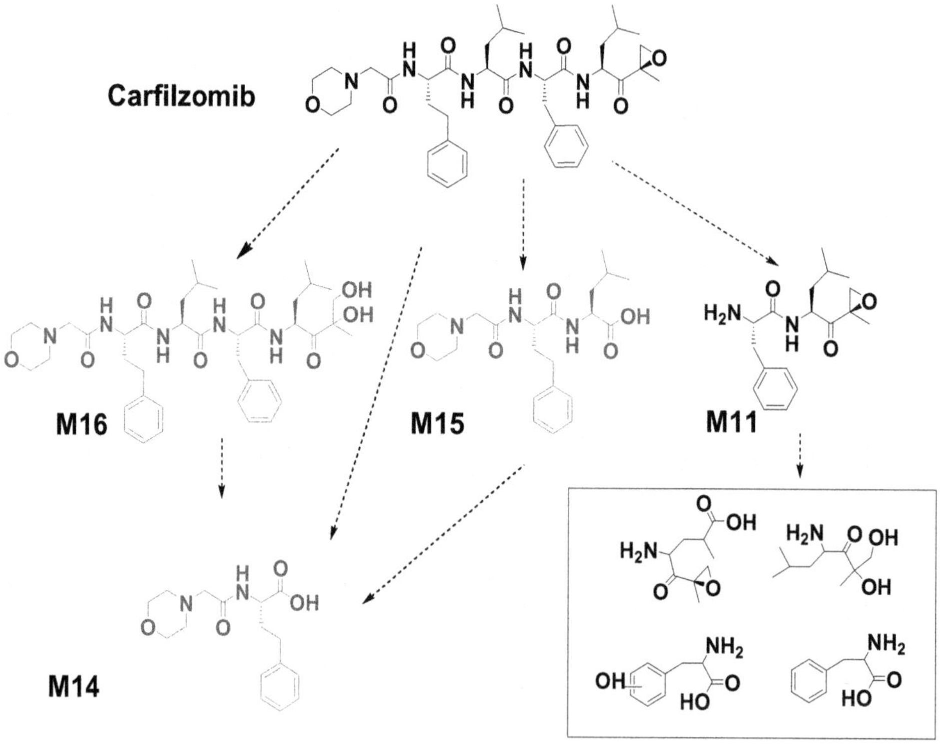

kidney, adrenal, and blood [47]. Interestingly, in vitro when carfilzomib was incubated in human liver microsomes (HLMs) in the presence of the cytochrome P450(CYP) co-factor nicotinamide adenine dinucleotide phosphate (NADPH), oxidative metabolites rather than hydrolysis products were predominant. However, these oxidative metabolites were either not detectable or presented at very low levels in plasma and urine samples from rats and humans. The lack of in vitro to in vivo correlation suggests liver microsome system is unlikely a relevant in vitro system to study the metabolism of peptide epoxyketone proteasome inhibitors.

Preclinical and clinical studies support that carfilzomib is primarily eliminated via hydrolysis both in liver and extrahepatic tissues [47]. Renal and biliary excretions are negligible with only minor level of parent compound detected in urine and bile samples from rats [47], and urine samples from patients (in-house unpublished data). The negligible role of renal clearance is further demonstrated by the lack of significant alteration of carfilzomib PK profile in patients with varying degrees of renal dysfunction [49,50]. We also examined the potential role of irreversible target binding in its high clearance considering proteasome is a ubiquitously expressed and an abundant protein target [36]. We compared carfilzomib PK in two cohorts of rats [47]: one pretreated with an IV bolus dosing of the vehicle (control group); the other pretreated with an IV bolus dosing of an analog tripeptide proteasome inhibitor oprozomib at a high dose to completely inhibit proteasome CT-L activity in blood and major tissues. Thirty minutes after the pretreatment, carfilzomib was given as an IV bolus at 2 mg/kg to both groups of animals. No significant difference in PK parameters were observed between the two groups. Furthermore, M16 (the diol metabolite), lacking the intact warhead to form a covalent adduct with proteasome active sites, also exhibited a CL higher than the hepatic blood flow in rats. These data support that irreversible target binding does not contribute significantly to the high systemic CL of carfilzomib. Finally, in vitro cross species blood/plasma partitioning ratio of carfilzomib ranged from 0.64 to 0.82 at relevant concentrations, suggesting red blood cell partitioning does not contribute to the observed high plasma clearance.

Despite a short half-life, carfilzomib induced rapid and sustained proteasome inhibition in preclinical species and in patients

The PK properties of carfilzomib is clearly distinct from conventional drugs, where low systemic clearance is often desirable. Metabolic stability is typically one of the tier one assays during lead optimization to prioritize those leads that potentially have good oral bioavailability, longer half-lives, and can elicit sustained target modulation. Carfilzomib is metabolically labile, not orally bioavailable, and was developed as an injectable drug. Nonetheless, understanding whether the short duration of exposure is adequate to engage its target was a key question at the early stage of its characterization. In vitro, the onset of proteasome inhibition by carfilzomib was rapid, occurred within seconds in cell-free systems and within minutes in cells [36]. A brief treatment (1 h) of tumor or non-transformed cells with carfilzomib followed by a 72-h washout period was used to mimic short duration of in vivo exposure. The short exposure to carfilzomib promoted accumulation of proteasome substrates and markers of apoptosis or stress response pathways. Carfilzomib was shown to be more cytotoxic to hematologic cell lines compared to solid tumor and non-transformed cells. In vivo, pharmacodynamics (PD) was evaluated in heathy animals due to wide expression of the proteasome in blood and normal tissues [47]. In rats at 1 h post a single IV bolus administration, dose dependent inhibition of CT-L activity, measured by a fluorogenic Leu-Val-Tyr-7-amino-4-methylcoumarin (LLVY-AMC) substrate-based assay, was observed in a variety of tissues examined except the brain. Liver was found to be less sensitive to the PD effect likely due to the competition between drug metabolism and target binding. Tissues were also examined at various time points to evaluate the recovery of proteasome activity. Except for whole blood, the CT-L activity recovered by 50%–100% within 24 h. A slow recovery in blood (with <50% recovery after 1 week of treatment) reflected the impact of an irreversible MOA in a cell type (erythrocytes) that cannot make new proteins. In all tissues, CT-L subunit inhibition significantly outlasted the systemic exposure to carfilzomib.

In the clinic, inhibition of proteasome activity was monitored mainly in blood and peripheral blood mononuclear cells (PBMCs). Bone marrow samples from a few studies [51] were also collected and used to confirm PD effect. In early clinical trials [52,53], CT-L activity was determined by LLVY-AMC assay. Dose dependent inhibition of CT-L proteasome activity was observed, with 70–80% inhibition at 15 mg/m^2 in whole blood and PBMCs, and approximately 90% inhibition at 27 mg/m^2 in PBMC following the first dose. Proteasome CT-L activity was consistently suppressed in whole blood between cycles. In PBMCs, deeper inhibition (>90% at 20 and 27 mg/m^2) was observed following the second dose and CT-L activity was essentially recovered at the beginning of the second cycle following a 12 day non-dosing period. The substrate-based LLVY-AMC assay, however, cannot differentiate CT-L activity between constitutive proteasomes and immunoproteasomes, both of which are expressed in MM cells. To obtain full proteasome active-site inhibition profile for better understanding the role of individual subunits in the anti-tumor effect, scientists at Onyx developed and validated a novel proteasome constitutive/immunoproteasome subunit enzyme-linked immunosorbent (ProCISE) assay [51]. The assay was used to quantify proteasome subunit activity and occupancy in patient samples from multiple phase 1/2 and phase 2 trials before and after treatment with carfilzomib. Consistent with results from the substrate-based assay, cumulative and sustained inhibition of CT-L subunits was observed in both whole blood and PBMCs, on average over 80% inhibition of $\beta 5$ and LMP7 was observed in patients treated with doses ≥ 15 mg/m^2 following repeat dosing. Dose dependent increases in MECL1 and LMP2 occupancy was observed at doses up to 45 mg/m^2. At a dose of 56 mg/m^2, carfilzomib produced near complete inhibition of LMP7, and was bound to, on average, more than 79% of all immunoproteasome active sites. Dose dependent inhibition of proteasome subunits was further demonstrated in CHAMPION-1 trial, where carfilzomib was administered on a weekly dosing schedule with dexamethasone [54]. Once weekly dose at 70 mg/m^2 (MTD) led to greater depth of inhibition on secondary immunoproteasome subunits MECL-1 and LMP2 and exhibited less recovery of proteasome inhibition on C2D1, compared with that from 20 or 36 mg/m^2 dose cohorts.

As TCIs gained broad attention, the field started to appreciate that PK of a covalent and irreversible inhibitor can be decoupled from PD responses when the resynthesis rate of the target is low. The PK profile or duration of exposure needed for a covalent inhibitor to engage its target depends on covalent bond formation kinetics and the rate of new target synthesis.

Covalent inactivation kinetics is defined by the ratio of maximum inactivation rate constant (k_{inact}) and the inhibitor concentration that causes half of the k_{inact} (K_I). To illustrate the unique PK/PD relationship for TCIs, Strelow [55] simulated in vivo covalent occupancy (for the target and a prospective off-target) over time for hypothetical covalent inhibitors with varying k_{inact}/K_I and PK profiles. For simplification, the rate of new protein resynthesis was assumed to be slow and negligible. In this model, a highly potent hypothetic covalent inhibitor, with a k_{inact}/K_I of 1.2×10^5 M^{-1} s^{-1} and a K_I of 10 nM for target protein B, was able to rapidly (within ~ 10 min) achieve nearly complete covalent occupancy. Target occupancy was maintained even after the inhibitor, with a high in vivo clearance (200 mL/min/kg), was cleared from circulation. In contrast, the inhibitor did not achieve significant occupancy for a prospective off-target (protein F) with a 1000-fold lower k_{inact}/K_I. On the other hand, a hypothetic inhibitor with a lower clearance (5 mL/min/kg) not only attained rapid engagement of target protein B, but it also induced significant occupancy for the off-target protein F. The example illustrates that a covalent and irreversible inhibitor with rapid on-target inactivation can provide PD effect that outlasts the duration of systemic exposure. In addition, high clearance may be a desirable PK property since it may help reduce potential off-target effects.

Carfilzomib is a real-world example with a rapid covalent kinetics (k_{inact}/K_I of 3.3×10^4 M^{-1} s^{-1} for CT-L subunit) and high clearance, yet it achieves rapid and prolonged in vivo target inactivation. Following carfilzomib treatment, the recovery of proteasome activity depends entirely on synthesis of new proteasomes (with a turnover half-life of about 24 h) [36,56]. It is worth to note that while a short systemic exposure of carfilzomib and bortezomib provides adequate proteasome inhibition for effective treatment of MM, both drugs have not shown significant efficacy in patients with solid tumors. Radhakrishnan et al. [57] hypothesized that utility of proteasome inhibitors for the treatment of patient with less sensitive cancers may be hampered by elevated proteasome synthesis upon proteasome inhibition in high eukaryotes [58–60]. Their study identified transcription factor erythroid derived 2-related factor 1 (Nrf1) as a mediator for the so called "bounce-back" response and suggested that prolonged inhibition of the proteasome by carfilzomib may be achieved by attenuating Nrf1 mediated proteasome recovery. Unlike carfilzomib, proteasome activity following bortezomib treatment recovers through both slowly reversible dissociating from the active sites of proteasome and new proteasome synthesis. Consequently, the lack of efficacy of bortezomib in less sensitive cancers will likely less readily to be rectified.

Carfilzomib has a low potential of CYP mediated DDI and its PK is not significantly altered in patients with hepatic impairment

Understanding drug-drug interactions (DDIs), both as a potential perpetrator or a victim, is important to mitigate adverse events or loss of effectiveness from unexpected exposure change in combination therapies. To ascertain appropriate product labeling and guide dose adjustment, PK of a new drug also needs to be evaluated in special populations (e.g. renal and hepatic impairment).

The DDI potential of carfilzomib was evaluated in vitro in HLMs and hepatocytes. In HLMs, carfilzomib showed direct and time-dependent inhibition (TDI) on CYP3A4, but not on other major CYP isoforms. Carfilzomib also decreased the expression of CYP3A4 mRNA and reduced the activities of CYP3A4 following a 3-day treatment in cultured human hepatocytes [46]. Other proteasome inhibitors also showed downregulation of CYP expressions in vitro but the mechanism remains to be elucidated [61]. These in vitro findings warranted a dedicated clinical DDI study to assess whether carfilzomib modulates CYP3A4 activity in patients. Patients with solid tumors received a single 2 mg oral dose of midazolam on

Day -7, followed by IV administration of carfilzomib at 27 mg/m^2 over 2–10 min on Days 1, 2, 8, 9, 15, and 16 of a single 28-day cycle. Patients also received a 2 mg oral dose of midazolam immediately after carfilzomib as Days 1 and 16. Carfilzomib after either a single or repeat dose administration did not significantly alter the PK of midazolam. As midazolam is a highly sensitive CYP3A4 substrate, the clinical DDI data support that carfilzomib will not interact with other CYP3A4 substrates in vivo. The lack of clinically significant DDI of carfilzomib is partly due to its high systemic clearance and short duration of exposure in vivo. Following IV administration, the mean plasma concentration of carfilzomib at 5 min post-infusion was approximately 20-fold of the mean C_{max} at the end of infusion and was further reduced to <1% by 30 min [46]. In addition, carfilzomib is highly bound to plasma proteins (97% bound), further limiting the exposure of CYP3A4 to free drug. Finally, in vitro data suggests carfilzomib is about 200-fold more potent against the proteasome compared to CYP3A4, with k_{inact}/K_I values of 3.3×10^4 and 1.5×10^2 M^{-1} s^{-1}, respectively. As discussed earlier, based on Strelow's model, the relatively slower covalent inactivation kinetics on CYP3A4 in combination with the high systemic clearance likely reduce the chance for carfilzomib to elicit modulation of CYP3A4 activity in patients.

The PK profile of Carfilzomib is also unlikely affected by concomitant medications that are strong CYP modulators. Although carfilzomib is primarily oxidized by CYP enzymes in HLMs, when evaluated in human hepatocyte suspensions in vitro, the presence of strong CYP inhibitors did not affect the rate of carfilzomib metabolism, supporting that CYP enzymes play only a minor role in the elimination of carfilzomib. The impact of hepatic impairment on carfilzomib (doses at 27 and 56 mg/m^2) PK was evaluated clinically in patients with relapsed or progressive advanced malignancies and varying degrees of impaired hepatic function [62]. Compared with patients with normal hepatic function, patients with mild and moderate hepatic impairment had 44%/45% (27/56 mg/m^2) and 26%/21% (27/56 mg/m^2) higher carfilzomib AUC_{0-last}, respectively. There was no consistent trend of increasing exposure resulting from increasing hepatic impairment severity (mild vs. moderate). Moreover, the level of increase in exposure is unlikely to be clinically significant, considering the high intrinsic PK variability (% CV in AUC_{0-last} of ~100%) and exposure–response relationship of carfilzomib. Taking together, these data support that no dose adjustment is needed when carfilzomib is co-administered with CYP activity modulators or in patients with hepatic impairment.

Evolution of carfilzomib dosing regimen

Optimization of dosing and schedule is an integral part of drug development. Carfilzomib dosing/schedule continued to evolve during clinical development, supported by insights gained from both preclinical and clinical PK/PD/efficacy and exposure/tolerability studies.

The anti-tumor activities of carfilzomib in preclinical xenograft models were dose and schedule dependent. Superior efficacy was observed when carfilzomib (5 mg/kg) was delivered via IV bolus twice weekly on Days 1 and 2 when compared to twice weekly administration at the same dose on Days 1 and 4, or weekly on day 1 at 10 mg/kg [36]. In addition, in rats, dosing on two consecutive days (QDx2 on Days 1, 2, 8, 9, 15, and 16 of a 28-day cycle) or five consecutive days (QDx5 on Days 1–5 of a 14-day cycle) led to cumulative inhibition of proteasome activity. Both QDx5 and QDx2 schedules were investigated clinically in early phase 1 trials [52,53] in patients with refractory hematological malignancies. In PX-171-001, carfilzomib was administered via a 1–2 min IV injection for five consecutive days (QD×5) followed by a 9-day rest (2-week cycle). This study produced promising preliminary clinical responses and the maximum tolerated dose (MTD) was 15 mg/m^2. In PX-171-002, carfilzomib was administered via a 1–2 min IV injection on two consecutive days (QD×2) on Days 1, 2, 8, 9, 15 and 16 every 28 days. MTD was not reached at doses up to 27 mg/m^2. At the highest dose tested (27 mg/m^2), one patient (out of six) had grade III hypoxia that met dose-limiting toxicity (DLT) criteria. In the expansion phase, a step-up dosing of 20/27 mg/m^2 (dose escalation from 20 to 27 mg/m^2 on day 8 of cycle 1) showed improved tolerability with no DLTs. Carfilzomib was associated with a first-dose infusion reaction variably characterized by a constellation of symptoms including fevers, chills, and/or dyspnea. The step-up dose regimen with a slower 2–10 min infusion and the addition of a low dose prophylactic dexamethasone (4 mg) helped to mitigate the first-dose effect. Due to favorable overall tolerability profiles, the QD×2 schedule with a step-up dosing of 20/27 mg/m^2 via a 2–10 min IV infusion was chosen as the recommended phase 2 dose/schedule (RP2Ds) for the phase 2 pivotal trial (PX-171-003-A1) [1], which led to the accelerated approval of carfilzomib as a single agent in patients with RRMM following great than three lines of therapy. The same RP2Ds of carfilzomib was adopted in combination with lenalidomide (Revlimid) and dexamethasone (KRd) in a randomized phase 3 study (ASPIRE) and led to the first full approval by the US FDA [10].

Concurrent with clinical development, additional preclinical studies demonstrated that a slower infusion significantly improved tolerability in rats [47]. At 8 mg/kg, a 30-min infusion was tolerated while IV bolus injection resulted in about 44% mortality. In a separate PK/PD study, the slower 30-min infusion decreased the C_{max} by about 28-fold but did not

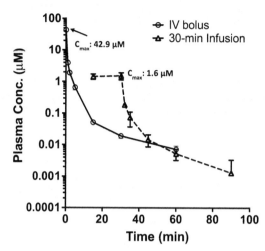

FIGURE 18.7 PK of carfilzomib following a single IV bolus or 30-min IV infusion to Sprague-Dawley rats at 8 mg/kg.

affect total exposure (AUC) compared to bolus injection in rats (Fig. 18.7). IV infusion and bolus injection induced comparable proteasome inhibition in blood and a variety of tissues, suggesting that AUC (i.e. total dose administered), rather than C_{max}, is the key driver for carfilzomib PD effects. On the other hand, the intolerability seems to be related to high C_{max}. The preclinical PK/PD/tolerability relationship provided basis for testing slower infusion in the clinic, aiming to maximize efficacy in patients by enabling higher total dose administration. The hypothesis was confirmed in a phase 2 study (PX-171-007) [63] in patients with RRMM. Carfilzomib was administered on a QDx2 schedule, with 20 mg/m² on days 1 and 2 of cycle one followed by dose escalation up to 56 mg/m² on day 8 of cycle one and thereafter. In this study, the MTD of carfilzomib was established as 20/56 mg/m², higher than that achievable with a 2–10 min infusion. At a dose of 20 mg/m², there was no significant difference in CT-L inhibition between patients receiving a 2–10 min infusion and those receiving a 30-min infusion while mean C_{max} was reduced by about 3-fold in patients with slower infusion.

Carfilzomib showed a dose dependent increase in inhibition of proteasome subunits. A pooled multivariate dose-response model derived using data from a few phase 2 studies [64] demonstrated that the odds of achieving a partial response or better for a given patient treated with 27 mg/m² was 4.08-fold higher (95% CI: 2.30–7.24, $P < .001$) than for a patient receiving 20 mg/m². When using average dose as a continuous variable and adjusting for study effect, the odds of a response increased by 1.28-fold (95% CI: 1.17–1.40, $P < .001$) for each 1 mg/m² increase in average carfilzomib dose. As discussed above, the ENDEAVOR study [11], in which high dose carfilzomib administered via a 30-min infusion in combination with dexamethasone (20/56 mg/m², Kd) showed significant improvement in PFS and OS compared to Vd, These results suggest that the simultaneous inhibition of all subunits to achieve near complete inhibition of immuno-proteasome contributed to the improvement in antitumor activity in patients with MM, including patients that are refractory to bortezomib, particularly given that approximately 75% of the proteasome in isolated myeloma cells are immunopro-teasome [51].

Despite the success of carfilzomib as monotherapy or in combinations, the twice-weekly IV administration schedule is quite burdensome for MM patients, particularly for those who are elderly, or who live far from the clinic. To improve patient convenience and potentially increase the duration of treatment, weekly carfilzomib schedule was tested in a phase 1/2 study (CHAMPION-1) in combination with dexamethasone [54]. The MTD of weekly dosing was further increased to 20/70 mg/m² and promising efficacy profile with an ORR of 60% was shown in a small number of patients. The effectiveness of once weekly carfilzomib dose regimen was further confirmed in a randomized phase III study (ARROW) in combination with dexamethasone [12].

The evolution of carfilzomib dose regimen exemplifies how preclinical research and a clear understanding of exposure-response relationship successfully translated into improved benefit to risk ratio and patient convenience for an oncology drug.

Reflection on carfilzomib discovery and development

Carfilzomib is a natural product inspired medicine that has benefited tens of thousands of patients since its first approval in 2012. The epoxyketone warhead and tetrapeptide backbone affords the delicate balance between the rates of covalent inactivation kinetics and metabolic clearance. The peptide backbone of the natural product epoxomicin was optimized to create carfilzomib with improved potency, selectivity, and aqueous solubility. The peptide backbone positions the warhead close to N-terminal Thr of the proteasome to enable efficient covalent bond formation. Truncating the peptide backbone of carfilzomib sequentially while maintaining the warhead resulted in significant loss of potency [48] supporting the importance of the non-covalent interaction. The epoxyketone warhead originated from epoxomicin is truly a gift from Mother Nature. The α-methyl group on the epoxide plays a critical role in tuning down warhead reactivity and rate of metabolism, likely due to the steric hindrance. In a follow-on program to develop selective inhibitors of the immuno-proteasome, analogs were made in which this α-methyl group was removed. Despite apparent increase in warhead reactivity, the removing of the α-methyl group resulted in significantly reduced proteasome inhibition in various tissues following IV administration in rats [unpublished data]. The result can be explained by the significantly increased rate of the metabolism of the warhead, thereby, tipping the balance between PK and PD.

Choosing relevant in vitro metabolism systems to evaluate peptide epoxyketone proteasome inhibitors has been instrumental in translating in vitro results and understanding clinic relevance. When evaluating metabolism in HLMs, CYP-mediated oxidative metabolites appeared to play a significant role in carfilzomib clearance. Moreover, in vitro CYP inhibition in HLMs also suggested carfilzomib is a potent time dependent inhibitor on CYP3A4 [46]. When studied in hepatocytes and in vivo, oxidative metabolites were minor and diol formation and peptide cleavage were major metabolites. Similar phenomenon was seen for the oral proteasome inhibitor oprozomib [65] and the selective immunoproteasome inhibitor KZR-616 [66], which are metabolized predominantly by microsomal epoxide hydrolases. Additionally, for both carfilzomib and oral proteasome inhibitor oprozomib, time dependent inhibition on CYP3A4 was not observed when evaluated in human hepatocytes, consistent with the lack of clinical DDI. The distinct observation in HLMs versus human hepatocytes might be due to significant loss of microsomal epoxide hydrolase (mEH) activity, which was found to be responsible for diol formation [65,66], during microsomal subcellular fractionation [67]. On the other hand, CYP activities are concentrated in the endoplasmic reticulum membrane, therefore may cause HLM incubation bias toward oxidation metabolism pathways mediated by CYP enzymes. Understanding of the in vitro to in vivo correlation provided valuable insight in choosing relevant in vitro systems for the selective immunoproteasome inhibitor discovery program. Instead of focusing on reducing oxidative metabolism, scientists focused on stabilize side chains on peptide backbone and used liver S9 in the absence of co-factor NADPH, a system with adequate peptidase and epoxide hydrolase activities, to guide lead optimization. A recent publication from scientists at Kezar Bioscience [66] further illustrates the importance of choosing relevant in vitro metabolizing systems in evaluating novel class of peptide epoxyketones, including KZR-616, a first-in-class selective immunoproteasome inhibitor currently being evaluated in phase 2 studies in autoimmune disorders.

Finally, it is important to recognize the utility and potential limitations in translating preclinical dosing regimens to humans. In carfilzomib development, all preclinical efficacy studies in mouse xenograft models were carried out via IV bolus administration. At the same total weekly dose, once weekly (D1) dosing of carfilzomib at 10 mg/kg has inferior anti-tumor activity compared to twice weekly (D1D2) dosing at 5 mg/kg. Highly doses were not tested to assess the potential of once weekly schedule due to intolerability at >10 mg/kg following IV bolus administration. In the clinic, a slower 30 min IV infusion resulted in higher MTD (56 mg/m^2) compared to that with 2—10 min infusion on a twice weekly (on Days 1 and 2) schedule, and the MTD was further increased to 70 mg/m^2 on a weekly (on Day 1) schedule. Increased dose intensity and total weekly dose translated into improved clinical outcomes in patients with RRMM. In small molecule oncology drug development, preclinical studies in xenograft models often provide insightful conceptual frameworks on schedule optimization. Nonetheless, careful consideration of practical issues such as convenience of dosing regimen is often necessary to improve compliance. Although not covered in this chapter, it is worth to noting that interspecies difference in PK also needs to be taking into consideration when translating an optimal preclinical dose schedule to the clinical settings.

References

[1] D.S. Siegel, T. Martin, M. Wang, R. Vij, A.J. Jakubowiak, S. Lonial, S. Trudel, V. Kukreti, N. Bahlis, M. Alsina, A. Chanan-Khan, F. Buadi, F.J. Reu, G. Somlo, J. Zonder, K. Song, A.K. Stewart, E. Stadtmauer, L. Kunkei, S. Wear, A.F. Wong, R.Z. Orlowski, S. Jagannath, A phase 2 study of single-agent carfilzomib (PX-171-003-A1) in patients with relapsed and refractory multiple myeloma, Blood 120 (!4) (2012) 2817—2825.

[2] P.F. Bross, R. Kane, A.T. Farrell, S. Abraham, K. Benson, M.E. Brower, et al., Approval summary for bortezomib for injection in the treatment of multiple myeloma, Clin. Cancer Res. 10 (2004) 3954—3964.

[3] J. Singh, R.C. Petter, T.A. Baillie, A. Whitty, The resurgence of covalent drugs, Nat. Rev. Drug Discov. 10 (2011) 307—317.

[4] Z. Pan, H. Scheerens, S.J. Li, B.E. Schultz, P.A. Sprengeler, L.C. Burrill, R.V. Mendonca, M.D. Sweeney, K.C. Scott, P.G. Grothaus, A.J. Douglas, J.M. Spoerke, L.A. Honigberg, P.R. Young, S.A. Darymple, J.T. Palmer, Discovery of selective irreversible inhibitors for Bruton's tyrosine kinase, ChemMedChem 2 (1) (2007) 58—61.

[5] L.A. Honigberg, A.M. Smith, M. Sirisawad, E. Verner, D. Loury, B. Chang, S. Li, Z. Pan, D.H. Thamm, R.A. Miller, The Bruton tyrosine kinase inhibitor PCI-32765 blocks B-cell activation and is efficacious in models of autoimmune disease and B-cell malignancy, Proc. Natl. Acad. Sci. 107 (29) (2010) 13075−13080.

[6] A. Yver, Osimertinib (AZD9291)-a science-drive, collaborative approach to rapid drug design and development, Ann. Oncol. 27 (6) (2016) 1165−1170.

[7] M.H. Potashman, M.E. Duggan, Covalent modifiers: an orthogonal approach to drug design, J. Med. Chem. 52 (2009) 1231−1246.

[8] A.S. Kalgutkar, D.K. Dalvie, Drug discovery for a new generation of covalent drugs, Expert Opin. Drug Discov. 7 (2012) 561−581.

[9] Q. Liu, Y. Sabnis, Z. Zhao, T. Zhang, S.J. Buhrlage, L.H. Jones, N.S. Gray, Developing irreversible inhibitors of the protein kinase systeinome, Chem. Biol. 20 (2013) 146−159.

[10] A.K. Stewart, S.V. Rajkumar, M.A. Dimopoulos, T. Masszi, I. Špička, A. Oriol, R. Hájek, L. Rosiñol, D.S. Siegel, G.G. Mihaylov, V. Goranova-Marinova, P. Rajnics, et al., Carfilzomib, lenalidomide, and dexamethasone for relapsed multiple myeloma, N. Engl. J. Med. 372 (2015) 142−152.

[11] M.A. Dimopoulos, P. Moreau, A. Palumbo, D. Joshua, L. Pour, R. Hajek R, et al., Carfilzomib and dexamethasone versus bortezomib and dexamethasone for patients with relapsed or refractory multiple myeloma (ENDEAVOR): a randomized, phase 3, open-label, multicenter study, Lancet Oncol. 17 (1) (2016) 27−38.

[12] M.A. Dimopoulos, R. Niesvizky, K. Weisel, D.S. Siegel, R. Hajek, M.-V. Mateos, M. Cavo, M. Huang, A. Zahlten-Kumeli, P. Moreau, Once-versus twice-weekly carfilzomib in relapsed and refractory multiple myeloma by select patient characteristics: phase 3 ARROW study subgroup analysis, Blood Cancer J. 10 (2020) 35−47.

[13] M. Dimopolous, H. Quach, M.V. Mateos, et al., Carfilzomib, dexamethansone, and daratunuman versus carfilzomib and dexamethansone for patients with relapsed or refractory multiple myeloma (CANDOR): results from a randomized, multicentre, open-label, phase 3 study, Lancet 396 (2020) 186−197.

[14] M. Hanada, K. Sugawara, K. Kaneta, S. Toda, Y. Nishiyama, K. Tomita, H. Yamamoto, M. Konishi, T. Oki, Epoxomicin, a new antitumor agent of microbial origin, J. Antibiot. (Tokyo) 45 (11) (1992) 1746−1752.

[15] N. Sin, K.B. Kim, M. Elofsson, L. Meng, H. Auth, B.H. Kwok, C.M. Crews, Total synthesis of the potent proteasome inhibitor epoxomicin: a useful tool for understanding proteasome biology, Bioorg. Med. Chem. Lett. 9 (15) (1999) 2283−2288.

[16] L. Meng, R. Mohan, B.H. Kwok, M. Elofsson, N. Sin, C.M. Crews, Epoxomicin, a potent and selective proteasome inhibitor, exhibits in vivo anitinflammatory activity, Proc. Natl. Acad. Sci. U. S. A. 96 (18) (1999) 10403−10408.

[17] D. Finley, Recognition and processing of ubiquitin-protein conjugation by the proteasome, Annu. Rev. Biochem. 78 (2009) 477−513.

[18] M. Groll, K.B. Kim, N. Kairies, R. Huber, C.M. Crews, Crystal structure of epoxomicin: 20S proteasome reveals a molecular basis for selectivity of alpha',beta'-epoxyketone proteasome inhibitors, J. Am. Chem. Soc. 122 (2000) 1237−1238.

[19] M. Elofsson, U. Splittgerber, J. Myung, R. Mohan, C.M. Crews, Towards subunit-specific proteasome inhibitors: synthesis and evaluation of peptide alpha', beta'-epoxyketones, Chem. Biol. 6 (11) (1999) 811−822.

[20] https://www.cancer.org/cancer/multiple-myeloma/about/key-statistics.html.

[21] P.G. Richardson, S. Zweegman, E.K. O'Donnell, J.P. Laubach, N. Raje, P. Voorhees, R.H. Ferrari, T. Skacel, S.K. Kumar, S. Lonial, Ixazomib for the treatment of multiple myeloma, Expert Opin. Pharmacother. 19 (17) (2018) 1949−1968.

[22] S.A. Holstein, P.L. McCarthy, Immunomodulatory drugs in multiple myeloma: mechanisms of action and clinical experience, Drugs 77 (5) (2017) 505−520.

[23] S. Afifi, A. Michael, A. Leskhin, Immunotherapy: a new approach to treating multiple myeloma with daratumumab and elotuzumab, Ann. Pharmacother. 50 (7) (2016) 555−568.

[24] T. Zhang, S. Wang, T. Lin, J. Xie, L. Zhao, Z. Liang, Y. Li, J. Jiang, Systematic review and meta-analysis of the efficacy and safety of novel monoclonal antibodies for treatment of relapsed/refractory multiple myeloma, Oncotarget 8 (20) (2017) 34001−34017.

[25] D.W. Sherbenou, T.M. Mark, P. Forsberg, Monoclonal antibodies in multiple myeloma: a new wave of the future, Clin. Lyphoma Myeloma Leuk 17 (9) (2017) 545−554.

[26] FDA approves first BCMA-targeted CAR-T cell therapy, Nat. Rev. Drug Discov., 20 (2021) 332.

[27] J. Adams, The development of proteasome inhibitors as anticancer drugs, Cancer Cell 5 (5) (2004) 417−421.

[28] Ciechanover, Proteolysis: from the lysosome to ubiquitin and the proteasome, Nat. Rev. Mol. Cell Biol. 6 (2005) 79−86.

[29] A. Hershko, A. Ciechanover, The ubiquitin system, Annu. Rev. Biochem. 67 (1998) 425−479.

[30] A. Ciechanover, A.L. Ashwartz, The ubiquitin-proteasome pathway: the complexity and myriad functions of proteins death, Proc. Natl. Acad. Sci. 95 (1998) 2727−2730.

[31] H. Hölzl, B. Kapelari, J. Kellermann, E. Seemuller, A. Sumegi, A. Udvardy, O. Medalia, J. Sperling, S.A. Muller, A. Engel, W. Baumeister, The regulatory complex of *Drosophila melanogaster* 26S proteasomes: subunit composition and localization of a deubiquitylating enzyme, J. Cell Biol. 150 (1) (2000) 119−129.

[32] S. Murata, H. Yashiroda, K. Tanaka, Molecular mechanisms of proteasome assesmbly, Nat. Rev. Mol. Cell Biol. 10 (2009) 104−115.

[33] K. Tanaka, The proteasome: overview of structure and functions, Proc. Jpn. Acad. Ser. 85 (2009) 12−36.

[34] J.B. Almond, G.M. Cohen, The proteasome: a novel target for cancer chemotherapy, Leukemia 16 (2002) 433−443.

[35] T. Hideshima, P. Richardson, D. Chauhan, V.J. Palombella, P.J. Elliott, J. Adams, K.C. Anderson, The proteasome inhibitor PS-341 inhibits growth, induces apoptosis, and overcomes drug resistance in human multiple myeloma cells, Cancer Res. 61 (2001) 3071−3076.

[36] S.D. Demo, C.J. Kirk, M.A. Aujay, J.T. Buchholz, M. Dajee, M.N. Ho, J. Jiang, G.J. Laidig, E.R. Lewis, F. Parlati, K.D. Shenk, M.S. Smyth, C.M. Sun, M.K. Vallone, T.M. Woo, C.J. Molineaux, M.K. Bennett, Antitumor activity of PR-171, a novel irreversible inhibitor of the proteasome, Cancer Res. 67 (13) (2007) 6383−6391.

[37] F. Parlati, S.J. Lee, M. Aujay, E. Suzuki, K. Levitsky, J.B. Lorens, D.R. Micklem, P. Ruurs, C. Sylvain, Y. Lu, K.D. Shenk, M.K. Bennett, Carfilzomib can induce tumor cell death through selective inhibition of the chymotrypsin-like activity of the proteasome, Blood 114 (2009) 3439–3447.

[38] W. Harshbarger, C. Miller, C. Diedrich, J. Sacchettini, Crystal structure of the human 20S proteasome in complex with carfilzomib, Structure 23 (2015) 418–424.

[39] E.M. Huber, M. Basler, R. Schwab, W. Heinemeyer, C.J. Kirk, M. Groettrup, M. Groll, Cell 148 (2012) 727–738.

[40] J. Schrader, F. Henneberg, T.A. Msta, K. Tittmann, T.R. Schneider, H. Stark, G. Bourenkov, A. Shari, Science 353 (6299) (2016) 594–598.

[41] M. Groll, C.R. Berkers, H.L. Ploegh, H. Ovaa, Crystal structure of the boronic acid-based proteasome inhibitor bortezomib in complex with the yeast 20S proteasome, Structure 14 (2006) 451–456.

[42] A.F. Smith, G.J. Morgan, F.E. Davies, Bortezomib (Velcade TM) in the treatment of multiple myeloma, Therapeut. Clin. Risk Manag. 2 (3) (2006) 271–279.

[43] P.G. Richardson, Q. Xie, C. Mitsiades, A.A. Shannan-khan, S. Lonial, H. Hassoun, D.e. Avigan, et al., Single-agent bortezomib in previously untreated multipole myeloma: efficacy, characterization of peripheral neuropathy, and molecular correlations with response and neuropathy, J. Clin. Oncol. 27 (21) (2009) 3518–3523.

[44] A.A. Kapur, J.L. Anderl, M. Kraus, F. Parlati, K.D. Shenk, S.J. Lee, T. Muchamual, M.K. Bennett, C. Driessen, A.J. Ball, C.J. Kirk, Non-proteasomal targets of the proteasome inhibitors bortezomib and carfilzomib: a link to clinical adverse events, Clin. Cancer Res. 17 (9) (2011) 2734–2743.

[45] J.D. Federspiel, S.G. Codreanu, S. Goyal, M.e. ALbertolle, E. Lowe, J. Teague, H. Wong, F.P. Guengerich, D.C. Liebler, Specificity of protein covalent modification by the electrophilic proteasome inhibitor carfilzomib in human cells, Mol. Cell. Proteasom. 15 (2016) 3233–3242.

[46] Z. Wang, J. Yang, C. Kirk, Y. Fang, M. Alsina, A. Badros, K. Papadopoulos, A. Wong, T. Woo, D. Bomba, J. Li, J.R. Infante, Clinical pharmacokinetics, metabolism, and drug-drug interaction of carfilzomib, Drug Metab. Dispos. 41 (1) (2013) 230–237.

[47] J. Yang, Z. Wang, Y. Fang, J. Jiang, F. Zhao, H. Wong, M.K. Bennett, C.J. Molineaux, C.J. Kirk, Pharmacokinetics, pharmacodynamics, metabolism, distribution, and excretion of carfilzomib in rats, Drug Metab. Dispos. 39 (2011) 1873–1882.

[48] H. Zhou, M.A. Aujay, M.K. Bennett, M. Dajee, S.D. Demo, Y. Fang, M.N. Ho, J. Jiang, C.J. Kirk, G.J. Laidig, E.R. Lewis, Y. Lu, T. Muchamuel, F. Parlarti, et al., J. Med. Chem. 52 (9) (2009) 3028–3038.

[49] A.Z. Badros, R. Vij, T. Martin, J.A. Zonder, L. Kunkel, Z. Wang, S. Lee, A.F. Wong, R. Niesvizky, Carfilzomib in multiple myeloma patients with renal impairment: pharmacokinetics and safety, Leukemia 27 (8) (2013) 1707–1714.

[50] H. Quach, D. White, A. Spencer, P.J. Ho, D. Bhutani, M. White, S. Inamdar, C. Morris, Y. Ou, M. Gyger, Pharmacokinetics and safety of carfilzomib in patients with relapsed multiple myeloma and end-stage renal disease (ESRD): an open-label, single-arm, Phase I Study Cancer Chemother. Pharmacol. 79 (2017) 1067–1076.

[51] S. Lee, K. Levisky, F. Parlati, M.K. Bennett, S. Kapur, L. Hellerman, T.F. Woo, A.F. Wong, K.P. Papadopoulos, R. Niesvizky, A.Z. Badros, R. Vij, S. Jagannath, D. Siegel, M. Wang, G.J. Ahmann, C.J. Kirk, Clinical activity of carfilzomib correlates with inhibition of multiple proteasome subunits: application of a novel pharmacodynamic assay, Br. J. Hawmatol. 173 (2016) 884–895.

[52] O.A. O'Connor, A.K. Stewart, M. Vallone, C.J. Molineaux, L.A. Kunkel, J.F. Gerecitano, R.Z. Orlowski, A phase 1 dose escalation study of the safety and pharmacokinetics of the novel proteasome inhibitor carfilzomib (PR-171) in patients with hematologic malignancies, Clin. Cancer Res. 15 (22) (2009) 7085–7091.

[53] M. Alsina, S. Trudel, R.R. Furman, et al., A phase I single-agent study of twice weekly consecutive-day dosing of the proteasome inhibitor carfilzomib in patients with relapsed or refractory multiple myeloma or lymphoma, Clin. Cancer Res. 18 (17) (2012) 4830–4840.

[54] J.R. Berenson, A. Cartmell, A. Bessudo, R.M. Lyons, Q. Harb, D. Tzachanis, R. Agajanian, R. Boccia, M. Coleman, R.A. Moss, R.M. Rifkin, P. Patel, S. Dixon, Y. Ou, J. Anderl, S. Aggarwal, J.G. Berdeja, CHAMPION-1, a phase ½ study of once-weekly carfilzomib and dexamethasone for relapsed or refractory multiple myeloma, Blood 127 (36) (2016) 3360–3368.

[55] J.M. Stelow, A perspective on the kinetics of covalent and irreversible inhibition, SLAS Discov. 22 (1) (2017) 3–20.

[56] E. Suzuki, S. Demo, E. Der, J. Keats, S. Kapur, P.L. Bergsagel, M.K. Bennett, C.J. Kirk, PLoS 6 (12) (2011) e27996.

[57] S.K. Radhakrishnan, C.S. Lee, P. Young, A. Beskow, J.Y. Chan, R.J. Deshaies, Mol. Cell 38 (1) (2010) 17–28.

[58] J. Lundgren, P. Masson, Z. Mirzaei, P. Young, Identification and characterization of a Drosophila proteasome regulatory network, Mol. Cell Biol. 25 (2005) 4662–4675.

[59] S. Meiners, D. Heyken, A. Weller, A. Ludwig, K. Stangl, P.M. Kloetzel, E. Kruger, Inhibition of proteasome activity induces concerted expression of proteasome genes and de novo formation of mammalian proteasomes, J. Biol. Chem. 278 (2003) 21517–21525.

[60] N. Mitsiades, C.S. Mitsiades, V. Poulaki, D. Chauhan, G. Fanouerakis, X. Gu, C. Beiley, M. Joseph, T.A. Libermann, S.P. Treon, et al., Molecular sequelae of proteasome inhibition in human multiple myeloma cells, Proc. Natl. Acad. Sci. U.S.A. 99 (2002) 14374–14379.

[61] R.C. Zangar, T.A. Kocarek, S. Shen, N. Bollinger, M.S. Dahn, D.W. Lee, Suppression of cytochrome P450 protein levels by proteasome inhibitors, J. Pharmacol. Exp. Ther. 305 (3) (2003) 872–879.

[62] J. Brown, R. Plummer, T.M. Bauer, S. Anthony, J. Sarantopoulos, F. De Vos, M. White, M. Schupp, Y. Ou, U. Vaishampayan, Pharmacokinetics of carfilzomib in patients with advanced malignances and varying degrees of hepatic impairment: an open-label, single-arm, phase 1 study, Exp. Hematol. Oncol. 6 (27) (2017).

[63] K.P. Papadopoulos, D.S. Siegel, D.H. Vesole, P. Lee, S.T. Rosen, N. Zojwalla, J.R. Holahan, S. Lee, Z. Wang, A. Badros, Phase I study of a 30-minute infusion of carfilzomib as single agent or in combination with low-dose dexamethasone in patients with relapsed and/or refractory multiple myeloma, J. Clin. Oncol. 33 (2015) 732–739.

[64] P. Squifflet, S. Michiels, D.S. Siegel, et al., Multivariate modelling reveals evidence of a dose-response relationship in phase 2 studies of single-agent carfilzomib, ASH Ann. Meet. Abstr. 118 (21) (2011) 1877.

[65] Z. Wang, Y. Fang, J. Teague, H. Wong, C. Morisseau, B.D. Hammock, D.A. Rock, Z. Wang, In vitro metabolism of oprozomib, an oral proteasome inhibitor: role of epoxide hydrolases and cytochrome P450s, Drug Metab. Dispos. 45 (7) (2017) 712–720.

[66] Y. Fang, H. Johnson, J.L. Anderl, T. Muchamuel, D. McMinn, C. Morisseau, B.D. Hammock, C. Kirk, J. Wang, Role of epoxide hydrolases and cytochrome P450s on metabolism of KZR-616, a first-in-class selective inhibitor of the immunoproteasome, Drug Metab. Dispos. 49 (9) (2021) 810–821.

[67] D. Levy, Membrane proteins which exhibit multiple topological orientations, Essays Biochem. 31 (1996) 49–60.

Chapter 19

Engaging diversity in research: does your drug work in overlooked populations?

Karen E. Brown[a,b] and Erica L. Woodahl[a,b]

[a]Department of Biomedical and Pharmaceutical Sciences, University of Montana, Missoula, MT, United States; [b]L.S. Skaggs Institute for Health Innovation, University of Montana, Missoula, MT, United States

Part 1: Awareness

Introduction

Racial and ethnic disparities among clinical trial participants is a long-standing issue demanding attention in the research community as advances in precision medicine increase. This exclusion from clinical trial enrollment has tangible consequences, preventing traditionally underserved populations from benefitting from health innovation and cutting-edge technologies. Further, pharmaceutical companies have historically gained approval to utilize their products at mass despite insufficient testing among participants representative of the target treatment population. Diversity is sorely lacking in both demographic (e.g., age, race, ethnicity, identified gender, geographic location) and non-demographic (e.g., comorbidities, organ dysfunction, weight extremes) factors. A commonality among these groups is they are often underserved and disproportionately affected by high disease burden. Aggregation of these populations into a generalized treatment population lends to the evident healthcare inequities we see today.

Current demographic data from clinical trial participants show a glaring inadequacy of efforts to diversify clinical trial enrollment to represent the diverse global population. The 2020 Drug Trials Snapshot, published by the United States (US) Food and Drug Administration's (FDA) Center for Drug Evaluation and Research, reported alarming statistics for clinical trial participation in newly approved drugs and biologics. Only 8% of all participants were African American, 11% Hispanic, and 6% Asian [1], while these ethnicities make up 12.4%, 18.7%, and 6% of the US population, respectively [2]. Real-world application of clinical trial results derived from studies that are overwhelmingly conducted in European descendant populations may be contributing to the health disparities that we see today and leaving minority-serving providers with data that they cannot feasibly translate to their patients.

Modern drug development is focused on genomics

Recent shifts toward precision medicine are shining a light on glaring underrepresentation in research, potentially leading to missed opportunities and inadequate treatment options. With advances in technology, genetic information forms the biological basis for potential treatment pathways through identification of specific drug targets. Further, the use of pharmacogenetics can inform clinical safety and efficacy parameters in drug development for genetic outliers in drug response and toxicity. Data derived from genomic research within populations of European descent have been utilized for disease risk scoring and drug development, yet translation to diverse ethnic populations is poor. There is a well-established lack of representation in human genome studies, with 96% of genetic study participants between 2000 and 2009 being of European descent and only a small improvement by 2021 of 86% [3,4]. Across all genome-wide association studies (GWAS) as of 2018, 78% of participants were of European descent despite making up only 16% of the global population [5]. The remaining participants were 10% Asian, 2% African, 1% Hispanic, and <1% in all other ethnicities combined. This exclusion creates a disconnect between research results and clinical utilization. The use of polygenic risk scores to predict disease risk is drastically less accurate for diverse populations relative to populations of European ancestry [6].

Overcoming Obstacles in Drug Discovery and Development. https://doi.org/10.1016/B978-0-12-817134-9.00020-9

Racial disparities are evident in every stage of drug development. In preclinical cancer research, the use of cancer cell lines that do not represent appropriate patient populations is evident. A genetic ancestry analysis of 1018 cancer cell lines from the Catalog of Somatic Mutations in Cancer (COSMIC) Cell Lines Project found that only 30% were annotated with ancestry or race information [7]. In the remaining cell lines, the study found 453 were predominately European, 215 East Asian, 30 African, 1 South Asian, and 1 cell line American Indian. In an evaluation of 32 human prostate cell lines available from suppliers ATCC, Sigma Aldrich, and ECACC, 97% were of European descent [8].

Beyond the recent initiatives among pharmaceutical manufacturers to combat this disparity, several key stakeholders in the life sciences field have publicly addressed the issue of inclusivity. In a recent editorial in *The New England Journal of Medicine*, the editors acknowledged this concern, announcing a new requirement for authors of research studies to include the representativeness of the study participants within a supplementary table as of January 1, 2022 [9]. The FDA in recent years has encouraged more patients to participate in clinical trials, with an emphasis on diverse patient populations, noting the evidence for variable response to medical products [10]. While correcting this issue is a complex path that will require efforts across the research ecosystem, there is an ethical responsibility in the industry to develop sustainable infrastructure that ensures equitable healthcare from the start—clinical trial participation.

L.S. Skaggs Institute for Health Innovation at the University of Montana: identifying opportunities to address health inequities through research in rural and underserved Montana

In 2007, Dr. Erica Woodahl returned to her hometown of Missoula, Montana to accept a faculty position at the University of Montana Skaggs School of Pharmacy. Returning after education and training in both the pharmaceutical sciences and humanities strengthened her ability to work with the underserved communities in the state. Her focus gradually shifted from bench research to discovering effective methods to work with the communities in Montana that would largely benefit from clinical and translational research.

Montana is the fourth largest state in the US with just over 1 million people and a population density of 7.8 people per square mile [11]. As a geographically remote state, Montana poses unique challenges in providing healthcare to its widely dispersed population. Each of the 56 counties in the state contain Mental Health and Primary Care Health Professional Shortage Areas (HPSAs) — as designated by the US Health Resources & Services Administration [12]. Further amplifying these resource limitations, health systems in rural areas have traditionally been late to implement health innovation when compared to their metropolitan counterparts. This gap in resource allocation contributes to the higher rates of mortality associated with several chronic disease states that are found in rural areas [13]. These characteristics and the absence of an academic medical center in Montana has created a research-naïve population. Between 2015 and 2019, only 158 participants in clinical trials conducted to support new molecular entities and original biologics were in Montana [14]. Similar participant numbers were found in states with corresponding population profiles, including Alaska (n = 7), North Dakota (n = 102), and Wyoming (n = 0). Throughout the industry, most of Montana is labeled as white space. Yet, as home to 12 American Indian tribes and 7 reservations, the Montana healthcare system supports an often overlooked, racially diverse population.

Part 2: Challenges and barriers to access

Participant access and burden

Improving clinical trial diversity is not a simple task. The costs incurred by a clinical trial sponsor associated with each patient and research site activation are substantial. From a financial standpoint, focusing clinical efforts on large, metropolitan areas may provide important cost-savings during drug development, as only 15% of the US population lives in rural areas, limiting the number of eligible trial participants [15]. Incongruent rates of disease burden and trial participation among diverse populations, however, may lead regulatory agencies to require further post-market studies, a substantial cost consideration.

Clinical trial design of randomized controlled trials, traditionally regarded as the gold standard for research, requires strict key inclusion and exclusion criteria to prove efficacy. These stringent eligibility criteria benefit the study by controlling for the innumerable amount of covariates that are found in real-world patient cases that may affect the statistical validation of the trial. Yet, patients with complex medical profiles will undoubtedly be treated with these medications after regulatory approval is achieved, but without the intensive monitoring included in the clinical trial participation process. Recommendations for performance of secondary effectiveness studies have been proposed to ensure similar results are found in a more representative sample of the treatment population [16].

Participant awareness

Significant facility infrastructure and trial support staff are required to recruit participants. Investigators in nonmetropolitan or minority-serving facilities often practice in already resource-limited and understaffed settings. Socioeconomic constraints among rural and underserved populations often contribute to the inability to access treatment centers that regularly conduct clinical research, leading to a general unawareness or even mistrust in research and the clinical trial process. Under current clinical trial models, researchers are also tasked with overcoming these cultural obstacles, educating populations about the benefits of clinical research and the impact of health innovation on their communities. The disconnect between industry sponsors and the researchers actively interacting with participants, particularly those in rural or underserved communities, is evident and changing this paradigm will require a top-down approach to provide researchers with the tools and support they need for thoughtful community engagement.

Participant perception

Beyond the infrastructural challenges posed, historical and recent unethical research has created a seemingly insurmountable barrier to diversifying research populations. Recently, vaccine reluctance among minority populations in the US amidst the COVID-19 pandemic shined a spotlight on the reality of this disparity [17]. Beyond COVID-19, there are a number of contemporary examples of injustices that have created distrust in researchers and the healthcare system, reaching well beyond the infamous cases of exploitation of African American men in the Tuskegee trials, the Havasupai people—which will be discussed further in this chapter—and the history of Henrietta Lacks [18—20]. Requital for the research injustices that continue to impact racial and ethnic minorities will never be accomplished. Actively excluding these groups from health innovation, however, is leading to critical gaps in care and disparities in health outcomes, for which the tides can still be turned.

L.S. Skaggs Institute for Health Innovation at the University of Montana: overcoming barriers through partnerships

Approximately 25 miles from the University of Montana sits the Flathead Reservation, home to the Confederated Salish and Kootenai Tribes (CSKT), with members and descendants that live in Missoula or regularly travel to the 80,000 population city for healthcare. In the historical context of generational trauma, fear of exploitation, and mistrust of researchers impacting Indigenous peoples, the concept of developing a genomic research partnership with the CSKT was fraught with complexities and barriers, especially given the rural and already resource-limited nature of the area. There were significant concerns for participation in genomics research—cultural, ethical, legal, and social—a justified response from healthcare professionals and researchers who understood the benefits of clinical research and supported the delivery of new health innovations.

Two important cases of unethical genomic research misconduct in Indigenous peoples—the Havasupai in Arizona (US) and Nuu-Chah-Nulth in British Columbia (Canada)—have shaped the views of biomedical research among many Indigenous communities [19,21]. In both cases, members of these tribal communities agreed to take part in genomic studies and later discovered their genetic samples and data had been grossly misused, with results published containing socially and culturally damaging information, without the knowledge or consent of the tribes. Several tribal governments formally condemned the researchers and the violation of tribal communities, with many tribes (e.g., the Navajo Nation) issuing moratoriums on genomic research [22]. A resolution of the National Congress of American Indians in 2005 reaffirmed tribal ownership of health-related data [23]. Legal implications of governance intended to protect the sovereign status of tribal nations may contradict federally-funded research guidelines that require data to be shared for use by other programs. Due to the inappropriate use and exploitation of these communities, negotiations between the research community, funding agencies, and tribal leadership regarding the use of data derived from research with these populations are required.

A collaborative effort with academic research partners in Alaska, Montana, Oregon, and Washington formed the Northwest-Alaska Pharmacogenomics Research Network (NWA-PGRN) [24,25]. The community-academic partnerships involved in the NWA-PGRN include Indigenous communities in Alaska and Montana. Through community-based participatory research (CBPR) practices, researchers in the NWA-PGRN identified unique concerns among their tribal partners and have built long-lasting research partnerships. While collection of the data is aligned with the health priorities of the communities and has been shown to provide important health information, transparency and accountability measures are required to continue to grow this collaboration [26]. One critical component of utilizing these methods is committing to research dissemination throughout the community. Locally, our community partners asked that we publish the results of our studies in the local tribal newspaper and work with our community advisory board to identify other sources for dissemination. A commitment to sharing research results prevents helicopter research, in which researchers are never to be heard from again, leaving participants and communities to wonder what resulted from their time and efforts participating in a study. Research dissemination is also an effective way to build trust in research and gain key-stakeholder buy-in with the broader community, tribal leaders, and local healthcare providers.

When the industry looks for solutions toward engaging research-naïve populations through the lens of researchers in areas lacking substantial biomedical research infrastructure, such as Montana, they'll find key individuals have developed the required roadmaps to overcome barriers in accessing underrepresented communities. Despite the history of misuse and unethical research conduct with Indigenous peoples, the NWA-PGRN community-academic partnerships have successfully overcome many of these barriers [24,25]. Further, by conducting pharmacogenetic research to identify outliers in safety and efficacy of drug treatment, the NWA-PGRN has successfully discovered ways to offer health benefits to their respective community partners. Through the process, we created a valuable opportunity to reframe the benefits of genomic research in an underserved population largely impacted by disproportionate health disparities and a historically negative viewpoint on clinical research reverberating throughout the community.

Part 3: Potential solutions

Development of a comprehensive roadmap

For companies in the beginning stages of these initiatives, concerted effort toward a critical evaluation of diversity within recent clinical trial programs can develop a baseline and help create realistic objectives [27]. Frameworks for promoting diversity in research are available to inform the process [28]. Setting clear ethnic and racial diversity goals in clinical trial programs is critical for success. In a perfect world, readily available epidemiologic and census data would be at the cornerstone of participant enrollment projections in a clinical trial. As demographic data on the diverse global population is readily available, target objectives for this initiative are lofty, yet clear. While various disease states disproportionately impact different populations, available epidemiologic data on real-world disease burden should be utilized to further hone diversity and inclusion goals. Overcoming the significant barrier of increasing diversity in the clinical trial landscape will require systemic changes to current site selection processes, reframing of benefit, and changes to current approaches of participant engagement. Various solutions to address diversity in clinical trial participation have been proposed and piloted among industry players.

New research sites and principal investigators

Many research sites are associated with academic medical centers and metropolitan areas, leaving a large portion of the population without access to clinical trials. Often, engagement of these research centers may be due to relationships with significant key opinion leaders with experience in serving as principal investigators. While utilizing these sites for a study may be appealing to a clinical trial manager or study sponsor, this often means that clinical trials will be repeatedly tapping into the same patient populations. A critical analysis of investigator databases and key opinion leader engagement strategies is required to identify opportunities to utilize community practitioners and minority-serving providers as investigators. Evaluating geographical areas and health systems for which commercial or medical affairs teams have already gained buy-in can identify low-hanging fruit. Physicians at these locations may have a desire to offer their patients new treatment options, take part in the advancement of medical technologies, and diversify their practice's income streams through industry-sponsored research opportunities, but do not know how to begin. Providing career development programs for these medical professionals may prove to be a successful intervention. Pharmaceutical company Bristol-Myers-Squibb (BMS), in partnership with the American Association for Cancer Research (AACR), recently hosted a multi-day virtual workshop intended to provide early-stage investigators with tools to increase the diversity of patient enrollment in clinical trials and a greater understanding of the clinical research process [29]. The workshop was the commencement of a long-term mentorship program for physician participants.

Profit-sharing models

In the age of precision medicine where there is a clear association between utilizing participants' medical information and biological samples to inform drug development—such as with immunomodulatory drugs and targeted gene therapies—financial reciprocity may be a potential pathway for increased diversity in research and community buy-in [22]. These solutions are likely to require extensive work for internal approval, however, reframing benefit in the context of the principles of CBPR and initiating open-minded dialogues may uncover potential for symbiotic relationships.

Hub-spoke partnership models

The development of relationships between a single, large institution with adequate research infrastructure and several community-based researchers with access to traditionally overlooked populations can provide a sustainable and complementary system to diversify clinical research populations. Several partnerships announced in recent years that follow this hub-and-spoke model aim to address the unique needs of various underrepresented and underserved populations. Stakeholders and agencies in cancer treatment and drug development have led the charge. Examples of unique models that are actively beginning implementation are discussed here.

In the summer of 2021, the Association of Community Cancer Centers (ACCC) launched the ACCC Community Oncology Research Institute (ACORI) after evaluating the lack of access to clinical trials in oncology community settings [30]. The Institute developed three primary domains involving advocacy for equity and inclusion, building capacity among community research settings, and diffusing clinical trial opportunities to these research programs.

Also in 2021, the Leukemia & Lymphoma Society (LLS) launched the Influential Medicine Providing Access to Clinical Trials (IMPACT) grant-funding program, partially supported by drug maker BMS [31]. This program aims to address the issue of diversity and inclusion by funding infrastructure diffusion at the Mayo Clinic, Vanderbilt University Medical Center, and Weill Cornell Medicine to their respective affiliates in smaller healthcare settings providing care to rural and underserved populations. The program has set a five-year initiative to increase trial enrollment within underrepresented communities to at least 20%.

In June of 2021, pharmaceutical manufacturer Genentech announced a major step in their 2025 Diversity and Inclusion Commitments strategy through the development of the Advancing Inclusive Research Site Alliance, an integration of founding partner sites in California, Texas, Alabama, and Tennessee [32]. The focus of this site integration is to enable the participation of underrepresented patient groups in oncology trials. The sites have a trusted track-record of success in clinical trial execution and are located in areas of higher populations of Black and Hispanic patients.

In 2018, the NIH's National Cancer Institute (NCI) collaborated with the Department of Veterans Affairs (VA) to develop the NCI and VA Interagency Group to Accelerate Trials Enrollment (NAVIGATE) program [33]. These large agencies work together to provide the necessary infrastructure required to execute externally-funded research programs, taking some of the clinical trial lift off the shoulders of the resource-limited local VA facilities. The program aims to increase enrollment of veterans with cancer into clinical trials.

The dynamic clinical trial landscape is in a phase of rapid evolution, and it is evident that beyond the deployment of novel technologies and regulatory guidance, there is a humanistic approach that manufacturers can and should utilize to addressing the lack of diversity in research. These partnerships may demonstrate success in improving participant enrollment and initiating research in diverse practice settings. The impact of these methods on improving clinical trial diversity will require future evaluation.

L.S. Skaggs Institute for Health Innovation at the University of Montana: facilitating research with traditionally overlooked populations

In the L.S. Skaggs Institute for Health Innovation case we present here, research partners in the NWA-PGRN that include the University of Montana, University of Washington, and Oregon Health & Science University support boots-on-the-ground efforts of partners in underserved communities in Alaska and Montana through collaborative community-engaged discussions and provision of critical lab infrastructure, such as biorepository storage and genomic sequencing, to support pharmacogenetic and precision medicine research [25].

Academia fosters collaborative, community-based, interdisciplinary efforts, and creates supportive working environments for future professionals that will continue to impact the next generation of researchers entering the industry. Engaging out-of-the-box partnerships can provide a unique perspective to drug makers actively seeking solutions for inclusivity in research. While the pharmaceutical industry is innovation-focused and efficiency-driven, the demands of the scientific clock are also felt among academia. Yet it takes time to foster community relationships and understand the unique barriers and facilitators for conducting research. Conversely, when we put on our ethical hats, slowing delivery of innovative technologies also comes at a cost that goes beyond a pharmaceutical company's bottom line. Health innovation opens the door to necessary improvements in patient care and at times even life-saving technologies. Partnerships can decrease change management timelines and provide novel treatments to underserved communities. Here we further describe the timeline and efforts made for the development of a community-academic research partnership.

Researchers at the University of Montana have a long history of partnering with rural and tribal populations. Our work began from conversations with healthcare providers located on the Flathead Reservation in the CSKT Tribal Health Department [25]. Developing these relationships improved local buy-in and allowed for important introductions and understanding of local processes and priorities. We presented to the CSKT Tribal Council on several occasions to gain tribal approval for our research. One of our first steps was establishing a community advisory board—the Community Pharmacogenetics Advisory Council (CPAC)—to provide an avenue for ongoing dialogue and relationship-building [34]. Prior to the COVID-19 pandemic, monthly in-person meetings were conducted with our advisory group where community members and researchers shared dinner, discussed research priorities, and were able to build trust for research. Since the start of the pandemic, these meetings have transitioned to virtual calls, however, engagement by community advisors has remained high and demonstrates the value of these methods, which offer insights on healthcare priorities, potential areas of research, and culturally-appropriate recruitment practices. The timeline from initial conversations with CSKT leadership about pharmacogenetics research to the publication of the first paper was 6 years [35]. This extended timeline helped develop a strong foundation of trust for our ongoing relationship with the CKST.

Utilizing constructs from the humanities and principles of CBPR, the partnership described here was developed as one of reciprocity and bidirectional learning [36]. This approach led to significant community buy-in and a symbiotic relationship in which the community and researchers are equal stakeholders, collectively providing input on the design and implementation of the program. Working directly with tribal partners strengthened and sustained a 15-year relationship that continues today.

Part 4: Impact

Concerted efforts to increase diversity in the COVID-19 vaccine studies

In the summer of 2020, amidst the COVID-19 pandemic and multi-stakeholder push for safe and effective vaccine development, there was significant vaccine hesitancy among racial and ethnic minority communities [37]. In one study, for example, researchers surveyed 1205 Arkansas adults in July and August of 2020 to evaluate COVID-19 vaccine hesitancy, selecting unlikely or very unlikely when asked if they would receive the COVID-19 vaccine. Among Black or African American populations, 50% of respondents showed hesitancy toward receiving the COVID-19 vaccine, compared to 18.37% of white respondents. Concerted efforts to include traditionally overlooked populations in clinical research ensures representation among these communities. Notably, on September 4, 2020, pharmaceutical manufacturer Moderna announced their intentions to slow enrollment in the Phase 3 study of their vaccine candidate to address the evident lack of diversity among trial participants—of whom only 24% were nonwhite—directing their research sites to focus on participation of minority volunteers [38]. This conscious decision led to a final participant pool of which 10.2% were Black or African American and 20.5% were Hispanic or Latino [39]. Pfizer had similar diversity results for their vaccine candidate studies [40]. The diversity in these studies stands in stark contrast to recent US-based vaccine studies, for which 78% of participants were white between 2011 and 2020 [41].

Opportunities in drug development stem from diversifying clinical trial populations

There is no more relevant example than the explosion of pharmacogenomic research to show that increasing engagement of diverse populations in clinical research is possible. In efforts to adequately capture biogeographic diversity, various consortia have deliberately focused on engaging non-European populations to characterize differences in genomic variation leading to variable drug response. Recent advancements in genomic medicine have allowed researchers to re-examine views on race and the use of race in research and healthcare, leaving an impact on the ways in which we approach clinical treatment [42,43]. Pharmacogenomics enables a departure from problematic race-based treatment guidelines. While self-reported race can correlate to ancestral origin and remains useful in capturing subjective information related to identity, population diversity is rapidly evolving. In the US, 2020 Census data, "Some Other Race alone or in combination" is the second-largest race group, increasing 129% from 2010 [44]. The dynamic landscape of racial categorization warrants a new approach in drug development—one that requires assessment of drug therapy in groups of diverse ancestry to allow for the necessary shifts we describe here in racial categorization.

L.S. Skaggs Institute for Health Innovation at the University of Montana: research results from a long-term commitment to relationship building

Like many minority populations disproportionately impacted by chronic disease states, Indigenous populations suffer from higher rates of diabetes, cardiovascular disease, and many cancers [45,46]. The science generated from our community-academic partnership described in this chapter is both incredibly innovative and desperately needed. Considering the novelty of pharmacogenomic research in the area, there was limited understanding of the importance of genetic variation in drug response. We sequenced genes responsible for coding cytochrome p450 enzymes and published the first paper in a tribal community in the US about genetic variation that leads to differences in drug response [35]. Through the collaboration of researchers in the NWA-PGRN, several additional studies have been completed and are underway to characterize genetic variation influencing drug disposition and response among Indigenous populations.

Our emphasis on community engagement and input proved valuable, and opportunities for mutually beneficial research began to emerge. One of the first community priorities that came to light involved a focus on anticancer agents and their utility in the CSKT populations [35]. Providers serving this group shared anecdotal results of patients not responding to traditional anticancer treatments and further discussions affirmed that cancer research was a community priority [34,47]. We conducted a pharmacogenetic study focused on the use of tamoxifen, a selective estrogen receptor modulator often used to reduce the risk of recurrence of breast cancer, in American Indian and Alaskan Native population [48]. As a prodrug requiring bioactivation to its active metabolite endoxifen via cytochrome P450 (CYP) drug-metabolizing enzymes—primarily medicated by CYP2D6—recommendations from worldwide resources have been published to avoid the use of tamoxifen in patients with *CYP2D6* genetic variation conferring intermediate or poor metabolizer status [49]. For participants in the CSKT population, 40% were found to be either CYP2D6 intermediate or poor metabolizers, 34% and 6% respectively. This decreased activity was associated with considerably lower concentrations of endoxifen, leading to an increased risk of cancer recurrence.

In our continued efforts to conduct research that can better inform the development of pharmacogenetic testing platforms for diverse populations, we used a candidate gene approach and identified a unique linkage disequilibrium pattern in the *CYP3A4* and *CYP3A5* genes among the CSKT population, with respect to the *CYP3A4*1G* allele [35]. We recently published our work characterizing the *CYP3A4*1G* allele and found a predicted increase in function, leading to higher metabolic activity, which was found at a frequency of 26.8% in the CSKT [50]. The Pharmacogene Variation Consortium (PharmVar) has assigned an official designation to the *CYP3A4*1G* star allele, which may pave the way for future incorporation into clinical guidelines [51,52]. Another significant finding produced through NWA-PGRN tribal partnerships was the identification of a novel variant in *CYP2C9* in the Yup'ik people of southwest Alaska leading to a Met1Leu (M1L) amino acid change [53,54]. The variant was relatively common in this population, with a minor allele frequency of 6.3%, more prevalent than the frequency of several well-defined alleles in the general population. This novel variant was predicted to be functionally disruptive, significantly slowing or stopping translation, and associated with CYP2C9 poor metabolizer status. These findings have a significant clinical impact. For example, several drugs spanning various therapeutic areas, including warfarin, phenytoin and many nonsteroidal anti-inflammatory drugs are predominantly metabolized by CYP2C9 [55–57]. Published pharmacogenetic guidelines for these medications commonly recommend significant decreases in dose or choosing an alternative agent in CYP2C9 poor metabolizers. For pharmacogenetic testing platforms that do not include the M1L variant, carriers are wrongly denoted as normal metabolizers by default, potentially leading to unoptimized drug treatment or adverse events. Significant improvements in diversifying clinical trial populations have yet to been seen, however, these findings represent the impact that a shift in this paradigm can have on the fields of clinical research and healthcare. The unique value added to the scientific literature base by our long-standing partnership described here is only one example of the vast potential for biomedical advances.

Part 5: Future directions

Aggregating needs and barriers among all minority and underserved populations is an unrealistic approach to improving inclusivity in clinical trials. There are many different cultural, geographical and socioeconomic factors that influence a community's decision to participate in clinical research. Engagement should always be initiated with open dialogues and respectful acknowledgment of another culture.

Several approaches have been attempted to address the issue of engaging diverse patient populations in clinical research with varying success. For far too long, processes in drug development have excluded overlooked populations from clinical research and health innovation, prioritizing speed over accuracy. Concerted efforts to engage underrepresented communities is required, yet time comes at a cost. The breadth of knowledge that has been developed over decades of fostering critical partnerships in some of the most challenging locations can be utilized and the principals of community-based participatory research should guide the process.

The community-academic partnership outlined in this chapter is one example of a successful collaboration that has been replicated through similar models in other Indigenous communities, however, as each unique community requires a custom approach tailored to varying cultures and values, the specific facilitators uncovered in this partnership do not directly translate to all minority communities, tribal or non-tribal, yet the methods we utilized to build sustainable and long-term relationships with targeted populations can be found across the globe. Expertize and strategic guidance for the engagement of diverse populations is likely to be found in unsuspecting places. Identification and investment into industry-sponsored partnerships with universities, community-based health systems, or other similar organizations that have existing relationships is a potentially scalable and ubiquitous solution. Intentional collaborations with organizations that can share benefit and bring informed perspectives to resolving the issue of diversifying clinical research participation are both a time and cost-saving approach.

L.S. Skaggs Institute for Health Innovation at the University of Montana: critical insights and new developments

In 2020, we launched the L.S. Skaggs Institute for Health Innovation (SIHI) at the University of Montana to improve access to emerging health innovations for rural and underserved communities in Montana [58]. The mission of SIHI is to be a statewide hub for health education, research, and outreach. Building upon the successful integration of research and clinical services in rural populations through existing University of Montana programs—namely the Precision Medicine Project, Improving Health Among Rural Montanans, and the Medication Therapy Management Center—SIHI is poized to serve as a global resource for rural and tribal community engagement.

Our pre-implementation efforts to understand effective strategies for the deployment of innovative clinical services have uncovered barriers that run parallel to the implementation of clinical research in diverse practice settings [36,47]. As a pillar of precision medicine, pharmacogenomics is one example of a health innovation ready for implementation. Implementation of pharmacogenomics into clinical practice has been troublingly uneven, with rural and minority communities left almost entirely behind. As with many examples of health innovation, disparities may continue to worsen under current models of care. Through SIHI, clinical and research expertize in pharmacogenomics can be accessed even amongst resource-limited communities. SIHI is poized to be the first in the US to implement pharmacogenetic testing in rural and tribal populations. Pharmacogenomics consultation will be integrated into clinical services in SIHI and offered statewide to healthcare professionals and patients via telehealth and virtual access. As the first to launch precision medicine implementation in these settings, SIHI will be a model for the country and will engage with partners both within and outside of Montana. Remaining true to their mission, SIHI continues to prioritize the development of programs that will support expansion of health innovation to often overlooked populations.

Part 6: Conclusions

Several barriers exist impeding access to diverse clinical trial populations. A concerted effort to develop processes for clinical trial site activation beyond metropolitan areas, to community practice settings and minority-serving physicians is required. When we critically evaluate the current models of the trial enrollment process, there are evident systemic missteps requiring correction. These issues were put on display during the COVID-19 pandemic. Now more than ever, the public is aware of the clinical trial process. Our hope is that this moment in drug development is not remembered as a missed opportunity. After years of efforts to bring health innovation to underserved communities and the groundwork completed by the pharmacogenomics community to improve translational research, the clinical research landscape is primed for disruption. Talented, emerging key opinion leaders practice in resource-limited areas every day and leading researchers continue their efforts toward improving the biomedical and healthcare infrastructure within their communities. Recreating the wheel isn't the answer, but awareness and open-ended dialogues with these key stakeholders is long overdue.

References

[1] FDA, 2020 Drug Trials Snapshot, 2021. Available from: https://www.fda.gov/drugs/drug-approvals-and-databases/drug-trials-snapshots. (Accessed 16 December 2021).

[2] N. Jones, R. Marks, R. Ramirez, M. Rios-Vargas. 2020 Census Illuminates Racial and Ethnic Composition of the Country. Available from: https://www.census.gov/library/stories/2021/08/improved-race-ethnicity-measures-reveal-united-states-population-much-more-multiracial.html. (Accessed 12 January 2021).

[3] A.B. Popejoy, S.M. Fullerton, Genomics is failing on diversity, Nature (London) 538 (2016) 161−164, https://doi.org/10.1038/538161a.

[4] S. Fatumo, T. Chikowore, A. Choudhury, M. Ayub, A.R. Martin, K. Kuchenbaecker, A roadmap to increase diversity in genomic studies, Nat. Med. 28 (2022) 243−250, https://doi.org/10.1038/s41591-021-01672-4.

[5] G. Sirugo, S.M. Williams, S.A. Tishkoff, The missing diversity in human genetic studies, Cell 177 (2019) 26−31, https://doi.org/10.1016/j.cell.2019.02.048.

[6] A.R. Martin, M. Kanai, Y. Kamatani, Y. Okada, B.M. Neale, M.J. Daly, Clinical use of current polygenic risk scores may exacerbate health disparities, Nat Genet. Springer Sci Bus Media LLC 51 (2019) 584–591, https://doi.org/10.1038/s41588-019-0379-x.

[7] M.D. Kessler, N.W. Bateman, T.P. Conrads, G.L. Maxwell, J.C. Dunning Hotopp, T.D. O'connor, Ancestral characterization of 1018 cancer cell lines highlights disparities and reveals gene expression and mutational differences, Cancer 125 (2019) 2076–2088, https://doi.org/10.1002/cncr.32020.

[8] S. Badal, K.S. Campbell, H. Valentine, C. Ragin, The need for cell lines from diverse ethnic backgrounds for prostate cancer research, Nat. Rev. Urol. 16 (2019) 691–692, https://doi.org/10.1038/s41585-019-0234-y.

[9] Striving for diversity in research studies. N. Engl. J. Med. 385 (2021) 1429–1430. doi:10.1056/NEJMe2114651.

[10] U.S. Food & Drug Administration, FDA Encourages More Participation, Diversity in Clinical Trials, n.d. Available from: https://www.fda.gov/consumers/consumer-updates/fda-encourages-more-participation-diversity-clinical-trials. (Accessed 16 December 2021.).

[11] US Census Bureau Montana QuickFacts. Available from: https://www.census.gov/quickfacts/MT. (Accessed 29 March 2022).

[12] HPSA Find. Available from: https://data.hrsa.gov/tools/shortage-area/hpsa-find. (Accessed 29 March 2022).

[13] S.C. Curtin, M.R. Spencer, Trends in Death Rates in Urban and Rural Areas: United States, 1999–2019. NCHS Data Brief, National Center for Health Statistics, Hyattsville, MD, 2021, pp. 1–8. Available from: https://stacks.cdc.gov/view/cdc/109049. (Accessed 5 April 2022).

[14] 2015–2019 Drug Trial Snapshots Summary Report Five-Year Summary and Analysis of Clinical Trial Participation and Demographics Contents, FDA, 2020. Available from: https://www.fda.gov/drugs/drug-approvals-and-databases/drug-trials-snapshots. (Accessed 16 December 2021).

[15] Rural Health. Available from: https://www.cdc.gov/ruralhealth/about.html. (Accessed 16 December 2021).

[16] L.M. Minasian, J.M. Unger, What keeps patients out of clinical trials? JCO Oncol Pract. 16 (2020) 125–127, https://doi.org/10.1200/JOP.19.00735.

[17] T. Beleche, J. Ruhter, A. Kolbe, J. Marus, L. Bush, B. Sommers, COVID-19 Vaccine Hesitancy: Demographic Factors, Geographic Patterns, and Changes over Time. Office of the Assistant Secretary for Planning and Evaluation, U.S. Department of Health and Human Services, 2021. Available from: https://www.census.gov/library/stories/2021/12/who-are-the-adults-not-vaccinated-against-covid.html. (Accessed 29 March 2022).

[18] The U.S. Public Health Service Syphilis Study at Tuskegee. Available from: https://www.cdc.gov/tuskegee/timeline.htm. (Accessed 29 March 2022).

[19] J. Bommersbach, Arizona's Broken Arrow: Did Arizona State University Genetically Rape the Havasupai Tribe? Phoenix Magazine, 2008, pp. 134–144. Available from: https://janabommersbach.com/arizonas-broken-arrow-did-arizona-state-university-genetically-rape-the-havasupai-tribe/. (Accessed 29 March 2022).

[20] The Legacy of Henrietta Lacks. Available from: https://www.hopkinsmedicine.org/henriettalacks/. (Accessed 29 March 2022).

[21] D. Wiwchar, Genetic Researcher Uses Nuu-Chah-Nulth Blood for Unapproved Studies in Genetic Anthropology, Ha-Shilth-Sa Canada's Oldest First Nation's Newspaper, July 22, 2013. Available from: https://www.hashilthsa.com/news/2013-07-22/genetic-researcher-uses-nuu-chah-nulth-blood-unapproved-studies-genetic. (Accessed 16 December 2021).

[22] R. James, R. Tsosie, P. Sahota, et al., Exploring pathways to trust: a tribal perspective on data sharing, Genet. Med. 16 (2014) 820–826, https://doi.org/10.1038/gim.2014.47.

[23] National Congress of American Indians, Resolution #TUL-05–059: Tribal Ownership of Health-Related Data. Available from: https://www.ncai.org/resources/resolutions/tribal-ownership-of-health-related-data. (Accessed 16 December 2021)

[24] B. Boyer, D. Dillard, E. Woodahl, R. Whitener, K. Thummel, W. Burke, Ethical issues in developing pharmacogenetic research partnerships with American Indigenous communities, Clin. Pharmacol. Therapeut. 89 (2011) 343–345, https://doi.org/10.1038/clpt.2010.303.

[25] E.L. Woodahl, L.J. Lesko, S. Hopkins, R.F. Robinson, K.E. Thummel, W. Burke, Pharmacogenetic research in partnership with American Indian and Alaska Native communities, Pharmacogenomics 15 (2014) 1235–1241, https://doi.org/10.2217/pgs.14.91.

[26] S.B. Trinidad, E. Blacksher, R.B. Woodbury, et al., Precision medicine research with American Indian and Alaska Native communities: results of a deliberative engagement with tribal leaders, Genet. Med. 24 (2021) 622–630, https://doi.org/10.1016/j.gim.2021.11.003.

[27] M. Rottas, P. Thadeio, R. Simons, et al., Demographic diversity of participants in Pfizer sponsored clinical trials in the United States, Contemp. Clin. Trials 106 (2021) 106421, https://doi.org/10.1016/j.cct.2021.106421.

[28] T.R. Rebbeck, J.F.P. Bridges, J.W. Mack, et al., A framework for promoting diversity, equity, and inclusion in genetics and genomics research, JAMA Health Forum 3 (2022) e220603, https://doi.org/10.1001/jamahealthforum.2022.0603.

[29] American Association for Cancer Research, AACR to Partner with the Bristol-Myers-Squibb Foundation on its Diversity in Clinical Trials Career Development Program, May 19, 2021. Available from: https://www.aacr.org/about-the-aacr/newsroom/news-releases/aacr-to-partner-with-the-bristol-myers-squibb-foundation-on-its-diversity-in-clinical-trials-career-development-program/. (Accessed 16 December 2021).

[30] Association of Community Cancer Centers News Release, Association of Community Cancer Centers Launches Institute to Diversify Cancer Clinical Trials, June 2, 2021. Available from: https://www.accc-cancer.org/home/news-media/news-releases/news-template/2021/06/04/association-of-community-cancer-centers-launches-institute-to-diversify-cancer-clinical-trials. (Accessed 16 December 2021).

[31] CISION PR Newswire, The Leukemia & Lymphoma Society Launches IMPACT Research Grants to Help Underserved Patients Access Clinical Trials, May 6, 2021. Available from: https://www.prnewswire.com/news-releases/the-leukemia—lymphoma-society-launches-impact-research-grants-to-help-underserved-patients-access-clinical-trials-301285367.html. (Accessed 16 December 2021).

[32] Genentech Media, Genentech Launches Oncology Clinical Trial Diversity Alliance, June 23, 2021. Available from: https://www.gene.com/media/statements/ps_062321. (Accessed 16 December 2021).

[33] National Cancer Institute, NCI and VA Collaborate to Boost Veterans' Access to Cancer Clinical Trials, July 10, 2018. Available from: https://www.cancer.gov/news-events/press-releases/2018/navigate-va-clinical-trials. (Accessed 16 December 2021).

[34] C.T. Morales, L.I. Muzquiz, K. Howlett, et al., Partnership with the confederated Salish and Kootenai tribes: establishing an advisory committee for pharmacogenetic research, Prog. Commun. Health Partnersh. 10 (2016) 173−183, https://doi.org/10.1353/cpr.2016.0035.

[35] A. Fohner, L. Muzquiz, M. Austin, et al., Pharmacogenetics in American Indian populations: analysis of CYP2D6, CYP3A4, CYP3A5, and CYP2C9 in the confederated Salish and Kootenai tribes, Pharmacogenetics Genom. 23 (2013) 403−414, https://doi.org/10.1097/FPC.0b013e3283629ce9.

[36] A.E. Fohner, K.G. Volk, E.L. Woodahl, Democratizing precision medicine through community engagement, Clin. Pharmacol. Therapeut. 106 (2019) 488−490, https://doi.org/10.1002/cpt.1508.

[37] D.E. Willis, J.A. Andersen, K. Bryant-Moore, et al., COVID-19 vaccine hesitancy: race/ethnicity, trust, and fear, Clin. Transl. Sci. 14 (2021) 2200−2207, https://doi.org/10.1111/cts.13077.

[38] M. Tirrell, L. Miller, Moderna Slows Coronavirus Vaccine Trial Enrollment to Ensure Minority Representation, CEO Says, CNBC Health and Science, September 4, 2021. Available from: https://www.cnbc.com/2020/09/04/moderna-slows-coronavirus-vaccine-trial-t-to-ensure-minority-representation-ceo-says.html. (Accessed 29 March 2022).

[39] L.R. Baden, H.M. El Sahly, B. Essink, et al., Efficacy and safety of the mRNA-1273 SARS-CoV-2 vaccine, N. Engl. J. Med. 384 (2021) 403−416, https://doi.org/10.1056/NEJMoa2035389.

[40] F.P. Polack, S.J. Thomas, N. Kitchin, et al., Safety and efficacy of the BNT162b2 mRNA covid-19 vaccine, N. Engl. J. Med. 383 (2020) 2603−2615, https://doi.org/10.1056/NEJMoa2034577.

[41] L.E. Flores, W.R. Frontera, M.P. Andrasik, et al., Assessment of the inclusion of racial/ethnic minority, female, and older individuals in vaccine clinical trials, JAMA Netw. Open 4 (2021) e2037640, https://doi.org/10.1001/jamanetworkopen.2020.37640.

[42] B.H. Davis, N.A. Limdi, Translational pharmacogenomics: discovery, evidence synthesis and delivery of race-conscious medicine, Clin. Pharmacol. Therapeut. 110 (2021) 909−925, https://doi.org/10.1002/cpt.2357.

[43] A.C.F. Lewis, S.J. Molina, P.S. Appelbaum, et al., Getting genetic ancestry right for science and society, Science (Am. Assoc. Adv. Sci.) 376 (2022) 250−252, https://doi.org/10.1126/science.abm7530.

[44] Y. Roman, The United States 2020 census data: implications for precision medicine and the research landscape, Pers. Med. 19 (2021) 5−8, https://doi.org/10.2217/pme-2021-0129.

[45] Indian Health Disparities. Available from: https://www.ihs.gov/newsroom/factsheets/disparities/. (Accessed 29 March 2022).

[46] E. Arlas, J. Xu, S. Curtin, B. Bastian, B. Tejada-Vera, Mortality profile of the non-Hispanic American Indian or Alaska native population, 2019, 70, US Department of Health and Human Services National Center for Health Statistics. National Vital Statistics Reports, 2021 Available from: https://www.cdc.gov/nchs/fastats/american-indian-health.htm. (Accessed 29 March 2022) 12.

[47] E.H. Dorfman, S. Brown Trinidad, C.T. Morales, K. Howlett, W. Burke, E.L. Woodahl, Pharmacogenomics in diverse practice settings: implementation beyond major metropolitan areas, Pharmacogenomics 16 (2015) 227−237, https://doi.org/10.2217/pgs.14.174.

[48] B.A. Khan, R. Robinson, A.E. Fohner, et al., Cytochrome P450 genetic variation associated with tamoxifen biotransformation in American Indian and Alaska Native people, Clin. Transl. Sci. 11 (2018) 312−321, https://doi.org/10.1111/cts.12542.

[49] M.P. Goetz, K. Sangkuhl, H. Guchelaar, et al., Clinical pharmacogenetics implementation Consortium (CPIC) guideline for CYP2D6 and tamoxifen therapy, Clin. Pharmacol. Ther. 103 (2018) 770−777, https://doi.org/10.1002/cpt.1007.

[50] A.E. Fohner, R. Dalton, K. Skagen, et al., Characterization of CYP3A pharmacogenetic variation in American Indian and Alaska Native communities, targeting CYP3A41G allele function, Clin. Transl. Sci. 14 (2021) 1292−1302, https://doi.org/10.1111/cts.12970.

[51] A. Gaedigk, M. Ingelman-Sundberg, N.A. Miller, J.S. Leeder, M. Whirl-Carrillo, T.E. Klein, The pharmacogene variation (PharmVar) consortium: incorporation of the human cytochrome P450 (CYP) allele nomenclature database, Clin. Pharmacol. Therapeut. 103 (2018) 399−401, https://doi.org/10.1002/cpt.910.

[52] A. Gaedigk, K. Sangkuhl, M. Whirl-Carrillo, G.P. Twist, T.E. Klein, N.A. Miller, The evolution of PharmVar, Clin. Pharmacol. Ther. 105 (2019) 29−32, https://doi.org/10.1002/cpt.1275.

[53] A. Fohner, R. Robinson, J. Yracheta, et al., Variation in genes controlling warfarin disposition and response in American Indian and Alaska Native people: CYP2C9, VKORC1, CYP4F2, CYP4F11, GGCX, Pharmacogenetics Genom. 25 (2015) 343−353, https://doi.org/10.1097/FPC.0000000000000143.

[54] L.M. Henderson, S.E. Hopkins, B.B. Boyer, T.A. Thornton, A.E. Rettie, K.E. Thummel, In vivo functional effects of *CYP2C9* M1L, a novel and common variant in the Yup'Ik Alaska Native population, Drug Metabol. Dispos. 49 (2021) 345−352, https://doi.org/10.1124/dmd.120.000301.

[55] J.A. Johnson, K.E. Caudle, L. Gong, et al., Clinical pharmacogenetics implementation consortium (CPIC) guideline for pharmacogenetics-guided warfarin dosing: 2017 update, Clin. Pharmacol. Ther. 102 (2017) 397−404, https://doi.org/10.1002/cpt.668.

[56] J.H. Karnes, A.E. Rettie, A.A. Somogyi, et al., Clinical Pharmacogenetics Implementation Consortium (CPIC) guideline for CYP2C9 and HLA-B genotypes and phenytoin dosing: 2020 update, Clin. Pharmacol. Ther. 109 (2021) 302−309, https://doi.org/10.1002/cpt.2008.

[57] K.N. Theken, C.R. Lee, L. Gong, et al., Clinical Pharmacogenetics Implementation Consortium guideline (CPIC) for CYP2C9 and nonsteroidal anti-inflammatory drugs, Clin. Pharmacol. Ther. 108 (2020) 191−200, https://doi.org/10.1002/cpt.1830.

[58] C. Evans, UM Creates New L.S. Skaggs Institute for Health Innovation, Missoulian, March 27, 2021. Available from: https://missoulian.com/news/local/um-creates-new-l-s-skaggs-institute-for-health-innovation/article_89b2bb20-3bb0-5ff7-be77-fcfd8d20bcb7.html. (Accessed 16 December 2021).

Chapter 20

PBPK modeling for early clinical study decision making

Arian Emami Riedmaier

PBPK Consultancy, Certara, Princeton, NJ, United States

Introduction

We are in an exciting era in drug discovery and development where novel targets and complex diseases have introduced a unique druggable space and opportunities for multi-specific medicines. In the past decade, research has moved toward more hard-to-treat diseases and the tolerance for safety and drug interaction risks has been significantly reduced, especially for indications where safe drugs are already on the market. Similarly, there is an expectation in the current landscape to be well-informed about the potential risks associated with developing a given drug prior to the initiation of first-in-human (FIH) studies, leaving little room for late-stage surprises. This has opened the door to novel opportunities for the application of model-informed drug development (MIDD) [1−3]. Regardless of the stage of drug development, a mechanistic approach can help to identify and evaluate risks associated with bringing a compound to the market, and if identified early in drug development, determine the key experiments that will provide crucial insights at later stages. One of the key elements of the MIDD handbook in drug discovery and development is physiologically based pharmacokinetic (PBPK) modeling. This chapter will focus on current applications of PBPK modeling, and the data required to answer critical questions at different stages of drug development. It will also highlight the challenges faced by PBPK modeling, and opportunities for expanding modeling capabilities in the upcoming years.

The concept of mechanistic PBPK modeling is not new. In the summer of 1937, Torsten Teorell, who is often referred to as the father of pharmacokinetics, submitted two scientific papers, which introduced the idea of deriving general mathematical relationships to describe the kinetics of distribution of substances in the human body [4]. Despite its early beginnings, the application of PBPK modeling within the pharmaceutical industry has been limited until more recently. This has, in part, been due to advances in computational power, but more importantly, due to the advancement in our understanding of *in vitro* to *in vivo* translation (IVIVE), thanks to the increasing availability of *in vitro* and *in silico* methods that have served as surrogates for *in vivo* absorption, distribution, metabolism, and excretion (ADME) processes [5−13]. A PBPK model is a mathematical representation that integrates drug data, as well as "systems" data related to the system being studied (i.e., data on species physiology and anatomy) to simulate the pharmacokinetic (PK) profile of a drug in plasma and all tissues [6,14]. System parameters include tissue volume, blood flow, microsomal protein, or hepatocyte count per gram of liver tissue, enzyme and transporter abundance, and glomerular filtration rate. Furthermore, physiological, and anatomical parameters specific to different human populations, such as variability and covariate relationships between these parameters, can be simulated. Populations can include healthy adults, pediatrics, smokers, obese, hepatic, and renal impaired, and more recently, cancer patients [6,7,15−19].

PBPK modeling in the context of MIDD

In its simplest form, a PBPK model is a compartmental model where each compartment is defined by a volume, blood flow rate, and tissue composition. These compartments are connected through assumptions that define tissue distribution and elimination, with the simplest models assuming a perfusion-rate limited distribution. PBPK modeling takes advantage of a "bottom-up" approach where compound-specific parameters are estimated based on *in vitro* data and sometimes, *in silico*

Overcoming Obstacles in Drug Discovery and Development. https://doi.org/10.1016/B978-0-12-817134-9.00014-3

methods, and used to predict *in vivo* PK in preclinical species and humans using an established relationship between these parameters, known as an IVIVE scalar [3,13,14,20]. This is in contrast to the complementary and more traditional approach of compartmental PK modeling that involves fitting to preclinical or clinical data using a direct mathematical relationship to allow identification of covariates that explain the variability in drug exposures [20].

PBPK and traditional compartmental modeling approaches serve different purposes in answering questions that may arise throughout the drug development process. Traditional compartmental models require less data and can be used to derive primary parameters where observed PK profiles are available. On the other hand, in cases where we expect mechanistic differences across species that drive the PK profile, PBPK models may be more representative. This general principle applies to both small and large molecules. In the case of antibody-drug conjugates (ADCs), the high affinity interaction with the target molecule can often manifest in non-linear PK, which is not well represented using traditional inter-species scaling approaches, but rather, requires a more mechanistic method [21,22]. In addition, PBPK models provide a holistic picture of all available mechanistic knowledge around a given molecule, which allows one to perform sensitivity analyses and hypothesis testing around various mechanisms as a compound moves from discovery to development [7,11,14,23]. The potential for performing iterative hypothesis testing that enables decision-making is what truly sets PBPK models apart from more traditional approaches, making PBPK a leading platform for identifying risks early and guiding study design throughout the drug discovery and development process.

Key criteria for a successful PBPK model

PBPK model building is centered around the systems pharmacology paradigm where physiological and anatomical data are utilized to parametrize the "system" or "population" component of the model and *in vitro* and *in silico* data are used to describe the ADME parameters for the drug of interest [6,16]. The ADME mechanisms are linked together using IVIVE scaling that has been ideally verified via a set of well understood reference compounds. Once a base model is built, it can be used to predict *in vivo* PK in preclinical species and humans. It is important at this stage to verify the model using available *in vivo* data [2,5,24–26]. Depending on the stage of drug development, only preclinical PK data may be available. At this point, it may be beneficial to apply the model assumptions in a PBPK model built in preclinical species and compare the outcome with *in vivo* studies. If there is a good match between the predicted and observed preclinical PK parameters, it provides more confidence around the assumptions and scaling approach utilized in the model building process. Small disconnects between predicted and observed values may be due to uncertainty in the input data. This is more likely at early discovery stages and models should be continuously refined with higher quality data as they become available throughout the drug development process [3,8,12,14,16,25–27]. On the other hand, a significant disconnect between the predicted and observed parameters may suggest that the model has failed to capture an important mechanism. This scenario should prompt further investigation into the mechanism of all the relevant processes involved in drug absorption and disposition across preclinical species and human. Thus, there are three key factors to be considered at every stage of drug development: (a) well-designed *in vitro* experiments and high-quality data, (b) a thorough mechanistic understanding of the compound of interest, and (c) continuous verification of model assumptions. Failure to correctly address these criteria can result in low confidence in the predictive ability of the PBPK model and potentially a significant mismatch between the predicted and observed parameters [3,5,8,12,28].

The road to establishing PBPK as a key modeling platform for predicting human ADME and DDI has not been a smooth one and we are still learning from ongoing research. In a lot of cases, the science required to understand the mechanism of action or the ADME behavior is still developing. In other cases, the methodology to capture these mechanisms has not yet been established. And yet in other cases, the connection between the *in vitro* or *in silico* and *in vivo* data remains to be elucidated [8,13,16,17,21,24,29]. In the upcoming sections, we will explore these challenges and discuss the approaches that have been utilized, in some cases, to overcome them.

Application of PBPK models

In the past decade, the use of PBPK modeling in drug development has gained a lot of momentum. PBPK models are now routinely utilized to address mechanistic questions starting in discovery to late-stage drug development [2,3,5,13,16,30]. Applications of PBPK modeling in the preclinical discovery and development space include prediction of human PK and efficacious dose, prediction of oral absorption, bioavailability and food effect, as well as modeling of DDI risk. In early clinical development through phase III and post-approval, PBPK models can be applied to predict PK and DDI in special subpopulations, including pediatrics and patients, with a focus on guiding the clinical development plan. At the different stages of drug development, PBPK models serve a variety of purposes, starting with influencing internal decision making, to influencing regulatory communications and gaining a mechanistic understanding of clinical observations. A key point to consider is that at the different stages of model development, different types of data will be available and different datasets can be used to build and validate PBPK models. Additionally, PBPK modeling is an iterative process of integrating mechanistic knowledge gained throughout the drug development process as we expand our understanding of the drug of interest [6,7]. In an ideal scenario, a model developed at drug discovery would incorporate new mechanistic knowledge as it is gained and could be extended to provide answers throughout the drug development process.

A review of the status of PBPK modeling in pharmaceutical industry summarizes areas of modeling where there is high confidence versus moderate and low confidence in utilizing PBPK modeling [3]. The categorization is mainly driven by potential uncertainty in key model parameters, either related to generation or translation of data. Since the publication of that review in 2015, there has been considerable progress in addressing some of the uncertainties, especially in the field of transporter research and biologics modeling [22,24,29−36]. Various models have been published that have used approximations and assumptions based on the available information as surrogates for the mechanistic data to enable model building. Here, we will discuss the various applications of PBPK modeling throughout drug development and the type of data available, as well as how certain challenges in obtaining or translating key data has been addressed in the literature.

Human PK and dose predictions

An accurate prediction of human PK requires a thorough mechanistic understanding of the ADME behavior of the molecule of interest. Successful models can be used to address a multitude of key questions in drug discovery and development, including whether the use of PBPK models can help reduce the need for preclinical species through accurate prediction of human exposure or food effect, for example. Furthermore, they can be used to guide expectations in FIH studies with respect to human PK, potential DDIs, and inter-individual variability related to pharmacogenetic effects. Since modeling of absorption will be discussed in the next section, the focus here will be on the distribution and elimination of the molecule of interest. The data required for the prediction of various ADME parameters are summarized in Table 20.1.

Distribution

For the prediction of distribution of small molecules, high quality measurements or *in silico* estimates of the physico-chemical properties is an essential input for all well-established distribution models [9,12,20,25,37,38]. The key challenge in predicting the human volume of distribution (V_{ss}) for small molecules is understanding the mechanism behind preferential tissue distribution that may be observed in preclinical species, and whether it will translate to humans. This question has introduced significant obstacles in preclinical PBPK modeling of small molecules. Accurate measurements of the blood to plasma ratio and protein binding behavior, including assessment of concentration-dependent binding, can help to understand the mechanism behind the distribution and ideally guide the species selection. Based on this data, if a specific species has been selected to be representative of human, building a PBPK model in the representative species and validating it using *in vivo* PK data from that species will provide significant insight into the tissue-specific scalars that should be used in human to get a more accurate prediction of V_{ss} [14,25,39]. While very resource intensive, it can also be helpful to measure tissue-specific drug concentrations in the preclinical species of interest to confirm the predicted distribution coefficients [9,38]. The decision to perform additional mechanistic studies in preclinical species can be guided by sensitivity analyses of the role of V_{ss} on human dose and exposure estimates and would be warranted for compounds with narrow therapeutic index and/or anticipated safety issues.

Accurately predicting distribution introduces additional challenges for the assessment of efficacy in PBPK-pharmacodynamic (PD) models of oncology [18,40]. Since tumor growth is normally assessed in mouse xenograft models, predictions normally rely on mouse PK. While mechanistic models that predict distribution have been published to relate distribution in different healthy organs and tumor based on work in tumor cells in xenografts, it is not well understood how implanted tumors behave compared to tumors in human tissue [41−43].

Moreover, attempts to predict the distribution of biologics, including monoclonal antibodies (mAbs) or antibody-drug conjugates (ADCs) using PBPK in recent years have introduced additional obstacles. Since the primary route of distribution and tissue uptake for antibodies is through convective transport, understanding the reflection coefficient, which is the fraction of antibody that is in the plasma/tissue and unable to pass through paracellular pores, as well as the rate of fluid movement into tissue will be essential for prediction of distribution [21,22,30]. In the absence of validated tissue-specific reflection coefficients, a fixed constant value representing the vascular reflection coefficient has been used for healthy tissue [44,45]. This assumption has performed well so far for predicting distribution in mice, but its performance remains to be seen in human models.

TABLE 20.1 Data required to address key questions in drug development using PBPK modeling and limitations and challenges faced in the process.

Key questions for PBPK modeling	Data required to address the question		Limitations and challenges	
	Small molecules	Biologics	Small molecules	Biologics
Understanding the absorption behavior, bioavailability, and food effect (if applicable)	• Physicochemical properties (e.g. LogP, pKa) • *In vitro* passive versus active permeability (i.e., through the use of MDCK or Caco-2 cell lines in the presence and absence of specific inhibitors) • Potential for efflux transport • pH-dependent solubility • Biorelevant solubility • Biorelevant dissolution • Low dose, oral and IV preclinical PK using a human-relevant formulation • Nice-to-have: preclinical food effect study in a representative species	For the development of mechanistic subcutaneous (SC) absorption models: • Fluid flow rate from the injection site, through the lymphatic system to the circulation • Expression of FcRN in cells in the lymphatics (incl. Lymph nodes)	Direct translation of bioavailability from preclinical species to human may be challenging if the compound is a substrate of active transport or has poor solubility. Studies in preclinical species are often aimed at achieving maximum exposure and are often run with enabling formulations, rather than with human-relevant formulations, which makes it very challenging to directly translate preclinical data to human. A mechanistic approach needs to be utilized to account for any species-specific effects and challenges.	Fluid flow rate and expression of receptors are often not reported with high confidence in the literature as this data is not easily generated. Current PBPK models that describe SC bioavailability of mAbs use an empiric approach to link the fraction of mAb going into the plasma from the lymph nodes to the FcRn binding affinity. While this approach has worked relatively well in predicting mouse bioavailability, its utility in human and higher species remains to be shown and has not been validated
Predicting the mechanism of distribution in human	• Physicochemical properties (e.g., LogP, pKa) • Concentration-dependent blood to plasma ratio • Plasma protein binding • Low dose, oral and IV preclinical PK • Nice-to-have: preclinical tissue distribution	• Understanding of the receptor quantity that is "available" for interaction • For tumor tissues: Understanding of the change in vascular permeability • Nice-to-have: tissue-specific vascular reflection coefficients	If species differences in tissue distribution is observed, mechanistic *in vivo* studies will have to be conducted to understand whether the behavior is expected in humans. These studies can be very resource intensive, and some gaps still exist with respect to translation of preclinical distribution mechanism to human (e.g., lysosomal trapping, and transporter-mediated distribution)	• The true reflection coefficient across tissues has proven challenging to measure. In the absence of this data, a fixed vascular reflection coefficient of 0.95 is used for healthy tissue. For tumor tissue, empirical scalars have been used to describe the change in vascular structure. • Furthermore, there is mounting evidence of inter-antibody differences in distribution, however, to date, a quantitative relationship has not

TABLE 20.1 Data required to address key questions in drug development using PBPK modeling and limitations and challenges faced in the process.—cont'd

Key questions for PBPK modeling	Data required to address the question		Limitations and challenges	
	Small molecules	Biologics	Small molecules	Biologics
				yet been established to describe the impact of physicochemical properties (e.g., charge of mAb) on PK.
Elucidating the key routes of elimination	• Microsomal and hepatocyte intrinsic clearance across species with in vivo PK data and human • Understanding of $f_{m,CYP}$ versus $f_{m,non-CYP}$ • Enzyme kinetics for key routes of metabolism and enzyme-specific scalars • Potential for uptake and/or efflux transport • If applicable, uptake and/or efflux kinetics, and transporter-specific scalars • Low dose, oral and IV preclinical PK • Bile duct cannulated studies in representative species to understand the contribution of renal and biliary routes of elimination • In vitro binding in test matrix	• Receptor expression data • Rate of uptake into endothelial cells • For describing target-mediated disposition: (1) target expression (in all tissue for human), and (2) turnover rate, ideally in the presence and absence of binding • Target shed rate	For many non-CYP enzymes and active transporters, there is a gap in validated in vitro to in vivo scaling factors due to the lack of clinical examples. Similarly, while animal models of biliary excretion exist, models with significant contribution of this mechanism will likely gain more confidence only once validated with human ADME data.	• Receptor expression data is not readily available and difficult to measure. Published PBPK models have relied on estimates of protein quantity, including model-generated estimates, mRNA expression data, quantitative protein expression data (western blot or mass spectroscopy), or a mixture of multiple methods • Target expression and turnover rate data is not readily available in the literature and not routinely measured, especially for higher species and humans • To get a rough estimate of target turnover, in vitro internalization data or pulse-chase studies can be used as a surrogate of direct measurement of membrane-bound target turnover in vivo
Predicting potential drug-drug interactions	• Understanding of $f_{m,CYP}$ versus $f_{m,non-CYP}$ as well as the percent contribution of additional routes of elimination, if any • IC_{50} values for relevant CYPs, UGTs, and uptake	• Understanding the impact of biologic treatment on tissue and tumor physiology (e.g., vascular and lymph flow rate, tumor vascular volume)	While the database of mixed-effect DDIs involving CYPs, non-CYPs, and transporters is growing, there is still moderate confidence around some mechanisms of drug-interaction due to lack	• The literature on the mechanism of drug-tumor interaction is still growing

Continued

TABLE 20.1 Data required to address key questions in drug development using PBPK modeling and limitations and challenges faced in the process.—cont'd

Key questions for PBPK modeling	Data required to address the question		Limitations and challenges	
	Small molecules	Biologics	Small molecules	Biologics
	and efflux transporters • Potential for time-dependent inhibition and kinetics, if applicable • Potential for induction and kinetics, if applicable	• For the small molecule component of ADCs, same dataset as for small molecule victim and inhibitor risk prediction	of clinical validation of preclinical models	

Further complicating the PBPK modeling of antibody distribution is the concept of inter-antibody differences linked to changes in antibody charge [46,47]. While quantitative relationships have not yet been published to describe the role of charge and other physicochemical properties on antibody PK, some models have demonstrated the use of empiric scaling factors to successfully describe the impact of inter-antibody differences [45]. Additional work in this area will allow modelers to capture this phenomenon more mechanistically in PBPK models and likely improve prediction performance.

Elimination

Understanding the elimination of small molecules has been one of the key focuses of PBPK models since their conception. There is currently a wealth of literature describing hepatic and microsomal clearance of compounds through cytochrome P450 enzymes (CYPs), expression and activity of these enzymes, as well as validated quantitative scalars to translate the *in vitro* data to human. A great review covering a wide range of industry examples is provided by Sager et al. [13]. Most commercial PBPK software have incorporated these mechanisms and scalars and there are no significant limitations around modeling CYP-mediated metabolism rate from *in vitro* systems [6]. The same cannot be said for non-CYP metabolically cleared substrates, such as compounds primarily cleared by glucuronidation (UGTs), acetylation (NATs), or sulfation (SULT). While a lot of progress has been made in the past years, especially with respect to establishing UGT expression patterns and scaling factors, for many non-CYP enzymes, there is a gap in validated *in vitro* to *in vivo* scaling factors in the absence of clinical data [48,49]. Nevertheless, an accurate measure of the percent contribution of the non-CYP pathways, using specific inhibitors in hepatocytes, for example, can provides a good assessment of the level of model uncertainty and can help with putting potential victim risk into perspective. Furthermore, recent advances in quantitative protein expression methods have enabled the quantification of protein expression with more accuracy, resulting in a better understanding of the *in vitro* to *in vivo* translation of clearance via non-CYP enzymes. A recent publication by Basit et al. is a great example of advances in this area [50].

Similarly, clearance of small molecules by active transport continues to be an area of moderate confidence due to the lack of transporter abundances and activity scaling factors [8,24,31]. As mentioned above, the rise of mass-spectrometry-based quantitative proteomics in recent years has introduced a sensitive and high-throughput tool for quantifying protein expression more rapidly and with more accuracy [32,51—53]. This has resulted in a steep incline in the emergence of scaling factors from many groups across the pharmaceutical industry. In many cases, while these scaling factors have shown variability across substrates and test systems, with appropriate verification using reference compounds and clinical data, they have provided a path forward for modeling mechanisms of transporter disposition and drug-interaction with increased confidence [29,31,32,34—36,53—56]. Since most molecules will involve a mixture of metabolism and transport mechanisms, it is important to understand the relative contribution of each pathway through IVIVE assessment using *in vitro* intrinsic clearance rates, *in vivo* clearance from preclinical species, and rate of uptake or efflux. These assessments can shed light on whether active transport will be a limiting factor in the clearance of the compound of interest and subsequently, the level of confidence in the PBPK model.

Understanding the elimination of small molecules via biliary and renal routes will rely more heavily on translation of preclinical data and understanding the elimination profile in preclinical species. While renal excretion is well-preserved across species, the involvement of active transport can complicate the translation. Current approaches for understanding these mechanisms of elimination include a multi-factorial approach using *in vitro* data and *in vivo* profiling in representative species [26,39]. These mechanisms are normally the first to be verified with FIH data once the compound has moved into the clinic.

While elimination of biologics is primarily mediated via catabolism, like small molecules, understanding protein expression and rate of uptake are also key to predicting clearance through PBPK modeling [30]. Antibodies that are bound to FcRn are protected from degradation and normally recycled, while unbound antibodies are directed to the lysosome for degradation. In PBPK models, this can be modeled using kinetic binding parameters, as well as measurements of target expression and rate of uptake into cells [21,22,30]. While receptor expression data is not abundant in the literature, several approaches have been used to obtain an estimate of protein quantity, including mRNA expression data, and quantitative protein expression data (e.g. Western blot) [44,57,58]. These approaches give an estimate of the total amount of receptor in tissue and not the physiologically relevant concentrations, introducing uncertainty in the model. Nevertheless, published examples suggest that these assumptions can enable acceptable predictions of antibody disposition [59].

An additional point to consider for large molecules is the potential for target-mediated disposition. Key to mechanistically modeling this phenomenon are measurements of target expression and turnover, neither of which is readily available in the literature nor routinely measured in the discovery stages of drug development, especially in monkey or human. Recent efforts have attempted to obtain this information from semi-quantitative immunohistochemical scores that can be converted into target concentrations [60,61]. Furthermore, estimates of target turnover have been obtained through *in vitro* internalization or pulse-chase studies. In the absence of quantitative data, these surrogate measures have successfully captured non-linear PK of several mAbs across species, providing a path forward for PBPK modeling of large molecule disposition.

PK/PD relationship

While accurately capturing the PK of the molecule is key to a successful PBPK model, the target exposure or PD is an equally important parameter that is often overlooked. The projected human dose is equally dependent on the PK as it is the PD of the molecule, and uncertainties in the target exposure can translate to significant mismatches in the predicted versus observed efficacious dose [3,7]. While the focus of this chapter is not PBPK/PD, it is important to be aware of the variability and uncertainty around the assumptions made in the PD model and ensure that they are transferred to the predicted efficacious dose.

Several publications have captured the data required in successfully predicting the clinical PK and dose of compounds in the preclinical space [2,5,13,14,25,39,52]. The publication by Chen et al. provides an in-depth analysis of the PBPK modeling process in the drug discovery space using four case studies and provides a good summary of the data required for correctly capturing the human PK parameters and profile [5].

Biopharmaceutics and food effect

Examples of PBPK modeling of oral absorption throughout drug development are widespread [23,27,62−73]. These models have been used to address key questions in drug development, such as the need for modified release formulations, as well as guiding clinical formulation design and selection. Recent advances in biorelevant methodology and improved understanding of the *in vitro* to *in vivo* translation has improved the accuracy of biopharmaceutics models and resulted in a surge in the use of PBPK for addressing biopharmaceutics questions from food effect to formulation design. Table 20.1 provides a summary of data required for successfully describing drug absorption through PBPK modeling. Recent publications show high confidence in the translation of *in vitro* data for biopharmaceutics classification system (BCS) I and III compounds, as long as a significant contribution of active transport can be ruled out [68,70,72]. The uncertainties in the translation of *in vitro* transporter kinetics and expression are outlined above. Furthermore, there is high confidence in predicting food effect for a subset of BCS II compounds where significant drug precipitation is not anticipated. The low confidence for this subset of compounds is related to a lack of bio-predictive experimental setups and established *in vitro to in vivo* translation of precipitation kinetics [65,68,72−74]. This is, arguably, one of the largest gaps in biopharmaceutics knowledge and several recent literature examples have assessed the potential for more biorelevant experimental setups, such as TNO Gastro-Intestinal Model (TIM), Ussing chamber, and biorelevant media to address these uncertainties [75−79].

Confidence in PBPK modeling of absorption is further reduced with BCS IV compounds where there is often a complex interplay of multiple factors, including solubility, dissolution, and active transport [63−65,68−70,72,73]. Even for BCS IV compounds, confidence needs to be assessed on a case-by-case basis depending on data availability and validity of the assumptions behind data translation. If the covariate interplay can be simplified through assumptions that can be validated through experimental data, then model uncertainties can be reduced. An example of this was shown for the BCL-2 inhibitor, venetoclax, where the potential for significant precipitation could be ruled out through assessment of the *in vitro* behavior of the drug, and the potential role of transporters was captured using uninhibited Caco-2 cells and validated through *in vivo* studies in rats [80]. In other cases, simplifying the interplay is not as straightforward and each mechanism will need to be verified independently with clinical data.

An additional route of absorption is through subcutaneous (SC) administration, a common route of administration for large molecules [22,30]. Mechanistic modeling of SC absorption requires measurements of the rate of fluid from the injection site to the circulation and the expression of receptor in lymphatic cells that the drug would pass through. Thus far, an example of a fully mechanistic SC absorption model is not available in literature. A published example in mice predicts antibody bioavailability by empirically linking the fraction of drug returning to the plasma from the lymph node to the target binding affinity. The utility of this approach in higher species has not yet been demonstrated [44].

Drug-drug interactions

DDI assessment is one of the first, and probably most validated, applications of PBPK modeling [8,12,13,16,81−87]. The assessment of enzyme- and transporter-mediated DDIs are highly relevant to the drug development process as they help drug developers understand and minimize the risk for potential changes in exposure and toxicity in the clinic. Furthermore, once a PBPK DDI model for a given pathway is verified, it may be used in lieu of additional clinical DDI studies, to predict additional DDI risk involving the same pathway. For example, a PBPK model built to predict DDI with a strong CYP inhibitor or inducer can be applied to predict moderate and weak inhibition and induction involving the same enzyme. CYP-mediated perpetrator interactions are very well studied and there have been numerous examples of successful prediction of these DDIs, which are thoroughly summarized in various review articles [3,8,13,15,16,81,85,87−89]. Therefore, there is generally high confidence around reversible inhibition, induction and time-dependent inhibition of CYPs. There have been some examples of lower confidence when multiple mechanisms of interaction occur at the same time, for example induction and reversible inhibition. In these instances, it can be difficult to tease apart the relative contribution of each mechanism and limited clinical data has been available to elucidate the *in vitro* to *in vivo* translation of data in such scenarios. Recently, more clinical examples of mixed-effect DDIs have become available and multiple consortia efforts have focused on the analysis of the predictive confidence of these examples [36,81,84,90,91]. The list of data required to model DDIs is outlined in Table 20.1. Perpetrator DDI assessment involving non-CYPs would require the generation of the same dataset, however, there is a significantly smaller database available to enable a retrospective evaluation of the performance of this data in PBPK models. Various key examples of the use of PBPK modeling in lieu of clinical studies are available in the literature [87]. Of note, is the modeling done for the hemoglobin S-polymerization inhibitor voxelotor (Oxbryta), approved for sickle cell disease, where the PBPK model was used to predict the victim risk in the presence of CYP3A4 inhibitors and inducers, as well as the risk of co-dosing voxelotor with CYP1A2, 2C19, 2C9, 2C8, and 2D6 substrates following multiple dose administration in healthy subjects and patients [87]. The labeling around dosage form and DDIs for this molecule dosed in adults was exclusively informed by PBPK modeling in lieu of clinical studies. Another example from the large molecule space is the PBPK modeling of polatuzumab vedotin (plivy) where the model was used to predict the effect of a strong CYP3A4 inhibitor and inducer on the PK of the unconjugated MMAE, as well as the impact of unconjugated MMAE on the PK of a sensitive CYP3A4 substrate [92].

Confidence around PBPK modeling of transporter-mediated perpetrator DDIs is more variable. In the case of apical active transport, perpetrator plasma concentrations drive the DDI and have, therefore, relatively high confidence if high quality IC_{50} values are available. For basolateral active transport where intracellular perpetrator concentrations drive the DDI, model confidence relies on the availability of high-quality transporter kinetics data and validated tissue scalars [13,29,31,32,51−53,91]. A great example of the use of PBPK modeling for predicting transporter mediated DDI is the work done on Simeprevir, a hepatitis C virus protease inhibitor. Due to the mechanistic nature of the model, it could be used to, not only, predict potential DDIs, but also explain the non-linear PK and inter-subject variability that is observed for this molecule in the clinic and help guide the drug development process [56].

Victim risk predictions rely on the same dataset required for predicting clearance and elimination, discussed earlier. It is important to understand the contribution of all mechanisms involved in the elimination of the drug in development for an accurate assessment of victim risk using PBPK. Several great examples of victim risk prediction via PBPK modeling are summarized in the publication by Sager et al. [13].

Pediatric and special populations dosing

Another powerful application of PBPK modeling is the prediction of expected exposure and exposure-response in patients and subpopulations (e.g. pediatrics, organ impairment, and patients) [17,19,82,93−96]. Unlike the previous examples, a key driver of PBPK models for these applications are "systems" data. This includes ontogeny, changes in expression of enzymes and transporters, as well as changes in physiology in the presence of disease, such as cancer. There has been increasing acceptance of pediatric and organ impairment PBPK modeling by the regulatory agencies and numerous publications have demonstrated the utility of these models as more clinical examples have become available [17,87,95].

Data collection and availability is more challenging for establishing a disease population. In the case of oncology, information on changes in physiology, for example tumor cell parameters, changes in interstitial space, blood cells, and plasma volume, need to be captured and will vary depending on the cancer type being modeled [18,40,45]. While great examples of oncology PBPK models have been published, their utility in specific cancer types remains to be seen [18,22]. More efforts are warranted across the pharmaceutical industry to parametrize the PBPK sub-compartments with cancer-type specific data in order to increase our confidence in PBPK predictions. Another important consideration for using PBPK models to predict changes in exposure due to disease is the ability to estimate tissue abundances. As discussed above with respect to transporters, emergence of quantitative proteomics has provided a path forward with respect to obtaining this data in a rapid and accurate manner.

Challenges and future opportunities

Advancements in our understanding of disease biology have helped identify new targets for previously hard to treat diseases. This increase in knowledge has given rise to increasing complexities in the mechanism of action of novel therapeutics, requiring a more holistic approach for drug discovery and development. The use of PBPK modeling has gained momentum across industry for enabling an integrated approach to dose optimization, formulation design, exposure-response analysis, clinical trial design, and risk assessment around potential drug interactions. Over the years, PBPK models have also become a platform for the aggregation of all available mechanistic knowledge for a given compound, making them exceedingly data intensive [3,6,11]. As a result, there has been a rise in the *in vitro*, *in silico*, and proteomics method development efforts to match the complex mechanisms of ADME and disease. Recent publications have demonstrated the importance of high-quality *in vitro* data and a good understanding of *in vitro* to *in vivo* translation to producing high confidence models that have been used to not only influence internal decisions, but also regulatory communications [87].

Yet, we continue to see more examples of rapidly emerging modalities, which could benefit, in the upcoming years, from robust PBPK models. These include bispecific antibodies, siRNAs and Chimeric Antigen Receptor T-Cell (CAR-T) treatments. For these applications, even more extensive knowledge and characterization of the "systems" data will be required to generate high impact models [97−100]. For bispecific antibodies, characterization of the sequential binding of the two targets and the impact that this would have on the downstream pharmacology will need to be correctly captured [100]. In the case of CAR-T therapies, PBPK modeling can support optimization of CAR expression and CAR affinity in new drug development, as well as aid dose selection and optimization [97]. We still have a long way to validated mechanistic models for these novel modalities, but advancements in our mechanistic knowledge and *in vitro* methodologies should help pave the path to developing models that capture the complexity of these new therapies.

References

[1] R. Madabushi, Y. Wang, I. Zineh, A holistic and integrative approach for advancing model-informed drug development, CPT Pharmacometrics Syst. Pharmacol. 8 (1) (2019) 9−11.

[2] R.L. Lalonde, et al., Model-based drug development, Clin. Pharmacol. Ther. 82 (1) (2007) 21−32.

[3] H.M. Jones, et al., Physiologically based pharmacokinetic modeling in drug discovery and development: a pharmaceutical industry perspective, Clin. Pharmacol. Ther. 97 (3) (2015) 247−262.

[4] T. Teorell, Kinetics of distribution of substances administered to the body. The extravascular modes of administration, Arch. Int. Pharmacodyn. Ther. (57) (1937) 205−225.

[5] Y. Chen, et al., Application of IVIVE and PBPK modeling in prospective prediction of clinical pharmacokinetics: strategy and approach during the drug discovery phase with four case studies, Biopharm. Drug Dispos. 33 (2) (2012) 85−98.

[6] M. Jamei, G.L. Dickinson, A. Rostami-Hodjegan, A framework for assessing inter-individual variability in pharmacokinetics using virtual human populations and integrating general knowledge of physical chemistry, biology, anatomy, physiology and genetics: a tale of 'bottom-up' vs 'top-down' recognition of covariates, Drug Metabol. Pharmacokinet. 24 (1) (2009) 53−75.

[7] H. Jones, K. Rowland-Yeo, Basic concepts in physiologically based pharmacokinetic modeling in drug discovery and development, CPT Pharmacometrics Syst. Pharmacol. 2 (2013) e63.

[8] T. Lave, et al., Challenges and opportunities with modelling and simulation in drug discovery and drug development, Xenobiotica 37 (10−11) (2007) 1295−1310.

[9] P. Poulin, F.P. Theil, A priori prediction of tissue: plasma partition coefficients of drugs to facilitate the use of physiologically-based pharmacokinetic models in drug discovery, J. Pharmaceut. Sci. 89 (1) (2000) 16−35.

[10] A. Rostami-Hodjegan, I. Tamai, K.S. Pang, Physiologically based pharmacokinetic (PBPK) modeling: it is here to stay!, Biopharm. Drug Dispos. 33 (2) (2012) 47−50.

[11] A. Rostami-Hodjegan, S. Toon, Physiologically based pharmacokinetics as a component of model-informed drug development: where we were, where we are, and where we are heading, J. Clin. Pharmacol. 60 (Suppl. 1) (2020) S12−S16.

[12] M. Rowland, C. Peck, G. Tucker, Physiologically-based pharmacokinetics in drug development and regulatory science, Annu. Rev. Pharmacol. Toxicol. 51 (2011) 45−73.

[13] J.E. Sager, et al., Physiologically based pharmacokinetic (PBPK) modeling and simulation approaches: a systematic review of published models, applications, and model verification, Drug Metab. Dispos. 43 (11) (2015) 1823−1837.

[14] K.R. Yeo, J.R. Kenny, A. Rostami-Hodjegan, Application of in vitro-in vivo extrapolation (IVIVE) and physiologically based pharmacokinetic (PBPK) modelling to investigate the impact of the CYP2C8 polymorphism on rosiglitazone exposure, Eur. J. Clin. Pharmacol. 69 (6) (2013) 1311−1320.

[15] K. Abduljalil, et al., Anatomical, physiological and metabolic changes with gestational age during normal pregnancy: a database for parameters required in physiologically based pharmacokinetic modelling, Clin. Pharmacokinet. 51 (6) (2012) 365−396.

[16] C. Perry, et al., Utilization of physiologically based pharmacokinetic modeling in clinical pharmacology and therapeutics: an overview, Curr. Pharmacol. Rep. (2020) 1−14.

[17] T. Heimbach, et al., Physiologically-based pharmacokinetic modeling in renal and hepatic impairment populations: a pharmaceutical industry perspective, Clin. Pharmacol. Ther. 110 (2) (2021) 297−310.

[18] S. Cheeti, et al., A physiologically based pharmacokinetic (PBPK) approach to evaluate pharmacokinetics in patients with cancer, Biopharm. Drug Dispos. 34 (3) (2013) 141−154.

[19] M. De Sousa Mendes, M. Chetty, Are standard doses of renally-excreted antiretrovirals in older patients appropriate: a PBPK study comparing exposures in the elderly population with those in renal impairment, Drugs R&D 19 (4) (2019) 339−350.

[20] S. Pilari, W. Huisinga, Lumping of physiologically-based pharmacokinetic models and a mechanistic derivation of classical compartmental models, J. Pharmacokinet. Pharmacodyn. 37 (4) (2010) 365−405.

[21] L. Hu, R.J. Hansen, Issues, challenges, and opportunities in model-based drug development for monoclonal antibodies, J. Pharmaceut. Sci. 102 (9) (2013) 2898−2908.

[22] D.K. Shah, A.M. Betts, Towards a platform PBPK model to characterize the plasma and tissue disposition of monoclonal antibodies in preclinical species and human, J. Pharmacokinet. Pharmacodyn. 39 (1) (2012) 67−86.

[23] M. Jamei, et al., Population-based mechanistic prediction of oral drug absorption, AAPS J. 11 (2) (2009) 225−237.

[24] H.M. Jones, et al., Mechanistic pharmacokinetic modeling for the prediction of transporter-mediated disposition in humans from sandwich culture human hepatocyte data, Drug Metab. Dispos. 40 (5) (2012) 1007−1017.

[25] R.S. Obach, et al., The prediction of human pharmacokinetic parameters from preclinical and in vitro metabolism data, J. Pharmacol. Exp. Therapeut. 283 (1) (1997) 46−58.

[26] C. Thiel, et al., A systematic evaluation of the use of physiologically based pharmacokinetic modeling for cross-species extrapolation, J. Pharmaceut. Sci. 104 (1) (2015) 191−206.

[27] V.K. Sinha, et al., From preclinical to human-prediction of oral absorption and drug-drug interaction potential using physiologically based pharmacokinetic (PBPK) modeling approach in an industrial setting: a workflow by using case example, Biopharm. Drug Dispos. 33 (2) (2012) 111−121.

[28] N. Parrott, et al., Best practices in the development and validation of physiologically based biopharmaceutics modeling. A workshop summary report, J. Pharmaceut. Sci. 110 (2) (2021) 584−593.

[29] L. Liu, K.S. Pang, The roles of transporters and enzymes in hepatic drug processing, Drug Metab. Dispos. 33 (1) (2005) 1−9.

[30] P.M. Glassman, J.P. Balthasar, Physiologically-based modeling of monoclonal antibody pharmacokinetics in drug discovery and development, Drug Metabol. Pharmacokinet. 34 (1) (2019) 3−13.

[31] R. Li, et al., A "middle-out" approach to human pharmacokinetic predictions for OATP substrates using physiologically-based pharmacokinetic modeling, J. Pharmacokinet. Pharmacodyn. 41 (3) (2014) 197−209.

[32] M. Meyer, et al., Using expression data for quantification of active processes in physiologically based pharmacokinetic modeling, Drug Metab. Dispos. 40 (5) (2012) 892−901.

[33] A. Tornio, et al., Glucuronidation converts clopidogrel to a strong time-dependent inhibitor of CYP2C8: a phase II metabolite as a perpetrator of drug-drug interactions, Clin. Pharmacol. Ther. 96 (4) (2014) 498−507.

[34] M.V. Varma, et al., Physiologically based modeling of pravastatin transporter-mediated hepatobiliary disposition and drug-drug interactions, Pharm. Res. 29 (10) (2012) 2860−2873.

[35] M.V. Varma, et al., Quantitative rationalization of gemfibrozil drug interactions: consideration of transporters-enzyme interplay and the role of circulating metabolite gemfibrozil 1-O-beta-glucuronide, Drug Metab. Dispos. 43 (7) (2015) 1108−1118.

[36] M.V. Varma, et al., Quantitative prediction of repaglinide-rifampicin complex drug interactions using dynamic and static mechanistic models: delineating differential CYP3A4 induction and OATP1B1 inhibition potential of rifampicin, Drug Metab. Dispos. 41 (5) (2013) 966−974.

[37] P. Poulin, A paradigm shift in pharmacokinetic-pharmacodynamic (PKPD) modeling: rule of thumb for estimating free drug level in tissue compared with plasma to guide drug design, J. Pharmaceut. Sci. 104 (7) (2015) 2359−2368.

[38] T. Rodgers, D. Leahy, M. Rowland, Physiologically based pharmacokinetic modeling 1: predicting the tissue distribution of moderate-to-strong bases, J. Pharmaceut. Sci. 94 (6) (2005) 1259−1276.

[39] F. Lombardo, et al., Comprehensive assessment of human pharmacokinetic prediction based on in vivo animal pharmacokinetic data, part 1: volume of distribution at steady state, J. Clin. Pharmacol. 53 (2) (2013) 167−177.

[40] M. Block, Physiologically based pharmacokinetic and pharmacodynamic modeling in cancer drug development: status, potential and gaps, Expert Opin. Drug Metabol. Toxicol. 11 (5) (2015) 743−756.

[41] P. Poulin, et al., Correlation of tissue-plasma partition coefficients between normal tissues and subcutaneous xenografts of human tumor cell lines in mouse as a prediction tool of drug penetration in tumors, J. Pharmaceut. Sci. 102 (4) (2013) 1355−1369.

[42] B.A. Ruggeri, F. Camp, S. Miknyoczki, Animal models of disease: pre-clinical animal models of cancer and their applications and utility in drug discovery, Biochem. Pharmacol. 87 (1) (2014) 150−161.

[43] J.L. Wilding, W.F. Bodmer, Cancer cell lines for drug discovery and development, Cancer Res. 74 (9) (2014) 2377−2384.

[44] Y. Chen, J.P. Balthasar, Evaluation of a catenary PBPK model for predicting the in vivo disposition of mAbs engineered for high-affinity binding to FcRn, AAPS J. 14 (4) (2012) 850−859.

[45] J.P. Davda, et al., A physiologically based pharmacokinetic (PBPK) model to characterize and predict the disposition of monoclonal antibody CC49 and its single chain Fv constructs, Int. Immunopharm. 8 (3) (2008) 401−413.

[46] C.A. Boswell, et al., Effects of charge on antibody tissue distribution and pharmacokinetics, Bioconjugate Chem. 21 (12) (2010) 2153−2163.

[47] T. Igawa, et al., Reduced elimination of IgG antibodies by engineering the variable region, Protein Eng. Des. Sel. 23 (5) (2010) 385−392.

[48] L. Docci, et al., Construction and verification of physiologically based pharmacokinetic models for four drugs majorly cleared by glucuronidation: lorazepam, oxazepam, naloxone, and zidovudine, AAPS J. 22 (6) (2020) 128.

[49] J. Zhou, U.A. Argikar, J.O. Miners, Enzyme kinetics of uridine diphosphate glucuronosyltransferases (UGTs), Methods Mol. Biol. 2342 (2021) 301−338.

[50] A. Basit, et al., Characterization of differential tissue abundance of major non-CYP enzymes in human, Mol. Pharm. 17 (11) (2020) 4114−4124.

[51] V. Kumar, et al., Quantitative transporter proteomics by liquid chromatography with tandem mass spectrometry: addressing methodologic issues of plasma membrane isolation and expression-activity relationship, Drug Metab. Dispos. 43 (2) (2015) 284−288.

[52] X. Qiu, H. Zhang, Y. Lai, Quantitative targeted proteomics for membrane transporter proteins: method and application, AAPS J. 16 (4) (2014) 714−726.

[53] Y. Uchida, et al., Quantitative targeted absolute proteomics of human blood-brain barrier transporters and receptors, J. Neurochem. 117 (2) (2011) 333−345.

[54] A. Emami Riedmaier, et al., More power to OATP1B1: an evaluation of sample size in pharmacogenetic studies using a rosuvastatin PBPK model for intestinal, hepatic, and renal transporter-mediated clearances, J. Clin. Pharmacol. 56 (Suppl. 7) (2016) S132−S142.

[55] R. Kikuchi, et al., Quantitation of plasma membrane drug transporters in kidney tissue and cell lines using a novel proteomic approach enabled a prospective prediction of metformin disposition, Drug Metab. Dispos. 49 (10) (2021) 938−946.

[56] J. Snoeys, et al., Mechanistic understanding of the nonlinear pharmacokinetics and intersubject variability of simeprevir: a PBPK-guided drug development approach, Clin. Pharmacol. Ther. 99 (2) (2016) 224−234.

[57] Y.Y. Fan, et al., Tissue expression profile of human neonatal Fc receptor (FcRn) in Tg32 transgenic mice, mAbs 8 (5) (2016) 848−853.

[58] T. Li, J.P. Balthasar, FcRn expression in wildtype mice, transgenic mice, and in human tissues, Biomolecules 8 (4) (2018).

[59] M.J. Eigenmann, et al., Quantification of IgG monoclonal antibody clearance in tissues, mAbs 9 (6) (2017) 1007−1015.

[60] P.M. Glassman, J.P. Balthasar, Physiologically-based pharmacokinetic modeling to predict the clinical pharmacokinetics of monoclonal antibodies, J. Pharmacokinet. Pharmacodyn. 43 (4) (2016) 427−446.

[61] P.M. Glassman, Y. Chen, J.P. Balthasar, Scale-up of a physiologically-based pharmacokinetic model to predict the disposition of monoclonal antibodies in monkeys, J. Pharmacokinet. Pharmacodyn. 42 (5) (2015) 527−540.

[62] A. Mitra, et al., Prediction of pH-dependent drug-drug interactions for basic drugs using physiologically based biopharmaceutics modeling: industry case studies, J. Pharmaceut. Sci. 109 (3) (2020) 1380−1394.

[63] B. Agoram, W.S. Woltosz, M.B. Bolger, Predicting the impact of physiological and biochemical processes on oral drug bioavailability, Adv. Drug Deliv. Rev. 50 (Suppl. 1) (2001) S41−S67.

[64] D. Fleisher, et al., Drug, meal and formulation interactions influencing drug absorption after oral administration. Clinical implications, Clin. Pharmacokinet. 36 (3) (1999) 233−254.

[65] F. Kesisoglou, et al., Physiologically based absorption modeling to impact biopharmaceutics and formulation strategies in drug development-industry case studies, J. Pharmaceut. Sci. 105 (9) (2016) 2723−2734.

[66] E.S. Kostewicz, et al., PBPK models for the prediction of in vivo performance of oral dosage forms, Eur. J. Pharmaceut. Sci. 57 (2014) 300−321.

[67] M. Li, et al., Predictive performance of physiologically based pharmacokinetic models for the effect of food on oral drug absorption: current status, CPT Pharmacometrics Syst. Pharmacol. 7 (2) (2018) 82−89.

[68] A.E. Riedmaier, et al., Use of physiologically based pharmacokinetic (PBPK) modeling for predicting drug-food interactions: an industry perspective, AAPS J. 22 (6) (2020) 123.

[69] E. Sjogren, H. Thorn, C. Tannergren, In silico modeling of gastrointestinal drug absorption: predictive performance of three physiologically based absorption models, Mol. Pharm. 13 (6) (2016) 1763–1778.

[70] C. Stillhart, et al., PBPK absorption modeling: establishing the in vitro-in vivo link-industry perspective, AAPS J. 21 (2) (2019) 19.

[71] S.C. Sutton, R. Nause, K. Gandelman, The impact of gastric pH, volume, and emptying on the food effect of ziprasidone oral absorption, AAPS J. 19 (4) (2017) 1084–1090.

[72] C. Tistaert, et al., Food effect projections via physiologically based pharmacokinetic modeling: predictive case studies, J. Pharmaceut. Sci. 108 (1) (2019) 592–602.

[73] C. Wagner, et al., Predicting the oral absorption of a poorly soluble, poorly permeable weak base using biorelevant dissolution and transfer model tests coupled with a physiologically based pharmacokinetic model, Eur. J. Pharm. Biopharm. 82 (1) (2012) 127–138.

[74] C. Wagner, et al., Use of physiologically based pharmacokinetic modeling for predicting drug-food interactions: recommendations for improving predictive performance of low confidence food effect models, AAPS J. 23 (4) (2021) 85.

[75] M. Minekus, The TNO gastro-intestinal model (TIM), in: K. Verhoeckx, et al. (Eds.), The Impact of Food Bioactives on Health: In Vitro and Ex Vivo Models, 2015, pp. 37–46. Cham (CH).

[76] T. van der Lugt, et al., Gastrointestinal digestion of dietary advanced glycation endproducts using an in vitro model of the gastrointestinal tract (TIM-1), Food Funct. 11 (7) (2020) 6297–6307.

[77] K. Kleberg, J. Jacobsen, A. Mullertz, Characterising the behaviour of poorly water soluble drugs in the intestine: application of biorelevant media for solubility, dissolution and transport studies, J. Pharm. Pharmacol. 62 (11) (2010) 1656–1668.

[78] C. Reppas, et al., Dissolution testing of modified release products with biorelevant media: an OrBiTo ring study using the USP apparatus III and IV, Eur. J. Pharm. Biopharm. 156 (2020) 40–49.

[79] B. Kisser, et al., The ussing chamber assay to study drug metabolism and transport in the human intestine, Curr. Protoc. Pharmacol. 77 (2017) 7 17 1–7 17 19.

[80] A. Emami Riedmaier, et al., Mechanistic physiologically based pharmacokinetic modeling of the dissolution and food effect of a biopharmaceutics classification system IV compound-the venetoclax story, J. Pharmaceut. Sci. 107 (1) (2018) 495–502.

[81] L.M. Almond, et al., Towards a quantitative framework for the prediction of DDIs arising from cytochrome P450 induction, Curr. Drug Metabol. 10 (4) (2009) 420–432.

[82] B. Feng, et al., Quantitative prediction of renal transporter-mediated clinical drug-drug interactions, Mol. Pharm. 10 (11) (2013) 4207–4215.

[83] C. Lu, et al., Assessment of cytochrome P450-mediated drug-drug interaction potential of orteronel and exposure changes in patients with renal impairment using physiologically based pharmacokinetic modeling and simulation, Biopharm. Drug Dispos. 35 (9) (2014) 543–552.

[84] B.S. Mayhew, D.R. Jones, S.D. Hall, An in vitro model for predicting in vivo inhibition of cytochrome P450 3A4 by metabolic intermediate complex formation, Drug Metab. Dispos. 28 (9) (2000) 1031–1037.

[85] R.S. Obach, R.L. Walsky, K. Venkatakrishnan, Mechanism-based inactivation of human cytochrome p450 enzymes and the prediction of drug-drug interactions, Drug Metab. Dispos. 35 (2) (2007) 246–255.

[86] J.G. Shi, et al., Predicting drug-drug interactions involving multiple mechanisms using physiologically based pharmacokinetic modeling: a case study with ruxolitinib, Clin. Pharmacol. Ther. 97 (2) (2015) 177–185.

[87] X. Zhang, et al., Application of PBPK modeling and simulation for regulatory decision making and its impact on US prescribing information: an update on the 2018-2019 submissions to the US FDA's office of clinical pharmacology, J. Clin. Pharmacol. 60 (Suppl. 1) (2020) S160–S178.

[88] K. Abouir, et al., Reviewing data integrated for PBPK model development to predict metabolic drug-drug interactions: shifting perspectives and emerging trends, Front. Pharmacol. 12 (2021) 708299.

[89] V. Arya, K. Venkatakrishnan, Role of physiologically based pharmacokinetic modeling and simulation in enabling model-informed development of drugs and biotherapeutics, J. Clin. Pharmacol. 60 (Suppl. 1) (2020) S7–S11.

[90] Y. Chen, et al., Physiologically-based pharmacokinetic model-informed drug development for fenebrutinib: understanding complex drug-drug interactions, CPT Pharmacometrics Syst. Pharmacol. 9 (6) (2020) 332–341.

[91] M.V. Varma, et al., Dealing with the complex drug-drug interactions: towards mechanistic models, Biopharm. Drug Dispos. 36 (2) (2015) 71–92.

[92] D. Samineni, et al., Physiologically based pharmacokinetic model-informed drug development for polatuzumab vedotin: label for drug-drug interactions without dedicated clinical trials, J. Clin. Pharmacol. 60 (Suppl. 1) (2020) S120–S131.

[93] M. Kiss, et al., Ontogeny of small intestinal drug transporters and metabolizing enzymes based on targeted quantitative proteomics, Drug Metab. Dispos. (2021).

[94] J. Lang, et al., Impact of hepatic CYP3A4 ontogeny functions on drug-drug interaction risk in pediatric physiologically-based pharmacokinetic/pharmacodynamic modeling: critical literature review and ivabradine case study, Clin. Pharmacol. Ther. 109 (6) (2021) 1618–1630.

[95] R. Leong, et al., Regulatory experience with physiologically based pharmacokinetic modeling for pediatric drug trials, Clin. Pharmacol. Ther. 91 (5) (2012) 926–931.

[96] B. Xia, et al., A simplified PBPK modeling approach for prediction of pharmacokinetics of four primarily renally excreted and CYP3A metabolized compounds during pregnancy, AAPS J. 15 (4) (2013) 1012–1024.

[97] A. Chaudhury, et al., Chimeric antigen receptor T cell therapies: a review of cellular kinetic-pharmacodynamic modeling approaches, J. Clin. Pharmacol. 60 (Suppl. 1) (2020) S147–S159.

[98] V.S. Ayyar, et al., Minimal physiologically based pharmacokinetic-pharmacodynamic (mPBPK-PD) model of N-acetylgalactosamine-conjugated small interfering RNA disposition and gene silencing in preclinical species and humans, J. Pharmacol. Exp. Therapeut. 379 (2) (2021) 134–146.

[99] K. Fairman, et al., Physiologically based pharmacokinetic (PBPK) modeling of RNAi therapeutics: opportunities and challenges, Biochem. Pharmacol. 189 (2021) 114468.

[100] H. Wong, T.W. Chow, Physiologically based pharmacokinetic modeling of therapeutic proteins, J. Pharmaceut. Sci. 106 (9) (2017) 2270–2275.

Chapter 21

Integrated pharmacokinetic/ pharmacodynamic/efficacy analysis in oncology: importance of pharmacodynamic/efficacy relationships

Harvey Wong

Faculty of Pharmaceutical Sciences, The University of British Columbia., Vancouver, BC, Canada

Introduction

Lack of efficacy remains the primary cause of drug attrition in recent reviews examining why drug fail [1,2]. Oncology, as a therapeutic area, accounted for the largest percentage of drug failures [2]. These reviews highlight a need to better understand drug efficacy at an earlier stage of oncology drug development. In the past, the dosing of anticancer agents in patients was often at the maximum tolerated doses making an understanding of an optimal dose schedule crucial to delivering the most efficacious dose while circumventing unwanted toxicities. More recently, the Food and Drug Administration's "Project Optimus" (https://www.fda.gov/about-fda/oncology-center-excellence/project-optimus) places emphasis on the importance of selecting of the optimal dose in addition to the optimal dose schedule. The move away from dosing at the maximum tolerated dose was likely in response to a larger number of molecular targeted agents being developed for use in oncology. "Project Optimus" further emphasizes the critical need to understand optimal dose and dose schedule for anticancer agents and places more importance on early characterization of exposure response relationships starting with nonclinical studies.

Immunodeficient mice bearing subcutaneous human tumors or xenograft mice are a "workhorse" model for the selection and characterization of anticancer drug candidates. By far, the primary advantage of xenograft models stems from the fact that tumors are of human origin and the relative ease at which antitumor activity can be monitored. Subcutaneous tumor growth can be monitored with common metrics such as tumor volume or other measurements of tumor dimensions. Further, tumor tissue can be harvested and measures of pharmacodynamic biomarker modulation can be assessed providing there is adequate tissue remaining following treatment with anticancer agent(s). Despite the utility of xenograft mice, much debate has occurred over their clinical predictive value [3-7]. However, tumor bearing mice, specifically xenograft mice, are used still widely used for assessments of preclinical antitumor activity and optimization of dose and dose schedule of novel anticancer agents. As such, tumor bearing mice supply much of the data that is used for the understanding of dose/exposure response relationships.

Preclinical pharmacokinetic/pharmacodynamic (PK/PD) modeling uses mathematical functions to quantitatively interrelate drug concentration and its' effects on a biological system of interest. It is an important tool in the drug discovery and development process by providing an integrated understanding of pharmacological relationships between drug concentrations in the body and efficacy, and enabling the translation of preclinical data to the clinic [8,9]. Species differences in factors such as plasma protein binding, pharmacokinetics, and/or in vivo drug potency can be adjusted for when using mechanistic PK/PD models for translation as these factors can be easily incorporated into models. Finally, establishment of PK/PD models enable simulations of scenarios other than those that were performed in the initial experiments. A need to reduce drug attrition due to a lack of efficacy has led to implementation of preclinical PK/PD modeling in drug discovery and development [10]. In a survey of pharmaceutical companies, it was reported that oncology was the therapeutic area where the most support was given to preclinical PK/PD modeling [11]. The primary objective of this chapter is to describe to readers application of a class of PK/PD model termed in this chapter as integrated pharmacokinetic/pharmacodynamic/efficacy (PK/PD/Efficacy) models and their applications in oncology drug development.

PK/efficacy, biomarker PK/PD, and integrated PK/PD/efficacy models

PK/PD models typically relate drug concentrations to a biological effect. In oncology, the biological effect usually refers to tumor shrinkage or modulation of a biomarker related to a biological pathway impacted by the drug. Common PK/PD models used to characterize drug concentration/effect relationships in oncology, typically in tumor bearing xenograft mice, include what we will refer to as PK/Efficacy models used to characterize relationships between drug concentrations and tumor growth inhibition (TGI) (Fig. 21.1A), and biomarker PK/PD models used to characterize drug's ability to modulate a pharmacodynamic biomarker (Fig. 21.1B) [10]. For PK/Efficacy models there is one component describing pharmacokinetics and one describing efficacy in the form of tumor growth inhibition. Similarly, for the biomarker PK/PD model there is one component describing pharmacokinetics and one describing efficacy but in this case PD biomarker modulation. The pharmacokinetics component is common between the two models (Fig. 21.1). The frequent application of PK/Efficacy and biomarker PK/PD models in characterizing oncology drug candidates speaks to their usefulness in characterization of in vivo potency and prediction of active dose and optimal dose schedule. The differential equations describing the entirety of these models are out of scope of this chapter. However, for illustrative purposes, representative differential equations showing how changes in the biological effect related to drug concentrations are shown below for the PK/Efficacy model (Eqs. 21.1 and 21.2) and the biomarker PK/PD model (Eq. 21.3).

$$\frac{d(\text{TV})}{dt} = k_{ng}(\text{TV}) - K(\text{TV}) \tag{Eq. 21.1}$$

$$K = \frac{K_{max} \times C^n}{KC_{50}^n \times C^n} \tag{Eq. 21.2}$$

where TV is defined as the tumor volume in mm^3, t is time, $d(\text{TV})/dt$ is the rate of change in tumor volume with time, k_{ng} is the net growth rate constant, C is the concentration of the anticancer agent, K is the rate constant describing the anti-tumor tumor effect, K_{max} is the maximum value of K, KC_{50} is the concentration of the anticancer agent where K is at ½ of K_{max}, and n is the Hill coefficient.

FIGURE 21.1 Representative PK/PD models used for oncology. (A) An indirect response model describing an irreversible effect of an anticancer agent on tumor growth [PK/efficacy model]. (B). An indirect response model describing the effect of an anticancer agent on a pharmacodynamics biomarker (in the diagram a model showing inhibition of biomarker production is shown) [biomarker PK/PD model]. "Oral" is the oral compartment, C represents the anticancer drug concentration, TV is tumor volume, PD is the pharmacodynamic biomarker, k_{ng} is the net tumor growth rate constant, K is the tumor elimination rate constant, k_{in} is the production rate of the PD biomarker, and k_{out} is the elimination rate constant of the PD biomarker. Forms of these PK/PD models are described in detail in Refs. [12–14].

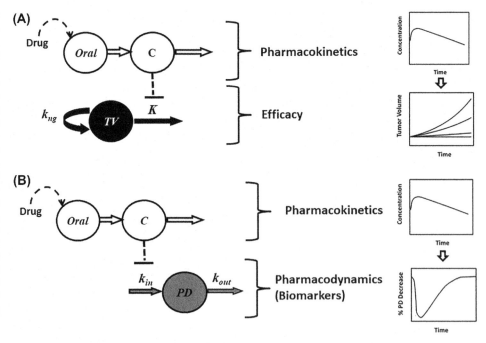

$$\frac{d(\text{PD})}{dt} = k_{\text{in}}\left(1 - \frac{I_{\max} \times C^n}{\text{IC}_{50}^n \times C^n}\right) - k_{\text{out}}(\text{PD})$$

Eq. 21.3

where PD is the biomarker level, $d(\text{PD})/dt$ is the rate of change in biomarker level with time, k_{in} is the production rate of the biomarker, $I_{\max}$ is the maximum inhibition of PD, IC_{50} is the concentration of the anticancer agent where the effect is at 50% of $I_{\max,}$ and k_{out} is the rate constant describing the elimination of the PD.

Drug concentration-effect relationships for tumor growth inhibition (TGI) are described by $K_{\max}$, KC_{50} and n in Eq. (21.2), and for PD biomarker reduction by $I_{\max}$, IC_{50} and n in Eq. (21.3). Separate PK/PD models with one describing tumor growth inhibition, and the other biomarker modulation similar to the models shown in Fig. 21.1 have been successfully applied in defining PD/Efficacy for anticancer agents such as crizotinib [15]. In the case of crizotinib, the concentration-effect curves for ALK (biomarker) inhibition and TGI from H3122 NSCLC cells or Karpas299 ALCL xenograft mice were extracted via PK/PD modeling and compared. The crizotinib EC_{50} concentration for ALK inhibition (233 ng/mL for H3122 and 666 ng/mL for Karpas299) was found to be similar to the EC_{50} for tumor growth inhibition (255 ng/mL for H3122 and 875 ng/mL for Karpas299). Crizotinib concentrations (in this case EC_{50} concentrations) provide a link between PD (biomarker modulation) and efficacy (tumor growth inhibition) as drug concentration (or PK) was the common element in both PK/PD models employed.

Integrated PK/PD/Efficacy models distinguish themselves from the PK/PD models shown in Fig. 21.1 in that they are comprised of three components; one describing pharmacokinetics, one describing pharmacodynamics, and one describing efficacy (Fig. 21.2). These three components are linked sequentially mimicking their inter-relationships in a biological system. As can be inferred from Fig. 21.2, drug concentrations perturb pharmacodynamic biomarker levels. In turn, modulation of the pharmacodynamic biomarkers is responsible for the biological effect (TGI). Integrated PK/PD/Efficacy models are more complex compared to models shown in Fig. 21.1 and require more work to construct and fit to experimental data. However, they bring additional value in that they provide a better understanding of biological relationships such as the PD/Efficacy relationship.

PD/efficacy relationship

The differentiating aspect of integrated PK/PD/Efficacy models compared to those described by Fig. 21.1 is the portion of the model describing the relationship between target PD biomarker modulation and TGI efficacy (PD/Efficacy relationship). Relationships between target modulation and efficacy, can be described by the same relationships associated with receptor pharmacology theory [16]. Fig. 21.3 shows two representative relationships between target modulation and biological effect. The curves shown in Fig. 21.3 can be described using equations that have used to describe concentration-response relationships such as logistic and Hill equations. For the purposes of discussion, in this chapter we will discuss the curves shown in Fig. 21.3A and B in context of the Hill equation (Eq. 21.4).

$$E = \frac{E_{\max} \times M^n}{\text{EM}_{50}^n \times M^n}$$

(Eq. 21.4)

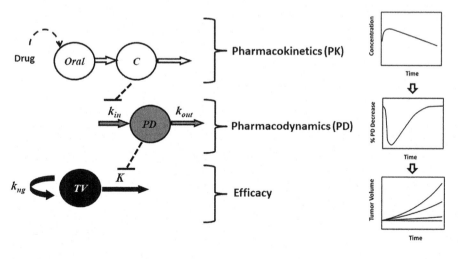

FIGURE 21.2 Representative integrated PK/PD/Efficacy model linking anticancer drug concentrations with pharmacodynamic response, and pharmacodynamic response with antitumor efficacy. "*Oral*" is the oral compartment, C represents the anticancer drug concentration, TV is tumor volume, PD is the pharmacodynamic biomarker, k_{ng} is the net tumor growth rate constant, K is the tumor elimination rate constant, k_{in} is the production rate of the PD biomarker, and k_{out} is the elimination rate constant of the PD biomarker. This PK/PD model is described in detail in Ref. [13].

Drug

Oral C

Pharmacokinetics (PK)

k_{in} k_{out}

PD

Pharmacodynamics (PD)

k_{ng} *TV* K

Efficacy

FIGURE 21.3 Representative curves describing the relationship between target modulation (% target inhibition) and effect where $n = 1$ (A) and $n > 1$ (B).

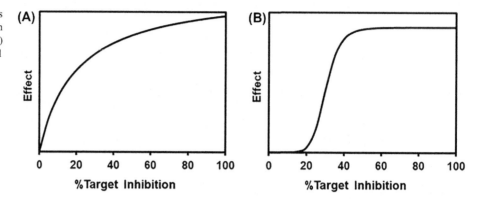

where E is the biological effect, E_{max} is the maximum value of E, M is the degree that the target (biomarker) is modulated, EM_{50} is the value of M where E is at ½ of E_{max}, and n is the Hill coefficient. In Fig. 21.3, M is expressed as %Target Inhibition. Fig. 21.3A shows biological effect rising linearly with increases in target inhibition until saturation of the effect begins where increases in effect no longer increase proportionally with increases in target inhibition. In the example, saturation of effect becomes more pronounced beyond approximately 20% target inhibition. Fig. 21.3A is described by a simplified form of Eq. (21.4) where $n = 1$. In cases where $n < 1$, biological effect similarly rises linearly with increases in target inhibition until saturation of the effect begins.

Fig. 21.3B differentiates from Fig. 21.3A in that it is sigmodal in shape ($n > 1$ in Eq. 21.4). The sigmoidal shape of this curve introduces a "threshold" target modulation that has to be achieved before an effect can be observed. In the representative Fig. 21.3B, this threshold is at approximately 20% target inhibition. It is only beyond this $\sim 20\%$ target inhibition threshold that effect is "turned on". In biology, this type curve with "threshold" or "switch-like" behavior is termed an ultrasensitive stimulus-response curves and has been observed for mitogen-activated protein kinase cascades [17].

In order to provide a more complete understanding of insights that can be obtained from examination of PD/Efficacy relationships, a more detailed description of the interpretation of E_{max} and EM_{50} from Eq. (21.4) in context of the integrated PK/PD/Efficacy model structure shown in Fig. 21.2 will be provided. In the integrated PK/PD/Efficacy model, the differential equation representing the change in tumor volume over time can be described by Eq. (21.1). In Eq. (21.1), tumor stasis (no change in TV) is achieved when $K = k_{ng}$ making the net change in TV to be "0". K is the effect (corresponding to E in Eq. 21.4) of the antitumor agent such that the change in tumor volume over time can also be described by Eq. (21.5) shown below where K in Eq. (21.1) is substituted with the mathematical expression describing E from Eq. (21.4).

$$\frac{d(\text{TV})}{dt} = k_{ng}(\text{TV}) - \left(\frac{E_{max} \times M^n}{\text{EM}_{50}^n \times M^n} \right)(\text{TV}) \qquad \text{(Eq. 21.5)}$$

Fig. 21.4, shows a representative plot of the target modulation versus effect curve in context of Eqs. (21.1) and (21.5) where K serves as the biological effect. In the example presented, $n > 1$ as the curve is clearly sigmoidal. E_{max} and EM_{50}

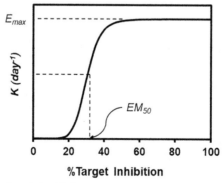

FIGURE 21.4 Representative curves describing the relationship between target modulation (% target inhibition) and antitumor effect (K) in context of an integrated PK/PD/efficacy model. In this plot, E_{max} is the maximum value of K and EM_{50} is the %target inhibition where K is at ½ of E_{max}. The Hill coefficient (n) in the representative plot is >1.

are also shown Fig. 21.4 and the overall shape of the relationship is determined by these two parameters as well as the value of n.

The relationship between $E_{\max}$ and k_{ng}, can provide biological insight into the biological activity of the antitumor agent on the tumor being studied. Table 21.1 presents three possible scenarios describing the relationship between parameters $E_{\max}$ and k_{ng}, the best antitumor response associated with each scenario, and the possible biological rationale. Of note, Table 21.1 lists "Best Antitumor Response" because the degree of target modulation is dependent on drug concentrations achieved in vivo. A lack of in vivo tolerability may limit concentrations and subsequent target modulation that can be achieved in vivo to the extent that $E_{\max}$ and EM_{50} in Eq. (21.5) cannot be estimated. If this is the case, it may be that only a linear relationship between target modulation and antitumor effect can be defined. Our discussion around $E_{\max}$ and k_{ng} that follows assumes that we are able to estimate these parameters.

As defined, k_{ng} is the net growth rate constant and is parameter specific to tumor types. This parameter can vary greatly depending on the tumor type that is implanted into mice. In contrast, $E_{\max}$ is a both a drug and tumor specific parameter and is linked to the biology that is represented. For molecular targeted agents, when $E_{\max} > k_{ng}$, the drug being tested is able to cause tumor regression in the xenograft model and has a maximum antitumor effect that is able to decrease tumor levels much faster than the growth. For molecular targeted anticancer agents, this suggests that tumor proliferation and survival is highly dependent on the biological pathway being inhibited by the targeted agent. When $E_{\max} = k_{ng}$ this suggests that modulation of the biological target mostly inhibits tumor growth but not tumor survival. In this scenario, the best response will be tumor stasis as the agent does not act to kill tumor cells. Finally, $E_{\max} < k_{ng}$ is associated with tumor growth delays and suggests that cancer cell growth and proliferation is not entirely dependent on signaling via the specific pathway that the anticancer agent is inhibiting. In the case of cytotoxic antitumor agents where drug action is more non-specific in nature, generally a higher $E_{\max}$ suggests that the tumor is more sensitive to the cytotoxic drug being evaluated.

Another important aspect of the PD/Efficacy relationship is that it is a "true biological relationship. If a first-in-class molecule is being evaluated using an integrated PK/PD/Efficacy model, the relationship between PD modulation and efficacy should be the same for all molecules targeting the same biological pathway. A requirement for this is that a proximal biomarker that is reflective of target occupancy/engagement is chosen to be the PD biomarker being monitored. In addition, molecules being evaluated are assumed to have no significant off target activity that contributes to the efficacy being monitored.

Finally, one important insight that is gained from examination of the PD/efficacy relationship is an understanding of the shape of the relationship and whether the relationship is a graded response (($n = 1$ or $n < 1$); Fig. 21.3A) or a "switch-like" response ($n > 1$; Fig. 21.3B). For pathways that show a "switch-like" or ultrasensitive stimulus-response curves, an understanding of the target modulation "threshold" value may be important and can be used to set PD endpoints in Phase I trials. In some cases, assays for proximal biomarkers that are directly reflective of target occupancy/engagement may not be available. For these instances, downstream biomarkers that are being monitored can be used for modeling. However, in this situation, one must mindful that modulation of downstream biomarkers may not be exclusive of the target being interrogated and may involve other biological pathways/processes.

Translational integrated PK/PD/efficacy modeling in oncology

The use of translational PK/PD modeling has increased as a consequence of continued drug candidate failures due to poor efficacy [1,2]. Oncology is a particularly challenging therapeutic area as many new oncology agents must demonstrate antitumor efficacy and improved survival when given in combination with standard of care. As such, an improved understanding of the biological mechanisms of action of new anticancer agents is advantageous to help determine the optimum dose and dose schedule required.

TABLE 21.1 Relationships between k_{ng} and $E_{\max}$.

Relationship	Best antitumor response	Possible biological rationale
$E_{\max} < k_{ng}$	Growth delay	Tumor growth and survival is not entirely dependent on signaling via pathway being modulated
$E_{\max} = k_{ng}$	Tumor stasis	Modulation of target impacts only tumor growth but not survival
$E_{\max} > k_{ng}$	Tumor regression	Modulation of target impacts tumor growth and survival.

As implied from the previous section, despite the additional complexity, there are beneficial insights provided by application of integrated PK/PD/Efficacy models (Fig. 21.2) as compared to using simpler PK/PD (Fig. 21.1B) and PK/Efficacy (Fig. 21.1A) models. This will be illustrated in case studies describing applications of integrated PK/PD/Efficacy modeling of inhibitors of the Raf/MEK/ERK [12,18] and Hedgehog signaling pathways [13].

RAF/MEK/ERK signaling pathway

The RAF/MEK/ERK signaling pathway is a highly conserved pathway and plays an important role in cell proliferation, survival, migration, cell cycle regulation, and angiogenesis [19–22]. Currently, three RAF kinase isoforms have been identified and are referred to as ARAF, BRAF and CRAF (also known as Raf-1) [23]. Activating mutations in BRAF have been frequently observed in several tumor types, including 50%–70% of malignant melanomas, 30% of papillary thyroid cancer, and 10%–15% of colorectal and ovarian cancers, among others [22,24–26]. The major mutation observed is in exon 15, which results in a Val600 Glu (V600E) amino acid substitution, leading to constitutive kinase activation [27]. Cancer cells harboring the V600E BRAF mutation have been shown to be particularly sensitive to inhibition of RAF and MEK (MEK1 and MEK2 isoforms). Currently, there are a handful of approved inhibitors of both RAF and MEK approved for cancer therapy [28]. In this first case study, learnings from the application of integrated PK/PD/Efficacy modeling of a BRAF inhibitor (GDC-0879 [12]; and Cobimetinib, a MEK inhibitor (GDC-0973; [18], will be discussed. Fig. 21.5 shows key components of this pathway as well as where BRAF and MEK inhibitors impact phosphorylation of pathway components. Phosphorylated MEK1 (pMEK1) and phosphorylated ERK (pERK) are biomarkers of the RAF/MEK/ERK signaling pathway that were monitored in our case studies.

GDC-0879 is a novel potent, selective BRAF inhibitor in various in vitro and cell-based assays with an IC_{50} estimate of 0.13 nM against purified BRAF V600E enzyme and a cellular pERK IC_{50} of 63 nM in the MALME-3M cell line [29]. In our preclinical investigations of GDC-0879, we aimed to characterized concentration-effect relationships for antitumor effect in A375 melanoma and Colo205 colorectal carcinoma (both V600E BRAF mutants) xenograft mice, and for PD biomarker modulation (pMEK1 inhibition) in A375 melanoma xenograft mice. As a final exercise, an integrated PK/PD/Efficacy model was used to characterize the PD/Efficacy relationship between pMEK1 inhibition in tumor (% Target Inhibition) and K (rate constant describing the antitumor tumor effect). A plot of the relationship in A375 (solid line) along with associated estimated pharmacodynamic parameters is shown in Fig. 21.6 and Table 21.2, respectively. A375 melanoma cells are known to have the V600E BRAF mutation (a sensitizing mutation) so it is no surprise that in A375 xenograft mice, the maximum effect (E_{max}) is far greater than the net tumor growth rate constant (k_{ng}). This is consistent with the tumor regressions in A375 xenografts observed at high GDC-0879 doses (>100 mg/kg once daily; [12]). Of note, the shape of the curve is sigmoidal with an estimated Hill coefficient of 8 (Table 21.2) indicating a very steep PD/Efficacy

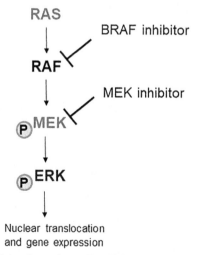

FIGURE 21.5 Components of the RAF/MEK/ERK signaling pathway. The "P" in circles indicate pathway components that are phosphorylated when pathway is activated. Inhibition of phosphorylated ERK (pERK) and phosphorylated MEK (pMEK) (specifically pMEK1 in our example) serve as biomarker measures of pathway inhibition. Pathway inhibition by BRAF and MEK inhibitors are shown. *Adapted from G. Bollag, J. Tsai, J. Zhang, C. Zhang, P. Ibrahim, K. Nolop, et al., 2012. Vemurafenib: the first drug approved for BRAF-mutant cancer. Nat. Rev. Drug Discov. 11, 873–886. https://doi.org/10.1038/nrd3847.*

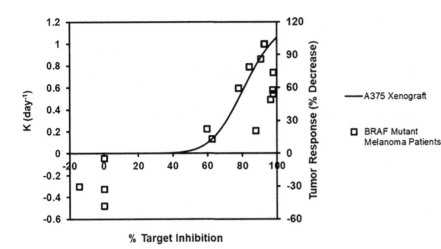

FIGURE 21.6 PD/efficacy relationship between %target modulation (pMEK1 inhibition) and effect (K) in A375 xenografts derived from GDC-0879 integrated PK/PD/efficacy analysis is shown as a solid line [12]. Squares represent observed % target modulation (pERK inhibition in cytoplasm) versus tumor response in BRAF mutant melanoma patients. *Digitized from G. Bollag, P. Hirth, J. Tsai, J. Zhang, P.N. Ibrahim, H. Cho, et al., 2010. Clinical efficacy of a RAF inhibitor needs broad target blockade in BRAF-mutant melanoma. Nature. 467, 596 −599. https://doi.org/10.1038/nature09454.*

TABLE 21.2 GDC-0879 pharmacodynamic parameters estimated using A375 xenograft mice.

PD parameter[a]	Estimate
k_{ng} (day^{-1})	0.079
E_{max} (day^{-1})	1.3
EM_{50} (% inhibition)	83
n	8.0

[a]PD parameters from Ref. [12] are re-expressed using terms in Eq. (21.5).

relationship. The curve was also right shifted with an EM_{50} of 83%. As a consequence, little to no antitumor effect is anticipated at target inhibition levels <40% [12]. At the time of the analysis, anecdotal data from the use of MEK inhibitors in the clinic suggested that a pathway knockdown of ~60% pERK knockdown would be required for tumor growth inhibition [30].

Shortly following the publication of results of the GDC-0879 integrated PK/PD/Efficacy modeling, clinical results for PLX4032, a BRAF inhibitor (vemurafenib, Zelboraf®), were published [31] which was followed by its approval for treatment of BRAF-mutated metastatic melanoma [32]. Of specific interest, the authors reported that decreases in cytoplasmic pERK correlated well with tumor response in BRAF mutant melanoma patients. Further, they observed that patients with tumor regressions were associated with >80% inhibition of cytoplasmic pERK concluding that a high degree of pathway inhibition was required for significant tumor response. Cytoplasmic pERK and tumor regression patient data from Ref. [31] was digitized and plotted along with the PD/Efficacy relationship estimated from A375 xenografts in Fig. 21.6. The observations in BRAF mutant melanoma patients were consistent and could be predicted based on the PD/Efficacy relationship established preclinically for A375 xenografts. The steep PD/Efficacy relationship along with the "right shifted" curve (Fig. 21.6) provides a rational explanation for observations a high requirement for pathway inhibition associated with tumor regression in BRAF melanoma patients. Based on the shape of the PD/Efficacy curve, a target inhibition "threshold" must be exceeded before antitumor activity is "switched on". Similarly, in BRAF mutant melanoma patients, a cytoplasmic pERK threshold of >60% inhibition must be achieved before tumor decreases were observed (Fig. 21.6).

Additional analysis using an integrated PK/PD/Efficacy model was performed in studies with the MEK inhibitor, cobimetinib (GDC-0973; Cotellic®), in A375 xenograft mice [18]. The integrated PK/PD/Efficacy model used to characterize cobimetinib preclinical xenograft studies was similar in concept to the model shown in Fig. 21.2 but included a tumor compartment as it was observed that cobimetinib resides for a prolonged period of time in tumor tissue. In addition, pERK inhibition in the tumor served as PD biomarker of pathway inhibition rather than pMEK1 inhibition in the example with GDC-0879. Despite these differences, the PD/Efficacy relationship obtained using cobimetinib was very similar to that obtained for GDC-0879 in that there was very little activity at 40% pERK inhibition in tumor. However, antitumor activity increased sharply as %pERK inhibition increased with maximal activity reached at 60 to 70 %pERK inhibition in the tumor. On the basis of early reports for MEK inhibitors, PD-0325901 and CI-1040, that suggested signs of activity at tumor %pERK decreases of >60% and 73%, respectively, we set >80% tumor pERK inhibition as our steady-state PD modulation target. Using patient pharmacokinetic data from cohort 1, the tumor pERK target of >80% inhibition, and preclinical PD estimates from additional xenograft models, we identified predicted cobimetinib doses (28−112 mg) that were anticipated to show clinical activity. Biological activity was observed in BRAF mutant melanoma patients at 60 and 100 mg which were fairly consistent with our predictions [18]. Our understanding of the shape of the PD/Efficacy relationship and the associated threshold for antitumor activity for BRAF and MEK inhibitors along with available information arising from MEK inhibitors in the clinic allowed us to set robust PD modulation targets allowing us to identify active doses in BRAF mutant melanoma patients.

Hedgehog signaling pathway

The hedgehog (Hh) pathway has been associated with a number of cancers including basal cell carcinoma (BCC) [33], medulloblastoma [34], colorectal, pancreatic [35], prostate [36], and lymphoma [37]. For BCC and medulloblastoma, Hh pathway activation occurs via mutational activation where aberrant cell proliferation is driven by ligand-independent cell autonomous Hh signaling. A larger set of cancers, driven by paracrine Hh signaling between tumor cells and the surrounding stroma, have been referred to as ligand-dependent cancers [38]. For ligand-dependent cancers, Hh ligands (Sonic, Indian, and Desert) bind to a transmembrane receptor, patched (PTCH) which, in the absence of ligand, inhibits the transmembrane protein, smoothened (SMO). In the presence of Hh ligand, the action of PTCH on SMO is relieved and SMO initiates signal transduction through the GLI family of transcription factors leading to induction of downstream targets which include GLI1 and PTCH forming both positive and negative feedback loops, respectively. For BCC $\sim$90% of sporadic cases are associated with inactivating mutations of the negative regulator PTCH leading to constitutive activation of the pathway [39] and up to 10% contain activating mutations in the positive regulator SMO [40]. Sporadic cases of medulloblastoma have also been associated with inactivating mutations in PTCH at a lower frequency of $\sim$30% of cases [41].

Interest in inhibitors of the Hh signaling pathway for the treatment of cancers led to the development of vismodegib (GDC-0449; Erivedge®), a potent, selective Hedgehog pathway inhibitor that targets SMO with an EC_{50} of 2.8 nM on a human palatal mesenchymal cell line (HEPM) stably expressing a GLI-responsive luciferase reporter gene [13]. During the development of vismodegib, we aimed to characterize the PK/PD/Efficacy relationship in models of both mutational (Ptch +/− medulloblastoma allograft) and ligand-dependent (patient-derived colorectal xenograft; D5123) Hh pathway activation with the goal of selecting an optimal dose and schedule for vismodegib in both cancer types. Similar to what was described for GDC-0879, an integrated PK/PD/Efficacy model similar to what is depicted in Fig. 21.2 was utilized to fit pharmacokinetic, pharmacodynamic and efficacy data from medulloblastoma allograft and D5123 xenograft studies with vismodegib. For vismodegib, inhibition of Gli1 mRNA served as the PD biomarker.

Estimated pharmacodynamic parameters for vismodegib in medulloblastoma and D5123 are presented in Table 21.3 and the PD/Efficacy relationship is shown in Fig. 21.7. For medulloblastoma allograft mice, $E_{max} > k_{ng}$ which is consistent with observed tumor regression resulting from vismodegib administration (see Table 21.1). In contrast, for D5123 colorectal xenograft mice, $E_{max} < k_{ng}$ which is consistent with the tumor growth delay observed in this model of ligand-

TABLE 21.3 Vismodegib pharmacodynamic parameters estimated using medulloblastoma allograft and D5123 xenograft mice.

PD parameter[a]	Medulloblastoma estimate	D5123 Estimate
k_{ng} (day^{-1})	0.154	0.0810
E_{max} (day^{-1})	0.589	0.0524
EM_{50} (% inhibition)	81.5	95.6
n	8.68	8.89

[a]PD parameters from Ref. [13] are re-expressed using terms in Eq. (21.5).

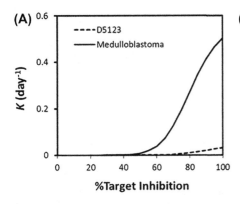

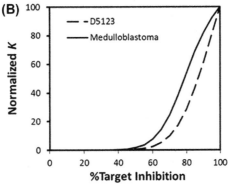

FIGURE 21.7 Vismodegib PD/Efficacy relationship between %target modulation (Gli1 mRNA inhibition) and K in medulloblastoma allograft mice and D5123 xenograft mice (A). Vismodegib PD/Efficacy relationship where K is normalized to the value of K at 100% Gli1 mRNA inhibition (B).

dependent cancer. The E_{max} estimated from medulloblastoma allograft mice was approximately 11-fold higher compared to the estimate from D5123 xenograft mice suggestive of medulloblastoma proliferation being more dependent on Hh pathway signaling compared to D5123. This is reflected in the lower amplitude of the PD/Efficacy relationship for D5123 in Fig. 21.7A. However, when K is normalized to the value of K at 100% Gli1 mRNA inhibition, curves describing the PD/Efficacy for medulloblastoma and D5123 show a similar sigmodal shape (Fig. 21.7B) characterized by a Hill coefficient of ∼9 (see Table 21.3). EM_{50}'s estimated for both cancer types are high >80% suggesting that very high levels of Gli1 mRNA inhibition are required to get maximal effect. To ensure maximal clinical benefit, this led us to target a minimum of 95% inhibition of Gli mRNA as our optimal PD modulation corresponding to unbound concentrations of 42−68 nM [13]. The recommended dose, 150 mg dose once daily, resulted in unbound concentrations that fulfilled this criteria (109 nM ± 0.058 SEM) [42].

As a consequence of this exercise, we gained insights on mechanisms of vismodegib drug resistance. Table 21.4 summarizes results of an efficacy study in an in vivo model of medulloblastoma (sg274 allograft mice) that contains a SMO mutant (D477G) that is largely resistant to vismodegib [13]. In medulloblastoma allografts containing wild type SMO that were used to obtain the PD/Efficacy relationship shown in Fig. 21.7, a dose of 25 mg/kg once daily was adequate for tumor regression (>100% TGI). In contrast, treatment with 100 mg/kg vismodegib twice daily (8-fold higher daily dose) resulted in 52% TGI in resistant sg274 allograft mice. In the same study, Hh-Antag (a second Hh pathway inhibitor), given at the same dose resulted in to slight regression of tumor in the sg274 model (>100% TGI). Tumor growth inhibition in sg274 allograft mice was associated with 76% inhibition of Gli1 mRNA in response to vismodegib and 99% inhibition in response to Hh-Antag (Table 21.4). The large reduction in efficacy with vismodegib administration despite a robust measurement of target modulation (76% inhibition of pathway) is consistent with the large drops in efficacy anticipated based on the PD/Efficacy relationship shown in Fig. 21.7. These data further supported our belief that high levels of pathway inhibition are required for optimal activity and that modest decreases in the inhibition of Gli1 can result in large losses of antitumor activity.

In the examples of integrated PK/PD/Efficacy modeling provided for the RAF/MEK/ERK and Hh signaling pathways, the extracted PD/Efficacy relationship were sigmoidal in shape resulting in rapid changes in antitumor efficacy (K) associated with modest changes in target modulation. These rapid changes in antitumor efficacy result in "thresholds" of target modulation that must be exceeded before antitumor efficacy can be observed. This behavior of PD/Efficacy relationships is not universal as work performed on the PI3 Kinas inhibitor, GDC-0941 (Pictilisib) [43] in MCF7.1 breast cancer xenografts (using pAKT inhibition as the measure of target modulation) resulted in a PD/Efficacy relationship with a more graded response with a shape more similar to what is depicted in Fig. 21.3A. Similarly, characterization of the PD/Efficacy relationship for a heat shock protein 90 inhibitor, PF04942847, in MDA-MB-231 breast cancer xenografts (using

TABLE 21.4 Tumor growth inhibition and target inhibition of vismodegib and Hh-Antag in sG274 allografts [13].

Hh pathway inhibitor	Daily dose	Anti-tumor efficacy	PD response (Gli1 mRNA)
Vismodegib	100 mg/kg BID	52% TGI	76% inhibition
Hh-Antag	100 mg/kg BID	Tumor regression (>100% TGI)	99% inhibition

AKT degradation as a measure of target modulation) resulted in a relationship that did not show rapid changes in efficacy with small changes in target modulation [44].

The use of integrated PK/PD/Efficacy models is not exclusive to the oncology therapeutic area. Integrated PK/PD/Efficacy analyses have been reported for BTK inhibitors and their use in preclinical rheumatoid arthritis models [45,46]. Application of integrated PK/PD/Efficacy models are not without its shortcomings. As with all modeling exercises, the outcome is only as good as the data that is used to build the model. An understanding of the relevance of the specific preclinical cancer model used in the integrated PK/PD/Efficacy analysis to the actual human disease is required to properly interpret and utilize information derived from the modeling exercise. Tumors in xenograft or allograft mice models that are used for preclinical PK/PD/Efficacy modeling are typically considered more homogenous when compared to the patient population in the cancer indication of interest. Further, constructing integrated models describing PK/PD/Efficacy relationship are more time consuming compared to construction of separate models describing PK/Efficacy and biomarker PK/PD relationships (Fig. 21.1). Despite this, integrated PK/PD/Efficacy models require far less labor and data when compared to more complex "full blown" systems pharmacology models that can provide similar biological insight. Overall, integrated PK/PD/Efficacy modeling and the resultant PD/Efficacy relationships allows for a more comprehensive understanding of target biology and aids in the identification of an optimal dose/and dose schedule and further refinement of clinical target concentrations/PD endpoints.

References

[1] H. Dowden, J. Munro, Trends in clinical success rates and therapeutic focus, Nat. Rev. Drug Discov. 18 (2019) 495–496, https://doi.org/10.1038/d41573-019-00074-z.

[2] R.K. Harrison, Phase II and phase III failures: 2013–2015, Nat. Rev. Drug Discov. 15 (2016) 817e8.

[3] J.I. Johnson, S. Decker, D. Zaharevitz, L.V. Rubinstein, J.M. Venditti, S. Schepartz, et al., Relationships between drug activity in NCI preclinical in vitro and in vivo models and early clinical trials, Br. J. Cancer 84 (2001) 1424–1431.

[4] L.R. Kelland, "Of mice and men": values and liabilities of the athymic nude mouse model in anticancer drug development, Eur. J. Cancer 40 (2004) 827–836.

[5] R.S. Kerbel, Human tumor xenografts as predictive preclinical models for anticancer drug activity in humans: better than commonly perceived-but they can be improved, Cancer Biol. Ther. 2 (2003) S134–S139.

[6] J.K. Peterson, P.J. Houghton, Integrating pharmacology and in vivo cancer models in preclinical and clinical drug development, Eur. J. Cancer 40 (2004) 837–844.

[7] T. Troiani, C. Schettino, E. Martinelli, F. Morgillo, G. Tortora, et al., The use of xenograft models for the selection of cancer treatments with the EGFR as an example, Crit. Rev. Oncol. Hematol. 65 (2008) 200–211.

[8] M. Danhof, J. de Jongh, E.C. De Lange, O. Della Pasqua, B.A. Ploeger, R.A. Voskuyl, Mechanism-based pharmacokinetic-pharmacodynamic modeling: biophase distribution, receptor theory, and dynamical systems analysis, Annu. Rev. Pharmacol. Toxicol. 47 (2007) 357–400.

[9] H. Wong, E.F. Choo, B. Alicke, X. Ding, H. La, E. McNamara, et al., Anti-tumor activity of targeted and cytotoxic agents in murine subcutaneous tumor models correlates with clinical response, Clin. Cancer Res. 18 (2012) 3846–3855.

[10] H. Wong, T. Bohnert, V. Damian-Iordache, C. Gibson, C.-P. Hsu, T. Heimbach, et al., Translational pharmacokinetic-pharmacodynamic analysis in pharmaceutical industry: an IQ consortium PK-PD discussion group perspective, Drug Discov. Today 22 (2017) 1447–1459, https://doi.org/10.1016/j.drudis.2017.04.015.

[11] E. Schuck, T. Bohnert, A. Chakravarty, V. Damian-Iordache, C. Gibson, C.P. Hsu, et al., Preclinical pharmacokinetic/pharmacodynamic modeling and simulation in pharmaceutical industry: an IQ consortium survey examining the current landscape, AAPS J. 17 (2015) 462–473.

[12] H. Wong, M. Belvin, S. Herter, K.P. Hoeflich, L.J. Murray, L. Wong, et al., Pharmacodynamics of 2-{4-[(1E)-1-(Hydroxyimino)-2,3-dihydro-1H-inden-5-yl]-3-(pyridine-4-yl)-1H-pyrazol-1-yl}ethan-1-ol (GDC-0879), a potent and selective B-Raf kinase inhibitor: relationships between systemic concentrations, pMEK1 inhibition, and efficacy, J. Pharmacol. Exp. Therapeut. 329 (2009) 360–367, https://doi.org/10.1124/jpet.108.148189.

[13] H. Wong, B. Alicke, K.A. West, P. Pacheco, H. La, T. Januario, et al., Pharmacokinetic/pharmacodynamic analysis of vismodegib in preclinical models of mutational and ligand-dependent hedgehog pathway activation, Clin. Cancer Res. 17 (2011) 4682–4692.

[14] H. Wong, S.E. Gould, N. Budha, W.C. Darbonne, E.E. Kadel 3rd, H. La, et al., Learning and confirming with preclinical studies: modeling and simulation in the discovery of GDC-0917, an IAP antagonist, Drug Metabol. Dispos. 41 (2013) 2104–2113.

[15] S. Yamazaki, P. Vicini, Z. Shen, H.Y. Zou, J. Lee, Q. Li, et al., Pharmacokinetic/pharmacodynamic modeling of crizotinib for anaplastic lymphoma kinase inhibition and antitumor efficacy in human tumor xenograft mouse models, J. Pharmacol. Exp. Therapeut. 340 (2012) 549–557, https://doi.org/10.1124/jpet.111.188870.

[16] I.L.O. Buxton, Pharmacokinetics and pharmacodynamics: the dynamics of drug absorption, distribution and elimination, in: L.L. Brunton, J.S. Lazo, K.L. Parker (Eds.), Goodman & Gilman's the Pharmacological Basis of Therapeutics, eleventh ed., L.L. McGraw-Hill, New York, 2006.

[17] C.Y. Huang, J.E. Ferrell Jr., Ultrasensitivity in the mitogen-activated protein kinase cascade, Proc. Natl. Acad. Sci. U. S. A. 93 (1996) 10078–10083.

[18] H. Wong, L. Vernillet, A. Peterson, J.A. Ware, L. Lee, J.F. Martini, et al., Bridging the gap between preclinical and clinical studies using PK-PD modeling: an analysis of GDC-0973, a MEK inhibitor, Clin. Cancer Res. 18 (2012) 3090–3099.

[19] M.S. Chapman, J.N. Miner, Novel mitogen-activated protein kinase kinase inhibitors, Expert Opin. Invest. Drugs 20 (2011) 209–220.

[20] B.B. Friday, A.A. Adjei, Advances in targeting the Ras/Raf/MEK/Erk mitogen-activated protein kinase cascade with MEK inhibitors for cancer therapy, Clin. Cancer Res. 14 (2008) 342–346.

[21] J.A. McCubrey, L.S. Steelman, W.H. Chappell, S.L. Abrams, E.W. Wong, F. Chang, et al., Roles of the Raf/MEK/ERK pathway in cell growth, malignant transformation and drug resistance, Biochim. Biophys. Acta 1773 (2007) 1263–1284.

[22] J.S. Sebolt-Leopold, R. Herrera, Targeting the mitogen-activated protein kinase cascade to treat cancer, Nat. Rev. Cancer 4 (2004) 937–947.

[23] S.V. Madhunapantula, G.P. Robertson, Is B-Raf a good therapeutic target for melanoma and other malignancies? Cancer Res. 68 (2008) 5–8.

[24] H. Davies, G.R. Bignell, C. Cox, P. Stephens, S. Edkins, S. Clegg, et al., Mutations of the BRAF gene in human cancer, Nature 417 (2002) 949–954.

[25] N. Li, D. Batt, M. Warmuth, B-Raf kinase inhibitors for cancer treatment, Curr. Opin. Invest. Drugs 8 (2007) 452–456.

[26] S.T. Yuen, H. Davies, T.L. Chan, J.W. Ho, G.R. Bignell, C. Cox, et al., Similarity of the phenotypic patterns associated with BRAF and KRAS mutations in colorectal neoplasia, Cancer Res. 62 (2002) 6451–6455.

[27] K.E. Mercer, C.A. Pritchard, Raf proteins and cancer: B-Raf is identified as a mutational target, Biochim. Biophys. Acta 1653 (2003) 25–40.

[28] R. Yaeger, R.B. Corcoran, Targeting alterations in the RAF-MEK pathway, Cancer Discov. 9 (2019) 329–341, https://doi.org/10.1158/2159-8290.CD-18-1321.

[29] J.D. Hansen, J. Grina, B. Newhouse, M. Welch, G. Topalov, N. Littman, et al., Potent and selective pyrazole-based inhibitors of B-Raf kinase, Bioorg. Med. Chem. Lett 18 (2008) 4692–4695.

[30] W. Tan, S.E. DePrimo, S.S. Krishnamurthi, J.J. Rinehart, L.M. Nabell, D. Nickens, et al., 2007. Pharmacokinetic (PK) and pharmacodynamic (PD) results of a phase I study of PD-0325901, a second generation oral MEK inhibitor, in patients with advanced cancer. American Association of Cancer Research-National Institute of Cancer-European Organization for Research and Treatment of Cancer Conference. October 2007, San Francisco, CA.

[31] G. Bollag, P. Hirth, J. Tsai, J. Zhang, P.N. Ibrahim, H. Cho, et al., Clinical efficacy of a RAF inhibitor needs broad target blockade in BRAF-mutant melanoma, Nature 467 (2010) 596–599, https://doi.org/10.1038/nature09454.

[32] G. Bollag, J. Tsai, J. Zhang, C. Zhang, P. Ibrahim, K. Nolop, et al., Vemurafenib: the first drug approved for BRAF-mutant cancer, Nat. Rev. Drug Discov. 11 (2012) 873–886, https://doi.org/10.1038/nrd3847.

[33] H. Hahn, J. Christiansen, C. Wicking, P.G. Zaphiropoulos, A. Chidambaram, B. Gerrard, et al., A mammalian patched homolog is expressed in target tissues of sonic hedgehog and maps to a region associated with developmental abnormalities, J. Biol. Chem. 271 (1996) 12125–12128.

[34] T. Pietsch, A. Waha, A. Koch, J. Kraus, S. Albrecht, J. Tonn, et al., Medulloblastomas of the desmoplastic variant carry mutations of the human homologue of Drosophila patched, Cancer Res. 57 (1997) 2085–2088.

[35] R.L. Yauch, S.E. Gould, S.J. Scales, T. Tang, H. Tian, C.P. Ahn, et al., A paracrine requirement for hedgehog signalling in cancer, Nature 455 (2008) 406–410.

[36] L. Fan, C.V. Pepicelli, C.C. Dibble, W. Catbagan, J.L. Zarycki, R. Laciak, et al., Hedgehog signaling promotes prostate xenograft tumor growth, Endocrinology 145 (2004) 3961–3970.

[37] C. Dierks, J. Grbic, K. Zirlik, R. Beigi, N.P. Englund, G.R. Guo, et al., Essential role of stromally induced hedgehog signaling in B-cell malignancies, Nat. Med. 13 (2007) 944–951.

[38] S.J. Scales, F.J. de Sauvage, Mechanisms of Hedgehog pathway activation in cancer and implications for therapy, Trends Pharmacol. Sci. 30 (2009) 303–312.

[39] M.R. Gailani, M. Ståhle-Bäckdahl, D.J. Leffell, M. Glynn, P.G. Zaphiropoulos, C. Pressman, et al., The role of the human homologue of Drosophila patched in sporadic basal cell carcinomas, Nat. Genet. 14 (1996) 78–81.

[40] J. Reifenberger, M. Wolter, R.G. Weber, M. Megahed, T. Ruzicka, P. Lichter, et al., Missense mutations in SMOH in sporadic basal cell carcinomas of the skin and primitive neuroectodermal tumors of the central nervous system, Cancer Res. 58 (1998) 1798–1803.

[41] Y. Lee, H.L. Miller, P. Jensen, R. Hernan, M. Connelly, C. Wetmore, et al., A molecular fingerprint for medulloblastoma, Cancer Res. 63 (2003) 5428–5437.

[42] P.M. Lorusso, C.M. Rudin, J.C. Reddy, R. Tibes, G.J. Weiss, M.J. Borad, et al., Phase I trial of hedgehog pathway inhibitor GDC-0449 in patients with refractory, locally-advanced or metastatic solid tumors, Clin. Cancer Res. 17 (2011) 2502–2511.

[43] L. Salphati, H. Wong, M. Belvin, K.A. Edgar, W.W. Prior, D. Sampath, et al., Pharmacokinetic-pharmacodynamic modeling of tumor growth inhibition and biomarker modulation by the novel PI3K inhibitor 2-(1H-Indazol-4-yl)-6-(4-methanesulfonyl-piperazin-1-ylmethyl)-4-morpholin-4-yl-thieno[3,2-d]pyrimidine (GDC-0941), Drug Metabol. Dispos. 38 (2010) 1436–1442, https://doi.org/10.1124/dmd.110.032912.

[44] S. Yamazaki, L. Nguyen, S. Vekich, Z. Shen, M.-J. Yin, P.P. Mehta, et al., Pharmacokinetic-pharmacodynamic modeling of biomarker response and tumor growth inhibition to an orally available heat shock protein 90 inhibitor in a human tumor xenograft mouse model, J. Pharmcol. Exp. Ther. 338 (2011) 964–973.

[45] F. Daryaee, Z. Zhang, K.R. Gogarty, Y. Li, J. Merino, S.L. Fisher, et al., A quantitative mechanistic PK/PD model directly connects Btk target engagement and in vivo efficacy, Chem. Sci. 8 (2017) 3434–3443, https://doi.org/10.1039/c6sc03306g.

[46] L. Liu, J. Di Paolo, J. Barbosa, H. Rong, K. Reif, H. Wong, Anti-arthritis effect of a novel Bruton's tyrosine kinase inhibitor in rat collagen-induced arthritis and mechanism-based pharmacokinetic/pharmacodynamic modeling: relationships between inhibition of BTK phosphorylation and efficacy, J. Pharmacol. Exp. Therapeut. 338 (2011) 154–163, https://doi.org/10.1124/jpet.111.181545.

Chapter 22

Predicting unpredictable human pharmacokinetics: case studies from the trenches of drug discovery

Zheng Yang[a],*

[a]Metabolism and Pharmacokinetics, Pharmaceutical Candidate Optimization, Bristol Myers Squibb, Princeton, NJ, United States

Introduction

Predicting human pharmacokinetics is a key activity for developability assessment in drug discovery. The outcome of human pharmacokinetic predictions forms the basis of human efficacious dose projections. The prediction results also influence drug designs during lead optimization and inform candidate differentiation and selection before advancing into the clinic. It suffices to say that human pharmacokinetic prediction is an integral part of drug discovery processes in finding better medicines for patients.

Over the past 2 decades, considerable progress has been made in experimental tools and prediction methodologies. Experimentally, advancements in the use of liver microsomes, cryopreserved hepatocytes, and long-term culture systems such as HepatoPac and HμREL [1,2] have moved human clearance predictions away from traditional animal in vivo data-based allometric scaling to the approaches oriented to human in vitro data. Methodologies-wise, the extrapolation of human in vitro data for clearance prediction based on the in vitro-to-in vivo correlation established in nonclinical species has been commonly adopted across the pharmaceutical industry. The extended clearance concept [3−5] that incorporates transporter-mediated active uptake and efflux into the human clearance prediction further provides a more mechanistic basis than the conventional metabolism-centric approaches. Development of in silico methods in predicting partition coefficients in tissues [6−8] and the commercialization of physiologically based pharmacokinetic (PBPK) modeling software, such as SimCYP, GastroPlus, and PK-Sim, have propelled the use of PBPK approaches in human pharmacokinetic predictions. PBPK modeling and Wajima's C_{ss}-MRT method [9] have been applied widely for predicting human pharmacokinetic profiles from nonclinical data.

With advancements in experimental approaches and prediction methodologies for human pharmacokinetic predictions, the industry has experienced success in reducing the attrition rate due to inadequate pharmacokinetic properties in the clinic. Waring et al. [10] reported the compilation and analysis of 812 oral small molecule drug candidates from four large pharmaceutical companies from 2000 to 2010. Out of 605 compounds that had been terminated, inadequate pharmacokinetic properties only accounted for 5% of the causes for the attrition and the failure rate was constant between 2000−5 and 2006−10. Consistent with the observation, Maurer et al. [11] recently analyzed the attrition causes of 43 Pfizer oral small molecules in the period of 2015−9 and found that pharmacokinetic issues accounted for only 5% of the overall attrition rate.

Accompanying the clinical success of drug candidates in pharmacokinetic attributes, various pharmaceutical companies over the years have published prediction methods and success rates in the prediction of human pharmacokinetics from nonclinical data. Obach et al. [12], to the author's knowledge, is the first paper from the industry that systematically evaluated various methodologies for the prediction of human pharmacokinetic parameters (clearance, steady-state volume of distribution (V_{ss}), half-life ($t_{1/2}$), and oral bioavailability (F_{po})) from nonclinical data using 50 Pfizer compounds from 1981

---

* Current affiliation: Drug Metabolism and Pharmacokinetics, Alnylam Pharmaceuticals, Inc., Cambridge, MA, United States.

Overcoming Obstacles in Drug Discovery and Development. https://doi.org/10.1016/B978-0-12-817134-9.00022-2

to 1994. Through this comprehensive evaluation, they found that the effective $t_{1/2}$ prediction ($=0.693 *$ clearance/V_{ss}), based on the clearance predicted from in vitro metabolic data without protein binding corrections and the V_{ss} predicted using multi-species allometry or the dog V_{ss} adjusted by plasma protein binding, allowed the successfully assigning compounds to appropriate dosing regimens 70%–80% of the time. De Buck et al. [13] from Janssen examined the use of PBPK modeling in predicting the human pharmacokinetic profiles of 26 proprietary compounds and concluded that the accuracy of prediction of the terminal $t_{1/2}$ within 2-fold was as high as 69% when the clearance was predicted from in vitro metabolism data without correction for binding and the V_{ss} was predicted from physicochemical properties and calibrated with in vivo rat tissue partition data. Huang et al. [14] from Bristol Myers Squibb reported the findings of prospective human pharmacokinetic predictions on 35 small molecule drug candidates from 1997 to 2005. Nearly 60% of compounds had the predicted human exposure (measured as the area under the curve, AUC) within 2-fold of the observed values. The paper also highlighted the use of Wajima's C_{ss}-MRT method for human pharmacokinetic profile predictions. At about the same time, Hosea et al. [15] studied 50 proprietary compounds (1998–2003) from Pfizer and evaluated single-species allometric scaling and the impact of clearance mechanism (i.e., clearance mediated mainly by P450 enzymes) on human pharmacokinetic predictions. They found that single-species allometric scaling using a power exponent of 0.75 performed as well as multiple-species scaling. The clearance predicted from human liver microsomes also worked well for drugs undergoing P450-mediated metabolism. When the human V_{ss} was predicted by assuming the same unbound V_{ss} between humans and individual animal species (rat, dog, or monkey) and the human clearance was predicted from the single-species allometry using a power exponent of 0.75, the within 2-fold success rate for the effective $t_{1/2}$ (predicted human $t_{1/2} = 0.693 *$ clearance/V_{ss}; observed human $t_{1/2}$ calculated from the AUC-based accumulation ratio) was 50%–66%. When the clearance predicted from human liver microsomes was used for drugs exclusively cleared by P450, the success rate was 60%–74%. In 2011, under the Pharmaceutical Research and Manufacturers of America (PhRMA) initiative, 12 PhRMA member companies participated the evaluation of 126 small molecule compounds (19 intravenous (IV) compounds and 107 oral compounds) for human pharmacokinetic predictions from nonclinical data [16,17]. Twenty-nine methods for predicting the clearance and twenty-four methods for predicting V_{ss} were examined. Among these methodologies examined, the maximum success rate for predicting the clearance, V_{ss}, and oral AUC within 2-fold was $\sim$78%. However, no specific methodology stood out in predicting the V_{ss} accurately for all compounds, and allometry-based clearance prediction methods performed slightly better than the approaches based on in vitro data. In the same year, Van den Bergh et al. [18] from Janssen published their evaluation of 35 compounds on the human oral pharmacokinetic profile prediction using the complex Dedrick plot and C_{ss}-MRT method with and without correction factors such as plasma protein binding, maximum life-span potential (MLP), and brain weight. The within 2-fold success rates for the AUC and terminal $t_{1/2}$ were 26%–51% and 43%–60%, respectively. At about the same time, the PBPK-based human pharmacokinetic profile predictions for 21 compounds in Pfizer were studied by Jones et al. [19]. The within 2-fold success rates for the AUC and terminal $t_{1/2}$ were 50% and 61%, respectively. In 2015, Zhang et al. [20] from Novartis reported their efforts of predicting the human pharmacokinetic profiles of 18 compounds by combining Wajima's C_{ss}-MRT method for the IV profile prediction with the advanced compartmental absorption and transit model for absorption kinetics. The within 2-fold success rates for the AUC and terminal $t_{1/2}$ were 65% and 65%, respectively. More recently, Peters et al. [21] from Merk KGaA reported that their success rate of predicting human exposure within 2-fold was 80% for 15 molecules, 5 of which were biologics. Davies et al. [22] from AstraZeneca summarized their success rate in human pharmacokinetic predictions over 2000–18 on 116 drug candidates. The within 2-fold success rates for the AUC and terminal $t_{1/2}$ were 60% and 64%, respectively. The cited references here are by no means to be comprehensive, but they show a general trend of the success rate of 60%–70% in the industry up to now.

Despite the success of human pharmacokinetic predictions, there is still room for improvement. On the absorption front, the oral data of clinically relevant dosage forms, as opposed to those from solution formulations typically used in the nonclinical setting, need to be incorporated for human pharmacokinetic predictions, especially if the peak concentration (C_{max}) is a critical consideration for human safety. There is also a need of improving our understanding of absorption mechanisms, particularly active transporter-mediated absorption for drugs that are charged at the gastrointestinal tract pH. On the disposition end, better in vitro systems need to be established to understand active transporter-mediated uptake and efflux for predicting the clearance and V_{ss}. Also, quantitative models and approaches for human clearance predictions need to be developed for the biotransformation pathways mediated by non-P450 enzymes (Phase II, amide hydrolysis, et al.). This is because challenges faced in transporter- and Phase II enzyme-mediated processes have commonly presented difficulties in the quantitative prediction of enterohepatic recirculation in humans. Understanding these processes also helps determine the fate of metabolites formed in hepatocytes and predict the circulating levels of pharmacologically active or toxic metabolites in humans. These challenges represent future opportunities in improving experimental systems and theoretical approaches for human pharmacokinetic predictions. In this regard, emerging microphysiological systems or organs on chips [23–25] may offer a promise of more integrated, in vitro platforms for studying these complex processes.

Additionally, the approaches developed using an in silico technique or machine learning may provide a new opportunity for early human pharmacokinetic predictions before the first synthesis of compounds [26,27], which could improve the efficiency of the overall drug discovery processes.

In this book chapter, the author wants to share some personal experiences of predicting human pharmacokinetics in the trenches of drug discovery. Three case studies on small molecule drug candidates are presented. The first case study highlights the difficulty and solution of predicting the human clearance of a low-turnover compound that had a narrow therapeutic index (TI). The second case study tells a story of a backup drug aiming for a short human $t_{1/2}$ after oral administration. It exhibited divergent nonclinical V_{ss} values (10-fold apart) that could not be attributed to plasma protein binding and affected its fate as a drug candidate for advancement into the clinic. The third story showcases the approaches of leveraging competitor molecule data for predicting the human pharmacokinetics of a long-lived drug candidate (human $t_{1/2} > 7$ days) and its active circulating metabolite. In all three cases, data- and mechanism-driven solutions were applied to resolve the issues and timely impacted the progression of drug candidates in discovery. In each case, the observed human pharmacokinetic data are also provided for comparisons and lessons learned.

General considerations in human pharmacokinetic predictions

Predicting human pharmacokinetics from nonclinical data is a scientific endeavor. Although experimental data are objective and factual, decisions made on prediction methodologies and approaches can be subjective and may affect the outcome of human pharmacokinetic predictions. This endeavor, therefore, not only involves science but also could be an art. As with any prediction, a human pharmacokinetic prediction can always be made by a range of tools and approaches. Using the human clearance prediction as an example, nine allometry-based methods and five variations in the in vitro-to-in vivo clearance extrapolation are available [28]. In this regard, what approach to use or how to treat different prediction results can be a matter of subjectivity. Achieving the desired accuracy of human pharmacokinetic predictions requires careful scientific thinking and understanding. For this reason, the author wants to share some personal and perhaps philosophical perspectives on the prediction of human pharmacokinetics.

First, concerted efforts are needed to understand what in vitro data means in the context of in vivo. The in vitro data include intrinsic clearance determinations in liver microsomes or hepatocytes. They can also be in vitro metabolic pathway evaluations or in vitro transporter data. For these data, in vitro systems or models reflect certain aspects of the in vivo setting, but they may not capture the entirety and/or complexity of a living system in terms of the enzyme or transporter expression and abundance, the interplay among metabolizing enzymes and transporters, non-specific binding, or dynamic changes in drug concentrations, et al. The best way to understand in vitro data for the in vivo context is to evaluate the in vitro-to-in vivo connectivity through nonclinical data. It is especially true when extrapolating the human in vitro data to predict human clearance. In this instance, one needs to determine whether metabolic pathways observed in an in vitro system are present in vivo using nonclinical data. One also needs to evaluate how well the clearances predicted from the in vitro data quantitatively correlated with the in vivo clearances in nonclinical species and assess whether there is consistency in the pattern of the predictions. It can be argued that, without the appropriate establishment of the in vitro-to-in vivo correlation in the clearance of nonclinical species, there should be no in vitro-to-in vivo extrapolation for the human clearance prediction. Simply put, understanding the in vivo context is the necessity of using any in vitro system for human pharmacokinetic predictions.

Second, the human relevance of nonclinical data needs to be well studied and understood. For example, when the F_{po} is $\leq 20\%$ in three of four nonclinical species, does it indicate that the F_{po} will not be high in humans? To address this question, one needs to understand what factor drives the incomplete F_{po} in nonclinical species as opposed to using the majority rule or the average value. Is the incomplete F_{po} due to limited absorption or extensive first-pass effect? If it is former and can be attributed to a low aqueous solubility or an inadequate passive permeability, then one would expect that the human F_{po} would be limited, because these factors are species-independent. On the other hand, if the extensive first-pass effect is responsible for the low F_{po} observed in nonclinical species and if the human clearance is anticipated to be low based on in vitro data and the in vitro-to-in vivo clearance correlation established in animal species, then one should expect a high F_{po} in humans and have confidence in moving the compound forward to the clinic. For the human clearance prediction, understanding the human relevance means that metabolic pathways observed in a human in vitro system (e.g., hepatocytes) are well represented in nonclinical species. As an example, hydrolysis is the major biotransformation pathway in human hepatocytes, whereas it is minor in the hepatocytes of nonclinical species. In this case, the in vitro-to-in vivo correlation established in nonclinical species is not meaningful as the metabolic pathway in humans is not reflected in animal species from a qualitative perspective. Quantitatively, hydrolysis may occur extrahepatically. Hence the clearance predicted from human hepatocytes likely underpredicts the human clearance. Because of the lack of hydrolysis in nonclinical species, allometry-based approaches that scale the clearances from nonclinical species are not expected to work well in human clearance prediction. The best approach to address the issue is to determine the enzymes responsible for hydrolytic reactions mechanistically and then leverage the human experience in the clearance of drugs that undergo the same biotransformation pathway. For the human volume of distribution prediction, understanding the human relevance implies that one needs to evaluate not only the extent of plasma protein binding in humans versus nonclinical species but also the binding affinity (i.e., how tightly a drug binds to human vs. animal plasma proteins) as well as the type of plasma proteins that the drug binds to. An example in the literature is UCN-01 [29]. In humans, it had a low V_{ss} of 0.11–0.13 L/kg, whereas the value was 6–17 L/kg in nonclinical species. An extremely high and tight protein binding to α1-acid glycoprotein unique to humans was attributed to the difference in the V_{ss} between humans and nonclinical species. In this example, the high and tight protein binding in humans also led to very low clearances (0.0012–0.0028 mL/min/kg) and very long terminal $t_{1/2}$ values (11–69 days). The incidence is not unique and has occurred in other compounds based on the author's experience.

Third, the approaches used for predicting human pharmacokinetics need to be determined by experimental evidence and mechanistic understanding. Applications of a global scaling factor or equations based on past success may not be adequate or appropriate for a specific asset of interest. It is because the nature of human pharmacokinetic predictions is quantitative. Here, detail matters. When making human pharmacokinetic predictions, one should consider factors such as modalities, indications, testing population (patients vs. healthy subjects in a first-in-human trial), and the therapeutic index (narrow vs. wide). These considerations may influence or justify the approaches used for human pharmacokinetic predictions. In some cases, these considerations call for a range of approaches in human pharmacokinetic predictions to capture different scenarios and uncertainty. Separately, when coming to the performance standard of human pharmacokinetic predictions, a prediction within a 2-fold of observed results is commonly used in the industry. However, in the case of monoclonal antibodies, a 2-fold underprediction in the human clearance may lead to a 2-fold overprediction in the $t_{1/2}$ (e.g., from 14 to 7 days), which could impact the selection of dosing regimens in the clinic. We recently experienced this situation. Based on the nonclinical data observed in cynomolgus monkeys, the human pharmacokinetics of a monoclonal antibody drug candidate was assumed to be the same as that in monkeys, as opposed to applying allometry scaling for the human clearance prediction. The observed human pharmacokinetic data proved the approach used, with the observed human pharmacokinetic profile nearly identical to that in monkeys. Had we used allometry for the human clearance prediction, we would underpredict the human clearance and overpredict the human $t_{1/2}$. This example illustrates the importance of applying data-driven approaches to human pharmacokinetic prediction.

Additionally, a clear understanding of the limitations and assumptions involved in the approaches and equations is needed when conducting human pharmacokinetic predictions. In this regard, the author wants to provide some perspectives on several methods commonly used.

(1) When using allometry-based methods for the human clearance prediction, one needs to understand the approaches are empirical, and the extrapolation of the clearance from animals to humans based on body weight bears little relevance to the actual mechanisms that govern drug clearance unless the clearance is high and organ blood flow-dependent. For this reason, the coefficient of determination (R^2) value of the linear regression line obtained from logarithmic-transformed data offers no confidence in the human clearance prediction. Also, because of the nature of the linear regression used in the allometric scaling, a small change in the mouse clearance at the low end of the regression line could lead to a change in the slope and alter the human clearance at the top end of the regression line. In some instances, the human clearance predicted from simple allometry can change from low to intermediate, even though all the nonclinical species evaluated show low clearance values and human in vitro systems show minimal drug turnovers. In the literature, it has been pointed out that allometry is infused with fundamental statistical errors and does not capture biological differences among species [30,31].

(2) Another consideration is the use of PBPK modeling for the prediction of human pharmacokinetic profiles. The approach has gained considerable attention because it is the model that is based on the anatomy and physiology of the body and can incorporate various aspects of the system- and drug-related parameters. However, as with any modeling approach, it requires a sound understanding of mechanisms that govern drug absorption and disposition as well as reliable data inputs. It is worth noting that one of the key data inputs to PBPK modeling for the prediction of human pharmacokinetic profiles is the predicted human clearance. As a result, if the human clearance cannot be predicted accurately, PBPK modeling suffers the same limitation as using the C_{ss}-MRT method [9] which is based on the superimposition of the normalized concentration-time data obtained from nonclinical species. Additionally, the tissue partition coefficients predicted in PBPK models need to be calibrated with nonclinical pharmacokinetic data to predict the V_{ss} and drug concentration-time profile in humans accurately [32]. Furthermore, it is the author's experience that, if the clearance and V_{ss} in humans can be predicted accurately, human systemic pharmacokinetic profiles can also be forecast accurately using Wajima's Css-MRT method. However, in the case of predicting tissue drug levels and dealing with complex kinetics (e.g., nonlinear pharmacokinetics), PBPK modeling has its advantages.

(3) For the prediction of human volume of distribution, the Øie-Tozer equation (see below) has been used widely for the prediction of human V_{ss} [33–35].

$$V_{ss} = V_p \times \left(1 + R_{E/I}\right) + V_p \times f_u \times \left(\frac{V_E}{V_p} - R_{E/I}\right) + V_R \times \frac{f_u}{f_{u,R}}$$

where V_P is the volume of plasma water; V_E is the volume of the extracellular fluid outside plasma (i.e., interstitial fluid); V_R is the volume of the rest of total body water outside the extracellular fluid (i.e., intracellular fluid); f_u is the unbound fraction in plasma; $f_{u,R}$ is the unbound fraction in the rest of total body water outside the extracellular fluid; $R_{E/I}$ is the ratio of the total number of drug-binding sites (or amount of drug-binding proteins) in the extracellular fluid outside plasma versus those in plasma. For the equation above, one needs to recognize the assumptions involved in deriving the equation. For example, the equation was derived by assuming that the unbound drug concentrations were the same across different fluid spaces (plasma, interstitial fluid, and intracellular fluid). Although it is true for passively diffused drugs, it does not apply to drugs that undergo active uptake and efflux, especially if active processes play an important role in drug disposition. Additionally, the $R_{E/I}$ assumed that drug-binding proteins were the same between plasma and interstitial fluid. The assumption is violated when significant drug binding to cell surface components occurs in the interstitial fluid space or the drug binds to components in the interstitial fluid space different from those in plasma. Furthermore, the Øie-Tozer equation was derived originally for the drugs exhibiting a small volume of distribution (less than 0.2 L/kg). When a drug exhibits a large volume of distribution that exceeds the volume of total body water (0.7 L/kg), an equation known as the Gillette equation (see below), first given by Wilkinson and Shand [36], is more applicable.

$$V_{ss} = V_p + V_T \times \frac{f_u}{f_{u,T}}$$

where V_T is the volume of total body water outside plasma and $f_{u,T}$ is the unbound fraction in total body water outside plasma. However, both Gillette and Øie-Tozer equations do not take into consideration of active processes that affect the assumption of equal unbound concentrations between plasma and tissues. Additionally, to predict the human V_{ss}, one needs to obtain the $f_{u,R}$ or $f_{u,T}$ from nonclinical species. When these values have a wide range, the cause of the discrepancy across nonclinical species and the relevance to humans need to be understood. This way, an appropriate approach for using $f_{u,R}$ or $f_{u,T}$ to predict the human Vss, as opposed to taking an average value, can be used.

Finally, keep it simple. Specifically, when predicting human clearance using in vitro data, considerations need to be given whether there is a need to include the unbound fraction in an in vitro incubation and blood. Scientifically, it is hard to know what binding numbers measured in a static system mean in the context of the in vivo situation. In liver microsomes, these binding values also include the binding to enzymes that are responsible for drug metabolism. In hepatocytes, the unbound fraction measured with no enzyme activity may not truly reflect the in vivo setting where a tighter binding to drug-metabolizing enzymes could compete against a non-specific weak binding. Operationally, each measurement is associated with experimental errors. The more variables are introduced to a prediction method, the more errors are propagated in the prediction results. Therefore, if a simple approach works in the in vitro-to-in vivo clearance correlation of nonclinical species without considering the unbound fractions, then there is no need to add complexity to human clearance predictions.

Methodologies for human pharmacokinetic predictions

General methodologies for human pharmacokinetic predictions have been extensively reviewed. Interested readers can refer to the publications by Zuo et al. [28,32]. The methodologies described below are the methods used by the author for the case studies described.

Prediction of human clearance

Allometric scaling is a commonly employed approach for human clearance prediction. The total body plasma clearances (CL_{tot}, in mL/min) observed in nonclinical species and the corresponding body weights (BW, in kg) are transformed in a logarithmic (log) scale. Linear regression is performed on the log-transformed data, from which the human CL_{tot} is extrapolated using the BW of 70 kg and the CL_{tot}-BW relationship established in nonclinical species. The Rule of Exponents developed by Mahmood and Balian [37] specifies that, when the slope of the regression line in a log scale (or the exponent in a linear scale) from simple allometry falls between 0.71 and 1.0, the product of clearance and MLP needs to be used against BW for the linear regression of the log-transformed data. When the slope of the regression line in a log scale from simple allometry is greater than 1.0, the product of clearance and brain weight should be used versus BW in the linear regression of the log-transformed data.

Another widely used method in the human clearance prediction is the extrapolation of the in vitro hepatic intrinsic clearance ($CL_{h,int}$) data determined from liver microsomes or hepatocytes [12,36,38,39]. The in vitro $CL_{h,int}$ from liver microsomal data is estimated as:

$$CL_{h,int} = \left(\frac{k_{microsomes}}{C_{protein}}\right) \times 45 \text{ mg protein per g liver weight} \times \text{x g liver weight per kg body weight}$$

where $k_{microsomes}$ is the disappearance rate constant (min^{-1}) obtained from the log-linear regression of the percent parent drug remaining versus time data in liver microsomes or the formation rate constant of a major metabolite determined from the initial formation rate divided by the product of the parent drug concentration at time zero and incubation volume; $C_{protein}$ is the protein concentration (mg proteins per mL) in liver microsomal incubations; x g liver weight per kg body weight is the liver weight relative to body weight in individual species. The value in mice, rats, dogs, monkeys, and humans is 90, 40, 32, 32, and 21 g/kg, respectively [40]. Similarly, the $CL_{h,int}$ from hepatocyte data is calculated as:

$$CL_{h,int} = \left(\frac{k_{hepatocytes}}{C_{cell}}\right) \times 120 \times 10^6 \text{ cells per g liver weight} \times \text{x g liver weight per kg body weight}$$

where $k_{hepatocytes}$ is the disappearance rate constant (min^{-1}) obtained from the log-linear regression of the percentage of the parent drug remaining-time data observed in hepatocyte incubations or the formation rate constant of a major metabolite determined from the initial formation rate divided by the product of the parent drug concentration at time zero and incubation volume; C_{cell} is the hepatocyte concentration (million cells per mL) in incubations. To predict the hepatic blood clearance ($CL_{h,blood}$), the following assumptions are made: (1) the drug of interest exhibits linear kinetics; (2) protein binding in an in vitro system is similar to that in blood and the two terms are canceled out in the calculation; (3) metabolic pathways and rates are similar between in vivo and in vitro (i.e., in vivo $CL_{h,int}$ = in vitro $CL_{h,int}$); and (4) the well-stirred model is adequate for hepatic clearance predictions. With these assumptions, the $CL_{h,blood}$ is calculated as follows:

$$CL_{h,blood} = \frac{Q_h \times CL_{h,int}}{Q_h + CL_{h,int}}$$

where Q_h is the hepatic blood flow with a value equal to 90, 70, 35, 44, and 20 mL/min/kg in mice, rats, dogs, monkeys, and humans, respectively [40,41]. Assuming that the liver is the major organ for elimination, the human CL_{tot} is predicted using the following equation:

$$CL_{tot} = CL_{tot,blood} \times \text{Blood-to-plasma concentration ratio} = CL_{h,blood} \times \text{Blood-to-plasma concentration ratio}$$

Prediction of human steady-state volume of distribution

Allometric scaling is generally used for the prediction of the V_{ss} in humans. Similar to allometry used in the clearance prediction, the V_{ss} (in liter) obtained in nonclinical species and the corresponding BW are transformed in a log scale. A linear regression on the log-transformed data is performed, from which the human V_{ss} is predicted using a BW of 70 kg. The same procedure can be applied to the unbound V_{ss} ($V_{ss,u}$), where the $V_{ss,u}$ is obtained after correcting for the unbound fraction (f_u) in plasma ($V_{ss,u} = V_{ss} \div f_u$).

Prediction of human oral bioavailability and absorption rate constant

The human F_{po} is predicted using the equation:

$$F_{po} = f_a \times f_g \times f_h$$

where $f_a \times f_g$ is the fraction of dose absorbed into the portal vein after oral administration; f_h is the hepatic availability. The $f_a \times f_g$ is estimated from nonclinical species as follows:

$$f_a \times f_g = \frac{F_{po,\text{nonclinical species}}}{1 - CL_{h,\text{blood,nonclinical species}}/Q_{h,\text{nonclinical species}}}$$

where the $CL_{h,\text{blood,nonclinical species}}$ is equal to the total body clearance of the drug from blood ($CL_{tot,blood}$) in the nonclinical species by assuming that the liver is the major organ for elimination. The $f_a \times f_g$ in humans is the average value of the nonclinical data. The human f_h is calculated using the following equation:

$$f_h = 1 - \frac{CL_{h,\text{blood,human}}}{Q_{h,\text{human}}}$$

where $CL_{h,\text{blood,human}}$ is the predicted hepatic blood clearance in humans.

The human absorption rate constant (k_a) is predicted as the average value observed in the nonclinical species studied. Assuming linear pharmacokinetics, the k_a in nonclinical species is estimated from the IV and oral data using the following equation:

$$k_a = \frac{1}{MRT_{po} - MRT_{iv}}$$

where MRT_{po} and MRT_{iv} are the mean residence time after oral and IV administration, respectively.

Prediction of human intravenous and oral pharmacokinetic profiles

The human pharmacokinetic profile following IV administration is predicted using the C_{ss}-MRT method developed by Wajima et al. [9]. In a nonclinical species, the C_{ss} is calculated as a dose divided by the V_{ss} from that species. The resultant C_{ss} is used to normalize the average plasma or blood concentrations observed in the same species at the dose used to calculate the C_{ss}. Similarly, the MRT obtained from that species is applied to normalize the time associated with the average plasma or blood concentration observed. The normalized IV pharmacokinetic profiles from individual nonclinical species are then combined and fitted with an appropriate pharmacokinetic compartment model. The fitted curve is converted back to a human IV pharmacokinetic profile using the C_{ss} (=dose ÷ V_{ss}) and MRT (=Vss ÷ CL_{tot}) predicted for humans. Alternatively, the normalized nonclinical IV data can be converted to the human profile using the predicted human C_{ss} and MRT and then fitted with an appropriate pharmacokinetic compartment model. Both approaches should result in similar human IV pharmacokinetic profiles predicted, from which the IV pharmacokinetic parameters in humans can be derived. The IV pharmacokinetic parameters are then coupled with the predicted human oral F_{po} and k_a to obtain an oral pharmacokinetic profile in humans.

Case studies

Case study 1. Compound with a low metabolic turnover in human in vitro systems

Background and critical question to be addressed

BMS-A was a small molecule drug candidate that exhibited a narrow TI in the nonclinical setting. It has a molecular weight of ∼500 Da and is a neutral compound in the pH range of 2–11. Metabolism is the primary clearance mechanism of BMS-A. Because of the narrow TI anticipated in the clinic, the IV route of administration was pursued to minimize variability in drug exposure for an oncologic indication. The critical project issue at the time was that BMS-A exhibited a low metabolic turnover in human liver microsomes and hepatocytes, rendering difficulties in predicting the human clearance that was critical to developing a narrow TI drug in the clinic. For example, the turnover $t_{1/2}$ determined based on the parent drug disappearance at a substrate concentration of 0.1 μM in human liver microsomes over a 120-min incubation was estimated to be 890 min. There was no apparent drug turnover in cryopreserved human hepatocytes at 2 million cells per mL over 2 h at the same substrate concentration, while the positive control midazolam performed as expected in the same experiment. The in vitro human systems, therefore, offered no confidence to predict the human clearance of BMS-A based on the parent drug disappearance. It is also worth noting that, at the time, the hepatocyte relay method was not established in the field [42]; nor was HepatoPac or HμREL system [1,2] available.

Additionally, BMS-A exhibited low clearance values across the nonclinical species studied. The hepatic extraction ratio, assuming that the CL_{tot} is equal to the $CL_{h,blood}$, was estimated to be 0.10 (mouse), 0.21 (rat), 0.01 (dog), and 0.25 (monkey), respectively. The simple allometry revealed a predicted human CL_{tot} of 1.1 mL/min/kg, with a power exponent of 0.66 (Fig. 22.1A). Using the Rule of Exponents [37], MLP or brain weight adjustment was not warranted for the human

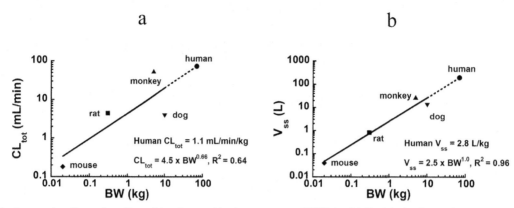

FIGURE 22.1 Interspecies allometric scaling of the pharmacokinetic parameters of BMS-A. (A) Total body plasma clearance and (B) steady-state volume of distribution.

clearance prediction because the power exponent from simple allometry was less than 0.70. If the adjustment was made, the predicted human CL_{tot} would be revised to 0.51 mL/min/kg (MLP) and 0.48 mL/min/kg (brain weight), respectively. However, despite the low clearance predicted from allometry, the approach lacked a mechanistic basis. Furthermore, it was suggested in the literature that allometry may not be appropriate for drugs that exhibit low clearances via metabolism [43]. Therefore, the critical question was how low the clearance of BMS-A would be in humans.

Issue resolution

To gain confidence in predicting human clearance using in vitro systems, the formation of metabolites was measured. This approach was taken because metabolite formation represented the appearance of a product that can be monitored readily. To adequately reflect the parent drug metabolism, the metabolite monitored needed to represent the major metabolic pathway of the compound of interest. Examining the metabolic profiles of BMS-A in liver microsomes and hepatocytes of human and nonclinical species revealed that an N-demethylated metabolite represented the major biotransformation pathway of BMS-A across the species studied. The relative abundance of metabolites formed was determined based on the LC/UV peak heights compared to that of BMS-A at the start of the incubation. The synthetic standard of the N-demethylated metabolite was subsequently made and used as a standard to quantify the metabolite concentration in the in vitro liver microsome and hepatocyte studies.

Prediction of human clearance

Using the N-demethylated metabolite as a way to monitor the turnover in liver microsomes and hepatocytes, the metabolism rate of BMS-A was studied in humans and nonclinical species. Fig. 22.2 shows the formation of the N-demethylated metabolite over time in β-nicotinamide adenine dinucleotide phosphate-fortified liver microsomes at a protein concentration of 1 mg/mL and a drug concentration of 0.1 μM. The rate of metabolite formation was different among species, with rats having the highest formation rate followed by mice, monkeys, humans, and dogs. Additionally, the rate of metabolite formation was linear between 0.1 and 1 μM in human liver microsomes. With the rate of metabolite formation determined and assuming that it represented the total turnover of BMS-A, the $CL_{h,blood}$ of BMS-A was predicted in humans and nonclinical species. The rate of metabolite formation was divided by the substrate concentration to obtain the total in vitro intrinsic clearance in the liver, after which the well-stirred model was applied to predict the $CL_{h,blood}$. Plasma protein binding (90%–94% bound in humans and 88%–96% bound in nonclinical species) was not used to obtain the protein binding in blood for the clearance prediction, nor was protein binding in the in vitro systems incorporated in the clearance prediction. Additionally, to compare with the in vivo clearance data, the CL_{tot} determined from the plasma concentration-time data was assumed to be equal to the $CL_{h,blood}$. The assumption was reasonable because the blood-to-plasma concentration ratio of BMS-A in humans and monkeys was approximately 1 and a minimal excretion of the parent drug in the urine of nonclinical species was observed.

Table 22.1 summarizes the in vitro $CL_{h,blood}$ predicted from liver microsomes in humans and nonclinical species as well as the observed $CL_{tot,blood}$ in nonclinical species. It is worth noting that the $CL_{h,blood}$ values of BMS-A predicted based on the parent drug disappearance from liver microsomes agreed with those calculated from the rate of the metabolite formation. Specifically, the human $CL_{h,blood}$ of BMS-A was predicted to be 0.71 mL/min/kg (based on the parent drug

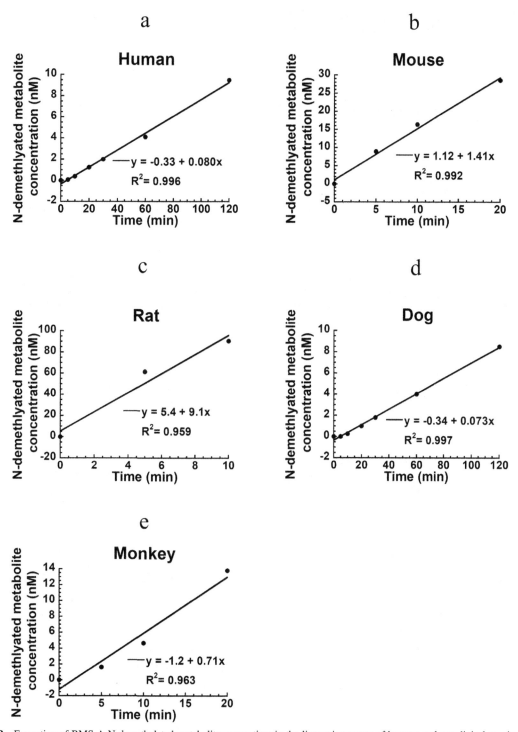

FIGURE 22.2 Formation of BMS-A N-demethylated metabolite versus time in the liver microsomes of humans and nonclinical species. (A) Human, (B) mouse, (C) rat, (D) dog, and (E) monkey. Only the linear portions of the concentration-time profiles are shown. Liver microsomes were fortified with β-nicotinamide adenine dinucleotide phosphate, and incubations were conducted at 37°C for 2 h using a microsomal protein concentration of 1 mg/mL and a substrate concentration of 0.1 nM.

disappearance) and 0.73 mL/min/kg (based on the metabolite formation). Furthermore, when the in vitro-in vivo correlation in the clearance was examined in nonclinical species, the ratio of the in vitro predicted $CL_{h,blood}$ versus the in vivo $CL_{tot,blood}$ was 3.4−3.5× in rodents, 2.3× in dogs, and 1.0× in monkeys, respectively. These results suggested clearances of nonclinical species correlated in vitro and in vivo, substantiating the use of liver microsomal data in the prediction of the

TABLE 22.1 In vitro-to-in vivo correlation in the clearance of BMS-A in nonclinical species and predicted human clearances.

Parameter	Mouse	Rat	Dog	Monkey	Human
In vitro predicted $CL_{h,blood}$ (mL/min/kg)[a]					
Based on parent drug disappearance	27	56	0.78	14	0.71
Based on metabolite formation	34	49	1.0	8.3	0.73
In vivo observed $CL_{tot,blood}$ (mL/min/kg)[b]	9.0	15	0.39	11	n.a.
Ratio of in vitro predicted versus in vivo observed clearance[c]	3.4	3.5	2.3	1.0	n.a.
Predicted human CL_{tot} (mL/min/kg)[d]	n.a.	n.a.	n.a.	n.a.	0.72 (monkey-scaling factor) 0.31 (dog-scaling factor) 0.21 (rodent-scaling factor)

n.a., not applicable.
[a]*The in vitro $CL_{h,blood}$ was predicted from liver microsome data generated at a drug substrate concentration of 0.1 μM and a microsomal protein concentration of 1 mg/mL, with an incubation time of up to 2 h.*
[b]*The in vivo $CL_{h,blood}$ was assumed to be the same as the in vivo CL_{tot} determined from the plasma concentration-time data, because the blood-to-plasma concentration ratio of BMS-A in monkeys and humans was near unity.*
[c]*The ratio was calculated using the average value of the in vitro $CL_{h,blood}$ from the two methods divided by the in vivo $CL_{tot,blood}$.*
[d]*Human CL_{tot} was predicted after correcting for the scaling factor determined based on the in vitro-to-in vivo correlation in the clearance of nonclinical species.*

human clearance of BMS-A. In comparison, the correlation of the hepatocyte-predicted clearance to the in vivo clearance was poor in the nonclinical species studied. For example, the clearance in mice was 13-fold over-predicted using mouse hepatocytes, whereas it was 3.4-fold under-predicted from dog hepatocytes. A lack of consistency in hepatocyte data for predicting the in vivo clearance in nonclinical species indicated that hepatocytes may not be a good system compared to liver microsomes in predicting the human clearance of BMS-A. This coupled with the fact that oxidative metabolism was dominant in the biotransformation of BMS-A in both human liver microsomes and human hepatocytes, justified the use of liver microsomal data in the prediction of the human clearance of BMS-A.

To predict the CL_{tot} of BMS-A in humans, several steps were taken. First, due to the anticipated narrow TI in the clinic, the scaling factors determined from the in vitro-to-in vivo clearance correlation in individual nonclinical species were used to adjust the $CL_{h,blood}$ (0.72 mL/min/kg) predicted from human liver microsomes. Second, as mentioned above, the $CL_{h,blood}$ predicted from human liver microsomes was assumed to be equal to the CL_{tot}, because of the blood-to-plasma concentration ratio of ~1 and a minimal renal clearance anticipated. Consequently, the human CL_{tot} of BMS-A was predicted to be 0.72 mL/min/kg (monkey-scaling factor), 0.31 mL/min/kg (dog-scaling factor), and 0.21 mL/min/kg (rodent-scaling factor), respectively (Table 22.1).

To assess the inter-subject variability associated with the human CL_{tot} of BMS-A, the Simcyp Population-based Simulator (version 9, Sheffield, UK) was employed. Reaction phenotyping studies with human liver microsomes and a panel of recombinant human cytochrome P450 enzymes demonstrated that the metabolism of BMS-A was primarily mediated via cytochrome P450 (CYP) 3A4 (73%) with some contribution from CYP2C9 (16%), 2C19 (5%) and 2C8 (6%). Using these data as inputs, 100 virtual trials with 10 virtual human healthy subjects per trial were conducted. The median percent coefficient of variation (%CV) in the clearance was determined to be 61%. The 5th and the 95th percentile of the %CV were 31 and 101%, respectively.

Prediction of human steady-state volume of distribution

The human V_{ss} of BMS-A was predicted to be 2.8 L/kg using simple allometry (Fig. 22.1B). The power exponent was determined to be 1.0, with an R^2 of 0.96.

Prediction of human pharmacokinetic profile following intravenous administration

Using the Css-MRT method developed by Wajima et al. [9], the IV pharmacokinetic profiles of BMS-A from nonclinical species were superimposed and are shown in Fig. 22.3A. With the predicted human CL_{tot} and the V_{ss} as inputs, the superimposed IV data of BMS-A were used to project the human plasma pharmacokinetic profile after IV administration (Fig. 22.3B). Based on the predicted human pharmacokinetic profiles, the terminal plasma $t_{1/2}$ of BMS-A in humans was

a

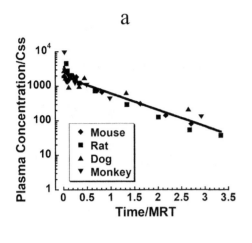

b

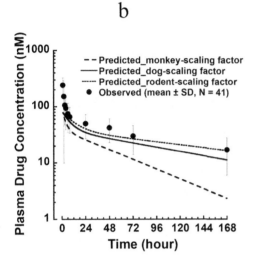

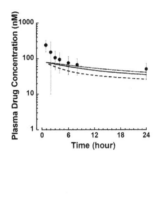

FIGURE 22.3 Prediction of the human pharmacokinetic profiles of BMS-A from nonclinical species. (A) Superimposed nonclinical IV plasma concentration-time profiles of BMS-A after data transformation using the C_{ss}-MRT method. The line represents the fitted curve. (B) Predicted versus observed human IV plasma concentration-time profiles of BMS-A at 4 mg. The symbols are the observed data (mean ± SD, N = 41); the lines show the predicted results with different clearance scaling factors based on individual nonclinical species.

estimated to be 37 h (monkey-scaling factor), 81 h (dog-scaling factor), and 124 h (rodent-scaling factor), respectively (Table 22.2). Furthermore, the nonclinical animal models indicated that maintaining the steady-state plasma concentrations above the protein binding-adjusted in vitro cellular IC_{50} (26 nM) for 48 h during a weekly treatment interval was required for robust efficacy while minimizing potential toxicity in the clinic. Using the information and assuming linear pharmacokinetics, the human efficacious dose given as a 1-h IV infusion in a weekly dosing regimen was projected to be 6 mg (monkey-scaling factor), 3 mg (dog-scaling factor), and 2 mg (rodent-scaling factor), respectively.

Predicted versus observed human pharmacokinetics

Table 22.2 summarizes the predicted versus observed human plasma pharmacokinetic parameters of BMS-A at a 4-mg dose, with the predicted and observed plasma concentration-time profiles shown in Fig. 22.3B. The human pharmacokinetics of BMS-A was reasonably predicted from the nonclinical data. The CL_{tot} values of BMS-A predicted using both dog- and rodent-scaling factors were in good agreement with the average observed value (0.8—1.2× vs. observed), whereas the monkey scaling factor led to 2.7× overprediction in the clearance. The predicted V_{ss} was 1.5× higher than the average observed result. Furthermore, the terminal $t_{1/2}$ predicted with dog- and rodent-scaling factors captured the average observed $t_{1/2}$ well (0.76—1.2× vs. observed), whereas the terminal $t_{1/2}$ obtained using the monkey-scaling factor was about 1/3 of the observed result because of the overprediction in the clearance. The shape of the observed average plasma concentration-time profile also matched up well with the ones predicted using the rodent- or dog-scaling factor. Importantly, using the observed average human pharmacokinetic data to project the human efficacious dose, the weekly dose was predicted to be 2.5 mg, which is in good agreement with the human efficacious doses (2—6 mg) projected using the nonclinical data. Moreover, the extent of variability in the CL_{tot} observed in the clinic, measured as the %CV, was 62%, well-aligned with the median results (61%) simulated from the virtual population using SimCYP.

TABLE 22.2 Predicted versus observed pharmacokinetic parameters of BMS-A after intravenous administration of a 4-mg dose to humans.[a]

Parameter	Predicted			Observed (mean ± SD, N = 41)
	Monkey-scaling factor	Dog-scaling factor	Rodent-scaling factor	
C_{max} (nM)	158 (0.58× vs. observed)	164 (0.60× vs. observed)	167 (0.61× vs. observed)	272 ± 135
T_{max} (h)	1 (1× vs. observed)	1 (1× vs. observed)	1 (1× vs. observed)	1 (median)
AUC_{tot} (nM × h)	2377 (0.27× vs. observed)	5520 (0.63× vs. observed)	8149 (0.93× vs. observed)	8791 ± 4778
CL_{tot} (mL/min/kg)	0.72 (2.7× vs. observed)	0.31 (1.2× vs. observed)	0.21 (0.80× vs. observed)	0.26 ± 0.16
V_{ss} (L/kg)		2.8 (1.5× vs. observed)		1.9 ± 0.84
Terminal $t_{1/2}$ (h)	37 (0.35× vs. observed)	81 (0.76× vs. observed)	124 (1.2× vs. observed)	107 ± 62

[a]Administered as a 1-h infusion; the average human body weight was assumed to be 70 kg.

Summary of case study 1

The formation of a metabolite, representing the major biotransformation pathway of a narrow TI drug, was used to overcome the issue of the slow metabolic turnover of the parent drug in the human in vitro systems. The results provided high-level confidence in the human clearance prediction for a low-clearance drug (<1 mL/min/kg) in humans. Efforts were also taken to understand the in vitro-to-in vivo correlation in the clearances of nonclinical species. Owing to the narrow TI anticipated in the clinic, the scaling factors derived from individual nonclinical species, as opposed to an averaged correction factor, were applied to predict the human in vivo clearance from the in vitro data. The range of predictions captured the uncertainty and led to a successful prediction of the human pharmacokinetics of BMS-A. The work greatly facilitated the clinical development plan on the anticipated human efficacious dose and regimen prospectively. It also impacted the formulation development for a compound that had a low aqueous solubility for parental administration.

Case study 2. Compound with divergent steady-state volume of distribution values in nonclinical species

Background and critical question to be addressed

BMS-B was a backup compound to BMS-A. Compared to BMS-A, it was aimed for the oral route of administration and to have a $t_{1/2}$ shorter than that of BMS-A in humans. Structurally, the differences between BMS-B and BMS-A were subtle. A methyl group in BMS-A was replaced with hydrogen in BMS-B, and hydrogen in another location of BMS-A was substituted with fluorine in BMS-B. Both were neutral compounds. The calculated logarithmic partition coefficient (clogP) of BMS-B was 5.12 versus 4.33 for BMS-A, suggesting that BMS-B was about 6-fold more lipophilic than BMS-A. On the other hand, the polar surface area of BMS-B was 113.65 $Å^2$ versus 104.86 $Å^2$ for BMS-A, indicating subtle differences on the surface associated with heteroatoms and polar hydrogen atoms that could also affect the permeability.

At the time, the human pharmacokinetics of BMS-A after IV administration were available. It was rewarding to see the approaches used for predicting human pharmacokinetics worked reasonably well for BMS-A. Namely, the rate of a major metabolite formation was used for predicting the clearance and simple allometry was employed for predicting the V_{ss}. Naturally, the same approaches could be extended to predict the human clearance and the V_{ss} of BMS-B. However, BMS-B exhibited significant species differences in the V_{ss}. For example, the V_{ss} of BMS-B in mice and dogs after IV administration was 1.9 and 1.4 L/kg, respectively. In comparison, the value in rats and monkeys was 7 and 15 L/kg, respectively. The differences in the V_{ss} among nonclinical species could not be readily explained by differences in plasma protein binding, where the unbound fractions in mice, rats, monkeys, dogs, and humans were found to be 0.048, 0.065, 0.10, 0.035, and 0.073, respectively. Furthermore, using simple allometry and f_u-adjusted allometry, the human V_{ss} of BMS-B was predicted to be 5.9 and 7.0 L/kg, respectively (Fig. 22.4A and B). Although simple allometry worked well in predicting the human V_{ss} of BMS-A, the large V_{ss} value predicted for BMS-B using allometry may mean that the backup compound could still have a long $t_{1/2}$ in humans, because the metabolic turnover of BMS-B in human liver microsomes or

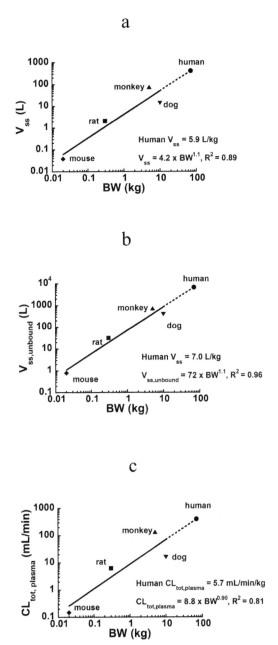

FIGURE 22.4 Interspecies allometric scaling of the pharmacokinetic parameters of BMS-B. (A) Steady-state volume of distribution, (B) unbound steady-state volume of distribution, and (C) total body plasma clearance.

hepatocytes was not distinctly faster than that of BMS-A. The critical question became whether the V_{ss} of BMS-B in humans was more like that in mice and dogs or more like that in rats and monkeys. Having a clear understanding of this aspect would determine the fate of BMS-B as the oral backup compound to BMS-A.

Issue resolution

To address the V_{ss} issue, an in vitro system was needed to rationalize the V_{ss} difference among nonclinical species and determine human relevance experimentally. Partitioning into red blood cells was first explored as an in vitro system to evaluate the species difference in the plasma V_{ss}. There was an encouraging trend as the dog exhibited the lowest blood-to-plasma concentration ratio of 0.67 followed by humans (0.81), rats (0.87), and monkeys (0.96). However, the dynamic range was not wide enough. Also, red blood cells represent a small organ mass and may not be sensitive enough to reflect

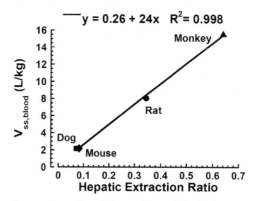

FIGURE 22.5 Correlation between the hepatic extraction ratio and the steady-state blood volume of distribution of BMS-B in nonclinical species.

the V_{ss} in the whole body. Subsequently, it was discovered that the V_{ss} correlated well with the clearance across nonclinical species. Specifically, a strong correlation ($R^2 = 0.998$) existed between the blood Vss ($V_{ss,blood}$) and the hepatic extraction ratio in nonclinical species (Fig. 22.5), where the hepatic extraction ratio was calculated as the $CL_{tot,blood}$ divided by the hepatic blood flow, with the assumption that the liver was the major organ for elimination. The assumption was reasonable because renal elimination was minor for BMS-B in nonclinical species. The result indicated that there was a common mechanism that governed the distribution and elimination of BMS-B, two independent pharmacokinetic processes. To further test the hypothesis on the correlation between the $V_{ss,blood}$ and the hepatic extraction ratio, a hepatocyte uptake study with ^{3}H-labeled BMS-B was performed in rats, monkeys, dogs, and humans. The results are shown in Fig. 22.6. In monkey and rat hepatocytes, drug-related radioactivity accumulated in cells, whereas it largely resided in the supernatant of human and dog hepatocytes. These results were consistent with the rank order of the V_{ss} in nonclinical species and provided evidence that hepatocytes were a suitable system in vitro to rationalize the V_{ss} differences in the nonclinical species evaluated. These data also suggested the human V_{ss} might be more like the dog V_{ss}, because of a similar distribution in the hepatocyte uptake study and the fact that the liver is one of the major organs in the body. Based on the experimental evidence, it was decided that hepatocytes, not liver microsomes, were used to study the intrinsic clearance of BMS-B in humans and nonclinical species. Even though the liver microsomal system worked well for BMS-A in predicting human clearance, hepatocytes were a more complete system that included drug distribution and elimination. Having both processes in place to study the intrinsic clearance of BMS-B was important, given the correlation between the two processes observed in vivo. After the human clearance was predicted with confidence, the human V_{ss} can then be predicted from the correlation established between the $V_{ss,blood}$ and the hepatic extraction ratio in nonclinical species. This unique approach offered the human V_{ss} prediction that was based on the experimental data and carried human relevance.

Prediction of human clearance

Leveraging the successful experience with BMS-A, the formation rate of a hydroxylated metabolite that was a major biotransformation product of BMS-B in human liver microsomes and hepatocytes was used to determine the intrinsic clearance of BMS-B in the hepatocytes of humans and nonclinical species. Table 22.3 summarizes the predicted versus observed clearances of BMS-B in nonclinical species as well as the predicted human clearance using scaling factors. It was apparent that the in vitro $CL_{h,blood}$ predicted from hepatocytes consistently underpredicted the in vivo $CL_{tot,blood}$ observed in the nonclinical species studied (CL_{tot} corrected for blood-to-plasma concentration ratio). The ratio of the predicted versus observed clearance in rats, dogs, and monkeys was 0.27, 0.53, and 0.20, respectively. Because the ratios from dogs and monkeys represented two extremes, they were used as the scaling factor for the human clearance prediction. As a result, the human CL_{tot} of BMS-B after applying the scaling factor and correcting for the blood-to-plasma concentration ratio (0.81) was predicted to be 0.81 mL/min/kg (dog-scaling factor) and 2.2 mL/min/kg (monkey-scaling factor) (Table 22.3). The prediction assumed that the liver was the major organ for the elimination of BMS-B in humans. By comparison, the human CL_{tot} predicted using simple allometry was 5.7 mL/min/kg (Fig. 22.4C), and it was 2.7 and 2.6 mL/min/kg using the MLP- and brain weight-adjusted methods, respectively.

Prediction of human steady-state volume of distribution

Several steps were taken to predict the human V_{ss} of BMS-B. First, the predicted human CL_{tot} of BMS-B was converted to the blood clearance (1.0 and 2.7 mL/min/kg for dog- and monkey-scaling factor, respectively) using the blood-to-plasma

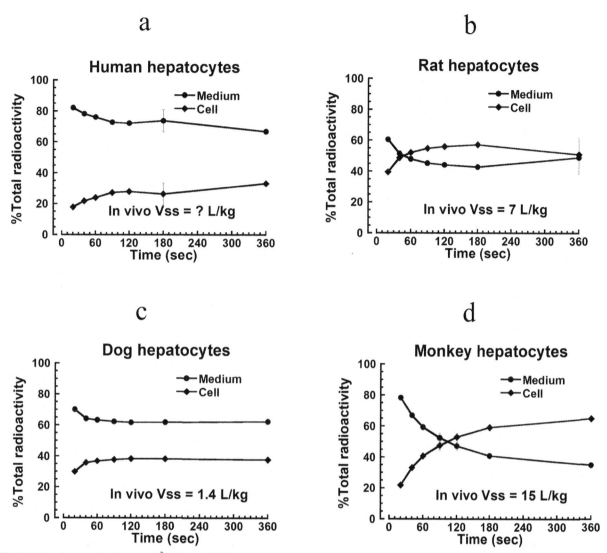

FIGURE 22.6 In vitro distribution of ^{3}H-labeled BMS-B in the medium and hepatocytes of humans and nonclinical species. (A) Human, (B) rat, (C) dog, and (D) monkey. Hepatocyte uptake experiments were conducted at 37°C for 5 min using a hepatocyte concentration of 1 million cells/mL and a substrate concentration of 0.2 μM. The medium and hepatocytes were separated using the oil-spin method, and radioactivity in respective matrices was measured using a liquid scintillation counter.

TABLE 22.3 In vitro-to-in vivo correlation in the clearance of BMSs-B in nonclinical species and predicted human clearances.

Parameter	Rat	Dog	Monkey	Human
In vitro predicted $CL_{h,blood}$ (mL/min/kg)[a]	6.7	1.8	5.7	0.53
In vivo observed $C_{tot,blood}$ (mL/min/kg)[b]	25	3.4	29	n.a.
Ratio of in vitro predicted versus in vivo observed clearance	0.27	0.53	0.20	n.a.
Predicted human CL_{tot} (mL/min/kg)[c]	n.a.	n.a.	n.a.	2.2 (monkey-scaling factor) 0.81 (dog-scaling factor)

n.a., not applicable.
[a]*The in vitro $CL_{h,blood}$ was predicted based on the formation of a hydroxylated metabolite in hepatocyte at a drug substrate concentration of 0.5 μM and a hepatocyte concentration of 1 million cells/mL, with an incubation time of 1 h. The hydroxylated metabolite was the major metabolite formed in vitro.*
[b]*In nonclinical species, the in vivo $CL_{tot,blood}$ was calculated as the in vivo CL_{tot} divided by the blood-to-plasma concentration ratio. The blood-to-plasma concentration ratio in rats, dogs, and monkeys was 0.87, 0.65, and 0.96, respectively.*
[c]*The human CL_{tot} was predicted by multiplying the hepatocyte-predicted $CL_{tot,blood}$ with the human blood-to-plasma concentration ratio of 0.81 and then corrected for the scaling factor determined in nonclinical species.*

concentration ratio. Assuming the total body clearance was entirely mediated by the liver, the hepatic extraction ratio was determined to be 0.05 (dog-scaling factor) and 0.13 (monkey-scaling factor). Second, using the correlation established between the $V_{ss,blood}$ and the hepatic extraction ratio in nonclinical species (Fig. 22.5) and with the predicted human extraction ratio as inputs, the human $V_{ss,blood}$ of BMS-B was predicted to be 1.4 L/kg (dog-scaling factor) and 3.5 L/kg (monkey-scaling factor). Third, the predicted human $V_{ss,blood}$ of BMS-B was multiplied by the blood-to-plasma concentration ratio to yield the human V_{ss} of 1.2 L/kg (dog-scaling factor) and 2.8 L/kg (monkey-scaling factor).

Prediction of human oral bioavailability and absorption rate constant

To predict the human F_{po}, it was assumed that there was no dissolution-limited absorption and the F_{po} obtained from a solution formation in nonclinical species was a reasonable approximation to the dosage form used in the clinic. Accordingly, the F_{po} observed in the nonclinical species along with the hepatic availability (f_h, $f_h = 1$ − hepatic extraction ratio) was used to estimate the percentage of dose absorbed into the portal vein (i.e., $f_a \times f_g$). The average $f_a \times f_g$ value in the nonclinical species was 56%. This value coupled with the predicted f_h in humans led to the predicted human F_{po} of 52% (dog-scaling factor) and 47% (monkey-scaling factor).

The rate of oral absorption in humans was assumed to follow first-order kinetics. The average value of the k_a in nonclinical species was 0.53 h^{-1}, which was used as the k_a in humans.

Prediction of human oral pharmacokinetic profile

Similar to what was done with BMS-A, the C_{ss}-MRT method [9] was used to superimpose the IV pharmacokinetic profiles of BMS-B in nonclinical species (Fig. 22.7A). With the predicted human CL_{tot} and V_{ss} as inputs, the superimposed IV data of BMS-B were converted to the human plasma pharmacokinetic profile after IV administration under two scenarios. The first scenario was based on the human CL_{tot} (0.8 mL/min/kg) derived from the dog scaling factor and the corresponding V_{ss} (1.2 L/kg) predicted from the correlation of the $V_{ss,blood}$ and the hepatic extraction ratio established in nonclinical species. The 2nd scenario used the human CL_{tot} (2.2 mL/min/kg) predicted from the monkey scaling factor and the corresponding V_{ss} (2.8 L/kg). The human IV PK curve was then fitted with a two-compartment model. The resultant PK parameters coupled with the predicted human F_{po} and k_a were then used to simulate the oral plasma pharmacokinetic profile of BMS-B in humans (Fig. 22.7B). The predicted plasma terminal $t_{1/2}$ in humans after oral dosing was 18 h (dog-scaling factor) and 16 h (monkey-scaling factor). These results suggested that BMS-B had a shorter $t_{1/2}$ than that (107 h) of BMS-A in humans, warranting its further advancement to early clinical development.

Predicted versus observed human pharmacokinetics

The human pharmacokinetics of BMS-B after oral administration was well predicted. The predicted versus observed human plasma pharmacokinetic profiles of BMS-B at a 2-mg dose are shown in Fig. 22.7B, and Table 22.4 summarizes the predicted versus observed pharmacokinetic parameters from plasma. The prediction made based on the dog-scaling factor captured the observed average pharmacokinetic curve well. The oral clearance, measured as the CL_{tot}/F_{po}, was 0.7× versus observed data using the dog-scaling factor and 2.1× with the monkey-scaling factor. The apparent V_{ss} (V_{ss}/F_{po}, 2.2−5.9 L/kg) predicted using dog- and monkey-scaling factors bracketed the observed data (4.2 ± 2.8 L/kg), suggesting the approach we took in the prediction of the human V_{ss} was reasonable. The T_{max} was also well predicted (1.7 h) versus the median value of 2 h observed. The C_{max} was underpredicted, 0.66× versus observed using the dog-scaling factor and 0.24× with the monkey-scaling factor. The plasma drug concentration at 24 h after the dose was within 2-fold of the observed data, 1.5× versus observed using the dog-scaling factor and 0.5× with the monkey-scaling factor. Importantly, the plasma terminal $t_{1/2}$ after oral administration was closely matched between the predicted (16−18 h) and observed data (23 h), indicating that BMS-B had a shorter human $t_{1/2}$ than that of BMS-A.

Summary of case study 2

A tailored approach was developed to predict the human V_{ss} based on the correlation established in the nonclinical species between the V_{ss} and the hepatic extraction ratio. The use of the approach was supported by the experimental evidence observed in hepatocyte uptake studies, where distinct differences were observed in drug accumulation in hepatocytes across species and correlated with the rank order of the V_{ss} in nonclinical species. The method overcame the challenge of the divergent V_{ss} values observed in nonclinical species that hindered the use of allometry and allowed a more mechanistic prediction of the human V_{ss}. The work was impactful in assessing the developability of BMS-B. Without it, BMS-B would not be advanced as an oral backup compound to BMS-A, because the project goal was to have a short $t_{1/2}$ than that of

a

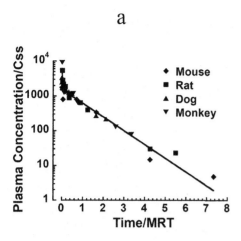

FIGURE 22.7 Prediction of the human plasma pharmacokinetic profiles of BMS-B from nonclinical species. (A) Superimposed nonclinical IV plasma concentration-time profiles of BMS-B after data transformation using the C_{ss}-MRT method. The line represents the fitted curve. (B) Predicted versus observed human oral plasma concentration-time profiles of BMS-B at 2 mg. The symbols represent the observed data (mean $\pm$ SD, N = 9); the lines are the predicted results under two scenarios. Scenario I was based on the human CL_{tot} (0.8 mL/min/kg) derived from the dog scaling factor and the corresponding V_{ss} (1.2 L/kg). Scenario II used the human CL_{tot} (2.2 mL/min/kg) predicted from the monkey scaling factor and the corresponding V_{ss} (2.8 L/kg).

b

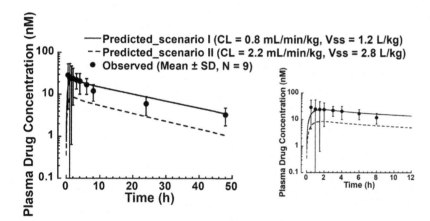

TABLE 22.4 Predicted versus observed pharmacokinetic parameters of BMS-B after oral administration of a 2-mg dose to humans.[a]

	Predicted		Observed
Parameter	Monkey-scaling factor	Dog-scaling factor	(mean $\pm$ SD, N = 9)
C_{max} (nM)	8.5 (0.24$\times$ vs. observed)	24 (0.66$\times$ vs. observed)	36 $\pm$ 22
T_{max} (h)	1.7 (0.85$\times$ vs. observed)	1.7 (0.85$\times$ vs. observed)	2 (median)
C_{24h} (nM)	3.0 (0.5$\times$ vs. observed)	8.7 (1.5$\times$ vs. observed)	6.0 $\pm$ 2.8
AUC_{tot} (nM $\times$ h)	194 (0.39$\times$ vs. observed)	576 (1.2$\times$ vs. observed)	498 $\pm$ 220
CL_{tot} (mL/min/kg)	2.2	0.81	n.a.
V_{ss}, (L/kg)	2.8	1.2	n.a.
F_{po} (%)	47	52	n.a.
CL_{tot}/F_{po} (mL/min/kg)	4.6 (2.1$\times$ vs. observed)	1.6 (0.7$\times$ vs. observed)	2.2 $\pm$ 1.4
V_{ss}/F_{po} (L/kg)	5.9 (1.4$\times$ vs. observed)	2.2 (0.54$\times$ vs. observed)	4.2 $\pm$ 2.8
Terminal $t_{1/2}$ (h)	16 (0.73$\times$ vs. observed)	18 (0.81$\times$ vs. observed)	23 $\pm$ 6.9

n.a., not available.
[a]The average human body weight was assumed to be 70 kg.

BMS-A in humans. Finally, the human pharmacokinetics of BMS-B was well predicted when compared with the observed data, vindicating the novel methodology used in the prediction of the human V_{ss}.

Case study 3. Compound having a variable oral bioavailability in nonclinical species, a long half-life, and a pharmacologically active circulating metabolite

Background and critical question to be addressed

BMS-986104 is a selective sphingosine 1-phosphate receptor 1 (S1P$_1$) modulator intended for the treatment of patients with autoimmune diseases [44]. The compound is a prodrug and needs to be phosphorylated to an active metabolite (BMS-986104-P). BMS-986104-P is an S1P$_1$ receptor agonist, but it serves as a functional antagonist of the receptor and prevents lymphocytes from egressing from lymphoid tissues into circulation. Pharmacologically, however, it is unclear which drug-related species in the circulation (BMS-986104-P, BMS-986104, or both) better relate to lymphopenia, the pharmaco-dynamic endpoint of S1P$_1$ modulators. This is because BMS-986104-P is charged at the physiological pH, which leads to low membrane permeability and likely a limited distribution to target tissues. It remains an open question as to how much BMS-986104-P in circulation reflects the tissue levels at the site of action. Additionally, the parent drug BMS-986104 is extensively distributed in the body due to its lipophilicity and can be phosphorylated in tissues for the intended pharmacological action. Furthermore, pharmacokinetic/pharmacodynamic modeling of the lymphopenia data of BMS-986104 in the nonclinical species revealed that the concentrations of either species correlated reasonably well with the PD response, suggesting the importance of predicting the concentrations of both the parent drug and the active metabolite in the clinic.

Nonclinically, BMS-986104 had a variable F_{po} from a solution formulation. The F_{po} in rats, dogs, and monkeys was 14%, 51%, and 71%, respectively. It exhibited a long terminal $t_{1/2}$. The terminal $t_{1/2}$ in rats, dogs, and monkeys after IV administration of 0.5 or 1 mg/kg was 162, 210, and 131 h, respectively. The total body blood clearance ($CL_{tot,blood}$) was low in the nonclinical species evaluated. The steady-state blood volume of distribution ($V_{ss,blood}$) was large, ranging from 13 to 30 L/kg. The pharmacologically active metabolite BMS-986104-P was also long-lived in the circulation, with the terminal $t_{1/2}$ parallel to that of the parent drug. The metabolite-to-parent (M/P) AUC ratio, compared in a molar unit, was variable among the nonclinical species studied. After IV administration at a dose of 0.5 or 1 mg/kg, the M/P AUC ratio in rats, dogs, and monkeys was 1.2, 2.4, and 0.7, respectively. The corresponding ratio following oral administration of 1 or 2 mg/kg was 2.5, 2.4, and 0.3, respectively. Additionally, at the time, it was not entirely clear about the underlying mechanisms involved in the formation of the phosphate metabolite, and whether or not the phosphorylation of the parent drug represented a major clearance pathway. These unique pharmacokinetic characteristics of BMS-986104 and BMS-986104-P in the nonclinical species made it challenging to predict their pharmacokinetics in humans.

Issue resolution

At the time when BMS-986104 was nominated as a clinical candidate, fingolimod (Gilenya, also known as FTY720 or FTY) as an S1P modulator was approved for the treatment of patients with relapsing forms of multiple sclerosis [45]. Examining the chemical structure and physicochemical properties of FTY revealed a remarkable similarity between FTY and BMS-986104 (Fig. 22.8). Experimentally, BMS-986104 resembled FTY in the $V_{ss,blood}$ and F_{po} in the nonclinical species studied (Table 22.5). Both compounds were highly protein-bound (>99%). Additionally, a human ADME study with FTY showed that oxidation (ω-hydroxylation at the octyl chain) was the major elimination pathway for FTY, with the FTY phosphate metabolite (FTY-P) eliminated mainly by dephosphorylation back to the parent drug [46]. The human ADME findings of FTY were consistent with the nonclinical results of BMS-986104, where the blood concentration-time

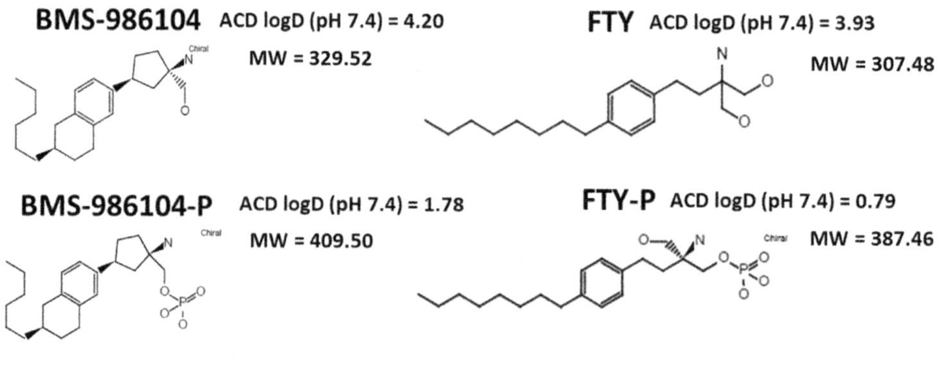

FIGURE 22.8 Chemical structures, molecule weights, and octanol-water distribution coefficients of BMS-986104, BMS-986104 phosphate metabolite (BMS-986104-P), fingolimod (FTY), and fingolimod phosphate metabolite (FTY-P). The octanol-water distribution coefficients at pH 7.4 were obtained from the software of Advanced Chemistry Development, Inc. (Toronto, Canada).

BMS-986104 ACD logD (pH 7.4) = 4.20 MW = 329.52

FTY ACD logD (pH 7.4) = 3.93 MW = 307.48

BMS-986104-P ACD logD (pH 7.4) = 1.78 MW = 409.50

FTY-P ACD logD (pH 7.4) = 0.79 MW = 387.46

TABLE 22.5 Pharmacokinetic parameters of BMS-986104 and fingolimod (FTY) in nonclinical species and humans.

Species	$CL_{tot,blood}$ (mL/min/kg)		$V_{ss,blood}$ (L/kg)		Terminal $t_{1/2,blood}$ (h)		Oral F_{po} (%)	
	BMS-986104	FTY[a]	BMS-986104	FTY[a]	BMS-986104	FTY[a]	BMS-986104	FTY[a]
Rat	1.6	7.0	14	16	162	36	14	47
Dog	0.8	7.9	13	14	210	25	51	39
Monkey	4.1	9.5	30	22	131	35	71	36
Animal Ave.	2.2	8.1	19	17	168	30	45	41
Human	n.a.	1.5	n.a.	17	n.a.	144	n.a.	94

n.a., not available at the time of the drug candidate nomination.
[a]*Pharmacokinetic parameters of FTY in nonclinical species were generated internally, while human values were obtained from the publication by Kovarik et al. [48].*

profiles were parallel between the parent drug and the phosphate metabolite. Also, the in vitro metabolic profiling of BMS-986104 in human, rat, dog, and monkey hepatocytes, as well as human liver microsomes, revealed that oxidation (hydroxylation at the alkyl terminus) was the primary metabolic pathway, similar to what was reported for FTY in humans [46,47]. Collectively, the experimental evidence generated nonclinically and clinically indicated that physicochemical properties and structures governed the absorption and disposition mechanisms of the two S1P modulators of interest. With this thinking in mind, efforts were spent exploring the methodologies for predicting the human pharmacokinetics of FTY and FTY-P using the nonclinical data generated internally. After the methodologies were established for FTY and FTY-P, the same approaches were then adopted to predict the human pharmacokinetics of BMS-986104 and BMS-986104-P.

Prediction of BMS-986104 human clearance

Because oxidative metabolism represented the major clearance mechanism of FTY in humans [46,47], liver microsomes were used to study the in vitro-to-in vivo correlation in the $CL_{tot,blood}$ among the nonclinical species studied and applied to predict the human $CL_{tot,blood}$ of FTY and BMS-986104 (Table 22.6). It is worth noting that metabolic turnovers were low for both FTY and BMS-986104. Despite the difficulty of measuring the parent drug disappearance in the liver microsomes, the $CL_{h,blood}$ predicted from liver microsomes reasonably captured the $CL_{tot,blood}$ observed in nonclinical species and humans for FTY, except for a discrepancy in dogs. Similarly, the $CL_{tot,blood}$ of BMS-986104 observed in nonclinical species was well predicted based on the liver microsomal data. ^{3}H-labeled BMS-986104 was also used to study the rate of total metabolite formation, which confirmed the parent drug disappearance results in human liver microsomes. Consequently, the $CL_{tot,blood}$ of BMS-986104 in humans, without the correction of protein binding in blood and the in vitro incubation, was predicted to be 0.7 mL/min/kg. Additionally, allometric scaling was attempted using simple allometry and

TABLE 22.6 In vitro-to-in vivo correlation in the clearance of fingolimod (FTY) and BMS-986104 in humans and nonclinical species.

Species	FTY[a]		BMS-986104[a,b]	
	Predicted $CL_{h,blood}$ from liver microsomes (mL/min/kg)	Observed $CL_{tot,blood}$ (mL/min/kg)	Predicted $CL_{h,blood}$ from liver microsomes (mL/min/kg)	Observed $CL_{tot,blood}$ (mL/min/kg)
Human	1.5	1.5	0.7	n.a.
Monkey	7.3	9.5	1.8	4.1
Dog	1.0	7.9	1.6	0.8
Rat	2.4	7.0	1.9	1.6

n.a., not available at the time of the drug candidate nomination.
[a]*The $CL_{h,blood}$ was predicted using the parent drug disappearance from liver microsomes without correcting for binding in blood and in vitro incubations.*
[b]*Total metabolite formation using ^{3}H-labeled BMS-986104 confirmed the results obtained from the parent drug disappearance in human liver microsomes.*

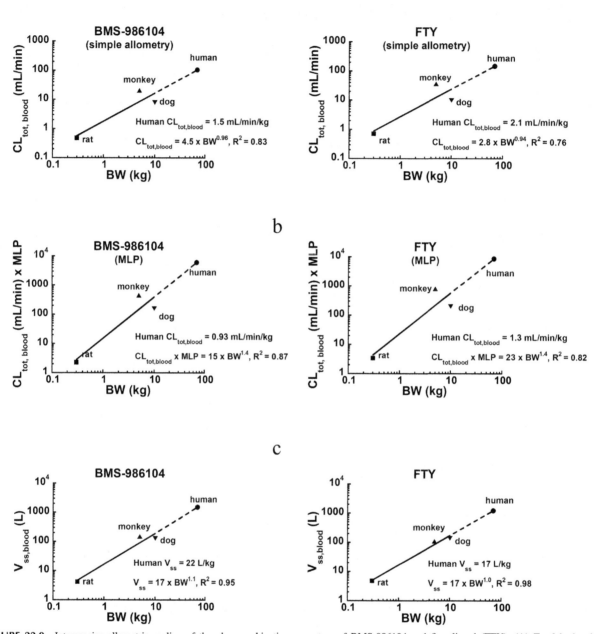

FIGURE 22.9 Interspecies allometric scaling of the pharmacokinetic parameters of BMS-986104 and fingolimod (FTY). (A) Total body plasma clearance, (B) product of total body plasma clearance and maximum life-span potential, and (C) steady-state blood volume of distribution.

MLP-adjusted allometry based on the Rule of Exponents [37]. The allometry using the MLP method well predicted the FTY $CL_{tot,blood}$ in humans (Fig. 22.9A and B). Using the same approach, the human $CL_{tot,blood}$ of BMS-986104 was predicted to be 0.93 mL/min/kg. Between the allometry-based and the in vitro-to-in vivo correlation methods, the predicted human $CL_{tot,blood}$ (0.7 mL/min/kg) from liver microsomes was used for predicting the human pharmacokinetics of BMS-986104. The use of human liver microsomes-derived clearance was based on the assumption that the elimination of BMS-986104 in humans was governed by oxidative metabolism and was supported by 3 pieces of evidence: (1) there was a good in vitro-in vivo correlation in the clearance of nonclinical species (Table 22.6); (2) FTY $CL_{tot,blood}$ in humans was well predicted from human liver microsomal data (Table 22.6); and (3) oxidative metabolism was the predominant biotransformation pathway of BMS-986104 in vitro and in nonclinical species.

Prediction of BMS-986104 human steady-state volume of distribution

The human $V_{ss,blood}$ of BMS-986104 was predicted to be 19 L/kg, the average value in animal species. This was supported by the fact that the $V_{ss,blood}$ of FTY in humans was similar to the average value in animal species (17 L/kg observed vs. 17 L/kg averaged from animal species). Additionally, simple allometry was used to predict the human $V_{ss,blood}$ of FTY and BMS-986104 from the nonclinical data (Fig. 22.9C). The results were in agreement with the $V_{ss,blood}$ averaged from animal data.

Prediction of BMS-986104 human oral bioavailability and absorption rate constant

For predicting the human F_{po} of BMS-986104, the human F_{po} (94%) observed with FTY was used [48]. Choosing the human F_{po} of BMS-986104 the same as that of FTY was based on the fact that the F_{po} averaged from animal species was similar between the two molecules (45% vs. 41%). The absorption rate constant k_a (0.10 h^{-1}) was obtained by averaging the values from animal data. Additionally, a lag time (1.5 h) observed in the human oral absorption of FTY was incorporated in predicting the human pharmacokinetics of BMS-986104 after oral administration.

Prediction of BMS-986104 human blood concentration-time profile after oral administration

To predict the human pharmacokinetic profile of BMS-986104, the $C_{ss,blood}$-MRT method [9] was first explored for FTY using the nonclinical data generated internally. Fig. 22.10A shows the superimposed blood concentration-time profiles of FTY obtained from rats, dogs, and monkeys. Using the predicted human $CL_{tot,blood}$ (1.5 mL/min/kg from human liver microsomes) and predicted human $V_{ss,blood}$ (17 L/kg, averaged from animal species), the human blood concentration-time profile of FTY after IV administration at 1 mg was predicted well (Fig. 22.10B), where the observed IV data were digitized from the publication [48]. With the predicted FTY IV pharmacokinetic data, the human oral pharmacokinetic profile of FTY at a dose of 1.25 mg was then predicted using the k_a (0.10 h^{-1}) averaged from nonclinical species and the F_{po} of either 41% (averaged from animal species, internally generated data) or 94% (determined in humans [48]). Additionally, a lag time (1.5 h) in the FTY oral absorption estimated from human data was used. Fig. 22.10C displays the predicted versus observed results for FTY, where the observed oral data were digitized from the publication [48]. Using the average bioavailability from nonclinical species, the results underpredicted the human oral pharmacokinetic profile of FTY. Based on this data and coupled with the fact that the average F_{po} of BMS-986104 was similar to that of FTY in the nonclinical species studied, the human F_{po} (94%) of FTY was used as the predicted human F_{po} of BMS-986104.

With a success in predicting human IV and oral pharmacokinetic profiles of FTY, the same approach was employed to predict the pharmacokinetics of BMS-986104 in humans. Fig. 22.11A shows the superimposed blood concentration-time profiles of BMS-986104 in nonclinical species. With the human $CL_{tot,blood}$ (0.7 mL/min/kg) predicted from liver microsomes and the human $V_{ss,blood}$ (19 L/kg) averaged from nonclinical species as the inputs, the human IV pharmacokinetic profile of BMS-986104 was predicted from the superimposed profile. Using the predicted human IV profile together with the k_a (0.086 h^{-1}) averaged from the animal data as well as the human F_{po} (94%) and the lag time (1.5 h) observed with FTY, the human oral pharmacokinetic profile of BMS-986104 was predicted and is shown in Fig. 22.11B. The predicted human T_{max} of BMS-986104 after an oral dose was 15 h, with a terminal $t_{1/2}$ predicted to be 455 h (19 days or 2.7 weeks).

Prediction of BMS-986104 phosphate metabolite human blood concentration-time profile after oral administration

To predict BMS-986104-P levels in humans, two approaches were taken. First, in vitro systems (platelet-enriched plasma and washed red blood cells) were explored to study the rates and species differences in the formation of the phosphate metabolites for BMS-986104 and FTY, based on the literature published at the time [49,50]. The in vitro systems allowed the assessment of the human relevance and provided an opportunity of building an in vitro-to-in vivo correlation in the phosphate formation in nonclinical species. The in vitro experimental data then served as a basis for predicting BMS-986104-P levels in humans. Second, FTY-P human pharmacokinetic data were closely leveraged to further inform the human relevance and helped to develop the prediction method from the nonclinical data.

In vitro phosphate metabolite formation and prediction of phosphate metabolite-to-parent molar AUC ratio in humans

Table 22.7 summarizes the formation rate (in pmol/h/million cells) of BMS-986104-P in platelet enriched plasma and washed red blood cells. It is clear that, across species, the active metabolite was largely formed in platelet enriched plasma but not much in washed red blood cells. Similar results were also found for FTY-P in the same experiments and are

a

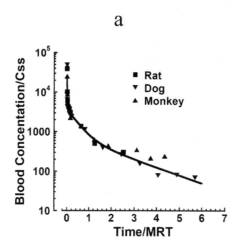

b

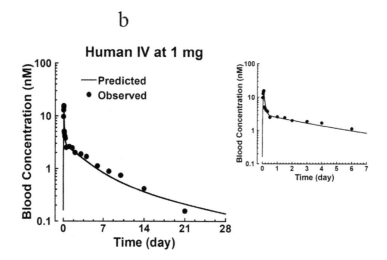

c

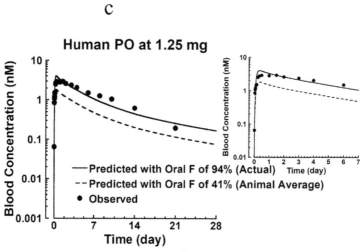

FIGURE 22.10 Prediction of the human blood pharmacokinetic profiles of fingolimod (FTY) from nonclinical species. (A) Superimposed nonclinical IV plasma concentration-time profiles of FTY after data transformation using the C_{ss}-MRT method. The line represents the fitted curve. (B) Predicted versus observed human IV blood concentration-time profiles of FTY at 1 mg. The symbols represent the observed data [48]; the line shows the predicted results. (C) Predicted versus observed human oral blood concentration-time profiles of FTY at 1.25 mg. The symbols display the observed data [48]; the line shows the predicted results.

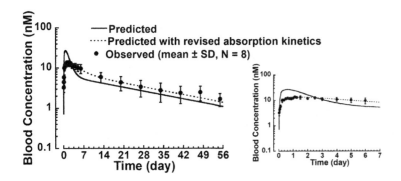

a

FIGURE 22.11 Prediction of the human blood pharmacokinetic profiles of BMS-986104 from nonclinical species. (A) Superimposed nonclinical IV plasma concentration-time profiles of BMS-986104 after data transformation using the C_{ss}-MRT method. The line represents the fitted curve. (B) Predicted versus observed human oral blood concentration-time profiles of BMS-986104 at 5.7 mg. The symbols represent the observed data (mean $\pm$ SD, N = 8); the solid line shows the originally predicted results and the dashed line displays the predictions after the revision of absorption kinetics based on the observed human data.

b

TABLE 22.7 In vitro rate of the fingolimod (FTY) and BMS-986104 phosphate metabolite formation in humans and nonclinical species.

	Rate of phosphate formation in platelet-rich plasma[a] (pmol/h/million cells)		Rate of phosphate formation in washed red blood cells[a] (pmol/h/million cells)	
Species	FTY	BMS-986104	FTY	BMS-986104
Human	0.3	0.03	0.005	0.001
Monkey	0.2	0.02	0.030	0.002
Dog	1.3	0.4	0.003	0.000
Rat	7.9	3.4	0.030	0.000

[a]Formation rate was determined at a drug concentration of 5 μM.

consistent with the literature reports [49]. These results suggest that the underlying mechanism for the formation of the active (phosphate) metabolite was similar between BMS-986014 and FTY. Based on the average concentrations of platelets and red blood cells in blood, the formation rate of BMS-986104-P and FTY-P in whole blood can be estimated. In humans, the in vitro formation rate of BMS-986104-P in blood was 6.8-fold less than that of FTY-P (Table 22.8). In nonclinical species, the formation rate of BMS-986104-P in blood was also smaller than that of FTY-P (Table 22.8).

When examining the in vitro-to-in vivo correlation in the phosphate metabolite formation, it was found that the in vitro ratio of FTY versus BMS-986104 correlated well with the in vivo ratio of FTY versus BMS-986104 (Table 22.8), where the in vivo ratio was determined using the M/P AUC ratio that was based on the molar concentrations. Based on the correlation established, the human M/P AUC ratio of BMS-986104 was predicted from the human FTY-P/FTY AUC ratio of 0.34−0.42 [51], using the following equation:

$$\text{BMS-986104 M/P AUC ratio} = \frac{\text{FTY human M/P AUC ratio}}{\text{In vitro phosphate formation ratio of FTY versus BMS} - 986104}$$

With the in vitro ratio of 6.8 between FTY and BMS-986104 determined in human blood, the human M/P AUC ratio of BMS-986104 was predicted to be 0.05−0.06.

One additional method was used to predict the M/P AUC ratio of BMS-986104 in humans. The method assumed that the in vitro phosphate formation in blood reflected the in vivo phosphate formation in circulation. Hence the fold difference between the human and a nonclinical species in the in vitro phosphate formation rate led to the same fold difference in the in vivo M/P AUC ratio between the human and that animal species. Based on this assumption, one could predict the human M/P AUC ratio with the following equation:

$$\text{Human M/P AUC ratio} = \frac{\text{M/P AUC ratio of a nonclinical species}}{\text{In vitro phosphate formation ratio of a nonclinical species versus humans}}$$

The approach was first explored to predict the human M/P AUC ratio for FTY. Using the FTY-P/FTY AUC ratio obtained in a nonclinical species and divided by the in vitro phosphate formation rate difference between that species and humans, the human M/P AUC ratio of FTY predicted from rats, dogs, and monkeys after oral administration was 0.05, 1.4, and 1.3, respectively. The geometric mean of these values yielded 0.45, similar to the observed human M/P AUC ratio (0.34−0.42) of FTY after oral dosing. Additionally, the human M/P AUC ratio of FTY after IV administration was estimated to be 0.37 (geometric mean of the values predicted from individual animal species). Taking the same approach, the M/P AUC ratio of BMS-986104 in humans predicted from rats, dogs, and monkeys after oral administration was 0.007, 0.3, and 0.2, respectively. Additionally, the human IV M/P AUC ratio of BMS-986104 predicted from rats, dogs, and monkeys was 0.004, 0.3, and 0.5, respectively. The geometric mean of either oral or IV datasets resulted in a predicted BMS-986104 human M/P AUC ratio of 0.08, similar to the first method that predicted a ratio of 0.05−0.06. With

TABLE 22.8 In vitro rate of the fingolimod (FTY) and BMS-986104 phosphate metabolite formation in humans and nonclinical species.

Species	In vitro rate of phosphate formation in blood[a] (pmol/h/µL blood)		In vivo phosphate metabolite-to-parent blood AUC ratio after oral administration		Ratio of FTY versus BMS-986104 in phosphate formation	
	FTY	BMS-986104	FTY	BMS-986104	In vitro	In vivo
Human	0.10	0.015	0.34−0.42[b]	n.a.	6.8	n.a.
Monkey	0.29	0.023	3.7	0.33	13	11
Dog	0.42	0.12	5.9	2.4 (PO)	3.5	2.5
Rat	12	5.1	5.6	2.5 (PO)	2.4	2.2

n.a., not available at the time of the drug candidate nomination.
[a]Rate of phosphate metabolite formation in blood was calculated by combining the rates determined in platelet-rich plasma and washed red blood cells with platelet and red blood cell counts in humans and nonclinical species (data from Table 22.7). The platelet counts in humans, rats, dogs, and monkeys were 0.28, 1.5, 0.30, and 0.47 million cells per µL blood, respectively. The red blood cell counts in humans, rats, dogs, and monkeys were 5.2, 7.8, 6.8, and 6.7 million cells per µL blood, respectively.
[b]Values reported by David et al. [51].

both approaches leading to similar results, a ratio of 0.08 was used for the human pharmacokinetic prediction of BMS-986104-P.

Prediction of presystemic formation of phosphate metabolite and methodology calibration with FTY phosphate metabolite

The FTY clinical data revealed that FTY-P peaked before FTY after oral administration FTY at 1.25 mg. The T_{max} of FTY and FTY-P was 12 and 6–8 h, respectively [51]. The result suggested that a portion of FTY-P was formed presystemically. If not considered, it would lead to a significant underestimation of the phosphate metabolite C_{max}. Having an accurately predicted C_{max} for the phosphate metabolite was important, because the phosphate metabolite concentration may be responsible for producing lymphopenia, the intended pharmacodynamic response, and possibly causing bradycardia, the adverse event associated with FTY in the clinic. Therefore, efforts were made to predict the presystemic formation of the phosphate metabolite in humans. To this end, a pharmacokinetic model was established to account for both systemically and presystemically formed metabolites (Fig. 22.12). In this case, the rate of changes in the phosphate metabolite blood concentration can be described using the following differential equation:

$$\frac{dC_{blood,m}}{dt} = k_{a,m} \times \frac{f_{presystemic,m} \times dose}{V_{d,blood,m}} + k_{form,apparent,m} \times C_{blood,parent\ drug} - k_{elim,m} \times C_{blood,m}$$

where $C_{blood,m}$ and $C_{blood,parent\ drug}$ are the blood concentrations of the metabolite and the parent drug, respectively; $f_{presystemic,m}$ is the fraction of the dose converting to the phosphate metabolite presystemically; $k_{a,m}$ is the absorption rate constant of the presystemically formed metabolite; $k_{form,apparent,m}$ is the apparent formation rate constant of the parent drug concentration in blood converting to the metabolite; $k_{elim,m}$ is the elimination rate constant of the metabolite; and $V_{d,blood,m}$ is the apparent volume of distribution of the metabolite in blood. At time zero, the amount of the presystemically formed metabolite was equal to the product of the dose administered and the $f_{presystemic,m}$. The phosphate metabolite was assumed to follow formation rate-limited kinetics. To model and simulate the phosphate metabolite data, the parent drug blood concentrations were used as a forcing function in the pharmacokinetic model (i.e., parent drug blood concentrations were not affected by phosphate metabolite concentrations in blood).

Using the pharmacokinetics model established, efforts were taken to explore using both in vitro and animal data to predict the human pharmacokinetics of FTY-P before applying the same approach to BMS-986104-P. The human FTY-P blood concentration-time data at the oral dose of 1.25 mg were simulated based on a population pharmacokinetic model published [52]. The observed human FTY data after a 1-mg IV dose and a 1.25-mg oral dose were also digitized from the published data [48]. To model the human data, a three-compartment pharmacokinetic model was first fitted simultaneously to the FTY human IV and oral data at 1 and 1.25 mg, respectively. The values of FTY human pharmacokinetic parameters were then fixed and used to model FTY-P human pharmacokinetic data. For the presystemically formed metabolite, the $f_{presystemic,m}$ was set as 0.06 ($1 - F_{po}$ of 0.94). The FTY-P human data were then fitted using the model described in Fig. 22.12. The $V_{d,blood,m}$ of FTY-P in humans was estimated to be 0.86 L/kg. The lag time in the oral absorption of the presystemically formed metabolite was determined to be 3 h.

Assuming that the FTY-P $V_{d,blood,m}$ in nonclinical species was the same as that in humans, the FTY-P nonclinical pharmacokinetic data generated internally were fitted using the model shown in Fig. 22.12. Using the FTY-P human

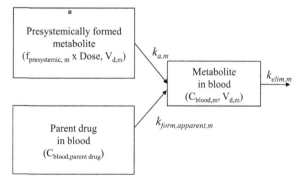

FIGURE 22.12 Schematic representation of the pharmacokinetic model of phosphate metabolite in the circulation. The model assumed that two sources contributed to the formation of the phosphate metabolite in blood. One came from the parent drug in blood and the other one was from the presystemically formed metabolite.

$V_{d,blood,m}$ value in the nonclinical species was a reasonable assumption, because FTY-P is charged at the physiological pH and its distribution is likely restricted and similar across the species due to limited membrane permeability. The step was also necessary to allow the $f_{presystemic,m}$ to be reliably estimated in nonclinical species. Similar to the modeling work conducted for the human data, the parent drug pharmacokinetic parameters in an individual animal species were first obtained and then applied as the fixed values for modeling the phosphate metabolite data in that species. From the modeling work of the nonclinical FTY-P data, the average value of the $f_{presystemic,m}$ estimated from rats, dogs, and monkeys was 0.16. The average $k_{a,m}$ and $k_{elim,m}$ from these nonclinical species was 0.23 and 0.27 h^{-1}, respectively.

With the pharmacokinetic parameters of FTY-P obtained in nonclinical species, efforts were then spent to leverage these parameters and use the model shown in Fig. 22.12 to predict the human pharmacokinetics of FTY-P. To do so, the $k_{form,apparent,m}$ of FTY-P in humans needed to be predicted. The average value from the nonclinical species cannot be used, because there was a significant species difference in the M/P AUC ratio for FTY (0.34−0.42 in humans vs. 3.7−5.9 in nonclinical species). However, the following pharmacokinetic equation exists after IV administration:

$$k_{form,apparent,m} = k_{elim,m} \times M/P \text{ AUC ratio}$$

The average $k_{elim,m}$ (0.27 h^{-1}) from nonclinical species coupled with the predicted human IV M/P AUC ratio can be used to predict the $k_{form,apparent,m}$ in humans. From the section above, the human IV M/P AUC ratio of FTY predicted from nonclinical species was 0.37 (geometric mean of the values predicted from individual animal species). As a result, the $k_{form,apparent,m}$ was calculated to be 0.10 h^{-1}.

To predict the human pharmacokinetic profile of FTY-P, the pharmacokinetic model shown in Fig. 22.12 was again used. The FTY human oral pharmacokinetic data predicted from nonclinical species served as an input to the FTY-P human blood concentrations. The other input was the presystemically formed metabolite, where the $f_{presystemic,m}$ (0.16) averaged from nonclinical species was employed together with a dose in a mole unit. To ensure the mass balance, the F_{po} of FTY was reduced to 0.84 (1 − 0.16). The average values of $k_{a,m}$ (0.23 h^{-1}) and $k_{elim,m}$ (0.27 h^{-1}) from nonclinical species were applied in the model, along with the $k_{form,apparent,m}$ (0.10 h^{-1}) calculated from nonclinical species. The FTY-P human $V_{d,blood,m}$ of 0.86 L/kg and a lag time of 3 h in the absorption of the presystemically formed metabolite were also used. With these parameters in place for the model, the human blood concentration-time profiles of FTY-P were predicted with and without the presystemically formed metabolite, and results are shown in Fig. 22.13. Compared to the observed data (the results simulated from a population pharmacokinetic model [52]), the approach developed for predicting the human blood pharmacokinetics of FTY-P worked reasonably well. Also, it was necessary to include the presystemically formed metabolite in the model; otherwise, the C_{max} of FTY-P in humans was underpredicted.

Prediction of human pharmacokinetics of BMS-986104 phosphate metabolite

With the successful prediction of FTY-P human pharmacokinetics from nonclinical data, the same approach was adopted for predicting the human blood concentration-time profile of BMS-986104-P. The nonclinical pharmacokinetic data of BMS-986104-P in rats, dogs, and monkeys were fitted using the model shown in Fig. 22.12, with the $V_{d,blood,m}$ assumed to be the same as that (0.86 L/kg) of FTY-P in humans. Similar to what was done for FTY-P, the parent drug blood concentrations of BMS-986104 predicted in humans were used as an input to predict the blood concentrations of BMS-986104-P. The presystemically formed metabolite was also included as another input for predicting the blood concentrations of BMS-986104-P. From the modeling of the nonclinical BMS-986104-P data, the average value of the $f_{presystemic,m}$ estimated from rats, dogs, and monkeys was 0.022. The value was 7-fold less than that of FTY-P and was consistent with the fold difference (6.8×) in the in vitro blood phosphate formation rate between FTY and BMS-986104. The average $k_{a,m}$ and $k_{elim,m}$ of BMS-986104 obtained from these nonclinical species was 0.17 and 0.018 h^{-1}, respectively. Like what was done for FTY-P, the $k_{form,apparent,m}$ (0.0014 h^{-1}) was calculated as the product of $k_{elim,m}$ and predicted human IV M/P AUC ratio (0.08) from nonclinical species. Additionally, the lag time in absorption (3 h) and the $V_{d,blood,m}$ (0.86 L/kg) were assumed to be the same as those of FTY-P in humans. With these parameters in place for the model, the human blood concentration-time profile of BMS-986104-P was simulated and is shown in Fig. 22.14A, and the predicted human pharmacokinetic parameters are summarized in Table 22.9. It is worth noting that the terminal $t_{1/2}$ of BMS-986104-P was predicted to be parallel to that of the parent drug.

Predicted versus observed human pharmacokinetics

The human blood pharmacokinetics of BMS-986104 was reasonably predicted from nonclinical data. The predicted versus observed human blood pharmacokinetic profiles of BMS-986104 are shown in Fig. 22.11B, with the pharmacokinetic parameters summarized in Table 22.9. After a single dose of 5.7 mg, the highest dose studied in a first-in-human trial, the

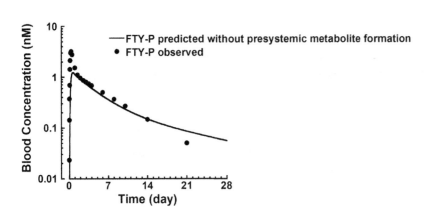

a

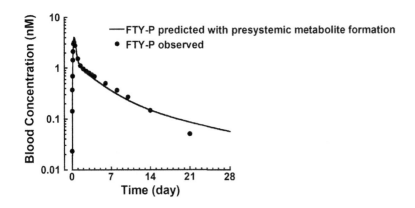

b

FIGURE 22.13 Prediction of the human blood pharmacokinetic profiles of fingolimod phosphate metabolite (FTY-P) from nonclinical species. (A) Predictions without the presystemic metabolite formation and (B) predictions with the presystemic metabolite formation. The symbols represent the observed data that were simulated from a population pharmacokinetic model [52]; the lines show the prediction results.

predicted blood $C_{max,blood}$ and $C_{24\ h,blood}$ were about 2-fold higher than the observed values. The predicted $AUC_{tot,blood}$, $CL_{tot,blood}/F_{po}$, and $V_{ss,blood}/F_{po}$ were all similar to the observed results. The predicted terminal $t_{1/2}$ was 455 h versus the average value of 432 h observed. Examining the average BMS-986104 blood concentration observed versus the predicted data, there was an overprediction at the initial time points but an underprediction after 7 days. Adjusting the original prediction parameters in absorption and the central compartment volume of distribution improved the prediction results, which is shown as the dashed line in Fig. 22.11B. The absorption rate constant k_a of BMS-986104 was changed from 0.086 h^{-1} (averaged value from a solution formulation in nonclinical species) to 0.018 h^{-1} for the first 24 h and 0.012 h^{-1} afterward. Additionally, the lag time of 1.5 h adopted from the FTY human data was removed. Finally, the central compartment volume of distribution was revised from 0.58 to 0.50 L/kg. These revisions in the prediction parameters led to the predicted blood concentration-time profile of BMS-986104 well matched with the average observed data.

The human blood pharmacokinetics of BMS-986104-P was overpredicted from the nonclinical data. At 5.7 mg, most BMS-986104-P blood concentrations were below the lower limit of quantification (LLOQ, 1.2 nM or 0.5 ng/mL), except for two subjects that had a phosphate metabolite level slightly above the LLOQ at two-time points. One subject had the BMS-986104-P blood concentration of 1.3 and 1.4 nM at 120 and 144 h post the dose, respectively; the other subject had 1.3 and 1.2 nM at 120 and 312 h after the dose, respectively, with a drug level below the LLOQ at 144 h. The predicted BMS-986104-P C_{max} at 5.7 mg was 5.3 nM, with the predicted T_{max} of 15–30 h (flat curve). Based on the observed data, the human C_{max} of BMS-986104-P was overpredicted by at least 4-fold. The phosphate metabolite-to-parent concentration ratio observed for the first subject was 0.11–0.14, and the concentration ratio for the second subject was 0.16–0.20. In

a

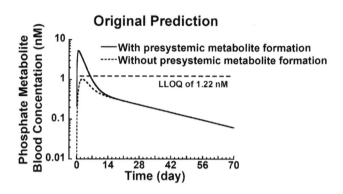

b

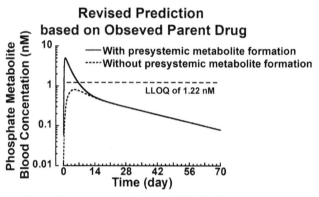

FIGURE 22.14 Prediction of the human blood pharmacokinetic profiles of BMS-986104 phosphate metabolite (BMS-986104-P) from nonclinical species. (A) Original predictions with and without the presystemic metabolite formation and (B) revised predictions with and without the presystemic metabolite formation. The revised predictions were made based on the observed parent drug pharmacokinetic data in humans that contributed as one of the two sources for the phosphate metabolite formation in blood. The *solid lines* are the predictions with the presystemic metabolite formation, the *dashed lines* represent the predictions without the presystemic metabolite formation.

comparison, the predicted phosphate metabolite-to-parent concentration ratio at 120, 144, and 312 h was 0.26, 0.22, and 0.097, respectively. These data suggested that the predicted metabolite-to-parent concentration ratios were reasonable in the two subjects that had concentration levels above the LLOQ. Furthermore, examining the predicted blood concentration-time profile of BMS-986104-P revealed that, when the presystemically formed metabolite was not incorporated into the prediction, the predicted blood concentrations were below the LLOQ (Fig. 22.14A and B), regardless of whether the revisions were made to the parent drug blood concentration-time profile. This observation suggested that the presystemic metabolite formation for BMS-986104 after oral administration may not be significant, which was different from FTY in humans. Had the LLOQ of BMS-986104 been improved by 5- to 10-fold or had BMS-986104 been dosed at a single dose higher than 5.7 mg, we would have known the human pharmacokinetic profile of BMS-986104-P with certainty.

Summary of case study 3

The prediction of the human pharmacokinetics of BMS-986104 and its active phosphate metabolite BMS-986104-P from nonclinical data presented significant scientific challenges on multiple fronts (variable F_{po}, long $t_{1/2}$, and the necessity of predicting active metabolite for efficacy and safety reasons), not mentioning a tight timeline at the time in delivering the results. The challenges were met with a solution of studying FTY, a drug for the same target. The human pharmacokinetic prediction methodologies for BMS-986104 were established by studying how the human pharmacokinetics of FTY and FY-P could be predicted from nonclinical data based on the internally generated nonclinical data as well as the observed

TABLE 22.9 Predicted versus observed blood pharmacokinetic parameters of BMS-986104 and its phosphate metabolite after oral administration of a 5.7-mg dose to humans.

Parameter	BMS-986104		BMS-986104 phosphate metabolite	
	Predicted	Observed[a] (mean ± SD, N = 8)	Predicted	Observed[a] (mean ± SD, N = 8)
$C_{max,blood}$ (nM)	26	14 ± 1.6	5.3[b]	1.3 and 1.4 nM in two subjects, with remaining subjects below LLOQ of 1.2 nM
Tmax (h)	15	29 (median)	15–30	n.a.
$C_{24h,blood}$ (nM)	25	12 ± 1.0	5.3[b]	<LLOQ of 1.2 nM
$AUC_{tot,blood}$ (nM × h)	6005	6607 ± 2521	837	n.a.
$CL_{tot,blood}$ (mL/min/kg)	0.70	n.a.	0.25	n.a.
$V_{ss,blood}$ (L/kg)	19	n.a.	0.86	n.a.
F_{po} (%)	94	n.a.	Not applicable[c]	n.a.
$CL_{tot,blood}/F_{po}$ (mL/min/kg)	0.74	0.71 ± 0.27	Not applicable	n.a.
$V_{ss,blood}/F_{po}$ (L/kg)	20	21 ± 3.3	Not applicable	n.a.
Terminal $t_{1/2,blood}$ (h)	455	432 ± 207	455	n.a.

n.a., not available.
[a]*The average human body weight of 70 kg was assumed.*
[b]*Flat phosphate metabolite curve between 15 and 30 h.*
[c]*Presystemic formation of phosphate metabolite in humans was assumed to be 2.2% of the oral dose administered, based on the average value of animal data.*

human results from the literature. Using FTY and FTY-P as calibrators for the methodology development was supported by similarities in physiochemical properties, in vitro metabolic profiles, and in vivo nonclinical pharmacokinetic data between FTY and BMS-986104. Nevertheless, the approach adopted was unique. As a result, two areas of high uncertainty in the human pharmacokinetic predictions of BMS-986104 and BMS-986104-P were highlighted at the time of the drug candidate nomination. One was the uncertainty of predicting the human F_{po} of BMS-986104, as the F_{po} was variable among nonclinical species and the in vitro permeability data in Caco-2 cells were not available due to low solubility. The other uncertainty was on the prediction of the phosphate metabolite formation in humans, particularly concerning the estimation of presystemically formed metabolite, because of the unknown mechanism. As we learned from the clinical data, the FTY-calibrated human prediction methodologies led to a reasonably good prediction of the human pharmacokinetics of BMS-986104, including the F_{po}. For BMS-986104-P, however, the human pharmacokinetics was overpredicted from the nonclinical data. Estimation of the presystemically formed metabolite likely contributed to the overprediction. In retrospect, the human pharmacokinetic prediction of BMS-986104-P should have been made in two scenarios (i.e., with and without the presystemically formed metabolite) to better inform the clinical development plan. Also, the bioanalytical assay sensitivity for the phosphate metabolite, a known challenge before entering the first-in-human trial, prevented us from evaluating the concentration-time profile of the phosphate metabolite at the top dose studied. These learnings from the clinic were valuable to inform the backup efforts and the human pharmacokinetic prediction of this class of compounds, which subsequently led to the discovery and clinical success of BMS-986166 [53,54].

Conclusion

Predicting human pharmacokinetics is an essential part of developability assessments in drug discovery. It serves as a cornerstone to human efficacious dose projections. As with any prediction, human pharmacokinetics can always be predicted from nonclinical data. However, the key to success in this endeavor is to focus on determining the mechanisms of absorption and disposition, understanding the in vivo context from in vitro data, and evaluating the relevance of nonclinical data to humans. In this book chapter, three case studies from the trenches of drug discovery are shared and predicted human pharmacokinetic results are compared with the observed clinical data. Each case has its unique scientific challenges. Despite differences, there is a common theme throughout the case studies in which tailored approaches were developed for human pharmacokinetic predictions based on mechanistic understanding and experimental evidence. The examples showcase scientific focuses and passion for finding solutions that impacted the projects, as work in drug discovery is often fast-paced and under a tight timeline. Also, human pharmacokinetic predictions may not be correct each time, but efforts should be made to experiment with approaches tailored to science and data. Mechanism-oriented human prediction methods allow for formulating different hypotheses and developing alternatives when a prediction is incorrect. The mindset differs from applying allometry for human pharmacokinetic predictions. Focusing on mechanisms and exploring data-driven approaches is how we advance the field of predicting human pharmacokinetics from nonclinical data. The author hopes these case studies may inspire others to do the same in finding innovative solutions to improve the accuracy of human pharmacokinetic predictions in drug discovery.

Acknowledgments

The author wants to thank the following individuals for their contributions to the case studies presented: Cliff Chen and Qian Ruan (Case study 1); Haiqing Wang, Hong Shen, and Qian Ruan (Case study 2); and Anthony Marino, Cliff Chen, Huadong Sun, Haiying Zhang, and Lois Lehman McKeeman (Case study 3).

Abbreviations

AUC_{tot}	total area under the plasma drug concentration-time curve
$AUC_{tot,blood}$	total area under the blood drug concentration-time curve
$C_{24\,h}$	drug plasma concentration at 24 h after dose
$C_{24\,h,blood}$	drug blood concentration at 24 h after dose
$C_{blood,m}$	metabolite blood concentration
$C_{blood,parent\,drug}$	parent drug blood concentration
$CL_{h,blood}$	hepatic blood clearance of drug
$CL_{h,int}$	hepatic intrinsic clearance of drug
CL_{tot}	total body plasma clearance of drug
$CL_{tot,blood}$	total body blood clearance of drug
C_{max}	maximum concentration of drug in plasma
$C_{max,blood}$	maximum concentration of drug in blood
C_{ss}	steady-state drug concentration in plasma (in Wajima's method, it is equal to dose divided by V_{ss})
$C_{ss,blood}$	steady-state drug concentration in blood (in Wajima's method, it is equal to dose divided by $V_{ss,blood}$)
$f_a \times f_g$	fraction of dose absorbed in the portal vein
f_h	hepatic availability
F_{po}	oral bioavailability
$f_{presystemic,m}$	fraction of dose converting to presystemically formed metabolite
f_u	unbound fraction in plasma
$f_{u,R}$	unbound fraction in the rest of total body water outside the extracellular fluid
$f_{u,T}$	unbound fraction in total body water outside plasma
IV	intravenous administration
k_a	absorption rate constant
$k_{a,m}$	absorption rate constant of presystemically formed metabolite
$k_{elim,m}$	elimination rate constant of a metabolite
$k_{form,apparent,m}$	apparent formation rate constant of parent drug concentration in blood converting to a metabolite
LLOQ	lower limit of quantification
M/P	metabolite-to-parent drug ratio
MLP	maximum life-span potential
MRT	mean residence time
MRT_{iv}	mean residence after intravenous administration
MRT_{po}	mean residence after oral administration
Q_h	hepatic blood flow
$R_{E/I}$	ratio of total number of drug-binding sites (or amount of drug-binding proteins) in the extracellular fluid outside plasma versus those in plasma

$t_{1/2}$	half-life of drug in plasma
$t_{1/2,blood}$	half-life of drug in blood
$V_{d,m}$	volume of distribution of a metabolite
V_E	volume of the extracellular fluid outside plasma (i.e., interstitial fluid)
V_P	volume of plasma water
V_R	volume of the rest of total body water outside the extracellular fluid (i.e., intracellular fluid)
V_{ss}	steady-state volume of distribution of drug in plasma
$V_{ss,blood}$	steady-state volume of distribution of drug in blood
$V_{ss,u}$	unbound steady-state volume of distribution of drug in plasma
V_T	volume of total body water outside plasma

References

[1] B. Bonn, P. Svanberg, A. Janefeldt, I. Hultman, K. Grime, Determination of human hepatocyte intrinsic clearance for slowly metabolized compounds: comparison of a primary hepatocyte/stromal cell co-culture with plated primary hepatocytes and HepaRG, Drug Metab. Dispos. 44 (2016) 527–533, https://doi.org/10.1124/dmd.115.067769.

[2] T.S. Chan, H. Yu, A. Moore, S.R. Khetani, D. Tweedie, Meeting the challenge of predicting hepatic clearance of compounds slowly metabolized by cytochrome P450 using a novel hepatocyte model, HepatoPac, Drug Metab. Dispos. 41 (2013) 2024–2032, https://doi.org/10.1124/dmd.113.053397.

[3] M. Chiba, Y. Ishii, Y. Sugiyama, Prediction of hepatic clearance in human from invitro data for successful drug development, AAPS J. 11 (2009) 262–276, https://doi.org/10.1208/s12248-009-9103-6.

[4] G.L. Sirianni, K.S. Pang, Organ clearance concepts: new perspectives on old principles, J. Pharmacokinet. Biopharm. 25 (1997) 449–470, https://doi.org/10.1023/a:1025792925854.

[5] M. Yamazaki, H. Suzuki, Y. Sugiyama, Recent advances in carrier-mediated hepatic uptake and biliary excretion of xenobiotics, Pharm. Res. 13 (1996) 497–513, https://doi.org/10.1023/a:1016077517241.

[6] P. Poulin, F.P. Theil, Prediction of pharmacokinetics prior to in vivo studies. 1. Mechanism-based prediction of volume of distribution, J. Pharm. Sci. 91 (2002) 129–156, https://doi.org/10.1002/jps.10005.

[7] T. Rodgers, D. Leahy, M. Rowland, Physiologically based pharmacokinetic modeling 1: predicting the tissue distribution of moderate-to-strong bases, J. Pharm. Sci. 94 (2005) 1259–1276, https://doi.org/10.1002/jps.20322.

[8] T. Rodgers, D. Leahy, M. Rowland, Physiologically based pharmacokinetic modeling 2: predicting the tissue distribution of moderate-to-strong bases, J. Pharm. Sci. 95 (2006) 1238–1257, https://doi.org/10.1002/jps.20502.

[9] T. Wajima, Y. Yano, K. Fukumura, T. Oguma, Prediction of human pharmacokinetic profile in animal scale up based on normalizing time course profiles, J. Pharm. Sci. 93 (2004) 1890–1900, https://doi.org/10.1002/jps.20099.

[10] M.J. Waring, J. Arrowsmith, A.R. Leach, P.D. Leeson, S. Mandrell, R.M. Owen, G. Pairaudeau, W.D. Pennie, S.D. Pickett, J. Wang, O. Wallace, A. Weir, An analysis of the attrition of drug candidates from four major pharmaceutical companies, Nat. Rev. Drug Discov. 14 (2015) 475–486, https://doi.org/10.1038/nrd4609.

[11] T.S. Mauer, M. Edwards, D. Hepworth, P. Verhoest, C.M.N. Allerton, Designing small molecules for therapeutic success: a contemporary perspective, Drug Discov. Today (2021), https://doi.org/10.1016/j.drudis.2021.09.017.

[12] R.S. Obach, J.G. Baxter, T.E. Liston, B.M. Silber, B.C. Jones, F. MacIntyre, D.J. Rance, P. Wastall, The prediction of human pharmacokinetic parameters from preclinical and in vitro metabolism data, J. Pharmacol. Exp. Therapeut. 283 (1997) 46–58.

[13] S.S. De Buck, V.K. Sinha, L.A. Fenu, M.J. Nijsen, C.E. Mackie, R.A. Gilissen, Prediction of human pharmacokinetics using physiologically based modeling: a retrospective analysis of 26 clinically tested drugs, Drug Metab. Dispos. 35 (2007) 1766–1780, https://doi.org/10.1124/dmd.107.015644.

[14] C. Huang, M. Zheng, Z. Yang, A.D. Rodrigues, P. Marathe, Projection of exposure and efficacious dose prior to first-in-human studies: how successful have we been? Pharm. Res. 25 (2008) 713–726, https://doi.org/10.1007/s11095-007-9411-4.

[15] N.A. Hosea, W.T. Collard, S. Cole, T.S. Maurer, R.X. Fang, H. Jones, S.M. Kakar, Y. Nakai, B.J. Smith, R. Webster, K. Beaumont, Prediction of human pharmacokinetics from preclinical information: comparative accuracy of quantitative prediction approaches, J. Clin. Pharmacol. 49 (2009) 513–533, https://doi.org/10.1177/0091270009333209.

[16] R.D. Jones, H.M. Jones, M. Rowland, C.R. Gibson, J.W. Yates, J.Y. Chien, B.J. Ring, K.K. Adkison, M.S. Ku, H. He, R. Vuppugalla, P. Marathe, V. Fischer, S. Dutta, V.K. Sinha, T. Björnsson, T. Lavé, P. Poulin, PhRMA CPCDC initiative on predictive models of human pharmacokinetics, part 2: comparative assessment of prediction methods of human volume of distribution, J. Pharm. Sci. 100 (2011) 4074–4089, https://doi.org/10.1002/jps.22553.

[17] B.J. Ring, J.Y. Chien, K.K. Adkison, H.M. Jones, M. Rowland, R.D. Jones, J.W. Yates, M.S. Ku, C.R. Gibson, H. He, R. Vuppugalla, P. Marathe, V. Fischer, S. Dutta, V.K. Sinha, T. Björnsson, T. Lavé, P. Poulin, PhRMA CPCDC initiative on predictive models of human pharmacokinetics, part 3: comparative assessment of prediction methods of human clearance, J. Pharm. Sci. 100 (2011) 4090–4110, https://doi.org/10.1002/jps.22552.

[18] A. Van den Bergh, V. Sinha, R. Gilissen, R. Straetemans, K. Wuyts, D. Morrison, L. Bijnens, C. Mackie, Prediction of human oral plasma concentration-time profiles using preclinical data: comparative evaluation of prediction approaches in early pharmaceutical discovery, Clin. Pharmacokinet. 50 (2011) 505–517, https://doi.org/10.2165/11587230-000000000-00000.

[19] H.M. Jones, I.B. Gardner, W.T. Collard, P.J. Stanley, P. Oxley, N.A. Hosea, D. Plowchalk, S. Gernhardt, J. Lin, M. Dickins, S.R. Rahavendran, B.C. Jones, K.J. Watson, H. Pertinez, V. Kumar, S. Cole, Simulation of human intravenous and oral pharmacokinetics of 21 diverse compounds using physiologically based pharmacokinetic modelling, Clin. Pharmacokinet. 50 (2011) 331−347, https://doi.org/10.2165/11539680-000000000-00000.

[20] T. Zhang, T. Heimbach, W. Lin, J. Zhang, H. He, Prospective predictions of human pharmacokinetics for eighteen compounds, J. Pharm. Sci. 104 (2015) 2795−2806, https://doi.org/10.1002/jps.24373.

[21] S.A. Peters, C. Petersson, A. Blaukat, J.P. Halle, H. Dolgos, Prediction of active human dose: learnings from 20 years of Merck KGaA experience, illustrated by case studies, Drug Discov. Today 25 (2020) 909−919, https://doi.org/10.1016/j.drudis.2020.01.002.

[22] M. Davies, R.D.O. Jones, K. Grime, R. Jansson-Löfmark, A.J. Fretland, S. Winiwarter, P. Morgan, D.F. McGinnity, Improving the accuracy of predicted human pharmacokinetics: lessons learned from the AstraZeneca drug pipeline over two decades, Trends Pharmacol. Sci. 41 (2020) 390−408, https://doi.org/10.1016/j.tips.2020.03.004.

[23] A. Herland, B.M. Maoz, D. Das, M.R. Somayaji, R. Prantil-Baun, R. Novak, M. Cronce, T. Huffstater, S.S.F. Jeanty, M. Ingram, A. Chalkiadaki, D. Benson Chou, S. Marquez, A. Delahanty, S. Jalili-Firoozinezhad, Y. Milton, A. Sontheimer-Phelps, B. Swenor, O. Levy, K.K. Parker, A. Przekwas, D.E. Ingber, Quantitative prediction of human pharmacokinetic responses to drugs via fluidically coupled vascularized organ chips, Nat. Biomed. Eng. 4 (2020) 421−436, https://doi.org/10.1038/s41551-019-0498-9.

[24] 2019 A. Roth, M.P.S.-W.S. Berlin, Human microphysiological systems for drug development, Science 373 (2021) 1304−1306, https://doi.org/10.1126/science.abc3734.

[25] C. Sakolish, Y.S. Luo, A. Valdiviezo, L.A. Vernetti, I. Rusyn, W.A. Chiu, Prediction of hepatic drug clearance with a human microfluidic four-cell liver acinus microphysiology system, Toxicology 463 (2021) 152954, https://doi.org/10.1016/j.tox.2021.152954.

[26] Danishuddin, V. Kumar, M. Faheem, K. Woo Lee, A decade of machine learning-based predictive models for human pharmacokinetics: advances and challenges, Drug Discov. Today (2021), https://doi.org/10.1016/j.drudis.2021.09.013.

[27] F. Miljković, A. Martinsson, O. Obrezanova, B. Williamson, M. Johnson, A. Sykes, A. Bender, N. Greene, Machine learning models for human in vivo pharmacokinetic parameters with in-house validation, Mol. Pharm. 18 (2021) 4520−4530, https://doi.org/10.1021/acs.molpharmaceut.1c00718.

[28] P. Zou, Y. Yu, N. Zheng, Y. Yang, H.J. Paholak, L.X. Yu, D. Sun, Applications of human pharmacokinetic prediction in first-in-human dose estimation, AAPS J. 14 (2012) 262−281, https://doi.org/10.1208/s12248-012-9332-y.

[29] E. Fuse, H. Tanii, K. Takai, K. Asanome, N. Kurata, H. Kobayashi, T. Kuwabara, S. Kobayashi, Y. Sugiyama, Altered pharmacokinetics of a novel anticancer drug, UCN-01, caused by specific high affinity binding to alpha1-acid glycoprotein in humans, Cancer Res. 59 (1998) 1054−1060.

[30] H. Tang, A. Hussain, M. Leal, E. Fluhler, M. Mayersohn, Controversy in the allometric application of fixed- versus varying-exponent models: a statistical and mathematical perspective, J. Pharm. Sci. 100 (2011) 402−410, https://doi.org/10.1002/jps.22316.

[31] H. Tang, M. Mayersohn, Controversies in allometric scaling for predicting human drug clearance: an historical problem and reflections on what works and what does not, Curr. Top. Med. Chem. 11 (2011) 340−350, https://doi.org/10.2174/156802611794480945.

[32] P. Zou, N. Zheng, Y. Yang, L.X. Yu, D. Sun, Prediction of volume of distribution at steady state in humans: comparison of different approaches, Expert Opin. Drug Metab. Toxicol. 8 (2012) 855−872, https://doi.org/10.1517/17425255.2012.682569.

[33] S. Mathew, D. Tess, W. Burchett, G. Chang, N. Woody, C. Keefer, C. Orozco, J. Lin, S. Jordan, S. Yamazaki, R. Jones, D. Li, Evaluation of prediction accuracy for volume of distribution in rat and human using in vitro, in vivo, PBPK and QSAR methods, J. Pharm. Sci. 110 (2021) 1799−1823, https://doi.org/10.1016/j.xphs.2020.12.005.

[34] S. Øie, T.N. Tozer, Effect of altered plasma-protein binding on ap-parent volume of distribution, J. Pharm. Sci. 68 (1979) 1203−12055, https://doi.org/10.1002/jps.2600680948.

[35] N.J. Waters, F. Lombardo, Use of the Øie-Tozer model in understanding mechanisms and determinants of drug distribution, Drug Metab. Dispos. 38 (2010) 1159−1165, https://doi.org/10.1124/dmd.110.032458.

[36] G.R. Wilkinson, D.G. Shand, Commentary: a physiological approach to hepatic drug clearance, Clin. Pharmacol. Ther. 18 (1975) 377−390, https://doi.org/10.1002/cpt1975184377.

[37] I. Mahmood, J.D. Balian, Interspecies scaling: predicting clearance of drugs in humans. Three different approaches, Xenobiotica 26 (1996) 887−895, https://doi.org/10.3109/00498259609052491.

[38] J.B. Houston, Utility of in vitro drug metabolism data in predicting in vivo metabolic clearance, Biochem. Pharmacol. 47 (1994) 1469−1479, https://doi.org/10.1016/0006-2952(94)90520-7.

[39] T. Iwatsubo, N. Hirota, T. Ooie, H. Suzuki, N. Shimada, K. Chiba, T. Ishizaki, C.E. Green, C.A. Tyson, Y. Sugiyama, Prediction of in vivo drug metabolism in the human liver from in vitro metabolism data, Pharmacol. Ther. 73 (1997) 147−171, https://doi.org/10.1016/s0163-7258(96)00184-2.

[40] B. Davies, T. Morris, Physiological parameters in laboratory animals and humans, Pharm. Res. 10 (1993) 1093−1095, https://doi.org/10.1023/a:1018943613122.

[41] R.P. Brown, M.D. Delp, S.L. Lindstedt, L.R. Rhomberg, R.P. Beliles, Physiological parameter values for physiologically based pharmacokinetic models, Toxicol. Ind. Health 13 (1997) 407−484, https://doi.org/10.1177/074823379701300401.

[42] D. Li, P. Trapa, R.S. Obach, K. Atkinson, Y.A. Bi, A.C. Wolford, B. Tan, T.S. McDonald, Y. Lai, L.M. Tremaine, A novel relay method for determining low-clearance values, Drug Metab. Dispos. 40 (2012) 1860−1865, https://doi.org/10.1124/dmd.112.046425.

[43] H. Tang, M. Mayersohn, A global examination of allometric scaling for predicting human drug clearance and the prediction of large vertical allometry, J. Pharm. Sci. 95 (2006) 1783−1799, https://doi.org/10.1002/jps.20481.

[44] T.G. Dhar, H.Y. Xiao, J. Xie, L.D. Lehman-McKeeman, D.R. Wu, M. Dabros, X. Yang, T.L. Taylor, X.D. Zhou, E.M. Heimrich, R. Thomas, K.W. McIntyre, B. Warrack, H. Shi, P.C. Levesque, J.L. Zhu, J. Hennan, P. Balimane, Z. Yang, A.M. Marino, G. Cornelius, C.J. D'Arienzo, A. Mathur, D.R. Shen, M.E. Cvijic, L. Salter-Cid, J.C. Barrish, P.H. Carter, A.J. Dyckman, Identification and preclinical pharmacology of BMS-986104: a differentiated S1P1 receptor modulator in clinical trials, ACS Med. Chem. Lett. 7 (2016) 283−288, https://doi.org/10.1021/acsmedchemlett.5b00448.

[45] Gilenya® (fingolimod) prescribing information. https://www.novartis.com/us-en/sites/novartis_us/files/gilenya.pdf. Accessed on December 6, 2021

[46] M. Zollinger, H.P. Gschwind, Y. Jin, C. Sayer, F. Zécri, S. Hartmann, Absorption and disposition of the sphingosine 1-phosphate receptor modulator fingolimod (FTY720) in healthy volunteers: a case of xenobiotic biotransformation following endogenous metabolic pathways, Drug Metab. Dispos. 39 (2011) 199−207, https://doi.org/10.1124/dmd.110.035907.

[47] Y. Jin, M. Zollinger, H. Borell, A. Zimmerlin, C.J. Patten, CYP4F enzymes are responsible for the elimination of fingolimod (FTY720), a novel treatment of relapsing multiple sclerosis, Drug Metab. Dispos. 39 (2011) 191−198, https://doi.org/10.1124/dmd.110.035378.

[48] J.M. Kovarik, S. Hartmann, M. Bartlett, G.J. Riviere, D. Neddermann, Y. Wang, A. Port, R.L. Schmouder, Oral-intravenous crossover study of fingolimod pharmacokinetics, lymphocyte responses and cardiac effects, Biopharm. Drug Dispos. 28 (2007) 97−104, https://doi.org/10.1002/bdd.535.

[49] Y. Anada, Y. Igarashi, A. Kihara, The immunomodulator FTY720 is phosphorylated and released from platelets, Eur. J. Pharmacol. 568 (2007) 106−111, https://doi.org/10.1016/j.ejphar.2007.04.053.

[50] A. Kihara, Y. Igarashi, Production and release of sphingosine 1-phosphate and the phosphorylated form of the immunomodulator FTY720, Biochim. Biophys. Acta 1781 (2008) 496−502, https://doi.org/10.1016/j.bbalip.2008.05.003.

[51] O.J. David, J.M. Kovarik, R.L. Schmouder, Clinical pharmacokinetics of fingolimod, Clin. Pharmacokinet. 51 (2012) 15−28, https://doi.org/10.2165/11596550-000000000-00000.

[52] K. Wu, F. Mercier, O.J. David, R.L. Schmouder, M. Looby, Population pharmacokinetics of fingolimod phosphate in healthy participants, J. Clin. Pharmacol. 52 (2012) 1054−1068, https://doi.org/10.1177/0091270011409229.

[53] J.L. Gilmore, H.Y. Xiao, T.G.M. Dhar, M.G. Yang, Z. Xiao, J. Xie, L.D. Lehman-McKeeman, L. Gong, H. Sun, L. Lecureux, C. Chen, D.R. Wu, M. Dabros, X. Yang, T.L. Taylor, X.D. Zhou, E.M. Heimrich, R. Thomas, K.W. McIntyre, V. Borowski, B.M. Warrack, Y. Li, H. Shi, P.C. Levesque, Z. Yang, A.M. Marino, G. Cornelius, C.J. D'Arienzo, A. Mathur, R. Rampulla, A. Gupta, B. Pragalathan, D.R. Shen, M.E. Cvijic, L.M. Salter-Cid, P.H. Carter, A.J. Dyckman, Identification and preclinical pharmacology of ((1 R,3 S)-1-amino-3-((S)-6-(2-methoxyphenethyl)-5,6,7,8-tetrahydronaphthalen-2-yl)cyclopentyl)methanol (BMS-986166): a differentiated sphingosine-1-phosphate receptor 1 (S1P 1) modulator advanced into clinical trial, J. Med. Chem. 62 (2019) 2265−2285, https://doi.org/10.1021/acs.jmedchem.8b01695.

[54] S. Singhal, I.G. Girgis, J. Xie, S. Dutta, D.E. Shevell, J. Throup, The safety and pharmacokinetics of a novel, selective S1P1R modulator in healthy participants, Expert Opin. Investig. Drugs 29 (2020) 411−422, https://doi.org/10.1080/13543784.2020.1742322.

Chapter 23

Esmolol (soft drug design)

Paul W. Erhardt

DUP Emeritus, Medicinal Chemistry, University of Toledo, Sylvania, OH, United States

Square pegs and round holes

Sydney Smith *circa* 1800 [1].

Overcoming Obstacles in Drug Discovery and Development. https://doi.org/10.1016/B978-0-12-817134-9.00018-0

Introduction

Case study's intent and related publications

Authors were asked to describe the hurdles that they encountered during their title drug's discovery and to explain how problems were solved. Further, the overall narrative should be more of a story rather than a technical report. Toward these ends I have discussed several hurdles in the order that they occurred during the discovery phase (Part 1) and, for the first time in print, during esmolol's development phase (Part 2). I have also included a separate section (Part 3) at the end of the story that discusses some take home lessons and provides brief follow-up information. For many problems I've included recollected dialogue so that readers can feel like they are actually present in the situation, i.e., as if reading the script for a stage play. High emotions were a significant aspect of esmolol's discovery and development. These potential "thrill of victory" or "agony of defeat" [2] moments have been captured by analogies to sporting events such as standing at bat during a baseball game, or to other stronger images which should be familiar to everyone even if unpleasant. I have occasionally used colloquial phrases previously in articles intended for international audiences and found that oftentimes these expressions required further clarification to be fully appreciated. Hence, for the many I have chosen herein to emphasize certain points or feelings (e.g., the two associated with reference items [1,2] above), I have also provided additionally helpful comments as reference citations that also attempt to acknowledge/credit the phrases' historical origins. Finally and perhaps most significant of all, I have personalized this description in terms of the overall importance of my family's critical role, something I have not been able to do in any of my previous writing efforts.

It should be acknowledged that beyond the original technical reports [3–6] and the first story version that I contributed to the ACS series entitled *Chronicles of Drug Discovery* [7], this will be my 15th publication pertaining to some aspect of esmolol's invention [8–16]. All of these have been done without royalties in response to requests for general discourses about soft drug discovery, or as part of textbook examples wherein highly abbreviated entries have been illustrative of specific drug design principles. Each publication has had different emphases and the version described herein will be the first to include a thorough description about esmolol's chemical development. When there is direct overlap of sentences or sections from one or more of my previous publications, they will be appropriately referenced.

As I now move into semiretirement, this will likely be my last rendition for technical audiences. I am delighted to have been asked yet one more time. I hope that readers will enjoy the unique nature of esmolol as a Goldilocks compound, its historical discovery and development parts as a Cinderella team story, and the eventual corporate rags-to-riches saga, all of which I will try to convey in my most personalized manner so far. While not short, I assure you that this is still an abridged narrative. I have included several headers and numerous sub-headers within each of the three major parts. I hope that these will be helpful to clear the hurdles and stay in the correct lane of the track that we are about to run on, for as you will soon see, the pursuit of esmolol did indeed become a race in itself. Likewise, at any point during your read, the table of contents (in simple list format above) may be useful to quickly see where you've been and where you have yet to go.

Finally toward further personalizing the present rendition, I would like to dedicate this chapter to my wife, children and grandchildren; as well as to some of my former birth family members who will always remain special to me because of their positive influence toward shaping my life. The composite of all of our circumstances eventually led to my role in the discovery of esmolol. By lineage, these special people are: (i) my 'uncle Paul' for whom I am a namesake and according to family lore, left my Swedish immigrant grandparents' humble farm in northern Minnesota to become a physician practicing plastic surgery on the front lines during WW II, but then was not able to live much longer thereafter; (ii) my mother 'Linnea' who obviously having this same brother atop one of her own pedestals, continually emphasized the importance of the medical sciences to me starting from a very young age; (iii) my father 'Bill' who totally committed himself toward supporting our family as a tradesman but died mid-life from cancer during a time when doctors had very few tools to address this dreaded disease; (iv) my older sister 'Carmen' who likewise exemplified selfless, dedicated support for her own family and also died mid-life from a lung disease that similarly lacked medical treatments; (v) my fiancé 'Judy' who while just beginning to envision our future family plans, encouraged taking the time and together making the sacrifices needed for me to pursue medicinal chemistry as a graduate student; and finally, (vi) especially again to my wife Judy and our five children ('Bill, Mike, Tricia, John and Christine') who have always provided the support needed during times when I, by no means a rocket scientist, truly had to struggle with my so-chosen, highly challenging professional career aimed at discovering new drugs. You will soon be meeting Judy and hearing about our children when they play important roles at some of the key turning points in the esmolol story.

Part 1. Discovery of a 'drug wannabe' called 'ASL-8052'

Introduction

Setting the clock and some of the stage

We'll need to go back to 1976, a little more than 150 years after Sydney Smith's original idiom as reiterated above [1], and a little less than 50 years before today. To appreciate some of the tools in our chemistry lab, let's take a quick peak using the eyes of a then young synthetic medicinal chemist. Advanced NMRs were 50 MHz. We felt very lucky to have one even though a good proton spectrum needed at least 10 mg of carefully weighed sample, and the instrument required iteratively fine-tuning its x-, y- and z-fields for about 20 min prior to each analysis. Applications like ^{13}C required outsourcing and today's ever-growing COSY et al. family of instrumental methods had not yet begun. Instead, one had to rely on additional NMR experiments by using shift reagents to glean more spectroscopic data [17]. To improve gravity column separations on a preparative scale, we were fiddling with home-made low-pressure pumping and refractive index detection systems, or with a first-ever medium-pressure commercial device [18] that would quickly produce liters of solvent waste unless optimal eluent selections/gradients were judiciously determined in advance by TLC. Thankfully, flash column methods would soon arrive [19] but then perhaps sadly, crystallization for the sake of purification would gradually become a dying art. Mass spec was just starting to evolve as a useful method for compound assessment during organic syntheses and its spectra often displayed base-line humps called "meta-stable peaks." Although now routinely eliminated electronically as part of background noise, at that time their presence could guide one's assignments about how a daughter peak likely arose from a preceding mass's peak [20]. Prodrug methodology was well established as a drug design option within a medicinal chemist's tool box [21], but the term 'soft drug' had not yet been coined, nor had even the concept of usefully deploying such a strategy become demonstrably instilled within the literature. The biotech revolution was yet to begin so its gradual inspiration for compound libraries to satisfy the appetite of HTS campaigns was completely absent. Small companies were still just around-the-corner of becoming fashionable, let alone eventually proving to have valuable roles in today's overall drug discovery enterprise and in CRO-assisted drug development activities.

Two early hurdles

Nothing close to identity crises, two identity clarifications should be discussed at the outset because they are also important to fully appreciate the atmosphere from which this story is about to unfold. One was corporate and the other was personal. Each is discussed below before moving into the main narrative. Consider us to be completing the stage set-up and then being introduced to one of the key actors just prior to opening the curtain to start the actual play.

Establishing a corporate identity

As mentioned above, small and virtual companies dependent upon CROs had not yet become fashionable, let alone legitimate players within the overall pharmaceutical enterprise. But then here we were as 'Arnar-Stone Laboratories' (ASL) with less than 10 employees working in research when I first joined: three pharmacologists, two synthetic chemists including myself, one formulation chemist, one toxicologist, one analytical chemist, and one bioanalytical chemist. Our administrative, business and sales-force folks totaled an even smaller number, although consumer sales were transferred to a larger, well-known distributer company. ASL's suburban Chicago location put us just North of two major pharmaceutical companies, at that time Searle and Abbott. Our feelings about this situation are conveyed by the depiction in Fig. 23.1 even though there was never any overt intimidation or ill-will ever expressed toward their fledgling neighbor by either of these well-established, legitimate pharmaceutical company players.

This corporate inferiority complex was addressed by two factors. The first involved our company's strategy. The latter was to focus upon critical care therapeutics since these smaller markets were of less interest to the larger companies who were typically busy in those days vying with each other for the 'next block-buster drug.' This decision can be attributed to a savvy administrative team. Our focus established both an effective business and technical niche in the marketplace and scientific arena. Because it naturally assumed a 'lay-low' working posture, it was also somewhat of a 'stealth operation' by

FIGURE 23.1 Our small, start-up company's view of its relationship to two, large and well-established neighboring companies while all three of us sought to operate successfully within the competitive environment of the global pharmaceutical enterprise dominated by big pharma. American Critical Care (ACC) is a new name soon to be given to ASL (see next section of text). The portrayal of these companies as a combination of buildings with human faces on structures also resembling both silos and gravestones depending upon which you choose to conjure-up in your own mind, is intentional in that the first of the latter attempts to convey the strict internalization of a company's intellectual property while the second of the latter attempts to capture and retain the spirit for this first scene from the story as the 'ghosts of esmolol past' [22]. Note that small biotechs would not become fashionable until nearly a decade later, and then finally recognized as important contributors until only after yet another several years had passed. ASL/ACC in reality now only a ghost from the past, was at this point in our esmolol story a vibrant albeit somewhat intimidated entity that was truly very, very much 'well-before its time.'

today's jargon, although there was never any attempt to remain secretive about our non-proprietary operations beyond those of the major players and how we were all similarly handling intellectual property (IP) at the time. In addition, the administrative-business team had also just negotiated the adoption of ASL by American Hospital Supply Corporation (AHSC) thereby gaining a strong financial parent along with a specialized sales force tailored for the hospital audience [7]. Eventually our name was changed to American Critical Care (ACC), reflecting this affiliation and our distinct mission to discover intravenous (iv), critical care therapeutics [7]. Indeed, ASL *via* AHSC was already marketing the endogenous renal vasodilator dopamine (Fig. 23.2) for use by the iv route to attenuate renal shutdown and delay death, thus allowing for longer treatment time during shock.

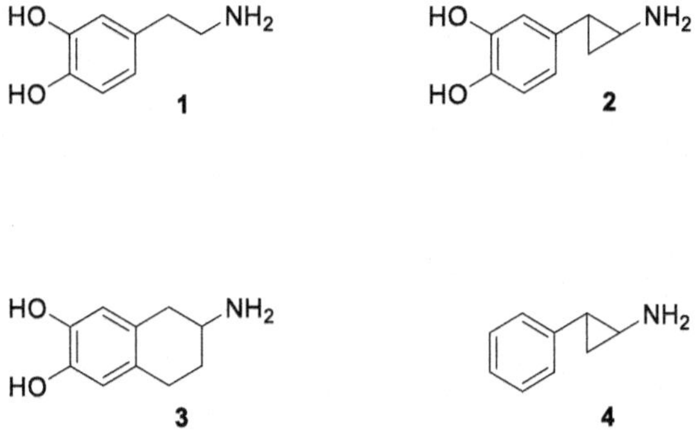

FIGURE 23.2 Chemical structures of dopamine (**1**), cyclopropyl-dopamine (**2**), another dopamine analog abbreviated ADTN (**3**), and tranylcypromine (**4**).

The second positive factor to address our corporate identity involved establishing and reinforcing an enthusiastic, entrepreneurial culture throughout our ranks. Likely well accepted within today's realm of small biotech and big pharma, I will still take a moment to submit that this element may be the most important of all because no matter how impressive and promising is a new technology in our particular field, initially maturing it in a timely manner across inevitable hurdles and eventually translating it to the clinic is not likely to occur without this factor imbedded at the forefront of a company's overall spirit and daily operations. In this regard we were somewhat lucky in that it was said that the initial founders, Arnar and Stone, had managed to discover a local anesthetic concoction while conducting formulation research in the corner of a garage [7]. Their lack of legitimate facilities and the sparsity of their resources left an image that was particularly relevant in our case and from which we could all rally forward. Thus, whatever we lacked in size and supplies, we were able to more than make up for with an entrepreneurial attitude by maintaining a connection to our founders' spirit. This factor can be attributed to the entire ACC workforce as it occurred from the grass roots up as much as it did from the administration down.

Establishing a personal identity I

My father was diagnosed and soon died from advanced cancer during my final year of undergraduate school at the University of Minnesota (UMN). This was well before the biotechnology-driven life sciences' revolution, so at that time his cancer's source could not even be confirmed, nor could his metastasized form be characterized in general, let alone in a gene-based personalized treatment plan like we are able to do today. Simply put, there was little that any of the doctors could do, and our plan to have a drink together on my 21st birthday did not occur. Rather than becoming a medical practitioner, it was then that I became determined to use my BA degree in chemistry with double minors in mathematics and psychology to pursue medical research. Thinking that with an advanced degree in a science field that could be used to potentially discover new therapeutic agents, I hoped that I might be able to enhance the medical profession's armamentarium to fight cancer. Still liking basic organic chemistry, I decided to seek a PhD in synthetic medicinal chemistry under the mentorship of Taito Soine in the College of Pharmacy at UMN. Professor Soine was internationally-recognized for his expertise in natural products and I was excited to join his research group. But then, during my first year of really enjoying graduate level courses, fate stepped-in and it appeared like it might have me destined to take a very different turn. In addition to being accepted to graduate school, I also received a much larger organization's official notification letter. The second letter informed me that my SSN drew a low draft number and 'Uncle Sam', in turn, was mandating that I immediately participate in our country's escalating war with Vietnam.

Some luck just in the nick-of-time

Thinking that my further education and professional goals were, minimally, about to be placed on a backburner, I was very lucky, however, to also be accepted by an Army Reserve unit that I had previously applied for. This third letter's official acceptance came just prior to the required report date for my regular army physical. With only a few days between, the Minnesota State board was able to maneuver my change in draft status just in the nick of time. Only God knows where the other turn may have taken me. At any rate, although I was still required to fly-off and say goodbye to my fiancée (see below) while *"Leaving on a jet plane"* was playing in the background [for real, see Ref. 23], this temporary departure would not be taking me to the front-lines in Vietnam. Instead, I underwent basic training and 'AIT' as a medic, and then my annual 2-week sessions of active duty were able to be performed in various states' military hospitals. Perhaps another story on another day, for now I'll only note here that the descriptions associated with my military experience would be filled with many sad images of badly injured young men returning home from the front lines—images much like what my uncle must have experienced every day when he was a surgeon for several years during WW II, and which now served to reinforce my commitment to pursue a medical-related career in research. My personal respect for my late uncle grew to what my mother had been feeling all along, and similarly but even more so for the young soldiers who continue to serve and sometimes sacrifice severely in our country's militaries today. My monthly weekend duties could be fulfilled at Fort Snelling in Minneapolis and, alternatively, these were actually somewhat upbeat, akin to the *"M*A*S*H"* episodes during the latter's slow-patient times [24]. For these, we trained to set-up large field hospital tents as quickly as possible while establishing and maintaining aseptic conditions. In the end, my several years of obligatory service as an army reservist became only a minimal disruption to the pursuit of my advanced degree in medicinal chemistry, and the overall experience actually strengthened my determination. Plus, what I can next describe as occurring across this same time period is all going to be very positive. So let's get moving along with that as I continue to mold a personal identity needed for you to appreciate my role and its' emotional connections within the esmolol story.

I met Judy during my third year of undergraduate studies when we were both working at the nearby St. Mary's Hospital, myself part-time as an orderly and she after recently completing her Associate Science Degree in X-ray technology. Our relationship continued as a pair of students and grew as a couple while I contemplated and entered graduate school, and she next converted her 2-year degree into a BS in biology also at the UMN. We became married during my second year of grad school and when I matriculated 3 years later, the Good Lord had already blessed us with two young children, Bill and Mike. It is difficult to emphasize enough just how important they were meant to be not only for the unfolding esmolol story but also in the truly 'bigger picture of things' in my life. However, with these blessings also came greater responsibilities as a father and, in those days, as the main provider for the family. Upon graduation, for the financial security of our family, I was committed to quickly finding a reasonably well-paying and secure/steady position. But the job market was very tight at the time and especially so for recently graduating medicinal chemists. Organic chemists were at the top rungs of research administration within most pharmaceutical companies, and when lab-based synthetic chemistry openings did become available, they tended to hire fellow organic chemists. In fairness to this practice at that time, because of their exposure to a broader range of biology-related subjects, medicinal chemists were not regarded as being as well trained in the conduct of pure synthetic chemistry. Simply put, we were not on the industry's preferred list for filling chemistry positions. Thus, my eyes shifted toward academic jobs where the prevailing sentiment instead emphasized "publish or perish" no matter what one's background or pedigree. The fastest path into academia would be to first undertake postdoctoral training, hopefully adding quickly to my publications list and thus enhancing my credentials for tenure-track employment, and potentially for within industry as well. Feeling that I had been afforded an excellent learning experience about how to design, synthesize and test molecules that were supposed to prompt some desirable effect in the body, I was curious and very interested in learning about what the body, in turn, does to such xenobiotics. The latter is phrased as such because this interest was well-before today's now commonly-practiced theme of early ADMET testing and responsive structural modification to enhance a drug candidate's overall profile. Little did I know how fortuitously the practical knowledge I gained from this curiosity-driven postdoctoral choice would eventually playout in the esmolol story, or for that matter, the field of drug discovery in general even further down-the-road.

A perfect position presented itself, namely a bioanalytical-PK-drug metabolism project working with Bob Smith in the Drug Dynamics Institute at the University of Texas, Austin. As a bioanalytical chemist, Bob had just the opposite view toward hiring a medicinal chemist who was trained in physical-organic synthetic chemistry. I was enthusiastically greeted while he hoped my chemical training might be used to address a stubborn problem in his analytical lab that involved trying to quantitatively assay apomorphine (APO) and its metabolites. APO is itself subject to rapid autooxidation so they were trying to measure something that Mother Nature had designed to inherently fall apart. Tuck that thought away for now as we keep moving along. I soon came up with a simple chemistry-related answer for this problem by judiciously deploying antioxidants, namely sodium bisulfite in aqueous media and dithiothreitol in organic phases. However, Bob was highly skeptical about having the group use my methods in the presence of the cytochrome P-450 enzymes (CYPs) because they required oxygen for their metabolic biotransformation reactions. Everyone thought it was a contradictory scenario (another sentiment to tuck away for now as we keep moving along). Thus, I first needed to deploy several standard compounds to demonstrate that the CYP-mediated, microsomal fraction-driven biotransformation reactions' competencies are not compromised by the addition of antioxidants. Much to Bob's and everyone's surprise, this worked beautifully. In fact, not only were the CYP-related oxidations maintained, the microsomal fractions could be deployed for longer study times, presumably because the rate of undesirable lipid peroxidation was diminished. Because both of us were young and eager to make a positive impact in the biomedical research arena, Bob and I managed to publish six papers associated with these novel findings after just 1-year of my postdoctoral studies [17,25−29]. That solid effort helped me to land a tenure-track, faculty position at Northeastern University in Boston. By many measures, I was now well on my way toward personally establishing a reputable scientific identity, and seemingly a secure financial situation from which to support our family.

However, between full-time teaching duties and grant writing efforts, I had little if any time to actually practice science the way I enjoyed it, namely hands-on experimentation to solve stubborn lab problems by working at the bench. I was not ready to leave that and become a teacher, as admirable as the latter may be and for how, many years later, I would eventually choose to finish-off my overall professional career. I became somewhat frustrated by this situation and the realization that a junior faculty's academic salary did not go very far in the Boston area with its high cost of living. Judy and I now had two young children plus a wonderful new baby girl, Tricia. We wanted to establish a home for our growing family, but the cost of housing in the Northeast at this time was simply prohibitive for us. Thus, when I was unexpectedly recruited to interview for a position within industry even before 1 year, and although the focus wouldn't be in the anti-cancer arena, it was an easy decision for Judy and I to at least 'take a look.' It was with a small company called Arnar-Stone Labs (ASL) located in the Midwest and, also importantly for us as the lone black sheep, much closer for visiting all of our kin that we had both left behind in Minneapolis. As a start-up, ASL had several positions and it was filling its ranks by a broader hiring philosophy than mentioned previously. Luckily, its management was impressed enough by the high productivity of my postdoctoral experience that they were willing to give this medicinal chemist a shot.

Ironically, my first assignment involved a challenging synthetic target. Really a very simple design, it was the cyclopropyl-dopamine analog depicted in Fig. 23.2. None of us, however, fully appreciated just how extremely challenging this particular target compound was. As my efforts bogged-down well into a multi-step synthesis, the sentiment about corporate credentials mentioned above not only returned but now became quite personal. I began to feel as if I was a mediocre participant like ACC in Fig. 23.1 and, by analogy, those having pure organic chemistry degrees were like the Searle and Abbott legitimate players. I was struggling. Could medicinal chemists really 'muster up' in the synthetic lab alongside organic chemists touting Harvard, Princeton or Yale pedigrees? Worse than such a general question, my own previously reputable career path suddenly seemed shaky and our family's financial security might even be in jeopardy right at a time when we had five mouths to feed: Judy, myself and our three wonderful children. With each experimental dead-end I became more stressed and this was working against me both in the lab and, unfortunately, when it remained on my mind as I came home each day. I was actually close to 'throwing-in-the-towel' but fearful that this would be perceived as a failure by both my professional colleagues and my family. Would the black sheep need to abandon the 'highfalutin' professional career path and shamefully wander back to Minneapolis? Both Judy and I had come from blue-collar-working parents where neither of our fathers were even able to finish high school during the country's 'great depression' years because at that time they had to take an actual job and contribute to their own birth family's finances. They had always encouraged our education and our entire families were proud of us to this point even though they were unhappy with our having to move away. Now, in the end, would we ultimately be letting all of them down on top of having had to make such upsetting moves in the first place?

Lake Alice

Luckily at this juncture, Judy and I had already been planning a trip to Minneapolis to visit both of our families. We also wanted to spend a few days at her folk's remote cabin on Lake Alice in Northern Minnesota so as to 'get away' for a while. Judy fully appreciated my stress and the gravity of the situation at ASL/ACC with its potential consequences upon our family's financial security. Her strength was evident and her overall perspective was 'right-on' as she insisted that perhaps such a break was exactly what was needed for all of us. Once we hit Lake Alice with its serenity, my life refocused within just a day or two. While Judy and the three kids were having fun and enjoying life, it became clear to me that they were my true supporters no matter what I did for a living or where we had to do it. They were much less concerned about what direction my professional career might take. Always hoping, of course, for only the best, it was also clear that they would be perfectly happy accepting whatever was to be for us financially as long as we all remained together wherever that might be. A view of the cabin and Lake Alice is shown in Fig. 23.3. The later popular, fictional 'Lake Wobegon' [30] was an actual reality for me, and our family visit championed by my wife had become a source of much needed inner peace and strength. But would this get me past my personal professional struggle and the organic synthesis hurdle in the lab? It's easy to make the easy compounds but when the tough ones come along, they can really wreak havoc with one's spirit if not kill your enthusiasm for the field altogether.

Establishing a personal identity II

I returned to work with a reinvigorated spirit and dogged determination to succeed for all of us. As I worked at the bench I pondered the scenario that not only does Mother Nature provide us with serene landscapes to enjoy, but that she sometimes feels compelled to balance those experiences with stormy weather conditions that can completely obscure them. Further, I considered that she's likely doing this exact same thing at the molecular level. Sometimes we just need to ride-out a storm to enjoy the horizon on another day, or similarly, to just go with her flow and try not to push things too hard or fast in the lab. Instead, for the really tough synthetic problems, it may be better to patiently proceed in a methodical manner while remaining open to what Mother Nature might be trying to show you. Following that path in this case led me not only to better defining the problem at hand, but also to devising some novel chemistry that was able to overcome the main hurdle. After that I soon accomplished the synthesis of the desired *trans*-target [31]. In addition, I even obtained its *cis*-version for SAR purposes [32]. This was a double victory. 'Push-pull' driven instability mechanisms had required that I finally devise some new chemistry that allowed Curtius conversion of acids to amines to occur under neutral conditions. That chemical method became a well-recognized paper in itself [33]. However, after all of that earlier frustration, in the end these compounds had disappointing activity [34]. I could only shake my head as ACC supplied compound requests to more than a dozen dopaminergic investigators around the world who apparently also had high hopes for this very specific, semi-rigid analog. While it was a great 'calling card' for ASL/ACC, nobody's results contradicted our findings including those

The cabin . . .

. . . on Lake Alice.

FIGURE 23.3 The seasonal cabin located on Lake Alice in Northern Minnesota. Appreciate the view and the calm that can come with it, truly a 'Lake Wobegon' well-before the latter's first publication [30] and thus also before the possibility to even just imaginatively enjoy such a fictional place ever became fashionable. Coincidentally, the latter was conveyed as the name of a small, rural town in Minnesota.

deploying isolated brain tissues and cells where positive results could have led to significantly larger clinical indications and markets. Alternatively, because of the successful syntheses, my stature within ASL/ACC was fully restored and even elevated. This helped to set a positive stage for what was about to come. Later, at a critical turning-point, everyone would be highly receptive to my novel, unprecedented notions that were eventually key to the molecular design of esmolol.

In fairness to the aforementioned situation technically, it turns-out that the cyclopropyl analog had been an evasive target not just among many of the academic-based 'dopaminergic folks' at the time, but it had also been escaping a team of synthetic chemists within large pharma interested in tranylcypromine analogs (Fig. 23.2). I finally learned this a few years later when I was the youngest scientist invited as an all-expenses-paid speaker to a prestigious international dopamine symposium held in Stockholm. I had proposed a reason for this compound's inactivity that was well-received [35] and between that and my original synthesis, I was one of the keynote speakers. While there I happened to join Carl Kaiser for dinner. Carl was director of research at Smith Kline & French Laboratories, very much one of the legitimate players within the international pharmaceutical enterprise. Carl had a motive for his invite of this young newcomer (me) to the dopaminergic field, namely he wanted to know every detail about my synthesis. In return, he eventually shared that "of all the many analogs protected by their tranylcypromine-related patents, my compound is noticeably absent." He further confided that after expending considerable effort themselves with a large team of organic synthetic chemists, "they had finally come to the conclusion that it could not be made at all due to its fragile nature and so it was carved-out from even being part of a Markush display so as to not jeopardize the validity of their patent overall". Some of this finally gratifying experience from this delicate compound is reflected in the two requested papers listed as references [36,37].

I should point-out that today's job market similarly represents a positive turn-around for medicinal chemists in general. Small companies have become well-accepted contributors and as such are very legitimate players amid the now oftentimes merged and even larger corporate entities. These small-pharma often need interdisciplinary team players with more diverse training than just synthetic organic chemistry. Likewise, the biotech revolution has gradually led to biologists and/or clinicians being a frequent discipline occupying the top rungs of the administrative research ladders within large pharma. 'Credentialized' medicinal chemists whether initially from medicinal or organic chemistry academic departments, are now in the upper tier of candidates being sought to support chemical-related operations during drug discovery and early pre-clinical development. Finally, since Judy and three of our children already have been mentioned while setting the stage for this narrative, to complete our family's part: we wound-up being blessed with two more children, John during the course of esmolol's discovery, and Christine during the course of esmolol's development. The trek that our growing family undertook across this period of time is depicted in Fig. 23.4.

Quickly, the factors and their sources remedying my personal identity clarifications included: (i) The notions that work in itself has merit and that a hard-work ethic coupled with the patience to make short-term sacrifices for the sake of longer-term goals would someday become fruitful, instilled most certainly by both Judy's and my parents' examples who had lived through circumstances far worse than anything mentioned here, e.g. both WW II and a major economic depression; (ii) A problem-solving spirit that is stimulated by scientific challenges and was then able to be methodically engaged in an analytical manner balanced between persistence and flexibility toward exploring alternative solutions, that was likely garnered across all of my years in the formal education system especially noting that one of my favorite subjects was always mathematics and gradually solving its advanced take-home problems; (iii) Some fortuitous choices decided by truly following my scientific interests and curiosities, wherein just as the word "fortuitous" implies, the eventually favorable consequences from which should probably be attributed to just plain luck; and finally but actually the most important of all, (iv) My commitment to support a family who fully had their trust and return support toward me, that consistently drove me forward during tough times and then past limits that I might not even have striven for if it had not been for them, coupled with their willingness to undertake major moves around the country so as to explore different employment options that might be best for all of us.

So, the timeframe has now been set and briefly depicted in the lab, as well as across the evolving culture of the pharmaceutical enterprise such that both our local presence and the story's place in a broader context can be appreciated for what they were like at the time. Our corporate stage has been described and a case made that it should be appreciated for its

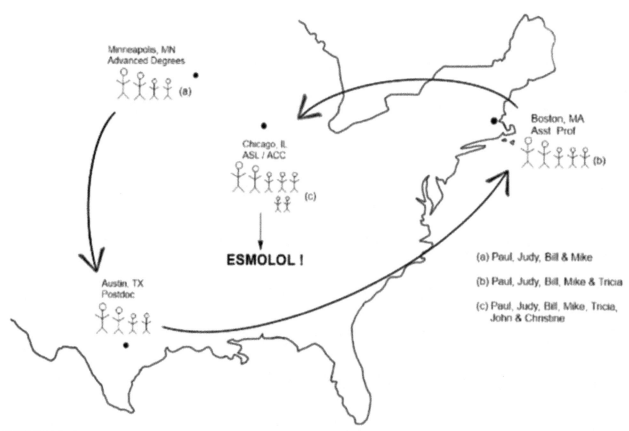

FIGURE 23.4 Trek taken by the Erhardt family leading to the discovery and development of esmolol. The use of stick-people is not meant to imply anything robotic about the family members, each of whom has most assuredly always been their own independently individualized personality, especially our five children. Instead, the figures are simply meant to account for the net number of us as the family grew in various locations until reaching our final tally. Our efforts toward such tallies not in any way like the similar counts taken in "The Sound of Music" [38], for neither my wife nor I ever found it necessary to deploy whistles and military lineups to account for all of our members, although I should confess that we may have approached that brink on more than one occasion at more than one location. See text for details.

savvy business/technical niche, and especially for its entrepreneurial spirit and enthusiasm in spite of its lack in size and resources. And finally, you have been introduced in a highly personalized manner to the cast's main character who you will soon see become responsible for nearly all of the chemical aspects associated with esmolol's discovery and translation to the clinic. During this description, certain developments along with both positive and negative personality traits have been exposed in an unabashed manner. Importantly, these will be shown to have a consequential impact upon esmolol's case study as the narrative unfolds. Some early, small but practical hurdles that needed to be accounted for, have already been addressed as well. Now, let the story begin.

Clinical, pharmacologic and initial drug targets

Enabling ER physicians

John Zaroslinski, a clinical pharmacologist and our VP of Research, should be credited with bringing the concept of an ultra-short-acting *beta*-adrenergic receptor blocking agent to everyone's attention. We all knew that a patient's response to chest pain associated with a mild to moderately severe myocardial infarction (MI) is to become anxious, if not fearful, about their situation. This prompts the body's fight-or-flight mechanism. Unfortunately, the resulting adrenergic storm that ensues across the heart exacerbates MI by whipping the sick heart muscles to work harder in terms of both chronotropic (heart rate or HR) and inotropic (muscle contraction force or CF) activity. This raises the muscles' need for oxygen while shortening the duration for its supply since the heart feeds itself during the brief relaxation period between beats. Administration of a *beta*-blocker (BB) can attenuate the adrenergic storm, thus lessoning tissue damage caused by low oxygen levels and potentially saving lives in more severe MIs. John went on to convey, however, "efforts to deploy BBs in this manner have led to instances of cardiac failure and even death [3]. This is because in these critical situations it is difficult to ascertain the extent that sick heart muscle is still able to rely on intrinsic beating capacity. If the adrenergic system is attenuated too far by a BB, the condition of patients with low intrinsic capacity can deteriorate rapidly to the point of total cardiac failure. What is needed is an ultra-short-acting (USA) BB that can be stopped and quickly cleared from the system whenever heart rate begins to fall to lower than beneficial rates." BBs were being designed at that time by several big pharma players to have long durations of action that allowed for once-a-day dosing while addressing the blockbuster market for antihypertensive agents. Taken together, this seemed like a perfect clinical indication for our corporate strategy. However, we noted that there could be a major hurdle in getting such an agent through clinical trials. How would we enlist MI patients in the middle of a health crisis of their own, how would we categorize them in terms of more detailed cardiac indices, and how would we demonstrate less loss of healthy tissue around the infarcts of treated patients?

Adjusting the clinical indication to practical therapeutic endpoints

Eventually it was decided to have the indication more simply directed toward lowering rapid heart rate in critical care settings, i.e. to be regarded as more of an antiarrhythmic agent. This does not preclude use in MI but instead focuses upon a practical endpoint, namely control of HR, that could have even broader utility across a range of other critical clinical conditions. Measurement of this endpoint is routine practice in these settings. This pragmatic decision can be attributed not only to ACC's research managers but especially to our panel of expert consultants which was represented by some of the top clinical research cardiologists in the country at that time.

Defining the pharmacological target

Clearly, our BB's most distinguishing feature needed to be an ultra-short duration of action (USA). Clinical experience with our marketed dopamine product suggested that a half-life of 10 min could also be ideal for the MI indication. Dopamine blood levels can be quickly altered by simply adjusting the drip-rate of its infusions during the critical treatment of advancing shock. Additional features that defined what we considered to be an optimal profile for our BB target included: (1) Reasonable potency (e.g. low μM) so as to not burden the body with high loads of drug and/or metabolites to deal with upon prolonged infusions; (2) No intrinsic (agonist) activity (i.a.) since even low levels of that could further exacerbate the heart muscles' need for oxygen; (3) No membrane depression (m.d.) since even low levels of that would interfere with regaining heart rate when BB activity is removed; and, (4) Non-selective or even better selective β_1-over β_2-adrenergic receptor blocking action since receptors on heart tissue are largely β_1 and those on the systemic vasculature are largely β_2. We all came together in regard to stereochemistry: Management being satisfied to follow the predominate strategy to market β-blockers as their less expensive racemic mixtures rather than pursuing single enantiomer drugs; Clinicians and pharmacologists suggesting that this practice did not seem to cause any added toxicity issues or place any extra burden upon clearance; and most certainly, We chemists who indicated that this would greatly simplify our synthetic efforts and more rapidly lead to potential candidate compounds, although the timing for the project had not yet been defined beyond it being sooner rather than later. A composite of our interdisciplinary team's clinicians' and pharmacologists' thoughts about the initial biological profile needed for the proposed USABB project is summarized in Fig. 23.5.

Bill Anderson and Rick Gorczynski, two close colleagues with PhDs in pharmacology, enthusiastically assumed responsibility for conducting the early screening activity for our new project. Bill ran our front-line or tier one panel of *in vitro* assays: (1) Guinea pig right atria (GPRA) spontaneously beating to assess i.a. and m.d. activity; (2) GPRA driven by isoproterenol to assess blockade of β_1-receptos and precisely determine potency as pA2 values; and, (3) Guinea pig trachea driven by isoproterenol to assess blockade of β_2-receptors and determine potency as pA2 values for comparisons of β_1-to β_2-receptor selectivity. Compounds having favorable profiles still needed to be tested for what was to us their most distinguishing feature, namely their duration of action. However, such testing becomes a bit of a hurdle because in our case this feature is still a front-line property and many compounds were being imagined for screening. Should we use a representative metabolic enzyme or group of selected enzymes in an *in vitro* fashion to assess the breakdown rates for our BB analogs; or do we need to go to an *in vivo* model? The former might not lead us down a correct path to the clinic and the latter will be cumbersome in terms of compound throughput. Plus, what species should be used for either approach? Appreciate that this is well-before the availability of isolated human enzymes or genetically humanized-enzyme rodent models.

Using the dog as a xenobiotic elimination 'black box' [39]

Eventually the group decided to go with an *in vivo* model despite its cumbersome nature. Our history with dopamine suggested that dog was preferable to cat and both were preferable to rodents in predicting outcomes in humans. Not at all a trivial situation, Rick took on the need to devise these tests within the context of β-adrenergic receptor blocking agents. Then with a newly-hired, able-assistant, Lee Preusser, he enthusiastically awaited the formidable task of conducting front-line screening for many anticipated analogs using an *in vivo* model. A tier 2 screening and tier 3 follow-up model were developed. Both involved isoproterenol infusions to elevate HR (ca. 2−2.5-fold), infusion of test drug to effect 50% blockade of HR, and then stopping test drug infusion while recording the time needed to have HR return to 80% (t80) of its pre-test-drug-administration, elevated HR. The first screen involved a 40-minute administration of test agent before stopping its infusion, while the Tier 3 model sought to achieve a pseudo-steady-state equilibrium of test agent concentration in the system by deploying a 3-h administration before stopping the infusion. For comparison, propranolol as a well-known BB with a long duration of action was used as a standard. It's 40 min protocol t80 was greater than 45 min which closely resembles the i.v. pharmacokinetic (PK) behavior observed in humans. Its 3-h administration protocol was even longer (>60 min). Alternatively, dopamine as our ultra-short acting standard, has a 40 min infusion PK-determined half-life of 10 min and this is retained after a 3 h infusion. Fig. 23.6 summaries the biological testing plan that was set-up by Bill and Rick to identify lead compounds for the USABB project. Initial aqueous solubility and stability testing for representative compounds was conducted by the chemists as part of their compound submission process. Criteria for moving compounds forward are also specified in Fig. 23.6.

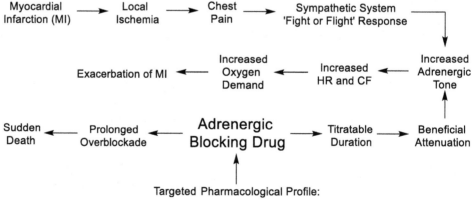

FIGURE 23.5 Clinical background and biological profile desired for the ultra-short acting β-blocker (USABB) project. *CF*, contractile force (of cardiac muscle); *HR*, heart rate. See text for further explanation.

Myocardial Infarction (MI) → Local Ischemia → Chest Pain → Sympathetic System 'Fight or Flight' Response → Increased Adrenergic Tone → Increased HR and CF → Increased Oxygen Demand → Exacerbation of MI

Sudden Death ← Prolonged Overblockade ← **Adrenergic Blocking Drug** → Titratable Duration → Beneficial Attenuation ↑

Targeted Pharmacological Profile:

(1) *beta*-Blocker preferably with selectivity for *beta*-1 receptors;
(2) No intrinsic activity and no membrane depression; and,
(3) Quick onset and ultra-short duration (1/2 life ca. 10 min)

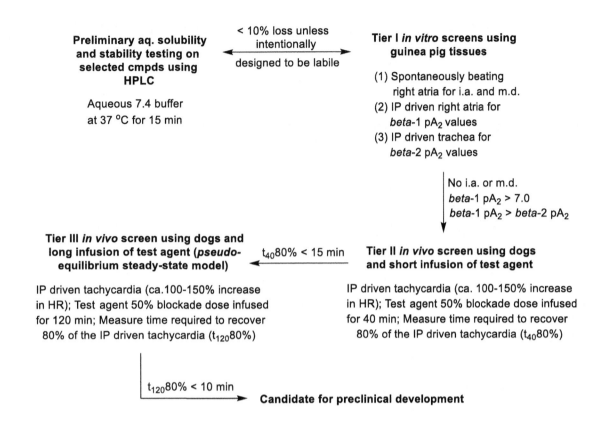

Prototypical *beta*-blocker: Propanolol has borderline aq. solubility, is stable with no i.a. and minimal m.d. activity, has similar *beta*-1 and *beta*-2 pA$_2$ values just over ca. 8.5, and durations of ca. 45 min and > 1 hr in the t$_{40}$ and t$_{120}$ 80% recovery protocols. Noteworthy is that propranolol's 45 min dog half-life is similar to its half-life after intravenous administration to humans.

FIGURE 23.6 Testing scheme used to characterize analogs prepared for the USABB project. Most test agents were designed to be substrates for the ubiquitous esterase enzymes, but a few were pursued where they were suspected to be inherently unstable. Since esters can be subject to spontaneous hydrolysis at pH 7.4, representatives for all structural types were checked in the preliminary aqueous solubility and stability assay. *i.a.*, intrinsic activity (agonist effect); *IP*, isoproterenol (a standard β-adrenergic receptor agonist that increases heart rate and contractile force); *m.d.*, membrane depression (local anesthetic type of effect); pA$_2$, negative log of antagonist concentration (BB dose) that requires a doubling of the agonist concentration (IP dose) to compensate for the action of the antagonist; the higher this value, the more potent the BB.

Was our decision to use an *in vivo* dog model as an enzymatic black box a lucky call? Absolutely, because while we knew that dopamine is subject to rapid metabolism by COMT for which the dog nicely models what also happens in humans, we had not yet established either a distinct metabolic or excretory pathway that would provide for a short duration in a BB analog. The prodrug literature (additionally discussed below) clearly demonstrates how esterases can quite generally be relied upon to effect rapid metabolism of ester substrates, but what testing paradigm for that might be the best for defining our BB compounds? For example, I learned somewhat later while surveying the published literature, that one of our nearby (legitimate player) neighbors had recently deployed a specific peptide prodrug appendage on dopamine to enhance its selective delivery to the kidney. They then used a correspondingly specific kidney peptidase isolated from rat for their assay only to eventually find that both their lead and backup compound failed miserably in the clinic because the human version of the rat enzyme had subtle differences in its structure-metabolism relationships (SMR). Our fledgling company could not afford one, let alone two clinical testing misfires. Such a looming hurdle in our case was circumvented by our research group's decision to use the *in vivo* dog model, coupled for sure by a bit of just plain luck, as well as by some technical precedent extrapolated from our own dopamine data.

Initial drug molecule targets

It was the chemist's turn to step up to the plate. As is common for medicinal chemists, we immediately had some thoughts about what might be tried and so, at the start, the targets' molecular design aspects did not seem to be a hurdle. Bob Borgman, the Director of Medicinal Chemistry, led off. He suggested that we could take two approaches toward the design of candidate molecules: polar compounds that might be rapidly excreted as such, and ester-containing structures in which the ester is strategically placed between the aryl and amino pharmacophore groups that are requisite for activity in all prototypical BBs such as propranolol [7]. The latter approach draws from the medicinal chemist's tool box involving prodrug design wherein the ubiquitous esterases are often relied upon to quickly liberate the active form of the drug [14–16,21]. In this case, however, esterase activity would lead to separation of the key pharmacophore groups and that, in turn, would result in a loss of activity. Likewise, there was some precedent from the arena of natural products wherein one could deduce from piecing together the associated literature that the moderate duration of cocaine was eventually manipulated into the ultra-short-acting, local anesthetic agent procaine upon reaching exactly such a structural end-point where an ester resided between requisite pharmacophore groups. Since the marketed BBs typically were racemic mixtures, we all again agreed that we could simplify our chemical effort by not needing to separate our target compounds into their individual enantiomers. The composite of the entire interdisciplinary team's thoughts about our initial internal ester target compounds are summarized in Fig. 23.7.

Bob decided to set up an extramural collaboration to have some representative structures for each approach made quickly. He also gave Dave Stoudt, my fellow chemist in our two-man lab, the task of exploring alternate synthetic routes to the ester compounds [7] while he simultaneously worked on the ADTN dopamine analogs project (Fig. 23.2). I was still heavily engaged in synthetic work directed toward preparing a cyclopropyl dopamine analog (Fig. 23.2) and as mentioned previously, I was under considerable pressure both company-wise and personally as my seemingly straight-forward synthetic project continued to bog down deeper and deeper into the intended synthesis.

Initial syntheses and testing efforts

All of the USABB project's *in vitro* and both *in vivo* models were quickly up-and-running. After approximately 6 months, several polar BBs had been prepared by our extramural collaborator. They proved to be weak inhibitors with only somewhat shortened durations of action, particularly when determined after the 3 h protocol. Therefore, this approach was

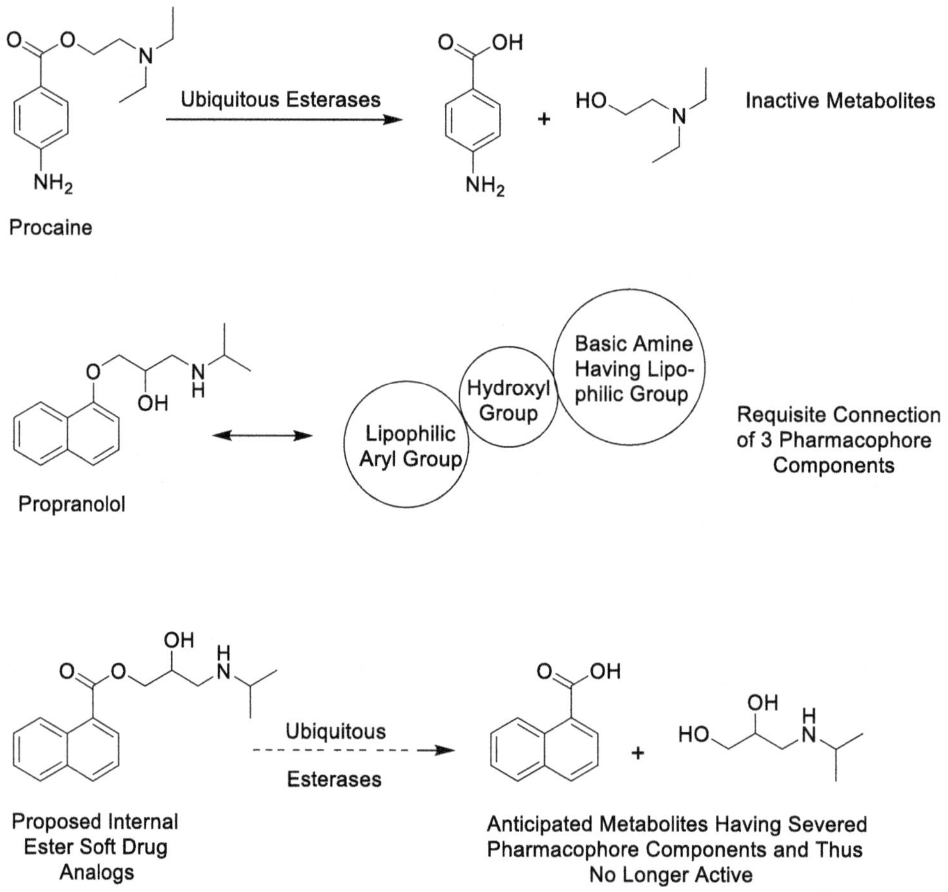

FIGURE 23.7 Internal ester concept. Procaine is a natural product derivative with a short duration of action resulting from rapid metabolism of its ester group to produce two inactive fragments of its requisite pharmacophore as present within its parent structure. Propranolol, marketed as its racemic mixture, is the prototypical β-adrenergic receptor blocking agent. Its classical pharmacophore is depicted immediately to the right. An internal ester version of propranolol is shown below. By analogy to procaine, rapid metabolism by esterases (dotted line) should sever the parent analog into two inactive fragments. Also see discussion within the text.

abandoned [7]. Later, after ACC had established that other chemical approaches did validate the therapeutic concept, and after an overall patent strategy had been initiated, this early BB effort was cleared for publication [40].

Unfortunately, the ester-containing targets were not lending themselves to synthetic efforts undertaken seriously by our collaborator or sporadically by Dave and Larry Black, a new support staff for Dave in our chemistry lab. Thus, for one reason or another, everyone in the ACC chemistry group and to a certain extent our colleagues in biology, were beginning to experience some degree of frustration and some level of heightened anxiety. Was our first real hurdle beginning to present itself for the USABB program?

Facing financial realities

Glen French was ACC's president. It was said that he had risen through the sales ranks of AHSC step-by-step after starting at the bottom wherein he had begun by peddling bed pans to hospitals. No doubt in all of our minds that he was a tough individual when such perseverance was coupled with his 'Rocky'-like physical appearance and manner. Periodically addressing all of ACC's staff in a state of the union fashion, he would often use one hand to gently jingle the coins in his pocket as he commanded the podium. This subliminal message about money when translated in our minds to the importance of maintaining profitability, was always loud-and-clear. On this particular occasion, however, Glen conveyed how our parent AHSC, as the source of ACC's research funding, was beginning to experience sticker shock. He explained that AHSC was, after all, a distribution company and that they had little patience for long R&D activities that were not delivering products to sell in the immediate future. They were not at all sympathetic about research activity woes. Enthusiasm goes a long way in our world of research operations, but results leading to marketable products do better in theirs. It was clear to all of us that we could not let our research projects continue to bog down. The sound of jingling coins had now become threatening. As stated earlier, this was all the more menacing to me with my own project bogged-down and a growing family to personally take care of in terms of financial security.

Identification of a preclinical candidate compound

Strike one!

After another 6 months, I had finally managed to complete my synthesis of the stubborn cyclopropyl compounds only to determine that they completely lacked the desired dopaminergic agonist activity. Instead, they proved to be α-receptor agonists. This profile was confirmed by several extramural investigators who requested samples for their own research studies, some of which involved the CNS as well as others with similar programs in the renal and peripheral vasculature. Between the latter's high level of interest and my consideration of the compounds as topographical probes that were able to identify certain steric features at the renal dopamine receptor [35–37], as mentioned earlier, at least ACC's reputation in the scientific community took a major step forward even if there were never any marketable products to emanate from this project.

The USABB project was even more unfortunate, however, because in this case there were still no ester compounds prepared for initial testing in the front-line screens. Frustration had grown to the point of discomfort, and anxiety had continued to mount. Jingling coins seemed to echo down the hallways as managers walked past the chemistry and biology labs expecting to learn something positive about the USABB project.

Time for a research meeting

Our meeting was called by Bob Lee, the new VP of research. It was attended by ACC's entire senior staff in biology and chemistry, all seven of us. Because Bob Borgman had moved into process chemistry, and Rich Krasula had shifted away from directing biology so as to better focus on toxicology, neither the medicinal chemistry or biology groups had managers at the time. Bob began by emphasizing that a clock was ticking. We had been working on the USABB project for about a year, with essentially no definitive results [7]. Medicinal chemistry had initially provided a few polar compounds that fell well-short of the desired profile, and they were failing to deliver any examples of the ester analogs in amounts for even just front-line, *in vitro* testing. This was harsh. Nobody likes to hear the word "failing" in regard to their efforts. Bob went on to suggest that "perhaps there is a logical inconsistency in attempting to synthesize a compound that is supposed to fall apart." To me this sounded a bit like my postdoctoral challenge which I was indeed able to successfully hurdle; but then Bob concluded with a question: "Gentlemen, are we trying to put a square peg in a round hole?" As we all discussed the situation, we chemists had to note that all of the short duration therapeutics, such as our dopamine product or procaine, were directly or indirectly derived from natural sources rather than being created by *ab initio* design from non-natural product compounds. Furthermore, because most companies were not interested in short acting compounds, there had been little industry effort in that direction, and so we had to admit that there was little precedent for the design and synthesis of such agents [7]. Bob's response to our summary was to immediately pose another negative question, again by starting with "gentlemen" which was beginning to hint that what was about to follow might not be what we wanted to hear: "Then can we really afford to spend more time in an unprecedented area that draws from speculative chemical considerations?" Undoubtedly, this was a critical strike against the ester approach. In my mind then and today, 'hand-waving' is a perfectly acceptable way for medicinal chemists to propose hypotheses and new compounds, but only as long as one can then 'make-em and test-em.' Our chemical strategies had just collapsed before our eyes because we couldn't make the probes. In fact, the entire USABB program appeared to have its head on the chop block with the guillotine poised to drop at the next moment [7]. Our impression of what might happen next is depicted in Fig. 23.8.

During the last stages of the cyclopropyl dopamine synthesis and scale-up runs for testing, I had begun to contemplate other approaches toward designing USABBs. I had already bounced my thoughts off of my closest biology colleague Rick and he seemed favorably impressed by my concept when accompanied by some enthusiastic hand-waving. The project definitely needed a shot-in-the-arm right-at-this-moment. It was time to share my thoughts and new idea even though I had not officially become a hands-on participant in the USABB project. I began by suggesting that there may be a different way to construct short acting BBs. We could still deploy ester arrangements, but do so in a completely different molecular context. I thought of the compounds as external esters compared to the internal esters that we had been trying to make thus far [7]. I explained that one shouldn't have to make internal esters to get inactive species after hydrolysis. Alternatively, if esters were simply placed close to either the amino- or aryl-pharmacophores, then when they were hydrolyzed, their carboxylic acids would become ionized at physiological pH. I proposed that this full-blown anionic charge would be too foreign to be recognized by the β-adrenergic receptor. In other words, the resulting anions could be used to mask, rather than separate, the requisite amino-group or the lipophilic aromatic system. Even if the full-blown anionic charge was relieved by the aqueous environment, the β-receptor when presented with a solvated, hydrogen-bound-cluster of water molecules should still reject such a species. I indicated that the external esters offered considerably more flexibility than the internal esters in terms of both designing compounds and being able to try different synthetic methods. Thus, we should be able to get to some actual probe compounds in short order. I concluded my hand-waving by returning to Bob's analogy. Instead of trying to modify either the peg or the hole, we could use this relationship to advantage. Upon hydrolysis, the external esters become square pegs that will no longer favorably interact with the pharmacophoric round holes present on the β-receptor. This simple version of the external-esters concept is shown in Fig. 23.9. Sometimes 'simple' is best and everyone seemed to be liking my idea and its practical design and synthesis aspects.

To this day I remain uncertain whether Bob Lee actually liked the idea per se, was impressed by my stubborn enthusiasm to keep trying, or maybe it might even have been just because I had picked-up on his own analogy. But whatever the reason or combination of reasons, he agreed to extend the program for another 3 months. Thus, this major hurdle reflecting a complete loss of confidence in the initial chemical strategies for the USA BB program, had at least temporarily been pushed off the track. We could once again try to move forward. In fairness to Bob's initial critique, he did

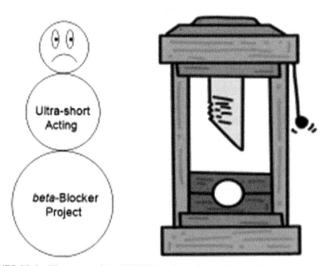

FIGURE 23.8 The status of the USABB project after 1 year of effort. See text details.

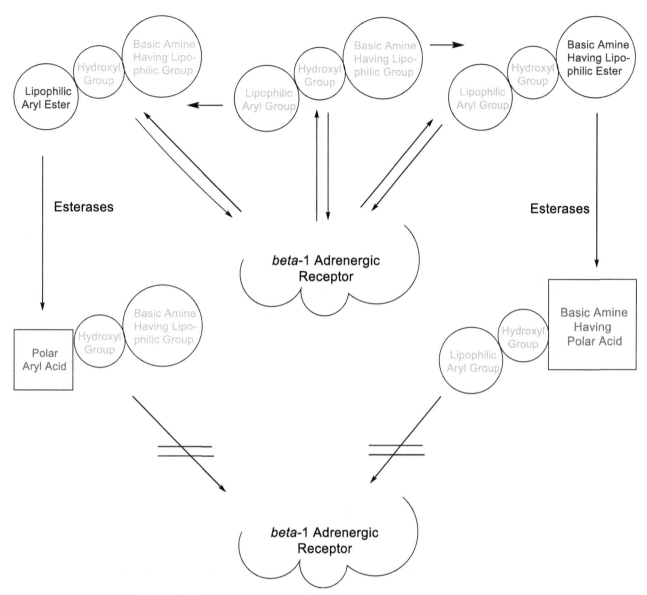

FIGURE 23.9 Simplified depiction of the external esters concept. See text for details.

not carry any coins in his pocket. Instead, he was himself a PhD pharmacologist with a soft spot for inquisitiveness rather than inquisitions. Then and now I still consider him as a true gentleman of basic science.

The USABB project was no longer on the chop block. In fact, it actually had gained in personnel resources. We now had the extramural collaborator and our entire medicinal chemistry staff of three PhD and one MS medicinal chemists. Our collaborator, Dave Stoudt and his new MS assistant Larry Black, and Sheung-Tsam Kam who was a brand-new hire PhD medicinal chemist from my alma mater, were assigned the task of continuing to explore syntheses for the internal esters. I was turned loose full-time to pursue syntheses of probes that I thought could validate my external esters concept. THANK YOU Mr. gentleman of science! Although we all had renewed enthusiasm, it was also clear to us that a firm deadline had been set. Feasibility would soon be ending unless we delivered some actual compounds with at least some testing-derived promise for eventual success. Most certainly a 'strike one' had just been called on the USABB project while the chemists were the ones 'at the plate.'

Given the urgency of the situation, I knew I needed to work even harder toward exploring the external esters concept. Trying to get a handle on the cyclopropyl dopamine project I had become accustomed to starting my 10-h days early so that I could 'make it home' each late afternoon just in time to still catch the 5:00 dinners with our entire family (the latter preceding their own activities which usually involved participation on at least one sports team for each of them—lotsa driving and split-spectating). Judy also appreciated the company's urgency and this project's importance to our family's security. We agreed that for two nights each week I could stay for a few hours more, and also do some Saturday half-days as long as I still made it home for lunch and the afternoon together. The rest of the weekends were all for family, and that faithfully included church on Sunday mornings (the adjective 'faithfully' being intentionally selected here for its double meanings).

Strike two!

Alkylations out of control

The first probes I designed were directed toward *N*-external esters placed on the framework of propranolol to determine if the esters would retain activity and if their hydrolyzed acids would become inactive. Distance from the amine was a key factor in my mind because placement further from the amine should have less impact upon desired activity while placement closer to the amine should be better for eliminating activity subsequent to hydrolysis. The initial target compounds and their proposed syntheses (dotted line) are shown in Fig. 23.10.

At least one methylene spacer was needed in the design to avoid creating a carbamate which I thought would detrimentally diminish the requisite basicity of the secondary amine pharmacophore. Presumably I could find an optimal distance residing somewhere between $n = 1-4$ after which folding of the added lipophilic substituent in an aqueous environment might be expected to complicate tracking SAR data. Syntheses of *secondary* aryloxypropanolamines can follow the "well-trodden path" [41] shown in Fig. 23.10 in a very well-behaved manner when deploying *primary* amine reagents containing at least some steric bulk *alpha* to the nitrogen, such as in isopropylamine for the case of propranolol [42]. However, I quickly learned that opening the key aryloxyepoxide intermediate using less hindered *primary* amines preferentially leads to dialkylations. Although I learned this the 'hard way,' it is not really surprising because the secondary amine after the first alkylation is more reactive than the primary amine reagent unless it is sterically crowded. In addition, prior literature associated with the discovery of practolol refers to low levels of this dialkylation issue even when using isopropylamine [43]. The hurdle in my case was that I did not want to add steric hindrance to this area because I wanted the esterases to have ready access to the neighboring ester adducts. In addition, I wanted to avoid creating a second asymmetric center which would lead to diastereomers that might add to the burden of reaction cleanups. Thus, I did not want to use $CH(CH_3)$-$(CH_2)_n$ types of spacers to jump the dialkylation hurdle while I felt that $C(CH_3)_2$-$(CH_2)_n$ spacers would be an overkill of steric impediment that would hinder nearby attack from the esterases. In addition, my hypothesis required that the full-blown anionic charge resulting after ester hydrolysis would be undesirable to the BB receptor normally expecting to interact with a lipophilic-substituted amine. If I added too much lipophilicity while seeking to add steric hindrance, the former might serve as a 'shield' from the anion's electronic effect that I was counting on to eliminate the parent compound's activity. Given all of the above, I decided to keep the initial targets simple, i.e. assemble links between the amine and ester that used straight-chain alkyl groups. Thus, I needed to get this chemistry to behave in a much more friendly manner if I was to have even a small family of probes to test my hypothesis. I tried a few routes and did produce several members of the desired series by sheer brute force methods. I was getting somewhere but this was cumbersome chemistry at best.

Richard Borch had served as a wonderful, truly exemplary mentor during my undergraduate chemistry studies and so, of course, one of the things I tried was his elegant method that deploys an aldehyde reagent with $NaBH_3CN$ [44,45] to control the degree of *N*-alkylation. While such chemistry did prove to be more amenable, the overall availability of various ester-containing aldehyde reagents was not as plentiful as I needed for my particular series. All of these syntheses are summarized in Fig. 23.11. In the end, I devised an alternate scheme that turned-out to be extremely practical for all types of *N*-external ester target compounds. This method involved preparation of an aryl-family of synthon reagents having transient *N*-benzyl groups that were readily removed by hydrogenation after an extremely well-controlled single alkylation step with a variety of readily available reagents. Turns-out that I had stumbled-upon and was revisiting a long-standing but sporadic approach in the literature also coincidentally examined during the discovery of practolol [43]. I methodically optimized it, even doubling the transient benzyl-adducts for cases involving two small alkyl-group types of products, and I demonstrated its very general and practical utility, all of which merited publication in itself [46]. Now that I think about it, maybe some of my enthusiasm for pursuing that method in such an in-depth manner can be attributed all-the-way-back to my undergraduate mentor Borch. This convenient route is also depicted in Fig. 23.11 along with some of the brute force methods that at least proved successful in small scale adequate for *in vitro* testing. Besides producing high overall yields of the desired products, the reactions using the *N*-benzyl synthon method were so clean that they could be performed in a back-to-back fashion with minimal cleanup being required between them. Fortuitously, minimizing cleanup manipulations also served to better preserve the desired ester linkages. Clearly, this chemistry became project enabling and I was now

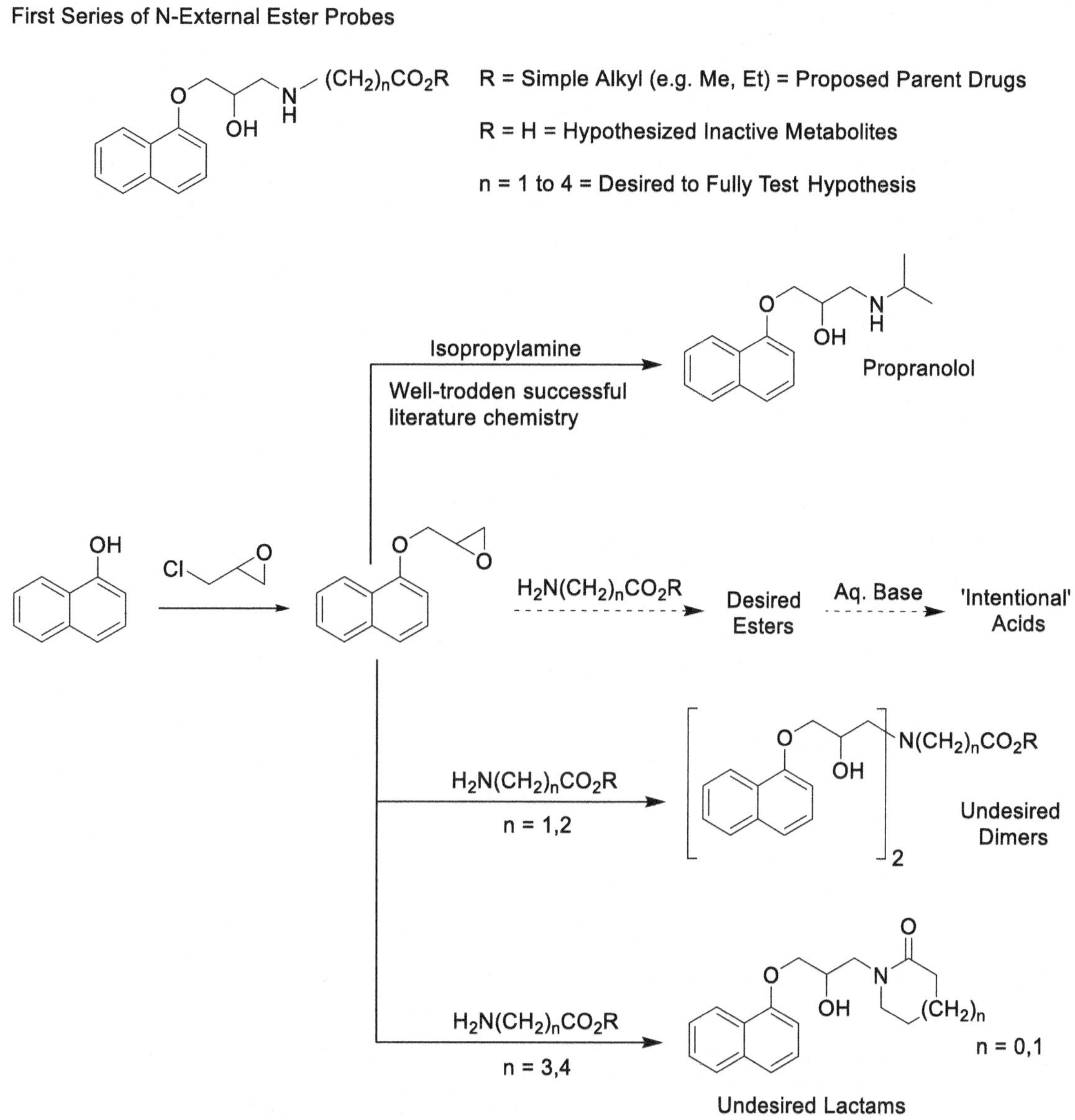

First Series of N-External Ester Probes

FIGURE 23.10 First series of *N*-external ester target compounds designed to probe this approach toward producing USABB agents. Also shown is the synthetic route commonly used to successfully prepare classical BBs like propranolol, and how it becomes riddled with hurdles when the alternative *N*-substituents having ester moieties attempt to gingerly step down this same path, let alone try to run down it like it's going to be an easy, fast track.

running down the track toward a family of *N*-external ester probes. A simply put lesson here: more reaction steps to get to the same target is not always a less desirable synthetic path. At any rate, while this small hurdle slowed me down a little at the start, it was not long enough to become a strike against the project. So, let's call this a 'ball one' because while ester compounds are now finally being prepared, they are still not yet being tested. And in that regard, let's also not fool ourselves here by thinking that a slow walk to first base is going to be adequate because we do need to have at least a 'double' to get into scoring position, or even better a 'home run' to really bring this project to fruition in the eyes of AHSC, and thus stop Glen from jingling his pocket change whenever he spots a researcher in the hallways.

"Your compounds are driving me nuts—they're behaving like bricks!"

Bill Anderson could not evaluate my first family of probes because I had added just enough alkyl species to convert the already lipophilic propranolol standard into unwieldly hydrophobic analogs that were essentially insoluble in his aqueous media. So much for all of the aforementioned chemistry fun. I went to bed that night thinking to myself 'nice job on the syntheses Paul but, SADLY, as pretty as the structures and my neat synthesis method are to me, these probes cannot even

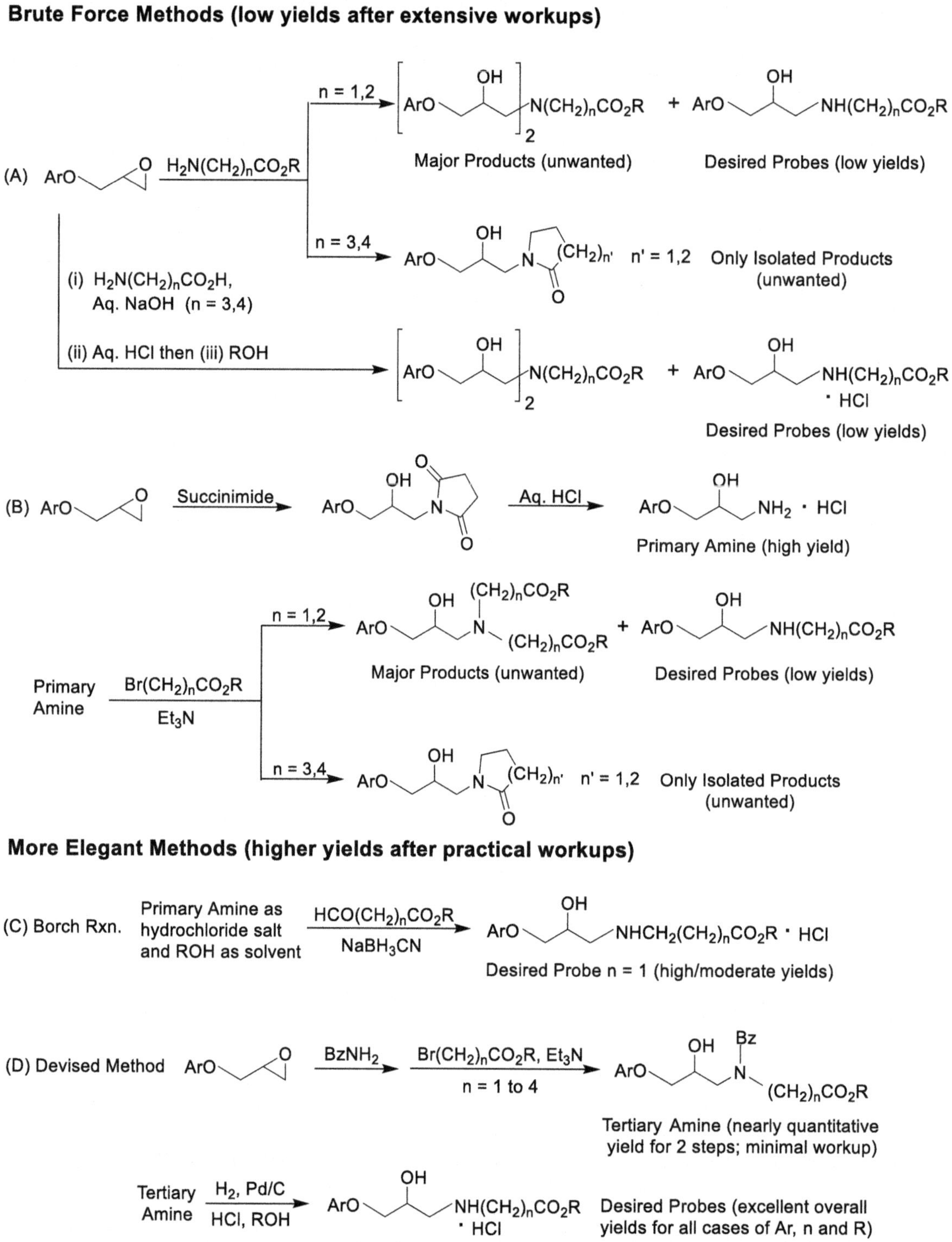

Brute Force Methods (low yields after extensive workups)

(A) AroO—epoxide + $H_2N(CH_2)_nCO_2R$

n = 1,2 → [ArO—CH(OH)—$N(CH_2)_nCO_2R]_2$ **Major Products (unwanted)** + ArO—CH(OH)—$NH(CH_2)_nCO_2R$ **Desired Probes (low yields)**

(i) $H_2N(CH_2)_nCO_2H$, Aq. NaOH (n = 3,4)

n = 3,4 → ArO—CH(OH)—N(lactam)$(CH_2)_{n'}$ n' = 1,2 **Only Isolated Products (unwanted)**

(ii) Aq. HCl then (iii) ROH

→ [ArO—CH(OH)—$N(CH_2)_nCO_2R]_2$ + ArO—CH(OH)—$NH(CH_2)_nCO_2R$ · HCl **Desired Probes (low yields)**

(B) ArO—epoxide $\xrightarrow{\text{Succinimide}}$ ArO—CH(OH)—N(succinimide) $\xrightarrow{\text{Aq. HCl}}$ ArO—CH(OH)—NH_2 · HCl **Primary Amine (high yield)**

Primary Amine $\xrightarrow[\text{Et}_3N]{Br(CH_2)_nCO_2R}$

n = 1,2 → ArO—CH(OH)—$N[(CH_2)_nCO_2R]_2$ **Major Products (unwanted)** + ArO—CH(OH)—$NH(CH_2)_nCO_2R$ **Desired Probes (low yields)**

n = 3,4 → ArO—CH(OH)—N(lactam)$(CH_2)_{n'}$ n' = 1,2 **Only Isolated Products (unwanted)**

More Elegant Methods (higher yields after practical workups)

(C) Borch Rxn. Primary Amine as hydrochloride salt and ROH as solvent $\xrightarrow[\text{NaBH}_3\text{CN}]{HCO(CH_2)_nCO_2R}$ ArO—CH(OH)—$NHCH_2(CH_2)_nCO_2R$ · HCl **Desired Probe n = 1 (high/moderate yields)**

(D) Devised Method ArO—epoxide $\xrightarrow{BzNH_2}$ $\xrightarrow[\text{n = 1 to 4}]{Br(CH_2)_nCO_2R, Et_3N}$ ArO—CH(OH)—N(Bz)$(CH_2)_nCO_2R$ **Tertiary Amine (nearly quantitative yield for 2 steps; minimal workup)**

Tertiary Amine $\xrightarrow[\text{HCl, ROH}]{H_2, Pd/C}$ ArO—CH(OH)—$NH(CH_2)_nCO_2R$ · HCl **Desired Probes (excellent overall yields for all cases of Ar, n and R)**

FIGURE 23.11 Methods used to prepare various of the *N*-external ester target compounds. Initially, Ar was a 1-naphthyl group like that present in the classical BB drug propranolol. As experiments continued, Ar was changed to a phenyl-ring and finally to a methodically selected substituted phenyl-ring which served as a surrogate scaffold optimized for testing purposes. The ester's R group was either a simple Me or Et for the parent target compounds and after intentional hydrolysis, R became H so as to allow for testing how the proposed esterase metabolite would also interact with the *beta*-adrenergic receptor. See text to specifically follow the transition of the aryl-moiety deployed in the 'maturing' probe compounds.

be used to address the key questions associated with my hypothesis. All of my extra-hours of focused work was for naught.' 'Maybe Bob Lee was right and we shouldn't be spending time trying to make drugs that are supposed to fall apart.' By now completely immersed in all of the BB literature, however, it quickly dawned on me that we didn't need the intact naphthalene ring system to achieve potent BBs. Indeed, it was the naphthalene that was largely causing the hydrophobicity issue, and it was not really my *N*-external ester constructs. My thoughts turned to 'quit second guessing my hypothesis and get back to the bench.' I was indeed charged-up the next morning and I immediately went down to Bill's testing lab. "Don't worry Bill, I think I know how I can fix this. The literature suggests that phenoxypropanolamines can be almost as potent as the naphthol aryl system used within the propranolol framework. These probes will have MUCH better aqueous solubility." This second series of target compounds is shown in Fig. 23.12. With the small synthetic hurdles already traversed above, these compounds were now quite friendly to make and, indeed, they had adequate aqueous solubility for testing. Since the clock kept ticking, this refined series was also quickly put to Bill's tests, so again no second strike here either and just another 'ball.' At this point we can set the project's count at "two and one," and then let's look at Bill's results.

"Your compounds are still driving me nuts—they're plagued with intrinsic activity!"

Bill's testing was quick but, alas, my second series again could not evaluate my concept very effectively because this time the initially desired BB profile for the ester-containing probes was scrambled by their also displaying sporadic but significant agonist activity. Alternatively and as desired, the probes for the proposed metabolite carboxylic acid versions did prove to be inactive in all regards. Thus, this series at least provided some support for the critical, second 'half' of my two-component concept, namely: esters active as BBs (hopefully) but acid metabolites not. Upon continued examination of the

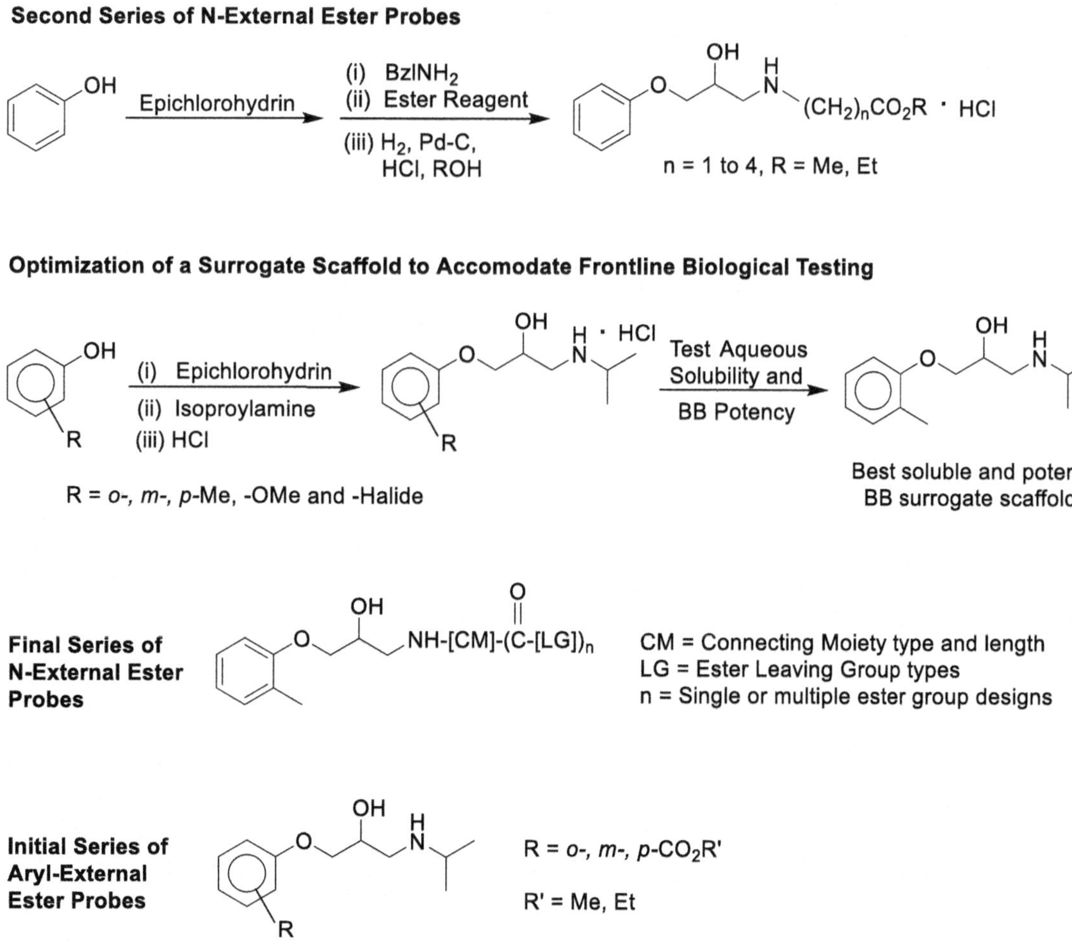

FIGURE 23.12 Second and final series of *N*-external ester probes, and initial series of aryl-external ester probes. Also shown is the series of non-ester compounds that was prepared to optimize a surrogate scaffold that could be deployed for *in vitro* testing purposes. See text for details.

extensive literature on BBs, I uncovered two citations in which intrinsic activity (i.a.) had been observed for other aryl-unsubstituted phenoxypropanolamine systems [47,48]. Appreciate that reviewing the literature in those days had no electronic files, and certainly no electronic search engines. Instead, all of such was done manually by using either hardcopy library collections or as library microfiche (still a hardcopy, manual searching system if you have never heard of it). Interestingly, I eventually was also able to discern that substitution anywhere on the aromatic ring with just about anything seems capable of completely removing the intrinsic activity/agonist problem [7].

Exploring surrogate scaffolds

By now I had lost my patience for deploying standard literature frameworks to assess my concept. Although it had seemed like the proper way to proceed scientifically by reducing the variables to only my added esters which, after all, was the focus of the specific question to address, this strategy was actually working against evaluating my hypotheses. Thus, I decided to step-back for a moment and first optimize my own BB nucleus for compatibility with Bill's *in vitro* models. With such a surrogate scaffold in-hand, I could then attach my esters on that framework so that we could finally proceed with our assessments of the hypothesis without all of these other distracting issues. At this time Chi Woo joined my group as an assistant chemist with an MS degree. He had been at Searle for several years and so he came with strong, lab-derived synthetic skills. Nevertheless, not really having any spare time to train a newcomer about the sensitive stability of our ester targets and their chemical idiosyncracies, I first gave him the assignment to prepare several non-ester (non-labile, non-fussy), aryl-substituted BB surrogate models using isopropyl amine to manage the potential unwanted multiple alkylation reactions. Within 2 weeks he had successfully prepared a group of about 10 standards having a variety of non-ester substitutions on the phenyl ring of the phenoxypropanolamine scaffold while having a simple isopropyl group on the amine (Fig. 23.12). In addition, I had made enough of the intermediate epoxide for many of the aryl systems to enable him to attempt several reactions with ethyl β-alanate [6]. Instead of deploying my newly devised route, Chi used brute force synthetic methods and his excellent lab skills for isolating the desired compounds before I could even tell him about all the trouble that I had previously experienced. Maybe that was for the better because not only did Chi produce the assigned isopropylamine-containing standard series, he also quickly delivered a couple examples of the $n = 2$, *N*-external ester targets as well [7]. As anticipated, none of these compounds had i.a. While Bill was measuring BB potency and i.a., Chi and I determined the standard series' aqueous solubilities in a quantitative manner. Picking the best blend of high BB potency and high aqueous solubility led to the *ortho*-methyl series shown in Fig. 23.12. Utilizing this framework as a constant, Chi and I then explored variables associated with the connecting chain (CM) length and type, ester leaving groups (LG), and multiple (M) *N*-external ester arrangements [7]. Shown in Fig. 23.12, this became our final test series for the *N*-external ester concept. Clock ticking, this series was assembled and tested very quickly. No more bricks, no more i.a. issues, just clean biological testing assessments. So 'ball three' here while our collaborative research team is finally able to accumulate and assess considerable SAR data relevant to at least my hypothesized approach and thus to the project overall. Internal esters were still not yet forthcoming but it was beginning to appear like just maybe the external esters might indeed be able to carry the project forward for at least some additional time.

While exploring the *N*-external esters with Chi, I was concurrently pursuing a few aryl-external esters as some first shots at this alternative design strategy toward external esters. These initial aryl-external ester probes are additionally shown at the bottom of Fig. 23.12. From my prior 'bad experience' with solubility issues, I went immediately to a phenyl-ring system rather than trying to deploy the highly lipophilic naphthyl-ring system. Plus for this series, because the phenyl ring would already be further substituted by the ester adducts, I felt that the prior i.a. problem would no longer be an issue. It was as though the aryl-external esters were meant to effectively dodge around my former off-target hurdles rather than having to leap over them. Indeed, Mother Nature seemed to be pointing me this way, although her present directions had required considerable effort on my part to now appreciate and effectively put into practice. On a similarly positive note, these syntheses proceeded very nicely along the well-trodden path while using isopropylamine to open the intermediate epoxides without detecting any formation of unwanted dimers. Clock always ticking, the aryl-external ester probes were thus assembled and tested very quickly along with the *N*-external esters. Unlike many of the initial members for the latter and exactly as suspected, the initial aryl-external esters did not present any testing problems. Thus, no new hurdles here, just plain solid synthetic medicinal chemistry coupled with effective, highly collaborative biological testing. As noted above, at this juncture the project's 'count' still remained at 'three and one' while both the chemists and the biologists working in tandem had to pinch-hit at the plate to accomplish our research team's goal of at least getting a man on base for the sake of the overall project.

Close but no cigar

Even though there was still no luck toward obtaining the internal ester compounds, we now had several probes available for testing that had external esters placed on either the amine or aryl pharmacophore units. For the N-external esters, BB potency appeared to be highest when the carbonyl was located β to the amine, i.e. CM $= CH_2CH_2$ in Fig. 23.12 [6,7]. This finding was similar to that reported for several structurally related amides [6,49,50]. Important to the concept, the N-external acids were found to be completely inactive in the front-line screen. Just as I had speculated, the round holes were not accepting the square pegs. Compounds were typically isolated as the hydrochloride salts of their amines. As encountered during synthesis under neutral and basic pH, at physiological pH when CM $= (CH_2)_3$ or $(CH_2)_4$, the free-amine esters were found to undergo spontaneous cyclization to their lactams [4,7]. Therefore, a corresponding δ-lactam was prepared and, not unexpectedly, was found to be inactive as a BB. Thus, these particular esters potentially provided a second, non-enzymatic pathway for their inactivation [4,7]. *In vivo* studies confirmed that the parent esters retained their BB properties while their acid forms were inactive; and for several probes, significantly shorter durations of activity had finally been obtained. For example, the probe having CM $= CH_2CH_2$, LG $= CH_2CH_3$ and $n = 1$ exhibited a 15 min t80 duration in our 40 min protocol model. That's ca. 1/3 as long-acting as propranolol. Clearly, we now had a couple of potentially winning 'runners on base.'

The aryl-external esters were similarly promising. The acids were inactive as BBs whereas their esters retained activity *in vitro* and *in vivo*. In addition, SAR relationships for the esters paralleled what would be expected from the BB literature [7]. For example, substitution in the *ortho*-position provided very potent compounds that were non-selective [5,7], whereas esters in the *para*-position yielded compounds that were less potent but tended to exhibit selectivity for β_1-over β_2-receptors [5,7]. The t80 durations for an *ortho*-methyl ester, a *para*-methyl ester and a *para*-ethyl ester using the 40 min infusion protocol were about 15, 30 and 60 min, respectively [7]. Further rallying around this additional promise we felt like the USA BB project now had the 'bases loaded' and was still very much 'alive at the plate.' Now with 'two outs' in the inning and its last hitter having a count of 'three balls' and just 'one strike,' either a "base hit" or even a slow 'walk' might win this game which now seemed to be dead-locked in a tie score that was teetering between having the project chopped into oblivion or successfully completed by delivery of a meritorious clinical candidate compound. On one hand the situation was exhilarating for the entire team; but on the other hand, while we were certainly getting close we also remained somewhat cautious just like the early 1800s American carnival idiom warns that until we actually hit our target there will be 'no cigar.'

Did Mother Nature just throw us a curve ball?

As it soon turned out, caution would have been the more prudent because our exhilaration suddenly changed when we moved on to test some of the most promising agents in the longer infusion protocol of 3 h so as to better represent a pseudo-steady-state equilibrium of the drug in the dog's body. Although still significantly shorter than propranolol, none of the compounds were able to retain their 15 min durations which, after all, wasn't quite at the precise target level of 10 min to begin with. Fall-off was somewhat less and thus better for the aryl-external-esters, but in practicality, we felt like we had just over-enthusiastically 'swung at the fences and completely whiffed over the top and to the side of a gradually dropping curve ball.' 'Strike two' reverberated loudly across all of our thinking. Had Mother Nature just been toying with us all along while we were 'at the plate' and had she actually set us up for this unexpected strike after a few intentional 'balls'? Had she used some of those pitches to prompt all of our aforementioned hard work and hustled efforts only to all now be for naught?

Lake Alice again

It was time for our annual trek home for a non-holiday visit with our two clans (whenever possible, we routinely did family visits for all of the major holidays as well). Again, both Judy and I sensed the need for some stress reduction and so we also planned for a few days "up at the lake." The serenity did indeed prove beneficial. One could not help but simply enjoy the esthetically pleasing views of sun rises and sun sets across the sparsely populated lake. I realized that there is a certain symmetry in what Mother Nature wants us to enjoy each day. She certainly wasn't throwing us any curve balls when it comes to this grand scale stuff, so maybe she wasn't doing so at the molecular level either. Yes, I had begun to think about 'work' at that particular moment, but it was in a very positive way and with the question: what was Mother Nature trying to tell us from the SAR that we had finally generated? It seemed like she had begun to take me down a path involving the aryl-external esters but now we were at a major fork in the road, if not yet another hurdle or an actual road block for the entire project. We returned home and I back to work, now in a positive mood but still wondering what exactly to do next.

Strike three?

Matters made worse

It was time for Bob Lee to call for a program decision meeting. His previous deadline of "another 3 months" had lapsed just prior to the end of all the efforts delineated above. He had already cut us some slack and he was really only now reluctantly getting to his duties as a responsible manager, rather than continuing to wait like a hopeful scientific practitioner stemming from the soft spot he did indeed carry for the rest of us. I'm sure that by this point, Glen with no hint of such a soft spot, had stopped by Bob's office on more than one occasion to jingle the coins in his pocket. It appeared that all of us in research could be left standing 'at the plate' while having a 'full count' with the 'bases loaded, two-outs in the last inning of a tied game' wherein the game itself had from the very start been somewhat of a tightrope walk across a 'live-or-die' precipice undertaken, perhaps from naivety, by our fledgling company. And all of these emotions were especially heightened for me since it was my concept about external esters that had continued to drive the project forward and further out onto the tightrope for the last several months. Clearly, at this point the project trying to rush across a tightrope having my name associated with it, were both on the guillotine's chop block. Was our USA BB game finally over? Certainly the clock's alarm was about to ring and we all suspected that it would trigger the drop of the guillotine's blade. We felt wood was being piled for a funeral pyre like the lyric in the classic tune by The Doors [51].

Molecular architectures and aesthetic symmetry

Luckily, to schedule a meeting of this importance with cross-departmental attendance took at least a couple of weeks even within our small organization. Personally, I felt I had just a little bit more time. It equated to only a couple of more 'chemical shots' at trying to optimize our initial findings. But then, within such a tight schedule of perhaps 2-weeks at best, what last couple of compounds to make? Several factors contributed to my decision. The more I thought about the possibilities while tossing-and-turning in bed one evening, I reminded myself that I had already decided that Mother Nature doesn't throw curve balls at all and that she wasn't toying with us. Instead, she had been revealing some insights to continue to guide us forward in a positive manner. But what was it that she was trying to show us? From the outset, we had recognized the benefit of a cardioselective BB in the various cardiac indications envisioned for our drug [3,7]. Both certain *N*-substituents and *para*-substituted-phenyl serving as the aryl-system, can bestow cardioselectivity, so I knew we could eventually achieve that benefit with either type of external ester approach. Alternatively, I was drawn by an aesthetic appeal that was unique to the symmetry afforded by the *para*-substituted phenyl ring that, in my mind, was appealing to me like the beauty that many of us can similarly find in Mother Nature's displays from a single crystalline snow flake's shape all-the-way to her displays of grand landscapes or cloud and star formations in the day and evening skies. This relationship deserves further acknowledgment. Perhaps in the end, it is a kindred spirit between medicinal chemists and pleasing molecular architectures afforded by Mother Nature alone or in conjunction with chemical syntheses, that encourages us to practice and enjoy our profession no matter how challenging the circumstances are for a given situation. Maybe medicinal chemists are as much molecular artists as we are molecular engineers and construction workers. Thus, my thinking became: if the project and my molecular design notions do have to go up in flame, then let me finally fuel this with a few chemical structures that at least bring me some aesthetically pleasing enjoyment. Simply put, I liked the beauty of the *para*-substituted aryl-external ester system. At the same time, however, I realized that these feelings were more aesthetic than technical. So how was I actually going to make that system work when it had already failed in our prolonged infusion, advanced testing model? Was I fooling myself here because this arrangement is really more pretty to me than practical to the project?

Steric factors to the rescue

Pertinent to technical considerations, I was intrigued by the significantly shorter duration of the *para*-methyl ester (30 min) in comparison to the *para*-ethyl ester (60 min). I wondered if simple steric effects could explain this remarkable difference [7]. Unfortunately, pondering this situation only led me to next conclude that since there was no smaller alcohol than methanol, it seemed like the 'esthetically pleasing' *para*-esters had already been minimized in terms of steric features. This quandary is depicted in Fig. 23.13. Pondering this view's image, however, also provides an answer that you too may quickly recognize. Take a look, just as I was doing. Can you see it? The answer itself is fun, plus its pursuit involves sound, physical organic chemistry with a biological twist, so even some more fun for a methodical medicinal chemist anxious to solve technical problems at the bench. If my hypothesis was to go down in flames, then at least these last shots at goal now also have some technical merit, and they were indeed going to be enjoyable to execute in both the synthesis and biological testing labs. I was becoming just as excited about this possible solution as are the positive lyrics "*try to set the night on*

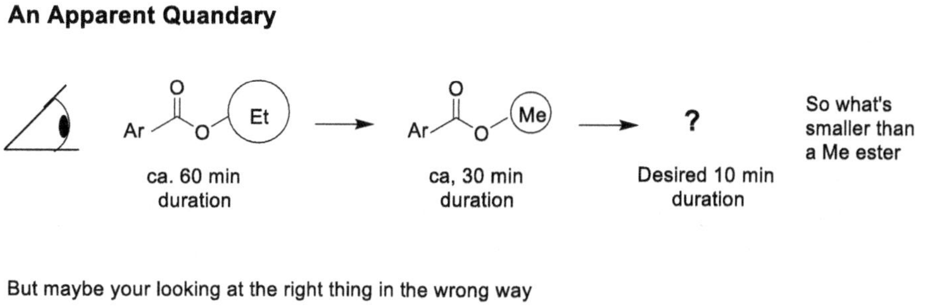

An Apparent Quandary

FIGURE 23.13 Promising data suggesting that esterase activity may be exquisitely related to steric bulk in an inverse manner. That's straightforward enough, but then the quandary becomes: what's smaller than a methyl ester? See text for details.

ca. 60 min
duration

ca, 30 min
duration

Desired 10 min
duration

So what's
smaller than
a Me ester

But maybe your looking at the right thing in the wrong way

fire" rather than the negative ones referring to a *"funeral pyre"* as was noted previously (both being borrowed from the Doors' rock song [51]).

For me the possible answer likely goes back to learning about metabolic enzymes during my postdoctoral training coupled with my more recent experience toward controlling the degree of *N*-alkylation by exploiting steric hindrance. It suddenly dawned on me like the proverbial 'light-bulb going-on,' that maybe it could be beneficial to push the bulky carboxyphenyl-group further away from the point of attack by the carboxylesterase enzymes. After all, that side of the ester was actually much larger than either a methyl or an ethyl group. This view and alternative strategy is depicted in Fig. 23.14.

I immediately ordered the chemical building blocks for such extensions as a homologous series of spacers, namely a single methylene spacer, an ethyl-spacer and an *n*-propyl-spacer. Luckily, my rush-order of the extended-acid starting materials arrived within just a few days and I quickly began to simultaneously prepare all three of their methyl esters. Fortuitously, my postdoctoral mentor Bob Smith happened to be in town on business and he joined my family for dinner at our suburban Chicago home [7]. After sharing the relevant data, I asked him what he thought about extending the *para*-carboxy group away from the bulky aromatic ring and using a simple methyl ester to potentially obtain a USABB [7]. His response was highly favorable. The next day, additionally armed with his encouragement at a time when I could definitely use it because there was no more time for debate, I was able to convince Bill and Rick to gear-up for quickly testing my last probes as soon as they became available. When I shared my idea with them, their enthusiasm was also extremely supportive. Because the project's clock was poised to have its final alarm go off, they even agreed to do the testing, both *in vitro* and *in vivo*, simultaneously rather than sequentially while also being set at the highest of priorities in each of their labs. I felt like we had two, not just one, anchormen reaching back for our team's baton compounds with both enthusiastically anxious to race full-speed to the finish line. I needed to make these final compounds quickly and pass them on to our team's anchormen. I hoped for all of our sakes, that at least one of my steric-hybridized, aryl-external ester probes would be successful and that our anchormen's sprint down the last length of what had become a grueling race would not be for naught.

I quickly completed syntheses and chemical quality control of the key steric probes shown in Fig. 23.15 along with the initial hit compound that lacked such extensions. *In vitro* and initial *in vivo* testing were undertaken simultaneously in an attempt to provide data for the upcoming research meeting [7]. As anticipated, the *in vitro* profiles were appropriate and perfectly acceptable. As I had hoped, the *in vivo* studies indicated that the durations after 40 min infusions were indeed reduced in a linear manner for the methylene and ethylene insertions: t80 values were 31, 20 and 12 min, respectively, for

A Possible Answer

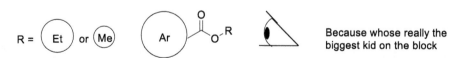

R = Et or Me

Ar

Because whose really the
biggest kid on the block

So let's focus on him and see if we can move him out of the picture by inserting some thin spacers

FIGURE 23.14 A possible answer for the quandary depicted in Fig. 23.13 emphasized here by taking an alternative view of the situation. While things often seem simple in hindsight (usually a perfect view in itself), let's not get too excited here yet because at this point this is still only another speculative hypothesis. Esthetically pleasing and now sounding good technically, we still really don't know if it will actually work. Am I just now waving my left hand rather than my right? Only one way to find out: I need to make em and my colleagues need to test em, and we all need to do this VERY QUICKLY!

FIGURE 23.15 Final series of aryl-external ester probes and data from testing them *in vivo* using the 40 min drug infusion protocol. The probe having $n = 2$ has indeed achieved the long-sought target of an ca. 10 min pharmacodynamic half-life. The interesting data for the probe having $n = 3$ is further discussed at a later point in the text. *Figure modified and used with permission from ACS P.W. Erhardt, C.M. Woo, W.G. Anderson, R.J. Gorczynski, Ultra-short-acting β-adrenergic receptor blocking agents. 2. (Aryloxy)propanolamines containing esters on the aryl function. J. Med. Chem. 25 (1982) 1408–1412.*

Final Series of
Aryl-External
Ester Steric
Probes

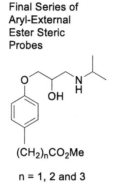

$(CH_2)_n CO_2 Me$

n = 1, 2 and 3

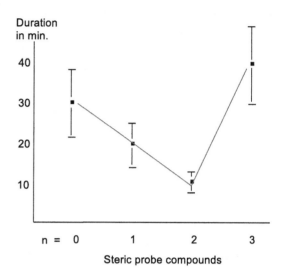

the $n = 0$ (parent hit compound prepared earlier as part of the first set of *ortho-*, *meta-* and *para-*aryl external ester series), $n = 1$ and $n = 2$ probes [6]. These promising results are also depicted in Fig. 23.15. However, before getting too excited here, the most discriminating biological study involving the 3-h drug infusion still needed to be completed. As Rick continued to simultaneously conduct these last studies, all of our programmatic efforts to date had led our team to the point where Mother Nature was now about to deliver her last pitch of the tied game. 'Digging-in at the back of the box,' I knew that this was going to be a fast ball like nothing I had ever seen before. I suspected that it would be down the middle, waist high, and that I needed to do more than just watch it go by. Mother Nature had given us all another chance and I didn't think she would throw any more curve balls. We agreed that our $n = 2$ probe should lead the way into our final round of advanced testing. It was our best shot, and as time would have it, it was going to be our last swing.

Most remarkable, personally elating and overall gratifying for me as a young scientist at this particular moment in the esmolol story was the retention of the t80 duration at ca. 10 min in the 3-h drug infusion protocol! Our entire research team was now enthusiastic and upbeat about the program rather than being initially hopeful and then ultimately fearful for its collapse. We appeared to finally have a lead structure that merited serious consideration as a preclinical development compound. It was called "ASL-8052" in our sequential designation of test agents going all the way back to our company's original name that had honored its founders. A side-by-side pharmacodynamic comparison of ASL-8052 with propranolol is depicted in Fig. 23.16. Bob Lee postponed his meeting that was being set-up to cancel the USABB project. There was no strike three called, instead we had made good contact with Mother Nature's pitch and the ball was soaring out-of-the-infield. Likewise, the guillotine was at least for now lowered and covered with a tarp. 'Out-of-sight and out-of-mind' [52] felt very good for that particular image at this point! However, there was still the sound of Glen jingling his coins. We were not there yet. We had a drug 'wannabe' but not a 'true drug' [13]. Our fly ball was indeed hit deep but it had not yet landed. We could not tell with certainty if it would be fair or foul, or if it would be caught, bounce into-play or, best of all, clear the outfield fence. Management, as well as the research team, were all on their feet to see just where this hit was going to go.

A true 'Goldilocks' compound [10,53]

Chi and I began to conduct initial process chemistry experiments for ASL-8052 with an eye toward eventual scaleup of raw drug, and just as we had for the external esters, we also spent the next couple of months exploring variables associated with the aryl external esters [7] with an eye toward further improvement of properties or for identifying a backup compound for ASL-8052. None of this additional work, however, produced a compound superior to ASL-8052 [7]. Various multiple esters were found to offer little, if any, improvements in duration [7]; and assembling esters that contained good leaving groups failed to shorten durations. Interestingly, the next higher homologue in my extended ester series ($n = 3$) exhibited a duration of 40 min, an abrupt departure from the straight line observed for the three lower homologues [7]. This last data point is strikingly evident in Fig. 23.15. Thus, neither the immediately longer or shorter homologues of ASL-8052 were able to meet the short-acting duration criteria that we had set as our target goal. ASL-8052 was 'in the middle' [7,10] structurally and only it was 'just right' [53] in terms of duration. It was indeed a 'Goldilocks' compound [53]. If I had not

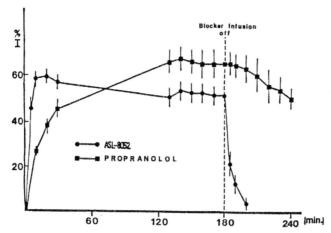

FIGURE 23.16 Comparison of the probe having $n = 2$ (aka ASL-8052) versus propranolol by testing them *in vivo* using the 3 h drug infusion protocol. The desired ultra-short duration was retained by ASL-8052 within this demanding biological model. *Figure used directly with permission from ACS P.W. Erhardt, C.M. Woo, W.G. Anderson, R.J. Gorczynski, Ultra-short-acting β-adrenergic receptor blocking agents. 2. (Aryloxy)propanolamines containing esters on the aryl function. J. Med. Chem. 25 (1982), 1408–1412.*

methodically examined 'methyl, ethyl and propyl' insertions and instead jumped immediately up to a propylene unit thinking I was taking an 'SAR shortcut', I may have erroneously concluded that this approach toward removing a steric impediment would not be worthwhile. My four hypotheses at that time and still today for the propylene's abrupt departure include: (i) The ester group is now far enough away from the pharmacophore such that the metabolite's negative effect upon binding to the *beta*-adrenergic receptor is minimized and the resulting acid retains significant activity (the square peg is too far away from the round hole to detract from favorable binding); (ii) There may also be a steric factor ca. 3 methylene units distal to the esterase(s)' active site machinery that is even more preclusive for binding and it prevents the phenyl-group from associating with the enzyme to an even greater degree than the lower homologues; (iii) There is a requisite motion associated with the overall active site's molecular machinery that is perturbed when a large steric factor like an aryl group is placed three methylene units away from a substrates' carboxy group; and/or finally, (iv) When the alkyl linker becomes three or more methylene units, it begins to fold-back upon the overall molecular framework due to hydrophobic collapse when placed in an aqueous environment, the resulting cluster then no longer dangles its ester group like an extended invitation for attack by the esterase. Nice academic considerations at this point but with Glen still jingling coins in his pocket and a good-looking preclinical candidate compound in his other hand, we were all pressed to move toward development of ASL-8052 ASAP. In addition, I appreciated that since we were dealing with a 'black box' of hydrolytic enzymes [39], any member of the overall participants could be affected in its own blend of any of these possibilities such that even for an academic endeavor, defining this situation could become an entire PhD thesis project. So the thinking remained for now, let's all push onward and upward as fast as possible with what we've now got in hand. Let's not lose sight of our fly ball and where it needs to come down.

Steric factors to the rescue again [7]

During this period, Sheung-Tsam ("Kam") had maintained the program's effort on the internal esters with diligence. I had suggested that he deploy a brute force synthetic method because it just might get at least some product while also divulging where things were going astray during some of the routes being undertaken by the other synthetic team members. He took my advice and through sheer persistence, he finally provided a key, internal-ester-containing probe that had evaded our inhouse and extramural participants for so long. Its structure is shown in Fig. 23.17. While the duration was short in the 40 min drug infusion model, overall its profile was similar to that for our *N*-external-ester-substituted phenoxypropanol-amines and thus it did not itself meet all of the specs set for our USABB target. With an example of this class of esters in-hand, we soon determined that one of its major chemical issues involved intramolecular attack between its secondary amine and the ester carbonyl moiety *via* transitioning a six-membered ring intermediate reminiscent of what I had pre-viously observed for analogous members within the *N*-external ester series that produced unwanted lactam products. By this time, I had become extremely aware of the advantages and disadvantages of steric factors during chemical synthesis [46] and during catabolism by enzymes [5]. I suggested to Kam that he might try employing a bulky *N*-alkyl substituent to hinder the problematic attack by the amine system. In addition, such functionality actually tends to increase blocking

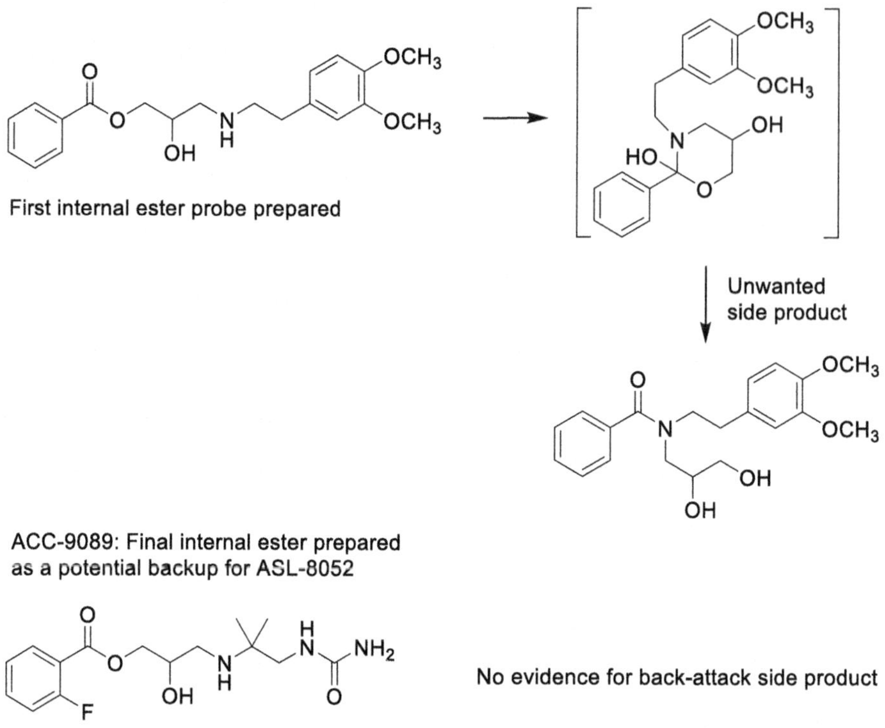

FIGURE 23.17 First compound (top) finally obtained as an example for the internal ester strategy, and the final version (bottom), ACC-9089 (flestolol), eventually selected as one of the potential backup compounds for ASL-8052 (esmolol; shown previously). Also shown here is the spontaneous pathway that likely was one of the major hurdles encountered during the initial attempts to synthesize internal esters.

First internal ester probe prepared

Unwanted side product

ACC-9089: Final internal ester prepared as a potential backup for ASL-8052

No evidence for back-attack side product

potency (e.g. α-gem-dimethyl substitution with tertiary-butyl vs. isopropyl), likely by both a direct enhanced interaction at β-adrenergic receptors and by diminishing their susceptibility as substrates for catabolism by monoamine oxidase. Though this suggestion required another run thorough his tedious synthesis, Kam immediately embarked on this effort. Eventually a potential backup compound for ASL-8052 was produced. It and some additional external ester possibilities produced by Chi and I in this same regard, were positioned to follow behind esmolol's development should the need arise. The structure of the most promising internal ester is also shown in Fig. 23.17. Its half-life of about 20 min persisted through both *in vivo* models but was somewhat longer when later studied in rabbits. It became number ACC-9089 and was eventually named 'flestolol' for the USABB program. Its associated efforts were later published in both medicinal and pharmacological journals [54–56] initially by our group and soon thereafter in a somewhat confirmatory manner by external investigators [57].

Part 2. Development of a drug called 'esmolol'

Introduction

Quickly resetting the stage and cast while the clock continues to run

Before opening the curtain for part 2, we'll need to quickly adjust our surroundings and introduce several new players. Practical process chemistry is now the foremost task at hand. Jumbo (multi-liter) glassware with 24/40 joints (and larger) began to out-populate my former 14/20 neck-ware that I can still relate to quite fondly, like a kid with some precious but fragile toys. Key to process chemistry was a completely new emphasis for me on RIGOROUS analytical chemistry and documentation. Given ACC's small size, it was up to Chi and I to do the initial chemistry optimization and scale-up syntheses activities. Really fun to be focusing upon just chemistry for its own sake and, importantly, we did have two analytical chemists with prior experience in drug development: James Carter at the management level, and Mike Baaske like us at a hands-on level in the lab. We also had several good folks in the drug metabolism and PK arena, just some who come immediately to mind being: Avraham Yacobi at the management level with Check Sum, Herman Stampfli and C. Y. Quon in the lab. As mentioned earlier, Rich Krasula was now dedicated to toxicology, and we did have several experienced lab folks to conduct preliminary formulation studies. Finally, Roger Stoll with a formulation and product development background will now be overseeing the ACC development effort similar to how Bob Lee had managed our previous basic research/discovery activities. I would now be reporting to Roger as much as to Bob Lee and Les Matier who had eventually taken-up the position of Group Leader for Medicinal Chemistry. Clearly, ASL-8052 was still soaring high in the air and despite what we may have imaginatively wanted, only clinical testing would actually show us where our precious lead compound would truly land. But to get to that we needed to first conduct rigorous preclinical development studies.

Chemical multitasking

Interdisciplinary interfacing

Overview

Fig. 23.18 summarizes the various chemical tasks that need to be undertaken during preclinical development of a small molecule, drug candidate compound. Depicted to display their sequence in clockwise order starting from one o'clock, many of these tasks are typically conducted simultaneously depending upon person-power. As medicinal chemists who had focused upon drug discovery, this was all very new to Chi and I. We did our best at multitasking but with just the two of us, our efforts were often forced into the depicted step-wise progression. This was not so much a hurdle but rather a steep hill that did not have any fix other than to 'keep our noses to the grindstone' [58], push forward and get our jobs done. Thankfully, we did have several interdisciplinary colleagues who were familiar with what was needed in each case. Their knowledge and guidance was invaluable, and interfacing with these scientists proved critical for moving ASL-8052 forward. As the inventing 'papa,' I knew it was time to hand-over and entrust 'my molecular baby' to other experts so that they could do 'their thing.' Letting-go was difficult given the 'baby's' history to this point, but solid teamwork would be the theme that was needed. My days of fighting like a bulldog to keep the project alive were over. Instead, now we were lucky to have several different types of scientists eager to join in the development of ASL-8052. But if only it was that simple.

Matters made worse again

This time it was Bob and Roger serving as co-chairs of the ASL-8052 'transition' (today's 'translational') team who had called a meeting. Bob, the gentleman of science, spoke first with a compliment that led immediately into his instructional intent, both delivered in his typically brief manner: "You've done a great job in producing a promising compound for the USA β-blocker program, but there's still a lot more that needs to be done to get it into the clinic." Roger immediately followed in his own manner: "And the bad news is that corporate is still wondering what's taking us so long to generate a marketable product. Honestly, it has taken us a long time to get to this point and their patience is wearing thin." So much for celebrating, not only could we again hear the clock, but it seemed to be ticking at an even louder and faster pace. Plus, even though Glen French was not present on this occasion, we could most certainly hear the coins yet once again jingling in his pockets; and just like the clock, the jingling was even louder and more rapid than before. Our research phase had been rough, to say the least; and now it was clear that the project's development phase was not going to be a picnic either

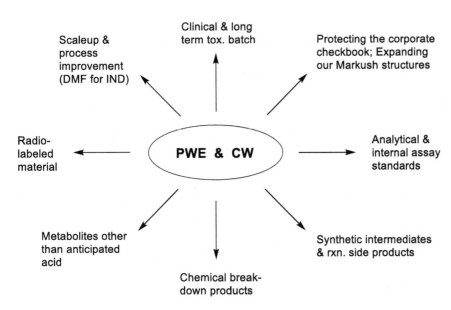

FIGURE 23.18 Chemical multitasking required in support of preclinical drug development. Markush structures refer to the scope of chemical composition (space) claimed in ongoing patenting activities. *DMF*, drug master file; *IND*, investigational new drug submission required for clinical testing within the US. The depicted steps 'around the clock' are usually undertaken in a simultaneous manner when adequate person-power and expertise are present. In this case only myself (PWE) and Chi Wu (CW) were available to conduct these pure chemistry, bench-level activities. Chi focused on the process chemistry while I was stretched rather thinly across all of these targeted areas. Luckily, there were interdisciplinary experts assessing the targets at the end of each of these small molecule drug development needs.

because of the critical need to get this work accomplished as fast as possible. No room for errors that might slow us down, was this phase going to be a similarly exhausting, up-and-down roller coaster ride of emotions?

Protecting the corporate checkbook

Needing to direct our efforts toward several of the steps depicted in Fig. 23.18, I decided to have Chi focus primarily on the scale-up chemistry while I worked as rapidly as possible on various of the other tasks. Since scale-up required close support from our analytical group, I gave their chemical needs the highest priority. This strategy placed our limited resources on the shortest path to clinical testing. Responding to the jingling coins, however, I also continued to synthesize new analogs to expand the SAR around these types of USA design motifs, and especially to define a broader scope for our patenting activities. I'll quickly wrap this up here because, even though proceeding at a backburner pace, it eventually led to some interesting results. In the end, ACC would hold 11 US. patents plus numerous closely translated patents in several other countries [59–69]. Three noteworthy aspects pertaining to SAR deserve brief mention. First, as mentioned earlier, our instillation of good leaving groups did not result in faster catabolism by esterases. My take-home lesson on this: Mother Nature has gradually evolved the carboxyl esterase mechanisms (plural because there are two major classes with many subclasses [14,16]) in an optimal manner that lowers the transition state energy for the hydrolysis to the point that it cannot be improved upon by having better leaving groups attached to the carbonyl. Second, there seems to be something special about carboxyl esterase substrates when heteroatoms, amides or electron rich systems (all providing dipoles) are located about two atoms away from either the oxygen or the carbonyl of the ester linkage because they tend to be more susceptible to hydrolysis. See Fig. 23.19 for speculation about the possible evolution of this observable SAR relationship, and also about how this observation later played-out in practical terms for not only our lead structure, but also for some of our potential backup compounds. Finally, while multiple *N*-external, aryl-external and combined *N*- and aryl-external esters could be constructed to have even shorter durations (e.g. 5 min), they proved to be too metabolically labile. From a practical standpoint, they were too difficult to manipulate/titrate even by careful intravenous infusion. My take-home: Not only was ASL-8052 a Goldilocks chemical compound, but our team's initial half-life target of ca. 10 min (rather than 5 min or 15 min) was, luckily, also a Goldilocks pharmacological profile 'just right' for successfully deploying USA compounds for these particular clinical indications.

Analytical and internal standards

Mike Baaske requested that I make an extremely pure batch of our lead compound that he could designate as THE analytical standard and "by the way, keep track of the specs like melting points etc. for all of your lots of ASL-8052 so that we can set appropriately practical numbers to stipulate during eventual GMP manufacture." He explained that high specs from the analytical standard are not as useful as the history of batch-to-batch specs. Setting too high specs could come back to haunt us down the road. Instead, he wanted the extremely pure batch to develop a validated, GLP-compliant quantitative HPLC assay that could serve as one of the primary analytical methods and be deployed in a practical manner to ascertain/confirm the purity of raw drug product. I'd already made several batches by now and so I'm thinking in response "now they tell me about the importance of recording these specs." Luckily, I could trace them all back to my original notebook page entries for each batch and find such data. Plus, Chi and I would be making at least another 15 batches by the time we wound-down our own in-house syntheses of ASL-8052 and enhancement of scaleup parameters. In the end, there would be plenty of batch history data for assembly of a Drug Master File (DMF). For the analytical batch I took his emphasis on 'THE' very seriously, likely overkill here but it didn't slow me down. I double-purified every intermediate: doing bulb-to-bulb distillations of II and vacuum distillations of III (Fig. 23.20) for the first time, and crystallization of IV as well as crystallization/recrystallization of the final product ASL-8052. Complete specs were compiled for every intermediate including commercial starting material I and each commercial reagent and solvent. Twenty grams of analytical standard was delivered along with ca. 1 g of each highly purified intermediate. Mike decided to checkout some of my earlier analogs as potential HPLC internal standards. An isopropyl ester (Fig. 23.20) proved useful for his raw drug assay and it additionally should have enhanced stability for potential use in future bioanalytical assay methods. I prepared several grams of this material for him and for ACC's PK folks along with the analytical standard materials mentioned above. Eventually a commercial material was selected as an analytical internal standard. Its unrelated structure (Fig. 23.20 compound 'CIS') produced a more convenient peak location for multiple assay runs and inter-run wash protocols.

The Grand Tetons

"Paul, your standard's melting point looks like the Grand Tetons." Was Mike really suggesting that my ASL-8052 material was not pure enough to be used as an analytical standard? Apparently, my beautiful baby was just plain ugly in his eyes.

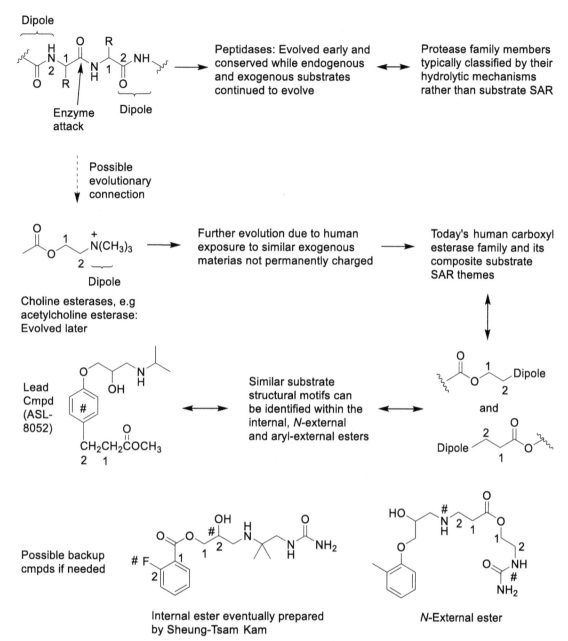

FIGURE 23.19 Carboxylesterase substrates' SAR theme derived from the USA BB research program. Dipole (also depicted as # in some of the specific structures) can be as simple as a heteroatom. The lead compound (ASL-8052) and its two potential backup compounds display this recurring structural motif. In this model, the phenyl ring in ASL-8052 endows lipophilicity preferred by β-adrenergic receptors while its subtle dipole enhances interaction with carboxylesterases. Also depicted is the possible connection of how carboxylesterases handling a range of xenobiotic substrates, may have evolved from hydrolytic enzymes associated with handling specific endogenous substrates. The symmetry of the SAR extending in either direction from the ester linkage is noteworthy (and thus esthetically pleasing to this author) whether or not derived by Mother Nature's supervision of the enzymes' evolution.

Egads, I thought to myself, this is somewhat insulting since I take considerable pride in the chemical quality of each and every one of my synthesized products, let alone this proposed analytical standard. My own data indicated a sharp melting point (mp) of 86–87°C. What kind of wrinkle is occurring now, will it become yet another chemical hurdle? I had exhausted myself chasing after ultimate purity for these materials. I really had no idea how to get them any purer than what I thought they already were by all of my own analyses. Turns out Mike was making a joke. When he thought of a melting point he had a very different notion in his head. He routinely uses differential scanning calorimetry (DSC) to very slowly examine a compound's mp. He was doing this on ASL-8052's mp range for the possibility of having different crystalline polymorphs present in the sample. He was able to see a couple of largely overlapped humps and exaggerated the situation

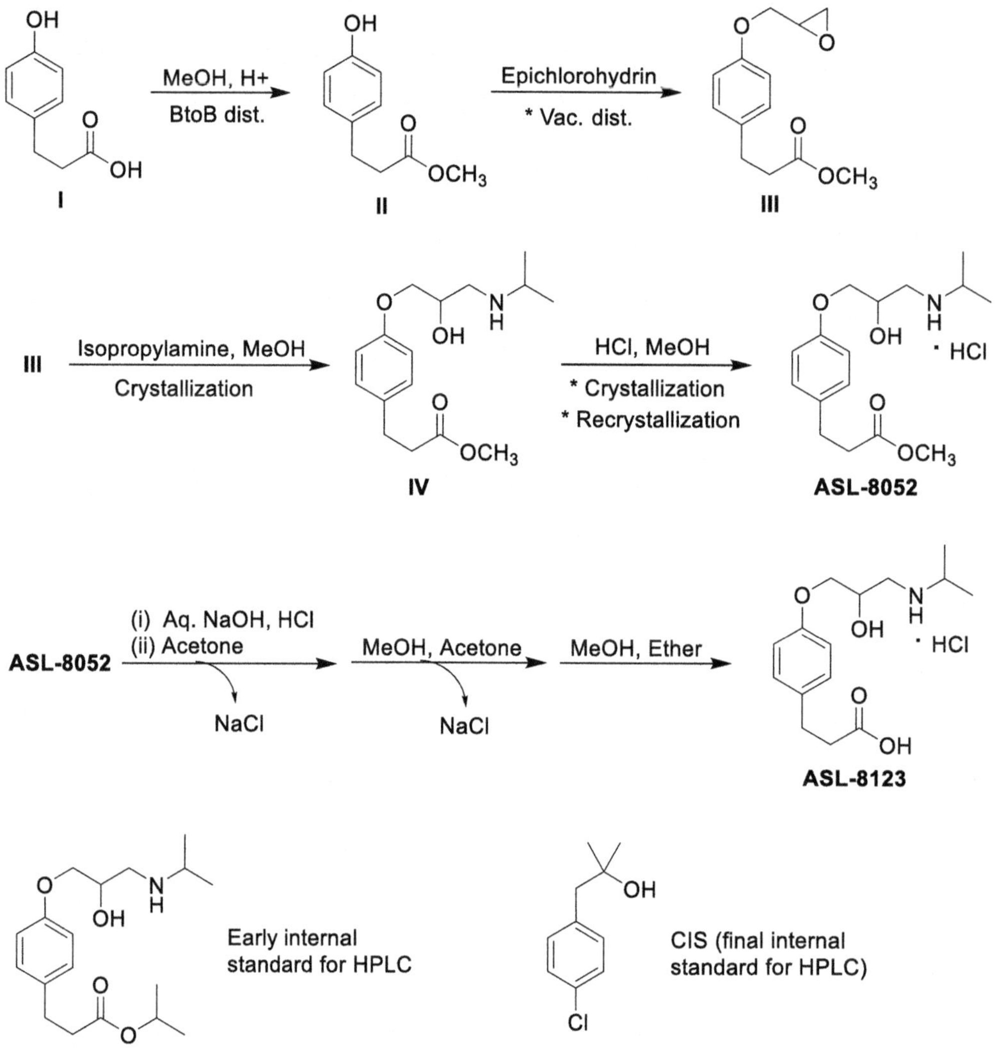

FIGURE 23.20 Synthesis of analytical standards for lead compound ASL-8052 and of its intended metabolite ASL-8123. Note that the steps marked by an asterisk (*) also became independent process chemistry steps in the final route used to prepare scaled-up (kg level) quantities of ASL-8052 raw drug. In the end the latter process required 11 distinct steps according to the chemical manufacturing flow chart specified within our eventual DMF because it also listed procedural steps for material manipulations such as evaporation of solvents, filtration-collection of solids, and drying of final product crystals. Such manipulations are not taken for granted when operating at multi-kilogram scale. Also shown are some of the internal standard compounds used for the HPLC assay method, namely the isopropyl ester version being prepared by us and the one finally selected, noted as 'CIS,' being commercially available in high-grade purity at reasonable cost.

just to have some fun with me. When DSC is run at 10°C/min a sharp mp is obtained at 89.5°C. He further explained that polymorphs would actually be a good thing to have because their presence could assist in faster dissolution of our product if we eventually go to market having a powder prepackaged in a vial for dilution with injectable saline immediately prior to use in the clinic. Mike went on to say that he would be tracking the polymorph possibilities for every one of our future batches and that his group along with the formulation folks expected to see subtle differences occurring throughout. Two independent techniques (not needing a known standard) were used to establish the material's purity, one being DSC and the other a non-aqueous titration of the secondary amine with a known amount of perchloric acid. Both methods indicated that the analytical standard for ASL-8052 (batch 10) was 98.9% pure. In addition to my routine analyses using mp, TLC in three different development systems, proton NMR, IR and C,H&N analyses (conducted by a vendor), Mike's group planned to conduct their own IR, UV, proton and ^{13}C NMR, MS, HPLC, C,H,N&Cl analysis (vendor), and DSC mp assays relative to the analytical standard. The latter material would now allow them to develop a validated GLP-compliant quantitative HPLC method for raw drug substance. But then Mike finally ended this part of our discussion by making another request.

We're definitely gonna need more stuff

Still recovering from his initial joke, "now what, how much material and what level of purity do you need" was all I could say at this point. Mike indicated that, in addition to the product, each of the synthetic intermediates and the internal standard, he would need to have a sample for any likely or even just possible side-products as well as for any chemical breakdown products. Although none of us thought that any of such materials would interfere with the ASL-8052 peak in his preliminary HPLC chromatogram, simply stating that opinion in the Drug Master File would not be adequate for the US FDA. As part of his assay validation, Mike needed to actually demonstrate that when such materials are 'spiked' into the analyte's milieu, they do not interfere with the desired quantitative assessment. The compounds I made in pure form for these reasons are shown in Fig. 23.21 while the possible breakdown mixtures that did not need to be highly purified or even fully characterized were produced by the formulation group as part of their major entry into the project. They were also able to take advantage of US FDA guidelines/approved protocols for the storage and accelerated breakdown assessments which, in turn, initiated some of the specific documentation that would eventually be needed from their field for our overall IND.

There's always a stubborn compound

Immediately coming to my mind as the most likely possibility for having a contaminant, is the free acid stemming from inadvertent hydrolysis of the ester at any of several steps during the overall synthesis, including especially during formation of the HCl salt at the end. In addition, since an acid is the proposed desirable metabolite of ASL-8052, we would need to have an analytical sample and multigram supply of this material so as to characterize it in parallel to the parent compound during development. Its synthesis as a highly pure material, however, was proving to be difficult and this was on the verge of becoming another hurdle among the various multitasks that I was trying to pursue as quickly as possible. The problem is that there is both an acidic carboxyl group and a basic amine present in a small molecule construct such that something is always ionized when one tries to partition between an organic phase and either an acid- or base-buffered

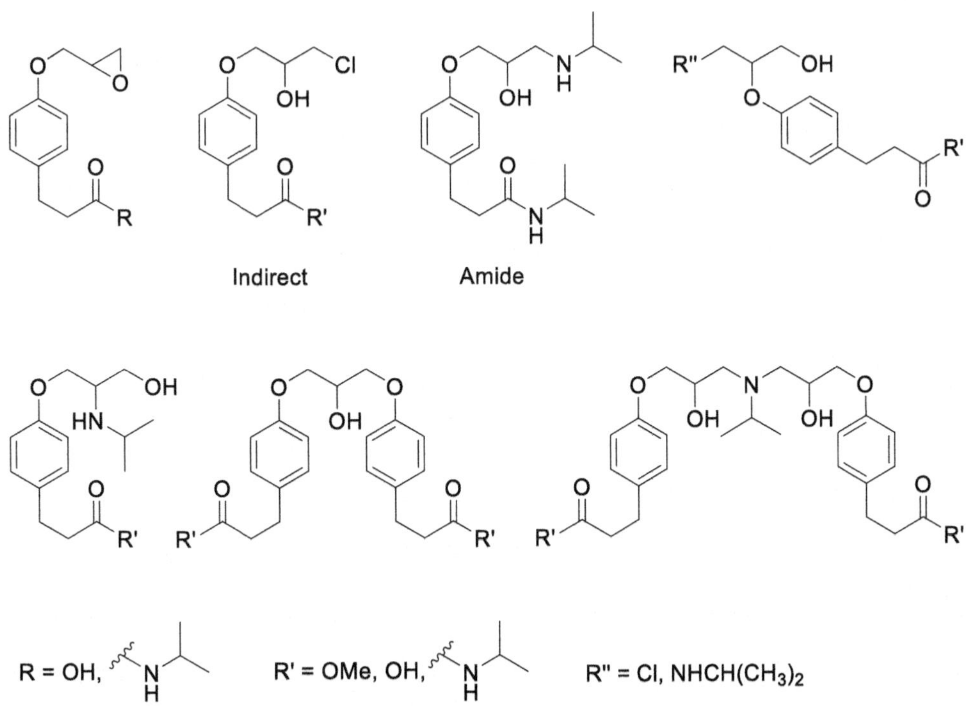

FIGURE 23.21 Potential side-products from the synthesis of ASL-8052 considered as possible trace contaminates in the final product. The acid resulting from hydrolysis (ASL-8123 shown in the preceding Fig. 23.20) and the compound designated as 'Amide' above were thought to be the most likely contaminate possibilities. Reaction of epichlorohydrin in acetone using potassium carbonate is thought to result in the intermediate depicted in Fig. 23.20 by a mixture of two mechanistic pathways: (A) Primarily by direct displacement of the halide; and, (B) by initial opening of the epoxide followed by collapse back to the epoxide from the transient chloro-hydroxy species. The transient compound is designated above as 'Indirect.' All of these compounds and several of the other possibilities were synthesized as potential side-product standards. There were no signs of any of these materials detected during either the synthesis of ASL-8052 or in the final, raw drug product.

aqueous phase as an otherwise easy and ideal way to purify compounds when either of such functional groups are present in just a singular manner. Through sheer persistence, I managed to produce pure material in multigram amounts (purification scheme also shown in Fig. 23.20). The workup was not at all pretty as it initially relied upon 'reverse crystallization' to remove NaCl (after hydrolysis of analytical grade ASL-8052 by 1 N NaOH followed by reacidification with dilute HCl) first by adding acetone and then by evaporation of the resulting aqueous mother liquor, re-dissolving in MeOH and again adding acetone to precipitate lingering NaCl. Finally, ether was added to crystalize pure de-esterified ASL-8052 which became ASL-8123 (notably 71 compounds after its parent's first synthesis). Since this program was started as an 8000 series, that's about 125 different structures made for the USA BB project to date, essentially all by Chi and I. I guess only one really stubborn compound among that size of a directed library is not so bad, but it just happened to come at a hectic time while we were busy chemical multitasking; and still hearing ticking clocks and jingling coins in the background. In addition to pure crystalline material, aqueous solutions of ASL-8123 having known molarity could readily be prepared directly from pure (analytical grade) ASL-8052 for use by the PK group. As an aside here I would like to note that several years later, when I shifted the latter stages of my career to academia, I did devise a more elegant synthesis of ASL-8123 that may be of general utility for purifying this type of reaction scenario wherein zwitterionic compounds are produced as the desired product [70]. The rest of the compounds that were synthesized as possible side-products did not cause any problems to prepare. In the end, none of the synthetic intermediates, potential side-products or the stressed mixtures produced by the formulation folks, interfered with the HPLC method undergoing GLP validation. Fig. 23.22 partially depicts these overall, very favorable analytical chemistry results.

Hydrogenations at negative pressure?

Avraham Yacobi was similarly quick to request that their drug metabolism/PK group also needed some special compounds for our now rapidly expanding development project. In addition to the parent USA βB, its metabolite ASL-8123 and the initial isopropyl ester internal standard which should be similar to ASL-8052 when trying to isolate the later from biological milieu, they "would really like to have" some radiolabeled material. Providing the first three items was now like "following well-trodden paths" [41]. For the radiolabel, I considered several possible routes on paper and decided to seriously look first at a route that I had already been exploring as part of our scale-up/process optimization efforts. It's depicted in Fig. 23.23. I worked-out the conditions wherein the final hydrogenation step was done at 50 psi over Pd-C as catalyst. I then used deuterium gas and that product proved itself to be useful for some MS-based bioanalytical studies. When I approached New England Nuclear (NEN) to use tritium gas on my penultimate intermediate, however, they indicated that due to the potential environmental hazard, they could only do tritiations under neutral and more preferably under slightly negative pressure. Amazed, I didn't even think hydrogenations would work when done in such a manner. Clearly, I really didn't know what I was doing in this specialized field of chemistry. Was this yet another hurdle that would slow us down, perhaps one I had created myself? NEN patiently explained that there's a useful compromise in that only very low percent reaction will occur initially with the tritium but then the reduction can be completed with hydrogen at higher pressure and, in-the-end, the product will still be so 'hot' that it will have to be mixed with 'cold' ASL-8052 to produce material suitable for the *in vivo* PK studies. That proved to be the case and our PK group was happy to have some tritium-labeled material to get started. Let's attribute the solution for this challenge to be the expertise and patience of the selected vendor with some just plain luck on my part for having spent time on this that, in-the-end, did not become wasted at a point when time was very precious for the project.

Next time, just call us first

NEN went on to say that they could readily incorporate a ^{14}C into ASL-8052 using my original route (Fig. 23.20). I also had devised some routes for ^{14}C labeling that looked very reasonable on paper, but their suggestion seemed ideal and I was intrigued by what they had in mind. Turns out that for another customer interested in an entirely different type of final product structure, they had already devised a way to produce my starting material I with ^{14}C incorporated into the carbon that attaches the propionic acid to the phenolic ring. In fact, not only did they have good specs for this material, they had plenty of left-over stock on-hand to use immediately if we so wanted. We jumped at this offer. But then their first batch fell short of the desired specs. Nothing's ever as simple as it seems. Nevertheless, after additional rounds of tech transfer discussions and, especially, further guidance about the epichlorohydrin reaction workup benefiting from a quick vacuum distillation, NEN's second batch proved to be perfect and our PK folks immediately put it to good use. The final and major lesson with regard to radiolabeling should be clear: call your experts before you invest much of your own lab time thinking that you're going to help them in advance—chances are they're already way ahead of you and a team approach from the get-go is the best way to proceed.

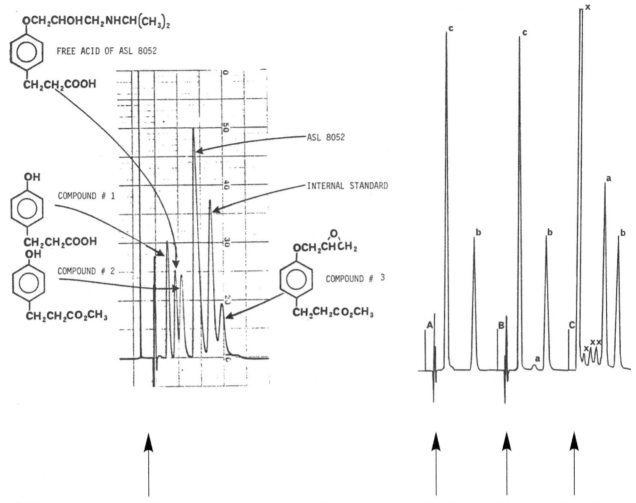

FIGURE 23.22 Reverse phase HPLC chromatograms. Vertical arrows indicate sample injections. The left panel depicts the resolution of all chemical intermediate peaks associated with the syntheses of ASL-8052 and ASL-8123 (free acid of ASL-8052). The right panel depicts the chromatograms for three different accelerated decomposition studies: (A) Boiling 1 h in 1 N NaOH; (B) Boiling 1 h in 1 N HCl; and, (C) Boiling 1 h in 30% hydrogen peroxide. For all three of the decomposition chromatograms, peak (a) is ASL-8052, (b) is the internal standard, (c) is ASL-8123, and peaks (x) are unknown degradation species. Both strong acid and strong base catalyze hydrolysis in a clean manner to produce ASL-8123. Oxidation likewise produces a highly polar species as the major product that does not interfere with the detection and quantification of ASL-8052, as well as several less polar materials in much smaller amounts that have peaks close to ASL-8052.

Having pure fun with process chemistry

Thanks to the many folks who preceded our entry into the βB field, Chi and I were already on solid ground for our scale up and process chemistry activities. First, our route simply followed the well-established literature method for preparing aryloxypropanolamines suitable for use in the clinic, i.e. preparing the classical βB scaffold [42]. Second, nearly all of the already marketed βBs were being used as their racemic mixtures. Intending to do the same with our USA βB removed the hurdle of needing to produce asymmetric material. Thus, we only needed to optimize the steps relative to our own chemical species, namely our distinct aryl system while insuring that its methyl ester adduct is not compromised during various modifications of the reaction/workup conditions. Within just a couple of months and after five internal reports demonstrating our improvements and setting specs for all chemical reactants and synthetic intermediates as well as for the final product, we had optimized our process from 15% to 20% overall yield to 30%—40%. Scale-up had started with 10 g runs and gradually been brought to a convenient level of 500 g runs of the epoxide intermediate III. Of the 11 steps in a flow-chart version of the synthesis and compound manipulation related activities, a vacuum distillation of III and the formation of crystalline HCl salt in MeOH/ether near the end represented potential challenges in our minds when going into actual manufacturing. We were well into discussions with two GMP production companies and both assured us that these

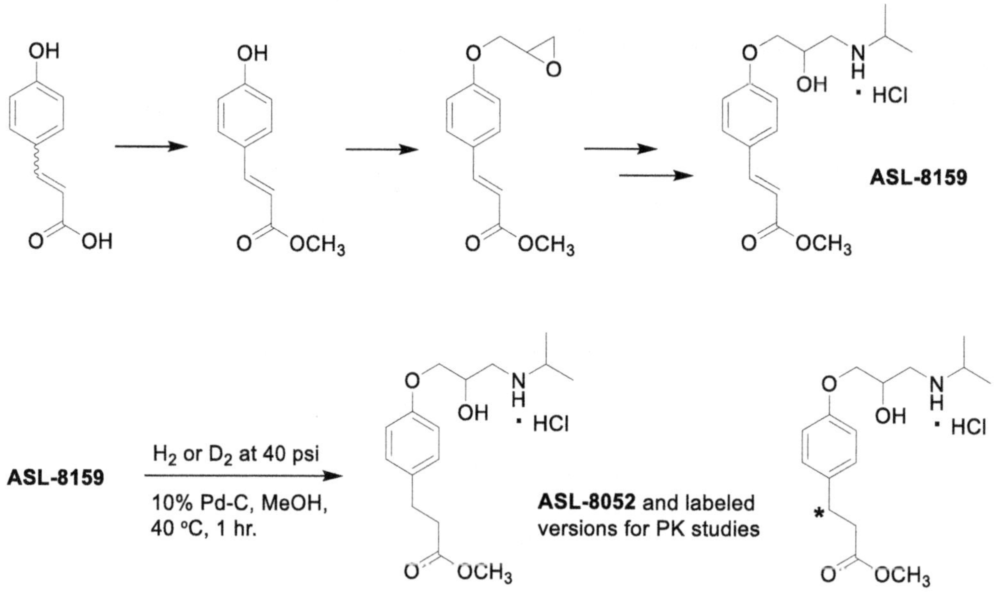

Note that a vendor performed tritiations at negative psi and room temp.; They also separately prepared a ^{14}C labeled material as shown by the asterisk on the ASL-8052 structure to the right.

FIGURE 23.23 Alternate synthetic route that was initially assessed during early syntheses of ASL-8052 and then reexamined later when considering radiolabeling chemistry. For large scale purposes, the less expensive *cis/trans-para*-hydroxycinnamic acid can be used because isomerization to the more thermodynamically stable, all-*trans* isomer occurs during the first esterification step. This eliminates any isomer ambiguity as the procedure continues.

processes would not be a problem for initial clinical/toxicology batches although attempts should be continued to preferentially avoid the use of ether. Due to the latter's high volatility and flammability, one of the companies indicated that their pilot plant reactor room would need to be hosed-down with water before addition of the ether to effect the crystallization, but even that was not an uncommon practice for them.

Stalagmites

With time, we later found that methylethylketone could be used in place of MeOH/Ether in the last synthetic step to provide crystals that grew like stalagmites in our 5 L flasks when placed in our walk-in refrigerator. A truly amazing and beautiful site provided by Mother Nature, I wish now that we had taken some pictures but appreciate that cell phones had not yet been invented so even getting some simple pics meant setting-up a camera and then going to a film-developing service. These mammoth crystalline towers with a slow twist reminiscent of DNA's spiral, were likewise highly pure and of even higher net yield for this key step followed by filtration and drying of the harvested material as the final two distinct process steps. Process chemistry flow charts set each of such physical manipulations as a distinct step, and rightly so when one is dealing with 500 gm to 1 kg quantities. Nothing is trivial at that scale so nothing should be taken for granted even if seemingly following a well-trodden path. Finally, we devised a synthesis of starting material I that resulted in about a 10-fold reduction of its cost. One of the commercial manufacturers that management had contacted early-on, was located in Canada. For now, I was encouraged to pursue them as our most preferred partner for eventual GMP manufacture of ASL-8052. While personally wondering "why them," I quickly increased the level and details associated with tech transfer to this organization. But this pure chemistry fun would soon come to an end. Things were about to turn very serious as time, itself, always remained of primary essence.

First in man study

The methanol scare

As we drew closer to a Phase I study, we began thinking about our drug's broader use in the clinic. While we intended that our USABB would be used for short periods in critical care situations (e.g. several hours at the long-end), we also considered that there could be circumstances where prolonged infusions (e.g. days or even weeks) might be beneficial or, alternatively, encountered by accidental usage. In those cases, we wondered if we might be gradually loading the body with methanol (ASL-8052's 'other' metabolite after ester hydrolysis) to the extent that the latter could eventually become toxic upon prolonged infusions. Having moved to head-up toxicology, Rich Krasula was the appropriate expert to join the 'infield' in order to catch this sudden 'line drive' that could potentially challenge our entire game plan just after things finally seemed like we were starting to pull ahead. Working with our biostatistician, Rich showed that even during prolonged infusions, methanol levels would level-off to a point well below that noted to have toxicity in humans [71,72]. Furthermore, these levels also fell below the normal ranges commonly equilibrated within humans from their ordinary daily diets wherein fruits and vegetables also supply methanol [73–75]. Humans form a healthy steady state of methanol intake, metabolism and excretion that runs higher than what ASL-8052 infusions will create no matter how long the administration. In the end, nothing serious from this 'scare', but then as indicated above, our efforts would soon be turning otherwise.

Before continuing the esmolol story, however, it should be pointed-out that much later we also decided to pursue a BB that could be administered by eye-drop to treat glaucoma and then likewise be metabolized and inactivated quickly upon entering the systemic circulation so as to avoid off-target cardiotoxicity. For that I insisted on designing ethyl rather than methyl esters as a further, upfront precaution given methanol's notorious reputation for causing blindness when methanol is consumed at high levels [76–78]. The fact that the eye enzymatically converts retinol to retinal and then uniquely uses the aldehyde as part of its light-sensing mechanism by actually forming an imine on the retina (really cool chemistry), seemed to me to be too much of a coincidence to not be taken as a serious warning from Mother Nature rather than as just being regarded as a potential red flag. While it has been suggested [78] that formaldehyde is not the culprit, this cautionary feeling remains the same for me today even though I have never found any reported evidence connecting these two intriguing mechanistic scenarios. Either way, methanol as the forerunner to ocular toxicity is certain and one can settle with a black box for the exact details of how that occurs. In the end, we never did identify an ethyl ester for this additional indication that was substantially stable in the eye fluids and, alternatively, was substantially labile in the systemic circulation. Notably, the eye itself appears to be loaded with a variety of aggressive esterases that not only make this a challenging approach, but also makes tracking SAR toward such an endpoint difficult.

The strategic planner

It was time for another Bob and Roger meeting, now being called "ASL-8052 development meetings" which I will confess that at least by title and for a few moments, brought a smile to my face. As usual, Bob spoke first: "Gentlemen, we need to get our compound into humans ASAP!" Then breaking-in from the back of the room came an unexpected and previously unnoticed late-joining attendee, Glen French himself: "Not only has corporate lost its patience with this program, they've suggested to us that their overall decision to fund a subsidiary research operation may have been a mistake. They appear to be in a state of complete 'research sticker shock.' They're thinking about settling back into being just a distribution company that immediately caters to a hospital's well-established product needs." So much for my smile. Clocks are again ticking loudly along with the sound of Glen's jingling coins whether or not he was actually doing so at the time. Roger was next: "I want to introduce you to our new consultant. I have known him for quite a while. He is with a strategic planning company and is an expert on IND submissions and bridging preclinical development activities into Phase I clinical studies. He is well-connected with international resources that we will need to tap if we want to move fast."

The strategic planner did indeed have a plan. As he moved to the front-center of the room, he began by conveying that "without an approved IND we cannot conduct a clinical study in the US; and given the mounting pressure from corporate, we do not have the time to put together such a submission and wait for an approval; so we need to set-up a human study outside of the US." After only a moment's pause he went on: "Not to worry though," as he had already gained approval from a physicians' group in Germany to do exactly such a study for us. Apparently, they were highly impressed by the information that he had forwarded to them and they were eager to take advantage of the 'physician's prerogative' option to clinically examine new medicines and herbals without a regulatory step as afforded to them at that time by German medical laws. In fact, they were already beginning to line up hospital beds and recruit human volunteers. The planner then continued with his plan: "And as many of you probably know, without an approved IND we also cannot manufacture raw drug in the States for a study to occur in any other foreign country. But not to worry." Now after two 'not too worries' I'm thinking this guy is definitely from Britain although likely a while back since no such accent was detectable. Whatever, his expression wasn't helping me any and I was indeed beginning to worry about where all of this is headed. I needed to interrupt and without trying to be sarcastic, I ask in his own tongue: "So why no worry?" Apparently he knew very well who I was because he looked directly at me and said: "Paul, the good news for this aspect of the plan is that I've already lined-up a licensed GMP manufacturer in Canada who is willing to work with us on getting the raw drug supply that will be needed." Suddenly understanding my previous thoughts about 'why a Canadian manufacturer,' I was now wondering just how long had this 'new' consultant really been working with Roger. Interrupting my thoughts, he went on: "but the bad news is that we don't have enough time to properly transfer the chemical technology into their own hands, and so we'll need you to join their lab and personally take charge of the scale-up while they insure that the proper GMP protocols and documentation takes place. They will oversee generation of a Drug Master File. They've fully agreed to all of this and will be very accommodating. And not too worry, Paul, you won't have to do the entire synthesis up there in an unfamiliar lab because US law stipulates only that we cannot manufacture the ACTIVE ingredient. Thus, you can perform all of the synthetic steps in your own lab up to the penultimate intermediate in your process chemistry scheme, namely to the free amine, ship that material to Canada and then complete only the last key chemical step where you make the hydrochloride salt that becomes our final, active ingredient product." All of the 'not too worries' in the world could not help me at this point because something about this plan did not sit right. I was indeed worrying and I was uncomfortable to the extent that I had become very restless in my chair.

What's gotten into Paul?

Then it came to me, so I stood and firmly stated: "I won't do that." Total silence fell across the room as all three of Glen, Bob and Roger slowly joined the strategic planner on the speaker's platform. A look of 'what's gotten into Paul' was on everyone's faces not just because an employee was balking at complying with what appeared to be a strategic directive like an order from the top, but because the employee was Paul who, on at least two previous occasions, had kept this program alive when the administration was on the verge of shutting it down. Why such a turn-around, and why is he expressing this so firmly and abruptly right in front of Glen French himself? This whole situation had become incredible. The looks on Glen, Bob and Roger's faces quickly turned from something inquisitive to something threatening. The room was not just silent now but also seemed for me to be very, very chilly. I realized that the guillotine was back in the room, I could feel it, and that this time it was not the program that was being led to the chop block but rather the possibility of my own neck, a highly uncomfortable position to say the least. See Fig. 23.24. Finally, the deafening silence (yes, as I learned in that exact moment, this can be a real thing) was broken by Bob who, just like the planner, looked directly at me and spoke just three words followed by my name. The direct looks were not welcoming to me, and the words were more significant than any of us at the meeting were ready to cope with: "and why not, Paul?" No echo, no whispers; again the deafening silence returned in the room to the point where one could hear a pin drop.

So let's pause this scene for a moment and close the curtain while I step through to deliver an 'aside' to the audience (you readers). Do you agree with all of the meeting's participants that there may be something wrong with me, or that maybe some outside factors are coming into play that are causing me to take such a contrary position in an abrupt manner? Or alternatively, is it the plan itself that is the negative influence? Is there something inherently wrong with this plan that will soon be revealed by my answer to Bob's question? Let's reopen the curtain, return to the scene and see what transpires.

Public speaking, let alone in an impromptu situation, not at all being one of my strongpoints, I think my reply was actually reasonably thoughtful and well-delivered. Given the awkward situation created by my challenge of management's

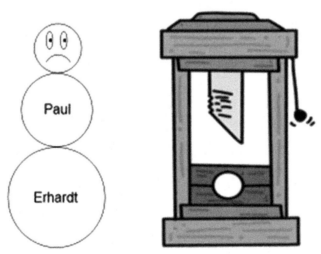

FIGURE 23.24 A highly uncomfortable situation for all and especially so for me. The picture should be self-explanatory—it's intended to convey just what you should be imagining even if unpleasant.

plan, at least I was able to speak. I began by trying for some early buy-in: "You and Roger will likely agree with me that when the hydrochloride salt form of our drug hits the bloodstream, it is immediately greeted by the body's phosphate buffering system. The same thing would happen to our penultimate intermediate arriving initially as a free amine such that both compounds result in the exact same ion pair with phosphate. Furthermore, both will have the exact same equilibrium between protonated ammonium and free amine as they then circulate and distribute throughout the body. Finally, it is actually the free amine equilibrium species that is able to traverse membranes and is thought to interact with the β-adrenergic receptor, perhaps re-protonating as part of its overall binding motif. The bottom line is that our free amine, penultimate intermediate is just as much an active ingredient as is the hydrochloride salt form." With that technical discourse said, I felt I also needed to clearly convey my strong feelings about the plan and this overall situation. So after just a short pause, I concluded with: "I cannot see myself saying anything otherwise if someday I am called upon to testify in a US court case." There was no argument from anyone. The silence in the room disappeared with various groups murmuring among themselves, including the group of four on the speakers' platform. After a few moments it became clear that our key leaders were all nodding in agreement that I was quite correct in my description; and although not as openly displaying their additional realization, that I also may have just saved all of their own 'you-know-whats.' It was Bob again who eventually spoke for all of them by asking: "So Paul, can YOU devise an alternative plan to generate the raw drug material in a timeframe that still meets the clinical study's schedule?" Emphasizing the 'you' in such a manner had the effect of removing the negative aspects of their own plan and, instead, somehow now laying them on my shoulders. And it didn't stop there: "Appreciate that the German clinicians are gearing up to start in just 3 months. They've already begun enrolling healthy volunteers. We cannot afford to miss their window. And you also need to know that according to the original plan, we'll additionally need 1 month subsequent to the synthesis in order to formulate our intended injectable product from the raw drug supply. That work is already set to be done at an approved facility in line with US law that is likewise located outside of the US, namely in France. They have requested 2 kg of raw drug for their formulation of our intended clinical product. So, the bottom line for YOU is: can YOU provide that amount of material in 2 months while taking advantage of the Canadian facility for synthesis? We can use both their and our own analytical capabilities for chemical quality control?" I was glad that I finally had heard a bit of encouragement in his last sentence when he chose to use 'we,' albeit done in a much softer tone, rather than another emphatic 'YOU.' This time my reply was positive, and it was delivered reasonably fast: "I'll try to devise such a plan and see where it takes me. I suggest that I involve Chi Woo to assist in the synthetic effort both here and in Canada." Glen was then quick to take-over the conversation and he soon concluded the meeting at that point in a very deliberate manner involving actual action toward a 'deliverable' accompanied by a timeframe: "I want to see Paul's scale-up plan on my desk by no later than early tomorrow afternoon." Now it was Chi's turn to be restless in his chair. While the room was emptying I explained to him that if this was going to happen in such a tight timeframe, it was going to take the two of us to do it, and that we'd likely be going to Canada for a week at a time during the course of a full month or more near the end. Accepting my judgment overall, Chi actually seemed like he was beginning to look forward to the travel part. Me, not at all but so be it. I honestly felt that we could indeed do this scaleup and still make the clinical study happen on schedule!

An alternate manufacturing plan

My plan was simultaneously delivered the next day to Bob and Roger with a quickly arranged short, late-morning discussion. They then had it on Glen's desk without any changes by Noon. It is summarized in Fig. 23.25. For the reasons iterated above, we needed to send epoxide intermediate III to Canada in order to remain in compliance with Federal regulations. Our prior process chemistry experience indicated that 500 g runs of epoxide + isopropylamine followed by formation of the hydrochloride salt and crystallization to provide our raw drug product ASL-8052 could be accomplished with high reproducibility in good yields having excellent purity (ca. 99%). Just in case one run conducted in the unfamiliar surroundings fell short in yield or purity, I decided that Chi and I should prepare in-house and ship ca. 3 kg of high-quality epoxide III to Canada so that we could perform six runs having 500 g in our race to get to the finish line with somewhere between 2 and 2.5 kg of product. The Canadian lab ordered the reagents and solvents for the last two steps, were prepared to perform chemical QC on them according to our specifications, and began to initiate paperwork for the final GMP protocol associated steps along with initiating the assembly of a Drug Master File. We already had all of the reagents we needed for our inhouse synthesis of epoxide III all the way up to at least 3 kg. Following our own well-trodden paths, we accomplished our inhouse work in just over two, 6-day weeks. Our intermediate epoxide III was shipped by AHSC's international network while taking advantage of the expertise associated with delivery of their numerous hospital supply products.

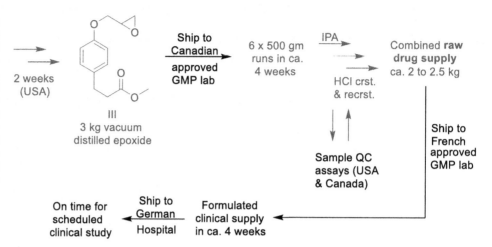

FIGURE 23.25 Modified plan to deliver raw drug supplies to France for preparation of the formulated material as premixed vials for injection to be used during clinical studies. Items marked in red are the critical activities that were undertaken by Paul and Chi within the US ACC lab and in the Canadian lab. *IPA*, isopropylamine. The IPA reaction leads to formation of ASL-8052's active ingredient. The subsequent HCl salt represents the final form of the raw drug product.

In practice versus on paper

A bag full of tricks

To reduce expenses, Chi and I rented a modest car and we shared a two-bed single room in a nice but not at all plush hotel that was near our Canadian contractor's lab in Montreal. When Chi opened his suitcase he had several spatulas laying on top of his clothing. "What's that?" I asked. "You never know what you might need" was his initial reply. "But I've already visited the pilot plant research area that they are going to let us use, and I told you that they have everything we will need or may even just want." Then Chi confided: "These are my lucky spatulas and I like using them when something becomes stubborn during chemical synthesis. For me they can be like magic." I had no reply for his superstition but mentally conceded to myself that we were going to need all of the luck that we could get and perhaps even some magic too, if we were indeed to pull this off. Chi was a lab veteran and I was happy to go with the flow for this superstition when the next morning he carried his spatulas to the lab.

Parlez-vous francais?

Our Canadian colleagues were extremely helpful, both at the management level and as friendly lab mates. They all spoke fluent English, and communications were never an issue, at least during our discussions and requests for assistance. Alternatively, the Canadian government had just mandated that French be learned in schools and that it should be their country's primary language. We witnessed three tiers of socializing among the workers during lunch and breaks. The tiers were based upon the quality of the French language that was being spoken by each group, 'Canadian French' being regarded as the lowest quality. Interestingly, our presence as 'yanks' from the States was just too alien to be caught-up by this issue and we were treated very nicely by all parties throughout our continuing visit, nicer than some of these folks were to each other even though we spoke no French at all. Tech transfer can be a challenge in itself, to the point of becoming a hurdle when communication is also difficult. Since we were conducting the synthetic and purification steps ourselves, tech transfer issues were never the case for us at this time, and when our technology was later transferred to this GMP facility to finally have them take-over, it was never an issue at that point either. I explained to Chi that in addition to our lucky alien nature in regard to their own language turmoil, we were also a bit like ambassadors during our visit for which another of our tasks would be to leave behind a positive relationship for the future transfer of our methods.

'The Sweetness' [79]

Chi and I typically flew to Montreal on a Sunday afternoon so that we could have a full work-week in the Canadian lab and return either late Friday or early Saturday. To be away this much was difficult for my entire family and especially for Judy who then had no help with the four kids (Bill, Mike, Tricia and John) plus our new baby (Christine). Judy fully understood, however, that the future of ACC and thus our own family's financial security, was very dependent upon successfully getting ASL-8052 into the clinic ASAP. Not only carrying the entire family load herself during my absences, she was extremely supportive to me when I would 'call home' each evening while gone. Just one quick example here. Since we both grew up in Minneapolis, Judy and I will always retain a soft spot in our hearts as fans for the Vikings, as well as for the Twins whose franchise was established there while we were in our middle-grades. Not so for Bill, Mike and John, however, who were quickly growing up in the Chicago suburb of Mundelein. Instead, they were turning into dedicated Bears fans. We had all been enjoying some of our Sunday afternoons together watching 'Da Bears' battle their way to at least some respectable seasons. This was fun family relaxation for all of us, especially the Bears versus Vikings games. I must admit that watching an athlete like Walter Payton (aka 'The Sweetness' as often called by Howard Cosell at the time [80]) run up-and-down the field like a deer when he was free and like a bull when someone was trying to tackle him, had also made me his fan right along with my three sons. And a few years later when several of the Bears' players did a rap song entitled 'The Super Bowl Shuffle' [81] which actually sounded pretty good to me as far as rap goes, I did become an entire Bears team fan. Any lessons here? Perhaps sacrificing for the future? Yes and yes. Chi and I spent several Sundays traveling to Montreal so as to complete our final batches of ASL-8052, a very hard decision for me given my loss of precious family time. Hard work ethic? Yes; and a full circle there because I can think of no one who worked harder at their 'trade' than the 'Sweetness', truly a model for everyone in this regard and also in regard to humility (how many premier running backs will fully commit to hard-nosed blocking when the 'call for the ball' goes to another back—rhetorical).

Crossing the border with white powders

Within a month, we had six ca. 400-plus gram batches of ASL-8052! The Canadian lab performed GLP analyses as each batch had been prepared, but I felt early-on that before combining our batches it would be equally important to likewise conduct our own in-house chemical QC measures (consider us a second-party check). This was also done after each batch was prepared. To insure the overall integrity for lots of this size, we needed to obtain at least five samples after tumbling their amber containers for several minutes between sampling. In the end, I hand-carried 5—10 vials of ca. 50 mg size white powders across the border in my briefcase on four different occasions. I had a letter from ACC's upper management, Bob and Roger, indicating who I was and the fact that I had non-commercial, research samples for analytical purposes back in the States. Luckily I was never challenged. The times have surely changed and I don't recommend this aspect of my now historical plan to be attempted by anyone today.

A freshly painted FitzMill

All six batches proved to have excellent specs. We had more raw drug material than had been requested. I thought for sure that our meeting back home in the States was going to be nothing but upbeat even though the clock was still ticking away. Not so. Roger, with his background in pharmaceutics, explained that before the Canadian lab transported the raw drug material to our partner in France to prepare the actual clinical formulation, we still needed to blend our batches into a single lot that would also be regarded as being homogeneous in terms of its physical form. "Not to worry" chimed the 'you know who' (would he ever give-up that expression, I thought), "I have already spoken to our Canadian partner in this regard as well, and they have assured me that they have a new FitzMill blender ready to accomplish this step." Of course his comment was again quickly followed by moving my personal work activities forward like a chess pawn: "Paul should immediately return over the next weekend for what should be his last rush visit to the Canadian facility. He can oversee the milling process. His visit should take only a couple of days next week." I couldn't help but recall that at least Glen had given me some opportunity for personal scheduling when he had previously requested me to devise a short-path plan for producing the raw drug supply—where did that type of opportunity go here? Whatever, we were indeed a team now and all of us were very much together in struggling to maintain our tight schedule. The best thing I could do at this time was to play my part rather than initiate any more controversy or start an argument over any details of who's doing what where. I needed to again put my 'nose to the grindstone' and this time that phrase [58] could actually be more than just an analogy. My eventual response was simple, an affirmative shake of my head. I was fated to once again make a trip to Canada tying-up yet another weekend that I might otherwise have enjoyed with my family, but this time tying-up a loose end that I had not created.

Our schedule allowed for just a couple of more days so there was time to accomplish this. But then, nothing's ever simple. As the Canadian lab's director opened the door to the dedicated blending room and pointed to the FitzMill in the exact middle under a bright overhead light, it was obvious to me that the blender was not all that 'new' and that it had just been freshly painted with a battleship gray coat. His smile and proud "wallah" moment at the room's entrance did not help me any, and instead made the situation even more troubling. This was my host who previously had been so gracious during our month of visits to perform chemical syntheses, but who now seemingly had drifted out of his own area of expertise in organic chemistry while still trying to be helpful to our overall ACC effort. First thinking to myself that there is no way am I going to send my white powders through this freshly painted, 'old' device and have them come out the other end as a nice homogeneous but potentially gray powder with highly compromised specs. Is this guy crazy? But then recalling my initial words to Chi that we should behave like ambassadors, I told the director in a controlled, softened tone that: "before scheduling our use of the room, I would like to again discuss and finalize our mixing plan with my own management."

Houston, we have a problem [82]

I called our gentleman of research: "Bob, this lab's blender is not new and worse, they've just given it a fresh coat of paint trying to be helpful to us. I don't want to have our batches be the first lot of research materials to go through this device. We don't have time for them to recertify the machine's specs and use by deploying some standard materials coupled with some protocol-driven cleanup procedure." No expert myself, I was guessing that type of GMP work with proper documentation and sequential sign-off can at best take several weeks in itself. Bob was obviously not happy and said he would immediately discuss the situation with Roger. No cell phones at the time, I should stay by the lab phone as he was prepared to yank Roger out of a meeting to have an immediate discussion and to also involve the strategic planner if needed. Perhaps our planner had another, and hopefully local partner within Canada, who could accomplish this step. As I waited for a return call I thought to myself: 'could we really afford adding time to the clock by involving yet another partner while trying to get this stuff to Germany *via* France? At least this time it wasn't me that was now going to hold things up. I felt I had made the right decision on not using the FitzMill, but now I'd leave how to move forward up to Bob and Roger. Let's hear what they come up with. Be patient Paul.' Tick, tick, tick.

Rural India

Roger was the one who finally called me back and within less than an hour at that: "Paul, you made the right call on not using the blender. It must be really old because the newer ones are now made of aluminum so that the metal itself never needs refurbishing. This mill may actually go back to our collaborator's earlier days when they worked with brewing companies and they were homogenizing various grains and hops. It may not even have been meant for fine pharmaceuticals. In any case, cleaning protocols require complete recertification of the machine prior to reuse and that can take several weeks. The good news is that it is permissible to hand-blend the materials through sieves having specified mesh sizes. You can do this in just an aseptic area rather than in a sterile manner. Sterile conditions will only be required for our actual formulator once they have received our certified GMP raw drug. The Canadian lab does have an aseptic space but as we now know, you'll have to look that over closely before you begin. You should wear surgical type gowns, head-face protection and gloves. They also claim to have all of this for you but, again, please look things over very carefully. Give me a call if you're not happy with anything along these lines. In the meantime I have alerted one of our folks in the pharmaceutics department to get the appropriate sieves up to you immediately, and he has agreed to stay to instruct and fully assist you in the hand-blending process. He is preparing to fly-out this afternoon, so please plan to pick him up at the airport later today." After receiving the flight information, I realized how much networking Bob and Roger had managed to accomplish in just the less than 1-h' time that I had waited for a reply. Quite impressive even by today's modern communication advantages. I never did ask Bob if he had to 'yank' Roger out of another meeting for their initial discussion, nor whether the strategic planner had to again be consulted. For all I know, the strategic planner may have, himself at that point, been standing by the guillotine, or maybe that's just my imagination now toying with me as our esmolol story gets held-up right at the finish line.

My pharmaceutics colleague was of India-Indian decent and outwardly retained considerable pride in such a heritage. I not only respected this but was happy to encourage it as we shared my two-bed, single hotel room for the night. However, I had to think seriously about his request the next day at the lab when he assured me that his pagri (Indian turban) had been freshly washed for just this occasion. Actually, the pagri did appear to be at least as protective as my surgical cap if not even better, and I will admit that it was more attractive. Although it seemed apparent as a process, I really knew nothing about the specific technique for how to properly blend solids through the sieves and so I was at his instructor's mercy in that regard. As manager, I went with the turban for him and a cap for me. Maybe the pagri was his version of Chi's spatula superstition and so if it helped him it helped us. Taught the proper shaking and powder capture technique, I gradually fatigued from the repetitive process after an hour or so while my Indian colleague continued to work at a steady pace at my side just a few feet away. Looking over at him standing in his turban, face mask, gown and gloves, while shaking sieve after sieve-load without pause, I could not help but picture the harvest of natural product drug materials being done in rural India. 'Kinda like' an ancient art going on here and the image was a far cry from the fancy lab I had found myself in just a few weeks before—but whatever or by however, the job that was needed at this particular moment in time was indeed getting done, mostly by my colleague. Thank God for this man in a turbin.

We finished in just less than a full day. Since anything not staying on our collection (filter) paper could not be gathered-up for inclusion in our final lot, we 'lost' a few grams. In my synthetic medicinal chemistry efforts where target/test compounds are initially prepared at the mg level, this seemed like an enormous loss of material. Most chemists will admit that after a few years of practicing chemistry, they may have had to perform at least one, if not more, 'benchtop ex-tractions.' However, sensing my desire to go after this material, my wise colleague quickly informed me that we had actually done a very good job in our net harvest and that our percent loss was really quite minimal as these processes go. Then he confided that when we collected our five analytical samples rotated from different locales across our final lot, we would need more than 250 mg for each because not only would we do our own complete chemical QC again, we would also be adding tests for pyrogens. The latter involved trying to spike temperatures in live rabbits done by a GLP-approved vendor who will need these larger samples. Our Canadian lab partner will be doing the same as part of their GMP-DMF documentation. Thus, another couple of grams would be needed for these last studies on our raw drug product. No problem, we had plenty of extra material. We gathered our samples and I once again made a border crossing carrying several vials of a white powder accompanied by paperwork similar to what I had carried previously. This time, however, the samples were considerably larger in that each was nearly 1 g. Again luckily, I was not challenged at the border.

What should we call this stuff?

Our final material passed all of our chemical QC specs, the Canadian lab's QC/DMF tests, and a commercial vendor's GLP pyrogenicity testing. On schedule according to our revised development plan, we now had the luxury to think about other matters like finalizing a proper name for the material beyond its internal designation as 'ASL-8052.' ACC's Director of Regulatory Affairs had already conducted a survey for name suggestions that could be sent to the US approval body for this, namely the United Stated Adopted Names (USAN) Council. Everyone knew that we needed to end our name in 'olol' since that had become the accepted standard format for all of the previous BBs on the market. I suggested that as the racemate of a compound with only one asymmetric center, no stereochemical designation needed to be indicated because that would be taken to be the case for us just as it has for the other already approved racemic BBs. Our two preferred suggestions were 'estolol' and 'promolol.' These were published for public opinion/comment and then discussed by the USAN Council. Both were rejected, the first because 'est' is reserved for estrogen-like compounds and the second because the prefix 'pro' is reserved for prodrugs. Replacing the 't' in our first suggestion with the 'm' from our second suggestion, the Council itself suggested 'esmolol HCl.' This was quite satisfactory to all of us, my own thought being that it also captured in part (although in reverse lingually) our drug's key structural feature, namely the methyl ester that endows ultrashort activity. I found a pleasing symmetry again to be present while casting my favorable vote on this matter.

On to Germany via France

My direct participation on this project was finally over. Given my focus and dedicated effort for such a long period, I felt as if 'my baby' was now grown and had just left home to head-off to college. Further hurdles did not arise, or at least of significance enough for the rest of us to hear about or of a chemical nature wherein I might have been consulted. In the end, our discovery and development teams had respectively survived and met our timeframes, and together we would all remain on schedule hereafter. Briefly, our Canadian partner used its courier services to deliver raw drug, esmolol HCl, to our French collaborator capable of producing GLP/GMP formulations. They produced the latter as premixed, sterile solutions in sealed ampules and then used their own courier services, in turn, to deliver the clinical supplies for the first-in-man study that then began immediately in Germany. The latter was done within 2 weeks, although completion of a final report proceeded for more than a month.

A Goldilocks grand slam, Cinderella rags-to-riches saga

Esmolol decreased heart rate in a pharmacology textbook relationship with dose (titration drip rate). It had a rapid onset with a distribution half-life of 2 min. As hoped, its elimination half-life was near 10 min even after prolonged infusions, actually even a little better as it was 9 min. It was evenly distributed in the body (3.4 L/kg volume of distribution) with a total clearance of 285 mL/kg/min. There were no significant signs of sympathomimetic (intrinsic) activity, membrane depression, cardio-toxicity or overt toxicity. Even when heart rate was significantly lowered to nearly a potentially threatening level, return to normal rhythm was immediate upon stopping the esmolol infusion and was without overall incident.

    After we've spent so much of our earlier part of the story 'at the plate' only to arrive at 'a full-count' and then having to wait and wait for this last 'pitch' before making solid contact that just leaves the ball 'hanging high-in-the-air,' it's now quite appropriate for us to finally rally with CONSIDERABLE ENTHUSIASM: Esmolol, our true Goldilocks compound [53] from among those in its close structural series, has just become a 'grand slam home run' [83] within the actual clinic. And given ACC's (formerly ASL's) stature as depicted in Fig. 23.1, this is truly a Cinderella story [84] as well, because the analogy in baseball would be to define ACC at the onset as an underdog team amid the major, highly rated teams, wherein it had then somehow made its way into the World Series (a 'Cinderella team') and it had just now won the playoff by 'one run' after 'a grand slam' that allowed them to come from behind with two outs in the bottom of the final inning of the final game.' All very exhilarating and finally, for the 'rags-to-riches' [85] theme, AHSC was soon purchased by Baxter-Travenol, another smaller but highly prospering medical supplies distribution company. Part of this arrangement involved re-selling AHSC's research arm, namely ACC, to Dupont and for that our story is probably best now conveyed by a direct quote from C&E News [86]: "The purchase of ACC by Dupont was made for $425 million, $190 million of which was dependent upon the progression of esmolol into the market." Now that was a nice amount of money back in 1987 for a compound based upon the, in hindsight simple, hypothesis that an external ester, upon metabolic hydrolysis, would no longer be welcome at β-adrenergic receptors even though the parent pharmacophore is still intact. It should be noted that only upper management held stock/options in ACC so I and my family did not financially benefit in any personal manner from this purchase, something I feel compelled to again mention later in Part 3 of the present, overall work. Alternatively, I did receive the ACC President's Award for Scientific and Technical Excellence which in addition to an inscribed plaque, provided an all-expense-paid trip for my family of seven to visit Cape Canaveral for a couple of days and then Disneyworld with 3-day passes for everyone. That award at least made up for some of those Sunday absences. I still use a pair of side-by-side pictures to decorate my office wall that together nicely couples these effort-award experiences from the esmolol story (Fig. 23.26). They also remind me of a theme conveyed by a Nobel prize laureate in C&E News that I came across somewhat later. This theme is also quite apropos for the pair of pictures and most certainly serves to help me stay 'grounded' as a scientist. According to this laureate, all of the organic chemistry-related science from the molecular to the planetary has already been thoroughly worked-out and there remains only fill-in delineation and practical applications. Thus, the esmolol story becomes just a simple application and, alternatively, truly basic chemical science efforts now reside beyond these two points, namely in the study of subatomic particles with its unexplained phenomena like quarks, and in the study of outer space with its unexplained phenomena like black holes.

To market, to market [88]

An IND was assembled shortly thereafter and it was able to include both the French formulation work and, quite gratifyingly to all of us, the German clinical study data and its favorable conclusions. No electronic filing at that time, it was submitted to the US FDA by FedEx delivery in March 1982 as a 14 volume set having 5250 pages weighing 45 pounds. The synthesis and process chemistry reports initially generated by Chi and I were integral components of the overall DMF, as was our final GMP production effort while working with ACC's key regulatory-approved Canadian partner. An NDA followed about 4 years thereafter and it gained FDA approval very quickly. Esmolol HCl entered the marketplace as 'Brevibloc®' in 1987. The clock had finally quit ticking and by now Roger had replaced Glen as President so the sound of

FIGURE 23.26 A range of chemistry from planetary to molecular. Left: souvenir picture purchased during family trip to Cape Canaveral as part of ACC's award for the discovery of esmolol. Right: space filling molecular model of esmolol used later for a book cover after some reorientation to better display the planar phenyl ring [87].

jingling coins was also completely absent. The programmatic and personal guillotines were gone. Instead, success parties were being held, and ACC's parent AHSC had begun to see dollars coming-in rather than just dollars going out for this project. Ironically however, as one of my chemistry colleagues pointed out to me, the parties seemed to fall short in some regards because 'esmolol's inventor' was no longer there. By then I had moved on to 'greener pastures' or perhaps better, to 'new prospecting territories' that held significantly greater resources for such endeavors (see next section).

Esmolol is still being used to save lives on a daily basis in critical care, emergency room situations for the very young, as well as adult and elderly patients. It is also commonly deployed in the perioperative setting to provide rapid control of ventricular rate in patients experiencing supraventricular tachycardia, atrial fibrillation or flutter. It is regarded as a class II antiarrhythmic agent with several additional indications where its short duration of action is beneficial such as preventing adrenergic storm during intubation or laryngoscopy. Periodic reviews are available [89–91] and an apropos summary is that "after more than 2 [now actually 3] decades of use, esmolol continues to provide an important therapeutic option in the acute care setting" [90]. Esmolol is marketed as premixed sterile saline solutions for use by injection or by iv drip administration either alone or in combination with other infusion materials providing it is titrated individually since its weakly acidic solutions are not compatible with basic buffering systems such as phosphate. A loading or 'push' dose of 0.5 mg/kg is typically administered for 1 min and then followed by a maintenance infusion of 0.05–0.2 mg/kg/min.

Part 3. Take home lessons and brief follow-ups

Take home lessons for today

Corporate-employee-family relationships

Corporate-employee interactions

I'm thinking that this section may be most useful for practitioners who are still at the early stages of their professional careers, just as I was during the esmolol story. More seasoned practitioners will hopefully nod in agreement as they quickly proceed with their read. My first suggestion is that an enthusiastically entrepreneurial spirit and hardworking culture can be much more important than the amount of company resources. Note that this point is not necessarily intended as a pitch for start-ups and small pharma over big pharma because the latter can certainly strive to create and maintain such an atmosphere within their ranks as well, and when that happens it really does become the best situation. Furthering this theme from an interviewee's perspective, consider asking as one of the more important questions to assess: how sincerely (not 'glitzy') excited do your potential coworkers seem to be about their daily jobs? Your coworkers' expertise is generally a given at most organizational levels but obviously another aspect to also consider/insure, perhaps the level of competency and experience being especially important at the management and upper-management levels in order to avoid the potential for future 'research sticker-price or time-clock shock.' Thus, since excitement alone is not going to get one there, also assess what is the level of pharmaceutical research savvy in the upper management ranks; and especially for small companies, also among the investors? The latter is something that you may have to separately explore on your own and sometimes it can be nearly impossible if they want to remain as 'silent investors.'

Similarly, does the organization operate as an overall 'team' that can 'pass the (track) baton' effectively between various resources as appropriate, particularly if certain resources need to be engaged in a proprietary manner as extramural partners, collaborators or contractors? Now this interviewee's third question is not intended as a pitch for big pharma with all their resources over small pharma because creating such interactions/exchanges in a seamless and expeditious manner within large organizations represents a true challenge in itself wherein 'bigger' likely often means 'harder' and/or 'slower.' Likewise, I can only hope that today's 'fashionable' academic-based 'drug discovery centers' also strive to optimize this theme despite their typical lack of financial resources to engage contractors as much as they might want/need to do.

Corporate or academic-based employees should visit the facilities and meet face-to-face with potential contractors and not just with potential partners and collaborators. I suggest that this needs to be done for every key step or study that they might participate in. This is time well spent, the alternative potentially resulting in something akin to one's precious compound undergoing homogenization in a freshly painted FitzMill. Good intentions and plans can abound among collaborators and CROs but they might not always be additionally accompanied by clear thinking. Expert consultants should obviously be contracted not just when you don't have adequate knowledge about a given situation, but also for second opinions about key strategies. However, these folks are not infallible and so remain on guard for potential flaws, especially when their suggestions appear to offer the expediency or urgency that your company is desperately seeking. Speed may be of the essence, but haste can also lead to waste. Before proceeding, step back, stop the clock for a few moments, muffle any jingling coins, and engage other staff in a non-stressful manner to carefully consider the consultant's recommendations.

Don't just accept them at face value because you've likely paid a premium price for their delivery. This is especially critical when the latter's advice intertwines with specific yet perhaps subtle details about legal and regulated aspects of the pharmaceutical business.

Finally, sticking with an interviewee's perspective for just one more moment, try to negotiate for stock or stock options as part of your pay, benefits or bonus plan discussions. I definitely learned this the hard way. However, I have no regrets about not sharing the wealth of ACC's sale to Dupont because without it I had to continue to work harder through the remainder of my career than I might have otherwise needed—but then that's only because I have indeed been able to continue to thoroughly enjoy basic/applied science as a hardworking profession in its own right, i.e. it's never been about the money for me other than to be a good provider for my family's basic needs. Alternatively, from a practical point of view, how can I not make such a suggestion to others because it can afford them even more options about how to proceed into the future in a financially secure manner should such a 'Goldilocks-Cinderella-rags-to-riches-saga' payday happen to occur for the company and thus also for them while holding stocks/options. Just because one does become rich in such a fashion doesn't mean they can't still continue to work hard at what they enjoy. Whatever, having become fashionable and important contributors today, I think most small companies and young investigators with much more business savvy than I had at the time, now recognize and appreciate the value in such corporate-employee relationships. And the latter is not just all financial because I think such a carrot is also a more effective way to establish the aforementioned enthusiastic corporate culture than are 'ticking clocks' and 'jingling coins.' While some of that also needs to be balanced in, the stress of 'project or employee guillotines' runs the risk of becoming counterproductive by potentially driving employees to spend a significant amount of their time and energy searching for another job, perhaps even another career. Plus, in the end, the general thought is that it can take an employer a year to refill a vacated position with a new top-notch employee. That's a lot of project down-time. Finally, stress can seemingly work for athletes during competitions and perhaps also for pharmaceutical companies in our highly competitive enterprise, but for the latter it must be carefully balanced at all times with the emotional state of the individuals on board, and that's most tolerable for them when the stress is spread evenly across the entire organizational team from top to bottom. ACC did have that spread going for it in general, although as you have also seen during the esmolol story, the guillotine did become a bit too personal for me at times.

Employee-family interactions

A people topic that's hard to address since I'm certainly no psychologist, sociologist or anything along those lines, but perhaps worthwhile within the context from my own experiences during the esmolol story, so please allow me to give this a shot. Obviously, researchers may be single, single-parents, or a couple of significant others with or without children. I submit that in all cases what I am about to convey can be applicable and may be extremely valuable. It is beneficial to have some type of support group/person for when an individual's times become seemingly tough and/or highly stressful. Tough (sometimes synonymous with meritorious) research problems can, without a doubt if you're serious about them to begin with, become stressful; and unfortunately more frequently than probably should be, one cannot necessarily count on having an understanding boss or organization wait patiently while little progress is being made. You've heard about this situation arising during the esmolol story on more than one occasion. And again here, for me that support group has always been my family, namely Judy and our children. Today, however, it's clear that it has become far more challenging just to raise a family because both spouses are likely to be working and trying to share house/family care while juggling between two, rather than just one, busy/demanding work schedules. Nevertheless, there are three important lessons which I learned that I would like to mention here because they can, hopefully, relate back to one's balance between work and family in a positive way for today, perhaps even more so for today. Most certainly these lessons were an integral part of esmolol's discovery and development story.

First if at all possible, try to sit down as a family for dinner together every late-afternoon/early-evening and let each of the children have a chance to relate something from their day's encounters in a casual manner. Starting while they're young surprisingly allows this practice to be just as fluid even when they become teens, although today one would seemingly have to firmly 'outlaw' cell phones during this family dining/chat period. For me this practice has translated to rising each day between 4 to 4:30 a.m. throughout my career in order to work for at least 10−12 h each day while still being able to make it home for a 5:30 to 6 p.m. dinner before next turning to the kids' evening activities and/or assistance with homework. Early on I thought I was doing this for them, but actually it was my growing family that became my own personal strength which kept me going, and it was this support group that pushed me to tackle my present job-related challenges as well as to strive for even greater personal heights in the future. Thus, this practice even if it at first seems like sacrifice, can indeed be equally beneficial for everyone in the long-run. And just so as to not scare-off any scientist wannabe students, I should make it clear that not all folks in research need to work this long of a day or seemingly as hard as conveyed by the esmolol story. I do not at all consider myself to be smarter than average folks, and Judy will be quick to testify that I am not fast at anything beyond certain sports (like ice hockey, baseball pitching and Golden Gloves boxing that I did while younger). In other words, the only special, professional thing I could bring to the competitive corporate table was the ability/willingness to 'work hard' for long hours, along with maybe some creative ('out-of-the-box') thinking at times. The many, many smarter and/or quicker-moving scientific folks that I have met in this field, can likely get my 10–12 h' worth of work stuff done in a typical 8-h day, maybe even less. Lucky for me, though, I loved the activities that I was doing, so all of it has never really ever seemed like 'work' anyway. The nature of the work itself has always inspired me to rise with anticipation/excitement at 4:00 or 4:30 each morning while experiencing only very limited moaning at the sink while splashing lukewarm water in my face. Finally, for our younger children, we kept our group get-togethers going into the evenings every Friday, Judy declaring that day to be 'family night.' They were indeed like a family party each time, with special snacks and drinks while we played games or watched television together a bit past their regular bedtimes. Today's corporate analogy would be the team building retreats which, quite disadvantaged, do not have the natural flow of a true family behind them and thus tend to feel artificial or contrived.

Second, if at all possible and along this same theme, try to practice in a unified family manner some major, positive religion. This can significantly reinforce and even enhance the wonderful benefits described above. For me as a very significant component, this meant attending Mass every Sunday morning as a family. I fully appreciate that it becomes rather challenging not to arrive late when seven people need to first reassemble themselves in the morning, especially when some have become teenagers—but it is well worth the time and effort. For this challenging effort the credit, and also make that a BIG KUDOS, must again go to Judy for pulling it off throughout our entire children-rearing period.

Third, when times get tough and stress mounts, everyone can benefit from having a 'get-away' place where they can find some peace and calm to clear their minds. The lesson is to find that place as an individualized/personalized version for yourself and then do go there when needed. It can be simple like a walking park, a gym, a yoga mat, or maybe a quiet coffee shop or just a special room or chair in your home. For me during the early period of the esmolol story when I was wondering if I would even be able to stay in the drug discovery profession at all, and to thus continue feeding my growing family, my place was Lake Alice. Not alone in my case, but rather with my family and their group strength led by Judy, but at this special get-away-time removed from each of our everyday noise and so 'free' to just relax and together enjoy each other and the remoteness of this outdoor setting in rural Northern Minnesota. I solved the tough chemical problem that I had been wrestling with in the lab shortly after returning from that type of get-away. It's still today for me, a special memorable trip where our young family of five just did nothing for a while except some swimming and fishing. It truly was a critical turning point in my professional career that kept me on the stage to eventually discover esmolol.

Medicinal chemistry

Soft drug – today's definition

Like 'prodrugs,' 'soft drug' terminology is now part of most pharmaceutical researchers' everyday repertoire. Today's internationally accepted definition is as follows [92,93]: a pharmacologically active agent that has been designed to be inactivated to one or more nontoxic metabolites in a predictable and controlled manner after achieving its therapeutic role. It is important to note that according to this definition, **a soft drug does not have to be short-acting** (discussed again later). Esmolol falls within this definition and it represents the most common type. From a historical perspective and from a design standpoint, esmolol is regarded as the prototypical soft drug. In its case, a specific metabophore (see later discussion) was appended to the classic pharmacophore for *beta*-adrenergic receptor blockade in order to program the resulting soft drug's metabolism according to a preselected metabolic pathway (esterase family) and biotransformation rate (that was further fine-tuned by steric considerations), into a metabolite that was no longer active at the *beta*-adrenergic receptor. As you have seen from the esmolol story, the resulting PK profile produced the desired therapeutic agent as an ultra-short acting *beta*-blocker that allows for moment-to-moment adjustment of adrenergic tone across the heart when it is administered by intravenous drip in either critical care or surgical settings. Fig. 23.27 further distinguishes the differences between a typical drug, a prodrug and a soft drug [14–16].

Soft drug ambiguity

While the deployment possibilities and design options for prodrugs have become reasonably straightforward across various disciplines engaged in drug discovery, this is not necessarily the situation for soft drugs in terms of either their design or deployment. Even within a medicinal chemist's toolbox, this situation remains somewhat ambiguous. As mentioned above, esmolol and its discovery have respectively served as the long-standing prototypical soft drug and classic textbook example. However, it was not I or anyone else at ACC who actually coined this two-word term. Instead, that credit goes

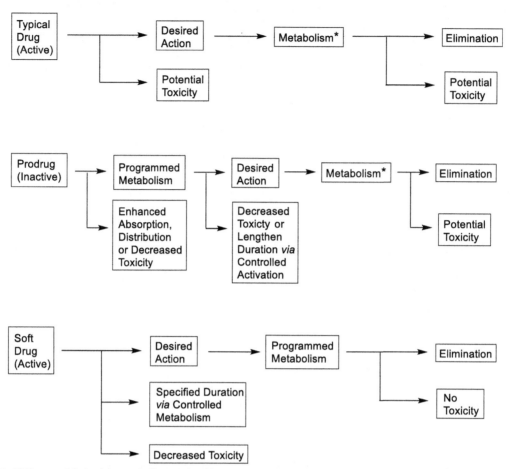

FIGURE 23.27   Different activity/toxicity metabolism relationships between a typical drug, a prodrug and a soft drug. Also highlighted are the potential benefits that can be gained by deploying prodrug and soft drug strategies. The asterisk (*) is meant to indicate that metabolism may or may not occur, the latter leading to direct excretion of the active agent. *Adapted from P.W. Erhardt, R. Khupse, J.G. Sarver, J.A. Trendel, Prodrugs: strategic deployment, metabolic considerations and chemical design principles, in: D. Abraham (Ed.) Burger's Medicinal Chemistry, Drug Discovery and Development, seventh ed., John Wiley & Sons: Hoboken, 2010, pp. 103–150; P.W. Erhardt, M.D. Reese, Soft drugs, in: Prodrugs and Targeted Delivery, Vol. 47. Methods and principles in medicinal chemistry. R. Mannhold, H. Kubinyi, G. Folkers (Series Eds.) and J. Rautio (Vol. Ed.), Wiley-VCH, STM Books, 2011, pp. 385–413; P.W. Erhardt, R. Khupse, J.G. Sarver, B.J. Kress, Prodrugs: strategic deployment, metabolic considerations and chemical design principles, in: Burger's Medicinal Chemistry, Drug Discovery and Development, eighth ed., D. Abraham, M. Myers (Eds.), John Wiley & Sons, Hoboken, 2021, pp. 1–105.*

back to Nicholas Bodor about 40 years ago [94] who, unknown to any of us at the time, had likewise been working on short-acting drugs as an academician. Although today's use of the term 'soft drug' [92,93] defines the mutually common pharmacological (and controlled PK-related) profile, Bodor's original intention was to define the term in contrast to Ariens' even earlier drug design concepts that relate to this topic. Ariens first used the phrase 'ultra-short-acting drugs' and the term 'hard drugs' in the mid-1960s [95] wherein hard drugs were intentionally designed to resist metabolic degradation. Thus, hard drugs could retain their desirable activities for longer periods of time or they could be used to avoid toxicity problems caused by reactive metabolites that are sometimes formed after *in vivo* administration of a standard drug" [15]. Notably, Bodor's design of soft drug compounds was significantly different than that used to discover esmolol. It involved the notion that when the point where a drug is metabolized is first determined *via* actual experimental testing, then this area of the pharmacophore can be considered a 'metabolic soft spot' that may be able to be converted to an ester linkage in order to achieve short-acting compounds. Bodor's strategy is closest to the internal esters approach for deactivation, but even for that, his instruction for such a design first requires obtaining metabolism data on the non-ester compound to serve as a guide for where the ester link should be placed. While quite rational in its own right, this is completely different from how the initial esmolol arrangements were designed in an *ab initio* manner prior to having experimental data relevant to metabolism. The difference is not always appreciated and hence some ambiguity can result. This is not to say that Bodor's data-derived strategy is not as useful as the *ab initio* design you have just read about, but only that it is distinctly different.

Both strategies require subsequent experimental data, sometimes considerable, to guide optimization of any originally designed soft drug motif. Bodor continued to published extensively about soft drugs during this early time period for our just evolving field [e.g. 96–99] but then he gradually turned to describing his strategy by using the term "retrometabolic drug design" which more aptly describes his method. Bodor did eventually produce some clinical candidates as well. For more recent reviews about his work see Refs. [100,101]. We soon became collegial colleagues, never really being competitors to begin with. At that time it was a situation something like the one I recounted previously with Carl Kaiser because here I was once again a 'young buck' accomplishing what the elder scientist had, so far, only been able to talk (hand wave) about. At any rate, with time Bodor and I became even closer friends, especially after I left industry and entered academe (later discussion).

It should be noted that in comparison to Bodor's retrometabolic drug design method, today's esmolol-related strategy is highly robust because its key design principles are wide-open to the imagination of a creative medicinal chemist who needs only to be thinking in terms of general physicochemical properties and what the parent drug's interaction with its receptor might entail, e.g. lipophilic (hydrophobic) versus hydrophilic forces etc.; and, of course, all thoughts always coupled with the importance of considering steric features. In both strategies, metabolism of an ester is assumed with reasonable confidence based upon reliable, long-standing knowledge derived from considerable work in the prodrugs field [14–16,102]. The key role played by steric factors in their relationship to esters and biotransformations in general, is further discussed below.

Before continuing with principles important to the chemical design of soft drugs, however, it is necessary to address one additional ambiguity that could arise around this phrase depending upon who you are talking to, namely its use 'on the street' as slang [103], or as a distinguishing legal definition in certain European countries [104]. In both of these situations 'hard drugs' are associated with greater, and 'soft drugs' with less, addicting properties relative to the specific, pharmacological context of narcotics. Those layperson and legal uses have nothing to do with the metabolic profiles of such compounds and they have nothing to do with our ongoing technical discussion herein which also emphasizes chemical structure and medicinal chemistry principles. Indeed, quite the opposite, in the medicinal chemistry context of barbiturates the shorter acting agents are usually the more potent (thus 'harder drugs' by these alternative definitions) while the longer-acting agents are typically less potent ('softer drugs'). That said and hopefully clarified, now back to the design of (the global pharmaceutical industry's accepted use of the term) 'soft drugs.'

Soft drug design

The design blueprint afforded by esmolol's success is simply: (1) Consider the ligand you want to devise so as to have a programmed metabolism (often times quick but not necessarily always so) leading to an inactive metabolite, and use either known data (e.g. X-ray, SAR, etc.) or a hypothesis to construct a working model about how it might bind to its biological surface of therapeutic interest (e.g. receptor or active site); (2) Place an ester (preferably a carboxylic acid ester) anywhere (within or adjacent to the perceived/hypothetical pharmacophore) on the ligand prioritized by your considerations undertaken in (1) and synthesize both it and its two hydrolyzed species one of which will be either the ester's acid partner (preferred with the other species then becoming an alcohol) or a hydroxy-group (and the other species an acid) retained near the pharmacophore or on either of the segmented pharmacophore components; (3) Test all three species in the efficacy assay to see if the placement shows promise, i.e. no matter which of the arrangements is operative, the ester should retain significant activity while neither of the hydrolyzed species should show significant efficacy; (4) Reiterate placement options until a promising site is identified; (5) Test the ester version in either a composite of hydrolytic enzymes (e.g. human esterases et al.) or in an *in vivo* model (preferably dog) so as to ascertain its rate of hydrolysis; (5) Adjust rate to perceived desirable level by either adding innocuous steric features to slow down metabolism (or eliminate spontaneous hydrolysis if observed), or reducing the effect of the existing steric features to speed up metabolism/spontaneous hydrolysis, the latter can be attempted by direct removal of the impeding bulk, or by distancing the ester from the steric features using a connecting chain optimized in an incrementally increasing fashion (e.g. methylene, ethylene, propylene). Interestingly, when considering both existing SAR and that generated during the soft drug campaign outlined above after several reiterations, it becomes useful to track neutral and negative SAR as well as the typical positive SAR. The role that such SAR can play during drug discovery in general is further discussed below. A simple pictorial version of one of the most fundamental applications taking from the soft drug design strategy iterated above is depicted in Fig. 23.28. Also see Fig. 23.29 in the subsequent SAR section that pertains to a more general situation of additionally considering efficacy along with several of the other ADMET parameters during target compound design and especially hybridization as useful positive, neutral and negative SAR accumulates for various of these parameters as well as that for metabolism and one's inherent knowledge about the latter as iterated above.

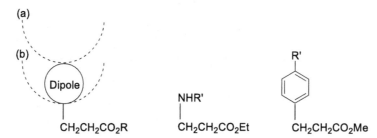

FIGURE 23.28 Fundamental application of the soft drug design strategy leading to a simple but highly useful metabophore species (far-left structure) when a programmed metabolism or short duration is a desired feature of the target compound. The dipole can be either pronounced like an amino (protonated ammonium) group (also see Fig. 23.19), or subtle like a simple phenyl ring. This useful metabophore can be appended to the pharmacophore (a) or when possible, be designed to be partially encompassed by the pharmacophore (b). If a short duration is desired, R should be methyl; if longer durations are desired, then R can be sequentially increased in size (steric features) while testing duration. The middle structure exemplifies a highly polar useful dipole linkage with considerable synthetic possibilities for merging with a pharmacophore. Its ethyl ester is meant to achieve a moderately short duration. The far-right structure exemplifies a highly lipophilic and subtle but useful dipole system. This arrangement was deployed within esmolol. For the latter, the phenyl ring is also part of esmolol's pharmacophore and R is a methyl that was needed for an ultra-short duration.

Metabolism's rule-of-one

Certain principles that I initially learned during the discovery of esmolol became even more firmly established while I continued to pursue my interests in drug metabolism as an advocate (see below) and then as a 'hobby' throughout the remainder of my career. I call them 'metabolism's rule-of-one' [14−16,92,93] by analogy and without meaning to diminish in any way Chris Lipinski's 'rule-of-five' [92,93,105]. Chris is a collegial colleague whom I introduced to the international lecture circuit many years ago while we were both early advocates of considering ADMET parameters during the early stages of drug discovery, my interest lying in "M". Although Chris quickly become famous for his "A" related rules, he will still argue in a friendly fashion with me about whether they should really be regarded as 'rules' or rather as just 'flags' (my view) during HTS campaigns or during early lead generation and hybridization exercises (appreciate that Pfizer already had huge compound libraries to survey even during that time which was still very much more recent, however, than our esmolol story). It should be noted that the methodological practice of using the rule-of-five continues to evolve [e.g. see 106].

Applicable to the metabolism of small molecule xenobiotics in general, the rule-of-one has five components which can be prioritized as follows: (1) If there is a simple ester present in the compound, it will typically get hydrolyzed as the predominant metabolic pathway unless it is sterically hindered; (2) All metabolic processes are exquisitely sensitive to steric features, where the rate for any given event is inversely proportional to the immediate steric environment at its biotransformation site; (3) Decreasing the electron density at the site of a CYP *P*-450-mediated biotransformation will generally attenuate aromatic hydroxylation, but have little impact on *N*- and *O*-dealkylation processes; (4) Replacing all of the hydrogens on the carbon *alpha* to a heteroatom by fluorines can completely block CYP-mediated *N*- or *O*-dealkylation at that location, while replacement of an aromatic hydrogen by fluorine may have little impact on hydroxylation at that location beyond that of electron withdrawal; and (5) as an often excepted parameter, increasing the xenobiotic's overall polarity will tend to decrease its metabolism, particularly with regard to oxidative pathways, and *vice versa* [as taken directly from 92, 93].

Five comments can help appreciate these principles [92,93]. First, the 'rules' derive from more than a 20-year review of small molecule drug metabolism information from a wide variety of public and private sector sources, including unpublished communications with numerous experts in the field. While there are five rules, their 'singular' name stems from the overwhelmingly high predictive probability [107,108] associated with the second rule compared to the other four where exceptions are not uncommon. Second, as a predictive tool pertinent for how a new drug and potential analogs might behave during *in vivo* drug metabolism studies, and ultimately upon administration to humans, no additional provisos are needed, as the rule's application already attempts to add probability assessments on top of the relevant metabolic possibilities [107,108]. Third, although not previously iterated in this manner, it is clear that the fields associated with prodrugs and drug targeting have completely embraced the theme of the first rule as the most prominent strategy toward preferentially allowing for quick release of the active agent [14−16,102]. Fourth, in addition to specific drug design strategies, however, the rules are also applicable in generally ranking the merits of compounds within large libraries and in virtual structural space or specific contexts, where assessment of metabolic probabilities, rather than just metabolic possibilities, becomes highly beneficial—make that critical [107,108]. Finally, it is also apparent that investigators sometimes are quick

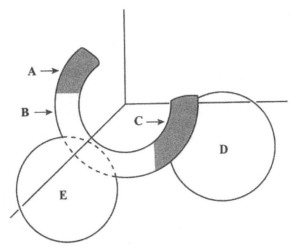

FIGURE 23.29 3D pattern recognition example illustrating the simultaneous consideration of efficacy and ADMET-related SAR parameters during drug design and lead selection. In this case, a useful acronym becomes SXR wherein $X = E$ for efficacy (typical pharmacophore relationships), Ab for absorption, D for distribution, M for metabolism (metabophore relationships as highlighted in this chapter), Ex is for excretion and T is for toxicity. SXR space can be mapped early-on by experimental results from HTS of a moderately sized, directed compound library wherein an E template has been identified. Compounds serving as probes of SXR space should be judiciously selected for *in vivo* testing based upon the structural information that they may be able to deliver in either a positive, neutral or negative manner relative to each X parameter. In this example molecular portions A and C represent requisite pharmacophoric features oriented in space by structural elements B. Lacking E and any distinguishing structural features associated with general metabophore relationships, B delivers neutral SAR during testing with regard to both E and M. Thus, B likely contributes toward prolonging the elimination half-life which, in turn, eventually increases T in off-target compartments. Although not necessary in the present example, confirmation for these suspicions can be tested by deploying just portion B of the parent's overall structure as a surrogate scaffold attached to groups having known $DMET$ profiles. This type of confirmation was done 'in reverse' (to remove unwanted properties) as part of the esmolol story because more than one variable was in question and one of those involved the key hypothesis itself. The reverse strategy can likewise be done in the present example as an effective working model without first establishing such a confirmation. Structural space D represents features that favorably contribute to Ab and initial D while space E represents favorable metabophoric space. Thus, in this case a range of suitable functionality defined by A can be used in the northwest region of the E pharmacophore while selected functionalities or bioisosteres that reside within the structural space defined by the overlap of C and D should be utilized in the southeastern region. The latter design motif optimizes Ab and initial D features while retaining E such that prodrug scenarios should not be needed to address these parameters. Alternatively, soft drug strategies should be contemplated to address the toxicity issue, especially since the SMR field of the overall 3D map, region E, indicates that there is some overlap with structural portion B. Lacking pronounced functionality, perhaps an unassuming phenyl group might be considered as a surrogate within or attached to this structural region, or perhaps an amino group if the B region is truly neutral to such modifications. In either case, the subtle or more pronounced dipole insertions could then be linked by two carbons to an ester group subject to metabolism whose rate can be predetermined in a manner inversely proportional to the degree of additionally inserted steric bulk. Note that in this example, a pure soft drug need not be the absolute target. Even if the acid resulting from esterase activity retains considerable E activity (then not a true soft drug by definition), if it leads to programmed elimination of the parent compound in a manner that reduces toxicity, then this target goal could still be regarded as successful. *Figure used directly with permission form P.W. Erhardt, Medicinal chemistry in the new millennium. A glance into the future, in: M.S. Chorghade (Ed.), Chapter 2 in Drug Discovery and Development, Vol. 1 Drug Discovery, John Wiley & Sons, Hoboken, 2006, pp. 17−102.*

to assume that replacement of an aryl-H by F will block hydroxylation at that site, and especially so when they have been successful experimentally. As iterated in rules 3 and 4, even those successes are likely a result of the net decrease in electron density prompted by such a substitution, rather than by an actual blockade of this particular metabolic event (e.g. see NIH-Shift [92,93,109]). Simply put, decreasing electron density within the ring attenuates aromatic hydroxylation.

Compound libraries [10]

While the attributes of a *"drug-like"* profile are in no way to be minimized, the first and foremost properties for a proposed test series during early drug discovery is certainly their *"assay-likable"* profile, i.e. if a compound can't be tested you won't get a result, or even worse, it may be perceived that one has an inactive compound and erroneously derive a negative SAR data point. Indeed, for the case of esmolol, the entire research program was almost halted when its first two series of target compounds were either too insoluble or too plagued by i.a. to be able to be effectively screened. To test my concept about external esters in this case required first synthesizing a series of related compounds just to identify a suitable surrogate scaffold. Although not foolproof for all new scenarios, the esmolol story provides evidence that its underlying hypothesis/concept can indeed work. Thus, this particular confirmatory step need no longer be undertaken as an investigation in itself. In the later follow-up section, you will see that esmolol's design concept has been subsequently used successfully by other investigators for several other marketed drugs. Similarly, while *"preferred scaffolds"* and *"privileged structures"* generally refer to the attributes of such molecules relative to their potential clinical performance as drug candidates, this concept need not be so restrictive. For example, it may be useful to think in terms of the various preclinical testing steps to exploit attributes to examine a specific hypothesis that will ultimately be reapplied to the actual lead series. This was done for esmolol when the N-external esters served as important testing surrogates to help confirm the merits of the overall "external esters hypothesis" and to firmly establish that it is not necessarily required to fragment a pharmacophore in order to eliminate activity.

Although the redundancy of close homologs within a compound library may detract from *"molecular diversity,"* their inclusion should not be precluded altogether, and certainly their pursuit should not be regarded as a mundane operation once a lead has been selected. Additional comments in this regard are provided below in the SAR category.

SAR [10,11]

The sole production of efficacy-associated *"positive hit"* data as typically derived from HTS methods can seriously detract from creative problem-solving medicinal chemistry. Note that verification of the key hypothesis leading to pursuit of the external esters was actually gleaned from the novel 'negative SAR' data found for the proposed carboxylic acid metabolites, with the anticipated 'neutral SAR' data associated with the esters also falling nicely into place. Thus, tracking positive, neutral and negative SAR data for at least efficacy, and whenever feasible also for as many of the ADME parameters as possible, can be extremely important for advancing and 'fixing' candidate compounds as they continue to progress toward development. A pictorial example of a scheme for tracking and utilizing such multiple data sets is depicted in Fig. 23.29 [11].

While all of hydrophilic/hydrophobic and/or substituent electronic properties may be important for various selected interactions with a given biological surface, steric effects are by far the most reliable and universally applicable parameter when trying to monitor and exploit SMR. Recall that the esmolol ester family was essentially nonresponsive to the electronics of the "leaving group." Simply put, I could not beat Mother Nature electronically. Alternatively, the esterases were exquisitely sensitive to localized steric parameters in terms of enzymatic hydrolysis rates. Indeed, the inverse relationship between the degree of steric bulk and the rate of drug metabolism within such localized vicinities, is so much more generally reliable compared to any of the other attempted physicochemical correlations, that it does indeed deserve to be considered as "metabolism's rule-of-one," just as was advocated during the earlier discourse of this topic. Ya gotta love the simple physics' principle of the situation: two bodies cannot occupy the same space at the same time; steric considerations 'rule.' But then again, perhaps one shouldn't get too adamant about even this SMR because of the potential for 'mutual molding' [110] (and that later also becoming 'induced fit' [see 111 for a recent and brief review]) between molecules (small and especially large) attempting to interact with one another in the biological realm; so maybe a big flag here instead when such movements are applicable. Thus, perhaps it's better to also just 'tuck-all-that-away' when considering steric effects and SMR—not too deeply, however, so still at the forefront of one's considerations.

Finally, the importance of pursuing methyl, ethyl, propyl etc. as a medicinal chemist fine-tunes a lead is worth mentioning again in this category, i.e. the *"Goldilocks"* nature of esmolol with its distinct 9 min half-life was found to reside only at $n = 2$ within its closely related series of analogs. With esmolol still saving lives daily within ERs across the globe, what more can be said about the potential merits of carefully conducting such systematic molecular scrutiny in a deliberately methodical manner? Never again succumb to the mindset "methyl, ethyl, futile" even if the phrase is being delivered by your boss because he/she thinks that such 'small step' efforts only slowdown the discovery process.

Process chemistry

If you're a drug discovery medicinal chemist in big pharma, be prepared to pass the baton to your internal experts in process chemistry and assist in any tech-transfer reports or actual lab activities that they may request. For the small pharma drug discovery scientist who is an organic chemist or a synthesis-inclined medicinal chemist, this 'work' can be just plain fun. In this regard, I feel very fortunate to have been able to have had first-hand experience in this aspect of drug development. But don't get carried away in that regard and try to take on too much by yourself. Lineup with a meticulous analytical chemist who knows GLP procedures right from the start of your own efforts. Proactively contact specialty experts such as radiolabeling services (contracted for small companies or present among the myriad of large company resources), perhaps after you've toyed with routes on paper but certainly before you venture into the lab in any serious manner. Contact, and if at all possible finalize, a relationship with a GMP-approved chemical manufacturing lab as early as feasible, e.g. you've considered some routes on paper and you have successfully utilized a reasonable route that is scalable to ca. 100-gram levels but have not yet spent a lot of time further optimizing it. Your GMP-approved partner may see something you didn't consider, and they will most likely have a better appreciation for the supply and cost issues associated with large amounts of various starting materials and reagents for any given route.

Biology

The obvious benefit of today's HTS campaigns is that they can work their way through huge libraries of test compounds to find initial 'hits,' and sometimes many of such, in short-order. Same for docking of virtual libraries, although we should instead call those virtual hits and thus today's version of hand-waving hypotheses that even when accompanied by rigorous computational considerations/reservations, still requires one to then 'make-em-and-test-em.' A downfall for HTS, however, is that historically it has not been very knowledge-generating beyond such efficacy assessments [9,11–13] although this finally appears to now be changing as more complexity is being added in a multi-assay-HTS comparative manner [112]. Perhaps more serious is sometimes a lack of also periodically checking low, medium and high hits as representatives for various structural templates in an *in vivo* setting as early as possible during the screening process. In addition to assessing the merits of a particular scaffold and confirming the relevance of the *in vitro* models in terms of efficacy, *in vivo* testing may reveal unwanted toxicity. This may be especially so if repetitive dosing can be undertaken *via* a few days study [8,113]. Interestingly, the discovery of esmolol represents an extreme version of the latter suggestion because it actually relied upon a dog model as a key component of the front-line screen to immediately ascertain overall metabolic stability. Although time consuming, this allowed the entire *in vivo* hydrolytic complement to be discerned as the outcome from a black box [39] of individual contributors, rather than quickly conducting a biochemical battery of discrete enzyme assays in an HTS manner. Had the latter been undertaken, SAR would have been very likely to cross back-and-forth from one test system to another for various molecular series, perhaps even to the extent of becoming non-interpretable as a composite of data relative to the key hypotheses being explored (net hydrolysis by this family of enzymes). When relying on esterase activity as part of the design of either prodrugs or soft drugs, consider dogs as a good *in vivo* model for the composite of such hydrolytic enzymes in humans. Furthermore, to this same point: ACC's early studies [e.g. 114] that primarily relied upon *in vitro* experiments are still frequently cited today wherein they suggest that esmolol's hydrolysis occurs almost exclusively by esterases present within human red blood cells. While the cited work is an excellent study/report, I remain somewhat skeptical that this is the complete answer. Here's my reason why. Again I'll begin by emphasizing that there is typically a myriad of enzymatic pathways (in this case esterases) eagerly standing-by to biodegrade a given xenobiotic such that even if during a battery of *in vitro* testing, one enzyme is significantly more active than all of the others, the suitability or preference of a substrate for a given enzyme (which is what such studies are actually assessing), is only one of five criteria leading to what will eventually happen *in vivo*. The other four criteria are: (1) The relative abundance of a suitable enzyme in various compartments; (2) The relative concentration of substrate achieved in various compartments having suitable enzymes; (3) The relative duration that a substrate may spend in a compartment having a suitable enzyme; and (4), The appreciation that any single enzyme selected as a major contributor must be compared to and **compete with the entire composite of all other enzymes** even if the latter are only weakly suitable as individual contributors, taking into account all of entries (1)−(3) for each of those as well. This is expressed in mathematical form within Fig. 23.30 wherein a simplified example is also recited. Bottom line: even a weakly acting enzyme as determined from a battery of *in vitro* assays, may become relevant *in vivo* when the weaker enzyme has higher relative concentrations in tissues where the substrate tends to accumulate and reside for longer periods of time; let alone considering how the higher acting enzyme may be able to compete against the summated cast of multiple, more weakly acting enzymes.

Now this is by no means meant to imply that *in vitro* metabolism studies are not worthwhile. Certainly if an enzyme shows no desire to react with a substrate at concentrations above what can be expected *in vivo* (or better at concentrations within the compartment where the enzyme resides), then it can likely be ruled-out as a contributor for producing at least a first generation metabolite. Likewise, once some specific enzymes have been determined to be relevant *in vivo*, then their assessment at the *in vitro* level for SAR (SMR) data can be highly valuable during further hybridization of the substrate's structure, e.g. removal or instillation of discrete steric features. Finally, referring to Fig. 23.30 above, it may be very useful to use *in vitro* methods to directly compare competing pathways that are suspected to be competitive with the desired metabolic pathway, especially if they can compromise the desired overall therapeutic activity profile. For this latter case, manipulating steric features can again be used in attempts to widen the margin between the competing pathways.

A final useful lesson pertaining to the biology arena was learned by accident from the esmolol story. Its ester construction leads to an acid metabolite where, fortuitously in general, such species can be considered as substrates for the organic anion transporter (OAT [92,93]) systems that serve to eliminate such natural and xenobiotic materials from the body. Unlike today, these transporters, or for that matter transporters in general, were not well-appreciated at that time. For esmolol, its metabolite was shown to be essentially inactive at its receptor. However, this ideal situation may not always be

Drug metabolism (DM) by isolated CYP enzymes as a function of time (f_t):

$$CYP_1 \ DM \ f_t = [D]_t \bullet CYP_1 \ Fit \bullet [CYP_1] \bullet [CoFE]_t$$

For example, experiments determine that drug's CYP_1 Fit is 80% of standard substrate that essentially undergoes complete metabolism under identical conditions of $[D]_t$ (t = 0), $[CYP_1]$, $[CoFE]_t$ (t = 0) and time (t).

Repeat experiments for 5 different CYPs, i.e. CYP_n where n = 2-6. For continuing simplified example, CYP Fits are respectively determined to be 20% for each of CYPs n = 2-5 and 0% for CYP_6 all relative to standard substrates specific for each CYP.

CYP_6 can be ruled-out as a significant contributor to overall biodegradation.

Extrapolating CYP_1's role (relative to all CYP contributions) toward initial DM *in vivo*:

Can assume $[CoFE]_t$ are adequate for each CYP and are not diminished as a function of time: $[CoFE]_t = 1$ and can be dropped as a multiplier in the equation.

CYP_6 need not be considered, leaving four CYPs to be additionally considered, so $\sum_2^5$ CYPs.

Consider CYPs initial metabolic contributions stemming primarily from three different compartments (intestinal mucosa, liver and lungs), so $\sum_1^3$ Tissues.

$$CYP_1 \ DM \ f_t = \frac{\sum_1^3([D]_t \bullet 80\% \bullet [CYP_1])}{\sum_1^3([D]_t \bullet 80\% \bullet [CYP_1]) + \sum_2^5 \sum_1^3([D]_t \bullet 20\% \bullet [CYP_n])}$$

Just as an example, assume: (i) Expression levels are the same for all of the selected CYPs in each of the selected tissues; and, (ii) Drug concentrations are about the same across all three tissues as a function of time. Then:

$$CYP_1 \ DM \ f_t = 240 \ / \ 480 = ca. \ 50\% \ of \ initial \ CYP\text{-}related \ biotransformations$$

FIGURE 23.30 Key parameters influencing the roles that drug metabolizing enzymes play during the biotransformation of a xenobiotic. Specifically shown is an example for a CYP enzyme studied at the *in vitro* level and the challenges associated with extrapolation of that data to the *in vivo* setting. Terms not already defined above: $[D]_t$ = drug concentration as a function of time; CYP_n Fit = drug's suitability as a substrate compared to standard agent that undergoes essentially linear, complete metabolism (e.g. say by t = 15 min which is the typical duration cap for common isolated CYP or microsomal fraction incubation studies [25,28,29]); and, $[CoFE]_t$ = concentration of requisite cofactors and energy supply as a function of time (more relevant for phase 2 glucuronidation/sulfation reactions where the conjugate partner supplies can be depleted with time during prolonged metabolism activities [92,93]). In the example, six CYPs were considered because only that many from this enormous enzyme family largely account for nearly all CYP-related metabolism of xenobiotics [92,93]. Similarly, only three tissues were considered for the initial period of a xenobiotic's entry into the systemic circulation after oral drug administration, namely the intestinal mucosa and liver as part of the first-pass [92,93] and the lungs as a *pseudo*-first-pass organ because it is also 'loaded' with xenobiotic-metabolizing CYPs [92,93]. After this initial exposure, continued blood flows to these tissues has been tabulated for various species including humans and their percentages (and the simplified example's assumption of [D]) should no longer be considered to be the same. Likewise, expression levels have been tabulated for several of the more prevalent CYPs in various tissues within various species including humans. Expression inherently varies considerably between tissues and so the tabulated data can be useful to better account for this factor. However, it is also altered by prior and ongoing exposures to xenobiotics and their metabolites which can be more difficult to account for. Thus, of the variables considered and simplified for the sake of the present example, this factor in practice may be the most subject to error. At any rate, the example demonstrates how an enzyme identified as a high metabolizer of a drug from an *in vitro* assessment may be only a moderate contributor when considered as part of the overall group of closely related enzymes that also participate and compete in the *in vivo* setting. For the esterases this situation is even more pronounced because as a family, many members are ubiquitous, aggressive and often display considerable overlaps of substrate selectivity.

the case such that an accumulation of the metabolite may eventually reach a level where the receptor can be activated by it. Likewise, while esmolol's metabolite also did not reach levels that exhibited off-target toxicity, this again may not always be the case. In either of such less than ideal situations, it may become useful to enhance the suitability of the metabolite for the OATs from the 'get go,' or to at least appreciate that this becomes another aspect of design that is available for a medicinal chemist to potentially manipulate (for example, also see Fig. 23.29 and its legend). If one does need to proceed into this aspect of design, then: (1) it is another situation where the *in vitro* study of the relevant enzymes and transporter systems could be very useful; and although perhaps unnecessary to again suggest, (2) steric manipulation might then once again prove to be advantageous.

Brief follow ups

American critical care

As indicated previously, AHSC/ACC was purchased by Baxter-Travenol who sold ACC to Dupont. That was the end of ACC as a name and of the company per se. When Dupont later merged with Merck, the niche critical care research effort was eventually phased-out for larger, blockbuster-drug programs. That was the end of the ACC theme as a corporate strategy, at least in the context of a direct lineage (see next section). Brevibloc continued to be marketed by Baxter International until esmolol became generic, after which several manufacturers around the world now provide clinical supplies. At last count, over 20 chemical suppliers provide esmolol HCl for non-clinical, research use purposes.

Esmolol HCl aka Brevibloc®

Esmolol stat!

As mentioned above, esmolol HCl is still being marketed today (as Brevibloc®) to save lives on a daily basis in critical care situations, plus for several other indications involving short term control of heart rate. Quite to my satisfaction and maybe I can also appropriately confess pride, a pharmacy student pointed out to me several years ago during a lecture I was giving about β-blockers, that one of the actors on 'ER' often shouted my drug's name at the start of the then popular television series [115]. Upon watching the show, I found this to be true and in its own way served as a layperson's testimonial reinforcing how esmolol can indeed save lives for the very young, as well as adult and elderly patients. Such a scene is captured in Fig. 23.31.

When I shortly thereafter had to travel to the LA/Hollywood area for some patent consulting activity, I proudly contacted the show's PR folks to see if I could get some free backstage passes for my wife and I. By this time, Judy was more interested in the possibility of personally meeting George Clooney rather than being associated with the discovery of esmolol. At any rate, the quick response that I received was: "Paul Earnhardt - who's that? - I've heard of Dale and Dale Junior but never you - listen, our passes are very limited so I'm afraid not - sorry", and then that was immediately followed

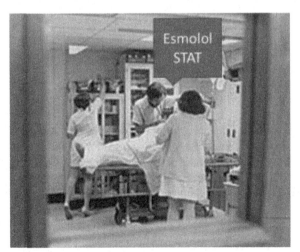

FIGURE 23.31 Picture of an opening scene from the popular television series 'ER' wherein they often yelled "esmolol STAT" [115]. I added the latter in this depiction as words coming from an emergency room physician like George Clooney who was one of the series' initial actors. *This particular picture having unidentified cast is courtesy of Wikimedia Commons: https://commons.wikimedia.org/w/index.php?search=Television+series+ER&title=Special:MediaSearch&go=Go&type=image. Opened 5/6/2022.*

by a 'click'/dial tone (which in those days of only land-phones was a hang-up without even a courteous goodbye). Thus, any personal pride I may have been deriving from that particular TV-related popularity and recognition of esmolol, proved to instead be quite limited to only our small group of drug discovery scientists and the pharmacy students required to attend my lectures.

Evolution to date

Now here's a few things I have been able to take some lasting pride in. More than 10,000 technical articles have been published about (not just referring to) esmolol. That's a rather large amount of print prompted by the simple hypothesis than an external ester, upon metabolic hydrolysis, would no longer be welcome in the lipophilic region of β-adrenergic receptors; and further, that the rate for this type of biotransformation in general, is exquisitely sensitive to its immediate steric environment such that the efficacious half-life for compounds designed in this manner can be strategically manipulated by the introduction or removal of simple molecular bulk. More personally, esmolol's success served as an initial lynch-pin that when coupled with my continuing interest in drug metabolism, led me several years ago to be one of the leading proponents for the then cutting-edge view toward considering ADMET properties during the early stages of small molecule drug discovery. Beyond being involved in an international lecture circuit for several years wherein I especially advocated such considerations relative to drug metabolism [e.g. 108,116−118], this culminated in an IUPAC book that I had the privilege to devise and edit after recruiting more than 50 experts as contributing coauthors [119]. Likewise for the initial 'terms and tutorial document' that I again had the privilege to organize as part of my involvement with the IUPAC [92]. The tutorial also recruited numerous international experts as coauthors and again focuses upon xenobiotic metabolism during small molecule drug design and development. It has now been republished in the latest (2021) ACS MEDI annual reviews in medicinal chemistry [93].

Moving from the literature into the practical realm of marketed drugs, after esmolol's arrival at least a dozen different soft drugs for a variety of other indications have been developed and introduced into the marketplace by several other organizations. Table 23.1 lists some of these agents entered during the period subsequent to when Brevibloc® was first introduced (1987) until 2010, a convenient timeframe allowing for efficient manual searching of new soft drugs entered into the marketplace [88]. Fig. 23.32 provides the chemical structures for this tabulated listing. Two recent reviews describe both some of that history such as the development of remifentanil [120] (see Table 23.1), and some of the more current developments in the soft drug arena such as what appears to be one of the latest US approvals in 2020 of the soft drug called remimazolam [121]. The first review [120], in particular, provides a nice, historical acknowledgment of the strategy employed to initially discover esmolol and then used again much later therein by their group to discover remifentanil. Discovered earlier by Glaxo Wellcome, remimazolam [121] was finally developed (Byfavo®) by PAION AG as the first ultra-short acting benzodiazepine for use as an anesthetic. The modifications of both of these agents' parent structures are shown in Fig. 23.33. As a medicinal chemist it is quite satisfying to quickly glance at many of these soft drug's chemical structures and immediately see the esmolol-derived metabophore that has been incorporated as part of their molecular frameworks so as to endow the desired PK profiles. For such 'fun' chemical comparisons see Table 23.1 and its accompanying Figs. 23.32 and 23.33. Most involve the general metabophore (ester - ca. 2 atom - dipole) and one clearly displays the explicit esmolol metabophore arrangement.

And into the future

Upon joining the University of Toledo (UT) a little more than 25 years ago (so about 10 years after working with ACC and then joining a big pharma company for the interim that also specialized in cardiovascular drugs—see next section), I considered two extensions of my earlier esmolol studies as side-projects. They were relegated to second priority, however, because for the first time I had an opportunity that results from sheer academic freedom. You should be able to guess what this opportunity was: Yes, I was finally able to focus my major research efforts upon anticancer drugs—hooray! On the downside, I now had to generate my own funding to actually conduct, rather than just think and handwave about, such research. But all of that's another story for another time, and so for now let's return, stay running on the track we started on many pages ago, and finish-off our story about esmolol as its themes continue to evolve into the soft drugs arena.

My first extension of the esmolol-related technologies involved its patent status. Since racemic esmolol would soon be going off patent, I had three MS students examine practical ways to produce only its active enantiomer [132−134]. Decreasing the amount of an inactive compound accompanying administration of an active agent, in this context sometimes referred to as 'unloading unnecessary ballast,' seemed like it might be a small but real therapeutic improvement over the original Brevibloc[Rx] product. For example, if half as much drug product was needed to deliver an equivalent efficacious potency, then half the amount of the HCl salt would need to be initially delivered at the administration site. This would be

TABLE 23.1 Soft drugs launched into the marketplace between 1988 (post esmolol in 1987) and 2010 identified from manual survey of NCE's reported in Annual Reports in Medicinal Chemistry (now Medicinal Chemistry Reviews) during this same period.

#/Name[a]	Trade Name[b]	Company[b]	Market Launch	Indication	Lead Ref.
1[c] Mivacurium	Mivacron	Wellcome	1992 USA	Muscle relax.	[122]
2 Betamethasone	Antebate	Torri	1894 Japan	Topical anti-inflam.	[123]
3 Rocuronium	Zemuron	Organon	1994 USA	Muscle relax.	[124]
4 Cisatracurium	Nimbex	Glaxo Well.	1995 USA	Muscle relax.	[125]
5 Remifentanil	Ultiva	Glaxo Well.	1996 USA	Analgesic	[126]
6 Loteprednol	Lotemax	Bausch&Lomb	1998 USA	Opthal. anti-inflam.	[127]
7 Rapacuronium	Raplon	Akzo Nobel	1999 USA	Muscle relax.	[128]
8 Landiolol	Onact	Ono	2002 Japan	Antiarrhythmic	[129]
9 Fluticasone	Veramyst	GSK	2007 USA	Antiallergy	[130]
10 Clevidipine	Cleviprex	AstraZeneca	2008 USA	Antihypertensive	[131]

[a]Specific salt partner has not been indicated. This is applicable to several of the agents.
[b]Proprietary name and organization name applicable at launch.
[c]Compounds numbered in order of introduction to the marketplace. These numbers are maintained so as to correspond with the structures depicted in Fig. 23.32. They are not meant to pertain to any structures shown in the prior text.

important because at least on infrequent occasion, irritation is sometimes observed at the site of administration (i.v. drip needle) due to the weakly acidic nature of the original product's premixed solutions. Because each enantiomer along with the racemic mixture were already part of the original patent's Markush disclosures, I regarded this type of 'new' product as an 'improved generic.' Thus, a highly practical (less expensive) route was imperative, and not just what I considered to potentially be a better version of our drug. Thinking I could call it "esmolol plus," I was disappointed when we found that the active enantiomer, that being the (S)-form like all of the other BBs, had a negative rotation. To obtain the latter we used each of the commercially available asymmetric epichlorohydrin enantiomers during initial syntheses [133]. These then served as standard targets to likewise try to hit by using more novel methods and less expensive reagents than chiral epichlorohydrin. Ultimately, we never did devise a less expensive route than that for the original compound, although we did have some success and fun with asymmetric chemistry while matriculating three MS students. The first student's chemistry, Cunyu Zhang [132], came full-circle and even beyond that of the esmolol story when he deployed chiral benzylamines as general synthons to control asymmetry at sites near the introduced amine (e.g. at the β-hydroxy position). From my earlier work [46] the chiral portion of the synthon could then be cleanly jettisoned by using well-behaved hydrogenolysis reactions to leave behind a primary or secondary amine adduct in high yields. This simple but practical route having general utility beyond β-blockers, is depicted in Fig. 23.34. However, like the optical rotation for the absolute configuration of esmolol's active enantiomer, preliminary studies with the chiral benzylamine synthons proved to be disappointing. The best diastereomeric selectivity that we were able to achieve never went higher than 25%. Alternatively, more classic synthetic routes involving asymmetric epichlorohydrin were pursued and found to be successful by another graduate student, Mike Reese [133]. Mike and especially Lei Fang [134], also tried several diastereomeric salt crystallizations and chiral chromatography experiments, along with stepping into the then somewhat new and now still interesting world of deploying enzymes during syntheses of small molecules. All three students were able to matriculate with an MS degree after having a range of chemical fun within their projects—ya gotta love academe for such purely, basic research endeavors even when they don't lead to practical synthetic methods/products. At any rate, the door to (S)-esmolol remains open. One can also imagine some additional therapeutic advantages for the single enantiomer version that would occur within humans, and thus not just the benefit associated with the surface site of infusion. However, it must be appreciated, favorably or unfavorably depending upon what's the end-game, that the critical care, niche market is not one that tends to draw a lot of generics when such a point arrives—for the same reasons mentioned in the esmolol story's introduction. An increase in consumer costs is still a factor to be reckoned with even for a small, critical care clinical indication, and especially so when associated with only modest improvements of the historical and still well-accepted agent's overall

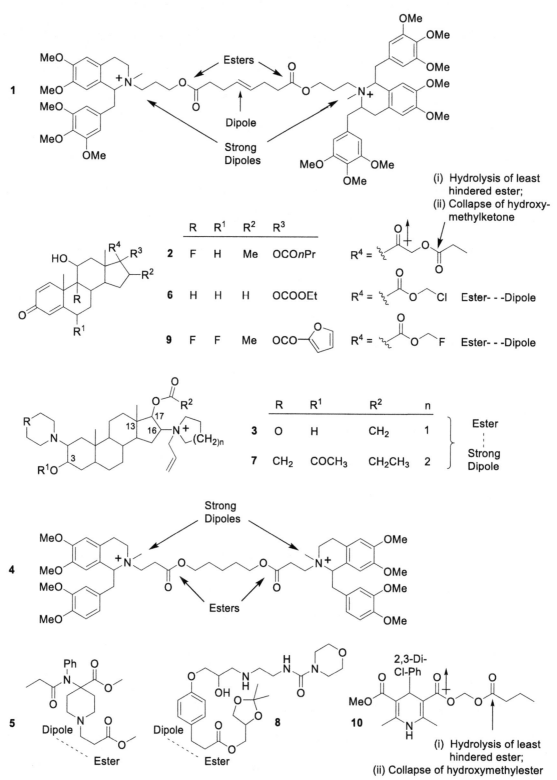

FIGURE 23.32 Structures of several new soft drugs introduced into the marketplace subsequent to the launch of esmolol. Stereochemistry and salt counterions are not shown. Numbering refers to the drug list in Table 23.1 and is not meant to correlate with numbers used for compounds discussed during the esmolol story conveyed in any of the prior text. Structure-metabolism relationships (SMR) similar to structural motifs identified during the discovery of esmolol are highlighted for each structure. Interestingly, compound 7 is a prodrug whose unhindered ester at position 3 on the steroid skeleton is metabolized first (note its two-atom distance from a nitrogen dipole) so as to quickly produce an active agent similar to compound 3. Both 3 and 7 are metabolized at a slower, programmed rate based upon a balance between their considerable steric impediments (flanking substitutions at positions 13 and 16) and metabolic enhancements from their very strong dipole (quaternary ammonium) species located 2 atoms away from the ester (position 17) where hydrolysis then leads to inactivation of the compounds. Eight of these structures are clearly external esters while drugs 1 and 4 can be considered to be both internal and external esters since a lone 'bulky quat' can still be regarded as a pharmacophore as can the 'bis-quat' skeleton common to many anticholinergic agents.

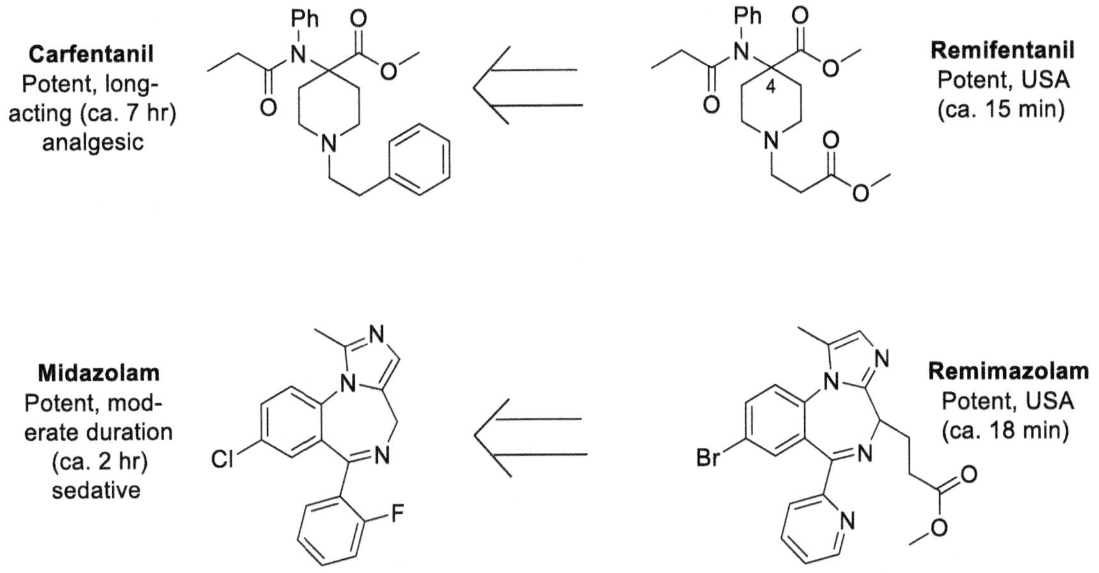

FIGURE 23.33 Structures of soft drugs highlighted in two recent review articles along with the parent drug templates from which they were designed [120,121]. Stereochemistry and salt counterions are not shown. *USA*, ultra-short acting. The exquisite sensitivity for steric inhibition of metabolism is clearly demonstrated by the stability of the methyl ester at position 4 in remifentanil compared to the methyl ester located two atoms away from the piperidine nitrogen dipole. The latter is a classical SAR motif derived from the esmolol story.

therapeutic profile. Thus, while this is likely a safe niche to go after, it will only be practical if one can keep costs the same as the least expensive generic, or better, also improve upon that aspect while simultaneously achieving the modest therapeutic gains.

For the second extension of potential soft drug projects, I generated a list of other (new use) indications derived from the esmolol-related technology based on my own thoughts and in conversations with several clinicians who I was able to contact through UT's close affiliation with the then Medical College of Ohio (then MCO and now fully merged with UT as part of a joint medical campus). One physician, Moustafa Aouthmany who was a specialist in neonatology, stepped forward with what I thought was the most compelling unmet medical need. There were some practical short-comings in the agents being used that might be fixed by deploying a soft drug strategy. The medical condition involved saving humankind's precious newborns from the potentially fatal syndrome of persistent pulmonary hypertension (PPHN where the 'N' stands for 'newborn'). One of the drug therapies being used at that time was tolazoline, an *alpha*-adrenergic blocker. Its vasodilator properties were beneficial but sometimes it seemed to worsen the situation. It was not a short-acting drug that could be quickly eliminated to recover from a worsened status of the newborn. Obviously, this is very reminiscent of John Z's earlier thoughts about the clinical need/benefit for a CV drug like esmolol. Undertaking what we today call a 'deep dive' into this situation, I could not find any definitive literature suggesting that the esterase capacity of newborns is necessarily fully competent compared to adults, or even at least adequate to expect the esmolol technology to work in an analogous fashion within newborn populations, and especially so if the newborns were premature deliveries. To address this critical point, I first had a MS student, Jing Liao [135], look at the esterase capacity of newborns by using esmolol as a standard to examine blood harvested by our neonatal physician from the baby's side of human placentas immediately after birth. Jing worked 'all hours of the day and night' to oblige our study-consenting mothers-to-be and our clinical colleague who was delivering babies and collecting/storing the placenta samples for us on ice for immediate pick-up because we needed whole blood samples (rather than the more conventional plasma samples which might have been able to be frozen while awaiting more convenient times for our assays). Importantly, we demonstrated that the newborn's esterase competency is fully comparable to that from mother's donated blood samples as well as from adults in general. Assays looked at both the quantitative disappearance of esmolol and the qualitative appearance of the acid metabolite, thanks to the work of another grad student, Cunyu, who prepared analytical grade standard materials for both analytes by using our well-established procedure for esmolol and a newly devised synthetic method to conveniently obtain its acid [70]. Jing then began to synthesize some initial probe compounds to define the parent analogs' efficacy, metabolic biodegradation/inactivation rates, and to explore the tolazoline-directed, soft drug library's SMR aspects (Fig. 23.35). Optimistically, this project was soon picked-up (in-licensed) by a corporate suitor who held our technology [136] for a few years but then,

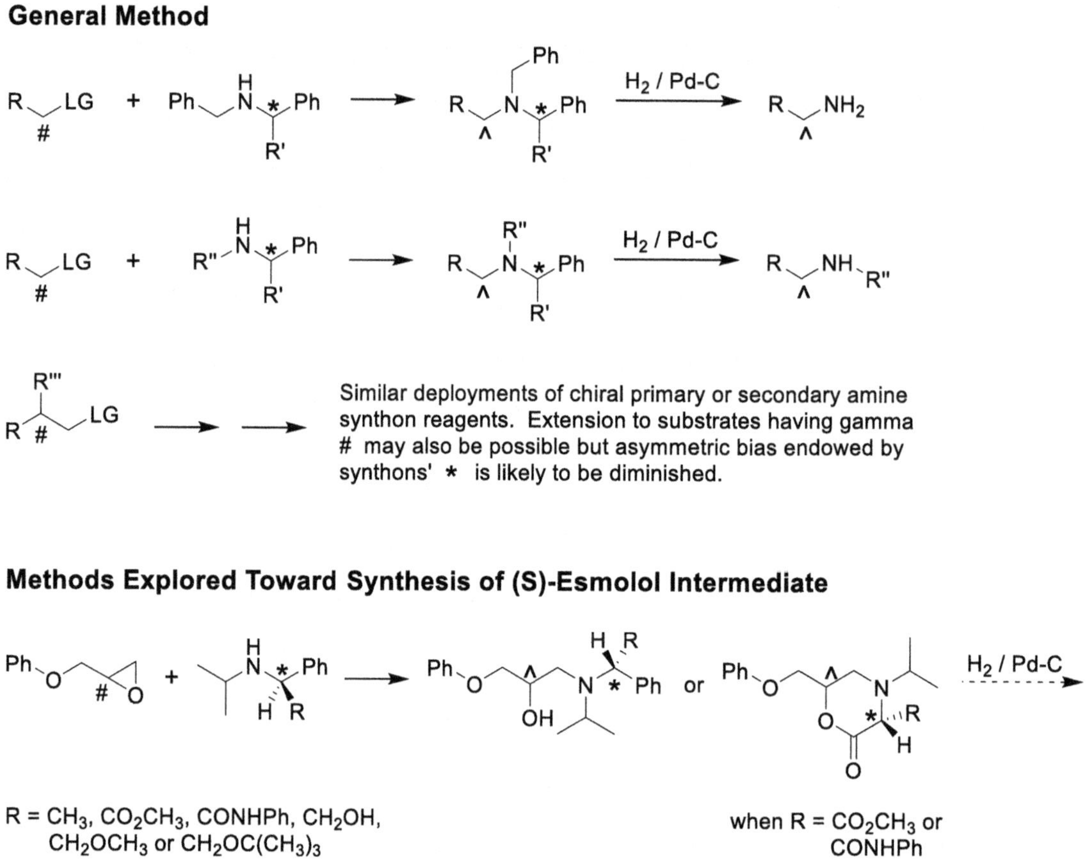

General Method

Similar deployments of chiral primary or secondary amine synthon reagents. Extension to substrates having gamma # may also be possible but asymmetric bias endowed by synthons' * is likely to be diminished.

Methods Explored Toward Synthesis of (S)-Esmolol Intermediate

R = CH₃, CO₂CH₃, CONHPh, CH₂OH, CH₂OCH₃ or CH₂OC(CH₃)₃

when R = CO₂CH₃ or CONHPh

FIGURE 23.34 General method proposed to introduce asymmetric bias into neighboring structural space while adding an amino-functionality onto a synthetic building block. Symbols: # = racemic mixture; * = pure enantiomer; and ∧ = asymmetrically biased mixture. Also depicted is the substrate utilized for producing β-hydroxy-amino-products and some of the synthon reagents explored for the specific case of constructing aryloxypropanolamines leading to esmolol. Isolation of the morpholin-2-one is reminiscent of the some of the back-attack ring forming reactions that plagued the early portion of the esmolol story and, likewise for the present cases, these did not lead to improved outcomes in terms of stereoselectivity. Note that in general, if high stereoselectivity cannot be achieved during the initial reaction or isolations leading to final enantiomeric products, then the intermediate compounds represent stabilized diastereomers that can be subjected to classical repeated crystallizations and/or regular (non-chiral) chromatography methods to further pursue the eventual enantiomeric products. While this, in itself, can be a useful consequence of the asymmetric synthon chemistry, appreciate that the yield for the desired enantiomer is then limited to only 50% from the starting moles of the racemic building block, something that is not attractive toward ultimately reducing process chemistry costs for larger batches of raw drug material.

disappointingly, never really advanced the project and eventually returned it to UT. Thus, like the asymmetric chemistry project discussed above, the door remains open to further explore this type of approach toward addressing this still unmet medical need. Furthermore, our preliminary metabolism studies demonstrate that various soft drugs for a range of different indications may also be possible within this very young, precious and delicate human population. Several other new uses for adult populations that stem from the clinical survey mentioned above are listed below in Table 23.2.

Some of the listed indications have now already been pursued by other companies, and from those, some have indeed led to marketed products as shown on Table 23.1 and in Figs. 23.32 and 23.33. Others remain open to still explore, noting here that their disclosure within the present context as possible new clinical indications, does not constitute a bar toward patenting either such uses or any structures that remain as yet to be designed [137]. For example, the situation is somewhat analogous to stating that it would be good to have a drug that can 'cure the common cold' without yet having such an actual agent in-hand. The esmolol strategy is by no means foolproof and it does not work in every molecular context even when existing SAR suggests that its requisite principles appear to be met for a given case. One still has to design the probe/candidate structures and then most importantly 'make-em-and-test-em' in the lab. Thus, specific molecular designs and creative reductions to practice remain, with perhaps only some support for the preliminary 'hand-waving' having been provided by the esmolol story and now by its follow-up.

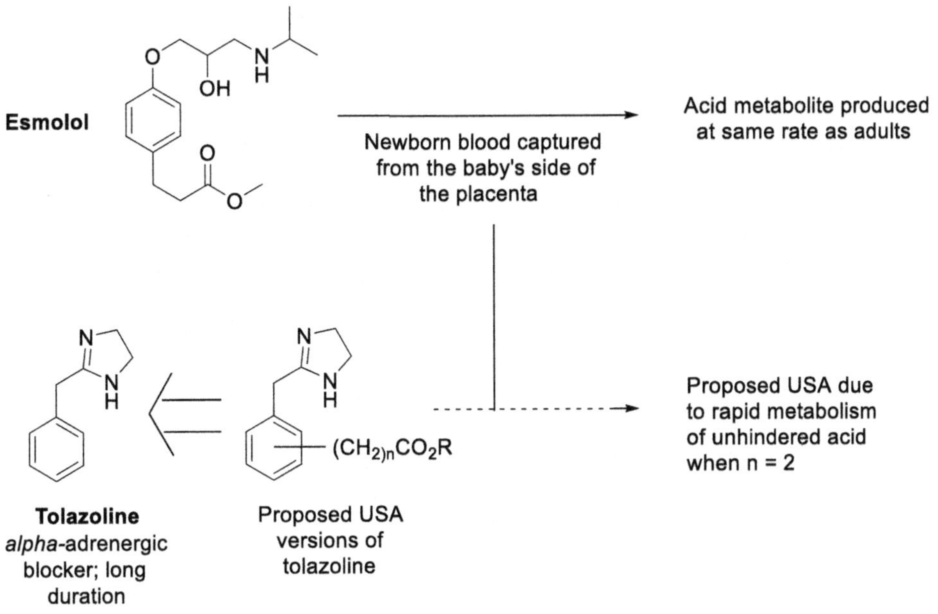

Esmolol

Newborn blood captured from the baby's side of the placenta

Acid metabolite produced at same rate as adults

Tolazoline
alpha-adrenergic blocker; long duration

Proposed USA versions of tolazoline

(CH₂)ₙCO₂R

Proposed USA due to rapid metabolism of unhindered acid when n = 2

FIGURE 23.35 Strategy to define USA agents that might be useful for treating persistent pulmonary hypertension in newborns (PPHN) while possessing an improved safety profile. SAR for this class of compounds exemplified by tolazoline, indicated that a variety of substituents can be placed at various locations on the aryl ring without detracting from vasodilation properties, some actually increasing activity. An acid moiety, however, had not yet been studied. Our suspicion was that the latter would significantly detract from activity, thus enabling an esmolol strategy to be deployed. Target compounds having an acid (as well as the methyl esters) were key probes that needed to be made early-on for this project.

TABLE 23.2 Clinical settings for which deployment of soft drug technologies could enhance existing therapeutic options.[a]

	Setting	Exemplary parent drugs
1	Localized antiglaucoma agent given by eyedrop	*beta*-Adrenergic blockers[b]
2	Weaning patients from a particular drug	Clonidine-like agents
3	Eye examination drops	Atropine
4	Neuromuscular blockade during surgery	Decamethonium, pancuronium
5	Hypertensive crises (Raynaud's)	Prazosin, indoramin
6	Consistent drug blood level when paired with sustained delivery technology	Phenytoin, carbamazepine
7	ACE inhibitor for ER use	Enalaprilat
8	Antihistamines for ER use	Diphenhydramine, famotidine
9	Bronchopulmonary crisis	Theophylline
10	Anti-inflammatory for ER use	Indomethacin
11	Antiarrhythmic (in addition to esmolol) for ER use	Lidocaine
12	Vasodilator for ER use	Nifedipine, verapamil
13	Localized action chemotherapeutics paired with localized administration or with photo-activation, sustained released implants, sutures, or wound healing preparations	Various anticancer drugs, sulfa- methoxazole, ampicillin, cepha- lexin, tetracycline
14	Numerous topical agents, e.g. psoriasis	Methotrexate
15	PPHN[c]	Tolazoline

[a]*Except for entry 1, this list was generated nearly 30 years ago when I first joined UT and surveyed several clinicians interested in discussing the need for specific short-acting or better-controlled duration drugs within their respective fields of expertise/practice. Not surprisingly, anesthesiologists were the most enthusiastic and prolific with suggestions. They were closely followed by ER emergency medicine physicians.*
[b]*See preceding discussion in text within the section entitled '**The methanol scare**.'*
[c]*Persistent pulmonary hypertension in newborns; see text for further discussion.*

Not yet exploited from this list but likely of high technical challenge (and so seemingly also of high scientific interest/curiosity) even amid today's advances in formulation technologies, is the possibility for generating prolonged delivery systems wherein steady state levels may be able to be sustained in selected compartments by matching/pairing the release of a soft drug to the latter's half-life in the same compartment, and/or its quick elimination upon leaving the desired compartment so as to reduce off-target toxicity. These interesting PK scenarios are depicted in Fig. 23.36. Release can be accomplished by either a localized formulation/device injection/implantation or a more generally circulating prodrug approach, all of for which have been programmed to provide a controlled rate desirable for achieving a specific therapeutic concentration range. Elimination is then accomplished by the soft drug strategy in a paired or matched rate programmed to hold or maintain this concentration during prolonged periods of sustained release from the delivery system.

Beyond the listing shown in Table 23.2, there is also a very intriguing possibility that the soft drug strategy could be useful in an exactly opposite manner. More speculatively, one can imagine combining the soft drug strategy of esmolol with that of Bodor (see earlier discussion in section entitled "Soft drug ambiguity") to address the most common of today's PK problems wherein one's lead compound exhibits too short of a duration of action. Typically, this fix involves

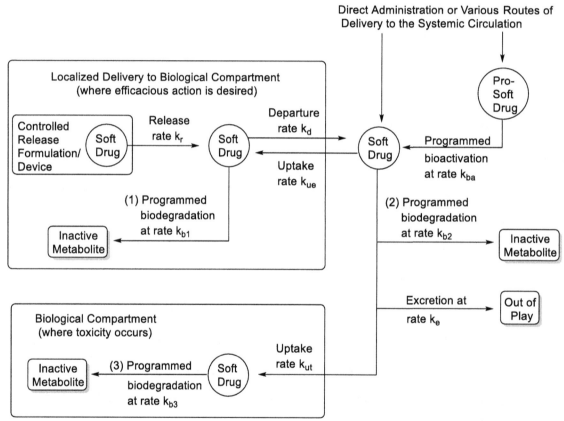

FIGURE 23.36 Using soft drug strategies to produce prolonged steady state drug concentrations in selected compartments while circumventing drug toxicity that may arise in other compartments. Although this simplified depiction captures only a small portion of the possibilities that might be derived from this theme, it does display enough complexity to exemplify the challenges that such strategies can encounter and potentially take advantage of. Note that the 'controlled release formulation' can also be a simple prodrug in which case "release rate k_r" would be the metabolic bioactivation rate (a tandem prodrug—soft drug scenario). Just a few, simple examples: (i) If after an initial loading dose having a rapid release, k_r can be matched with k_d or with the sum of k_d plus all inherent, compartment-related bio-deactivation metabolic pathways, then a steady state of active drug will be obtained in that compartment and one then has options to prompt complete bio-deactivation in either the systemic circulation (k_{b2}; most common approach taken to date), in the compartment where toxicity is known to occur (k_{b3}), or as a combination of the two; (ii) clearly, the most simple case exists when a standard drug absorbed into the circulation already achieves a reasonably long, steady-state concentration within a range adequate for prolonged therapy and there is knowledge about the uptake rate K_{ut} and metabolic activities for a compartment known to harbor toxicity from the drug's exposure such that if k_{b2} (providing steady-state is not compromised) or especially k_{b3} can be programmed to be faster than K_{ut}, then toxicity can be circumvented; and, (iii) if k_d is too slow to be useful, then k_{b1} may be one's only option other than an extremely slow, pulsed release rate k_r. 'Out of play' might only be temporary if enterohepatic recycling can be intentionally prompted as a means to provide pulsed levels of drug reentry/therapy after just a single dose, another completely under-investigated potential strategy despite the body's effective use of this pathway for recycling its endogenous steroids in terms of conserving molecular mass if not always regaining full activity.

identifying the culprit metabolic 'hot spot' in the lead compound (or 'soft spot' in Bodor's jargon), followed with attempts to eliminate or attenuate the bioconversion by altering electronic or steric effects at or near that site. However, often times the more successful this practice is, the greater the propensity for 'metabolic switching' [138,139] to occur to an entirely different location at a nearly equal or still unwanted pace of too rapid degradation. To possibly avoid the latter (an Erhardt finish here for which I will take full blame for any failures should you try this highly speculative approach), one might first add an ester to focus metabolic activity/fate to either that same site or directed to another location if needed. Since the ester placement must be tolerated for activity, the retained site or directed site substitutions should reflect efficacy neutral SAR. Retaining the same site would take advantage of acknowledging/recognizing both the overall molecule's initial metabolic hot spot plus the ubiquitous esterases' aggressive metabolic behavior, while direction to another site would potentially allow the investigator to be in control of the metabolic switch while also taking advantage of the esterases. The next step would be to slow-down the rate of ester hydrolysis by fine-tuning intentionally added steric features in a somewhat umpolung (reversed) fashion relative to the esmolol story. This overall strategy is depicted in Fig. 23.37 by way of a simple example using structural arrangements that should now look quite familiar to you. Admittedly, the premise for this is very academic and thus seemingly merits investigation in itself, perhaps by manipulating molecular constructs having well-precedented metabolic outcomes. Basically, the hypothesis would be that there may be certain molecular themes that lend themselves to preferential bioconversion pathways independent of the metabolic rates that may be forthcoming thereafter (an initial general metabolic recognition and molecular categorization/prioritization of xenobiotic surfaces that may occur before engaging them in discrete relationships with specific enzyme active sites). If that's the case, ester links may be one of those themes such that their presence may not just lend the molecule to esterase pathways but also serve to attenuate the scaffold's potential to visit (switch to) other possibilities. Alternatively, and as is what is usually thought (our present dogma), if this is not the case and there is no initial bias among any of the potentially competing pathways other than the suitability of a given substrate for each given enzyme participant at their discrete interactive levels, then this last, quite speculative 'open door' may not have really ever been open in the first place. Whatever, there's a lot left to explore within the arena of xenobiotic metabolism at the basic research level even for a sequence of several MS and PhD thesis students.

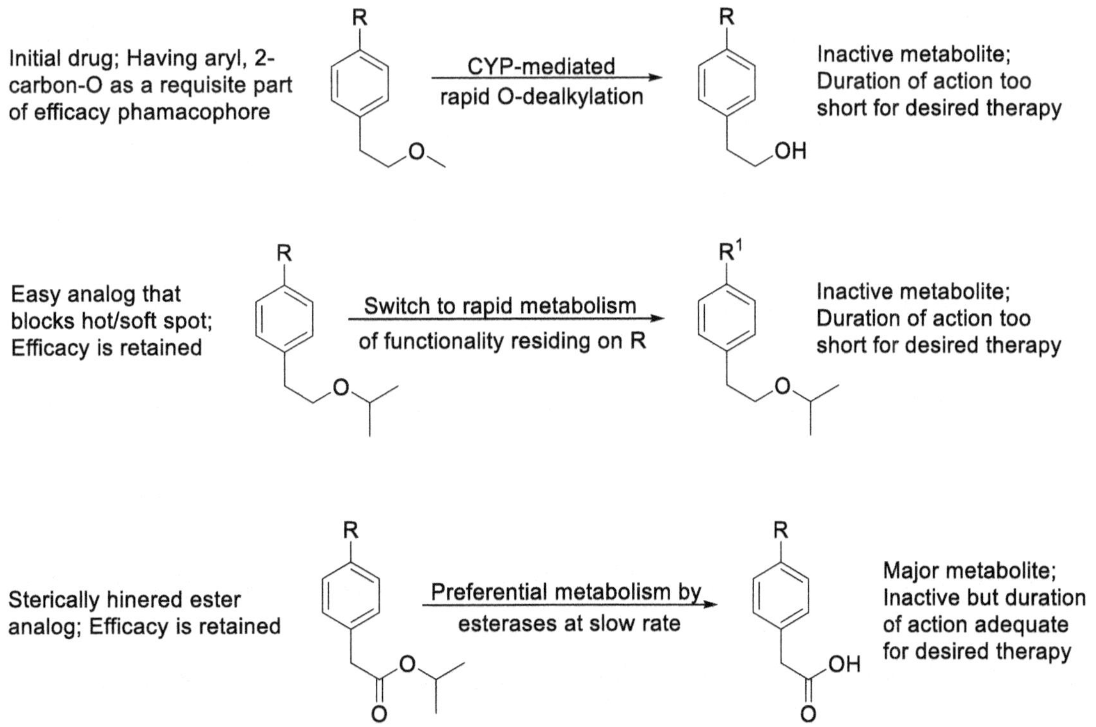

FIGURE 23.37 Using sterically hindered ester functionality to avoid metabolic switching while lengthening the duration of efficacy-related activity. In this simplified example, the original metabolism hot spot (aka soft spot) is taken advantage of in the new design, although this need not be the case. See text for more details and the speculative rationale for why this strategy may be possible.

The Erhardt family

Professionally

As suggested in the previous section about 'take home lessons,' practicality (maybe just plain common sense) dictates that one should try to get stock or stock options as part of their hiring package when going into industry as a career, and especially so if one's employer is a small pharma. That now resaid, however, I want to make it very clear that despite my own early naivety about these business arrangements which ultimately prevented us from receiving such payouts, our family has never been 'in need' financially. Bottom line: this profession has served all of us very, very well through the years in terms of food on the table and a roof over our heads if not much more than that in terms of luxury—and appreciate that's for a family of seven where for many years there was only a single source of income while Judy had her hands full with a mix of five young children and early teenagers. Alternatively, there were times when moving our family created considerable social challenges that were often difficult for each of us to manage in our own ways. In every case, our moves seemed like the most prudent path for our family to follow at the time. Taken together with mutual support, always held strongly together by Judy, we forged through such challenges as a family unit on more than one occasion (see update below that will add to our already mentioned family moves and see Fig. 23.38 which displays a complete tally of such). Making new friends in different parts of the country was not difficult because of the graciously accepting spirit that we always encountered in both the east coast and mid-west. Instead, the difficulty became having to physically leave these so-established friends upon each next move. However, no move is ever harder than the initial departure from one's clan of extended relatives who can, as in our case, consider you to be black sheep departing from the flock that, even to this date and its own continued growth, has essentially all remained in the Minnesota area. Heaven forbid that anyone should ever leave.

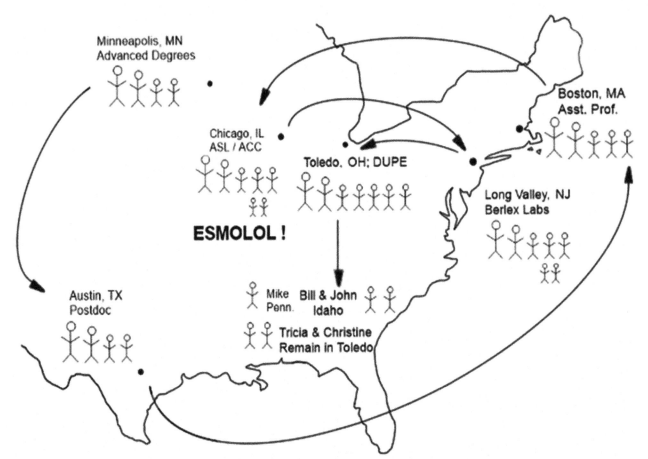

FIGURE 23.38 The Erhardt family and the moves that it made during Paul's professional science career always dedicated to the pursuit of discovering new small molecule therapeutic agents. DUPE = Distinguished University Professor Emeritus. See text for the 'ups and downs' associated with such moves. Note that all of the five Erhardt 'kids' have now married and are themselves very busy raising children of their own; thus Paul and Judy now have 10 grandchildren, five of whom live close-by in the Toledo suburbs.

Beyond providing financial security for a family, one can only hope that the work they do is of some value to others, or is at least somehow appreciated by them. This can be as basic as being able to rightfully take some pride in a restaurant table's state after bussing some dishes and wiping with a cloth (been there, done that), such that when the arrival of the next party sits down they appreciate its cleanliness. Thus, it's not so much what you do but rather how you do it that can be important here, and if something extra special is accomplished as a result of your efforts, then so much the better. As a practicing medicinal chemist/drug discovery scientist, one has an opportunity to experience both of these feelings, perhaps the second one arriving only after a bit of luck has also been thrown into the mix of the effort. In my case, the personally gratifying discovery of esmolol and then becoming a cutting-edge leader who advocated for the consideration of ADMET properties during the early stages of compound characterization and identification of initial leads, eventually did lead to prestigious recognitions by both the IUPAC [140] and the ACS. Along with my teaching efforts and research in academia (see below), the IUPAC award, in turn, contributed to my later recognition as a DUP by UT [141]. Like the latter, the ACS award is equally fulfilling since it also represents an overall career type of recognition that involved induction into the ACS MEDI's Hall of Fame [142]. While nothing like the popularly recognized football hall of fame (so there's no point in becoming too inflated by any of this), it is a distinction well-recognized and appreciated by at least my own professional peers. In any case, both the IUPAC and ACS MEDI recognitions are nice rewards for something I always thought of as a side-line or useful hobby to accompany the hard work entailed by bench-level synthetic medicinal chemistry and the extremely high odds that even one's best candidate compounds will likely never see the actual clinic.

As the younger children grew into their early school years, Judy was able to return to work while still insuring that all of our 'Humpty Dumpties' [143], that distinctive title being especially applicable to our teenagers, were off to a proper start each morning. The latter is no small task in itself and if you happen to have occasion to ask any of the "king's horses or men," they will quickly testify to this 'fact' [143]. Initially, Judy worked as one of our Church's parish secretaries, and then after another of our family moves, she became a parochial school secretary. Upon updating and renewing her teaching credentials she then became involved with elementary, junior and senior high school substitute teaching, including doing so for public schools wherein she, similarly rising very early in the morning, had to call-in one's availability/willingness to fill a vacant, suitable position on any given day. While still performing the numerous daily activities required by our family of seven around the house including the morning assemblies of our Humpty Dumpties as mentioned above, at this point Judy was also significantly adding to the family's financial security and contributing toward our eventual retirement. In addition, it should be clear from her line of professional activities, that her job satisfaction came from interacting with people under positive circumstances, the hope that she could help them get to the latter when they needed it, and the almost always successful endpoints that she did achieve toward accomplishing that end. Simply put, Judy likes working with people while I like working in a lab with molecules. Both are complicated by individual dynamics and so problem solving for either case requires creative thinking, perhaps sometimes accompanied by a bit of luck as well that's at least equally so for the case of people versus molecules. Okay, let's face it fellow chemical scientists even though we may not be quick to admit it, the behavior of people is much, much more complicated than the behavior of molecules. And, in the end, hopefully both very different types of efforts can be equally appreciated and acknowledged by others.

After discovering esmolol, the Erhardt family moved to New Jersey where I joined a big pharma CV company, namely Berlex Labs Inc. which at that time was the new US subsidiary of Schering AG. I was now a Section Head with two tiers of about ten synthetic medicinal chemists reporting to me, several hired from neighboring 'big name' (pedigree) schools like Harvard, Princeton and Yale. I thought surely that with all of these additional laboratory resources and the highly trained and talented synthetic power, we would be able to discover and move several new compounds into the marketplace. After 10 years we had generated three INDs but none of the associated compounds ever made it through clinical testing, one due to toxicity issues only uncovered during late stage testing (perhaps itself a story with an important lesson for another day), and the other two because of business decisions resulting from a change in our development cost analyses and marketing perspectives. After that I joined UT as a tenured, full professor and Director of the Center for Drug Design and Development (CD3). Like esmolol's initial ASL, the CD3 was well ahead of its time [144,145], noting that today academic-based drug discovery centers now abound across the US and Europe. During the last 25 years, we out-licensed six different technologies to companies planning to bring them to the clinic, and the latter did happen for one of them. However, that particular technology has recently been returned to UT wherein an alternate indication is now being pursued. Clearly, while esmolol became a success, the next nine agents that I discovered and translated to the point of clinical testing all fell short and never made it to the marketplace for various reasons. Ironically, a 10% market success rate for new small molecule therapeutics is a ballpark figure that is often part of the investment communities thinking and decision-making when funding early-stage technologies. I do feel very lucky to have been associated with one success story because if one then extrapolates that same figure (although perhaps this is then a bit like 'apples and oranges' [146]) to medicinal chemists in general, maybe only 10% of us can also hope to ever make such a drug discovery claim? One's gota love practicing (actually working at) this profession (scientific endeavor) for the sheer process itself with the possibility of delivering something that might contribute to moving the field forward while not stressing about achieving either its grand successes or big financial payouts, otherwise, in the end, you may be very much disappointed after your professional trip.

In my role as an educator, I have been blessed by 26 excellent graduate students (most on the PhD track) who chose me to be their professional career advisor/mentor. It has been my honor in every case to be able to do this, and I've experienced considerable satisfaction/gratification in seeing each of them go-off to succeed in their own career. As mentioned above, based upon both my internationally-recognized research and my more recent teaching/mentoring activities, UT awarded me the title of DUP [141]. I am now semiretired as an Emeritus Distinguished University Professor, a "DUPE" so-to-speak with lotsa title but no UT-direct salary—although I do have plentiful lab and office space at no cost to me, so absolutely no complaints here. I am only involved in research. I'm now conducting the latter with postdocs who are supported by extramural funding that I have, in this very different realm compared to industry, also been lucky enough to have garnered in a steady manner for several years. I presently have three different collaborative research projects with two 'pokers in the fire' [147] in terms of potential new drug candidates. Hey, I'm well on my way into another new set of 10 possibilities, so maybe one more will catch fire again and make it into the marketplace. Even if not, though, I am still very much enjoying the process and thus the overall trip which, for me, is not quite over.

Personally

As mentioned during its story, by the time esmolol's discovery/development was coming into fruition, our family had grown to five children. As they quickly matured through school accompanied by involvement in numerous team sport activities, each took-on part time jobs during their senior years of high school so as to start saving for their anticipated college expenses. This was expected and each did this eagerly. Our family move from New Jersey to Toledo (corporate to academic employment for me) at that time was accompanied by nearly a 50% reduction in salary. I had gradually 'moved-up the ladder' into middle-management (now three tiers away from the lab) by then, and wherein I was once again feeling alienated from the actual practice of research that drives me to get-outta-bed early each day. There was no way my high salary could be matched by anything less than a Dean's salary as a faculty member in academe. I had no credentials for academic administration and that was just the opposite of what I was seeking anyway. It just seemed too similar to research administration—already been there, done that, not enjoyed the process and now wanting to make a change. Alternatively, there was also a perk that by this time I was no longer too naïve to not have it also seriously considered into our family plans. The perk was free tuition for faculty member dependents which, for our family, equated to a little more than a half-million dollars sign-up bonus even in those days [148]. So how to make this happen to everyone's satisfaction? Judy and I offered each of our young adults two choices as they reached this point in their own academic lives: go to UT (which does indeed provide a good education for one's buck) but with the additional option to still live on their own in a dorm or apartment using mostly their own money for that; or go to whatever other school that they wanted while having to pay nearly all of the costs themselves. 'Getting out of the house' was as appealing to them as anything else, plus the practicality of the 'good-bang-for-a-buck' education that, as mentioned above, UT offered then and still continues to offer today. In the end, four graduated from UT gaining their undergraduate degrees without having to take-out any student loans. Our oldest son Bill had already started at East Stroudsburg University (ESU) by then but he, too, was able to attend UT as a transient student during his final year of college and his courses were then credited by ESU. Judy and I then gently nudged all of them out of the nest by enticing them to drive away in their own cars even though the latter were 'family trickle-down,' quite well-used vehicles. Still adequately functional and safe, however, these used cars' real appeal drew from the fact that they no longer required further loan payments.

Two of our three sons, Bill and John, went west: from Ohio to Idaho pursuing professions related to their degrees in environmental science. Who knew our earlier days of fun camping trips and creating temporary safe-habitats for reptiles like toads which can be fed fireflies so as to become truly psychedelic with throats glowing like strobe lights for half-the-night, could have had such an impact at a later date. Both have now achieved MS degrees related to this field from the University of Idaho while working full time to help support their own families. In addition to the wide-open spaces of the high plains and mountains, they enjoy skiing and fly fishing. Indeed, while we joke with Bill about his glowing work involving cleaning-up/moving our nation's historical pile of nuclear waste to more environmentally safe and sound locations, we likewise kid John about his fishing-for-a-living since he works with the Idaho Fish & Wildlife Conservation Office, US Fish & Wildlife Service. Alternatively, Mike chose to go back east: pursuing a profession related in various ways to his BA degree in entrepreneurial business. He enjoys serving as a coach for one of his passions as a former wrestler. Like his brothers, Mike is an avid fisherman but really quite special in his own right and almost always unchallenged by the rest of us whenever we can get out for a trip together. Ironically, he builds yard-size decorative ponds on-the-side with his son which also seems to come full circle with our earlier days of camping trip habitat assemblies. Our 2 daughters have stayed in the Toledo area. Tricia, honored as the best math major at UT's graduation ceremony, manipulated her BA degree to become the head of information technology at a small healthcare company located in Southern Michigan. She enjoys encouraging her two children in the musical and performing arts. Christine utilized her BA degree in pre-K to third-grade education to become a teacher at a local private school. Like Mike, Christine maintains one of her passions for spots, namely soccer by coaching in junior and participating in senior leagues. She was the first high school girl from the Toledo area to be invited into Ohio's Olympic Development Program, something that only then began to occur on a regular basis. All five 'kids' became married within a few years after college, although our two sons in Idaho did not move quite as fast in that regard. From this composite, Judy and I now have 10 grandchildren, five of which reside in the Toledo area. Fig. 23.39 is a pic of our extended family posing near our lake home in Southern Michigan. Yes, Judy and I have been fortunate enough to establish another 'get-away' (Fig. 23.40) similar to the one that was so important during the esmolol story (Fig. 23.3). We now hope that it can serve as a similar refuge whenever that might be needed by any of us at any time as each of us continues, and sometimes may struggle, with our own lives and our own families.

While we all have been blessed with good health, it does seem fitting to mention that I now have a pacemaker to traverse a completely blocked A-V node; and I take a β-blocker daily to lower my blood pressure (long-acting version but ironically close enough). Likewise, one of my precious grandchildren, Allie, takes a daily β-blocker as a preventative to keep her prolonged QT interval from becoming a critical issue. Before closing I want to acknowledge the enormous pride that I have for this wonderful family while also noting that Judy and I recently celebrated our 50th wedding anniversary by gathering everyone for a week-long festivity along the Florida Keys. Simply put, all the esmolol stories in the world cannot compare.

Epilogue

To close this chapter, I will once again [11] string together three older quotes that have been separately recited more recently by others relative to some important interdisciplinary developments associated with the field of medicinal chemistry; and I'll add a bit of my own sentiment as a one-liner finish:

> "We have scarcely as yet read more than the title page and preface of the great volume of nature, and what we do know is nothing in comparison with that which may be yet unfolded and applied."[a] *And as we continue to go forth and* "see further, then it will be by standing on the shoulders of the giants,"[b] *as well as on the shoulders of the many others like us who have gone before and who have thus brought us to where we are now. For* "we shall not cease from exploration. And the end of all of our exploring will be to arrive where we started, and know the place for the first time."[c] *Hopefully, we will have also enjoyed the process itself and thus had plenty of fun along the way.*[d]

[a] *Joseph Henry, more than 100 years ago, as quoted more recently by Jacobs [149].*

FIGURE 23.39 Today's Erhardt clan now grown to include 10 grandchildren stemming from five new families as the original children have each continued through life on their own paths, Tricia becoming a Seddon and Christine becoming a Marker along the way. Left-to-right: Top row Mike & son Matthew, Bill & wife Jessy, Tricia and husband Charlie Seddon; middle row: Mike's daughter Lilly, Grandma Judy, Bill's daughter Julia, Grandpa Paul, Bill's daughter Sarah, and Tricia's son Andrew; Bottom row Jon Marker with son Will and daughter Allie, Christine Marker with daughter Leah, John's wife Brenda with son Ben, John, and finally Brooke Seddon. Picture taken in 2019.

The lake home . . .

. . . on Goose Lake.

FIGURE 23.40 The year-round cabin located on Goose Lake in the Irish Hills area of Southern Michigan. A little over 1-h away from Toledo, this can be enjoyed across a regular weekend unlike the several hours drive from Minneapolis to the earlier lake cabin which required a long-weekend minimally to be able to enjoy. Thus, a convenient 'Wobegon' setting.

[b]*Isaac Newton, about 300 years ago, as quoted more recently by Wedin [150].*

[c]*T. S. Eliot, more than 100 years ago, as more recently quoted by the International Human Genome Sequencing Consortium in their report on initially deciphering the human genome [151]. Interestingly, the completion of the entire (no gaps) human genome was finally reported [152] just as I was crafting this last page for the esmolol story.*

[d]*I've added this last sentence because as I now look back from a position of semi-retirement, I feel very fortunate to have had a job that was never really 'work' at all but rather just a long, 'fun' trip made challenging at times by hurdles that although annoying or stressful for a while, actually served to avoid job complacency from setting-in and which in-the-end, did become surmountable when met with some creative thought and extra-effort that then made the overall experience even that much more meaningful and satisfying.*

Fig. 23.41, immediately below, is meant to provide a series of images that serve to summarize and conclude the esmolol story in a visual manner. As such it needs no additional caption. I hope you've enjoyed this overall read as much as I've enjoyed assembling it; and I hope this final pic will, at this point, prompt a smile as you leave the chapter.

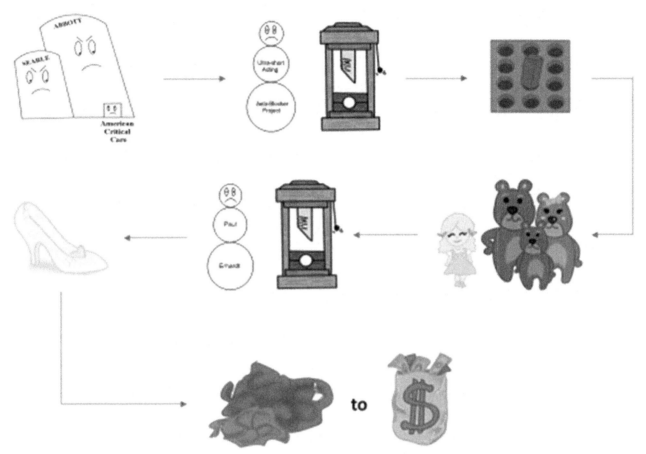

FIGURE 23.41 A visual summary of the esmolol story.

Acknowledgments

The following readers provided useful comments that sharpened the first draft of this manuscript: my six immediate family members, whom you have already met during the esmolol story, as non-chemists; two chemistry graduate students, Mathieu Geremia and Geraud Valentin, as early lab-practitioners; a postdoctoral medicinal chemistry research investigator, Divya Andy, as a mid-career lab-practitioner, and a tenured chemistry faculty, Peter Andreana, as a veteran research practitioner. Contributing to the figures were: grandson Andrew Seddon for the two cabin/lake pics in 3 and 40; both graduate students who took particular interest toward enhancing some of the figures with Geraud directly contributing to the 'Erhardt travel' depictions in 4 and 38; especially granddaughter Brooke Seddon who personally drew the guillotine diagram needed for 8 and 24, as well as creating several of the other cartoon pics needed for the summary Fig. 23.41; and finally, Divya for helping to capture a shot of my contrasting moon/molecule pictures needed for Fig. 23.26.

References

[1] S. Smith, Elementary sketches of moral philosophy. Delivered at the Royal Institution, in the years 1804, 1805 and 1806 (London, 1850). Quoted by Alan Bell in Sydney Smith: A Life; Oxford UP: Oxford, 1980. https://en.wikipedia.org/wiki/Square_peg_in_a_round_hole. Accessed 3/8/2022.

[2] J. McKay, Spoken in the Show Wide World of Sports, 1961. https://www.shmoop.com/quotes/the-thrill-of-victory-and-the-agony-of-defeat.html. Narration (line) written by Stanley Ross. https://en.wikipedia.org/wiki/Wide_World_of_Sports_(American_TV_pro-gram). Both accessed 3/8/2022.

[3] J. Zaroslinski, R.J. Borgman, J.P. O'Donnell, W.G. Anderson, P.W. Erhardt, S.T. Kam, R.D. Reynolds, R.J. Lee, R.J. Gorczynski, Ultra-short acting β-blockers: a proposal for the treatment of the critically ill patient, Life Sci. 31 (1982) 899−907.

[4] P.W. Erhardt, C.M. Woo, R.J. Gorczynski, W.G. Anderson, Ultra-short-acting β-adrenergic receptor blocking agents. 1. (Aryloxy)propanolamines containing esters in the nitrogen substituent, J. Med. Chem. 25 (1982) 1402−1407.

[5] P.W. Erhardt, C.M. Woo, W.G. Anderson, R.J. Gorczynski, Ultra-short-acting β-adrenergic receptor blocking agents. 2. (Aryloxy)propanolamines containing esters on the aryl function, J. Med. Chem. 25 (1982) 1408−1412.

[6] P.W. Erhardt, C.M. Woo, W.L. Matier, R.J. Gorczynski, W.,G. Anderson, Ultra-short-acting β-adrenergic receptor blocking agents. 3. Ethylenediamine derivatives of (aryloxy)propanolamines having esters on the aryl function, J. Med. Chem. 26 (1983) 1109−1112.

[7] P.W. Erhardt, Esmolol, in: D. Lednicer (Ed.), Chronicles of Drug Discovery, ACS Books, Washington, D.C., 1993, pp. 191−206.

[8] P.W. Erhardt, Case studies: a prodrug and a soft drug, in: P.W. Erhardt (Ed.), Drug Metabolism: Databases and High Throughput Testing during Drug Design and Development, IUPAC/Blackwell, Geneva, 1999, pp. 62−69.

[9] P. Erhardt, Medicinal chemistry in the new millennium. A glance into the future, J. Pure Appl. Chem. 74 (2002) 703−785.

[10] P.W. Erhardt, Case study: "Esmolol stat.", in: J. Fischer, C.R. Ganellin (Eds.), Analog-based Drug Discovery, Wiley-VCH, Weinheim, 2006, pp. 233−246.

[11] P.W. Erhardt, Medicinal chemistry in the new millennium. A glance into the future, in: M.S. Chorghade (Ed.), Chapter 2 in Drug Discovery and Development, Vol. 1 Drug Discovery, John Wiley & Sons, Hoboken, 2006, pp. 17−102.

[12] P.W. Erhardt, J.R. Proudfoot, Drug discovery: historical perspective, current status and outlook, in: J.B. Taylor, D.J. Triggle, P.D. Kennewell (Eds.), Comprehensive Medicinal Chemistry II, Volume 1, vol 1, Elsevier, Oxford, 2007, pp. 29−96.

[13] P.W. Erhardt, Drug discovery, in: M. Hacker, W. Messer, K. Bachmann (Eds.), Pharmacology: Principles and Practice, Elsevier, Oxford, 2009, pp. 475−560.

[14] P.W. Erhardt, R. Khupse, J.G. Sarver, J.A. Trendel, Prodrugs: strategic deployment, metabolic considerations and chemical design principles, in: D. Abraham (Ed.), Burger's Medicinal Chemistry, Drug Discovery and Development, seventh ed., John Wiley & Sons, Hoboken, 2010, pp. 103−150.

[15] P.W. Erhardt, M.D. Reese, Soft drugs, in: Prodrugs and Targeted Delivery, Vol. 47. Methods and principles in medicinal chemistry. R. Mannhold, H. Kubinyi, G. Folkers (Series Eds.) and J. Rautio (Vol. Ed.), Wiley-VCH, STM Books, 2011, pp. 385−413.

[16] P.W. Erhardt, R. Khupse, J.G. Sarver, B.J. Kress, Prodrugs: strategic deployment, metabolic considerations and chemical design principles, in: D. Abraham, M. Myers (Eds.), Burger's Medicinal Chemistry, Drug Discovery and Development, eighth ed., John Wiley & Sons, Hoboken, 2021, pp. 1−105.

[17] R.V. Smith, P.W. Erhardt, D.B. Rusterholz, C.F. Barfknecht, NMR study of amphetamines using europium shift reagents, J. Pharm. Sci. 65 (1976) 412−417.

[18] Early Waters' "Prep-500" device for which many companies now offer much more efficient (solvent sparing) medium pressure chromatography systems such as Teledyne's commonly used "CombiFlash" series of instruments.

[19] W.C. Still, M. Kahn, A. Mitra, Rapid chromatographic technique for preparative separations with moderate resolution, J. Org. Chem. 43 (1987) 2923−2925.

[20] T.O. Soine, A. Zhelva, M.M. Mahandru, P. Erhardt, L. Bubeva-Ivanova, Natural coumarins VII: isolation and structure of a new coumarin, peuruthenicin, from *Peucedanum ruthenicum* M.B, J. Pharm. Sci. 62 (1973) 1879−1880.

[21] T. Higuchi, V. Stella (Eds.), Pro-drugs as Novel Drug Delivery Systems. ACS symposium series 14, American Chemical Society, Washington, D.C., 1975.

[22] This phrase is a take-off from the 'spirits of Christmas past, present and yet-to-come,' which are ghostly characters in the novella written by Charles Dickens entitled A Christmas Carol that was first published in 1843 by Chapman & Hall: London. The popular book has never been out of print. The story has been adapted many times for stage, opera and film in numerous countries around the world. Its plot revolves around the fictional character Ebenezer Scrooge who was an unhappy miser (note today's use of his name as a synonym for miser) that becomes a happy, generous man after being sequentially visited one night by the ghosts of his former business partner and the three spirits mentioned above. https://en.wikipedia.org/wiki/A_Christmas_Carol. Accessed 3/29/2022.

[23] Written and first recorded by John Denver in 1966, this song became highly popularized shortly thereafter by the folk group Peter, Paul and Mary. https://www.google.com/search?gs_ssp=eJzj4tFP1zcsNM1KLoo3zzVg9BLLSU0sy8xLV8jPU0hUyEotUSjIScxLBQDp3Qx9&q=leaving+on+a+jet+plane&rlz=1C1GCEB_enUS964US964&oq=leaving+&aqs=chrome.1.69i57j46i512j46i433i512l2j0i512j0i433i512j0i512l3.6690j0j15&sourceid=chrome&ie=UTF-8. Accessed 3/9/2022.

[24] An American comedy-drama television series about a frontline field hospital during the Korean war that aired on CBS from 1972−1983 based on the 1968 novel by Richard Hooker (MASH: A Novel About Three Army Doctors) and adapted from the subsequent film having the title M*A*S*H. MASH is an acronym for Mobile Army Surgical Hospital. https://en.wikipedia.org/wiki/M*A*S*H_(TV_series). Accessed 3/9/2022.

[25] R.V. Smith, P.W. Erhardt, S.W. Leslie, Microsomal O-demethylation, *N*-demethylation and aromatic hydroxylation in the presence of bisulfite and dithiothreitol, Res. Comm. Chem. Path. 12 (1975) 181−184.

[26] R.V. Smith, P.W. Erhardt, Nash determination for formaldehyde in the presence of bisulfite, Anal. Chem. 47 (1975) 2462−2464.

[27] P.W. Erhardt, R.V. Smith, T.T. Sayther, J.E. Keiser, Thin-layer chromatography of apomorphine and its analogs, J. Chromatogr. 116 (1976) 218−224.

[28] R.V. Smith, P.W. Erhardt, J.L. Neumeyer, R.J. Borgman, Metabolism *in vitro* of potential apomorphine prodrugs, Biochem. Pharmacol. 25 (1976) 2106−2107.

[29] J.P. Rosazza, M. Kammer, L. Youel, R.V. Smith, P.W. Erhardt, D.H. Truong, S.W. Leslie, Microbial models of mammalian metabolism. O-Demethylations of papaverine, Xenobiotica 7 (1977) 133−143.

[30] G. Keillor, Lake Wobegon Days, Viking, Minneapolis, 1985. ISBN 0670805149.

[31] R.J. Borgman, P.W. Erhardt, R.J. Gorczynski, W.G. Anderson, (±)-(E)-2-(3,4-Dihydrox-yphenyl)cyclopropylamine hydrochloride (ASL-7003): a rigid analog of dopamine, J. Pharm. Pharmacol. 30 (1978) 193−195.

[32] P.W. Erhardt, R.J. Gorczynski, W.G. Anderson, Conformational analogues of dopamine: synthesis and pharmacological activity of (E)- and (Z)-2-(3,4-dihydroxyphenyl)cyclopropylamine hydrochlorides, J. Med. Chem. 22 (1979) 907−911.

[33] P.W. Erhardt, Curtius conversion of acids to amines under neutral conditions *via* an anthrylmethyl carbamate, J. Org. Chem. 44 (1979) 883.

[34] R.J. Gorczynski, W.G. Anderson, P.W. Erhardt, D.M. Stout, Analysis of the cardiac stimulant properties of 2-(3,4-dihydroxyphenyl)cyclopropylamine (ASL-7003) and 2-amino-6,7-dihydroxy-1,2,3,4-tetrahydronaphthalene (A-6,7-DTN), J. Pharmacol. Exp. Therapeut. 210 (1979) 252−258.

[35] P.W. Erhardt, Topographical model of the renal vascular dopamine receptor, J. Pharm. Sci. 69 (1980) 1059−1061.

[36] P.W. Erhardt, (E)-2-(3,4-Dihydroxyphenyl)cyclopropylamine and renal vascular dopamine receptor topography. Refinement of a receptor model, in: A. Carlsson, J.L.G. Nilsson (Eds.), Acta pharm suec., supp. 1983 (2), Symposium on dopamine receptor agonists, Swedish Pharmaceutical Press, Stockholm, 1983, pp. 56−64.

[37] P.W. Erhardt, Renal vascular dopamine receptor topography. Structure-activity relationships that suggest the presence of a ceiling, in: C. Kaiser, J.W. Kababian (Eds.), ACS Symposium Series, 224, Dopamine Receptors, American Chemical Society, Washington, D.C., 1983, pp. 275−280.

[38] A 1965 American musical-drama film called *The Sound of Music*, about a Catholic postulant serving as a governess for an Austrian family all of who survived WW II. The film version was written by Ernest Lehman and produced/directed by Robert Wise after adapting it from a 1959 stage play written by Lindsay and Crouse with music by Richard Rogers and Oscar Hammerstein. All are based on a true story taken from the 1949 memoirs "*The Story of the Trapp Family Singers*" recorded by Maria von Trapp. https://en.wikipedia.org/wiki/The_Sound_of_Music_(film). Accessed 3/10/2022.

[39] This phrase stems from slang initially used by the Royal Airforce during the mid-1940s to describe a pilot's navigational instruments; and later extended to convey any sort of test system from which the output derives from mechanisms that are undefined to the user. https://www.etymonline.com/word/black%20box. Accessed 3/14/2022.

[40] J.P. O'Donnell, S. Parekh, R.J. Borgman, R.J. Gorczynski, Synthesis and pharmacology of potential β-blockers, J. Pharm. Sci. 68 (1979) 1236−1238.

[41] R.B. Woodward, F.E. Bader, H. Bickel, A.J. Frey, R.W. Kierstead, The total synthesis of reserpine, J. Am. Chem. Soc. 78 (1956) 2023−2025.

[42] A.F. Crowther, L.H. Smith, β-Adrenergic blocking agents. II. Propranolol and related 3-amino-1-naphthoxy-2-propanols, J. Med. Chem. 11 (1968) 1009−1013.

[43] A.F. Crowther, R. Howe, L.H. Smith, β-Adrenergic blocking agents. 10. (3-Amino-2-hydroxypropoxy)anilides, J. Med. Chem. 14 (1970) 511−513.

[44] R.F. Borch, D. Bernstein, H.D. Durst, Cyanohydridoborate anion as a selective reducing agent, J. Am. Chem. Soc. 93 (1971) 2897−2904.

[45] R.F. Borch, A.I. Hassid, New method for the methylation of amines, J. Org. Chem. 37 (1972) 1673−1674.

[46] P.W. Erhardt, Benyzylamine and dibenzylamine revisited. Synthesis of *N*-substituted aryloxypropanolamines exemplifying a general route to secondary aliphatic amines, Synth. Commun. (1983) 103−113.

[47] J. Augstein, D.A. Cox, A.L. Ham, P.R. Leeming, M. Sanrey, β-Adrenoceptor blocking agents. 1. Cardioselective 1-aryloxy-3-(aryloxyalkylamino) propan2-ols, J. Med. Chem. 16 (1973) 1245−1251.

[48] L.H. Smith, Cardio-selective β-adrenergic blocking agents, J. Appl. Chem. Biotechnol. 28 (1978) 201212.

[49] M.S. Large, L.H. Smith, β-Adrenergic blocking agents. 19. 1-Phenyl-2[[(substituted-amido)alkyl]amino]ethanols, J. Med. Chem. 23 (1980) 112−117.

[50] J.J. Barlow, B.G. Main, H.M. Snow, *beta*-Adrenergic stimulant properties of amidoalkylamino-substituted 1-aryl-2-ethanols and 1-(aryloxy)-2-propanols, J. Med. Chem. 24 (1981) 315−322.

[51] "Funeral pyre" is a lyric borrowed from the song "*Light My Fire*" released in 1967 by the rock band 'The Doors,' one of the most successful American rock bands as a quartet from 1965-1971 and then as a trio until 1973.

[52] This epigram is credited to the English author/playwright John Heyward in 1542 and as recorded in his 1546 work A dialogue conteinyng the nomber in effect of all the prouerbes in the English tongue. https://en.wikipedia.org/wiki/John_Heywood. Accessed 3/14/2022.

[53] The phrase 'Goldilocks effect' is used by several different disciplines. I have used it in numerous lectures about esmolol's discovery and eventually published it in that context as well [10]. In my case it is intended to mean 'just right' amid a series of lower and higher molecular homologs. The phrase is taken for this type of meaning from various English stories written in the mid-1800s about 'Goldilocks and the Three Bears' all of which are probably best credited to being derived from a much earlier Anglo-Saxon fairy tale for which historical tracking becomes difficult, https://owlcation.com/humanities/goldilocks-and-three-bears. (Accessed 14 March 2022).

[54] S.-T. Kam, W.L. Matier, K.X. Mai, Arylcarbonyloxypropanolamines I. Novel β-blockers with ultra-short duration of action, J. Med. Chem. 27 (1984) 1007−1016.

[55] R.J. Gorczynski, A. Voung, Cardiovascular pharmacology of ACC-9089 − a novel, ultra-short acting *beta*-adrenergic receptor antagonist, J. Cardiovasc. Pharmacol. 6 (1984) 555−564.

[56] V.S. Murthy, T.-F. Hwang, L.B. Rosen, R.J. Gorczynski, Controlled β-receptor blockade with flestolol: a novel ultrashort-acting β-blocker, J. Cardiovasc. Pharmacol. 9 (1987) 72−78.

[57] J.G. Grohs, G. Fischer, G. Raberger, Effects of flestolol, an ultra-short acting β-adrenoceptor antagonist, on hemodynamic changes produced by treadmill exercise or isoprenaline stimulation in conscious dogs, J. Cardiovasc. Pharmacol. 15 (1990) 175−181.

[58] This idiom derives from millers during the 1400s who used their noses to check if the stones on their grindstones/millstones were overheating while they laboriously pedaled foot-driven devices to grind grains and cereals. Its first citation appears in the 1532 publication "*A Mirror or Glasse to know thyself*" written by John Firth. https://www.phrases.org.uk/meanings/keep-your-nose-to-the-grindstone.html. Accessed 3/14/2022.

[59] P.W. Erhardt, R.J. Borgman, J.P. O'Donnell, Method for the treatment or prophylaxis of cardiac disorders, 1983, pp. 1–9. U.S. Patent 4,387,103.

[60] S.-T. Kam, P.W. Erhardt, R.J. Borgman, J.P. O'Donnell, Method for the treatment or prophylaxis of cardiac disorders, 1983, pp. 1–14. U.S. Patent 4,405,642.

[61] P.W. Erhardt, R.J. Borgman, Compounds and method for treatment or prophylaxis of cardiac disorders, 1984, pp. 1–13. U.S. Patent 4,450,173.

[62] W.L. Matier, P.W. Erhardt, G. Patil, Esters of 3-(3-substituted-amino-2-hydroxy-propoxy)-4-substituted-1,2,5-thiadiazole derivatives, 1985, pp. 1–12. U.S. Patent 4,508,725.

[63] P.W. Erhardt, C. Woo, Ethylenediamine derivatives of aryloxypropanolamine aryl esters having various medicinal properties, 1985, pp. 1–6. U.S. Patent 4,556,668.

[64] P.W. Erhardt, R.J. Borgman, J.P. O'Donnell, Method for the treatment or prophylaxis of cardiac disorders, 1986, pp. 1–9. U.S. Patent 4,593,119.

[65] S.-T. Kam, P.W. Erhardt, R.J. Borgman, J.P. O'Donnell, Compounds for treatment or prophylaxis of cardiac disorders, 1986, pp. 1–13. U.S. Patent 4,604,481.

[66] P.W. Erhardt, W.L. Matier, Esters of thiadiazole oxypropanolaine derivatives and pharmaceutical uses, 1986, pp. 1–20. U.S. Patent 4,623,652.

[67] P.W. Erhardt, W.L. Matier, Esters of aryloxypropanolamine derivatives and medicinal uses, 1987, pp. 1–20. U.S. Patent 4,692,446.

[68] P.W. Erhardt, W.L. Matier, Esters of aryloxypropanolamine derivatives, 1989, pp. 1–21. U.S. Patent 4,804,677.

[69] P.W. Erhardt, W.L. Matier, Esters of aryloxypropanolamine derivatives, 1990, pp. 1–21. U. S. Patent 4,906,661.

[70] C. Zhang, P. Erhardt, Hitting a soft drug with a hard nucleophile: preparation of esmolol's metabolite by treatment with bis(tributyltin)oxide, Synth. Commun. 42 (2012) 722–726.

[71] C.M. Lai, R.W. Krasula, Steady-state concentrations of methanol and formic acid, 1981, pp. 1–5. Unpublished internal report (eventually submitted to the US FDA as part of esmolol IND).

[72] R.W. Krasula, Production of methanol as a metabolite of ASL-8052, 1981, pp. 1–6. Unpublished internal report (eventually submitted to the US FDA as part of esmolol IND).

[73] R.W. Krasula, Production of methanol as a metabolite of ASL-8052, 1981, pp. 1–8. Summary. Unpublished internal report (eventually submitted to the US FDA as part of esmolol IND).

[74] K.E. McMartin, J.J. Ambre, T.R. Tephly, Methanol poisoning in human subjects, Am. J. Med. 68 (1980) 414.

[75] L.D. Stegink, N.C. Brummel, K.E. McMartin, G. Martin-Amat, L.J. Filer Jr., G.L. Baler, T.R. Tephly, Blood methanol concentrations in normal adult subjects administered abuse doses of aspartame, J. Toxicol. Environ. Health 7 (1981) 281–290.

[76] M.S. Hayreh, S.S. Hayreh, G.L. Baumbach, P. Cancilla, G. Martin-Amat, T.R. Tephly, K.E. McMartin, A.B. Maker, Methyl alcohol poisoning: III. Ocular toxicity, Arch. Opthalmol. 95 (1977) 1851–1858.

[77] G. Martin-Amat, K.E. McMartin, S.S. Hayreh, et al., Methanol poisoning: ocular toxicity produced by formate, Toxicol. Appl. Pharmacol. 45 (1978) 201–208.

[78] K.E. McMartin, G. Martin-Amat, P.E. Noker, et al., Lack of role for formaldehyde in methanol poisoning in the monkey, Biochem. Pharmacol. 28 (1979) 645–649.

[79] Nickname for Walter Payton for which different origins have been indicated by various sources. I put most weight on his brother's view as expressed in the book "Walter & Me: Standing in the Shadow of Sweetness" Eddie Payton, Paul Brown and Craig Willey and published by Triumph Books, Chicago, 2012, pp. 1–256. ISBN 9781600787638.

[80] Howard Cosell (2007 inductee into the U.S.'s Sports Broadcasting Hall of Fame) promulgated Walter Payton's nickname of 'The Sweetness' [78] while hosting Monday Night Football with cohosts Frank Gifford and Don Meredith from 1970 to 1983. https://www. sportsbroadcastinghalloffame.org/inductees/howard-cosell/. Accessed 3/16/2022.

[81] Performed as a song by the Chicago Bears football team in 1985 prior to their Super Bowl victory in 1986. It was released through Capitol Records' Red Label imprint achieving number 41 on the Billboard Hot 100 list and eventually earned a Grammy nomination for Best R&B Performance by a Duo or Group with Vocals in 1987. https://en.wikipedia.org/wiki/The_Super_Bowl_Shuffle. Accessed 3/16/2022.

[82] Phrase in the 1995 film *Apollo* 13 spoken by actor Tom Hanks. Screenwriter William Broyles, Jr. adapted/modified it from words actually conveyed by astronaut John Swigert during the 1970 spaceflight. https://www.google.com/search?q=houston+we+have +a+problem+movie&rlz=1C1GCEB_enUS964US964&oq=houston%2C+we+have+a+problem&aqs=chrome.3.69i57j0i512l6j46i512j0i512l 2.20086j0j15&sourceid=chrome&ie=UTF-8. Accessed 3/16/2022.

[83] Although applicable to several different sports, for the sport of baseball: A 'grand slam' is a hit that goes over the playing field's fence while otherwise remaining in fair-play (in bounds) when the bases are already loaded with players (runners) on first, second and third base. This 'ultimate hit' for the game results in 4 points and the hitter and runners need only to trot around the bases rather than having to run quickly so as to avoid a play of the ball being made against any of them to negate the hit and possibly result in one or more outs for their team's half-inning (half-segment of standard 9 innings professional game).

[84] The Cinderella story is a folk tale with many variants throughout the world having the general theme of a young woman living in forsaken circumstances that are suddenly changed to remarkable fortune, commonly in the Western world to the throne via marriage with a Prince that has returned her glass slipper that she left behind after attending a royal ball disguised as belonging to the 'upper class' of the day. Based on the story of Rhodopis as recounted by Strabo sometime between 7 BC and AD 23 about a Greek slave girl who marries the King of Egypt, the first literary European version was written in Italy by Giambattista Basile in his Pentamerone published in 1634. Its most common, present version was largely popularized by the Brothers Grimm in their folk tale collection Grimm's Fairy Tales in 1812. https://en.wikipedia.org/wiki/Cinderella. Accessed 3/16/2022. Extrapolation to sports, intends to convey that a team regarded as having essentially no chance to be competitive against its opposing teams, goes on to have a much higher rate of success/wins than was initially anticipated. In an extreme case, the Cinderella team not only achieves a

winning record but eventually goes on to win the final tournament and become the sole champion, all while remaining an underdog throughout the entire season and playoff series. https://en.wikipedia.org/wiki/Cinderella_(sports). Accessed 3/16/2022.

[85] This expression typically refers to a situation where a person rises from poverty to wealth or alternatively from obscurity to heights of fame and celebrity—sometimes suddenly. It is a common archetype of early literature such as in fairy tales like Cinderella [84] and Aladdin, or in novels like Charles Dickens' Oliver Twist, as well as remaining part of modern popular culture as exemplified by the writings of Horatio Alger, Jr. and by numerous real-life examples throughout recent history and still occurring today. https://en.wikipedia.org/wiki/Rags_to_riches. Accessed 3/16/2022. Although the definitive origin of this exact phrase/idiom is unknown, the stories of the American author Horatio Alger, Jr. (1834−1899) are generally regarded as at least a highly popular recognized source. https://www.idioms.online/from-rags-to-riches/. Accessed 3/16/2022.

[86] Business concentrates. DuPont heart drug approved, in: M. Heylin (Ed.), Chem. Eng. News 65 (2) (1987) 13.

[87] P.W. Erhardt, J.G. Sarver, Design and molecular modeling, in: P.W. Erhardt (Ed.), Cover on Drug metabolism − Databases and High-Throughput Testing during Drug Design and Development, IUPAC/Blackwell, Geneva, 1999.

[88] Taken from repeating new chapters having this title in series Annual Reports in Medicinal Chemistry/now Medicinal Chemistry Reviews. J.J. Bronson, Present Editor-In-Chief. Now available on-line via the ACS MEDI homepage. https://www.acsmedchem.org/. Accessed 3/16/2022.

[89] D.B. Wiest, Esmolol. A review of its therapeutic efficacy and pharmacokinetic characteristics, Clin. Pharmacokinet. 28 (1995) 190−202.

[90] D.B. Wiest, J.S. Haney, Clinical pharmacokinetics and therapeutic efficacy of esmolol, Clin. Pharmacokinet. 51 (2012) 347−356.

[91] K.P. Garnock-Jones, Esmolol: a review of its use in short-term treatment of tachyarrhythmias and the short-term control of tachycardia and hypertension, Drugs 72 (2012) 109−132.

[92] P. Erhardt, K. Bachmann, D. Birkett, et al., Glossary and tutorial of xenobiotic metabolism terms used during small molecule drug discovery and development (IUPAC technical report), Pure Appl. Chem. 93 (2021) 273−403.

[93] P. Erhardt, K. Bachmann, D. Birkett, et al. Glossary and tutorial of xenobiotic metabolism terms used during small molecule drug discovery and development (IUPAC technical report). Republished from Pure Appl. Chem. 2021, 93, 273 in Med. Chem. Rev. J.J. Bronson, Editor-In-Chief. ACS: Washington, D. C., 2022, pp. 461−471 hardcopy with entire document (pp. 461−651) available on-line via the ACS MEDI homepage https://www.acsmedchem.org/. Accessed 3/17/2022.

[94] N. Bodor, Soft drugs, in: E.B. Roche (Ed.), Design of Biopharmaceutical Properties through Prodrugs and Analogs, Academy of Pharmaceutical Sciences, Washington, D.C., 1977, pp. 98−135.

[95] E.J. Ariens, A.M. Simonis, Drug transference: drug metabolism, in: Molecular Pharmacology, the Mode of Action of Biologically Active Compounds. Vol. 3 − I. In Medicinal Chemistry, a Series of Monographs. G. DeStevens, Series Ed. and E.J. Ariens, Vol. Ed. Academic Press: New York/London, 1964, pp 53−118.

[96] N. Bodor, Soft drugs. 1. Labile quaternary ammonium salts as soft antimicrobials, J. Med. Chem. 23 (1980) 469−474.

[97] N. Bodor, Designing safer drugs based on the soft drug approach, Trends Pharmacol. Sci. 3 (1982) 53−56.

[98] N. Bodor, Y. Oshiro, T. Loftsson, M. Katovich, W. Caldwell, Soft drugs VI. The application of the inactive metabolite approach for the design of soft β-blockers, Pharmaceut. Res. 1 (1984) 120−125.

[99] N. Bodor, The soft drug approach, Chemtech 14 (1984) 28−38.

[100] N. Bodor, P. Buchwald, Soft drug design - general principles and recent applications, Med. Res. Rev. 20 (2000) 58−101.

[101] N. Bodor, P. Buchwald, Retrometabolism-based drug design and targeting, in: D.J. Abraham (Ed.), Burger's Medicinal Chemistry, Drug Discovery and Development, sixth ed., John Wiley & Sons, Hoboken, 2003, pp. 533−608.

[102] B. Testa, J.M. Mayer, Hydrolysis in Drug and Prodrug Metabolism − Chemistry, Biochemistry, and Enzymology, Wiley VCH, Zurich/Weinheim, 2003, pp. 1−780.

[103] T. Nordegren, The A−Z Encyclopedia of Alcohol and Drug Abuse, T. Brown Walker Press/Universal Pub., Boca Raton, 2002, p. 327.

[104] M. Veiligheid, How Does the Law Distinguish between Soft and Hard Drugs?. https://www.government.nl/topics/drugs/how-does-the-law-distinguish-between-soft-and-hard-drugs. (Accessed 16 May 2019).

[105] C. Lipinski, Drug-like properties and the causes of poor solubility and poor permeability, J. Pharmacol. Toxicol. Methods 44 (2000) 235−249.

[106] P. Leeson, Drug discovery: chemical beauty contest, Nature 481 (2012) 455−456.

[107] P. Erhardt, Statistics-based probabilities of metabolic possibilities, in: P. Erhardt (Ed.), Drug Metabolism: Databases and High Throughput Testing during Drug Design and Development, IUPAC/Blackwell, Geneva, 1999, pp. 185−191.

[108] P.A. Erhardt, Human drug metabolism database: potential roles in the quantitative predictions of drug metabolism and metabolism-related drug-drug interactions, J. Curr. Drug Metabol. 4 (2003) 411−422.

[109] G. Guroff, J. Daly, D. Jerina, J. Reson, B. Witkop, S. Undenfriend, Hydroxylation-induced migration: the NIH shift. Recent experiments reveal an unexpected and general result of enzymatic hydroxylation of aromatic compounds, Science 157 (1967) 1524−1530.

[110] E.J. Ariens, The structure-activity relationships of *beta*-adrenergic blocking drugs, Ann. N. Y. Acad. Sci. 136 (1967) 606−631.

[111] S.A. Belorkar, S. Jogaiah, Chapter 1. Enzymes − past, present and future, in: S.A. Belorkar, S. Jogaiah (Eds.), Protocols and Applications in Enzymology, Elsevier, Amsterdam, 2022, pp. 1−15.

[112] J.W.M. Nissink, S. Bazzaz, C. Blackett, M.A. Clark, O. Collingwood, J.S. Disch, D. Gikunju, K. Goldberg, J.P. Guilinger, E. Hardaker, E.J. Hennessy, R. Jetson, et al., Generating selective leads for Mer kinase inhibitors − example of a comprehensive lead-generation strategy, J. Med. Chem. 64 (2021) 3165−3184.

[113] K.J. Shaw, P.W. Erhardt, A.A. Hagedorn III, C.A. Pease, W.R. Ingebretsen, J.R. Wiggins, Cardiotonic agents. 7. Prodrug derivatives of 4-ethyl-1,3-dihydro-5-[4-(2-methyl-1*H*-imidazol-1-yl)benzoyl]-2*H*-imidazol-2-one, J. Med. Chem. 35 (1992) 1267−1272.

[114] C.Y. Quon, H.F. Stampfli, Biochemical properties of blood esmolol esterase, Drug Metab. Dispos. 13 (1985) 420−424.

[115] An American medical-drama television series that aired on NBC from 1994 to 2009. It was created by novelist and physician Michael Crichton and produced by Constant C Productions and Amblin Television. The plot follows the characters' responses to critical issues faced by an emergency room (ER) in a fictional hospital located in Chicago - thus coincidentally located near the ACC research facility where esmolol was discovered and underwent preclinical development. https://en.wikipedia.org/wiki/ER_(TV_series). Accessed 3/30/2022 (also coincidentally on the fifth birthday of my granddaughter Leah).

[116] T.T. Wilbury, Comparison of commercially available metabolism databases during the design of prodrugs and codrugs, in: P. Erhardt (Ed.), Drug Metabolism: Databases and High Throughput Testing during Drug Design and Development, IUPAC/Blackwell, Geneva, 1999, pp. 208–222. Note that 'T. T. Wilbury' is a fictional, composite name for the following coauthors of this work: P. Erhardt, G. Grethe, B. Snyder, D. Hawkins, J. Hayward, G. Klopman, F. Darvas, S. Marokhazi, P. Kormos, G. Kulkarni, H. Kalasz and A. Papp. All authors were seasoned experts successfully practicing in the fields of xenobiotic metabolism and/or computational chemistry. Our composite name, intending to reflect the voluntary spirit of such seasoned experts, was derived from the name of a rock band called "The Traveling Wilburys" [117] where, at that point in each of their highly successful individual careers, the band's members were similarly working together at their 'trade' in a voluntary manner just for the sheer fun of the group's performances and individual riffs therein.

[117] A British-American, rock-music group formalized in early 1988 that consisted of seasoned, individual super-stars (alphabetically) Bob Dylan, George Harrison, Jeff Lynne, Roy Orbison and Tom Petty. They released one highly successful album prior to Orbison's death in late 1988 followed by another successful song and then eventually another album. The band continued in a less formal manner into the early 1990s and then faded into silence as a group shortly thereafter. https://en.wikipedia.org/wiki/Traveling_Wilburys. Accessed 3/30/2022.

[118] P. Erhardt, Metabolism prediction, in: F. Darvas, G. Dorman (Eds.), High-throughput ADMETox Estimation: In Vitro & In Silico Approaches, Eaton Pub, Westborough, 2002, pp. 41–48.

[119] P. Erhardt (Ed.), Drug Metabolism: Databases and High Throughput Testing During Drug Design and Development, IUPAC/Blackwell, Geneva, 1999 pp. viii–ix, 1–340.

[120] P.L. Feldman, Insights into the chemical discovery of remifentanil, Anesthesiology 132 (2020) 1229–1234.

[121] G.J. Kilpatrick, Remimazolam: non-clinical and clinical profile of a new sedative/anesthetic agent, Front. Pharmacol. 12 (2021) 1–18.

[122] S.R. Wrigley, R.M. Jones, A.W. Harrop-Griffiths, M.W. Platt, Mivacurium chloride: a study to evaluate its use during propofol-nitrous oxide anesthesia, Anesthesia 47 (1992) 653–657.

[123] Y. Koshiyama, Y. Maekawa, T. Kojima, K. Kariya, T. Muto, H. Ohtani, N. Ueda, S. Kanno, H. Uchiyama, M. Tamegaya, M. Oda, Topical anti-inflammatory activity with weak systemic side effects of betamethasone butyrate propionate (BBP) on paper disk granuloma in rats, Oyo Yakuri (Pharmacometrics) 47 (1994) 489–493.

[124] T.C. Wicks, The pharmacology of rocuronium bromide (ORG 9426), AANA J. 62 (1994) 33–38.

[125] J.M. Hunter, New neuromuscular blocking drugs, N. Engl. J. Med. 332 (1995) 1691–1699.

[126] P.L. Feldman, M.K. James, M.F. Brackeen, J.M. Bilotta, S.V. Schuster, A.P. Lahey, M.W. Lutz, M.R. Johnson, H.J. Leighton, Design, synthesis, and pharmacological evaluation of ultrashort- to long-acting opioid analgesics, J. Med. Chem. 34 (1991) 2202–2206.

[127] S.J. Dell, D.G. Shulman, G.M. Lowry, J. Howes, A controlled evaluation of the efficacy and safety of loteprednol etabonate in the treatment of seasonal allergic conjunctivitis, Am. J. Ophthalmol. 123 (1997) 791–797.

[128] S.V. Onrust, R.H. Foster, Rapacuronium bromide: a review of its use in anesthetic practice, Drugs 58 (1999) 887–918.

[129] A. Sugiyama, A. Takahara, K. Hashimoto, Electrophysiologic, cardiohemodynamic and β-blocking actions of a new ultra-short-acting β-blocker, ONO-1101, assessed by the *in vivo* canine model in comparison with esmolol, J. Cardiovasc. Pharmacol. 34 (1999) 70–77.

[130] L.A. Sorbera, N. Serradell, J. Bolos, Fluticasone furoate, Drugs Future 32 (2007) 12–16.

[131] J. Varon, Clevidipine (antihypertensive), Drugs 68 (2008) 283–285.

[132] C. Zhang, Benzylamine-related Chiral Synthetic Reagents: Asymmetric Opening of Terminal Epoxides. MS degree thesis, University of Toledo, 1999, pp. 1–121.

[133] M. Reese, Drug Design (STAT5 Modulators), Development (Glyceollin I) and Improvement (Esmolol Plus). MS degree thesis, University of Toledo, 2008, pp. 1–65.

[134] L. Fang, Stereoselective Synthesis of Esmolol and in Vitro Pharmacokinetic Study of Esmolol and its Acid Metabolite. MS degree thesis, University of Toledo, 2009, pp. 1–120.

[135] J. Liao, Development of Soft Drugs for the Neonatal Population. MS degree thesis, University of Toledo, 2000, pp. 1–147.

[136] P.W. Erhardt, M.M. Aouthmany, Method and compositions for treating persistent pulmonary hypertension, 2004, pp. 1–25. U. S. Patent 6,756,047 B2.

[137] PWE became a certified patent agent after passing the US PTO bar exam administered in NYC in 1994 subsequent to one-year of self-study guided by two, one-week short-courses.

[138] M.G. Horning, K.D. Haegele, K.R. Sommer, J. Nowlin, M. Stafford, Metabolic switching of drug pathways as a consequence of deuterium substitution, in: E.R. Klein, P.D. Klein (Eds.), Int. Conf. on Stable Isotopes, Argonne Nat. Lab, Oak Brook, 1975, pp. 41–54. Text available online at, https://www.osti.gov/servlets/purl/1603304. (Accessed 31 March 2022).

[139] Z. Zhang, W. Tang, Drug metabolism in drug discovery and development, Acta Pharm. Sin. B 8 (2018) 721–732.

[140] PWE received the IUPAC appreciation of service award for outstanding contributions to the advancement of worldwide chemistry in 2007. IUPAC in Torino, Italy. Chemistry International-Newsmagazine for IUPAC 2007, 29 (6), 4–9. https://doi.org/10.1515/ci.2007.29.6.4. Accessed 4/1/2022.

[141] PWE awarded University of Toledo Distinguished University Professorship (DUP) in 2012. https://www.utoledo.edu/offices/provost/academic-honors-committee/distinguish-university-professor.html. Accessed 4/1/2022. A link to my later DUP technical lecture can also be found at this site.

[142] PWE inducted into the ACS MEDI Hall of Fame in 2018. https://www.acsmedchem.org/medi-hall-of-fame-inductees-acs. Accessed 4/1/2022.

[143] 'Humpty Dumpty' is a fictional character most often depicted as a humanized hen's egg for which the related-story of today originates from an English nursery rhyme of an undefined early date. An early written versions goes back to lyrics recorded by James William Elliot in National Nursery Rhymes and Nursery Songs (1870). The story/rhyme involves Humpty falling off a wall and breaking into pieces, after which "all the king's horses and all the king's men . . . couldn't put Humpty together again." Humpty, in such a dilemma, is referenced in many works and cultures, including a popular Broadway play in the U.S. that ran during the late 1860s. https://en.wikipedia.org/wiki/Humpty_Dumpty. Accessed 4/1/2022.

[144] P. Erhardt, Drug design and development. A research center more than twenty years in the making, Chem. Int. 36 (6) (2014) 8−13, 27.

[145] P. Erhardt, Drug design and development. Part II: reflections from an academic-based center, Chem. Int. 37 (3) (2015) 12−15.

[146] This idiom is thought to have been first derived from John Ray's written works Proverb Collection of 1670 wherein he used the expression 'apples to oysters' to emphasize two things that are not/should not be comparable/compared. It is used in this same sense quite universally while varying the second object across many different languages and cultures. https://www.theidioms.com/apples-to-oranges/. Accessed 3/31/2022.

[147] An idiom originating from the early blacksmith's trade indicating by today's usage that one is involved with more than one (usually many) different projects. It can be used in a positive manner to suggest that one's activities may provide multiple alternatives toward moving forward; or in a negative manner to indicate that because of the many ongoing projects, one is simply too busy or split too thinly to be able to accomplish things/end-points in a timely manner. The use will depend upon and be made clear by the context of a given sentence. https://funkyenglish.com/idiom-too-many-irons-in-the-fire/. Accessed 4/1/2022.

[148] For example: 5 kids × 5 years (average for 4-year degree when elongated by having to also work part-time throughout) x $15 K/year (actually low side here since some of our better 'students' among the bunch were being accepted to ivy league schools who had tuitions of at least $25 K/year even a few year's ago) = $375K + income tax payment at ca. 30% of actual salary needed to net this amount = $ 536 K.

[149] M. Jacobs (Ed.) Chem. Eng. News, 77 (9) (1999) 5.

[150] R. Wedin, Chemistry 1 (2001) 17−20.

[151] International Human Genome Research Team (having over 100 participating coauthors). Initial sequencing and analysis of the human genome, Nature 409 (2001) 860−921.

[152] Telomere-to-Telomere (T2T) Consortium (having about 100 participating coauthors). The complete sequence of a human genome, Science 376 (2022) 44−53.

Index

'*Note:* Page numbers followed by "f" indicate figures and "t" indicate tables.'

Printed in the United States
by Baker & Taylor Publisher Services